The Legal Environment of Business

Seventh Edition

Roger E. Meiners
University of Texas at Arlington

Al H. Ringleb
Consortium International MBA

Frances L. Edwards
Clemson University

WEST **West Legal Studies in Business**
an International Thomson Publishing company I T P®

Cincinnati • Albany • Boston • Detroit • Johannesburg • London • Madrid • Melbourne • Mexico City
New York • Pacific Grove • San Francisco • Scottsdale • Singapore • Tokyo • Toronto

Team Director: *Jack W. Calhoun*
Senior Acquisitions Editor: *Rob Dewey*
Acquisitions Editor: *Scott Person*
Senior Developmental Editor: *Jan Lamar*
Marketing Manager: *Michael Worls*
Production Editor: *Sandra Gangelhoff*
Manufacturing Coordinator: *Georgina Calderon*
Production House: *Shepherd, Inc.*
Internal design: *Ellen Pettengell Design, Chicago*
Cover design: *Kim Torbeck, Imbue Design, Cincinnati*
Cover photo: *copyright Tony Stone Images*
Printer: *World Color—Versailles, KY*

Printed in the United States of America.

3 4 5 6 7 8 9 10

International Thomson Publishing Europe
Berkshire House
168-173 High Holborn
London, WC1V7AA, United Kingdom

Nelson ITP, Australia
102 Dodds Street
South Melbourne
Victoria 3205 Australia

Nelson Canada
1120 Birchmount Road
Scarborough, Ontario
Canada M1K 5G4

International Thomson Publishing Southern Africa
Building 18, Constantia Square
138 Sixteenth Road, P.O. Box 2459
Halfway House, 1685 South Africa

International Thomson Editores
Seneca, 53
Colonia Polanco
11560 México D.F. México

International Thomson Publishing Asia
60 Alberta Street #15-01
Albert Complex
Singapore 189969

International Thomson Publishing Japan
Hirakawa-cho Kyowa Building, 3F
2-2-1 Hirakawa-cho, Chiyoda-ku
Tokyo 102, Japan

Library of Congress Cataloging-in-Publication Data

Meiners, Roger E.
    The legal environment of business / Roger E. Meiners, Al H.
Ringleb, Frances L. Edwards. — 7th ed.
        p.   cm.
    Includes index.
    ISBN 0-324-00423-0 (alk. paper)
    1. Industrial laws and legislation—United States.   2. Commercial
law—United States.   I. Ringleb, Al H.   II. Edwards, Frances L.
III. Title.
KF1600.M43   20000   99-23199
346.7307—dc21   CIP

This book is printed on acid-free paper.

This book is dedicated to:
Thomas Anderson Roe,
innovator in business and philanthropy
and a dear friend

R.E.M.

Brief Contents

Contents

Appendices

Table of Cases

Preface

Courses on the legal and regulatory environment of business provide important background for students preparing for a variety of careers. One faces legal, social, political, and ethical issues in any profession. Most are simple situations, that can be handled with common sense, but in many situations ignorance of the principles of business and law can result in problems.

This textbook presents the legal environment from the perspective of the professional non-lawyer. Few students who take this course will become lawyers, and most will not take additional courses in law. This course offers the opportunity to learn key points of the law from the standpoint of a working professional.

We have received excellent feedback from professors and students who have used the six previous editions of this book and have pointed out both its shortcomings and its strong points. We have taken these comments into account in preparing this edition to make the book even more helpful and practical as we study the complex legal environment that businesses face in an increasingly international setting.

Basic Organization

A one-semester course in the legal environment of business faces the problem of determining what to cover in such a short time. It is like a physician giving a one-semester course to teach students what they need to know about medicine—so many topics, so little time. There is agreement that the key elements of the legal system must be covered. This is done in Part One of the book, Elements of Law and the Judicial Process. Part Two, Elements of Traditional Business Law, reviews the major areas of the common law (broadly defined) that apply to business. Part Three, The Regulatory Environment of Business, covers the major regulatory laws that managers are likely to face and reviews major points of international business law.

Key Features

EDITED CASES

A primary way to learn law is to read real cases that the courts had to resolve. Each major case presented here has the background facts and legal proceedings, up to the time of the case reported here, summarized by the authors under the label **Case Background.** Then the court's holding, legal reasoning, and explanation of the law as it applies to the facts at hand are presented in the words of the court in the **Case Decision.** Since most decisions are quite long, we present only the key portions of the holding. Material that has been deleted is indicated by asterisks (* * *) for lengthy pieces of text and periods (. . .) for shorter amounts. Finally, some **Questions for Analysis** are offered for the reader to consider or for class discussion (answers are provided in the *Instructor's Resource Guide*).

INTERNATIONAL PERSPECTIVES

This feature discusses how similar aspects of the law covered at certain points in the chapter are handled in other countries. As globalization reaches more businesses, managers must know how to deal with different legal systems and cultures. This feature makes clear that the rules of the game are different in other nations and that managers must be prepared to operate and resolve problems in a complex legal environment.

JURISPRUDENCE?

These short features add a light or humorous touch to the topic at hand by discussing an actual case or legal situation that is fairly unusual. While law and business are serious, odd things happen in our lives and in the legal environment that remind us that trouble can come from very unexpected places, that the results of the legal process can be quite surprising, that scoundrels are among us, and that truth can be stranger than fiction.

ISSUE ARTICLES

An article, usually from a major business publication such as *The Wall Street Journal*, that discusses a political, regulatory, or ethical issue related to the legal subject matter of the chapter appears at the end of each chapter. The article illustrates how the law directly impacts business operations and provides a good vehicle for class discussion of issues important in today's legal environment of business. Each article ends with *Issue Questions* that can be the basis of class discussion (the *Instructor's Resource Guide* presents answers to the questions).

CYBERLAW

This new feature presents short discussions of application of the law to the many developments arising from computers and new forms of telecommunication. E-commerce and e-mail mean new legal issues for the courts to resolve as they apply traditional legal principles to never-before-heard-of ways of doing business, transmitting information, and communicating with friends and strangers.

SUMMARY

The text of each chapter is summarized in bullet format that provides a quick review of the major points of law and the major rules covered and serves as a self-test of points that will be covered in examinations.

REVIEW AND DISCUSSION QUESTIONS

The student is first asked to review major terms used in each chapter. (Term meanings are provided in the *Glossary.*) A couple general questions are then asked about major subjects covered in the chapter, followed by *Case Questions.* Questions 5 and 7 in each chapter are answered at http://meiners.swcollege.com/. We have attempted to keep them short to encourage their use for class discussion or for use as a study tool. A few *Policy Questions* to spur discussion of controversial political or social issues affecting the legal environment and some *Ethics Questions* that pose problems that managers could face are then asked. Some chapters have *Internet Assignments* that pose legal environment questions that can be answered by searching materials available on the Internet. All questions are answered in the *Instructor's Resource Guide.*

New to This Edition

All chapters have been revised, but some more than others. Chapters 2 and 3, on the judicial process and trial process, have been reorganized to be more user-friendly in sequence of learning the information. Chapter 5, on the Constitution, has an expanded discussion of equal protection and its application in the case of minority set-asides in government contracts in the Supreme Court's *Adarand* case on that point.

The two torts chapters have been redesigned; the first chapter focusing on an overview of intentional torts and negligence; the second chapter focuses on torts that tend to be particular to business, including a new discussion of misrepresentation (fraud) and a business case that illustrates how the issue often arises.

The two contracts chapters have been extensively revised. Chapter 10 on the traditional common law of contracts has been streamlined and has a greater focus on real-world contract issues that arise. The second chapter, which previously was a general review of the Uniform Commercial Code, is now Chapter 11, *Domestic and International Sales.* It gives a new overview of Article 2 on sales and then looks at international sales, with a focus on the U.N. Convention on Contracts for the International Sale of Goods, which is becoming more commonly used in international trade.

The chapter that was called *Debtor/Creditor Relations* has been revised and is now called *Negotiable Instruments, Credit, and Bankruptcy*, indicating that it now gives an introduction to UCC Article 9, and then goes on to give a general overview of the credit-debt relationship in business, including the bankruptcy process.

As noted previously, a new feature called *Cyberlaw* has been added in appropriate chapters, showing applications of legal principles to new issues arising in the "information age," such as electronic commerce and e-mail. Legal cases in many chapters have been replaced and many *Issue* readings are new, so that feature stays timely in terms of application of law, ethics, and social issues in business.

Ancillaries

- Professor Lynda S. Hamilton of Georgia Southern University has again revised the *Student Study Guide* to provide a variety of knowledge testing to reinforce key material learned in the text and to help prepare for examinations. Quicken Business Law Partner® 3.0 CD-ROM is now included in the back of the study guide.

- The *Instructor's Resource Guide* is revised and expanded. As before, it answers all questions in the book. It also provides a detailed outline of each chapter, summarizing the content of the text, including all cases. The instructor can refer quickly to this guide to remember the points the students have covered in the text. The guide also provides numerous additional summarized cases that the instructor can use to illustrate key points of law. Additional material, such as more discussion of certain points and examples of the law in practice, is provided as lecture and discussion enhancements.
- The *Test Bank* has about 3,000 questions and is available in computerized form for users of IBM PCs and compatibles in Thomson World Class Learning Testing Tools software. Every test question, whether a direct question of information or an application question, is referenced to the main text page. More questions based on fact have been added to test critical thinking ability.
- A set of *Transparency Acetates* keyed to the text and the *Instructor's Resource Guide*. Also, *PowerPoint* slides will be available.
- Many other West Publishing Company ancillaries are available: *Business Law and the Legal Environment Video Library*, *WestLaw*, *You Be the Judge* software, *West's Regional Reporters*, *Contracts: An Interactive Guide*, *UCC Article 2 Sales: An Interactive Guide*, Court TV Trial Stories, and CNN Legal Issues Video update. Please ask your West Representative for the qualification details for these supplements.

Acknowledgments

The authors thank the adopters and reviewers from around the country who sent helpful comments and materials for the seventh edition. Much of the credit for the improvements belongs to them. The reviewers for this edition include:

Thomas M. Apke
California State University, Fullerton

Susan Boyd
The University of Tulsa

Melville T. Cottrill
Southern Connecticut State University

Elaine C. Daniels
Central Michigan University

Howard Ellis
Millersville University

Jerry L. Furniss
The University of Montana

Gamewell Gantt
Idaho State University

Frederick J. Pinne
Central Missouri State University

John L. Roberts
Colorado State University, Fort Collins

Lee Ruck
George Mason University

Michael G. Walsh
Villanova University

The authors also extend thanks to the professionals in business, law, and government who assisted in making this textbook as up-to-date and accurate as possible.

Finally, we thank the editors and staff of West Legal Studies in Business. In particular, we thank the sales representatives who continually give us valuable information on the day-to-day perceptions of the textbook—information provided by the instructors and students who are using it. We thank Sandy Gangelhoff, whose diligence and determination got us through the production process on schedule. Special thanks also goes to our developmental editor, Jan Lamar, who tolerates us with good humor. The efforts of our new editors, Rob Dewey and Scott Person, who manage huge tasks, are much appreciated.

We welcome and encourage comments from the users of this textbook—both students and instructors. By incorporating those comments and suggestions, we can make this text an even better one in the future.

Roger E. Meiners
Al H. Ringleb
Frances L. Edwards

The Legal Environment of Business

Seventh Edition

PART 1

Elements of Law and the Judicial Process

Part One reviews the major components of the legal system and provides the framework for understanding the material presented in the other two parts of the book. Just as people in business must understand the elements of accounting, finance, management, and marketing, it is important that they also know how the legal environment plays a critical role in the way business and the economy function. Law changes as the structure of business changes, as social pressures produce changes in political policy that is reflected in the rules under which business operates, as the ethical expectations of business increase, and as the economy becomes more interwoven in international operations.

The chapters in this part review the major components of the legal system: the origins of law, constitutional law, the role of law in society and business, the structure and functioning of the court system and of administrative agencies, and the use of alternative forms of dispute resolution. This serves as a structural background for the rest of the text, which reviews substantive laws that impact business.

CHAPTER 1

The Modern Environment of Business The legal, social, and ethical pressures that businesses face today in a complex international political economy are discussed. Chapter includes the purposes, sources, and structure of law and the legal system.

CHAPTER 2

The Court System The structure and powers of the court systems are reviewed, followed by a discussion of how a case gets to which court and what powers the courts have over the parties to a case.

CHAPTER 3

The Trial Process The steps in litigation from the time a party has a complaint for which the law may offer relief, the kinds of relief that the courts may offer, the stages of litigation, and the appeals process are discussed.

CHAPTER 4

Alternative Dispute Resolution Most lawsuits are not resolved through the public court systems; they are settled prior to trial. In civil disputes between private parties and with government agencies, private dispute resolution—including negotiation, mediation, and arbitration—has become ever more important.

CHAPTER 5

The Constitution: Focus on Application to Business Congress is provided nearly unlimited authority by the Constitution to regulate business. However, limits on governmental powers are provided by civil liberty protections for persons and businesses against an over-reaching state.

CHAPTER 6

Government Agencies and Administrative Process Regulatory agencies have grown ever more important as a source of substantive law as legislatures grant agencies significant powers to make and enforce laws that greatly impact business operations.

CHAPTER 1

The Modern Environment of Business

Life can be good, as Barbara Fong knows. She is only thirty-four, but her company, Gnof, is hot. Two years earlier, the game software company had gone public with a stock offering, making Fong and a couple of her close friends, who had been with Gnof since the start, instant millionaires, at least on paper. Living in San Diego, cranking out hot software that had wide appeal, and sneaking in ski trips to Montana in the winter meant that every good thing Barbara could imagine had happened while she was young.

But recently, grief seemed to await her at work instead of programming difficulties. When the stock market fell in 1998, and Gnof stock dropped too, some unhappy shareholders sued, claiming that their lost profits were due to mismanagement. Their lawyers have offered a settlement to be determined in arbitration that could clean out most cash in the firm and her bank account; but it at least provides relief from the trial preparation that has been dragging on for over a year and consumes legal and expert fees as well as valuable time.

A hacker got into Gnof's system and stole some software that was under development. Some of Fong's associates think they have identified the hacker and, perhaps more importantly, think the stolen material appears in slightly altered form in a game just released by a competitor. They are pushing Fong to take legal action against the hacker and the competitor. The fact that every new Gnof game is pirated and sold for next to nothing in over half the world is infuriating, but it is possible that the cost of attacking the problem will be more than the income lost.

Dope smoking is not unknown among software writers, and Fong had ignored the issue other than having made it clear that there was to be no such activity on company property. One employee who spent more time high than working was fired. He has sued Gnof for violation of the Americans with Disabilities Act. Another programmer came to see Fong last week and threatened to sue for sexual harassment due to actions by one of Fong's senior managers. The manager says that the claims are nonsense, that he will not stay with the company if he is "hung out to dry," and that nothing better be said about the matter.

Last week, a suit was filed by the parents of a twelve-year-old who supposedly cut his hand badly when messing with a Gnof game CD. In fact, the CDs do seem to have a rather sharp edge, but the company that produces the CD for Gnof claims that the contract does not require them to make the more costly, better-trimmed CDs that would not have such sharp edges. "We can do it," the CD-maker rep said, "but Gnof will have to pay 3 percent more per CD." She also mentioned to Fong that the company was being questioned by the EPA about wastewaters emitted by the plant that may contain higher-than-approved emission levels of the chemicals used in making CDs.

Barbara muses about the good old days, four years ago, when she and three friends sat in a crummy office and produced their first successful game—broke, but a lot happier. Now she has little time to think about software details, let alone dream up whole new concepts. Her life is filled with managerial, marketing, financial, and legal issues that are not unique to Gnof.

Every company deals with an array of issues, including legal matters that can wipe out a firm, especially a smaller one. Few lawsuits will do that, but legal issues permeate all aspects of business operations. As a business becomes global in scope, legal issues become even more complex. While Fong thinks they are wrong, she is troubled by the complaints by some "children advocacy" groups that claim Gnof software, among others, is not educational in content and contains too much violence. The product content is clearly legal, but should Gnof products meet the social or ethical standards that some people believe are important?

Because the environment of business is now so complex, ethical, legal, social, political, and international issues all impact company operations. As Exhibit 1.1 indicates, whether your field is human resources, banking, advertising, or software development, you must be familiar with a wide range of subjects to have the skills needed to be aware of possible problems and to recognize potential opportunities that someone with a limited view of the world would be likely to miss. This book, which focuses on the legal environment of business, helps to fit one large piece into the complicated puzzle of the modern business world.

The study of the legal environment of business begins with an overview of the nature of law and the legal system. Composed of law from several sources, the legal environment is influenced by the needs and demands of the business community, consumers, and government. This chapter provides an understanding of the functions of law in society, the sources of U.S. law, and the classifications of law. It then considers some of the major ethical issues that play an even larger role in the modern environment of business.

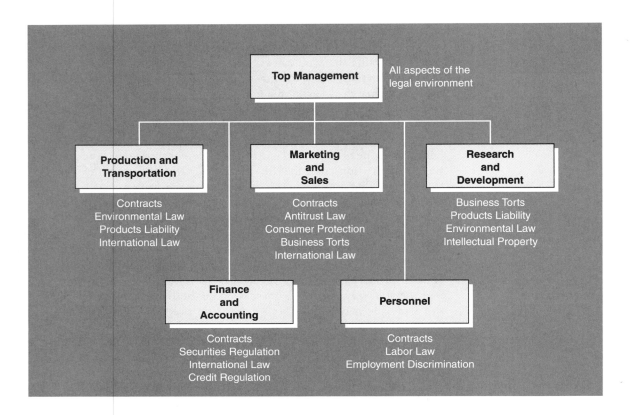

EXHIBIT 1.1

*Overview of a Business's
Legal Environment*

Law and the Key Functions of the Legal System

In the legal environment of business, *law* refers to a code of conduct that defines the behavioral boundaries for business activity. A precise definition of law is elusive. Law is an abstract term. Consider the following definitions. *Black's Law Dictionary*, an authoritative legal dictionary, defines law as follows:

1. Law, in its generic sense, is a body of rules of action or conduct prescribed by controlling authority, and having binding legal force.
2. That which must be obeyed and followed by [members of a society] subject to sanctions or legal consequences is a law.

Oliver Wendell Holmes, a legal scholar and supreme court justice, offered the following definition:

> Law is a statement of the circumstances, in which the public force is brought to bear . . . through the courts.

In his book *Growth of Law*, the jurist Benjamin Nathan Cardozo defined law as follows:

A principle or rule of conduct so established as to justify a prediction with reasonable certainty that it will be enforced by the courts if its authority is challenged.

Thus, law may be viewed as a collection of rules or principles intended to prescribe and direct human behavior. Through enforcement, such rules or principles provide a measure of predictability and uniformity to the boundaries of acceptable conduct within a society. Nations have both *formal rules*, that is, what are commonly called laws, and *informal* or *implicit rules* that come from a society's history, values, customs, commercial practices, and ethics.

Law and the legal system serve several key functions in society. The most important functions include influencing the behavior of the members of a society, resolving disputes within the society, maintaining important social values, and providing a method for social change. The *International Perspectives* feature discusses the efforts in the country of Chad to develop a legal system that is attractive to business development. Its experience, which is not unique, reminds us how difficult it would be to do business in a country without a workable legal system.

ENHANCING SOCIAL STABILITY BY INFLUENCING BEHAVIOR

The legal system helps to define acceptable behavior and to control unacceptable behavior. Law and the legal system instruct members of a society on what may and may not be done in various circumstances. The law thus imposes a structure on society by limiting activities that are detrimental to the "public interest" and encouraging beneficial activities. The law restricts business practices that are viewed as dishonest or otherwise outside the ethical and social norms of a society. At the same time, the law can encourage transactions and practices that further society's goals.

The business of raising and selling marijuana in Amsterdam (Holland) is legal because the government decided that legalizing marijuana would eliminate the criminal element in the drug trade and would make it less likely that people would use harsher drugs that are still illegal, such as cocaine. In the United States, raising and selling marijuana is illegal and can be punished by long prison terms. But, in the United States, the production and sale of alcoholic beverages, with certain controls, is legal in most of the country. In Saudi Arabia, people have been executed for being involved in the alcohol business. The laws in these countries reflect social norms and are intended to control behavior.

CONFLICT RESOLUTION

The next important function of the law is the resolution of disputes within a society. Disagreements are inevitable, since societies are made up of individuals with differing desires and social preferences. Karl N. Llewellyn, a legal theorist, states:

> What, then, is this law business about? It is about the fact that our society is honeycombed with disputes. Disputes actual and potential, disputes to be settled and disputes to be prevented; both appealing to law, both making up the business of law. . . . This doing of something about disputes, this doing of it reasonably, is the business of law.

Chad: A Third-World Country Looks to Create a Legal System

 Chad is located in north-central Africa. It is three times the size of California, has a population of six million people, and has a per capita income of about $200 per year.

The country seeks outside assistance to develop its economy. A conference on the promotion of the private sector in Chad found that the country lacked an effective legal system and that no accepted rule of law existed. Chad's citizens are not willing to use the existing court system, wherein judges often receive orders from the governing authority on how to decide cases. Disputes are largely resolved through an unauthorized system of "courts" established by the police and military authorities. National law is often in conflict with the customs and traditions of the various ethnic groups in the society and is largely ignored. The lack of a predictable legal system is a significant deterrent to the development of the country's commercial base.

To help resolve these difficulties in the legal system, Professor Louis Alcoin recommended the following reforms:

Reform the court system to improve dispute resolution, with emphasis on ensuring that judges are independent of the governing authority.

Establish a separate court to be used only to resolve commercial disputes.

Write and publish the civil and commercial codes.

Reform the areas of enforcing judgments, business registrations, the investment code, property law, government contracts, and banking.

Publish new legislative acts with the understanding that none would take effect until they are published.

In undertaking these legal reforms, include laws that reflect the country's customs and traditions to the extent appropriate.

The governing authority and the business community in Chad understand the need for such reforms. Chad must develop a legal system more attractive to the business community. In the absence of these reforms, the country will not overcome the barriers to development that result from the lack of a reliable or respected legal system.

One formal mechanism for the resolution of disputes is the court system, which is used for resolving *private disputes* between members of society and *public disputes* arising between a person and the government. Our court system is intended to provide a consistent mechanism for resolving disputes. As we will see in Chapter 4, businesses are increasingly turning to legal conflict resolution processes outside of the courts.

SOCIAL MAINTENANCE

A society is shaped by its values, customs, and traditions. It is not surprising, then, that law plays a crucial role in maintaining the social environment. Honesty and integrity are reflected by the enforceability of contracts; respect for other people and their property is reflected in tort and property law; and some measures of acceptable behavior are reflected in criminal laws. For example, federal law makes it illegal for a U.S. company to pay a bribe to an official of a foreign government to obtain business. Few other countries have such a law, reflecting differences in approaches to acceptable business practices in different countries.

SOCIAL CHANGE

The legal system provides an effective way to bring about changes in "acceptable" behavior. Behavior that was acceptable at one time may not serve society well today, or in the future, as circumstances make certain actions less acceptable. For example, to help alter behavior, laws have been enacted to prohibit racial discrimination in decisions to hire, promote, or discharge a worker. In the past, racial discrimination may have been an accepted—or at least a tolerated—norm of business behavior for which no sanctions were imposed. Such behavior is no longer considered acceptable to society.

Sources of Law in the United States

The oldest source of law in this country is the *common law*—law that is made and applied by judges as they resolve disputes between private parties. The common law in the United States dates to colonial times, when English common law governed most internal legal matters. To maintain social order and to encourage commerce, the colonists retained the common law when the United States became an independent nation.

In addition to the judge-made common law, the most fundamental source of law is the U.S. Constitution, through which other laws are created. The Constitution creates the branches of government—each of which has the ability to make law. Congress—the legislative branch of government—has used its constitutionally granted powers to create what is often referred to as the fourth branch of government, that is, the administrative agencies, a source of law of great importance to business. Similarly, state constitutions determine the structure of government within a state and establish procedures and certain rights.

COMMON LAW

The origin of our law and legal system can be more easily understood by considering the origin, workings, and functions of English common law. In 1066, the Normans conquered England. William the Conqueror and his successors began the task of unifying the country. An important element in unification was the establishment of King's Courts, called *Curia Regis*. Those courts developed and applied a common or uniform set of rules for the entire country. The set of rules that gradually evolved marked the beginning of English *common law*.

Case Law

Under the common law, a judge's resolution of any particular dispute generally follows earlier judicial decisions that resolved similar disputes. For hundreds of years now, the decisions in important cases have been gathered and recorded in books called case reporters. To settle disputes that are similar to past disputes, judges use recorded cases for guidance for their decisions. A previously decided case provides legal principle, called *precedent*, that can be applied to the facts of a new case under consideration.

To settle unique or novel disputes, judges create new common law. New laws, however, are based on the general principles suggested by many previously recorded decisions. Since common law is state law, there are differences across the states in the interpretation of common law principles, but the judges in one state often look to cases from other states to help resolve disputes that do not have clearly established rules.

Doctrine of Stare Decisis

The practice of deciding new cases by referencing decisions is the foundation of the English and American judicial processes. The use of precedent in deciding present cases forms a doctrine called *stare decisis*, meaning in Latin "to stand on decided cases." Under this doctrine, judges are encouraged (but not forced) to stand by precedents. According to Judge Richard Posner:

> Judge-made rules are the outcome of the practice of decision according to precedent (stare decisis). When a case is decided, the decision is thereafter a precedent, i.e., a reason for deciding a similar case the same way. While a single precedent is a fragile thing . . . an accumulation of precedents dealing with the same question will create a rule of law having virtually the force of an explicit statutory rule.

Value of Precedent

Stare decisis promotes several useful functions in our legal system. First, consistency in the legal system enhances the ability to plan business transactions. People have reasonable expectations about the enforcement of agreements and the legal standards that apply. Second, as a rule is applied in many disputes involving similar facts, people will be increasingly confident that the rule will be followed in the resolution of future disputes. Finally, the doctrine creates a more just legal system by neutralizing the prejudices of individual judges. If judges use precedent as the basis for decisions, they are less influenced by their personal biases and beliefs.

Changes in Society

An advantage of dispute resolution through the common law is its ability to change with the times. As changes occur in technology or in social values, the common law can evolve and provide new rules that better fit the new environment. Although most cases are decided on the basis of stare decisis, judges are not prohibited from changing legal principles if conditions warrant. A judge may modify or reverse an existing legal principle. If that decision is appealed to a higher court for review, the higher court may accept the new rule as the one to be followed.

In recent years, there have been rapid changes in the manner in which we can communicate with one another. While the mail and telephone calls dominated in the past, businesses now need many communications systems to be competitive. E-mail and faxes have often replaced the former method of personally signed documents. The law adapted to accept new communication methods.

CONSTITUTIONS

A *constitution* is the fundamental law of a nation. It establishes and limits the powers of government. The U.S. Constitution (Appendix C) allocates the powers of government between the states and the federal government. Powers not granted to the federal government are retained by states or are left to the people.

The U.S. Constitution

The U.S. Constitution is the oldest written constitution in force in the world. It sets forth the general organization, powers, and limits of the federal government.

Specifically, the Constitution creates the legislative, executive, and judicial branches of the U.S. government.

This division in governmental power as established by the Constitution is referred to as the *separation of powers*. It arose out of a fear by the founders of this country that too much power might become concentrated in one governmental branch. The separation of powers means that each branch of government has functions to perform that can be checked by the other branches. The government structure that has developed is illustrated in Exhibit 1.2.

The U.S. Constitution clearly establishes itself as law that is supreme over state or federal laws that go beyond what the Constitution permits. According to Article VI:

> This Constitution, and the Laws of the United States which shall be made in Pursuance thereof; and all Treaties made, or which shall be made, under the Authority of the United States, shall be the supreme Law of the Land; and the Judges in every State shall be bound thereby, any Thing in the Constitution or Laws of any State to the Contrary notwithstanding.

State Constitutions

The powers and structures of all state governments are based on written constitutions. Like the federal government, the state governments are divided into legislative, judicial, and executive branches. The constitutions specify how state officials are chosen and removed, how laws are passed, how the court systems run, and how finances and revenues are paid and collected. Each state constitution is the highest form of law in a state. Some state constitutions, unlike the U.S. Constitution, are very long and are filled with details that are difficult to change because amending constitutions is more difficult than revising a law passed by a legislature.

LEGISLATURES

Congress and the state legislatures are the sources of *statutory law*. Statutes or legislation include much of the law that significantly affects business behavior, such as regulations. Federal courts review statutes passed by Congress to ensure that they do not violate the U.S. Constitution. The courts in each state review statutes passed by their legislature to ensure that they do not violate the constitution of the state or of the United States. If a state legislature passes a statute that violates the U.S. Constitution, and a state court does not strike down the statute, the statute may be stricken by a federal court.

United States Congress

Article I, Section 1, of the U.S. Constitution provides that all power to make laws for the federal government is given to Congress, a legislature consisting of a Senate and a House of Representatives. The process of enacting a law through the federal legislative process is illustrated in Exhibit 1.3. Of the 20,000 pieces of legislation proposed in each session of Congress, fewer than 200 usually reach the House and Senate floors for debate.

State Legislatures

Each state has lawmaking bodies similar to Congress in their functions and procedures. With the exception of Nebraska, all states have a two-part legislature containing a House of Representatives (sometimes called a House of Delegates or an

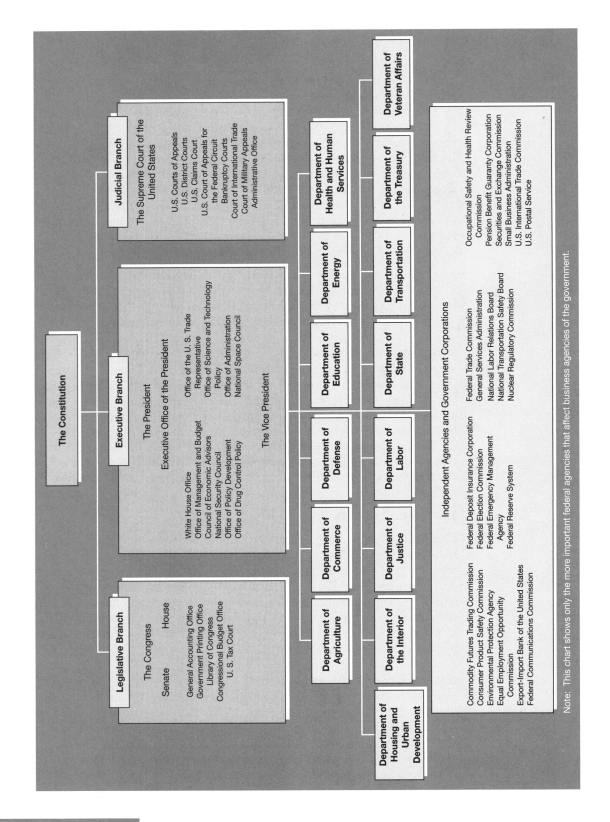

The Constitution

Legislative Branch

The Congress

Senate   House

General Accounting Office
Government Printing Office
Library of Congress
Congressional Budget Office
U. S. Tax Court

Executive Branch

The President

Executive Office of the President

White House Office
Office of Management and Budget
Council of Economic Advisors
National Security Council
Office of Policy Development
Office of Drug Control Policy

Office of the U. S. Trade
  Representative
Office of Science and Technology
  Policy
Office of Administration
National Space Council

The Vice President

Judicial Branch

The Supreme Court of the
United States

U.S. Courts of Appeals
U.S. District Courts
U.S. Claims Court
U.S. Court of Appeals for
  the Federal Circuit
Bankruptcy Courts
Court of International Trade
Court of Military Appeals
Administrative Office

Department of
Agriculture

Department of
Commerce

Department of
Defense

Department of
Education

Department of
Energy

Department of
Health and Human
Services

Department of
the Interior

Department of
Justice

Department of
Labor

Department of
State

Department of
Transportation

Department of
the Treasury

Department of
Veteran Affairs

Department of
Housing and
Urban
Development

Independent Agencies and Government Corporations

Commodity Futures Trading Commission
Consumer Product Safety Commission
Environmental Protection Agency
Equal Employment Opportunity
  Commission
Export-Import Bank of the United States
Federal Communications Commission

Federal Deposit Insurance Corporation
Federal Election Commission
Federal Emergency Management
  Agency
Federal Reserve System

Federal Trade Commission
General Services Administration
National Labor Relations Board
National Transportation Safety Board
Nuclear Regulatory Commission

Occupational Safety and Health Review
  Commission
Pension Benefit Guaranty Corporation
Securities and Exchange Commission
Small Business Administration
U.S. International Trade Commission
U.S. Postal Service

Note: This chart shows only the more important federal agencies that affect business agencies of the government.

EXHIBIT 1.2

*The Government of the
United States*

EXHIBIT 1.3

Legislative Process

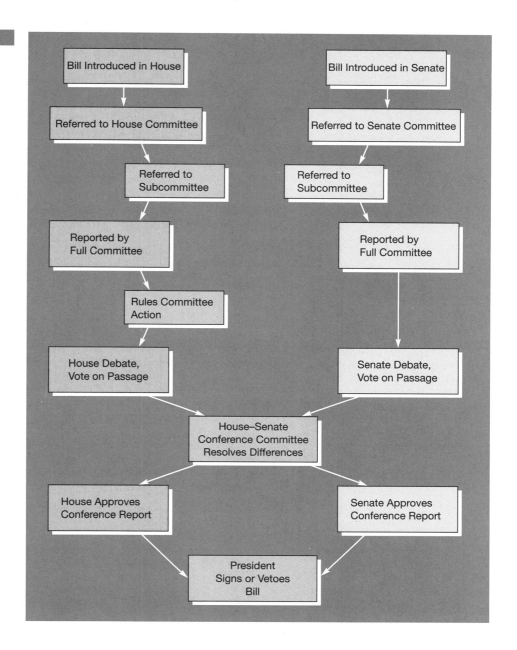

Assembly) and a Senate. The lawmaking process in state legislatures is similar to the procedure followed by the Congress as illustrated in Exhibit 1.3. Note, however, that in some states voters may directly propose or enact legislation through the voting process in referendums or initiatives.

An important state law affecting business is the Uniform Commercial Code (UCC). The UCC was prepared by the National Conference of Commissioners on Uniform State Laws with the assistance of law professors, the business community, and several legal organizations. It is designed to ease the legal relationship between parties involved in commercial transactions by making commercial laws uniform among the various states (and U.S. territories). The UCC as it applies to the sale of goods is discussed in more detail in Chapter 11. Another law adopted by most state legislatures is the Uniform Partnership Act, covered in Chapter 14.

ADMINISTRATIVE AGENCIES

An administrative agency is created when the legislative or executive branch of the government delegates some of its authority to an agency. Congress (or the state legislature) enacts a law that specifies the duties of the agency.

With congressional delegation, administrative agencies can exercise broad powers to enact regulations, supervise compliance with those regulations, and adjudicate violations of regulations. Regulations flowing from administrative agencies are among the important sources of law affecting the legal environment of business. The procedures of administrative agencies are discussed in Chapter 6.

THE JUDICIARY

As previously discussed, common law is the foundation of the legal environment of business. In addition to contributing to common law, the judiciary interprets and enforces laws enacted by legislative bodies. As we will see, some statutes, such as the antitrust laws, are not precise and require significant court interpretation. The judiciary also reviews actions taken by the executive branch and administrative agencies. The next two chapters deal with the courts in detail.

THE EXECUTIVE

In addition to being the one who signs (or vetoes) bills passed by Congress, the president is another source of law affecting the legal environment. The lawmaking authority of the president is limited by the Constitution. However, the president can create law by issuing *executive orders*, requiring federal agencies to do certain things within the president's scope of authority, such as an order to give preference to buying recycled products.

JURIS **prudence?**

The Law Is the Law

 Under the Mining Law of 1872, rights to hardrock minerals (not coal, gas, or oil) on public lands sold for $2.50 to $5.00 an acre. While Congress and the Clinton Administration argued about how to amend the law to update the mineral rights prices, in 1995, ASARCO paid $1,745 to obtain the rights to minerals on public lands with an estimated market value of $3 billion. The year before, mineral rights worth an estimated $11 billion were sold for a similar pittance to two foreign corporations.

Secretary of the Interior Bruce Babbitt, who under the 1872 law was required to sell the mineral rights, said that while amendments to the law are being considered, "This process has gone from distasteful to obscene. Let's call this exactly what it is: corporate welfare."

Source: Department of Interior News Release

The president can also indirectly influence the degree to which administrative agencies undertake their duties and responsibilities. One administration may not pursue environmental, antitrust, or international trade regulation as strongly as another administration. Thus, some businesses may face a more hostile legal environment under one administration and a more permissive one under another.

INTERNATIONAL SOURCES OF LAW

Companies conducting business in other countries must be as concerned with those countries' laws and regulations as with the U.S. domestic legal environment. The principal sources of international law affecting business include the laws of individual countries, the laws defined by treaties and trade agreements among countries, and the rules enacted by multinational regional or global entities—such as the World Trade Organization.

Article II, Section 2, of the U.S. Constitution requires approval by two-thirds of the Senate before a treaty (international agreement) executed by the president becomes binding on the U.S. government. Treaties of some significance to business include the United Nations Convention on Contracts for the International Sale of Goods (which can govern the sale of goods between parties from different countries) and the United Nations Convention on the Recognition and Enforcement of Foreign Arbitral Awards (which assists in the enforcement of arbitration clauses in international contracts). Treaties and other laws particular to the international legal environment are discussed in Chapter 21 and at various points in other chapters.

Classifications of Law

Law can be classified in several ways, such as whether it originated from a constitution, a legislative body, the judiciary, or the executive branch of government. The more common classification systems, however, classify law on the basis of whether it is public or private, civil or criminal, or procedural or substantive. Laws may fall into more than one classification. For example, the sale of automobile insurance is affected by private law (a contract between the company and the buyer) and public law (state regulation of insurance, which could result in civil or criminal penalties for insurance sellers who break state law).

PUBLIC AND PRIVATE LAW

Some examples of public and private law are provided in Exhibit 1.4. Public law is concerned with the legal relationship between members of society—businesses and individuals—and the government. Public law includes statutes enacted by Congress

EXHIBIT 1.4

Examples of Public and Private Law

Public Law	Private Law
Administrative Law	Agency Law
Antitrust Law	Contract Law
Constitutional Law	Corporation Law
Criminal Law	Partnership Law
Environmental Law	Personal Property
Labor Law	Real Property
Securities Regulation	Torts

Sources of Law in Japan

 The various legal systems from around the world can be placed into groups or "families" based on similarities in structure and substance. The legal system of the United States and most other English-speaking countries belongs to the family of legal systems based on the common law, discussed earlier in this chapter. Another family would include the *religious law* traditions—Islam and Judaism.

The largest family includes countries that follow a *civil-law* approach. In this group are the countries of Western Europe (France, Germany, Italy, and Spain) and of Eastern Europe (Poland and Hungary). Civil law has been adopted in countries in Latin America, Africa, and parts of the Middle East.

An important member of the civil-law family is Japan, which adopted much of the German civil-law legal system in the late 1800s to be more attractive to Western businesses. Like its civil-law counterparts, Japan's basic source of law is its codes. In contrast to common-law systems where many basic laws are developed by judges, civil-law codes are enacted by the government—in Japan, the Diet, or national parliament. The codes arrange categories of law in an orderly and comprehensive way. In Japan, the basic codes are the Civil Code, the Commercial Code, the Penal Code, and Procedural Codes such as the Code of Criminal Procedure and the Code of Civil Procedure.

To illustrate, under common law, judges have developed rules in tort law imposing liability for intentional and negligent acts. Article 709 of the Japanese Civil Code is quite similar. It states:

> A person who violates intentionally or negligently the right of another is bound to make compensation for damages (for injuries to the person, his liberty, or reputation as well as his property) arising therefrom.

The Japanese courts apply codes very strictly. The application of a code provision to a dispute is influenced by past applications, particularly those of the highest courts. Because the Japanese rely more on informal dispute resolution, many parts of the codes have not been litigated. In such situations, Japanese lawyers rely on interpretations of the codes by legal scholars. If no specific code provision applies to a dispute that has arisen, the court may look to traditions and equity in reaching a decision, or it may apply a code provision intended to apply to another type of dispute. Through this process—and the enactment of new code provisions by the Diet—Japan's civil-law legal system adjusts to societal and technological changes.

and state legislatures and regulations issued by administrative agencies. It influences the behavior of members of society and brings about social change.

Private law sets forth rules governing the legal relationships among members of society. It helps to resolve disputes and to provide a way for the values and customs of society to influence law. Private law is primarily common law and is enforced primarily through the state court systems. Unlike public law, which at times makes major changes in legal rules, private law tends to be quite stable and changes slowly.

CIVIL AND CRIMINAL LAW

When a legislative body enacts a law, it decides whether the law is to be civil, criminal, or both. Unless a statute is designated as criminal, it is considered civil law. Examples of civil and criminal law are provided in Exhibit 1.5.

Criminal law concerns legal wrongs or crimes committed against the government. As determined by federal or state statute, a crime is classified as a *felony* or a *misdemeanor.* A person found guilty of a criminal offense may be fined, imprisoned,

	Civil Law	Criminal Law
EXHIBIT 1.5 *Examples of Civil and Criminal Law*	**Contract Law** Auto Repairs Buying Airline Tickets Forming a Business Sale of Clothing House Insurance **Tort Law** Assault and Battery Defamation Invasion of Privacy Strict Liability Trespass	**Misdemeanor Offenses** Assault and Battery (Simple) Disturbing the Peace Larceny (Petit) Public Intoxication Trespass **Felony Offenses** Burglary Homicide Larceny (Grand) Manslaughter Robbery

or both. To find a person guilty of a crime, the trial court must find that the evidence presented showed *beyond a reasonable doubt* that the person committed the crime. The severity of punishment depends in part on whether the offense was a felony or a misdemeanor. Generally, those offenses punishable by imprisonment for more than a year are classified as felonies. Misdemeanors are generally less serious crimes, punishable by a fine and/or imprisonment for less than a year.

The objective of criminal law is to punish the wrongdoer for violating the rules of society. Although the victim may have been killed, injured, or otherwise wronged because of the criminal act of the wrongdoer, criminal law is not designed to provide restitution for the victim of the crime. Individual restitution is a matter for civil law.

Civil law is concerned with the rights and responsibilities that exist among members of society or between individuals and the government in noncriminal matters. A person or business found liable for a *civil wrong* may be required to pay money damages to the injured party or to do or refrain from doing a specific act or

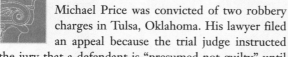

JURIS prudence?

Say What?

Michael Price was convicted of two robbery charges in Tulsa, Oklahoma. His lawyer filed an appeal because the trial judge instructed the jury that a defendant is "presumed not guilty" until proven guilty. What the judge should have said is that a defendant is "presumed innocent" until proven guilty. Price's two sixteen-year sentences were overturned, and a new trial was ordered.

Properly charged, the jury in the second trial understood that Price was "presumed innocent" until they found him guilty. Price was found guilty and sentenced to two thirty-year terms.

Source: *Tulsa World* (Ok.)

EXHIBIT 1.6		
Examples of Substantive and Procedural Law	**Substantive Law**	**Procedural Law**
	Antitrust Law	Administrative Procedure
	Contract Law	Appellate Procedure
	Criminal Law	Civil Procedure
	Environmental Law	Court Orders
	Labor Law	Criminal Procedure
	Securities Regulation	Rules of Evidence

both. In finding the wrongdoer liable, the jury (or the judge in a nonjury trial) must find that the *preponderance* (majority) *of the evidence* favored the injured party.

SUBSTANTIVE AND PROCEDURAL LAW

Substantive law includes common law and statutory law that define and establish legal rights and regulate behavior. *Procedural law* determines how substantive law is enforced through the courts by determining how a lawsuit begins, what documents need to be filed, which court can hear the case, how the trial proceeds, and so on. A criminal case, for example, must follow criminal procedural law. The appropriate appellate procedure must be followed when a lower-court decision is appealed to a higher court for review. Similarly, agencies enforcing administrative laws and regulations must follow appropriate procedures. While most of our focus will be on substantive law, it is important to keep in mind that proper procedure must be followed by all participants in the formal legal system. Examples of substantive and procedural laws are provided in Exhibit 1.6.

Ethics and Business

The public image of business has been slipping since the 1960s. According to a poll conducted in 1966, 55 percent of the American people had a "great deal of confidence" in American business executives. In recent years, that percentage has dropped to about 20 percent. Surveys indicate that confidence in business leaders is low—especially with regard to honesty and ethical standards. (Confidence in political leaders and institutions is even lower.)

One possible explanation is that personal and corporate ethical standards have fallen. Stories of insider trading, product-content deceptions, bribery, pollution, and other business misconduct can be seen as confirmation of the public perception. But it is more likely that some of the decline in image is due to increased concern about ethical issues by the public. The public simply expects more from business now than it did in the past.

PERCEPTIONS OF ETHICS AND RESPONSES

In response to declining public image and real internal problems, most corporations now have written codes of ethics. But studies indicate that the development of corporate codes of ethics has done little to improve corporate culture. Professor William Frederick found that corporations with codes of ethics were cited for legal infractions by federal regulatory agencies more frequently than corporations without codes. In corporations making a special effort to improve corporate ethics by

Provisions Usually Included in Codes	Frequency	Provisions Usually Excluded from Codes	Frequency
Relations with Government	86.6%	Personal Characteristics	93.6%
Customer/Supplier Relations	86.1	Product Safety	91.0
Political Contributions	84.7	Environmental Affairs	87.1
Conflicts of Interest	75.3	Product Quality	78.7
Honest Records	75.3	Civic Affairs	75.2

Source: Marilynn Cash Matthews, Washington State University

EXHIBIT 1.7

A Survey of Company Codes of Ethics

placing more people asserted to have a socially conscious perspective on their boards of directors, relatively little change in the corporate culture was found.

Exhibit 1.7 summarizes the results of a codes-of-ethics survey of 202 large companies. As the exhibit illustrates, the provisions most commonly included emphasize improving the "bottom line"—relations with the government, customer/supplier relations, and conflicts of interest. Most of the codes of ethics surveyed failed to mention product safety, environmental concerns, and product quality.

Many companies now hire ethics specialists in an effort to improve their practices and public perceptions about them. Managers are increasingly provided with incentives to be more concerned about ethics and to comply with company codes of conduct. Several major forces are at work that contribute to the push for changes in corporate culture:

- Pressure comes from changes in management structure. As companies become less hierarchical, they place more emphasis on shared responsibility or teamwork, increasing the incentives for managers to monitor each other's actions, since all can be held responsible, rather than let blame fall on one person in the chain of command. On the other hand, many employees have learned that corporate loyalty to employees is weak when it is time to reorganize or downsize.
- Pressure comes from the U.S. Sentencing Guidelines, which are followed by federal judges when they assess fines and prison sentences for violation of federal laws. Punishment is reduced if a company can show that it has an in-house program to comply with the law. That is, evidence of serious effort by a company to have the organization obey the law and behave ethically (such as cooperate voluntarily in investigations) reduces punishment when violations occur.
- Pressure comes from the boards of directors. A survey of more than 700 corporate directors showed that the top reasons for dismissal of a company president are financial malfeasance (95 percent agree) and ethical or moral malfeasance (94 percent agree), compared to just one percent stating that they would fire a president for earning lower than expected profits in any given year.

ETHICS AND MORALS: DEFINITIONS AND APPLICATIONS

When considering standards of behavior, a distinction can be made between morals and ethics. The term *morals* refers to generally accepted standards of right and wrong in a society. The term *ethics* refers to more abstract concepts that might be encountered in the study of the standards of right and wrong in philosophy and theology. For purposes of our practical discussion of business, the terms *morals* and *ethics* are interchangeable.

Morals and ethics should not be confused with etiquette or good manners. Since statements about either can use terms such as *should* or *ought*, this confusion is tempting. A person may say, "You should not slurp your soup," or "You ought to introduce yourself when you enter a home for a party." While these statements prescribe conduct just as ethical statements do, they are considered part of good manners, not moral or ethical behavior. Morals and ethics are more important than etiquette. Most of us would take a violation of a rule such as "You should not lie to your father" as more serious than a violation of a rule such as "You should compliment your host after a good dinner."

Ethics and the Law Compared

Moral and ethical statements should not be confused with rules of law. The fact that an action is legal does not mean that it is moral and ethical. Suppose management is informed that the company is emitting a toxic pollutant into the atmosphere. The pollutant is not regulated, so no law is being violated. Company scientists believe the pollutant will eventually cause health problems. Should management decide to stop emitting the pollutant? Should it wait until the government makes the emission illegal? Just because emitting the pollutant is legal does not make it moral and ethical.

Questions about legality and morality are not necessarily the same. The court faces this issue in the *Soldano* case. The plaintiff asserts that if the defendant had acted, a life would have been saved. Although the defendant's refusal to act may have been unethical or immoral, the court is asked to decide whether it was illegal.

Soldano v. O'Daniels
California Court of Appeal
141 Cal.App.3d 443, 190 Cal.Rptr. 310 (1983)

CASE BACKGROUND *Villanueva entered Happy Jack's Saloon, pulled a gun, and threatened to kill Soldano. A patron of Happy Jack's ran across the street to a bar called the Circle Inn, told the bartender (the defendant) about the incident at Happy Jack's, and asked the bartender to call the police or allow him to make the call. The bartender refused. Soldano was killed by Villanueva. Soldano's child (the plaintiff) brought a wrongful death action against the bartender.*

On the grounds that a person cannot be liable for nonactions, the trial court dismissed the plaintiff's action. The plaintiff appealed to the court of appeal, arguing that the case should have been allowed to go to trial.

CASE DECISION Andreen, Associate Justice.

* * *

Does a business establishment incur liability for wrongful death if it denies use of its telephone to a good samaritan who explains an emergency situation occurring without and wishes to call the police?

* * *

There is a distinction, well rooted in the common law, between action and nonaction. It has found its way into the prestigious *Restatement Second of Torts* (hereafter cited as "*Restatement*"), which provides in section 314:

> The fact that the actor realizes or should realize that action on his part is necessary for another's aid or protection does not of itself impose upon him a duty to take such action.

The distinction between . . . active misconduct [causing] injury and failure to act to prevent [injury] not brought on by the defendant, is founded on "that attitude of extreme individualism so typical of anglo-saxon legal thought."

Defendant argues that the request that its employee call the police is a request that it do something. He points to the *established rule* that one who has not created a peril ordinarily does not have a duty to take affirmative action to assist an imperiled person. It is urged that the alternative request of the patron from Happy Jack's Saloon that he be allowed to use defendant's telephone so that he personally could make the call is again a request that the defendant do something—assist another to give aid. Defendant points out that the *Restatement* sections which impose liability for negligent interference with a third person giving aid to another do not impose the additional duty to aid the good samaritan.

The refusal of the law to recognize the moral obligation of one to aid another when he is in peril and when such aid may be given without danger and at little cost in effort has been roundly criticized. Prosser describes the case law sanctioning such inaction as a "refus(al) to recognize the moral obligation of common decency and common humanity" and characterizes some of these decisions as "shocking in the extreme. . . . Such decisions are revolting to any moral sense. They have been denounced with vigor by legal writers." A similar rule has been termed "morally questionable" by our Supreme Court. . . . It is time to re-examine the common law rule of nonliability for [nonaction] in the special circumstances of the instant case.

* * *

The employee's conduct displayed a disregard for human life that can be characterized as morally wrong (Footnote 9. The moral right of plaintiff's decedent to have the defendant's bartender permit the telephone call is so apparent that legal philosophers treat such rights as given and requiring no supporting argument. The concept flows from the principle that each member of a community has a right to have each other member treat him with the minimal respect due a fellow human being): he was callously indifferent to the possibility that Darrell Soldano would die as the result of his refusal to allow a person to use the telephone. Under the circumstances before us the bartender's

burden was minimal and exposed him to no risk: all he had to do was allow the use of the telephone. It would have cost him or his employer nothing. It could have saved a life. Finding a duty in these circumstances would promote a policy of preventing future harm. A citizen would not be required to summon the police but would be required, in circumstances such as those before us, not to impede another who has chosen to summon aid.

* * *

The words of the Supreme Court on the role of the courts in a common law system are well suited to our obligation here:

> The inherent capacity of the common law for growth and change is its most significant feature. Its development has been determined by the social needs of the community which it serves. It is constantly expanding and developing in keeping with advancing civilization and the new conditions and progress of society, and adapting itself to the gradual change of trade, commerce, arts, inventions, and the needs of the country. . . .

In short, as the United States Supreme Court has aptly said, "This flexibility and capacity for growth and adaptation is the peculiar boast and excellence of the common law."

* * *

The possible imposition of liability on the defendant in this case is not a global change in the law. It is but a slight departure from the "morally questionable" rule of nonliability for inaction absent a special relationship. It is one of the predicted "inroads upon the older rule.". . . However small it may be it is a step which should be taken.

We conclude that there are sufficient justiciable issues to permit the case to go to trial and therefore reverse.

QUESTIONS FOR ANALYSIS

1. Under the "established rule," was the bartender obligated to provide assistance? Is the established rule overly broad?
2. What factors motivated the court to modify the established rule in this case?

Just as legality does not imply morality, illegality does not always imply immorality. The fact that an action is illegal does not necessarily mean it is immoral or unethical. If the speed limit is 65 mph, is it unethical to go 68 mph? The moral status of the civil rights activities of the 1960s is not settled by the fact that some of those activities were illegal. In his *Letter from Birmingham Jail*, Martin Luther King, Jr., said, "I can urge [people] to disobey segregation ordinances, for the [ordinances] are morally wrong."

Laws designed to restrict opportunities for minorities were common until the time of the civil rights movement. The moral force used to oppose those laws was a key reason many of the laws were stricken and segregation was declared illegal. However, some laws remain on the books that restrict economic opportunities. For example, the Davis-Bacon Act, passed in the 1930s, requires building contractors in projects receiving federal money to pay "prevailing wages." In practice, prevailing wages is union scale. The Davis-Bacon Act was passed by northern members of Congress who had strong union support and members of Congress from southern states. Northern all-white unions did not like the competition from building contractors who hired blacks who were willing to do the jobs for lower wages to get out of the rural South. African-Americans were glad to get out of the South and have economic opportunities in the North. Southern politicians did not want blacks to leave the South because it reduced the supply of black farm workers. The Act is still law and still reduces economic opportunities for new entrants into the construction industry, often nonunion minorities who would like to compete for government contracts. Can such restrictions on economic competition be justified as moral, even though clearly legal?

Should the courts uphold laws that produce immoral results? In the *Soldano* case we saw a moral problem caused by a legal rule that affects decisions of private citizens. What about statutes that produce immoral results? If the statutes do not violate constitutional rights, the courts tend to leave them alone. Otherwise, judges become legislators. Consider the ethical aspects of the issues raised in the *Stanley* case.

United States v. Stanley
United States Supreme Court
483 U.S. 669, 107 S.Ct. 3054 (1987)

CASE BACKGROUND *Stanley was an Army sergeant who volunteered in 1958 to participate in a program he was told would test the effectiveness of protective clothing against chemical warfare. The volunteers, unknown to them, were given doses of LSD. The Army wanted to test the effects of that drug. For years afterward, Stanley suffered hallucinations, memory loss, and periods of incoherence; could not work well; and on occasion would "awake from sleep at night and . . . violently beat his wife and children, later being unable to recall the entire incident." Stanley left the Army in 1969 and was divorced. In 1975, the Army contacted him and asked him to cooperate in a study of the long-term effects of LSD*

on "volunteers" from the 1958 test. That was the first time Stanley knew he had been given the drug.

Stanley sued the Army for compensation, but the claim was denied. Stanley then filed suit under the Federal Tort Claims Act. The district court ruled for the government because Stanley "was at all times on active duty and participating in a bona fide Army program during the time the alleged negligence occurred. . . . [T]he government is not liable under the Federal Tort Claims Act for injuries to servicemen where the injuries arise out of or are in the court of activity incident to service." The court of appeals upheld this judgment. Stanley appealed.

CASE DECISION Scalia, Justice.

* * *

. . . [T]he Constitution explicitly conferred upon Congress the power . . . "[t]o make Rules for the Government and Regulation of the land and naval Forces," U.S. Const. Art. I, §8, cl. 14, thus showing that "the Constitution contemplated that the Legislative Branch have plenary control over rights, duties, and responsibilities in the framework of the Military Establishment. . . ."

[The dismissal of Stanley's claim was upheld; he had no case under the Federal Tort Claims Act or under the laws written by Congress concerning the rights of members of the Armed Forces.]

* * *

Justice Brennan . . . dissenting in part.

In experiments designed to test the effects of lysergic acid diethylamide (LSD), the Government of the United States treated thousands of its citizens as though they were laboratory animals, dosing them with this dangerous drug without their consent. One of the victims, James B. Stanley, seeks compensation from the Government officials who injured him. The Court holds that the Constitution provides him with no remedy, solely because his injuries were inflicted while he performed his duties in the Nation's Armed Forces. If our Constitution required this result, the Court's decision, though legally necessary, would expose a tragic flaw in that document. . . .

Before addressing the legal questions presented, it is important to place the Government's conduct in historical context. The medical trials at Nuremberg in 1947 deeply impressed upon the world that experimentation with unknowing human subjects is morally and legally unacceptable. The United States Military Tribunal established the Nuremberg Code as a standard against which to judge German scientists who experimented with human subjects. Its first principle was:

"1. *The voluntary consent of the human subject is absolutely essential.*

"The duty and responsibility for ascertaining the quality of the consent rests upon *each individual* who initiates, directs or engages in the experiment. *It is a personal duty and responsibility which may not be delegated to another with impunity.*" *United States* v. *Brandt* (The Medical Case), 2 Trials of War Criminals Before the Nuremberg Military Tribunals Under Control Council Law No. 10, pp. 181–182 (1949) (emphasis added).

The United States military developed the Code, which applies to all citizens—soldiers as well as civilians. . . .

Having invoked national security to conceal its actions, the Government now argues that the preservation of military discipline requires that Government officials remain free to violate the constitutional rights of soldiers without fear of money damages. What this case and others like it demonstrate, however, is that Government officials (military or civilian) must not be left with such freedom. . . .

* * *

[Brennan argued that Stanley should be allowed to sue the officers who conducted the experiments, but not the U.S. government.]

QUESTIONS FOR ANALYSIS

1. A report issued by Congress expressed outrage at what had happened. Besides express outrage, what else could Congress have done?
2. Brennan would give Stanley the right to sue the people in charge of the experiment but not the right to sue the government. Details of the legal rules aside, is that decision more moral than the one to give Stanley no cause of action?
3. Should the courts be in the business of applying ethical principles rather than enforcing laws held to be constitutional?

Corporate Social Responsibility

The debate over corporate ethics often focuses on corporate social responsibility. Are corporations the kinds of entities that can be praised or blamed for their actions much like people are praised or blamed? Corporations exhibit "behavior" that resembles that of people: they pay taxes, enter into legal arrangements, exercise certain rights of freedom of speech, and own property. On the other hand, unlike people, corporations are strictly liable for the injuries caused by their products, do not have the right to vote, and are artificial entities created and destroyed by contract. So, while corporations are not real persons, are they moral agents in the sense of being entities that can be held morally accountable for their actions?

ARE CORPORATIONS MORAL AGENTS? NO

Philosopher John Ladd argues that corporations are not moral agents that can be held morally accountable for their actions. Ladd holds that corporations are controlled by their structures. Corporations can act only in accordance with specified organizational goals. In the case of a corporation, those goals include the company's survival and growth.

According to Ladd, an organization is "rational" when it works to achieve its goals. Morals are relevant insofar as they relate to the organization's goals. Thus, if the public finds a television commercial sponsored by a corporation morally offensive, the corporation might decide to eliminate the commercial. The reason, however, would be that the commercial might result in a boycott of company products and a reduction in profits—not because the company has moral ideals.

Ladd concludes that organizations with "formal structures" cannot have moral obligations and hence "cannot have moral responsibilities in the sense of having obligations towards those affected by their actions or subject to their actions. . . . Organizations have tremendous power, but no responsibilities." Thus, corporations cannot govern themselves by moral principles but must be controlled by law. The government must see to it that corporations do not act in a way that is detrimental to society.

ARE CORPORATIONS MORAL AGENTS? YES

Many writers do not accept the view that the corporate structure precludes moral responsibility. Ethical principles can be corporate goals—along with self-preservation and profit. Many corporate policy statements include moral objectives. It is possible that such statements are only window dressing and do not express operating policy. But the presence of such statements suggests that corporations can be morally responsible.

Philosopher Kenneth Goodpaster provides support for the view that it makes sense to attribute moral responsibility to corporations. Goodpaster isolates four elements of moral responsibility—perception, moral reasoning, coordination, and implementation—and finds analogies to each of them in corporate life.

Perception
Rational decision making begins with a moral agent's perception of his or her environment. Corporations exhibit this characteristic when they gather information before making a decision. There is no reason executives cannot take into account the moral as well as the economic and legal dimensions of a decision.

Moral Reasoning
A moral agent must be able to move from assumptions to conclusions about what ought to be done. Similarly, a corporation's managers and directors can weigh alternatives with attention to such considerations as injustice to employees or the community.

Coordination

A moral agent integrates the moral evaluation with various nonmoral considerations, such as self-interest, the law, economics, and politics. A corporation can engage in similar deliberations. Goodpaster believes that this is where considerable moral failure occurs in corporate life. Corporations often trade moral for nonmoral considerations and end up in undesirable moral compromises. In the *Grimshaw* case, did the management of Ford Motor trade safety for the cost savings imposed by fuel-efficient imports in its inexpensive Pinto?

Grimshaw v. Ford Motor Company
California Court of Appeals
119 Cal.App.3d 757, 174 Cal.Rptr. 348 (1981)

CASE BACKGROUND *The plaintiffs, Grimshaw and the heirs of Lilly Gray, brought a product liability action against Ford Motor. The Grays bought a Ford Pinto hatchback. Six months and 3,000 miles later, the car stalled on a freeway, was struck in the rear by another car, and burst into flames. Lilly Gray, the driver, died as a result of burns from the accident. Grimshaw, a passenger, suffered burns over his body.*

Ford had done cost-benefit analyses before marketing the Pinto. The costs of redesigning the fuel tank had been weighed against possible liability if the design remained unchanged. Management decided that the cost of the change would exceed the liability costs likely to arise from accidents. On that basis, the Pinto was sold without the safety features that the plaintiffs alleged could have prevented their injuries.

The jury awarded more than $3 million in compensatory and $125 million in punitive damages. Although the punitive damages were reduced by the trial judge to $3.5 million, Ford appealed, arguing that the punitive damages awarded were excessive.

CASE DECISION Tamura, Judge.

* * *

Ordinarily marketing surveys and preliminary engineering studies precede the styling of a new automobile line. Pinto, however, was a rush project, so that styling preceded engineering and dictated engineering design to a greater degree than usual. Among the engineering decisions dictated by styling was the placement of the fuel tank. It was then the preferred practice in Europe and Japan to locate the gas tank over the rear axle in subcompacts because a small vehicle has less "crush space" between the rear axle and the bumper than larger cars. The Pinto's styling, however, required the tank to be placed behind the rear axle leaving only 9 or 10 inches of "crush space," far less than in any other American automobile or overseas subcompact. In addition, the Pinto was designed so that its bumper was little more than a chrome strip, less substantial than the bumper of any other American car produced. The Pinto's rear structure also lacked reinforcing members . . . [making] the Pinto less crush resistant than other vehicles. Finally, the differential housing selected for the Pinto had an exposed flange and a line of exposed bolt heads. These protrusions were sufficient to puncture a gas tank driven forward against the differential upon rear impact.

* * *

When a prototype failed the fuel system integrity test, the standard of care for engineers in the industry was to redesign and retest it. The vulnerability of the production Pinto's fuel tank at speeds of 20 and 30-miles-per-hour fixed barrier tests could have been remedied by inexpensive "fixes," but Ford produced and sold the Pinto to the public without doing anything to remedy the defects. Design changes [could have been implemented] that would have enhanced the integrity of the fuel tank system at relatively little cost per car. . . . Equipping the car with a reinforced rear structure, smooth axle, improved bumper and additional crush space at a total cost of $15.30 would have made the fuel tank safe in a 34 to 38-mile-per-hour rear end collision.

* * *

Harley Copp, a former Ford engineer and executive in charge of the crash testing program, testified that the highest level of Ford's management made the decision to go forward with the production of the Pinto, knowing that the gas tank was vulnerable to puncture and rupture at low rear impact speeds creating a significant risk of death or injury from fire and knowing that "fixes" were feasible at nominal cost. He testified that management's decision was based on the cost savings which would inure from omitting or delaying the "fixes."

* * *

Through the results of the crash tests Ford knew that the Pinto's fuel tank and rear structure would expose consumers to serious injury or death in a 20 to 30-mile-per-hour collision. There was evidence that Ford could have corrected the hazardous design defects at minimal cost but decided to defer correction of the shortcomings by engaging in a cost-benefit analysis balancing human lives and limbs against corporate profits. Ford's institutional mentality was shown to be one of callous indifference to public safety. There was substantial evidence that Ford's conduct constituted "conscious disregard" of the probability of injury to members of the consuming public. . . .

There is substantial evidence that management was aware of the crash tests showing the vulnerability of the Pinto's fuel tank to rupture at low speed rear impacts with consequent significant risk of injury or death of the occupants by fire. There was testimony from several sources that the test results were forwarded up the chain of command. . . . While much of the evidence was necessarily circumstantial, there was substantial evidence from which the jury could reasonably find that Ford's management decided to proceed with the production of the Pinto with knowledge of test results revealing design defects which rendered the fuel tank extremely vulnerable on rear impact at low speeds and endangered the safety and lives of the occupants. Such conduct constitutes corporate malice.

* * *

[The court of appeals affirmed the trial court's ruling.]

QUESTIONS FOR ANALYSIS

1. What was the court's principal objection to Ford's decision-making process?
2. Has the court found all managerial trade-offs between safety and profits to constitute "corporate malice"? If not, when does corporate malice begin? Would it differ by industry?
3. Suppose the Pinto could be designed to withstand a 60-mph impact but the design would greatly increase its price. Thus, the auto would become safer for those who could afford it but deprive others who could not afford the auto of its useful benefits. Would consumers be willing to pay a lower price for less safety equipment and accept more of the risk of accidents? Should they be allowed to do so?

Implementation

A moral agent carries out a decision by understanding the environment, implementing the strategy, and guiding it toward realization. A corporation can implement its decisions in a similar way.

Since the decision-making process used by corporations is strongly analogous to that of morally responsible agents, Goodpaster concludes that there is nothing illogical about holding corporations morally responsible. The question now arises: What should corporate moral responsibilities include?

CORPORATE RESPONSIBILITY: THE NARROW VIEW

One view of corporate responsibility is called the *narrow* or the *agents-of-capital view*. According to Nobel laureate Milton Friedman, perhaps the best-known advocate of the narrow view, the social responsibility of business executives (and hence of a corporation) is "to make as much money as possible while conforming to the basic rules of the society, both those embodied in law and those embodied in ethical custom."

The Self-Interest Motivation

Friedman believes that corporations often do things that have the appearance of altruism but are simply in their self-interest. A corporation might open a day-care center to improve the morale of employees or to attract a higher-quality work force. For similar reasons, it might improve safety in a factory beyond that required by law. Friedman asserts that management does these things when they are in the economic interest of shareholders.

Friedman argues that executives work for the shareholders. Since the corporate goal is to maximize profits over time, a management decision to spend shareholders' money for purposes other than meeting that goal is not justified. If management designates funds for other purposes, it is infringing on the rights of shareholders. If executives donate to the symphony in the city where the company is headquartered, does that benefit the company, or does it benefit the social status of the executives?

If shareholders and executives want to promote a social cause, they can make contributions out of the profits and salaries they receive from the corporation. In this way, they will honor their own moral agency without infringing on the rights of other shareholders, who either may not want to contribute to social causes or may want to contribute in a different way.

Friedman points out that corporate managers are not trained in social policy or elected to public office. Managers are not the best equipped people to deal with social problems. Further, social well-being can be effectively pursued if business does what it does best—provide goods and services and make a profit for its shareholders. This argument is the so-called invisible hand argument. Adam Smith, the eighteenth-century Scottish economist, maintained that when people are left to pursue their economic self-interest, they produce more good for society than when they are motivated by claiming altruistic concerns. According to Smith in *The Wealth of Nations:*

> It is not from the benevolence of the butcher, the brewer, or the baker that we expect our dinner, but from their regard for their own interests. Following their own interests, it is as if they were led by an invisible hand to produce greater overall utility.

CORPORATE RESPONSIBILITY: THE BROAD VIEW

In contrast to Friedman, Melvin Anshen maintains that there is a "social contract" between business and society. This contract represents an implicit understanding of the proper goals and responsibilities of business. In the nineteenth century, the major social goal was rapid economic growth. Accordingly, the function of business was to promote growth in an atmosphere of unfettered competition and minimal government regulation. Today, society has concerns beyond economic growth, particularly regarding the quality of life and the integrity of the environment. Anshen asserts that the social contract between business and society has changed and the narrow view of corporate responsibility is no longer appropriate.

Professor Keith Davis agrees: "One basic proposition is that social responsibility arises from social power." The economic and political power of corporations means that the actions of corporations vitally "affect the interests of others." In a speech to the Harvard Business School, Henry Ford II stated a similar idea:

> The terms of the contract between industry and society are changing. . . . Now we are being asked to serve a wider range of human values and to

What Does Business Do When a Government Is Immoral?

 China, like a number of other nations in Asia, Africa, and the Middle East, is controlled by a government that is basically immoral. Harry Wu, a research fellow at Stanford's Hoover Institution, spent twenty years in prison labor camps in China for his political activities. He estimates that millions of people are imprisoned in labor camps, many for political "crimes." Prisoners face torture and very harsh working and living conditions, sometimes making products for government-controlled operations that are used in joint ventures with U.S. firms. Chrysler denies that prison products are being used in its Beijing Jeep plant, but human rights advocates say there is good evidence of the practice.

Levi-Strauss and Timberland both stopped producing products in China (and other countries) because of human rights abuses. Other companies operate in China and claim that by acting ethically they will lead by example. The major drawback to progress is that the Chinese government is entangled in business and is at the root of corruption. To operate, one must deal with corrupt authorities.

A terrible paradox is presented. By working with a corrupt government, companies are given legitimacy and revenues. Withdrawal from the market reduces the chances for economic advancement by ordinary people. Orville Schell, a fellow at the Freedom Forum at Columbia University, notes, "Only the rule of law keeps state enterprises from riding roughshod over people in business. Without protection of individual rights, you can't protect business."

Source: *Business Ethics*

accept an obligation to members of the public with whom we have no commercial transactions.

The "Social Contract"

If one believes that a social contract exists, then individuals are obligated to respect equally the rights of all people and should agree to have their less-basic rights infringed to protect the more-basic rights of others. An example of this can be found in the *Soldano* case. Most would agree that the defendant had an obligation to help by at least allowing his phone to be used to call the police. His obligation grows out of the fact that he may have saved a life with little cost to himself. Similarly, perhaps corporations should be morally obligated to assist in solving social problems—if they can do so with relatively little infringement on their own general well-being.

According to Adam Smith's invisible-hand argument, corporations can contribute more to the public good if left to do what they do best, namely make a profit within the bounds of the law and basic moral guidelines. Critics of the narrow view cite a number of problems.

First, business will try to pass off some of its costs to the general public. These costs (called "externalities" by economists) are evident in the area of the environment.

Second, it is argued that the quality of life for employees and the community can erode if the narrow view is embraced. For example, a corporation will improve working conditions for its employees only when it is in its self-interest to do so. It will be concerned with product safety only when the law or competitive conditions force it to do so.

Third, if the narrow view is followed by corporations, laws may be passed to force "corporate responsibility." Laws often do not apply well to novel or particular circumstances. Once in place, laws may not change with the times and can cause inefficiency.

THINKING ABOUT CORPORATE RESPONSIBILITY

The debate about the extent of corporate responsibility continues. Business is expected to be more active in carrying out social responsibilities and to be more assertive in seeking changes in the political and social environments. "Public interest" representatives are being placed on corporate boards of directors to help review management decisions. Codes of conduct and corporate policy statements are being developed and promoted to clarify what is ethical activity within the corporation.

However, it is generally agreed that improving corporate social responsibility ultimately depends upon changing something much more nebulous. This usually goes under the title of "corporate culture" and refers to the values and attitudes that pervade the corporate workplace, which reflects society in general. But corporate culture is also set by top management and boards of directors. Encouraging future managers and board members to think clearly about ethical issues is one way to ensure their support.

Summary

- The modern environment of business means that managers in all firms face a variety of ethical, legal, social, political, and international issues that make business increasingly complex.
- Law is a collection of principles and rules that establish, guide, and alter the behavior of members of society. Rules include both the formal rules (law) of society and the informal rules as dictated by customs, traditions, and social ethics.
- Law and the legal system serve important functions in an orderly society. Law helps to define acceptable behavior. To ensure order, the legal system provides a formal means through which disputes can be resolved. The law maintains the important values of a society. Finally, the legal system provides a way to encourage changes in social consciousness.
- Judge-made or common law is the original source of law in this country. Derived from English common law, our common-law system encourages judges to use prior decisions—precedents—for guidance in deciding new disputes.
- Other sources of law include the U.S. and state constitutions, Congress and the state legislatures, the judiciary, the executive branch (the President at the federal level and the governors at the state level), state and federal administrative agencies, and multiple sources that form the international legal environment of business.
- Law can be classified on the basis of whether it is public or private, civil or criminal, or substantive or procedural.
- Over the past thirty years, the public image of business and of other institutions has declined. Dishonesty is believed to be more prevalent than it was in years past. To overcome real and perceived problems, the business community is encouraging codes of ethics.

- The terms *ethics* and *morals* are generally interchangeable. These terms should not be confused with statements about etiquette or good manner or with rules of law.
- The responsibilities of corporations beyond those required by law and by the profit motivations of their shareholders have been heavily debated. Some scholars assert that corporations are not moral agents and thus cannot have moral responsibilities. Others assert that corporate life has all the elements of moral responsibility and corporations should therefore be considered as moral agents.
- The two competing theories of social responsibility are the agents-of-capital view and the social contract view. The agents-of-capital (narrow) view asserts that the corporation has the responsibility to maximize profits while conforming to the rules of society. Under the social contract (broad) theory, it is claimed that society has moved beyond an emphasis on economic growth so that corporations should now focus more on quality of life and environmental concerns.

Issue

Should Firms Constantly Bend to Political Pressures?

The opportunity to do business in other countries can mean not only adjusting to other sets of laws, but also adjusting to local political sensitivities. Many countries are run by regimes that make it clear that certain topics should be avoided to get along in the country. Apple Computer changed an ad campaign in Asia to avoid possibly offending Chinese government officials over the issue of repression in Tibet. The author questions the trade-off of ethics and profit opportunities.

APPLE SHOULD 'THINK DIFFERENT' ABOUT ASIA

Michael Judge

Mr. Judge is an editorial page writer for *The Asian Wall Street Journal*. Reprinted by permission of *The Wall Street Journal* © 1998 Dow Jones & Company, Inc. All rights reserved worldwide.

After days of prevarication, Apple Computer finally came clean last week about why it dropped the Dalai Lama's picture from the Asian edition of its "Think Different" advertising campaign. In an attempt to associate itself with historical figures who triumphed against the odds, the company put together a medley of "great thinker" portraits, and the version running in the U.S. and Aus-

tralia includes the Tibetan spiritual leader alongside such figures as Alfred Hitchcock and Pablo Picasso. What began Apple's PR fiasco was the decision to purge the Dalai Lama from its Asian edition, where he will be replaced by the American aviator Amelia Earhart.

Apple's Asia-Pacific marketing director, Vincent Lum, first tried to explain away the decision by suggesting that Earhart is a more "easily recognized" figure in Asia—even though her sole connection to the region is that her plane plunged into the Pacific in 1937. When that explanation failed, the company fessed up. "Where there are political sensitivities, we did not want to offend anyone," said Sue Sara, a spokeswoman for Apple's Asia-Pacific division. "We needed to decide on images that were appropriate across the region."

So much for thinking different. Apparently the folks at Apple have been taking night classes at the Rupert Murdoch school of free speech. Lesson No. 1: Free speech is fine and dandy, unless it jeopardizes your access to a massive and potentially lucrative market. Apple's market share in China is negligible. It may have decided that ads featuring the Dalai Lama—whom Chinese officials once reviled as a "political insect" and recently compared to the Branch Davidian cult leader, David Koresh—would not be good for business.

But if there is anything more dispiriting than Apple's decision to pull the Dalai Lama ad, it is the company's decision to try to cash in on him in the first place. While Buddhism, Tibet and the Dalai Lama are the latest craze in advertising and Hollywood—witness "Little Buddha," "Seven Years in Tibet" and "Kundun"—they represent a way of life (and death) for millions of Asians, who take their faith and their struggle for freedom seriously. Apple's mistake was trying to hitch itself to a religious and political movement, mixing it indiscriminately with an American-style celebrity list.

While Apple's spin doctors were scrambling for excuses, many Asians were struggling to persuade China to amend its current Tibet policy. After meeting in Kyoto, Japan, this month with Buddhist leaders from 15 Asian countries to discuss ways to rejuvenate the ancient religion, the Dalai Lama called for a dialogue with China to reach a "mutually satisfactory agreement." Unlike the oversimplified slogan—"Free Tibet!"—emblazoned on the T-shirts and minds of U.S. undergraduates, the lama stated his case rationally and with great humility: "I am not seeking independence for Tibet," he told an audience of more than 700 in Tokyo. "I am just hoping for general autonomy."

Meanwhile, six Tibetan activists have been on a "death fast" in New Delhi since March 10 to protest Chinese repression in their homeland. The hunger strikers, led by 71-year-old Kun Sang, are demanding that the United Nations address the Tibet issue in the General Assembly, name a special envoy to Tibet and appoint a special representative to investigate human-rights violations in the country. China invaded Tibet in 1950, and the Communists have since destroyed most of its monasteries. Despite increased international "awareness," repression has intensified over the past year. More than 600 Tibetans are currently being detained for peacefully

advocating greater autonomy for Tibet. And there are widespread reports of political prisoners—Buddhist nuns among them—having died in Chinese jails, allegedly as a result of torture or negligence.

Earlier this month, Chinese dissident Wei Jingsheng voiced his support for the hunger strikers and appealed to the international community to support the Tibetan cause: "I fully support and respect their struggle for the rights of Tibetan people and the future of Tibet," said Mr. Wei, who understands the brutality of China's regime, having spent most of the past 18 years in prison before being feed in November and exiled to the U.S.

At the launch of the "Think Different" campaign, Steve Jobs, Apple's one-time boy wonder and current "interim" CEO, said, " 'Think Different' celebrates the soul of the Apple brand—that creative people with passion can change the world for the better." But by using a religious and political leader to sell computers, and then only where he is not a threat to the status quo, Apple runs the risk of rendering words like "soul," "creative" and "passion" meaningless. Perhaps Mr. Jobs and his friends at Apple should change the name of their latest ad campaign from "Think Different" to just plain "Think."

ISSUE QUESTIONS

1. Allowing free trade with countries that have poor records on human rights is controversial. Are companies that do business in such countries and change their ads and other activities so as to placate authorities acting in an unethical manner, or does trade lead to more freedom?

2. Suppose Apple had never used the Dalai Lama in any ads. Would anyone have ever known they wanted to avoid irritating Chinese government officials?

REVIEW AND DISCUSSION QUESTIONS

1. Define the following terms:

law	constitution
informal rules or principles	substantive law
common law	ethics
precedent	morals
stare decisis	corporate social responsibility

2. Compare and contrast the following:
   a. Civil law and criminal law
   b. Felony and misdemeanor
   c. Substantive law and procedural law
   d. Preponderance of the evidence and beyond a reasonable doubt
   e. Ethics and etiquette
   f. Ethics and the law
3. Should the common-law maxim "Ignorance of the law is no excuse" apply to a foreigner who does not speak English?

CASE QUESTIONS

4. Consider the following fact situation:
[T]he crew of an English yacht . . . were cast away in a storm on the high seas . . . and were compelled to put into an open boat belonging to the said yacht. That in this boat they had no supply of water and no supply of food. . . . That on the eighteenth day . . . they . . . suggested that one should be sacrificed to save the rest. . . . That next day . . . they . . . went to the boy . . . put a knife into his throat and killed him then and there; that the three men fed upon the body . . . of the boy for four days; that on the fourth day after the act had been committed the boat was picked up by a passing vessel, and [they] were rescued, still alive. . . . That they were carried to the port of Falmouth, and committed for trial . . . That if the men had not fed upon the body of the boy they would probably not have survived to be so picked up and rescued, but would within the four days have died of famine. That the boy, being in a much weaker condition, was likely to have died before them. . . . The real question in this case [is] whether killing under the conditions set forth . . . be or be not murder. [*Regina* v. *Dudley and Stephens*, 14 Queens Bench Division 273 (1884)] In deciding this case, what factors should the judge take into account?

5. The evidence is clear that smoking is a serious health hazard. Should cigarette manufacturers be liable for the serious illnesses and untimely deaths caused by their products—even though they post a warning on the package and consumers voluntarily assume the health risks by smoking? [*Cipollone* v. *Liggett Group, Inc.*, 644 F. Supp. 283 (D.N.J., 1986)]

6. Two eight-year-old boys were seriously injured when riding Honda mini-trail bikes provided by their parents. The boys were riding on public streets and ran a stop sign when they were hit by a truck. One boy was not wearing a helmet. The bikes had clear warning labels on the front stating that they were only for offroad use. The owner's manual was clear that the bikes were not to be used on public streets and that riders should wear helmets. The parents sued Honda. The supreme court of Washington said that there was one basic issue. "Is a manufacturer liable when children are injured while riding one of its mini-trail bikes on a public road in violation of manufacturer and parental warnings?" What do you think the court held? Is it unethical to make products like minibikes that will be used by children? [*Baughn* v. *Honda Motor Co.*, 727 P.2d 655 (Sup. Ct., Wash., 1986)]

7. In 1982, Johnson Controls adopted a "fetal protection policy" that women of childbearing age could not work in the battery-making division of the company. Exposure to lead in the battery operation could cause harm to unborn babies. The company was concerned about possible legal liability for injury suffered by babies

of mothers who had worked in the battery division. The Supreme Court held that the company policy was illegal. It was an "excuse for denying women equal employment opportunities." Is the Court forcing the company to be unethical by allowing pregnant women who ignore the warnings to expose their babies to the lead? [*United Auto Workers* v. *Johnson Controls*, 499 U.S. 187 (1991)]

POLICY QUESTION

8. Does the common law produce "better" law than that which would exist if only the Congress or the state legislatures were allowed to enact law?

ETHICS QUESTIONS

9. The local opera company visits your company's headquarters. It asks for a donation of $10,000, claiming that without such corporate support the opera will close. What factors do you consider in making a recommendation to your company about such a donation?

10. Migrant farm workers are at about the bottom of our employment force and quality-of-life standards. They work very hard, do not make much money, and live with their families in what are often miserable conditions. You run a large vegetable farm operation that hires migrant workers an average of four weeks per year. You pay the going wage rate for the workers, who rent dumps to live in while they work in your area before moving north. Do you have an ethical responsibility to pay more than the market wage so that these workers could live in better conditions? Do you have a responsibility to provide housing to the workers you employ? If you pay above-market rates, your neighbor farmers will be mad at you and point out that—as you know—most of the farm operations run on thin margins as it is, so that much higher wages could drive you all out of business. Assuming these to be facts, what responsibilities do you think you have? Closing the Mexican border will reduce the number of migrant workers, which will drive up the wage rate. The migrant workers in the United States will be better off, but those who used to cross from Mexico will be worse off. Is it ethical to close the border?

11. The ABC Company has been supplying widgets to your XYZ Company for many years. The widgets are needed in the production of gidgets. ABC has always been a fair company to deal with. When problems have arisen, ABC has usually resolved them to your satisfaction. Now the LMN firm from Singapore has approached you, saying it will provide widgets to you for 10 percent less than you were paying ABC. ABC tells you that there is no way it can cut its prices and, if you cut it off, it will have to pare back production so that fifty people will be fired. Should you stick with ABC to protect American jobs? What other considerations may be involved?

INTERNET ASSIGNMENT

Along with the executive and legislative branches, the federal judiciary is a constitutionally co-equal branch of the U.S. Government. The federal trial and appellate courts themselves are, in essence, the storefronts for the federal judiciary, the offices through which the courts provide dispute resolution services. Less well known are the various agencies, each created by statute, responsible for the managerial and administrative functions of the third branch. These agencies, known collectively as the National Agencies of Federal Judicial Administration, are:

(a) The Judicial Conference of the United States (28 U.S.C. §331),

(b) The Administrative Office of the U.S. Courts (28 U.S.C. §§601–612),

(c) The Judicial Councils of the Circuits (28 U.S.C. §332),

(d) The Judicial Conferences of the Circuits (28 U.S.C. §333), and

(e) The U.S. Sentencing Commission (28 U.S.C. §§991–998).

The role of these agencies is far more important to the law than one might at first imagine. For example, the federal courts' basic venue provisions, 28 U.S.C. §§ 1391–1447, have significant implications for litigants, they are part of the federal legal landscape. These provisions are not found in the Constitution, nor were they drafted by Congress, however. They were promulgated by the Judicial Conference of the United States, and submitted to Congress as a proposed bill. The same is true for the Federal Rules of Civil Procedure and the Federal Rules of Appellate Procedure. Recommendations of the Judicial Conference of the United States regarding the rules of court ordinarily become law with very few, if any, changes made by the legislature. Thus, understanding the federal courts' operation and organization requires at least a passing knowledge of the functions of the judicial agencies.

Using the World Wide Web to find your information (and giving the URL for each source actually used), for each of the above-listed agencies describe briefly: (a) its purpose and/or mandate, and (b) its organizational structure.

See Appendix B.

CHAPTER 2

The Court System

Folley's Metal Fabrication of California advertises and sells its products in several western states. Its products are all manufactured in California. If a customer in Arizona buys a Folley's product after seeing a Folley's advertisement, and is then injured using it, can that injured customer bring the lawsuit in the Arizona state court systems for resolution? Must the dispute be decided in a California state court because the business is located in that state? Or are there circumstances in which such a dispute must be decided in the federal court system? Does the law of Arizona or California apply? In any dispute, parties must understand and resolve these questions before they can effectively use our court system.

This chapter provides an overview of the American court system and discusses how an injured party can seek relief in the courts. In their operations, businesses may face disputes with competitors, suppliers, customers, and government agencies. Many disputes are resolved by the parties with no serious disruption in business relationships or activities. A significant number, however, require resolution in our court system—through civil litigation.

A business that has a civil dispute going to litigation must first answer the question, Which court has the power and the authority to decide the case? That is, which court has the jurisdiction to take the case for resolution? Today, many businesses operate in several states—and often in several countries. As a consequence, the choice of the appropriate court may not be clear, or more commonly, the parties may be in a position to choose among several appropriate courts.

The Federal Court System

The federal court system was created in response to the following declaration in the U.S. Constitution:

> The judicial Power of the United States, shall be vested in one supreme Court and in such inferior Courts [courts subordinate to the Supreme Court] as the Congress may from time to time ordain and establish.

After a long period of adjustment, the federal court system developed into a three-level system. It consists of the U.S. district courts, the U.S. courts of appeals, and the U.S. Supreme Court. Each court has its own distinct role within the federal court system.

FEDERAL DISTRICT COURTS

The U.S. district courts are the courts of original jurisdiction in the federal system. As the trial courts of the federal system, the U.S. district courts are the only courts in the system that use juries. Most cases involving questions of federal law originate in these courts. The geographical boundaries of a district court's jurisdiction will not extend across state lines. Thus, each state has at least one federal district court; the more populated states are divided into two, three, or—as in California, New York, and Texas—four districts. In addition, there are federal district courts in the District of Columbia, Puerto Rico, Guam, and the Virgin Islands.

FEDERAL APPELLATE COURTS

Federal district court decisions may be reviewed in the U.S. courts of appeals. Established in 1891, the U.S. courts of appeals are the intermediate-level appellate courts in the federal system. There are now twelve courts of appeals, one for each of the eleven circuits into which the United States is divided and one for the District of Columbia. The division of the states into circuits and the location of the U.S. courts of appeals are presented in Exhibit 2.1.

As appellate courts, the U.S. courts of appeals exercise only appellate jurisdiction. If either party to the litigation is not satisfied with a federal district court's decision, it has the *right* to appeal to the court of appeals for the circuit in which that district court is located. The Fourth Circuit U.S. Court of Appeals in Richmond, Virginia, for example, will hear appeals only from the federal district courts in the states of Maryland, North Carolina, South Carolina, Virginia, and West Virginia. The *one exception* is the U.S. government, which does not have the right to appeal a decision involving a criminal dispute.

The U.S. courts of appeals assign three-judge panels to review decisions of the district courts within their circuits. They also review orders of federal administrative agencies when a party appeals the final decision of a regulatory agency. As a practical matter, because it is so difficult to obtain review by the U.S. Supreme Court, the courts of appeals make the final decision in most cases.

EXHIBIT 2.1

The Federal Judicial Circuits

SPECIALIZED FEDERAL COURTS

Although the U.S. Supreme Court, courts of appeals, and district courts are the most visible federal courts, there are a few important courts with limited or special jurisdiction within the federal court system. These courts differ from other federal courts in that their jurisdictions are defined in terms of subject matter rather than by geography.

The most prominent of these courts is the Court of Appeals for the Federal Circuit, created in 1982. Although its territorial jurisdiction is nationwide, its subject-matter jurisdiction is limited to appeals from the U.S. district courts in patent, trademark, and copyright cases and in cases where the United States is a defendant; appeals from the U.S. Claims Court and U.S. Court of International Trade; and the review of administrative rulings of the U.S. Patent and Trademark Office. As in the U.S. courts of appeals, three-judge panels preside over cases before the Court of Appeals for the Federal Circuit.

U.S. SUPREME COURT

The U.S. Supreme Court is the highest court in the country, as we see in Exhibit 2.2. Created by the U.S. Constitution, the Supreme Court is primarily an appellate review court. Cases reaching the Court are usually heard by nine justices, one of whom is the Chief Justice. The term of the Court begins, by law, on the first Monday in October and continues as long as the business of the Court requires. The Court sits in Washington, D.C.

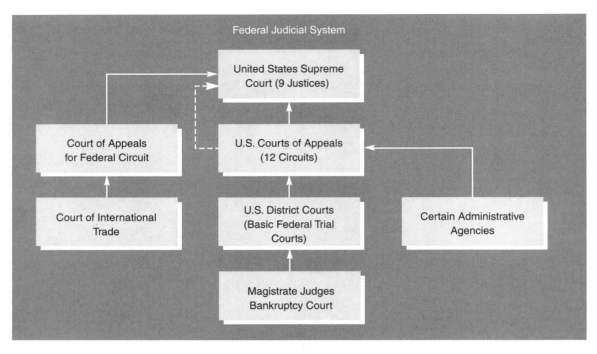

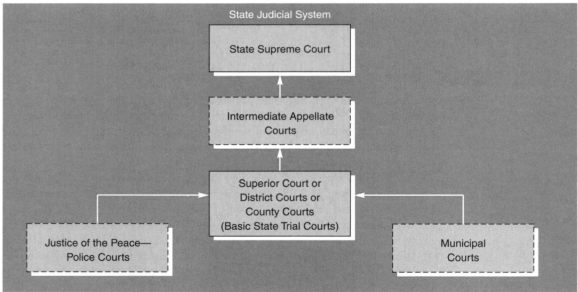

As an appellate court, the Supreme Court may review appeals from the U.S. district courts, the U.S. courts of appeals, and the highest courts of the states. In rare instances, such as in the case of a dispute between two state governments, the U.S. Supreme Court has *original and exclusive jurisdiction*. Although the Congress may change the Court's appellate jurisdiction, it cannot change the Court's original jurisdiction conferred upon it by the Constitution.

Appellate review is normally obtained by petitioning the court for a *writ of certiorari*. Under the Supreme Court Selections Act of 1988, nearly all appeals to the

The French Court System

Like most European countries, France is a civil law country—its legal system is based on written (code) law rather than on judge-made common law. The structure of the French system appears similar to that of the U.S. federal court system. The French system consists of a supreme court (*cour de cessation*), a court of appeals (*cour d'appel*), and a lower court of general jurisdiction (*tribunal d'instance*).

The appellate process in France, however, is considerably different from that in the United States. In contrast to the powers held by the U.S. Supreme Court, the *cour de cessation* does not have the authority to pronounce judgment. Rather, it has power either to reject an appeal or to invalidate the decision and return the case to the court of appeals for reconsideration. The court's power to impose a judgment is limited because the intent of the post-Revolution founders was to give the high court far

less power than the royal pre-Revolution courts had held.

In the event the appeal is rejected, the proceedings are finished. If, on the other hand, the decision of the *cour d'appel* is invalidated, the court then reconsiders the case before a five-judge panel. However, the judges are not bound by the higher court's determination of the law as they would be in the United States. They may either accept or reject it. They may also consider new facts.

If the case is then appealed a second time to the *cour de cessation*, the case is heard by a panel of twenty-five judges consisting of the senior and leading members of the court. If this appeal is rejected, the proceedings end; if the *cour d'appel* decision is invalidated, the case is returned to the panel for reconsideration. On the second appeal, however, the judges of the *cour d'appel* must follow the higher court's decisions on points of law.

Supreme Court are at the Court's discretion. The members of the Court determine which cases they wish to review; at least four justices must agree to review a case before a writ is granted. In the event the Court does not grant certiorari, the decision of the lower court becomes final. If certiorari is granted, the Supreme Court issues the writ directing the lower court to send up for the review its record in the case. Although it receives thousands of such petitions each term, the Court accepts less than two hundred. Most petitions granted involve an issue of constitutional importance or a conflict between the decisions of two or more U.S. courts of appeals. Concerns about the way in which the Supreme Court selects cases for review are discussed in the "Issue" article at the end of this chapter.

Despite differences in substantive law, foreign courts are often similar in basic structure, but not in procedure, to those in the United States. The International Perspectives feature compares the court system in France with the U.S. court system.

The Litigation Process

Civil litigation involves the use of the law and the legal process to resolve disputes among individuals, businesses, and governments. It is a formal process involving a mechanism provided by the government—the court system—to allow for impartial dispute resolution. Litigation provides one way to resolve disputes without resorting to acts of violence or coercion.

The civil litigation process serves society through three principal functions. First, civil litigation is designed to bring a peaceful resolution to disputes that do not involve crimes. No orderly society could exist without a formal dispute resolution process. Second, the legal process not only decides who is right and wrong but also provides a mechanism for enforcing its decisions. Those legal mechanisms ensure that corrective measures can be undertaken to remedy wrongs. Finally, the courts not only apply the law of the society but also develop it. As society changes, the courts help to modify laws in response to those changes.

RULES OF CIVIL PROCEDURE

From the moment the *plaintiff*—the party who claims to have suffered an injury that the law can remedy—brings an action, a lawsuit is governed by a detailed set of procedural rules. These rules force the parties to define the issues in the dispute. The rules also control the manner in which the parties to the dispute—the plaintiff and the *defendant* (the party who allegedly injured the plaintiff)—present evidence and arguments in support of their positions.

Although the states are free to develop their own procedural rules, most have adopted the *Federal Rules of Civil Procedure* or rules similar to them. The Federal Rules were developed by an advisory committee appointed by the U.S. Supreme Court, became effective in 1938, and have been modified over the years. The Federal Rules govern the procedural aspects of the litigation process, including the pleadings, discovery, trial procedures, and relevant motions. The purpose of the Federal Rules of Civil Procedure is to facilitate the litigation process:

> These rules . . . shall be construed to secure the just, speedy, and inexpensive determination of every action.

Note that these rules govern only civil litigation; somewhat different procedures are used in criminal and administrative litigation.

The Federal Rules of Civil Procedure are contained in the United States Code, Title 28. In addition to establishing trial procedural rules, Title 28 establishes the organization of the federal courts, judicial agencies, and important rules governing jurisdiction and venue. This chapter concentrates on jurisdiction and the organization of the American court system. Chapter 3 examines basic trial procedures and processes.

Jurisdiction

The literal meaning of the term *jurisdiction* is the power to speak of the law. A court's jurisdiction defines the limits within which it may declare, expound, administer, or apply the law. The basic limitations imposed upon a court by a constitution and the statutes that created it determine what kinds of legal disputes it may resolve, depending on who the parties to the dispute are.

When a plaintiff files a lawsuit, the correct court must be chosen to resolve the dispute. While there may be a number of courts from which to choose, the plaintiff's choices are limited to the court or courts having appropriate jurisdiction. In bringing the lawsuit, the plaintiff must select a court that has both:

1. Jurisdiction over the subject matter of the dispute
2. Jurisdiction over either the person of the defendant or the property of the defendant

If a court should rule in a particular case and it is later determined that jurisdiction was lacking, the judgment of that court will be declared null and void upon appeal. Without appropriate jurisdiction a court cannot exercise authority.

SUBJECT-MATTER JURISDICTION

Subject-matter jurisdiction is created by a constitution or a statute regarding the types of disputes a court can resolve. Subject-matter limitations might include minimum requirements on the amount in controversy or restrictions on the types of disputes a court can hear. For example, state statutes might restrict disputes in district (trial) courts to civil cases involving more than $2,000, or they might require that all cases involving wills be heard by a probate court. In such situations, the state legislature has placed limitations on the subject-matter jurisdiction of its courts.

Organization of the Court System

The court system consists of two related systems: the federal court system and the court systems that exist in all states. The state and federal court systems both have lower courts of *original jurisdiction*, where disputes are initially brought and tried, and courts of *appellate jurisdiction*, where the decisions of a lower court can be taken for review. In both systems, the courts of original jurisdiction are trial courts. In almost all cases, one judge presides over the proceeding. The court's principal function is to determine the true facts in the dispute and to apply the appropriate law to those facts in rendering a decision (judgment). As we discuss in the next chapter, the jury is responsible for deciding the facts in a case; if there is no jury in a case, the judge decides the facts.

Appellate courts are concerned with errors in the application of the law and in the procedural rules applied during the trial court proceeding. Normally three judges review decisions at the intermediate appellate court level. Five or more judges are used in the highest appellate state courts. The basic structure of the American court system is illustrated in Exhibit 2.2.

Subject-Matter Jurisdiction: The State Courts

Although the names and organization differ somewhat from state to state, the state court systems are quite similar in general framework and jurisdictional authorities. Like the federal system, the state court system is usually a three-level court system. In addition, the state court system has several important local courts of special or limited jurisdiction.

State Courts of Original Jurisdiction Each state court system has courts of *original jurisdiction*, or trial courts, where disputes are initially brought and tried. These courts usually consist of one set of courts of *general jurisdiction* and several courts of *limited* or *special jurisdiction*. The courts of general jurisdiction have authority to decide almost any kind of dispute and are able to grant virtually every type of relief. In many states, the amount in controversy, however, must generally exceed a specific amount, typically $2,000 to $5,000.

The state courts of general jurisdiction, or trial courts, are usually organized into districts, often comprising several counties. These district courts have different names in different states, although their jurisdictional limitations are very similar. In some states, the courts of general jurisdiction are called superior courts. The same courts in Pennsylvania and Ohio are called the Courts of Common Pleas, and in Oregon, the Circuit Courts. In Kansas, Louisiana, Maine, and other states, the courts of general jurisdiction are called district courts.

The state courts of limited or special jurisdiction include municipal courts, justice of the peace courts, and other more specialized courts (such as probate courts, which handle only matters related to wills and trusts). The jurisdiction of the municipal courts is similar to that of the district courts, except the claims they hear

JURIS **prudence?**

Thanks for the Help, Judge

During a murder trial in a Pennsylvania state court, the prosecutor wanted to introduce in evidence a tape recording made by a police informant talking to the defendant. The judge ruled that the tape could not be used in the trial. The prosecutor was upset at the ruling and engaged in a "caustic and disrespectful confrontation." The judge called a recess. The prosecutor telephoned the Pennsylvania Supreme Court chief justice, who contacted the trial judge and told him he should admit the tape in evidence.

After the defendant was convicted, his attorney appealed to the federal court of appeals, claiming that due process had been violated in Pennsylvania courts. The federal appeals court agreed; the trial judge and chief justice should not have carried on such a conversation. A new trial was ordered. The chief justice refused to comment.

Source: *Yohn* v. *Love*, 76 F.3d 508 (3rd Cir., 1996)

typically involve less money. Litigants who are not satisfied with the decision of the limited-jurisdiction court often appeal to the court of general jurisdiction. On appeal, the parties will get a whole new trial or, in legal terminology, a *trial de novo*.

Similarly, many states provide *small claims courts*, which have very limited jurisdiction. Restrictions are imposed on the subject matter these courts can hear and the amount in controversy. For example, the amount in controversy in many small claims courts must not exceed $5,000, and the subject matter is limited to debts and contract disputes. Small claims courts are particularly advantageous for collecting small debts because procedure requirements are much less formal and representation by an attorney is not necessary and usually not permitted. Small claims courts are a much faster (and less expensive) forum than the district courts, with disputes generally being heard within a month or two after their filing date.

State Courts of Appellate Jurisdiction Every judicial system provides for the review of trial court decisions by a court with *appellate jurisdiction*. Generally, a party has the right to appeal any judgment to at least one higher court. When a court system contains two levels of appellate courts, appeal usually lies as a matter of right to the first level and at the discretion of the court at the second. The highest appellate court will often limit its review to those cases having legal issues of broad importance to the state. The most common issues reaching the highest court in a state typically involve the validity of a state law, the state constitution, or a federal law as it is affected by a state law. A party seeking further review from the highest state court may seek review from the U.S. Supreme Court, but that is not granted very often.

Subject-Matter Jurisdiction: The Federal Courts

Under the U.S. Constitution, the federal courts may hear only those cases within the judicial power of the United States. That is, federal courts have the judicial power to hear cases involving a *federal question*:

> The judicial Power shall extend to all Cases . . . arising under this Constitution, the Laws of the United States, and Treaties made, or which shall be made, under their Authority. . . .

International Perspective

London's Commercial Court

When international contracts are signed, the parties can specify how future disputes will be resolved, including the choice of a court. If a court is not agreed upon initially, parties can agree at the time of a dispute where to resolve the matter. The Commercial Court in London has become a popular forum; almost all of its cases involve parties from more than one country.

Formed in 1895, the ten-judge court is often chosen because London is a major business city, most firms have assets in London that the court can easily control, and the judges are all experienced in commercial matters. Each trial is handled by one judge; there is no jury. Trials usually occur within a year and are finished rather quickly; the losing party pays the winner's attorney fees. Since English courts are respected, their judgments are more likely to be enforced in other countries, and the remedies used by the court have been innovative and relevant to commercial matters.

This includes cases based on the relationship of the parties involved:

> [The judicial Power shall extend] to all Cases affecting Ambassadors, other public Ministers and Consuls . . . to Controversies between two or more States;—between a State and Citizens of another State;—between Citizens of different States . . . and between a State, or the Citizens thereof, and foreign States, Citizens or Subjects.

When federal jurisdiction is based on the parties involved, most of the litigation is generated (1) by cases in which the United States is a party to the suit or (2) by cases involving citizens of different states. The original purpose for allowing federal jurisdiction when a legal dispute arises between citizens of different states—commonly referred to as *diversity-of-citizenship* jurisdiction—was to provide a neutral forum for handling such disputes.

State courts might be biased in favor of their own citizens and against "strangers" from other states. To obtain *diversity jurisdiction*, there must be total diversity among the parties. That is, all parties on one side of the lawsuit must have state citizenship different from the parties on the other side of the lawsuit. To establish federal jurisdiction in a diversity case, the parties must also show two things: (1) that they are from different states and (2) that the *amount in controversy* (the sum the plaintiff is suing the defendant for) is more than $75,000. (In federal question cases, there is no dollar amount requirement.)

Territorial Jurisdiction

Once it is established that the court of preference has subject-matter jurisdiction, the plaintiff must next meet the territorial jurisdiction requirements of that court. A court's jurisdictional authority is generally limited to the territorial boundaries of the state in which it is located. Territorial jurisdiction usually does not become an issue unless the defendant is not a resident of the state in which the plaintiff wishes to bring the lawsuit. In such a case, the plaintiff must determine how to bring the defendant—or the defendant's property—before the court.

EXHIBIT 2.3

A Typical Summons

United States District Court
for the
Southern District of California

Civil Action, File Number **80151**

Elena Gori
Plaintiff

v.   Summons

Tom Eyestone
Defendant

To the above-named Defendant:

You are hereby summoned and required to serve upon *Carol Chapman,* plaintiff's attorney, whose address is *3620 San Felipe, San Diego, California,* an answer to the complaint which is herewith served upon you, within 20 days after service of this summons upon you, exclusive of the day of service. If you fail to do so, judgment by default will be taken against you for the relief demanded in the complaint.

Gloria Hernandez
Clerk of Court

[Seal of the U.S. District Court]

Dated 2/5/00

JURISDICTION OVER THE PERSON

A court's power over the person of the defendant is referred to as *in personam jurisdiction*. It is usually established by serving the defendant with a *summons*—a notice of the lawsuit (see Exhibit 2.3). That is, after selecting the appropriate court, the plaintiff must officially notify the defendant of the action filed by *service of process*, which consists of a summons. The summons directs the defendant to appear before the court and to defend against the plaintiff's allegations. The court will issue a *default judgment* against a defendant who fails to appear.

Service of process is usually achieved by *personal service*. The summons is physically delivered to the defendant (or left at the defendant's home or place of business) by either the plaintiff, the plaintiff's attorney, a private process server, or a public official such as a sheriff or a U.S. marshal. If the defendant cannot be located, courts allow the limited use of *substituted service*, such as publication of the pending lawsuit in a newspaper for a certain period of time. The U.S. Supreme Court has repeatedly emphasized that substituted service must be of a kind reasonably calculated to alert the defendant of the action.

JURISDICTION OVER OUT-OF-STATE DEFENDANTS

If both parties to a lawsuit are residents of the same state, the courts of the state clearly have jurisdiction over both persons. But if the defendant is a resident of another state, obtaining jurisdiction can be more difficult. The most obvious method for obtaining in personam jurisdiction over nonresident defendants is to

JURIS prudence?

We Want the Piggy Bank, Your Honor

When nine-year-old Johnny Lupoli was warming up on the sidelines for a Little League game, he accidentally threw a wild pitch. The ball hit Carol LaRosa, the mother of a teammate, in the face, causing a wound that required sixty stitches. LaRosa sued Johnny for $15,000.

Superior Court Judge Fraccasse dismissed the suit. For the benefit of LaRosa's lawyer, the judge noted that Connecticut does not allow children, alone, to be the plaintiff or defendant in a lawsuit. Johnny's lawyer said he was considering filing suit against LaRosa. "They've really hassled Johnny. . . . They've probably harmed him emotionally."

Source: *National Law Journal*

serve them with process while they are within the state. The nonresident defendant need only be passing through the state to be legally served with a summons. Note that although nonresident defendants need not have intended to return to the state for process to be served, they cannot be tricked into coming into the area for the purpose of being served.

It is difficult to obtain jurisdiction over nonresident defendants when they have no need to return to the state. While it would seem as though businesses could avoid lawsuits under such circumstances, the court can still exert its jurisdiction by several means. If the defendant has committed a wrong (such as causing an automobile accident) within the court's territorial boundaries or has done business within the state, the court can exercise jurisdiction under the authority of the state's *long-arm statute* (see Exhibit 2.4). A long-arm statute is a state law that permits the state's courts to reach beyond the state's boundaries and obtain jurisdiction over nonresident defendants. Long-arm statutes make it much easier for plaintiffs to sue nonresident defendants.

Jurisdiction Over Out-of-State Business Defendants

Long-arm statutes are aimed primarily at nonresident businesses. They give courts a basis for exercising their jurisdiction over nonresident businesses that they may not use when dealing with nonresident private defendants. Do business defendants receive less favorable treatment by courts when it comes to jurisdiction than do private defendants? It is often claimed that courts are more hostile to business defendants, viewing them as potentially powerful and unscrupulous parties, against whom the state's citizens need protection. True nor not, courts may exercise jurisdiction over a corporation in the following three situations:

1. The court is located in the state in which the corporation was incorporated.
2. The court is located in the state where the corporation has its headquarters or its main plant.
3. The court is located in a state in which the corporation is doing business.

The first basis for jurisdiction relies on the corporate law idea that state governments, by issuing charters, create corporations, which are treated as "persons" under the law. One of the requirements in obtaining a corporate charter from a

EXHIBIT 2.4

Long-Arm Statute: Revised Statutes of Ohio

Sec. 2307.382 Personal Jurisdiction

(A) A court may exercise personal jurisdiction over a person who acts directly or by an agent, as to a cause of action arising from the person's:

(1) Transacting any business in this state;

(2) Contracting to supply services or goods in this state;

(3) Causing tortious injury by an act or omission in this state;

(4) Causing tortious injury in this state by an act or omission outside this state if he regularly does or solicits business, or engages in any other persistent course of conduct, or derives substantial course of conduct, or derives substantial revenue from goods used or consumed or services rendered in this state;

(5) Causing injury in this state to any person by breach of warranty expressly or impliedly made in the sale of goods outside this state when he might reasonably have expected such person to use, consume, or be affected by the goods in this state, provided that he also regularly does or solicits business, or engages in any other persistent course of conduct, or derives substantial revenue from goods used or consumed or services rendered in this state;

(6) Causing tortious injury in this state to any person by an act outside this state, committed with the purpose of injuring persons, when he might reasonably have expected that some person would be injured thereby in this state

(7) Causing tortious injury to any person by a criminal act, any element of which takes place in this state, which he commits or in the commission of which he is guilty of complicity.

(8) Having an interest in, using, or possessing real property in this state;

(9) Contracting to insure any person, property, or risk located within this state at the time of contracting.

(B) For purposes of this section, a person who enters into an agreement, as a principal, with a sales representative for the solicitation of orders in this state in transacting business in this state. . . .

(C) When jurisdiction over a person is based solely upon this section, only a cause of action arising from acts enumerated in this section may be asserted against him.

---

state is the designation of a registered office and an agent within the state. This office is a place where the corporation can always be served with process.

The second basis for jurisdiction relies on the corporation's status as an in-state resident. When a corporation is physically located within a state, the plaintiff can serve the corporation with process without having to use extraordinary measures. A company facility is effectively the residence of a business within a state.

The third basis for jurisdiction—doing business in a state—has been subject to close constitutional scrutiny by the U.S. Supreme Court. In attempting to reach out-of-state corporate defendants, states have relied heavily upon long-arm statutes. As Exhibit 2.4 demonstrates, those statutes often list "transacting business" within the state as a basis for jurisdiction. According to the Supreme Court in *International Shoe Company* v. *Washington* (66 S.Ct. 154, 1945), a state's long-arm statutes must identify certain *minimum contacts* between the corporation and the state where the suit is being filed to qualify as transacting business.

In the following case, the court is asked to consider whether the activities of a university qualify as minimum contacts sufficient to allow the court to exercise personal jurisdiction.

CYBERLAW

The Long Arm of the Internet

Businesses that offer services or products via the Internet can have instant access to the national market. That raises the question, When does a web site advertiser become subject to jurisdiction in other states? Some cases on this issue have arisen to give some insights.

In general, a vendor using a web site that Internet users must track down and contact has not done enough to create the minimum contacts necessary to invoke long-arm jurisdiction. In the case *Cybersell* v. *Cybersell* (130 F.3d 414), an appeals court held that "it would not comport with 'traditional notions of fair play and substantial justice' for Arizona to exercise personal jurisdiction over . . . [a] Florida web site advertiser who has no contacts with Arizona other than maintaining a home page that is accessible to Arizonans, and everyone else, over the Internet . . ."

However, if a service provider actively solicits business, then the long-arm statute may apply. For example, in *Minnesota* v. *Granite Gate Resorts* (568 NW2d 715), a Minnesota appeals court held that a Nevada provider of Internet gambling service was subject to personal jurisdiction in Minnesota for advertising an illegal service (gambling in Minnesota) as being available for Minnesota residents.

State of Oregon v. Lillard
California Court of Appeals, Second District
24 Cal.App.4th 1550 (1994)

CASE BACKGROUND *Earnest Killum was a high school basketball player from California. Coaches from Oregon State University visited Killum and his mother, Thelma Lillard, at their home in California. Killum decided to attend Oregon State and began school in September 1990. During his summer break in July 1991, Killum was home playing basketball with some friends. During the game, he suffered a minor stroke, for which he was treated at UCLA Medical Center. Doctors placed him on anticoagulant medication and told him to avoid contact sports and other physically demanding activities until doctors could determine that he was well enough to resume activities.*

The OSU athletic trainer called Lillard and assured her that if Killum returned to OSU he would receive the best medical treatment available. Lillard also spoke with the university's athletic director, who gave her similar assurances. Killum returned to OSU, and in December 1991, doctors at OSU reduced his level of anticoagulant medication. This cleared Killum to begin playing basketball with the OSU team. In January 1992, Killum traveled with the team to Los Angeles to play UCLA and USC. Killum suffered a stroke and died.

Lillard brought suit for wrongful death against the university (represented by the state in this case) based on negligent medical treatment. She filed her case in a California state court. Oregon moved to have the case dismissed based on a lack of personal jurisdiction. The trial court denied the motion to dismiss. Oregon appealed the decision.

CASE DECISION Epstein, Judge.

* * *

California's long-arm statute authorizes California courts to exercise jurisdiction over nonresidents on any basis not inconsistent with the federal or state Constitution. The Due Process Clause of the United States Constitution permits personal jurisdiction over a party in any state with which the party has "certain minimum contacts . . . such that the maintenance of the suit does not offend 'traditional notions of fair play and substantial justice.' "

* * *

Ms. Lillard's showing in this case was that OSU, through its agents, came to California and recruited her son Earnest while he was a high school student in California. . . . After he suffered a mild stroke in California that summer, agents from OSU spoke with Earnest and with Ms. Lillard, assuring both of them that Earnest would receive proper medical care and treatment if he returned to OSU.

[OSU] "purposefully directed" activities at Earnest and his mother, both residents of California, through the initial recruitment of Earnest during his senior year and his "re-recruitment" the following summer after his first stroke. . . . [OSU], having undertaken recruitment activities directed at a specific California resident, could reasonably expect to be subject to liability in California for injury resulting from these activities.

* * *

[OSU argues] that Oregon is the more convenient forum because all the medical care giving rise to this action was rendered there. Equally significant is that both of Earnest Killum's strokes occurred and were treated in California. . . . While petitioners may be inconvenienced by the need to travel to Cali-

fornia to defend this action, they nevertheless will be motivated to make that journey. In contrast, [Ms. Lillard] has no means to secure attendance at the trial in Oregon of the California medical practitioners who treated her son.

Moreover, California has a strong interest in protecting the rights of its residents who are allegedly victims of medical malpractice.

* * *

[W]e conclude that it is fair and reasonable to subject petitioners to the jurisdiction of the California courts.

QUESTIONS FOR ANALYSIS

1. The court held that recruiting activities create the minimum contacts with a state that a plaintiff must establish to use a long-arm statute. Should amateur sports be different from the kinds of commercial activities usually associated with minimum contacts?

2. Would the outcome of this case have been any different had the coaches never visited Killum in California but simply recruited him over the telephone? Why?

JURISDICTION BASED UPON POWER OVER PROPERTY

When a court is unable to obtain jurisdiction over the person of the defendant, it still has limited authority to establish jurisdiction based on the existence of the defendant's property within the state's territorial boundaries. In such cases, the court exercises jurisdiction because the plaintiff sues the defendant's property.

In Rem Jurisdiction

In lawsuits based on a dispute over property, a court in the area where the property is located has jurisdiction to resolve claims against that property—whether the defendant property owner is there or not. In such situations, the court is said to have *in rem jurisdiction*. The basis of *in rem* jurisdiction is the presence of the property in question within the territorial jurisdiction of the court.

Property in an *in rem* proceeding can include tangible property—real estate and personal property—and intangible property—bank accounts and stocks. To satisfy the minimum contacts standard, however, the courts cannot properly exercise jurisdiction over property that has been forcibly removed from another state where it is usually kept.

Quasi in Rem Jurisdiction

A court obtains *quasi in rem* jurisdiction when the defendant's property within a state is attached (or seized) to secure payment for an unrelated matter. For example, Roth may owe AutoBody $2,000 for painting her automobile. Unable to col-

The "Long Arm" of the Law

Dr. Humberto Alvarez-Machain was a citizen and resident of Mexico who practiced medicine in Guadalajara, Mexico. The U.S. Drug Enforcement Agency (DEA) believed that Alvarez took part in the torture and murder of one of its agents.

Alvarez was kidnapped in Guadalajara and taken to El Paso, Texas, where DEA agents arrested him for violating U.S. criminal law. The men who kidnapped Alvarez were not U.S. agents but had the approval of the U.S. government for their acts. At his trial, Alvarez argued that the federal court should dismiss his case because the U.S. government did not have personal jurisdiction over him, based on a U.S./Mexico extradition treaty. The court agreed, dismissed the case, and ordered Alvarez be returned to Mexico.

The Supreme Court reversed the lower courts, finding that the extradition treaty did not apply to the case. Hence, the Court could then consider whether or not the U.S. government's approval of the kidnapping violated U.S. or international law. U.S. law was not violated, because the Supreme Court had found forcible abductions in another country legal in an earlier case. Nor, the Court held, was the abduction illegal under principles of international law. Thus, Alvarez could be forced to stand trial for violating U.S. criminal law.

Source: *U.S.* v. *Alvarez-Machain*, 112 S.Ct. 2188; 1992.

---

lect its fee from Roth, AutoBody sues her. AutoBody cannot serve Roth personally with process because Roth lives in another state. AutoBody discovers that Roth has property in the territorial jurisdiction of the court. To gain jurisdiction, AutoBody attaches (or seizes) Roth's property to satisfy the debt. The court bases its jurisdiction on the fact that Roth owns property in the state. In this case, the court is said to have *quasi in rem jurisdiction*, and the decision it renders binds the parties. As in an *in rem* proceeding, the property involved can be either tangible or intangible.

Notification Limitations

If a plaintiff uses the defendant's property as a basis for jurisdiction, the plaintiff must notify the defendant, or someone who represents the defendant, of the legal action. In the past, *constructive notice*—such as publication of a legal notice in a newspaper for a specified time period—was considered sufficient. Because it has become so easy for both people and businesses to move from state to state, constructive notice alone has been held to be unconstitutional by the U.S. Supreme Court. Many states have since enacted statutes providing for mail or personal service when jurisdiction is based on the defendant's property.

Relations between the Court Systems

The jurisdiction relationships between state and federal court systems are illustrated in Exhibit 2.5. Some disputes can be resolved only in the state courts, some disputes only in the federal courts, and some disputes in either the federal or the state court systems.

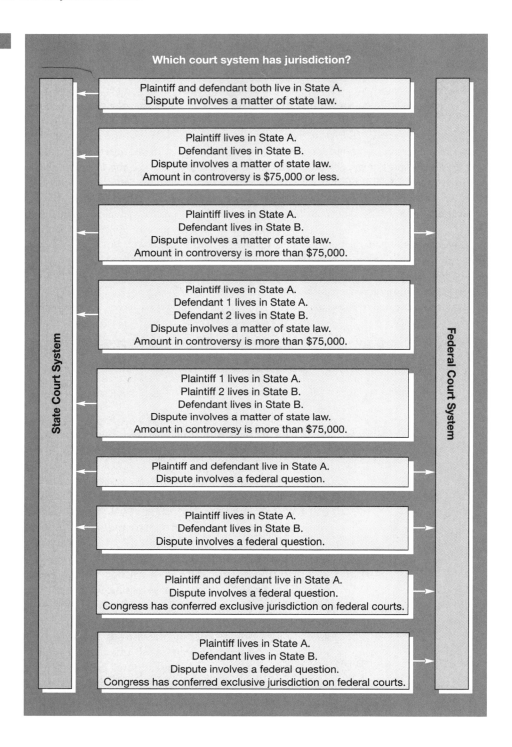

EXHIBIT 2.5

Jurisdiction Relationships between Court Systems

Which court system has jurisdiction?

State Court System

Federal Court System

Plaintiff and defendant both live in State A.
Dispute involves a matter of state law.

Plaintiff lives in State A.
Defendant lives in State B.
Dispute involves a matter of state law.
Amount in controversy is $75,000 or less.

Plaintiff lives in State A.
Defendant lives in State B.
Dispute involves a matter of state law.
Amount in controversy is more than $75,000.

Plaintiff lives in State A.
Defendant 1 lives in State A.
Defendant 2 lives in State B.
Dispute involves a matter of state law.
Amount in controversy is more than $75,000.

Plaintiff 1 lives in State A.
Plaintiff 2 lives in State B.
Defendant lives in State B.
Dispute involves a matter of state law.
Amount in controversy is more than $75,000.

Plaintiff and defendant live in State A.
Dispute involves a federal question.

Plaintiff lives in State A.
Defendant lives in State B.
Dispute involves a federal question.

Plaintiff and defendant live in State A.
Dispute involves a federal question.
Congress has conferred exclusive jurisdiction on federal courts.

Plaintiff lives in State A.
Defendant lives in State B.
Dispute involves a federal question.
Congress has conferred exclusive jurisdiction on federal courts.

EXCLUSIVE JURISDICTION

Courts in the federal system have *exclusive jurisdiction* over certain kinds of legal disputes. State courts do not have subject matter jurisdiction over these cases and so may not try them. Congress usually specifies by statute (but not always, as discussed later in federal question cases) matters over which the federal courts have exclusive jurisdiction. For example, federal courts have exclusive jurisdiction in cases involving federal crimes, bankruptcy, patents, and copyrights.

Similarly, state courts have exclusive jurisdiction over disputes such as divorce, adoption, and other matters controlled by the state government. A state government may confer exclusive jurisdiction on its courts as long as it does not infringe on the supremacy of federal law. If a plaintiff seeks relief for such a state matter in a federal court, the case would be dismissed for lack of jurisdiction. The plaintiff would need to refile the case in the appropriate state court.

With exclusive jurisdiction, the court hearing the case—whether a federal court or a state court—applies its procedural rules and follows its substantive law. If the court with jurisdiction is a state court in California, for example, it follows California procedural rules and applies the laws of the state of California. If the court is a federal court, it follows federal rules of procedure and applies federal law.

CONCURRENT JURISDICTION

As Exhibit 2.5 illustrates, both the federal and the state court systems have jurisdiction in some disputes. When both systems have the power to hear a case, *concurrent jurisdiction* exists. As Exhibit 2.5 also illustrates, both systems have jurisdiction when either of the following is the case:

1. There is diversity of citizenship and the amount in controversy exceeds $75,000.
2. The dispute involves a federal question and Congress has not conferred exclusive jurisdiction on the federal courts.

Federal Question Jurisdiction

The concurrent jurisdiction of the two court systems is understandable in cases where there is diversity of citizenship. An out-of-state defendant may worry that the state courts in the plaintiff's state might be biased in favor of the plaintiff. However, the rationale for state courts to exercise jurisdiction in federal question cases is less clear and has required consideration by the Supreme Court:

> We start with the premise that nothing in the concept of our federal system prevents state courts from enforcing rights created by federal law. Concurrent jurisdiction has been a common phenomenon in our judicial history, and exclusive federal court jurisdiction over cases arising under federal law has been the exception rather than the rule. *Charles Dowd Box Co.* v. *Courtney*, 368 U.S. 502 (1962).

However, as the court has explained, Congress may state "explicitly or implicitly" that state courts do not have jurisdiction over a particular matter of federal law. In explicit cases, Congress provides by statute that federal courts have exclusive jurisdiction over the matter. In implicit cases, Congress provides exclusive jurisdiction "by unmistakable implication from the legislative history, or by a clear incompatibility between state-court jurisdiction and federal interests." In such cases, only the federal court system has jurisdiction over the case. If a plaintiff seeks relief for such a matter in a state court, the case would be dismissed for lack of jurisdiction. The plaintiff would be required to refile the case in a federal court.

Concurrent Jurisdiction and Removal

When concurrent jurisdiction exists, the plaintiff may bring suit in either the state court or the federal court system. If the plaintiff chooses the state court system, the defendant has the right to have the case removed from the state court to a federal court. Defendants also have the right to remove cases based on diversity of citizenship from state to federal courts. In both cases, this right of *removal* is intended to protect out-of-state defendants from state courts that might be biased in favor of their own citizens. Since this reason does not apply if the plaintiff brings suit in federal court, there is no right of removal by the defendant from a federal court to a state court.

A plaintiff considers several issues when deciding which court system best suits her legal needs. For example, the rules of procedure in federal and state courts may be different, and the plaintiff's attorney may be more familiar with (and more successful using) one set of rules than the other. Potential jurors may be a consideration. In state courts, jury members might be drawn from a smaller area and so may be more likely to know a party than are jurors in a federal court, who are drawn from a larger area. Finally, local politics may be an issue for state judges. The plaintiff can do little to prevent the defendant from removing the case to the federal court if the defendant wants to do so.

If the federal court's jurisdiction is based on diversity of citizenship, the plaintiff may be tempted to name a citizen of her own state as a defendant to the lawsuit. Then the federal court would not have jurisdiction, because the citizenship of all parties on the defendant's side would not be different from the citizenship of all parties on the plaintiff's side. The plaintiff cannot simply name a person a defendant without good reason. The court requires the plaintiff to show that a defendant is a *real and substantial party* to the lawsuit. In other words, the plaintiff is not allowed to name a defendant simply to destroy the federal court's diversity jurisdiction over the case.

APPLYING THE APPROPRIATE LAW IN FEDERAL COURT

When there is diversity of citizenship, and the plaintiff has chosen or the defendant has removed the case to the federal court system, the central question becomes, Which body of substantive law should the court apply to resolve the dispute—federal law or state law?

Suppose that Smith and Jones were involved in a contract dispute and Smith sued Jones in California. If Smith and Jones were both from California, the case would be tried in a California state court, and California law would be applied to resolve the dispute. However, if Smith was from Arizona and Jones was from California (and the amount in controversy exceeded $75,000), the dispute could be decided by a federal court because of diversity of citizenship. If the issue in dispute was governed by statutory law, federal and California courts would apply the same law (the statutory law of California), and the outcomes very likely would be the same. But what would happen if the case involved common-law issues and if the federal courts had their own version of the common law? In this situation, a federal court and a state court hearing similar cases might reach different decisions. This is what used to happen in the United States until the Supreme Court decided the landmark 1938 case of *Erie* v. *Tompkins*.

In *Erie* v. *Tompkins*, the Supreme Court overturned an earlier case, *Swift* v. *Tyson*, and held that except in matters governed by the federal Constitution or by acts of Congress, federal courts must apply state law. Thus, federal judges must apply both a state's common law and a state's statutory law when deciding diversity-of-citizenship cases. The federal court, however, follows federal procedural law.

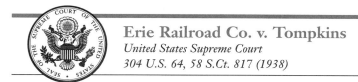

Erie Railroad Co. v. Tompkins
United States Supreme Court
304 U.S. 64, 58 S.Ct. 817 (1938)

CASE BACKGROUND *Tompkins was injured on "a dark night" by something protruding from a passing freight train owned by Erie Railroad Company, as Tompkins stood next to the tracks. He claimed the accident occurred because of negligent operation of the train. Tompkins was a citizen of Pennsylvania, and Erie was a company incorporated in New York. Tompkins (the plaintiff) brought suit in federal district court in New York. Erie argued that the court, in deciding the case, should apply the law of Pennsylvania. Under Pennsylvania common law, Tompkins would be a trespasser, and Erie would not be liable for his injuries. Tompkins argued that because no statute existed on the subject in Pennsylvania, federal common law should apply. Under federal common law, Erie could be liable for Tompkins's injuries.*

The trial court agreed with Tompkins, and the jury awarded him $30,000 in damages. The decision was affirmed by the circuit court of appeals. Erie appealed to the U.S. Supreme Court, arguing that in diversity-of-citizenship cases federal courts must apply the appropriate state statutory and common law.

CASE DECISION Brandeis, Justice.

* * *

First. *Swift* v. *Tyson*, held that federal courts exercising jurisdiction on the ground of diversity of citizenship need not, in matters of general jurisprudence, apply the unwritten law [the common law] of the State as declared by its highest court; that they are free to exercise an independent judgment as to what the common law of the State is—or should be. . . .

* * *

Second. Experience in applying the doctrine of *Swift* v. *Tyson*, had revealed its defects. . . . Diversity of citizenship jurisdiction was conferred [by the Constitution] in order to prevent apprehended discrimination in state courts against those not citizens of the State. *Swift* v. *Tyson* introduced grave discrimination by non-citizens against citizens. It made rights enjoyed under the [state's common law] vary according to whether enforcement was sought in the state or in the federal court. . . . Thus, the doctrine rendered impossible equal protection of the law. In attempting to promote uniformity of law throughout the United States, the doctrine had prevented uniformity in the administration of the law of the State.

* * *

Third. Except in matters governed by the Federal Constitution or by Acts of Congress, the law to be applied in any case is the law of the State. And whether the law of the State shall be declared by its Legislature in a statute or by its highest court in a decision is not a matter of federal concern. . . . Congress has no power to declare substantive rules of common law applicable in a State. . . . And no clause in the Constitution purports to confer such a power upon the federal courts.

* * *

Fourth. The defendant contended that by the common law of Pennsylvania . . . the only duty owed to the plaintiff was to refrain from wilful or wanton injury. . . . The Circuit Court of Appeals . . . declined to decide the issue of state law. As we hold this was error, the judgment is reversed and the case remanded to it for further proceedings in conformity with our opinion.

Reversed.

CASE NOTE The concept of federal common law in diversity-of-citizenship cases was ended. Hence, Tompkins was a trespasser and Erie was not liable for his injuries.

QUESTIONS FOR ANALYSIS

1. Why had the decision in *Swift* v. *Tyson* prevented uniformity in the administration of the law of the state?
2. After *Erie*, which court's procedural law must be applied in a diversity-of-citizenship case?

EXHIBIT 2.6		
Conflict-of-Law Rules Frequently Affecting Businesses	**Substantive Law Issue**	**Apply State Law from State**
	Contract Disagreement	In which contract was formed or in which contract was to be performed or most significantly affected by the contract or designated in the contract
	Liability Issues Arising from Injury	In which injury occurred
	Workers' Compensation	Of employment or in which injury occurred

APPLYING THE APPROPRIATE LAW IN STATE COURT

When a state court hears a case involving incidents that took place in more than one state or entirely in a different state, a conflict-of-law problem may arise. The state court determines whether its own law or the law of another state should be applied. To help courts in such situations, states have enacted statutes that provide *conflict-of-law* rules. Some general conflict-of-law rules that affect businesses are presented in Exhibit 2.6.

Conflict-of-law rules vary according to the nature of the dispute. In contract cases, for example, the traditional rule is that the law of the state in which the contract was made determines the interpretation of the contract. In tort cases, the traditional rule is that courts apply the substantive law of the place where the tort occurred. However, the rules are not always simple. Some courts evaluate the interests of the states involved in a dispute. The state with the most "significant interest" in the case would be the state whose law would be applied.

There is no consensus among the states as to the best approach. However, the approaches used share several important concerns. They try to account for the interests of parties in the fair resolution of the dispute, for the interests of the governments in the effective application of their laws and the policy rationales upon which they are based, and for the benefits that result from the ability of citizens to predict the legal consequences of their actions. The most popular approach is that outlined in the *Restatement (Second) of Conflict of Laws*, which is applied in half the states. The following case discusses how a court goes about applying the *Restatement's* approach in conflict-of-law cases.

Beattey v. College Centre of Finger Lakes

District Court of Appeal of Florida, Fourth District

613 So.2d 52 (1992)

CASE BACKGROUND *Richard Beattey, Jr., was driving in the Bahamas when he collided head-on with a truck owned by College Centre of Finger Lakes and driven by its employee, Zeakes. College Centre was a New York corporation with an office in the Bahamas. Two passengers in Beattey's vehicle, both Indiana residents, died at the scene. Beattey was flown to Fort Lauderdale, Florida, but died en route from his injuries.*

Beattey's parents, Indiana residents at the time of the accident and representatives of their son's estate, filed this

action for wrongful death in a Florida state court against College Centre. College Centre conceded that it was liable for the negligence of its driver, Zeakes. If Bahamian law applied, the Fatal Accidents Act of the Bahamas would control this case. The act limits recovery in a wrongful death action to funeral expenses. Under the law of any U.S. state, plaintiffs could sue for much more.

The trial court applied a "significant relations" conflict-of-law test and found that the Bahamas had the most significant interest in the case and that Bahamian law should thus be applied. The Beatteys appealed the decision, arguing that the court did not apply the conflict-of-law test appropriately.

CASE DECISION Hersey, Judge.

* * *

The first step in conflict of laws analysis is to ascertain the nature of the problem involved: e.g. torts, contracts, property, divorce, etc. The instant case clearly sounds in tort because [Beattey Jr.'s] estate and parents are suing for wrongful death due to [College Centre's] negligence.

The second step in any conflict of laws analysis is to determine the [proper] choice of law rule. Florida's choice of law rule is the significant relationships test as provided by the *Restatement (Second) of Conflict of Laws*. . . .

The final step in the analysis is to determine which state's interest is most significant, and "(s)ignifican(t) in this context denotes the competing interests of the conflicting states in the determination of a particular issue."

* * *

We first address the relationships Indiana, Florida, Bahama, and New York have to the subject occurrence, then apply the criteria from the *Restatement* rules.

Indiana

Appellants Richard Beattey Sr. and Laurel Beattey were residents of Indiana at the time of their son's death; however, they since have moved to West Germany and do not intend to return to the United States as residents. The decedent [Richard, Jr.] also held a driver's license issued by the state of Indiana at the time of his death. (Additionally, the two other people who were killed in the decedent's vehicle were residents of Indiana; however, this need not be considered as they are not parties to this appeal.)

Florida

The lawsuit was initiated in Florida and the decedent died of his injuries en route to Ft. Lauderdale. The autopsy was performed in Florida, as well as a brief investigation into his death.

Bahamas

The collision occurred in the Bahamas. At the time of the accident, [College Centre] had a field office in the Bahamas. Both vehicles involved in the accident were registered through the Bahamas, and the decedent's vehicle insurer engaged a Bahamian agency to investigate the accident.

New York

[College Centre] is a corporation with its principal place of business in New York. Also, [College Centre's] corporate charter was granted by the State of New York's Education Department. [College Centre's] insurance was issued through a New York agency, and the insurance contract has several provisions pertaining to New York law. Furthermore, at the time of his death, the decedent was living in New York while attending college. Therefore, the decedent, [College Centre], and [College Centre's] insurance company have New York as a common denominator.

Secondly, we apply . . . the *Restatement* to weigh the above factors properly:

(2) a. the needs of the interstate and international systems. All parties involved are/were American citizens with expectations of being protected by American laws. When all of the parties are of one citizenship, then that country has a significant interest in the litigation which outweighs the competing interest of another country. . . .

b. the relevant policies of the forum. The forum here is Florida because the litigation was initiated in Ft. Lauderdale. The current policies here are the significant relationships test . . . and the corresponding rules from the *Restatement*.

c. the relevant policies of other interested states and the relative interests of those states in the determination of the particular issue. This factor clearly indicates New York. New York has an interest in this case because a corporation formed in its state is being held liable, and more importantly, the insurance for the corporation was issued through a New York agency, and the rates were based on New York data. "In regard to insurance contracts, the choice of law rule generally accepted in Florida is that a contract of insurance is governed by the law of the state where the contract was finally consummated."

* * *

e. the basic policies underlying the particular field of law. The particular field of law underlying the instant case is tort law. . . . Application of Bahamian law would seem repugnant to Florida public policy where there is no recovery allowed for wrongful death in Bahamian law, under which a party may recover only funeral expenses.

Additionally, it would seem that the Bahamas would have no particular interest in the outcome of litigation between two parties from New York. . . .

f. certainty, predictability and uniformity of result. The application of New York law here would serve to protect New York residents who may rely on and expect New York insurance coverage to apply even when traveling out-of-state.

g. ease in the determination and application of the law to be applied. While the [law of the] place of injury would be easier to apply since it is the location of the accident and it simply provides no recovery, New York law would best serve the overall interests of the parties in these circumstances.

Based upon the criteria . . . , it is clear that New York has the most significant relationships to the occurrence, and thus its law should govern here.

* * *

We reverse and remand for further appropriate proceedings.

QUESTIONS FOR ANALYSIS

1. Under the approach taken by the court, what are the basic steps that state courts go through in solving conflict-of-law issues? What would have been the result in this case if the traditional rule had been applied?
2. In considering the various countries/states related in some way to the occurrence—Indiana, Florida, New York, Bahamas, and West Germany—which had the strongest relationship with the parties?
3. Of the criteria set forth in the *Restatement*, which tended to favor New York?

Venue

Not every court that has jurisdiction over both the subject matter and the person of the defendant will hear a case. It is also necessary that the lawsuit be brought in a court having proper *venue*. On the basis of fairness, state statutes generally provide that a lawsuit be brought in a court located in the county in which either the plaintiff or the defendant lives. Similarly, the defendant can be sued in a federal court only in a district where either the defendant or the plaintiff lives or where the dispute arose.

CHANGE OF VENUE

In some controversial or well-publicized cases, defendants request a *change of venue* from the court where the plaintiff filed the case. In such cases, defendants worry that because of the publicity surrounding their case, they will be unable to get a fair trial. Once such fairness requirements are met, the court selected has jurisdiction and venue.

FORUM NON CONVENIENS

A legal doctrine closely related to venue is the doctrine *forum non conveniens* (the forum is not suitable). A party that relies on this doctrine asks the court to dismiss the case and transfer it to another court, even though the original court does have jurisdiction. The moving party argues that the dismissal should be granted because there is another, more convenient court that could hear the case. When considering whether or not to grant the motion, a court considers where the actions related to the case took place, where the witnesses are located, whether the parties will be

Justice Can Have a Bite to It

 When West Virginia judge Troisi became irritated with a rude defendant, he stepped down from the bench, took off his robe, and bit the defendant on the nose. A report prepared for the state Supreme Court found that the judge frequently lost his temper in court. Troisi resigned and pleaded no contest to battery charges. He spent five days in jail and was put on probation. After he was released, he yelled at a court clerk who had testified against him. That violated his probation, so it was back to jail for six months. "Mr. Troisi just doesn't get it," said Judge Recht.

Source: *National Law Journal*

unfairly burdened by using a particular court, and whether problems of conflicts of law might be avoided by transferring the case. In state courts, this doctrine is used to transfer cases to the courts of other states or to federal court, whereas a motion for change of venue is used to transfer cases within the state. In federal courts, this doctrine is used to transfer cases to federal district courts in different states.

Judicial Officials

As the main link between law and society in the judicial system, judges perform several important functions. Most obviously, judges resolve disputes. For the system to work well, judges must apply the law evenly and consistently and not be swayed by public opinion. Judges also uphold the dignity of the law and the legal system. It is their responsibility to maintain the legal system's reputation for honesty and impartiality. Also, judges enhance the legal culture of society by maintaining respect for the law and the legal system.

FEDERAL JUDICIAL OFFICIALS

Federal judges are nominated by the president and confirmed by a majority vote in the U.S. Senate. Since the Constitution guarantees federal judges the right to serve "during good behavior," they enjoy a secure lifetime appointment. There are approximately 1,200 federal judges. According to the Constitution, federal judges may be removed from office only if the Congress impeaches them for treason, bribery, or other high crimes and misdemeanors. The impeachment process includes the actual impeachment (indictment) by the House of Representatives, followed by a trial before the Senate. If at least two-thirds of the senators vote for removal, the judge is removed from office. This happens only rarely.

While Congress may change the structure of the federal court system, it may not reduce a judge's salary or term of office once an appointment has been made. The writers of the Constitution gave federal judges job security because they

The Judge Is In On the Plot, Too!

Teri Smith Tyler filed suit in federal court. Named as defendants, among others, were Bill Clinton, Jimmy Carter, Ross Perot, IBM, and NASA. Tyler alleged a "conspiracy involving the defendants to enslave and oppress certain segments of our society. Plaintiff contends she is a cyborg, and that she received most of the information . . . through 'proteus' . . . some silent, telepathic form of communication. . . . Defendants are involved in the 'Iron Mountain Plan,' which provides for the reinstitutionalization of slavery and 'bloodsports' (which she identifies as death-hunting and witch-hunting), and the oppression of political dissidents, herself included."

Tyler contended the defendants had her college dorm room attacked by airplanes and helicopters and that other students whispered about her and avoided her socially. "Plaintiff additionally contends that the Gulf War against Iraq was undertaken so that America could restock its sexual slavery camps, which had been depleted."

A U.S. attorney requested the court dismiss Tyler's request for $5.6 billion in damages, the end of the cyborg program run by NASA, and an end to the organ-donor program, among other things. The judge agreed. "A plaintiff asserting fantastic or delusional claims, should not, by payment of a filing fee, obtain a license to consume limited judicial resources and put defendants to effort and expense."

Source: *Tyler v. Carter,* 151 F.R.D. 537

wanted to guarantee that judges would be independent, nonpartisan, and free from the pressure of politics. In reaching decisions, it is important that judges be independent decision makers protected from political pressures in the event of a controversial dispute.

STATE JUDICIAL OFFICIALS

State judges are chosen by a variety of methods. They are elected, appointed, or chosen by a method that mixes the election and appointment processes. In several of the states with the mixed system, the state bar association has a committee to recommend qualified attorneys for the bench. The governor then appoints a judge from its list. The judge selected then serves until the next election, at which time the public is asked to vote *for* or *against* him. This system for selecting judges is referred to as the *Missouri System.*

In contrast to the position enjoyed by federal judges, most state judges serve for a fixed term whether they are appointed or elected. Terms range from one year for judges in some Midwestern states to a fourteen-year term for judges in New York. Massachusetts and New Hampshire appoint judges to serve until they reach age seventy; only Rhode Island provides a lifetime term of office.

Some observers claim that appointed judges are of higher average quality than elected judges. Others claim that elected judges work harder than appointed judges. No clear evidence exists, however, that convincingly demonstrates that one approach is more effective than another. Exhibit 2.7 shows the selection process for judges to the highest court in the states. Note that some appointed judges must stand for retention election, when voters say yes or no to their remaining on the bench.

Selection of State Supreme Court Judges

Initial Selection Process	States
Appointment Systems	
Merit Selection by Committee	Alaska, Arizona, Colorado, Delaware, Florida, Hawaii, Indiana, Iowa, Kansas, Maryland, Massachusetts, Missouri, Nebraska, New York, Oklahoma, South Dakota, Utah, Vermont, Wyoming (19)
Government Appointment	California, Connecticut, Maine, New Hampshire, New Jersey, Rhode Island, South Carolina, Virginia (8)
Election Systems	
Nonpartisan Election	Georgia, Idaho, Kentucky, Louisiana, Michigan, Minnesota, Montana, Nevada, North Dakota, Ohio, Oregon, Washington, Wisconsin (13)
Partisan Election	Alabama, Arkansas, Illinois, Mississippi, New Mexico, North Carolina, Pennsylvania, Tennessee, Texas, West Virginia (10)

Source: American Judicature Society, Chicago, IL 60606

JUDICIAL IMMUNITY

Under the common law *doctrine of judicial immunity*, a judge is absolutely immune from suit for damages for judicial acts taken within or even in excess of his or her jurisdiction. This immunity applies even when the judge acts maliciously. There are several justifications for the doctrine. It is generally asserted that in the absence of the doctrine, judges would face undue influence on their judicial decisions. As a consequence, judges would lose their ability to be independent decision makers. In addition, it is asserted that judicial immunity protects judges from the burden of defending retaliatory suits by unsuccessful litigants. By protecting judges from such suits, the doctrine of judicial immunity serves to bring disputes and the litigation process to a close.

Summary

- Civil litigation involves the use of the law and the legal process to resolve disputes among businesses, individuals, and governments. Litigation through the court systems provides a means of resolving those disputes without the need to resort to force.
- The court system is made up of the state court systems and the federal court system. Most courts follow the Federal Rules of Civil Procedure in governing the important procedural aspects of the litigation process.
- Civil litigation has three important functions: to bring a peaceful resolution to a dispute, to provide a mechanism to enforce decisions, and to develop law as society changes.
- In the study of the court system, the most basic notion is the concept of jurisdiction. The term *jurisdiction* means the power to speak of the law. A court must have jurisdiction to hear and resolve a dispute. A court's jurisdiction is divided into two basic categories: subject-matter jurisdiction and territorial jurisdiction.

- Subject-matter jurisdiction is a constitutional or statutory limitation on the types of disputes a court can resolve. Typical subject-matter constraints include minimum requirements on the amount in controversy in the dispute and restrictions on the types of disputes the court has authority to resolve.
- The subject-matter jurisdiction of a court varies according to its position in the court system and the court system it is in. Courts of original jurisdiction in the federal and the state court systems are trial courts. They have authority to hear virtually any kind of dispute and provide any kind of relief. Courts with appellate jurisdiction have the power to review cases decided by courts below them. Most state court systems and the federal court system have two levels of appellate courts. The highest appellate court in the federal system is the U.S. Supreme Court.
- The federal court system has limited subject-matter jurisdiction. The federal courts are limited by the U.S. Constitution to cases involving a federal question or diversity of citizenship where the amount in controversy exceeds $75,000. The state court systems can hear most disputes, including federal question cases where Congress has not limited jurisdiction to the federal court system.
- In addition to meeting the subject-matter jurisdictional requirements of a court, the parties—the plaintiff and the defendant—must meet territorial jurisdictional requirements of the court. A state court's territorial jurisdiction is generally limited to the boundaries of its state.
- Territorial jurisdiction normally is not an issue unless the defendant is not a resident of the state in which the plaintiff wants to bring the action. Jurisdiction of the court over the defendant is obtained by personal service of process. For out-of-state defendants, however, the court may need to exercise jurisdiction under authority of the state's long-arm statute. Generally, the plaintiff must show that the out-of-state defendant is transacting business or has some other interest in the state.
- When the court is unable to establish its jurisdiction through personal service on the defendant, the court may be able to establish jurisdiction over property owned by the defendant that is located within the state.
- The federal courts in diversity-of-citizenship cases must apply the appropriate state common and statutory law.
- In state court cases, when the incident in question took place in another state, the court must look to the forum state's conflict-of-law rule to determine what substantive law will apply to resolve the dispute.
- Most U.S. judges are attorneys. It is their responsibility to uphold the legal system's reputation for honesty and impartiality. Federal judges are nominated by the president and confirmed by the Senate. They enjoy lifetime employment once appointed. State judges are variously appointed and elected, depending upon state procedures.

Is High-Tech Justified in the Courtroom?

Most courtrooms look a lot today like they did a century ago. While some trials are shown on television, and videotaped testimony is used at times, the courts have not adopted many of the information age visual and data presentation methods possible. The article discusses an experiment with high-tech in the courtroom.

TECHNO-JUSTICE

James D. Zirin

Zirin is a senior partner in the New York law firm of Brown & Wood. Reprinted by permission of *Forbes* Magazine © Forbes Inc., 1998.

The State Supreme Court, at 60 Centre Street in Manhattan, resides in a magnificent century-old building. Adorned by a Corinthian colonnade, the courthouse symbolizes our justice system. Inside, the judges, Old Glory at their back, tower over lawyers, spectators, witnesses and the jury box. Here, in our litigious society, people get even and wealth is reallocated.

Courtroom 228 is, at first glance, very traditional. But under the floor sits an intricate web of conduits connecting an integrated high-tech system of video, audio and "real time" transcription technology that converts the venerable chamber into Courtroom 2000. In real time, the transcripts are projected on a screen. Powerful real time search engines allow an immediate review of any portion of the testimony or trial record.

Courtroom 2000 is a pilot program wherein complex commercial trials are conducted in a technologically integrated courtroom. Lawyers for Arthur Andersen wanted to prove at a recent trial that the DeLorean motorcar project in Northern Ireland had failed because there was no market for the car. Onto the flat screen flashed former British prime minister Margaret Thatcher, archly testifying to that effect on a videotaped deposition. Financial statements were projected for the jury on state-of-the-art monitors. When the lawyers wanted to emphasize a portion of a document, they zoomed in on the relevant text.

The Courtroom 2000 approach is ideal for trying complex commercial cases. In jury trials, particularly in long commercial cases, jurors have appeared inattentive to prolonged readings from documents and depositions. It is not unknown for them to nod off.

Courtroom 2000 technology makes it possible to keep jurors alert and interested by using modern presentation techniques. A seasoned trial lawyer once told me: "Remember what is in the jury's head, and speak to that." The average juror, it has been estimated, spends more than four hours a day in front of a television screen. Technology has made the distinction between virtual reality and true reality seamless. At a trial in Courtroom 2000, otherwise dull evidence can come alive. Counsel can highlight a passage in a document, play a segment of a deposition, use animation, draw a picture on a whiteboard, explain a chart or otherwise demonstrate that one picture is worth a thousand words. A witness on the stand can likewise use a light pen to highlight areas of text, with the document and the highlighting appearing on the panel screens for the jury to consider. There is also a "kill" switch that enables the judge to turn off the jury monitors so that the judge and counsel alone can view contested items of evidence.

How much will it cost to convert our justice system to high technology? The cost of the equipment used in Courtroom 2000 is about $100,000, but New York City has had to spend just $5,000, and that was to rip up the floors to install cables. The equipment is all on loan from technology vendors eager to promote their wares. The vendors see a big market in U.S. litigation. In addition to America's thousands of courtrooms, much of the equipment could be readily used in lawyers' offices for trial preparation or for alternate dispute resolution such as arbitration or mediation.

This technology, along with changes in jury selection, can do wonders for our creaky justice system. Court reform encourages broader jury selection: Accountants, lawyers, doctors (not on call), state and federal judges and even the governor and the mayor sometimes get called. Excuses routinely accepted in the past from busy individuals are now carefully scrutinized. With modern juries, better presentation technology becomes particularly important.

The work of a trial lawyer is essentially that of a storyteller. Storytelling in the next century will be high tech and more visual. Older attorneys, accustomed to relying on their verbal and dramatic skills, may resist these changes. But in the justice system, as in so many other areas of life, communications technology is changing the world, and for the better.

ISSUE QUESTIONS

1. Should legislatures make significant investments in courtrooms so they have available the kinds of tech-nical equipment mentioned in the article? Will it make trials more effective?

2. Suppose one party in a suit is willing to invest in expensive high-tech presentations, while the other party cannot afford such costly presentations. Should such differences in presentation be allowed? Will glitzy presentations give a bigger advantage to the wealthier party?

REVIEW AND DISCUSSION QUESTIONS

1. Define the following terms:

plaintiff	in personam jurisdiction
defendant	summons
jurisdiction	service of process
general jurisdiction	in rem jurisdiction
limited jurisdiction	quasi in rem jurisdiction
appellate jurisdiction	conflict-of-law
diversity of citizenship	venue
writ of certiorari	

2. Compare and contrast the following:
    a. Service of process and substituted process
    b. Appellate jurisdiction and original jurisdiction
    c. Federal question jurisdiction and diversity-of-citizenship jurisdiction
    d. Jurisdiction over the person and jurisdiction over property

CASE QUESTIONS

3. Smith, a Tennessee resident, was sued in federal court in Arkansas by an Arkansas resident in a contract dispute involving an Illinois corporation. Smith was given his summons to appear in the court in Arkansas while flying on a commercial flight from Memphis to Dallas while the plane was over the state of Arkansas. Did that constitute legal service of summons? [*Grace* v. *MacArthur*, 170 F.Supp. 442 (E.D., Ark., 1959)]

4. Burger King (BK) is headquartered in Miami. Its franchise contracts are governed by Florida law. Franchise policy is determined in Miami, but day-to-day monitoring of franchisees is done by district offices that report to Miami. Rudzewicz had a Michigan franchise that was not doing well. BK terminated the franchise and told Rudzewicz to vacate the restaurant. Rudzewicz refused and kept running the operation. BK filed suit in federal court in Florida, claiming that Rudzewicz was in breach of contract and sued for damages and for an injunction. Rudzewicz claimed that the Florida federal court did not have jurisdiction because he was a Michigan resident and the subject of the case, the restaurant, was in Michigan. The district judge held that under Florida's long-arm statute, the con-

tract Rudzewicz signed made him subject to litigation in Florida. The court of appeals reversed, ruling that fairness and due process did not allow jurisdiction in Florida. What did the Supreme Court hold? [*Burger King* v. *Rudzewicz*, 105 S.Ct. 2174 (1985)]

5. Burlington is a Delaware corporation with its principal place of business in North Carolina. Maples is an Alabama corporation with its principal place of business there. Maples bought machines from BVA, an Arkansas company. Maples made the contract with BVA in Alabama; it sent no employees to Arkansas and it has no operations in Arkansas. Burlington sued Maples, claiming that the machines it bought contained Burlington trade secrets. Can Burlington bring suit against Maples in Arkansas? [*Burlington Industries* v. *Maples Industries*, 97 F.3d 1100 (8th Cir., 1996)]

6. The officers of a Maryland savings and loan that went bankrupt were sued in Maryland state court by depositors who lost money. Among the claims made against the officers were that they violated a federal statute, Racketeer Influenced and Corrupt Organizations Act (RICO). Before the case came to trial, some depositors filed another suit in federal district court against the same officers, claiming that the federal court had to hear the complaint that the officers violated RICO. The federal trial court dismissed the case, ruling that the state trial court could hear the case and rule on the matters involving possible violations of state law as well as RICO, the federal law. Was this correct? [*Tafflin* v. *Levitt*, 110 S.Ct. 792 (1990)]

7. Charlotte Chambers and thirty-four other South Dakota residents chartered a bus in Sioux Falls, South Dakota, from Dakotah Charter, a South Dakota corporation, to attend a Tae Kwon Do tournament in Arkansas. While en route from South Dakota to Arkansas, the bus stopped, among other places, in Missouri. Chambers fell on the steps in the bus and broke her ankle. She sued for personal injury, claiming that Dakotah failed to maintain the bus in a safe condition. Dakotah denied her claims and contended that her own carelessness caused her injury. Which law should apply to the case—the law of South Dakota (where the contract was made), Missouri (where the injury occurred), or Arkansas (where the contract was ultimately to be performed)? [*Charlotte Chambers* v. *Dakotah Charter*, 488 N.W.2d 63 (Sup.Ct., S.D., 1992)]

8. Michelle West was born in Georgia in 1972. Her parents were divorced in 1974. Their divorce decree, issued by a Georgia court, required Michelle's father to pay child support until Michelle turned 18. The decree did not require Michelle's father to contribute toward a college education. When Michelle became 18, she was living in South Carolina. She applied to and was accepted by a private college in South Carolina. Michelle's father lived in Georgia but worked and paid income taxes in South Carolina. Michelle filed suit in a South Carolina state court against her father, seeking support payments beyond her eighteenth birthday, to help cover the costs of her college education. Under South Carolina law, Michelle's father could be made to contribute to her education. Under Georgia law, Michelle's father would not be responsible for any of her expenses after she turned eighteen. Which law should the court apply in this case? [*West* v. *West*, 419 S.E.2d 804 (Ct.App., S.C., 1992)]

9. The Vons Companies process meat for use by fast-food restaurants. Some of Vons' meat was bought by Washington state Jack-in-the-Box restaurants. This meat was tainted by *E. coli* bacteria. Jack-in-the-Box customers who consumed the

meat suffered serious illness, and several died. Vons sued the owners of two Jack-in-the-Box franchises in California court, seeking damages and repayment, for money it was forced to pay to the food-poisoning victims. Vons claimed that because Jack-in-the-Box restaurants did not cook the meat properly, the *E. coli* outbreak occurred. The franchise owners responded that the California court did not have personal jurisdiction over them based on insufficient contacts with the state. The owners based this claim on the fact that they had assigned their rights to run the two restaurants to third parties, who operated the restaurants. Thus, they argued, the link between the harms caused by improper cooking and the relationship of the franchise owners to California was too remote. The franchise agreements were signed in California and were governed by California law. The contracts between the Jack-in-the-Box owners and the operators were signed in Washington state. Is there a sufficient connection between the owners and the people actually running the restaurants (the operators) to the state of California to allow the court to exercise jurisdiction? [*The Vons Companies* v. *Seabest Foods*, 37 Cal.App.4th, 1090 (Ct.App., Cal., 1995)]

10. Juanita Partin, a Louisiana citizen, was rear-ended by Dolby, a citizen of Delaware, in Delaware. Partin was driving a friend's car that was registered in Louisiana. Partin suffered serious injuries. She sued Dolby, Dolby's insurance company, and her own insurance company, Allstate. Partin settled her case against Dolby and Dolby's insurer for $100,000. However, Partin claimed that her injuries exceeded this amount, and so she filed suit in Louisiana against Allstate to recoup more money. Partin's suit was based on the "underinsured" motorist provisions of her auto insurance contract with Allstate. That contract was issued to her while she was a resident of Georgia. It stated that Georgia law applied to all claims arising out of the contract. If Georgia law applies, Partin will not be able to recover any extra money from Allstate, because Dolby would not qualify as an "underinsured motorist." However, if Louisiana law applies, Partin could collect an additional sum from Allstate because Dolby's insurance was insufficient to cover all of Partin's medical needs. If Delaware law applies, Partin is also unable to collect from Allstate. Which of these three possible choices of law should the Louisiana court use? [*Partin* v. *Dolby*, 652 So.2d 670 (Ct.App., La., 1995)]

11. Tracy Prows had a contract with Pinpoint to sell computers. Under the agreement, Prows worked with companies to develop computer specifications for their needs. Pinpoint would make the computers based on the specifications and sell the computers to Prows at wholesale prices. Prows would resell the computers to the customer at retail prices, making a profit. Flying J and Prows wrote specifications for computers to meet Flying J's needs. Then Flying J went right to Pinpoint and bought directly from the manufacturer, cutting Prows out. Prows sued Pinpoint for breach of contract in Utah court. Prows and Flying J are residents of Utah, and the contract between Prows and Pinpoint was signed in Utah. Pinpoint moved to dismiss the case for improper venue because the contract stated that all claims arising from the contract would be tried in New York, using New York law. What should the Utah court do? The Second Restatement of Conflict of Laws says that when parties specify a particular legal forum, that choice should be honored unless the forum "has no substantial relationship to the parties." [*Prows* v. *Pinpoint Retail Systems*, 868 P.2d 809 (S.Ct., Ut., 1993)]

12. A group of minors brought suit in California state court against a group of pharmaceutical companies, alleging that their grandmothers ingested the drug

diethylstilbestrol (DES) while pregnant (which the defendants manufactured), and that taking the drug caused them, the grandchildren, assorted harms. All but one of the plaintiffs lived in New York or New Jersey. The case was originally filed in New York, but the New York court dismissed the case because New York law does not recognize legal harms that involve third-generation plaintiffs. California law does not limit tort claims in this way. One plaintiff lived in California, and the California court was asked to try the case. The trial court dismissed the case based on forum non conveniens. Plaintiffs appealed. How should the appellate court rule? If motion to dismiss is upheld, the plaintiffs would have no other forum in which to bring their cases. [*Boaz* v. *Boyle & Company*, 40 Cal.App.4th 700 (Ct.App., Cal., 1995)]

13. Colemill Enterprises, a South Carolina company, purchased an airplane from Southeastern Flight Services, a Georgia company. The purchase price included a maintenance package that required Southeastern to keep the airplane in top operating condition. Shortly after the purchase, and while carrying Colemill's top executive, the airplane crashed and all passengers and crew were killed. There was evidence that the aircraft had been defectively manufactured and improperly maintained. The airplane was manufactured in Michigan and maintained in Georgia; the crash occurred in South Carolina. In a subsequent wrongful death action brought in Georgia, which state's law will apply? [*Risdon Enterprises, Inc.* v. *Colemill Enterprises*, 324 S.E.2d 738 (Ct.App., Ga., 1984)]

14. Ruth Creech, an Ohio resident, filed an action for malpractice against the City of Faith Hospital and physician McGee, both residents of Tulsa, Oklahoma. The claims arose out of injuries suffered while Creech was a patient at the City of Faith Hospital in Tulsa. Creech had heard of the hospital through the "Expect a Miracle" television program featuring Oral Roberts. Broadcast around the United States, the program invited people to come to the hospital for treatment. The case was tried in federal court in Ohio. The court found for Creech. The hospital and McGee appealed on the ground that the federal court could not exercise jurisdiction over them under the Ohio long-arm statute. They contended that they did not have sufficient minimum contacts with Ohio to confer jurisdiction. Assuming that Ohio's long-arm statute is similar to the one in Exhibit 2.4, was the court's exercise of jurisdiction reasonable? [*Creech* v. *Roberts*, 908 F.2d 75 (6th Cir., 1990)]

15. A married couple filed a complaint against the husband's former wife for stalking them. When the couple appeared before Judge Winchell, he directed them to change the charges against the ex-wife and then assisted them in filing the complaint against the woman, who was then arrested. The county prosecutor determined that the complaint was frivolous and recommended it be dismissed, but Winchell refused to dismiss the case. He was removed from the case by a superior judge because of his bias against the ex-wife. She sued Winchell for violation of her civil rights. Could she go forward with such a suit? [*Barnes* v. *Winchell*, 105 F.3d 1111 (6th Cir., 1997)]

POLICY QUESTION

16. Why are there appellate courts? Should judicial officers be required to take a competency examination before taking the bench? Should they be appointed or elected? Should they serve a lifetime term or some fixed number of years like most elected officials?

ETHICS QUESTIONS

17. Sylvia Eyestone, a California resident, was invited to Utah by the West States Refining Company to negotiate a dispute. When discussions proved fruitless, West had process served on Eyestone before she could leave the state. Should the service be allowed to stand? Is this a sound business decision?

18. Should judges consider the social consequences of their decisions? What if the case involves an individual who has committed a hideous crime and the judge is being asked to release the individual on a technicality?

INTERNET ASSIGNMENT

Along with the executive and legislative branches, the federal judiciary is a constitutionally co-equal branch of the U.S. Government. The federal trial and appellate courts themselves are, in essence, the storefronts for the federal judiciary, the offices through which the courts provide dispute resolution services. Less well known are the various agencies, each created by statute, responsible for the managerial and administrative functions of the third branch. These agencies, known collectively as the National Agencies of Federal Judicial Administration, are:
(a) The Judicial Conference of the United States (28 U.S.C. §331),
(b) The Administrative Office of the U.S. Courts (28 U.S.C. §§601–612),
(c) The Judicial Councils of the Circuits (28 U.S.C. §332),
(d) The Judicial Conferences of the Circuits (28 U.S.C. §333), and
(e) The U.S. Sentencing Commission (28 U.S.C. §§991–998).

The role of these agencies is far more important to the law than one might at first imagine. For example, the federal courts' basic venue provisions, 28 U.S.C. §§ 1391–1447, have significant implications for litigants, they are part of the federal legal landscape. These provisions are not found in the Constitution, nor were they drafted by Congress, however. They were promulgated by the Judicial Conference of the United States, and submitted to Congress as a proposed bill. The same is true for the Federal Rules of Civil Procedure and the Federal Rules of Appellate Procedure. Recommendations of the Judicial Conference of the United States regarding the rules of court ordinarily become law with very few, if any, changes made by the legislature. Thus, understanding the federal courts' operation and organization requires at least a passing knowledge of the functions of the judicial agencies.

Using the World Wide Web to find your information (and giving the URL for each source actually used), for each of the above-listed agencies describe briefly: (a) its purpose and/or mandate, and (b) its organizational structure.

See Appendix B.

CHAPTER 3

The Trial Process

Litigation has increased substantially over the past two decades. The news media report regularly on major lawsuits dealing with consumer injuries caused by products, medical malpractice, blown business deals, copyright infringement, and other disputes. Kim Basinger was ordered by a court to pay $9 million for failing to appear in a movie—even though there was no written contract. General Motors was ordered to pay more than $100 million to the family of a young man killed in an accident while driving a GM pickup that had a design defect. Exxon was ordered to pay $5 billion in damages for an oil spill off the Alaska coast.

While these lawsuits make the news, tens of thousands of seemingly less significant lawsuits are filed each year. Such suits can become a significant cost of doing business. To control costs, businesses are trying to reduce present and future legal expenses. Some companies conduct "legal audits" to evaluate their activities and determine potential sources of liability. On the basis of the audits, efforts are made to reduce legal expenses where possible and to make managers and employees aware of legal issues. Lawyers are playing more active roles in evaluating new activities to try to determine future legal problems in an effort to reduce litigation expenses.

This chapter discusses the nature of a lawsuit and the factors involved in litigation. It discusses the procedures and processes of litigating a dispute—from the pleadings through the discovery, trial, and appellate stages.

The Adversary System

A distinctive element of our judicial system is that it is an *adversary system of justice.* It requires the parties to argue their positions before a court. Parties may bring only actual, not potential or hypothetical, controversies before courts. This means that the responsibility for bringing a lawsuit, shaping its issues, and presenting convincing evidence rests upon the parties to the dispute. The adversary system reflects the belief that the best way to discover the truth in a case is by allowing the evidence and legal theories of the plaintiff to compete against the evidence and legal theories of the defendant.

Courts play a small role in establishing the facts of a case. Unlike in many countries, judges do not investigate either the parties or the facts of the case. Instead, the court applies the legal rules to the facts that the parties establish. By doing this, the court hopes to resolve the case peacefully. Given the adversarial nature of our legal system, individuals and businesses should weigh several factors before bringing a lawsuit. Here, we focus on the business perspective.

BUSINESS AS PLAINTIFF

Just as with individuals, a business typically does not file a lawsuit unless it believes it has suffered harm. However, since the law does not compensate all harms, a business must first decide whether the law provides relief for its injury. If the injury is not the kind the law protects against, the suit will be dismissed by the court.

A business incurs real costs, for example, when the marketing department works for weeks to persuade a major account to buy its product, only to see the sale go to a competitor. Similarly, if a finance department goes to great lengths and expense to hire a qualified new graduate, only to see the student accept a job offer with a competitor, the business has suffered a harm, but not one that the law recognizes. If, as in these situations, a grievance is not redressable by a court of law, a lawsuit would be a fruitless and wasteful undertaking.

What Is the Probability of Winning the Lawsuit?

Even if a firm decides that its grievance can be redressed by the courts, it must consider the probability of winning the lawsuit. In making this estimation, the business must consider several important factors. Can it find and bring the defendant into court? Can it produce the necessary witnesses and documents that will prove its case? Will the *finder of fact*—the *jury* or, if there is no jury, the *judge*—believe the evidence presented? Further, will the defendant be able to justify its conduct or prove the existence of a *defense*—a legal excuse—for its conduct? Finally, does the attorney's estimate of how the case will cost seem reasonable? After all, the parties to a case, not the attorneys, pay the bills.

Would the Relief Provided Make the Lawsuit Worthwhile?

Perhaps most important, a potential litigant must consider whether the relief the court might provide is worth the time, effort, and money. The party must weigh these costs against alternatives to the suit: settlement, arbitration, self-help, or simply letting matters rest. If a case involves monetary damages, the business must consider whether the defendant will be able to pay. Even if the defendant can pay, collecting the court's award may be difficult and expensive. Further, in the event collection is possible, the potential plaintiff must be concerned about whether anything would be left after paying attorney's fees, court costs, and other litigation expenses.

A business must also consider the effect on its operations. It must take into account the likely impact on its reputation and its goodwill as a result of bringing the action. A business may decide to ignore an injury because a lawsuit would open up its operations to close scrutiny by the public. The necessary evidence at the trial, for example, may require the disclosure of a company trade secret or of confidential financial data. A business may decide that, in such circumstances, litigation is not in its interest.

BUSINESS AS DEFENDANT

The questions and concerns confronting a business as defendant are not much different from those confronting a business as plaintiff. A manager asks legal counsel to determine the suit's likelihood of success and to estimate the costs of defending the company against the suit and of a judgment against the company. After accounting for any available insurance coverage (which usually means the insurance company becomes involved in litigation decisions), the business plans its response to a lawsuit. Throughout this process, managers should consider several other important issues.

How Will Litigation Affect the Company's Goodwill?

A defendant business must be concerned with the impact a lawsuit will have on its reputation and goodwill. In some cases, the impact of litigation is so negative that a company will avoid the publicity of a lawsuit by settling the case in private out of court.

In some cases, litigation may threaten a company's survival, so it has no option other than litigation. The cigarette industry, for example, has taken a very strong posture with regard to lawsuits alleging that it is liable for the injury to health caused by smoking cigarettes. Each such lawsuit has been litigated vigorously. The firms know that even a single judicial decision imposing liability invites more lawsuits.

How Important Is the Business Relationship?

A defendant must consider the importance of its relationship with the plaintiff. If the plaintiff and the business have an ongoing relationship—for example, as a supplier or wholesale customer—management may decide that continuing the relationship is more important than prevailing in court. The business may then find its best option is to settle the case or suggest using alternative dispute resolution, even though the company believes it could win the case if it went to court. Maintaining friendly, trusting business relations and a reputation for doing so is an important business strategy.

When natural gas and other energy prices fell sharply in the 1980s, Natural Gas Pipeline Company (NGP) found that it was unable to fulfill contractual commitments to natural gas producers. Several hundred producers filed suit against NGP and other pipeline companies, alleging breach of contract. The management of NGP believed it could win these lawsuits by arguing that upholding the contracts would violate important public policy concerns. Rather than litigate, however, NGP renegotiated its contracts to preserve valuable business relationships. Had it litigated, it may never have established the trust needed to form long-term, profitable relationships.

Is Settlement a Viable Alternative?

In some cases, a company may decide that its best course of action is to *settle* a dispute with a plaintiff rather than litigate. That is, the company pays the plaintiff some money (or takes other action the plaintiff wants) in return for an agreement to drop the lawsuit. In such cases, the defendant determines that the costs of settling the dispute are less than the costs of litigation. To estimate the costs of litigating the dispute, the company considers not only the direct costs of litigation—attorney's fees, expert witness fees, and court costs—but also costs associated with lost productivity as executives prepare for trial and the potentially negative impacts on its reputation. If these costs are higher than the costs of settling, the company considers settlement a viable alternative to litigation. Most lawsuits are settled out of court.

Defending Spurious Lawsuits

Many businesses suffer from so-called nuisance actions. In such cases, a plaintiff files a claim that is essentially baseless in hopes of gaining a settlement payment from the company. Litigation is expensive and risky, and nuisance plaintiffs bet that these factors will cause defendants to settle rather than litigate the claims they file. Depending on the nature of the claim, it generally costs corporations $10,000 to $50,000 to defend against a single nuisance action.

A company might find itself confronted not only with legal expenses but also with internal managerial expenses associated with efforts to defend against baseless lawsuits. The lure of potentially large settlements leads some people to undertake behavior that has serious consequences. For example, a man claimed that the inside of his mouth had been seriously burned by drinking a tainted can of Pepsi. Even though the company was sure the claim was false, to minimize possible risks to others and because of media attention, Pepsi responded immediately by withdrawing its products from stores in the area, at high cost. Later the police and the company determined that the man had inflicted the damage upon himself and then claimed it was Pepsi's fault.

To discourage nuisance actions and fraudulent claims, many companies have a policy to litigate such claims. These policies send a signal to would-be plaintiffs (and their attorneys) that they should not sue unless they are serious.

Rational Lawsuits

There may be times when a company encourages a lawsuit as the lower-cost option. Suppose, for example, that Richland Foods enters into a long-term contract with Scharmato to buy tomato paste. When the world price of tomato paste falls, Richland decides that the terms of the contract are no longer acceptable and could hurt the company financially. Scharmato refuses to renegotiate the contract. Richland then decides to breach the contract. It waits until the harvest season, when supplies are abundant, then informs Scharmato it will not accept further shipments of tomato paste. Scharmato sues Richland for breach of contract. Richland has decided that a breach of contract suit is likely to be less expensive than purchasing tomato paste under the terms of the contract. While this behavior raises ethical questions, it is nonetheless a fairly common practice in the business community.

RESOLVING DISPUTES THROUGH THE COURTS

The basic trial procedures in lawsuits involving a business do not differ significantly from lawsuits involving nonbusiness parties. With rare exception, all parties must follow the procedural rules of the court system to resolve a dispute. However, there are differences between business and nonbusiness cases:

1. The typical business case is more complex.
2. It generally involves more documents and exhibits as evidence.
3. It relies more heavily on expert testimony.
4. It takes more time.
5. The damage award is larger if the business loses.

Complex Facts and Issues

The legal issues in a business dispute are often more complex than in a nonbusiness dispute. Business activities can involve intricate fact situations that require complex evidence to unwind. In an antitrust case, for example, the presiding judge required both sides to write out in detail what they intended to prove. Even after the judge ordered several refinements, the response was nearly 5,000 pages long. Given that degree of complexity, it is not uncommon for several teams of attorneys to be involved in preparing and presenting the case.

Greater Use of Documents and Exhibits

In a complex dispute, thousands of documents and exhibits could be presented at trial. More important, the documents involved may be part of a series of related documents, adding to the complexity. For example, there may be a series of related papers, correspondence, internal memos, or an exchange of letters that allegedly make up a contract. In such a case, the judge and the jury will have a difficult task just understanding the documents. A dispute between Texaco and Borden produced more than 500,000 documents, many of which were interrelated.

Heavier Reliance on Expert Testimony

The testimony of expert witnesses often is an important part of a lawsuit. Even relatively simple disputes can require expert testimony on fundamental economic and finance issues. In environmental cases, for example, the issues may require testimony from various experts, including scientists, medical doctors, engineers, and economists. In complex cases, expert testimony can involve complicated statistical models presented by experts. The cost of that testimony can be significant, running into millions of dollars in some cases.

Longer Trials

Because of the complexity of the issues involved, business litigation is often longer than nonbusiness litigation. While a simple trial might last a day, a more complex case might take weeks or months to complete. Each party could call many witnesses and enter thousands of documents and exhibits into evidence. In addition, it is not uncommon for several years to pass before the dispute even reaches the trial stage. During all of this, senior management must devote some time to reviewing litigation issues and strategies.

Larger Damage Awards

In litigation, where the remedy sought is usually monetary damages, businesses are often viewed as "deep pockets." That is, the jury may award more money to a party injured by a business than to a party injured in the same way by another person. A business is viewed by the jury as having more than enough resources to compensate injured victims. A jury study found that injured plaintiffs who sue businesses receive awards that are four times larger, on the average, than awards to plaintiffs with similar injuries who sue individuals.

JURIS **prudence?**

Realistic Evidence

Vincent Morrissey charged New Haven, Connecticut, police with brutality. At the trial, police officer Ralph Angelo, on the witness stand, claimed that Morrissey started the fight by swinging at him. Morrissey's attorney asked Angelo to show the jury how hard Morrissey had swung at him. Angelo slugged the lawyer on the chin, dropping him and forcing the trial into recess.

Source: *Times Union* (Albany, NY)

THE GROWTH OF BUSINESS LITIGATION

Over the past decades, the United States has experienced rapid growth in business litigation. As Exhibit 3.1 shows, more than 100,000 business-related lawsuits—about 500 suits every working day—are filed in the federal district courts alone. In over 50,000 of those disputes, the interpretation, implementation, or application of a federal regulatory law is at the heart of the dispute. However, litigation in federal court is only the tip of the iceburg. Each year, about 20 million civil cases are filed in state courts. Not only has the number of lawsuits increased, so has the size of judgments. According to Jury Verdict Research, jury awards in product liability cases average over $1 million.

The costs associated with both resolving and preventing disputes have become a significant cost of doing business. While some managers have always carefully monitored their legal environments, it was not until recent years that the importance of such monitoring became apparent, in small as well as large businesses.

Basic Trial Procedures

As discussed in the opening section, the American legal system is an adversary system of justice. That is, the responsibility for bringing a lawsuit, shaping its issues, and presenting convincing evidence rests with the parties to the dispute. This section discusses the major procedural rules governing the civil litigation process. A summary of the stages of a typical lawsuit is presented in Exhibit 3.2.

EXHIBIT 3.1

Business Litigation, U.S. District Courts, 1996

Nature of Dispute	Number of Cases Filed
Contracts	33,413
Real Property	6,276
Product Liability	38,170
Asbestos	6,760
Environmental Matters	1,158
Patent, Copyright, Trademark	6,800
Labor Laws	15,068
Employment Discrimination	22,150
Securities and Commodities	1,741

Source: *Statistical Abstract of the United States*

EXHIBIT 3.2

Stages of a Typical Lawsuit

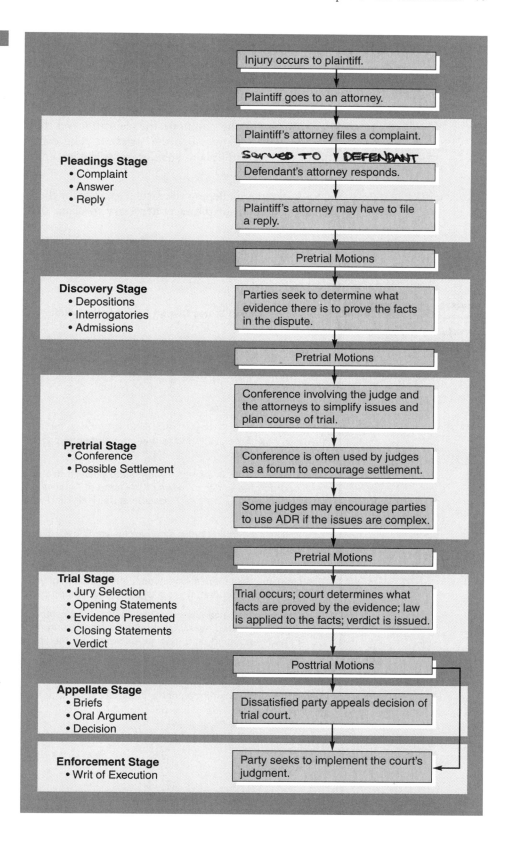

Injury occurs to plaintiff.

Plaintiff goes to an attorney.

Pleadings Stage
- Complaint
- Answer
- Reply

Plaintiff's attorney files a complaint.

Served to ↓ Defendant

Defendant's attorney responds.

Plaintiff's attorney may have to file a reply.

Pretrial Motions

Discovery Stage
- Depositions
- Interrogatories
- Admissions

Parties seek to determine what evidence there is to prove the facts in the dispute.

Pretrial Motions

Pretrial Stage
- Conference
- Possible Settlement

Conference involving the judge and the attorneys to simplify issues and plan course of trial.

Conference is often used by judges as a forum to encourage settlement.

Some judges may encourage parties to use ADR if the issues are complex.

Pretrial Motions

Trial Stage
- Jury Selection
- Opening Statements
- Evidence Presented
- Closing Statements
- Verdict

Trial occurs; court determines what facts are proved by the evidence; law is applied to the facts; verdict is issued.

Posttrial Motions

Appellate Stage
- Briefs
- Oral Argument
- Decision

Dissatisfied party appeals decision of trial court.

Enforcement Stage
- Writ of Execution

Party seeks to implement the court's judgment.

PLEADINGS STAGE

To begin his or her lawsuit, the plaintiff must first determine which court has both subject-matter jurisdiction and jurisdiction over the parties to the dispute. The plaintiff gives notice to the defendant by *service of process*, typically consisting of a *summons*, an example of which was presented in Exhibit 2.3.

Along with the summons, the plaintiff serves the defendant with the first of the *pleadings*, commonly called the *complaint*. The complaint is a statement that sets forth the plaintiff's claim against the defendant. As illustrated in Exhibit 3.3, the complaint contains

- A statement alleging the facts necessary for the court to take jurisdiction
- A statement of the facts necessary to claim that the plaintiff is entitled to a remedy
- A statement of the remedy the plaintiff is seeking

EXHIBIT 3.3

Example of a Typical Complaint

United States District Court for the Southern District of California

Civil No. 2–80151

Callie O'Keefe
Plaintiff

v.   Complaint

William Hitchcock, Inc.
Defendant

Comes now the plaintiff and for her cause of action against the defendant alleges and states as follows:

1. The plaintiff is a citizen of the state of California and defendant is a corporation incorporated under the laws of the state of Delaware, having its principal place of business in the state of Massachusetts. There is diversity of citizenship between parties.

2. The amount in controversy, exclusive of interest and costs, exceeds the sum of $75,000.

3. On January 10, 2000, in a public highway called Petty Street in Charlotte, North Carolina, defendant's employee, John Kluttz, negligently drove a motor vehicle owned by defendant against plaintiff who was properly crossing said highway.

4. As a result, plaintiff was hit and knocked down and had her leg broken and was otherwise injured, was prevented from transacting her business, suffered great pain of body and mind, and incurred expenses for medical attention and hospitalization.

5. The costs plaintiff incurred included: $15,000 in medical care, $100,000 in lost business, and $100,000 in pain and suffering.

WHEREFORE, plaintiff demands, judgment against defendent in the sum $215,000 and costs.

by
Linda Johnson
Attorney for Plaintiff
5450 Tower of the Americas
San Diego, CA 92138

Dated: 7/19/00

RESPONSES TO THE COMPLAINT

Following the service of the plaintiff's complaint, the defendant must file a responsive pleading. If the defendant does not respond, the court will presume the claims of the plaintiff are true and grant the plaintiff's requests. Depending on the circumstances, the defendant may file (1) a motion to dismiss, (2) an answer with or without an affirmative defense, or (3) a counterclaim.

Motion to Dismiss

A *motion to dismiss* by the defendant asks the court to dismiss the action because it does not have jurisdiction over either the subject matter of the dispute or the defendant's person. This motion may challenge the venue (location of the court) or the sufficiency of the service of process.

The defendant may also file a *motion to dismiss for failure to state a claim or cause of action* or a *demurrer.* (Note that the rules of civil procedure in some states do not use the term *demurrer;* they use only the term *motion to dismiss.*) The motion to dismiss for failure to state a claim is an allegation by the defendant that even if the facts are true, the injury claimed by the plaintiff is one for which the law furnishes no remedy. In addition, the defendant may file this motion if the plaintiff has failed to include an important part of the case in the pleadings. That is, the plaintiff's pleadings are inadequate to meet the minimum requirements under the rules of civil procedure.

Answer

If the defendant's motion to dismiss is denied or if the defendant does not make such a motion, the defendant must file an *answer* with the court. In this pleading, the defendant admits or denies the allegations made by the plaintiff in the complaint. If the defendant admits the allegations in the plaintiff's complaint or fails to deny the claims, a judgment is entered for the plaintiff. If the defendant denies the allegations, the trial process continues.

Counterclaim

The defendant can deny the plaintiff's allegations in an answer and assert his own claim against the plaintiff. The defendant's claim is known as a *counterclaim.* In many cases, the defendant will base his counterclaim on the same events that the plaintiff bases her complaint on. The counterclaim is in essence a complaint by the defendant, and the plaintiff must respond to it just as the defendant responded to the original complaint.

Affirmative Defenses

In answering the complaint, the defendant may admit to some or all of the plaintiff's allegations but may assert additional facts that should result in the action being dismissed. Called an *affirmative defense,* the defendant admits that he injured the plaintiff but that the additional facts he asserts constitute a defense (a legal excuse) to the plaintiff's complaint. The defendant could admit to being in a car accident involving the plaintiff but could assert that the claim is now barred by the statute of limitations; that is, the plaintiff waited too long to file suit. Other examples of affirmative defenses include self-defense, insanity, excessive vagueness of the plaintiff's complaint, and failure to state a claim that the law recognizes.

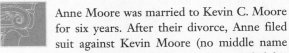

I Said No, No, No, It Ain't Me, Babe!

Anne Moore was married to Kevin C. Moore for six years. After their divorce, Anne filed suit against Kevin Moore (no middle name and no relation), demanding that she be awarded his house and that she see his bank records. When Anne failed to appear at a court hearing on her motion, Kevin's attorney convinced the court to throw out her claim because Kevin Moore is not Kevin C. Moore. The judge ordered Anne to pay Kevin's attorney fee of $996 (which she did not pay).

Anne filed another motion seeking access to Kevin's bank records, claiming "Kevin Moore of Sunrise is Anne Moore's ex-husband despite his previous statement that he was not." She also claimed that Kevin C. Moore (who cannot be found) owns the house occupied by Kevin Moore and is letting Kevin stay in the house to cheat her out of it. Anne told a reporter, "Apparently there's more going on here than meets the surface."

Source: *Sun-Sentinel* (Fort Lauderdale, Florida)

Reply

In most court systems, the pleadings stage ends after the answer. Any new matters raised by the defendant's answer are automatically taken as denied by the plaintiff. When the defendant does file a counterclaim, the plaintiff may answer it with an additional pleading, called a *reply*, which is an answer to the counterclaim.

The complaint, answer, and, if present, the counterclaim and reply form the *pleadings*. The purpose of the pleadings is to notify each of the parties of the claims, defenses, and counterclaims of the other side. The pleadings focus the issues, helping to remove the element of surprise from the resolution of the dispute. By so doing, the pleadings allow the advocates in this adversarial system to state their arguments for the court, thus assuring that a truer decision will be reached.

Motion for Judgment on the Pleading

After the pleadings are completed, either party may file a *motion for judgment on the pleadings*. This motion is essentially the same as a motion to dismiss, but it occurs after the pleadings have been completed. Like the motion to dismiss, the probability of its being granted varies directly with the substance of the argument and the degree of detail required in the pleadings. Essentially, the plaintiff is claiming that the defendant has no defense and the judge should rule immediately for the plaintiff; or the defendant is claiming that the plaintiff failed to state a case and the case should be dismissed.

DISCOVERY STAGE: OBTAINING INFORMATION BEFORE TRIAL

After the pleadings, the litigation enters the discovery stage. During this stage, the parties use various legal tools to obtain evidence about the dispute. The attorneys are particularly interested in gathering information from the opposing parties and their witnesses and experts. The process of obtaining information is known as *discovery*. The Federal Rules of Civil Procedure and the corresponding state procedural codes set down the guidelines and limits for the discovery process.

Purpose of Discovery

Discovery serves several important functions. Years ago, disputes moved from the pleadings stage directly to the trial stage. As a result, the parties had little information about the specific evidence the other party was going to use. The evidence presented often caught the opposing party by surprise—a "trial by ambush." The discovery process prevents surprises by giving the parties access to information that might otherwise remain hidden.

Discovery also preserves evidence of witnesses who might not be available at the time of the trial, as well as the testimony of witnesses whose memory may fade with the passage of time, or who may later attempt to change their testimony.

Finally, by allowing both parties the opportunity to become knowledgeable of the facts, discovery encourages pretrial settlements. Often, after a determination of the facts, both parties can assess the strengths of both sides and can estimate what a reasonable out-of-court settlement would be. Most cases are settled, but if settlement efforts are unsuccessful, the discovery process narrows the issues of the dispute so that the trial can focus on the important questions in the case.

Tools of the Discovery Process

The discovery rules offer several ways to get information from an opposing party. Discovery allows attorneys to gather the testimony of parties and witnesses and to gather relevant documents and other kinds of evidence. The tools of discovery include depositions, written interrogatories, orders for production of documents, requests for admissions, and orders for a mental or physical examination. According to the Federal Rules of Civil Procedure, a party seeking information must select a discovery tool that is not "unduly burdensome" to the other party. In practice, parties can force out nearly any information related to the legal issues. The opposing party cannot refuse to comply just because of the burden of compliance.

Depositions and Interrogatories The principal discovery tool is the *deposition*—the sworn testimony of a witness recorded by a court official. In this procedure, the person whose deposition is taken is questioned by attorneys from both sides. The questions and the answers are recorded, sworn to, signed, and transcribed.

The deposition is useful in finding information relevant to the resolution of the dispute, including leads to other witnesses or documents. It is also useful during the trial to impeach—or challenge—a witness who attempts to change his or her story at the trial. Finally, the deposition of a witness who is unavailable at the time of the trial may be allowed in place of live testimony.

A useful discovery tool is *written interrogatories*—written questions submitted by the opposing party. The party receiving the interrogatories prepares written answers with the aid of an attorney and signs them under oath. The main difference between written interrogatories and depositions with written questions is that the interrogatories may be addressed only to a party to the suit and not to other witnesses. Although the interrogatories lack the spontaneity of a deposition, they require the party to provide information from his or her records and files—the kind of information not carried in one's head.

Orders for the Production of Documents An order for the production of documents allows a party access to information in the sole possession of the other party. The kinds of information that are often the subject of such an order are medical bills, business records, letters, and repair bills. The party seeking the information usually has the right to gain access for the purposes of inspection, examination, and reproduction. If a trade secret or other confidential information is involved, a company can get a *protective order* to ensure confidentiality. The court may impose severe sanctions (penalties) on a party found to have violated a protective order.

Requests for Admissions Either party can serve the other with a written request for an admission of the truth in matters relating to the dispute. Requests for admissions are used to force admissions of facts about which there are no real disputes between the parties. Their purpose is to eliminate the need to establish at the trial those facts about which there is no real controversy. For example, in a contract dispute over the price of a product, one party may ask the other to admit that deliveries were made and accepted according to the terms of the contract. If admitted, these facts will not have to be proven at trial.

Mental and Physical Examinations In a dispute in which the physical or mental condition of a party is an issue, the court may be asked to order that party to submit to an examination. Because of concerns for that party's right to privacy, the party requesting the order must show a greater need for the information than in requests for other forms of discovery. Generally, the party requesting the order specifies the exact type of mental or physical examination desired and the time, the place, and the specialists who are to conduct it.

Sanctions for Failing to Respond to a Discovery Request Under the Federal Rules of Civil Procedure and the procedural codes of most states, courts have broad powers to impose sanctions against a party who fails to comply with discovery requirements. If a party fails to comply with the requirements of a deposition, written interrogatories, or a request, the court may issue an order directing the party to comply. If the party does not comply with the order, the court may order a *default judgment* granting victory to the other party or find the noncomplying party in *contempt of court* and order the party to jail or impose a fine.

Discovery: Impacts on Business

Discovery can impose significant costs on businesses and managers. Businesses can be forced to endure the expense and the disruption of their staff while employees answer questions and produce documents. In one regulatory dispute between Ford Motor Company and the Federal Trade Commission, it cost Ford $4 million just to copy required documents. The burdens imposed by depositions are particularly heavy when executives have to take time to prepare for and provide a deposition. In disputes involving technical matters or significant detail, the deposition of the manager responsible for the project or the most knowledgeable about it may take two weeks or more.

It is not uncommon for the chief executive of a corporation to get a subpoena requesting that he appear for a deposition. In most cases, the information being sought is in the hands of subordinates, not of the chief executive. Courts protect executives if the purpose of a deposition is to harass them, but their participation is not uncommon. This expense is one more reason out-of-court settlement is likely.

In some cases, the courts examine the circumstances and recommend an alternative discovery tool. Plaintiffs seeking damages for injuries from an alleged defective design in a Dodge van sought the deposition of Lee Iacocca, then the chairman of Chrysler. The court held that although "[Iacocca's] prestigious position is an unimpressive paper barrier shielding him from the judicial process, . . . he is a singularly unique and important individual who can be easily subjected to harassment and abuse. . . . Therefore, . . . an orderly discovery process will be best served by resorting to interrogatories at this time. . . ." In the following case, the court is confronted with a similar request for a deposition of executives.

Wauchop v. Domino's Pizza, Inc.
United States District Court, N.D. Indiana
143 F.R.D. 199 (1992)

CASE BACKGROUND *This case was filed as a wrongful death action by the family of a woman killed in an automobile accident involving a delivery vehicle owned by a Domino's Pizza franchisee. The plaintiffs filed the suit against Domino's Pizza; Thomas Monaghan, the president of Domino's; the franchise owner; and the Domino's delivery vehicle driver. The plaintiffs charged Domino's with negligence based on its thirty-minute delivery guarantee, claiming that the policy caused delivery personnel to drive dangerously. According to the guarantee, if a pizza was not delivered on time, it was free. At the time of this lawsuit, twenty deaths had been attributed by the news media to driving practices brought about by the guarantee.*

The plaintiffs had filed a motion for default judgment against Monaghan because he refused to give a deposition. Monaghan filed a motion for summary judgment, stating that he was not responsible for the injuries in this case. In this ruling on the motion, the court decides whether Monaghan must attend the deposition.

CASE DECISION Miller, Judge.

* * *

[Previously] the court ordered the parties to complete all outstanding written discovery and all previously noticed depositions by February 28. Mr. Monaghan's deposition previously had been noticed. The court also afforded the plaintiffs until March 16, to file a response to Mr. Monaghan's motion for summary judgment. During the status conference, counsel for Domino's and Mr. Monaghan stated that she would have a problem producing Mr. Monaghan for deposition.

Mr. Monaghan had moved for summary judgment on August 5th [of the previous year], contending that he should not be held personally liable for the accident that forms the basis of this action. His motion is supported by his own written statement, which stated that he was not personally involved in the operation of the

franchise, . . . that he never had any dealings with [the driver], and that his only conduct in relation to the 30-minute guarantee was in his capacity as a corporate director or officer. In his written statement, Mr. Monaghan states that the 30-minute guarantee policy went through corporate channels and was implemented after discussions with franchisees. He also states that the guarantee stresses safe driving.

* * *

The plaintiffs planned to test the assertions in Mr. Monaghan's written statement by deposing Mr. Monaghan and other employees of Domino's. Mr. Monaghan, however, has refused to make himself available for deposition for several reasons. Mr. Monaghan's motion to strike the notice of his deposition reiterates the arguments in his summary judgment motion; he claims that he is not personally liable to the plaintiffs because the only allegations against him relate to his implementation of the 30-minute policy in his capacity as a director, shareholder, and chief executive officer of Domino's. He further reiterates that he was never directly involved with [the driver] or with the operation of the franchise. . . .

Mr. Monaghan also claims, surprisingly, that the 30-minute policy is not an issue in this case. He states . . . that no reasonable trier of fact could find that [the driver] was trying to comply with the 30-minute policy when the accident occurred, because at the time of the accident [he] was returning to the store from a pizza delivery. Further, Mr. Monaghan claims that the 30-minute policy could be an issue only if [the driver] was speeding at the time of the accident, and that the only evidence that [he] was speeding is [a passenger's] speculation during his deposition. . . . Finally, Mr. Monaghan argues that he has no knowledge of the policies and procedures of Domino's that cannot be obtained through written discovery or deposition of other Domino's employees.

* * *

The plaintiffs are entitled to take Mr. Monaghan's deposition to inquire into his role in the development of the 30-minute policy, a topic central to the plaintiffs' theory of Mr. Monaghan's liability and central to Mr. Monaghan's written statement. The plaintiffs point to discovery material that lends support to their contention that Mr. Monaghan was directly involved in implementation of Domino's policies.

* * *

Under the discovery rules as they exist, Mr. Monaghan has raised no viable impediment to the taking of his deposition. . . . The court cannot avoid the conclusion that Mr. Monaghan is willing to delay and frustrate discovery indefinitely, notwithstanding the previous orders regarding the discovery of the relationship between the 30-minute policy and the accident in this case.

* * *

[T]he court will not enter default against Mr. Monaghan at this time, but will afford him an opportunity to rectify his failure to comply with the court's previous orders relating to discovery. The order found at the conclusion of this memorandum requires Mr. Monaghan to appear in Chicago for his deposition and to pay the plaintiff's fees.

* * *

QUESTIONS FOR ANALYSIS

1. Why would Mr. Monaghan and Domino's Pizza not want to give the deposition in this case? Why was his deposition needed?
2. In general, in what situations would the depositions of lower-level employees be sufficient? When would the depositions of higher-level employees be necessary?

PRETRIAL STAGE

Either party or the court may request a *pretrial conference*. These commonly held conferences involve the attorneys and the judge, but may also involve the parties themselves. The purpose of the conferences is to simplify the issues and plan the course of the trial. To ensure more efficient trials, judges may request that the parties seek additional admissions of facts or limit the number of witnesses.

At pretrial conferences, judges encourage settlements (as we discuss in Chapter 4). A survey of settlement policies of judges in the Second Circuit found that most judges are actively involved in settling cases. Most judges see their role in pretrial conferences both as a trial judge and as a "peacemaker." As trial judges, they discuss with the parties the costs and risks of going to trial. As peacemakers, judges work openly for settlements.

Recent decisions tend to increase judges' authority to encourage pretrial settlements. For example, in *G. Heileman Brewing Co.* v. *Joseph Oat Corp.* (871 F.2d 648), the Seventh Circuit Court of Appeals held that a district court may order the parties to appear in person at a pretrial conference for the purpose of discussing the settlement of their case. The court stated:

> This litigation involved a claim for $4 million—a claim which turned upon the resolution of complex factual and legal issues. The litigants expected the trial to last from one to three months and all parties stood to incur substantial legal fees and trial expenses. This trial also would have preempted a large segment of judicial time—not an insignificant factor. Thus, because the stakes were high, we do not believe that the burden of requiring a corporate representative to attend a pretrial settlement conference was out of proportion to the benefits to be gained, not only by the litigants but also by the court.

Summary Judgment

If the parties determine at the close of discovery that they do not disagree about the facts of the case, either party may move for a *summary judgment*. Because there is no dispute about facts, a party asks the judge to apply the law to these facts and resolve the dispute. If a motion for summary judgment is granted, the case is over. The defendant is either released from the matter, or the plaintiff has won. Summary judgments for defendants are more common than for plaintiffs. The judge's decision to grant or deny a motion for summary judgment may be appealed. In reaching a decision, the judge is free to consider evidence not contained in the pleadings, such as affidavits. The judge's ruling has the same legal effect as a decision of the trial court. Motions for summary judgment may be made before or during the trial, but they are granted only if there are no disagreements about the key facts to a dispute.

TRIAL STAGE

After discovery is complete, if there has been no dismissal, summary judgment, or settlement, the dispute is set for *trial*. In many court systems, the trial calendar is quite long. Delays of up to three years before a noncriminal case comes to trial are not uncommon.

The Jury

The Seventh Amendment of the U.S. Constitution as well as state constitutions provides for the right to a *jury* in certain cases. In the federal court system, this right is guaranteed if the amount in controversy exceeds $20 and involves a common-law claim. Most state court systems have similar guarantees, although the minimum amount in controversy may be higher. The state of Iowa requires that the amount in controversy be at least $1,000. There is no right to a jury trial in cases in which the plaintiff requests an equitable remedy rather than monetary damages.

Decision to Use a Jury The right to a jury trial does not have to be exercised. If a jury is not requested, the judge determines the true facts in the dispute and applies the law to resolve it. Several important considerations enter into the decision whether or not to request a jury trial, including the judge's perceived temperament,

---

JURIS prudence?

The Dog Ate My Summons

Trying to avoid jury duty is common. The Harris County (Houston, Texas) District Court Clerk compiled the following list of excuses offered by jury duty dodgers:

"I have to feed my bird during the day."

"I take care of three cats during the day."

"I have to pee—a lot."

"I shot holes in my daughter's boyfriend's car."

"My wife killed someone."

"I had something removed from my head this morning."

Source: *National Law Journal*

the complexity of the evidence, and the degree to which the emotions of the jury are likely to affect the judgment.

Selection of the Jury   The jury selection process formally begins when the clerk of the court sends a notice requesting individuals to appear for jury duty. From this group (jury pool), the judge selects the jury that will hear the case. The importance of selecting a jury has led to the birth of a new profession: jury consultants. These consultants help attorneys understand the communities from which jurors come. They use focus groups and surveys to build a picture of a particular community. Attorneys are most likely to use jury consultants in complex or controversial cases.

Voir Dire   The screening process used to select jury members is called *voir dire*. Depending upon the court, either the judge or the attorneys conduct voir dire. The purpose of this screening process is to determine whether a prospective juror is likely to be so biased or prejudiced that he or she could not reach an objective decision based on the evidence to be presented. If such a determination is made, the attorney may *challenge for cause*, and that person is disqualified. Attorneys are allowed a limited number of peremptory challenges that permit an attorney to reject a prospective juror without stating a reason why. Juries traditionally involve a panel of twelve persons, although in many states, panels of fewer than twelve—frequently six—are used.

The Trial

Although judges have some freedom to change the structure of a trial, most follow the general order summarized in Exhibit 3.4. Although jury and nonjury trials are handled in much the same way, they have a number of important procedural differences. In nonjury trials, the judge may put more limits on the attorneys' opening statements and closing arguments. The following discussion details the steps involved in a typical jury trial.

Opening Statements   After the jurors have been sworn in, both attorneys make *opening statements*. In those statements, the attorneys tell the jury what the crucial facts are and how they will prove that those facts support their positions. Opening

EXHIBIT 3.4	**Jury Trial**	**Nonjury Trial**
Summaries of Typical Jury and Nonjury Trials	1. The selection of a jury 2. Plaintiff's opening statement 3. Defendant's opening statement 4. Plaintiff's presentation of direct evidence 5. Defendant's presentation of direct evidence 6. Plaintiff's presentation of rebuttal evidence 7. Defendant's presentation of rebuttal evidence 8. Opening final argument by the plaintiff 9. Defendant's final argument 10. Plaintiff's closing argument 11. Instructions to the jury 12. Jury deliberation and verdict	1. Plaintiff's opening statement 2. Defendant's opening statement 3. Plaintiff's presentation of direct evidence 4. Defendant's presentation of direct evidence 5. Plaintiff's presentation of rebuttal evidence 6. Defendant's presentation of rebuttal evidence 7. Defendant's final argument 8. Plaintiff's closing argument 9. Judge's deliberation and verdict

statements are generally limited to twenty minutes. The plaintiff's attorney normally presents the first statement.

Presentation of Direct Testimony Following the opening statement, the plaintiff's attorney calls witnesses. The plaintiff goes first and has the burden of proving that his or her claims are correct. Each witness is first questioned by the plaintiff's attorney; this is called *direct examination*. The defendant's attorney then examines that witness on *cross-examination*. Cross-examination may be followed by *re-direct examination* by the plaintiff's attorney and then by *re-cross-examination* by the defendant's attorney. The judge controls the length and the course of these latter examinations.

Motion for Directed Verdict After having called and examined all witnesses, the plaintiff *rests*. The defendant's attorney may then ask for a *directed verdict* on the grounds that the plaintiff has not presented sufficient evidence to support the claims—that is, he or she has not met the burden of proof, and the judge should dismiss the case at this point. If the motion is granted, the defendant "wins" the trial (although the plaintiff may appeal this decision). If the motion is denied, the defendant must present his or her direct case. In addition, after both parties rest, either may, at that time, move for a *directed verdict*. If the motion is denied, the case goes to the judge or jury for a verdict. As the following case illustrates, the plaintiff must be able to demonstrate to the court that the defendant's actions could possibly be found to have caused the injuries.

May v. Hall County Livestock Improvement Association
Supreme Court of Nebraska
216 Neb. 476, 344 N.W.2d 629 (1984)

CASE BACKGROUND *May, the plaintiff, slipped and fell at a racetrack owned by Hall County, the defendant. May brought an action against Hall County for the injuries she incurred in that fall. At the close of the plaintiff's case, the trial court sustained the defendant's motion for a directed verdict. The court asserted that although the plaintiff proved she was injured, she did not prove that the defendant could be responsible. The plaintiff appealed, arguing that her evidence was sufficient to sustain a jury verdict against the defendant.*

CASE DECISION Cambridge, District Judge.

This is an appeal in a slip and fall case. The trial court sustained the defendant's motion for a directed verdict at the close of the plaintiff's case. As we must, we assume the truth of the material and relevant evidence presented by the plaintiff, find every controverted fact in her favor, and give her the benefit of every reasonable inference deducible from the evidence.

On April 12, 1977, the plaintiff attended the horseraces at Fonner Park Racetrack, Grand Island,

Nebraska. The defendant owned and operated the park. The plaintiff . . . paid for admittance into a reserved area . . . where there were tables and chairs from which the races could be observed. The area had a cement floor. Food, soft drinks, and beer, purchased either at concession stands located in the area or from waitresses who served the tables, were consumed in the area. The plaintiff sat at one of those tables, and on various trips from and to the table [said] she saw "slippery places" and liquid on the cement in the areas around her table but not near her table; she never looked under her own table before the accident to see if there was any liquid under the table or around her chair. The plaintiff stood up for most, if not all, of the sixth race, and when she saw that the horse she had bet was going to win, she started to take steps to go, and her left foot slipped; she tried to break her fall by catching the leg of the table with her right foot, but did not succeed. After regaining consciousness the plaintiff recalled that the bottom or lower part of her right pantleg was wet. According to the food concession manager, who arrived on the scene while the plaintiff was still lying on the floor and who remained there until the plaintiff had left, there were no spills, liquids, or debris of any kind on the floor where the plaintiff had fallen, and the floor was dry. . . . As a result of the fall, the plaintiff sustained head injuries and a broken right hip with complications in the healing of that fracture.

* * *

It is well-established law in this state that a possessor of premises is under a duty to use reasonable care to make his premises safe for a business visitor or to give him adequate warning to enable him to avoid harm when certain conditions are true.

* * *

It is apparent from the foregoing recital of facts that the plaintiff failed to produce any evidence which could have reasonably satisfied the jury that the physical harm suffered by the plaintiff was caused by a condition or activity on the defendant's premises. Giving full weight to all of the plaintiff's evidence and all inferences reasonably deducible therefrom, it can be

concluded that such conditions and activities did in fact exist on the defendant's premises at the time in question, but there is literally no evidence in the record establishing that any one of them was the proximate cause or a proximately contributing cause of the plaintiff's slip and fall and the physical harm which resulted therefrom.

Where the facts presented to sustain an issue are such that but one conclusion can be drawn when related to the applicable law, it is the duty of the court to decide the question as a matter of law and not submit it to a jury.

* * *

Affirmed.

QUESTIONS FOR ANALYSIS

1. What are the requirements placed on the court in sustaining a directed verdict?
2. What basic element of the plaintiff's case was missing in her presentation of the evidence?
3. Would this case have made it to trial if the plaintiff had been required to detail her legal arguments at the pleading stage?

Closing Arguments Before the case goes to the jury, the attorneys each present a *closing argument.* The attorneys try to summarize the evidence for the jury in a manner most favorable to their case. Normally, the plaintiff may present closing arguments both before and after the defendant. As in the opening statement, the judge limits the amount of time available to the attorneys for their closing arguments. It is improper for an attorney to discuss in closing argument a matter that was excluded from the trial.

Instructions to the Jury Before the jury retires to deliberate and reach a verdict, the judge gives the jury *instructions* (or *charges*). In the instructions, the judge tells

JURIS prudence?

You Got Me There, Counselor!

The editor of the Massachusetts Bar Association's *Lawyers Journal* has kept a collection of courtroom bloopers by lawyers when questioning various parties. Among them:

"Were you present when your picture was taken?"
"Are you qualified to give a urine sample?"

"Did he kill you?"
"Were you alone or by yourself?"
"How many times have you committed suicide?"

Source: *Wall Street Journal*

the jury the applicable law, summarizes the facts and issues of the dispute, and states which of the parties has the *burden of persuasion*. After the instructions have been given, the jurors are placed in the custody of the *bailiff* or other court official, who oversees them during their deliberations and whose responsibility it is to see that they remain together and that there is no jury misconduct.

Reaching a Verdict The jury deliberates to reach an agreement and find for either the plaintiff or the defendant. In a civil trial, the parties must prove their contentions by a *preponderance of the evidence*. If jurors are unable to resolve an issue, they should find against the party who has the burden of persuasion for that issue. In such cases, juries are simply unable to reach a unanimous decision. The jury is said to be *hung*, and a new trial before a different jury is necessary. The jury is discharged and a *mistrial* declared.

Because of the cost and delay associated with a new trial, courts are reluctant to allow hung juries. Although many jurisdictions still require a unanimous jury decision, some allow verdicts in civil disputes to be less than unanimous. In Minnesota, a less than unanimous verdict is permitted, but only after the jury has deliberated for a specified period of time.

After the jury has reached a verdict, the verdict is read in open court by the foreman of the jury or by the judge or the clerk of the court. The judgment is then entered. In some cases, the jury deliberates a second time to determine damages to be awarded if they find for the plaintiff.

Motions After the Verdict After the verdict has been presented, the parties have the opportunity to challenge it with certain *posttrial motions*. The challenging party (the loser) can move for a *judgment notwithstanding the verdict* or *judgment n.o.v.* This motion raises the same question as the motion for a directed verdict. The party moving for the judgment n.o.v. is stating that a reasonable jury would not have found for the other party. That is, the jury's verdict is not supportable by the evidence presented at the trial. If the judge agrees, the jury's verdict is reversed.

The losing party can also move for a new trial. There are several grounds for this motion. Most commonly, an attorney argues that the judge erred in admitting certain evidence or that the judge's instructions to the jury were inappropriate. It can also be argued that there was misconduct by the attorneys, the parties, or the jurors; or the monetary damages awarded were either excessive or inadequate. The party requesting the motion is asking the court to set aside the current verdict and hold a new trial. A new trial may also be granted if new and important evidence, a clerical mistake, or fraud is discovered subsequent to the trial. However, the granting of a new trial under these circumstances is rare. The following case considers the issue of jury misconduct.

Powell v. Allstate Insurance Co.
Supreme Court of Florida
652 So.2d 354 (1995)

CASE BACKGROUND *Powell was injured when his car collided with another vehicle. Powell collected $10,000 from the other driver, the limit of that driver's liability coverage. Powell then sued Allstate, his insurance com-* *pany, for over $200,000 under provisions of his underinsured motorist coverage. The case was tried by a jury, which awarded Powell $29,320. The day after the trial, one juror informed Powell's attorney and the trial judge* *that certain jury members had made racial jokes and seemingly racist statements about Powell during the trial. The juror stated that she believed that the verdict reflected racial bias. (Powell is African-American, and all jurors were white.) Powell requested a new trial. The trial court denied the request. Powell appealed the denial. The appellate court also denied a new trial. Powell appealed the decision that upheld the trial court's denial of a motion for a new trial based on jury misconduct.*

CASE DECISION Anstead, Justice.

* * *

The authority of a trial court to grant a new trial derives in part from the equitable principle that neither a wronged litigant nor society itself should be without a means to remedy a palpable miscarriage of justice.

* * *

[W]e adopted the test used by the Fifth Circuit [Federal Court of Appeals] . . . which limits the trial court's inquiry in jury misconduct cases to objective demonstration of extrinsic factual matter disclosed in the jury room. Having determined the precise quality of the jury breach, if any, the [trial] court must then determine whether there was a reasonable possibility that the breach was prejudicial to the defendant.

* * *

[W]hen appeals to racial bias are made openly among the jurors, they constitute overt acts of mis-

conduct. . . . [T]he conduct alleged herein, if established, [is] violative of the guarantees of both the federal and state constitutions which ensure all litigants a fair and impartial jury and equal protection of the law.

* * *

It is not by chance that the words "Equal Justice Under Law" have been placed for all to see above the entrance to this nation's highest court. . . . The justice system, and the courts especially, must jealously guard our sacred trust to assure equal treatment before the law.

* * *

Accordingly, we . . . remand with instructions for the trial court to conduct an appropriate hearing to ascertain whether racial statements were made as asserted. If the trial court determines that such statements were made, it shall order a new trial.

QUESTIONS FOR ANALYSIS

1. The court in this case suggests that when jurors make offensive remarks about the race, religion, or ethnic origin of a party to lawsuit in the juror room, this may constitute jury misconduct. Can you think of any other groups that should be covered by this rule?
2. Does this case illustrate a situation in which use of a jury consultant might have been advisable? If so, why?

REMEDIES AVAILABLE IN CIVIL LITIGATION

Most civil disputes are settled outside the court system. The expense of a lawsuit, long delays before the dispute actually goes before the court, and concerns about how the dispute will be resolved by the court encourage litigants to settle before trial. If the dispute does go to trial, however, the persons involved are seeking resolution of the dispute in the form of a specific remedy provided by the court. Within the American court system, the remedies awarded by courts in civil disputes are classified as either *equitable remedies* or *monetary damages*. The large majority of cases are for monetary damages, but in some cases a remedy in equity is more appropriate. Exhibit 3.5 summarizes the remedies available in civil litigation.

Monetary Damages

If a court finds that a party has suffered a legally recognized harm, the court may award the party monetary damages. The general categories of monetary damage awards are compensatory, punitive, and nominal damages. As disputes have become more and more complex and the expertise for assessing damages has improved and

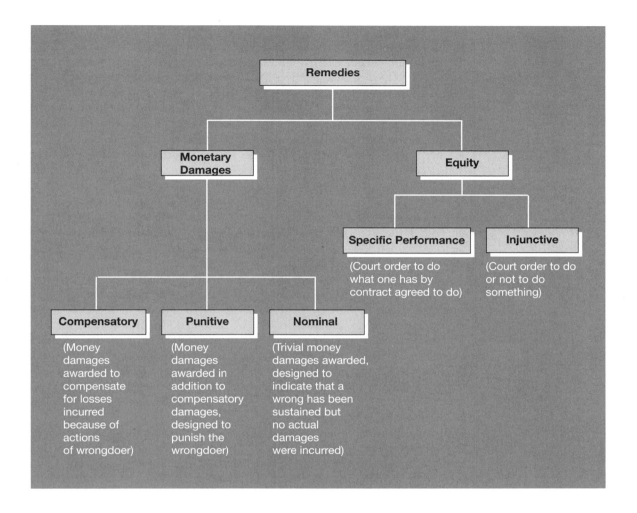

Equitable Remedies and Monetary Damages

become more reliable, the courts have developed new approaches for providing compensation to injured parties.

Compensatory Damages *Compensatory damages* are intended to give injured parties enough money to restore them to the economic position they were in before the injury or to cover the costs incurred because of the injury. These are the most common monetary damages. Compensatory damages may be awarded for loss of time and money, pain and suffering, injury to reputation, and mental anguish.

Suppose Album Shipping contracts to sell pasta to Camerican International for $20,000. In the event Album does not deliver and Camerican must buy its pasta from another source for $25,000, Camerican is entitled to $5,000 in compensatory damages from Album. It has suffered a net loss of $5,000 in the purchase. In Chapter 10, on contracts, we will review the issues involved in and alternative forms of compensatory damages.

Punitive Damages In those situations where the wrongdoer's actions were particularly reprehensible or in situations where the defendant's conduct was willful or malicious, the court may award the injured party *punitive* or *exemplary damages* in addition to compensatory damages. The court's intent in awarding punitive damages is to punish the wrongdoer and discourage others from similar conduct in the future. Punitive damages have become a major concern for businesses.

An Atlanta jury awarded $4.24 million in compensatory damages to a family whose teenage son was killed when his General Motors pickup truck erupted in flames after being broadsided by a drunk driver. The jury also "sent a message to General Motors" to fix the gasoline tanks it determined were the cause of the death—in the form of an additional $100 million in punitive damages. As we will see in Chapter 5, the Supreme Court has reviewed some of the constitutional issues that can relate to punitive damages.

Nominal Damages If a plaintiff suffers a technical injury but has not suffered actual damages to his person or property (or the damages are considered trivial by the court), the court may award *nominal damages*. The plaintiff may recover as little as one dollar plus court costs. Note, however, that while the damages imposed may be trivial, the court costs can still be significant.

In a case brought by the failed United States Football League (USFL) against the National Football League (NFL), a federal court found that the NFL had violated antitrust laws. The court found the damages suffered by the USFL as a consequence were trivial and awarded the USFL one dollar in nominal damages. The NFL owner's relief with the decision was short-lived, however, as the judge awarded attorneys' fees and court costs to the USFL in excess of $6 million. Furthermore, the court held that technical injuries such as those caused by the NFL's activities are recognized at law, thereby upholding the importance of legal obligations.

Equitable Remedies

Over the centuries, courts recognized that there were times when monetary damages were not practical or effective. Money may not be relevant or the defendant may not be solvent, yet could do certain things to help rectify a wrong. Using the broad powers of equity that courts have, they devised *remedies in equity* that can be imposed when remedies at law, such as monetary damages, are inadequate.

A remedy in equity may be called for when money damages cannot cover what was promised, such as a unique item, or when the damages would be difficult to estimate. Similarly, if equitable relief will help prevent further monetary losses, it may be ordered, as would be the case if the defendant could not pay damages but could offer something in equity.

Specific Performance In equity, courts can order *specific performance* as a remedy and require the offending party to do what he had promised to do. This remedy is frequently applied under the law of contracts in circumstances where monetary damages would not adequately compensate the wronged party or where the subject matter is unique. If the owner of a unique piece of land has a contract to sell the land and then changes her mind, a court may order her to perform as promised and transfer title to the land to the buyer for the promised payment. This is particularly the case when the subject matter is land or rare properties, such as art, antiques, or even baseball cards, because such items may be unique and irreplaceable, or because the other party may have incurred substantial expense in expectation of the deal being upheld.

Injunction An *injunction* is a court order directing a person to do something, not to do something, or to stop doing something. Injunctions can be temporary or permanent. In a *temporary injunction*, the court imposes conditions on the activities of the alleged wrongdoer until the rights of the parties have been determined or the wrongdoer has made changes or alterations in the activity to make them less offensive. In ordering a *permanent injunction*, the rights of the parties generally have been determined and the court has found that the activities of the wrongdoer are incompatible with the rights of the injured party and that they cannot be corrected or modified to satisfy the court.

Suppose that Amacher decides to store low-level radioactive wastes on his farm. His neighbor may ask the court for a temporary injunction stopping Amacher from undertaking the activity until the potential or actual harmful effects on the neighborhood can be determined. If the activity is determined by the court to be harmful, the court may then issue a permanent injunction ordering Amacher to stop the storage operation and move it elsewhere.

Courts rarely issue injunctions ordering someone to perform personal services. Suppose Dali had agreed to paint your portrait, but then refused to do it. A court would not issue an injunction ordering Dali to paint the portrait, because courts do not want to become involved in supervising services, such as making sure that Dali does the job and does it to your satisfaction. Courts also do not want to force people into involuntary servitude—doing work they do not want to do.

APPELLATE STAGE

The decision in a case may be appealed if one of the parties believes an *error of law* was made during the trial. The parties cannot, however, appeal the factual determinations made at the trial. Common bases for appeal include errors made by the trial court judge in admitting evidence that should have been excluded, refusals to admit evidence that should have been heard, improper instructions given to the jury, and the granting or denying of motions to dismiss the case. Appellate courts ensure the fairness of trials; that is, they ensure that the trial court judge correctly applied the law.

Arguments before Appeals Courts

The parties present their arguments to the appellate court through *written briefs* and *oral arguments*, which discuss the law, not the facts in the case. Always more than one judge hears an appeal, with three being the most common number of judges for the first appeal. In reviewing the trial court's decision, the appellate court has the authority to review any ruling of law by the trial judge. It has the power to *affirm*, *reverse*, or *modify* the judgment of the trial court. In essence, the judges "vote" for the decision they most favor. The governing decision of the appellate court is that decision that receives the majority vote of the judges.

Decisions by Appeals Courts

The appellate court's majority decision—and the decision that decides the case—is presented in written form and is referred to as the court's written or *majority opinion*. This majority opinion sets forth the legal rationale for the court's decision. It also provides guidance to judges, attorneys, and society in general for the resolution of similar disputes in the future. In addition, the court may issue *concurring opinions* (an opinion written by a judge [or judges] who agrees with the majority decision but for a different reason) or *dissenting opinions* (an opinion written by a judge [or judges] who strongly disagrees with the decision of the majority). While

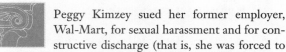

JURIS prudence?

Thanks for the Help, Counselor

Peggy Kimzey sued her former employer, Wal-Mart, for sexual harassment and for constructive discharge (that is, she was forced to quit because of the harassment). The jury found in her favor, awarding her $35,000 in damages for harm from sexual harassment and $1 in damages for harm from constructive discharge, and it added $50 million in punitive damages. Wal-Mart appealed.

Reducing the award to $5 million, the judge noted, "The jury's assessment of actual harm clearly bore no real relationship to the punitive damages awarded. More than likely, the disparity arose from the aggravating behavior of defense counsel at trial. For example, while cross-examining the plaintiff, counsel approached, waived 'the finger' in her face, and shouted, 'f*** you'."

Source: *Kimzey* v. *Wal-Mart Stores, Inc.*, 907 F.Supp. 1309

---

concurring and dissenting opinions may influence future thinking about the dispute, the majority decision decides the case and has the force of law.

When the appellate court's majority opinion agrees with the trial court's decision, the appellate court has *affirmed* that decision. When the majority opinion disagrees with the trial court, the appellate court's decision *reverses* the trial court's decision. Not infrequently, the appellate court affirms the decision but *modifies* it in some way—for example, by reducing the monetary damages awarded by the trial court. On occasion, the appellate court may disagree with a trial court's application of the law in one part of the case. However, in contrast with cases when the appellate court reverses the trial court's decision because of error, it is not clear to the appellate court how the case would turn out if that error were corrected. In this situation, the appellate court is likely to *remand* the case—return the case—to the trial court for retrial. The trial court must then retry the case, being careful to take into account the appellate court's ruling.

ENFORCEMENT STAGE

After a dispute has been tried at the trial level, if no appeal is taken or if no further appeal is available, the *judgment* becomes final. The same dispute cannot be considered again in this or any other forum. It is *res judicata*—literally, a thing decided.

The judgment may be a monetary award to the plaintiff, a declaration of the rights between the parties, or an order requiring or prohibiting some activity on the part of the defendant. When the defendant wins, the judgment generally does not involve an award of money. It states that the defendant is not responsible for the plaintiff's injuries. In some instances, the court may require that the losing party pay the other party's legal expenses.

Enforcing Judgments

When the plaintiff recovers a monetary damage award, it is the plaintiff's responsibility to collect from the defendant. In the event the defendant does not pay, the plaintiff can seek a *writ of execution*. The writ commands an official such as the sheriff to seize the property of the defendant and, if necessary, to sell the property to satisfy the judgment.

German Trial Procedure

The rules governing trial procedures can vary substantially from country to country. In Germany, trials are conducted much differently from trials in the United States. Perhaps most striking to U.S. observers is the fact that judges in Germany play a much more active role in the trial process than do American judges. In Germany, civil procedure is governed by rules called the Zivilprozessordnung (ZPO). Under these rules, the judge holds hearings to gather evidence to help him reach a decision in the case. The trial progresses informally (compared to trials in the U.S.) through these hearings.

In the United States, the role of the judge is usually limited to applying the law to the facts of the case. In Germany, the judge decides the facts of the case and then applies the law to those facts. The judge, not the lawyers, decides which witnesses to call. The judge, not the lawyers, interrogates the witnesses and records their testimony. Judges may ask questions only about the evidence that the parties to the case present themselves. And what is presented is much more limited than what is typically presented at U.S. trials. This is so because German courts protect many more confidential relationships than do U.S. courts.

If the judgment concerns specific property, then the writ will instruct the sheriff to grab that property. Otherwise, sufficient property must be seized to allow the judgment to be satisfied. However, in each state, certain property is exempt from seizure, such as personal clothing, tools of a trade, and a minimum amount of money. Courts may also order *garnishment* of a debtor's property, which usually involves an order for a certain amount of the debtor's paycheck to be paid on a regular basis to the judgment winner.

Although obtaining a writ of execution to enforce a judgment may be relatively easy, it is often difficult to collect a judgment. If a party does not have any valuable property to seize, or if the losing party flees the jurisdiction taking his property with him, it may be nearly impossible for the plaintiff to collect his judgment. In other cases, the losing party, by stalling or otherwise failing to comply with the writ of execution, makes it as difficult as possible for the plaintiff to collect. The following case discusses one difficult defendant and shows that flagrant behavior can be costly.

New Maine National Bank v. Nemon

Supreme Judicial Court of Maine
588 A.2d 1191 (1991)

CASE BACKGROUND *Nemon borrowed $125,000 from New Main National Bank. He signed a promissory note that stated that, in case he did not pay, he (Nemon) would pay all costs associated with collecting this debt, including attorneys' fees. Nemon defaulted on his loan. The bank demanded that Nemon pay the balance due.*

Nemon did not pay, and the bank sued for breach of contract. The bank moved for a summary judgment against Nemon. The trial court granted the motion, stating that the bank was entitled to the balance due on the loan, accumulated interest, and attorneys' fees, plus $3,000 extra to cover the anticipated costs of collecting the money from

Nemon. After the court entered its judgment, the bank sought and obtained a writ of execution against Nemon.

Nemon did not comply with the writ and repeatedly failed to produce documents that the court ordered him to produce concerning his debt to the bank. Nemon also repeatedly failed to appear at scheduled court dates. The court charged Nemon with contempt and authorized a civil order of arrest but stayed the sentence so that Nemon could absolve himself of the contempt charge. Nemon failed to appear at court to absolve himself. Thereafter, the court issued an arrest warrant. The next day, Nemon paid the outstanding balance due on his judgment. Four months later, the bank moved to collect additional sums from Nemon to cover the costs of its numerous post-writ-of-execution expenses. The court granted the motion. Nemon appealed.

CASE DECISION The decision of the court was issued *per curiam.*

* * *

Arthur J. Nemon appeals from a judgment in the Superior Court granting the plaintiff, Maine National Bank, relief . . . in the form of $8,000 in additional attorney fees incurred in the post-judgment collection process.

* * *

Following Nemon's default in payment, the Bank demanded the balance due. . . . The court granted summary judgment for the Bank for the amount of the principal balance due, accumulated interest, and attorney fees . . . plus costs estimated to be incurred in the collection of said amount. A writ of execution in the amount of $144,130.47 followed. Then began a merry chase.

* * *

We review the Superior Court's [decision].

* * *

Nemon contends . . . that the . . . motion was beyond the court's discretion to grant because it was really an untimely motion to alter or amend the judgment. . . . That argument lacks merit.

* * *

Nemon contends . . . that the court abused its discretion in granting relief because Maine National Bank did not present adequate evidentiary support for its motion. The record does not support his assertion. The Bank submitted extensive affidavits detailing its efforts to collect the judgment and the fees and disbursements involved in those efforts. Nemon belatedly argues that an itemized bill should have been required. We find no abuse of discretion in the court's reliance on the Bank's affidavits.

* * *

We find Nemon's appeal "egregious" and conclude that it "is obviously without any merit and has been taken without any reasonable likelihood of prevailing, and results in delayed implementation of the judgment of the [Superior Court]; increased costs of litigation; and dissipation of the time and resources of the Law Court.". . . Accordingly, we assess sanctions pursuant to [Maine's code of civil procedure]. Judgment affirmed. Treble costs are awarded to New Maine National Bank.

QUESTIONS FOR ANALYSIS

1. The bank did not collect its judgment just because a writ of execution was issued. Is there anything parties can do to prevent this kind of collection problem?
2. The court awarded the bank treble (triple) damages, which means Nemon pays $24,000 instead of the $8,000 the bank originally requested. What is the rationale for the court's increase of the damages award?

Summary

- The American legal system is an adversary system of justice. The responsibility for bringing and presenting a lawsuit rests upon the litigants. The system reflects the belief that truth is best discovered through the presentation of competing ideas.
- Several considerations, including the probability of winning and the likelihood of collecting a judgment, are fundamental to the decision to bring a lawsuit.

Most business lawsuits are more complex, use more documents and evidence, rely more on expert testimony, take longer, and result in larger damage awards than most nonbusiness lawsuits. Business litigation has increased over time. Large judgments—some for billions of dollars—have forced several large companies into bankruptcy.

- Litigation begins with pleadings. The plaintiff must notify the defendant by service of process that a complaint has been filed with a court. The defendant must answer the complaint with a motion to dismiss, a defense, or a counterclaim, or the plaintiff wins by default. The plaintiff may respond to the defendant's answer with a reply.

- Before trial, the discovery process allows both parties to gather legal evidence. Depositions or interrogatories may be taken from both the parties and the witnesses. The discovery process allows both parties to know what the trial is to be about so that few surprises arise. Gathering evidence may cause the parties to settle the case as the likely outcome becomes clear.

- At most trials, the defendant has the right to ask for a jury trial. Attorneys discuss with clients the advisability of a jury trial or a trial where the judge hears and determines the entire matter. When a jury is used, it is the finder of fact.

- At trial, after opening statements by both parties, the plaintiff presents witnesses and evidence to prove the facts of her case. Witnesses are questioned by both sides. After the cases have been stated, either party can request that the judge give a directed verdict to end the case. In most cases, the matter goes to the jury after closing arguments and instructions by the judge. The jury determines the facts of the case and applies the law as explained by the judge.

- The remedies awarded by the courts in resolving civil disputes include monetary damages and equitable relief. Monetary damages include compensatory, punitive, and nominal damages. Equitable remedies include specific performance and injunctions.

- The judge can set aside the verdict of a jury, but this is rare. A party unhappy with the result may appeal the decision. The court of appeals reviews the case to determine whether any errors were made in the application of the law to the facts (as they were determined by the judge or jury). The court of appeals may affirm, reverse, or modify the trial court's decision.

- Plaintiffs winning judgments are responsible for attempting to collect the judgment, which is difficult if the defendant leaves the state or has few assets. The plaintiff may have to return to the court to obtain further orders to force compliance with the judgment. A writ of execution allows the property of the defendant to be seized to satisfy the judgment.

Issue

Should Perjury Be Treated More Harshly?

The impeachment charges against President Clinton were largely based, legally, on perjury—that he lied under oath about his relationship with Monica Lewinsky. Arguing about the definitions of "is" *and "sex," Mr. Clinton crafted his answers under oath so as to skirt possible claims of perjury. Legal proceedings can often appear to be a liars' contest. When two sides tell opposite stories, it is not uncommon that one party is lying under oath.*

Yet perjury charge are rarely brought. This reading asks if the quality of judicial proceedings would improve if parties knew there were likely to be greater penalties in case of lying.

IN U.S. COURTS, THE WHOLE TRUTH IS OFTEN ANYTHING BUT

Richard B. Schmitt

Mr. Schmitt is a staff reporter. Reprinted by permission of *The Wall Street Journal* © 1998 Dow Jones Company, Inc. All rights reserved worldwide.

When it comes to truth and justice, the American way can involve some pretty big lies.

A case in point: Esther Rodriguez vs. Mars Inc., maker of candy bars. Ms. Rodriguez, a custodial worker at a Snickers plant in Chicago, filed a federal lawsuit in 1996 against Mars alleging sexual harassment. During the proceedings, Mars lawyers asked her how she had spent her time during certain intervals of her career. She replied, in a sworn deposition, that she had been caring for her sick father. Later, Mars discaovered that during the time in question she had been in prison, convicted of felony theft.

In Congress, lawmakers are debating President Clinton's sworn statements about his relationship with Monica Lewinsky. But outside Washington, lawyers and judges are talking about a trend in the rest of the country: Lying in court is getting common.

"It happens all the time," says Samuel B. Kent, a U.S. district judge in Galveston, Texas. Last month, the judge prevailed upon the plaintiff in an insurance case to drop his suit after it became clear that he had a history of filing suspicious fire claims and, according to the judge, "very likely burned down his own house."

The case didn't get far enough to determine for certain whether the judge was right. But he says lying "is becoming a remarkably common aspect of modern litigation." Last year, the National Law Journal, a newspaper for the legal profession, identified "spoliation of evidence"—hiding or destroying crucial court documents—as one of the top 10 new litigation trends of 1997.

By any name, concealing the truth often goes unpunished. Mark Perlmutter, an Austin, Texas plaintiffs' attorney who just published a book titled "Why Lawyers (and the Rest of Us) Lie and Engage in Other Repugnant Behavior," says one reason perjury prosecutions aren't undertaken more often is that lying has become so generally accepted in court proceedings.

"You can catch people red-handed doing things, and nobody seems to care too much," says Patrick Malone, a Washington, D.C., plaintiffs' lawyer specializing in medical-malpractice suits. He once had evidence that a doctor erased a crucial entry in some medical records to conceal an error. The erasure constituted potential obstruction of justice; but the doctor, who claimed he couldn't remember the episode, was never penalized, according to Mr. Malone.

Perjury—defined as the intentional misrepresentation of a material fact—is tough to prove and usually not a priority for prosecutors operating on a limited budget. Still, some perjury cases are vigorously prosecuted, and some courts do come down hard on those who lie. This past summer, a psychiatrist at the Boise (Idaho) Veterans Administration Hospital was convicted of obstructing justice and sentenced to home detention and probation after lying about a sexual liaison with a patient who had sued the hospital for malpractice. And in Washington, D.C., an orthopedic surgeon who had been a much-used expert witness for plaintiffs in car-wreck cases just finished up an 18-month term in a federal prison camp and halfway house for falsifying his credentials.

Ethicists and lawyers say big jury awards in personal-injury cases have prompted suits based on fabricated allegations. Indeed, many lies seem to be the product of wishful thinking by plaintiffs charging deep-pocketed companies with inflicting personal harm. Recently, a couple in Brazil, Ind., sought a $50,000 settlement from Tricon Global Restaurants Inc. because, they claimed, they had discoavered a withered frog in some fast food purchased at one of Tricon's Taco Bell restaurants. Not so, said the court, which last month convicted the couple of fraud. They face up to three years in jail.

Historically, lying has been most common in criminal cases, where defendants pull out all the stops in a last-ditch effort to retain their freedom. Now it is creeping into civil cases with some regularity.

Today, "there is at least as much lying in civil cases as in criminal cases," says Robert Feldman, a Palo Alto, Calif., litigator and former federal prosecutor. He says he considers it refreshing when someone whose deposition he is taking decides to "just tell the truth for a half-hour."

In the case of Ms. Rodriguez, the candy-company worker who lied about being in jail, the judge, as a sanction, struck her answers in the deposition. That, in turn, led to the dismissal of her harassment case last year.

"This was a clear case of perjury," says Jody Moran, a Chicago labor lawyer who defended Mars. If Ms.

Rodriguez had told the truth about her record, Ms. Moran says, Mars likely wouldn't have been able to use her conviction to challenge her character and credibility because her crime was several years in the past.

Will she be prosecuted for lying? Terrance Norton, a Chicago law professor who represented Ms. Rodriguez, believes his client's lie was more the product of deep embarrassment than evil intent, and therefore, he says, he would be surprised by a perjury prosecution. Besides, he adds, "It wouldn't be practical to indict all the people who lie under oath."

ISSUE QUESTIONS

1. Is is possible for two parties to tell opposite stories, but both believe they are telling the truth?
2. Why are perjury charges rarely brought? What are the practical reasons for bringing perjury charges?

REVIEW AND DISCUSSION QUESTIONS

1. Define the following terms:

pleadings	judgment n.o.v.
complaint	damages
motion	compensatory damages
answer	punitive damages
counterclaim	nominal damages
affirmative defense	equity
deposition	specific performance
interrogatory	injunction
voir dire	dissenting opinion
directed verdict	writ of execution

2. Compare and contrast the following concepts:
   a. Motion to dismiss and a motion for directed verdict
   b. Deposition and written interrogatories
   c. Voir dire and challenge for cause
   d. Direct examination and cross-examination
   e. Briefs and oral argument

CASE QUESTIONS

3. Effron bought a ticket for a cruise to South America on the *Stella Solaris* from Sun Line Cruises (SLC), a New York corporation. *Stella Solaris* was owned by a Greek corporation, Sun Line Greece (SLG). During the cruise, Effron fell and was injured. She filed a personal injury suit in New York federal court against SLC and SLG. SLG argued that the case against it should be dismissed based on a forum selection clause in Effron's ticket. The clause stated that any disputes between the ticket holder and SLG would be litigated in Greece. Effron argued that if this clause were enforced she would not get her day in court because she was unable to bring suit in Greece. SLC argued that it should be granted a summary judgment, because it was acting on behalf of SLG and was, therefore, not liable for Effron's harms. Effron argued that no one had made it clear that SLC was acting on behalf of SLG, and so she should be able to sue. How should the court rule on SLG's motion to dismiss the case? Would it be fair to subject a foreign corporation to personal jurisdiction in U.S. courts if the corporation expressly tried to prevent this outcome? How should the court rule on SLC's motion for summary judgment? [*Effron* v. *Sun Line Cruises, Inc.*, 857 F.Supp. 1079 (S.D.N.Y., 1994)]

4. Bybee and her husband are opera singers. Bybee met Del Monaco, general manager of the Bonn (Germany) Opera Company (BOC). After an audition, Del Monaco and the BOC offered Bybee and her husband positions with the company in Germany. Bybee accepted the offer and signed an employment contract; her husband did not. The BOC failed to honor the contract because, Bybee alleged, of her husband's refusal to sign. Bybee, a resident of New York, filed suit against the BOC and Del Monaco in New York federal court. The defendants argued that the case should be dismissed based on the doctrine of forum non conveniens. Bybee claimed that litigating in Germany would be too burdensome for her and that she had witnesses to the contract in New York. The BOC and Del Monaco argued that litigating in New York would be too burdensome for them and that the contract was signed in Germany and written in German and their witnesses were in Germany. What should the court decide in this case? [*Bybee* v. *Oper der Standt Bonn*, 899 F.Supp. 1217 (S.D.N.Y., 1995)]

5. Dollar Rent-a-Car alleged that Ford Motor violated antitrust laws. Ford gave Hertz and Avis—but not Dollar—a guaranteed resale price after using Ford cars in their rental businesses. Dollar sought to take the depositions of Ford's president and vice president. Ford refused to produce the executives, claiming that Dollar was demanding the depositions "solely for the purpose of harassment and oppression, and not because the additional depositions were reasonably calculated to lead to the discovery of admissible evidence." Dollar asserted that there was an important connection between the executives and the issues in the case because of the importance of the clients and the size of the deal. Dollar requested the federal district court to order Ford to produce the executives. Was Ford required to do so? [*Travelers Rental* v. *Ford Motor*, 116 F.R.D. 140 (1987)]

6. Amy and Robert Bohl filed a suit in an Ohio state court, alleging that Dr. Vigh, committed malpractice in the orthodontic care of the Bohls. The Bohls attempted to take the deposition of Dr. Vigh, but twice the doctor failed to appear. Notice of the depositions was properly filed and served on Vigh. The Bohls filed a motion for sanctions. Neither Vigh or his counsel appeared for the hearing on the motion for sanctions. The trial court has discretion to impose a variety of sanctions, including an order to appear for a deposition, a fine and/or imprisonment, or a default judgment that includes an award for compensatory damages and attorneys' fees. Under these circumstances, what would you suggest? [*Bohl* v. *Vigh*, 1995 WL 31527 (Ohio App. 12 Dist.)]

7. Brungart and her husband sued for personal injuries she suffered while shopping at a K Mart in Baton Rouge, Louisiana. Brungart alleged that through no fault of her own, a heavy rug fell off a high shelf in the store, hit her on the head, and knocked her to the ground, at which point another rug fell on her. A store manager, who came to the scene, found the rug display in good order. At trial, Brungart claimed that she had touched and moved only rugs on a lower shelf. According to the store manager, Brungart had told him that she had moved some oriental rugs (which were only on the high shelves) immediately before her accident. The jury found Brungart 80 percent responsible for her harms. Brungart's husband's claims were denied entirely. Brungart and her husband made a motion for judgment n.o.v. In Louisiana, a judgment n.o.v. may be granted only if "the facts and inferences point so strongly and overwhelmingly in favor of the moving party that reasonable men could not arrive at a contrary verdict." The trial court granted the motion, and K Mart appealed. Should the appeals court uphold the decision of the trial court? [*Brungart* v. *K Mart Corp.* 668 So.2d 1335 (Ct.App., La., 1996)]

8. Sarah Slaughter took English 102 from Michael O'Gorman at Waubonsee Community College. Slaughter went to talk with O'Gorman about how she could raise her final grade. She alleged that O'Gorman told her he would raise her grade in exchange for sexual favors. She reported the incident to college officials. Waubonsee established a panel to investigate her claim, and it determined that although O'Gorman had sexually harassed Slaughter, the stories of O'Gorman and Slaughter were so different that the panel could not say exactly what had happened. Slaughter filed suit against the school for sexual harassment. The school argued that under applicable federal law it was liable to Slaughter only if she could prove that the school had participated in or ignored her harassment. Because the school had set up the panel, it claimed that it was not liable to Slaughter. The school moved for a summary judgment. Should the court grant this motion? [*Slaughter* v. *Waubonsee Community College*, 1995 WL 579296 (N.D.Ill., 1995)]

9. Hulvey was injured while operating a Caterpillar forklift. He sued Caterpillar for his injuries. Hulvey lost, but the decision was set aside because of juror misconduct. Caterpillar appealed the decision to set aside the verdict of the jury. Hulvey claimed that the verdict should be set aside because one of the jurors (Olmstead) was an attorney, who "swayed" the other jurors with his knowledge of the law. Olmstead made derogatory comments about people who file personal injury suits, noting that despite his claims of pain, Hulvey could sit in a chair at court for long periods of time. Should the appeals court uphold the decision concerning juror misconduct? Should courts inquire into the discussion in the jury room? [*Caterpillar Tractor Co.* v. *Hulvey*, 353 S.E.2d 747 (Sup. Ct., Va., 1987)]

10. Folsom was injured while unloading potatoes at A&P's warehouse. He sued A&P, alleging that the company was responsible for his injuries. At the close of a two-and-one-half-day trial, the jury deliberated thirty-five minutes and found for A&P. Folsom alleges jury misconduct and moves for a new trial. What result? [*Folsom* v. *Great Atlantic & Pacific Tea Co.*, 521 A.2d 678 (Me. 1987)]

POLICY QUESTIONS

11. The parties to a dispute often reach a settlement before trial. In such cases, it is not uncommon for the parties to agree to keep the terms of the settlement secret—often referred to as protective orders. Is it in the interest of the general public that settlements be kept secret?

12. Legal proceedings in the court system are heavily subsidized by the government, particularly when the case involves a jury. Costs easily run into the tens of thousands of dollars, but the parties to the case pay only trivial filing fees. Should fees be raised substantially so the parties bear more of the costs of litigation?

ETHICS QUESTION

13. In giving instructions to the jury, should judges be allowed to comment on the evidence presented at the trial? Consider the following charge a judge provided to the jury:

. . . I am going to tell you what I think of the defendant's testimony. You may have noticed, Mr. Foreman and ladies and gentlemen, that he wiped his hands during his testimony. It is rather a curious thing, but that is almost always an indication of lying. Why it should be so we don't know, but that is a fact. I think that every single word that man said, except when he agreed with the government's testimony, was a lie.

INTERNET ASSIGNMENT

Over ninety percent of all civil litigation is settled or otherwise resolved before trial. In large measure this is attributable to the pretrial discovery process. Civil discovery under the Federal Rules of Civil Procedure is highly effective in assisting all the parties to a dispute in identifying and understanding the strengths and weaknesses of their respective positions. Accordingly, as a practical matter, the discovery process itself is perhaps the single most important and consequential aspect of litigation. Hence, understanding the scope and limitations of discovery is essential to anyone who can reasonably expect to be involved in litigation. Using the World Wide Web to find your information (and giving the URL for each source actually used) state, with citation to any applicable discovery rules from the Federal Rules of Civil Procedure.

(a)   The (1) general scope and (2) limits of permissible pretrial discovery,

(b)   The conditions under which depositions may be taken before an action is filed,

(c)   Who must be given notice that a deposition will be taken, and what information must be contained in the notice,

(d)   Under what conditions must a party to a lawsuit obtain the court's permission to take a deposition using written questions,

(e)   When and by whom may a deposition be used in court proceedings,

(f)   Who may serve interrogatories, and when, and upon whom may interrogatories be served,

(g)   Who may serve requests for the production or inspection of documents, and upon whom, and what is the permissible scope of this form of discovery,

(h)   The conditions under which a person may be compelled to submit to a physical or mental examination,

(i)   Who may serve discovery in the form of written requests for admissions, and upon whom, and what is the permissible scope of this form of discovery, and

(j)   What recourse does a party have if a person upon whom discovery is served fails to respond, in whole or in part, to the party's discovery requests.

CHAPTER 4

Alternative Dispute Resolution

When Barbara Fong's software company, Gnof, was sued by unhappy stockholders who lost money when stock prices dropped, it is likely that the case was settled out of court. As in other areas of litigation, suits brought by shareholders are almost always settled, which includes suits being dropped. Of all civil cases filed in court, about 90 percent are resolved before a judgment is entered at trial.

Why resolve a suit out of court? Experienced lawyers can make pretty good estimates of the outcome of most cases that go to trial, so they can recommend resolution that heads off costly litigation. Cases that are litigated consume more hours of attorneys' time, are more likely to need expert witnesses, and consume more time of company personnel. Barbara Fong would rather concentrate on business rather than spend two weeks preparing for a deposition and, later, for possible testimony at trial. As former Chief Justice Warren Burger said:

> We, as lawyers, know that litigation is not only stressful and frustrating but expensive and frequently unrewarding for litigants. . . . Commercial litigation takes business executives and their staffs away from the creative paths of . . . development and production and often inflicts more wear and tear on them than the most difficult business problems.

Over the past several decades, the average time required for civil cases to get into court has lengthened, adding to the cost and uncertainty of the litigation process. Criminal cases have priority over civil cases, and court dockets are loaded, so civil

EXHIBIT 4.1

Comparing Disputant Control under Various ADR Processes

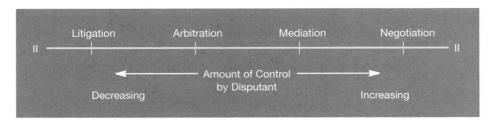

Source: Adapted from Larry Ray, "Emerging Options in Dispute Resolution," *ABA Journal,* June 1989

litigation can easily be put off for years. Most judges strongly encourage cases to be settled rather than consume valuable court time. Disputes can be mediated, arbitrated, or negotiated quickly if both parties are interested in doing so. Even if a party is on the losing side of a matter, often there is value in knowing what cost must be borne, rather than having a liability of uncertain size hanging around for years.

Since most disputes are resolved under the rule of law but outside of the courtroom, it is as important to know the settlement process as it is to understand the trial process. As we will see, different formats may be used to resolve disputes outside of court. This chapter considers negotiation, mediation, arbitration, and other forms of *alternative dispute resolution (ADR)*. Judges often pressure parties to resolve disputes before trial and encourage the use of alternatives to traditional litigation to reduce the time spent in court.

The choice of an alternative to litigation in resolving disputes must be agreed upon by the parties. Often parties include a clause in a contract calling for the parties to submit to a particular alternative method of dispute resolution should a dispute arise. As Exhibit 4.1 illustrates, negotiation offers the parties the most control over the process. That is, parties can walk away from negotiations, unlike litigation or arbitration. Of course, walking away rarely resolves anything.

Arbitration

Arbitration is the most widely recognized form of ADR. It is a process in which two or more persons agree to allow a neutral person (or panel) to resolve their disputes. The advantages of using a neutral expert, called an *arbitrator,* or *arbiter* are twofold: (1) because he is mutually agreed upon by the parties, the arbitrator has the trust of both parties, and (2) because the arbitrator is already an expert in the subject matter, less time is needed to educate him about the dispute. This usually results in a faster resolution of the dispute and a decision respected by both parties.

In the *Federal Arbitration Act (FAA)*, Congress states in the strongest terms that agreements to arbitrate must be upheld. The FAA states that a "written provision in any . . . contract evidencing a transaction involving commerce to settle by arbitration a controversy thereafter arising out of such contract or transaction . . . shall be valid, irrevocable, and enforceable, save upon such grounds as exist at law or in equity for the revocation of any contract" (9 U.S.C. §2). If a party tries to avoid arbitration, the courts are instructed by the FAA to compel and enforce arbitration.

Europe Emerges as the Arbitration Forum of Choice

 Few companies care to litigate matters in another country, so in international business there is even more incentive to arbitrate matters than there is in disputes involving domestic parties. Multinational firms have found that arbitration in Europe tends to work well and is trusted by businesses throughout the world.

Knowing the value of attracting commercial arbitration, most European nations have changed their laws to provide a predictable, user-friendly environment for international arbitration. Switzerland, England, and Sweden are among the countries that have adopted laws similar to the United Nations Commission on International Trade Law (UNCITRAL) rules for effective arbitration.

In each country, private organizations—such as the International Chamber of Commerce, the London Court of International Arbitration, and the Stockholm Chamber of Commerce—have established rules for arbitration procedure and frameworks for resolving conflicts and have developed reputations for providing fair arbitration standards and assistance. Parties to international contracts made anywhere in the world can bind themselves to arbitrate disputes under the arbitration rules and organization of their choosing.

Similarly, a majority of the states have adopted the *Uniform Arbitration Act (UAA)*, which has provisions very similar to those in the FAA. States that have not adopted the UAA generally have laws that are quite similar in effect. These state laws strongly uphold the integrity of the arbitration process.

The decision of an arbitrator is binding on the parties and can be appealed to the courts only under specific and limited circumstances. Appeals are limited because arbitration is a voluntary process by which the parties contractually bind themselves not to litigate. The courts uphold such voluntary agreements. If the parties do not view the arbitration decision as final, they merely add another step to the litigation process. The number of commercial disputes going to arbitration for resolution has increased steadily over the years.

THE ARBITRATION PROCESS

It is common for parties to provide for arbitration of future disputes by inserting an arbitration clause in a contract, such as this standard arbitration clause:

> Any controversy or claim arising out of or relating to this contract, or the breach thereof, shall be settled by arbitration administered by the American Arbitration Association under its Commercial Arbitration Rules, and the judgment on the award rendered by the arbitrator(s) may be entered in any court having jurisdiction thereof.

Similarly, parties to a dispute not already covered by an arbitration clause, may agree to submit the dispute to arbitration. A sample submission form from the American Arbitration Association is seen in Exhibit 4.2. Arbitration begins when a party files a *submission* to refer a dispute to arbitration. The time in which a dispute must be filed is usually much shorter than the time in which a lawsuit must be filed. Some commercial arbitration clauses require that cases must be filed within a couple months of the claim or the right to contest the matter is lost.

American Arbitration Association
Submission to Dispute Resolution

The named parties hereby submit the following dispute for resolution under the _____
_____ Rules* of the American Arbitration Association:

Procedure Selected: ☐ Binding arbitration   ☐ Mediation
                           ☐ Other (Please describe) _____

The Nature of the Dispute:

The Claim of Relief Sought (the Amount, if Any):

Type of Business: Claimant_____ Respondent _____

Place of Hearing: _____

We agree that, if binding arbitration is selected, we will abide by and perform any award rendered
hereunder and that a judgment may be entered on the award.

To Be Completed by the Parties

_____	_____
Name of Party	Name of Party
_____	_____
Address	Address
_____	_____
City, State, and ZIP Code	City, State, and ZIP Code
( ) _____ ( ) _____	( ) _____ ( ) _____
Telephone Fax	Telephone Fax
_____	_____
Signature†	Signature†

_____	_____
Name of Representative for Party	Name of Representative for Party
_____	_____
Name of Firm (if Applicable)	Name of Firm (if Applicable)
_____	_____
Representative's Address	Representative's Address
_____	_____
City, State, and ZIP Code	City, State, and ZIP Code
( ) _____ ( ) _____	( ) _____ ( ) _____
Telephone Fax	Telephone Fax
_____	_____
Signature†	Signature†

Please file three copies with the AAA.
* If you have a question as to which rules apply, please contact the AAA.
† Signatures of all parties are required for arbitration.

EXHIBIT 4.2   Source: American Arbitration Association

*Form Used to Submit a
Dispute to Arbitration*

Selection of Arbitrators

When a case goes to court, the parties to the case usually have no control over who the judge will be, as most trial court systems have many judges and various case assignment methods are used. Under arbitration, the parties agree on who the arbitrator will be, or they agree to a selection method under the arbitration rules specified in their arbitration agreement. Most matters are arbitrated by one arbitrator, but panels of three arbitrators are not unusual.

Arbitrators are often attorneys, but that is not a general requirement. Rather, arbitrators are required to be impartial, which means that they must avoid even the appearance of conflicts of interest and should uphold the integrity of the arbitration process as spelled out in various codes of ethics for arbitrators. Since arbitration is common in many areas, such as labor disputes, the parties generally insist upon arbitrators with training and experience in the field. Arbitration associations help to ensure the quality of the arbiters, as the associations want to maintain a reputation for quality dispute resolution. Hence, arbitrators often have more expertise in their case area than do most judges, who may hear certain kinds of cases only rarely.

The Hearing

After the submission and the selection of an arbitrator, a hearing is scheduled. The parties set the rules of the hearing either with or without assistance of the arbitrator and give the arbitrator the power to enforce the hearing rules. The hearing is normally a closed-door proceeding conducted much like a trial but without some of a trial's more restrictive procedural aspects. For example, the manner in which evidence can be presented in an arbitration hearing is generally less rigid. Since the arbitrator is an expert in the field, he is less likely to be persuaded by improperly presented evidence.

The Award

After the close of the hearing, the arbitrator reaches a decision. Called an *award*, this decision must generally be delivered by the arbitrator within thirty days of the close of the hearing. The award is usually in writing. However, whereas the court system often requires written legal opinions, under arbitration, the arbitrator need not state his findings of fact or the legal basis of the decision unless the parties have requested that they be provided (and are willing to pay for that extra work).

In most arbitration, the arbitrator makes an award based on an evaluation of the evidence presented. Besides deciding if one party owes the other party cash, goods, or something else, the allocation of compensation for the arbitrator and administrative fees is decided by the arbitrator. In some arbitration, the arbitrator does not construct an award but chooses between the claims of the two parties. For example, in salary disputes in Major League Baseball, the arbitrator picks either the salary requested by the player or the salary offered by the baseball team.

Appealing the Award

Just as parties who lose in court may be dissatisfied, parties who lose in arbitration may want to carry the matter further. Just as attacks on judges are very unlikely to be acceptable, attacks on arbitrators are rarely successful. The belief that arbitrators should be protected from attacks was expressed long ago by the highest court in Massachusetts in *Hoosac Tunnel Dock & Elevator Co.* v. *O'Brien* (137 Mass. 424; 1884):

> An arbitrator is a quasi judicial officer, under our laws, exercising judicial functions. There is as much reason in his case for protecting and insuring his

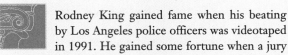

Arbitrate or Take a Beating?

Rodney King gained fame when his beating by Los Angeles police officers was videotaped in 1991. He gained some fortune when a jury awarded him $3.8 million in damages for the incident. As in many such lawsuits, King's attorney, Milton Grimes, was to collect 25 percent of the jury verdict plus, he asserted, court-awarded fees for King's attorney, which were $715,000. Grimes said he was never paid.

To head off litigation, King and Grimes agreed to have the dispute arbitrated by a former California supreme court justice. Going into the arbitration over Grimes's 1.6-million-dollar claim, King said, "These attorneys, man, are just like vultures or hyenas." Grimes responded that "Mr. King . . . refuses to face reality." The arbitration award was confidential.

Source: *National Law Journal*

impartiality, independence, and freedom from undue influences, as in the case of a judge or juror. The same considerations of public policy apply, and we are of the opinion that the same immunity extends to him.

Furthermore, errors of fact or law by an arbitrator are not reviewable by the courts. According to the Federal Arbitration Act, there are four grounds for overturning an award. These occur when

1. The award was obtained by corruption or fraud.
2. There was evidence of partiality or corruption by an arbitrator.
3. An arbitrator was guilty of serious procedural misconduct, such as refusing to hear relevant evidence, that prejudiced the rights of a party.
4. An arbitrator exceeded his power, and an award was made on a subject not relevant to the proceeding.

As the Second Circuit Court of Appeals ruled in *Merrill Lynch* v. *Bobker* (808 F.2d 930; 1986), for the courts to be justified in overruling an award:

> The [arbitrator's] error must have been obvious and capable of being readily and instantly perceived by the average person qualified to serve as an arbitrator. [The arbitrator must know of] the existence of a clearly governing legal principle but decides to ignore or pay no attention to it.

Under the doctrine of *res judicata*, the final judgment on the merits of a case by a court prevents an issue from being relitigated. This doctrine also holds to arbitration awards. While this doctrine has certain limitations in arbitration cases (especially in the area of employment rights), in general, an arbitration award is final and the matter cannot be litigated again or appealed.

VOLUNTARY AND COMPULSORY ARBITRATION

Traditionally, arbitration is a voluntary process. The parties submit their dispute to an arbitrator for a decision rather than go to court. This agreement can occur at the time of a dispute or, more commonly, is required as a part of a contract that preceded the dispute. Labor contracts (between a union and an employer) and individual employment contracts often include arbitration requirements. Many commercial contracts include standard terms about arbitration. Most stockbrokers require their customers to sign a contract stating that in the event of a dispute over their account the matter will be arbitrated. Many insurance contracts require arbitration of disputes. Hence, arbitration is a common feature in modern contracts.

An arbitration agreement can include many details about how the arbitration is to be conducted, or it can leave the details open. For example, professional baseball player contracts require final offer arbitration to be used when a salary dispute occurs. That is, both the player and the team owner submit a "final offer" to the arbitrator, who must, by the rules of that kind of arbitration, choose only one offer or the other. This gives the parties an incentive to be realistic in their negotiations and offers in arbitration. Arbitration is usually voluntary, but in certain situations it is compulsory.

Public Sector Employment

Many states require compulsory arbitration for some or all public sector employees. Police officers, firefighters, and public school teachers may not be permitted to strike. Rather, public employees—usually through their unions—and their employer—usually a city or other local government—must arbitrate the terms of employment: wages, hours, and working conditions. When such arbitration is mandatory, legislation usually requires the awards to have a written record and decision so that judicial review can ensure that the awards are supported by the evidence.

Medical Malpractice

To help constrain medical costs, some states require medical malpractice claims to be arbitrated before a suit may be filed in court. Suits are not prohibited, but many cases are settled by arbitration that might not have been settled had they not been forced to go that route first. Other states allow medical service providers to offer voluntary but binding arbitration agreements to their patients; decisions from such cases cannot be appealed to the courts.

Court-Annexed Arbitration

Some state and federal courts require arbitration as a pretrial requirement. Called *court-annexed arbitration* (or judicial arbitration), these programs are limited to disputes in which the amount in controversy is relatively small. Eligible cases are referred to mandatory pretrial arbitration (or voluntary in some states), which is conducted by an attorney, a retired judge, or, in some court systems, a panel of three attorneys. The procedure employed usually consists of a quasi-judicial hearing leading to a resolution of the dispute.

Either party may reject the decision and insist on a court trial. Relatively few cases submitted to the process, however, proceed to trial. Courts using this process have reductions in case backlogs and case processing time. In Pittsburgh, for example, this arbitration process ends nearly three-quarters of all disputes referred to it. In addition, the average delay before an arbitration hearing is only three months, in contrast to the eighteen-month delay before a trial. The federal district courts are empowered to use arbitration and other ADR techniques both by the Federal Rules of Civil Procedure and as a part of the court's inherent power to manage its cases. Challenges to arbitration decisions occur as parties test the limits of the process. The Supreme Court discusses several arbitration issues in the *Gilmer* decision, which notes how far-reaching arbitration may be.

Gilmer v. Interstate/Johnson Lane Corp.

United States Supreme Court
500 U.S. 20, 111 S.Ct. 1647 (1991)

CASE BACKGROUND *As a condition of employment, Gilmer was required by his employer, Interstate, to register as a securities representative with the New York Stock Exchange (NYSE), which required him to arbitrate employment controversies by NYSE rules. When Gilmer was fired at age sixty-two, he sued in federal court, claiming a violation of the Age Discrimination in Employment Act (ADEA). Interstate moved to compel arbitration under Gilmer's employment contract and the Federal Arbitration Act (FAA). The district court ruled for Gilmer that the matter must be tried in court. The appeals court reversed, ordering arbitration. Gilmer appealed.*

CASE DECISION White, Justice.

* * *

The FAA was originally enacted in 1925 and then reenacted and codified in 1947 as Title 9 of the United States Code. Its purpose was to reverse the longstanding judicial hostility to arbitration agreements that had existed at English common law and had been adopted by American courts, and to place arbitration agreements upon the same footing as other contracts.

* * *

It is by now clear that statutory claims may be the subject of an arbitration agreement, enforceable pursuant to the FAA. Indeed, in recent years we have held enforceable arbitration agreements relating to claims arising under the Sherman Act [antitrust law]; §10(b) of the Securities Exchange Act of 1934 [securities fraud]; the civil provisions of the Racketeer Influenced and Corrupt Organizations Act (RICO); and §12(2) of the Securities Act of 1933 [improper sale of securities]. In these cases we recognized that "[b]y agreeing to arbitrate a statutory claim, a party does not forgo the substantive rights afforded by the statute; it only submits to their resolution in an arbitral, rather than a judicial, forum."

Although all statutory claims may not be appropriate for arbitration, "[h]aving made the bargain to arbitrate, the party should be held to it unless Congress itself has evinced an intention to preclude a waiver of judicial remedies for the statutory rights at issue." In this regard, we note that the burden is on Gilmer to show that Congress intended to preclude a waiver of a judicial forum for ADEA claims. If such an intention exists, it will be discoverable in the text of the ADEA, its legislative history, or an "inherent conflict" between arbitration and the ADEA's underlying purposes. . . .

Gilmer concedes that nothing in the text of the ADEA or its legislative history explicitly precludes arbitration. He argues, however, that compulsory arbitration of ADEA claims pursuant to arbitration agreements would be inconsistent with the statutory framework and purposes of the ADEA. Like the Court of Appeals, we disagree.

* * *

In arguing that arbitration is inconsistent with the ADEA, Gilmer also raises a host of challenges to the adequacy of arbitration procedures. Initially, we note that in our recent arbitration cases we have already rejected most of these arguments as insufficient to preclude arbitration of statutory claims. Such generalized attacks on arbitration "res[t] on suspicion of arbitration as a method of weakening the protections afforded in the substantive law to would-be complainants," and as such, they are "far out of step with our current strong endorsement of the federal statutes favoring this method of resolving disputes." Consequently, we address these arguments only briefly.

Gilmer first speculates that arbitration panels will be biased. However, "[w]e decline to indulge the presumption that the parties and arbitral body conducting a proceeding will be unable or unwilling to retain competent, conscientious and impartial arbitrators." In any event, we note that the NYSE arbitration rules, which are applicable to the dispute in this case, provide protections against biased panels. The rules require, for example, that the parties be informed of the employment histories of the arbitrators, and that they be allowed to make further inquiries into the arbitrators' backgrounds. In addition, each party is allowed one peremptory challenge and unlimited challenges for cause. Moreover, the arbitrators are required to disclose "any circumstances which might preclude [them] from rendering an objective and impartial determination." The FAA also protects against bias, by providing that courts may overturn arbitration decisions "[w]here there was evident partiality or corruption in the arbitrators." There has been no showing in this case that those provisions are inadequate to guard against potential bias.

Gilmer also complains that the discovery allowed in arbitration is more limited than in the federal courts, which he contends will make it difficult to prove discrimination. It is unlikely, however, that age discrimination claims require more extensive discovery than other claims that we have found to be arbitrable. . . . Although those procedures might not be as extensive as in the federal courts, by agreeing to arbitrate, a party "trades the procedures and opportunity for review of the courtroom for the simplicity, informality, and expedition of arbitration." Indeed, an important counterweight to the reduced discovery in NYSE arbitration is that arbitrators are not bound by the rules of evidence.

A further alleged deficiency of arbitration is that arbitrators often will not issue written opinions, resulting, Gilmer contends, in a lack of public knowledge of employers' discriminatory policies, an inability to obtain effective appellate review, and a stifling of the development of the law. The NYSE rules, however, do require that all arbitration awards be in writing, and that the awards contain the names of the parties, a summary of the issues in controversy, and a description of the award issued. . . .

It is also argued that arbitration procedures cannot adequately further the purposes of the ADEA because they do not provide for broad equitable relief and class actions. As the court below noted, however, arbitrators do have the power to fashion equitable relief. Indeed, the NYSE rules applicable here do not restrict the types of relief an arbitrator may award, but merely refer to "damages and/or other relief." The NYSE rules also provide for collective proceedings. But "even if the arbitration could not go forward as a class action or class relief could not be granted by the

arbitrator, the fact that the [ADEA] provides for the possibility of bringing a collective action does not mean that individual attempts at conciliation were intended to be barred." Finally, it should be remembered that arbitration agreements will not preclude the EEOC from bringing actions seeking class-wide and equitable relief.

An additional reason advanced by Gilmer for refusing to enforce arbitration agreements relating to ADEA claims is his contention that there often will be unequal bargaining power between employers and employees. Mere inequality in bargaining power, however, is not a sufficient reason to hold that arbitration agreements are never enforceable in the employment context. Relationships between securities dealers and investors, for example, may involve unequal bargaining power, but we nevertheless held in [earlier cases] that agreements to arbitrate in that context are enforceable. As discussed above, the FAA's purpose was to place arbitration agreements on the same footing as other contracts. Thus, arbitration agreements are enforceable "save upon such grounds as exist at law or in equity for the revocation of any contract." "Of course, courts should remain attuned to well-supported claims that the agreement to arbitrate resulted from the sort of fraud or overwhelming economic power that would provide grounds 'for the revocation of any contract.'" There is no indication in this case, however, that Gilmer, an experienced businessman, was coerced or defrauded into agreeing to the arbitration clause in his registration application. As with the claimed procedural inadequacies discussed above, this claim of unequal bargaining power is best left for resolution in specific cases.

* * *

We conclude that Gilmer has not met his burden of showing that Congress, in enacting the ADEA, intended to preclude arbitration of claims under that Act. Accordingly, the judgment of the Court of Appeals is Affirmed.

QUESTIONS FOR ANALYSIS

1. Can Gilmer expect to get the same kind of fair treatment before an arbitrator that he would get before a federal judge?
2. Does arbitration destroy the right to jury trial?

Negotiation

The least formal form of ADR is *negotiation;* it is almost always voluntary and, unlike arbitration, has no mandatory procedure, although there can be legal consequences from lying. Negotiation occurs when parties decide to settle a matter between themselves; the use of lawyers or representatives is not required but is often a good idea.

Negotiation has risen in popularity in recent years. For example, Georgia-Pacific Corp. set up an in-house ADR program in 1993. After five years of experience, they report that the program saves the company at least a million dollars a year in litigation expenses by keeping dozens of cases a year out of court. Direct negotiation is the form of ADR that experience has shown to be the most successful. Motorola similarly reports that negotiation is regarded as the most successful and cost-effective form of ADR. Over 4,000 firms have signed a pledge to the CPR Institute for Dispute Resolution to seek ADR. The Institute's experience is that negotiation is generally the cheapest form of ADR and resolves about 90 percent of disputes.

ISSUES IN NEGOTIATION

Whenever people bargain for something, they are engaged in negotiation. Many contracts are formed after negotiation. A negotiated settlement of a dispute is usually a contract that, like other contracts, is enforced by the courts. When parties enter into formal negotiation, it may be to make a deal, that is, looking forward to forming a contract to do business. Negotiations need not involve attorneys, but negotiations to resolve disputes over past events are more likely to involve attorneys who try to settle the matter before it ends up in litigation. The *Red Owl* case in Chapter 10 is a famous example of business negotiations that were not handled properly and resulted in litigation.

STAGES OF NEGOTIATION

While the steps of negotiation may be the same in negotiating a contract, negotiation in a dispute involves parties at odds with one another. Since the parties to the dispute are unlikely to be experienced negotiators and may be influenced by their anger about what has happened, negotiation to settle a dispute is often handled by an attorney or other experienced person. The negotiator is the agent of the party who authorizes the agent to represent her. As we will see in Chapter 13, the agent works for the party who hired her and must follow her instructions even if she wants to do something the negotiator may think is foolish.

The first stage of negotiation involves studying the issues and planning for negotiation. To do a good job, just as in litigation, a party should gather facts and relevant information (not just go on personal opinions), understand the weak points, consider the objectives of negotiation, know the law that would be applied to the situation if litigated, know the alternative routes that can be taken, and decide how to handle the negotiation process, such as whether the parties to the dispute will be present.

Next, the parties must exchange information. At this point, the style of the negotiator plays a role. Some negotiators are combative "tough guys," while others are thoughtful problem solvers in their approach. In either case, the negotiator must know what information to present, such as an offer to settle.

While one negotiation strategy is to state (and mean) that the first offer is the final offer, most negotiators expect to compromise. Some concessions are planned in advance to help get the parties closer to a realistic settlement. Since the courts encourage negotiation, settlement offers presented in negotiation may not be used as evidence in court. If a negotiation is properly run, almost nothing said in the negotiation can be later used in court if the negotiation fails. The fact that a negotiation that fails will not come back to haunt a party in court encourages the integrity of the process. Finally, if an agreement is reached, it is usually spelled out in writing and becomes a contract that can be enforced in court. The courts have a strong policy of enforcing negotiated settlements.

ETHICAL DUTIES

Anyone involved in negotiation must be careful not to misrepresent the truth, which can constitute fraud. Fraud that involves lying to someone and misleading them to their detriment can lead to a tort suit, as discussed in Chapters 7 and 8. Misleading someone in contract negotiation can also be a breach of contract, which also leads to litigation. Thus, parties to negotiation face legal constraints on their behavior. While all parties to negotiation should be constrained by ethical considerations, attorneys, like other professionals, are bound by codes of ethics or codes of professional responsibility. Attorneys who violate their ethical responsibility may suffer discipline by their bar association.

Mediation

Unlike negotiation, where the parties to a dispute or their representatives meet to settle a matter, in *mediation* a neutral third party is always used to help the parties to a dispute reach a resolution. Mediation or conciliation usually is used to solve one situation by reaching a mutually acceptable agreement. Unlike arbitration, where the arbitrator imposes an award on the parties, the mediator cannot impose a decision but can only help facilitate resolving a conflict.

The American Arbitration Association suggests the following provision be included in contracts:

> If a dispute arises out of or relates to this contract or the breach thereof and if the dispute cannot be settled through negotiation, the parties agree first to try in good faith to settle the dispute by mediation administered by the American Arbitration Association under its Commercial Mediation Rules before resorting to arbitration, litigation, or some other dispute-resolution procedure.

Mediation is the most common form of ADR used to resolve disputes that start out in the courts. About half of the federal district courts require that mediation be attempted before trial or at least offer the alternative. In most state courts, mediation is actively encouraged or required before parties to civil litigation go to trial. Surveys indicate that attorneys prefer to go to mediation rather than to arbitration when pressured to go to ADR.

Mediation is also often used to help resolve labor disputes. The Federal Mediation and Conciliation Service was established to help unions and employers bargain to a contract. Mediation is also commonly used to help resolve marital

Global Acceptance of Arbitration

International business contracts usually contain arbitration clauses. Over one hundred nations have signed the United Nations Convention on the Recognition and Enforcement of Foreign Arbitral Awards, which binds signatory nations to uphold the validity of arbitration awards. The gap between the formal law and local legal reality has often been large.

Although China signed the Convention in 1988, Chinese courts had a reputation for not enforcing arbitration decisions. For example, one non-Chinese company won an award for $4.9 million in arbitration at the Swedish Chamber of Commerce. The Shanghai company that lost the case did not pay. When the foreign firm sued in court in China to enforce the award, the courts refused to enforce the arbitration decision. In 1995, China's supreme court held that lower courts in China could not reverse arbitration awards without permission of the supreme court.

India has also had a reputation as a country where foreign awards are nearly impossible to enforce through Indian courts. The government of India adopted the Indian Arbitration Act of 1996 to encourage the use of arbitration. In the first case under the Act, the Bombay High Court upheld an arbitration award from London against a Bombay company. The court held that under the law, Indian courts cannot review the merits of foreign arbitration unless the party has substantial proof of bias or the award otherwise violates public policy.

Other developed nations have acted to come more into line with international standards. In 1998, Germany adopted a new arbitration law to replace the arbitration provisions of the 1877 German Civil Procedure Code. The new law has broad coverage and meets the latest standards of the U.N. Commission on International Trade Law.

---

problems and, if not successful, to set the terms of divorce. In such cases, mediation is a voluntary process that helps avoid litigation. As Professor Lon Fuller explained, mediation has the "capacity to reorient the parties toward each other, not by imposing rules on them, but by helping them to achieve a new and shared perception of their relationship, a perception that will direct their attention toward each other." (*Mediation*, 44 S.Cal.L.Rev. 305; 1971)

THE MEDIATOR

Some states do not have requirements about who may serve as a mediator, but most people want a person trained or experienced in mediation, as the results are more likely to be successful and the parties may have more confidence in the mediator. Some states require those offering their services as mediators to be trained professionals. The law in Massachusetts states:

> [A] "mediator" shall mean a person not a party to a dispute who enters into a written agreement with the parties to assist them in resolving their disputes and has completed at least thirty hours of training in mediation and who either has four years of professional experience as a mediator or is accountable to a dispute resolution organization . . . or one who has been appointed to mediate by a judicial or governmental body. (M.G.L.A. ch. 233 §23C)

The Society of Professionals in Dispute Resolution is an organization that helps to train and govern the credentials of mediators. The Society identifies the skills that a mediator should possess and the steps that should be taken in proper mediation.

Those who offer their services as mediators and fail to act in a professional manner may be subject to liability by a party to the dispute unhappy with the outcome.

MEDIATION PROCESS

A mediator, when agreed upon by both parties, must review the issues involved to prepare to handle the matter. The mediator explains the process involved and makes clear that she is a neutral party. The mediator collects information, outlines the key issues, listens, asks questions, observes the parties, discusses options, and encourages compromise. If successful, the mediator helps draft an agreement between the parties that settles the dispute. Properly drafted, the agreement is an enforceable contract and, therefore, settles the matter.

One decision that the mediator must get the parties to agree upon is whether they want confidentiality, which is usually the case. If confidentiality is agreed upon, nothing said in the mediation can be made public or be used in court as evidence if mediation should fail and a suit follows. Regardless of what the parties agree upon, there is a presumption in law that information revealed during negotiation or mediation should not be used in evidence. Otherwise, parties could say in court that the other side offered this or that during negotiation, which could be seen as evidence of accepting responsibility. To encourage honesty in negotiation and mediation, most discussions are privileged, and mediators cannot be required to testify later in court. Some states, including Colorado, have made this a firm rule by statute:

> Mediation proceedings shall be regarded as settlement negotiations, and no admission, representation, or statement made in mediation not otherwise discoverable or obtainable shall be admissible as evidence or subject to discovery. In addition, a mediator shall not be subject to process requiring the disclosure of any matter discussed during mediation proceedings. (Colo. Rev.Stat. 13-22-307)

The possible consequences of violating the confidentiality of mediation proceedings and settlement are made clear in the *Paranzino* case.

Paranzino v. Barnett Bank of South Florida, N.A.
District Court of Appeals of Florida, Fourth District
690 So.2d 725 (1997)

CASE BACKGROUND *Paranzino claimed that she went to a Barnett bank with $200,000 in cash to obtain two certificates of deposit, each for $100,000. She claimed that she was issued only one certificate for $100,000. She sued the bank for breach of contract. The bank denied having received $200,000 and noted that Paranzino was given a receipt for $100,000 and that her monthly statements reflected that fact for several months before she made her claim. While litigation was pending, the parties and their counsel attended court-ordered mediation and signed a mediation agreement that included a confidentiality statement.*

At mediation, Paranzino was offered $25,000 by Barnett to settle the matter. Paranzino rejected the offer and called the newspaper, which ran a story about the matter. The bank then moved the trial court to strike Paranzino's pleadings and for sanctions on the grounds that she and her attorney had breached the confidentiality of the mediation proceedings by disclosing information concerning the settlement offer and by making statements concerning the bank's alleged motivation for making the offer. The trial court granted the bank's motion to strike and dismissed the case with prejudice. Paranzino appealed.

CASE DECISION Shahood, Judge.

* * *

By violating the court-ordered mediation and the confidentiality provision of the Mediation Report and Agreement, the appellant ignored and disregarded the court's authority. The mediation order was entered by the court at appellant's request and the mediation report and agreement signed by all of the parties specifically stated that the mediation proceedings were to be confidential. In addition, the agreement further provided that the mediation was governed by the . . . Florida Rules of Civil Procedure.

Rule 1.420(b) . . . permits a court to involuntarily dismiss an action. The rule specifically provides in pertinent part, the following:

> (b) Involuntary Dismissal. Any party may move for dismissal of an action or of any claim against that party for failure of an adverse party to comply with these rules or of any order of court.

In granting appellee's motion, the trial court made the following findings: This court finds that, in the instant case, all parties were aware of the precedent condition of absolute confidentiality regarding the mediation proceedings. The evidence presented reveled that the Plaintiff and her attorney willfully and deliberately disregarded the confidentiality agreement by exposing confidential information, namely the settlement offer, to the media. Indeed, the very basis of court-ordered mediation is that parties can rely upon the confidentiality of all oral or written statements. This was clearly violated with their disclosure of the settlement offer.

In addition, the trial court further based its ruling on strong public policy concerns in finding that appel-

lant's breach of confidentiality violated the parties' confidentiality stipulation, and that the acts of appellant ran "afoul of the statutory language of Fla.Stat. 44.102(3)."

[It] provides in relevant part:

> Each party involved in a court-ordered mediation proceeding has a privilege to refuse to disclose, and to prevent any person present at the proceeding from disclosing, communications made during such proceeding . . . all oral or written communications in a mediation proceeding . . . shall be confidential and inadmissible as evidence in any subsequent legal proceeding, unless all parties agree otherwise. . . .

* * *

In this case, the trial court found that the actions of appellant and her attorney "willfully and deliberately disregarded the confidentiality agreement by exposing confidential information, namely the settlement offer, to the media." Such a finding by the court cannot be said to constitute an "abuse of discretion.". . .

We accordingly affirm the order of the trial court striking appellant's pleadings and dismissing the case with prejudice.

Affirmed.

QUESTIONS FOR ANALYSIS

1. Since the mediation was private, not in the courtroom, why did the rules of civil procedure apply?
2. Suppose mediation proceedings were always public. What would be the effect on mediation?

CREATIVE BUSINESS USE OF MEDIATION

One party cannot force another party to enter into mediation, but experience indicates that offers to mediate, even though not binding, can resolve many problems and thereby reduce litigation and the bad press that can go with it. For example, Ford Motor has a mediation program through which a mediator can offer solutions to consumers' complaints without costly litigation. Consumers must first discuss complaints with their dealer and local district office. If a problem is not resolved, a complaint may be filed with the Ford Consumer Appeals Boards. The board's decision is binding on Ford and dealers but not on consumers, who retain all legal remedies. Ford has learned that the process, in addition to solving most complaints that reach this level, encourages dealers to be more responsive to consumer problems.

Creative Dispute Resolution

The Church of the Immortal Consciousness is headed by Trina Kamp in Tonto Village near Payson, Arizona. The church was the subject of assorted rumors, such as devil worship and baby selling. It sued a Payson couple for slander for supposedly starting the rumors.

At a pretrial hearing to try to mediate the matter, Arizona judge Flournoy allowed Kamp to "channel" testimony from Dr. Pahlvon Duran, a fifteenth-century Englishman who is Kamp's inspiration for the church. While church followers sang Beatles songs, Kamp's voice changed and Duran, speaking through Kamp, said he wanted "to get on with the show." Duran/Kamp explained that the church is about loving and giving and caring. Then Duran had to leave because of an appointment in Russia.

The parties agreed to drop the case. "I believe it's a judge's job to help people settle their differences," said Judge Flournoy. "It was interesting."

Source: *The Arizona Republic*

Innovative Forms of ADR

Negotiation, mediation, and arbitration are the oldest and most established forms of ADR, but parties are free to agree upon other forms that allow them to settle their dispute in a peaceful manner (duels are not legal for settling disputes). Some forms of ADR have been invented by private parties, while others have been implemented by courts and private parties looking for ways to reduce the time and costs of litigation and reduce the burdens imposed on the taxpayer-supported judicial system.

MINITRIAL

Despite its name, the *minitrial* is not a trial but a structured settlement process that can blend negotiation, mediation, and arbitration. The parties to the process decide its structure, which varies from case to case. The parties usually agree to confidentiality. They must agree about the scope of discovery, that is, how much information each side will present. A neutral adviser is usually picked to help move things along. Organizations such as the American Arbitration Association (see http://www.adr.org) have guidelines for conducting minitrials.

Phases of a Minitrial

Unlike in trials, where discovery can consume years of work, minitrial discovery is limited to what is needed for each side to know the key issues involved. The parties trade position papers, key documents, and lists of witnesses and testimony expected.

A hearing, called an "information exchange," is held where attorneys summarize the case, usually with senior executives present from both sides who have authority to settle the matter. The rules of evidence do not apply, but the parties are in an adversarial position, making summary arguments for their sides. The executives often understand the matter better by hearing the give-and-take by the attorneys for both sides.

The mediator or party hired to help with the matter is usually requested to evaluate the case and give an opinion as to the likely outcome if the case were to go to trial. Since the mediator is respected and experienced, the opinion given often carries great weight with both parties as they consider settlement.

The parties may quit the proceedings at any time, but there is usually a settlement process that may be negotiated or mediated. The information exchange allows the parties to get to the heart of the matter and bargain over the toughest issue. Even when litigation follows a minitrial, the effect of the minitrial is often to shorten the litigation, because evidence and issues that do not much matter have been reviewed and discarded.

The Minitrial in Business Disputes

Minitrials have successfully resolved large disputes. For example, Union Carbide used the minitrial format to settle eighteen personal-injury suits arising from factory workers' exposure to an industrial chemical. One of the largest cases settled using the minitrial procedure was a 200-million-dollar antitrust and breach-of-contract claim between Texaco and Borden. Although the actual minitrial did not lead to the resolution, it did bring the executives together to discuss the problem. The solution involved the renegotiation of a seemingly unrelated contract. Both parties praised the solution, calling it one "anticipated by no one and impossible to achieve in court."

The Minitrial and the Courts

"Court-supervised" minitrial projects have been implemented in several federal district courts. The District of Massachusetts, for example, adopted the minitrial format to manage a complex patent/antitrust case expected to consume eight weeks of trial time. The judge served as a neutral adviser in the minitrial, and after one day of presentations, the seven-year-old case was settled. In a multimillion-dollar contract dispute between two natural gas companies, the parties followed their own discovery rules and conducted a two-day in-court minitrial. They resolved their dispute less than eight months after the case was filed.

SUMMARY JURY TRIAL

The summary jury trial was developed for use in the federal court system by federal district judge Thomas Lambros of Ohio. A *summary jury trial* is the jury equivalent of a minitrial. It generally takes place after discovery has been completed and shortly before trial and when it appears that a case will not be settled before trial.

The summary trial begins with the selection of six advisory jurors who do not know that the trial is not binding. Each side is given a short time to summarize its case. Presentations in court generally (but not always) are limited to evidence admissible at trial and based on depositions, discovered documents, expert reports, and other discovery material. Witnesses usually do not participate. After the presentations, the judge gives the jury abbreviated instructions on the law. The jury then reaches its decision. After the proceeding, a judicial officer (and frequently the jury) meets with the parties to discuss the decision and encourage settlement.

If one or both parties are not satisfied with the result of the summary trial, which usually takes one day, they may still take the dispute to a full trial with no punishment from the court. Nothing learned at the summary trial may be used as evidence at trial. However, the federal court in Ohio reported that of the 200 cases assigned to summary jury trial, 193 settled prior to a full trial. In those summary trial cases that have gone on to a full trial, the trial decision has been consistent with the summary trial decision. While the courts have leeway to put pressure on parties to settle cases before trial, ADR is a voluntary process, as the court noted in the *NLO* decision.

In re NLO, Inc.
United States Court of Appeals, Sixth Circuit
5 F.3d 154 (1993)

CASE BACKGROUND *NLO ran a uranium-processing facility. It was sued by former employees who claimed they suffered injuries because "NLO had intentionally or negligently exposed them to hazardous levels of radioactive materials, increasing their risk of cancer and subjecting them to emotional distress." The trial court ordered that a summary jury trial be held and that it would be open to the public. NLO petitioned the appeals court to vacate the district court order to participate in the summary jury trial before the matter could be tried in regular court.*

CASE DECISION Merritt, Chief Judge.

* * *

A summary jury trial is a non-binding minitrial designed to give the attorneys and their clients an indication of what they may expect at a full-blown trial on the merits. The parties exchange evidence before the summary jury trial has commenced, and are limited to the evidence thus disclosed. A jury is selected from the regular jury pool. The parties then present opening statements, summarize the evidence which would be presented at a full trial (no live testimony is permitted), and present closing statements. The jury is then instructed on the law and asked to respond to a series of interrogatories concerning liability and damages.

* * *

District courts unquestionably have substantial inherent power to manage their dockets. That power, however, must be exercised in a manner that is in harmony with the Federal Rules of Civil Procedure.

* * *

Rule 16(a) gives district courts the power to compel attendance at pretrial conferences. Rule 16(c) gives guidance concerning "subjects to be discussed" at those conferences:

The participants at any conference under this rule may consider and take action with respect to . . . (7) the possibility of settlement or the use of extrajudicial procedures to resolve the dispute; . . . (10) the need for adopting special procedures for managing potentially difficult or protracted actions that may involve complex issues, multiple parties, difficult legal questions, or unusual proof problems. . . .

The Advisory Committee notes to Rule 16(c)(7) indicate that no compulsory authority exists:

[I]t is not the purpose of Rule 16(c)(7) to impose settlement negotiations on unwilling litigants. . . . The rule does not make settlement conferences mandatory. . . . In addition to settlement, Rule 16(c)(7) refers to exploring the use of procedures other than litigation to resolve the dispute. This includes urging the litigants to employ adjudicatory techniques outside the courthouse. . . .

District courts struggle to deal effectively with caseloads expanding at a precipitous rate. The utilization of procedures designed to facilitate settlement whenever possible is expressly encouraged by Rule 16, for a case that settles obviously consumes much less of the court's scarce resources than a case that proceeds to a full trial on the merits. Although judges should encourage and aid early settlement, however, they should not attempt to coerce that settlement. "Rule 16 . . . was not intended to require that an unwilling litigant be sidetracked from the normal course of litigation." Requiring participation in a summary jury trial, where such compulsion is not permitted by the Federal Rules, is an unwarranted extension of the judicial power.

* * *

If summary jury trials aid parties in realistically assessing their potential liability or award and facilitate settlement talks, then litigants will voluntarily participate in order to avoid the expenses associated with lengthy trials. . . . Judges who require particular lawyers or litigants to participate in additional and unconventional settlement procedures unnecessarily call their own impartiality into question . . . undermin[ing] the atmosphere of fairness and justice in the federal courts.

Requiring participation in a pre-trial conference, even if settlement is explored, is permitted under Rule 16(a), and justifiably so, for it may facilitate settlement at very little expense to the parties and the court. A jury trial, even one of summary nature, however, requires at minimum the time-consuming process of assembling a panel and (one would hope) thorough preparation for argument by counsel, no matter how brief the actual proceeding. Compelling an unwilling litigant to undergo this process improperly interposes the tribunal into the normal adversarial course of litigation. It is error.

* * *

Accordingly, we . . . vacate that portion of the district court's order . . . ordering a summary jury trial.

QUESTIONS FOR ANALYSIS

1. Since summary jury trials save time and expense, why should they not be mandatory when the judge believes they have a high chance of ending a suit?
2. Why do you suppose NLO did not want to have a summary jury trial?

Confidential Proceedings

One of the largest settlements reached as a result of a summary jury trial involved a dispute between General Electric and Cincinnati Gas and Electric, a public utility company. Cincinnati Gas built a large nuclear power plant using a design supplied by General Electric. It sued in federal court seeking $360 million in compensatory damages and $1 billion in punitive damages for cost overruns and delays allegedly caused by GE's plant design. After a two-week, nonbinding summary trial in which the jury found General Electric not liable, the parties settled the case for $78.3 million.

An issue that arose from the case was the confidentiality of the proceeding. The *Cincinnati Post* claimed that it had the right to attend the summary jury trial, just as the press has the right to attend regular court trials. The Sixth Circuit rejected this claim, as did the two parties to the case. The court held that "settlement techniques have historically been closed to the press and public." The summary jury trial is not an adjudication; it is an effort to help parties settle. The judge does not issue an opinion, and the finding of the jury is advisory. Rejecting the right of access of the press, the court noted that "the public would have no entitlement to observe any negotiations leading to a traditional settlement of the case, and the parties would be under no constitutional obligation to reveal the content of the negotiation." (854 F.2d 900; 1988)

EXPANDING THE USE OF ADR

Congress has encouraged the use of ADR originally in the Federal Arbitration Act, and recently in the Judicial Improvements Act and the Administrative Dispute Resolution Act. States have been changing their rules of civil procedure to encourage the use of ADR techniques. The objective is to reduce the costs and delays associated with the state and federal court systems.

The Judicial Improvements Act of 1990

The Judicial Improvements Act of 1990 encourages and in some cases requires the use of ADR by federal district courts. It requires every federal district court to study its caseload and to develop a caseload management plan to reduce delay and congestion. The plans developed suggest the use of a broad variety of ADR and caseload management techniques. Under the law, the federal courts have wide latitude in developing and implementing their plans. The law allows courts to refer cases to ADR programs. In response, several courts developed projects to test the viability of expanded ADR techniques. A report by the RAND Institute for Civil Justice in 1998 found that there had been little impact on caseload speed or cost to parties.

The Administrative Dispute Resolution Act of 1990

The Administrative Dispute Resolution Act authorizes the use of ADR by federal administrative agencies. The Act does not mandate ADR in all cases but requires federal agencies to adopt an ADR policy. The Act amends the Administrative Procedures Act (discussed in Chapter 6).

The Act applies to most disputes brought by or against a federal administrative agency. The Act outlines the ADR that may be used, including settlement negotiation, mediation, minitrials, and arbitration. An important restriction included in the Act is the requirement that all parties, public and private, consent to the use of an ADR technique. An executive order issued by the president in 1996 expanded the use of binding arbitration by federal agencies.

PROS AND CONS OF ADR TO BUSINESSES

The use of ADR by the business community has grown rapidly. Businesses have used these processes to resolve large and small disputes with other businesses, consumers, and the government. Several important motivating factors contribute to this increase in the use of ADR by business. The following are some of the more important factors:

1. The avoidance of high-cost litigation (By eliminating or reducing discovery and formal trial presentations, the costs of discovery, experts, staff time, and attorney's fees are significantly reduced.)
2. The fear that litigation will result in an outcome far more adverse than reasonably anticipated, that is, a greater degree of certainty in the outcome and more control over the process
3. Much quicker resolution of the matter
4. The desire to maintain the business relationship
5. The parties' agreement to keep it confidential (Important when adverse publicity might injure the reputations of the parties.)

As the number of cases that the court systems face continues to grow, it is likely that ADR will be used more and more and that it will become recognized by the general population as a reasonable alternative to the public courts.

A primary objection to ADR to settle business disputes is the confidentiality that the parties to the dispute prefer. When a case is tried in court, the facts, arguments, and reasoning of the court become public knowledge. The individual case matters less than what we learn from observing problems that arise and how the courts resolve them. The ability to learn law and learn from the mistakes of others is largely lost when public litigation is replaced by private settlements.

Summary

- Parties have always been free to resolve disputes out of court, but in recent years, alternative dispute resolution (ADR) has increased because the courts are clogged with litigation. Civil litigation comes behind criminal cases, further delaying the resolution of noncriminal disputes. ADR allows parties to agree to the process they want to use to resolve a matter.
- Arbitration is the most formal ADR process. A decision to enter into arbitration is a binding contract. The parties who agree to arbitration choose an arbitrator, a neutral party who arbitrates the dispute and issues a binding decision, called an award, much like a judge resolves a case.
- Arbitration hearings are run much like a trial, but the rules of evidence are not as strict. Each side presents its case to the arbitrator and may call witnesses and experts to testify. An arbitrator's award need not be justified in writing. Appeals of awards to the courts are rarely successful because the parties have agreed to be bound by the decision. Unless fraud or other misconduct by the arbitrator can be shown, the courts are unlikely to intervene.
- Arbitration is often a standard part of employment contracts, insurance and commercial sale contracts, and agreements with stockbrokers. Such arbitration clauses are becoming more common. Arbitration is required of certain state employees who may be denied the right to strike.
- Negotiation is the least formal form of ADR. The two parties deal directly with each other or do so through their attorneys or other agents who represent them in talks to resolve a matter. The parties usually study the issues, exchange information, make offers, compromise, and move toward a formal settlement. Misrepresentation in negotiation may result in a suit for tort or breach of contract.
- Mediation is a more structured form of negotiation; a neutral mediator helps the parties come to a resolution of a dispute. A mediator must be agreed upon by both parties, who do not grant the power to resolve the matter to the mediator. A mediator gets the parties to agree on a process, explains the rules to them, gathers information, outlines key issues, talks to and listens to the parties, suggests options, encourages compromise, and may help draft an enforceable settlement.
- Minitrials are a form of mediation in which the parties exchange information, present their arguments before attorneys and executives from both sides, get input from the mediator about likely results, and often then move toward a settlement. Some courts encourage and supervise minitrials before trial to encourage settlement.
- Summary jury trials are used by some state and federal courts to encourage parties to settle before trial. A brief, nonbinding trial with a real jury is held. The decision that results from the summary trial usually leads to a settlement, as the parties have good insight about how the case would be resolved after a regular, more costly, trial.
- ADR processes are usually confidential, although the parties agree upon that issue at the start. Since what the parties reveal cannot be used against them in court if it would not otherwise have been evidence, the parties are more likely to speak freely. Mediators and arbitrators cannot be called as witnesses in subsequent trials, except in unusual situations, and they are rarely subject to liability for their participation in an ADR process.

- While parties cannot be forced to settle cases, federal and state laws strongly encourage the use of ADR processes to reduce the costs of the public court systems. Businesses, like other participants in ADR, generally prefer the results of ADR to the expense and uncertainty of the trial process.

Issue

Will There Be Any Cases Left for the Courts

The rapid growth of ADR means that private dispute resolution handles many cases that previously would have gone to the courts. The American Arbitration Association alone handles more than 60,000 cases per year. Attorney General Janet Reno stated that the Department of Justice would assign 170,000 civil cases a year to private arbitrators. Aggressive use of ADR has cut the number of civil suits filed in Los Angeles County about in half in less than ten years. As the following article indicates, even more suits, in the area of employment law, will be headed to arbitration. Some critics assert that this may not be a good move.

COMPANIES TRY TO PREVENT FIRED EXECUTIVES FROM SUING

Joann S. Lublin

Reprinted by permission of *The Wall Street Journal* © 1995 Dow Jones & Company, Inc. All rights reserved worldwide. Lublin is a staff reporter for the *Journal*.

Big bosses often demand big money when they sue over lost jobs. But a growing number of companies are trying to figure out how to prevent those suits.

They have plenty of reason to worry. There has been a rising tide of unfair dismissal lawsuits filed by ousted executives.

* * *

Now some companies are establishing alternative dispute mechanisms, such as arbitration or mediation, to avoid just such situations. More than 100 big companies have litigation-alternative programs covering at least some employees, up from about 10 a decade ago, estimates James Henry, president of the nonprofit CPR Institute for Dispute Resolution in New York. Among them: Northrop Grumman Corp., General Motors

Corp.'s Hughes Aircraft Co. and Aetna Life & Casualty Co.

Most of the new alternative dispute-resolution programs apply to nearly every nonunion employee from the highest officer on down. "The motivation is all the greater" for companies to cover higher-ranking executives "because the stakes are higher," Mr. Henry says.

Chrysler Corp. instituted such a program . . . for all nonunion salaried employees—including the chief executive officer. Initially, a group of managers from the individual's functional area hear the employee's complaint. The employee may then appeal to a corporate panel of human resources officials, and, finally, to an outside arbitrator whose decision is binding.

Eckerd Corp. recently began testing a new grievance procedure for terminated hourly employees at a Houston distribution center. If the pilot program succeeds, Eckerd officials want to extend the program to management. Workers at the nonunion company may appeal their discharge to a review panel of four other employees. If the panel reaches a tie vote, binding arbitration can follow.

"Over the past ten years, we've had a number of management dismissals that led to litigation," says James Sidman, employee relations attorney for the Clearwater, Fla., retail-drug concern. "It makes sense for [the procedure] to be all-encompassing."

Certain companies try to avoid lawsuits in a less sweeping fashion, insisting that senior executives' employment contracts mandate arbitration. That's true for two top officers at Eastman Kodak Co. More than half of all executive contracts require that arbitrators settle contractual grievances, up from about 25% five years ago, pay consultants say.

The rise partly reflects executives' increased acceptance of the idea. "The company used to want to go to arbitration, and the executive wanted to go to court," says Pearl Meyer, who heads her own executive compensation firm in New York. "The reason arbitration is catching on [with executives] is because it's less costly and more timely." Wrongful-discharge suits sometimes drag on for three to six years.

Rockwell International Corp. used a more unusual approach to promote arbitration for resolving most of its executives' employment disputes. In May 1992, the diversified high-technology concern gave its nearly 900 senior managers a choice: Accept an arbitration agreement or forgo any more stock options.

A handful of managers balked, forfeiting their options that year. Most later changed their minds, recalls Marilyn Maledon, an assistant general counsel for the Seal Beach, Calif., company. She immediately signed the arbitration accord, because, she adds, there aren't "any substantive rights given up. You give up your rights to a jury trial. But that doesn't bother me."

Rockwell now requires the arbitration agreements for anyone joining or advancing into management. When top officers were mulling the widened mandate, Ms. Maledon warned that superstars opposed to arbitration might spurn their job offers. Her colleagues stood firm, and she says they haven't lost any job candidates over the policy.

However, many plaintiffs' attorneys oppose employers' move toward requiring arbitration. "You are giving away your rights upfront," says Joseph Golden, an employment lawyer in Southfield, Mich. Unfairly dismissed managers get a fairer shake from a jury, he insists. "You can make a more emotional appeal . . . and have a lot more impact."

* * *

ISSUE QUESTIONS

1. When employees are told that a condition of employment is that they must agree to ADR in the event of a dispute, is there really a choice in the matter?

2. In cases of unfair dismissal, is an "emotional appeal" to a jury really a more fair way to settle a dispute?

REVIEW AND DISCUSSION QUESTIONS

1. Define the following terms:

alternative dispute resolution   mediation
arbitration   minitrial
award   summary jury trial
negotiation

CASE QUESTIONS

2. A franchise agreement (contract) between the parent company franchisor and the franchisees who operated 7-Eleven stores said that any dispute between the franchisor and franchisees would be settled by arbitration. A franchisee sued the franchisor in state court, claiming that some actions of the franchisor were in violation of state law concerning franchises. The state supreme court ruled that the issues covered by the state law could be tried in state court and did not have to be submitted to arbitration. What did the U.S. Supreme Court hold about the choice between arbitration and litigation? [*Southland Corp.* v. *Keating*, 465 U.S. 1 (1984)]

3. Broadway Realty sold Hembree a house. The purchase contract provided as follows: "Any controversy or claim arising out of or relating to this contract, or the breach thereof, shall be settled by arbitration in the city of contract origin, in accordance with the rules of the American Arbitration Association." Hembree found that the home had a defective roof. His claim came before an arbitrator. The arbitrator found for Hembree on the theory of implied warranty and awarded him

damages. In applying the theory, however, the arbitrator made an error in the application of the law. Since Broadway was the developer and not the builder, it should not be liable to Hembree on an implied warranty theory. On that basis, Broadway appealed the arbitrator's decision. How will the state court rule? [*Hembree* v. *Broadway Realty and Trust Co.*, 728 P.2d 288 (Ct. App., Az., 1986)]

4. Cooper worked at a plant run by Misco. He operated hazardous machinery. Misco's contract with Cooper's union stated that any grievances would go to binding arbitration. One basis for firing an employee was for possession or use of illegal drugs on company property. Cooper was suspected of drug use. While he was at work, the police searched his home and found marijuana. They also watched him at work get into another worker's car with two other workers at the Misco plant. When the two other workers went back into the plant, the police found Cooper in the back seat of the car, which was filled with marijuana smoke and had a lit marijuana cigarette in the front ashtray. Misco fired Cooper, who appealed for arbitration. The arbitrator ordered Cooper reinstated because he was not found in possession of marijuana on company property, nor was he seen smoking marijuana. Misco appealed; the district court and court of appeals reversed the arbitrator, holding that he exceeded his authority by ordering Cooper reinstated and, further, that the award was in violation of public policy. Cooper's union appealed to the Supreme Court. What holding? [*United Paperworkers International Union* v. *Misco, Inc.*, 108 S.Ct. 364 (1987)]

5. Chube was a supervisor in a "safety sensitive position" at an Exxon chemical plant. Under company drug policy, employees in such positions were subject to random drug tests. An employee who failed the test could be disciplined or fired. Chube tested positive for cocaine and was fired. He was later sentenced to prison for selling cocaine. Chube's union protested the dismissal, and the case went to arbitration. The arbitrator held that Chube was improperly dismissed, because there was no evidence of drug usage on the job. Hence, Chube must be reinstated in his job (when released from prison) and paid back wages. Exxon appealed to federal court. What result? [*Exxon Corp.* v. *Baton Rouge Oil and Chemical Workers Union*, 77 F.3d 850 (1996)]

6. Mago worked for E. F. Hutton. When the company was bought by Shearson, she was asked to sign a standard employment agreement that she would arbitrate any employment dispute. She later sued Shearson for sexual discrimination in employment in violation of Title VII of the Civil Rights Act of 1964. The district court refused to enforce the arbitration agreement because arbitrators cannot settle employment discrimination matters that can have judicial remedies. Was the district court correct? [*Mago* v. *Shearson Lehman Hutton*, 956 F.2d 932 (9th Cir., 1992)]

7. AT&T's labor agreement with a union stated that most disputes would go to arbitration. Article 9 of the agreement said that AT&T "is free to exercise certain management functions, including the hiring, placement, and termination of employees." Article 20 of the agreement states which workers will be laid off when "lack of work necessitates Layoff." AT&T laid off seventy-nine workers in Chicago, claiming that under Article 9, its decision was a management function not subject to arbitration. The union claimed that under Article 20, AT&T had to submit the layoffs to arbitration. The union sued in federal court for a court order enforcing the arbitration agreement. The district court and court of appeals held that it was for the arbitrator to decide whether the union's interpretation of the

contract was correct and whether there must be arbitration. Is that correct? [*AT & T Technologies* v. *Communications Workers of America*, 106 S.Ct. 1415 (1986)]

8. An employer and a union disputed what happened at an arbitration hearing. The employer challenged the arbitration award in federal court and subpoenaed the arbitrator to testify about what happened at the arbitration at which he presided. Could the arbitrator be required to testify? [*Main Central Railroad Co.* v. *Brotherhood of Maintenance of Way Employees*, 117 F.R.D. 485 (U.S. Dist. Ct., Me., 1987)]

9. Mediator Hammond assisted in negotiations between a union and a company. After mediation, the union declared that an agreement had been reached. The employer denied that an agreement had been reached and refused to sign the union contract. The union filed an unfair labor practice complaint with the National Labor Relations Board. The company claimed that it had the right to call the mediator as a witness in the unfair labor practice complaint. Could the mediator be called to give testimony in the case? [*National Labor Relations Board* v. *Joseph Macaluso, Inc.*, 618 F.2d 51 (9th Cir., 1980)]

10. Thomas sued his former employer for racial, sexual, and national origin discrimination in violation of two civil rights laws. During pretrial negotiations, the employer offered Thomas his job back "without prejudice," meaning that it would not affect some of his claims in the lawsuit, such as for mental distress, but if he returned to work, he could not claim he was owed back wages from the date from which he could have started working. Thomas refused the offer. The employer asserted that it should have the right to present testimony to the jury about its offer that was rejected. Thomas said that the negotiations were completely confidential and there could be no testimony. Who was right? [*Thomas* v. *Resort Health Related Facility*, 539 F.Supp. 630 (U.S. Dist. Ct., E.D.N.Y., 1982)]

11. Lightwave Technologies and Corning Glass Works were involved in extended litigation involving many issues. The parties agreed to hold a minitrial to see whether a settlement could be reached with respect to the antitrust claims Lightwave had made against Corning. Lightwave's attorney told Corning that he had authority to settle the matter. After the minitrial, a deal was struck, which Corning presumed was final. Lightwave's president rejected the deal and stated that the attorney did not have authority to bind Lightwave to a deal without his permission. Corning sued to enforce the settlement worked out at the minitrial, because it acted in good faith, presuming that Lightwave's attorney had the authority to settle the matter. Who won? [*Lightwave Technologies* v. *Corning Glass Works*, 725 F.Supp. 198 (U.S.Dist. Ct., S.D.N.Y., 1989)]

POLICY QUESTION

12. How much authority should judges have to force parties into ADR? This has become a controversial issue, as some courts have become quite insistent that parties try to work out a settlement to avoid trial even when at least one of the parties states that it is not interested. Not having a trial generally produces decent results with respect to the merits of a case, but there is a presumption that parties have a right to a day in court if they insist on it.

ETHICS QUESTION

13. Because litigation is so expensive, time-consuming, and risky for large firms, many firms offer to settle cases that are largely bogus. The firms know that there is little merit to the cases, but rather than risk large sums, they negotiate a settlement for $10,000 to $50,000 just to get out of the problem. Obviously, it is not ethical to bring dubious suits just to extract some cash, but is it ethical for firms to negotiate their way out of these suits instead of litigating them and defeating those who tend to specialize in bringing such suits?

CHAPTER 5

The Constitution: Focus on Application to Business

George Washington presided over a convention in Philadelphia from May to September 1787, at which the Constitution of the United States was drafted. The Constitution became effective in March 1789, when it had been ratified by the legislatures in nine of the thirteen original states. It is composed of the preamble and seven articles. The preamble reads:

> We the People of the United States, in Order to form a more perfect Union, establish Justice, insure domestic Tranquility, provide for the common defence, promote the general Welfare, and secure the Blessings of Liberty to ourselves and our Posterity, do ordain and establish this Constitution for the United States of America.

The Articles are divided into sections:

I. Composition and powers of Congress

II. Selection and powers of the president

III. Creation and powers of the federal judiciary

IV. Role of the states in the federal system

V. Methods of amending the Constitution

VI. Declaring the Constitution to be supreme law of the land

VII. Method for ratifying the Constitution

The process of amending the Constitution began almost immediately as there was concern that there was not enough protection for individual rights. In 1791, the first ten amendments (the *Bill of Rights*) were ratified by the states after having been approved by the First Session of Congress. The Twenty-seventh Amendment, restricting changes in pay for members of Congress, was ratified in 1992. A proposed amendment may be proposed by a two-thirds vote in the House and Senate and then be ratified by three-fourths of the state legislatures, or it may be proposed by two-thirds of the state legislatures by calling for a constitutional convention, the results of which must be ratified by three-fourths of the state legislatures. The Constitution is reprinted in Appendix C.

Some rights are clearly expressed, but most of the Constitution is written in general terms or in terms that can be interpreted in different ways. Justice Story noted this in 1816 in *Martin* v. *Hunter's Lessee* (14 U.S. 304):

> The constitution unavoidably deals in general language. It did not suit the purposes of the people, in framing this great charter of our liberties, to provide for minute specifications of its powers, or to declare the means by which those powers should be carried into execution. It was foreseen that this would be a perilous and difficult, if not an impracticable, task. The instrument was not intended to provide merely for the exigencies of a few years, but was to endure through a long lapse of ages, the events of which were locked up in the inscrutable purposes of Providence. It could not be foreseen what new changes and modifications of power might be indispensable to effectuate the general objects of the charter; and restrictions and specifications which, at the present, might seem salutary, might, in the end, prove the overthrow of the system itself. Hence its powers are expressed in general terms, leaving to the legislature, from time to time, to adopt its own means to effectuate legitimate objects, and to mold and model the exercise of its powers, as its own wisdom and the public interest should require.

All citizens are affected by the Constitution. Court rulings about the rights of individuals when they are accused of crimes draw the most popular attention. The Constitution provides safeguards against overzealous law enforcement agencies, primarily through the Bill of Rights. Supreme Court interpretation of the rights of persons accused of crimes and of other constitutionally protected rights changes over time. The Court has reversed itself on major constitutional issues over the years, reading the same words in an opposite manner. Some would say this means the Court is political; it may reflect changes in technology, social values, economic conditions, and political realities.

The Commerce Clause

This chapter focuses on constitutional law that affects business. While all parts of the Constitution have application to business and to individuals, certain provisions have a particular impact on business. In that respect, perhaps the most important part of the Constitution is Article I, Section 8: "The Congress shall have Power . . . To regulate Commerce with foreign Nations, and among the several States, and with the Indian Tribes; . . ." Known as the *commerce clause*, these few words have been interpreted to give Congress the power to enact most of the federal regulation of business discussed in this text.

The clause might be reduced to "regulate Commerce . . . among the several States" to show the essential basis of federal regulation. The authority granted to Congress in the commerce clause, when combined with the necessary and proper clause, gives Congress tremendous regulatory power. Before we return to the commerce clause, let's consider this companion clause.

THE NECESSARY AND PROPER CLAUSE

The Constitution enumerates a list of specific congressional powers (including collecting taxes, regulating commerce, and providing for national defense). At the end of the list, clause 18 of Article I, Section 8, gives Congress power "to make all Laws which shall be necessary and proper for carrying into Execution the foregoing Powers, and all other Powers vested by this Constitution in the Government of the United States, or in any Department or Officer thereof." This is the *necessary and proper clause.*

The necessary and proper clause, along with the commerce clause, has been held to provide justification for broad congressional control of commerce. It is unusual for a law to be struck down by the Supreme Court for not being "necessary and proper." The clause gives Congress power to deal with matters beyond the list of specified federal concerns as long as control of those matters helps Congress to be more effective in controlling matters of national interests.

McCulloch v. Maryland

Chief Justice Marshall gave a broad reading to the necessary and proper clause in 1819 in *McCulloch* v. *Maryland* (17 U.S. 316). In that case, the state of Maryland questioned whether Congress had the right to establish a national bank, since banking was not a power of Congress "enumerated" in the Constitution. The Supreme Court upheld the constitutionality of the bank chartered by Congress under the necessary and proper clause. The Court held that the clause expands the power of Congress; the necessary and proper clause does not restrict Congress to control of enumerated powers:

> 1st. The clause is placed among the powers of Congress, not among the limitations on those powers.
> 2nd. Its terms purport to enlarge, not to diminish the powers vested in the government. It purports to be an additional power, not a restriction on those already granted.

Over the years, the Supreme Court has upheld a wide range of federal statutes as necessary and proper, even though the subject of the legislation could not have been contemplated when the Constitution was written. For example, the Court upheld a federal statute limiting liability that would arise from nuclear accidents as necessary and proper to achieve the government's objective of encouraging the development of private nuclear power plants.

Federal Supremacy

Another key point made in the *McCulloch* decision is that when the federal government has the power to act under the Constitution, its actions are supreme; that is, they take precedence over the actions of other governments. The state of Maryland argued that even if the federal government had the right to establish a national bank, the state could regulate the bank, such as impose taxes on it, as it did on other banks. The Court struck down the Maryland tax as in violation of Article VI, Paragraph 2, the *supremacy clause:* "The Constitution, and the Laws of the United States . . . shall be the supreme Law of the Land; and the judges in every State shall be bound thereby. . . ." If Congress did not want Maryland to tax a bank created by Congress, Maryland could not do so because, so long as they are constitutional, federal laws are supreme over state laws.

DEFINING "COMMERCE AMONG THE SEVERAL STATES"

Although most federal regulation of business evolved since the 1930s, Congress has had broad regulatory powers since the early days of the Republic. In 1824, Chief Justice Marshall established some of the basic guidelines of the commerce clause in *Gibbons* v. *Ogden* (22 U.S. 1). He held that commerce among the states means *interstate commerce,* that is, commerce that concerns more than one state. Further, Justice Marshall held:

> What is this power? It is the power to regulate; that is, to prescribe the rule by which commerce is to be governed. This power, like all others vested in Congress, is complete in itself, may be exercised to its utmost extent, and acknowledges no limitations other than are prescribed in the Constitution.

Exclusive power over regulation of foreign commerce also resides with Congress.

Interstate Commerce Broadly Defined

Just because the effect of a business on interstate commerce is small does not mean that the business is exempt from federal regulation. For example, in the 1942 Supreme Court decision *Wickard* v. *Filburn* (317 U.S. 111), federal controls on the production of wheat were held to apply to a small farm in Ohio that produced only 239 bushels of wheat for consumption on the farm. The Court reasoned that Congress intended to regulate the wheat industry. To control wheat prices effectively, there could not be an exemption for small intrastate producers. Although one farmer would not make a difference, all the small farmers added together would have an impact on the wheat market. Therefore, all wheat production could be regulated.

In another decision, *Perez* v. *United States* (402 U.S. 146; 1971), the Supreme Court upheld federal regulation of local loan-sharking activities. The Court held that even though the activity may be local, in sum it may be substantial, and the funds behind local loan sharks are often interstate in origin, since they may come from organized crime, which is a national concern. This decision provides a commerce clause basis for the federalization of criminal law, which is traditionally a state police power.

In the *Katzenbach* v. *McClung* decision, the Court used the commerce clause to extend nondiscrimination requirements of the 1964 Civil Rights Act to local operations.

Katzenbach v. McClung
United States Supreme Court
379 U.S. 294, 85 S.Ct. 377 (1964)

CASE BACKGROUND *Ollie's Barbecue was a family-owned restaurant in Birmingham, Alabama. It had 220 seats for white customers. Although most of the employees were black, black customers were allowed to buy food only at a take-out window. The Department of Justice (Attorney General Katzenbach) sued the restaurant for violating Title II of the 1964 Civil Rights Act, which prohibits racial segregation in places of public accommodation. This includes restaurants that offer "to serve interstate travelers or [if] a substantial portion of the food which it serves . . . has moved in interstate commerce." Ollie's (McClung) contended that since its customers were local, not traveling interstate, it should be exempt from the law. The government noted that almost half of the food Ollie's bought came from out of state, which was enough to make the business interstate.*

A three-judge district court concluded that there was no rational relationship between food purchased by McClung in interstate commerce and food sold in a restaurant, so it refused to enforce the Act. The government appealed to the Supreme Court.

CASE DECISION Clark, Justice.

* * *

. . . [T]here was an impressive array of testimony that discrimination in restaurants had a direct and highly restrictive effect upon interstate travel by Negroes. This resulted, it was said, because discrimination practices prevent Negroes from buying prepared food served on the premises while on a trip, except in isolated and unkempt restaurants and under most unsatisfactory and often unpleasant conditions. This obviously discourages travel and obstructs interstate commerce for one can hardly travel without eating. Likewise, it was said, that discrimination deterred professional, as well as skilled, people from moving into areas where such practices occurred and thereby caused industry to be reluctant to establish there.

* * *

[Much] is said about a restaurant business being local but "even if appellee's activity [is] local and though it may not be regarded as commerce, it may still, whatever its nature, be reached by Congress if it exerts a substantial economic effect on interstate commerce." *Wickard v. Filburn.*

This Court has held time and again that this power extends to activities of retail establishments, including restaurants, which directly or indirectly burden or obstruct interstate commerce.

* * *

Confronted as we are with the facts laid before Congress, we must conclude that it had a rational basis for finding that racial discrimination in restaurants had a direct and adverse effect on the free flow of interstate commerce. Insofar as the sections of the Civil Rights Act here relevant are concerned, Congress prohibited discrimination only in those establishments having a close tie to interstate commerce, i.e., those, like McClung's, serving food that has come from out of the State. We think in so doing that Congress acted well within its power to protect and foster commerce in extending the coverage of Title II only to those restaurants offering to serve interstate travelers or serving food, a substantial portion of which has moved in interstate commerce.

The absence of direct evidence connecting discriminatory restaurant service with the flow of interstate food, a factor on which the appellees place much reliance, is not, given the evidence as to the effect of such practices on other aspects of commerce, a crucial matter.

The power of Congress in this field is broad and sweeping; where it keeps within its sphere and violates no express constitutional limitation it has been the rule of this Court, going back almost to the founding days of the Republic, not to interfere. The Civil Rights Act of 1964, as here applied, we find to be plainly appropriate in the resolution of what the Congress found to be a national commercial problem of the first magnitude. We find in it no violation of any express limitations of the Constitution and we therefore declare it valid.

The judgment is therefore reversed.

QUESTIONS FOR ANALYSIS

1. Might the Court have found differently if the restaurant could have shown that all of its food was produced in the state?

2. Suppose evidence showed that when restaurants were required to integrate, they often closed their doors and refused to do more business. Does this go against the argument that the law enhances interstate commerce?

FEDERAL/STATE REGULATORY RELATIONS

The legal environment contains a vast array of state and federal laws and regulations. As Exhibit 5.1 illustrates, the responsibility for regulating a particular activity may be the responsibility of a state governing body or a federal governing body, or it may be shared by state and federal governments. Federal environmental regulation, for example, requires the Environmental Protection Agency to set national pollution control standards. Given the federal standards, state environmental regulations provide specific requirements to be met within a state.

States often legislate on a subject matter on which Congress has legislated. When can state law exist along with federal law? Federal regulation takes precedence over state regulation that contradicts or reduces the standards imposed by federal law. States may not enact laws that burden interstate commerce. The primary justification for most state regulation is to protect public health and safety, but those concerns are not to be a ruse for restricting competition.

In some areas, such as postal authority, Congress has preempted the power of the states to regulate at all. States may not pass laws in such areas even if the laws do not contradict federal laws. In many areas, states may add their own rules to strengthen the impact of a federal rule, so long as the rules do not conflict with the intent of the law and do not impede interstate commerce. For example, states may pass air pollution regulations to apply to their industries that are stricter than the

EXHIBIT 5.1

State and Federal Regulatory Responsibilities

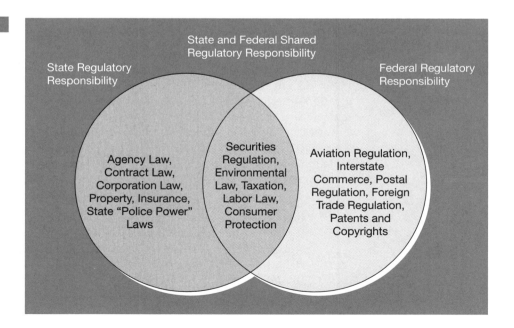

JURIS **prudence?**

Great Constitutional Moments

Arkansas required trucks to have straight mudflaps. Illinois required trucks to have mudguards that "contour the rear wheel, with the inside surface being relatively parallel to the top 90 degrees of the rear and 180 degrees of the whole surface. . . . [and] must be installed not more than 6 inches from the tire surface . . . and must have a lip or flange on its outer edge of not less than 2 inches." Trucks on interstate highways could be ticketed in either state for having the wrong flap.

The Supreme Court held that the Arkansas flaps were more common and so, "the heavy burden which the Illinois mudguard law places on the interstate movement of trucks and trailers seems to us to pass the permissible limits of safety regulations."

Source: *Bibb* v. *Navajo Freight Lines, 79 S.Ct. 962*

federal air pollution rules. However, unless specifically allowed by Congress, states may not pass rules less strict than the federal rule. In some areas, such as insurance, Congress has specifically authorized states to regulate the business within state borders.

When State Law Impedes Interstate Commerce

In 1911, the Supreme Court, in *Southern Railway Co.* v. *Arizona* (222 U.S. 20), had to consider Arizona regulations that for "safety considerations" required trains to be shorter in Arizona than in other states. Although the Arizona law was not intended to conflict with the federal rules about train length, the effect of the Arizona safety requirement was to impede interstate commerce. At the Arizona border, trains had to be shortened.

The Supreme Court struck down the Arizona law. Chief Justice Stone said, "The decisive question is whether in the circumstances the total effect of the law as a safety measure in reducing accidents and casualties is so slight or problematical as not to outweigh the national interest in keeping interstate commerce free from interferences which seriously impede it."

Since there are numerous Supreme Court cases in this area, the exact boundaries of the constitutional rules are constantly being probed. But the Supreme Court consistently takes a hard line against state regulations that restrict interstate commerce or are designed to help local businesses at the expense of out-of-state competitors:

- In *Chemical Waste Management* v. *Hunt* (504 U.S. 334; 1992), the Court held that it was a violation of the commerce clause for Alabama to impose a higher fee for hazardous waste generated outside the state than it charged for hazardous waste generated within the state when both were disposed at commercial disposal facilities in Alabama.
- In *Morales* v. *Trans World Airlines* (504 U.S. 374; 1992), the Court held that the Airline Deregulation Act of 1978 prohibits the states from regulating airline rates, routes, or services. Therefore, state attorney general may not sue the airlines under state consumer protection statutes even though they contend that airline fare advertising is injuring consumers.

- Oklahoma required coal-burning power plants in the state to burn at least 10 percent Oklahoma-mined coal. Wyoming challenged the regulation because it meant less Wyoming coal was sold to Oklahoma. The Court held in *Wyoming v. Oklahoma* (502 U.S. 437; 1992) that the Oklahoma law was discriminatory and interfered with interstate commerce.

The states have a legitimate interest in protecting public health, safety, and other public policies. When such goals are the real or stated reason for a state regulation, the regulation chosen must be designed to achieve its legitimate interest with minimal impact on interstate commerce, as discussed in the *Hughes* decision.

Hughes v. Oklahoma
United States Supreme Court
441 U.S. 322, 99 S.Ct. 1727 (1979)

CASE BACKGROUND *To protect natural minnows—ones that live in state waters—Oklahoma prohibited shipping or selling minnows out of state. Hughes was convicted of transporting minnows from Oklahoma to Texas. He bought the minnows from a dealer licensed to do business in Oklahoma. If the minnows had been captured and sold within the state, it would have been legal. It was illegal to take the fish across the state line. The Oklahoma supreme court upheld the statute and Hughes's conviction as constitutional for, among other things, Oklahoma's interest in protecting its natural resources. Hughes appealed.*

CASE DECISION Brennan, Justice.

* * *

The few simple words of the Commerce Clause—"The Congress shall have Power . . . To regulate Commerce . . . among the several States . . ."—reflected a central concern of the Framers that was an immediate reason for calling the Constitutional Convention: the conviction that in order to succeed, the new Union would have to avoid the tendencies toward economic Balkanization that had plagued relations among the Colonies and later among the States under the Articles of Confederation. The Commerce Clause has accordingly been interpreted by this Court not only as an authorization for congressional action, but also, even in the absence of a conflicting federal statute, as a restriction on permissible state regulation. The cases defining the scope of permissible state regulation in areas of congressional silence reflect an often controversial evolution of rules to accommodate federal and state interests.

* * *

We turn then to the question whether the burden imposed on interstate commerce in wild game by [the Oklahoma law] is permissible under the general rule articulated in our precedents governing other types of commerce. Under that general rule, we must inquire (1) whether the challenged statute regulates evenhandedly with only "incidental" effects on interstate commerce, or discriminates against interstate commerce either on its face or in practical effect; (2) whether the statute serves a legitimate local purpose; and, if so, (3) whether alternative means could promote this local purpose as well without discriminating against interstate commerce. The burden to show discrimination rests on the party challenging the validity of the statute, but "[w]hen discrimination against commerce . . . is demonstrated, the burden falls on the State to justify it both in terms of the local benefits flowing from the statute and the unavailability of nondiscriminatory alternatives adequate to preserve the local interests at stake." Furthermore, when considering the purpose of a challenged statute, this Court is not bound by "[t]he name, description, or characterization given it by the legislature or the courts of the State," but will determine for itself the practical impact of the law.

[The Oklahoma law] on its face discriminates against interstate commerce. It forbids the transportation of natural minnows out of the State for purposes of sale, and thus "overtly blocks the flow of interstate commerce at [the] State's borders." Such facial discrimination by itself may be a fatal defect, regardless of the State's purpose, because "the evil of protectionism can reside in legislative means as well as legislative ends." At a minimum such facial discrimination invokes the strictest scrutiny of any purported legitimate local purpose and of the absence of nondiscriminatory alternatives.

Oklahoma argues that [its law] serves a legitimate local purpose in that it is "readily apparent as a conservation measure." The State's interest in maintaining the ecological balance in state waters by avoiding the removal of inordinate numbers of minnows may well qualify as a legitimate local purpose. We consider the States' interests in conservation and protection of wild animals as legitimate local purposes similar to the States' interests in protecting the health and safety of their citizens.

* * *

Far from choosing the least discriminatory alternative, Oklahoma has chosen to "conserve" its minnows in the way that most overtly discriminates against interstate commerce. The State places no limits on the numbers of minnows that can be taken by licensed minnow dealers; nor does it limit in any way how these minnows may be disposed of within the State. Yet it forbids the transportation of any commercially significant number of natural minnows out of the State for sale. [Its law] is certainly not a "last ditch" attempt at conservation after nondiscriminatory alternatives have proved unfeasible. It is rather a choice of the most discriminatory means even though nondiscriminatory alternatives would seem likely to fulfill the State's purported legitimate local purpose more effectively.

[This decision] does not leave the States powerless to protect and conserve wild animal life within their borders. Today's decision makes clear, however, that States may promote this legitimate purpose only in ways consistent with the basic principle that "our economic unit is the Nation," and that when a wild animal "becomes an article of commerce . . . its use cannot be limited to the citizens of one State to the exclusion of citizens of another State."

Reversed.

QUESTIONS FOR ANALYSIS

1. The dissent argued that the burden on commerce from such a regulation was minimal and that more weight should be given to the legitimate interest of protecting natural resources. Where should such a line be drawn?
2. Suppose Oklahoma got other states to agree on such a restriction on the shipment of minnows and that Oklahoma similarly agreed on shipments in the other direction to help other states protect their resources. Would that be a reasonable compromise?

Imitators Not Allowed

The states may not necessarily imitate federal regulations if such imitation inhibits interstate commerce. Consider the following situation. Since the 1920s, Congress has required that timber removed from federal lands in Alaska may not be shipped out of state unless processed in Alaska. Unprocessed logs could not be shipped out of Alaska; they had to be cut into boards first. The state of Alaska imitated the federal rule in 1980, requiring that timber cut on state lands be processed in the state before shipment out of state.

The Supreme Court struck down the state law in a 1984 case, *South-Central Timber Development* v. *Wunnicke* (467 U.S. 82). "Although the Commerce Clause is by its text an affirmative grant of power to Congress to regulate interstate and foreign commerce, the Clause has long been recognized as a self-executing limitation on the power of the States to enact laws imposing substantial burdens on such commerce." That is, although Congress could impose such a requirement on timber, the state could not do so, too, unless authorized to do so by Congress. "In light of the substantial attention given by Congress to the subject of export restrictions on unprocessed timber, it would be peculiarly inappropriate to permit state regulation of the subject."

The Taxing Power

Congress is given the power to "lay and collect Taxes, Duties, Imposts and Excises" by Article I, Section 8, clause 1, of the Constitution. Although this text does not investigate federal taxation (since it is a complex topic requiring specialized courses), keep in mind that taxation is a potent tool of regulation. Taxes can be used for more than simply raising revenue to pay for government services. They can deter and punish certain behavior. For example, a tax may be tied to a requirement to keep detailed records about goods subject to the tax. In this manner, goods such as explosives, firearms, drugs, and liquors can be kept under close federal supervision.

FEDERAL TAXATION

The Supreme Court rarely questions the constitutionality of federal taxing schemes. In 1937, the Court noted in *Sonzinsky* v. *U.S.* (300 U.S. 506):

> Inquiry into the hidden motives which may move Congress to exercise a power constitutionally conferred upon it is beyond the competency of courts. . . . We are not free to speculate as to the motives which moved Congress to impose it, or as to the extent to which it may operate to restrict the activities taxed. As it is not attended by offensive regulation, and since it operates as a tax, it is within the taxing power.

The Court has upheld taxes on illegal gambling, narcotics, and marijuana. This enhances the ability of the government to prosecute those involved in illegal activities. If the income from such activities is reported, the government has evidence of illegal dealings. If the income is not reported and money is found, then the tax laws have been violated. As the Court held in *U.S.* v. *Kahriger* (345 U.S. 22; 1953), "It is axiomatic that the power of Congress to tax is extensive and sometimes falls with crushing effect on businesses deemed unessential or inimical to the public welfare, or where, as in dealings with narcotics, the collection of the tax also is difficult."

STATE TAXATION

Since most commerce is interstate, what can the states tax? The intent of the Constitution is to protect interstate commerce from discriminatory state taxes. As the Court ruled in the 1959 case *Northwestern States Portland Cement Co.* v. *Minnesota* (358 U.S. 450):

> [A] State "cannot impose taxes upon persons passing through the state or coming into it merely for a temporary purpose." . . . Moreover, a State may not lay a tax on the "privilege" of engaging in interstate commerce. . . . Nor may a State impose a tax which discriminates against interstate commerce either by providing a direct commercial advantage to local business . . . or by subjecting interstate commerce to the burden of "multiple taxation." . . . States, under the Commerce Clause, are not allowed "one single tax-dollar worth of direct interference with the free flow of commerce."

Consider the following cases in which the Supreme Court reviewed state taxing schemes to decide whether they interfered with interstate commerce:

- The state of Hawaii imposed a 20 percent tax on all alcoholic beverages except for local products. The Court struck this down in 1984 (*Baccus Imports* v. *Dias*, 468 U.S. 263), holding that the tax imposed on alcoholic products had to be the same regardless of origin.
- Michigan exempted from state income taxes the retirement benefits paid to Michigan government employees. The state taxed all other retirement income, such as retired federal government employees' benefits. The Supreme Court struck this down in *Davis* v. *Michigan Dept. of Treasury* (489 U.S. 803; 1989) as discriminatory. State income taxes must apply equally to all government retirement benefits.
- In *Quill Corp.* v. *North Dakota* (504 U.S. 298; 1992), state sales taxes imposed on out-of-state firms doing mail-order business with North Dakota residents were stricken as a violation of the commerce clause. Mail-order firms that do not have a physical presence in the state may not be taxed without permission of Congress.
- Illinois imposes a 5 percent tax on all long-distance calls to or from the state. If a taxpayer can show that another state has billed the call, the Illinois tax is refunded. This tax was held not to violate the commerce clause in *Goldberg* v. *Sweet* (488 U.S. 252; 1989) because it satisfies a four-part test of the constitutionality of state tax schemes that the Court announced in *Complete Auto Transit* v. *Brady* (430 U.S. 274; 1977):

  1. The tax applies to an activity having a substantial nexus (connection) with the state.
  2. The tax is fairly apportioned (to those inside and outside the state).
  3. The tax does not discriminate against interstate commerce.
  4. The tax is fairly related to services provided by the state.

Apportioning State Tax Burden

The Supreme Court has held that the income of businesses may be taxed by the states—so long as the proceeds are fairly apportioned among the states—using formulas that account for the intrastate share of interstate commerce.

The apportionment issue generates substantial litigation because firms often have manufacturing and distribution facilities that involve activities in many states and purchase inputs from many sources. It is difficult to know how to assign the various costs to the different portions of an operation—different accounting techniques produce different legitimate results. The federal courts are concerned with whether the tax imposes greater burdens on transactions that cross state lines than on those that occur entirely within a state.

State Taxes May Not Impede Foreign Trade

Although the power of Congress to tax is nearly unlimited, the states may not interfere with interstate commerce through their taxing schemes. Further, since the Constitution gives Congress the power to regulate international trade, as it does interstate commerce, the states may not interfere with international commerce.

The Supreme Court emphasized that point in the 1979 case *Japan Line, Ltd.* v. *County of Los Angeles* (441 U.S. 434). Several California cities and counties imposed a property tax on cargo-shipping containers owned by Japanese companies. The containers were used only in international commerce on Japanese ships.

The California taxes were levied on the containers in the state during loading and unloading. The Supreme Court held the tax to be unconstitutional. The commerce clause reserves to Congress the power over foreign commerce. Foreign commerce may not be subject to state taxes, or the states could effectively regulate foreign trade. Only the federal government may speak on foreign trade and tax matters.

Business and Free Speech

The First Amendment prohibits congressional encroachment on *freedom of speech:* "Congress shall make no law . . . abridging the freedom of speech. . . ." This right is not absolute. As Justice Holmes said in *Schenck* v. *U.S.* (249 U.S. 47; 1919), "The most stringent protection of free speech would not protect a man in falsely shouting fire in a theatre and causing a panic." The Constitution prohibits laws "abridging the freedom of speech," but it does not prohibit all laws restricting communication. For example, as the Supreme Court noted in *Ward* v. *Rock Against Racism* (491 U.S. 781; 1989), the City of New York could require a city sound technician to be present to regulate the volume at which music was played at an outdoor concert, but the technician could not control the content of the sound at the concert.

Do commercial speech (advertisements) and political statements by corporations (statements about public issues) deserve the same freedoms? In both cases, the parties are trying to convince some people about something—to buy soap or to support a political program. The Constitution does not distinguish between the two kinds of speech, but traditionally there have been many more restrictions on commercial speech than on political speech by business. The Supreme Court has helped to resolve the issue of First Amendment protection of business speech.

BUSINESS AND POLITICAL SPEECH

First National Bank of Boston v. *Bellotti* (435 U.S. 765; 1978) provided the Supreme Court the opportunity to address the issue of *political speech* by corporations and First Amendment freedoms. A Massachusetts statute prohibited corporations from making contributions or expenditures "for the purpose of . . . influencing or affecting the vote on any question submitted to the voters, other than one materially affecting any of the property, business or assets of the corporation." Some businesses wanted to make contributions to help defeat a proposition to amend the Massachusetts constitution to allow the legislature to impose a graduated personal income tax.

The U.S. Supreme Court struck down the statute: "The speech proposed . . . is at the heart of the First Amendment's protection. The freedom of speech . . . guaranteed by the Constitution embraces at the least the liberty to discuss publicly and truthfully all matters of public concern without previous restraint or fear of subsequent punishment. . . ." The Court could

> find no support in the First or Fourteenth Amendments . . . for the proposition that speech that otherwise would be within the protection of the First Amendment loses that protection simply because its source is a corporation. . . . [I]t amounts to an impermissible legislative prohibition of speech based on the identity of the interests that spokesmen may represent in public debate over controversial issues.

The Court reemphasized the right of free speech on political issues by business in the *Consolidated Edison* decision. In the case, the Court explained the test that restrictions must pass to be allowed to regulate such speech.

Consolidated Edison Company v. Public Service Commission of New York
United States Supreme Court
447 U.S. 530, 100 S.Ct. 2326 (1980)

CASE BACKGROUND *Consolidated Edison, the appellant, inserted material in favor of nuclear power in its billing envelope. The Public Service Commission of New York then ruled that Consolidated Edison could not discuss its opinions on controversial issues of public policy in its monthly bills. The commission held that utility customers who receive bills containing inserts are a captive audience who should not be subjected to the utility's views.*

The New York Court of Appeals (New York's highest court) upheld the commission's prohibition. Consolidated Edison appealed. The issue is whether the First Amendment of the Constitution is violated by an order of the Public Service Commission that prohibits the inclusion in electric bills of inserts discussing controversial public policy issues.

CASE DECISION Powell, Justice.

* * *

The Commission's ban on bill inserts is not, of course, invalid merely because it imposes a limitation upon speech. We must consider whether the State can demonstrate that its regulation is constitutionally permissible. The Commission's arguments require us to consider three theories that might justify the state action. We must determine whether the prohibition is (1) a reasonable time, place, or manner restriction, (2) a permissible subject-matter regulation, or (3) a narrowly tailored means of serving a compelling state interest.

* * *

A restriction that regulates only the time, place or manner of speech may be imposed so long as it's reasonable. But when regulation is based on the content of speech, governmental action must be scrutinized more carefully to ensure that communication has not been prohibited "merely because public officials disapprove the speaker's views."

* * *

The Commission does not pretend that its action is unrelated to the content or subject matter of bill inserts. Indeed, it has undertaken to suppress certain bill inserts precisely because they address controversial issues of public policy. The Commission allows inserts that present information to consumers on certain subjects, such as energy conservation measures, but it forbids the use of inserts that discuss public controversies. The Commission . . . justifies its ban on the ground that consumers will benefit from receiving "useful" information, but not from the prohibited information. The Commission's own rationale demonstrates that its action cannot be upheld as a content-neutral time, place, or manner regulation.

The Commission next argues that its order is acceptable because it applies to all discussion of nuclear power, whether pro or con, in bill inserts. The prohibition, the Commission contends, is related to subject matter rather than to the views of a particular speaker. Because the regulation does not favor either side of a political controversy, the Commission asserts that it does not unconstitutionally suppress freedom of speech.

The First Amendment's hostility to content-based regulation extends not only to restrictions on particular viewpoints, but also to prohibition of public discussion of an entire topic. . . .

To allow a government the choice of permissible subjects for public debate would be to allow that government control over the search for political truth.

* * *

Where a government restricts the speech of a private person, the state action may be sustained only if the government can show that the regulation is a precisely drawn means of serving a compelling state interest.

* * *

The State Court of Appeals largely based its approval of the prohibition upon its conclusion that the bill inserts intruded upon individual privacy. The court stated that the Commission could act to protect the privacy of the utility's customers because they have no choice whether to receive the insert and the views expressed in the insert may inflame their sensibilities. But the Court of Appeals erred in its assessment of the seriousness of the intrusion.

* * *

Where a single speaker communicates to many listeners, the First Amendment does not permit the government to prohibit speech as intrusive unless the "captive" audience cannot avoid objectionable speech.

Passengers on public transportation or residents of a neighborhood disturbed by the raucous broadcasts from a passing soundtruck may well be unable to escape an unwanted message. But customers who encounter an objectionable billing insert may "effec-

tively avoid further bombardment of their sensibilities simply by averting their eyes." The customer of Consolidated Edison may escape exposure to objectionable material simply by transferring the bill insert from envelope to wastebasket.

* * *

Reversed.

QUESTIONS FOR ANALYSIS

1. Should a distinction be drawn between political speech paid for by private persons and that paid for by customers who may not want the speech? The political inserts in this case were paid for by Con Ed customers who buy electricity from that company.
2. Would you distinguish between speech that addresses issues and corporate political speech that endorses particular candidates for office?

The Supreme Court held in the 1987 case *Board of Airport Commissioners of Los Angeles* v. *Jews for Jesus* (482 U.S. 569) that blanket restrictions on speech in commercial establishments is not allowed by the First Amendment. The Court held that the airport authority could not impose an outright ban on all political and other controversial speech in the Los Angeles International Airport. However, the Court indicated, as in *Consolidated Edison*, that restrictions as to time, place, and manner may be allowed but will be reviewed for reasonableness.

CYBERLAW

Freedom of Speech on the Net

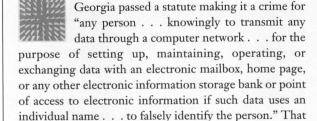

Georgia passed a statute making it a crime for "any person . . . knowingly to transmit any data through a computer network . . . for the purpose of setting up, maintaining, operating, or exchanging data with an electronic mailbox, home page, or any other electronic information storage bank or point of access to electronic information if such data uses an individual name . . . to falsely identify the person." That is, there could be no anonymous communications.

In *American Civil Liberties Union of Georgia* v. *Miller* (977 F. Supp. 1228), the federal court issued an injunc-

tion preventing Georgia from enforcing the statute. Statutes that regulate speech must be narrowly tailored to survive First Amendment challenges. The Georgia statute was too sweeping in its coverage to stand. Similarly, the Supreme Court, in *Reno* v. *American Civil Liberties Union* (117 S.Ct. 2329), struck down the Communications Decency Act of 1996. While the supposed intent of the law was to restrict pornography for children on the Web, the court held that the act went too far in restricting First Amendment rights; it was like "burning the house to roast the pig."

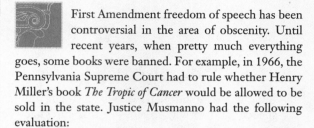

JURIS prudence?

Don't Care for the Book, Huh?

First Amendment freedom of speech has been controversial in the area of obscenity. Until recent years, when pretty much everything goes, some books were banned. For example, in 1966, the Pennsylvania Supreme Court had to rule whether Henry Miller's book *The Tropic of Cancer* would be allowed to be sold in the state. Justice Musmanno had the following evaluation:

"[T]he defendants say that *Cancer* is entitled to immunity under the First Amendment because court decisions have declared that only worthless trash may be proscribed as obscene. To say that *Cancer* is worthless trash is to pay it a compliment. *Cancer* is the sweepings of the Augean stables, the stagnant bile of the slimiest mudscow, the putrescent corruption of the most noisome dump pile, the dreggiest filth in the deepest morass of putrefaction."

The majority ruled in favor of allowing the book to be sold.

Source: Commonwealth of Pennsylvania, v. Robin, 218 A.2d 546

An example of a legitimate restriction comes from the 1990 decision *Austin v. Michigan Chamber of Commerce* (494 U.S. 652). In that decision, the Supreme Court allowed states to prohibit the use of general corporate money for supporting or opposing political candidates. The compelling government interest that allows this regulation is the desire to eliminate distortions caused by corporate spending for this purpose out of general corporate funds, as opposed to corporate spending for this purpose that comes from corporate money that has been set aside for specific political purposes.

BUSINESS AND COMMERCIAL SPEECH

Drawing the line between *commercial speech*—such as advertising a product for sale—and political speech by a corporation can be difficult. In many cases, the intent is the same: to increase the expected profits of the business. In one case, it is done by trying to convince people to buy a product. In another case, it is done by trying to influence governmental policy in a way that will favor the business or to reduce prospects of passage of a law that would hurt the business. The Supreme Court recognizes that free speech applies to both commercial speech and political speech by business.

Speech and Competition

The modern commercial speech doctrine began to evolve in the 1970s. It first came about as restrictions on advertising were attacked as anticompetitive. Some commercial speech restrictions—such as prohibitions on advertisements—violated antitrust laws, but almost all such restrictions violated the rights of sellers of legal products and services to inform citizens of the availability and merits of their products and services.

In 1975, in *Bigelow* v. *Virginia* (421 U.S. 809), the Supreme Court reversed the conviction of a Virginia newspaper editor who published ads about the availability of low-cost abortions in New York City. A Virginia law prohibited publications from encouraging abortions. The Court held that speech that is related to products or services has value in the marketplace of ideas.

The following year, in *Virginia State Board of Pharmacy* v. *Virginia Citizens Consumer Council* (425 U.S. 748), the Court struck down a Virginia law prohibiting the advertising of prices of prescription drugs. "It is clear . . . that speech does not lose its First Amendment protection because money is spent . . . as in a paid advertisement. . . ." The Board of Pharmacy argued that the restrictions on advertising were needed to protect the public from their own ignorance about drugs. The Court responded:

> There is, of course, an alternative to this highly paternalistic approach (of prohibiting advertising of drug prices). That alternative is to assume that this information is not in itself harmful, that people will perceive their own best interests if only they are well enough informed, and that the best means to that end is to open the channels of communication rather than to close them.

While commercial speech that is not truthful may be regulated (unlike political speech), the Court now finds little justification for extensive controls on truthful commercial speech. In the *Central Hudson Gas & Electric* decision, the Court established a four-part test that must be met to justify restrictions on commercial speech.

Central Hudson Gas & Electric Corporation v. Public Service Commission of New York

United States Supreme Court
447 U.S. 557, 100 S.Ct. 2343 (1980)

CASE BACKGROUND *The winter of 1973–74 was difficult because of the Organization of Petroleum Exporting Countries (OPEC) oil embargo, shortages of natural gas, and public perceptions about rapidly declining energy supplies. The Public Service Commission of New York ordered electric utilities in New York to end all advertising that "promotes the use of electricity." The order was based on the commission's finding that New York utilities did not have sufficient capacity to furnish all customer demands for the winter. The commission declared all promotional advertising contrary to the national policy of conserving energy. It offered to review any proposed advertising that would encourage energy conservation. The New York high court upheld the constitutionality of the Commission's regulation. The utility appealed to the Supreme Court.*

CASE DECISION Powell, Justice.

* * *

The Commission's order restricts only commercial speech, that is, expression related solely to the economic interests of the speaker and its audience. . . . The First Amendment, as applied to the States through the Fourteenth Amendment, protects com-

mercial speech from unwarranted government regulation. Commercial expression not only serves the economic interest of the speaker, but also assists consumers . . . in the fullest possible dissemination of information. In applying the First Amendment to this area, we have rejected the "highly paternalistic" view that government has complete power to suppress or regulate commercial speech. "[P]eople will perceive their own best interests if only they are well enough informed and . . . the best means to that end is to open the channels of communication, rather than to close them. . . ." Even when advertising communicates only an incomplete version of the relevant facts, the First Amendment presumes that some accurate information is better than no information at all.

Nevertheless, our decisions have recognized "the 'common-sense' distinction between speech proposing a commercial transaction, which occurs in an area traditionally subject to government regulation and other varieties of speech." . . . The Constitution therefore accords a lesser protection to commercial speech than to other constitutionally guaranteed expression. The protection available for particular commercial expression turns on the nature both of the expression and of the governmental interests served by its regulation.

The First Amendment's concern for commercial speech is based on the informational function of advertising. Consequently, there can be no constitutional objection to the suppression of commercial messages that do not accurately inform the public about lawful activity. The government may ban forms of communication more likely to deceive the public than to inform it, or commercial speech related to illegal activity.

If the communication is neither misleading nor related to unlawful activity, the government's power is more circumscribed.

*   *   *

In commercial speech cases . . . a four-part analysis has developed. [1] At the outset, we must determine whether the expression is protected by the First Amendment. For commercial speech to come within that provision, it at least must concern lawful activity and not be misleading. [2] Next, we ask whether the asserted governmental interest is substantial. If both inquiries yield positive answers, [3] we must determine whether the regulation directly advances the governmental interest asserted, and [4] whether it is not more extensive than is necessary to serve that interest.

We now apply this four-step analysis for commercial speech to the Commission's arguments in support of its ban on promotional advertising.

The Commission does not claim that the expression at issue either is inaccurate or relates to unlawful activity.

*   *   *

The Commission offers two state interests as justifications for the ban on promotional advertising. The first concerns energy conservation. Any increase in demand for electricity—during peak or off-peak periods—means greater consumption of energy. The Commission argues . . . that the State's interest in conserving energy is sufficient to support suppression of advertising designed to increase consumption of electricity. In view of our country's dependence on energy resources beyond our control, no one can doubt the importance of energy conservation. Plainly, therefore, the state interest asserted is substantial.

*   *   *

We come finally to the critical inquiry in this case: whether the Commission's complete suppression of speech ordinarily protected by the First Amendment is no more extensive than necessary to further the State's interest in energy conservation. The Commission's order reaches all promotional advertising, regardless of the impact of the touted service on overall energy use. But the energy conservation rationale, as important as it is, cannot justify suppressing information about electric devices or services that would cause no net increase in total energy use. In addition, no showing has been made that a more limited restriction on the content of promotional advertising would not serve adequately the State's interests.

*   *   *

Reversed.

QUESTIONS FOR ANALYSIS

1. Since the Court found that the state had a substantial interest in the subject in question (electricity conservation), why did it find the ad restrictions to be unconstitutional? What part of the four-part test was not met?
2. Suppose the commission had said that only advertising designed to promote energy conservation was allowed. Would that have met the Supreme Court test?

The Supreme Court has ruled in several cases that First Amendment rights may be violated by restrictions on advertising for professional services, such as by lawyers or doctors. The Court addressed the issue in the 1988 case *Shapero* v. *Kentucky Bar Association* (468 U.S. 881) when it held that the bar association violated the First Amendment by prohibiting lawyers from soliciting business by sending truthful letters to prospective clients known to face possible legal action. If an attorney engages in misleading or deceptive solicitation practices, the attorney may be punished by the bar for doing so, but the bar may not act as a barrier to commercial speech.

The Court further discussed the regulation of commercial speech in the 1989 case *Board of Trustees of the State University of New York* v. *Fox* (492 U.S. 469). The standard for judging commercial speech regulation is one that is "not necessarily perfect but reasonable" and one "narrowly tailored to achieve the desired objective." The basis of the regulation must be a substantial state interest in controlling an undesirable activity, balanced against the cost imposed by the restrictions. When regulations are challenged, the state bears the burden of justifying restrictions on commercial speech.

Freedom to Criticize

Freedom of speech can mean that a business will find itself criticized in a commercial setting. The Supreme Court upheld this right in the 1984 decision *Bose Corp.* v. *Consumers Union* (466 U.S. 485). Consumers Union published a report in *Consumer Reports* that was critical of the quality of a stereo speaker made by Bose. Bose sued, claiming product disparagement.

The Supreme Court held that for a public figure, such as a corporation selling products, to recover damages for a defamatory falsehood, the trial court must find clear and convincing evidence that there was actual malice in publishing a knowing or reckless falsehood. Since actual malice was not shown in this case, the suit was dismissed.

> The First Amendment presupposes that the freedom to speak one's mind is not only an aspect of individual liberty—and thus a good unto itself—but also is essential to the common quest for truth and the vitality of society as a whole. Under our Constitution "there is no such thing as a false idea. However pernicious an opinion may seem, we depend for its correction not on the conscience of judges and juries but on the competition of other ideas." Libelous speech is limited by the First Amendment, but the standard is strong.

The right to criticize is not the right to make false statements that injure another. As the Court noted in the 1990 case *Milkovich* v. *Lorain Journal Co.* (497 U.S. 1), a business such as a newspaper is not protected by the First Amendment when it makes false statements as fact that defame someone. If a reasonable person can conclude that there is injury to reputation, it does not matter whether the false information is stated as an opinion rather than as fact.

Other Key Parts of the Bill of Rights

The Bill of Rights contains the first ten amendments to the Constitution. Some of these amendments, while providing important rights for citizens, have little special impact on business. Most of the rest of the amendments, numbered eleven through twenty-seven, also have no special impact on business, although we will see later in the chapter that the Fourteenth Amendment has had important consequences. No amendment was written specifically to address a business issue. Some just happen to have an impact on the legal environment of business.

UNREASONABLE SEARCH AND SEIZURE

The Fourth Amendment reads: "The right of the people to be secure in their persons, houses, papers, and effects, against unreasonable searches and seizures, shall not be violated, and no Warrants shall issue, but upon probable cause. . . ." Most cases arising under this amendment are criminal and concern the proper method of search and seizure of suspected criminals and evidence. However, searches by government agents to help enforce regulations that rarely result in criminal charges are also subject to limits. In Fourth Amendment cases, a key question is whether or not proper search and seizure procedures were used by government authorities. A major issue is whether a person has a constitutionally protected reasonable expectation of privacy. Essentially, closed places, such as homes and businesses, are not subject to random police searches.

Limits on Searches and Inspections

If a government inspector shows up at a business and asks to inspect the premises or search company records for some purpose related to the law's being enforced by the inspector, does the business have to allow admission? Not without a warrant, the Supreme Court held in *Marshall* v. *Barlow's* (436 U.S. 307; 1978). In that case, an inspector for the Occupational Safety and Health Administration (OSHA) arrived at Barlow's plant in Pocatello, Idaho, and asked to search the work areas. Barlow asked the inspector whether he had a warrant. Since he did not, Barlow refused admission to the plant. OSHA asked the Court to require businesses to admit inspectors to conduct warrantless searches.

The Court refused, saying that warrantless searches are generally unreasonable and that this rule applies to commercial premises as well as homes. The government argued that if inspectors had to obtain warrants, businesses would have time to hide safety and health defects on worksites. The Court responded:

> We are unconvinced . . . that requiring warrants to inspect will impose serious burdens on the inspection system or the courts, will prevent inspections necessary to enforce the statute, or will make them less effective. In the first place the great majority of businessmen can be expected in normal course to consent to inspection without warrant; the Secretary (of Labor) has not brought to this Court's attention any widespread pattern of refusal.

As the Court predicted, in fact, most businesses allow warrantless searches; the requirement to obtain a warrant when demanded has not become burdensome or much affected law enforcement. Warrantless searches are allowed in cases of "closely regulated" businesses, as the Court discussed in the *Burger* decision. Since the *Burger* decision, more and more businesses have been held to be "closely regulated" and so subject to warrantless search.

New York v. Burger
United States Supreme Court
482 U.S. 691, 107 S.Ct. 2636 (1987)

CASE BACKGROUND *Burger ran an automobile junkyard, where cars were dismantled and the parts sold. Because many stolen cars are sold, junkyards are licensed and are required to keep records of cars and parts that are received. A New York statute allowed warrantless inspections of junkyards. Police officers entered Burger's junkyard and asked to see Burger's license and records. Burger told the police that he had*

neither. The police then said they would search the place, which they did without his objection. They found stolen cars and parts. Burger was charged with possession of stolen property.

At trial, Burger moved to suppress the evidence obtained during the inspection on the ground that the inspection statute was unconstitutional. The court denied the motion to suppress the evidence. The motion was reversed by the New York Court of Appeals, which held that the statute violated the Fourth Amendment's prohibition of unreasonable searches and seizures. The decision of the high court of New York was appealed to the Supreme Court to determine whether the statute was unconstitutional.

CASE DECISION Blackmun, Justice.

* * *

The Court long has recognized that the Fourth Amendment's prohibition on unreasonable searches and seizures is applicable to commercial premises, as well as to private homes. An owner or operator of a business thus has an expectation of privacy in commercial property, which society is prepared to consider to be reasonable. This expectation exists not only with respect to traditional police searches conducted for the gathering of criminal evidence but also with respect to administrative inspections designed to enforce regulatory statutes. An expectation of privacy in commercial premises, however, is different from, and indeed less than, a similar expectation in an individual's home. This expectation is particularly attenuated in commercial property employed in "closely regulated" industries. The Court observed in *Marshall v. Barlow's, Inc.*, "Certain industries have such a history of government oversight that no reasonable expectation of privacy could exist for a proprietor over the stock of such an enterprise."

* * *

Because the owner or operator of commercial premises in a "closely regulated" industry has a reduced expectation of privacy, the warrant and probable-cause requirements, which fulfill the traditional Fourth Amendment standard of reasonableness for a government search, have lessened application in this context. Rather, we conclude that, as in other situations of "special need," where the privacy interests of the owner are weakened and the government interests in regulating particular businesses are concomitantly heightened, a warrantless inspection of commercial premises may well be reasonable within the meaning of the Fourth Amendment.

This warrantless inspection, however, even in the context of a pervasively regulated business, will be deemed to be reasonable only so long as three criteria are met. First, there must be a "substantial" government interest that informs the regulatory scheme pursuant to which the inspection is made. . . .

Second, the warrantless inspections must be "necessary to further [the] regulatory scheme." . . .

Finally, "the statute's inspection program, in terms of the certainty and regularity of its application, [must] provid[e] a constitutionally adequate substitute for a warrant." In other words, the regulatory statute must perform the two basic functions of a warrant; it must advise the owner of the commercial premises that the search is being made pursuant to the law and has a properly defined scope, and it must limit the discretion of the inspecting officers.

* * *

The New York regulatory scheme satisfies the three criteria necessary to make reasonable warrantless inspections. . . . First, the State has a substantial interest in regulating the vehicle-dismantling and automobile-junkyard industry because motor vehicle theft has increased in the State and because the problem of theft is associated with this industry. . . .

Second, regulation of the vehicle-dismantling industry reasonably serves the State's substantial interest in eradicating automobile theft. . . .

Third, [the statute] provides a "constitutionally adequate substitute for a warrant." The statute informs the operator of a vehicle-dismantling business that inspections will be made on a regular basis. Thus, the vehicle dismantler knows that the inspections to which he is subject do not constitute discretionary acts by a government official but are conducted pursuant to statute. . . .

Finally, the "time, place, and scope" of the inspection is limited to place appropriate restraints upon the discretion of the inspecting officers.

* * *

Accordingly, the judgment of the New York Court of Appeals is reversed. . . .

QUESTIONS FOR ANALYSIS

1. Suppose that during such a warrantless search the police found evidence of another crime, such as a stash of cocaine. Should such evidence be allowed to be used?

2. If one goes into the junkyard or other "closely regulated" business, one must accept the possibility of warrantless searches. What businesses are not "closely regulated" and therefore not subject to such searches?

Restrictions on Use of Evidence

Evidence that is improperly gathered by law enforcement officials is in violation of the Fourth Amendment rights regarding search and seizure and may not be used in court under the *exclusionary rule*. Generally, this has meant that evidence gathered from a private home or business without a warrant was improper and could not be used. As the *Burger* decision indicates, the Court gives business fewer constitutional rights in this respect than persons in their homes. There have been few Supreme Court cases on this issue, but the trend is in favor of warrantless searches of regulated businesses, which can include employees.

In *Skinner* v. *Railway Labor Executives' Ass'n* (489 U.S. 602; 1989), the Court approved of warrantless searches of railroad employees involved in train accidents or in safety violations. The searches consist of blood, breath, and urine tests for evidence of alcohol or other drug use. These searches are not in violation of the Fourth Amendment, because they are in a "closely regulated" industry, are based on compelling public interest in safety, and may be used only in specific situations. The employees know they are subject to this requirement as a part of their employment, so the limited invasion of privacy is acceptable.

SELF-INCRIMINATION

The Fifth Amendment protects individuals against *self-incrimination:* "No person shall be . . . compelled in any criminal case to be a witness against himself." This protection applies to persons, not to corporations. Although corporate executives cannot be made to testify against themselves, business records that might incriminate the corporation (and executives) must be produced, since such records are not protected by the Fifth Amendment.

That corporations are not due the same Fifth Amendment protection as are individuals was noted by the Supreme Court in *Braswell* v. *United States* (487 U.S. 99; 1988). Braswell was president and sole shareholder of a corporation. Claiming Fifth Amendment privilege against self-incrimination, he refused to produce company records ordered under a federal grand jury subpoena. The Court rejected this claim, holding that the corporation was an entity not protected by the Fifth Amendment; hence, Braswell had to produce corporate records, even though the records might incriminate him.

JUST COMPENSATION

The Fifth Amendment states, ". . . nor shall private property be taken for public use, without just compensation." Termed the *just compensation or takings clause*, its traditional primary use was to require governments to pay for property the government required someone to sell because public officials determined that the property should be used for some specific purpose, such as for the construction of a highway, oil pipeline, or military base.

The Supreme Court appears to have broadened the application of the just compensation clause in recent decisions. Local governments, where most land-use requirements are determined, have broad powers to change zoning and land-use requirements without paying compensation, even though the value of the land is affected by changes in land-use rules. When new land-use rules reduce property values, must the government compensate the property owners?

CYBERLAW

No Right of Privacy in Chat Rooms

 An FBI agent monitored on-line chat rooms to uncover distribution of child pornography. He would enter the chat rooms, so his user name was seen, but he would not participate. Based on his observations, Charbonneau was accused of distributing child pornography to contacts made in the chat room. He contended that this method of collecting evidence violated his Fourth Amendment right to a reasonable expectation of privacy.

A federal court held that the evidence collected was good. "The expectation of privacy in E-mail transmissions depends in large part on both the type of E-mail sent and recipient of the E-mail." Messages sent to a chat room, unlike personally addressed E-mails, lose their privacy, so the evidence may be used against him.

Source: *U.S. v. Charbonneau* (979 F.Supp. 1177)

Regulatory Takings

A 1987 Supreme Court decision, *Nollan* v. *California Coastal Commission* (483 U.S. 825), addressed compensation in land-use rules. The Nollan's wanted to tear down their house and build a larger one on their beach property in Ventura, California. The Coastal Commission said that their permit would be granted only if they agreed to allow the public an easement (access) to the private land that was their backyard. The high-tide line determines the lot's oceanside boundary. The Coastal Commission wanted the public to have the right to use what had been the Nollans' backyard—above the high-tide line—along the beach. This was a common requirement that had been imposed for several years whenever private property owners requested a building permit.

The Supreme Court held that the takings clause of the Fifth Amendment had been violated. The state could not tie a rebuilding permit to an easement (land use) that it would have to pay for if it simply imposed the easement. "California is free to advance its 'comprehensive program,' if it wishes, [of increased beach access] by using its power of eminent domain for this 'public purpose,' but if it wants an easement across the Nollans' property, it must pay for it." The *Dolan* decision was the next major decision in this area of law.

 ## Dolan v. City of Tigard
United States Supreme Court,
512 U.S. 374, 114 S.Ct. 2309 (1994)

CASE BACKGROUND *Florence Dolan, owner of a plumbing and electric supply store in the business district of Tigard, Oregon, applied for a permit to double the size of her store and to pave the store's gravel parking lot. As a part of its master plan, the city approved Dolan's building permit on the condition that Dolan dedicate about one-sixth of her land to the city. The land would be part of a public recreational greenway in the floodplain along Fanno Creek, which ran next to her property, and would be part of a pedestrian/bicycle pathway intended to relieve traffic* *congestion. Dolan protested this loss of her property as a condition of getting the building ordinance. The Oregon courts upheld the city's determination; Dolan (petitioner) appealed to the Supreme Court.*

CASE DECISION Rehnquist, Chief Justice.

* * *

Without question, had the city simply required petitioner to dedicate a strip of land along Fanno Creek for public use, rather than conditioning the grant of her permit to redevelop her property on such a dedication, a taking would have occurred [that would have required compensation] . . .

On the other side of the ledger, the authority of state and local governments to engage in land use planning has been sustained against constitutional challenge as long ago as our decision in *Euclid v. Ambler Realty Co.*, 272 U.S. 365 (1926) [which appears in Chapter 9]. "Government could hardly go on if to some extent values incident to property could not be diminished without paying for every such change in the general law." A land use regulation does not effect a taking if it "substantially advance[s] legitimate state interests" and does not "den[y] an owner economically viable use of this land." . . .

Under the well-settled doctrine of "unconstitutional conditions," the government may not require a person to give up a constitutional right—here the right to receive just compensation when property is taken for a public use—in exchange for a discretionary benefit conferred by the government where the property sought has little or no relationship to the benefit.

Petitioner contends that the city has forced her to choose between the building permit and her right under the Fifth Amendment to just compensation for the public easements. Petitioner does not quarrel with the city's authority to exact some forms of dedication as a condition for the grant of a building permit, but challenges the showing made by the city to justify these exactions. She argues that the city has identified "no special benefits" conferred on her, and has not identified any "special quantifiable burdens" created by her new store that would justify the particular dedications required from her which are not required from the public at large.

* * *

[B]ecause petitioner's property lies within the Central Business District, the Community Develop-

ment Code already required that petitioner leave 15% of it as open space and the undeveloped floodplain would have nearly satisfied that requirement. But the city demanded more—it not only wanted petitioner not to build in the floodplain, but it also wanted petitioner's property along Fanno Creek for its Greenway system. The city has never said why a public greenway, as opposed to a private one, was required in the interest of flood control. . . .

[T]he city wants to impose a permanent recreational easement upon petitioner's property that borders Fanno Creek. Petitioner would lose all rights to regulate the time in which the public entered onto the Greenway, regardless of any interference it might pose with her retail store. Her right to exclude would not be regulated, it would be eviscerated.

If petitioner's proposed development had somehow encroached on existing greenway space in the city, it would have been reasonable to require petitioner to provide some alternative greenway space for the public either on her property or elsewhere. But that is not the case here. We conclude that the findings upon which the city relies do not show the required reasonable relationships between the floodplain easement and the petitioner's proposed new building. . . .

Dedications for streets, sidewalks, and other public ways are generally reasonable exactions to avoid excessive congestion from a proposed property use. But on the record before us, the city has not met its burden of demonstrating that the additional number of vehicle and bicycle trips generated by the petitioner's development reasonably relate to the city's requirement for a dedication of the pedestrian/bicycle pathway easement. The city simply found that the creation of the pathway "could offset some of the traffic demand . . . and lessen the increase in traffic congestion." . . .

No precise mathematical calculation is required, but the city must make some effort to quantify its findings in support of the dedication for the pedestrian/bicycle pathway beyond the conclusory statement that it could offset some of the traffic demand generated.

Cities have long engaged in the commendable task of land use planning, made necessary by increasing urbanization particularly in metropolitan areas such as Portland. The city's goals of reducing flooding hazards and traffic congestion, and providing for public greenways, are laudable, but there are outer limits to how this may be done. "A strong public desire to improve the public condition [will not] warrant achieving the desire by a shorter cut than the constitutional way of paying for the change."

The judgment of the Supreme Court of Oregon is reversed. . . .

QUESTIONS FOR ANALYSIS

1. The city's action would have reduced the value of Dolan's property by a fraction. Regulatory changes often have such an effect. Could this decision substantially restrict the ability of state and local governments to change building requirements?

2. Is there a difference between a direct taking of property, such as the city's ordering Dolan to give it one of her six acres, and a regulatory taking, such as the city's ordering Dolan to dedicate the use of one acre for public purposes?

RIGHT TO TRIAL

The Sixth Amendment addresses the right of persons to trial by jury in criminal cases. The Seventh Amendment provides for the right to jury trial in common-law cases. Although the law is well established about the constitutional right to jury trial in criminal cases and common-law cases, what about cases in which a business is charged with a violation of a statute that regulates the business? If the charge is criminal, the right to request a jury trial remains. What if the charge is civil? The Supreme Court explained the difference in *Tull* v. *U.S.* (481 U.S. 412; 1987).

Tull, a real-estate developer, was charged by the government with violating the Clean Water Act by damaging wetlands. The government sought an injunction to force Tull to stop work and asked for $23 million in civil penalties. Tull requested a jury trial, which was denied. At the bench trial, Tull admitted not having the required permits and dumping fill dirt where the government claimed. He claimed, however, that the lands in question were not wetlands, so he was not liable. The district court held that the lands were wetlands and ordered Tull to restore the lands to their original condition and to pay several hundred thousand dollars in civil penalties.

On appeal, the Supreme Court ruled that Tull was due a jury trial under the Seventh Amendment with respect to the issue of whether or not he was liable because the lands were wetlands. If the only question was that of imposing civil penalties, no right to jury trial existed. Since civil penalties are imposed by statute, there is no constitutional right to trial on such matters. There is a right to jury trial on the question of the liability of the defendant only when there is the "substance of the common-law right of trial by jury." That is, when the legal issue involved is close to that of a common-law right, jury trial rights exist. If the legal issue is one of statutory law only, there is no right to jury trial.

EXCESSIVE FINES

The Eighth Amendment is most famous for its restriction on "cruel and unusual punishments," but it also holds that "no excessive fines" may be imposed. Since large jury awards have become more common in recent years, as we will see when we study torts and product liability, defendants have questioned whether the Eighth Amendment offers protection against huge punitive damage awards.

A jury awarded the plaintiff in a tort suit $51,146 in compensatory damages and $6 million in punitive damages. The defendant appealed to the Supreme Court, claiming that the huge punitive damage award violated the Eighth Amendment. In

Constitutional Law in Foreign Jurisdictions

The United Kingdom, unlike the United States and most other nations, does not have a written constitution, yet it has a body of constitutional law. The courts there recognize three kinds of rules: statutory law, case law, and custom or constitutional convention. Statutory law, which comes from Parliament, is potentially unlimited in scope.

The courts may not strike down statutes because of constitutional restrictions, as may U.S. courts. There is no official separation of powers; the courts in the United Kingdom cannot use constitutional custom to overrule parliamentary law. By custom, the monarch cannot veto laws.

The United Kingdom is a democratic nation with a high regard for civil liberties. While that nation works well without a formal constitution, it was that lack of fixed constitutional protections that convinced the founders of the United States that a written constitution

was desirable. In the United Kingdom, constitutional customs change over time, just as the U.S. Supreme Court at different times infers different standards from the Constitution, often reflecting changes in social values and economic realities.

It should be remembered that U.S. constitutional rights do not protect American citizens if they are subject to legal action in another nation. Similarly, U.S. constitutional rights do not always extend to noncitizens not in the United States. The Supreme Court, in U.S. v. *Verdugo-Urquidez* (494 U.S. 259; 1990), held that the Fourth Amendment does not apply to the search and seizure by U.S. agents of property located outside the United States that is owned by a non-U.S. citizen. The Amendment protects people in the United States against arbitrary action by the government; it does not restrain the federal government's actions against aliens outside American territory.

1989, in *Browning-Ferris Industries* v. *Kelco Disposal* (492 U.S. 257), the Court held that the excessive fines clause does not apply to punitive damage awards in cases between private parties. Reaching back as far as the Magna Carta, the Court found that the purpose of the Eighth Amendment was to restrict the potential for governmental abuse of prosecutorial power by the imposition of excessive fines. The Eighth Amendment does not apply to private litigation. The issue of high punitive damages, which is of great concern to many businesses, was next attacked as a violation of the Fourteenth Amendment, as we see in the following section.

Recently, the claim of excessive fines has been raised in a number of civil suits that allow the government to press for large damages. For example, when illegal drug dealing occurs on private property, the property may be confiscated. Even if the property is worth a thousand times what the drugs were worth, this has generally been held not to be an excessive fine in violation of the Eighth Amendment, so long as the fines are part of a rational and consistent scheme to deter certain behavior.

One of the few restrictions to be imposed on forfeiture came in the 1998 Supreme Court case, *U.S.* v. *Bajakajian* (118 S.Ct. 2028). The Bajakajians were leaving the country with $357,144 in cash. The money was legally earned in their business; they were taking the money to repay relatives who had given them money to start their gasoline station. While it was legal to take the money out of the country, the Bajakajians failed to report that they were leaving with more than $10,000. Government agents seized all the money, contending that it could be kept because it was an "instrumentality" of the crime committed. In a five to four vote, the Court held that the forfeiture was an "excessive fine" in violation of the Eighth Amendment as it was grossly disproportional to the gravity of the offense.

Fourteenth Amendment

The Fourteenth Amendment holds, in part, "No State shall . . . deprive any person of life, liberty, or property, without due process of law; nor deny to any person within its jurisdiction the equal protection of the laws." This amendment has been a powerful device for extending federal constitutional guarantees to the states and preventing states from passing laws that diminish federal constitutional protections.

The Fourteenth Amendment, which was passed after the Civil War, has two key provisions concerning substantive and procedural law: the *due process clause* and the *equal protection clause*. Substantive due process comes into play whenever the courts review the ability of the government to restrict the freedoms of life, liberty, or property. Equal protection comes into play when the courts are called on to review a classification of persons established by a government.

In general, substantive due process claims can be stated two different ways. First, substantive due process is violated when the state infringes on fundamental liberty interests without narrowly tailoring that infringement to serve a compelling state interest. Second, substantive due process is offended when state action either shocks the conscience or offends judicial notions of fairness and human dignity.

Suppose a state prohibited all persons from riding motorcycles in the state. A challenge to the law could be based on due process. The person claiming he or she should be allowed to ride a motorcycle would claim that the Fourteenth Amendment was violated because the substance of the law, not the procedures used to enforce the law, restricted the freedom of all persons in the state without a constitutionally legitimate rationale. However, when governments restrict the rights of citizens, unless a fundamental constitutional liberty is at stake (would that include motorcycle riding?), the law needs to relate rationally to a legitimate government interest, such as public safety, to satisfy due process requirements.

Now suppose a state changed its law to prohibit people under age twenty-five or over age sixty from riding motorcycles. A challenge to the law would be brought by someone under age twenty-five or over age sixty claiming that the equal protection

---

JURIS **prudence?**

No Hammer Locks, Ladies

Jerry Hunter was arrested for violating an Oregon law prohibiting women from participating in a "wrestling competition." The Oregon Supreme Court addressed the constitutionality of the law in a 1956 decision:

"[T]he Fourteenth Amendment to the U.S. Constitution does not protect those liberties [to be in a public wrestling match]. . . . [The legislature] intended that there should be at least one island on the sea of life reserved for man that would be impregnable to the assault of woman. . . . In

business . . . in the professions, in politics, as well as in almost every other line of human endeavor, she had matched her wits and prowess with those of mere men, and, we are frank to concede, in many instances had outdone him. . . . is it any wonder that the legislative assembly took advantage of the police power of the state in its decision to halt this ever-increasing feminine encroachment upon what for the ages had been considered strictly as manly arts and privileges?"

Source: *State of Oregon* v. *Hunter*, 300 P.2d 455

clause of the Fourteenth Amendment had been violated. That is, persons in those age groups belong to the class of persons affected by the law, which they claim is constitutionally wrong because it creates a class that suffers a loss of freedom. To uphold such a law that classifies persons, the court must find a valid governmental interest, such as public safety. While it may be rational to have age restrictions on motorcycle drivers, there could be no safety rationale for racial restrictions on driving motorcycles.

As interpreted in recent decades, the Fourteenth Amendment has become very important for persons. From it, the Supreme Court has broadened constitutional protections and recognized such things as a right of privacy that includes sexual relations and abortion, matters that used to be subject to far more state controls. The courts are less generous in extending Fourteenth Amendment protection to economic legislation that affects business. Unless a basic constitutional right is at stake, economic regulations will not be stricken as in violation of the Fourteenth Amendment unless there is no rational basis for the law.

DUE PROCESS

Does the Fourteenth Amendment's due process clause act as a check on unlimited jury discretion to award punitive damages in the absence of any express statutory limit? The Supreme Court considered this issue several times, but the *BMW* case was the first time it directly limited punitive damages for violating due process.

BMW of North America v. Gore
United States Supreme Court
517 U.S. 559, 116 S.Ct. 1589 (1996)

CASE BACKGROUND *Gore bought a new BMW from a dealer in Alabama for $40,750. Nine months later, when the car was being waxed, it was pointed out to Gore that it had been repainted. Gore's car, like others, suffered acid rain damage to the finish before delivery, so it was repainted. BMW's policy was that if repairs to a new car cost less than 3 percent of the sale price, it would not be mentioned to the customer. If repairs cost more than 3 percent, the car would be put in company service for a while and then sold as used. Since Gore's paint job cost $600, or 1.5 percent of the sale price, he was not told of that repair work.*

Gore sued BMW. He asserted at trial that the paint job made the car worth $4,000 less and that, since BMW had repainted about 1,000 cars over the years, it had inflicted $4 million in losses on customers. BMW claimed the repair policy was in good faith and that there was no attempt to impose losses on customers. The jury awarded Gore $4,000 in compensatory damages and $4 million in punitive damages. The Alabama supreme court cut the punitive damages in half; BMW appealed.

CASE DECISION Justice Stevens delivered the opinion of the Court.

* * *

Punitive damages may properly be imposed to further a State's legitimate interests in punishing unlawful conduct and deterring its repetition. . . . Only when an award can fairly be categorized as "grossly excessive" in relation to these interests does it enter the zone of arbitrariness that violates the Due Process Clause of the Fourteenth Amendment. For that reason, the federal excessiveness inquiry appropriately begins with an identification of the state interests that a punitive award is designed to serve. We therefore focus our attention first on the scope of Alabama's legitimate interests in punishing BMW and deterring it from future misconduct. No one doubts that a State may protect its citizens by prohibiting deceptive trade practices and by requiring automobile distributors to disclose presale repairs that affect the value of a new car. But the States need not, and in fact do not, provide such protection in a uniform manner.

* * *

We think it follows from these principles of state sovereignty and comity that a State may not impose economic sanctions on violators of its laws with the intent of changing the tortfeasors' lawful conduct in other States. Before this Court Dr. Gore argued that the large punitive damages award was necessary to induce BMW to change the nationwide policy that it adopted in 1983. But by attempting to alter BMW's nationwide policy, Alabama would be infringing on the policy choices of other States. To avoid such encroachment, the economic penalties that a State such as Alabama inflicts on those who transgress its laws, whether the penalties take the form of legislatively authorized fines or judicially imposed punitive damages, must be supported by the State's interest in protecting its own consumers and its own economy. Alabama may insist that BMW adhere to a particular disclosure policy in that State. Alabama does not have the power, however, to punish BMW for conduct that was lawful where it occurred and that had no impact on Alabama or its residents. Nor may Alabama impose sanctions on BMW in order to deter conduct that is lawful in other jurisdictions.

* * *

Elementary notions of fairness enshrined in our constitutional jurisprudence dictate that a person receive fair notice not only of the conduct that will subject him to punishment but also of the severity of the penalty that a State may impose. Three guideposts, each of which indicates that BMW did not receive adequate notice of the magnitude of the sanction that Alabama might impose for adhering to the nondisclosure policy adopted in 1983, lead us to the conclusion that the $2 million award against BMW is grossly excessive: the degree of reprehensibility of the nondisclosure; the disparity between the harm or potential harm suffered by Dr. Gore and his punitive damages award; and the difference between this remedy and the civil penalties authorized or imposed in comparable cases. We discuss these considerations in turn.

Degree of Reprehensibility

Perhaps the most important indicium of the reasonableness of a punitive damages award is the degree of reprehensibility of the defendant's conduct. As the Court stated nearly 150 years ago, exemplary damages imposed on a defendant should reflect "the enormity of this offense."

In this case, none of the aggravating factors associated with particularly reprehensible conduct is present. The harm BMW inflicted on Dr. Gore was purely economic in nature. The presale refinishing of the car had no effect on its performance or safety features, or even its appearance for at least nine months after his purchase. BMW's conduct evinced no indifference to or reckless disregard for the health and safety of others. To be sure, infliction of economic injury, especially when done intentionally through affirmative acts of misconduct, or when the target is financially vulnerable, can warrant a substantial penalty. But this observation does not convert all acts that cause economic harm into torts that are sufficiently reprehensible to justify a significant sanction in addition to compensatory damages.

* * *

Ratio

The second and perhaps most commonly cited indicium of an unreasonable or excessive punitive damages award is its ratio to the actual harm inflicted. . . . The principle that exemplary damages must bear a "reasonable relationship" to compensatory damages has a long pedigree.

* * *

The $2 million in punitive damages awarded to Dr. Gore by the Alabama Supreme Court is 500 times the amount of his actual harm as determined by the jury. Moreover, there is no suggestion that Dr. Gore or any other BMW purchaser was threatened with any additional potential harm by BMW's nondisclosure policy.

* * *

Sanctions for Comparable Misconduct

Comparing the punitive damages award and the civil or criminal penalties that could be imposed for comparable misconduct provides a third indicium of excessiveness. . . .

The maximum civil penalty authorized by the Alabama Legislature for a violation of its Deceptive Trade Practices Act is $2,000; other States authorize more severe sanctions, with the maxima ranging from $5,000 to $10,000. . . .

The sanction imposed in this case cannot be justified on the ground that it was necessary to deter future misconduct without considering whether less drastic remedies could be expected to achieve that goal.

* * *

The fact that BMW is a large corporation rather than an impecunious individual does not diminish its entitlement to fair notice of the demands that the several States impose on the conduct of its business. Indeed, its status as an active participant in the national economy implicates the federal interest in preventing individual States from imposing undue burdens on interstate commerce. While each State has ample power to protect its own consumers, none may use the punitive damages deterrent as a means of imposing its regulatory policies on the entire Nation.

* * *

The judgment is reversed, and the case is remanded for further proceedings not inconsistent with this opinion.

QUESTIONS FOR ANALYSIS

1. The Court said it would not provide a "mathematical bright line" for the acceptable ratio between compensatory and punitive damages. Why not?
2. The four dissenters in this case argued that it is up to the states to control punitive damages, not the federal courts. What kind of problems can one state cause for businesses?

It was previously noted that foreigners cannot ask for U.S. constitutional protection for events that happen outside the United States. However, when foreign parties are subject to litigation in the United States, they are protected. This point is made in the *Asahi Metal* decision, which concerns a foreign business that was sued in California.

Due process, on one hand, concerns the fairness of law enforcement procedures, as in the *Asahi* decision. The substance of due process, however, concerns the content of legislation. All laws must be constitutional so as not to violate the due process clause. If a law restricts a fundamental constitutional right, there must be a compelling interest for it. As we have seen already, when it comes to the regulation of business, most regulations will meet constitutionality tests.

Asahi Metal Industry Co. v. Superior Court of California

United States Supreme Court
480 U.S. 102, 107 S.Ct. 1026 (1987)

CASE BACKGROUND *Asahi, a Japanese company, did worldwide business, but only a trivial amount in California. It sold component parts to a Taiwanese manufacturer (Cheng Shin), who sold its finished products in California. Cheng Shin was sued in California in a product liability suit. It settled the case but sued Asahi in California for indemnity for its losses. Asahi argued that California courts could not exercise jurisdiction over Asahi and force it to appear in court in this matter. The California Supreme Court held that because some of Asahi's parts ended up in a product in commerce in California, Asahi was subject to jurisdiction under California's long-arm statute. Asahi appealed to the U.S. Supreme Court.*

CASE DECISION O'Connor, Justice.

* * *

There is no evidence that Asahi designed its product in anticipation of sales in California. . . . On the basis of [this and other] facts, the exertion of personal jurisdiction over Asahi by the Superior Court of California exceeds the limits of Due Process.

The strictures of the Due Process Clause forbid a state court from exercising personal jurisdiction over Asahi under circumstances that would offend "traditional notions of fair play and substantial justice." . . . A court must consider the burden on the defendant, the interests of the forum State, and the plaintiff's interest in obtaining relief. It must also weigh in its determination "the interstate judicial system's interest in obtaining the most efficient resolution of controversies; and the shared interest of the several States in furthering fundamental substantive social policies."

* * *

Certainly the burden on the defendant in this case is severe. Asahi has been commanded by the Supreme Court of California not only to traverse the distance between Asahi's headquarters in Japan and the Superior Court of California in and for the County of Solano, but also to submit its dispute with Cheng Shin to a foreign nation's judicial system. The unique burdens placed upon one who must defend oneself in a foreign legal system should have significant weight in assessing the reasonableness of stretching the long arm of personal jurisdiction over national borders.

When minimum contacts have been established, often the interests of the plaintiff and the forum in the exercise of jurisdiction will justify even the serious burdens placed on the alien defendant. In the present case, however, the interests of the plaintiff and the forum in California's assertion of jurisdiction over Asahi are slight. All that remains is a claim for indemnification asserted by Cheng Shin, a Taiwanese corporation, against Asahi. The transaction on which the indemnification claim is based took place in Taiwan; Asahi's components were shipped from Japan to Taiwan. Cheng Shin has not demonstrated that it is more convenient for it to litigate its indemnification claim against Asahi in California rather than in Taiwan or Japan.

* * *

Considering the international context, the heavy burden on the alien defendant, and the slight interests of the plaintiff and the forum State, the exercise of personal jurisdiction by a California court over Asahi in this instance would be unreasonable and unfair. . . .

* * *

Reversed. . . .

QUESTIONS FOR ANALYSIS

1. The California court argued that jurisdiction was just, because any firm that places goods into commerce knowing that they end up in California should know that consumers of those products are due the same protection they receive from producers of other products. To not allow jurisdiction over Asahi would encourage firms to evade potential legal liability by hiding in foreign places, which may lead to more injuries to consumers. Does this seem correct?

2. Should foreign producers be treated any differently than domestic producers located in other states?

EQUAL PROTECTION

The Fourteenth Amendment, as previously noted, says, "No state shall . . . deny . . . the equal protection of the laws." The *equal protection clause* has come to mean that governments must treat people equally. However, equal protection does not extend to all government activities. Some actions by government that discriminate are held to tougher standards than others. Over the years, the equal protection clause of the Fourteenth Amendment has been tied to the due process clause of the Fifth Amendment to strengthen due process requirements, as we see in the *Adarand* case.

Government action that intends to discriminate on the basis of race is held to a standard of strict scrutiny. Hence, government programs that discriminate on the basis of race are not likely to meet a Fourteenth Amendment challenge unless there is a compelling state interest. This meant, of course, that "Jim Crow" laws that discriminated against minorities were stricken as unconstitutional. In more recent years, the issue has been whether governments may intentionally discriminate in favor of certain minorities or disadvantaged individuals. In the *Adarand* case, the Supreme Court indicated that affirmative action programs would be subject to more strict scrutiny.

Adarand Constructors, Inc. v. Pena
United States Supreme Court
515 U.S. 200, 115 S.Ct. 2097 (1995)

CASE BACKGROUND   *The Department of Transportation requires that prime government contractors, such as highway construction firms, hire subcontractors that are certified by the Small Business Administration as being controlled by socially and economically disadvantaged individuals, which must include minorities. In one highway subcontract for guardrails, Adarand, the low bidder, was passed over by the contractor in favor of a higher-bidding certified disadvantaged subcontractor. Adarand sued, claiming that the race-based presumptions used in subcontractor choice violated the equal protection component of the Due Process Clause. The suit was dismissed by the district court. The appeals court upheld the dismissal, holding that the constitutionality of the federal race-based action was subject to a lenient standard of scrutiny. Adarand appealed.*

CASE DECISION   O'Connor, Justice.

* * *

Adarand's claim arises under the Fifth Amendment to the Constitution, which provides that "No person shall . . . be deprived of life, liberty, or property, without due process of law." Although this Court has always understood that Clause to provide some measure of protection against arbitrary treatment by the Federal Government, it is not as explicit a guarantee of equal treatment as the Fourteenth Amendment, which provides that "No State shall . . . deny to any person within its jurisdiction the equal protection of the laws." Our cases have accorded varying degrees of significance to the difference in the language of those two Clauses.

* * *

Despite lingering uncertainty in the details, [previous cases] had established three general propositions with respect to governmental racial classifications. First, skepticism: "'[a]ny preference based on racial or ethnic criteria must necessarily receive a most searching examination,'". . . . Second, consistency: "the standard of review under the Equal Protection Clause is not dependent on the race of those burdened or benefited by a particular classification," i.e., all racial classifications reviewable under the Equal Protection Clause must be strictly scrutinized. And third, congruence: "[e]qual protection analysis in the Fifth Amendment area is the same as that under the Fourteenth Amendment." Taken together, these three propositions lead to the conclusion that any person, of whatever race, has the right to demand that any governmental actor subject to the Constitution justify any racial classification subjecting that person to unequal treatment under the strictest judicial scrutiny.

* * *

The principle of consistency simply means that whenever the government treats any person unequally because of his or her race, that person has suffered an injury that falls squarely within the language and spirit of the Constitution's guarantee of equal protection. It says nothing about the ultimate validity of any particular law; that determination is the job of the court applying strict scrutiny. The principle of consistency explains the circumstances in which the injury requiring strict scrutiny occurs. The application of strict scrutiny, in turn, determines whether a compelling governmental interest justifies the infliction of that injury.

Consistency does recognize that any individual suffers an injury when he or she is disadvantaged by the government because of his or her race, whatever that race may be.

* * *

Finally, we wish to dispel the notion that strict scrutiny is "strict in theory, but fatal in fact." The unhappy persistence of both the practice and the lingering effects of racial discrimination against minority groups in this country is an unfortunate reality, and government is not disqualified from acting in response to it. . . . When race-based action is necessary to further a compelling interest, such action is within constitutional constraints if it satisfies the "narrow tailoring" test this Court has set out in previous cases.

* * *

[Reversed and remanded]

QUESTIONS FOR ANALYSIS

1. The Court appears in this decision to strike down quota systems that would require a certain percentage of state business be given to particular groups. What kind of affirmative action programs might meet the strict scrutiny test?

2. Congress and the office of the president has generally ignored this decision. Few federal set-aside programs have been changed. How can such programs continue in place?

State classifications based on sex are also subject to scrutiny. To be allowed to stand, such laws must substantially relate to important government objectives and provide "exceeding persuasive justification," as the Supreme Court held in the 1996 case, *U.S.* v. *Virginia*. It held that the state of Virginia violated the equal protection clause by excluding women from the Virginia Military Institute.

Subject to less scrutiny under the equal protection clause are economic regulations. For example, in a case in 1988, *Pennell* v. *City of San Jose* (485 U.S. 1), the Supreme Court upheld a rent control ordinance. The claim that the rent control was taken under the Fifth Amendment that violated the equal protection clause was rejected because the controls were "rationally related to a legitimate state interest." Since economic regulations often are not directly intended to be discriminatory on the basis of race or sex, they are more likely to stand judicial review as not in violation of equal protection.

Summary

- The commerce clause and the necessary and proper clause give Congress nearly unlimited discretion to regulate and tax business. Unless a statute specifies that certain businesses are exempt, regulations apply to all, since even local (intrastate) business has been held to affect interstate business.

- States may impose regulations that do not conflict with federal regulations or may impose regulations in areas in which Congress gives them specific regulatory authority, but states may not impose burdens on interstate commerce. Numerous state regulatory and taxing schemes have been limited because they violate the commerce clause of the Constitution.

- The taxing power of the federal government is nearly unlimited. Taxes may be used for purposes other than just to raise revenues. They may be discriminatory or used to regulate and may be punitive in nature. The Supreme Court rarely questions the taxing schemes of Congress. State taxing schemes may not discriminate against interstate or international commerce.

- Commercial speech is afforded a high level of First Amendment protection. Businesses have the right to participate in political discussion whether or not it concerns an issue that directly affects business.

- Restrictions on commercial speech are subject to constitutional guidelines concerning strong public necessity. Truthful speech about lawful activities may be regulated only if the regulation would advance a substantial governmental interest and the regulation is no more extensive than is necessary.

- Since companies have Fourth Amendment guarantees against unreasonable searches and seizures, law enforcement authorities can be required to obtain warrants for most inspections. The main exception is in the case of closely regulated industries. The business sensibility of requiring an inspector to obtain a warrant for a routine inspection is dubious.

- Companies may not withhold documents or testimony requested by prosecutors on the grounds that the evidence might incriminate the company; only individuals may invoke that Fifth Amendment right. Efforts to evade the requirement to testify by holding corporate evidence out of the country will not necessarily work.
- When government agencies prevent property from being used in a legitimate manner because of long, unjustified procedural delays, or if agencies impose rules that substantially change the property value, compensation may be sought under the just compensation clause of the Fifth Amendment.
- The Supreme Court has held that large damage awards (including punitive damages) by juries against businesses do not violate the Eighth Amendment protection against excessive fines, nor do they violate Fourteenth Amendment due process clause protections of fair play and substantial justice.
- The due process clause of the Fourteenth Amendment has been used to extend constitutional protections to matters subject to state regulation. Economic regulations must be shown to be related to a legitimate government interest, such as public safety. The clause is also used to ensure fairness in law enforcement procedures.
- The equal protection clause of the Fourteenth Amendment is used to protect individuals from suffering a loss of freedom from state laws that discriminate against a class of persons when there is no compelling governmental interest in the law, such as public health or safety.

Issue

Should Free Speech Rights Apply at the Workplace?

To reduce discrimination in employment, suits have been filed against employers and unions for speech or practices that are claimed to inflict injury on some persons based on sex, race, national origin, or religion. The reading here questions how such concerns should be balanced against the right to free speech, which is traditionally given very high protection in the United States.

HARASSMENT LAW FLIRTS WITH SPEECH SUPPRESSION

Eugene Volokh

Reprinted by permission of *The Wall Street Journal* © 1995 Dow Jones & Company, Inc. All rights reserved worldwide. Volokh is a professor of constitutional law at UCLA law school.

It's becoming increasingly clear that sexual harassment law, racial harassment law and religious harassment law

can suppress free speech. And courts are beginning to notice.

Take the case of Sylvia DeAngelis, the first female sergeant in the El Paso, Texas, Police Department. From 1987 to 1990, an anonymous columnist in the police union newsletter would occasionally write sexist things about her and about female officers generally. A typical example: "Do you remember when there were no women workin' the streets? (Ah yes, those were the good days! . . . Sorry gals, truth hurts!)"

Ms. DeAngelis sued the union, claiming the columns created a "hostile and sexually abusive working environment." The jury agreed, and awarded her $10,000 in compensatory damages and $50,000 in punitive damages. All for publishing a newsletter column.

On May 10 [1995], a federal appeals court overturned the verdict. Ten columns in a newsletter over three years, Judge Edith Jones wrote, weren't "severe or pervasive" enough to create a hostile environment (the legal test for workplace harassment). Occasional offensive comments, the court concluded, do not harassment make.

But even more significantly, the court acknowledged that, where speech is involved, harassment law "steers into the territory of the First Amendment," adding, "It is no use to deny or minimize this problem." When a sexual harassment claim is founded solely on offensive statements, "the statute imposed content-based, viewpoint-discriminatory restrictions on speech."

The DeAngelis case is far from the only instance where harassment law potentially conflicts with free speech. But it's one of the few court decisions that acknowledges the conflict. Consider some examples:

• A state court concluded it was "religious harassment" for a Christian-owned company to put Bible verses on paychecks and religious articles in the company newsletters.

• A federal trial court said that use of "sexist" job titles like "draftsman" instead of "draftsperson," might be sexual harassment. A Kentucky state agency has actually gotten a company to change its "Men working" signs (at a cost of over $35,000) on the theory that the signs "perpetuat[e] a discriminatory work environment and [are] unlawful."

• The Equal Employment Opportunity Commission sued an employer over an ad campaign that used samurai, kabuki and sumo wrestling to allude to its Japanese competitors, and that referred to its Japanese competitors—not to any of its workers—as "Japs." The EEOC claimed that both the slurs and the ads created a hostile environment for a Japanese-American employee. The case was settled before trial, "for undisclosed monetary terms and other commitments."

• A federal court ordered an employer and its employees to "refrain from any racial, religious, ethnic, or other remarks or slurs contrary to their fellow employees' religious beliefs."

• Another federal court characterized an employee's hanging "pictures of the Ayatollah Khome[i]ni and a burning American flag in Iran in her own cubicle" as "national-origin harassment" of an Iranian employee who saw the pictures.

Of course, in many workplaces harassment cases, there's simply no First Amendment issue involved. Bosses trying to extort sexual favors from subordinates, unwanted sexual touching by co-workers, stalking that

leads victims to fear for their safety—all of this appalling conduct is clearly punishable and should be punished.

Likewise, there shouldn't be much problem with restricting one-on-one statements, such as repeated unwanted sexual propositions, or face-to-face slurs. When there's only one listener, the listener should be entitled to say, "Stop, I don't want you to say this to me anymore." The speaker will still be able to speak his mind to others, he'll just have to leave this one listener alone.

But that's not what's going on in the DeAngelis case, or in the others described above. The speech in these cases—Bible verses on paychecks, criticism (even offensive criticism) of foreign businesses or leaders, "remarks contrary to fellow employees' religious beliefs," and even sexist comments in a union newsletter—is at the core of the First Amendment's protections.

What's more, the government is trying to restrict this speech precisely because it expresses a viewpoint that's offensive and that the government dislikes. The government isn't restricting all offensive speech—only offensive speech that's arguably bigoted. Harassment law, said one federal court, is aimed at "informing people that the expression of racist or sexist attitudes in public is unacceptable," so that "people may eventually learn that such views are undesirable in private, as well." Doubtless this is a laudable end; but the means—punishment of speech—seem constitutionally troublesome.

Of course, there's no question that speech can hurt. One wouldn't want to be in Ms. DeAngelis's shoes; she must have struggled hard to become El Paso's first female police sergeant, and being publicly derided because of her sex must have stung terribly. The columnist was being inexcusably rude.

The same goes for many of the above examples. One can certainly sympathize with employees who are offended by various sexually, racially or religiously themed comments. Many people don't go to work to get involved in political debates; they want to do their jobs, get paid and go home without enduring insults or even petty insensitivities.

But at the same time, most of us spend more waking hours at work than anywhere else. The workplace is where we most often talk about important political and social issues. And that goes double for job-related issues, such as whether women officers are as good as men.

The government can't, consistently with the First Amendment, suppress speech like this. The DeAngelis court realized this; perhaps other courts soon will, too.

ISSUE QUESTIONS

1. Is it realistic to think that a person in a minority at a workplace will tell those in the majority, which may include one's supervisor, to stop offensive talk?

2. Government intervention aside, what position should employers voluntarily take about such matters? Should it be legal for employers to dismiss employees who make offensive remarks?

REVIEW AND DISCUSSION QUESTIONS

1. Define the following terms:

   commerce clause   self-incrimination
   interstate commerce   just compensation (takings) clause
   necessary and proper clause due process clause
   political speech   equal protection clause
   commercial speech

2. Congress requires, via the Internal Revenue Service, that you report to the IRS any income from illegal activities, such as drug dealing. If you report the income, you reveal your illegal activities. If you do not report the income and the dealing is discovered, you can be charged with income tax evasion. Does this violate the Fifth Amendment? If not, why not?

CASE QUESTIONS

3. Many states prohibit their lottery tickets from being sold out of the state, so Pic-A-State would have its agents buy lottery tickets in various states and hold them there; someone in Pennsylvania would buy a claim on the tickets held in the other states. Congress passed a law prohibiting interstate transmission of lottery ticket information to be used for lottery ticket sales. Pic-A-State, which was being put out of business, challenged the law as unconstitutional. Was it correct? [*Pic-A-State Pa. v. Reno*, 76 F.3d 1294 (3rd Cir., 1996)]

4. Plaistow, New Hampshire, passed an ordinance prohibiting truck traffic during late-night hours at a truck terminal loading and unloading facility. It did so to reduce noise and fumes for the benefit of town residents. The truck terminal had been in operation several years. Most of the trucks came five miles from an interstate highway to change loads. The truckers contested the regulation as a restriction on interstate commerce and illegal for regulating an area (interstate trucking) subject to federal regulations. Were the truckers right? [*New Hampshire Motor Transport Assn. v. Town of Plaistow*, 67 F.3d 326 (1st Cir., 1995)]

 5. Taylor sold live minnows as fishing bait in Maine. He imported some minnows into Maine from another state in violation of Maine law. He was then indicted under a federal law that makes it illegal to move fish in interstate commerce in violation of state law. Taylor claimed that the indictment should be dismissed because the Maine statute unconstitutionally burdened interstate commerce. Maine argued that it needed the statute to protect the state's fisheries from diseases and undesired varieties of fish. The U.S. Court of Appeals sided with Taylor, and the state of Maine appealed to the Supreme Court. Do the indictment and the statute stand? [*Maine v. Taylor*, 477 U.S. 131 (1986)]

6. The state of Iowa had a statute limiting to 55 feet the length of trucks on its highways. This made it illegal for commonly used double-trailer trucks 65 feet long to use Iowa highways. The shippers had to either use shorter trucks or go around the state. Iowa justified the regulation on the basis of safety on the highways and because the bigger trucks caused more damage to its highways. Was this regulation constitutional? [*Kassel* v. *Consolidated Freightways Corp.*, 450 U.S. 662 (1981)]

7. When margarine was invented, it cut into the butter market. The dairy lobby begged Congress for help and got it in the form of a federal tax on margarine of one-quarter of a cent per pound on white margarine and ten cents per pound on yellow margarine. Obviously, since people were used to yellow butter, white margarine was unattractive and less competitive. This discriminatory tax on margarine, especially yellow margarine, was challenged. What result? [*McCray* v. *U.S.*, 195 U.S. 27 (1904)]

8. Montana imposed a tax on coal that ran as high as 30 percent of its value. The tax generated as much as 20 percent of all state revenues. Since over 90 percent of the coal was shipped to other states, the tax was mostly borne by non-Montanans in higher utility prices. Was this tax constitutional? [*Commonwealth Edison* v. *Montana*, 453 U.S. 609 (1981)]

9. Massachusetts imposed a tax on all milk sold in the state. The tax proceeds, collected by the state, were distributed to dairy farmers in Massachusetts. Milk buyers who bought milk from out-of-state dairies contested the tax as unconstitutional for interfering with interstate commerce. Were they correct? [*West Lynn Creamery* v. *Healy*, 114 S.Ct. 2205 (1994)]

10. The California Public Utilities Commission required Pacific Gas and Electric Company to include in its monthly billing envelope, which often included political editorials and other materials, material prepared by a group that often opposed positions taken by PG&E, so long as the added material did not increase the weight of the envelopes so that more postage would have to be paid. Did PG&E have to include this material so that its customers could see alternative views? [*Pacific Gas & Electric* v. *Public Utilities Comm.*, 475 U.S. 1 (1986)]

11. The city of Cincinnati, for reasons of the safety and appearance of its streets and sidewalks, would not allow new racks on public property that distributed "commercial handbills" (free newspapers and advertising papers). Regular newspapers were allowed to have racks. The publishers of the free circulars sued the city for violating their First Amendment rights. Did they win? [*Cincinnati* v. *Discovery Network*, 113 S.Ct. 1505 (1993)]

12. An employee heard a news report that an attempt was made on the president's life. The employee said to other employees: "If they go for him again, I hope they get him." The employer fired the employee for the statement. Is the statement protected by the First Amendment? What if the employee made the statement in public, such as by a letter to the editor of the newspaper? [*Rankin* v. *McPherson*, 483 U.S. 378 (1987)]

13. Under the Hazardous Materials Transportation Act, the Secretary of Transportation regulates the transportation of hazardous materials. The regulatory scheme includes warrantless, unannounced inspections of property and records involved in transporting hazardous materials. A propane gas dealer contested the constitutionality of surprise, warrantless inspections of its transport facilities. The

government sued to force such inspections. Was that position upheld? [*U.S.* v. *V-1 Oil Co.*, 63 F.3d 909 (9th Cir., 1995)]

14. Albert Wild was served a summons by the Internal Revenue Service to appear and testify about the tax records of Air Conditioning Supply Company, of which Wild was owner and president. He appeared but refused to produce the records, claiming Fifth Amendment protection against self-incrimination. The IRS wanted to force him to produce the records of the company. Could they do so? [*Wild* v. *Brewer*, 329 F.2d 924 (9th Cir. 1964)]

15. A church owned land in a rural area that it used as a retreat center and a recreation area for disabled children. A fire in the area destroyed vegetation, allowing flooding to occur. The land was flooded. To protect public safety, the county adopted a temporary ordinance prohibiting any new building in the area until it determined what to do. The church request to rebuild was denied for six years while the county pondered what the building code, if any, should be for the area. The church sued for loss of use of the land. Could it recover under the just compensation clause of the Fifth Amendment? [*First English Evangelical Lutheran Church of Glendale* v. *Los Angeles County*, 482 U.S. 304 (1987)]

16. Levin was convicted of making two cocaine sales for $250 from his home; he was given probation and had to pay a small fine. The drug laws allowed the government to seize and sell his home (worth $68,000 in equity value to Levin). Levin protested that this was an excessive fine in violation of the Eighth Amendment. Did he get his home back? [*U.S.* v. *Certain Real Property*, 954 F.2d 29 (2nd Cir., 1992)]

17. The New York City Transit Authority ruled that methadone (a narcotic) users (who are usually recovering from heroin addiction) would not work for it in any job capacity. The district court held that this violated the equal protection clause by unfairly excluding methadone users, even from jobs that were not safety sensitive, such as drivers. The Transit Authority appealed to the Supreme Court. Was there a violation of the equal protection clause? [*New York City Transit Authority* v. *Beazer*, 440 U.S. 568 (1979)]

18. The state of West Virginia imposed a tax on property that was supposed to be in proportion to the value of the property. Taxpayers whose property was assessed at eight to thirty-five times more than comparable neighboring property, so that they were required to pay eight to thirty-five times as much in property tax as were other owners of similar property, sued the state for violation of the equal protection clause. Would such economic regulation be in violation? [*Allegheny Pittsburgh Coal Co.* v. *County Commission of Webster County*, 488 U.S. 336 (1989)]

POLICY QUESTION

19. Would a constitutional restriction on political speech that is sponsored by commercial interests produce a less biased, more fair system of political decision making?

ETHICS QUESTIONS

20. Since it is legal for physicians and other professionals to do some commercial advertising, a physician puts an ad in the newspaper telling people that the flu

season could be bad this year and that the flu kills hundreds of people every year (which is true). She urges people to come to her office to get a flu shot to protect themselves. Is this ethical? The medical associations used to hold such ads unethical.

21. A firm subject to OSHA inspections requires an OSHA inspector who shows up unexpectedly one day to get a warrant before engaging in the search. The firm owner knows that the inspector is a genuine inspector and that there is no question that the warrant to search will be issued. However, requiring the inspector to get the warrant takes half a day of the inspector's time (which is paid for by taxpayers). Is it ethical to bar such inspections?

INTERNET ASSIGNMENT

Law schools typically use the Supreme Court's commerce clause cases to teach students about the demise of federalism. Indeed, the Supreme Court has, since the mid-1930s taken great pains to read the commerce clause very expansively. *See, e.g.,* *Wickard* v. *Filburn*, 317 U.S. 111 (1942), *Katzenbach* v. *McClung*, 379 U.S. 294 (1964). The last chapter of the commerce clause saga has not been written, however, and the commerce clause may be experiencing a measure of judicial resuscitation.

Using the World Wide Web to find your information (and giving the URL for each source actually used) locate and read the Supreme Court's opinion in *United States* v. *Lopez*, Docket 93-1260, April 26, 1995. What do you think best explains the Supreme Court's seemingly conflicting opinions in these three cases? In *Wickard* v. *Filburn*, Justice Jackson began from the premise that the Court's recognition of the relevance of economic effects made unfeasible the application of legal formulas in commerce clause analysis. In *United States* v. *Lopez*, however, Chief Justice Rehnquist began his analysis from the premise that "We start with first principles. The Constitution creates a Federal Government of enumerated powers." Justice Rehnquist then continued with reference to James Madison and the Federalist Papers, ultimately finding that the government's commerce clause arguments were too attenuated to withstand constitutional scrutiny. How, if at all, can these very different approaches to commerce clause jurisprudence be reconciled?

Assume a publicly owned corporation, WidgetCo, Inc., has its principal place of business and manufacturing plant in Michigan. Suppose further that, unbeknownst to WidgetCo's shareholders, the managers and employees of WidgetCo have been using the company's Michigan plant at night as a marginally-illegal casino, in violation of state law. In due course, WidgetCo's Michigan plant is raided by the Michigan police, who seize not only the illegal gambling equipment, but also WidgetCo's plant. In addition, Michigan declares WidgetCo a public nuisance, seizes the equitable title to all the shareholders' shares of stock, and files suit to abate (make void) the shareholders' equity interests in the company. The shareholders, who had no knowledge of any illegal activity, defend on the grounds that the abatement violates both their due process and takings clause rights.

Using the World Wide Web (and giving the URL for each source actually used) locate and read the Supreme Court's opinions in: (1) *Bennis* v. *Michigan*, Docket 94-8729, March 4, 1996, and (2) *BMW of North America, Inc.* v. *Gore*, Docket 94-896, May 20, 1996. What results for WidgetCo's shareholders?

CHAPTER 6

Government Agencies and Administrative Process

Administrative agencies have a significant impact on the legal environment of business. Many federal and state agencies have or share responsibilities for regulating a wide range of business activity. Changes in technology and the ways in which business is done often lead to the development of new regulations to supervise the activities of the new industry. Decades ago, regulations were imposed on railroads, truckers, and airlines as the transportation industry developed. In recent years, as the transportation industry has matured, many of the regulatory constraints have been removed. Worker safety, discrimination, environmental, and other social issues are now regulated in many ways by administrative agencies. As the Internet has grown, some believe it should be regulated too.

This chapter begins with a discussion of the development of administrative agencies. It then considers the powers delegated to the agencies by Congress, including their legislative, investigative, adjudicatory, and enforcement powers. The discussion finally turns to the concept of judicial review—the power of the judicial branch of government to review an agency's actions or decisions.

Administrative Agencies

Administrative agencies have become a fundamental part of modern U.S. government. They are the primary tool through which local, state, and federal governments perform regulatory functions. In the words of the Supreme Court in *F.T.C. v. Ruberoid Company* (1952):

> The rise of administration bodies probably has been the most significant legal trend of the last century and perhaps more values today are affected by their decisions than by those of all the courts. . . . They have become a veritable fourth branch of the government. . . .

The first federal agency was the Interstate Commerce Commission (ICC), created in 1887 to regulate railroads. Early in the 1900s, the Federal Trade Commission (FTC), which handles antitrust cases, and the Food and Drug Administration (FDA) were created. During the Great Depression in the 1930s, many agencies were created, such as the Securities and Exchange Commission (SEC) and the Federal Communications Commission (FCC). In the late 1960s and early 1970s, a number of agencies were created, including the Environmental Protection Agency (EPA) and the Equal Employment Opportunity Commission (EEOC). Today, more than fifty independent agencies and the fourteen cabinet departments issue about 80,000 pages of regulations each year.

Exhibit 6.1 is a list of a few agencies and their web site addresses. Almost all agencies can be easily found on the web. Some agencies are included in a larger agency. For instance, the Food and Drug Administration is part of the Department of Health and Human Services.

CREATING AN ADMINISTRATIVE AGENCY

An *administrative agency* is an authority of the government—other than a legislature or a court—created to administer a particular law. An agency generally performs at least some functions of the three constitutional branches of government: legislative, judicial, and executive. Congress gives an agency power and authority through a *legislative delegation*. It delegates to an agency the power to perform its regulatory purpose, which is to formulate, implement, and enforce policy relevant to its area of authority. A statute delegating those powers to the agency is an *enabling statute*.

EXHIBIT 6.1	
Selected Federal Administrative Agencies and Web Sites	Commodity Futures Trading Commission (CFTC); *www.cftc.gov* Consumer Product Safety Commission (CPSC); *www.cpsc.gov* Department of Commerce (DoC); *www.doc.gov* Department of Labor (DoL); *www.dol.gov* Equal Employment Opportunity Commission (EEOC); *www.eeoc.gov.* Food and Drug Administration (FDA); *www.fda.gov* Federal Trade Commission (FTC); *www.ftc.gov* Health and Human Services (HHS); *www.hhs.gov* Occupational Safety and Health Administration (OSHA); *www.osha.gov.* Securities and Exchange Commission (SEC); *www.sec.gov*

JURIS **prudence?**

Just in Case You Were Not Sure

 The Consumer Product Safety Commission regulates the fabrics used in children's sleepwear. To make sure people know what that means, the commission explains it in a regulation, §1616.2 Definitions.

(a) "Children's sleepwear" means any product of wearing apparel size 7 through size 14, such as nightgowns, pajamas, or similar or related items, such as robes, intended to be worn primarily for sleeping or activities related to sleeping. Underwear and diapers are excluded from this definition.

(b) "Sizes 7 through 14" means the sizes defined as 7 through 14 in Department of Commerce Voluntary Product Standards PS 54-72 and PS 36-70, previously identified as Commercial Standards, CS 153-48, "Body Measurements for the Sizing of Girls' Apparel" and CS 155-50, "Body Measurements for the Sizing of Boys' Apparel," respectively.

Source: *Code of Federal Regulations*

Why Create an Agency?

Administrative agencies are generally created when a problem requires expertise and supervision in working toward solutions. By 1970, for example, Congress decided the federal government should address the issue of air quality. But as an institution, Congress has neither the time nor the expertise to determine how such a law might be applied to numerous industries and thousands of different sources emitting air pollutants. Congress also lacks the ability to handle law enforcement compliance directly. Hence, when Congress enacted the Clean Air Act, it delegated primary responsibility for it to the Environmental Protection Agency. The EPA has the legislative, investigative, adjudicatory, and enforcement powers to accomplish the task. The EPA can consider technical details more effectively than can Congress and can monitor industry on a continuous basis. Congress closely monitors the EPA (and all other agencies) and can change how it operates if Congress is not satisfied with the results.

ADMINISTRATIVE LAW

Administrative law consists of legal rules that define the authority and structure of administrative agencies. The primary sources of *administrative law* include the following:

1. The enabling statutes of administrative agencies
2. The Administrative Procedures Act
3. Court decisions that review the validity of agency actions and that enforce the law

The primary structure of administrative law is determined by the *Administrative Procedures Act (APA)*. Enacted by Congress in 1946, the APA defines the procedural rules and formalities for all federal agencies. An agency must abide by APA requirements unless Congress specifically imposes different or additional requirements on the agency.

EXHIBIT 6.2

Administrative Agencies: Summary of Regulatory Powers

Regulatory Power	Definition	Advantages of Agencies
Legislative or Rulemaking Power	The ability to develop administrative rules for the implementation of the agency's regulatory policies	Agencies can employ experts to consider technical details.
Investigative Power	The ability to obtain the necessary information to ensure that the statute and the agency's rules are observed	Agencies can monitor regulated industries continuously—whether or not there has been a violation.
Adjudicatory Power	The ability to resolve disputes and violations through a judicial type of proceeding	Agencies can bring actions quickly and enjoy flexibility and informality in their procedures.
Enforcement Power	The ability to impose sanctions to encourage compliance with statutes, the rules developed by an agency, and an agency's adjudicatory outcomes	Agencies enjoy flexibility in imposing sanctions, including fines, prohibitions, restrictions on licenses and permits, and the threat of public exposure.

Congress has authority under the commerce clause and the necessary and proper clause in the Constitution to create regulatory agencies and give them powers to enact rules. Agencies are also granted the authority to investigate violations of their rules and to prosecute violators. Although specific powers differ from agency to agency, we can generalize a "typical" administrative agency. A summary of agency regulatory powers is provided in Exhibit 6.2.

RULEMAKING

Most agencies have authority to engage in *rulemaking*. By the rulemaking process, an agency develops administrative rules and states its regulatory policy. Agencies use their own terminologies. The Treasury Department, for example, calls its rules "decisions"; other agencies refer to their rules as standards, guidelines, regulations, or opinions.

TYPES OF RULES

The Administrative Procedures Act defines an agency rule as

> The whole or part of an agency statement of general or particular applicability and future effect designed to implement, interpret, or prescribe law or policy describing the organization, procedure, or practice requirements of an agency.

To be more precise, administrative rules are classified as being substantive (legislative), interpretative, or procedural.

Substantive or Legislative Rules

Substantive rules or *legislative rules* are administrative laws with the same force of law as statutes enacted by Congress. That is, when an agency issues a substantive rule under its grant of authority by Congress, the rule is federal law. Contrary to popular misimpression, substantive regulations are not a "lower form" of law than the laws written directly by Congress. Before issuing such rules, an agency is generally required by the APA to provide public notice and the opportunity for interested parties to comment. In some circumstances, an agency conducts a formal hearing to allow interested parties to present evidence and arguments for or against the proposed rule. Procedural requirements and agency rulemaking processes are discussed in more detail in the next main section.

Interpretative Rules

Interpretative rules are statements issued by an agency to provide its staff and the public with guidance regarding the interpretation of a substantive rule or a congressional statute. Interpretative rules range from informal general policy statements to authoritative rulings that are binding on the agency.

In contrast to legislative rules, interpretative rules are exempt from the notice and comment requirements of the APA. As a consequence, an agency may issue interpretative rules without inviting input from interested parties. However, parties affected by rules may challenge an agency's interpretative rule by arguing that it is really a legislative rule. If the challenge is successful, the agency must provide public notice. Interested parties then have the opportunity to comment. Thus, the ability of an agency to distinguish between the two types of rules is important. The distinction is discussed in the *United Technologies* decision.

United Technologies Corp. v. U.S. Environmental Protection Agency
United States Court of Appeals, District of Columbia Circuit
821 F.2d 714 (1987)

CASE BACKGROUND *The Resource Conservation and Recovery Act (RCRA) regulates the disposal of hazardous waste. Congress authorized the EPA to administer and enforce the statute. When RCRA was amended by Congress in 1984, it instructed the EPA to require all hazardous waste disposal facilities, such as landfills, to meet certain design and operating requirements. The EPA issued new Final Rules in 1985 that detailed how the 1984 law was to work in practice. The regulations imposed tougher standards on all hazardous waste disposal sites. Various industrial groups challenged the new rules because the EPA issued them as interpretative rules without public notice or comment. The petitioners requested the court of appeals to declare the rules to be legislative rules that must have public review before they are issued.*

CASE DECISION Edwards, Circuit Judge.

* * *

A. "Interpretative" versus "Legislative" Rules
[1] The APA specifically excludes "interpretative" rules from its notice and comment procedures. The meaning of this exclusion was amplified by the court [in an earlier case] in which certain general principles were set forth to be used in determining whether or not a rule is interpretative. As a starting point, the court found that the agency's characterization of a rule is "relevant," although not necessarily "dispositive." As a more general principle, however, the court offered the following test to distinguish between interpretative and legislative rules: "An interpretative

rule simply states what the administrative agency thinks the [underlying] statute means, and only '"reminds" affected parties of existing duties.' On the other hand, if by its action the agency intends to create new law, rights or duties, the rule is properly considered to be a legislative rule." . . . Stated slightly differently, "'interpretative rules are statements as to what the administrative officer thinks the statute or regulation means,'" whereas legislative rules have "effect[s] completely independent of the statute."

Turning to the Final Rule in the instant case, we find that most if not all of it is properly viewed as interpretative. The Agency clearly so viewed it. It saw the "principal purpose" of the Final Rule as being "to codify the new statutory requirements" of the 1984 Amendments. In the preamble to the Final Rule, the EPA explained and interpreted its regulations, not by reference to whether the Agency was reasonably exercising its delegated power to promulgate rules, but by reference to "its view of what Congress intended these new requirements to be. Such statements of statutory interpretation are derived from the legislative history and EPA's view of Congressional purposes for the new requirements." Indeed, the EPA carefully segregated out proposed rules which "deal with issues that are logical outgrowths of the new provisions rather than matters addressed directly by the statutory language,"

and has subjected those rules to notice and comment procedures.

* * *

[W]hat distinguishes interpretative from legislative rules is the legal base upon which the rule rests. If the rule is based on specific statutory provisions, and its validity stands or falls on the correctness of the agency's interpretation of those provisions, it is an interpretative rule. If, however, the rule is based on an agency's power to exercise its judgment as to how best to implement a general statutory mandate, the rule is likely a legislative one. Here, there is no question that the Final Rule is an attempt to construe specific statutory provisions. The validity of the regulations depends on whether or not the Agency has correctly interpreted congressional intent as expressed in the 1984 Amendments. As such, it is clearly an interpretative rule.

* * *

QUESTIONS FOR ANALYSIS

1. Why would EPA prefer to have rules issued as interpretative rules rather than as legislative or substantive rules?
2. Why did the petitioners from industry want the rules declared to be legislative rules?

Procedural Rules

Procedural rules detail an agency's structure and describe its method of operation and its internal practices. The power to enact such rules is authorized by the agency's enabling statute. Once procedural rules are issued, the agency is bound by them. A challenge to an agency decision is usually upheld if the challenging party can show that the agency did not comply with its own procedural rules in reaching a decision.

RULEMAKING PROCEDURE

Legislative or substantive rules draw the most attention, since they tend to be of the greatest consequence as an agency determines the primary requirements of how a statute is to be applied in practice. When an agency makes or amends a legislative rule, the APA allows it to use informal and formal rulemaking procedures. Exhibit 6.3 outlines the two methods. Proposed rules are drafted by agency staff, are reviewed internally, then approved by the head of the agency for public consideration. In either case, the APA requires the agency to publish the proposed rule in the *Federal Register*. Such notice also states how the rulemaking is to proceed, such as when comments from interested parties must be received and where any hearings will be held.

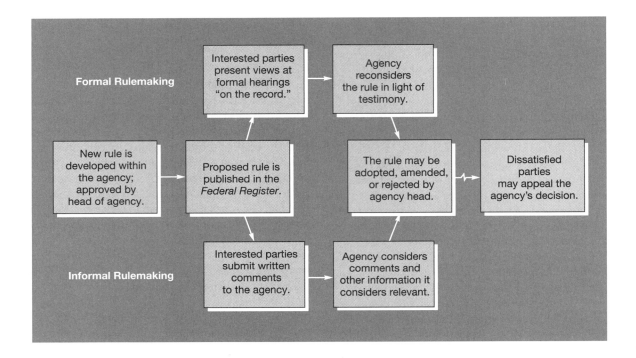

Formal Rulemaking

Interested parties present views at formal hearings "on the record."

Agency reconsiders the rule in light of testimony.

New rule is developed within the agency; approved by head of agency.

Proposed rule is published in the *Federal Register*.

The rule may be adopted, amended, or rejected by agency head.

Dissatisfied parties may appeal the agency's decision.

Informal Rulemaking

Interested parties submit written comments to the agency.

Agency considers comments and other information it considers relevant.

EXHIBIT 6.3

Agency Procedures: Formal vs. Informal Rulemaking

Informal Rulemaking

If the rulemaking is informal, the APA provides that interested parties may submit written comments to the agency stating their position. In addition, in deciding whether the rule or regulation should be enacted, the agency is free to consider sources of information other than the written comments submitted by interested parties.

Formal Rulemaking

Under some statutes, rules must be made "on the record." The agency is required to hold formal hearings. Interested parties may introduce exhibits and call witnesses, who may be subject to examination and cross-examination. Only a small number of federal statutes require rulemaking proceedings "on the record." Formal rulemaking may provide interested parties with a greater opportunity to be heard, but the costs can be considerably greater than under informal rulemaking.

Parties dissatisfied with the rule that is issued, whether rulemaking was formal or informal, may seek review of the rule as with other agency decisions. Parties first must appeal to the agency. Then, after agency procedures have been exhausted, they may seek review with the appropriate federal court, usually the U.S. Court of Appeals and especially the Court of Appeals for the District of Columbia.

Enforcing Rules

Writing rules is only a part of the task of administrative agencies. The main job of most agencies is to enforce laws written by Congress or by the agencies under the authority granted them by Congress. Enforcement means that agencies must gather information or investigate. Agencies have various ways of doing this; rule

```
C Y B E R L A W
```

Do Old Regulations Apply to New Forms of Competition?

 The growth of technology related to the Internet raises tricky issues for regulators. If a new form of technology competes with existing regulated firms, and the new technology is not covered in the regulations that govern existing competitors, are the new competitors covered?

Bandwidth expansion allows Internet telephony and video—new forms of communication not covered by existing regulations. Existing firms want the new competitors to be subject to rules so that they cannot expand

so quickly. Even if the regulators agree with existing competitors, the way the laws were written, and the regulations that implement the statutes, they did not envision the new inventions.

In many cases, if regulation is to be maintained, Congress will have to act. Such actions—as in the case of the Communications Decency Act of 1996, which was unanimously struck down by the Supreme Court as unconstitutional—indicate that Congress must not act too hastily or be defeated in its intent to control a new medium.

violations are handled in a number of different ways, as we will see when we discuss enforcement powers.

INVESTIGATIVE POWERS

Without information about compliance with federal laws, administrative agencies could not perform their responsibilities. Some information is obtained through staff analysis and agency records, but agencies must rely on their statutory authority to seek most needed information. Congress gives most agencies broad investigative power. Agencies obtain most information in three basic ways:

1. Regulated businesses are required to self report.
2. Direct observation is made by inspections to determine whether a business is meeting a law's requirements.
3. Agency subpoena power is used to require a business to produce documents.

Requiring Monitoring and Self-Reporting

Agencies may require businesses to monitor their own behavior. Those subject to a regulation are required to report certain information to an agency at set times, such as monthly, or when certain events (often a violation) occur. The Clean Air Act, for example, requires businesses to monitor air pollution emissions and report the data to the Environmental Protection Agency:

> The Administrator may require any person who owns or operates any emission source . . . to (A) establish and maintain such records, (B) make such reports, (C) install, use, and maintain such monitoring equipment or methods, (D) sample such emissions, and (E) provide such other information as the Administrator may reasonably require. . . .

Reporting information of violations can lead to fines and agency sanctions. If, for example, the information reported indicates that a firm has emitted too much pollution, the EPA can impose a fine. Businesses have contested fines resulting from mandatory self-reporting of violations, arguing that reporting of self-incriminating evidence violates the Fifth Amendment. However, as pointed out in Chapter 5, the Supreme Court has ruled that the self-incrimination privilege of the Fifth Amendment applies only to individuals and does not protect corporations and other legal entities. Failing to report or reporting false information almost always leads to heavier fines and more severe agency sanctions than when a party volunteers violations.

Direct Observation by Agencies

Agencies also acquire information by direct observation of regulated activities. Examples include on-the-spot worksite safety inspections by OSHA inspectors and testing by the EPA for excessive air pollution emissions. As discussed in Chapter 5, the Supreme Court has imposed limits on warrantless searches by administrative agencies. Unless a firm is in a "closely regulated" industry, agencies can be required to obtain warrants for routine inspections. The warrants are simple to obtain. However, no warrant is required if an agency's evidence is obtained from an "open-field" observation. That is, a warrant is not required if the evidence is gathered by an inspector by observations from areas where the public has access, as the *Dow Chemical* decision discusses.

Dow Chemical Company v. United States
United States Supreme Court
476 U.S. 227, 106 S.Ct. 1819 (1986)

CASE BACKGROUND *Dow Chemical sued to prohibit the EPA's aerial observation and photography of its industrial complex. The EPA had requested an on-site inspection of the plant, but Dow denied the request. Instead of seeking an administrative search warrant, the EPA hired a commercial aerial photographer, who took photographs of the facility from various altitudes, all within the lawful airspace.*

Dow sued in federal district court, alleging that the EPA's action violated the Constitution's Fourth Amendment protections against unlawful searches and seizures. The district court ruled for Dow, but the Court of Appeals reversed in favor of the EPA. Dow appealed to the U.S. Supreme Court.

CASE DECISION Burger, Chief Justice.

* * *

The photographs at issue in this case are essentially like those commonly used in map-making. Any person with an airplane and aerial camera could readily duplicate them. Dow claims EPA's use of aerial photography was a "search" of an area . . . and that it had a reasonable expectation of privacy from such photography protected by the Fourth Amendment.

Congress has vested in EPA certain investigatory and enforcement authority. . . . When Congress invests an agency with enforcement and investigatory authority, it is not necessary to identify explicitly each and every technique that may be used in the course of executing the statutory mission.

* * *

Regulatory or enforcement authority generally carries with it all the modes of inquiry and investigation traditionally employed or useful to execute the authority granted. Environmental standards such as clean air and clean water cannot be enforced only in libraries and laboratories, helpful as those institutions may be.

* * *

Dow's inner manufacturing areas are elaborately secured to ensure they are not open or exposed to the public from the ground. Any actual physical entry by EPA into any enclosed area would raise significantly different questions, because "(t)he businessman, like the occupant of a residence, has a constitutional right to go about his business free from unreasonable official entries upon his private commercial property."

The narrow issue raised by Dow's claim of search and seizure, however, concerns aerial observation of a 2,000-acre outdoor manufacturing facility without physical entry.

We pointed out in [another case] that the Government has "greater latitude to conduct warrantless inspections of commercial property" because "the expectation of privacy that the owner of commercial property enjoys in such property differs significantly from the sanctity accorded an individual's home." We emphasized that unlike a homeowner's interest in his dwelling, "(t)he interest of the owner of commercial property is not one in being free from any inspections." And with regard to regulatory inspections, we have held that "(w)hat is observable by the public is observable, without a warrant, by the Government inspector as well."

* * *

It may well be, as the Government concedes, that surveillance of private property by using highly sophisticated surveillance equipment not generally available to the public, such as satellite technology, might be constitutionally proscribed absent a warrant. But the photographs here are not so revealing of intimate details as to raise constitutional concerns.

Although they undoubtedly give EPA more detailed information than naked-eye views, they remain limited to an outline of the facility's buildings and equipment. The mere fact that human vision is enhanced somewhat, at least to the degree here, does not give rise to constitutional problems. An electronic device to penetrate walls or windows so as to hear and record confidential discussions of chemical formulae or other trade secrets would raise very different and far more serious questions.

* * *

We hold that the taking of aerial photographs of an industrial plant complex from navigable airspace is not a search prohibited by the Fourth Amendment. Affirmed.

QUESTIONS FOR ANALYSIS

1. If the Court had decided differently, how could the EPA have obtained the same information?
2. Are there disadvantages associated with using administrative search warrants that are so serious that agencies must undertake alternative activity, such as aerial photography, without notifying the other party?

Agency Subpoena Power

An agency may also obtain information by issuing a *subpoena*, a legal instrument that directs the person receiving it to appear at a specified time and place to testify or to produce documents. The Clean Air Act provides an example of a congressional authorization of the power to issue subpoenas and the procedure for enforcing them:

> [F]or purposes of obtaining information . . . the Administrator may issue subpoenas for the attendance and testimony of witnesses and the production of relevant papers, books, and documents, and he may administer oaths. . . . In case of . . . refusal to obey a subpoena served upon any person . . . , the district court for any district in which such person is found or resides or transacts business . . . shall have jurisdiction to issue an order requiring such person to appear and give testimony before the Administrator . . . and any failure to obey such an order may be punished by such court as a contempt thereof.

Unless the request for information by the agency is vague, or if the burden imposed on the business outweighs the possible benefits to the agency, the business must comply with the subpoena. Even trade secrets and other confidential information cannot necessarily be kept from the agency. If a business asserts that the information requested by a subpoena deserves confidential treatment, an agency usually respects the request or the business may seek a court order providing protection.

ENFORCEMENT POWER

Congress grants agencies an array of enforcement tools. These tools are used to encourage voluntary compliance with the law, the rules of an agency, and an agency's decisions. The EPA, for example, can ensure compliance with air pollution control requirements by seeking civil and criminal penalties and injunctions, if necessary. In the Clean Air Act, for example, Congress provided that

> The Administrator shall commence a civil action for a permanent or temporary injunction, or to assess and recover a civil penalty of not more than $25,000 per day of violation, or both, whenever [the owner or operator of a major stationary source of pollution] . . . violates or fails to comply with any order. . . .

In addition to having the authority to sue in federal court to seek civil and criminal penalties, agencies have authority to impose other types of sanctions. To illustrate the wide range of sanctions available to an agency, consider the examples offered by the APA in its definition of *sanction:*

1. Prohibition, requirement, limitation, or other condition affecting the freedom of a person
2. Withholding of relief
3. Imposition of a penalty or fine
4. Destruction, taking, seizing, or withholding of property
5. Assessment of damages, reimbursement, restitution, compensation, costs, charges, or fees
6. Requirement, revocation, or suspension of a license
7. Taking other compulsory or restrictive action

Enforcement methods vary among agencies. Most rely on a mix of formal and informal ways to obtain compliance with regulatory requirements. Our discussion here focuses on agency procedures, but when an agency brings criminal charges against a party, it works with the Department of Justice (office of the Attorney General), which usually handles the prosecution of criminal cases that must be heard in federal court.

Informal Agency Procedures

Agencies rely heavily on *informal procedures* that allow considerable discretion in forcing compliance. Since informal procedures generally require less time and are less costly than formal procedures in bringing about compliance, agencies prefer to use them when possible.

Informal procedures include tests and inspections, processing applications and permits, negotiations, settlements, and advice in the form of advisory opinions. Publicity, or the threat of it, can also be considered an informal procedure through which an agency can coerce industry compliance with its rules and regulations.

In many cases, agencies act on the spot. For example, an OSHA inspector, upon finding a situation that endangers workers, may order immediate changes. Many such incidents are handled this way rather than involving formal procedures. The existence of an agency and its rules may produce desired industry behavior.

For example, manufacturers "voluntarily" withdraw products from the shelves and destroy them when a problem is discovered that would likely result in formal action by an agency.

Review of Informal Procedure Decisions A business dissatisfied with an agency action involving informal procedures may seek review. The decision is first reviewed by the agency head. If dissatisfied with the agency's final decision, parties may seek review by the federal court. In reviewing agency procedures, the courts are generally most concerned with whether the agency procedure was fair and the decision was consistent with the legislative intent of Congress.

Formal Agency Procedures

Among the *formal procedures* used by most regulatory agencies are adjudicatory hearings. The manner in which the hearings are defined and conducted is dictated by the APA. In some instances, an agency's enabling statute may require procedures that differ somewhat from those provided by the APA.

Adjudicatory Hearings An *adjudicatory hearing* is a formal agency process under APA rules, which are similar to those followed in a regular trial. As Exhibit 6.4 illustrates, an adjudicatory hearing is usually initiated by the agency filing a complaint against a firm. The complaint may come about from information provided by members of the public, competitors, agency investigation, or other law enforcement organizations. The business must respond to the complaint that

EXHIBIT 6.4

Formal Agency Procedure: Adjudicatory Hearing

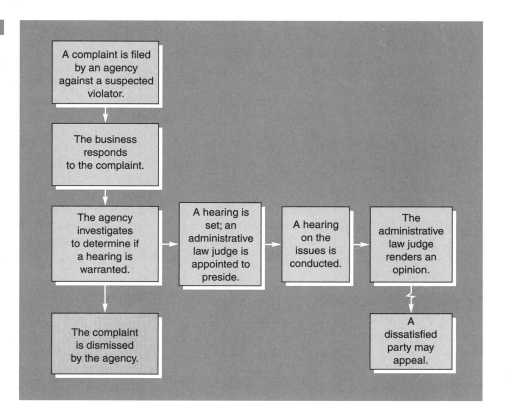

Administrative Agencies in Japan

One of the most worrisome areas of Japanese law and legal culture for an American company is the body of administrative "law" known as "administrative guidance" (*gyosei shido*). This term includes all the procedural tools Japanese agencies can use to exert formal and informal regulatory authority over businesses. An administrative agency, for example, may issue guidance by direction (*shiji*), request (*yobo*), warning (*keikoku*), encouragement (*kansho*), or suggestion (*kankoku*).

The power basis of administrative guidance is in the government's control of foreign trade. In theory, businesses are not forced to comply with administrative guidance. But a business that ignores a government suggestion might find that its quota of imported materials has been reduced, that it cannot get permission for

needed foreign exchange, that it is being denied government financing for future expansions, or that some other sanction is imposed.

The Foreign Exchange Control and Foreign Investment Acts, for example, require that any agreement involving expenditures abroad must be approved by the Foreign Investment Council. A business that has not complied with an agency's request that a pollution control device be installed might find that a contract requiring expenditures abroad has not been approved.

The Japanese judiciary has taken a hands-off policy toward administrative guidance. As long as the agency action is within its discretion, the action will not be reviewed unfavorably even if it is abusive. This gives Japanese administrative agencies considerably more power than U.S. agencies.

alleges violation of the law enforced by the agency. If the matter is not settled by negotiation, a hearing may be necessary.

An *administrative law judge* (*ALJ*) from the agency presides over the hearing. The ALJ is a civil service employee of the agency. The agency is represented by its counsel, who presents the agency's evidence in support of the complaint; the business then presents its evidence. Witnesses may be cross-examined, just as in a trial court, but the procedure is less formal than a court trial. The hearing must conform to the procedural due process guarantees of the Constitution, but litigants in an adjudicatory hearing are not entitled to a jury trial. There is no right to a jury trial in agency adjudicatory hearings because the Seventh Amendment does not apply since these are not criminal or common-law cases.

After a hearing, the ALJ issues a written decision. If the business does not object to the decision, the agency normally adopts the decision. If the business is dissatisfied with the ALJ's decision and seeks review, the agency head (commissioners or administrator) review the decision in the same manner as an appellate court. If the business is dissatisfied after this final agency review, it may then proceed to the federal courts for further review.

Judicial Review

The APA sets the procedural requirements for a party seeking court review of an agency decision. Most appeals concern the legitimacy of regulations and whether a penalty issued by an agency for a violation was justified. If those requirements are met, the party may challenge an agency decision with an appeal to the federal court of appeals. That appeal is referred to as *judicial review*, an external check on agency power. Its existence ensures that agencies follow required procedures, do not go beyond the authority granted them by Congress, can justify their actions, and respect constitutional rights.

WHEN JUDICIAL REVIEW CAN OCCUR

Before a court will accept a request to review an agency's action, that party making the request must satisfy several procedural requirements. Without such requirements, the courts could intrude into areas of agency responsibility and would be flooded with more cases. The most important of these procedural requirements are summarized in Exhibit 6.5.

Jurisdiction

As in any lawsuit, the party challenging an agency action must select a court that has authority to hear the case. Most regulatory statutes declare which court has *jurisdiction* to review agency actions. Suppose, for example, that the EPA enacts a rule requiring metal fabrication plants to install certain technology to control air pollution. A company challenges the rule because it believes that the EPA's required technology will not work on older plants. The company must bring the challenge to the appropriate court. To determine the appropriate court, the company must consult the Clean Air Act, which provides the following:

> A petition for review of an action of the Administrator in promulgating any national ambient air quality standard . . . or any other nationally applicable regulation . . . may be filed only in the United States Court of Appeals for the District of Columbia. A petition for review of the Administrator's actions in approving or promulgating any . . . regulation . . . or any other final action . . . which is locally or regionally applicable may be filed only in the United States Court of Appeals for the appropriate circuit. . . . Any petition for review . . . shall be filed within sixty days from the date of notice of such promulgation . . . or action.

EXHIBIT 6.5 *Judicial Review of Agency Actions: Procedural Requirements*	

Procedural Requirement	Definition
Jurisdiction	The aggrieved party may seek judicial review only in courts that have the power to hear the case. Most statutes specify which courts have jurisdiction to hear an appeal from an agency action.
Reviewability	An appellate court has the ability to reconsider an agency decision to determine whether correction or modification is needed.
Standing	A party seeking judicial review must demonstrate that it incurred an injury recognized by law as a result of the agency's action.
Ripeness	There can be no judicial review until the agency's decision is final so that the court will have the final issues in the case before it and not hypothetical question or unresolved dispute.
Exhaustion	This is a "gatekeeping" device, requiring that a party seeking judicial review must have sought relief through all possible agency appeal processes before seeking review by the courts.

JURIS prudence?

Regulators Protecting Consumers?

 Like most countries, Japan and Germany have regulations claimed to protect consumers that appear to do the opposite. German law does not allow stores to be open more than 68.5 hours per week; they must close by 6:30 P.M. on weekdays, at 2 P.M. on Saturdays, and may not open at all on Sunday. In Japan, stores must take twenty-four days of "holiday" each year, that is, close two days every month.

Japan's antitrust "watchdog," the Fair Trade Commission, does not allow retailers to give discounts below the listed price on CDs, books, or magazines. Discount

coupons may not be issued because they might "confuse" consumers. One Japanese retailer tried to import small plastic food containers from Thailand. The customs agency required every carton to be opened and the containers and their lids tested to make sure they worked. Now the company buys locally made containers. They do not have to be tested and cost consumers three to four times as much as the "untrustworthy" imports.

Source: *The Wall Street Journal*

Reviewability

The party challenging an agency action must determine whether the action is *reviewable* by the courts. Administrative agencies must follow required procedure rules or risk being found by the reviewing courts to have acted arbitrarily. Further, agencies may not exceed their regulatory objectives or risk being found to have violated the duties they were assigned by Congress. For these reasons, the APA authorizes the courts to review most agency actions. However, judicial review is not available if (1) judicial review is prohibited by statute or (2) the agency action is committed to agency discretion.

Review Prohibited by Statute Just as Congress may specify in a statute which court has jurisdiction for judicial review, it can prohibit judicial review. Consider, for example, the following statutory provision regarding the authority of the Secretary of Veteran Affairs:

> [T]he decisions of the [Secretary] on any question of law or fact under any law administered by the [Department of Veterans Affairs] providing benefits for veterans and their dependents or survivors shall be final and no other official or any court of the United States shall have the power or jurisdiction to review any decision.

Thus, if a party seeks review of an administrative decision from the Department of Veteran Affairs, the court will dismiss the challenge as not being reviewable. Congress can include such an exception in a statute as long as the exception does not violate constitutional rights.

Agency Action Committed to Agency Discretion In addition to statutory exceptions to judicial review, there are also exceptions for actions committed to agency discretion for practical reasons. Some agency actions require speed, flexibility, and secrecy in decision making, which may be inconsistent with judicial review. For example, decisions affecting the national defense and foreign policy have been found to be committed to agency discretion and therefore nonreviewable. Such

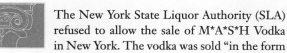

A Little Dignity in Booze, Please

The New York State Liquor Authority (SLA) refused to allow the sale of M*A*S*H Vodka in New York. The vodka was sold "in the form of an intra-venous ('IV') feeding device" that included "a metal contrivance permitting hookup of the bottle in the inverted position above the patient's head." The SLA ruled that "the proposed label and bottling is misleading, deceptive, offensive to the commonly and generally accepted standards of fitness and good taste, is not dignified . . . approval would not be conducive to proper regulation."

A New York court overturned the regulatory decision. "The court has inspected the bottle produced in open court and finds that it unmistakably labels its contents as 80-proof vodka. . . . No rational person could believe that a serious medicinal application of the product was intended. . . . this is a case for the application of the maxim: *"de gustibus non disputandum"* [There is no disputing over personal tastes.]. One of the prized qualities of vodka is its tastelessness."

Source: *Hawkeye Distilling Co.* v. *NYSLA*, 460 NYS2d 696

agency actions cannot be challenged through the courts. Exceptions to judicial review rarely apply to regulations that directly affect business.

Standing

A party seeking a court challenge to an agency action must have *standing* to seek judicial review. The standing requirement is rooted in Section 2 of Article III of the Constitution, which limits the judicial power to *actual cases or controversies*. Federal courts cannot hear complaints from parties who have no direct stake in a real dispute or who raise only hypothetical questions. Administrative law generally restricts the right of review to parties who can show an injury recognized by law as being entitled to protection.

The U.S. Supreme Court addressed the standing issue in *Lujan* v. *Defenders of Wildlife* (504 U.S. 555; 1992). In that case, environmental groups argued that U.S. aid to Egypt helped to build dams on the Nile River that endangered the rare Nile crocodile. Plaintiffs asserted that the agencies providing the aid should comply with the Endangered Species Act. The Court refused to hear the challenge because the plaintiffs lacked standing—they had suffered no "injury in fact." The Court stated that disagreement with an agency's policy is not the same as showing a concrete injury to the complaining party resulting from the policy.

Ripeness

The *ripeness doctrine* is concerned with whether the agency action is final so as to warrant judicial review. That is, rules or agency decisions that are not finalized are not ripe for review because they could be changed. According to the Supreme Court in *Abbott Labs* v. *Gardner* (387 U.S. 136; 1967), the doctrine is designed to

> [prevent courts] from entangling themselves in abstract disagreements over administrative policies, and to protect agencies from judicial interference until an administrative decision has been formalized and its effects felt in a concrete way by the challenging parties.

Exhaustion

The *exhaustion doctrine* requires a party to complete all agency appeals procedures before turning to a court for review. That is, parties may not resort to the courts for assistance until they have exhausted all internal agency review procedures regarding newly issued rules or disciplinary actions under a rule. An action must be considered final by an agency before proceeding to court.

SCOPE OF JUDICIAL REVIEW

When all procedural requirements have been met, the court of appeals can review an agency action. The court's *scope of review* determines how far it can go in examining the action. The scope of review depends on whether the issue before it involves a question of substantive law, statutory interpretation, or procedure. Each imposes different requirements on the reviewing court.

Review of Substantive Determination

A court's review of an agency's substantive determination is generally provided the lowest scope of judicial review. That is, as a rule, the courts yield to the agency's judgment in technical and scientific matters in working out the details of regulations. The courts generally will not find that an agency's actions or decisions are *arbitrary, capricious, or an abuse of discretion* if the following are true:

1. The agency has sufficiently explained the facts and its policy concerns.
2. Those facts have some basis in the agency's record.
3. On the basis of those facts and concerns, a reasonable person could reach the same judgments the agency has reached.

We see an example of a court review of an agency regulation in the *Georgia-Pacific* case, where an OSHA regulation instructed workers how to drive forklifts.

Georgia-Pacific Corp. v. Occupational Safety and Health Review Commission
United States Court of Appeals, Eleventh Circuit
25 F.3d 999 (1994)

CASE BACKGROUND *At a Georgia-Pacific (G-P) plant in Talladega, Alabama, a forklift was carrying a load of plywood. When it turned a corner, it struck and killed an employee who was squatting down, working out of sight of the forklift driver.*

An investigation by the Occupational Safety and Health Administration (OSHA) resulted in G-P's being issued a citation for violating an OSHA regulation concerning "Powered Industrial Trucks," 29 C.F.R. §1910.178(n)(4): "The driver shall be required to slow down and sound the horn at cross aisles and other locations where vision is obstructed. If the load being carried obstructs forward view, the driver shall be required to travel with the load trailing." The citation imposed a fine of $480.

After the accident, G-P followed the regulation, requiring operators to drive in reverse when carrying loads that obstructed the forward view. Plant managers received many complaints from forklift drivers that driving backwards was difficult and unsafe. G-P then decided to contest the OSHA citation on the basis that the rule was unenforceably vague. The administrative law judge (AJL) ruled that the standard was not vague but held that G-P had not violated it and reversed the citation. OSHA's Review Commission reviewed the ALJ's finding and held that the standard was not vague but that G-P had violated the regulation. G-P appealed.

CASE DECISION Per curiam.

* * *

When considering remedial legislation such as the OSH Act and its implementing regulations, the purported vagueness of a standard is judged in the light of its application to the particular facts of the case. To pass constitutional muster a regulation must provide a fair and reasonable warning of what it prohibited.

We recognize "that an agency's construction of its own regulations is entitled to substantial deference," if the [agency's] interpretation is "consistent with the regulatory language and is otherwise reasonable." . . . However, where the [agency's] interpretation of a regulation is either unconstitutionally vague as applied or unreasonable given the regulated activity, we may refuse to accept the [agency's] interpretation.

* * *

The primary purpose of the particular regulation at issue in this case is to ensure that forklifts, when carrying a load in the workplace, are operated in the manner that is most safe. We must therefore determine whether the [agency's] interpretation of the phrase "obstructs forward view" contained in 29 C.F.R. §1910.178(n)(4) is consistent with the regulatory language and reasonable given the intent of the regulation. . . .

[T]he various interpretations of the phrase "obstructs forward view" put forth by [OSHA] would give rise to several illogical and unreasonable results. First, we believe that such strict interpretations would require all forklifts, regardless of the size of the load carried or the degree of obstruction, to travel with the load trailing. We find this unreasonable because it is clear that in certain situations it would be safer to travel in the forward direction with a partially obstructed view than it would be to travel with the load trailing. In fact, the uncontradicted evidence in this case supports this fact. Second, such interpreta-

tions would often result in the operation of a forklift with the load trailing even though the operator's field of vision to the rear is more limited than it is to the front. We think it unreasonable . . . to construe the standard so strictly concerning the forward operation of forklifts without taking into consideration the degree of obstruction that may exist to the rear of the forklift. Finally, it would be equally unreasonable to interpret such a regulation in a way that would for all practical purposes ban the use of forklifts. . . .

A statute or regulation is considered unconstitutionally vague under the due process clause of the Fifth or Fourteenth Amendments if it "forbids or requires the doing of an act in terms so vague that men of common intelligence must necessarily guess at its meaning and differ as to its application." . . .

In the instant case, the issuance of the citation and the litigation which has ensued demonstrates the vagueness of the regulation. Neither [OSHA] nor the experts have been able to settle upon a single definition of the phrase "obstructs forward view."

* * *

Because we find [OSHA's] interpretation of the phrase "obstructs forward view" unreasonable and because we find the regulation as applied void for vagueness, we REVERSE the ruling of the Review Commission, vacate the citation, and leave it up to [OSHA] to promulgate a reasonable and specific standard.

QUESTIONS FOR ANALYSIS

1. Should an agency be able to presume that its rules will be applied with common sense, or should the rules be so precise that they cover situations with clarity?
2. Why did G-P spend a large sum contesting a fine of $480?

Review of Statutory Interpretation

A court's review of an agency's statutory interpretation is given a greater scope of review. In contrast to the technical judgments required of the agency in implementing a statute, the courts have primary responsibility for the interpretation of the reach and meaning of statutes enacted by Congress. That is, the courts determine whether an agency has gone beyond the authority it was granted by Congress. Although the courts will give great weight to the interpretation of a statute by the agency responsible for its implementation, they will reject that interpretation if it does not comply with interpretations by established principles of statutory construction.

Review of Procedural Requirements

The court's review of an agency's procedural requirements is provided the most intense scope of review. The court is responsible for ensuring that the agency has not acted unfairly or in disregard of statutorily prescribed procedures. The courts have been regarded historically as the authority in procedural fair play.

Congressional Restrictions on Agencies

In addition to having checks imposed on them by judicial review, agencies are checked by Congress. Just as it delegates powers to an agency, Congress may revoke those powers since agencies are creations of Congress. This section discusses measures that Congress uses or has considered using in providing those checks.

DIRECT CONGRESSIONAL CHECKS ON AGENCIES

Public awareness and concern about the costs and effectiveness of regulation, as well as pressure from special interest groups, have prompted various responses from Congress. The most immediate control mechanism enjoyed by Congress is the ability to control agency activity through the budget process. In addition, members of Congress have proposed bills calling for, among other things, *sunset provisions* and mandatory *cost-benefit analysis*.

Agency Appropriations and Reporting Requirements

Administrative agencies depend on public funding to support their programs. Congress requires agencies to report progress on programs and activities on a regular basis, and congressional committees frequently hold oversight hearings. Administrative agencies submit budget requests annually for review by the president and by Congress. The president or Congress can recommend cuts in an agency's budget if either is opposed to some of the agency's activities. The final budget, which is very detailed, is agreed upon by the House, the Senate, and the president. Through budget appropriations, Congress can mandate that an agency address specific issues and can prohibit an agency from working on other specific issues. Thus, budget control gives the president, and especially Congress, the ability to control agency regulatory policy.

Sunset Laws

Congress has considered including mandatory sunset provisions in federal regulatory laws. A sunset provision requires Congress to review an agency's regulations, programs, or general usefulness on a regular basis. If it is determined that the agency is no longer needed, it goes out of existence; that is, the sun is allowed to set upon it. Sunset provisions would require Congress to rethink the basic justification for agencies since it must reauthorize the agency. While not common at the federal level, some states have routine sunset review of their agencies.

Cost-Benefit and Risk Analysis

Mandatory cost-benefit analysis requires agencies to weigh the costs and benefits of new regulations. When the costs exceed the benefits derived from a regulation, the regulation is more easily challenged for reasonableness. The aim of cost-benefit analysis is to make the decision-making process more cost-effective. The same holds true for risk-assessment requirements that estimate the risk reduction achieved by regulations that affect health and safety. In the absence of an explicit requirement by Congress, an agency is not required to undertake a cost-benefit analysis or risk assessment of the regulations it issues.

INDIRECT CONGRESSIONAL CHECKS ON AGENCIES

Congress has passed several laws that can have the effect of indirectly controlling the power of administrative agencies. Through those acts, which include the Freedom of Information Act, the Privacy Act, and the Government in the Sunshine Act, Congress made it easier for parties outside an agency to obtain information in the possession of the agency.

Freedom of Information Act

The *Freedom of Information Act* (*FOIA*) makes most documents held by federal agencies available to the public. Unless the document falls within certain exempted categories, it must be released upon a request by a citizen. Exempted are trade secrets, documents related to national security, and documents that would, if disclosed, invade personal privacy.

Privacy Act

The *Privacy Act* is intended to give citizens more control over what information is collected about them and how that information is used. It requires that unless an exception applies, notice and prior consent are required before an agency can disclose information that concerns and identifies an individual. Individuals are given the right to access agency records and to request amendments to correct inaccuracies. The act provides that individuals can enforce their rights in federal district courts.

Government in the Sunshine Act

Congress enacted the *Government in the Sunshine Act* to limit secret meetings by agencies. Under the act, the public is entitled to at least one week's notice of the time, place, and subject matter of any agency meeting. The agency must specify whether the meeting is to be open or closed to the public.

The act lists situations in which meetings may be closed. An open meeting is not required, for example, when the meeting might concern matters to be kept secret in the interest of national defense or disclosure of trade secrets or protected financial information.

Federal courts have authority to enforce the provisions of the Government in the Sunshine Act. An agency action taken at a meeting in violation of the act is not invalid merely because of such violation; some other basis for overturning an agency action would have to be established. The court may grant an injunction against future violations of the act and may order an agency to publish transcripts or recordings of the meeting.

Summary

- Administrative agencies are created by Congress and granted legislative, investigative, adjudicatory, and enforcement powers.

- The first federal agency was the Interstate Commerce Commission, established by Congress in 1887 to regulate railroads. The most significant growth periods of agencies took place during the Great Depression of the 1930s and the "social reform" era of the 1960s and 1970s.
- Administrative law consists of legal rules defining the authority and structure of administrative agencies, specifying procedural requirements, and defining the roles of government bodies (particularly the courts) in their relationship with agencies. The primary administrative law is the Administrative Procedures Act (APA).
- Administrative regulations are classified as legislative (substantive), which are major regulations issued under grants of power from Congress; interpretative, which help to explain legislative regulations and statutes; and procedural, which detail the steps an agency uses in its rulemaking procedures and enforcement.
- Agencies may require businesses that are subject to regulation to volunteer information related to the regulations on a regular basis, including reporting violations.
- Agencies may also watch for violations, including inspecting business property, and can gather information that is provided when requested or may be forced from a business by use of subpoena.
- Agencies perform regulatory responsibilities by the use of informal and formal procedures. Informal procedures, which consist of tests and inspections, are not subject to the procedural requirements of the APA. Formal procedures, which include adjudicatory hearings, must meet the APA's procedural requirements.
- Agencies may issue fines, citations, or other penalties to rule violators. The violators can accept a penalty or contest it at an agency hearing before an administrative law judge, whose decision can be reviewed by the head of an agency and then by the federal courts of appeals. Criminal charges by an agency must be filed in federal court.
- Judicial review imposes a check on agency actions. To obtain review, the party challenging the action must meet the procedural requirements of jurisdiction, reviewability, standing, ripeness, and exhaustion.
- Congress provides direct and indirect checks on the administrative agencies. The direct checks provided by Congress include control over agency appropriations, reporting requirements, sunset laws, and cost-benefit analysis. Indirect checks include such acts as the Freedom of Information Act, the Privacy Act, and the Government in the Sunshine Act.

Issue

Should Rental Housing Be "Closely Regulated"?

The courts grant regulatory agencies great leeway to make inspections of regulated businesses. In the name of protecting public health and safety and the environment, regulatory inspections may be expanding into more and more areas, including homes.

IS YOUR HOME A CASTLE?
NOT IF YOU'RE A RENTER

Scott Bullock

Reprinted by permission of *The Wall Street Journal* © 1996 Dow Jones & Company, Inc. All rights reserved worldwide.

Bullock is an attorney with the Institute for Justice, a public interest law firm that filed suits on behalf of tenants in Park Forest and Kalamazoo.

When Ken Black heard the fateful knock on the door of his home in a suburb of Chicago last October, he couldn't have known that it signaled the latest episode in the government's assault on property rights.

Nursing a back injury, Mr. Black struggled to the front door to find a police officer and a local official bearing a search warrant. Mr. Black said they had no right to enter his home and told them to go away. Reluctantly they did, but vowed to return.

That same month, Debra Taylor, a woman who lives a few blocks up the street, came home from work to discover a notice plastered on her door. It declared that the village had a search warrant for her home and would return sometime in the next 30 days.

Why is the Village of Park Forest, Ill., demanding entry to the homes of Ken Black and Debra Taylor? Suspicion of drug-dealing? Allegations of child abuse? No. The village demands entry to satisfy itself that there are no infractions of its housing code—a demand it makes only upon those who rent, as Mr. Black and Ms. Taylor do. Two years ago the village passed an ordinance authorizing a government inspector to search single-family rental homes at "all reasonable times" to ensure compliance with the housing code. It makes no similar demands on owners.

The village is serious about exercising this power. A few weeks after Mr. Black and Ms. Taylor received their unexpected visits, notices arrived in the mail informing them that they were being taken to court. The village asked a Cook County Circuit judge to hold the tenants and their landlord, Rick Reinbold, in contempt of court and to imprison all of them for at least a 24-hour period so that the village could conduct its inspections. Also named in the suit was Ms. Taylor's 12-year-old daughter, Aftan. After seeing the notice, Aftan asked her mother how the government could jail them merely for wanting to keep strangers out of their home.

Aftan is not alone. Most Americans believe that their home is a castle—the one place where government unquestionably must respect their privacy and property rights.

Although the Fourth Amendment is usually thought of as dealing only with those accused of illegal activity, it broadly guarantees one of the most fundamental aspects of American liberty and private property rights: the right to keep unwanted intruders off one's property. It prohibits government officials from entering a home without either an individual's consent or a valid search warrant issued by a judge and based on some reasonable belief ("probable cause") that the law is being violated.

As Park Forest tenants have learned, however, the village has canceled these protections for individuals who rent their homes. When conducting housing code inspections, the village does not have to seek consent from the tenants before demanding entry into the houses, nor does it have to show any cause for the inspection. Instead, it orders landlords to provide access to rented homes, cutting the tenants entirely out of the process. Most landlords comply, and let government inspectors roam through the bedrooms and bathrooms of the houses they rent out.

Mr. Black and Ms. Taylor, however, happened to have a landlord who objected to these searches, maintaining that the inspections violated his tenants' right to privacy. Mr. Reinbold, a former Navy diver and Vietnam veteran, told the Chicago Tribune: "Being a veteran, you swear to defend the Constitution against all enemies, foreign and domestic. Until this happened, the 'domestic' part of the oath never clicked for me. This is a clear violation of privacy rights, a domestic attack on the Constitution." For this principled stand, the village fined him $1,500.

Last June a judge dismissed the fine, declaring that the village must obtain search warrants before conducting the inspections. The village immediately obtained two warrants based not on probable cause—the usual standard—but merely on the official's word that the inspections were necessary to preserve public health and safety.

The Park Forest situation is the latest in a series of recent attacks on one of the most fundamental yet often overlooked tenets of property ownership: the right to exclude. Increasingly, this right is treated with cavalier disregard by governments. From rules in New Jersey requiring access to leafleteers in private shopping malls, to a Minnesota law converting private wetlands into "public waters," governments are trying to destroy the right to keep intruders off one's property.

Perhaps nowhere has the right to exclude been more undermined than in the context of administrative inspections. In order to search private property, government officials normally must obtain a search warrant based on probable cause that a law is being violated. In *Davis v. U.S.* (1946), however, the Supreme Court carved out an exception to this requirement for "administrative" inspections of businesses and other commercial property.

The standard for administrative inspections is based merely on an official's word that a search is necessary to protect public health and safety or because a period of time has elapsed since the last inspection. What was once a narrow exception in constitutional jurisprudence has today been expanded into the virtually unchecked authority of administrative officials to intrude onto private property against an owner's wishes.

The expansion of administrative inspections is especially apparent in the enforcement of environmental laws, as government officials trespass on private, noncommercial property to confirm that federal environmental regulations are being enforced.

Few people notice or perhaps care when such inspections are directed at commercial enterprises. But as the Park Forest case and a similar ordinance in Kalamazoo, Mich., demonstrate, the administrative search doctrine is now used to invade the privacy of the home.

Park Forest officials justify their inspections on the basis of preserving "the housing stock of the community," a purpose that if upheld by the courts could just as easily apply to all residential property. Before government inspectors arrive on all our porches demanding entry, we must halt this creeping erosion of property rights.

Note: In 1998, federal judge Joan Gottschall struck down the Park Forest rule as unconstitutional, noting that "This court can't find nothing in the record to indicate why the Village undertook such an invasive program solely for single-family homes and can find nothing that limits in any way the scope of inspections" (*Black* v. *Village of Park Forest*, 20 F.Supp.2d 1218). It took three years of costly litigation that was, fortunately for the residents, largely covered by the public interest law firm.

ISSUE QUESTIONS

1. Should constitutional protections that require search warrants to be issued for good cause be restricted when business is involved?
2. If a business such as rental property can be subject to random searches, why not also be able to search the person and workstations of employees on the job? How do you draw a consistent line between personal rights and business interests?

REVIEW AND DISCUSSION QUESTIONS

1. Define the following terms and concepts:
   enabling statute judicial review
   rulemaking standing
   substantive rules ripeness
   interpretative rules exhaustion
   procedural rules
2. What advantages does an agency have over the judicial system in monitoring business behavior?
3. Congress gives some regulatory agencies it creates very general mandates. Congress may say something to the effect of "go regulate the environment in the public interest." The agencies then devise regulations to execute the "intent" of Congress. Should Congress be more specific when it creates agencies?

CASE QUESTIONS

4. The Consumer Products Safety Commission had a substantive rule called the "Small Parts Rule" that banned small parts from children's toys that could be choked on. The rule as originally written said it excluded "paper, fabric, yarn, fuzz, elastic and string" that might be attached to a small piece. Later, the Commission issued an interpretative rule stating that "paper, fabric, etc." could also be banned. The interpretative rule was challenged as improper because it was really a substantive rule that was issued without proper notice and public comment. Was the

challenge proper? [*Jerri's Ceramic Arts* v. *Consumer Products Safety Comm.*, 874 F.2d 205 (4th Cir., 1989)]

5. Prison inmates sentenced to die by lethal injection sued the Food and Drug Administration for refusing to take action against the makers and users of the drugs used for lethal injection. That is, the prisoners claimed that the drugs violated FDA standards and thus should be subject to an enforcement action to prevent violations of FDA rules. The FDA claimed that it did not have to review drugs or undertake enforcement actions that it did not think necessary. The prisoners claimed that the FDA had to hold all drugs to the same standards and that enforcement action had to be taken. Were the prisoners correct? [*Heckler* v. *Chaney*, 470 U.S. 821, 105 S.Ct. 1649 (1985)]

6. Dewey owned a mine in Wisconsin. He refused to allow agents of the Department of Labor to inspect the mine without a search warrant. The Department of Labor wanted to determine whether violations discovered in a previous search had been corrected. The Federal Mine Safety and Health Act authorizes a specific number of warrantless inspections, but it does not dictate the procedures that inspectors must follow. Did the warrantless search violate Dewey's Fourth Amendment rights? [*Donovan* v. *Dewey*, 452 U.S. 594, 101 S.Ct. 2534 (1981)]

7. The U.S. Department of Transportation (DOT) adopted a regulation that would require new cars to have either air bags or automatic seat belts (the kind that strap you to the seat when you get in the car). The carmakers protested that this would be too expensive and would not work. In 1981, DOT, under new leadership, repealed the regulation, saying that since it had evidence that people would unhook the seat belts, the regulation was not effective. Car insurance companies sued DOT, claiming that the agency could not repeal the regulation. The court of appeals held that since the repeal was not based on sufficient evidence, the regulation must be reimposed. What did the Supreme Court have to say? [*Motor Vehicle Manufacturers Assn.* v. *State Farm*, 463 U.S. 29, 103 S.Ct. 2856 (1983)]

8. The EPA proposed expensive new pollution control regulations for coal-burning electricity plants. After receiving comments in the public review period from those who opposed the higher electricity prices that would result from the pollution controls, and informal feedback from members of Congress, the EPA published its final regulations, which were not as strict as originally proposed. Some environmental groups sued, claiming the EPA had been influenced by informal comments and that such comments to agency heads are illegal or should be in the public record. Did the regulation stand? [*Sierra Club* v. *Costle*, 657 F.2d 298 (D.C. Cir., 1981)]

9. The Sierra Club sued the Secretary of the Interior for allowing the lease of federal land to be used for a ski resort (after studying the issue and deciding such use was appropriate). The club claimed that the change in the use of the land would adversely change the area's aesthetics and ecology. The court of appeals held that the club did not have standing to sue. Was that correct? [*Sierra Club* v. *Morton*, 405 U.S. 727, 92 S.Ct. 1361 (1972)]

10. Under the Immigration Reform and Control Act of 1986, an alien illegally present in the United States who wanted to get permission to reside in the country permanently had to apply for temporary resident status by showing that he had a continuous physical presence in the country for a certain time period. The Immigration and Naturalization Service issued regulations concerning "continuous

physical presence" and other terms of the statute. Class actions were filed on behalf of aliens who would not be eligible for legalization under the regulations issued. Could the suits go forward? [*Reno* v. *Catholic Social Services*, 509 U.S. 43, 113 S.Ct. 2485 (1993)]

11. A freedom of information request was filed with the Nuclear Regulatory Commission for information about nuclear plant operations that had been provided voluntarily by the plants to the commission on the agreement that the information be kept confidential, even though it did not involve trade secrets. The commission refused to release the information, claiming it would injure its working relationship with the plant operators. Was this a proper reason to refuse the information request? [*Critical Mass Energy Project* v. *Nuclear Regulatory Comm.*, 731 F.2d 554 (D.C. Cir., 1990)]

POLICY QUESTION

12. Are the regulatory reform measures—cost-benefit analysis and sunset laws— good ideas, or are they likely to cause more problems than they solve? Do they allow private interests to have more say in the continued existence of regulations?

ETHICS QUESTIONS

13. Most regulatory matters are settled informally; only a small number result in litigation. When a company is in a dispute with a federal agency, it knows that if it does not reach a settlement, there can be costly litigation. From the perspective of the government agency, the litigation is costless—the taxpayers foot the bill. Agencies know that the threat of costly litigation enhances their chance of extracting a settlement from the company. Should the government use this leverage to extract more in a settlement than it knows it would be likely to get in a court-resolved dispute?

14. Suppose you are an administrator at the Environmental Protection Agency. It has been reported that a plant in a small town is in violation of the environmental laws. If you enforce the laws' requirements, the plant will be forced to shut down. The plant is the major source of employment for the town, and its closure would impose severe economic hardships. Should that fact play a role in regulatory enforcement?

15. The Environmental Protection Agency requires your company to self-report pollution discharges daily. It is your job to make those reports. The reports could be easily fudged if the company exceeded its designated limits. Excessive discharges would cost the company $25,000 for each day its limit is exceeded. One morning, your superior forgot to start the pollution control device, and the designated amount of pollution was exceeded. Your superior strongly implies that you should fudge the figures. You are worried that if you don't, you might be fired. Should you report the correct figures to the EPA? Would your answer be different if you knew whether or not the excessive pollution caused any damage?

INTERNET ASSIGNMENT

Most people probably are not aware of the scale of government agencies' role in modern commercial life. Unless an agency far exceeds its statutory mandate, its actions can carry the force of law. *See, e.g., Chevron, U.S.A., Inc.* v. *Natural Resources Defenses Council, Inc.*, 467 U.S. 837 (1984). To gain a sense of the number and scope of federal agencies, use your Web browser to look around in the Federal Web Locator site maintained by Villanova University (http://www.law.vill.edu/ Fed-Agency/fedwebloc.html) and follow some of the hyperlinks found there. Once you have a basic familiarity with the names and mandates of the various agencies, answer the following questions.

Suppose you plan to start a new business, say a medium-sized manufacturing facility on the outskirts of a medium-sized city. Your plan is to raise most of your start up money from commercial sources (through debt and equity instruments), to acquire and develop roughly ten acres of idle land, appoint it with appropriate improvements and equipment, hire roughly fifty to one hundred employees, and to then set about the business of manufacturing your products for sale in interstate commerce. Even before your first widget rolls off the line, how many federal agencies, and which ones, will have some measure of regulatory jurisdiction over your enterprise? Suppose the land you select has a small creek along the back boundary, and that some twenty-five years ago your site, while it was still a farm, was the final resting place for several old automobiles and some farm operating equipment. Assume also that your proposed site is the home of several indigenous species of animal life—perhaps rabbits, field mice, birds, minnows and frogs. What is the scope of agency regulation for your proposed site even before you start hiring workers and manufacturing your products? Which agencies will acquire additional regulatory oversight over your operations once you are ready to begin hiring and manufacturing? As regards future agency action—formal and informal rule making, public comment opportunities, policy changes, enforcement actions—how will you determine for which agencies you will need to retain counsel to advise you?

PART 2

Elements of Traditional Business Law

Common-law rules evolved over centuries as judges and juries responded to changes in business and social norms. The common law is the traditional basis of private legal relationships that dominate the business legal environment. While the common law evolved differently than the major codes of other nations, the basic elements of how private relationships are governed are similar around the world. Over the years, the common law has been modified and codified in various statutes and regulations.

These chapters review the core topics of what traditionally has been called business law. This part of the law concerns the rights and obligations of parties to each other in business formation and in various working relationships.

Contracts, especially those formed in domestic and in international sales of goods, are a key part of business relationships. To make contracts work, credit is often extended and various forms of negotiable instruments are often used. We begin by studying tort law—the common-law obligations and rights we have to protect the sanctity of each others' person and property. We also study the law of property itself—physical property and, of rapidly growing importance, intellectual property.

CHAPTER 7

Intentional Torts and Negligence Torts, legal wrongs for which remedies may be sought, provide common-law protection for our persons and our property. The two major branches of tort law and the categories of torts within the branches are covered.

CHAPTER 8

Business Torts This chapter focuses on torts that are peculiar to business. Of all the possible torts that may arise, the one area that involves the most money and has changed rapidly is that of product liability.

CHAPTER 9

Property Real property, such as land and buildings, is the kind of property that was considered the most important historically. However, in recent decades, as the information age has evolved, intellectual property has become the most important asset of most people and businesses.

CHAPTER 10

Contracts Business relationships are based on contracts. This chapter considers the key elements the courts look for when a contract is contested to determine the rights and obligations that may have been created.

CHAPTER 11

Domestic and International Sales The Uniform Commercial Code dominates the law of sales in the United States, so we see how these rules can differ from traditional contract law, and we see how the rapidly growing area of international sales is often governed by particular contract rules.

CHAPTER 12

Negotiable Instruments, Credit, and Bankruptcy Most business contracts involve payment by one of the common forms of negotiable instruments that evolved over time to facilitate exchange. Similarly, businesses often grant credit, which can have a variety of terms and, at times, be associated with the difficult problem of bankruptcy.

CHAPTER 13

Agency Business often involves the delegation of authority to various parties to perform certain duties. In recent years, the use of independent contractors has increased in importance, so we must distinguish that role from that of an employee.

CHAPTER 14

Business Organizations Businesses are, at base, a set of contractual obligations. The major forms of business, including partnerships and corporations, are arrangements that evolved to suit the needs of parties doing business. The range of organizational opportunities for businesses is explored.

CHAPTER 7

Intentional Torts and Negligence

The law of torts is the most quickly changing part of the common law. Like other parts of the common law, the law of torts evolves through case decisions that reflect social values, community standards, and the way we deal with each other in the current environment. In recent years, tort law has become a major issue for business; tort liability is a significant expense, and some claim that tort judgments bear little relation to reality.

The biggest jury verdict in history was a tort case. In 1984, Pennzoil agreed to buy a large share of Getty Oil. Texaco, knowing of the agreement, offered more money for Getty and got Getty's owners to refuse Pennzoil's offer in favor of Texaco's. Pennzoil then sued Texaco for the common-law tort of inducement of breach of contract. A Houston jury awarded Pennzoil $10.5 billion in damages. Texaco did not have that much cash and could not raise it, so a settlement of about one-third the verdict was agreed upon. While the dollars in that case are huge, the point we see in many tort cases is the same—juries often place a high value on the enforcement of legal rights.

The Scope of Tort Law

Tort has many definitions. The word is derived from the Latin *tortus* (twisted) and means "wrong" in French. Although the word faded from common use years ago, it has acquired a technical meaning in the law. A *tort* is generally defined as a civil wrong, other than a breach of contract, for which the law provides a remedy. Tort is a breach of a duty owed to another that causes harm. That is, liability is imposed for conduct that unreasonably interferes with the interests of another.

ROLE OF TORT LAW

Many accidents occur each year that result in personal injury and property damage. To have a legal action in tort, the injury sustained to person or property must legally be the consequence of the actions of another. In a tort action, the person or business whose interests have been invaded sues the party allegedly responsible for losses suffered.

As discussed in Chapter 1, one act may result in both a criminal case and a tort case. The criminal action is brought by the government against the alleged wrongdoer for violating a rule imposed by the legislature. The victim of the crime is a witness in the criminal case. The victim may be happy to see the criminal prosecuted, but the criminal case does not provide compensation to the injured party. That party would be the plaintiff in the tort suit, hiring an attorney to bring suit to seek compensation for injuries wrongfully inflicted by the defendant (the accused criminal in the criminal case). In practice, it is not common for there to be both a criminal case and a tort case evolving from the same incident, since most criminals do not have enough assets to be worth suing in tort.

Like all areas of the common law, tort law is determined in each state (although individual suits may be tried in federal court). The rules vary from state to state, but the principles are similar among all states. Tort law is private law. It is intended, as the Alaska Supreme Court has said, to place an injured party "as nearly as possible in the position he would have occupied had it not been for the defendant's tort." It is also expected that fear of payment for torts will deter injurious behavior by others. In a small percentage of tort suits, punitive damages are awarded in addition to compensation for injury. Punitive damages are intended to punish the defendant (financially) for malicious behavior and to send a message that such behavior will not be tolerated.

BUSINESS AND TORTS

As we are about to review, torts are classified on the basis of how the harm was inflicted: intentionally, negligently, or without fault (strict liability). Regardless of how a tort is classified, businesses become involved in a tort action in one of three ways: (1) a person is harmed by the actions of a business or its employees, (2) a person is harmed by a product manufactured or distributed by the business, or (3) a business is harmed by the wrongful actions of another business or person. The principles of tort law covered in this chapter are applicable to persons in everyday life, but the focus is on business applications. Chapter 8 discusses torts that are peculiar to business.

Intentional Torts against Persons

A major category of tort liability is based on the intent of the defendant to interfere with the plaintiff's interests. *Intentional torts* are classified on the basis of the interests the law seeks to protect: personal rights and property rights. We first review intentional torts against persons and then look at intentional torts against property. As would be expected, the law imposes a greater degree of responsibility on tortfeasors (persons who commit torts) for intentional acts that harm protected interests than for unintentional acts. As Justice Holmes said, it is the difference between kicking a dog and tripping over a dog. In both cases, the dog gets kicked, but one case is intentional, while the other case is careless.

ESTABLISHING INTENT

Several elements are needed to establish the legal requirement of *intent*. First is the state of mind of the defendant, which means that the person knew what he was doing. Second is that the person knew, or should have known, the possible consequences of his act. Third is having in mind the knowledge that certain results are likely to occur.

While these elements are wrapped together, there may be legal differences between act, intent, and motive. To be liable, a defendant must have acted. That is, there must have been voluntary physical actions. An act is to be distinguished from its consequences. Intent is the fact of doing an act, such as firing a gun. The motive—why the person wanted to fire the gun—is legally distinct from the act. If Donna points a gun and fires into a crowd of people, that is a wrongful act for which she may be held liable regardless of her motives. For her to say that she had no bad motive—that when she fired the gun she really wished no one would be hurt—does not relieve her of liability. Under tort law, she acted voluntarily, she should have known what the consequences of her act could be, and she is presumed to have intended the consequences of her act.

Intentional torts are based on *willful misconduct*—acts that invade protected interests. Intentional torts occur when a jury finds that, under the circumstances, a reasonable person would have known that harmful consequences were likely to follow from the act. Intent matters much less than the act of invading the interests of another person. Even in cases in which the defendant did not have a bad motive (i.e., was playing a trick), if the tortfeasor intended to commit the act that inflicted injury on another, the required intent would be present for tort liability.

Business Liability

A business is most likely to become involved in a lawsuit for an intentional tort through the wrongful actions of an employee. As discussed further in Chapter 13, a business is liable under the law of agency if a tort results from an activity carried out within the scope of a worker's employment.

Intentional torts involving interference with personal rights include assault, battery, false imprisonment, infliction of emotional (mental) distress, invasion of privacy, and defamation. However, since the law of tort is always evolving, many cases have arisen over the years that do not clearly fit in a particular category.

ASSAULT

Assault is intentional conduct directed at a person that places the person in fear of immediate bodily harm or offensive contact. The protected interest is freedom from fear of harmful or offensive contact. Actual contact with the body is not necessary. For example, pointing a gun or swinging a club at a person can constitute an assault. The requirement of "fear" is satisfied if a reasonable person under the same or similar circumstances would have apprehension of bodily harm or offensive contact. An essential element of this tort is that the person in danger of harm or injury must know of the danger and be apprehensive of its threat. If, for example, a person points a gun at another while the other person is sleeping, there is no assault since there was no fear of harm while sleeping.

BATTERY

Battery, which is the issue in the *Funeral Services by Gregory* case, is an unlawful touching—intentional physical contact without consent. The protected interest is freedom from unpermitted contact with one's person. One's person includes clothing and other things identified as a part of a person. The contact is not limited to direct touching of another. Contact may be made with anything used by the tortfeasor, such as a stick or a gun. Even if the touching does not cause actual physical harm, it is unlawful if it would offend a reasonable person's sense of dignity.

Funeral Services by Gregory, Inc. v. Bluefield Community Hospital
Supreme Court of Appeals of West Virginia
186 W.Va. 424, 413 S.E.2d 79 (1991)

CASE BACKGROUND *"John Doe" died of AIDS at Bluefield Community Hospital. The hospital did not tell the mortician, plaintiff Gregory, of the cause of death. Since an autopsy had been done at the hospital, the body was very bloody but Gregory was not concerned because the death certificate did not list AIDS or infectious disease as cause of death. He wore protective clothing while embalming Doe and, when finished, burned the clothing and washed his hands and arms with Clorox. Later the hospital told Gregory the cause of death.*

Gregory asserted that had he known the truth, he would have recommended cremation and a closed-casket funeral without embalming or would have used more careful procedures if embalming was requested by the family. Gregory sued the hospital for battery for its knowingly allowing him to be touched by an AIDS-infected body. He and his wife also sued for mental distress because of their fear of being infected with AIDS. The trial court dismissed their claims, and they appealed.

CASE DECISION Brotherton, Justice.

* * *

The *Restatement (Second) of Torts*, §13(a) and (b) (1965), states that: "[a]n actor is subject to liability to another for battery if (a) he acts intending to cause a harmful or offensive contact with the person of the other or a third person, or an imminent apprehension of such a contact, and (b) a harmful contact with the person of the other directly or indirectly results." The word "intent" in the *Restatement* denotes that "the actor desires to cause the consequences of his act, or that he believes that the consequences are substantially certain to result from it."

In this case, the hospital simply released the body to the plaintiff's funeral home for preparation. The plaintiff alleges that this act resulted in an "offensive touching" which constituted a battery, because he was subsequently "exposed to body fluids and mucus membranes of the deceased 'John Doe' which were infected with the AIDS virus thereby being exposed by the extreme and outrageous conduct of the defendants intentionally or recklessly to the AIDS virus. . . ." However, the plaintiff does not allege that the hospital acted with the intention of causing him a harmful or offensive contact, nor is there any evidence which might support such a charge. . . .

We also note that the plaintiff did not allege that he suffered actual physical impairment as a result of what he refers to as an "exposure" to the AIDS virus. All of the plaintiff's claims are based solely on a fear of contracting the AIDS virus. However, Gregory has been tested for AIDS antibodies on four occasions with negative results. Thus, there is no evidence that Gregory has been infected with the Human Immunodeficiency Virus (HIV), a retrovirus that causes AIDS.

* * *

[W]e conclude that if a suit for damages is based solely upon the plaintiff's fear of contacting AIDS, but there is no evidence of an actual exposure to the virus, the fear is unreasonable, and this Court will not recognize a legally compensable injury.

* * *

For the reasons set forth above, the orders of the Circuit Court of Mercer County dismissing the appellants' claims are hereby affirmed.

QUESTIONS FOR ANALYSIS

1. Suppose, as happens to hospital workers, the mortician cut himself while embalming the body, thereby infecting him with the virus. Would he have a claim?
2. Why was there no claim of assault in this case?

Assault and Battery

Assault and battery are often linked, although they are separate offenses in many jurisdictions. The principal distinction is the difference between the requirements of apprehension of an offensive physical contact for an assault and of actual physical contact for a battery. The two torts may exist without each other. An individual may strike another who is asleep, for example, thus committing battery but not assault. On the other hand, an individual may shoot at another and miss, thereby creating an assault but no battery. In common discussion, and in some courts, the term *assault* is used to cover assault and battery.

Defenses

There are situations in which assault and battery are permitted. The law recognizes that a person allegedly committing these torts may have a *defense*—a legally recognized justification for the defendant's actions—that relieves a person of liability. Common defenses to assault and battery are consent, privilege, self-defense, and defense of others and of property. These defenses can be used in any tort but are most common in cases of assault.

Consent occurs when the injured party gives permission to the alleged wrongdoer to interfere with a personal right. Consent may be either expressed or implied by words or conduct. An example of consent in battery includes voluntary participation in a contact sport such as boxing or football.

A *privilege* can give immunity from liability. It can excuse what would have been a tort had the defendant not acted to further an interest of social importance that is entitled to legal protection. For example, the acts of judges are done under authority of law and so, even if malicious, are immune from tort.

Self-defense is a privilege based on the need to allow people who are attacked to take steps to protect themselves. The force allowed is that which a reasonable person may have used under the circumstances. A person may take a life to protect his own life, but the measures used in self-defense should be no more than are needed to provide protection. If an assailant has been stopped and made helpless, a person has no right to inflict a beating at that point.

Similarly, *in defense of others* or *in defense of property* one may use force reasonable under the circumstances. If someone is being threatened with an attack, other persons have a privilege to defend the victim by using force against the assailant. We have the right to defend our property—to keep others from stealing or abusing it—but again, the force used must be reasonable under the circumstances. Since the law places a higher value on human life than on property, it is unlikely that killing or inflicting serious bodily injury on someone invading property will be allowed. It is not reasonable to shoot a person stealing hubcaps from your car.

FALSE IMPRISONMENT

The tort of *false imprisonment* (or *false arrest*) is the intentional holding or detaining of a person within boundaries if the person is harmed by such detention. The protected interest is freedom from restraint of movement. The detention need not be physical; verbal restraints, such as threats, may be the basis of an action for false imprisonment.

Businesses face false imprisonment suits from the detention of suspected shoplifters. It is not uncommon for a suspected shoplifter who is innocent to sue the business for false imprisonment. Shoplifters cost stores billions of dollars each year, but such suits deter stores in their attempts to catch shoplifters.

Defense

As a result of business lobbying, most states have antishoplifting statutes, which provide businesses with an affirmative defense to a charge of false imprisonment for detaining a shoplifter. The store must have reasonable cause to believe the person has shoplifted, and the person must be delayed for a reasonable time and in a reasonable manner. That defense failed K-Mart in the following case.

Caldwell v. K-Mart Corp.
Court of Appeals of South Carolina
306 S.C. 27, 410 S.E.2d 21 (1991)

CASE BACKGROUND *A store security employee watched Patricia Caldwell while she shopped at K-Mart. Caldwell carried a large purse and was seen studying various small items. At times, she bent down out of sight of the guard, who thought she was putting things in her purse. When she left the store, the guard approached her in the parking lot and said he thought she had store merchandise in her purse, although he did not know what specific items. Caldwell opened her purse, and although the guard saw no store merchandise, he asked her to come back into the store with him. Caldwell and the guard walked around the store for about fifteen minutes to the areas where Caldwell had been shopping. The guard said six or seven times that he had seen Caldwell put things in her purse. Caldwell left the store when another employee said she could go. Caldwell sued K-Mart for false imprisonment. The jury awarded her $75,000 in damages plus $100,000 in punitive damages. K-Mart appealed.*

CASE DECISION Cureton, Judge.

* * *

False imprisonment is defined as a deprivation of a person's liberty without justification. To establish a cause of action, the evidence must demonstrate (1) the defendant restrained the plaintiff, (2) the restraint was intentional, and (3) the restraint was unlawful.

* * *

Caldwell's counsel conceded at oral argument that the initial stop in the parking lot was probably justified but asserted the actions of the guard in walking Caldwell through the store and continuing to accuse her of taking merchandise were not justified as part of a reasonable investigation. We think these facts created an issue for the jury to resolve and the trial judge properly denied the motions of K-Mart for directed verdict, judgment notwithstanding the verdict, and new trial based upon the weight of the evidence.

During the course of the trial Caldwell sought to introduce portions of the K-Mart loss prevention manual into evidence. The portion in question dealt with shoplifting arrests. K-Mart argued the manual was not relevant because the [shoplifting defense] statute, and not the manual, governed the standard by which its conduct was to be judged. The court admitted the manual into evidence. We find no abuse of discretion.

Evidence is relevant when it logically tends to prove or disprove a material issue in dispute. One of the material issues in dispute was the reasonableness of K-Mart's actions in investigating the suspected shoplifting. The manual contained guidelines for employees in making shoplifting arrests. For example, it stated as a basic step that before making an apprehension the employee "must see the shoplifter take our property." It also stated the employee should watch the suspected shoplifter continuously and only apprehend the person after he has had an opportunity to pay and is outside the store. Any apprehension should be made in the presence of a witness. Further, any interrogation should be done in privacy in the Loss Prevention Office.

While each case must be dealt with on its own facts, the loss prevention manual was relevant on the material issue of the reasonableness of K-Mart's actions.

* * *

The jury awarded Caldwell $75,000 actual damages and $100,000 punitive damages in the false imprisonment claim. K-Mart contends the amount of the verdict necessarily demonstrates the jury was motivated by caprice, passion, and/or other considerations not supported by the evidence. It, thus, argues the trial court erred in denying its motion for remittitur or alternatively a new trial based upon the excessiveness of the verdict.

As to actual damages, the evidence indicates Caldwell was detained for approximately fifteen minutes. She was not touched or searched. After merchandise was not found in her pocketbook outside the store, she was escorted through the store in the various areas in which she had been shopping. During this time she testified the security guard continued to state to her that she had taken K-Mart merchandise. Testimony indicates she was emotionally upset for several days and continued to be upset by the incident. There was testimony Caldwell experienced discomfort in going into stores up to the time of trial. Testimony also indicated the incident caused Caldwell to move her residence from Newberry to Columbia.

* * *

When a party seeks a new trial based upon the amount of the jury verdict, the trial court and appellate court are guided by certain principles. If a verdict is excessive in the sense it may be considered unduly liberal, the trial judge alone has the power and responsibility to set aside the verdict absolutely or reduce it by granting a new trial nisi. The appellate court will not set aside a verdict for undue liberality. On the other hand if a verdict is so grossly excessive and shockingly disproportionate that it indicates the jury was motivated by passion, caprice, prejudice, or other consideration not founded on the evidence then it is the duty of the trial court and the appellate court to set aside the verdict absolutely.

Although this is undoubtedly a large verdict, we are not convinced it was motivated by caprice, passion, prejudice, or other improper considerations. Affirmed.

QUESTIONS FOR ANALYSIS

1. K-Mart argued that, as a matter of law, it was not reasonable for the jury to find that fifteen minutes spent walking around the store discussing the matter was false imprisonment. Would you agree that if the time is short and there is no force there should be no tort action?
2. When arguing for damages, Caldwell's attorney told the jury that K-Mart was worth $5 billion. Should the worth of the defendant be taken into consideration in damage estimation?

INFLICTION OF EMOTIONAL DISTRESS

The tort of *infliction of emotional distress* (*mental distress*) involves intentional conduct by a person that is so outrageous it creates severe mental or emotional distress in another. The protected interest is peace of mind. This cause of action protects a person from conduct that goes way beyond the bounds of decency, but not from

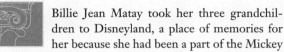

Oh, No! Goofy Lost His Head

Billie Jean Matay took her three grandchildren to Disneyland, a place of memories for her because she had been a part of the Mickey Mouse Club troupe that performed at Disneyland's 1955 opening. After their day at the park, Matay and her grandchildren were robbed by a gunman when they returned to their car. Security guards took them to back offices for questioning. There, the grandchildren discovered "the reality that the Disney characters were, in fact, make-believe." Matay sued Disneyland for emotional distress for the trauma of seeing the Disney characters out of costume and for poor security.

Source: *National Law Journal*

annoying behavior, petty insults, or bad language. Courts used to be reluctant to find this tort without some physical injury. Most courts moved away from that requirement as better understanding of psychological harm developed. Many states also provide compensation to third parties based on emotional distress. For example, a Louisiana court provided compensation for emotional distress to a wife who found that her comatose husband had suffered rat bites while in bed at a hospital where he was being treated.

Bill collectors, landlords, and insurance adjusters are often involved in emotional-distress suits. Badgering, late-night phone calls, profanity, threats, and name-calling lay the groundwork for potential emotional-distress suits. Employers have been sued more often in recent years for the distress suffered by employees who have been subjected to extreme statements or harassment at work. The *Monsanto* case is an example of an employee subjected to profane treatment.

White v. Monsanto Company
Supreme Court of Louisiana
585 So.2d 1205 (1991)

CASE BACKGROUND *Irma White, a church-going woman in her late forties with grown children, worked at a Monsanto refinery. She and other employees were waiting for safety equipment so they could transfer a chemical from a large container into smaller ones. Shop rules required employees to clean up an area while waiting for equipment. White did cleanup work, but the other employees sat waiting for the equipment. Supervisor McDermott saw that the group was idle and yelled at the workers, referring to them as "m***f***s," accusing them of sitting on their "f***ing asses," and threatening to "show them the gate." The tirade lasted about a minute, and McDermott left the area.*

White was upset and experienced pain in her chest, pounding in her head, and difficulty breathing. She went to McDermott's office to discuss the incident. McDermott said he apologized to her; she said he did not. White went to the company nurse, who suggested that she see a doctor. Her physician met her at the hospital. White had chest pains, shortness of breath, and cold, clammy hands. Fearing a heart attack, the doctor admitted White to the hospital for three days for tests and observation. A heart attack was ruled out, and the diagnosis was acute anxiety reaction—a panic attack.

White returned to work. She was paid her regular pay while on sick leave. Her medical bills of $3,200 were *paid by the company's medical benefits program. White becomes upset thinking or dreaming about the incident and has taken prescribed medicine.*

White sued Monsanto and McDermott, alleging that McDermott's conduct inflicted mental anguish and emotional distress. The jury awarded White $60,000. Defendants appealed to the court of appeal, which affirmed. Defendants appealed.

CASE DECISION Hall, Justice.

* * *

One who by extreme and outrageous conduct intentionally causes severe emotional distress to another is subject to liability for such emotional distress, and if bodily harm to the other results from it, for such bodily harm.

Thus, in order to recover for intentional infliction of emotional distress, a plaintiff must establish (1) that the conduct of the defendant was extreme and outrageous; (2) that the emotional distress suffered by the plaintiff was severe; and (3) that the defendant desired to inflict severe emotional distress or knew that severe emotional distress would be certain or substantially certain to result from his conduct.

The conduct must be so outrageous in character, and so extreme in degree, as to go beyond all possible bounds of decency, and to be regarded as atrocious and utterly intolerable in a civilized community. Liability does not extend to mere insults, indignities, threats, annoyances, petty oppressions, or other trivialities. Persons must necessarily be expected to be hardened to a certain amount of rough language, and to occasional acts that are definitely inconsiderate and unkind. Not every verbal encounter may be converted into a tort; on the contrary, "some safety valve must be left through which irascible tempers may blow off relatively harmless steam." . . .

Liability can arise only when the actor desired to inflict severe emotional distress or where he knows that such distress is certain or substantially certain to result from his conduct. . . . The conduct must be intended or calculated to cause severe emotional dis-

tress and not just some lesser degree of fright, humiliation, embarrassment, worry, or the like.

Applying these precepts of law to the facts of the instant case, we find that plaintiff has failed to establish her right to recover from the defendants for an intentional tort.

The one-minute outburst of profanity directed at three employees by a supervisor in the course of dressing them down for not working as he thought they should does not amount to such extreme and outrageous conduct as to give rise to recovery for intentional infliction of emotional distress. . . . Such conduct, although crude, rough and uncalled for, was not tortious. . . . The brief, isolated instance of improper behavior by the supervisor who lost his temper was the kind of unpleasant experience persons must expect to endure from time to time. The conduct was not more than a person of ordinary sensibilities can be expected to endure. The tirade was directed to all three employees and not just to plaintiff specifically. . . .

The duty here was to not engage in extreme or outrageous conduct intended or calculated to cause severe emotional distress. The duty was not breached because the conduct was not extreme or outrageous to a degree calculated to cause severe emotional distress to a person of ordinary sensibilities and the supervisor did not intend to inflict emotional distress of a severe nature, nor did he believe such a result was substantially certain to follow from his conduct.

For the reasons expressed in this opinion, the judgments of the district court and court of appeal are reversed, and judgment is rendered in favor of defendants dismissing plaintiff's suit, at plaintiff's cost.

QUESTIONS FOR ANALYSIS

1. Would it have made any difference if White had suffered a heart attack? What if she had suffered no physical distress, but only mental distress?
2. Should men and women be held to different standards in such matters? More women than men are likely to be upset by such instances. Should courts take into account differences in sensitivities?

INVASION OF PRIVACY

The tort of *invasion of privacy* is a fairly recent development in tort law. The concept behind the tort is a person's right to solitude and to be free from unwarranted public exposure. The tort of invasion of privacy may be committed in a number of ways:

1. The use of a person's name or picture without permission (which can make advertisers and marketing companies liable)
2. The intrusion into a person's solitude (illegal wiretapping or searches of a residence; harassment by unwanted and continual telephoning)
3. The placing of a person in a false light (publishing of a story with serious misinformation)
4. The public exposure of facts that are private in nature (such as public disclosure of a person's drug use or debts)

Defenses

In addition to providing common-law protection, some states have statutes to recognize a right to privacy. In either case, the right to privacy is largely waived when a person becomes a public figure, such as an entertainer, a politician, or a sports personality. In addition, the publication of information about an individual taken from public files and records does not constitute an invasion of privacy. The *Globe International* case concerns invasion of privacy; the claim of emotional distress is included, which is common in privacy cases.

Peoples Bank & Trust Company of Mountain Home v. Globe International, Inc.
United States District Court, W. Dist. of Arkansas
786 F.Supp. 791 (1992)

CASE BACKGROUND *Nellie Mitchell ran a newsstand on the town square of Mountain Home, Arkansas. When she was ninety-five years old, the Sun, a supermarket tabloid paper published by Globe, published a photograph of her, taken from a ten-year-old news story, with a story entitled:*

SPECIAL DELIVERY
World's oldest newspaper carrier, 101, quits because she's pregnant!
I guess walking all those miles kept me young

The story, written as if fact, is about "papergal Audrey Wiles" in Stirling, Australia, who had been delivering papers for ninety-four years. Readers are told that Wiles became pregnant by "Will," a "reclusive millionaire" she met on her newspaper route. "I used to put Will's paper in the door when it rained, and one thing just kind of led to another." A photograph of Nellie "trudging down the road with a large stack of papers under her arm" is used in conjunction with the story.

Testimony at trial was that most of defendant's articles are created "TOH," or "top of the head," in the words of the editor of the Sun. That is, the authors, none of whom use their real names, are given a headline and a picture and then "make up" the accompanying stories.

When the picture of Mrs. Mitchell was selected, it was assumed she was dead.

The jury found that defendant's conduct had invaded Mitchell's privacy by placing her in a false light and was an intentional infliction of emotional distress by the tort of outrage. The jury awarded $650,000 in compensatory damages and $850,000 in punitive damages. Defendant moved for new trial or for damage awards to be overturned or for verdict to be set aside as a matter of law.

CASE DECISION Waters, Chief Judge.

* * *

With regard to the extent of emotional distress suffered by Mrs. Mitchell, she testified that she was mad, upset, embarrassed, and humiliated by the article. Further, Mrs. Mitchell indicated she had been teased about being pregnant. Betty Mitchell, Nellie Mitchell's daughter, testified that her mother "almost suffered a stroke." There was also testimony to the effect that Mrs. Mitchell attempted to buy up the papers so others could not see them. . . . Defendant argues that Mrs. Mitchell never went to a doctor, didn't miss work, and in general did not alter her normal daily activities. . . .

But the answer to the argument lies in the fact that the essence of the tort of outrage is the injury to the plaintiff's emotional well-being because of outrageous treatment by the defendant. If the conduct is sufficiently flagrant to give rise to the tort, then the injury the law seeks to redress is the anguish itself and it need not rest . . . on more demonstrative loss or injury. . . .

It may be, as defendant in essence argues, that Mrs. Mitchell does not show a great deal of obvious injury, but a reasonable juror might conclude, after hearing the evidence and viewing the *Sun* issue in question, that Nellie Mitchell's experience could be likened to that of a person who had been dragged slowly through a pile of untreated sewage. After that person had showered . . . there would be little remaining visible evidence of the ordeal which the person endured . . . but few would doubt that substantial damage had been inflicted by the one doing the dragging. This court is certainly in no better position to determine what that is "worth" than 8 jurors picked from the citizenry of . . . Arkansas to hear and decide the case.

* * *

The right to recover for an invasion of privacy is conditioned upon the complaining party's demonstrating that (1) the false light in which he was placed by the publicity would be highly offensive to a reasonable person, and (2) that the defendant had knowledge of or acted in reckless disregard as to the falsity of the publicized matter and the false light in which the plaintiff would be placed. . . .

The court cannot say as a matter of law that the article is incapable of being interpreted as portraying actual events or facts regarding the plaintiff. The "facts" conveyed are not so inherently impossible or fantastic that they could not be understood to convey actual facts. Nor can we deny that no person could take them seriously. Moreover, even if the headline and certain facts contained in the article could not be

reasonably believed, other facts e.g., the implication of sexual promiscuity, could reasonably be believed. . . .

The defendant could very easily indicate to its readers in some fashion that the material conveyed in the *Sun* is fiction if it really intended that its readers recognize that the articles are false and made up fantasy. . . . [I]t could be inferred from the manner or publication that the defendant intends its readers to believe its articles are conveying actual facts or at the very least leave the reader in doubt as to what portions are factual and what portions are pure fantasy.

* * *

. . . the defendant's motion will be denied.

CASE NOTE   The court of appeal upheld the verdict but found the compensatory damage award to be "shockingly inflated," since there was "no evidence of adverse effects on Mitchell's health and no evidence of lost earnings, permanent injury, medical expenses, diminution of earning capacity, or future pain and suffering." Mitchell was "angry, upset, humiliated, embarrassed, depressed and disturbed" by the article. The trial court was ordered to reconsider compensatory damages. Punitive damages were upheld as within the discretion of the jury and judge.

QUESTIONS FOR ANALYSIS

1. Is it sensible for the judge to say that a jury could find it believable that a 101-year-old woman could be pregnant? Would not a reasonable person know the story was nonsense, like other stories in the same issue of the *Sun*, such as "Farmer Becomes a Millionaire Making Whips for Wife Beaters," "Students Kill Teacher with Voodoo Doll," and "Farmer Kills Self by Breathing Cow Gas"?

2. Can the damages be justified? What relationship is there between the compensatory damages of $650,000 and the invasion of privacy suffered?

DEFAMATION

The tort of *defamation* is an intentional false communication that injures a person's reputation or good name. If the defamatory communication was spoken, *slander* is the tort. If the communication was in the form of a printing, a writing, a picture, or a radio or television broadcast, the tort is *libel*. The elements that must be shown to exist for both torts to be actionable are

1. Making a false or defamatory statement about another person
2. Publishing or communicating the statement to a third person
3. Causing harm to the person about whom the statement was made

Some statements are considered *defamation per se*. That is, they are presumed by law to be harmful to the person to whom they were directed and therefore require no proof of harm or injury. Statements, for example, that a person has committed a crime, has a sexually communicable disease, or has been improper in carrying out business activities can be dafamatory per se.

Workplace Defamation

Communications by employers about the work performance of past or current employees is a notable source of defamation suits. Whether the suit has merit, as in the *Buck* case, or not, the costs of defending against such actions can be substantial. As a result, many companies have a policy not to provide any information—good or bad—about employees, whether they request it or not.

Frank B. Hall & Company, Inc. v. Buck

Court of Appeals of Texas, Fourteenth District
678 S.W.2d 612 (1984)

CASE BACKGROUND *Buck was a successful insurance salesman when he was hired by Frank B. Hall & Company. During the next several months, Buck generated substantial business and brought several major accounts to the firm. Eckert, Hall's office manager, abruptly fired Buck. Buck sought employment at other insurance firms, but his efforts were fruitless. He hired an investigator, Barber, to discover why Hall had fired him. On the basis of statements made by Eckert, Buck sued Hall for defamation. The jury found for Buck and awarded $605,000 in actual damages and $1.3 million in punitive damages, plus interest, attorney's fees, and court costs. Hall appealed.*

CASE DECISION Junell, Justice.

* * *

Eckert told Barber that Buck was horrible in a business sense, irrational, ruthless, and disliked by office personnel. He described Buck as a "classical sociopath," who would verbally abuse and embarrass Hall employees. Eckert said Buck had stolen files and records from [his previous company]. He called Buck "a zero," "a Jekyll and Hyde person" who was "lacking . . . in scruples."

. . . Burton [president of another insurance firm] testified that Buck had contacted him in the summer of 1977 to discuss employment possibilities. When asked why he was no longer with Frank B. Hall & Co., Buck told Burton that he "really (didn't) know." Because he was seriously interested in hiring Buck, Burton telephoned Eckert to find out the circumstances surrounding Buck's termination. Eckert told Burton, "Larry didn't reach his production goals." Burton, who was very familiar with Buck's exceptional record as a good producer in the insurance business, was surprised at Eckert's response. When pressed for more information, Eckert declined to comment, stating, "I can't go into it." Burton then asked if Eckert would rehire Buck, to which Eckert answered, "No.". . .

Burton testified that Eckert made the statements and that because of Eckert's comments, he was not willing to extend an offer of employment to Buck. He stated, "When I talked to Mr. Eckert at Frank B. Hall agency, he led me to believe that there was something that he was unable to discuss with me" and "(t)here was something that he was unwilling to tell me about that I had to know."

Hall argues . . . there is no evidence . . . that Burton attached any defamatory significance to Eckert's statements. We find the evidence sufficient to show that Burton reasonably understood them in a defamatory sense. . . .

Here, the jury found (1) Eckert made a statement calculated to convey that Buck had been terminated because of serious misconduct; (2) the statement was slanderous or libelous; (3) the statement was made with malice; (4) the statement was published; and (5) damage directly resulted from the statement. The jury also found the statements were not substantially true. The jury thus determined that these statements, which were capable of a defamatory meaning, were understood as such by Burton. The jury is the exclusive judge of the credibility of witnesses and the weight to be given their testimony. In resolving contradictions and conflicts, they may choose to believe all or part or none of the testimony of any one witness in arriving at the finding it concluded was the most reasonable under the evidence.

* * *

The judgment of the trial court is affirmed.

QUESTIONS FOR ANALYSIS

1. What evidentiary requirements do fired employees need to meet in establishing defamation of character?
2. How could Hall have avoided liability for defamation in this case?

Defenses

Truth and privilege are defenses to an action for defamation. If the statement that caused harm to person's reputation is in fact the truth, some states hold that truth is a complete defense regardless of the purpose or intent in publishing the statement. *Truth* is an important defense to a defamation suit.

Depending on the circumstances, three privileges—absolute, conditional, and constitutional—may be used as a defense to a defamation action. *Absolute privilege* is an immunity applied in those situations where public policy favors complete freedom of speech. For example, state legislators in legislative or committee sessions, participants in judicial proceedings, and state and federal government executives in the discharge of their duties have absolute immunity from liability resulting from their statements.

A *conditional privilege* eliminates liability when the false statement was published in good faith and with proper motives, such as a legitimate business purpose.

CYBERLAW

Tort Liability for Internet Servers

 Internet users will do things that are illegal or violate the rights of others. Are the Internet servers liable? In general, no, so long as they were not aware of, or had no reason to be aware of, the improper activity occurring on their system.

In *Zeran* v. *America Online* (129 F.3d 327), a federal appeals court held that AOL cannot be sued for tort liability for a defamatory message that an AOL user sent. The sender may be liable, but AOL was not.

However, in *Marobie-FL, Inc.* v. *Natl. Assn. of Fire Equipment Distributors* (983 F.Supp. 1167), a federal court held that the improper use (infringement) of copyrighted clip art that was distributed by a Web Page owner could result in liability if the server was aware of the infringement and took no steps to prevent distribution of the infringed material. It was to be determined at trial if the server "monitored, controlled, or had the ability to monitor or control the contents of [the violating Web Page]."

Libel in Foreign Courts

 Unlike the United States, many countries do not have constitutional freedom of speech. The news media in the United States can communicate defamatory material about public officials or persons of legitimate public interest as long as the material is provided without actual malice. In the United Kingdom, the news media do not have this extensive privilege. Plaintiffs need show only that the defamatory statement was communicated in the United Kingdom and that their reputation was damaged. To avoid liability, a defendant must demonstrate that the statements made were true or that they had been made either in court or in Parliament.

As a result of this difference in the law of defamation, a number of U.S. communications companies find themselves in foreign courts defending against defamation suits. Although the broadcasts in question may have originated in the United States and may have been rebroadcast in the foreign country without the consent of the U.S. company, the company will not be relieved of liability on that basis alone.

The need to defend libel actions in foreign jurisdictions is not the only issue. U.S. publishers' concern is also with the growing number of libel suits filed by individuals who file them outside the United States to take advantage of the more favorable laws. Most such cases would not likely prevail in U.S. courts. *Time* magazine, NBC, and Dow Jones have faced serious actions in foreign jurisdictions. In each case, the plaintiff selected the foreign court knowing that it could not prevail in the U.S. courts.

Businesses have a privilege to communicate information believed to be true. However, if the plaintiff can show, as in the *Buck* case, that there was malice involved or that broadcasting of false information was intentional, then there is no privilege. Individuals have a conditional privilege to publish defamatory matter to protect their legitimate interests, such as to defend their reputation against defamation by another.

As discussed in Chapter 5, the First Amendment to the Constitution guarantees freedom of speech and freedom of press. This *constitutional privilege* protects members of the press who publish "opinion" material about public officials, public figures, or persons of legitimate public interest. This privilege is lost only if the statement was made with *actual malice*, that is, the false statement was made with reckless disregard for the truth.

MALICIOUS PROSECUTION

Parties who have been defendants in tort suits and have won may have a tort action for *malicious prosecution* against their former plaintiff. This tort may be heard only after the previous tort matter has been settled in court. The party bringing the malicious prosecution claim must show legal malice, that the legal system was used as a weapon, such as filing false charges with the police that result in an innocent person's being arrested or bringing baseless tort actions against someone. As one court said, the essence of malicious prosecution "is the putting of legal process in operation for the mere purpose of vexation or inquiry." As the *Fust* decision shows, the courts do not like to be used as tactical weapons in a dispute that does not relate to genuine legal issues.

Fust v. Francois
Missouri Court of Appeals, Eastern District, Division Three
913 S.W. 2d 38 (1995)

CASE BACKGROUND *Francois owned land in St. Louis next to land owned by Carl and Rita Fust. Francois requested rezoning of his property from residential use to commercial use so that he could build a commercial development. The Fusts, who lived on their land next to the proposed development, actively campaigned against the rezoning. Francois's request was rejected by the county council. Later, Francois offered to buy some of the Fusts' property, which would make his planned development more likely, but his offer was rejected. The two parties had several nasty exchanges of letters threatening assorted legal actions.*

Francois sued the Fusts for trespass on his property, demanding $150,000 in damages. He sued the Fusts for harassment and mental anguish for inciting the neighbors to oppose the development, demanding $450,000 in damages. He sued the Fusts for defamation, claiming that a letter they wrote him and showed to others was an effort to embarrass him and to force him to offer the Fusts a high price for their property; he demanded $400,000 in damages. At trial, the case was dismissed for Francois's failure to comply with the Fusts' discovery requests. Francois then sent the Fusts a letter threatening further legal action.

The Fusts sued for malicious prosecution. The jury awarded $1.1 million in compensatory damages and $1.65 million in punitive damages. The judge reduced the damages to $440,000 compensatory and $660,000 punitive. Francois appealed.

CASE DECISION Rhodes, Judge.

* * *

To succeed in an action for malicious prosecution, the plaintiff has the burden of showing the following: (1) commencement of an earlier suit against plaintiff; (2) instigation of the suit by defendant; (3) termination of the suit in plaintiff's favor; (4) lack of probable cause for the suit; (5) malice by defendant in instituting the suit; and (6) damage to plaintiff resulting from the suit. Francois argues the Fusts failed to satisfy the fourth element.

Probable cause for initiating a civil suit means "a belief in the facts alleged, based on sufficient circumstances to reasonably induce such belief by a person of ordinary prudence in the same situation, plus a reasonable belief by such person that under such facts the claim may be valid under the applicable law."

. . . it is evident Francois made only a minimal attempt to gather the facts and legitimize his claim thereby making his belief unreasonable.

* * *

Looking at the record, there is sufficient evidence that Francois pursued the lawsuit against the Fusts because of an improper motive. The evidence suggests the suit was instituted to get back at the Fusts for their public campaign efforts against the proposed development and their interference with the building of the fence. There is also evidence of Francois' desire to purchase the Fusts' property to facilitate the completion of the project and his initiation of the suit was a way to pressure them to sell. Upon their refusal to sell, a letter was sent at Francois' direction warning of possible environmental problems and threatening liability. When campaigning continued, Francois filed suit. There were no efforts on the part of Francois to resolve the dispute amicably. Rather, the jury could infer that Francois used the courts as a weapon to get the Fusts to conform. When the Fusts denied the settlement proposal, the suit was expanded to add Rita Fust. Upon the involuntary dismissal of the suit, another letter was written by Francois to the Fusts ordering them to stop their activities and threatening another lawsuit if they did not. This evidence taken in totality supports a finding of legal malice. . . .

The judgment is affirmed.

QUESTIONS FOR ANALYSIS

1. Suppose that when Francois sued the Fusts he had presented evidence to the court that showed that they had trespassed on his property. Would that have been enough of a serious prosecution to avoid the outcome of this case?
2. Could the Fusts have sued Francois if he had repeatedly threatened to sue them and told them they were breaking the law but did not actually file suit against them?

Intentional Torts against Property

Some wrongs do not harm people but do harm their property or property interests. Property refers to *real property*—land and things attached to it, such as buildings; *personal property*—a person's possessions other than an interest in land; and *intellectual property*—interests in property created by thinking, such as trade secrets. We discuss the different forms of property in Chapter 9; here we review the torts that interfere with the right to enjoy and control one's property. Tort actions that may be initiated for intentional violations of the property rights of another include trespass to land, nuisance, trespass to personal property, conversion, and misappropriation.

TRESPASS TO LAND

The tort of *trespass to land* is an unauthorized intrusion by a person or a thing on land belonging to another. If the intruder intended to be on another's property, it is irrelevant if the intruder mistakenly thought she owned the land or had permission to be on it. It is not necessary for the property owner to demonstrate actual injury to the property. For example, shooting a gun across another's property may be a trespass to land despite the fact that no physical damage occurs. Land owners have a right of peaceful enjoyment of their property. If, however, a person enters another's property to protect it from damage or to help someone on the property who is in danger, that is a defense against the tort of trespass to land.

The original idea of possession of land included dominion over a space "from the center of the earth to the heavens." A trespass could be committed on, beneath, or above the surface of the land. That rule is much more relaxed today. An airplane flying over a property owner's airspace does not create an action in trespass so long as it is flying at a reasonable altitude.

NUISANCE (PRIVATE AND PUBLIC)

The common law of torts recognizes two kinds of nuisance: private nuisance and public nuisance. A *private nuisance* is an activity that substantially and unreasonably interferes with the use and enjoyment of land. The interference may be physical,

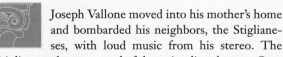

JURIS **prudence?**

Expensive Boom Box

Joseph Vallone moved into his mother's home and bombarded his neighbors, the Stiglianeses, with loud music from his stereo. The Stiglianeses kept a record of the noise disturbances. Over three years, they recorded 100 instances in which Vallone's music was between 60 and 100 decibels in their home. They called the police fifty-one times and finally sued for damages due to private nuisance. The judge imposed $100,000 in damages on Vallone for loss of enjoyment of property and for drop in property value to the Stiglianeses but reduced the damages to $25,000 compensatory and $5,000 punitive because of the court's jurisdiction limit in damages.

Source: *National Law Journal*

such as vibration, the destruction of crops, or the throwing of objects upon the land. The interference may cause discomfort or a health risk from pollution, odors, excessive noise, dust, or noxious fumes. A nuisance may include offensive conditions on neighboring land that injures the occupants' mental peace through the problems those conditions create or threaten to create, or simply through their offensive nature. Most people would find, for example, that the use of the house next door for drug deals is upsetting to their mental peace while in their own houses.

Common-law nuisance actions have been useful for challenging environmental damage. In fact, nuisance actions have challenged virtually every major industrial activity that causes some form of pollution, as we will see in Chapter 17. As the *Pendoley* decision shows, even legitimate businesses may be shut down as a result of nuisance.

Pendoley v. Ferreira
Supreme Judicial Court of Massachusetts, Essex (1963)
345 Mass. 309, 187 N.E.2d 142

CASE BACKGROUND *The Ferreiras started a pig farm in 1949 on twenty-five acres. By 1960, the farm had 850 pigs, 225 piglets, and 10 employees. When the farm was started, the area was sprinkled with residences. By 1960, at least thirty new homes had been built within smelling distance of the farm. Pendoley and other homeowners joined to sue Ferreira for damages for nuisance from the smell of the pig operation and requested an injunction to force the farm to be closed. Trial court awarded nine homeowners an average of $300 each in damages and enjoined the Ferreiras "from operating their piggery . . . in such an unreasonable manner as to cause a stench to emanate therefrom which materially interferes with the reasonable enjoyment of the property of a large number of people living in the vicinity." Ferreira appealed for reversal of the trial court decision; Pendoley appealed for a stronger injunction against the farm operation. (Note that the court had appointed a master, an expert, to gather information about the matter to assist it in its findings.)*

CASE DECISION Cutter, Justice.

* * *

The master's conclusion that a nuisance exists is consistent with common knowledge that the offensive odors of a piggery with a large number of pigs ordinarily cannot be confined to a small area, here twenty-five acres. These owners of residences within a distance to which substantial piggery odors carry are entitled to specific relief against the frequently recur-

rent smells which interfere substantially with the enjoyment of their property 'to the discomfort and annoyance of a large number of residents.' . . .

It can hardly be contended that damages alone will be adequate compensation for the affront to the senses of a large group of homeowners and their families from the nauseating piggery odors. In the circumstances established by the master's report, there exists a substantial, unreasonable interference with the proper enjoyment of their residences which calls for explicit injunctive relief.

* * *

Upon the facts appearing in the master's report, the Ferreiras cannot be expected to correct the offensiveness of the piggery. The master has found that the piggery is very well operated. Substantial and effective improvement can hardly be expected in such a piggery. The Ferreiras' difficulty lies in the inherently offensive aspects of any piggery in a residential neighborhood and in the material discomfort which piggeries cause to others.

. . . we think that the plaintiffs are entitled to have the offensive operation terminated entirely within a reasonable time. Due consideration, however, must be given to the Ferreiras' economic interest in an orderly, rather than a hurried, liquidation of their pigs, and to affording them opportunity to find new premises. Accordingly, a permanent injunction against any operation of the piggery is to be granted, but the final decree is to provide (a) a reasonable opportunity for the Ferreiras to dispose of, or to move, the pigs, structures, and equipment, and (b) that the injunction is to take effect completely only at a specified future date, with provisions for the protection of the plaintiffs in the interim in some practicable manner. . . .

So ordered.

QUESTIONS FOR ANALYSIS

1. The court said that due consideration must be given to the losses the Ferreiras would incur from having to move their legitimate business operation, but then ordered them out within one year. Was this really consideration?

2. A defense raised in nuisance cases such as this one is that the plaintiffs were "coming to the nuisance." That is, since the owners all knew that the pig farm was there when they built their homes, they should not be able to claim a nuisance, unlike if the pig farm had come later. Should this have applied in this case?

A *public nuisance* is an unreasonable interference with a right held in common by the general public. A public nuisance usually involves interference with the public health and welfare. For example, an illegal gambling establishment, bad odors, and the obstruction of a highway would be grounds for a public nuisance action. In addition to having the common law, states have statutes that define various activities as being public nuisances.

Whether an action creates a private or a public nuisance depends upon who is affected by it. The pollution of a well by a factory, for example, is a private nuisance if it interferes only with the rights of landowners living next to the plant. The suit will be brought by those landowners against the owners of the plant. However, if the pollution hurts the public water supply, it is a public nuisance. In such circumstances, the legal representative of the community, such as the county attorney, will bring the action on behalf of the citizens against the polluters.

TRESPASS TO PERSONAL PROPERTY

The intentional and wrongful interference with possession of personal property of another without consent is a *trespass to personal property*. An important element in this tort is that someone has interfered with the right of the owner to exclusive possession and enjoyment of personal property. Liability usually occurs when the trespasser damages the property or deprives the owner of the use of the property for a time. However, if the interference with the personal property of another is warranted, there is a defense to the trespass. Many states have statutes that allow motel operators to hold the personal property of guests who have not paid their bills.

CONVERSION

The tort of *conversion* is an intentional and unlawful control or appropriation of the personal property of another. In contrast to trespass on personal property, conversion requires that the control or appropriation so seriously interferes with the owner's right of control that it justifies payment for the property. Several factors are considered in determining whether the interference warrants a finding of conversion: the extent of dominion or control, the duration of the interference, the damage to the property, and the inconvenience and expense to the owner. As with trespass to land, mistake is not a defense to conversion.

Generally, one who wrongfully acquires possession of another's personal property—by theft, duress, or fraud—is said to have committed the tort of conversion. In most court systems, a bona fide purchaser (a good-faith purchaser who thought the seller was the rightful owner of the property) is liable for conversion if the property was purchased from a thief.

MISAPPROPRIATION

Some forms of intellectual property, including trademarks and trade secrets (valuable information that is protected from revelation to others), are protected by tort law from *misappropriation* or *theft* by others. We will discuss intellectual property in detail in Chapter 9 and will see that much of it is covered by statutes that specify the civil damages that may be had when such property is taken by others without permission. As with other forms of property, owners may sue those who invade their property rights for damages and may ask a court to issue an injunction against further unauthorized use of the property.

Negligence

Unlike intentional torts, torts based on *negligence* protect individuals from harm from others' unintentional but legally careless conduct. As a general rule, we have a duty to conduct ourselves in all activities so as to not create an unreasonable risk of harm or injury to others. Persons and businesses who do not exercise due care in their conduct will be liable for negligence in a wide range of torts if the following elements can be shown by an injured party:

1. The wrongdoer owed a duty to the injured party (often known as the duty of ordinary care).
2. The duty of care owed to the injured party was breached through some act or omission on the part of the wrongdoer (often this breach itself is termed negligence).
3. There is a causal connection between the wrongdoer's negligent conduct and the resulting harm to the injured party.
4. The injured party suffered actual harm or damage recognized as actionable by law as a result of the negligent conduct.

Broadly defined, *negligence* is conduct—an act or omission (failure to act)—by a person that results in harm to another to whom the person owes a duty of care. In contrast to an intentional tort, in negligence the harmful results of a person's conduct are not based on an intended invasion of another person's rights or interests. If the person's conduct creates an *unreasonable risk of harm* to others, such conduct may be termed negligent even though there was no intent to cause harm. Thus, the person who intentionally runs over another person while driving has committed the intentional tort of battery. A person who unintentionally runs over another while driving carelessly may have committed a tort of battery based on negligence.

DUTY OF CARE

In determining whether a person's conduct is negligent, that is, violates the duty of care in any given situation, the law applies a standard of reasonableness. The

Tort Liability in France

In France, as in other code nations, a wrong-doer's liability is established in the Civil Code. In general, the Civil Code makes a wrongdoer liable for damages that result from his or her negligence. In particular, the Civil Code specifically permits recovery for economic loss arising from negligent conduct (quasi-delit). The only limitations on damages are that they must be the immediate and direct consequence of the tort.

The wrongdoer's liability, however, is conditioned on finding the specific elements of the tort. The tort must be defined in the Civil Code, which is more restrictive than the general common-law standards.

First, the harm, either physical or economic, must be specific and certain. Second, there must be a finding of fault on the part of the negligent party. The U.S. doctrine of strict liability in tort is not present to any significant extent in the French system. Third, there must be a finding of causality, and the courts use the notion of proximate cause. Finally, the extent of the harm and the recoverable loss is determined by a judge and not by a jury.

standard is usually stated as *ordinary care* or *due care* as measured against the conduct of a hypothetical person—the *reasonable person*.

The reasonable person represents a standard of how persons in the relevant community ought to behave. If the person is a skilled professional, such as a doctor, financial consultant, or executive, the standard is that of a reasonably skilled, competent, and experienced person who is a qualified member of that profession. In determining whether a person's conduct was negligent, the question is, What would a reasonable qualified person have done under the same or similar circumstances? If the conduct was not that of a reasonable person in the eyes of the jury or the judge, the person has failed the reasonableness test and has acted negligently.

The reasonableness standard or the reasonable person standard is a theoretical concept in law. It describes a person who acts in a reasonable manner under the circumstances. Although the law does not require perfection, errors in judgment must be reasonable or excusable under the circumstances, or negligence will be found, as the *Bethlehem Steel* decision indicates.

Bethlehem Steel Corp. v. Ernst & Whinney
Supreme Court of Tennessee (1991)
822 S.W.2d 592

CASE BACKGROUND *Ernst & Whinney, a national accounting firm, prepared an audited financial report for E.L. Jackson Manufacturing. Ernst knew that Jackson needed the report for Bethlehem to show that Jackson's finances were strong enough so that Bethlehem would sell it steel on credit. The report overstated the financial status of Jackson, which went into bankruptcy owing Bethlehem a substantial sum. Bethlehem sued* *Ernst for damages resulting from negligent preparation of its audit report. The jury awarded Bethlehem $400,000 in damages, but the judge set aside the verdict and ordered a new trial. The court of appeals reversed the order setting aside the damages and affirmed the grant of a new trial. Parties appealed.*

CASE DECISION Reid, Chief Justice.

* * *

The classes of non-clients who might rely on information provided by an accountant include creditors, investors, shareholders, management, directors, and regulatory agencies. The varying relationships are on a single continuum, and the slices of the continuum encompassing liability may vary in thickness depending upon the factual situation. Public policy considerations determine the extent along the continuum to which accountants will be held liable for inaccurate audits. . . .

[I]n fairness accountants should not be liable in circumstances where they are unaware of the use to which their opinions will be put. Instead, their liability should be commensurate with those persons or classes of persons who they know will rely on their work. With such knowledge the auditor can, through purchase of liability insurance, setting fees, and adopting other protective measures appropriate to the risk, prepare accordingly.

A majority of jurisdictions have adopted the rule set forth in §552 of the Restatement (Second) of Torts (1977), which provides, in part:

(1) One who, in the course of his business, profession or employment, or in any other transaction in which he has a pecuniary interest, supplies false information for the guidance of others in their business transactions, is subject to liability for pecuniary loss caused to them by their justifiable reliance upon the information, if he fails to exercise reasonable care or competence in obtaining or communicating the information.

(2) . . . the liability stated in Subsection (1) is limited to loss suffered
    (a) by the person or one of a limited group of persons for whose benefit and guidance he intends to supply the information or knows that the recipient intends to supply it; and
    (b) through reliance upon it in a transaction that he intends the information to influence or knows that the recipient so intends or in a substantially similar transaction.

* * *

Tennessee has adopted the Restatement (Second) of Torts §552 as the guiding principle in negligent misrepresentation actions against other professionals and business persons. . . . [This] Court held that a subcontractor, despite lack of privity, may pursue an action against a construction manager based on negligent misrepresentation. . . . [Another] case . . . found that an attorney may be liable to a third party for negligence even if no attorney-client relationship was intended. The . . . Court recognized, as follows, that the Restatement principles could extend to all professions . . . .

[This] Court adopted the principles later approved by the American Law Institute in Restatement (Second) of Torts 2d, §552 (1977) in connection with the liability of business or professional persons who negligently supply false information for the guidance of others in their business transactions. These principles, of course, could apply to attorneys as well as to land surveyors, accountants, or title companies.

The conclusion is that Section 552 of the Restatement is the appropriate standard for actions by third parties against accountants based on negligent misrepresentation in this state.

* * *

The judgment of the Court of Appeals is affirmed, and the case is remanded for a new trial consistent with this opinion. Costs are adjudged one-half to the appellant and one-half to the appellee.

QUESTIONS FOR ANALYSIS

1. How does a court determine whether an accountant or other professional has exercised reasonable care in the preparation of work?
2. In some states, only parties that have a direct contractual relationship with an accountant (or other professional) may sue if they suffer a loss because of negligence in preparation of professional work. That is, Bethelehem could not have recovered in those states. Does it make sense that liability for negligence should apply only if the professional has a direct relationship with the party using its work?

CAUSATION

A basic element of a tort in negligence is a *causation* between one party's act and another's injury. For a party to have caused an injury to another and be held negligent, the act must have been the cause in fact and the proximate cause of the other's injury.

Cause in Fact

Cause in fact is established by evidence showing that a person's conduct is the actual cause of an event because the event would not have occurred without it. Courts express this in the form of a rule commonly referred to as the *but for* or *sine qua non* rule. That is, the injury would not have occurred *but for* the conduct of the tortfeasor. A hotel's failure to install a proper fire escape, for example, is not the cause in fact of the death of a person who suffocated in bed from smoke. The person would have died regardless of whether the hotel had a proper fire escape.

Proximate Cause

In many jurisdictions, the injured party must prove that the defendant's act was not only the cause in fact of the injury but also the proximate cause of the injury. *Proximate cause* limits liability to consequences that bear a reasonable relationship to the negligent conduct. Consequences that are too remote or too far removed from negligent conduct will not result in liability.

A person's act may set off a chain of events and injuries that were not *foreseeable*. The principal cause in fact of the Great Chicago Fire of 1871 that destroyed much of the city may have been Mrs. O'Leary's negligent conduct of leaving an oil lamp in the barn for her cow to kick, but no court would hold her liable for the full consequences of her initial act. The chain of events must be foreseeable, as the court discusses in the famous *Palsgraf* decision.

Palsgraf v. Long Island Railroad Company
Court of Appeals of New York
248 N.Y. 339, 162 N.E. 99 (1928)

CASE BACKGROUND *Helen Palsgraf was waiting on a platform to catch a train. As another train began to leave the station, a man carrying a package ran to catch it. He jumped on the train, but looked like he might fall off. A guard, holding the door open for him on the train, reached to help him, while another guard, standing on the platform, pushed the teetering man from behind. The man dropped the package onto the rails. The package contained fireworks that exploded. The shock from the explosion caused some scales located on the platform to fall, striking the plaintiff and injuring her seriously.*

Palsgraf sued the railroad for the negligence of its employees during this event. The jury found in her favor, and the appellate division affirmed the jury's decision. The defendant appealed.

CASE DECISION Cardozo, Chief Justice.

* * *

The conduct of defendant's guard . . . was not wrong in its relation to the plaintiff, standing far away. Relative to her it was not negligence at all. Negligence is not actionable unless it involves the invasion of a legally protected interest, the violation of a right. "Proof of negligence in the air, so to speak, will not do." "Negligence is the absence of care, according to the circumstances." The plaintiff, as she stood upon the platform of the station, might claim to be protected against intentional invasion of her bodily security. Such invasion is not charged. She might claim to be protected against unintentional invasion by conduct involving . . . an unreasonable hazard that such invasion would ensue. . . . If no hazard was apparent to the eye of ordinary vigilance, an act innocent and harmless . . . with reference to her did not take to itself the quality of a tort because it happened to be a wrong, though apparently not one involving the risk of bodily insecurity, with reference to someone else. "In every instance, before negligence can be predicated of a given act, back of the act must be sought and found a duty to the individual complaining, the observance of which would have averted or avoided the injury. The ideas of negligence and duty are strictly correlative."

* * *

The argument for the plaintiff is built upon the shifting meanings of such words as "wrong" and "wrongful" and shares their instability. What the plaintiff must show is a "wrong" to herself; i.e., a violation of her own right, and not merely a wrong to someone else, nor conduct "wrongful" because unsocial. . . .

The range of reasonable apprehension is at times a question for the court, and at times, if varying inferences are possible, a question for the jury. Here, by concession, there was nothing in the situation to suggest to the most cautious mind that the parcel wrapped in newspaper would spread wreckage through the station. If the guard had thrown it down knowingly and willfully, he would not have threatened the plaintiff's safety, so far as appearances could warn him. His conduct would not have involved, even then, an unreasonable probability of invasion of her bodily security. Liability can be no greater where the act is inadvertent.

Negligence, like risk, is thus a term of relation. Negligence in the abstract, apart from things related, is surely not a tort, if indeed it is understandable at all. Negligence is not a tort unless it results in the commission of a wrong, and the commission of a wrong imports the violation of a right, in this case, we are told, the right to be protected against interference with one's bodily security. But bodily security is protected, not against all forms of interference or aggression, but only against some. One who seeks redress at law does not make out a cause of action by showing without more than that there has been damage to his person. If the harm was not willful, he must show that the act as to him had possibilities of danger so many and apparent as to entitle him to be protected against the doing of it though the harm was unintended.

* * *

The judgment of the Appellate Division and that of the Trial Term should be reversed, and the complaint dismissed, with costs in all courts.

QUESTIONS FOR ANALYSIS

1. For the plaintiff to recover, what is the court requiring that she demonstrate?
2. Why did the plaintiff sue the railroad company? Could she have made a better case against the owner of the fireworks?

Most courts stand by *Palsgraf* today. Various state supreme courts have restated the proposition. The Missouri court has held that the duty owed by the plaintiff to the defendant "is generally measured by whether or not a reasonably prudent person would have anticipated danger and provided against it. . . ." The New Mexico court explained: "A duty to the individual is closely intertwined with the foreseeability of injury to *that individual* resulting from an activity conducted with less than reasonable care. . . ." And the Texas court stated that "before liability will be imposed, there must be sufficient evidence indicating that the defendant knew of or should have known that harm would eventually befall a victim."

Intervening Conduct

One issue in determining proximate cause is the possibility of *intervening conduct*. If the causal connection between a person's act and the resulting harm to another is broken by an intervening act or event, there is a *superseding cause*. If the causal relationship between the defendant's act and resulting harm is in fact broken by the intervening act, which was unforeseeable under the circumstances, the defendant will likely not be liable.

Suppose Cantwell Construction has dug a ditch across a public sidewalk to lay some pipe. When the workers quit for the night, they negligently leave the ditch uncovered and do not place any warnings. That night, if Boudreaux intentionally shoves Yandle into the ditch and Yandle is hurt, Boudreaux's conduct is intervening conduct that relieves Cantwell of liability. However, suppose Yandle had accidentally fallen into the ditch at night and was drowning because it was filled with rainwater. Frierson dives into the ditch to save Yandle, and Frierson drowns; Cantwell Construction will be liable to Yandle and Frierson. Because *danger invites rescue*, the common law holds the negligent party responsible for the losses suffered by those who attempt to save people who are in danger as the result of the torts of others.

Substantial Factor

Proximate cause has been criticized as difficult to understand and apply. The California Supreme Court, in *Mitchell* v. *Gonzales* (819 P.2d 872; 1991), joined some other states in replacing the *proximate cause rule* in negligence actions in favor of the *legal cause rule*, which uses the *substantial factor test*.

The substantial factor test, which was developed by the *Restatement (Second) of Torts* and is believed to be clearer to juries, says: "A legal cause of [injury] is a cause which is a substantial factor in bringing about the [injury]." That is, as the Pennsylvania Supreme Court has explained, the jury is asked to determine whether a defendant's conduct "has such an effect in producing the harm as to lead reasonable men to regard it as a cause, using that word in the popular sense" (379 A.2d at 114). As Exhibit 7.1 indicates, defendants could be liable even if their negligent behavior was only one factor contributing to an injury, so long as it was found to be a substantial factor.

EXHIBIT 7.1

Elements of Negligence

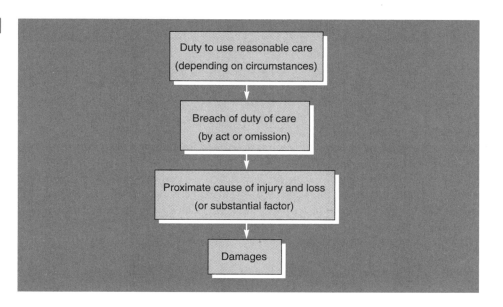

DEFENSES TO A NEGLIGENCE ACTION

Even if an injured party has established the required elements of negligence, the party may be denied compensation if the defendant establishes a *valid defense*. As a general rule, any defense to an intentional tort is also available in a negligence action. In addition, other defenses are available to defendants in negligence actions, including assumption of risk and comparative negligence.

Assumption of Risk

An injured party who voluntarily assumed the risk of harm arising from the negligent or reckless conduct of another may not be allowed to recover compensation for such harm. Such action by the injured party is called *assumption of risk* and creates a defense for the negligent defendant. The defense requires that the injured party knew or should have known of the risk and that the risk was voluntarily assumed. Thus, spectators at sporting events such as baseball games assume the risk for injuries that result from the usual playing of the game and the reaction of the crowd.

Assumption of risk is an affirmative defense. It must be specifically raised by the defendant to take advantage of it. When established, assumption of risk usually bars the plaintiff from recovery, even if the defendant was negligent.

Comparative Negligence

Almost all states have adopted the doctrine of *comparative negligence* (that replaced an old rule called contributory negligence). Under comparative negligence, damages are reduced by the percentage of the injuries caused by the plaintiff's own negligence. We see an example of the effects of comparative negligence in the *Wassell* decision.

Wassell v. Adams
United States Court of Appeals, Seventh Circuit
865 F.2d 849 (1989)

CASE BACKGROUND *Susan Wassell was visiting her fiancé, who lived just north of Chicago. She stayed at a small motel, owned by the Adamses. At 1:00 A.M. she was awakened by a knock on the door. Thinking it was her fiance, she looked through the peephole, did not see anyone, but opened the door anyway. A strange man asked for "Cindy" and asked for a drink of water. While Wassell went to get it, the man came into the room. He told her the water was not cold enough and he wanted money. She said she had $20 in the car. The man went to the bathroom to get more water; while he was in there Wassell hid her purse (there was no phone in the room). The man emerged naked from the waist down. Wassell ran out of the room screaming; apparently no one heard her. The man caught her, dragged her back to her room, and raped her. The man was never caught.*

A psychologist testified at trial that the rape induced stress that has "blighted her life." Wassell sued the motel owners with negligence for failing to warn her to take
more precautions, since the motel was near a high-crime area and a rape had occurred before.

"A jury composed of four women and three men found that the Adamses had indeed been negligent and that their negligence had been a proximate cause of the assault, and the jury assessed Susan's damages at $850,000, which was the figure her lawyer had requested in closing argument. But in addition the jury found that Susan had been negligent too—and indeed that her negligence had been 97 percent to blame for the attack and the Adamses' only 3 percent. So, following the approach to comparative negligence [in Illinois] . . . the jury awarded Susan only $25,500 in damages." Wassell asked the trial judge to grant judgment in her favor notwithstanding the verdict, claiming "that she had been nonnegligent as a matter of law or . . . that the jury's apportionment of negligence was contrary to the manifest weight of the evidence." The trial judge refused; Wassell appealed.

CASE DECISION Posner, Circuit Judge.

* * *

. . . [T]here is no methodology for comparing the causal contributions of the plaintiff's and of the defendant's negligence to the plaintiff's injury. In this case, either the plaintiff or the defendants would have avoided that injury. . . .

It is careless to open a motel or hotel door in the middle of the night without trying to find out who is knocking. Still, people aren't at their most alert when they are awakened in the middle of the night. . . . As innkeepers (in the increasingly quaint legal term), the Adamses had a duty to exercise a high degree of care to protect their guests from assaults on the motel premises. And the cost to the Adamses of warning all their female guests of the dangers of the neighborhood would have been negligible. . . .

But this analysis is incomplete. It is unlikely that a warning would have averted the attack. Susan testified that she thought the man who had knocked on the door was her fiance. Thinking this, she would have opened the door no matter how dangerous she believed the neighborhood to be. . . . Of course, if the Adamses had told her not to open her door in the middle of the night under any circumstances without carefully ascertaining who was trying to enter the room, this would have been a pertinent warning and might have had an effect. But it is absurd to think that hoteliers are required to give so obvious a warning, any more than they might warn guests not to stick their fingers into the electrical outlets. Everyone, or at least the average person, knows better than to open his or her door to a stranger in the middle of the night.

* * *

We are not supposed to speculate about the jury's reasoning process. . . . The issue for us is not whether this jury was rational and law-abiding but whether a rational jury could, consistently with the evidence, have returned the verdict that this jury did.

If we were the trier of fact, persuaded that both parties were negligent and forced to guess about the relative costs to the plaintiff and to the defendants of averting the assault, we would assess the defendants' share at more than 3 percent. But we are not the trier of fact, and are authorized to upset the jury's apportionment only if persuaded that the trial judge abused his discretion in determining that the jury's verdict was not against the clear weight of the evidence. We are not so persuaded. It seems probably wrong to us, but we have suggested an interpretation of the evidence under which the verdict was consistent with the evidence and the law. And that is enough to require us to uphold the district judge's refusal to set aside the verdict.

CASE NOTE Illinois, like some other states, now holds that if the plaintiff is 50 percent or more at fault, the plaintiff recovers nothing. Other states have the rule that existed in Illinois at the time of this case, allowing the damages to be split according to percentage of fault assigned to the parties.

QUESTIONS FOR ANALYSIS

1. Should the law take into consideration the sophistication or "street smarts" of the parties to a case? Wassell, young and from a rural area, was unsophisticated and had never been in a big city like Chicago before.
2. The law in Illinois now holds that if the plaintiff is more than 50 percent at fault, no recovery will be allowed. Is this a sensible rule?

Summary

- Tort law concerns legal wrongs inflicted by one party on another by interfering with an interest protected by common law. Tort law changes over time as social values, technology, and business practices change. The primary purpose of tort law is to compensate the injured party and to put the burden on the tortfeasor to return the injured party to his original position.
- Intentional torts are based on willful misconduct that invades a right of another and causes injury. The rights can be the rights of persons to be safe and secure in their person or in their property. Wrongdoers will be expected to pay damages to compensate for injuries.

- Intentional interference with personal rights includes assault—when a person is placed in fear of bodily harm or offensive contact; battery—unlawful physical contact without consent; false imprisonment—detaining someone within boundaries against his or her will; emotional distress—caused by outrageous conduct; invasion of privacy—a violation of a person's right to be free from unwanted exposure; defamation—false communication that injures a person's reputation, including slander and libel; and malicious prosecution—unjustified use of the law to injure another.

- Intentional interference against property includes trespass to land—an intrusion on real property belonging to another; nuisance—interference with the use and enjoyment of private land or interference with a right held in common by the public; trespass to personal property—interference with a person's right to use his or her personal property; conversion—unlawful control over another person's personal property; and misappropriation—unauthorized use or theft of one's intellectual property.

- Tort liability for negligence arises when the duty of ordinary care—the care expected of a reasonable person under the circumstances—to another person is breached, usually by an act that is the proximate cause (or substantial factor) of harm to the other person.

- Defenses raised in tort lawsuits include that of truth in defamation cases; consent—that the plaintiff had approved of the interference that led to injury; privilege—that the defendant had a right to take the actions now challenged, including self-defense in case of assault; inflicting injury on another to defend someone else being attacked; and physically defending property. Force used should be no more than is reasonable under the circumstances. The law places a higher value on human life than on property. In negligence cases, defenses also include assumption of the risk by the plaintiff and negligence by the plaintiff, which may be compared to the negligence of the defendant.

Issue

Are Greedy Consumers Causing the Punitive Damage "Crisis"?

For over a decade, industry groups have lobbied Congress for statutory restrictions on punitive damage awards. They cite such cases as the Alabama doctor who was upset with the paint job on his new BMW and was granted $4 million in punitive damages. But are greedy consumers and huckster lawyers driving the system, or are other forces at work?

WHY BUSINESSES SOMETIMES LIKE PUNITIVE AWARDS

Richard B. Schmitt*

Reprinted by permission of *The Wall Street Journal* © 1995 Dow Jones & Company, Inc. All rights reserved worldwide. Schmitt is a staff reporter.

It sounds like just the sort of runaway jury verdict that businesspeople love to hate.

But when a federal appeals court upheld a $30 million punitive-damage award earlier this year against a unit of Occidental Petroleum Corp., executives at at least one company cheered. They work for Continental Trend Resources Inc., an Enid, Okla., oil company that was the plaintiff.

Despite business groups' complaints about high punitive damages, these days businesses themselves are winning many such awards, which are intended to punish and deter wrongdoers. "If they are the ones seeking them, they have no objection at all," says Houston lawyer Joseph Jamail, who won the biggest punitive-damage award ever, $3 billion, in a suit by Pennzoil Co. against Texaco Inc. in the 1980s. Mr. Jamail says executives call him all the time with questions about how to win punitive damages.

The trend points up a paradox in the current debate over overhauling the civil justice system. In Congress, where a House-Senate conference may soon take up the issue of federal tort legislation, the focus has been on limiting punitive damages in cases launched by injured consumers against manufacturers of defective products. The bill passed by the Senate would apply only to product-liability cases, which tend to be brought by consumers, while the House version would limit damages in a broader array of cases.

The likely compromise would continue to allow large damages in many other cases—including contracts, unfair competition and misleading advertising—the bulk of which are filed by businesses.

To consumer groups, this sounds unfair. "The business community wants to limit consumer rights but maintain unfettered access to the courts for themselves," says Richard Vuernick, legal policy director at Citizen Action, a consumer lobbying group. "It is just blatant hypocrisy."

Business groups seeking the punitive-damage caps contend that most companies would prefer broader limits on punitive damages, even if it might hurt them in isolated cases where they were the ones filing suit. "People we represent understand there is a much greater likelihood that you are going to be the victim than the beneficiary of the current system," says Theodore Olson, a Washington lawyer for a group of Fortune 500 companies seeking damage limits.

But businesses frequently are the beneficiaries: In fact, punitive-damage awards appear to be more common in cases brought by businesses than in disputes arising from personal injuries. A study this year of 75 local court systems by the National Center for State Courts shows that punitive damages were awarded 13% of the time in victorious contract cases—many of which are business actions—compared with just 4% in tort cases.

Moreover, the median award in contract cases is higher, at $56,000, than the $38,000 median award in

tort cases. The amount of punitive damages typically awarded tends to be higher where the harm is financial rather than physical, says Stephen Daniels, a senior research fellow at the American Bar Foundation in Chicago. "The awards can be very high, because businesses are fairly good at documenting their losses," he says, adding that the sheer size of some business litigants means that "any type of court award is likely to be very, very high."

Last month, for instance, a company in Mississippi won a $400 million punitive-damage award against a Canadian funeral-home chain over an aborted merger. Punitive damages have been recently awarded in several big cases where businesses have sued insurance companies in claim disputes, including a $14 million award against Liberty Mutual Insurance Co., which has sought review by the U.S. Supreme Court. The $30 million award in the Continental case was equal to more than 100 times the company's actual losses.

With such high potential rewards, companies seem to be requesting punitive damages almost routinely. Last month, Scott Paper Co. sued Procter & Gamble Co., seeking punitive damages in a dispute over paper-towel ads. Previously, P&G requested punitive damages against Bankers Trust New York Corp. in connection with losses from investing in derivatives. Quaker Oats Co. recently requested punitive damages when it sued Borden Inc. to rescind Quaker's purchase of two Brazilian pasta companies.

"It is a growing, growing trend" for companies to seek punitive damages, says William Shernoff, a Claremont, Calif., plaintiffs' lawyer who specializes in winning punitive damages from insurance companies that refuse to pay claims on time. Mr. Shernoff made a name in the 1970s representing individual policyholders; today, he says about 25% of his clients are businesses.

Of course, companies on the losing end of such cases aren't fans of punitive damages. Mark Greenwold, an attorney in Washington for Occidental, says the $30 million award in the Continental case, coming in a dispute over interpreting natural gas contracts, was something of a travesty. "For anybody who cares about the concept of rationality in the administration of justice, this has to be very disturbing," he says. Occidental has also sought U.S. Supreme Court review.

But Eric Eissenstat, a lawyer for Continental, says punitive damages play an important role in business litigation. "Our country is founded on a free-market system," he says. Punitive damages, he says, send a strong message to companies who "don't want to play by the rules."

ISSUE QUESTIONS

1. Should juries be subject to strict guidelines about when punitive damages can be imposed? Should there be a relationship between the amount of compensatory damages and the amount of punitive damages?

2. Since the purpose of punitive damages is to punish the tortfeasor, not enrich the plaintiff, should punitive damages go partly or completely to the government instead of to the plaintiff?

REVIEW AND DISCUSSION QUESTIONS

1. Define the following terms:

tort	libel
assault	malicious prosecution
battery	trespass
consent	nuisance
privilege	conversion
false imprisonment	negligence
emotional distress	proximate cause
invasion of privacy	comparative negligence
defamation	ultrahazardous activity
slander	

2. Are most accidents and injuries covered by tort law?

CASE QUESTIONS

3. Milo Vacanti took his CD player to Master Electronics for repairs. Vacanti presumed that the repairs would be covered by warranty, but he did not discuss the matter with the staff at Master. When he returned to pick up the player after it had been repaired, he was presented a bill, which he refused to pay. He grabbed the player and started to leave the store. Two employees yelled at him and then scuffled with him to get the player back. Vacanti claimed he suffered injuries to his hand, ribs, neck, and lip. He sued for assault and battery, presenting medical bills for $3,150. Did he win? [*Vacanti* v. *Master Electronics*, 514 N.W.2d 319 (Sup. Ct., Neb., 1994)]

4. Ahron Leichtman, an antismoking advocate, was invited to appear on a radio talk show in Cincinnati to discuss smoking on the day of the Great American Smokeout. While he was in the studio, another talk show host lit a cigar and repeatedly blew smoke in Leichtman's face. Leichtman sued the radio station for battery and for invasion of privacy. Did he have a case? [*Leichtman* v. *WLW Jacor Comm.*, 634 N.E.2d 697 (Ct. App., Ohio, 1994)]

5. Charlotte Newsom worked as a cashier at a store. One day she was told to report to the manager's office, where she was accused by two security staff members of stealing $500. She denied stealing the money. The meeting lasted two hours. The security staff asserted to have evidence of theft, although Newsom constantly denied the claim. Whenever Newsom stated that she wanted to leave, the staff told her she would be arrested for theft if she left. Finally, Newsom wrote a statement

about the matter, denying the charge. She was fired on the spot and left the store. Did she have a case for false imprisonment? [*Newsom* v. *Thalhimer Brothers*, 901 S.Wd.2d 365 (West. Dist. Ct. App., Tenn., 1994)]

6. While Rouse was looking at new cars at a dealership, he gave his car keys to a sales rep so that his car could be examined for its trade-in value. When Rouse decided to leave without buying, the keys were hidden from him—supposedly lost—for about a half hour. The sales rep thought this was a joke. Rouse sued and was awarded $5,000 in punitive damages. What was the tort claimed? Would the damages be allowed on appeal? [*Russell-Vaughn Ford* v. *Rouse*, 206 So.2d 371 (Sup.Ct., Ala., 1968)]

7. A patron at a casino in Nevada got into a fight with another customer. The bouncer went to throw out the patron and got into a fight with him. The bouncer took the patron to a back room to photograph him (they keep photos of trouble-makers), which resulted in another fight in which the patron suffered significant injury to his arm. What torts could the patron bring against the casino? [*Cerminara* v. *California Hotel and Casino*, 760 P.2d 108 (Sup. Ct., Nev., 1988)]

8. Jerry Katz, a politician, stated that he would not raise taxes if elected. The local newspaper supported Katz, who won the election. At his first board meeting, Katz moved to raise taxes. His actions prompted an editorial that began "Jerry Katz is a liar. He has lied to us in the past, and he will lie to us in the future." Katz sued the newspaper. What would that action be, and what would be the likely result? [*Costello* v. *Capital Cities Communications*, 505 N.E.2d 701 (App. Ct., Ill., 1987)]

9. Rubin contracted to build a hydroelectric facility for Sterling. Later the parties got into a fight over things going on at the operation. Sterling falsely told the bank that loaned Rubin $1 million that Rubin had defaulted on the contract, which was not true. Presuming that Rubin was in default, the bank raised the interest rate on the loan because it faced a higher risk. What action does Rubin have against Sterling? [*Rubin* v. *Sterling Enterprises*, 674 A.2d 782 (Sup. Ct., Vt., 1996)]

10. Kelly-Springfield (K-S) agreed to sell some land to D'Ambro. The deal was to be completed on a specified date, but D'Ambro failed to make any payment by the due date. K-S then began talking to other parties who had expressed an interest in the property. D'Ambro filed suits in state and federal court, claiming that K-S failed to live up to the sale agreement, and demanded damages or that K-S be required to sell the property to D'Ambro. Because of the litigation, the interested parties backed away from the K-S property. What action can K-S bring against D'Ambro? [*Kelly-Springfield Tire Co.* v. *D'Ambro*, 596 A.2d 867 (Super. Ct., Pa., 1991)]

11. Willis worked at a DuPont plant in Texas. Under work rules, he had to submit to random drug tests. The tests were performed for DuPont by Roche Biomedical Labs. Roche reported to DuPont that Willis had failed a test. Following normal procedures, Willis's work was restricted, and Willis had to attend counseling and submit to further drug tests. Roche then determined that the initial test was wrong; the test was a false positive. Willis was reinstated and paid all back wages. He sued Roche and DuPont for defamation and for negligence in drug test procedures. Was either claim valid? [*Willis* v. *Roche*, 61 F.3d 313 (5th Cir., 1995)]

12. Unknown to him, Greg Gazelle's wife bounced ten checks for $860 at a grocery store from their joint checking account. Gazelle's wife had signed his name to the checks. After trying unsuccessfully to collect, the store filed a criminal complaint against Gazelle, who was arrested and spent a week in jail. Charges were

dropped when it was discovered that he had not written the checks. Did Gazelle have a tort action for malicious prosecution against the store? [*Winn-Dixie Stores v. Gazelle*, 523 So.2d 648 (First Dist. Ct. App., Fla., 1988)]

13. Dun & Bradstreet, a company that reports on the credit history of businesses, incorrectly stated that Greenmoss Builders had once gone bankrupt when in fact it had not. Greenmoss claimed it lost business because of the incorrect report, which was sent to prospective customers. Greenmoss sued for damages for defamation and won. Dun & Bradstreet said that since there was no "actual malice" in what was said, it could not be held liable. What did the U.S. Supreme Court say? [*Dun & Bradstreet v. Greenmoss Builders*, 472 U.S. 749, 105 S.Ct. 2939 (1985)]

14. Tomato growers in Tennessee bought a product called Frostguard from a California company. The company claimed the product would protect tomatoes from the harmful effects of frost. The growers applied Frostguard as directed but suffered substantial crop losses as a result of a frost. They sued the maker of Frostguard for negligence in advertising. Could they win such a tort action? [*Ritter v. Custom Chemicides*, 912 S.W.2d 128 (Sup. Ct., Tenn., 1995)]

15. The basement of the Girone home was flooded with raw sewage that overflowed from a city sewer line. Walking across the odorous floor, Mrs. Girone slipped and fell, breaking her hip. She sued the city for negligent maintenance of the sewage line and for trespass. The city contended she was negligent for not being more careful walking on the slippery floor. Who won? [*City of Winder v. Girone*, 462 S.E.2d 704 (Sup. Ct., Ga., 1995)]

16. Members of Earth First! demonstrated in a forest against logging. Several protestors chained themselves to logging machinery owned by a private company. Logging operations had to be ceased for a day because of the protest and occupation of machinery (which was not damaged). What cause of action does the logging company have against the protesters? [*Huffman and Wright Logging Co. v. Wade*, 857 P.2d 101 (Sup.Ct., Ore., 1993)]

17. McKenzie lived next to a gas station run by Yommer. Unknown to Yommer, a gas storage tank developed a leak, polluting McKenzie's well water, making the water unfit for drinking or bathing. Yommer replaced the storage tank, but the problem with McKenzie's water persisted, and McKenzie sued. What tort was claimed? What, if any, is the basis for liability? [*Yommer v. McKenzie*, 257 A.2d 138 (Ct.App., Md., 1969)]

POLICY QUESTION

18. An area of the law that is currently in question is whether Internet servers, including America Online and Prodigy, can be sued for defamation by persons who are defamed by a user of their service. The Internet servers argue that they are like telephone companies in that they only provide electronic communication services and do not control the truth of all communications. Should the servers be liable in tort for the truthfulness of speech on the Internet?

ETHICS QUESTIONS

19. Businesses have become more aggressive at suing publications that report negative news about them or make negative comments. A cigarette company sued CBS

for interviewing a disgruntled former executive; an infomercial producer sued *Forbes* for $420 million for a negative article about infomercials, and ABC paid $15 million and made on-the-air apologies to settle a suit by two tobacco companies for $10 billion for a report about "spiking" cigarettes with nicotine. It has been claimed that such suits are primarily to scare the media from negative reporting. Since the suits have possible merit, there is no malicious prosecution, but the use of the law seems to be mostly strategic—to discourage the media from being critical of company practices. Is this a defensible business tactic?

20. An employee at the supermarket you manage mopped one of the aisles in the store and placed signs at the ends of the aisles to warn people not to use the aisle until the floor dried. One customer walked around the sign, slipped, fell, and suffered serious injuries. Her lawyer comes to you with the following story. He says he is going to sue the store for negligence that led to her injuries. However, he says he doubts he can win, since case law in the state makes it clear that the sign is considered a reasonable warning so that contributory negligence by the customer would eliminate liability of the store. This means the customer will get nothing, but one can never be completely sure. The worst part is that the customer has no insurance, has incurred large hospital bills, cannot work for several months, and has no source of support. The lawyer makes the following deal. He will forgo any fee for the case and will sue only for an amount equal to the medical costs incurred and the wages lost if you will agree to testify there was no sign in place to warn that the floor was wet. The payment will be made by the insurance company. This will not affect your position with the insurance company, and you will save attorney's fees. Should you make such a deal? What if you knew that the law in most states would provide an award because their law held that warning signs were not sufficient and a complete physical barrier had to be in place?

INTERNET ASSIGNMENT

Texas courts have long held that gambling debts are not recoverable by action, as against public policy. Texas does, however, follow the general common law of fraud. The elements of a claim for fraud are: (1) a material misrepresentation; (2) that was false; (3) that the speaker knew to be false when made; (4) that was made so that the other party would act upon the misrepresentation; (5) the other party in fact acted in reliance on the misrepresentation; and (6) as a result suffered injury. *See Jackson v. Speer*, United States Court of Appeals for the Fifth Circuit, No. 92-1419, October 14, 1992 (http://www.law.utexas.edu/us5th/us5th.html).

During a January 1987 visit to the Bahamas, Aubin, a businessman, frequent gambler, and Texas resident, visited Cable Beach Hotel and Casino, which was owned and operated by Carnival Leisure, a Bahamian corporation. After gambling away all the money he had brought to the casino, Aubin asked that credit be extended to him so that he could continue gambling. The casino issued six "markers" to Aubin, which he signed, totaling $25,000. Markers may be used by a patron to obtain credit at the casino. It is undisputed that Aubin obtained $25,000 in gambling chips with his markers.

Aubin contends that he signed markers which did not contain the name of his Houston bank, his account number, the date, etc. He contends that the casino added this information to the markers before presenting them for payment. He denies that he had authorized the completion or presentation of the markers for payment. The forms signed by Aubin contained the following language in small type:

> I represent that I have received cash for the above amount and that said amount is on deposit in said financial entity in my name, is free and clear of claim and is subject to this check and is hereby assigned to payee, and I guarantee payment with exchange and costs in collecting.

At the time Aubin signed the markers, he did not have the $25,000 on deposit at his Houston bank. Aubin lost the entire $25,000 playing blackjack. When Aubin did not redeem the markers within thirty days and the drafts were presented for payment at Aubin's Houston bank, the casino learned that Aubin had stopped payment on the bank drafts. After unsuccessful collection attempts, Carnival Leisure sued Aubin to enforce the debt and for fraud. What result? *See Carnival Leisure Industries, Ltd.* v. *Aubin*, United States Court of Appeals for the Fifth Circuit, No. 93-2878, June 2, 1995 (http://www.law. utexas.edu/us5th/us5th.html).

CHAPTER 8

Business Torts

There is no such thing as a "business tort," but many torts involve businesses as defendants, and some torts, by definition, involve only businesses. This chapter focuses on the areas of tort law that are of particular concern to business. About 5 percent of all civil suits are tort actions, but the money involved in some tort cases draws attention to this area of law. Consider some statistics about tort cases:

- Plaintiffs win about 52 percent of personal injury suits and 41 percent of product defect suits.
- The median award in product liability suits has been about $400,000.
- The median award in personal injury suits is over $60,000.
- Ten percent of personal injury suit awards are for over $1 million.
- The median jury award for back strain, the most common injury, is $9,500.
- The median jury award for food poisoning is $12,000.
- The average jury award for a rape on business property is $1.8 million.
- The median jury award for paraplegia is $6.5 million.

Defendants who expect to be found liable usually settle out of court. Since little information is available about such settlements, the magnitude of tort litigation is not known. However, a number of products (including ladders) and services (e.g., baby delivery) are estimated to cost about 20 percent to 30 percent more because of expected liability claims.

Tort Law and Business

As reviewed in Chapter 7, there are many categories of intentional torts. Those torts occur when the tortfeasor is found to have intended to invade a protected interest and the tortfeasor knew or should have known of the consequences of the act that resulted in an injury. Such willful misconduct can be against persons or property.

Other torts involve negligence, which we also studied in Chapter 7. Torts based on negligence do not require willful misconduct. Negligence is carelessness in a legal sense: when people fail to act the way they are obligated to behave and, as a result, their actions affect others. Persons in business are presumed to have a certain level of expertise that will hold them to a higher level of care than may be expected of a nonprofessional in the same situation.

While businesses may be defendants in suits for assault, such actions are not as peculiar to business as are the tort actions covered in this chapter. These actions mostly involve only business, are involved in cases that most frequently concern business, and tend to be instrumental in the most common big-dollar cases. As we will see, many suits involve both claims of intentional tort and claims of negligence—plaintiffs make as many plausible claims in one case as they can. As we will study later in the chapter, other cases involve strict liability in tort.

COSTS OF TORT LITIGATION

Each year about one-half million lawsuits involving tort claims are filed in our nation's court systems, most in state courts. As Exhibit 8.1 illustrates, compensation for injured parties—the main purpose of tort law—accounts for less than half of the total cost. The costs of tort litigation, both the process itself and the damages paid, have prompted concern about the ability of the court system to effectively and efficiently compensate innocent parties who are injured.

EXHIBIT 8.1

The Distribution of Tort Litigation Costs

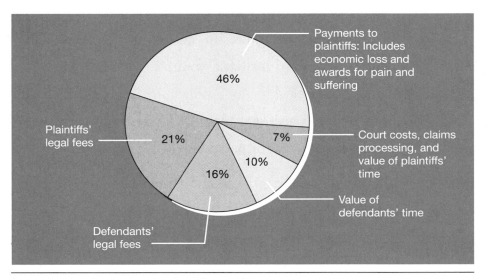

Source: Institute for Civil Justice, Rand Corporation

The cost of the tort system is difficult to calculate. Estimates of the direct costs range from about $40 billion to $150 billion per year. Business organizations have lobbied Congress since the 1980s to impose federal statutory limits on tort damages. They claim that many of the awards are excessive or unjustified and that the cost is making American business less competitive in international markets, since most nations have far fewer tort cases and less generous damage awards. Over a dozen states have enacted limits on pain and suffering awards and on punitive damage awards, as those two categories are alleged to be the most abused areas of tort. Some of these damage caps have been stricken by state supreme courts as violation of constitutional rights. While torts are a part of the common law, increasingly, as with other areas of the common law, statutes are playing an ever more important role in determining legal standards. We next look at some areas of tort law that tend to be peculiar to business and, in the case of product liability, involve massive sums of dollars.

MISREPRESENTATION

When a person suffers an injury due to deliberate deception, there may be a tort of *fraud*, *misrepresentation*, *fraudulent misrepresentation*, or *deceit*. When this issue arises in a business relationship, there is often a breach of contract or some other tort issue present. Misrepresentation is a broad concept and may be held to be an intentional tort or to be a tort based on negligence.

Intentional Misrepresentation

When misrepresentation is an intentional tort, there must be proof, as the House of Lords expressed in a famous case in 1889, "that a false representation has been made (1) knowingly, or (2) without belief in its truth, or (3) recklessly, careless whether it be true or false" (*Derry v. Peek*, 14 A.C. 337 at 374). While misrepresentation is a common-law rule subject to different interpretations in different jurisdictions, as the law has evolved the following key elements have generally been agreed upon to establish fraud or intentional misrepresentation.

1. A material misrepresentation of a fact: false important information was passed.
2. *Scienter* or intent to defraud: the defendant knew there was a misrepresentation of information being passed.
3. Intent to induce reliance: the defendant wanted the plaintiff to believe the falsehood.
4. Justifiable reliance by the plaintiff on the misinformation: the plaintiff had good reason to believe the misrepresentation offered by the defendant.
5. Relationship between the parties: the plaintiff and defendant were engaged in some relationship that created a legal obligation.
6. Causation: a logical link existed between reliance on the misstatement and the losses that were then suffered by the plaintiff.
7. Damages: losses were suffered by the plaintiff due to reliance on the fraud.

As with other torts, the relationship of the parties can be significant in determining whether legal responsibility is created. If a stranger walking down the street tells you to invest all of your money in Fly-by-Night Company stock, you will not have a cause of action against the stranger when all of your money is lost when the company collapses, because there is no justification to believe a stranger about such a decision, nor is there a business relationship—it was just friendly, stupid advice. But if your stockbroker tells you to invest all of your money in Fly-by-Night Company stock and tells you it is a safe, sure investment, when she knows it is a highly risky venture and she is getting kickbacks for sending clients to invest in the stock, then your reliance may be justified and she and her employing company may well be responsible for your losses when the company goes broke.

Negligent Misrepresentation

A tort action for misrepresentation can occur due to negligence of the other party, which almost only occurs when there is a business or professional relationship. For example, if an attorney fails to file some documents on time and a case is lost due to that careless error, there was not intent to do harm, but there was negligence that caused a loss. Instances in which there is a reliance on information or services provided by professionals who fail to meet the duty of care expected of a professional are the basis of most negligent misrepresentation actions. The *Squish La Fish* case discusses such an instance.

Squish La Fish, Inc. v. Thomco Specialty Products, Inc.
United States Court of Appeals, Eleventh Circuit
149 F.3d 1288 (1998)

CASE BACKGROUND *Squish La Fish holds a patent on a plastic device called "Tuna Squeeze" that is used to squeeze oil and water from cans of tun. It received an order from a distributor for two million units. Squish hired ProPack to affix each Tuna Squeeze to preprinted cardboard "point of purchase" cards for display in stores. ProPack brought in Thomco to advise it as to the kind of adhesive that should be used to make the Tuna Squeeze stick to the cardboard. The Thomco representative recommended a 3M adhesive called "Extra High Tack Adhesive Transfer" and, according to the Squish representative, said that the adhesive would easily wash off of the Tuna Squeeze in warm water. The Thomco representative testified that he said he "thought" the adhesive would wash off. ProPack and Squish relied on Thomco's advice and did not test to see if the adhesive would wash off.*

After 8,600 units had been produced, it was discovered that the adhesive would not wash off of the Tuna Squeeze and the distributor was not happy with the results. The adhesive was replaced with two-sided tape, but the distributor wanted a guarantee that the product would be delivered on time and that there would not be adhesive problems. Squish could not make the promise because there were still problems with finding a good adhesive. The distributor canceled the contract.

Squish sued Thomco for negligent misrepresentation. The district court granted summary judgment for Thomco; Squish appealed.

CASE DECISION Cohill, Senior District Judge.

* * *

The Georgia Supreme Court adopted the "negligent misrepresentation exception" from the *Restatement (Second) of Torts* §522 (1977). Under this now well-established . . . rule,

[O]ne who supplies information during the course of his business, profession, employment, or in any transaction in which he has a pecuniary interest has a duty of reasonable care and competence to parties who rely upon the information in circumstances in which the maker was manifestly aware of the use to which the information was to be put and intended that it be so used. This liability is limited to a foreseeable person or limited class of persons for whom the information was intended, either directly or indirectly.

The elements of this cause of action have recently been formulated as follows: (1) the negligent supply of false information to foreseeable persons, known or unknown; (2) such persons' reasonable reliance upon that false information; and (3) economic injury approximately resulting from such reliance.

* * *

We find that the district court committed an error of law when it failed to acknowledge that Squish La

Fish's indirect reliance, through ProPack, on Thomco's alleged representations concerning the . . . adhesive, were sufficient to bring the company within the negligent misrepresentation . . . rule.

Because the district court granted summary judgment on the ground that indirect reliance on Thomco's alleged misrepresentation did not permit Squish La Fish to plead negligent misrepresentation, it did not address whether any disputed issues of material fact remained for trial regarding the elements of plaintiff's claim. Applying the three-part test for negligent misrepresentation to the facts before the district court, it is clear that Squish La Fish, as the manufacturer of the product being affixed by Thomco's adhesive, was a foreseeable user of Thomco's representations concerning that adhesive. The parties dispute the remaining two prongs of the

analysis: whether any false information was conveyed about the adhesive's removability, and whether Squish La Fish indirectly relied upon any such information. The record shows that disputed issues of material fact remain for trial as to both issues.

* * *

Reversed and remanded.

QUESTIONS FOR ANALYSIS

1. Why did Squish not sue Thomco for breach of contract instead of the tort of negligent misrepresentation?
2. Would Thomco have a good defense that ProPack and Squish should have had the sense to try the adhesive to make sure it worked properly before putting it into production?

INTERFERENCE WITH CONTRACTUAL RELATIONS

One of the more common business torts is *intentional interference with contractual relations*. The basis of the claim is that the injured business's contractual relations were wrongfully interfered with by another party. The elements of this tort are

1. the existence of a contractual relationship between the injured business and another party
2. that was known to the wrongdoer, who
3. intentionally interfered with that relationship.

When a wrongdoer intentionally causes another party to break a good contract, the motive does not matter. The point is that breaking the contract is done to benefit the tortfeasor. This causes injury to the party who suffers the breach of contract. The party who suffers the breach may sue both the party who breached the contract for breach and the wrongdoer for the tort of interference with the contract. The *Robi* case gives an example of this tort.

Robi v. Five Platters, Inc.
United States Court of Appeals, Ninth Circuit
918 F.2d 1439 (1990)

CASE BACKGROUND *The Platters singing group was formed in 1953. The five original Platters performed together on television and in concert from 1954 to 1960. They were the dominant pop music group in 1955–56 before Elvis Presley burst on the scene. They had twelve gold records, including "Only You," "Smoke Gets in Your Eyes," "Great Pretender," and "Twilight Time." Their manager, Buck Ram, formed a corporation named The Five Platters, Inc. (FPI). During the 1960s the group broke up, and Ram bought all shares of FPI stock and put a new group on the road under The Platters' name.*

Robi, an original member of the group, continued to perform under the name "The Platters," which resulted in lawsuits between Robi and Ram (owner of FPI) starting in 1972. In this case, Robi sued FPI for, among other things, intentional interference with contractual relations and was awarded over $3.5 million in damages at district court. FPI appealed.

CASE DECISION Pregerson, Judge.

* * *

To establish a claim of intentional interference with contractual relations under California law, Paul Robi had to show (1) that he had valid and existing contracts; (2) that FPI had knowledge of his contracts and intended to induce their breach; (3) that the contract was in fact breached; (4) that the breach was caused by FPI's wrongful conduct; and (5) that Robi suffered damage.

Ample evidence existed to support the district court's findings that FPI defendants damaged Paul Robi's business and professional reputation, including:

1) Over 50 letters and telegrams written by parties associated with FPI to numerous trade magazines, booking agents, promoters, and performance venues claiming that Robi had no right to perform as The Platters and threatening to sue anyone who hired or promoted Robi. The evidence included correspondence sent by FPI after the district court entered its preliminary injunction enjoining such activity.
2) Testimony of three music producers who stated that FPI representatives told them that Robi's

group was phony and had no rights to the name "The Platters"; that the representatives threatened to put Robi out of business and threatened them with litigation; and that but for FPI's actions, they would have hired and promoted Robi in more frequent and lucrative bookings.
3) Testimony of Paul and Martha Robi regarding the income and business opportunities lost as a result of FPI's interference.

. . . Robi . . . [presented] ample written evidence of FPI's harassing behavior, which the court determined was intended to and did discourage parties from hiring or promoting him.

* * *

Affirmed.

CASE NOTE The court returned the name The Platters to Robi. Since Robi died prior to this decision, the damages and the rights to the name The Platters were assigned to his wife.

QUESTIONS FOR ANALYSIS

1. Since a disagreement existed about the use of the name The Platters, and if FPI was serious about suing anyone who allowed Robi to use the name The Platters, why should FPI not be allowed to interfere with Robi's contracts that used the name of the group?
2. Why should such cases come under tort law instead of contract law?

INTERFERENCE WITH PROSPECTIVE ADVANTAGE

Similar to the tort of interference with contractual rights is the tort of *interference with prospective advantage* (also called interference with prospective economic advantage and interference with prospective contractual relationship). Businesses may devise countless schemes to attract customers, but it is a tort when a business attempts to improve its place in the market by interfering with another's business in an unreasonable and improper manner. An employee of Elaine's Hot Threads, for example, cannot be positioned at the entrance of Runners Sportswear to tell customers to go to Elaine's. Most courts define such conduct as predatory behavior. If this type of activity were permitted, Elaine's could reap the benefits of Runners' advertising and goodwill. If the behavior of the defendant is merely competitive and not predatory in nature—for example, the defendant is so effective in advertising that customers are drawn from the losing business—the courts do not find improper interference. In the *Monette* case, the court found interference.

Monette v. AM-7-7 Baking Company, Ltd.

United States Court of Appeals, Sixth Circuit
929 F.2d 276 (1991)

CASE BACKGROUND *September 30, 1988, Monette bought a bread route from Picarella for $28,000. He received a truck and a list of customers serviced on the delivery route. Two thirds of the bread products Monette sold to his customers were bought from AM-7-7 Baking. The other third of Monette's products were from other bakers. Since Monette had no contract with AM-7-7, Monette and AM-7-7 were under no obligation to do business with each other. "The parties merely had an ongoing relationship in which they voluntarily transacted business—the sale and purchase of bread products—from day to day."*

Monette and AM-7-7 did not get along. After a few weeks, AM-7-7's owner told the previous bread route owner that "he did not like Monette and stated that he was "going to boot him out of here." In November, an AM-7-7 employee accompanied Monette on his route, claiming he would help him increase bread sales. He made a list of Monette's customers and told him it was only evidence for his boss that he had done his job. In February 1989, AM-7-7 refused to sell Monette bread. The same day, company representatives used Monette's customer list to visit his customers, telling them they were taking over the route, would sell them bread directly, and would sell them the bread products Monette had brought them from other bakers. Monette was forced to abandon his route,

Monette sued AM-7-7 for intentional interference with prospective economic advantage. He won and was awarded $60,000 in damages. AM-7-7 appealed.

CASE DECISION Forester, Judge.

* * *

Monette's theory is that he proved all the elements of the tort of intentional interference with prospective economic advantage. Defendants' main arguments are that no evidence was introduced at trial that defendants pressured Monette's retail customers to cease buying bread from Monette, and, in any event, that AM-7-7 . . . was justified in terminating its relationship with Monette because he was not servicing the route effectively.

Monette responds that . . . he merely needed to prove that defendants intentionally committed acts

that caused Monette's customers to discontinue their business relationships with Monette and that such interference by defendants was improper or unjustified. . . . Evidence was presented that defendants used fraudulent and deceptive means to coerce Monette into disclosing his customers to defendants so that defendants could take over the bread route for their own benefit.

* * *

The tort of intentional interference with contractual relations differs from intentional interference with prospective economic advantage. The former centers on interference with an actual contractual relationship, whereas the latter tort does not require the existence of an enforceable contract. In fact, "[i]t is not necessary that the prospective relation be expected to be reduced to a formal, binding contract." *Restatement (Second) of Torts* §766B comment © (1979).

In order to establish interference with a prospective economic advantage, the plaintiff must show:

1. the existence of a valid business relation (not necessarily evidenced by an enforceable contract) or expectancy;
2. that defendant knew of the business relationship;
3. that defendant intentionally interfered by improperly inducing or causing a breach or termination of the relationship or expectancy;
4. that defendant's improper or unjustified interference resulted in injury to the plaintiff.

* * *

The judgment of the district court is affirmed.

QUESTIONS FOR ANALYSIS

1. AM-7-7 had no obligation to continue to sell Monette bread; why should it be a tort for it to approach Monette's customers to offer them a better deal?
2. Monette paid $28,000 for the route; he offered to sell it to AM-7-7 for $15,000. How could compensatory damages be $60,000?

PREMISES LIABILITY

Businesses have long been liable for accidents on their property as a result of negligence of the business. "Slip-and-fall" suits are common. They occur when someone suffers an injury from slipping and falling on a wet floor (or some other unsafe area) that was not barricaded to keep patrons away from the safety hazard. Since the public has been "invited" to come onto business property, it is presumed that the property is safe for public admission.

A newer area of premises liability is the liability of a business that does not provide sufficient security to help prevent crimes from occurring on its property. For instance, in 1995 Supreme Court of Connecticut case, *Stewart v. Federated Department Stores* (662 A.2d 753), the court upheld a 1.5-million-dollar verdict in favor of the heirs of a woman who was robbed and murdered in the parking garage of a Bloomingdale's department store. The store was found negligent for not having a security guard on duty at the time of the murder. The store was in a high-crime area, and other customers had been robbed in the garage. *Ann M.*, the leading California case on this subject, discusses the duty of a property owner.

Ann M. v. Pacific Plaza Shopping Center
Supreme Court of California
6 Cal.4th 666, 863 P.2d 207 (1993)

CASE BACKGROUND *Ann M. was working alone at a San Diego photo-processing store in Pacific Plaza, a strip mall with twenty-five stores. After she opened the store for business at 8 A.M., a man armed with a knife entered the store, raped her, robbed the store, and fled (he was not caught). Ann M. sued the shopping center for negligence for failing to provide adequate security to protect her from an unreasonable risk of harm. Ann M. contended that the security patrols that drove through the mall area three or four times a day were inadequate; she claimed that there should have been more continuous patrols of the mall because transients in the area posed a threat. Several purse snatchings and other crimes had taken place at the mall or in the area. The trial court granted Pacific Plaza summary judgment, holding that it did not violate its duty of care to Ann M. The appeals court affirmed. Ann M. appealed to the California Supreme Court.*

CASE DECISION Panelli, Associate Justice.

* * *

It is now well established that California law requires landowners to maintain land in their possession and control in a reasonably safe condition. In the case of a landlord, this general duty of maintenance, which is owed to tenants and patrons, has been held to include the duty to take reasonable steps to secure common areas against foreseeable criminal acts of third parties that are likely to occur in the absence of such precautionary measures.

* * *

[We] turn to the heart of the case: whether Pacific Plaza had reasonable cause to anticipate that criminal conduct such as rape would occur in the shopping center premises unless it provided security patrols in the common areas. For, as frequently recognized, a duty to take affirmative action to control the wrongful acts of a third party will be imposed only where such conduct can be reasonably anticipated.

In this, as in other areas of tort law, foreseeability is a crucial factor in determining the existence of duty. . . .

Unfortunately, random, violent crime is endemic in today's society. It is difficult, if not impossible, to envision any locale open to the public where the occurrence of violent crime seems improbable.

* * *

Turning to the question of the scope of a landlord's duty to provide protection from foreseeable third party crime, we observe that . . . the scope of the duty is determined in part by balancing the foreseeability of the harm against the burden of the duty to be imposed. . . .

While there may be circumstances where the hiring of security guards will be required to satisfy a landowner's duty of care, such action will rarely, if ever, be found to be a "minimal burden." The monetary costs of security guards is not insignificant. Moreover, the obligation to provide patrols adequate to deter criminal conduct is not well defined. "No one really knows why people commit crime, hence no one really knows what is 'adequate' deterrence in any given situation." Finally, the social costs of imposing a duty on landowners to hire private police forces are also not insignificant. For these reasons, we conclude that a high degree of foreseeability is required in order to find that the scope of a landlord's duty of care includes the hiring of security guards. We further conclude that the requisite degree of foreseeability rarely, if ever, can be proven in the absence of prior similar incidents of violent crime on the landowner's premises. To hold otherwise would be to impose an unfair burden upon landlords and, in effect, would force landlords to become the insurers of public safety, contrary to well established policy in this state.

Turning to the facts of the case before us, we conclude that violent criminal assaults were not sufficiently foreseeable to impose a duty upon Pacific Plaza to provide security guards in the common areas.

* * *

We, therefore, conclude that Pacific Plaza was entitled to summary judgment on the ground that it owed no duty to Ann M. to provide security guards in the common areas.

The judgment of the Court of Appeal is affirmed.

CASE NOTE Ann M. also filed a workers' compensation claim against her employer and was awarded benefits. Since such benefits are by state law an exclusive remedy, Ann M. dropped her employer as a defendant in this suit.

QUESTIONS FOR ANALYSIS

1. Ann M. argued that a bank robbery in the shopping mall and assorted other crimes such as purse snatching, along with the presence of transients in the area, were sufficient warning of foreseeable danger. Is that correct, or are more serious crimes necessary to establish danger?

2. The owner of Pacific Plaza discussed the possibility of additional security with the mall tenants and told them that because of the expense of full-time security, rents would have to be increased. Instead, the tenants paid for a security service to drive by a couple of times a day. Should responsibility for security be in the control of the tenants or the landlord?

Product Liability

Product liability is a general term applied to an area of the law that is primarily tort law but also involves some contract law and statutory law. This area of law concerns the liability that producers and sellers of goods have to those injured by defects in a product. Since some cases involve thousands of people and billions of dollars, it is an area of the law that gets considerable public attention and is controversial. Several major companies have been bankrupted by product liability decisions. The primary political issue is whether the law has become so tough in assigning liability to producers that the legislature should intervene and set limits on the liability that can be incurred.

Louis Brandeis, who later sat on the U.S. Supreme Court, said, "Political, social, and economic changes entail the recognition of new rights, and the common law, in its eternal youth, grows to meet the demands of society" (*Harvard Law Review*, 1890). The evolution of product liability law in the past century certainly reflects how the common law changes. This section reviews the history of the law because, while new rules have evolved over time as expectations about safety and

Is Japan Really Different?

Some politicians want legislation to restrict tort litigation. They often cite Japan as an example of where there is less litigation and fewer lawyers. This is supposed to make the Japanese more competitive than people in the United States, where tort cases are claimed to be out of control.

The United States has twenty-five times more lawyers per person than Japan because the government of Japan allows only between 300 and 500 new attorneys each year. However, Japanese universities produce 50 percent *more* legal specialists per person than do American universities. These Japanese "nonlawyers" do all legal work except represent clients in court for a fee. Although the nonlawyers are not called lawyers, they are paid to do what Americans call legal work.

A study of fatal traffic accidents in Japan by UCLA law professor Mark Ramseyer and Hitotsubashi Univer-

sity law professor Minoru Nakazato found that the American and Japanese tort systems do not look all that different. The systems are organized differently because of the small number of people in Japan called lawyers, but the results are surprising for those who think that Americans are the only people in the world who file lawsuits and that American juries are too sympathetic to plaintiffs. The authors found that Japanese plaintiffs win a higher percentage of tort liability suits than do American plaintiffs. They also found the payments to Japanese plaintiffs to be very close to those given to American plaintiffs in similar tort suits.

Many of the rules in Japan are different from those in the United States, but a close examination makes the actual operation of the two tort systems look more alike than is often claimed.

responsibility changed, the old law is still generally good law and in some cases is the basis of suits filed today. This section also allows us to study the evolution of the common law in a specific area.

CONSUMER PRODUCTS AND NEGLIGENCE

In the nineteenth century, the courts adopted the rule that a manufacturer was liable for injuries caused by defects in its products to parties with whom the manufacturer had a contractual relationship regarding the product. The term *privity of contract* refers to the relationship that exists between two contracting parties. It is essential to a legal action involving a contract that privity exist between the parties. Since consumers rarely bought products directly from manufacturers, there was no privity between consumer and producer. Producers were effectively isolated from liability for most product-related injuries.

Rule of Caveat Emptor

Parties injured by defective products who did not have privity of contract with the manufacturer operated under the rule of *caveat emptor*, which means "let the buyer beware." According to the U.S. Supreme Court, the rule of caveat emptor "requires that the buyer examine, judge, and test [the product] for himself." Thus, a consumer without privity took the risk that a product was of adequate quality. If a product did not meet safety expectations and injury resulted, the financial burden of the injury fell on the consumer.

In a product injury case, an injured party would contend that the manufacturer was under a duty to provide reasonably safe products. However, if no privity existed, the courts held that no legal duty existed between the manufacturer and the consumer. Thus, the manufacturer could not be found negligent in the construction or design of its product in cases brought by an injured consumer who lacked privity.

Negligence in Tort

Justifying the privity rule, the courts reasoned that it would place too heavy a burden on manufacturers to hold them responsible to numerous consumers whose identity they did not know. The rule often left innocent injured consumers without redress. In response to the harsh result the rule could impose, the courts began to recognize exceptions. Finally, in 1916, in the famous *MacPherson* decision, New York struck down the privity rule and held a manufacturer liable in tort for negligence for a product-related injury.

MacPherson v. Buick Motor Company
Court of Appeals of New York
217 N.Y. 382, 111 N.E. 1050 (1916)

CASE BACKGROUND *Buick produced cars and sold them to dealers. MacPherson bought a new Buick from a dealer in New York. The wheels on MacPherson's Buick were made by another company for Buick. Not long after he bought the car, one of the wheels suddenly collapsed, causing an accident that injured MacPherson, who sued Buick. MacPherson's suit against Buick traditionally would have been barred because of lack of privity; that is, Buick sold the car to the dealer, who in turn sold it to MacPherson. The dealer had privity with MacPherson but was not responsible for the defect. The trial court and the appellate division ruled for MacPherson, finding Buick liable in tort for injuries caused by the defect. Buick appealed to the highest court in New York.*

CASE DECISION Cardozo, Justice.

* * *

One of the wheels was made of defective wood, and its spokes crumbled into fragments. The wheel was not made by the defendant; it was bought from another manufacturer. There is evidence, however, that its defects could have been discovered by reasonable inspection, and that inspection was omitted. There is no claim that Buick knew of the defect and willfully concealed it. . . . The charge is one, not of fraud, but of negligence. The question to be determined is whether the defendant owed a duty of care and vigilance to anyone but the immediate purchaser.

* * *

If the nature of a thing is such that it is reasonably certain to place life and limb in peril when negligently made, it is then a thing of danger. Its nature gives warning of the consequences to be expected. If to the element of danger there is added knowledge that the thing will be used by persons other than the purchaser, and used without new tests, then, irrespective of contract, the manufacturer of this thing of danger is under a duty to make it carefully. That is as far as we are required to go for the decision of this case. There must be knowledge of a danger, not merely possible, but probable. It is possible to use almost anything in a way that will make it dangerous if defective. That is not enough to charge the manufacturer with a duty independent of his contract. Whether a given thing is dangerous may be sometimes a question for the court and sometimes a question for the jury. There must also be knowledge that in the usual course of events the danger will be shared by others than the buyer. Such knowledge may often be inferred from the nature of the transaction. But it is possible that even the knowledge of the danger and of the use will not always be enough. The proximity or remoteness of the relation is a factor to be considered. We are dealing now with the liability of the manufacturer of the finished product, who puts it on the market to be used without inspection by his customers. If he is negligent, where danger is to be foreseen, a liability will follow.

* * *

We think the defendant was not absolved from a duty of inspection because it bought the wheels from a reputable manufacturer. It was not merely a dealer in automobiles. It was a manufacturer of automobiles. It was responsible for the finished product. It was not at liberty to put the finished product on the market without subjecting the component parts to ordinary and simple tests. Under the charge of the trial judge nothing more was required of it. The obligation to inspect must vary with the nature of the thing to be inspected. The more probable the danger the greater the need of caution.

* * *

The judgment should be affirmed.

QUESTIONS FOR ANALYSIS

1. Buick argued that it should not be liable because it did not make the wheels—some other company did. Why not make the injured party sue the producer of the defective part?
2. Buick argued that this was the only wheel out of 60,000 sold that had been shown defective. Should 1/60,000 be sufficient to establish negligence?

By eliminating the requirement of a contractual relationship between the manufacturer and the consumer (privity), manufacturers are held responsible for product safety to consumers by fact of a sale. Manufacturers must therefore produce products using proper care to eliminate foreseeable harm, or they risk being found negligent in tort if a consumer is injured by a defective product. The rule originating with *MacPherson* and adopted by the courts in every state provided that

> The manufacturer of a product is liable in the production and sale of a product for negligence, if the product may reasonably be expected to inflict harm on the user if the product is defective.

The Negligence Standard When liability is based on negligence, a manufacturer is required to exercise *reasonable care* under the circumstances in the production of its product. The circumstances include the probability of a defect, magnitude of the possible harm, cost of effective inspection, and standards of the industry. Liability may be imposed on a manufacturer for negligence in the preparation of the product—for failing to inspect or test the materials, for below-normal-quality workmanship, or for failing to discover possible defects. Defects and dangers must be revealed, even if the manufacturer becomes aware of them only after the sale of the product to the consumer. Reasonable care must also be taken in presenting the product to the public—through advertisements or other promotions—to avoid *misrepresentation*. If a causal connection can be established between the failure of the manufacturer to exercise reasonable care in any of these areas and an injury suffered by a consumer, liability for damages may be imposed on the manufacturer by the court.

For fifty years after *MacPherson*, negligence was the universal law of product liability. Beginning in the early 1960s, however, the courts began also to apply a strict liability doctrine to manufactured products. Despite the dominance of strict liability, a plaintiff who can show in a product liability suit that the defendant has been negligent may have a stronger case and be more likely to receive punitive damages.

CONSUMER PRODUCTS AND STRICT LIABILITY

Over time, experience showed that negligence in tort did not resolve some product-related injury cases. Consumers had difficulties establishing that a manufacturer had not exercised reasonable care in the production of its product. The *strict liability* doctrine, in contrast, holds manufacturers liable to consumers injured by defective products even though the manufacturer exercised all reasonable care. Thus, the injured party is not required to attack the reasonableness of the conduct of the manufacturer, but rather focuses on problems with the product.

Strict liability was first applied to product-related injuries through a warranty theory under contract law. As we will see, this proved to be too restrictive, and the courts began to develop the rule of strict liability in tort. Later, the adoption of strict liability in tort by the American Law Institute in authoritative *Second Restatement of Torts* helped spur the adoption of strict liability in tort in product-related injury cases throughout the country.

Product Liability under Contract Law

Strict liability under contract law is based on the relationship between the injured party and the manufacturer because of the existence of a *warranty*. Warranty is based upon a manufacturer's assurance to the consumer that a product will meet certain quality and performance standards. Such warranties may be either express or implied.

Strict Liability Based on Implied Warranty The first major application of the doctrine of strict liability for defective consumer products was in the area of food and drink. For example, in a 1913 case from Washington State, *Mazetti* v. *Armour* (135 P. 633), the court disregarded the privity of contract requirement: "a manufacturer of food products . . . impliedly warrants his goods when dispensed in original packages." Consumer injury caused by defective food or drink is a breach of implied warranty, and the manufacturer is strictly liable for the injury. For decades now, the courts have imposed strict liability based on an implied warranty of safety (see Exhibit 8.2) in defective food and drink cases.

In 1960, the Supreme Court of New Jersey extended implied warranty of safety to other consumer products. In *Henningsen* v. *Bloomfield Motors, Inc.* (161 A.2d 69), the New Jersey court held the manufacturer of an automobile strictly liable to the purchaser's wife (who was driving the car when the brakes failed and an accident occurred) for her injuries on the basis of an implied warranty of safety. This was the key decision to expand the implied warranty theory beyond its application in food and drink cases. *Henningsen* had a dramatic impact on the liability rules:

> What followed [the *Henningsen* case] was the most rapid and altogether spectacular overturn of an established rule in the entire history of the law of torts. There was a deluge of cases in other jurisdictions following the lead of New Jersey, and finding an implied warranty of safety as to a wide assortment of products. (Prosser and Keeton on Torts, 5th ed., p. 690)

EXHIBIT 8.2

Implied Warranty

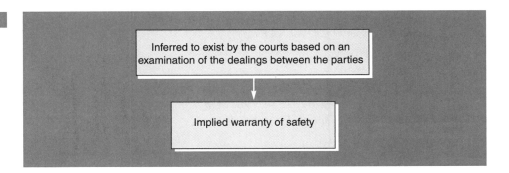

EXHIBIT 8.3

Express Warranty

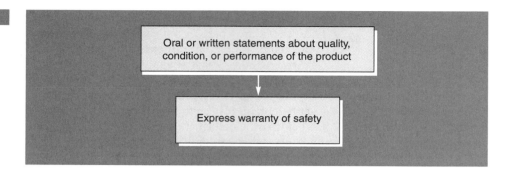

Statutory Implied Warranty In addition to creating implied warranties of safety under the common law of contract, the *Uniform Commercial Code (UCC)* (a statute we study in Chapter 11 that has been adopted by the states) creates implied warranties governing quality and performance of certain products. As we will study in detail in Chapter 11, under Section 2–314, the UCC provides that if the seller of a product is a merchant under the Code—defined as one who deals in the kinds of products sold to the consumer—the products are statutorily warranted as *merchantable*. A product is considered merchantable if it is fit for the purpose for which it is being sold. In addition, Section 2–315 of the UCC provides that when the seller knows the purpose the buyer has for the product, and the buyer relies on the seller's expertise to supply a suitable product, there is an implied warranty that the goods will be fit for that particular purpose.

Strict Liability Based on Express Warranty Strict liability under contract law is also applied in cases in which a manufacturer makes an *express representation* about its product to consumers. A manufacturer, for example, could advertise quality or performance characteristics of its product. To the extent the claim becomes a part of the bargain between the manufacturer and the consumer, the manufacturer is held to have a duty of performance as to that representation (see Exhibit 8.3).

Strict liability based on express warranty does not require that injured consumers have purchased the product directly from the manufacturer. As the decision in *Baxter* v. *Ford Motor Company* illustrates, the courts can disregard privity of contract and allow the consumer to sue the manufacturer, not the retail dealer. Injured consumers are not required to prove fault because the law requires manufacturers to guarantee the truthfulness of their representations. Hence, *misrepresentation* about a product may be the basis for strict liability in tort.

Baxter v. Ford Motor Company

Supreme Court of Washington
168 Wash. 456, 12 P.2d 409 (1932)

CASE BACKGROUND *Baxter purchased a new Model A from a Ford dealer in May 1930. Printed material from Ford, distributed by the dealer, stated that the* windshield was "Triple Shatter-Proof Car's Glass." This innovation was advertised by Ford as a safety feature, because the windshield "will not fly or shatter under the *hardest impact . . . it eliminates the dangers of flying glass." In October 1930, as Baxter was driving the car, a pebble from a passing car hit the windshield, causing a small piece of glass to fly into Baxter's left eye, resulting in its loss.*

Baxter sued Ford because the windshield was not shatter-proof glass. The trial court did not allow the advertising to be admitted in evidence, held there was no privity of contract between the parties, and entered judgment for Ford. Baxter appealed.

CASE DECISION Herman, Justice.

* * *

Ford Motor Company contends that there can be no implied or express warranty without privity of contract, and warranties as to personal property do not attach themselves to, and run with, the article sold.

* * *

In the case at bar the automobile was represented by the manufacturer as having a windshield of non-shatterable glass "so made that it will not fly or shatter under the hardest impact." An ordinary person would be unable to discover by the usual and customary examination of the automobile whether glass which would not fly or shatter was used in the windshield. In that respect the purchaser was in a position similar to that of the consumer of a wrongly labeled drug, who has bought the same from a retailer, and who has relied upon the manufacturer's representation that the label correctly set forth the contents of the container. For many years it has been held that, under such circumstances, the manufacturer is liable to the consumer, even though the consumer purchased from a third person the commodity causing the damage. The rule in such cases does not rest upon contractual obligations, but rather on the principle that the original act of delivering an article is wrong, when, because of the lack of those qualities which the manufacturer represented it as having, the absence of which could not be readily detected by the consumer, the article is not safe for the purposes for which the consumer would ordinarily use it.

* * *

Since the rule of caveat emptor was first formulated, vast changes have taken place. . . . Methods of doing business have undergone a great transition. Radio, billboards, and the products of the printing press have become the means of creating a large part of the demand that causes goods to depart from factories to the ultimate consumer. It would be unjust to recognize a rule that would permit manufacturers of goods to create a demand for their products by representing that they possess qualities which they, in fact, do not possess, and then, because there is no privity of contract existing between the consumer and the manufacturer, deny the consumer the right to recover if damages result from the absence of those qualities, when such absence is not readily noticeable.

* * *

The nature of nonshatterable glass is such that the falsity of the representations with reference to the glass would not be readily detected by a person of ordinary experience and reasonable prudence. Baxter, under the circumstances shown in this case, had the right to rely upon the representations made by Ford Motor Company relative to qualities possessed by its products, even though there was no privity of contract between Baxter and Ford Motor Company.

* * *

The trial court erred in taking the case from the jury and entering judgment for respondent Ford Motor Company. It was for the jury to determine, under proper instructions, whether the failure of respondent Ford Motor Company to equip the windshield with glass which did not fly or shatter was the proximate cause of appellant's injury. . . .

Reversed, with directions to grant a new trial with reference to respondent Ford Motor Company. . . .

QUESTIONS FOR ANALYSIS

1. Ford claims there was no contract upon which Baxter could base his claim, because the purchase documents said nothing about shatter-proof glass. Does that argument have merit? Would Baxter have bought the car anyway had he known that it did not have shatter-proof glass?
2. Suppose a passenger riding in Baxter's car was injured by the flying glass. Would the passenger have had a claim against Ford on the basis of express warranty in contract?

Statutory Express Warranty As in the case of implied warranties, the UCC also creates express warranties as we will see in Chapter 11. Section 2–313 provides that promises or statements the seller makes about a product become part of the bargain for sale; an express warranty is created. As under the common law, the UCC provides that the seller need not use the word *warranty* or *guarantee* for an express warranty to be created.

The Supreme Court reaffirmed the availability of these bases for liability in the 1992 case, *Cipollone* v. *Liggett Group* (112 S.Ct. 2608). The heirs of Rose Cipollone, who began smoking in 1942 and had died of lung cancer in 1984, claimed that cigarette manufacturers were liable for her death. The Court held that there may be a cause of action based on breach of express warranty under Section 2–313 of the UCC, which reads, in part:

> Any affirmation of fact or promise made by the seller to the buyer which relates to the goods and becomes part of the basis of the bargain creates an express warranty that the goods shall conform to the affirmation or promise.

The Cipollones claimed that cigarette advertisements in the 1940s and 1950s stated that smoking did not cause health problems. Since that is not true, and the cigarette makers should have known that smoking was not healthy, there was a breach of warranty. The Court also noted that a cause of action may exist under the common law for misrepresentation. Liability may be imposed if it can be shown that the cigarette makers hid the truth about the dangers of smoking or created a false impression that smoking was safe.

Strict Liability in Tort

When asked to impose strict liability under contract law, the courts can be faced with the difficulty of determining what constituted a warranty. In addition, the courts frequently faced express limits on liability that manufacturers wrote in their warranties. In response to such difficulties, the courts simplified the legal basis for injured plaintiffs by adopting the rule of *strict liability in tort*. The Supreme Court of California was the first court to adopt strict liability in tort in product injury cases with its 1963 decision in *Greenman*.

Greenman v. Yuba Power Products, Inc.

Supreme Court of California
59 Cal.2d 57, 27 Cal.Rptr. 697, 377 P.2d 897 (1963)

CASE BACKGROUND *Greenman's wife bought him a Shopsmith—a power tool that could be used as a saw, drill, and wood lathe. Greenman had studied material about the product and asked his wife to buy it. Two years later, Greenman was using the machine as a lathe. After working on the same piece of wood several times without incident, the wood suddenly flew out of the machine and struck Greenman on the forehead, inflicting serious injuries.*

Greenman sued the manufacturer, Shopsmith, and the retail dealer, Yuba Power, alleging breaches of war-

ranties and negligence. The verdict in Greenman's favor against Shopsmith was appealed.

CASE DECISION Traynor, Justice.

* * *

Plaintiff introduced substantial evidence that his injuries were caused by defective design and construction of the Shopsmith. His expert witnesses testified that inadequate set screws were used to hold parts of the machine together so that normal vibration caused the tailstock of the lathe to move away from the piece of wood being turned permitting it to fly out of the lathe. They also testified that there were other more positive ways of fastening the parts of the machine together, the use of which would have prevented the accident.

* * *

A manufacturer is strictly liable in tort when an article he places on the market, knowing that it is to be used without inspection for defects, proves to have a defect that causes injury to a human being. Recognized first in the case of unwholesome food products, such liability has now been extended to a variety of other products that create as great or greater hazards if defective.

* * *

We need not recanvass the reasons for imposing strict liability on the manufacturer. . . . The purpose of such liability is to insure that the costs of injuries resulting from defective products are borne by the manufacturers that put such products on the market rather than by the injured persons who are powerless to protect themselves. Sales warranties serve this purpose fitfully at best. In the present case, for example, the plaintiff was able to plead and prove an express warranty only because he read and relied on the representations of the Shopsmith's ruggedness contained in the manufacturer's brochure. Implicit in the machine's presence on the market, however, was a representation that it would safely do the jobs for which

it was built. Under these circumstances, it should not be controlling whether plaintiff selected the machine because of the statements in the brochure, or because of the machine's own appearance of excellence that belied the defect lurking beneath the surface, or because he merely assumed that it would safely do the jobs it was built to do. It should not be controlling whether the details of the sales from manufacturer to retailer and from retailer to Greenman's wife were such that one or more of the implied warranties of the sales act arose. "The remedies of injured consumers ought not to be made to depend upon the intricacies of the law of sales." To establish the manufacturer's liability it was sufficient that plaintiff proved that he was injured while using the Shopsmith in a way it was intended to be used as a result of a defect in design and manufacture of which plaintiff was not aware that made the Shopsmith unsafe for its intended use.

* * *

The judgment is affirmed.

QUESTIONS FOR ANALYSIS

1. Why did the court move to strict liability in tort rather than do as the New Jersey court had done a few years previously and hold that strict liability could be imposed on the basis of implied warranty in contract?
2. Would strict liability be imposed on the manufacturer if a friend of Greenman's had used the machine and was hurt while using it?

Section 402A The principal author of the *Second Restatement of Torts*, the American Law Institute, adopted a strict liability in tort rule in product injury cases similar to that imposed in *Greenman*. This helped bring about nationwide acceptance of the strict liability in tort rule. The *Restatement's* strict liability in tort rule is found in Section 402A:

(1) One who sells any product in a defective condition unreasonably dangerous to the user or consumer or to his property is subject to liability for physical harm thereby caused to the ultimate user or consumer, or to his property, if
   (a) the seller is engaged in the business of selling such a product, and
   (b) it is expected to and does reach the user or consumer without substantial change in the condition in which it is sold.
(2) The rule stated in Subsection (1) applies although
   (a) the seller has exercised all possible care in the preparation and sale of his product, and

EXHIBIT 8.4

Elements of Strict Liability

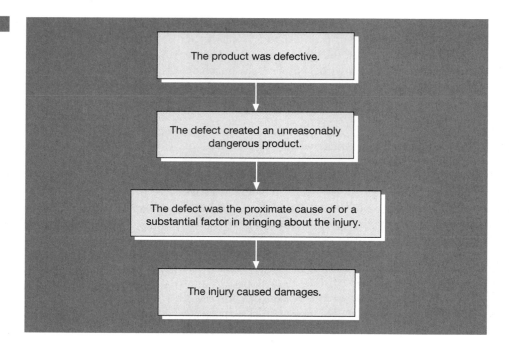

The product was defective.

↓

The defect created an unreasonably dangerous product.

↓

The defect was the proximate cause of or a substantial factor in bringing about the injury.

↓

The injury caused damages.

(b) the user or consumer has not bought the product from or entered into any contractual relation with the seller.

Applications of Strict Liability

Exhibit 8.4 outlines the chain of events needed to establish strict liability in tort. Cases in which there is a flaw in the product when it is sold that causes an injury are the simplest use of the rule. Since the *Greenman* decision, the application of the doctrine has expanded to include three other primary areas: (1) the manufacturer failed to warn the consumer of risks of use or of known hazards in certain uses of the product, (2) the product is poorly designed (as opposed to being defectively manufactured), and (3) the product produces latent injuries (injuries that occur years after the consumer has used the product).

Failure to Warn A manufacturer's *failure to warn* consumers of dangers involved in the use of a product, or to instruct consumers about proper procedures in using a product, has long been actionable. In recent years courts have expanded the range of what may constitute failure to warn that can result in strict liability. *Morales v. American Honda Motor Co.* illustrates failure to warn.

Morales v. American Honda Motor Co.

United States Courts of Appeals, Sixth Circuit
71 F.3d 531 (1995)

CASE BACKGROUND *Nine-year-old Gary Thompson drove his Honda Z50R motorcycle into the* *path of a pickup truck as he left an unpaved farm road and drove onto a paved public road in Kentucky. The*

driver of the pickup was not at fault because her view of the dirt road was obstructed by bales of hay and she had the right-of-way. Gary suffered severe injuries, including permanent brain damage. Medical expenses at the time of trial were over $320,000. Gary's mother, who brought suit on his behalf, had bought him the cycle. The owner's manual stated that the cycle was "designed for junior riders" and was "not recommended for children under 7 years old." The small cycle, which could go up to 40 mph, was stated not for use on public roads: "It is illegal to ride this motorcycle on public streets. . . . It must be ridden only in off-road areas where such activities are permitted. If it becomes necessary to cross a public roadway, remember to get off the motorcycle and push it across."
On the cycle itself was a printed warning:

IMPORTANT NOTICE

THIS VEHICLE IS DESIGNED AND MANUFAC-TURED FOR OFF-THE-ROAD USE ONLY. IT DOES NOT CONFORM TO FEDERAL MOTOR VEHICLE SAFETY STANDARDS AND OPERA-TION IN PUBLIC STREETS, ROADS, OR HIGH-WAYS IS ILLEGAL.

REMEMBER

—PRESERVE NATURE—RIDE SAFELY—ALWAYS WEAR A HELMET—READ OWNER'S MANUAL CAREFULLY BEFORE RIDING.

Gary's mother said she had told Gary the safety rules many times, including on the day he was hit. Among her claims against Honda was that the "warnings were inade-quate, because Honda did not explain the potential conse-quences of a child riding this motorcycle on the road in terms a child could understand."

The district court granted Honda's motion for sum-mary judgment, ruling that "even if the owner's manual contained a stronger and more explicit statement warning the rider that a car could hit him if he rode on the road, no reasonable jury could find that Gary would have fol-lowed that warning." Gary's mother appealed.

CASE DECISION   Holschuh, District Judge.

* * *

With respect to failure to warn, the character of warnings that accompany the product is generally an evidentiary consideration in deciding whether a prod-uct is unreasonably unsafe. . . .

Kentucky's highest court held that a product was unreasonably unsafe if there was a failure to provide

adequate warnings to the ultimate user. Under Ken-tucky law, the duty to warn extends to the dangers likely to result from foreseeable misuse of a product. Further, the . . . court held that in the absence of an adequate warning, the defendant cannot shift to the plaintiff the burden of proving that he would not have misused the product regardless.

The . . . court noted that the fact that reasonable minds could differ as to the adequacy of the warnings made the issue of negligence a jury question.

* * *

[A] factual question is presented as to whether the warnings given with the motorcycle constituted a sub-stantial factor in contributing to the cause of the acci-dent. The only warning that Honda gave was that it was illegal to ride this motorcycle on public roads. No warning was given that specifically pointed out [spe-cific] dangers. . . . Honda cannot shift to plaintiff the burden of proving that the product would not have been misused had the product contained stronger warnings. A factual question is raised as to whether Honda's failure to give adequate warnings, admitted for the purpose of the summary judgment motion, was a substantial factor in causing the accident. This is properly a jury question that precludes the entry of summary judgment by the trial court.

* * *

In this case, there is sufficient evidence which, when viewed in the light most favorable to plaintiff, would permit the reasonable inference that Honda's alleged design defect and/or failure to warn was a sub-stantial factor in bringing about Gary's harm. Accord-ingly, we vacate the district court's grant of summary judgment and remand for further proceedings consis-tent with this decision. . . .

QUESTIONS FOR ANALYSIS

1. Knowing that seven-year-olds are not likely to pay attention to warnings, is there any way Honda could avoid liability regardless of how many warn-ings were given? That is, could Honda be held liable for most accidents?

2. Gary's mother also argued that the cycle was defective because it did not have a red flag on a flexible pole that would stand up at about six feet to make the cycle more visible to drivers. Is that evidence of an unreasonably dangerous product that should be subject to strict liability?

Manufacturers must warn of possible dangers in the use, storage, and handling of their products. For example, although household cleansers are dangerous and not intended for consumption, manufacturers know that parents often leave such products in places where children might get them. Thus, liability may be imposed for not warning people sufficiently of such dangers and for not taking steps to reduce possible tragedies, such as by using containers that are not attractive to children, using hard-to-remove caps, and putting danger labels or symbols on the containers. How far does the failure-to-warn liability in tort extend? While the limits of the application are still being defined by the courts, the following cases serve as examples:

- A Pennsylvania court found that a gun manufacturer that failed to warn users of possible damage to their hearing from long-term exposure to gunfire was liable for injuries.
- The Supreme Court of Alaska upheld a verdict against a diet food producer that failed to provide adequate warnings about using the adult diet food as baby food. Because the food was safe for dieting adults but not for infants, the company should have stated so on its product rather than assume that adults would not use the product as baby food.
- The high court of New York held liable the producer of a commercial pizza dough roller machine for injuries suffered by a worker who stuck his hands in the machine when he tried to clean it. Although the machine had a safety switch to be used when cleaning the machine, the worker had turned off the safety switch so that he could stick his hands in the machine. The manufacturer failed to warn when it did not clearly explain the dangers of turning off the safety switch.
- The Eleventh Circuit Court of Appeals held that the warnings printed on a bottle of Campho-Phenique, an external medicine, stating "Keep out of reach of children," "For external use," and "in case of ingestion—seek medical help and call poison center" were not strong enough to explain the dangers. A four-year-old child drank the medicine and suffered severe injuries. The suit proceeded on the basis of failure to warn.
- A jury in a federal court ordered Johnson & Johnson to pay $8.85 million to a man who had had a liver transplant because years of drinking alcohol and taking Tylenol had destroyed his liver. J&J had not warned Tylenol users that there was evidence that serious liver damage could occur to regular drinkers who also took regular doses of Tylenol.

Design Defects Unlike defective product cases, *design defect* cases are not concerned with a product that has been poorly manufactured, been sold to a consumer, and then caused injury. Rather, such cases focus on the determination of whether an injury to users could have been prevented by differently designing and producing the product. In that regard, consider the following design defect cases:

- In a Washington State case, a worker received a $750,000 judgment for the loss of a leg. While repairing a machine, coworkers had removed a metal plate from the top of the machine. After repairing the machine, the workers failed to replace the metal plate and covered the machine with cardboard. The plaintiff later walked on what he thought was the metal plate, as was customary, and fell into the machine. The court held that a design defect had allowed the machine to be able to run when the metal plate was removed.

- A restaurant employee was seriously burned when he tried to retrieve something that fell out of his shirt pocket and into a commercial French fryer machine. The D.C. Circuit Court of Appeals held that a jury could find that a safer alternative design of the machine was possible, in which case it could impose liability.
- A child pushed the emergency stop button on an escalator, causing a person to fall and be injured. The Seventh Circuit Court of Appeals ruled that it was a design defect both to make the button red, because that color is attractive to children, and to place the button so that it was accessible to children.
- In an Eleventh Circuit Court of Appeals case, the plaintiff was injured when he took his riding mower up a hill that was too steep; the mower rolled over, and the plaintiff was cut by the whirring blades. The court held that there was technology in existence when the mower was built that would have caused the mower to shut off automatically when it came off the ground or when the rider let go of the controls. Because such technology was not included in the product's design, the manufacturer was strictly liable for the plaintiff's injuries.

The court in the *Brunswick* decision reviewed a claim of design defect that had been rejected at trial.

Pree v. The Brunswick Corporation
United States Court of Appeals, Eighth Circuit
983 F.2d 863 (1993)

CASE BACKGROUND *Pree was injured when he fell from the back of a friend's pleasure boat that was powered by twin Mercury Marine 330-horsepower engines produced by defendant. It was raining and lightning, the water was choppy, and the boat was being docked at about 1:30 A.M. after a day of drinking and partying on the Lake of the Ozarks. As Pree was standing on the back of the boat trying to grab the dock, the boat lurched and Pree fell off and was severely injured by the unguarded, rotating propeller blades.*

Pree sued Brunswick, claiming that the propeller was defective and unreasonably dangerous because it was not covered by a propeller guard. The jury ruled for Brunswick. Pree appealed, claiming that evidence about his drinking should not have been allowed and, even if the evidence were allowed, that the propellers without guards were defective to the ordinary consumer.

CASE DECISION McMillian, Circuit Judge.

* * *

Strict tort liability applies to product liability actions arising out of the way a product was designed. In order to recover under the theory of strict liability

in tort for a defective design, Missouri law requires that a plaintiff prove the following elements:

(1) [the] defendant sold the product in the course of its business;
(2) the product was then in a defective condition unreasonably dangerous when put into a reasonably anticipated use;
(3) the product was used in a manner reasonably anticipated;
(4) [the] plaintiff was damaged as a direct result of such defective condition as existed when the product was sold.

Because there are no real disputes as to the other three elements, we predicate our decision on the second element: whether the twin motors were in a defective condition unreasonably dangerous because they were designed without propeller guards. Whether a product is unreasonably dangerous is the determinative factor in a design defect case. . . . [A] product is defectively designed if it "creates an unreasonable risk of danger to the consumer or user when put in normal use."

* * *

[Experts hired by Pree testified that the propellers were unreasonably dangerous and that propeller guards should have been installed. Experts hired by Brunswick testified that propeller guards were not a good idea.]

* * *

James Getz testified that as Chairman of the National Boating Safety Advisory Council's Propeller Guard Subcommittee he compiled data and evaluated various propeller guarding devices. Getz testified that after the Propeller Guard Subcommittee conducted hearings and testing, it concluded that it could not recommend a propeller guard because they presented problems with respect to entrapment, blunt trauma and hydrodynamic issues. He testified that the United States Coast Guard had adopted the findings and recommendations of the Propeller Guard Subcommittee not to require or recommend propeller guards.

* * *

Additionally, although Pree forcefully argues that appellee could have employed a safer alternative design for their propellers, there was no evidence that such a design existed at the time the propellers were manufactured.

* * *

After viewing the record in the light most favorable to Pree, we conclude that the evidence was insufficient to show that appellee's engines were unreasonably dangerous, and the district court should have declared as a matter of law, that the engines were not defective and directed a verdict for appellee.

* * *

Accordingly, the judgment of the district court is affirmed.

QUESTIONS FOR ANALYSIS

1. Why did the court not address the issue of Pree's drinking?
2. Spinning propellers are obviously dangerous. Are some products so dangerous that they are not subject to strict liability for injuries they inflict?

Unknown Hazards The largest dollar volume and number of product liability cases are based on *unknown hazards* or latent defects—dangers that were not known or not fully appreciated at the time the product was manufactured. Since the hazard associated with the product may not be learned for years, neither the producer nor the consumer may be able to do anything to prevent injury.

Billions of dollars have been awarded in thousands of suits (often joined as class actions) involving the health effects of asbestos, injuries caused by IUDs, and damage caused by drug side effects that did not appear for years. The first major area of litigation for unknown hazard involved asbestos; asbestos makers have paid billions of dollars to tens of thousands of plaintiffs. At one point, more than two-thirds of all product liability suits filed in federal court were asbestos related. Companies in the asbestos industry have devoted more than $10 billion to help resolve litigation, which has been proceeding for more than twenty years. Although more than 100,000 plaintiffs have agreed to class action settlements, thousands more have not reached settlements. The *Borel* decision was one of the most important in opening the way for asbestos litigation.

Borel v. Fibreboard Paper Products Corp.
United States Court of Appeals, Fifth Circuit
493 F.2d 1076 (1973)

CASE BACKGROUND *Borel was exposed to asbestos from 1936 through 1969 as he worked at various indus-* *trial insulation jobs. In 1964, an X ray showed his lungs to be cloudy. His doctor advised him to avoid asbestos dust. In*

1969, a lung biopsy revealed pulmonary asbestosis. The following year, Borel had a lung removed because of mesothelioma, a lung cancer caused by asbestosis. Shortly thereafter, Borel died.

Borel's heirs continued with litigation that Borel had begun against eleven manufacturers of asbestos insulation materials he had used over the years. Four manufacturers settled out of court, and one was dismissed at trial, leaving six manufacturers, including Fibreboard and Manville. The jury found the defendants liable under strict liability. The manufacturers appealed.

CASE DECISION Wisdom, Circuit Judge.

* * *

The evidence . . . indicated . . . that during Borel's working career no manufacturer ever warned contractors or insulation workers, including Borel, of the dangers associated with inhaling asbestos dust. . . . Furthermore, no manufacturer ever tested the effect of their products on the workers using them or attempted to discover whether the exposure of insulation workers to asbestos dust exceeded the suggested threshold limits.

* * *

As the plaintiff has argued, insulation materials containing asbestos may be viewed as "unavoidably unsafe products." . . . As a practical matter, the decision to market such a product requires a balancing of the product's utility against its known or foreseeable danger. . . . [E]ven when such balancing leads to the conclusion that marketing is justified, the seller still has a responsibility to inform the user or consumer of the risk of harm. The failure to give adequate warnings in these circumstances renders the product unreasonably dangerous.

* * *

Furthermore, in cases such as the instant case, the manufacturer is held to the knowledge and skill of an expert. This is relevant in determining (1) whether the manufacturer knew or should have known the danger, and (2) whether the manufacturer was negligent in failing to communicate this superior knowledge to the user or consumer of its product. The manufacturer's status as expert means that at a minimum he must keep abreast of scientific knowledge, discoveries, and advances and is presumed to know what is imparted thereby. But even more importantly, a manufacturer has a duty to test and inspect his product. The extent of research and experiment must be commensurate with the dangers involved. A product must not be made available to the public without disclosure of those dangers that the application of reasonable foresight would reveal. Nor may a manufacturer rely unquestioningly on others to sound the hue and cry concerning a danger in its product. Rather, each manufacturer must bear the burden of showing that its own conduct was proportionate to the scope of its duty.

* * *

The Petition for Rehearing is denied. . . .

QUESTIONS FOR ANALYSIS

1. The levels of asbestos that Borel was exposed to were usually within "safe" levels established by government studies. Should adherence to such studies or regulations relieve a manufacturer of liability?
2. Borel was exposed to asbestos on the job. Should liability be imposed on employers who expose employees to dangerous products or on producers of the products used on the job?

Also ongoing are efforts to resolve silicone-breast-implant litigation. Two million women had such implants before the implants were banned in 1992 because of health problems alleged to be associated with silicone leaks. A three-billion-dollar settlement funded by implant makers was approved in 1995. But with more than 220,000 women already requesting compensation, the ability of the fund to handle claims is uncertain. Further, thousands of women have opted to file suit individually. Confusion in the litigation, and increasing doubts about the evidence that the silicone causes health problems, has kept the matter unresolved.

Market Share Liability

An intriguing development in product liability arose in a 1980 California Supreme Court case, *Sindell* v. *Abbott Laboratories* (607 P.2d 924). The case pioneered the

JURIS prudence?

It's Nerf Basketball for the Ivy League

Cornell University freshman Darren Traub was playing pickup basketball when he tried to dunk the ball, which he had never been able to do. Traub ran at the hoop, his hand hit the rim, he fell down, and hurt both wrists. He sued the university and the basketball hoop maker for negligence and strict liability, contending that the rigid rims caused or enhanced his injuries.

The defendants moved for summary judgment, claiming that Traub assumed the risk inherent in playing basketball with a rigid hoop, noting that "what goes up must come down." Judge Pooler disagreed and held that the suit would go forward. The danger that occurs "when a player's fingers, hands, and wrists come into contact with a rigid basketball hoop," which can make a controlled landing difficult, is not well known, so Traub may not have assumed the risk. Further, a rigid hoop may be defective compared to a breakaway hoop that might have been installed instead.

Source: *Traub* v. *Cornell*, 1998 WL 187401

notion of *market share liability* or *enterprise liability*. Such liability arose in response to suits filed involving the daughters of women who had taken DES (diethylstilbestrol) during pregnancy. DES is responsible for cancer in the reproductive systems of (now adult) daughters of women who took DES before it was banned. Because DES was produced by numerous companies and was ingested twenty or more years ago, plaintiffs could not identify the manufacturer of the drug taken by their mothers. The California court allowed plaintiffs to sue all drug manufacturers who marketed DES and said that those manufacturers would share liability according to their share of the market for the drug.

Rules somewhat similar to that adopted in the *Sindell* decision appeared in a 1984 case, *Abel* v. *Eli Lilly* (343 N.W.2d 164). The Supreme Court of Michigan adopted a "DES-modified alternative liability" that allows plaintiffs to sue any or all manufacturers of the drug in question at the time it was taken by the plaintiffs' mothers. In response to such litigation, about 300 cases brought by women claiming injury from DES were consolidated in a market-share settlement approved by the New York courts. Eli Lilly's share ranged from over 50 percent when the drug was first used in the 1940s down to about 20 percent in the 1960s, when there were many more producers. Other drug makers pay proportionate shares of the damages determined at trial.

Joint and Several Liability

The Wisconsin Supreme Court addressed the same question in *Collins* v. *Eli Lilly*. It rejected the market-share liability terminology but held that plaintiff(s) could sue any or all manufacturers and that the manufacturers could bring in other manufacturers as defendants so they would share the liability. This is the more traditional *joint and several liability* rule, which has been abolished in some states, that allows any defendant to be held responsible for all damages. In mass tort cases such as DES and asbestos, where numerous producers are involved, in practice the litigation tends to look like market-share liability but that terminology has not been adopted by any other states.

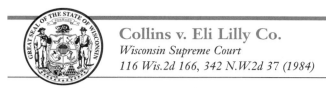

Collins v. Eli Lilly Co.
Wisconsin Supreme Court
116 Wis.2d 166, 342 N.W.2d 37 (1984)

CASE BACKGROUND *Collins was born in 1958. Her mother had taken DES (diethylstilbestrol) during pregnancy, as prescribed, to prevent miscarriage. DES was banned in 1971 when its cancer risks to the reproductive organs of adult women whose mothers had taken the drug during pregnancy with their daughter(s) became known. Collins had radical cancer surgery in 1975. Like at least 1,000 other cancer victims, she attributed the cancer to the DES taken by her mother and sued a dozen producers of DES. Under tort law as it existed, Collins would be unlikely to recover damages because of the lack of ability to prove which specific drug company had produced the pills her mother consumed. The Supreme Court of Wisconsin had to decide how to handle this kind of case.*

CASE DECISION Callow, Justice.

* * *

We recognize that DES cases pose difficult problems. The entirely innocent plaintiffs may have been severely harmed by a drug they had no control over, and they may never know or be able to prove with certainty which drug company produced or marketed the DES taken by their mothers. The defendants are faced with possible liability for DES which they may not have produced or marketed. We conclude, however, that as between the plaintiff, who probably is not at fault, and the defendants, who may have provided the product which caused the injury, the interests of justice and fundamental fairness demand that the latter should bear the cost of injury. Accordingly, we have formulated a method of recovery for plaintiffs in DES cases in Wisconsin. We note that this method of recovery could apply in situations which are factually similar to the DES cases.

Although the defendants in this case may not have acted in concert under the concert of action theory, all participated in either gaining approval of DES for use in pregnancy or in producing or marketing DES in subsequent years. Each defendant contributed to the risk of injury to the public and, consequently, the risk of injury to individual plaintiffs such as Therese Collins. Thus each defendant shares, in some measure, a degree of culpability in producing or marketing

what the FDA, many scientists, and medical researchers ultimately concluded was a drug with possibly harmful side effects. Moreover, as between the injured plaintiff and the possibly responsible drug company, the drug company is in a better position to absorb the cost of the injury. The drug company can either insure itself against liability, absorb the damage award, or pass the cost along to the consuming public as a cost of doing business. We conclude that it is better to have drug companies or consumers share the cost of the injury than to place the burden solely on the innocent plaintiff. Finally, the cost of damages awards will act as an incentive for drug companies to test adequately the drugs they place on the market for general medical use. This incentive is especially important in the case of mass-marketed drugs because consumers and their physicians in most instances rely upon advice given by supplier and the scientific community and, consequently, are virtually helpless to protect themselves from serious injuries caused by deleterious drugs.

* * *

Thus, the plaintiff need commence suit against only one defendant and allege the following elements: that the plaintiff's mother took DES; that DES caused the plaintiff's subsequent injuries; that the defendant produced or marketed the type of DES taken by the plaintiff's mother; and that the defendant's conduct in producing or marketing the DES constituted a breach of a legally recognized duty to the plaintiff. In the situation where the plaintiff cannot allege and prove what type of DES the mother took, as to the third element the plaintiff need only allege and prove that the defendant drug company produced or marketed the drug DES for use in preventing miscarriages during pregnancy.

* * *

At the trial of this case the plaintiff will have to prove each of these elements to the satisfaction of the trier of fact. . . .

[C]ause remanded for trial and further proceedings consistent with this opinion. . . .

QUESTIONS FOR ANALYSIS

1. Why would Collins be allowed to sue for something that occurred thirty years before?

2. Compare this ruling to that of the Supreme Court of California, which held that the major drug companies would pay the damages on a proportionate share according to their share of the drug market in question. Are these different in impact?

Defenses in Product Liability Suits

Strict liability holds manufacturers to a high standard of product safety. It does not mean absolute liability. Manufacturers are not liable if the consumer has engaged in improper activity that increases the risk of injury. Most courts recognize product misuse and assumption of risk as defenses in product-related injury cases. Some other defenses to tort actions were discussed in Chapter 7. The rules vary somewhat from state to state, and regulations may also affect liability.

Product Misuse If it can be shown that the product was misused, combined with another product to make it dangerous, used in some improper and unforeseen manner, or not maintained properly, the negligence of the consumer may preclude recovery for damages. If proper instructions concerning the use of the product (especially in a situation where the consumer could be expected to pay attention to warnings) are ignored by the consumer and lead to injury, it is possible that liability will not be imposed on the manufacturer because the consumer was negligent. As we saw before, the courts will compare the negligence the plaintiff contributes to a situation to the fault of the defendant.

In one case, the court barred recovery by plaintiffs who were injured when the blowout of a fairly new tire was shown to be caused by plaintiff overinflating the tires. The court noted, "To hold otherwise would be to convert a strict liability cause of action into one of absolute liability." In another case, drunkenness by a consumer was held to have led to product misuse that resulted in injury.

Assumption of Risk As we saw in the last chapter, one may consent to assume risk. Playing contact sports, riding horses, and engaging in many other activities that can lead to injury are voluntary choices that include a chance of injury. Certain consumer products are unavoidably dangerous such that, so long as the consumer understands the risk, the consumers are presumed to accept the bad with the good. Medicinal drugs are understood to be inherently dangerous. Most have known side effects about which physicians and consumers should be informed, but we must accept the fact that given the current state of scientific knowledge, these beneficial products cannot be made safer.

Another class of goods, which are much more controversial, are products such as tobacco and alcohol that inflict well-known undesirable side effects. If a person smokes cigarettes for forty years and contracts lung cancer, should the cigarette producer be liable? If a person drinks large quantities of alcohol for years and contracts cirrhosis of the liver, should the liquor industry be liable? In general, the courts have said no; the persons using the cigarettes and alcohol know of the risks involved and should bear the costs. It is not hard to imagine the impact on the liquor and cigarette industries if they were held liable for health problems believed to be associated with the use of their products.

Strict Liability Goes Global

The United States has always had the toughest liability product standards in the world. U.S. manufacturers have claimed that this puts them at a competitive disadvantage. But as Europe and Japan move to a strict liability standard, the fact that American producers are used to meeting high quality standards may enhance their global competitiveness.

As Professors Hurd and Zollers of Syracuse University discuss in an article in the *American Business Law Journal*, the European Union (EU) is forcing common product liability law to be adopted by all major nations in Europe. The standard is one of strict liability for injuries caused by defective consumer goods. Most member nations have accepted that standard. Similarly, Japan is expected to have strict liability in force through its civil code by the end of the 1990s. As in other areas of law, countries understand that common standards enhance their ability to have their products accepted around the world.

The major difference between the United States and other countries will be not the strict liability standard for products but the incentives to litigate. There are fewer damages to sue for in many countries because those countries have comprehensive social programs that compensate injured consumers. Juries are rarely used outside of the United States; judges in other countries tend to give much smaller judgments than similar cases might produce here. The United States is the only major country that allows the contingency fee in litigation, which allows attorneys to carry most of the risk of the cost of litigation. Most countries also use the "loser pays" rule that requires the losing party to cover the attorney fees for the winning party; this discourages suits with a small chance of victory.

Sophisticated Purchaser The *sophisticated purchaser* or *knowledgeable purchaser* defense usually applies in business settings. It has long been held that there is no need for the producers of obviously dangerous products, such as knives, to warn consumers of the dangers of knives, but what about products that are not obviously dangerous and that are used in the workplace? A sophisticated purchaser is one who by experience and expertise is aware of the possible health hazards associated with the use of a product and who has an obligation to inform its employees and customers of potential hazards.

A company that constantly buys inputs for use in manufacturing does not need to be fully informed at each purchase about all dangers. The supplier has a duty to inform the user of all known dangers, but once the communication has been made, unless something new comes to the attention of the supplier, the supplier does not need to constantly repeat warnings.

For example, in the 1998 case *Akin* v. *Ashland Chemical Co.* (10th Cir., 156 F.3d 1030), a group of Air Force employees at Tinker Air Force Base in Oklahoma sued several suppliers of chemicals to the Air Force for toxic tort arising out of exposure to chemicals. The appeals court upheld the dismissal of the case. "Because of the wealth of research available, the ability of the Air Force to conduct studies, and its extremely knowledgeable staff, we find that the Air Force easily qualifies as a 'knowledgeable purchaser' that should have known the risks involved with low-level chemical exposure. Employees of the Air Force are also deemed to possess the necessary level of sophistication, so that defendants had no duty to warn the Air Force or its employees of the potential hazards."

Statutory Limits on Liability

Various laws are specifically designed to limit potential tort liability:

- Worker compensation statutes usually make that program the exclusive remedy for injured workers, unless an intentional tort was involved.
- Federal regulations that prescribe maximum allowable radiation exposure levels set the standard of care upon which liability is based.
- As government contractors, manufacturers of products for the government made to government specifications are generally immune from product liability.
- Products that must follow federal regulations regarding label requirements, including warnings of possible injuries, are not subject to common-law failure-to-warn actions.
- State laws may specify limits on liability, such as Colorado's statutory limits on the liability of ski resorts for injuries suffered by skiers.

ULTRAHAZARDOUS ACTIVITY

Long before the development of strict liability for defective products, the common law had developed a rule of strict liability for injuries resulting from *ultrahazardous activity*. This rule, which is in effect in almost all states, goes back to the 1868 British case, *Rylands* v. *Fletcher*. The *Restatement of Torts* defines such activity as one that "necessarily involves a risk of serious harm to the person, land or chattels of another which cannot be eliminated by the exercise of the utmost care" and "is not a matter of common usage."

This rule has applied to such things as blasting with explosives, allowing chemicals to seep into water supplies, crop dusting, and transporting chemicals in a city. Actually, most of these activities are not all that uncommon, but they are ultrahazardous. The party in charge of such acts is generally responsible for whatever happens. For instance, in the 1992 Florida case, *Old Island Fumigation, Inc.* v. *Barbee* (604 So.2d 1246), Old Island fumigated two of the three buildings in a condominium complex. Old Island was told that the third building was sealed from the other two, but, in fact, it was not, and residents of the third building were made ill. Even though Old Island could not reasonably have been expected to find the opening that let the fumes into the third building (the opening was a mistake made by the architect or contractor who built the buildings), the court of appeals ordered summary judgment against Old Island. Because fumigation is an ultrahazardous activity, Old Island was liable for injuries "regardless of the level of care exercised in carrying out this activity." The negligence of other parties is irrelevant to the imposition of strict liability in such cases.

DOES PRODUCT LIABILITY NEED REFORM?

Manufacturers are pushing for statutes that would limit strict liability for producers. They claim that liability costs make America less competitive in world markets. The annual cost to the economy is said to be in the hundreds of billions of dollars, consuming as much as 2.5 percent of GDP, compared to about as little as 0.5 percent of GDP in some other developed nations. The threat of liability forces good products off the market in the United States and results in less research for new products. As a result, liability insurance in the United States often costs more than what it costs for similar businesses in Canada, Japan, or Europe because, in the United States, liability awards are higher and liability suits are easier to bring.

Organized opposition to the proposed legislation mostly comes from trial lawyers associations, which assert that liability is a reflection of our society's belief that if you injure people, you should pay for the costs of their injuries. In any event, the cost estimates are overstated. If mass torts cases such as asbestos are subtracted, there has been little change in the number of product liability suits filed annually in the past twenty years. While there are some large punitive damage awards, they are relatively rare and do serve to punish companies that have not been responsible.

A Middle Ground?

Trial lawyers argue for no changes in the product liability system. Business groups want to limit damages, limit the bases for liability, and return some product cases to the rule of negligence instead of strict liability. Many states passed laws to restrict liability and to put caps on damages. Some of these laws have been struck down as unconstitutional, but caps on damages for "pain and suffering" have been upheld in California, Florida, Illinois, Indiana, Maryland, and several other states.

Perhaps a middle ground is provided by the prestigious American Law Institute, which produced a report by leading legal scholars recommending liability reform. Among the recommendations:

- Awards for pain and suffering would be for severely injured plaintiffs only.
- Juries would be given a scale setting dollar amounts for specific injuries to determine damages.
- Payment received by a plaintiff from private insurance would offset jury awards to prevent double collection.
- Compliance with government standards would be a strong defense in a lawsuit and provide a bar against punitive damages.
- Defendants would pay the legal fees of successful plaintiffs.

Summary

- Misrepresentation, or fraud, is a general category of tort that can be intentional or based on negligence. When intentional, it must be shown that there was an intent to provide misleading information to convince someone to do something they would not have otherwise, and that the party had good reason to rely on the deceit, which was then the cause of a loss suffered. Most negligent misrepresentation occurs in a professional setting, when a party suffers a loss due to failure to live up to the standard of care expected of a person in the field of expertise in question.
- The tort of interference with contractual relations occurs when ongoing contractual deals are wrongfully and knowingly interfered with by another party who wants the existing contract to be broken.
- Interference with prospective advantage (or prospective economic advantage) is an unreasonable interference in another party's business dealings so as to prevent an ongoing relationship from succeeding.
- Businesses are liable for injuries that occur on their property as a result of negligence in the care of the premises. An important extension of premises liability in recent years is liability for injuries suffered by victims of criminal attacks on business property.

- The rule of negligence in tort dominated product liability the first half of this century. Still good law, it requires producers to take the care of a reasonable person when making products to prevent foreseeable injury. The reasonable person is held to the skill of an expert in the industry.
- Strict liability for defective products began in contract law based on implied warranty inferred by the courts from a review of the parties' dealings or based on express warranty about the quality of a product. The Uniform Commercial Code also imposes liability for products that are warranted to be merchantable or have guaranteed quality.
- Strict liability in tort became widely accepted after the 1963 *Greenman* decision in California. Section 402A of the *Second Restatement of Torts* imposes strict liability on the manufacturer when a "product in a defective condition unreasonably dangerous to the user or consumer or to his property" is sold. Unlike negligence, it does not matter how much care was used in the preparation of the product prior to sale. Besides a flaw in the product, common reasons for the imposition of strict liability are failure to warn of hazards in using the product and defects in the design of the product that make it less safe than it should be.
- Many strict liability suits have concerned unknown hazards, such as those associated with asbestos, where the danger did not become known until many years later. When claims of thousands of persons exceed all funds of defendants, the claims may be joined together for settlement. When many companies have made the same product, they may be held joint and severally liable, potentially requiring all producers to pay compensation.
- A defense that may be raised in product liability suits is negligence by the user, which can include product misuse. There also can be assumption of risk by the consumer, especially for products such as medicinal drugs that are beneficial but have unavoidable side effects and products such as tobacco and alcohol that are legal but have known bad effects. Producers do not have to constantly warn sophisticated buyers, such as producers, about all dangers in products. Statutes and regulations can also limit the liability of producers.
- Strict liability in tort has long been imposed on those who engage in ultrahazardous activities, such as using explosives, and on those who handle unusually dangerous substances, such as toxic chemicals. If the party involved in the ultrahazardous activity causes an injury to an innocent party, regardless of the degree of care taken to prevent harm, liability is imposed.

Issue

What Would Tort Reform Lead To?

Business associations have been lobbying Congress for over a decade to pass "tort reform." They seek legislation that would restrict common-law tort rights, in particular, legislation that would limit the size of judgments juries can award, limit the bases for tort liability suits, and impose other restrictions that would reduce the number of tort cases and the size of judgments. In this article, Professor Grady argues that the tort system serves to discipline careless actors. If that discipline is restricted, there may be increased calls for more direct government regulation of businesses that inflict injuries on citizens.

TORTS: THE BEST DEFENSE AGAINST REGULATION

Mark F. Grady

Grady is Dean of the law school at George Mason University. Reprinted by permission of *The Wall Street Journal* © 1992 Dow Jones & Company, Inc. All rights reserved worldwide.

The essential guarantors of liberty and prosperity are free speech, free markets and common law. Nevertheless, in recent years . . . critics of the litigation explosion [have] become openly hostile to America's civil justice system and to the common law that is its heart. Many conservatives lament judges who have run amok and a system out of control.

But the common law goes with free markets the same way that free markets go with free speech. A society whose affairs are governed by truly liberal ideals must always prefer judge-made law to legislation, at least in the normal course of things. The common law is a subtle and sophisticated system of social control that has evolved over centuries—through a pattern of judicial decisions. Although the decisions of individual judges may sometimes be unwise, their collective efforts usually work out better than those of legislators (or price regulators). Bad judicial decisions often prompt a correction by other judges.

The Chicago Flood of 1992 offers a good example of why the tort system was created and should be maintained. Critics . . . may point to cases of excessive recovery and decry a system out of whack. But the main purpose of the tort system is the reduction of accident costs for society—or the deterrence of negligence. At the same time, the system sets reasonable standards of blame regarding accidents that are bound to occur in this complex, technological age.

Negligence seems to have played a major role in the Chicago River crisis. Chicagoans this spring learned a difficult lesson about its consequences as the river rushed through a hole in a tunnel system located just below it and then forced its way into a surrounding maze of underground systems—including the subway and sublevels of downtown buildings such as Marshall Field's.

Suddenly, an aging underground railroad tunnel that currently houses major utility systems became big news as many of Chicago's downtown businesses were brought to a sloppy halt. To make matters worse, some insurance companies have refused to pay for the economic losses because they say that they were caused by negligence.

The losses were enormous, and it would be easy for the tort system to send a crippling message to the parties responsible—the city and its contractor. Nonetheless, as the system has evolved, crushing liability is unlikely. Negligence law creates a difference between "economic losses" and physical losses. Only the physical losses are recoverable. Thus, if Marshall Field's had Frango mints in its flooded basement, the value of that inventory would be recoverable, but the goods that it could not sell during the time its doors were closed would not be. Critics of the civil liability system sometimes argue that this type of legal distinction illustrates how far out of touch from economic realities judges have grown.

The economic logic behind the distinction is sounder than it may first appear. First, it is difficult to measure the lost business of the firms affected by the flood, since some purchases will simply be deferred. Second, business is rarely lost to the economy. When firms such as Marshall Field's lose business, other firms gain it—what the law of negligence calls unrecoverable "economic loss" economists call "mere wealth transfers." It would be inefficient to induce people to take precautions against transfers within the economy. Finally, to allow recovery for economic losses would really turn the tort system into an insurance system.

Making the city and the contractor liable for the physical losses would send a strong enough message that more precaution by them is desirable. Any further recovery would put the tort system in a position in which it would compete with the private offering of business interruption insurance—a contest that the courts could not win.

The late economist Friedrich Hayek, a Nobel Prize winner lauded in Journal editorials, compared the common law to markets and language—two other systems that regulate our affairs in a decentralized and sophisticated way. Negligence law, part of the common law, is American society's basic response to the social problems that technology creates.

Legislation, which is the Hayekian opposite of the common law, develops through influence trading that is completely absent in common law evolution. Individual judges have about as much influence on the development of the common law as an individual trader has on the spot price of potatoes. Only with new bodies of law can individual judges—or a group of judges—have a measurable influence.

Many people who believe that markets and language embody important social knowledge have difficulty imagining that the common law also does so. But it seems doubtful that Congress would have adopted negligence law's subtle distinction between recoverable physical losses and unrecoverable economic ones if it were developing legislation to deter a future bursting forth of the fountains of the deep. Which member of Congress would have the courage to say that the optimum precaution against wealth transfers between Marshall Field's and other stores is zero?

[Former Vice President Quayle] pointed to the vast increase in civil justice claims. For instance, negligence claims against doctors have risen from one per 100 doctors (per year) in 1960 to 17 per 100 doctors in the mid-1980s. Mr. Quayle says that this admittedly staggering increase reflects either a society crazy with litigation or a ridiculous expansion of the (judge-made) liability rules.

It is a little-known fact, however, that the first negligence explosion occurred during the 1875–1905 period. In that time of industrial revolution, claims increased by fully 800%, and the negligence rule did not change significantly. When machines abound, negligence claims increase. Put differently, a doctor who forgot to perform a modern fetal health procedure could not have been liable in 1960, before the procedure was invented. When technology is ambitious, negligence claims increase. That is the purpose—to regulate the technology and to make it safer. The negligence explosion did not kill the Industrial Revolution, and it will not kill the modern medical one.

The 1990s, like prior decades, have produced strange alliances. Still, it would be a disaster if . . . reformers were to substitute legislation for the common-law order. The reformers need to understand that it will not be a social victory if the net result of abolishing the tort system is more safety regulations of the type associated with the FDA, the Consumer Product Safety Commission and OSHA. Surely the [reformers] would not want that inevitable result.

ISSUE QUESTIONS

1. Would it be more efficient to eliminate tort actions and have government regulators set standards for all actions?
2. Why might business prefer government regulation to common-law tort?

REVIEW AND DISCUSSION QUESTIONS

1. Define the following terms:
   disparagement   implied warranty
   interference with contractual relations   design defect
   interference with prospective advantage   failure to warn
   caveat emptor   unknown hazard
   strict liability   market share liability
   express warranty sophisticated purchase
2. Refer to §402A of the *Second Restatement of Torts:* What does "the seller is engaged in the business of selling such a product" mean? Who is excluded by this? What does "it is expected to and does reach the user or consumer without substantial change in the condition in which it is sold" mean? What situations does this cover? What is the difference between the idea that the rule applies although "the seller has exercised all possible care in the preparation and sale of his product" and the rule of negligence? What does "the user or consumer has not bought the product from or entered into any contractual relation with the seller" mean?
3. Should purchasers be allowed to sign away their right to sue in tort by contract? That is, assuming both parties are informed of the risks, should it be legal for a buyer of a good or service to sign a purchase contract agreeing not to sue in tort if any injuries occur?

CASE QUESTIONS

4. The buyers of residential property mistakenly believed that the 3.5 acres of land included the well attached to the house, which they later found out was not on the property. The previous owner and the real estate agent had pointed out the well, but had not stated that it was on the property. The buyers did not examine the existing survey of the property nor did they order a new survey done, either of which would have shown that the well was not on the property. Did the buyers have a basis for a suit for fraud? [*Crawford* v. *Williams*, 375 S.E.2d 223 (Sup. Ct., Ga., 1989)]

5. Fourteen "disciples" of self-proclaimed yoga guru Amrit Desai worked for Desai at his large "retreat center for holistic health and education," some for as long as twenty years. The disciples had given Desai much of their wealth and worked for him for very low wages as they attempted to follow his teachings of poverty and chastity. They sued Desai for fraud when they allegedly discovered that Desai had huge quantities of cash and assorted sexual relations over many years. Could this be the basis for a fraud action to recover for lost wages and donations? [*Dushkin* v. *Desai*, 18 F.Supp.2d 117 (D. Mass., 1998)]

6. Dorothy Zimmerman owned a condo at Winding Lake II. Shortly after moving in, she began to experience difficulties with cold, dampness, and mildew on various interior walls. The builder's efforts to remedy the situation proved fruitless. Zimmerman and other occupants stationed themselves in front of the sales office to the condo complex and proceeded to walk about carrying signs and talking to passersby. One sign read: "Open House, See Mildew, Feel Dampness, No Extra Charge." Several prospective buyers left the project without visiting the sales office. No new units were sold during the time in which the occupants picketed. The company sued Zimmerman and others who participated. What will be the action alleged and what will be the result? [*Zimmerman* v. *D.C.A. at Welleby, Inc.* 505 So.2d 1371 (Dist. Ct. App., 4th Dist., Fla., 1987)]

7. Florida land developer Lehigh would show prospective buyers Lehigh Acres and have the buyers stay at its motel. Competitor Azar would watch for the buyers, contact them at the motel, tell them that under federal law they had three days to cancel any contract with Lehigh, and then show them less expensive property that he was selling. Lehigh wanted a court order to keep Azar away from its customers because Azar was interfering with business relationships. Will the court tell Azar to stay away? [*Azar* v. *Lehigh Corp.*, 364 So.2d 860 (Dist. Ct. App., 2d Dist., Fla., 1978)]

8. Joe Washington was shot in the head during a robbery at a dry cleaning store at a strip mall in Dallas. Security at the mall consisted of security guards a few hours per week hired by the mall owner. Washington sued the mall owner for failure to provide sufficient security. The dry cleaning store had been robbed ten times before the robbery in question. Does Washington have a case against the mall owner? [*Washington* v. *RTC*, 68 F.3d 935 (5th Cir., 1995)]

9. Many crimes involve the use of cheap handguns. Producers and sellers of such handguns know that some of these guns will be used in crimes by the purchaser of the gun or by a criminal who steals the gun. Could the producers and retailers of such handguns be held liable for the injuries suffered by persons shot during a crime? That is, could such a producer be held strictly liable or negligent for selling

a "defective" product in that one of its known end uses is crime? [See *Patterson* v. *Rohm Gesellschaft*, 608 F.Supp. 1206 (N.D.Tex., 1985)]

10. A rainstorm blew water into a grocery store every time the door was opened by a customer going in or out, and customers tracked water into the store. The manager had an employee frequently mop up the water around the door. Nevertheless, a woman entering the store slipped in the water on the floor inside the door, fell, and was injured. No sign had been posted to warn customers of the water. Was the store liable for the woman's injuries? [*H.E. Butt Grocery Company* v. *Hawkins*, 594 S.W.2d 187 (Civ. App., Tex., 1980)]

11. A four-year-old child used a Bic lighter to start a house fire that killed a two-year-old. The lighter had a warning: "KEEP OUT OF REACH OF CHILDREN." The dead child's parents sued Bic for strict liability due to inadequate warning and because the lighter was unreasonably dangerous. What was the result? [*Todd* v. *Societe Bic*, 21 F.3d 1402 (7th Cir., 1994)]

12. Two experienced welders were working inside a barge. A gas hose leading to the welding torch developed a leak that the workers apparently could not smell because of "nasal fatigue" from having inhaled so much gas. One worker lit a cigarette, igniting the gas, killing both workers. The workers' heirs sued the gas and gas hose producers in strict liability. Was either company liable? [*Little* v. *Liquid Air Corp.*, 37 F.3d 1069 (5th Cir., 1994)]

13. An infant was given St. Joseph Aspirin for Children. The infant had the flu, and the aspirin triggered Reye's syndrome, leaving the child quadriplegic, blind, and profoundly mentally retarded. The product contained a warning, approved by the Food and Drug Administration, about the dangers of giving aspirin to children with the flu or chicken pox, but the child's guardian in the Los Angeles area could read only Spanish. The product was advertised in Spanish, but the warning was not published in Spanish. Was strict liability imposed for failure of duty to warn? [*Ramirez* v. *Plough, Inc.*, 25 Cal.Rptr.2d 97 (Sup. Ct., Cal., 1993)]

14. Brandon Branco, an experienced BMX (bicycle motorcross) racer, suffered severe injuries when he crashed at Kearny Moto Park's BMX course in San Diego. He had complied with all safety rules and claimed that the park was negligent in its design of one jump. His expert witness testified that the jump (two hills in a row) required a very high degree of expertise not likely to be had by most riders at the park. Given that everyone had the chance to observe the jump and other riders successfully go over it, could there be negligence? [*Branco* v. *Kearny Moto Park*, 43 Cal. Rptr.2d 392 (Ct. App., 4th Dist., Cal., 1995)]

15. A three-year-old child turned on the hot water in a bathtub. His eleven-month-old sister climbed into the tub and was severely burned before being rescued by her mother. The child died from the burns. The mother sued the hot water tank maker for installing a thermostat that allowed the water to reach 170 degrees, which was the industry standard. Is that a design defect? [*Williams* v. *Briggs Co.*, 62 F.3d 703 (5th Cir., 1995)]

16. Ralph Fisher died from brain cancer apparently caused by exposure on the job to polychlorinated biphenyls (PCBs) that Monsanto manufactured and sold to Fisher's employer, Westinghouse, which used PCBs in making electrical transformers. PCBs were known to be highly toxic. Fisher's estate claimed that Monsanto should be held liable either for negligence or in strict liability for failure to

warn Fisher of the dangers involved. What defense would Monsanto have? [*Fisher v. Monsanto*, 863 F.Supp. 285 (W.D., Va., 1994)]

17. Residents and businesses in a Pennsylvania town sued the owners and operators of a nuclear power plant (Three Mile Island) for personal injuries and for loss of business they claim they suffered because of an accident at the nuclear plant that released radiation into the atmosphere. What defense would the power plant have? [*In re TMI*, 67 F.3d 1103 (3rd Cir., 1995)]

POLICY QUESTION

18. In recent years, drug companies have been held liable for side effects of drugs that are widely distributed for public health reasons. Our population receives shots for polio, whooping cough, and other diseases that used to kill thousands of people each year. However, some people who receive the shots will either die from them or suffer permanent injuries. The shots they receive are not defective, and it is not possible to predict who will suffer such horrible consequences. Should drug companies and doctors be required to tell all potential shot users—including parents of children who get shots—about the risk involved and let them decide whether they want the shots or not? If everyone else gets the shots, the person who does not is probably safe from the disease because no one else will carry it. Some people know this, so they avoid the shots and let everyone else provide the public health benefit by getting the shots. Should public policy considerations take precedent over personal wishes? That is, should we all be forced to get the shots, or do we let everyone choose, even though that increases the risk of disease for many more people? Given that some people will be injured or killed by the shots, what should the policy be—nothing (tough luck), the producer of the shots pays the victims, or the government has a special fund for such things?

ETHICS QUESTIONS

19. Various industries have lobbied for legislative restrictions on tort liability. For instance, the nuclear power industry has long been protected by a statute that limits its upper-dollar liability in the event of a serious accident that is much lower than the potential losses from such an accident. Also, the industry cannot be held liable in tort for radiation releases so long as federal guidelines are not exceeded. Many companies in other industries would like similar protection. Is it ethical to seek statutory limits on liability? Is it ethical for legislators to grant such protection? What limits would be acceptable?

20. You are an executive with a drug company that has recently been selling a highly effective, FDA-approved prescription drug that greatly reduces the pain of migraine headaches. This patented drug is earning a high rate of return for your company and is expected to do so for several years. One of the research scientists comes to you and reports that she thinks that the drug may have long-term effects that lead to brain tumors. She says that tests on rats and mice are not conclusive and probably will not be. There will have to be long, expensive tests run on other animals to determine whether this is the case, but the scientist believes that the results are likely to be bad. She claims that a small percentage of the users will develop tumors after about twenty years. Since no one else is likely to run the tests needed to determine whether this is possibly true, if you do nothing, there may be

no consequences for twenty years. Since it may not be true, there may never be any consequences. You know that twenty years from now you will no longer be where you are and, in any event, cannot be held liable for what happens. You can do nothing, order more rat and mice tests, or order expensive testing on other animals. You know that if word gets out, sales may be likely to drop and your job security may be threatened. Suppose you think tests should be started, but your superiors say no. What should you do?

INTERNET ASSIGNMENT

Pratt & Whitney-Canada, Ltd., a subsidiary of United Technologies Corporation, manufactured and sold a PT-6 aircraft engine to the Cessna Aircraft Company. After installing the engine in a Cessna Caravan Aircraft, Cessna sold the aircraft to the Federal Express Corporation, the first purchaser. The fifth and last purchaser was Martinaire, Inc. On a routine flight a defective engine component failed and the airplane crashed. There were no personal injuries. However, there was damage to the aircraft and damage on the ground to property owned by a third party for which the Martinaire, Inc. and American Eagle Insurance Company, became legally responsible. The aircraft was subsequently destroyed and sold for salvage.

A service policy between Federal Express and Pratt & Whitney-Canada, Ltd., disclaimed implied warranties, liability in tort and contract, and limited remedies to repair or replacement. The policy also contained an express warranty against defects in the engine. By its own terms, the warranty expired before the crash.

Martinaire, Inc. and American Eagle Insurance filed suit against Pratt & Whitney-Canada, Ltd. and United Technologies Corporation alleging negligence, strict product liability, and breach of implied warranty. What result? *See American Eagle Insurance Company and Martinaire, Inc. v. United Technologies Corporation and Pratt & Whitney-Canada, Ltd.*, United States Court of Appeals for the Fifth Circuit, No. 93-1841, February 24, 1995 (http://www.law.utexas.edu/us5th/us5th.html).

CHAPTER 9

Property

Microsoft and Coca-Cola are both worth tens of billions of dollars. Much of the value in the companies is from the property they own. Yet neither firm owns much real estate: both have rather modest holdings in buildings and land. Much of the companies' value is in knowledge, which can be owned in various forms of private property. Microsoft has copyrights on software programs; Coca-Cola owns the secret formula for Coke as well as the commercial use of the prized trademarks Coke and Coca-Cola.

Before the information age, highly valued companies had large physical property holdings in land, machinery, or minerals. One's wealth was usually measured in terms of physical assets. Now the most valuable asset of many companies is knowledge, which includes intellectual property that is protected by the law. As the economy becomes less industrial and more service and knowledge oriented, intellectual property will continue to grow in importance.

This chapter reviews the major forms of property. It begins with a discussion of the more traditional category of property, real property, such as real estate. Another major category is personal property, which includes *chattel* (movable property such as clothing and furniture). More importantly for our discussion, we will study forms of property that can be represented only by pieces of paper recognizing their existence, such as patents, copyrights, trademarks, trade secrets, and goodwill. These forms of property are described later in the chapter.

Real Property

Real property refers to land, things under the land, such as oil and minerals, and things solidly attached to the land, such as buildings, trees, and other natural vegetation; at least that is the most common way to visualize property. At law, *property* is a legally protected expectation of being able to use a thing for one's advantage. That is, it is not physical composition of the land that matters so much as the right to use the land for one's purposes. A person who has no expectation of legally being able to use a piece of land for any purpose has few or no rights with respect to the land. If someone has a right to use the land however she likes, or if she has a right to use the land for certain purposes, her expectations of drawing advantages from the land change because of her legal interest in the land.

The review of tort law was concerned mostly with personal interests protected by the law. Property interests differ from personal interests in that property refers to physical things, such as land and objects, and other things in which one can have a recognized interest against other persons. That is, a person has the right to deny others the use of the "things" in which he has an interest. One's interest in things that are protected by property law can be very general interests, or they can be restricted to a few interests or rights.

HISTORICAL ORIGINS

Some of the terms that describe the law regarding real property appear a bit peculiar because the terms and concepts come from the common law as developed in England from the twelfth to the sixteenth centuries. While some terms are old, the substance of the law has changed greatly over the years. The common law has been modified by statutory law, although many of the statutes primarily provide procedures for enforcing common-law property rules.

When William the Conqueror invaded England from Normandy and became king in 1066, he took control of land held by the losing Saxons and distributed it to his Norman barons and lords, who were called tenants in chief. The tenants in chief were required to provide services to the king in exchange for their land holdings. Most provided knights for military service as requested by the king; others paid rent to the king either in money or in agricultural products. The tenants in chief often granted parcels of land to a knight, called a knight's fee, or a subtenant. The peasants who lived on the land worked for the knights and the lords; it was a feudal society.

While the system started with grants of tenancies for life, so that the tenant or subtenant had the right to occupy and use the land for life, by the twelfth century, it became customary for the tenancy in the land to pass at death to the eldest son of the tenant (or whoever the tenant designated as his heir). This became a recognized right of inheritance. Rather than have the property return to the king upon the death of the lord, the property passed to the tenant's heirs. Eventually, the tenant became complete owner of the land, having the right to sell part or all of the land to anyone at any time. Since by 1600 feudalism had disappeared in England, it never took hold in the North American colonies. Individual landownership was recognized; the property system we have today was becoming well established.

DEEDS AND TITLES

Ownership of land is evidenced by various documents. The deed and the title are among the most important. A *deed* is the most common way to transfer ownership interests in property. Deeds identify the original owner(s), describe the land, identify the new owner(s), and state that ownership is being transferred, possibly subject to certain conditions.

The *title*, which comes from receipt of a valid deed, is the means by which the owner of property has legal possession of the property. It is the formal right of ownership. A clear title means that no other persons can claim ownership. Titles may be held by one or more persons or by a business. Titles to land are recorded by state officials, usually at the county level. Title recording provides a public record of who owns what and of limitations or claims on titles, such as the claim that mortgage lenders often hold on real estate.

Rights Are Not Unlimited

Ownership of land does not mean an owner has unlimited rights. The common law and many statutes restrict what we do with or on our land. As we saw in Chapter 7, the law of nuisance prevents us from interfering unreasonably with the use of others' property, which includes doing obnoxious things on our property that impose costs on our neighbors. State and local laws also restrict the uses of land by various zoning restrictions and building regulations. The idea is that the law should protect all landowners and the public at large from the effects of land "misuse" as a result of one landowner's inconsiderate decisions. Outside of such limitations, property owners have great leeway to change the use of their property temporarily or permanently. Next we consider the most important forms of property ownership and control.

FEE SIMPLE

The law often refers to one's interest in real property as an *estate*. According to the *Property Restatement*, an estate is "an interest in land which (a) is or may become possessory and (b) is ownership measured in terms of duration." That is, one may have possession of land now or may have the right to take possession of land at some point in the future. There are time limits on the length of ownership. Ownership may be for life, which is uncertain in length, but one cannot take property to the grave—one's interests in an estate must pass to other persons.

The most common form of real property ownership is *fee simple* or *fee simple absolute*. Fee simple means the right to exclusive possession of a particular piece of land for an indefinite time as well as the right to dispose of the land as the owner pleases. Traditionally, ownership in fee simple was said to extend to the skies, but air travel limited that concept. Ownership is also said to extend "to the center of the earth," meaning fee simple ownership includes the right to minerals and oil under the land. Those assets, like other features of land, can be sold or rented separately from the main piece of property. Most real estate in the United States is in fee simple, meaning it may be inherited, transferred to others, or sold in part or in whole and, in general, is the strongest form of real property control.

Evolving Property Law: Condominiums

While property law is old in origin, it adapts to changes in society. Condominiums were not seen much before the 1960s, but the fee simple estate applies to such living arrangements. Each living space in a building may be owned in fee simple (with numerous conditions attached), yet the land the building sits on, as well as common areas such as elevators and lobbies, is held in common (for the benefit of the condo owners) by another person or a group of persons. To hasten the adoption of property law to such arrangements, all states have statutes that simplified the legal process of having condos and other modern living arrangements consistent with traditional property law.

LIFE ESTATES

The restrictions that owners can place on the transfer of their fee simple property are too numerous to mention, but one of the most common is the *life estate*, which is particularly common in wills. In such cases (or in a sale of fee simple property with such a condition), the title to the property does not pass until a beneficiary has used the property for life. This is a common feature in a will where one spouse has fee simple title to a couple's home and wants the surviving spouse to have the home for life.

Life estates may be granted to whomever the owner designates. For example, Bruce and Dot own their home in fee simple. They intend to keep it until death, and they want their children to inherit the property, but they are also concerned for the well-being of their impoverished cousin Teresa. They provide in their wills that fee simple title passes to their children, but while Teresa is alive, after Bruce and Dot's deaths, Teresa has use of the property (as *life tenant*) because of the life estate the couple created for her. Teresa's *beneficial interest* in the property means she may use it however she sees fit, including renting it to others, but she may not ruin the property. When she dies, Bruce and Dot's children take possession of the property in which they have fee simple ownership.

SERVITUDES

Servitudes are a large category of positive and negative requirements imposed by an owner upon his property. Servitudes may be positive, as when the owner of an estate obliges his estate to permit something to be done on his property by another. Servitudes may also be negative, as when the owner of an estate obligates her estate to be prevented from certain uses. This odd definition should become clearer when we consider the most important forms of servitudes, easements and covenants.

Easements

An *easement* is a right to enter land in possession of another and make certain use of it or to take something from land that is owned by others. It is not ownership of an estate but a "burden" on another person's estate. The legal document that creates an easement is much the same as a deed: it explains the use of certain property that is conveyed from the property owner to the easement owner. Easements are very common; we see them all the time in the form of roads, sidewalks, and underground utilities. Positive easements allow the easement owner to go on the estate for certain purposes. An example of a negative easement would be giving up a right that the owner of an estate would normally have, such as agreeing with your neighbor not to build a second story on your house that would interfere with the neighbor's view. One may also give or sell someone the right to remove valuable things from one's estate, such as oil, mineral, or trees; this right may be referred to as a *profit*.

An easement (or a profit) means that a limitation exists on the right of exclusive possession and use of one's property. Unless the easement is for a set time period, it will be a condition attached permanently to the property if given or sold to another. As with ownership arrangements, parties are generally free to agree upon any kind of easement they wish. Almost all homes have easements for utilities, such as gas lines, to be buried on the property and easements for public sidewalks that may be built along the street. Once an easement is granted, the property owner may not interfere with it unless the easement holder agrees. That is, the sidewalk may not be blocked or removed, and if the gas line needs to be dug up for repair, the gas company has the right, doing as little damage as possible, to dig up the yard to get to the pipe.

Easements are often sold to a neighbor who needs the use of someone else's property. If Ben buys twenty acres in the woods to build a cabin and the property is behind Margaret's land, which faces the road, to have access to his property, Ben will need to get an easement from Margaret to build a road across her property. It is obviously a good idea to get needed easements to property settled before buying an estate that needs easements for accessibility. If Ben doesn't obtain the easement, he might have to get on and off his land by helicopter.

Adverse Possession

A peculiar form of easement is called *easement by prescription*, or *adverse possession*. Unlike other easements, this is a hostile use of another person's land; that is, someone who has no right to occupy or use an estate does so without permission. The use may be in the form of an easement, such as driving across another's property regularly, or may be actual possession, such as building a house and living on another's property. In such cases, the user of the property may obtain a legally recognized easement, such as the right to continue driving across the land, or may obtain title to the land on which the house is built.

The general conditions needed for adverse possession are that it must be

1. Actual: the adverse user in fact uses or possesses the property in question.
2. Open: the use or possession must be visible so that the owner is on notice.
3. Hostile: the use or possession is without permission of the owner.
4. Exclusive: the use or possession is not shared with others who also have no right.
5. Continuous: the use or possession must go on without major interruption for as much time as required by law to obtain the easement by prescription or title by adverse possession.

All states have rules, called *statutes of limitation*, for the number of years the adverse possession must occur before it becomes a legally protected possession. Issues involving easement and adverse possession are seen in the *Hickerson* case.

Hickerson v. Bender
Court of Appeals of Minnesota
500 N.W.2d 169 (1993)

CASE BACKGROUND *The Fagans owned two lots in a subdivision on Gull Lake, Minnesota. They sold one lot in 1955 to the Beckers. The deed for that lot included an easement "for the purpose of ingress to and egress from Gull Lake over the easterly Fifteen (15) feet" of the lot* *that the Fagans kept, "on condition that this easement shall perpetually benefit all of the property heretofore and now owned by the grantors . . . the present and future owners of any part of such property so owned by the grantors being entitled to share equally in this easement."*

The Beckers sold the property with the easement to Tichner, who conveyed it to Swisher, who conveyed it to Hickerson in 1990. Nothing had been built on the lot. The Fagans sold their lot to the Benders in 1958, who immediately built a home. The deed from Fagan to Bender did not mention the easement. The Benders' garage and concrete patio, various trees, and a retaining wall all blocked the easement. Hickerson sued the Benders, claiming the easement is valid, for monetary damages. Testimony at trial indicated that before Hickerson bought the property, previous owners had walked on the easement in 1967 and in about 1977.

The trial court held that the easement had been extinguished by abandonment and adverse possession before Hickerson bought the property, so Hickerson no longer had an easement. Hickerson appealed.

CASE DECISION Harten, Judge.

* * *

Did the trial court err in determining that the easement was extinguished by both abandonment and adverse possession?

* * *

1. Abandonment. Abandonment of an easement is generally a question of fact.

To have the effect of divesting title and reinvesting the same in the grantor of the easement, the abandonment must amount to something more than mere [nonuse], for there must appear to have been an intentional relinquishment of the rights granted. . . . This intention need not appear by express declaration, but may be shown by acts and conduct clearly inconsistent with an intention to continue the use of the property for the purposes for which it was acquired.

* * *

Here, the trial court determined that the Hickersons' predecessors' (Swishers') acquiescence to the Benders' improvements was evidence of intent to abandon. . . . The failure of the easement holders to object to the Benders' obstruction to the easement is "conduct clearly inconsistent" with the use of the easement.

* * *

2. Adverse Possession. The trial court also concluded that the easement was extinguished by adverse possession. To extinguish an easement by adverse possession, the possessor must prove, by clear and convincing evidence, an exclusive, actual, hostile, open, and continuous possession for the statutory fifteen year period. Adverse possession must be "inconsistent with continuance of the easement." The trial court's factual findings satisfy the elements of adverse possession.

The Hickersons argue that the improvements were not "open, notorious, and hostile" because the improvements may not have been visible to their predecessors in title from adjoining Green Gables Road. We construe "open," however, to mean visible from the surroundings, or visible to one seeking to exercise his rights. . . . [Hickersons'] argument is refuted by the trial court's finding that "the improvements were obvious obstructions [of] which anyone who claimed rights adverse to the interest of the [Benders] would have been aware." . . . The improvements here are also not consistent with continued use of the easement. The trial court's findings support the conclusion that the Benders extinguished the easement by adverse possession.

The trial court's findings support the determination that the easement was extinguished by abandonment and adverse possession.

Affirmed.

QUESTIONS FOR ANALYSIS

1. Why was walking on the easement now and then not enough to keep it good?
2. Should the prior owners be liable to Hickerson, since they passed him a deed that claimed to have an important easement?

Covenants

A *covenant*, or a *covenant running with the land*, is not a legal interest in an estate but may be thought of as a contract with an estate. Of course, only people can bind property to certain promises. Estates cannot form promises, but the agreement made in a covenant will "run" with the land. That is, the covenant is a binding promise that goes with an estate when it is transferred to a new owner, who must abide by the covenant. The covenant may impose a positive obligation for the

You Can't Smoke in Your House!

David Dworkin rented the top half of a house. During his second year, the bottom-floor tenant moved out and the landlord, who smoked, moved in. Dworkin asked that the landlord seal the two floors so that he could not smell the smoke. The landlord refused, noting that the lease said nothing about smoking.

Dworkin sued, contending that the landlord breached the covenant of quiet enjoyment, so that

Dworkin should be allowed to move out without losing his deposit. The trial court ruled for the landlord, but the appeals court held that the case should go to trial for a jury to determine if secondhand smoke was grounds for terminating a lease.

Source: *Dworkin v. Paley* (638 N.E.2d 636)

---

estate owner to do something, or it may impose a negative obligation to refrain from doing something that would, in the absence of the covenant, be allowed.

Most covenants impose a benefit on an estate; otherwise why would many people agree to them? The most common forms are residential subdivision covenants; for example, only single-family homes will be allowed, every home will have at least 2,000 square feet, no prefabricated homes will be allowed, no dog kennels will be allowed, no businesses may operate from a home, and all homes must be painted pastel colors. Such covenants ensure certain attributes to a subdivision that the owners of the homes think desirable. The covenants are essentially restrictions that attach to the deed when a home is sold, because the subdivision covenants pass to the new owner. Covenants in conflict with public policy are not enforceable.

LANDLORD AND TENANTS

Historically, renting property was not nearly as common as it has become in our mobile society. When we rent, the property rented is called a *leasehold*. The landlord has an interest of some length in the property that is rented. The property may be owned in fee simple by the landlord, but that is not necessary to create a leasehold with a tenant. A *tenant* is a party with a possessory estate for a fixed time period or at will as determined by the landlord. That is, the leasehold gives the tenant certain rights to occupy and use the property. The tenant has possession of the estate; the landlord has the right to reclaim the estate in the future. Unless prohibited by the leasehold, the tenant may lease all or a portion of the property to a subtenant.

Leases

A *lease* is an agreement that creates a leasehold out of an estate and contains various *covenants* or conditions, such as how much rent is to be paid and what restrictions have been placed on the use of the property. All leases are subject to a large body of statutory and common law that sets boundaries on what is legal in a leasehold and on how a dispute about any issue is to be resolved.

Many states have adopted all or part of the Uniform Residential Landlord and Tenant Act to modernize and clarify standard terms of leases. Although state laws may require certain terms, in general, the courts want leases to:

1. Identify the parties
2. Describe the premises (address or legal description of the property) being leased
3. State how long the lease is to be in effect
4. State how much rent is to be paid

Note that a lease does not have to end at a specific date but can go from month to month. Most leases also specify who is responsible for utility bills, tell when and where the rent is to be paid, note the terms of a damage deposit, and state the tenants' responsibility for wear and tear of the property.

Rights of a Tenant

A tenant has a legal interest in the property rented and has the right of possession during the term of the lease. Other parties may be excluded, including the landlord, with some exceptions. The landlord has a privilege to enter the premises to make needed repairs. Leases often state that the landlord has the right to enter the property to inspect it or to show it to future tenants, but there is no general right to pop in anytime the landlord wants. If a landlord fails to make essential repairs in a timely manner, such as keep the air conditioning working during the summer, or otherwise allows the premises to be uninhabitable, there may be "constructive eviction," as occurred in the *Barton* case. In such cases, the landlord has broken the lease, and the tenant has the right to terminate the tenancy, leave, and, in some cases, sue to recover costs incurred by the untimely move.

Barton v. Mitchell Co.
District Court of Appeals, Florida
507 So.2d 148 (1987)

CASE BACKGROUND *Barton leased premises for five years from the Mitchell Company to operate a store selling patio furniture. Two years into the lease, Mitchell leased an adjacent space in the shopping center to Body Electric, an exercise studio. Loud music, screams, shouts, and yells accompanied the operation of Body Electric during business hours. The intensity and volume of such noise impacted the operation of Barton's business. The noise caused the walls to vibrate, causing a painting to fall off the wall. It became difficult, if not impossible, for Barton to conduct her business. She lost customers and salespersons because of the noise. She repeatedly complained to the landlord, who made promises but did nothing for eight months, at which point Barton vacated the premises.*

Mitchell sued Barton for breaking the lease. The trial court awarded Mitchell $18,930, the balance of the rent due for the remainder of the lease. Barton appealed.

CASE DECISION Walden, Judge.

* * *

The landlord says that it has no responsibility for the inability of Ms. Barton to operate her business on account of the noise and vibration coming from the adjacent tenant's premises because of paragraph 20 of the lease:

Landlord shall not be liable to Tenant or any other person for any damage or injury caused to any person or property by reason of the failure of Landlord to perform any of its covenants or agreements hereunder, . . . or for any damage arising from acts or negligence of other tenants or occupants of the Shopping Center. Tenant agrees to indemnify and save harmless the Landlord from and against any and all loss, damage, claim, demand, liability or expense by reason of any damage or injury to property or person which may be claimed to have arisen as a result of or in connection with the occupancy or use of said Premises by Tenant.

We disagree with the landlord's interpretation because here no one is seeking to sue or impose liability or collect damages from the landlord.

As we view it, the dispositive lease proviso is paragraph 40 entitled Quiet Enjoyment:

Tenant, upon paying the rents and performing all of the terms on its part to be performed, shall peaceably and quietly enjoy the Demised Premises subject nevertheless, to the terms of this lease and to any mortgage, ground lease or agreements to which this lease is subordinated or specifically not subordinated as provided in Article 29(b) hereof.

When there is a constructive eviction such constitutes a breach of the covenant of quiet enjoyment. A constructive eviction occurs when a tenant is essentially deprived of the beneficial enjoyment of the leased premises where they are rendered unsuitable for occupancy for the purposes for which they are leased.

Since this was a large shopping center, we assume, we hope correctly, that all leases were similar. In paragraph 11 of the printed lease, it was stated that, "nor shall tenant maintain any loud speaker device or any noise making device in such manner as to be audible to anyone not within the premises."

Thus, from our overview, we hold, according to the mentioned authorities, that Ms. Barton was constructively evicted from the premises at the time of her departure and, therefore, has no responsibility for rent thereafter. Here, the landlord was advised of the difficulty. The landlord acknowledged responsibility and agreed to remedy the situation and had the means to do so. The terms of the lease with reference to noise could have been enforced against Body Electric. The walls could have been insulated. Yet the landlord did nothing. Despite the damage to her business, Ms. Barton waited a reasonable time for the landlord to act.

The judgment on appeal is REVERSED.

QUESTIONS FOR ANALYSIS

1. Suppose Mitchell had installed good quality sound insulation on the wall but the thumping from the stereo in the exercise studio still created a somewhat unpleasant environment. Could Barton have left then?
2. Since Barton lost business and had to bear the cost of moving, should she have been able to recover damages from Mitchell?

Duties of a Tenant

The tenant has the right to use the property but not to abuse it by making changes that will affect the property beyond its lease term. Abuse can come from negligence—careless failure to prevent damage from problems such as a leaking pipe, or careless damage by the tenant—or take the form of "waste"—intentional destruction or the removal of valuable property, such as trees, from the premises. The tenant may not be a nuisance to neighbors and may not engage in illegal activities on the premises.

PUBLIC CONTROL OF REAL PROPERTY

States have many statutes that modify the common law. Some statutes make property law operate better by providing offices for the registration of titles to private property, for listing loans taken out against property, and for noting claims made against property (often called *liens*) that are filed by people who assert they are owed money by the property owner, such as for failure to pay for putting a new roof on a house. Governments also have strong powers to affect the use of private property. Most important are the power of eminent domain and the broad police powers that include such things as control of property by zoning rules.

Eminent Domain

Governments at all levels may use tax dollars to buy private property, or they may use their power of *eminent domain* to force the sale of property or the granting of an easement. Eminent domain is the power to take private property for public use without the consent of the owner. As the U.S. Supreme Court noted in 1875 in

Landlord-Tenant Law in India

 An old saying in India is "Fools build houses and wise men live in them." Arvind Khanna understands that very well. He owns a two-bedroom apartment in the center of New Delhi built by his grandfather fifty years ago. The apartment is still occupied by members of the original tenant's family, and the occupants still pay the same rent, fifteen rupees a month, which is about forty cents.

Landlord-tenant law in India is oriented to giving tenants most of the benefits, which means that few people now want to risk being a landlord. Since the law says, in effect, that a tenant cannot be evicted and that the rents cannot be raised, landlords rarely expect to get their property back. Tenants can obtain what is called a statutory tenancy, which gives them—and their heirs—the right to stay on the property long past the term of any lease.

The effect of the law is to discourage new building. As a result, what should be very valuable property in downtown Bombay, given the high demand for office space, is occupied by run-down old buildings. Landlords have little incentive to keep property in repair that they do not expect to control in the future.

When new buildings are built, landlords charge higher prices than they would get in Tokyo or New York. Further, landlords demand several million dollars as a security deposit, which they hold without paying interest as a way of insuring that building costs are covered. The lack of strong rights for commercial property owners means a shortage of rental property for business. Some foreign companies run operations out of hotel rooms that cost $250 per night rather than rent office space. Other firms have given up opening an office because the cost was so high. Arthur Andersen has so little space in its office that it encourages its employees to work at the offices of its clients.

Kohl v. *U.S.* (91 U.S. 367), "The right of eminent domain always was a right at common law. It was not a right in equity, nor was it even the creature of a statute. The . . . right itself was superior to any statute." That is, it comes from the right of the government as sovereign to control property for its purposes.

This power of eminent domain may also be used to benefit private parties when the government declares that the activities of the private party, such as a railroad obtaining track right-of-way or a utility company obtaining easements for laying utility lines, are in the public interest. That is, the power of eminent domain may be delegated to private companies.

The Fifth Amendment to the Constitution states that "private property" shall not "be taken for public use, without just compensation." The same rule applies to state and local governments, which are allowed to force a private property owner to give up title to part or all of his land or to force a property owner to give an easement on the land for some public purpose. These governments must, however, offer compensation, which is generally determined by statutes that allow "fair market value" to be paid for the property interests taken by the government.

Police Powers

Eminent domain is government taking of land, but government also controls private land use by regulation. Except for environmental regulations, most land regulation is done at the state and local level. This is generally called the *police power* to regulate behavior to protect or promote the "general welfare." While the general welfare usually means health or safety, in practice it means very general power to control private use of property.

JURIS prudence?

Get Out of the Way, You Old Coot!

Julius James has lived his life on a small peanut and cattle farm he inherited from his slave ancestors. The Florida Department of Transportation ordered him out of his house, which sits on 21 acres the state is taking to expand a freeway near Ocala. He was offered $2 million for the eminent domain taking, and the state bought him a nicer house nearby.

But after 109 years of living in the same house, James said, "I don't want to move at all. This is home." Ordered by the state to vacate his home, James won an emergency appeals court order four days before he was to be evicted, allowing him to remain in his home. State officials were left to ponder their next move.

Source: *National Law Journal*

A key issue is often not whether or not there is such a power to regulate but whether government must provide compensation when land use controls reduce property values. No one questions that when the government takes property by eminent domain it must pay for the property. But in general, even when the government greatly reduces the value of property by regulation, compensation might not be due. As we saw in Chapter 5, the Supreme Court has declared that when almost all value of property is destroyed by regulation, it is protected by the Fifth Amendment rule of just compensation. But when regulation causes property to lose a lot of its value, compensation is rarely provided, so long as the government can show a rational reason for the police power that caused the economic damage and show that there was no violation of due process with respect to the injured property owner. While this has become a big issue in recent years due to the Endangered Species Act, as we will see in Chapter 17, the concept is not new, as the *Euclid* case illustrates.

Village of Euclid v. Ambler Realty
United States Supreme Court
272 U.S. 365, 47 S.Ct. 114 (1926)

CASE BACKGROUND *Ambler owned sixty-eight undeveloped acres in Euclid, Ohio, an incorporated village near Cleveland with fewer than 10,000 residents. In 1922 the village council adopted an ordinance that established comprehensive zoning. The plan zoned the village into six land-use districts, three building-height districts, and four minimum-lot-size districts. Ambler had planned to develop its property into an industrial park with an estimated value of $10,000 per acre. The zoning plan put part of Ambler's land into the lowest valued residential category, multifamily units (apartments). The rest of Ambler's land was zoned for the least desirable industrial use, including "sewage disposal, . . . garbage and refuse incineration, scrap iron, junk, . . . crematories, penal and correctional institutions, insane and*

feeble-minded institutions." Ambler estimated that the value of its property had fallen to $2,500 per acre because of the zoning and sued in federal court, claiming that the ordinance deprives it of "liberty and property without due process of law." The district court agreed and declared the ordinance unconstitutional. Euclid appealed.

CASE DECISION Sutherland, Justice.

* * *

Is the ordinance invalid, in that it violates the constitutional protection 'to the right of property in the appellee by attempted regulations under the guise of the police power, which are unreasonable and confiscatory'? . . .

The ordinance now under review, and all similar laws and regulations, must find their justification in some aspect of the police power, asserted for the public welfare. The line which in this field separates the legitimate from the illegitimate assumption of power is not capable of precise delimitation. It varies with circumstances and conditions. A regulatory zoning ordinance, which would be clearly valid as applied to the great cities, might be clearly invalid as applied to rural communities. In solving doubts, the maxim 'sic utere tuo ut alienum non laedas,' [so use your own property that you do not injure another] which lies at the foundation of so much of the common law of nuisances, ordinarily will furnish a fairly helpful clue. And the law of nuisances, likewise, may be consulted, not for the purpose of controlling, but for the helpful aid of its analogies in the process of ascertaining the scope of the power. Thus the question whether the power exists to forbid the erection of a building of a particular kind or for a particular use, like the question whether a particular thing is a nuisance, is to be determined, not by an abstract consideration of the building or of the thing considered apart, but by considering it in connection with the circumstances and the locality. A nuisance may be merely a right thing in the wrong place, like a pig in the parlor instead of the barnyard. If the validity of the legislative classification for zoning purposes be fairly debatable, the legislative judgment must be allowed to control.

There is no serious difference of opinion in respect of the validity of laws and regulations fixing the height of buildings within reasonable limits, the character of materials and methods of construction, and the adjoining area which must be left open, in order to minimize the danger of fire or collapse, the evils of overcrowding and the like, and excluding from residential sections offensive trades, industries and structures likely to create nuisances.

* * *

We have nothing to do with the question of the wisdom or good policy of municipal ordinances. If they are not satisfying to a majority of the citizens, their recourse is to the ballot—not the courts. The matter of zoning has received much attention at the hands of commissions and experts, and the results of their investigations have been set forth in comprehensive reports. These reports which bear every evidence of painstaking consideration, concur in the view that

the segregation of residential, business and industrial buildings will make it easier to provide fire apparatus suitable for the character and intensity of the development in each section; that it will increase the safety and security of home life, greatly tend to prevent street accidents, especially to children, by reducing the traffic and resulting confusion in residential sections, decrease noise and other conditions which produce or intensify nervous disorders, preserve a more favorable environment in which to rear children, etc.

* * *

If these reasons, thus summarized, do not demonstrate the wisdom or sound policy in all respects of those restrictions which we have indicated as pertinent to the inquiry, at least, the reasons are sufficiently cogent to preclude us from saying, as it must be said before the ordinance can be declared unconstitutional, that such provisions are clearly arbitrary and unreasonable, having no substantial relation to the public health, safety, morals, or general welfare.

* * *

Under these circumstances, therefore, it is enough for us to determine, as we do, that the ordinance in its general scope and dominant features, so far as its provisions are here involved, is a valid exercise of authority, leaving other provisions to be dealt with as cases arise directly involving them.

* * *

This process applies with peculiar force to the solution of questions arising under the due process clause of the Constitution as applied to the exercise of the flexible powers of police, with which we are here concerned.

Decree reversed.

QUESTIONS FOR ANALYSIS

1. Given the broad coverage allowed by the zoning controls, is there any land use that government cannot control under its general police powers?
2. Suppose Ambler had been declared an area in which no development was allowed; would it have had a better case?
3. Sutherland says that if the zoning laws are not good policy, it is up to the voters to toss out the elected officials responsible for them. But if the majority wishes to use zoning laws to injure the property of the minority, how could the minority ever hope for justice?

JURIS **prudence?**

Bite the Hand That Feeds You

Schlotzsky's Deli, a fast-food restaurant head-quartered in Austin, Texas, planned to build an outlet in Raleigh, North Carolina. It chose a piece of land next to a strip mall and a condo development. The land needed to be rezoned by the city council for approval as a restaurant site. Requests to rezone property are posted for public notice.

The rezoning was supported by the strip mall owners, the condo owners, and the city planning commission. Only one party—the North Carolina Restaurant Associ-ation, which had its office next door to the proposed restaurant site—opposed the zoning approval.

Although none of the other neighbors seemed concerned, the restaurant association complained that having Schlotzsky's located next to it would make traffic worse in the area. The head of the Raleigh planning commission responded, "It's a restaurant, for Pete's sake. You would think they would say, 'Welcome to the neighborhood.'"

Source: *News & Observer* (Raleigh, N.C.)

Zoning

Governments have long mandated controls on land use, such as regulations over 200 years ago stating that dangerous businesses such as gunpowder factories and stinky businesses such as slaughterhouses must be located away from residential areas. In more recent times, *zoning* has become the primary method of local land control. All under the general police powers of the state, zoning rules commonly limit building height and size, require green areas, set population density limits, decide what kinds of buildings and businesses can be built where, and set numerous rules about the quality and type of construction that must be used. So long as such regulations do not violate a provision of the Constitution, such as free speech, or violate due process rules, the zoning rules are likely to be upheld.

Intellectual Property

Physical property—such as houses, land, and cars—is obvious because it is visible or tangible. We can see it, hold it, stand on it, or sit in it. Intellectual property is another form of property, sometimes called *intangible property* because it is not as easy to see, may be impossible to hold, and is harder to value. The term *intellectual property* is used because such property is produced mostly by thinking, not by physical labor.

Major forms of intellectual property include trademarks, trade names, copyrights, patents, and trade secrets. The common law has a long tradition of providing protection for intellectual property, and the Constitution expresses its importance: Article I, Section 8, authorizes Congress "To promote the Progress of Science and useful Arts, by securing for limited Times to Authors and Inventors the exclusive Right to their respective Writings and Discoveries." Today, the Commissioner of Patents and Trademarks annually issues more than 100,000 patents—half to Americans and half to foreigners—and annually registers more than 60,000 trademarks and more than 600,000 copyrights.

Just as the common law protects real property, it also works with various statutes to protect intellectual property by allowing property owners to sue in case

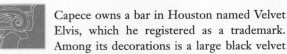

Don't Step on His Estate's Velvet Shoes

Capece owns a bar in Houston named Velvet Elvis, which he registered as a trademark. Among its decorations is a large black velvet portrait of the king of rock and roll, Elvis Presley. Capece advertises the bar as a "monument to the excesses of American culture."

Unamused, Elvis Presley Enterprises of Memphis sued Capece, demanding that he remove both the name Elvis and commercial references and representations of Presley from the bar. It contended that the decorations are trademark infringements and violate the Presley Enterprise publicity rights to Elvis, just as it requires Elvis impersonators to obtain licenses. Capece vowed to fight the "Elvis police," although he had considered calling the bar The Lava Lamp.

Capece won round one in federal court. The judge held that customers would not be misled into thinking that the club was associated with Elvis Presley Enterprises. Presley won round two when the appeals court reversed in its favor and issued an injunction against the use of the mark "The Velvet Elvis." There was a likelihood of confusion, especially since Presley runs an Elvis-theme nightclub in Memphis and is considering expanding.

Sources: *National Law Journal* and *Elvis Presley Enterprises v. Capece*, 141 F.3d 188

of *infringement*. That is, wrongful, unauthorized use of intellectual property in violation of the owner's rights is the basis for a tort action. When intellectual property is infringed upon, damages may be awarded to the property holder and an injunction against further unauthorized use may be issued. This protection has been enhanced by various statutes. How important is protection of intellectual property? The U.S. government estimates that counterfeit and fraudulent use of intellectual property costs business more than $60 billion a year.

TRADEMARKS

A *trademark* is a commercial symbol—a design, logo, distinctive mark, name, or word—that a manufacturer prints on its goods so they can be readily identified in the marketplace. That is, it is a brand name. Producers may not imitate genuine trademarks. Since companies spend large sums so that consumers will recognize their products and trust their products' quality, the common law has long recognized the right to protect this property. This common-law protection was made a part of federal law by the *Lanham Act*. Federal trademark law allows trademarks to be registered if they are distinctive and nonfunctional. As long as the owner continues to use and protect the trademark, the trademark's exclusive use can be perpetual.

Traditionally, trademark protection was created by priority of use. The first person to use a symbol in a business or geographic area has the right to stop others from using the same or very similar trade symbol in that business or area. The Lanham Act allows a person to register a symbol with the Patent and Trademark Office in Washington, D.C. The Trademark Revision Act of 1988 allows nationwide claim to a mark from the moment it is registered, so long as sincere intent exists to use the symbol in commerce.

The advantages of registration of trademarks with the U.S. Patent and Trademark Office, rather than relying only on common-law protection of trademarks, include

1. Nationwide notice of the trademark owner's claim
2. Evidence of ownership of the trademark in event of dispute
3. Federal court jurisdiction, if desired
4. Forming the basis for obtaining registration in other nations
5. Filing the registration with U.S. Customs Service to help prevent importation of foreign goods that infringe on the trademark

Registration

The registration process includes payment of a fee ($245 in 1999), submission of a copy of the mark (a specimen), a description of the goods that will use the mark, and a declaration that to the best of the applicant's knowledge the mark does not conflict with other marks (see http://www.uspto.gov). The applicant is responsible for doing a search of existing trademarks to make sure there is no confusion on infringement with existing marks. The process usually takes about a year. A trademark examiner reviews the request to make sure the mark does not conflict with existing marks, is not descriptive, and does not claim too much coverage. That is, if you are trademarking a word for a brand of perfume, you cannot register the word *perfume*, because that is too descriptive. If the word *Charlie* is registered as a trademark for perfume, other people may be allowed to use the word in other contexts, such as Charlie's Motel.

Registration is good for ten years, after which it must be renewed. You can make sure people know a mark is protected by stating "Registered in U.S. Patent and Trademark Office" or using the circle-R (®). You also see the symbol "TM," which puts people on notice but is not specified in the Lanham Act. However, lack of notice that a mark is a trademark does not mean the owner of the mark is not due legal protection for the mark. Since 1995, international protection of trademarks has been encouraged by the World Trade Organization.

Classifications of Trademarks

Trademarks are classified as arbitrary and fanciful, suggestive, descriptive, or generic (see Exhibit 9.1). *Arbitrary and fanciful* are most favored because they are inherently distinctive (arbitrary), such as made-up names like *Exxon*, or they are names not related to the product (fanciful), such as *Black and White* for a Scotch

EXHIBIT 9.1	Arbitrary and Fanciful	Suggestive	Descriptive	Generic (No Longer Trademarks)
Types of Trademarks	Polaroid	Orange Crush	Raisin Bran	Trampoline
	Lexus	Roach Motel	Holiday Inn	Nylon
	Virginia Slims	Dairy Queen	Musky (Perfume)	Thermos
	Ivory (Soap)	Passion (Perfume)		Shredded Wheat
				Zipper

CYBERLAW

Who Owns What Domain Name?

 Network Solutions Inc. (NSI) was chosen years ago by the National Science Foundation to be in charge of issuing and controlling domain names, such as www.WestBusLaw.com. Only one entity can have that name so that the Web is not confounded by multiple persons claiming the same domain name. Delta.com could link one to Delta Airlines, but Delta, the faucet maker, beat the airline to the name and, since Delta faucet is a genuine business, it could claim the name, and the airline is Delta-air.com. First come, first serve, among legitimate users.

Cybersquatters have grabbed control of many names, since registration of a name only costs $100 initially. The long distance phone company Sprint claimed mci.com, knowing it would block its competitor MCI. That was not fair under the rules, so NSI turned mci.com over to MCI. Some cybersquatters have registered many names on the expectation that they would later be desired.

A cybersquatter named Toeppen registered many trademarks as his domain names. Such registrations are not challenged initially. Panavision, a movie equipment maker, sued Toeppen when he demanded $13,000 to sell the company panavision.com and panaflex.com, another of its trademarks. Panavision won the case, but many companies simply paid to have the rights to the name transferred rather than go to the cost and time of litigating the matter.

whiskey and *Stork Club* for a restaurant. *Suggestive* marks hint at the product, such as *Chicken of the Sea* for canned tuna and *Roach Motel* for a roach (bug) trap. *Descriptive* marks are not as favored by the law and must be shown to have acquired customer recognition to be allowed protection. Examples of successful descriptive marks are *Raisin Bran* for breakfast cereal containing raisins and bran, *Bufferin* for aspirin with acid buffering, and *Holiday Inn* for motels. *Generic* marks are words that are common and do not refer to products from a specific producer. Some words that were once trademarks have been lost to become generic marks: *thermos* for vacuum-insulated bottles, *aspirin* for acetylsalicylic acid, and *escalator* for moving stairways.

Most colleges have trademarks for their name or a distinctive use of letters in their name and for their sports team name and mascot. Collegiate Licensing is a licensing agent for many universities and the manufacturers that make clothing and various items with university logos. This allows colleges to collect royalties from and control the use of their trademarks so that the trademarks are not used in ways the colleges do not approve.

Trademark protection applies to a wide range of creative property other than the names of products. Trademark law applies to titles of movies, advertising slogans, titles of comic books, and fictional characters, such as Batman. This allows the producers of highly popular movies and cartoon characters to license use of the names, such as Disney's Hunchback of Notre Dame, which shows up in toys and premiums at fast-food restaurants. The extent of trademark protection depends on how well known the mark is and whether a similar mark would be confused with the original mark in nonrelated markets. Firms must be protective of their trademarks, or they can lose them, but, as the *Harley-Davidson* case indicates, a challenge to a user can result in consideration of the validity of a trademark.

Harley-Davidson, Inc. v. Grottanelli
United States Court of Appeals, Second Circuit
164 F.3d 806 (1999)

CASE BACKGROUND *Grottanelli runs The Hog Farm, a motorcycle repair shop in western New York. He used the word "hog" in connection with events he sponsored and products he sold. He also used variants of Harley's bar-and-shield logo.*

Harley sued to enjoin Grottanelli from using the word "hog" in reference to his service and products and from using a logo that incorporates a part of Harley's bar-and-shield logo. The district court held in Harley's favor. Grottanelli appealed.

CASE DECISION Newman, Circuit Judge:

* * *

<u>The word "Hog" Applied to Motorcycles</u>
Public use of the word "hog". In the late 1960s and early 1970s, the word "hog" was used by motorcycle enthusiasts to refer to motorcycles generally and to large motorcycles in particular. The word was used that way in the press at least as early as 1965, and frequently thereafter, prior to the 1980s when Harley first attempted to make trademark use of the term. Several dictionaries include a definition of "hog" as a motorcycle, especially a large one. The October 1975 issue of Street Chopper contained an article entitled "Honda Hog," indicating that the word "hog" was generic as to motorcycles and needed a tradename adjective.

Beginning around the early 1970s and into the early 1980s, motorcyclists increasingly came to use the word "hog" when referring to Harley-Davidson motorcycles. However, for several years, as Harley-Davidson's Manager of Trademark Enforcement acknowledged, the company attempted to disassociate itself from the word "hog." The Magistrate Judge drew the reasonable inference that the company wished to distance itself from the connection between "hog" as applied to motorcycles and unsavory elements of the population, such as Hell's Angels, who were among those applying the term to Harley-Davidson motorcycles.

Harley-Davidson's use of the word "hog". In 1981, Harley-Davidson's new owners recognized that the term "hog" had financial value and began using the term in connection with its merchandise, accessories, advertising, and promotions. In 1983, it formed the Harley Owners' Group, pointedly using the acronym "H.O.G." In 1987, it registered the acronym in conjunction with various logos. It subsequently registered the mark "HOG" for motorcycles. That registration lists Harley-Davidson's first use as occurring in 1990.

Grottanelli's use of the word "hog". Grottanelli opened a motorcycle repair shop under the name "The Hog Farm" in 1969. Since that time his shop has been located at various sites in western New York. At some point after 1981, Grottanelli also began using the word "hog" in connection with events and merchandise. He has sponsored an event alternatively known as "Hog Holidays" and "Hog Farm Holidays," and sold products such as "Hog Wash" engine degreaser and a "Hog Trivia" board game.

<u>The Bar-and-Shield Logo</u>
Harley-Davidson's use of the logo. Since approximately 1909, Harley-Davidson has used variations of its bar-and-shield logo—a shield traversed across the middle by a horizontal bar. The words "Motor" and "Cycles" (or sometimes "Company") appear at the chief and base of the shield, respectively, and the name "Harley-Davidson" appears on the horizontal bar. Variations of the bar-and-shield logo were registered with the United States Patent and Trademark Office in 1982 and thereafter.

Grottanelli's use of the logo. By 1979, Grottanelli had begun using variants of Harley-Davidson's bar-and-shield logo. His 1979 advertisements include a hand-drawn copy of the bar-and-shield logo, with the name "Harley-Davidson" displayed on the horizontal bar. Since 1982, in response to letters of protest from Harley-Davidson, Grottanelli has replaced the words "Harley-Davidson" on the horizontal bar of his logo with the words "American-Made." He has also placed a banner at the bottom of his logo with the words "UNAUTHORIZED DEALER."

* * *

The District Court . . . enjoined Grottanelli from making various trademark uses of the word "hog." Harley-Davidson acknowledged at oral argument that its . . . claim fails if "hog" is generic as applied to large motorcycles. No manufacturer can take out of the language a word, even a slang term, that has generic meaning as to a category of products and appropriate it for its own trademark use. . . .

We have observed that newspaper and magazine use of a word in a generic sense is "a strong indication of the general public's perception" that the word is generic. In this case, media use of "hog" to mean a large motorcycle began as early as 1935 and continued thereafter.

However, rather than recognize that the word "hog," originally generic as applied to motorcycles, cannot subsequently be appropriated for trademark use, the Magistrate Judge upheld Harley-Davidson's anti-dilution claim on the ground that its "HOG" mark has become a strong trademark. This was error. Even the presumption of validity arising from federal registration cannot protect a mark that is shown on strong evidence to be generic as to the relevant category of products prior to the proprietor's trademark use and registration.

Supporting the generic nature of "hog" as applied to motorcycles is Harley-Davidson's aversion to linking the word with its products until the early 1980s, long after the word was generic.

* * *

For all of these reasons, Harley-Davidson may not prohibit Grottanelli from using "hog" to identify his motorcycle products and services. Like any other manufacturer with a product identified by a word that is generic, Harley-Davidson will have to rely on all or a portion of its tradename (or other protectable marks) to identify its brand of motorcycles, e.g., "Harley Hogs."

Bar-and-Shield Logo

Parody defense. Grottanelli admits that his use of his bar-and-shield logo "purposefully suggests an association with Harley," but argues that his use is a protectable parody. We have accorded considerable leeway to parodists whose expressive works aim their parodic commentary at a trademark or a trademarked product, but have not hesitated to prevent a manufacturer from using an alleged parody of a competitor's mark to sell a competing product. Grottanelli uses his bar-and-shield logo on the signage of his business, in his newsletter, and on T-shirts. The signage on his business is, in effect, trademark use for a competing service, since Harley-Davidson offers motorcycle repair service through its authorized dealers, and Grottanelli's placement of his bar-and-shield logo on his newsletter and T-shirts promotes his repair and parts business. In this context, parodic use is sharply limited.

* * *

Disclaimer defense. Grottanelli gains no protection by coyly adding to his version of the bar-and-shield logo the wording "UNAUTHORIZED DEALER."

* * *

For all of these reasons, Grottanelli was properly enjoined from using his current bar-and-shield logo and any mark that so resembles Harley-Davidson's trademarked logo as to be likely to cause confusion.

Conclusion
The judgment of the District Court is affirmed to the extent it enjoined Grottanelli's use of his bar-and-shield logo and reversed to the extent that it enjoined his use of the word "hog." No costs.

QUESTIONS FOR ANALYSIS

1. Since Grottanelli was using the word "hog" commercially before Harley-Davidson used it commercially, could he not sue Harley for infringement on his trademark?
2. Since "hog" is generic, does that mean it cannot be a trademark for, say, a brand of perfume?

Counterfeiting

Counterfeiting of trademarks owned by universities, Major League Baseball, and well-known companies such as Nike, Disney, and Levi Strauss means that the owners must work to protect their property. Levi's has seized millions of pairs of counterfeit pants. Not only are profits lost to counterfeiters, but also, since counterfeit goods are usually low quality, consumers might think the trademarks do not represent quality, and the reputation of the owner can suffer.

Note that even if people are told that the counterfeit goods are counterfeit—so that no one is being fooled—the trademark has still been counterfeited. For example, Ferrari makes very expensive cars with distinctive body designs. Ferrari

JURIS prudence?

Chicken Beats Stuffing out of Barney

The creator and owner of Barney describes the stuffed character as "a purple, highly stylized 'Tyrannosaurus Rex' type dinosaur character with a friendly mien, a swath of green down his chest and stomach, and green spots on his back." Ted Giannoulas, otherwise known as The Chicken, appears in comic performances at baseball, basketball, and hockey games. The Chicken would use a character with "a rounded purple body with an oversized, rounded head, a swatch of contrasting color down the chest and stomach, a strip of white around the mouth resembling teeth, and a friendly, smiling demeanor." The crowd knew the purple character was a spoof on Barney. The Chicken would attack Barney and engage in assorted skits with the "putative Barney."

Barney's owners sued the Chicken for trademark infringement, false description, unfair competition, and dilution of trademark. The federal court dismissed the suit with prejudice, holding that "Although plaintiff does not appreciate defendants' intent, there is no doubt that parody is intended. Defendants' act is not an effort to confuse consumers, but rather to amuse."

Source: *Lyons Partnership, L.P.* v. *Giannoulas*, 14 F.Supp.2d 947

---

sued companies that made fiberglass imitations of its car bodies that could be placed on car frames. Even though everyone knew the bodies were not Ferrari and there was a name other than Ferrari on the bodies, the distinctive design of Ferrari was held to be a trademark that could be protected against imitations.

Trade Dress

A commercial symbol also protected by trademark law and the Lanham Act is *trade dress*, which has been given more attention in recent years, although it is often not registered. Trade dress concerns the "look and feel" of products and of service establishments. This includes the size, shape, color, texture, graphics, and even certain sales techniques of products. This has been applied to many products such as teddy bears, luggage, greeting cards, romance novels, and folding tables.

The Supreme Court supported a trade dress claim in the 1992 case, *Two Pesos* v. *Taco Cabana* (112 S.Ct. 2753). One Mexican-style restaurant could not copy its competitor's decor, which included distinctive exterior decorations and interior design. Trade dress that is "inherently distinctive" is protected under the Lanham Act and by common-law principles concerning unfair competition. Similarly, in the 1995 case, *Qualitex Co.* v. *Jacobson* (115 S.Ct. 1300), the Supreme Court noted that "Color alone . . . can meet the basic legal requirements for use as a trademark." The color of a product can be trademarked when it acts as a symbol to distinguish one brand from others.

Other Marks

The Lanham Act also recognizes *service marks*. These marks, denoted by "SM," apply to services rather than to goods, but the law is the same as it is for trademarks. Service marks apply to services such as advertising, insurance, hotels, restaurants, and entertainment. For example, the International Silk Association uses the motto "Only silk is silk." That is a service mark. "Burger King" is a trademark. The phrase "Home of the Whopper" is a service mark that is owned by Burger King.

A *certification mark* is any word, symbol, device, or any combination of these that is used, or intended to be used, in commerce to certify regional or other geographic origin ("Made in Montana"). It may also be the type of material used, mode of manufacture, quality, accuracy, or other characteristics of someone's goods or services, or that the work was performed by members of a union ("Union Made in the USA") or another organization.

A trademark or service mark that is used in commerce by members of a cooperative, an association, or other collective group or organization is a *collective mark*. This includes a mark that indicates membership in a union, an association, or other organization.

Trade Names

A *trade name* is the name of a company or a business. Some products, such as Coca-Cola, have the same trademark as the trade name of their producer. Trade names cannot be registered under the Lanham Act, but they are protected by the common law. About one-half of the states allow trade names to be registered, but the rule is that trade name protection belongs to the first to use the name in a given area of business. The general rule is that the first to use the name in a particular business in a geographic area has the ownership right to the name.

Protection applies to the areas in which the name has meaning; national protection of the name cannot be claimed unless there might be confusion. For example, because Coca-Cola operates and is known worldwide, no one may use the trade name in any business, such as by opening a Coca-Cola Motel. Even though Coca-Cola is not in the motel business, its name is protected in all uses. Because the name Coca-Cola has tremendous goodwill value, the company could license its use to motel operators. Usage of the good name of the company is thus prohibited without the company's permission. Similarly, Rollerblade, Inc. has been careful to protect its name from becoming the generic term for in-line skates.

COPYRIGHT

Copyrights are the easiest form of intellectual property protection to obtain and are strong protection. Of the more than 600,000 items copyrighted each year, about half are books and articles and half are musical works. The federal Copyright Act has been generally consistent with the common-law standards for protection that have existed for many years. The Copyright Act of 1976 (amended several times since) protects original expression automatically from the time it is fixed in expression—printed, sung, used in a computer, or whatever form expression takes. The length of copyright protection depends on when the work was produced, as Congress has changed the terms of protection numerous times. For many years, works were protected by copyright for the life of the author plus fifty years. However, the Sonny Bono Copyright Term Extension Act of 1998 added twenty years to the life of copyrights that would have expired that year. Hence, since 1999, most copyrighted materials in the United States have the same protection term, life of the author plus seventy years, as is the case in the European Union.

The Copyright Act gives a copyright owner five exclusive rights over copyrighted works:

1. The right to reproduce the work.
2. The right to publish or distribute the work.
3. The right to display the work in public.
4. The right to perform the work in public.
5. The right to prepare derivative works based on the original work.

CYBERLAW

Infringement on the Net

 Frena operated a bulletin board system (BBS). His subscribers could upload and download copies of photos from *Playboy* magazine. The photos had the BBS name attached. Playboy Enterprises sued Frena for trademark infringement. He claimed that his subscribers were responsible for uploading and downloading the photos. The court was not impressed and granted *Playboy* summary judgment. By placing the name of the BBS on photos, there was an effort to pass off the photos as if they were Frena's, which is infringement. Whether or not he was responsible for every photo on the BBS, he was clearly involved in the activity since he ran the BBS.

Similarly, the MAPHIA bulletin board posted unauthorized Sega games that were bootlegged from prerelease copies. The games appeared with the Sega name. The court ruled for Sega that there was trademark infringement and that there was also a likely violation of the Lanham Act, since this was unfair competition and the public could be confused by the presence of the Sega name on the bootleg programs.

Sources: *Playboy Enterprises* v. *Frena* (839 F.Supp. 1552) and *Sega Enterprises* v. *MAPHIA* (857 F.Supp. 679)

The 1990 amendment added what are called moral rights, which include the right of the author to have proper attribution of authorship and to prevent unauthorized changes in or destruction of an artist's work.

Copyrighted work must be original. You cannot copyright a 200-year-old song, because you did not create it; the song is in the public domain and may be used, performed, or reproduced by anyone. The Supreme Court noted that copyrighted works must be original in its 1991 decision *Feist Publications* v. *Rural Telephone Service Co.* (111 S.Ct. 1282), in which one company copied the white-page telephone listings of another company. The Court ruled that there is nothing original in listing telephone user names, addresses, and phone numbers alphabetically; it is "devoid of even the slightest trace of creativity." Public facts not presented in an original manner cannot obtain copyright protection. There must be an original element in the work.

Registration

Copyright registration is simple. Fill out an application form from the Copyright Office in Washington, D.C.; send two copies of the copyrighted work; and pay a $20 fee. The Copyright Office simply records the registration; it does not check to make sure that the material is in fact original or that all the information provided is accurate. The registration process provides important evidence of copyright ownership in event of an infringement suit. A notice of copyright consists of the circle-C ©, the year of first publication, and the name of the copyright owner. Notice is not required but is encouraged by the Copyright Act because it helps provide proof of ownership in case of a dispute.

Infringement and Fair Use

We have all made copies of copyrighted works without getting permission. Is that illegal infringement? The Copyright Act allows *fair use* of original material "for

Global Copyright Protection

There is no such thing as an "international copyright" that protects copyrighted materials around the world. Copyright protection is a matter of national law. However, most countries protect foreign works via two international copyright conventions, the Berne Convention and the Universal Copyright Convention (UCC).

The United States has been a member of the Berne Convention since 1989 and of the UCC since 1955. Under both conventions, if one holds a protected work in a nation that is a member, then protection applies in all countries that are members of the conventions. The UCC requires use of the copyright symbol, ©, along with the name of the copyright owner and the year of publication. The Berne Convention is the same as U.S. law, which has no formal notice requirements, but, as in the

United States there are advantages for publishing a copyright notice to help defeat claims of innocent infringement. The United States has treaties with some other nations that are not members of either convention. In other countries, one would have to follow national law.

International copyright protection was further strengthened by the World Intellectual Property Organization (WIPO), which added to the Berne Convention protection for "works in digital form." Protection for digital on-line materials was strengthened and clarified in U.S. copyright law by the Digital Millennium Copyright Act of 1998.

For a discussion of U.S. and international copyright laws, see http://lcweb.loc.gov/copyright/.

---

purposes such as criticism, comment, news reporting, teaching, . . . scholarship, or research." When considering whether a use is fair, as in the *Campbell* case, the courts apply four factors:

1. The purpose and character of the copying (for commercial use or for nonprofit educational use)
2. The nature of the copyrighted work
3. The extent of the copying
4. The effect of the copying on the market for the work

In the 1984 Supreme Court case, *Sony Corp. v. Universal City Studios*, 104 S.Ct. 774, the fact that VCR owners may copy copyrighted television programs for personal use was held to be covered by the fair-use exception. Similarly, it is fair use to use a copyrighted work as the basis for another work in some circumstances, as 2 Live Crew discovered.

Campbell v. Acuff-Rose Music, Inc.
United States Supreme Court
510 U.S. 569, 114 S.Ct. 1164 (1994)

CASE BACKGROUND *"Oh, Pretty Woman" was written by Roy Orbison and William Dees and recorded by Orbison in 1964. Rights to the song were sold that year to Acuff-Rose Music, which registered the song for copyright.*

Acuff-Rose earns income from the licensing of "cover" recordings and other derivative works. Luther Campbell (also known as Luke Skyywalker), lead vocalist and songwriter of the rap group 2 Live Crew, wrote a version of the song in 1989, which he entitled "Pretty Woman." Campbell stated that he intended to create a parody "through comical lyrics, to satirize the original work. . . ." Campbell released his song as one of ten tracks on the album "As Clean As They Wanna Be." The credits recognize Orbison and Dees as the writers of the original song and Acuff-Rose as its publisher.

After the album was released, Campbell wrote to tell Acuff-Rose of 2 Live Crew's parody of "Oh, Pretty Woman" and stated that proper credit was given and that royalties would be paid. Acuff-Rose responded that it refused use of the song for parody purposes and would not grant a license for use. The album was sold anyway; Acuff-Rose sued. The district court held that the use of the song was fair use and that Campbell did not have to pay royalties. The court of appeals reversed, finding that an infringement occurred for which damages would be paid. Campbell appealed.

CASE DECISION Souter, Justice.

We are called upon to decide whether 2 Live Crew's commercial parody of Roy Orbison's song, "Oh, Pretty Woman," may be a fair use within the meaning of the Copyright Act of 1976.

* * *

It is uncontested here that 2 Live Crew's song would be an infringement of Acuff-Rose's rights in "Oh, Pretty Woman," under the Copyright Act of 1976, 17 U.S.C. §106, but for a finding of fair use through parody. From the infancy of copyright protection, some opportunity for fair use of copyrighted materials has been thought necessary to fulfill copyright's very purpose, "[t]o promote the Progress of Science and useful Arts. . . ." U.S. Const., Art. I, §8, cl. 8.

* * *

Like less ostensibly humorous forms of criticism, [parody] can provide social benefit, by shedding light on an earlier work, and, in the process, creating a new one. We thus line up with the courts that have held that parody, like other comment or criticism, may claim fair use under [the Copyright Act].

* * *

[P]arody, like any other use, has to work its way through the relevant factors, and be judged case by case, in light of the ends of the copyright law. . . .

[W]e think it fair to say that 2 Live Crew's song reasonably could be perceived as commenting on the original or criticizing it, to some degree. 2 Live Crew juxtaposes the romantic musings of a man whose fantasy comes true, with degrading taunts, a bawdy demand for sex, and a sigh of relief from paternal responsibility. The later words can be taken as a comment on the naivete of the original of an earlier day, as a rejection of its sentiment that ignores the ugliness of street life and the debasement that it signifies. It is this joinder of reference and ridicule that marks off the author's choice of parody from the other types of comment and criticism that traditionally have had a claim to fair use protection as transformative works.

* * *

It is true, of course, that 2 Live Crew copied the characteristic opening bass riff (or musical phrase) of the original, and true that the words of the first line copy the Orbison lyrics. But if quotation of the opening riff and the first line may be said to go to the "heart" of the original, the heart is also what most readily conjures up the song for parody, and it is the heart at which parody takes aim. Copying does not become excessive in relation to parodic purpose merely because the portion taken was the original's heart.

* * *

Evidence of substantial harm to it would weigh against a finding of fair use, because the licensing of derivatives is an important economic incentive to the creation of originals. Of course, the only harm to derivatives that need concern us, as discussed above, is the harm of market substitution. The fact that a parody may impair the market for derivative uses by the very effectiveness of its critical commentary is no more relevant under copyright than the like threat to the original market. . . .

[T]here was no evidence that a potential rap market was harmed in any way by 2 Live Crew's parody, rap version.

* * *

It was error for the Court of Appeals to conclude that the commercial nature of 2 Live Crew's parody of "Oh, Pretty Woman" rendered it presumptively unfair. No such evidentiary presumption is available to address either the first factor, the character and purpose of the use, or the fourth, market harm, in determining whether a transformative use, such as parody, is a fair one. The court also erred in holding that 2 Live Crew had necessarily copied excessively from the Orbison original, considering the parodic purpose of the use. We therefore reverse the judgment of the Court of Appeals and remand for further proceedings consistent with this opinion.

QUESTIONS FOR ANALYSIS

1. Justice Kennedy said that he thought this opinion went too far. If one asserts that something is a parody of an original work and thereby avoids copyright law, recording artists could put out slightly altered versions of Beethoven's symphonies and claim it all to be a parody, greatly reducing the use of copyright. Where should the line be drawn?

2. As Justice Souter notes, the 2 Live Crew version is mostly "degrading taunts" of women and "a bawdy demand for sex" and being glad for a lack of financial responsibility for fathering children. None of that has anything to do with the original song. Is the 2 Live Crew version a parody? Is it, as the Constitution notes, something that promotes "useful arts"?

PATENTS

A *patent* is a grant from the government to an inventor for "the right to exclude others from making, using, offering for sale, or selling" the invention for twenty years after the inventor files a patent application. According to the statute, a person who "invents or discovers any new and useful process, machine, manufacture, or composition of matter, or any new and useful improvement thereof, may obtain a patent." A *process* generally means an industrial or technical process, act, or method. *Manufacture* refers to articles that are made by manufacturing, and *composition of matter* relates to chemical compositions and other mixtures of ingredients. For something to be *useful* means the invention must have a use and be operative, not just be a theory.

Key conditions for an invention to be patented, as the *Richardson-Vicks* case discusses, are originality and novelty. The statute states that an invention cannot be patented if "(a) the invention was known or used by others in this country, or patented or described in a printed publication in this or a foreign country, before the invention thereof by the applicant for patent," or "(b) the invention was patented or described in a printed publication in this or a foreign country or in public use of no sale in the country more than one year prior to the application for patent in the United States." That means that even if the inventor is the first to describe the invention or to show it in public, if a patent application is not filed within one year of publication, the right to a patent is lost.

A major advantage of patents is the strong protection provided. For the life of the patent, its owner has the right to exclude all others from making or using the patented invention. For example, Polaroid won a billion-dollar judgment against Kodak for infringement on its instant camera and film patents. However, the patent process has drawbacks. The application process is technical, expensive, and time-consuming. The approval process usually takes about two years. Once approved by the Patent Office, the patent application, which contains all the details, is made public. That means competitors can gain a lot of valuable information. As a result, inventors prefer to use trade secrets for some innovations. More than one hundred years ago, the Coca-Cola company decided to keep the formula for Coke a secret. Had it obtained a patent instead, the formula could have been used by anyone after about 1907. Some firms use a combination of trade secrets and patents to protect their innovations.

The Federal Circuit Court of Appeals has primary responsibility for reviewing patent cases. As the *Richardson-Vicks* case indicates, patents may be stricken when challenged if the court determines that the patent office did not apply the proper standards when issuing a patent. This can have significant consequences for competitors in the same area of commerce.

A Move to Uniform Patents?

The World Trade Organization (WTO), which became operational in 1995, not only watches over trade restrictions such as tariffs but also helps protect intellectual property based on Trade-Related Aspects of Intellectual Property Rights (TRIPS) covered in the treaty that established the WTO.

The members of WTO, which includes most nations, have agreed to grant and enforce patents lasting twenty years from the time the patent request is filed in one of the countries. The U.S. Patent Office changed its rules to comply with this system. The goal is to make patent standards the same around the world so that a patent issued in one country is accepted in all countries and an inventor doesn't have to apply for a patent in every country.

An inventor should file a patent application in the United States as soon as possible to establish proof of being the first to invent. Then a Patent Cooperation Treaty (PCT) application, which is good in most developed nations, is filed to help establish patent priority around the world. An international searching authority, such as the European Patent Office (EPO), is paid to search for relevant prior art, that is, existing patents that cover the patent application, so the application can be amended or withdrawn so as not to infringe on existing patents. The patent application then can be reviewed by the U.S. Patent Office or the EPO. After a patent is issued, there is a strong presumption in other countries that it is valid, but application must still be made in other countries for local patent protection.

Patents issued by the EPO are good in most European nations; patents issued in the United States, Canada, or Mexico are good in all of North America (under the North American Fair Trade Agreement). Patents are more costly to obtain from Japan, but its standards are becoming more like those of the United States and Europe. Patents in South America, Africa, and the Middle East are often hard to obtain and mean little.

For data on international patent applications, see the World Intellectual Property Organization's web site: http://pctgazette.wipo.int.

Richardson-Vicks Inc. v. Upjohn Company
United States Court of Appeals, Federal Circuit
122 F.3d 1476 (1997)

CASE BACKGROUND *Richardson-Vicks (RVI) owns the right to patent 4,522,899, issued in 1985, for an over-the-counter (OTC) medicine that combines the analgesic ibuprofen and the decongestant pseudoephedrine. It is sold for the relief of cough, cold, and flu symptoms. In 1990, Upjohn and other competitors of RVI requested reexamination of the patent by the patent office. They contended that the patent was invalid because it was very similar to prior inventions and was for something obvious. In 1992, a reexamination certificate was issued, upholding the validity of the patent.*

Richardson-Vicks then sued Upjohn and other firms for patent infringement because they sold products that consisted of the same formula as covered by the patent. The defendants claimed that the patent was invalid for obvi- *ousness and prior invention. The jury ruled for RVI and awarded it a royalty of 7 percent of the infringing sales. The judge overturned the jury verdict, holding that there was "no legally sufficient evidentiary basis for a reasonable jury to have found for plaintiff on the issues of obviousness and prior invention." RVI appealed. [Note that the key part of the patent focuses on "claim 36," the combination of the two ingredients used by RVI and its competitors in their OTC medicine.]*

CASE DECISION Plager, Circuit Judge.

* * *

Claim 36 defines a cough and cold medication comprising two ingredients—ibuprofen and pseudoephedrine—in "combinatory immixture." The question then is whether this composition would have been obvious in view of the prior art. . . .

The trial court reviewed the claims, the written description, and the prosecution history, and concluded that the phrase "combinatory immixture" required "the two ingredients in a single form such as a tablet or elixir." Neither party seriously disputes this definition. Having conducted a similar review of the evidence relevant to claim construction, we find no error in this definition and adopt it as our own.

The obviousness issue therefore boils down to whether one of ordinary skill in the art would have combined the two ingredients into a single form. . . . [W]e remain cognizant of the statutory presumption of validity, 35 U.S.C. §282, as well as that "the facts to support a conclusion of invalidity must be proven by clear and convincing evidence. . . . The obviousness of a patent claim is determined "at the time the invention was made."

* * *

In this case we agree with the trial court that, when all the factors are considered, the claims would have been obvious to one of ordinary skill in the art. The prior art combinations of an analgesic (aspirin or acetaminophen) and a decongestant (pseudo-ephedrine) in a single unit dosage were known to be particularly effective for treating sinus headaches because both drugs help to alleviate the associated pain. Ibuprofen was a known analgesic that was interchangeable with either aspirin or acetaminophen. Moreover, ibuprofen was prescribed in combination with pseudoephedrine by the doctors who testified. The only difference between the prescribed combination and the patented invention is that the prescription was not contained in a single tablet. Such a combination was clearly suggested by the prior art including CO-TYLENOL®, which combined an analgesic with pseudoephedrine into a single tablet. In fact, it was so combined by a third party, AHP, in October 1983, prior to the date of invention. The unexpected results and commercial success of the claimed invention, although supported by substantial evidence, do not overcome the clear and convincing evidence that the subject matter sought to be patented is obvious.

There also exists another fact that created a strong motivation to combine the two ingredients into a single unit dosage, i.e., in "combinatory immixture." In 1983, numerous prior art publications announced that the Food and Drug Administration ("FDA") would approve ibuprofen as an over-the-counter medicine, subject to voluntary compliance with certain advertising restrictions. Those publications indicated that the FDA would likely approve dosages in the range of 200 to 400 mg, precisely within the range of the claimed invention. The OTC industry anticipated that ibuprofen would quickly begin displacing acetaminophen and aspirin as the preferred analgesic because ibuprofen was known to be as or more effective a pain reliever and also produced "fewer gastrointestinal effects than aspirin." The motivation to substitute ibuprofen for either acetaminophen or aspirin in the prior art "combinatory immixtures" to produce the claimed combination would have been particularly strong for the ibuprofen manufacturers because it allows them to strengthen the name brand recognition through so-called "line extensions." These line extensions allow the ibuprofen manufacturers to use their brand names under which ibuprofen is sold (e.g., Motrin IB®) in other products (e.g., Motrin IB Sinus®) and thereby increase the name recognition of the underlying ibuprofen product.

The evidence of commercial success is equally unpersuasive. Even if we infer that the jury found that the claimed invention was a "commercial success," this evidence does not convince us that the invention was not obvious. The advantages of ibuprofen were well known by doctors and patients alike. Those advantages included reduced gastrointestinal side effects and greater pain relief than aspirin. It is not surprising then that the claimed invention was highly successful and may have displaced the prior art combinations because consumers preferred ibuprofen to aspirin or acetaminophen.

* * *

On the basis of the record before us, the judgment of the trial court is affirmed.

QUESTIONS FOR ANALYSIS

1. What is the rationale in the patent law for requiring inventors to reveal to the public the method used to get the invention being patented?
2. Why does the court not take into account the commercial success of a product when its patent is being challenged after it has become a success?

TRADE SECRETS

Coca-Cola has kept a valuable secret for more than 100 years—the formula for Coke. Businesses have many *trade secrets*. Information such as the Coke formula could have been patented. Other proprietary information, such as computer software, could be copyrighted, but firms may prefer to keep the information secret. Some information may not be eligible for patent or copyright protection but is still a valuable secret. Tort law protects such information. The *Restatement (2d) of Torts* defines such information as follows: "A trade secret may consist of any formula, pattern, device, or compilation of information which is used in one's business, and which gives him an opportunity to obtain an advantage over competitors who do not know or use it."

Information is a trade secret if

1. It is not known by the competition.
2. The business would lose its advantage if the competition were to obtain it.
3. The owner has taken reasonable steps to protect the secret from disclosure.

If the trade secret is stolen by a competitor, either by the abuse of confidence of an employee or by trespass, electronic surveillance, or bribery, the courts can provide relief to the injured business in the form of damages and an injunction against further use of the secret.

Generally, businesses with trade secrets protect themselves by having employees agree in their employment contracts not to divulge those secrets. Still, the classic example of a theft of a trade secret involves an employee who steals a secret and then uses it in direct competition with the former employer or sells it to a competitor for personal gain. As the *Buffets* decision notes, however, obtaining what someone thinks is proprietary information is not enough to be found to have committed a theft.

Buffets, Inc. v. Klinke

United States Court of Appeals, Ninth Circuit

73 F.3d 965 (1996)

CASE BACKGROUND *Buffets does business as Old Country Buffets (OCB), cafeteria-style, all-you-can-eat restaurants. Dennis Scott, a founder, developed OCB menus and the practice of "small-batch cooking" to ensure freshness. After OCB opened a restaurant in Vancouver, Washington, Scott met the Klinkes, who were experienced in the restaurant business, and gave them a tour of OCB. Klinke asked Scott if they could buy an OCB franchise to run, but OCB did not sell franchises. Klinke then asked a friend, Miller, who worked at OCB, to hire another Klinke friend, Bickle. Miller and Bickle got Klinke a copy of OCB's recipes and its employee manual. The Klinkes' son, Greg, also worked at OCB for a while, after lying on his application about his background. The Klinkes then*

opened a buffet restaurant, Granny's, at which they used the OCB employee manuals and recipes. OCB sued for trade secret theft, but the district court granted summary judgment in favor of the Klinkes.

CASE DECISION Nelson, Circuit Judge.

* * *

[Washington law] defines a trade secret as "information, including a formula, pattern, compilation, program, device, method, technique or process that:

(a) Derives independent economic value, actual or potential, from not being generally known to, and not being readily ascertainable by proper means by, other persons who can obtain economic value from its disclosure or use; and

(b) Is the subject of efforts that are reasonable under the circumstances to maintain its secrecy."

. . . [T]he Washington Supreme Court makes the important distinction between copyright law and trade secrets law, noting that "[c]opyright does not protect an idea itself, only its particular expression. . . . By contrast, trade secrets law protects the author's very ideas if they possess some novelty and are undisclosed or disclosed only on the basis of confidentiality."

* * *

The district court did not hold, as OCB contends, that the recipes were not trade secrets merely because they had their origins in the public domain, but also because many of them were "basic American dishes that are served in buffets across the United States." This finding was certainly not erroneous. The recipes were for such American staples as BBQ chicken and macaroni and cheese and the procedures, while detailed, are undeniably obvious. Thus, this is not a case where material from the public domain has been refashioned or recreated in such a way so as to be an original product, but is rather an instance where the end-product is itself unoriginal.

* * *

[T]he alleged secrets here at issue were found to be so obvious that very little effort would be required to "discover" them.

* * *

The district court held that the job manuals were not trade secrets as they were not the subject of reasonable efforts to maintain their secrecy. Commenting upon OCB's security measures, the court observed that "[g]iven the limited tenure of buffet employees, and the fact that they often move from restaurant to restaurant, a company which allows its employees to keep job position manuals cannot be heard to complain when its manuals fall into the hands of its rivals."

We see no error in the district court's ruling. . . . [T]he Uniform Trade Secrets Act [states] that "[r]easonable efforts to maintain secrecy have been held to include advising employees of the existence of a trade secret, limiting access to a trade secret on a 'need to know basis', and controlling plant access." . . . [T]he fact that employees were advised of neither the manuals' status as secrets, nor of security measures that should be taken to prevent their being obtained by others, suggests that OCB's interest in security was minimal.

The court made no findings concerning whether the manuals were generally known or readily ascertainable, but even a cursory review of them suggests that they fail this prong of the trade secret test as well. The manuals contain little more than such food service truisms as "[w]hen tasting foods, never use a cooking utensils [sic]" and "[f]ollow each recipe exactly." Thus, while it may have been reasonable to conclude that OCB obtained value from the manuals, there is little to suggest that any value was obtained from the manuals being kept secret.

Finally, OCB argues that since the Klinkes illegally obtained the manuals, the question of whether the security measures taken to protect them were reasonable is irrelevant. This argument, however, misses the mark, as the issue of whether security measures were reasonable pertains to the preliminary question of whether the material is in fact a trade secret.

* * *

[T]he Klinkes may be liable for stealing something, but they cannot be liable for misappropriation of trade secrets.

* * *

The judgment of the district court is affirmed.

QUESTIONS FOR ANALYSIS

1. What if OCB had kept its recipes and employee manuals under tight security and had warned all employees of the proprietary nature of the information?

2. The court speaks as if anyone could do what OCB has done. If that is so, why was OCB doing well when other restaurants were failing? Would it not be presumed that its recipes and employee training were significant factors in its success?

Summary

- Real property refers to land, things attached to the land, such as buildings and trees, and things under the land, such as minerals. Property law determines the protected interests one has in certain property. Interests are usually evidenced by a deed, a title, a leasehold, or other document establishing the transfer of property interests.

- Rights to property are restricted by statutory law, such as zoning restrictions and building regulations, common-law rules regarding nuisance, and limitations established by the document establishing interests in certain property.

- Property law often refers to one's property as an estate. The most common form of ownership is fee simple, the right to exclusive possession of the property for an indefinite time. A life estate usually grants exclusive possession of property for the remainder of one's life but may restrict the use of the property, such as for residential use only.

- Servitudes are requirements imposed by owners on their property. One class of servitudes is the covenant, a binding promise that goes (runs) with an estate. Most common are restrictive building covenants in residential subdivisions that set limits on what kind of house may be built.

- An easement is a right to enter another's estate for a particular purpose, such as to drive across another's property to get to one's own property. Easements may be obtained by adverse possession, which is actual, open, hostile, exclusive, and continuous use of another's property for a required number of years that results in a permanent right to use the property.

- Property owners may form a leasehold with a tenant so that the tenant has a possessory estate for a fixed time. Most leases contain numerous conditions limiting the use of the property, and landlord-tenant leases are subject to state statutes. Tenants generally have a right to exclusive possession during the lease except for needed entry by the landlord for repairs or some other special purpose.

- Eminent domain allows government to force the sale of property or the granting of easements to the government or to another private party. The police powers of government allow extensive regulation of land use, such as through zoning, which determines such details as what can be built on property and how large structures can be.

- Intellectual property is usually intangible property, that is, protected property created mostly by mental effort. The scope of interests in intellectual property is determined by a mix of common law and statutory law that restricts infringement by others.

- Trademarks are designs, logos, distinctive marks, or words that manufacturers put on their goods for identification by consumers. The first producer to use a mark in a given area establishes priority of use. Under the Lanham Act, marks may be registered with the Patent and Trademark Office. Rights to a mark continue for as long as the mark is used and protected.

- The strongest trademarks are arbitrary and fanciful, which includes made-up words or real words applied to a product not related to the word as commonly used. Suggestive marks that hint at the kind of product are also provided strong protection. Less protection is available for descriptive marks, where the mark implies the good. Generic marks are words that were once protected trademarks but were lost as a result of lack of protection and common usage.

- Counterfeiting of marks, even when admitted, is prohibited. The same is true of trade dress, which is trademark law applied to the look and feel of a product, such as a distinctive color or design. Service marks are the same as trademarks but apply to services instead of goods. Trade names are business names and are protected in the relevant market in which the business is recognized.

- Copyrights allow exclusive control over original written works, musical compositions, art, and photography. Control extends to reproduction, publication, displays, performances, or derived works. While copyright exists at common law, registration under the Copyright Act provides clear evidence of ownership and is good for fifty years plus the life of the creator. Fair use of copyrighted works is not infringement and usually applies to personal use and educational applications that do not diminish the value of the work.

- Patents are exclusive statutory grants to protect an invention, design, or process that is genuine, useful, novel, and not obvious. Protection runs for twenty years from the time of patent application, which reveals to the public all details about the innovation.

- Trade secrets are formulas, patterns, devices, or compilation of information used in business that gives an economic advantage over competitors who do not have the information. They are protected by tort law from theft. Trade secret owners must take reasonable steps to protect the information from disclosure, including employee agreements not to reveal the information.

Issue

Should Retailers Help Enforce Intellectual Property Rights?

Piracy of intellectual property protected by a patent, copyright, trade secret or trademark is common but would not be nearly as successful if retailers would refuse to sell pirated goods. While the intellectual property rights holder can sue those who violate their rights, and can ask various government agencies for assistance, these measures are expensive and only partly effective. While Coca-Cola has the resources to go after those who pirate the name Coke, the problem can drive a small firm out of business. In the following reading, a small business owner stresses the importance of retailers being ethical in their dealings with pirates.

HOW (NOT) TO PEDDLE NEW IDEAS

Georgena Terry

Reprinted by permission of *The Wall Street Journal* © 1996 Dow Jones & Company, Inc. All rights reserved worldwide. Ms. Terry is founder and CEO of Terry Precision Bicycles for Women, Inc., in Macedon, N.Y.

Sitting across from me is something all the intellectual property laws, all the common law rights and all the most experienced attorneys in the U.S. can't do anything about: a competitor's bicycle saddle. Not that I mind competition, but this one looks suspiciously like my own patented saddle. It has the same cover, the same steel rails, the same plastic base, the same shape, the same hallmark cut-out in the front that makes it ever so comfortable for women, and it was made by the same foreign manufacturer that makes my saddle. The foam padding on the inside is slightly different from mine, but feels the same to the touch. The tag accompanying it even asserts that it was designed by a woman—I guess they mean me. In stores where it's sold, it's referred to as a "Terry" saddle.

My company designs and distributes products for female cyclists. In 1991, I designed and ultimately patented this women's bicycle saddle, which successfully addresses the conflict between the hard nose of most bicycle saddles and the female rider's tender anatomy. I found a foreign manufacturer to make my saddle and watched sales grow by leaps and bounds as we made models for casual and serious riders and (yes!) even men.

At a 1994 trade show, I was more than a little surprised to find my saddle, with my name on it, at a competitor's booth. My manufacturer told me this was a mistake—she didn't mean to send saddles with my name on them; they should have been unmarked. Apparently she saw nothing wrong with selling this design to others. Further investigation revealed that she'd shipped 4,000 such saddles to another distributor on the assumption that I would bless this project. On learning of my dismay, she assured me that, with my OK, she planned to keep faithful records of all saddles sold and to pay me a royalty. I gave no OK, but she continued to sell saddles and never paid any royalties.

Soon the saddle began to appear everywhere, wreaking havoc in domestic and foreign markets alike. From New Zealand to Britain, we were putting out fires right and left. And throughout the chaos, my manufacturer steadfastly asserted that each "event" was a mistake that would never happen again. But the problem still persists; just this month, the heavily discounted saddle was offered in a national mail-order catalog. My legal eagles sympathize, but they tell me there's not much I can do. And the little I can do will take years and more than a few bucks.

Our front line in this battle should be the 2,000 independent bicycle dealers who sell our products. But when presented with a knock-off saddle that's "just like a Terry, only cheaper," they embraced it with open arms. Like Coke, Kleenex and Frigidaire, Terry became the name for an entire class of products, no matter who makes them—in my case, a woman's saddle with a certain look and function. From a bottom-line analysis, who can blame them? They can buy these saddles for less than a "real" Terry and sell them for a higher margin.

Sounds fine until you remember the saddle is a Terry. Dealers called us by the dozens: "Hey, did you know so-and-so is distributing your saddle? They even call it a Terry," or "Did you know so-and-so is using your saddle on their bicycles?" Even after we told them the product was being sold without our permission, not one of them said, "I won't carry this saddle because I know it's yours and I don't feel right about selling it. This isn't how I like to earn my money."

Forced to fight back, I've responded by finding a new manufacturer and then introducing new designs. It'll take me a little time, but I'll gradually get back the market share I lost to these interlopers. I firmly believe that she who laughs last laughs best.

But try as I might, I can't let this rest. It goes beyond patent protection, the Supreme Court's doctrine of equivalents for patents or trademark issues. It reaches to the core of the morality of business, the caretaking of products, and holding the higher ground.

Listen up, all of you retailers who moan and groan because products have turned into commodities and your customers are beating you up for lower prices: Creative competition, the kind that propels a concept ever upward, is about ideas that exist on a higher scale, ideas that visit at unexpected moments, making us burn with enthusiasm and boundless energy. It's not about knock-offs and sinister back-room moves.

A successful product is the outcome of someone's genius and vision. Like a work of art, it's presented to the market with great pride and expectation—and more than a little trepidation. These are the products that distinguish your store from the store down the street. Once in your hands, you have a responsibility to make sure their value (and yours) is not debased. If you're lucky enough to come across such a product, respect it and nurture it. Don't let it become a commodity. And don't ever assume you'll lose customers because you took the higher ground.

ISSUE QUESTIONS

1. Is it unethical for retailers to buy and sell goods they know or suspect are pirated copies of originals that are supposed to be protected?
2. What could be done to make enforcement work better? Is it worth the effort?

REVIEW AND DISCUSSION QUESTIONS

1. Define the following terms:

real property	intellectual property
fee simple	trademark
life estate	trade dress
covenant	trade name
easement	copyright
adverse possession	fair use
leasehold	patent
eminent domain	trade secret

2. A century or more ago, landlord-tenant law held the tenant responsible for major repairs to property, such as roof repairs. Today it is presumed that such repairs are the responsibility of the landlord. Why might the law have changed in this regard?

CASE QUESTIONS

3. The Eagles owned 100 acres of mountain land in Virginia. Their neighbor, White, claimed ownership of 919 acres, including 103 acres that the Eagles wanted to buy but White did not want to sell. The Eagles did careful research about title to White's land and discovered that title to the 103-acre parcel had never been issued to anyone in the history of Virginia and that White had never paid taxes on the land. The land was declared to be "waste and unappropriated." Who gets the land, the Eagles or White? [*Black* v. *Eagle*, 445 S.E.2d 662 (Sup. Ct., Va., 1994)]

4. When David married Jean, he was sole owner of the property in question in this case. In 1967, he wrote a document saying that David and Jean give a life estate in the property to David's parents and "at their death said property will return in fee simple to [David and Jean], their heirs and assigns." David and Jean divorced in 1980; the divorce decree divided their property but made no mention of the property in question here. David married Laura in 1984; David died in 1992, leaving his property to Laura. Jean sued Laura, claiming that the 1967 document gave her fee simple one-half interest in the property, subject to the life estate. Does Jean own half of the property in question? [*Wilson* v. *Butts*, 1995 WL 705294 (Ct. of Civ. App., Ala., 1995)]

5. Hausman bought industrial property in Dayton, Ohio, for his business, MMI. BancOhio gave MMI a mortgage to assist in the purchase. Three years later, MMI was bankrupt and defaulted on the mortgage. As provided by the mortgage, BancOhio attempted to sell the property, but there were no buyers. The vacant property was subject to looting, arson, and vandalism. The city declared the property a public nuisance under city law and ordered the property owners to clean up the problem. Since BancOhio was the only party related to the property with money, the city held it responsible. Could the mortgage holder be liable? [*Hausman* v. *City of Dayton*, 653 N.E.2d 1190 (Ohio Sup. Ct., 1995)]

6. Peterson owns and operates a private golf course in Sioux Falls, South Dakota. In 1964, Peterson sold property adjoining the golf course, including a restaurant and parking lot, to AL. The parking lot was used by the golfers on Peterson's golf course and by restaurant patrons. In 1978, AL sold the property containing the parking lot to VBC. Peterson had always maintained the parking lot. In 1992, VBC demanded Peterson pay rent for the use of the parking lot by the golfers. Peterson

sued, claiming title to the parking lot by adverse possession. Is Peterson right? [*Peterson* v. *Beck*, 537 N.W.2d 375 (Sup. Ct., S.D., 1995)]

7. The Causbys owned a chicken farm near Greensboro, North Carolina. The farm was located in the path of the flyway to a military landing strip 2,000 feet away during World War II. Bombers, transports, and fighter aircraft used the field, often flying just above treetops over the Causby farm. Chickens died of fright and quit laying eggs; the value of the chicken operation dropped to zero. The peace and tranquility of the Causbys in their home was also disturbed. The Causbys sued the U.S. government. The Court of Claims held that the United States had taken an easement over the property and that the value of the easement and value of the property destroyed was $2,000. Did the judgment stand? [*U.S.* v. *Causby*, 66 S.Ct. 1062 (1946)]

8. Baxter rented a house from Milheim in Denver for a term of one year. As Milheim knew, Baxter intended to live in the house and rent rooms to boarders. When Baxter moved in, she discovered that the house next door, also owned and leased by Milheim, was a house of ill repute, "where immoral men and women were constantly meeting for immoral purposes . . . she was greatly annoyed by the vulgar and indecent conduct of the tenants." Baxter moved out after two weeks and sued Milheim for the income she lost as a result of not being able to rent rooms. A jury awarded her $2,180. Milheim appealed, claiming that Baxter had no reason to break the lease. Who is correct? [*Milheim* v. *Baxter*, 103 P. 376 (Sup. Ct., Colo., 1909)]

9. Hormel is the maker of SPAM luncheon meat, trademarked since 1937. SPAM is a distinctive widely recognized name. Over $5 billion worth of SPAM has been sold over the years. Hormel sued Jim Henson Productions for trademark infringement for using a Muppet character "Spa'am" in its *Muppet Treasure Island* movie. "Spa'am is the high priest of a tribe of wild boars that worships Miss Piggy as its Queen Sha Ka La Ka La. . . . Henson hopes to poke a little fun at Hormel's famous luncheon meat by associating its processed, gelatinous block with a humorously wild beast." The district court denied Hormel's request for an injunction against the name Spa'am. Did Hormel win on appeal? [*Hormel Foods* v. *Jim Henson Productions*, 73 F.3d 497 (2nd Cir., 1996)]

10. The Self-Realization Fellowship Church sued a competitor, the Ananda Church of Self-Realization, for trade name and trademark infringement. The district court refused to issue an injunction against the use of the term *Self-Realization* and ordered the trademark registration to be invalidated. Did this decision stand on appeal? [*Self-Realization Fellowship Church* v. *Ananda Church of Self-Realization*, 59 F.3d 902 (9th Cir., 1995)]

11. Scientists employed by Texaco routinely photocopied articles in scientific journals to enhance their knowledge in their areas of specialization. Publishers of the journals sued Texaco, claiming that such copying infringes their copyrights. Texaco defended by saying that this was fair use. Who wins? [*American Geophysical Union* v. *Texaco Inc.*, 37 F.3d 881 (2d Cir., 1994), order amended and superseded 60 F.3d 913 (2d Cir., 1994)]

12. An American company imported video game cartridges from China that were pirated from the copyrighted originals made by Nintendo. The pirated copies also were sold with the Nintendo name on them. What laws have been violated, and what are the damages? [*Nintendo of America* v. *Dragon Pacific Intl.*, 40 F.3d 1007 (9th Cir., 1994)]

13. United States Gypsum developed a new putty to use on walls and ceilings to cover cracks. A key ingredient in the compound was a silicon product made by another company. The patent application did not list that as an ingredient in the putty. When a competitor started to make and sell the same putty and the two companies ended up in court, could USG win for patent infringement? [*United States Gypsum Co.* v. *National Gypsum Co.*, 74 F.3d 1209 (Fed. Cir., 1996)]

14. Defendant flew his plane over a chemical plant being built by duPont and took numerous photos of the construction. Although the plant was guarded on the ground from outsiders, it was not guarded from aerial inspection. The photographs revealed a lot about secret processes. Defendant said that if duPont cared, it would have covered the construction site. Does duPont have a legitimate trade secret action against the photographer? [*E. I. duPont deNemours & Co.* v. *Christopher*, 431 F.2d 1012 (5th Cir., 1970)]

15. Metro Traffic sold traffic reports to radio stations in the Los Angeles area. Its reporters had an employment contract that could be ended anytime but said that the employee would not go to work for a competitor in the LA area for two years because of the "confidential and proprietary" information learned at Metro. Station KFWB was a client. It let its contract with Metro expire in favor of working with Shadow Traffic, which also produced traffic reports. Shadow hired several of Metro's reporters. Metro sued Shadow and its former employees for use of trade secrets. The trial court ruled for Shadow and the employees. Did the appeals court agree? [*Metro Traffic Control* v. *Shadow Traffic Network*, 27 Cal.Rptr.2d 573 (Cal. Ct. App., Sec. Div., 1994)]

POLICY QUESTIONS

16. Zoning and other statutory-based control of property is determined mostly at the local level under grants of power from the state government. An important area in which this is no longer true is environmental protection. Many of the rules, such as those regarding protection of endangered species and the level of toxic waste that may be dumped, are primarily set at the federal level. Would it make more sense to have standard property rules for the entire nation rather than allow different locales to treat similar property differently?

17. The purpose of patents is to encourage and reward investors. That being the case, why should the protection be limited to twenty years? Why should it not be permanent, just as title to real property is presumed to be permanent?

ETHICS QUESTIONS

18. Many copyrighted books are published each year that list a famous person, such as a president or would-be president, as the author. In fact, the famous person did not write the book but merely talked to a good writer, who wrote the book and split the payment for the book with the famous person. Should book publishers always inform us that ghost authors actually wrote the book? Some book serials are published with the name of a well-liked author who has died or no longer writes. Obviously the "author" who is listed did not participate in writing the book at all. Are these practices unethical?

19. An unhappy employee from a competitor offers to sell your company secret information from the other company. Having the information will save you a lot of money and, at the least, keep you more competitive with the other company—which could mean lower prices for consumers because of the added competition. While it is illegal, is it unethical to buy the information if it leads to lower prices? What if the employee offers to *give* you the information?

INTERNET ASSIGNMENT

Using the World Wide Web to find your information (and giving the URL for each source actually used) answer each of the following questions. Hint: find the Oppedahl & Larson Patent Law Web Server.

(a) Where is the patent FAQ prepared by the U.S. Patent and Trademark Office?

(b) What is an orphan drug?

(c) What is the Berne Convention?

(d) What is the Paris Convention?

(e) What is the PCT (Patent Cooperation Treaty)?

(f) What is the EPC (European Patent Convention)?

(g) What is a CIP (continuation-in-part) patent application?

(h) What is an FWC (file wrapper continuation) patent application?

(i) How do I order copies of patents?

(j) What is ITU (intent to use)?

(k) What is the SPI (Software Patent Institute)?

(l) What is the WIPO (World Intellectual Property Organization)?

(m) What should I do if I am about to publish something about my invention?

(n) What should I do if I am about to sell (or offer for sale) a new product that might be patentable?

(o) What should I do if I am about to reveal something to the public that might be patentable?

(p) What is the difference between a patent attorney and a patent agent?

(q) What is an Invention Disclosure Document and how does it differ from a patent application?

(r) The name of my company was approved when I incorporated. Doesn't that mean I am free to use that name as a trademark?

(s) What is "patent prosecution"?

(t) What is the pass rate for the patent bar exam?

CHAPTER 10

Contracts

Several years ago, actress Kim Basinger agreed to star in a movie, *Boxing Helena*. Her agent thought the movie would be terrible and did not want her to appear in it. Before filming started, she backed out. Main Line Pictures then made the movie with a lesser-known actress, and it flopped, losing money. Main Line sued Basinger for breach of contract.

Main Line claimed there was a good contract based on her oral agreement, made over lunch with the producer of the movie and based on several drafts of an agreement written by Basinger's attorney, though were not signed by both parties. Main Line claimed that the reason the movie lost money was that it did not have a big-name star, such as Basinger. She contended that there was not a valid contract. She testified that she did not firmly commit to making the movie and that there were only background discussions about the concept, which she finally decided against.

The jury believed Main Line, found a contract to have existed, which Basinger breached, and awarded damages of $9 million. The suit was later settled out of court; Basinger paid Main Line $3.8 million.

That case points out the fact that sometimes, as perhaps was the case with Basinger, one may enter into what the law determines to be a binding obligation, or at least have another person believe a deal exists, when that was not the intent. The *law of contracts* gives us great leeway in our ability to deal with others. There are specific rules that involve the creation of a contract. The *freedom of contract*, which is a hallmark of the law, means that there are also responsibilities imposed on parties who commit to binding relationships. Next we study the key elements of the creation of contracts and the rights and duties that accompany common-law contracts.

Contract Law

Contract law is primarily state common law. It has developed through centuries of judicial opinions that have resolved virtually every kind of contract dispute. When English courts began to resolve contract disputes, they made express reference to the law merchant (*lex mercatoria*), which were commercial rules that merchants devised over centuries of doing business in Europe. Hence, contract law reflects real business experience. Today, the *Restatement (2d) of Contracts* is an authoritative document that provides a summary of the common law of contract as we know it.

Contract law is also subject to various statutes. Of particular importance is Article 2 of the *Uniform Commercial Code* (*UCC*). The UCC is a statute adopted in similar form in all states except Louisiana, which only adopted part of the UCC. Article 2 of the UCC applies to sales of goods. The UCC was designed to promote uniformity of the laws relating to commercial sales of goods. The next chapter studies the role of this law in detail.

DEFINITION OF A CONTRACT

Sir William Blackstone, a famous English jurist, defined a *contract* as "an agreement, upon sufficient consideration, to do or not to do a particular thing." Modern definitions center on a *promise*—the element common to all contracts. Section I of the *Restatement (2d) of Contracts* defines a contract as "a promise or a set of promises for the breach of which the law gives a remedy, or the performance of which the law in some way recognizes as a duty." It defines a promise as "a manifestation of the intention [of a party] to act or refrain from acting in a specified manner."

A contract, then, is the legal relationship that consists of the rights and duties of the agreeing parties growing out of promises. Contract law governs the enforceability of that relationship.

Not all promises, however, are enforceable contracts. A promise may be either binding (contractual) or nonbinding (noncontractual). For a promise to be binding, and thus enforceable, it must meet the essential requirements of a contract. If a party fails to properly perform a nonbinding promise—that is, if the party is in breach of the promise—contract law will not provide a remedy. This concept is important because it emphasizes the necessity of meeting the requirements of a contract when the parties want their exchange of promises to be binding. The essence of a contract is illustrated in Exhibit 10.1.

SOURCES OF CONTRACT LAW

Contract law is a part of the common law that has evolved for hundreds of years. Since contract law is judge-made law at the state level, there are some differences in contract rules across the states, but the basic rules are similar in all states. Unlike common-law countries, many countries rely on code law for their basic legal

EXHIBIT 10.1

Essence of a Contract

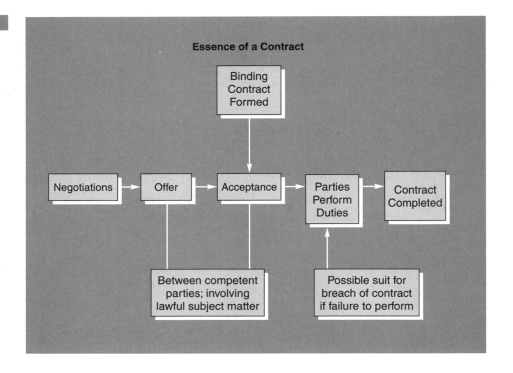

framework. Most of these countries have civil codes that contain the elements of contract law. There are not great differences between common-law rules of contract and civil-code law of contract. Both evolved from the way business was done in practice. As we will study in the next chapter, there is code law for contracts in the United States as in the civil-law countries. The Uniform Commercial Code governs many contracts for the sale of goods in the United States. It, too, is quite similar to the civil codes that govern contract law in non-common-law nations. In this chapter, we focus on the common law of contracts.

Types of Contracts

Years ago, many contracts had to show evidence of great formality. Some had to be "sealed" with wax as proof of validity. Over the years, such formalities have gone by the way as the courts look for evidence of intent to make a promise with legal consequences. Before we look at the key elements of contracts, we consider the different types of contracts that exist.

EXPRESS AND IMPLIED CONTRACTS

An *express contract* is a contract created by a direct statement by the parties of a promise or promises to each other. The statement may be either oral or in writing. If Simone offers to sell her car for $2,000 to Leonardo, who tells her he will buy it for that price, an express oral contract has been created for selling the automobile for $2,000. If Simone makes the same offer in a letter and Leonardo accepts by letter, an express written contract has been created.

In an *implied contract*, the parties do not directly state the promises to one another. Rather, the promises are inferred from the behavior of the parties or the circumstances in which they find themselves. Words, conduct, and gestures may be found to imply the existence of certain contracts. Suppose you pay Posh Spice every Saturday to wax and detail your car. After a while, she just shows up on Saturday, does the job, and you pay her. Many times you two do not even talk to each other. One Saturday, as usual, she shows up and does the work. When she comes in to get paid, you tell her to get lost and that you owe her nothing because you did not ask her to do the work this Saturday, so there is no contract. A court is likely to infer from the conduct of the parties that there is an implied contract, so payment must be made.

BILATERAL AND UNILATERAL CONTRACTS

Most contracts are *bilateral contracts*. That is, there are two promises or an exchange of promises. Each party to the contract is a *promisor*, one making a promise, and is also a *promisee*, the recipient of the other's promise. When Simone agreed to sell her car to Leonardo for $2,000, she was promising to deliver her car to him in the condition in which he saw it and with good title, and he was promising to give her $2,000 when he received the car. Either party could break its promise and then, possibly, be responsible for reasonable losses incurred by the other party who relied on the promise.

Some contracts are *unilateral contracts*, although some states no longer use this term. That is, the promise goes one way. It is a promise in exchange for performance of an act. For example, you tell Posh Spice that you will pay her $100 if she shows up and waxes and details your car on Saturday. She says nothing, but shows up on Saturday and does the job. You made a promise that she accepted by doing the work. If she had not shown up to do the work, she would not have breached a promise to you because there was no exchange of promises. There was a promise that could be accepted only by doing the work requested.

EXECUTORY AND EXECUTED CONTRACTS

Some contracts are classified on the basis of when they are performed. *Executory contracts* are contracts that have not been fully performed by either party. *Executed contracts* are those that have been fully performed by both parties. Contracts fully performed by one party but not by the other are partially executed or partially performed. The difference is important because it affects the remedies available to the parties in case the contract is breached. The remedies available depend on whether the party has performed fully or partially under the terms of the contract.

VALID, VOID, VOIDABLE, AND UNENFORCEABLE CONTRACTS

A *valid contract* is one in which all the necessary elements to form a contract are present. Such contracts are enforceable at law. A *void contract* is one that does not exist at law. A void contract would include a contract about an illegal subject matter, such as a contract to sell cocaine.

A *voidable contract* is a contract where one of the parties to the contract has the right to avoid legal obligation without incurring liability. For this reason, the contract is not void but is voidable, or capable of becoming void at one party's option.

Contract Rights in Eastern Europe

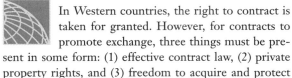

In Western countries, the right to contract is taken for granted. However, for contracts to promote exchange, three things must be present in some form: (1) effective contract law, (2) private property rights, and (3) freedom to acquire and protect information.

Under communism, there were few private property rights in Eastern Europe. Most property was owned by the government. Production decisions and the allocation of resources were made by the government. The countries' business and legal systems had little need for contracts or contract law.

Since the fall of communism, the countries of Eastern Europe have attempted, with varying degrees of success, to implement a democratic form of government. To attract foreign investors and encourage business, most are working to create open market systems. Many production decisions are now made by private citizens.

The new governments have tried to develop contract law. Investments require contracts. One party—usually the foreign partner—contributes money, and the other party works to pay it back over time. Investors will not invest unless they believe that contracts will be enforced. Most countries have invited Western legal scholars and practitioners to teach contract law to local lawyers.

Another serious roadblock has been the lack of private property. It is risky to enter into a contract if the contracting party does not have clear legal rights to the property involved. Each of the countries has a process to place property into the hands of citizens. While the Czech Republic acted quickly, some countries found the process difficult and bogged down in political fights. Should each family be given the house it is living in? Should workers be given equal shares in a factory where they have been working? If the government took the property years ago from its owners, such as from Jews kicked out or killed in World War II, should the property be returned to their heirs? Clearly it will be some time before many of these roadblocks to the freedom to contract are resolved and the benefits of business based on voluntary contracts can be appreciated.

Most contracts entered into by a person below the legal age (a minor), for example, are voidable contracts. The contracts are treated as valid if the minor elects to keep the contracts in force, but may become void at the minor's option. Similarly, a contract is voidable if there is fraud involved. Suppose Simone sells Leonardo her car for $2,000, after telling him that the car had never been in an accident. Upon inspection, he discovers that the car had recently been in a major wreck but had been repaired. He can walk away from the contract because her lie made it voidable.

An *unenforceable contract* exists when there is no remedy for a contract that was initially valid because performance of the contract becomes illegal or contrary to public policy. For example, when the U.S. government declared that no Americans could do business with Iraq, contracts related to business in that country became unenforceable. Similarly, if Madonna offered to sell RodMan her house for $2 million, and he agreed to buy, the contract would be unenforceable if the agreement was not in writing because the Statute of Frauds requires that contracts for the sale of land be in writing. A contract may also become unenforceable because the statute of limitations has expired. That is, the time allowed to the party who suffered from a breach of contract to bring a suit has passed, so the court will no longer accept a case about a breach.

QUASI CONTRACTS

A *quasi contract* is not a true contract. The courts created the concept of quasi contract to give relief to innocent parties, or to prevent injustice, even though no "true" contract exists. In the words of New York's highest court in *Bradkin* v. *Leverton*, 309 N.Y.S.2d 192, (1970):

> Quasi contracts are not contracts at all. . . . The contract is a mere fiction, a form imposed in order to adapt the case to a given remedy. . . . Briefly stated, a quasi-contractual obligation is one imposed by law where there has been no agreement or expression of assent, by word or act, on the part of either party involved. The law creates it, regardless of the intention of the parties, to assure a just and equitable result.

A quasi contract, which is also called *quantum meruit*, is used by the courts to avoid injustice. Something of value has been provided but there either was no contract—such as a doctor providing emergency medical assistance to an injured child without first getting permission of the parents—or a contract was not completed, but breach of contract is not the remedy. For example, in *Burke* v. *McKee* (304 P.2d 307; 1956), the Oklahoma supreme court ordered a contractor paid for work he had completed. The contractor had promised to clear eighty acres of land. He quit when he had finished about half the work, due to some dispute with the landowner. The owner refused to pay unless he finished all the work. The court ordered the contractor be paid the value of his work done to the point at which he quit. The landowner was not to get the value of the work for nothing, as that would be *unjust enrichment*, and he could hire another contractor to finish the job at no higher cost.

Elements of a Contract

A contract provides parties with reasonable confidence that bargained-for exchanges will be enforceable. This section discusses the basic elements necessary for a bargain between two or more parties to form a valid contract. While most business contracts consist of standardized forms, the basic elements of a contract are constant. The elements include agreement, consideration, legal capacity of the parties to contract, lawful subject matter, and genuine consent to the contract (see Exhibit 10.2). In addition, compliance with the Statute of Frauds may be necessary.

EXHIBIT 10.2

Elements of a Contract

A. An Agreement
  1. Offer
  2. Acceptance
B. Consideration
C. Contractual Capacity
D. Legality
E. Genuine Consent

THE AGREEMENT

In contract law, an *agreement* means that there is a mutual understanding between the parties as to the substance of the contract. This agreement between the parties is reached through a process of *offer* and *acceptance*.

The Offer

An *offer* is a promise to do something or to refrain from doing some specific thing. More formally, as defined in the *Restatement (2d) of Contracts*, "An offer is the manifestation of willingness to enter into a bargain, so made as to justify another person in understanding that his assent to that bargain is invited and will conclude it." The party making an offer is called the *offeror* or *offerer*; the *offeree* is the party to whom the offer is made.

That is, the offer to obligate oneself to a contract can be to do something positive or negative. An example of a positive obligation would be to agree to sell your car to someone for $5,000. An example of a negative obligation would be to agree to give up the right to sue someone. Since the offeror is allowing the offeree the opportunity to create a binding promise by making a valid acceptance of the offer, at common law the offeror controls the terms of the offer made. To be an effective offer, three requirements must be met:

(1) there must be a clear present intent by the offeror to become contractually bound,
(2) the terms and conditions of the offer must be clear and certain, and
(3) the offer must be properly communicated.

Manifestation of Intent In making an offer, the offeror must have the definite *intent* to be bound to the contract, and that intent must be clearly expressed or manifested. *Preliminary negotiations* are not offers but are invitations to negotiate or to make an offer. Dickering with a salesperson about the price of a car is negotiation, not an offer.

A person's intent is tested by an objective standard. The court decides from the evidence whether a reasonable person familiar with the business being transacted would be justified in believing an offer had been made. If, under the circumstances, the court decides that intent was lacking, a contract could not be formed. For example, if Marie says, "I would like to sell my car for $5,000," there is no firm offer to sell that allows Tara to form a contract by saying, "Sold. I will pay you $5,000."

Many things that are stated as being for sale are not regarded as definite offers that can be accepted to create a contract. For example, when a jacket worn by Elvis Presley is put on the auction block, unless otherwise stated, it is an invitation for people to submit offers on the jacket. If no offers are high enough, the owner of the jacket can withdraw it.

Similarly, most advertisements are regarded as invitations for others to submit offers to buy. If a catalog lists a particular model of laser printers for $499.99 each, it is most likely that if you order one the order will be accepted and a contract formed. But the seller listing the printers for sale can reject such offers to buy, as such lists are usually considered to be requests for offers to buy, rather than offers themselves. However, as the *Chang* case indicates, in some instances an advertisement can be an offer that can be accepted to create a contract. The case also discusses other elements needed to create a contract.

Chang v. First Colonial Savings Bank
Supreme Court of Virginia
410 S.E.2d 928 (1991)

CASE BACKGROUND *Chia and Shin Chang saw an ad in a Richmond newspaper that stated: "Saving at First Colonial is a very rewarding experience. In appreciation for your business we have Great Gifts for you to enjoy NOW—and when your investment matures you get your entire principal back PLUS GREAT INTEREST. . . . Plan B: 3 1/2 Year Investment. Deposit $14,000 and receive two gifts: a Remington Shotgun and GE CB Radio, OR an RCA 20" Color-Trac TV, and $20,136.12 upon maturity in 3 1/2 years. Substantial penalty for early withdrawal. . . . Rates shown are 8 3/4% for Plan B. . . ."*

The Changs deposited $14,000 in January 1986. They received the color TV and a certificate of deposit. Three and one-half years later, when they redeemed their certificate, they were told that the ad had an error and that they should have deposited $15,000 to get the $20,136.12 at redemption. The bank paid them $18,823.93, which was 8 3/4% interest on $14,000 for 3 1/2 years. The Changs sued for the $1,312.19 difference. They won at trial court, but the appeals court held that the ad did not constitute an offer but was an invitation to bargain, so it held for First Colonial. The Changs appealed.

CASE DECISION Hassel, Justice.

* * *

The general rule followed in most states, and which we adopt, is that newspaper advertisements are not offers, but merely invitations to bargain. However, there is a very narrow and limited exception to this rule. '[W]here the offer is clear, definite, and explicit, and leaves nothing open for negotiation, it constitutes an offer, acceptance of which will complete the contract.' As Professor Williston observed: In any event there can be no doubt that a positive offer may be made by even an advertisement or general notice. . . . The only general test which can be submitted as a guide is an inquiry whether the facts show that some performance was promised in positive terms in return for something requested.

Applying these principles to the facts before us, we hold that the advertisement constituted an offer which was accepted when the Changs deposited their $14,000 with the Bank for a period of three and one-half years. A plain reading of the advertisement demonstrates that First Colonial's offer of the television and $20,136.12 upon maturity in three and one-half years was clear, definite, and explicit and left nothing open for negotiation.

Even though the Bank's advertisement upon which the Changs relied may have contained a mistake caused by a typographical error, under the unique facts and circumstances of this case, the error does not invalidate the offer. First Colonial did not inform the Changs of this typographical error until after it had the use of the Changs' $14,000 for three and one-half years. Additionally, applying the general rule to which there are certain exceptions not applicable here, a unilateral [one-sided] mistake does not void an otherwise legally binding contract.

First Colonial further argues that even if the newspaper advertisement was an offer, it was a unilateral offer unsupported by consideration, and it was withdrawn before the date the Changs deposited their $14,000. We disagree.

An offer, which is usually but not always a promise, is a manifestation of a willingness to enter into a bargain. The offer identifies the bargained for exchange and creates a power of acceptance in the offeree.

It is true that an offer that is not supported by consideration may be withdrawn any time before it is accepted. However, First Colonial was required to communicate the withdrawal of the offer to the Changs before they accepted it. As we have noted, First Colonial did not inform the Changs that the offer had been withdrawn or that the advertisement purportedly contained a typographical error until the Bank had used their $14,000 for three and one-half years.

We also reject First Colonial's argument that the advertisement did not create a contract because there was no meeting of the minds. . . .

The offerer has a right to prescribe in his offer any conditions as to time, place, quantity, mode of acceptance, or other matters, which it may please him to insert in and make a part thereof, and the acceptance to conclude the agreement must in every respect meet and correspond with the offer, neither falling within or going beyond the terms proposed, but exactly meeting them at all points and closing with these just as they stand.

When the Changs tendered their $14,000 to First Colonial for three and one-half years, they complied with all of the conditions in First Colonial's offer. Hence, there was a meeting of the minds and an enforceable contract.

Accordingly, we will reverse the judgment of the circuit court and enter final judgment here in favor of the Changs for $1,312.19 plus interest.

Reversed and final judgment.

QUESTIONS FOR ANALYSIS

1. Since the ad stated that the interest rate to be paid was 8 3/4 percent, which the bank did pay on the Changs' money, why did the truth of that promise not allow the bank to pay the amount of interest that it actually paid?
2. Suppose the error in the ad were more obvious because the ad had said that if you deposit $1,400 you get a TV and $20,000. Would the bank still have been forced to pay that amount?

Definite Terms and Conditions Not every tiny detail of an offer must be present for it to be a valid offer. Under the common-law rule, terms of an offer must be sufficient so that each party's promises are reasonably certain. An offer that has unclear major terms, or is missing important terms, cannot serve as the basis for a contract. Sometimes the courts supply missing terms if they are minor, so that the offer does not fail for *indefiniteness*. That prevents a party from backing out of a contract after the fact, claiming that there never was an offer because some trivial point was not clear.

Communication of the Offer Exhibit 10.3 summarizes the timing of communication of offer and acceptance. An acceptance requires *knowledge of the offer* by the offeree. The case of a person who captures a fugitive and later learns of a reward is a good example of an offer failing for lack of communication. Because the communication of the offer occurred after the act of acceptance (capturing the fugitive), a proper acceptance did not take place. A contract cannot be formed by accepting an unknown offer.

Terminating an Offer

Termination of an offer can occur either through the action of the parties or by the operation of law. The parties can *terminate* an offer by withdrawing it (by the offeror) or rejecting it (by the offeree) or through lapse of time (by the inaction of the offeree). An *option contract* is different because it is one where a binding promise has been created to keep an offer open for a specified period of time. Termination of an offer by operation of law can occur through intervening illegality, destruction of the subject matter of the offer, or death or insanity of the offeror or the offeree.

Termination by the Parties Offerors can terminate most offers by withdrawing an offer before it has been accepted by the offeree. The withdrawal of the offer by the offeror is a *revocation*. To be effective, the revocation must be communicated to the offeree. Generally, the offeror may revoke the offer anytime before acceptance. An offer can also state that it must be accepted within a designated time period. The expiration of that time period terminates the offer.

After an offer has been made, the offeree can create a contract by accepting the offer or can terminate the offer by rejecting it. One important form of rejection is a *counteroffer*—a proposal by the offeree to change the terms of the original offer. For example, if Warisch offers to buy Kohl's old laptop computer for $500 and Kohl says that he will sell it for $600, a counteroffer has been made. The original

EXHIBIT 10.3

*Legal Effect of Offer
and Acceptance
Communications*

Communication	Time Effective	Legal Effect
By Offeror		
1. Offer	When received by offeree	Offeree has the power to accept
2. Revocation	When received by offeree	Ends offeree's power to accept
By Offeree		
1. Rejection	When received by offeror	Terminates the offer
2. Counteroffer	When received by offeror	Terminates the offer
3. Acceptance	When sent by offeree	Forms a contract

offer by Warisch is terminated by the counteroffer. The offeree now has to wait for the offeror's acceptance or rejection of the counteroffer to determine if a contract resulted. That is, by making a counteroffer, Kohl became the offeror and Warisch became the offeree.

Finally, an offer may terminate through *lapse of time*. If an offer does not state a specific period for acceptance, the passage of a reasonable length of time after the offer has been made will terminate it. What is reasonable depends upon the circumstances. An offer to buy stock in a company at a set price terminates through lapse of time very quickly, while an offer to sell a building expires after a longer time. It depends on the normal practices of the businesses involved.

Termination by the Operation of Law An offer that terminates by operation of law through *intervening illegality* occurs when a court decision or legislation makes an offer illegal after it has been made. Suppose Horace Grant starts a business that offers to sell PowerBall lottery tickets to people in South Carolina. South Carolina enacts a law forbidding the sale of any lottery tickets in the state. Grant's offer to sell Power Ball lottery tickets in South Carolina is terminated by an intervening illegality.

An offer also terminates by law if the *subject matter is destroyed*. Suppose Espinoza offers to sell Washburn her car. Before Washburn accepts Espinoza's offer, the car is wrecked in an accident. The offer terminated when the accident occurred.

The *mental or physical incapacity or death of the offeror or the offeree* also terminates an offer by operation of law. An offer is terminated by mental or physical disability because the person does not have the mental capacity to enter into or fulfill a contract, and physical limitations, such as a severe injury, may make a party unable to perform a contract that requires certain skills or abilities. Similarly, a dead offeror or offeree cannot execute a contract.

The Acceptance

In contract law, *acceptance* is an offeree's expression of assent or agreement to the terms of the offer. In most contracts, this means the offeree accepts by making a promise, although for a unilateral contract, acceptance occurs by performing the service requested. To be effective, an acceptance must be unconditional, unequivocal, and properly communicated. A supposed acceptance that lacks one of these elements will generally not bring about a binding contract.

Must Be Unconditional An offeree must accept an offer as presented by an offeror. In effect, the acceptance must be the *mirror image* of the offer. The common-law rule is that a supposed acceptance that adds conditions to the original offer is a counteroffer. By changing the terms of the offer, there is not unconditional acceptance; the offeree rejects the offer. This is a key issue in the *Normile* case.

Normile v. Miller
Supreme Court of North Carolina
326 S.E.2d 11 (1985)

CASE BACKGROUND *Miller offered her property for sale through real estate agents. The property was shown to Normile and Kurniawan (N&K) by a realtor, Byer, who helped N&K prepare a written offer to buy Miller's property. N&K used a standard form real estate contract. They filled in the blanks for the key terms of the offer. One clause stated: "OFFER & CLOSING DATE: Time is of the essence, therefore this offer must be accepted on or before 5:00 P.M. Aug. 5th, 1980. A signed copy shall be promptly returned to the purchaser." Byer took the offer to Miller on August 4. Miller made several changes in the terms of the offer, signed it, and returned it. Byer presented the counteroffer to N&K the evening of the fourth. N&K told Byer they wanted to think about it.*

The next day, at noon of the fifth, Segal signed an offer to buy Miller's property. Miller accepted that offer without change and signed the contract that afternoon. Byer told N&K that the property had been sold. N&K then signed Miller's counteroffer of the day before, accepting it without any changes, but Miller sold to Segal. N&K sued Miller, claiming they had the right to buy the property up until 5:00 P.M. on the 5th. The trial court and appeals court held that Segal was to get the property. N&K appealed.

CASE DECISION Frye, Justice.

* * *

In the instant case, the offerors [N&K] submitted their offer to purchase defendant's property. This offer contained a Paragraph 9, requiring that "this offer must be accepted on or before 5:00 P.M. Aug. 5th 1980." Thus the offeree's power of acceptance was controlled by the duration of time for acceptance of the offer. "The offeror is the creator of the power, and before it leaves his hands, he may fashion it to his will . . . if he names a specific period for its existence, the offeree can accept only during this period."

This offer to purchase remains only an offer until the seller accepts it on the terms contained in the original offer by the prospective purchaser. If the seller does accept the terms in the purchaser's offer, he denotes this by signing the offer to purchase at the bottom, thus forming a valid, binding, and irrevocable purchase contract between the seller and purchaser.

However, if the seller purports to accept but changes or modifies the terms of the offer, he makes what is generally referred to as a qualified or conditional acceptance. Such a reply from the seller is actually a counteroffer and a rejection of the buyer's offer.

These basic principles of contract law are recognized not only in real estate transactions but in bargaining situations generally. It is axiomatic that a valid contract between two parties can only exist when the parties "assent to the same thing in the same sense, and their minds meet as to all terms." This assent, or meeting of the minds, requires an offer and acceptance in the exact terms and that the acceptance must be communicated to the offeror. "If the terms of the offer are changed or any new ones added by the acceptance, there is no meeting of the minds and, consequently, no contract." This counteroffer amounts to a rejection of the original offer. "The reason is that the counteroffer is interpreted as being in effect the statement by the offeree not only that he will enter into the transaction on the terms stated in his counteroffer, but also by implication that he will not assent to the terms of the original offer."

The question then becomes, did Miller accept [N&K's] offer prior to the expiration of the time limit contained within the offer? We conclude that she did not. The offeree . . . changed the original offer in several material respects, most notably in the terms regarding payment of the purchase price. This qualified acceptance was in reality a rejection of [N&K's] original offer because it was coupled with certain modifications or changes that were not contained in the original offer. Additionally, Miller's conditional acceptance amounted to a counteroffer to [N&K]. "A counter-offer is an offer made by an offeree to his offeror relating to the same matter as the original offer and proposing a substituted bargain differing from that proposed by the original offer." Between [N&K] and Miller there was no meeting of the minds, since the parties failed to assent to the same thing in the same sense. . . .

Thus, the time-for-acceptance provision contained in [N&K's] original offer did not become part of the terms of the counteroffer. And, of course, if they had accepted the counteroffer from Miller, a binding purchase contract, which would have included the terms of the original offer and counteroffer, would have then resulted.

* * *

Therefore . . . we conclude that Miller made no promise or agreement to hold her offer open. Thus, a necessary ingredient to the creation of an option contract, i.e., a promise to hold an offer open for a specified time, is not present. Accordingly, we hold that defendant's counteroffer was not transformed into an irrevocable offer for the time limit contained in the original offer because the defendant's conditional acceptance did not include the time-for-acceptance provision as part of its terms and because defendant did not make any promise to hold her counteroffer open for any stated time.

* * *

It is evident from the record that after [N&K] failed to accept defendant's counteroffer, there was a second purchaser, . . . Segal, who submitted an offer to defendant that was accepted. This offer and acceptance between the latter parties, together with consideration in the form of an earnest money deposit . . . ripened into a valid and binding purchase contract.

By entering into the contract with . . . Segal, defendant manifested her intention to revoke her previous counteroffer to [N&K]. "It is a fundamental tenet of the common law that an offer is generally freely revocable and can be countermanded by the offeror at any time before it has been accepted by the offeree." The revocation of an offer terminates it, and the offeree has no power to revive the offer by any subsequent attempts to accept.

Generally, notice of the offeror's revocation must be communicated to the offeree to effectively terminate the offeree's power to accept the offer. It is enough that the offeree receives reliable information, even indirectly, "that the offeror had taken definite action inconsistent with an intention to make the contract."

In this case, [N&K] received notice of Miller's revocation of the counteroffer in the afternoon of August 5, when Byer saw Normile and told him, "[Y]ou snooze, you lose; the property has been sold." Later that afternoon, [N&K] initialed the counteroffer and delivered it to Byer, along with their earnest money deposit of $500. These subsequent attempts by [N&K] to accept defendant's revoked counteroffer were fruitless, however, since their power of acceptance had been effectively terminated by the offeror's revocation. Since defendant's counteroffer could not be revived, the practical effect of [N&K's] initialing defendant's counteroffer and leaving it at the broker's office before 5:00 P.M. on August 5 was to resubmit a new offer. This offer was not accepted by defendant since she had already contracted to sell her property by entering into a valid, binding, and irrevocable purchase contract with . . . Segal.

For the reasons stated herein, the decision of the Court of Appeals is . . . AFFIRMED.

QUESTIONS FOR ANALYSIS

1. N&K never rejected Miller's counteroffer; they merely held it until 5 P.M. the next day while thinking about it. Does the law require that a party answer instantly to avoid losing a contract?
2. Were Byer's actions ethical? He knew that N&K would decide what to do on the fifth, yet he took another offer to Miller, knowing it could leave N&K out of the picture.

Must Be Unequivocal Acceptance must be unequivocal or definite. Suppose an offeree receives an offer to buy a car for $10,000. If the offeree says "I see" or "What a good idea," either expression fails the unequivocal test. There is no acceptance.

While the words "I accept" are a clear indication of an offeree's acceptance, any words or conduct expressing the offeree's intent to accept the offer is an effective acceptance. When negotiations take place, however, much is expressed in words and conduct that is not a complete rejection or a clear acceptance. In such cases, the courts look at the offeree's expressions to determine whether a reasonable person would consider them as an acceptance of the offer.

As a general rule, silence is not considered acceptance for the simple reason that it is not unequivocal. It could mean either yes or no to the offeree. However, the past business dealings of the offeror and the offeree may allow silence by the

EXHIBIT 10.4

Alternative Results

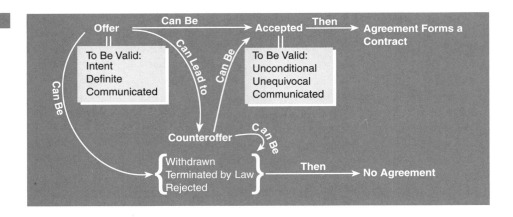

offeree to be acceptance. For example, if a company has serviced a copier for a customer every week, there does not need to be an express statement every week that copier service is desired.

Must Be Properly Communicated The final requirement of acceptance is that it is properly communicated to the offeror (unless it is a unilateral contract that is accepted by performance). Three factors can be important in meeting this requirement: (1) the method of acceptance, (2) the timeliness of acceptance, and (3), in some cases, performance as acceptance. Exhibit 10.4 summarizes the elements of offer and acceptance.

The general rule in communicating an acceptance is that any reasonable method is adequate. Problems arise when the offeror authorizes one way to communicate acceptance but the offeree uses another. If, for example, the offeror requires that acceptance be made by letter, a response by telephone will not create an acceptance. If no method of acceptance is specified, the offeree may use any reasonable means to communicate. The safest approach is to use the method used by the offeror in communicating the offer.

The timeliness of acceptance is important, especially when the value of goods or services being offered changes rapidly. To deal with time problems, the courts created the general rule that if the method of acceptance is reasonable under the circumstances, the acceptance is effective when it is sent.

In some circumstances, an offeror has attempted to revoke an offer before receiving the offeree's acceptance. This led to the *mailbox rule*, which states that acceptance is effective when it is mailed (sent) and revocation is effective when it is received by the offeree. For example, the offeror sends the offer June 1, and the offer is received by the offeree on June 3. The offeror sends a revocation of the offer on June 2, and the revocation is received by the offeree on June 4. If the offeree had sent an acceptance to the offeror on June 3 and the acceptance had reached the offeror on June 5, would there be a valid acceptance? Applying the mailbox rule, the answer is yes, since the acceptance is effective upon being sent by the offeree (June 3), while the revocation is effective upon receipt (June 4).

Special considerations govern the acceptance of what some states call unilateral contracts. A unilateral contract exists when a promise is made in exchange for a performance. Thus, a unilateral contract offer is accepted by *performance*. For example, if your dog is lost and you announce a $100 reward for its return, anyone can accept your offer by finding the dog and returning it for the reward. The finder does not need to promise you they will find the dog, they just do it to accept the offer of the reward. Courts usually require that the performance be completed for the acceptance to take place. Some courts take the view that once performance starts, the offeror loses the right to revoke the offer.

CONSIDERATION

Consideration is something of value or something bargained for in exchange for a promise. It is the element of a contract that keeps it from being gratuitous (a gift). If consideration is absent, neither party can enforce the promise or agreement.

The traditional rule is that an exchange is consideration if it creates a legal detriment to the *promisee* (the party to whom a promise is made) or a legal benefit to the *promisor* (the party making a promise). A *legal detriment* is an act, or a promise to act, or the refraining from an action, such as giving up a legal right. A *legal benefit* to the promisor exists when the promisor acquires some legal right through the promisee's act, promise to act, or refraining from doing some act.

Consideration requires either a legal detriment to the promisee or a legal benefit to the promisor, although both usually occur at the same time. Suppose Shaftel buys a watch from SwissWatch for $100. Shaftel suffers a legal detriment (gives up the right to keep $100) in exchange for a benefit (the watch). SwissWatch suffers a legal detriment (gives up the watch) in exchange for a benefit ($100). As the following famous case illustrates, courts use this *detriment-benefit test* to determine whether there is consideration for a contract.

Hamer v. Sidway
Court of Appeals of New York, Second Division
124 N.Y. 538, 27 N.E. 256 (1891)

CASE BACKGROUND *William E. Story, Sr., was the uncle of William E. Story II. At a celebration at which guests were present, Story Sr. promised his sixteen-year-old nephew that he would pay him $5,000 if he would refrain from "drinking, using tobacco, swearing, and playing cards or billiards for money" until he was 21 years old. Upon turning 21, the nephew wrote to the uncle, telling him that he had performed his part of the agreement and wished to be awarded the $5,000. The uncle wrote a letter to the nephew stating, "Your letter . . . came to hand all right, saying that you had lived up to the promise made to me several years ago. I have no doubt but you have, [and] you shall have five thousand dollars, as I promised you."*

Two years later the uncle died, without having paid the nephew the $5,000. The executor of Story Sr.'s estate refused to pay the $5,000, stating that there had been no consideration by the nephew for the money. Here the court reviews the agreement and discusses the element of consideration as a part of the contract.

CASE DECISION Parker, Judge.

The question [before us] . . . is whether by virtue of a contract . . ., William E. Story became indebted to his nephew, William E. Story, II, on his twenty-first birthday in the sum of $5,000. . . .

The defendant contends that the contract was without consideration to support it, and therefore invalid. He asserts that the nephew, by refraining from the use of liquor and tobacco, was not harmed, but benefited; that that which he did was best for him to do, independently of his uncle's promise, and insists that it follows that, unless the promisor was benefited, the contract was without consideration, a contention which, if well founded, would seem to leave open for controversy in many cases whether that which the promisee did or omitted to do was in fact of such benefit to him as to leave no consideration to support the enforcement of the promisor's agreement. Such a rule could not be tolerated, and is without foundation in the law. [We have] defined "consideration" as follows:

"A valuable consideration, in the sense of the law, may consist either in some right, interest, profit, or benefit accruing to the one party, or some forbearance, detriment, loss, or responsibility given, suffered, or undertaken by the other."

Courts "will not ask whether the thing which forms the consideration does in fact benefit the promisee . . ., or is of any substantial value to any one. It is enough that something is promised, done, forborne, or suffered by the party to whom the promise is made as consideration for the promise made to him. In general a waiver of any legal right at the request of another party is a sufficient consideration for a promise. Any damage, or suspension or forbearance of a right will be sufficient to sustain a promise. . . . 'Consideration' means not so much that one party is profiting as that the other abandons some legal right in the present, or limits his legal freedom of action in the future, as an inducement for the promise of the first."

Now, applying this rule to the facts before us, the [nephew] used tobacco, occasionally drank liquor, and he had a legal right to do so. That right he abandoned for a period of years upon the strength of the promise of [his uncle] that for such forbearance he would give him $5,000. We need not speculate on the effort which may have been required to give up the use of those stimulants. It is sufficient that he restricted his lawful freedom of the action within certain prescribed limits upon the faith of his uncle's agreement, and now, having fully performed the conditions imposed, it is of no moment whether such performance actually proved a benefit to the promisor [the uncle], and the court will not inquire into it; but, were it a proper subject of inquiry, we see nothing in this record that would permit a determination that the uncle was not benefited in a legal sense.

* * *

QUESTIONS FOR ANALYSIS

1. What was the consideration in this case?
2. Was it important that the activities the nephew refrained from did not harm but benefited him?
3. What detriment did the nephew incur?

Adequacy of Consideration

For the most part, courts do not like to inquire into the *adequacy of consideration* given in a contract. In a business transaction, the bargaining is the responsibility of the parties to the contract. Even if one party bargains poorly and the values of the items to be exchanged are very unequal, the courts generally do not interfere. Courts support contracts that are bargained for, even if the consideration is not related to market value, as the *Hamer* case explained.

Preexisting Duty and Past Consideration

Consideration is a present *detriment* to the promisee or a present *benefit* to the promisor. An obligation that existed before a new agreement (*preexisting duty*) does not constitute consideration. The reason is that the promisee has not incurred a detriment if there was already an obligation to perform; without a detriment, there can be no consideration.

Consider a professional baseball player who becomes unhappy with his contract because similar players are now making more money than he is. Suppose his team wants to make him happy and will give him a salary increase. An agreement to provide the increase, given an existing contract, would not be supported by consideration by the athlete. Since only the team would be incurring a detriment, the increase would be a gift, not a bargain. The athlete had already agreed to perform for the club at the original contract amount (past consideration). To provide consideration, the team will require the player to agree to a contract extension. The team's detriment is the additional salary, and the athlete's detriment is the additional time he agrees to play for the team at the new salary.

Similarly, promises made that are based on *past consideration* are usually unenforceable because there is no new consideration given in exchange. Such promises

My Lawyer Should Be Responsible for My Breach of Contract!

Latrell Sprewell, a $10-million-a-year-plus basketball player for the Golden State Warriors, was kicked off the team and had his contract torn up for physically attacking his coach twice. First Sprewell sued the National Basketball Association, claiming they could not suspend him from playing. A federal judge threw the case out. Sprewell than sued his agent for not including a term in his contract with Golden State that would have made the team pay him regardless of his personal conduct.

Source: *Wall Street Journal*

are usually gifts, and promises to make a gift are generally not enforceable. In the previous example, if the baseball player had a great season and the team owner said he was going to give him $100,000 for having played so well, there is no contract because there is no consideration. The $100,000, if paid, is a gift; that is, it is not paid in exchange for services yet to be performed. If the money is not paid, the player has no suit for breach of promise.

Enforceable Promises without Consideration

Circumstances exist where consideration for a promise is not required by the courts for the promise to be enforceable. Suppose a business makes a promise to a customer who needs a particular product for a renovation project. The customer will not start the project without the product. The business tells the customer that it can deliver the product at a certain price so he does not need to order it from another seller. On that basis, but without a firm contract, the customer begins the renovation. The court may find that business is bound by its promise if it later refuses to deliver the product to the customer. The doctrine used by the courts to bind such a promisor is called *promissory estoppel* (or *detrimental reliance*). The rationale for the doctrine is that it will avoid an injustice due to the promisee's reasonable reliance on the promisor's promise.

Under the doctrine, the promisor is *estopped* (prevented) from denying his previous promise. The *Restatement (2d) of Contracts* explains promissory estoppel this way: "A promise which the promisor should reasonably expect to induce action or forbearance on the part of the promisee . . . and which does induce such action or forbearance is binding if injustice can be avoided only by enforcement of the promise."

This is not a rule imposed lightly by the courts. One area in which promissory estoppel arises not infrequently is that of promises to charities. Suppose an art museum is raising $50 million for an expansion. It collects promises from various donors, but none of the money is collected until there are enough promises to make the project feasible. Once that happens, if a donor backs out after the building is underway, the courts may rule that promissory estoppel applies and the gift must be made. The building contract was entered into on reliance of the donation being made. The well-known *Red Owl* case is a good example of how the rule can arise in a business setting.

Hoffman v. Red Owl Stores, Inc.
Supreme Court of Wisconsin
26 Wis.2d 683, 133 N.W.2d 267 (1965)

CASE BACKGROUND *Hoffman owned a bakery but wanted to own a grocery store. He contacted Red Owl, which operated a chain of supermarkets. Several conversations between Hoffman and Red Owl took place, leading to the idea that they might establish a Red Owl store in Wautoma, Wisconsin. In September 1960, Lukowitz continued negotiations for Red Owl. It was discussed that Hoffman would need $18,000 capital to invest in the business. Upon the advice of Lukowitz to get more experience, Hoffman leased a building, bought inventory and fixtures, and began operating a grocery store in Wautoma.*

After three months, Lukowitz advised Hoffman to sell the store, which was making a profit, assuring Hoffman that Red Owl would find a larger store for him. Hoffman sold the fixtures and inventory in June 1961. Before Hoffman sold the store, he told Red Owl that he had $18,000 for the start-up costs of the Red Owl franchise. Red Owl selected a site, and at its suggestion, Hoffman made a $1,000 down payment. Upon the assurances of the representative of Red Owl that the business was ready to begin, Hoffman sold the bakery for $10,000, incurring a $2,000 loss.

In November, Lukowitz and Hoffman met to discuss Hoffman's financial standing. A document titled "Proposed Financing for an Agency Store" stated that Hoffman was to contribute $24,100 instead of $18,000. Through a series of loans, Hoffman came up with the required money. A week later, Hoffman was told that if he could get another $2,000, the deal would be made for $26,000. Hoffman objected to this new requirement and other demands by Red Owl, and negotiations ended.

Hoffman sued Red Owl for breach of contract. Red Owl defended that no contract existed because of a lack of consideration. There was no franchise agreement and no financing plan agreed upon by the parties. Hoffman contended that Red Owl was liable under the theory of promissory estoppel. The trial court held for Hoffman, stating that an "injustice would result if plaintiffs were not granted damages." The defendants appealed.

CASE DECISION Currie, Chief Justice.

* * *

Many courts of other jurisdictions have seen fit over the years to adopt the principle of promissory estoppel, and the tendency in that direction continues. . . .

[T]he development of the law of promissory estoppel "is an attempt by the courts to keep remedies abreast of increased moral consciousness of honesty and fair representations in all business dealings."

* * *

The record here discloses a number of promises and assurances given to Hoffman by Lukowitz in behalf of Red Owl upon which plaintiffs relied and acted upon to their detriment.

Foremost were the promises that for the sum of $18,000 Red Owl would establish Hoffman in a store. After Hoffman had sold his grocery store and paid the $1,000 [toward land purchase for the store], the $18,000 figure was changed to $24,100. Then in November, 1961, Hoffman was assured that if the $24,100 figure were increased by $2,000 the deal would go through. Hoffman was induced to sell his grocery store fixtures and inventory in June, 1961, on the promise that he would be in his new store by fall. In November, plaintiffs sold their bakery building on the urging of defendants and on the assurance that this was the last step necessary to have the deal with Red Owl go through.

We determine that there was ample evidence to sustain the answers of the jury . . . with respect to the promissory representations made by Red Owl, Hoffman's reliance thereon in the exercise of ordinary care, and his fulfillment of the conditions required of him by the terms of the negotiations had with Red Owl.

* * *

We conclude that injustice would result here if plaintiffs were not granted some relief because of the failure of defendants to keep their promises which induced plaintiffs to act to their detriment.

* * *

Order affirmed.

QUESTIONS FOR ANALYSIS

1. How could Red Owl have avoided the outcome in this case?
2. How could Hoffman have protected himself against being placed in this position?

EXHIBIT 10.5	Incapacity	Degree of Incapacity	Legal Effect on Contract
A Summary of Contractual Capacity	Minor	Partial Capacity	Voidable
	Intoxicated Person	Partial Capacity	Voidable
	Mentally Insane:		
	Adjudicated	No Capacity	Void
	Insane in Fact	Partial Capacity	Voidable

CAPACITY TO CONTRACT

One essential element of a contract is *contractual capacity*, or legal ability, to create a contract. The term *capacity* refers to a party's ability to perform legally valid acts, acquire legal rights, and incur legal liabilities. Generally, minors, intoxicated persons, and the insane have limited capacity to contract. A party claiming incapacity has the burden of proving it.

Most individuals have complete capacity to contract. If a person, perhaps as a result of mental disability does not have capacity to contract, the contract entered into is void. If a person has *partial capacity*, the contract is enforceable unless the person with partial capacity exercises the right to disaffirm the contract. Contracts created by those with partial capacity are voidable. A summary of the legal effects on contracts resulting from less-than-complete capacity is presented in Exhibit 10.5.

Minors

A *minor* is a person under the legal age of majority. The traditional age of majority was 21 for men and women, but all states have statutes that set the age at 18 for most contracts and younger for some, such as for student loans. At common law, the general rule is that a minor may enter into contracts but the contracts are voidable at the option of the minor. This *right to disaffirm* contracts stems from the traditions of the English courts wishing to protect the young from the results "of their own folly." A company that enters into a contract with a minor—knowingly or unknowingly—may find itself with relatively few rights if the minor disaffirms the contract.

After a minor reaches the age of majority, most states provide that the person may *ratify* contracts made while a minor. The person must generally show an intent to be bound. Ratification may be either expressed through words or a writing or implied by the person's conduct, such as continued use of an automobile. The right to disaffirm extinguishes after a reasonable time. If a minor disaffirms a contract after receiving benefits, such as a 16-year-old driving a car for six months, *restitution* must be paid for the value of the benefit received, provided the minor is able to do so.

There are some contracts, however, that minors may not disaffirm. Enlistment contracts to join the Army and marriage contracts are classic examples of *nonvoidable contracts*. Further, some states have statues that do not allow minors to disaffirm certain contracts, such as for insurance, educational loans, medical care loans, and bank account agreements.

Mentally Impaired and Intoxicated Persons

If a person is *intoxicated* (or under the influence of drugs) at the time a contract is made, most courts hold that the contract is voidable. The test is whether the person was too intoxicated to understand the nature of the agreement. When the person becomes sober, he or she may disaffirm the contract.

Contract law classifies mentally impaired persons as either adjudicated insane or insane in fact. A person is *adjudicated insane* if a court rules that the person is not competent to carry on contractual activities. A contract entered into by a person who is adjudicated insane is void. A person not adjudicated insane but who lacks the capacity to enter into a contract is *insane in fact* and has the right to disaffirm a contract. The right to disaffirm or to ratify a contract arises after a mentally impaired person is restored to competency or after a *guardian* is appointed to act on that person's behalf. A guardian may disaffirm or ratify an existing contract and may enter into a new contract on behalf of the impaired person. Some states do not allow disaffirmance of a contract made by an impaired person if the contract is just and reasonable.

LEGALITY

For a contract to be valid, its *subject matter* must be *lawful*. The contract will be illegal and unenforceable if its subject matter violates a state or federal statute or the common law or is contrary to public policy. The terms *illegal bargain* and *illegal agreement* rather than illegal contract may be more proper because contract by definition refers to a legal and enforceable agreement.

Illegal Agreements

Bargains or promises that violate state or federal statutes are illegal agreements that the courts will not recognize as enforceable contracts, regardless of the intent of the parties. Statutes prohibit a variety of activities, so attempts to contract for such activities violate the statutes. Deals to trade in prohibited drugs, such as cocaine, are illegal agreements, as are other contracts to engage in criminal activities. State law strictly controls some activities, such as gambling and the sale of alcoholic beverages. Hence, gambling contracts are often illegal and the person who won an illegal wager cannot seek help from the courts. Many professions are regulated by the states. In some states, one must have a license to practice law or to clip poodles; to offer services for sale without the license would be an attempt to create an illegal contract. Similarly, some states have limits on interest rates that can be charged on certain types of loans; attempts to charge rates above the maximum allowed is called *usury* and illegal. When a court is asked to enforce a contract and it finds it to be in violation of law, the court may strike the entire bargain as unenforceable or only strike the part of the bargain that concerns illegal subject matter.

Contracts Contrary to Public Policy

Some contracts are unenforceable because their subject matter is *contrary to public policy*. A contract may not violate any particular statute yet may have a negative impact on public welfare. Some contracts that courts have held to be contrary to public policy are exculpatory agreements, unconscionable contracts, contracts with public servants, and contracts in restraint of trade.

Exculpatory Agreements An *exculpatory agreement* releases one party from the consequences brought about by wrongful acts or negligence. An example of an exculpatory agreement is an employment contract with a clause stating that the employee will not hold the employer liable for any harm to her caused by the employer while on the job. With such a clause, the employer is no longer con-

JURIS prudence?

Speaking of Unconscionable Actions . . .

Because of a dispute, Cambers Cable television company dropped the ABC affiliate station that carried, among other programs, *Monday Night Football.* Cable subscriber Phillip Schlenker of Novato, California, sued for breach of contract. He argued that the company claimed that it would carry all major networks, but it no longer did, depriving him of watching *Monday Night Football.*

Being forced to go to a bar to drink during five games, Schlenker ran up a $75 bar tab, which the court awarded him in damages, plus attorney fees. After all, "You cannot sit in a tavern and watch a game without buying something from the bar," said Schlenker. The Federal Communications Commission reported that the case appeared to be precedent setting.

Source: *Gannett News Service*

cerned about being sued for tortious acts. Such clauses are generally held to violate public policy and are not enforceable.

Unconscionable Contracts The courts usually do not concern themselves with the fairness of a bargain struck by contracting parties. But in some cases, if a contract is grossly unfair to an innocent party, the courts, in equity, will not enforce it. Such contracts are called *unconscionable contracts* and occur when one of the parties, being in a strong position, takes advantage of the other party. The stronger party convinces the other party to enter into a contract contrary to his well-being. Such agreements may violate public policy and may not be enforceable.

Contracts with Public Servants A contract to influence a public servant to violate the duty the government employee owes to the public is contrary to public policy. For example, if a lobbyist contracts to pay a legislator if a bill is passed or not passed, the contract would be unenforceable. It also violates public policy to pay regulators or police officials to give special favors.

Contracts in Restraint of Trade Contracts that restrain trade or unreasonably restrict competition are considered contrary to public policy and are not enforced by the courts. Part of the common law on this subject became part of modern antitrust law, discussed later in the text.

Even if a contract does not violate a statute, it still may be an unenforceable restraint of trade. A *covenant not to compete*, for example, may be a restraint of trade if it does not meet certain guidelines. A covenant not to compete typically arises in contracts for the sale of a business and for employment. The employee (or seller) agrees not to compete with the employer (or buyer). If the covenant is limited to a reasonable time and territory, courts generally find it enforceable, but the rules vary quite a bit from state to state. Contracts between businesses often restrict the parties from interfering with other existing business relationships that become known by virtue of the parties now working together, as we see in the *General Commercial* case.

General Commercial Packaging, Inc. v. TPS Package Engineering, Inc.
United States Court of Appeals, Ninth Circuit
126 F.3d 1131 (1997)

CASE BACKGROUND *General Commercial provides packing services for businesses in Florida and California. Its longtime customer, Walt Disney, hired it to package materials for shipment to EuroDisneyland. General Commercial hired TPS as a subcontractor to help with that work.*

To protect its business with Disney, General Commercial required TPS to sign a contract that included a clause that TPS would not during the contract or for one year afterward deal directly with Disney. If TPS worked with Disney without permission, it would pay General Commercial 25 percent of its revenues from that business. TPS ignored the provision and began working directly for Disney.

General Commercial sued for breach of contract. The district court held that the contract violated California's prohibition against contracts in restraint of trade. General Commercial appealed.

CASE DECISION   Per Curiam.

* * *

Under California law, "every contract by which anyone is restrained from engaging in a lawful profession, trade, or business of any kind is to that extent void." Cal.Bus. & Prof.Code §16600. Although TPS raised no objection to the clause which precluded it from dealing directly with Disney—thereby cementing a highly profitable subcontracting relationship with General Commercial—it now claims that section 16600 renders its promise void. TPS reads section 16600 to nullify "every part of every contract that restricts a person from pursuing, in whole or in part, any trade, business or profession." The contract it signed, TPS concludes, is invalid because it prohibits TPS from infiltrating Disney's corner of the packing and shipping market.

We [previously] rejected this strict interpretation of section 16600. . . . Section 16600 does not impair General Commercial's contract with TPS unless it entirely precludes TPS from pursuing its trade or business.

* * *

TPS claims that [the] rule is, at bottom, a rule of reasonableness, and that California courts have refused to interpret section 16600 as imposing such a rule. . . . However, determining whether a contract precludes a party from engaging in a trade or business is not an inquiry into its reasonableness. A "rule of reason" compares the costs and benefits of a restraint of trade, and permits even significant restrictions if the benefits outweigh the costs. . . .

General Commercial's contract with TPS is therefore valid unless it "completely restrain[s]" TPS from plying its trade or business. . . . In considering this question, we recognize that a contract does not have to impair a party's access to every potential customer to contravene section 16600. Because most businesses cannot succeed with only a handful of customers, a contract can effectively destroy a signatory's ability to conduct a trade or business by placing a substantial segment of the market off limits. This explains why courts have been less tolerant of contracts that prohibit employees from soliciting all of their former employers' customers, and of wholesale covenants not to compete.

TPS has never disputed General Commercial's claim that the contract "does not prohibit TPS from engaging in the crating and packing business." Nor could it. The agreement only precludes TPS from dealing with Disney and those other firms which General Commercial "has introduced to and contracted with TPS to perform packing and crating subcontracting services." Apart from Disney, TPS was not barred from soliciting work from any firm with which it had a prior relationship. The contract thus only limits TPS's access to a narrow segment of the packing and shipping market.

The district court's order granting TPS's motion for summary judgment on Count I of its complaint is reversed. The breach of contract claim is remanded to the district court for consideration of any remaining defenses which TPS may have raised.

* * *

QUESTIONS FOR ANALYSIS

1. Would a large firm be able to use contract terms as existed in this contract to limit a company that contracts with it not to deal with competitors?

2. Under a rule of reason, what kinds of restrictions that extend beyond the immediate matter of the contract itself could be imposed on the other party to a contract?

REALITY AND GENUINENESS OF CONSENT

The concept of freedom of contract is based on the right of individuals to enter into the bargains of their choice. The courts assume that if a person entered into a contract, there was a desire to do so and the other party may rely on the bargain. Under some circumstances, however, a person may enter into an agreement without knowledge of all relevant information surrounding the transaction. Without knowledge, there is no *reality of consent* or *genuine consent* by the parties, and the contract is void or voidable depending on the circumstances. It is often said that there must be a *meeting of the minds* for there to be consent to the contract.

A famous case from 1887 in Michigan, *Sherwood* v. *Walker* (33 N.W. 919), illustrates the effect of mutual mistake. A cow, Rose 2d of Aberlone, was sold for about one-tenth of what she would have been worth had she not been believed to be sterile. After the sale, when she was found to be pregnant, the seller wanted to void the contract but the buyer refused. The high court of Michigan held the transaction was void because the parties thought they bargained for a sterile cow, not a much more valuable breeding cow, so the deal was made under false assumptions. In any contract, parties take certain risks, but they do not take risks about presumed facts materially affecting their bargain.

Statutory Exceptions

In some circumstances, reality or genuineness of consent is governed by statute. Some statutes deal with high-pressure selling techniques by door-to-door salespeople. These "home solicitation" statutes allow contracts to be voided if the innocent party entered into the contract under extreme pressure by a salesperson that amounts to duress or undue influence. Under federal law, the Federal Trade Commission's cooling-off rule allows purchasers of door-to-door sales with a value over twenty-five dollars to void the contract in writing within three business days.

Fraud and Misrepresentation

A person who "agrees" to a contract due to *fraud, misrepresentation, duress,* or *undue influence* has the right to disaffirm the contract because there was not genuine consent. Duress and undue influence are not common in contractual matters, but contracts formed under either are voidable. Duress occurs when someone is "forced" to sign a contract; that is, the contract is made because of a threat that gave no easy out. In the case of undue influence, a person enters into a contract because they are so dominated by another person, or have so much trust in the other person, that they are subject to improper persuasion. This happens sometimes to elderly people who have to rely on a "trusted" caretaker.

Fraud A contract induced by fraud may be rescinded. If the contract is rescinded before any losses are incurred, then there is not likely to be a cause of action for damages. But it is possible that the person who committed the fraud may be sued in tort. To establish common-law fraud, the injured party must show that:

1. There was a *misstatement* of an important fact; that is, false information was presented as fact in the making of the contract. The misstatement must be about a key fact relevant to the contract. Unimportant or unrelated misstatements, such as claiming that Abraham Lincoln was president during World War I, cannot be the basis of fraud. Hyping a product—such as by saying "This is the most fun computer game every invented" or "Now is the best time to buy"—is not sufficient to indicate an intent to defraud.

2. There must be *scienter* or intent to defraud; that is, the party wanted to mislead the other party and intentionally deceived him. Scienter means that the court finds that there is something rotten about the deal (has a bad scent) about which the seller could not be ignorant.

3. The seller must know, or have reason to know, that the statement she is making is false. If you sell your car, which you bought used, and you assert that the mileage is correct, when in fact the odometer had been turned back by the person who owned it before you, you do not know you are not telling the truth.

4. The recipient of the false information must justifiably rely on that information in making the decision to go ahead with the deal. If a seller tells you false information intending to deceive you, but you are not fooled and you go ahead with the deal anyway, there is no fraud. On the other hand, if you are very naive and believe information that you should know to be false, such as a claim that the engine in a car is made out of gold, there is no justifiable reliance.

5. There must be *privity* between the parties; that is, they must have been in a contractual arrangement. A third party observing fraud cannot sue.

6. There must be *proximate cause*. The fact that there was false information that caused the contract to be formed must be related to losses that were suffered for there to be a cause of action for damages. That is, if one is lied to but there are no consequences, then it does not matter much.

7. There must be *damages* that were caused by the fraud. That is, even if there is fraud in the making of a contract, if there are no damages that result, there should be no award.

Misrepresentation   In practice, misrepresentation and fraud are quite similar and often occur together. But there can be misrepresentation that does not reach the level of fraud. Misrepresentation requires a false statement to significantly influence the making of a contract. A false statement can be made in innocent ignorance or can be intentional. If a false statement is made innocently, the contract may be voidable if the misstatement was *material*, or key, to the decision to make the contract and the value of the contract. If the misrepresentation of a material fact is intentional, then there is clearly fraud that will be grounds for rescinding a contract. However, there are unlikely to be damages in the case of innocent misrepresentation. The *Johnson* case discusses fraud and misrepresentation in a case involving the sale of a house.

Johnson v. Davis
Supreme Court of Florida
480 So.2d 625 (1985)

CASE BACKGROUND   *The Davises entered into a contract to buy the Johnson's three-year-old home. The contract required a $5,000 deposit payment and an additional $26,000 deposit within five days. A clause in the contract stated: "Buyer shall have the right to obtain a written report from a licensed roofer stating that the roof is in watertight condition. In the event repairs are required . . . seller shall pay for said repairs which shall be performed by a licensed roofing contractor."*

Before paying the $26,000, the Davises noticed water damage. Johnson said that was from a window problem that had been corrected and that there had never been any problems with the roof. The $26,000 payment was made, and the Johnsons moved out. A couple days later, the Davises saw water coming into the house during a rain storm. Roofers hired by Johnson said the problem could be fixed for $1,000. Roofers hired by Davis said the roof was defective and needed $15,000 in repairs. The Davises sued for breach of contract, fraud, and misrepresentation, and sought rescission of the contract and return of their deposit. Johnson counterclaimed to keep the deposit as damages. The district court and the court of appeals held for the Davises. The Johnsons appealed.

CASE DECISION Adkins, Justice.

* * *

We also agree with the district court's conclusions under a theory of fraud and find that the Johnsons' statements to the Davises regarding the condition of the roof constituted a fraudulent misrepresentation entitling respondents to the return of their $26,000 deposit payment. In the state of Florida, relief for a fraudulent misrepresentation may be granted only when the following elements are present: (1) a false statement concerning a material fact; (2) the representor's knowledge that the representation is false; (3) an intention that the representation induce another to act on it; and, (4) consequent injury by the party acting in reliance on the representation. . . .

The record reflects that the statement made by the Johnsons was a false representation of material fact, made with knowledge of its falsity, upon which the Davises relied to their detriment as evidence by the $26,000 paid to the Johnsons.

The doctrine of caveat emptor does not exempt a seller from responsibility for the statements and representations which he makes to induce the buyer to act, when under the circumstances these amount to fraud in the legal sense. To be grounds for relief, the false representations need not have been made at the time of the signing of the purchase and sales agreement in order for the element of reliance to be present. The fact that the false statements as to the quality of the roof were made after the signing of the purchase and sales agreement does not excuse the seller from liability when the misrepresentations were made prior to the execution of the contract by conveyance of the property. It would be contrary to all notions of fairness and justice for this Court to place its stamp of approval on an affirmative misrepresentation by a wrongdoer just because it was made after the signing of the executory contract when all of the necessary elements for actionable fraud are present. Furthermore, the Davises' reliance on the truth of the Johnsons' representation was justified . . . "a recipient may rely on the truth of a representation, even though its falsity could have been ascertained had he made an investigation, unless he knows the representation to be false or its falsity is obvious to him." . . .

That is, where failure to disclose a material fact is calculated to induce a false belief, the distinction between concealment and affirmative representations is tenuous. Both proceed from the same motives and are attended with the same consequences; both are violative of the principles of fair dealing and good faith; both are calculated to produce the same result; and, in fact, both essentially have the same effect.

* * *

Modern concepts of justice and fair dealing have given our courts the opportunity and latitude to change legal precepts in order to conform to society's needs. Thus, the tendency of the more recent cases has been to restrict rather than extend the doctrine of caveat emptor. The law appears to be working toward the ultimate conclusion that full disclosure of all material facts must be made whenever elementary fair conduct demands it. . . .

Accordingly, we hold that where the seller of a home knows of facts materially affecting the value of the property which are not readily observable and are not known to the buyer, the seller is under a duty to disclose them to the buyer. This duty is equally applicable to all forms of real property, new and used. . . .

Affirmed.

QUESTIONS FOR ANALYSIS

1. The dissent argued that, since the Johnsons were not experts on roofs and had only agreed to pay for repairs if the Davises ordered an inspection, at most Johnson should be responsible for the cost of repairs as the contract stated. The contract did not allow the Davises to back out if there were found to be roof problems. Is that reasonable?

2. When there is conflicting testimony as to who said what about the roof, should that allow the matter to rise to the level of fraud?

Digital Signatures Can Create Valid Documents

 The American Bar Association has issued Digital Signature Guidelines to "establish a safe harbor—a secure, computer-based signature equivalent—which will (1) minimize the incidence of electronic forgeries, (2) enable and foster the reliable authentication of documents in computer form, (3) facilitate commerce by means of computerized communications, and (4) give legal effect to the general import of the technical standards for authentication of computerized messages." There are few legal barriers to creating binding contracts by electronic communication.

Many state legislatures have passed a statute such as the Utah Digital Signature Act (Utah Code Ann. §46-3-101). These laws provide that a digital signature is "as valid as if it had been written on paper." A digital signature using a public key from a government-approved certificate authority, such as VeriSign (see www.verisign.com), "is a legally valid signature" unless the presumption can be rebutted by evidence.

CONTRACTS IN WRITING AND THE STATUTE OF FRAUDS

In contract law, the general rule is that an express or implied contract, written or oral, is enforceable. Written contracts are a good idea because they are difficult to deny and courts prefer written documents over conflicting oral claims. Some contracts, however, must be in writing and signed to be enforceable. Such contracts are subject to the *Statute of Frauds*, which evolved from a 1677 English statute called "An Act for the Prevention of Frauds and Perjuries." The purpose was to prevent parties from committing fraud by claiming that a contract existed when in fact it did not. To reduce such fraud, the statute requires that for certain contracts to be enforceable, they must be in writing.

Virtually every state has a statute similar to the English act. Most states have six types of contracts that are covered by the Statute of Frauds and that must therefore be evidenced by a writing to be enforced by a court in the event of a dispute:

1. Contracts for the sale of real property (land)
2. Contracts that cannot be performed within one year
3. Promises to pay the debt of another
4. Promises by an administrator to personally pay estate debts
5. Promises made in consideration of marriage
6. Contracts for the sale of goods for $500 or more under the UCC

Sufficiency of the Writing

For a writing to be *sufficient* under the Statute of Frauds, it must set out the material terms of the contract and be signed by at least the defendant. Courts usually require the writing to contain the names of the parties, the consideration offered by the parties, the subject matter of the contract, and other material terms. However, confirmations, invoices, E-mails, sales orders, and even checks may satisfy the sufficiency of the writing requirement. Without a necessary writing, the alleged contract cannot be enforced.

Parol Evidence Rule

A contract is often preceded by negotiations. The parties may exchange letters or other communications before signing the actual contract. Occasionally, parties omit from the final contract items agreed upon in negotiations. In a subsequent lawsuit, if the parties disagree about those items, oral evidence about the items generally will not be admitted into evidence by the court. The evidence is excluded on the basis of the parol evidence rule.

The *parol evidence rule* restricts the use of evidence in a lawsuit when the evidence is contrary to the terms of a written contract. Oral evidence cannot contradict, change, or add terms to a written contract. Oral or parol evidence may be introduced when the written contract is incomplete or ambiguous; when it proves fraud, mistake, or misrepresentation; or when the parol evidence explains the written instrument through previous trade usage or course of dealing. The parol evidence rule is also a part of the law of sales under the UCC.

Performance, Discharge, and Breach of Contracts

Eventually contracts come to an end. When the obligations of a contract have been *performed*, the contract is terminated or *discharged*. Just as there are rules to govern the creation of contracts, there are rules to govern the performance and discharge of contracts. Many of the various ways in which a contract can be discharged are summarized in Exhibit 10.6.

EXHIBIT 10.6

Discharge of a Contract and Its Effect on the Parties

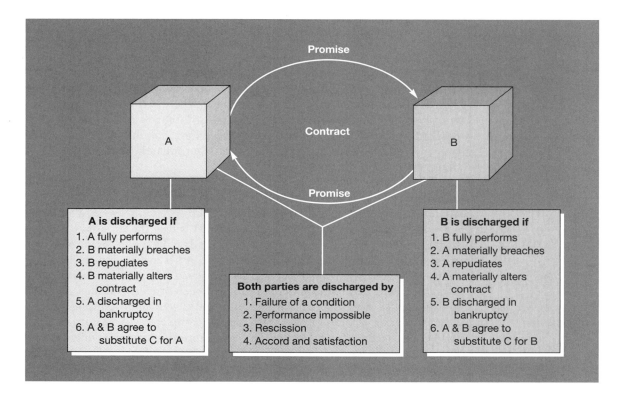

ASSIGNMENT AND DELEGATION

A contract may end up being performed by another party. A transfer of contract rights to a third party is *assignment;* a transfer of contractual duties to a third party is a *delegation.* Some contracts are primarily for personal services that cannot be assigned. Shaquille O'Neill cannot, without approval, delegate his duty to play center for the Los Angeles Lakers to any other person. If a dentist has agreed to cap your teeth, you cannot assign your right to have your teeth capped to someone else.

However, many contracts are capable of being assigned or delegated to third parties. Unless the contract, or a statute or public policy, prohibits such transfer, it often does not matter who gets the job done, so long as it is done according to the terms of the deal. The assignment or delegation creates a new contract that may be enforced as any other contract in the event of problems. If the third party performs according to the terms of the contract, the original contractual duty is discharged. The consideration the performing party is entitled—that promised in the original contract or in the assignment—depends on the details of his contract.

Third-Party Beneficiaries

A *third-party beneficiary* is a party who is not part of an original contract who acquires rights under the contract. For example, suppose Sting loans Marilyn $5,000. In consideration for the loan, Marilyn promises to pay $5,000 to Garth, to whom Sting already owes $5,000. If Marilyn fails to pay Garth, he may sue Marilyn to collect the $5,000, even though Garth and Marilyn did not enter into a contract. Garth is a third-party beneficiary of the contract between Sting and Marilyn.

PERFORMANCE

Most contracts come to an end by the complete *performance* of the parties' obligations under the contract. Contracts may be for one sale or for a long-term provision of a service. Suppose IBM buys 100,000 copies of a Microsoft program. When the programs specified in the contract have been delivered and IBM has paid, the contract is terminated. Both parties completed their part of the bargain. If a contract is to be completed over time, such as for Night Staff to clean the offices in BigBank's office building for two years, once Night Staff has done the cleaning for two years and BigBank has paid, the contract terminates. No further legal obligation is owed by either party.

Substantial Performance

Suppose, in the preceding examples, that Microsoft ships 99,220 of the 100,000 copies of a computer program ordered by IBM within the time stated in the contract, but 780 of the copies arrive a month late. Has Microsoft performed its obligation so that IBM must pay, or is there a lack of performance such that IBM may refuse or can sue Microsoft for breach of contract? In most contracts, *substantial performance* means that the contract basically has been properly fulfilled and payments must be made. The parties are expected to act in *good faith.* Refusing to pay when over 99 percent of the contract was properly completed would not be acceptable. IBM could delay payment on the last copies until they arrive or might even reject them if they are too late for use, but there is not a justification for IBM to rescind the agreement for lack of performance by Microsoft. Of course, if IBM incurs costs due to the late arrival, Microsoft is liable for those damages. The difference between a breach where there has been substantial performance and a *material breach* of contract can be a judgment call, so if a party wants to make sure things will be done according to strict specifications, that must be made clear in the contract.

DISCHARGE BY BREACH

When a party to a contract does not perform as the contract requires, there is a *breach of contract*. The party injured by the breach may be entitled to a remedy (discussed in the next section). To determine the remedy that may be provided, the court will look to determine the extent of the breach.

Material Breach

If the performance provided by a party is substantially less than the requirements of the contract, there is a *material breach*. Suppose that Microsoft fails to deliver the 100,000 program copies to IBM on time or that it delivers an earlier version of the software. As a result, IBM must scramble for replacements and cannot deliver its PCs because it has no software or the wrong software. IBM would have a cause of action against the breaching party, Microsoft, for any damages. It would be discharged from its performance promised under the contract and would not have to accept delivery of the wrong version of the program or the correct version when they arrive late.

Anticipatory Breach

Before the performance of the contract is to take place, an *anticipatory breach*, or *repudiation*, occurs if one party indicates inability or lack of desire to perform the contract. Sometimes the breaching party will not volunteer that it is going to breach, but the fact that the contract will not be performed becomes clear. If Microsoft was scheduled to ship 100,000 program copies to IBM for delivery by August 1, but IBM learns on July 25 that the copies were destroyed in a fire at the Microsoft production facility, and there are no replacement copies, IBM does not have to wait until August 1 to look for replacements.

The doctrine of anticipatory breach discharges the duties of the nonbreaching party under the contract and allows the nonbreaching party to sue for damages incurred from the repudiation. However, until the nonbreaching party treats the expression not to perform as a repudiation, the breaching party may retract the repudiation, and the duties of the contract will be reinstated.

DISCHARGE BY AGREEMENT OF THE PARTIES

Just as parties have the freedom to contract, they also have the freedom to agree to modify or to terminate their obligations under the contract. *Discharge by agreement* between the parties can take various forms. Among the most important are rescission, novation, and accord and satisfaction.

Rescission

A mutual *rescission* occurs when both parties agree that their contractual relationship should be terminated without performance. A rescission discharges completely the obligations of both parties under the contract. Suppose Ordan Trading contracts with Alimenta to buy ten million pounds of pasta from a factory that Alimenta promises to build. Although the parties negotiated the contract in good faith, events cause Alimenta to become nervous about building the factory as planned. Ordan can buy the pasta elsewhere, and it agrees to let Alimenta cancel the deal. Thus, the parties agree to rescind—cancel—the contract. That rescission discharges the obligations of both parties.

Novation

In a *novation*, all the parties agree to discharge one party from the contract and create a new contract with another party who is to become responsible for the discharged party's performance. Suppose, for example, that Greenwood Mills has a contract to provide L. L. Bean with pullover sweaters for five years. Greenwood wants to turn the job over to Beasley Textiles. If Bean agrees that Beasley will perform Greenwood's obligations under that contract, the new agreement will be called a novation. The effect of the agreement is to release Greenwood from the original contract and replace it with Beasley.

Accord and Satisfaction

Another way parties may agree to discharge their duties to one another under a contract is through *accord and satisfaction*. An *accord* is an agreement by the parties to give and accept some performance different from that originally bargained for. *Satisfaction* is the actual performance of the new obligation. The original obligation is discharged when the new consideration is provided.

Suppose Spielberg owes DiCaprio $1,000. If Spielberg offers to direct a movie for DiCaprio in place of paying him the $1,000, and DiCaprio accepts, then there is an executory accord. If Spielberg then directs a movie for DiCaprio, there is accord and satisfaction. The new consideration discharges the original claim. Had Spielberg failed to direct a movie, then DiCaprio could still have sued him for the $1,000 because there was no satisfaction of the accord.

DISCHARGE BY OPERATION OF LAW

The occurrence of certain legal events may terminate the obligations of the parties to a contract. This termination is called *discharge by operation of law*. A bankruptcy proceeding often results in the discharge of contractual obligations of the bankrupt party. For example, if Night Staff declares bankruptcy and suspends operations, BigBank is discharged from its contract by bankruptcy law and may hire another firm to provide cleaning services for its office building.

DISCHARGE BY CONDITION

A party's duty to perform under a contract is not always certain. Sometimes the duty of the party is conditioned on the occurrence or nonoccurrence of some event. The *condition* is often stated expressly in the contract. The contract might state, for example, that the party will perform as promised "if the price of a product rises above three dollars" or "as soon as a warehouse is built." Contract law defines three kinds of conditions: *conditions precedent*, where some stated event must take place before the promises of the parties become operative; *conditions subsequent*, where some event expressly terminates the duties of the parties to the contract; and *conditions concurrent*, where performance of the promise of the parties to the contract occurs at the same time.

Failure of a Condition Precedent

Contracts may be discharged by the *failure of a condition precedent*. For example, suppose the businesses along a street agree that "If the city paves the street in front of our shops by March 19, 2002, we agree to plant trees between the sidewalk and the street in front of our shops by May 1, 2002." The businesses have created a contract based on a condition precedent. The city must pave the street by March 19 before the businesses must begin performance—planting the trees. If the city does not pave the street, the contract among the businesses will be discharged by failure of the condition precedent.

Express Condition Subsequent

Contracts may also be discharged by an *express condition subsequent*. For example, contracts between U.S. and German firms in 1939 stated: "In case of declared war between our nations, this contract will become null and void." The outbreak of war between the United States and Germany in 1941 (the express condition subsequent) terminated the obligations of the parties under existing contracts.

Condition Concurrent

Duties under a contract that occur simultaneously are termed *concurrent conditions*. A sales contract for a house between a buyer and a seller is a good example of the performance of concurrent conditions. If either party does not perform, such as not deliver good title or not deliver payment, the other party's duty does not arise.

DISCHARGE BY IMPOSSIBILITY

The doctrine of *discharge by legal impossibility* is used to end the obligations of the parties to a contract (or excuse nonperformance) when an event occurs that makes performance impossible. In determining whether the parties are discharged from their duties, the courts distinguish between objective impossibility (or true impossibility) and subjective impossibility.

Objective impossibility occurs when a party who was to provide personal services dies or is incapacitated, a law is passed making performance of the contract illegal, or the subject matter of the contract is destroyed (the factory where the Microsoft programs are made burns down). Objective impossibility discharges the obligations of the parties to the contract.

Subjective impossibility generally does not discharge the obligations of the parties. Events such as shortages of supplies, strikes by workers, or loss of profits anticipated from a contract will rarely be termed by the courts as objective impossibilities. The rationale behind this rule is that businesses must assume the risk of foreseeable occurrences in any business transaction. The *Busse* decision discusses this issue.

F. J. Busse, Inc. v. Dept. of General Services

Commonwealth Court of Pennsylvania
408 A.2d 578 (1979)

CASE BACKGROUND *Busse contracted with the General State Agency (GSA) to build a fountain at a state park in Pittsburgh where the Allegheny and Monongahela Rivers join to form the Ohio River, an area of frequent flooding. After Busse began work, Hurricane Agnes dumped on the construction site over six* *inches of silt that had to be removed to complete the job. Busse was granted more time to complete the job but was not paid the additional $85,000 in costs incurred as a result of the storm damage. Busse appealed the refusal of the state Board of Arbitration Claims to pay the additional costs.*

CASE DECISION MacPhail, Judge.

* * *

We think that the GSA has succinctly stated the narrow issue to be decided by this Court—who must bear the loss from a destruction of part of the unfinished work which the contractor had contracted to do where that destruction is caused by an act of God through no fault of either of the contracting parties?

* * *

Our law is to the effect that where one of two innocent persons must sustain a loss, the law will place that burden on the party that has agreed to sustain it. In their carefully researched briefs, both counsel have referred us to cases where the courts have come down on both sides of the question now before us, but in nearly all of those cases, the decisions reached depended on which party the terms of the contract imposed the risk of loss. In the instant case the Board found that the contract placed the risk of flooding on Busse by virtue of the language found in . . . the contract.

* * *

Even in the absence of contractual language imposing the risk on Busse, our law is that a con-tractor is presumed to have assumed the risk of unforeseen contingencies arising during the course of the work unless performance is rendered impossible by an act of God. There is no dispute that a hurricane is an act of God, but the flooding did not make performance of the contract impossible as that term has been construed under the law. Legal impossibility means not only strict [objective] impossibility, but impracticability because of extreme and unreasonable difficulty, expense, injury or loss involved. Here, flood damage did not make performance impracticable, even though it did make it more expensive.

* * *

Order affirmed.

QUESTIONS FOR ANALYSIS

1. Is there logic in the rule used in this case, rather than a rule that holds the buyer liable for unexpected increases in costs, such as the costs of dealing with an unexpected hurricane? After all, the buyer gets the benefit of the final results; it is just another job to the contractor.
2. How could Busse have avoided the problem encountered in this situation?

Impracticability

A modern extension of impossibility is impracticability, which applies to UCC sales and to common-law contracts. In some jurisdictions, impracticability has replaced the notion of impossibility. The *Restatement (2d) of Contracts* holds, at §262, that impracticability may be applied because of "extreme or unreasonable difficulty, expense, injury or loss. . . ." The *Busse* case would probably also fail the test of impracticability in most courts; the term means more than unexpected difficulty and cost. It usually applies due to wartime shortages, crop failures, or loss of needed supplies due to international embargos. In general, if the defendant could have taken steps to have avoided the problem that arose later, impracticability is not a good defense. Courts generally expect at least part performance even if full performance is excused by impracticability.

Remedies

Parties to contracts usually perform their obligations as required. Interestingly, even when one of the parties does not perform appropriately, relatively few contract disputes end up in court. Professor Lawrence Friedman found an explanation for this phenomenon in a study by a sociologist:

> Macaulay explored the behavior of businessmen in Wisconsin. He found that many of them tended to avoid or sidestep formal contract law and contract

Contracting with the Japanese

A typical U.S. view is that a contract defines the rights and responsibilities of the parties and seeks to cover all possible contingencies. The traditional Japanese view is that a contract is secondary in a business transaction; the basis upon which two parties do business is an ongoing relationship, with both parties committed to the pursuit of similar objectives. Consequently, relationships, not contracts, are negotiated in Japan.

The specific details of a Japanese contract are seldom negotiated. Legal documents are usually brief and flexible. This is important to accommodate the evolving relationship between the parties. Contracts are often viewed as tentative agreements to be redefined as circumstances between the parties change. Long legal agreements drafted by one side, especially a foreign firm, are viewed with suspicion. The relationship should take precedence over formal rights and obligations. Practical problems can be resolved by compromise. Reflecting this belief, the Japanese often include a good-faith clause in contracts with Westerners. The clause states that disputes are to be resolved through good-faith discussions among the parties. This desire to establish and maintain mutual trust as a basis for a business relationship may account for the longer time it takes to negotiate an agreement.

Japanese contract-negotiating teams are generally larger than American teams. Depending on the transaction, there may be ten or more people on the Japanese side. It is common for there to be a small number on the U.S. side. Members of the Japanese group may excuse themselves during a session so they can caucus. By discussing an issue among themselves, they work for a consensus within the team and the company. As a rule, negotiations proceed slowly. The Japanese do not appear to operate with the urgency typical of Americans. The Japanese take the time they need until they are sure of a decision and have reached consensus among themselves.

doctrine. They especially shied away from suing each other, even when they had a "good case" according to law. The reason was not at all mysterious. Businessmen depended upon each other; they lived and worked in networks of continuing relationships. A manufacturer might buy paper clips, pens, and office supplies from the same dealer, year in and year out. Suing at the drop of a hat, or arguing excessively, or sticking up for abstract "rights," was disruptive; it tended to rip apart these valuable relationships. Also, there were norms, practices, and conceptions of honor and fairness that businessmen customarily followed. These were more subtle, more complicated, than the formal norms of the lawyers. (Friedman, *American Law*, p. 143)

Still, thousands of contract disputes must be resolved every year. In the resolution of such disputes, there is a basic premise that after a breach, innocent parties should be placed in an economic position they would have enjoyed had the contract been performed. If, however, the circumstances are such that the legal remedy of monetary damages is inadequate, the court may grant the injured party an appropriate equitable remedy. The types of remedies available to the parties are presented in Exhibit 10.7.

DAMAGES

The remedy usually granted for breach of contract is monetary damages. The innocent party seeks a money judgment for the thing contracted for, for lost profit, and for any other damages incurred. A variety of damage awards is available to the

EXHIBIT 10.7

Contract Remedies

Monetary Damages	Equitable Remedies
Compensatory Damages	Specific Performance
Expectancy Damages	Injunction
Liquidated Damages	Restitution
Nominal Damages	Reformation
Punitive Damages	
Special Damages	

courts, including compensatory, expectancy, liquidated, nominal, and special damages. Punitive damages may be awarded if there is a tort related to the breach of contract.

In general, the rule is that *damages* should put the party who suffered from the breach of contract by the other party in the same economic position as if the contract had been performed. That is, there can be a claim for losses suffered and for any gains (profits) prevented, less any cost savings incurred. The protected interests have been classified as *restitution interest*, or recovery of value given; *reliance interest*, or costs incurred depending on the contract to be fulfilled; and *expectation interest*, or lost profits that could have been earned if the contract had been fulfilled.

Calculating Damages

Suppose Microsoft and IBM contract for Microsoft to develop a special program that will only be used on IBM-brand computers. IBM agrees to pay $50 million for the exclusive rights to the program. As work progresses, Microsoft gives IBM $2 million worth of specialized software. After six months, IBM decides the software will have little value in the future, so rather than go forward with a deal that could lose tens of millions of dollars, it cancels the contract. Microsoft could sue for damages to recover for its restitution interest, the $2 million worth of software given to IBM; its reliance interest, the costs incurred at Microsoft due to a staff of programmers and other employees who worked for months on the project, plus the value of Microsoft facilities consumed during the time spent working on the IBM project (assume these costs total to $8.1 million); and its expectation interest, the $12.6 million it estimated it would earn in profits from the project. Microsoft might recover $22.7 million, plus interest.

Was IBM foolish to breach? Not if it decided that the whole project was foolish. Better to breach and pay the $22.7 million than spend over $50 million. This is referred to as *efficient breach*. Also note that if the work Microsoft did on the software for IBM has alternative use with market value, then it may not be able to recover all costs it incurred in development from IBM. But it may be very difficult for IBM to prove the link between such costs and a product that appears later in another form. This is not the same as if a contract to buy laptop computers was breached; there it is very clear how much the seller obtains from its next best sale. Other, special forms of damages arise in some cases, as are reviewed next.

Liquidated Damages

Liquidated damages are damages specified in the contract to be paid in the event of breach. Liquidated damages are not allowed if the court finds that they are so excessive that they actually impose a penalty. That is, the damages specified in the

JURIS **prudence?**

Miss New York Courts

Miss New York 1995, Helen Goldsby, was replaced by the first runner-up during her year reign. Goldsby's crown was lifted for her alleged failure to fulfill the obligations of being Miss New York. She was expected to live in Watertown but abandoned the small town in favor of New York City, where she worked as an understudy in a Broadway play. Such regular employment also was a violation of royal office, as was being named as "the other woman" in divorce papers filed by the wife of a Wall Street banker. The pageant director explained that not being of good moral character, such as by having an affair with a married man, would be a breach of contract.

Goldsby claimed she was forced to work on Broadway because her income as Miss New York was so low she could not pay her rent. She sued for breach of contract and demanded $2 million damages. Her suit never went anywhere, but a similar situation involving Miss Colorado 1997 (minus the sex charge) resulted in a jury verdict for her of $153,000.

Source: *The Associated Press*

contract must be related to actual losses that could be suffered. For example, if an office building is supposed to be completed by May 15 for occupancy, the contract may require the builder to pay liquidated damages of $500 per day after May 15 until the building is ready. But the contract could not call for "damages" of $1 million per day, that would be a penalty, which is not allowed.

Nominal Damages

When a plaintiff has suffered a breach of contract but has not suffered an actual loss, a court may award *nominal damages.* The amount of recovery to the injured party may be as little as a dollar, but often court costs are also awarded. Such awards can be important because proof of breach may be related to other legal issues.

Punitive Damages

Punitive or *exemplary damages* are usually awarded when the wrongdoer's conduct has been willful or malicious. They punish the wrongdoer by allowing the plaintiff to receive relief beyond compensatory or expectancy damages. Punitive damages are intended to discourage the wrongdoer and others from similar conduct in the future. As a rule, punitive damages are not awarded in contract actions; the basis for these damages is a tort related to the breach.

MITIGATION OF DAMAGES

When a breach of contract does occur, the injured party is required to undertake reasonable efforts to *mitigate,* or lessen, the losses that may be incurred. If Microsoft fails to deliver promised software to IBM, IBM must take steps to get a replacement, if possible. The injured party may not recover for losses that could have been avoided. In the *Copenhaver* case, the plaintiff avoided the loss but attempted to recover damages as though he had not.

Copenhaver v. Berryman
Texas Court of Civil Appeals
602 S.W.2d 540 (1980)

CASE BACKGROUND *Berryman owned an apartment complex. He contracted for Copenhaver to own and operate the laundry facilities in the complex. With four years remaining on a five-year contract, Berryman terminated the contract and removed Copenhaver's machines on March 10, 1977. By September 10, 1977, Copenhaver had put the equipment into use in other locations.*

Copenhaver sued, claiming that he was entitled to run the facility for the length of the contract. If he had been allowed to do so, he would have earned a net profit of $13,886.58. The trial court awarded Copenhaver $3,525.84 for the damages suffered from March to September. Copenhaver appealed the decision.

CASE DECISION Ney, Chief Justice.

* * *

While the defendant is liable for the pecuniary loss sustained by the party injured by the breach, the party so injured must exercise, as a general rule, reasonable efforts in an attempt to minimize his damages. As stated by our Supreme Court:

> Where a party is entitled to the benefits of a contract and can save himself from the damages resulting from its breach at a trifling expense or with reasonable exertions, it is his duty to incur such expense and make such exertions.

Although the injured party has a duty to minimize his loss, the burden of proof as to the extent to which the damages were or could have been mitigated lies with the party who has breached the contract.

* * *

We are of the opinion that there is evidence in the record to support the finding of fact that the plaintiffs suffered no damage from September 10, 1977, to the date of trial. After September 10, all of the equipment was in use in other locations. There is also some evidence . . . that plaintiffs were generating at least as much income, if not more, from the operation of the machines in question after September 10, 1977.

* * *

The testimony concerning the plaintiff's over-all business is vague, speculative, and conclusory. The only evidence we can find to substantiate this contention is some general testimony to the effect that plaintiffs acquired some 14 to 15 new locations after the breach. Plaintiffs admitted they did not even know where the machines in question were ultimately placed. Nor, did the plaintiffs introduce evidence from which it could be reasonably concluded that they would have expanded to each new location even had defendants not breached the contract in question and that defendants' breach somehow limited their expansion.

We are of the opinion that the trial judge could reach no reasonable conclusion other than to find plaintiffs had not proved they were damaged beyond the six-month period, after which the machines were in use in other locations.

* * *

The judgment of the trial court is affirmed.

QUESTIONS FOR ANALYSIS

1. How did the plaintiff mitigate the losses stemming from the defendant's breach in this case?
2. Suppose the plaintiff had not been able to move the machines into other locations. How would he have then mitigated the losses?
3. What is the purpose of this mitigation of losses rule?

EQUITABLE REMEDIES

If money damages are inadequate to compensate for the injury caused by a breach of contract or do not resolve the problem properly, *equitable remedies* such as specific performance or an injunction may be available. These remedies are available to injured parties only at the discretion of the court. They generally will not be granted where an adequate damage remedy exists or where enforcement would impose a great burden to the defendant.

Specific Performance

In some circumstances, a plaintiff in a contract action may be entitled to specific performance. *Specific performance* is an order by the court requiring the party who created the wrong to perform the obligations she had promised in the contract. The remedy is granted for breach of a contract in those circumstances where the payment of money damages is inadequate. Contracts for the sale of a particular piece of real property (land) or of a unique good, such as a piece of art, are the types of contract where specific performance may be granted by the courts. Courts will not order people to perform personal service—do some particular job—because it would be involuntary servitude. Damages would be proper in such cases.

Injunction

As with the remedy of specific performance, the remedy of injunction is allowed by the courts in circumstances where the payment of damages does not offer a satisfactory substitute for the performance promised. An *injunction* is an order by the court that requires a party to do or to refrain from doing certain acts. Suppose a partnership agreement had a clause stating that a partner who quits to go into business for herself will not compete against the partnership for three years. If a partner quits the partnership to start a new competing firm, the payment of damages may be an inadequate remedy for the partnership. The court, through the granting of an injunction, may order the departed partner to not compete with the partnership.

REFORMATION

The remedy of *reformation* is not common. It means that a court rewrites some terms in a contract. Obviously there can be a mistake made in the writing of the contract. The problem is that one party claims there was no mistake and the other insists that there was a mistake when the written document was prepared. The courts do not like to go against written documentation in favor of parol evidence, because we are presumed to have read the documents we have agreed to, but it can be done.

RESTITUTION

The remedy of *restitution* may be used by the courts to prevent *unjust enrichment.* That is, if one party has unjustly enriched himself (received a benefit not paid for) at the expense of another party, the court can order payment to be made or the goods involved to be returned.

One form of restitution that we noted previously in the chapter is that of quasi contract or contract implied in law. This can happen when one party confers a benefit, in good faith, on another party when there was not a valid contract. The party who knowingly received the benefit may be required to pay the other party for the costs incurred in providing the benefit. Again, this remedy is not common in practice, but reflects the authority the courts have to prevent significant injustices from hiding behind formal contractual requirements.

In the next chapter, we examine some of the contract issues covered in this chapter, but with a more specific focus on domestic and international sales of goods.

Summary

- Basic to the law of contracts is freedom of contract. Every business has the freedom to enter into most contracts they desire. Because of public policy goals, state and federal laws place some restrictions on the kinds of contracts businesses can enter into.
- Contract law is basically common or judge-made law. The *Restatement of Contracts* is an authoritative document providing a summary of the common law of contract. Additional contract law is provided by the Uniform Commercial Code.
- A contract is a promise or set of promises that creates an agreement between parties. It creates legal rights and duties enforceable under the law.
- Contracts may be classified as express or implied; bilateral or unilateral; executory or executed; valid, void, voidable, or unenforceable contracts; and quasi contracts. A contract may fall into several categories; for example, a contract may be express, bilateral, executed, and valid.
- Under the common law, enforceable contracts have several elements in common:

  1. There must be an agreement (offer and acceptance).
  2. The parties to a contract must provide consideration.
  3. The parties must have the legal capacity to contract.
  4. The subject matter of the contract must be legal.
  5. The consent of the parties must be genuine.

- Some contracts must be in writing to fulfill requirements of the Statute of Frauds. They include contracts for the sale of land and real property, contracts that cannot be completed within one year, promises to pay the debt of another, and contracts for goods over $500 under the UCC.
- Contracts may be discharged—or terminated—in several ways: by performance, through a breach by one or both of the parties to the contract, by the failure of a condition precedent or the occurrence of an express condition subsequent, by the impossibility of performance, by operation of law, or by mutual agreement of the parties.
- In the event of a breach of contract, the injured party may ask the court for relief. To a reasonable extent, the injured party has the responsibility to minimize losses from the breach. For the remaining losses, the courts can award monetary damages or provide equitable relief.

Issue

Should Contracts Be Tossed Out When There Is a Pattern of Problems?

Contract law presumes that parties are competent adults who read and understand the terms of the deals they make, especially in business relationships where there are two sophisticated *parties dealing with each other. However, vague terms can cause problems, as can reliance on oral claims made by representatives that are not consistent with what is in the contract.*

Despite the common use of contracts, they are often largely ignored as parties go about their business on a good faith basis, changing terms over time, and presuming that both sides are honorable and want to continue good relations over time. As the reading indicates, sophisticated firms can get in serious trouble when attention is not paid to unclear terms.

READ THE FINE PRINT IS LESSON OF DISPUTES WITH COMPUTER LESSOR

John R. Emshwiller

It seemed like a straightforward deal: leasing about $1.5 million worth of computer equipment. But for the customer, Millar Elevator Service of Holland, Ohio, it has turned into a painful lesson in Consumer Behavior 101: Read the fine print.

Millar leased the equipment from a company called Amplicon Inc. James Frey, Millar's vice president of finance, says an Amplicon salesperson told him over the phone that buying the hardware and software at the end of the lease, as Millar intended to do, would cost up to about $200,000.

But as the lease approached expiration, Amplicon pointed to language in the written contract saying the price had to be a "mutually agreeable" one, say Millar officials. Then it quoted a price agreeable to Amplicon: $550,000.

Crucially, Mr. Frey says he didn't have Amplicon's earlier oral assurance incorporated into the lease. "I didn't think I needed to. I thought they were operating in good faith," he says. "Shame on me."

Amplicon, based in Santa Ana, Calif., denies that it lacked good faith, or did anything at all wrong. It says its salespeople are schooled that any price agreements have to be incorporated into the contract.

The case, now being fought over in court, isn't an isolated one. Since 1990, more than 100 leasing clients have ended up in litigation over leases with Amplicon, including Ingersoll-Rand Co., James River Corp., U.S. Robotics Inc. and a Donald Trump partnership.

A number of litigants have said that at the lease's end, they found themselves on the hook for money they didn't expect to owe, and some claim this was because of oral assurances from Amplicon that weren't reflected in the written lease contract.

This raises two questions: Why rely on oral assurances? And if you do receive such assurances, why not make sure the written contract contains them?

Sometimes, people in the leasing business say, the answer may have to do with accounting. A written option to buy gear at the end of a lease, at a set price, can be a liability the client has to book. Some clients try to avoid this by having oral side agreements, leasing executives say.

In other cases, the explanation is more benign: simple inattention. The contract is relatively small, and the corporate legal department is very busy. "People are naive if they believe that there is a high level of review of this kind of stuff in corporate America," says David Cole, Millar's in-house counsel. He concedes that he, like Mr. Frey, didn't closely study the Amplicon lease before signing it.

* * *

Amplicon is largely the creation of 47-year-old Patrick Paddon, a Michigan native who co-founded it in 1977. "I couldn't believe the profit margins" in leasing, he says. He has built Amplicon into a public company that had $300 million in revenue in the fiscal year ended June 30, 1997, and earned $15.7 million. He owns over 50% of its stock, a stake worth more than $100 million.

* * *

Mr. Paddon says that litigation is a normal part of the leasing business and that Amplicon has done thousands of transactions in its history, with many satisfied customers. The company urges clients to read the leases carefully before signing them, he says.

* * *

In any case, Amplicon's methods aren't winning it friends in some of its accounts. Take Ingersoll-Rand, which leased computer software from a unit of Amplicon. In paying $375,000 to settle a lease dispute, Ingersoll-Rand wrote a clause into the settlement papers laying out a procedure to ensure that in the future it would "never do business with Amplicon" or "with any company in which Patrick Paddon owns a controlling interest."

An attorney for Ingersoll-Rand had read over the lease, according to the court records and someone familiar with the case, but missed the import of the section giving Amplicon the right to extend the lease if the two sides couldn't agree on what to do with the gear at the end of the term. Amplicon officials say they believe Ingersoll-Rand fully understood the lease but just didn't want to pay.

* * *

Officials of Amplicon acknowledge that its strategy is to offer low lease rates, with the idea that it has the chance to make additional money at the end of the term. A customer, says Amplicon General Counsel Neil Kenduck, may simply be focusing on the low monthly lease rate. But "you can't have it both ways. You can't negotiate a great deal and then thumb your nose at the end to the lessor," he says.

In the course of all the litigation, some Amplicon customers haven't come out looking so great themselves. The practice of discussing the purchase price of equipment orally, but not putting it in writing, "is sort of slimy, but it's beneficial for both sides," says Thomas E. McCurnin, a Los Angeles lawyer who represents several leasing companies but not Amplicon. The leasing company closes the deal, he explains, and the client gets some idea what it will be paying at the end of the lease—but without any balance-sheet consequences.

One client Amplicon sued, Baltimore wholesale grocer B. Green & Co., argued in court that it had had oral price assurances from Amplicon. But Judge Robert Thomas of California state court in Santa Ana granted a judgment to Amplicon and excoriated the grocer, saying such an oral side deal was "reprehensible" and "constitutes illegal conduct by making misrepresentations" about a lease to a company's auditors and lenders. B. Green denies any intent to deceive, noting that it is privately held and explaining that it didn't even have any lenders at the time. It is appealing the judgment.

Millar Elevator's Mr. Frey also says he had no thought of misleading anyone when he got oral assurances from Amplicon about what it would cost to buy the computer equipment at the end of the lease. He says he wasn't thinking all that much about the deal, which he began negotiating with an Amplicon salesperson in late 1992. The transaction "wasn't minute, but it wasn't the biggest thing we had at the time" he says.

He says he didn't fully appreciate the lease's language saying an eventual purchase price had to be mutually agreeable to Amplicon and Millar, a unit of Schindler Holding AG in Ebikon, Switzerland.

Mr. Frey says that when sending back some lease documents to Amplicon in late 1994, he attached a cover letter stating that Millar anticipated buying the equipment when the lease ended in 1997 for about what he thought was the agreed-upon price of 10% to 12% of the original cost, which would come to roughly $200,000. Mr. Frey says he didn't hear back about the letter, and "I didn't think I had to."

That was another assumption he says he now has reason to rue. Amplicon contends it never received any such letter from Mr. Frey. It recently wrote to Millar saying Amplicon has "good reason to believe" Mr. Frey's letter had been "fabricated" after the fact. Mr. Frey vehemently denies this.

Millar has sued Amplicon in Santa Ana state court, seeking damages and cancellation of the lease. Amplicon has countersued, also seeking damages. The companies say they are trying to negotiate a settlement.

Mr. Frey is still trying to figure out how a little lease deal got so messy. "This whole thing boggles my mind," he says.

ISSUE QUESTIONS

1. If one company is involved in many suits, all relating to the same contractual issue, should the courts use their powers of equity to reform the terms that end up in dispute?
2. What would be the case for making companies stick to the contracts they sign?

REVIEW AND DISCUSSION QUESTIONS

1. Define the following terms and expressions:

offer
acceptance
consideration
breach of contract
promissory estoppel
legal capacity
unconscionable contract

mutual mistake
parol evidence rule
discharge
impossibility
damages
mitigation of damages

2. Mr. Jones walks into a grocery store, puts fifty cents down on the counter, and says, "A Coke please." Under contract law, what has just occurred? If the grocery store owner hands him a Coke and takes the fifty cents, what type of contract has been agreed upon?

CASE QUESTIONS

3. Three armed men robbed the First State Bank of Kentucky of more than $30,000. The Kentucky Bankers Association provided and advertised a reward of $500 for the arrest and conviction of the bank robbers. The robbers were later captured and convicted. The arresting officers and the employees of the bank who provided important information leading to the arrest have all claimed the reward. Is there a contract between these parties and the Bankers Association? [*Denney* v. *Reppert*, 432 S.W.2d 647 (Ct. App., Ky., 1968)]

4. Barry hired Anglin to produce engineering drawings for work it was doing at a brewery. Anglin said it would charge "street" rates for the work, which meant $35 an hour for regular work, $40 an hour for overtime work, and $45 an hour for his time. Barry gave Anglin a "purchase order" for the work, but no rate was specified. Barry paid bills for two months but then quit paying. Barry insisted that the work be done but constantly complained about the rates and did not pay bills for four months. Anglin sued for $98,618, the amount it was due for work at the "street" rate. Barry claimed there was no contract because there was no meeting of the minds about the rate to be paid. Who prevails? [*Anglin* v. *Barry*, 912 S.W.2d 633 (Ct. App., Mo., 1995)]

5. Houston Lighting & Power Company sent a brochure that the company "will offer to subdivision developers . . . [of] single family dwellings" underground residential electrical service without construction charge. The brochure also stated, "At Company option certain lots adjacent to overhead distribution facilities will be served from the overhead distribution" that "Developer will provide required easements . . . and install conduit to Company's specifications" and other specifics. A mobile home park developer stated that he was willing to do what was required and demanded the underground service be installed to the mobile home sites. The company refused. The developer claimed that he had accepted an offer; the company claimed the brochure was merely an invitation to discuss the matter. Who was right? [*Edmunds* v. *Houston Lighting & Power*, 472 S.W.2d 797 (Ct. Civ. App., Tx., 1971)]

6. Cantu was a teacher for the San Benito School District. August 18, right before the start of the schoolyear, she hand delivered a letter of resignation, effective August 17, and requested that her final paycheck be sent to an address fifty miles away. The superintendent received the letter on August 20 and immediately wrote and mailed a letter accepting the resignation. On August 21, Cantu hand delivered a letter withdrawing her resignation. She was given a copy of the letter that had been mailed the day before and was told she would not be rehired. Was her resignation effective or not? [*Cantu* v. *Central Education Agency*, 884 S.W.2d 565 (Ct. App., Tx., 1994)]

7. At the end of a two-year lease, landlord and tenant discussed a new lease. The tenant sent a letter to the landlord stating that it would pay rent of $1,800 per month and that "all other terms and conditions of the [original] lease including, taxes, insurance, utilities, etc., shall remain the same." The letter also said that it

was to be advised "by confirmation letter if the terms of the two-year lease extension are acceptable to [the lessor]." The lessor never responded. The tenant paid rent for a couple months, then moved out. The landlord sued for breach, claiming there was an oral agreement evidenced by the letter from the tenant; the tenant claimed there was no contract. Who is correct and why? [*Valiant Steel* v. *Roadway Express*, 421 S.E.2d 773 (Ct. App., Ga., 1992)]

8. Mary Lowe, in the presence of her son David and Allen Amdahl wrote: "January 26, 1987. I Mary Lowe in the presence of David Lowe received from Allen Amdahl $1.00 in cash binding the sale of my farm (of 880 acres) for the amount of $210,000 with final payment due Nov. 1, 1989. Terms of Agreement have been mutually agreed to by both parties. Contract drawn up as soon as possible." She signed this statement, and David Lowe witnessed it. Amdahl wrote on the back of the paper a payment schedule between then and November 1989 but did not sign the paper. When he returned with a formal contract, Lowe refused to sign. Amdahl sued. Was there an enforceable contract? [*Amdahl* v. *Lowe*, 471 N.W.2d 770 (Sup. Ct., N.D., 1991)]

9. Rose, a minor, purchased a new car from Sheehan Buick for $5,000. Rose later, while still a minor, elected to disaffirm the purchase and notified Sheehan of her decision. She also requested a full refund of the purchase price. Sheehan refused, and Rose brought an action to invalidate the contract and to seek a refund of the purchase price. What will be the likely result? [*Rose* v. *Sheehan Buick, Inc.*, 204 So.2d 903 (Fla.App., 1967)]

10. To help in a fund-raising drive for a hospital, Burt executed a pledge for $100,000 that provided, "In consideration of and to induce the subscription of others, I promise to pay to Mount Sinai Hospital of Greater Miami, Inc. the sum of $100,000 in ten installments." Burt made two installment payments of $10,000 each before his death. The hospital filed a claim for the unpaid balance against his estate. Is this a contract for which the estate is now liable? [*Mount Sinai Hospital* v. *Jordan*, 290 So.2d 484 (Sup. Ct., Fla., 1974)]

11. Smith contracted to build a gymnasium for Limestone College. About the time the building was finished, an "extraordinarily heavy rainfall" caused the sewer system to back up into the gymnasium, doing damage that cost Smith $37,000 to repair. Smith billed the city sewer system for the work done. The city refused to pay, claiming there was no contract. Smith claimed an implied contract existed; was he right? [*Stanley Smith & Sons* v. *Limestone College*, 322 S.E.2d 474 (Ct. App., SC, 1984)]

12. A contract stated: "Contractor shall transport in the Contractor's trucks such tonnage of beets as may be loaded by the Company from piles at the beet receiving stations of the Company, and unload said beets at such factory . . . as may be designated by the company. The term of this contract shall be from October 1, 1980, until February 15, 1981." Contractor was to be paid solely on the basis of the amount of beets he hauled. The company had identical contracts with other independent truckers. After two months, company told contractor that his services were no longer needed even though there were more beets to haul. Contractor sued, claiming he had the right under the contract to haul beets with the other truckers who may be there until all beets had been hauled or until February 15. Was he right? [*De Los Santos* v. *Great Western Sugar*, 348 N.W.2d 842 (Sup. Ct., Neb., 1984)]

13. By oral contract, Olson sold Wilson thirty head of cattle for slaughter. Wilson sent Olson a check for $9,373 "in full payment of . . . cattle, 30 head. . . ." Olson claimed that he was promised 35 cents per pound, which would have been $10,725. Wilson said that it promised to pay based on "grade and yield," a common industry practice. Olson cashed the check and sued for the difference in price. Could he collect? [*Olson* v. *Wilson & Co.*, 58 N.W.2d 381 (Sup. Ct., Iowa, 1953)]

14. A builder constructed a house according to plans provided by the owner. The contract specified that only Reading brand pipe was to be used in the plumbing. After the house was completed, the owner discovered that another brand of pipe had been used. The owner refused final payment and demanded that the pipe be replaced with Reading pipe, which would have involved major reconstruction. Evidence at trial was that the two brands of pipe were of the same general quality. Did the owner have to make final payment, or did the pipe have to be replaced? [*Jacob & Youngs* v. *Kent*, 129 N.E. 889 (Ct. App., N.Y., 1921)]

15. Lewis Cudd had a life insurance policy that named his mother as beneficiary. During World War II, his ship was missing and "presumed lost" by the Navy, which issued a "Certificate of Presumptive Death." The insurance company paid Mrs. Cudd the value of the policy. Later it was discovered that Lewis was a prisoner of war; Lewis returned home after the war. The life insurance company sued to recover the insurance benefits. On what basis did it recover? [*Pilot Life* v. *Cudd*, 36 S.E.2d 860 (Sup. Ct., S.C., 1945)]

16. GE contracted to provide kitchen appliances for an apartment complex for $93,500. Several months later, GE discovered that a mathematical error had been made in the bid and that the bid should have been for an additional $30,150. GE demanded rescission of the contract. Did it get it? [*General Electric Supply* v. *Republic Construction*, 272 P.2d 201 (Sup. Ct., Ore., 1954)]

17. Employer Engelcke Manufacturing asked one of its employees, Eaton, to design electronic plans for Whizball, a game it planned to produce and sell. Eaton said he thought he could do the job after work for about $1,500. During the next year, the project became more complicated, and Eaton devoted substantially more time to it than had been expected. Engelcke said it would pay him for his work. When the project was mostly done, Engelcke fired Eaton and refused to pay him because the electronic plans were not completed. Engelcke claimed Eaton breached an express contract and that it got nothing of value. Was there a contract? Could there be damages? [*Eaton* v. *Englecke Manufacturing, Inc.*, 681 P.2d 1312 (Ct. App., Wash., 1984)]

18. Transatlantic agreed to ship a load of wheat from the United States to Iran for $305,842. While the ship was enroute, a war caused the Suez Canal to be closed. Transatlantic had to turn around and sail all the way around Africa to get to Iran. It sued for the additional $44,000 it cost to go the extra distance. Could it collect? [*Transatlantic Financing* v. *U.S.*, 363 F.2d 312 (D.C.Cir., 1966)]

ETHICS QUESTION

19. Michele works long and hard to develop the perfect recipe for chocolate-covered ants. After perfecting the method, she has it patented but fails to sell much of her product. Web buys the patent rights from Michele for $100. The next year

there is a craze for chocolate-covered ants. Web makes a fortune; Michele gets nothing. The contract between the two was legal in every respect. Should Web give Michele some portion of the profits? Suppose, instead, that Michele had promised to supply Web all the boxes of chocolate-covered ants that he wanted for one dollar a box for a five-year period. Because of the subsequent craze for chocolate-covered ants, Web can sell the boxes for ten dollars each. Should he share the unexpected profits with Michele? Suppose the price of chocolate and ants rose so that Michele lost one cent on each box supplied to Web but Web continued to make high profits; should Web be forced to rewrite the terms of the deal? Should he, as an ethical businessman, voluntarily do so?

INTERNET ASSIGNMENT

Floors is a carpet retailer and dealer that sells carpet to residential and commercial customers in North Texas. Fieldcrest is a carpet manufacturer that markets its product through dealers like Floors. Fieldcrest's practice was to market its "Karastan" line of carpeting only through a limited number of authorized dealers.

According to Floors, it entered into an oral agreement with Fieldcrest in 1982 whereby Floors became an authorized dealer for Fieldcrest's "Karastan" line. Floors alleged that the agreement required it to acquire carpeting, carpet samples, display racks, and promotional material from Fieldcrest. The agreement allegedly required Floors to sell and advertise Fieldcrest's product in conformity with certain rules promulgated by Fieldcrest. Floors claimed that Fieldcrest agreed not to terminate the contract (and, therefore, Floors' designation as an authorized "Karastan" dealer) except for "good cause," specifically, for Floors' failure to comply with Fieldcrest's strict marketing requirements. At trial the parties acknowledged that Floors was not required to buy any minimum quantity of carpet or to meet any continuing sales quotas or goals to retain its dealership.

In 1993, Fieldcrest terminated its eleven-year relationship with Floors, unilaterally and without explanation. That Floors never violated any of Fieldcrest's marketing requirements was undisputed.

Floors sued Fieldcrest in Texas state court, alleging breach of contract, promissory estoppel, and breach of fiduciary duty. What result? Is an indefinite term contract, terminable only for good cause, required to be in writing under the statute of frauds? See *Floors Unlimited, Inc.* v. *Fieldcrest Cannon, Inc.*, United States Court of Appeals for the Fifth Circuit, No. 94-10680, June 15, 1995 (http://www.law.utexas.edu/us5th/us5th.html).

See Appendix B.

CHAPTER 11

Domestic and International Sales

Amerada Hess contracted to supply Orange and Rockland Utilities with "all of its fuel oil requirements" for five years. The contract fixed the price at $2.14 per barrel. Hess thought the contract was good until the market price of oil began to increase. When the price rose, Orange and Rockland more than doubled its use of Hess fuel oil. The price was so low that Orange and Rockland profited by reselling the Hess oil to other utilities at market prices. Was Hess required to continue to sell more oil to Orange and Rockland under the contract? Or could Hess break the contract because the price was now unfavorable to it?

These are the types of questions addressed in this chapter on the sale of goods under the *Uniform Commercial Code* (*UCC*). *Article 2* of the UCC governs the law of commercial sales. Since buying and selling goods is the primary activity of many commercial enterprises, it is not surprising that the law of sales is an important part of the legal environment of business. This chapter provides an overview of the law of sales in Article 2 of the UCC. It considers the nature of sales contracts under the UCC and the requirements the UCC places upon merchants. The chapter then examines some key aspects of international commercial sales.

Introduction to the UCC

The Uniform Commercial Code is the law that governs many contracts for the sale of goods. Like the common law of contract, commercial law is primarily state, not federal, law. The UCC is a "model statute," meaning that it provides a guide for states to follow in adopting their own rules for commercial transactions. Each state has adopted some version of the UCC.

HISTORY OF COMMERCIAL LAW

People have traded for thousands of years. Commercial law consists of rules that govern such trade. Commercial rules governing trade—"codes"—existed more than 2,000 years ago in Greece. Over a thousand years later, in medieval Europe, merchants developed an elaborate set of rules governing trade issues such as sales, payment, insurance, and shipping. These rules were known as the *lex mercatoria* or *law merchant*. The law merchant was international law in that it applied the same rules to transactions in different countries. For example, a fourteenth-century merchant who sold bolts of woolen cloth would be likely to see the same contract rules if the sale took place in London, England; Marseilles, France; or Prague, Bohemia. Merchants themselves, rather than governments, generally enforced this law.

By the eighteenth century, judges in England decided to incorporate the customary law merchant into the common law of England. From that point forward, commercial law became a matter of national law. After it became independent, the United States continued to employ both English common law and English commercial law. As the economy developed during the nineteenth century, so too did commercial law. As new technologies—railroads, steam ships, telegraphs—emerged, commercial law was modified to accommodate the changing needs of merchants.

In the early part of the twentieth century, each state in the United States had a different, but related, set of commercial laws. At the same time, as transportation and communication improved, companies were better able to do business in many states, and international trade increased. One of the costs of doing business in different states was dealing with the different rules of commercial law. By the 1940s, some legal scholars and people in business decided that it would be more efficient to have a more consistent set of rules governing commercial transactions to reduce the differences across the states.

In 1942, two groups, The National Conference of Commissioners on Uniform State Laws and the American Law Institute, began drafting a national commercial law. After ten years of work, under the direction of law professor Karl Llewellyn, the groups presented the Uniform Commercial Code to the states. Every state has adopted at least part of the UCC, although Louisiana has not adopted Article 2. There is no single, identical commercial law in the state, but the fifty versions of the UCC adopted by the states are much the same. Over the years, the UCC has been modified to reflect changes in the way businesses operate. Exhibit 11.1 notes the major sections of the UCC.

APPLICATION OF THE UCC

We refer here, except when noted otherwise, to the "model" UCC and cite specific sections (§) of it. The UCC states that its purpose is "to simplify, clarify and modernize the law governing commercial transactions" (§-102).

	Article Number and Title	Coverage
EXHIBIT 11.1 *The Articles of the Uniform Commercial Code*	**1: General Provisions**	Purpose of the UCC; general guidance and definitions
	2: Sale of Goods	Applies to sale of goods (and leases of goods)
	3: Negotiable Instruments	Use of checks, promissory notes, and other financial instruments
	4: Bank Deposits and Collections	Rights and duties of banks and their clients
	5: Letters of Credit	Guaranteed payment by a bank that extends credit on behalf of client
	6: Bulk Transfers	Sale of large part of a company's material
	7: Warehouse Receipts, Bills of Lading, and Other Documents of Title	Papers proving ownership of goods being shipped
	8: Investment Securities	Rights and duties related to stock or other ownership interests
	9: Secured Transactions	Sales in which seller holds a financial interest in goods sold

This chapter primarily concerns Article 2 of the UCC, which deals with the sale of goods. When does the UCC apply, rather than the common law of contracts? The UCC applies when "the item involved is movable and is not money or an investment security" (§2-102). Examples of movable goods include wristwatches, computers, and airplanes. Land is not movable, nor are houses or most other buildings. Article 2 covers the sale of *goods*, not services, so, for example, if you contract with a lawyer to represent you, that would be under the common law of contracts, as do contracts deal with intangible personal property such as patents, copyrights, and stocks.

If, as often happens, a contract involves the sale of both goods and services, the rules that govern the contract are determined by figuring out what the predominant purpose of the contract is. That is, if a contract is primarily for goods but includes some services, then it is governed by the UCC. For example, if you buy a new computer for $2,000, and the price includes a three-year warranty, the warranty is a service, but since most of the value is in the machine, it is a contract for goods covered by the UCC. The issue of which law governs—common law or the UCC—can be important for a variety of reasons, one of which is the basis of the *Zartic* case.

Southern Tank Equipment Co. v. Zartic, Inc.
Court of Appeals of Georgia
471 S.E.2d 587 (1996)

CASE BACKGROUND *"Southern quoted a price of $77,000 to supply Zartic with a chemical mixing tank and an associated pump and sump. Southern would install* *it, but excavation, foundation, and electrical work would be supplied by other contractors. Further discussions resulted in Southern agreeing to supply an associated* *'water treatment assembly' composed of a system of pipes and valves to specifications, for an additional $62,000, resulting in a total price of $139,000. Southern contends the project was substantially completed in September 1987, but Zartic claims the work was not completed. The parties agree that . . . Southern's cause of action arose in September 1987. The contract is evidenced by a variety of documents including letters and an order signed by both parties."*

"The contract called for staggered payments, and Southern received $100,000, but not the final $39,000. Suit to recover that amount, plus interest, attorney fees, and costs, was filed February 12, 1993. The [trial] court held that the contract was for the sale of goods and thus suit was barred by the four-year statute of limitation found in [UCC §2-725]. Southern contends the contract was not for the sale of goods, the applicable [common-law contract] statute of limitation is . . . within six years of the contract's completion."

The trial court held that since the UCC applied, the statute of limitations had expired and the suit was dismissed on summary judgment. Southern appealed.

* * *

CASE DECISION Beasley, Chief Justice

As the trial court noted, this contract calls for a mixed sale of goods and services . . . "When the predominant element of a contract is the sale of goods, the contract is viewed as a sales contract and the UCC applies 'even though a substantial amount of service is to be rendered in installing the goods.' When, on the other hand, the predominant element of a contract is the furnishing of service, the contract is viewed as a service contract and the UCC does not apply." . . .

Factors to be considered in determining the predominant element of a contract include the proportion of the total contract cost allocated to the goods and whether the price of the goods are segregated from the price for services. A smaller proportion of the total price assignable to services, or a failure to state a separate price for services rendered, suggest a contract for the sale of goods with services merely incidental.

* * *

The parties agree that the contract initially called only for sale, delivery, and installation of a chemical mixing tank, which evidence showed had a quoted price of $77,000. Southern does not dispute that this alone would be a contract for the sale of goods. Thus over half the total contract price was allocated to this purchase, predominately for one piece of equipment, with the remaining $62,000 including both goods and services.

* * *

The trial court properly concluded from the evidence that the contract was for the sale of goods, governed by the UCC, and that the suit was barred by the failure to file within four years of September 1987.

Judgment affirmed.

QUESTIONS FOR ANALYSIS

1. Southern argued that it was buying a "system" that required a lot of service; the goods themselves were of little value if not installed and running properly. Why did that not make this primarily a service contract?
2. Why might the UCC have a shorter statute of limitations than common-law cases?

SALES, TITLES, GOODS, AND MERCHANTS UNDER THE UCC

Sales

Article 2 applies to contracts for the *sale* of goods. A sale occurs when there is a "passing of title from the seller to the buyer for a price," §2-106(1). Hence, the sale must involve the *title* to goods being passed. The title represents the legal rights to ownership of a thing, such as a car or a computer. If legal title does not pass, there has not been a sale under the UCC. Article 2 does not apply to the lease of goods, such as the lease of a car, but most states have adopted Article 2A, a new Code article dealing with certain leases of personal property.

Titles

How do we determine who holds title to goods? A person may hold legal title to a good if (1) the good exists, and (2) the good has been identified (such as by the serial number on a car) to the contract, meaning that the seller has specified which goods are being sold to the buyer. If these conditions hold, UCC §2-401 allows title to be passed however the parties see fit. For example, the UCC would allow title to pass in any of the following situations, if that is what the parties desire, as determined by contract language, custom, or past practices between the parties:

- When the goods arrive for shipment at a train yard
- When the goods arrive for shipment at a port
- When the goods arrive at the buyer's warehouse
- When the goods leave the seller's warehouse
- When the goods are halfway between the seller's factory and the buyer's warehouse

If the parties should disagree about whether or not title passed, or they failed to specify when title passed, then the courts look to the rules of the UCC (§2-401), which states that (1) title passes to the buyer when the seller completes all her obligations regarding delivery of the goods; or (2) title passes to the buyer when the seller delivers the title documents, if the goods did not have to be moved.

If a seller "sells" stolen goods, then good title does not pass to the buyer. For example, if someone steals a computer from a university and sells the computer to a buyer who does not know it is stolen, if the university finds the stolen property, it gets it back. A thief has no title, or void title, and so can not pass good title.

Goods

The UCC defines *goods* as "all things (including specially manufactured things) which are movable at the time of identification to the contract for sale," §2-105(1). In other words, the subject matter of a sales contract is not considered a good under Article 2 unless it is movable and tangible. A good is *movable* if it can be carried from one location to another. A good is *tangible* when it has a physical existence—that is, it can be seen and touched. Thus, services and intangible interests—such as stocks, bank accounts, patents, and copyrights, which are called intangible forms of personal property—are not goods under Article 2. A contract involving such items would be governed by the common law of contracts or possibly by another part of the UCC.

Merchants

Section §1-203 holds all parties who enter into an Article 2 sales contract to a standard of *good-faith*, or honest, dealing. Good-faith dealing is defined by UCC §1-201 as "honesty in fact in the conduct or transaction incurred." Article 2 places a higher duty of conduct on merchants, who are treated differently from other parties because they possess more business expertise. A merchant is recognized by §2-104 as a person who

1. Regularly deals in goods of the kind involved in the transaction,
2. By occupation presents himself as having knowledge or skill specialized to the transaction, or
3. Employs an agent who holds herself out as having particular knowledge or skill about the goods involved.

Forming a Sales Contract

As we noted previously, contracts are governed by the common law of contracts unless the UCC changes or modifies the rule. In most instances, the changes imposed by the UCC reduce the formality of contract law. The UCC requires less formality because it recognizes that most business deals are not highly formal and UCC rules are used to "fill the gap" when a contract is silent on an issue. This section considers the effect of UCC Article 2 on general contract principles. As you read the section, keep in mind the basic differences between the UCC and the common law of contracts, some of which are outlined in Exhibit 11.2.

EXHIBIT 11.2

Offer and Acceptance: Comparing the UCC and the Common Law of Contracts

INTENT TO CONTRACT

Under the common law, a contract cannot be formed until the offer is accepted. The offer-acceptance rule is rather strictly applied. Article 2 relaxes this rule; §2-204 provides that a contract "may be made in any manner sufficient to show

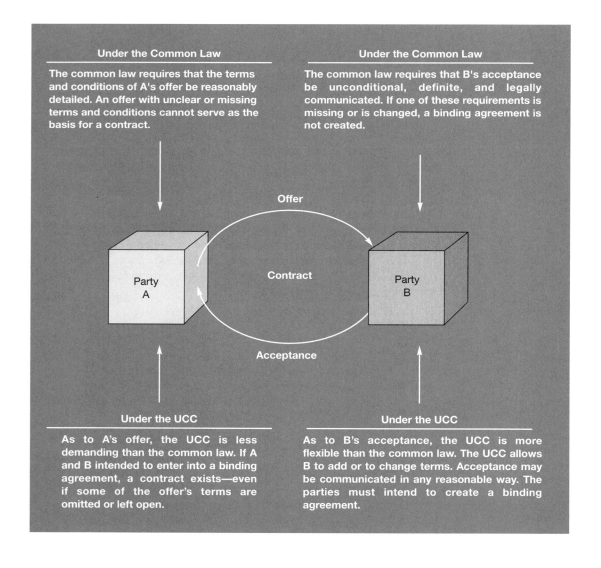

Under the Common Law

The common law requires that the terms and conditions of A's offer be reasonably detailed. An offer with unclear or missing terms and conditions cannot serve as the basis for a contract.

Under the Common Law

The common law requires that B's acceptance be unconditional, definite, and legally communicated. If one of these requirements is missing or is changed, a binding agreement is not created.

Offer

Contract

Party A

Party B

Acceptance

Under the UCC

As to A's offer, the UCC is less demanding than the common law. If A and B intended to enter into a binding agreement, a contract exists—even if some of the offer's terms are omitted or left open.

Under the UCC

As to B's acceptance, the UCC is more flexible than the common law. The UCC allows B to add or to change terms. Acceptance may be communicated in any reasonable way. The parties must intend to create a binding agreement.

agreement" between the parties. For example, suppose a buyer and seller have been doing business together for months. Every Tuesday, the seller delivers restaurant supplies to the buyer's restaurant. Every Thursday, the buyer pays the invoice by mail. Under the UCC, a contract has been formed by the conduct of the parties. It does not matter that the moment of contract formation is uncertain.

An Indefinite Offer

The common law requires that an offer specify all relevant terms. Article 2 is less demanding. If the parties intended to enter into a binding agreement on the basis of the offer, a contract exists. This is the case even though some of the offer's major terms—such as price, delivery, or payment terms—might be omitted or are left open for later determination. A contract does not fail for indefiniteness "if the parties have intended to make a contract and there is a reasonably certain basis for giving an appropriate remedy."

When terms are left open by the parties, Article 2 provides rules for determining the terms. For example, as a general rule the buyer and seller must agree on the quantities of goods to be exchanged or the agreement is too indefinite to be a contract. Exceptions arise in two instances: (1) when the buyer has agreed to purchase the total output of the seller (called an *output contract*) and (2) when the seller has agreed to supply the full requirements of the buyer (called a *requirements contract*). In either case, a contract for the sale of goods need not specify a definite quantity. Relying on the good faith of the parties, Article 2 fixes the contract quantity at the actual output of the seller or the actual requirements of the buyer. Such UCC rules encourage businesses to enter into contracts that provide more flexibility than does common-law contract law. But this flexibility is not to be abused. The following case considers an open-quantity term in a requirements contract.

Orange and Rockland Utilities, Inc. v. Amerada Hess Corporation
Appellate Division of the New York Supreme Court
59 A.D. 2d 110, 397 N.Y.S.2d 814 (1977)

CASE BACKGROUND *In December 1969, Amerada Hess agreed to supply Orange and Rockland Utilities (O&R) with "all of the fuel oil required for its Lovett Generating Plant until September 30, 1974." The contract included estimates of O&R's annual fuel oil requirements and fixed the price at $2.14 per barrel. Several months later, the market price of fuel oil began increasing. By May 1970, it had reached $3.00 per barrel. O&R notified Hess of increases in its fuel oil requirements. Additional supplies were needed because O&R was substituting oil for more costly natural gas as a boiler fuel and then selling the extra electricity to neighboring utilities.*

By June 1970, O&R's demand was 63 percent over the original estimate. Hess refused to meet the revised requirements but did increase supplies 10 percent above the contract estimates. O&R then bought additional fuel

oil from other suppliers at considerably higher prices. By 1971, its purchases of fuel oil were more than double the estimates in the original contract.

O&R sued Hess for the difference between what it paid for fuel oil in the open market and what its costs would have been if Hess had supplied all its oil at the $2.14 contract price. The trial court denied recovery, finding a lack of good faith by O&R. O&R appealed.

CASE DECISION Margett, Justice.

This action, for damages as a result of an alleged breach of a requirements contract, raises related but distinctly separate issues as to whether the plaintiff buyer's requirements occurred in good faith and whether those requirements were unreasonably disproportionate to the estimates stated in the contract.

* * *

It is noted at the outset that the parties agreed, pursuant to their contract, that New Jersey law should apply. The governing statute is section 2-306 of the Uniform Commercial Code (UCC), which provides, in relevant part:

> A term which measures the quantity (to be supplied by a seller to a purchaser of goods) by the . . . requirements of the buyer means such actual . . . requirements as may occur in good faith, except that no quantity unreasonably disproportionate to any stated estimate or in the absence of a stated estimate to any normal or otherwise comparable prior . . . requirements may be . . . demanded.

There is . . . a good deal of . . . case law on the requirement of "good faith." It is well settled that a buyer in a rising market cannot use a fixed price in a requirements contract for speculation. Nor can a buyer arbitrarily and unilaterally change certain conditions prevailing at the time of the contract so as to take advantage of market conditions at the seller's expense.

There is no judicial precedent with respect to the meaning of the term "unreasonably disproportionate" which appears in . . . section 2-306 of the UCC. . . .

Turning . . . to the facts of the instant case, we conclude that, at least as to the year in which this controversy first arose, there was ample evidence to justify a finding of lack of good faith on plaintiff's part. . . . The following picture emerges: non-firm sales from plaintiff's Lovett plant, presumably in large part to the New York Power Pool, increased nearly sixfold from 67,867 megawatt hours in 1969 to 390,017 megawatt hours in 1970. The significance of that increase in non-firm sales lies in the fact that such sales did not enter into the budget calculations which formed the basis of the estimates included in the contract. Even

assuming that a prudent seller of oil could anticipate some additional requirements generated by non-firm sales, an increase of the magnitude which occurred in 1970 is unforeseeable. That increase, of 322,150 megawatt hours, translates into the equivalent of over 500,000 barrels of oil. The conclusion is inescapable that this dramatic change in plaintiff's relationship with the New York Power Pool came about as a result of the subject requirements contract, which insured it a steady flow of cheap oil despite swiftly rising prices. O&R's use of the subject contract to suddenly and dramatically propel itself into the position of a large seller of power to other utilities evidences a lack of good faith dealing.

* * *

We hold that under the circumstances of this case, any demand by plaintiff for more than double its contract estimates, was, as a matter of law, "unreasonably disproportionate" to those estimates. We do not adopt the factor of more than double the contract estimates as any sort of an inflexible yardstick. Rather, we apply those standards . . . which are calculated to limit a party's risk in accordance with the reasonable expectations of the parties. . . .

The quantities of oil utilized by plaintiff during the period subsequent to 1970 were not within the reasonable expectations of the parties when the contract was executed, and accordingly we hold that those "requirements" were unreasonably disproportionate to the estimates.

Judgment . . . affirmed, with costs.

QUESTIONS FOR ANALYSIS

1. What was O&R's motivation in increasing its requirements under the contract?
2. Why was the case decided under the UCC and not the common law of contracts?

Merchant's Firm Offer

Article 2 also modifies the contract rules governing when an offer may be revoked. Under the common law, an offer can be revoked anytime before acceptance. The principal common-law exception is the option contract, under which the offeree gives consideration for the offeror's promise to keep the offer open for a stated time period. Section 2-205 provides another exception: If a merchant-offeror gives assurances in a signed writing that the offer will remain open for a given period, the merchant's *firm offer* is irrevocable. More important, the merchant's firm offer is irrevocable without the need for consideration. If the period is not stated in the offer, the offer stays open for a reasonable time not to exceed three months.

International Sales of Goods

American businesses involved in international business for the first time are often most surprised by contract-law issues. Some countries that were under communist rule have little if any form of modern contract law. Several of the countries have received assistance in developing contract law from leading American legal organizations. Other well-developed civil-law countries (such as Italy, France, Germany, and Japan) have contract rules—but those rules can be very different from American rules.

Differences in contract rules can be managed to some extent by including the *United Nations Convention on the International Sale of Goods* in international contracts for the sale of goods (which we study later). The

Sales Convention resulted from long negotiations among sixty-two countries. Since civil-law countries are dominant, it is not surprising that the Convention follows civil-law concepts more closely than Anglo-American common-law concepts. Thus, the Convention can be a trap for unwary American businesses. For example, the Convention does not include a Statute of Frauds. Thus, it allows for the enforcement of both oral and written contracts for the sale of goods. Perhaps more interesting is that the Convention does not require consideration for the creation of a contract. Clearly, American businesses want to be very careful in drafting international business contracts to avoid confusion and potentially serious legal consequences.

ACCEPTANCE

Article 2 modifies the common-law rules for acceptance in several important ways. To bring the rules of acceptance more in line with business practices, the UCC provides greater flexibility in the way acceptance can be communicated. If the offeror does not clearly demand a particular method of acceptance, Section 2-206 holds that a contract is formed when the offer is accepted in any reasonable manner under the circumstances. This flexibility allows the legal rules governing acceptance to keep pace with new modes of communication.

The UCC provides that an acceptance may be valid even if the offeree includes additional terms or changes existing terms in an offer. Under the common law, an acceptance cannot deviate from the terms of the offer without being considered either a rejection or a counteroffer. Article 2 makes an acceptance valid when the parties intend to form a contract—even though the offeree's acceptance contains different terms from those in the offer.

Conflicting Terms

It is not uncommon for an offeror to send an offer on a standard company form or in a letter that lists standard terms, such as when payment is due. The offeree may accept the offer but send acceptance on its own standard form or in a letter that does not contain all the terms that were stated in the offer. UCC §2-207(1) states that in such cases there is a valid acceptance. However, the contract is based on the offeror's terms. The different terms contained in the acceptance become a part of the contract only if the offeror accepts the terms posed by the offeree in acceptance.

If the offeree wants its terms included in the contract, it must make acceptance "expressly conditional on assent to the additional or different terms." It would be enough to say in the reply to the offer something such as "I accept the offer, but only if you agree to the following terms," which are then listed. If the offeror then says nothing, but goes ahead with the deal, the changed terms from the offeree are assumed to be a part of the contract unless the changed terms materially affect the contract; then there must be acceptance of the changes. Similarly, if the offeror's offer states that no changes are allowed unless approved, then there must be a specific reply to the changes. If the parties forget or fail to specify certain terms in the contract, and a dispute arises, then the courts may have to apply the UCC to "fill the gaps."

FILLING THE GAPS

Like the common law of contracts, the UCC allows parties to form contracts that may differ from ordinary practice. But unlike common-law contracts, the UCC fills in parts of sales contracts that are left open, are unclear, or otherwise must be settled to make a contract complete. This handles the reality of business dealings where contracts are often not complete or circumstances force changes to occur. The UCC instructs the courts how to resolve certain situations that arise that are not resolved by the terms of the contract.

In Section 1-205, the Code states that when parties have had regular dealings, their previous conduct will be looked to as the basis for understanding the current situation. Further, the courts will look to *trade usage*—the regular practice and methods of dealings in a given trade—for how to resolve an unsettled transaction. In addition, the UCC addresses several common areas of contractual disputes, a few of which are reviewed here.

Price

While price is usually specified, in some contracts it is not clear or is expected to be set over time as the parties work together. If price is unclear when a contract is found to exist, §2-305 directs the courts to determine "a reasonable price." Reasonable price may or may not be "fair market value," depending on the past dealings and conduct of the parties. If the price referred to in the contract relies on benchmarks, such as "the price of wheat on August 15" or "cost plus 10 percent," disputes may arise as to whether the price of wheat included delivery or the "cost" was determined in good faith. In such cases, the courts attempt to determine what the parties intended when they formed the contract and what would be the most reasonable method, given usual business practices, to determine the price to fulfill the contract.

Quantity

The UCC generally requires that a contract specify in writing a quantity to be purchased in order to satisfy the statute of frauds. But some contracts are requirements (or exclusive dealing) contracts, as we saw in the *Orange and Rockland* case. When the quantity to be supplied is not detailed, the courts apply §2-306, which requires the parties to use best efforts to supply the goods and to use or resell the goods. The court looks to the apparent intent of the parties and trade customs. Abuses, such as the quantity increase in the *Orange and Rockland* case, where one party exploits the other, do not satisfy the UCC test of good-faith dealing.

Delivery Terms

Most sales contracts specify how goods are to be delivered and who is responsible for the cost of transportation. At some point, responsibility for transportation and control of the goods switches from the seller to the buyer. Sections 2-319 to 2-324 detail the definition of delivery terms, such as "free on board" (F.O.B.), often used in contracts. If delivery is not specified, the UCC fills the gap so long as a contract

German Law Favors Smaller Companies

Germany's Law on General Business Terms (AGBG) is its commercial code most like the UCC. It applies to commercial dealings among merchants and with consumers. Unlike the UCC, however, the AGBG is more concerned about the relative bargaining power of two parties in a contract between merchants. It also prohibits certain contract terms quite common in the United States. Hence, U.S. firms must be sure that they know what law will govern a contract in the event of a dispute.

A common term in U.S. commercial contracts is a disclaimer that the parties are not liable for lost profits as a result of problems that arise. If bargained for, this provision is legal in the United States but prohibited in Germany. More sweeping in effect, the AGBG holds void any clause that violates good faith by imposing an "unfair burden" on the other party. The AGBG does not look favorably on enforcing boilerplate terms in a contract "imposed" by a large firm on a smaller firm. When such provisions are stricken, a contract that was desirable can suddenly become unfavorable.

The AGBG also prohibits clauses that disclaim liability for acts of gross negligence. It may void contracts that are for unusually long periods of obligations and generally prohibits clauses that give the seller the right to increase prices, except in limited circumstances. Hence, as is the case in most international business, one cannot presume that U.S. commercial practices will necessarily be valid, and care in contracting is essential.

exists. Section 2-309 states that the time for delivery is to be a "reasonable time." What is reasonable depends, of course, on factors such as trade custom, the apparent intentions of the parties, and the availability of transportation services. If the parties do not state what is to determine the time of delivery, §2-311 states that "specifications or arrangements relating to shipment are at the seller's option." As would be expected, Section 2-503 requires the seller to tender delivery "at a reasonable hour." Similarly, if not specified, Section 2-308 presumes that delivery is to be at the seller's place of business. When the seller turns goods over to a shipping company, Section 2-504 holds that it has a duty to assure that the carrier is competent and that all parties understand who bears the risk of loss at various points before the buyer gets possession of the goods.

CONTRACT MODIFICATION

Under the common law, contract modifications must be supported by new consideration to be binding on the parties. The UCC §2-209 makes a significant change in the common-law rule by providing that the parties need not provide new consideration to modify an existing sales contract. Such a modification to a sales contract, however, must meet the UCC's test of good-faith dealing and usually must be in writing.

STATUTE OF FRAUDS

Article 2 §2-201 provides a *statute of frauds* provision. The basic rule is that a contract for the sale of goods for $500 or more is not enforceable unless it is in writing and signed by the party against whom enforcement is sought. In comparison to the common law, the UCC relaxes the requirements for the sufficiency of a writing to satisfy the Statute of Frauds.

Under Article 2, the writing need not specify every material term in the contract. The key element is that there is some basis for believing that the parties made a contract for the sale of goods. For example, suppose a buyer sends a letter to a seller indicating an intent to buy shipping cartons. Later, because other sellers offer lower prices, the buyer wants to get out of the deal. If the buyer indicated an intent to enter into an agreement by writing and signing the letter, the writing is "sufficient" under Article 2 to be binding. The letter must be signed by the buyer, since the seller is seeking enforcement against the buyer.

Failure to Respond to a Writing

The UCC recognizes that it is not uncommon in business for contract writings to be incomplete. This is especially the case when parties discuss a deal, and one sends a writing to confirm what was discussed, but the other party does not send a written reply. Hence, in some situations, even when there is a failure to respond to a writing signed by the other party, there may be a good contract.

Section 2-201(2) states: "Between merchants if within a reasonable time a writing in confirmation of the contract and sufficient against the sender is received and the party receiving it has reason to know its contents, it satisfies the [writing] requirements . . . against such party unless written notice of objection to its contents is given within ten days after it is received." This only applies to contracts between merchants; the writing must be complete as to essential terms; and the writing must be sent soon (and received) after the contract has been formed.

Parol Evidence

Since the UCC is more generous than contract law in presuming contracts to exist when terms are not all necessarily set, oral testimony is more likely to be needed to clarify disputes over terms of a contract subject to the UCC. Section 2-202 states that written documents may not be contradicted by oral testimony but that such testimony may be used to explain customary trade dealings or the meaning of certain terms. Parol evidence may not be used "if the court finds the writing to have been intended also as a complete and exclusive statement of the terms of the agreement."

Performance and Obligations

Once a buyer and a seller have formed a contract for the sale of goods, both parties must perform their obligations under that contract or risk being found in breach. The general duties and obligations assumed by each party to a contract for the sale of goods include those specified by the contract, imposed by the UCC, and, where necessary, provided by trade custom. The *Ashe* case illustrates several aspects of the UCC in practice.

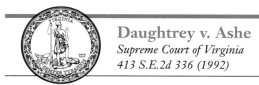

Daughtrey v. Ashe
Supreme Court of Virginia
413 S.E.2d 336 (1992)

CASE BACKGROUND *Ashe offered to sell Daughtrey a particular bracelet for $15,000. When Ashe showed the bracelet, he said he knew that the diamonds were v.v.s. quality (one of the highest grades assigned to diamonds). When Daughtrey bought the bracelet, Ashe filled out an appraisal form that was "for insurance purposes only,"* *saying that the appraised value was $25,000 and that the diamonds were v.v.s. quality.*

Later, Daughtrey discovered that the diamonds were not v.v.s. quality. Ashe refused to replace the diamonds with ones of v.v.s. quality but offered a refund of the purchase price. Since diamonds had risen in value, Daughtrey refused the refund and sued for specific performance, demanding diamonds of v.v.s. quality or damages equal to the difference in the value of the diamonds he had and v.v.s. diamonds.

The trial court denied Daughtrey's claim because the appraisal form was not a term or condition of the sale nor a warranty of the value of the bracelet. Daughtrey appealed.

CASE DECISION Whiting, Justice.

* * *

First, [Ashe says] the "appraisal on its face stated that it was for insurance purposes only." However, . . . Ashe's description of the grade of the diamonds should be treated as any other statement he may have made about them . . .

Second, the Ashes contend that Ashe's statement of the grade of the diamonds is a mere opinion and, thus, cannot qualify as an express warranty under [the UCC]. . . .

However . . . Ashe did more than give a mere opinion of the value of the goods; he specifically described them as diamonds of "H color and v.v.s. quality."

Ashe did not qualify his statement as a mere opinion. And, if one who has superior knowledge makes a statement about the goods sold and does not qualify the statement as his opinion, the statement will be treated as a statement of fact.

Nor does it matter that the opinions of other jewelers varied in minor respects. All of them said, and the trial judge found, that the diamonds were of a grade substantially less than v.v.s. . . .

Given these considerations, we conclude that Ashe's description of the goods was more than his opinion; rather, he intended it to be a statement of fact. Therefore, the court erred in holding that the description was not an express warranty under [UCC §2-313].

Next, the Ashes maintain that because the description of the diamonds as v.v.s. quality was not discussed, Daughtrey could not have relied upon Ashe's warranty and, thus, it cannot be treated as "a part of the bargain."

In our opinion, the "part of the basis of the bargain" language of [UCC §2-313] does not establish a buyer's reliance requirement. Instead, this language makes a seller's description of the goods that is not his mere opinion a representation that defines his obligation.

* * *

Ashe introduced no evidence of any factor that would take his affirmation of the quality of the diamonds out of the agreement. Therefore, his affirmation was "a part of the basis of the bargain." Accordingly, we hold that the Daughtreys are entitled to recover for their loss of bargain, and that the court erred in ruling to the contrary. . . .

Reversed and Remanded.

QUESTIONS FOR ANALYSIS

1. It is common for jewelers to give customers an "appraisal form" that will help them get a generous payment from their insurance company in case the jewelry is stolen. If that was the real purpose of the form Ashe gave Daughtrey, why should the form be taken seriously as to the terms of the bargain itself?
2. Why would not a full refund allow Daughtrey to be placed in the position he was in before the deal had been entered into?

SELLER'S RIGHTS AND OBLIGATIONS

The seller's basic obligation under the UCC is to transfer and deliver conforming goods to the buyer. The seller must be concerned about the appropriate manner and timeliness of delivery, the place of tender, and the quality of tender. The proper tender of goods to and their acceptance by the buyer entitles the seller to be paid according to the contract.

Under the common law, a doctrine developed called the *perfect tender rule*. Under this doctrine, the seller's tender of delivery was required to conform in detail to the terms of the agreement between the parties. In the absence of perfect tender, the buyer either rejected the entire delivery or accepted it. The UCC §2-601 restates the perfect tender rule:

> [I]f the goods or the tender of delivery fail in any respect to conform to the contract, the buyer may:
> (a) reject the whole;
> (b) accept the whole; or,
> (c) accept any commercial unit or units and reject the rest.

This modifies the common-law rule by allowing the buyer to accept less than the entire shipment. It allows buyers to reject goods that do not conform completely to the contract. The rationale for the rule is that buyers are entitled to receive the goods they have bargained and paid for—and not something less.

On the other hand, allowing a buyer to reject a shipment when the nonconformities are slight may enable the buyer to escape payment obligations. This is a problem particularly when the market price of the goods is falling. The buyer can find some nonconformity, cancel the contract, and purchase the goods at a lower price from another seller. Article 2's general policy of enforcing contracts when reasonable discourages such unfair behavior. The UCC allows modifications to the buyer's common-law right to reject the seller's goods for failure to comply with the perfect tender rule.

Right to Cure by the Seller

UCC §2-508 provides some opportunities for a seller to *cure* an improper tender of goods that has been rejected by the buyer. After the buyer has rejected a shipment as not conforming to the contract, the seller may cure the defective tender or delivery if

(1) The time for the seller's performance under the contract has not yet passed;
(2) The seller notifies the buyer in a timely manner of an intent to cure the defect; and
(3) The seller properly repairs or replaces the defective goods within the time allowed for his performance.

In the following case, the buyer rejected nonconforming goods and provided the seller with an extended period in which to cure the improper tender.

Ramirez v. Autosport
Supreme Court of New Jersey
88 N.J. 277, 440 A.2d 1345 (1982)

CASE BACKGROUND   *On July 20, 1978, Mr. & Mrs. Ramirez bought a van from Autosport. The van cost $14,100, and Autosport gave the Ramirezes $4,700 for their old van as a trade-in. The Ramirezes agreed to turn in their old van immediately and to take delivery of the new van on August 3. On August 3, the Ramirezes tendered payment. However, the new van was not ready: it had paint scratches, missing electric and sewer hookups,* *and damaged hubcaps. Autosport agreed to cure the problems. After repeated phone calls from the buyers, Autosport promised delivery on August 14.*

On the 14th, the van was still not ready. This time, the repainted surfaces were not dry, and the seat cushions were wet because the windows had been left open during a storm. A third delivery date was set for September 1, but the new van was still not ready for delivery. Finally, in

October, the Ramirezes returned with their attorney and canceled the contract. They also demanded the return of their old van, but Autosport had sold it to another customer.

The Ramirezes filed suit against Autosport for rescission of the contract and recovery of the value of their old van. Autosport counterclaimed for breach of contract. The trial court found for the Ramirezes. Autosport appealed.

CASE DECISION Pollock, Judge.

This case raises several issues under the Uniform Commercial Code ("the Code" and "UCC") concerning whether a buyer may reject a tender of goods with minor defects and whether a seller may cure the defects.

* * *

To the extent that a buyer can reject goods for any nonconformity, the UCC retains the perfect tender rule. Section 2-601 states that goods conform to a contract "when they are in accordance with the obligations under the contract." Section 2-601 authorizes a buyer to reject goods if they "or the tender of delivery fail in any respect to conform to the contract." The Code, however, mitigates the harshness of the perfect tender rule and balances the interests of buyer and seller. The Code achieves that result through its provisions for revocation of acceptance and cure.

* * *

Underlying the Code provisions is the recognition of the revolutionary change in business practices in this century. The purchase of goods is no longer a simple transaction in which a buyer purchases individually-made goods from a seller in a face-to-face transaction. Our economy depends on a complex system for the manufacture, distribution, and sale of goods, a system in which manufacturers and consumers rarely meet. Faceless manufacturers mass-produce goods for unknown consumers who purchase those goods from merchants exercising little or no control over the quality of their production. In an age of assembly lines, we are accustomed to cars with scratches, television sets without knobs and other products with all kinds of defects. Buyers no longer expect a "perfect tender." If a merchant sells defective goods, the reasonable expectation of the parties is that the buyer will return those goods and that the seller will repair or replace them.

Recognizing this commercial reality, the Code permits a seller to cure imperfect tenders. Should the

seller fail to cure the defects, whether substantial or not, the balance shifts again in favor of the buyer, who has the right to cancel or seek damages. In general, economic considerations would induce sellers to cure minor defects. Assuming the seller does not cure, however, the buyer should be permitted to exercise his remedies under [the UCC]. The Code remedies for consumers are to be liberally construed, and the buyer should have the option of cancelling if the seller does not provide conforming goods.

To summarize, the UCC preserves the perfect tender rule to the extent of permitting a buyer to reject goods for any nonconformity. Nonetheless, that rejection does not automatically terminate the contract. A seller may still effect a cure and preclude unfair rejection and cancellation by the buyer.

The trial court found that Mr. and Mrs. Ramirez had rejected the van within a reasonable time under [UCC] 2-602. The court found that on August 3, 1978 Autosport's salesman advised the Ramirezes not to accept the van and that on August 14, they rejected delivery and Autosport agreed to replace the cushions. Those findings are supported by substantial credible evidence, and we sustain them. . . . [W]e find that Autosport did not effect a cure. Clearly the van was not ready for delivery during August, 1978 when Mr. and Mrs. Ramirez rejected it, and Autosport had the burden of proving that it had corrected the defects. Although the Ramirezes gave Autosport ample time to correct the defects, Autosport did not demonstrate that the van conformed to the contract on September 1. In fact, on that date, when Mr. and Mrs. Ramirez returned at Autosport's invitation, all they received was discourtesy.

* * *

Affirmed.

QUESTIONS FOR ANALYSIS

1. What is the underlying purpose of the seller's right to cure? Was that purpose met in this case?
2. The judge asserts that "Buyers no longer expect a 'perfect tender.'" Are these notions still valid today, given the movement by managers toward total quality management? To the extent that they are not completely valid, how would you expect the total quality movement to be reflected in future UCC decisions regarding defective products?

BUYER'S RIGHTS AND OBLIGATIONS

In general, a buyer's obligations begin when the seller tenders delivery of goods that conform to the sales contract. The buyer is required by §2-507 to accept conforming goods and to pay for them according to the contract. The decision by the buyer to accept or reject the goods determines how the seller will continue to perform. If the buyer accepts the goods, the seller will await payment. If the buyer rejects the goods as nonconforming, the seller may need to remedy the problem or may have to consider suit for breach of contract.

Buyer's Right of Inspection

Unless the parties have otherwise agreed, under §2-513 the buyer has a right to inspect the goods before accepting or paying for them. Inspection allows the buyer to verify that the goods received are those the seller had agreed to deliver. The buyer must pay for any expenses associated with an inspection. However, the expenses can be recovered from the seller as damages if the goods do not conform to the contract.

Buyer's Right of Rejection

According to §2-601 and §2-602, a buyer who receives goods that are nonconforming may reject them as a breach of contract and withhold payment. The buyer may also cancel the contract and recover from the seller any prepayments made. The buyer must notify the seller of a rejection in a timely manner to allow the seller to either cure the nonconformity, if realistic, or reclaim the goods.

Installment Contracts

An *installment contract* is one contract that provides for delivery in two or more separate lots. Under §2-612 each lot is to be accepted and paid for separately. In an installment contract, a buyer can reject an installment—but "only if the nonconformity substantially impairs the value of that installment and cannot be cured." The entire installment contract is breached only when one or more nonconforming installment "substantially" impairs the value of the "whole contract." If the buyer subsequently accepts a nonconforming installment and fails to notify the seller of cancellation, the contract is reinstated.

Buyer's Duty of Acceptance

When the seller has properly tendered conforming goods, the buyer has a duty to accept them. That is, under §2-606 and §2-607, the buyer has a duty to become the owner of goods properly tendered by the seller. If the goods are nonconforming, but have been accepted under §2-608, the buyer may later revoke acceptance only if the nonconformity "substantially impairs" the value of the goods. Of course, if the buyer accepts nonconforming goods, they must be paid for.

Obligation of Payment

Unless otherwise agreed, section 2-507 requires payment at the time and place at which the buyer receives the goods. Even when the contract calls for the seller to deliver the goods to a transportation company for shipment to the buyer, the buyer's payment for the goods is not due until the goods are received. Payment upon receipt gives the buyer a chance to inspect the goods before paying for them. The *Hoover* case discusses several issues that can arise when a problem occurs in delivered goods.

Hoover Universal, Inc. v. Brockway Imco, Inc.

United States Court of Appeals, Fourth Circuit

809 F.2d 1039 (1987)

CASE BACKGROUND *Hoover was interested in buying an Imco process for making plastic bottles known as ORB VI, which Imco developed, patented, and had in operation. After various trips, inspections, and discussions, including being given all materials related to the machines, production, and cost of operation, Hoover paid $3.5 million for the eleven machines. Both parties failed to notice that an error in the handouts overstated the bottles that would be produced by about 20 percent.*

Paragraph 2(d) of the contract stated: "Since Hoover has reviewed the Business and will inspect the Purchased Assets and become familiar with and satisfy itself concerning the same, with the exception of specific representations and warranties set forth in Paragraph 10 hereinafter, Imco makes no representation or warranty to Hoover with respect to the financial condition or prospects of the business, or the merchantability, condition or workmanship of the purchased assets or any part thereof . . . , the absence of any defects therein, whether latent or patent. . . . Hoover shall be responsible, and assumes all risk and liability, for the consequences of its purchase, ownership, use and possession of the Purchased Assets and the conduct of the Business after closing by or on behalf of Hoover."

When Hoover began to operate the machinery, the error in the handouts on the rate of production was discovered; Hoover sued for breach of warranty and fraud. The trial court held that the comprehensive nature of the written agreement barred both claims. Hoover appealed.

CASE DECISION Hall, Circuit Judge.

* * *

Assuming for the purposes of decision that Imco's handout was either an affirmation of fact or a description of the goods, it does not follow that summary judgment was improperly granted. As the district court implicitly recognized, any effort by Hoover to prove that the handout was part of the basis of the bargain would have inevitably foundered on the barrier raised by the existence of a detailed written contract. The parol evidence Rule, as codified in the [UCC] §2-202, states that:

Terms with respect to which the confirmatory memoranda of the parties agree or which are otherwise set forth in a writing intended by the parties as a final expression of their agreement with respect to such terms as are included therein may not be contradicted by evidence of any prior agreement or of a contemporaneous oral agreement but may be explained or supplemented (a) by course of dealing or usage of trade (§1-205); . . . and

(b) by evidence of consistent additional terms unless the court finds the writing to have been intended also as a complete and exclusive statement of the terms of the agreement.

The district court did not explicitly apply the language of §2-202(b). Its reference, however, to a "merged contract" and to the fact that any liability would have to be discovered "within the four corners of the instrument" leave no doubt that the court found the Asset Purchase Agreement to be a "complete and exclusive statement" of the agreement between Hoover and Imco. In light of the detailed nature of the contract, including the well-drafted merger clause, we can see no error in that conclusion.

It follows, therefore, that §2-202 precludes any effort by Hoover to establish through the handout a warranty relating to the ORB VI cavitation capacity even in the unlikely eventuality that the warranty could be construed as a consistent additional term.

* * *

Hoover argues that the [production] capacity described in the handout was a substantial motivating factor in its decision to buy the ORB VI. Its detrimental reliance on that misrepresentation established, in Hoover's view, a prima facie case of either actual or constructive fraud.

* * *

[A] seller who misrepresents a material fact in connection with a sale may be liable for fraud in the inducement. However, in circumstances where a prudent buyer would have conducted an investigation and, thereby, discovered the seller's misstatement, a buyer who fails to make such an investigation may not assert fraud based on the factual misrepresentation. A buyer who fails to conduct a proper investigation may still recover if the seller's conduct intentionally diverts the buyer from engaging in a reasonable inquiry.

As the district court recognized in its opinion, Hoover not only should have made a prudent investigation, it expressly agreed in paragraph 2(d) of the contract that it would "inspect" and "become familiar" with the ORB VI. It is undisputed that a timely investigation would have revealed the error in the handout. Furthermore, Hoover alleged no conduct by Imco that could reasonably be construed as an effort to forestall further inquiry by Hoover.

Hoover's clear failure to fulfill the duty of inspection imposed by both the operation of law and contract precludes its effort to assert reliance on Imco's prior statement.

* * *

Affirmed.

QUESTIONS FOR ANALYSIS

1. The contract did not specify the productive capacity of the machines, so why did the court not integrate into the contract the handout that stated the production ability?
2. If the contract had not contained the disclaimer paragraph, would the result have been different?

Sales Warranties

Broadly speaking, a *warranty* is a statement or representation made by a seller that the goods being sold conform to certain standards of quality, safety, performance, and title. If the goods do not conform to the standards created by the warranty, the seller can be held liable in damages for breach of warranty. Article 2 provides five types of warranties (which are summarized in Exhibit 11.3).

WARRANTY OF TITLE

Under §2-312, a seller in a sales contract warrants that good title is being transferred to the buyer and that the goods will be delivered free of any claims against them, such a liens, unless those have been revealed to the buyer. As the UCC explains in its official comments, the purpose of this is that a buyer gets "a good, clean title" in a legal manner and that the buyer "will not be exposed to a lawsuit in order to protect it." This means that a seller is responsible to the buyer even if the seller innocently sells a good that does not have good title, such as a stolen property.

Warranty of title also means that the seller, if a merchant, ordinarily warrants that goods being sold are free of any claim of infringement, such as if a patented good has been copied. If a seller has infringed on a trademark, copyright, or patent owned by a third party, the seller is responsible for expenses incurred by a buyer who is ignorant of the infringement as a result of the infringement.

EXPRESS WARRANTIES

An *express warranty* is created by a seller's promise or guarantee as to the quality, safety, performance, or durability of goods being sold. During negotiations, a seller may help induce a buyer to purchase goods by making representations about the goods that become warranties. Section 2-313 lists three circumstances where an express warranty may be created:

1. A seller provides a sample or model of the good that the buyer relies upon as evidence of what the goods will be like,
2. A seller describes attributes about the goods to the buyer, or
3. A seller makes specific oral or written statements or promises to the buyer about the goods that are a part of the basis of the bargain.

EXHIBIT 11.3

Summary of Warranties under the UCC

Warranty of Title §2-312	Seller is the rightful owner of the goods, the goods are free of any liens, and there are no infringements.
Express Warranty §2-313	Seller's promise as to quality, safety, or performance. May be created by the seller's statements, description, or models.
Implied Warranties	Imposed on the seller by the UCC:
Merchantability §2-314	Requires that the goods are reasonably fit, and safe for the purposes they are being sold for; also applies to packaging and labeling.
Fitness for a Particular Purpose §2-315	If the buyer relies on the seller's skill or judgment in selecting goods for a particular purpose, the goods must be able to perform that purpose.
Trade Usage §2-314	The seller must provide the goods to the buyer in the manner customary in the trade.

Statements about goods are more likely to be held to be express warranties when the claims are specific, not general statements about "how nice" the goods are or other general happy talk (puffery). Similarly, an express warranty is created if statements are made about attributes of the goods that are not obvious, such as claims about the quality of steel used in production of a good, or it is a case in which the buyer has good reason to rely on the expertise of the seller. Obviously, when statements are made in writing, as in the *Daughtrey* v. *Ashe* case, they are more likely to be held to be express warranties. It does not matter that a seller does not intend to create an express warranty by making claims about a product; if it is reasonable that the buyer rely on the seller's claims, then they are likely to be express warranties.

IMPLIED WARRANTIES

An *implied warranty* is a minimum quality and safety standard that is imposed by Article 2. This part of the UCC has important implications, for it establishes a standard similar to that imposed by product liability law in tort. Implied warranties exist at law. Unlike express warranties, which are based on representations made by the seller, implied warranties are automatically imposed on sellers unless they specifically disclaim them.

Implied Warranty of Merchantability

Section 2-314 states that unless the parties to the contract expressly agree otherwise, an *implied warranty of merchantability* accompanies every sale by a merchant. This provision of the UCC applies to sellers who are merchants of the goods of the kind in question. That is, it applies to those who routinely deal in such goods or offer their expertise to others about such goods, such as jewelers selling jewelry and furniture stores selling furniture.

Merchantable means, according to the UCC, that the good "must be of a quality comparable to that generally acceptable in that line or trade." That is, industry standards must be met. Obviously, for such things as jet engines, industry standards are very high and the seller must offer products of current standards. If the product is a common one, such as bushels of #2 winter wheat, the quality must be average; one cannot pass off a load of bottom-of-the-silo, moldy, rat-dropping-infested wheat. Further, the goods must be able to do the tasks expected of the goods in question. If the goods are one-ton trucks, they must be able to carry the loads expected of such trucks. Also, goods must be adequately packaged and labeled and be in conformance with claims made on labels or sales materials. This issue is discussed in the *Reid* case.

Reid v. Eckerds Drugs, Inc.
North Carolina Court of Appeals
40 N.C. App. 476, 253 S.E.2d 344 (1979)

CASE BACKGROUND *Frankie Reid bought an aerosol can of deodorant from Eckerds Drugs. The label on the can included the following statement:*

WARNING: Use only as directed. Do not apply to broken, irritated or sensitive skin. If rash or irritation develops discontinue use. Never spray towards face or flame. Do not puncture or incinerate can. Do not expose or store at temperature above 120° F. Intentional misuse by deliberately concentrating and inhaling the contents can be harmful or fatal. Keep out of reach of children.

One morning, Reid liberally sprayed his underarms and neck with the deodorant. He put the can down, walked across the room, and lit a cigarette. He burst into flames and was severely burned on his upper body where the deodorant had been applied. He sued the seller, Eckerds, and the manufacturer, the J.P. Williams Company, alleging breach of the implied warranty of merchantability.

At trial, the defendants showed that the deodorant could not be ignited unless an open flame was within ¼ inch of the surface coated with it. They also showed that large quantities of the deodorant had been sold without injuring other consumers. The trial court granted defendants' motion for summary judgment. Reid appealed.

CASE DECISION Martin, Judge.

* * *

In its pure form, an action for breach of implied warranty of merchantability under [UCC] 2-314 entitles a plaintiff to recover without any proof of negligence on a defendant's part where it is shown that (1) a merchant sold goods, (2) the goods were not "merchantable" at the time of sale, (3) the plaintiff (or his property) was injured by such goods, (4) the defect or other condition amounting to a breach of the implied

warranty of merchantability proximately caused the injury, and (5) the plaintiff so injured gave timely notice to the seller. The action is akin to strict liability in tort. . . .

Two things are apparent with reference to the aerosol deodorant can: (1) the product contained therein was not available to the ultimate consumer, and it was not useable by him as it was constituted, without the assistance of the pressurized aerosol can and its propellant. Hence, any effort to distinguish between the deodorant and its aerosol applicator is unrealistic and specious; (2) the directions for use of the product clearly contemplate the use of the product as contained and dispensed by the aerosol can. The warnings of the label are easily understood to refer to the can itself and its proper use. No specific warnings about the use and formulation of the deodorant itself are given. Therefore, when it is assumed that both the can and its contents are components of the product for the ultimate consumer, it must also be assumed that the labeling and packaging of the whole product should fairly be expected to warn of any dangerous properties of both contents and container, especially where the normal and proper use of the product dictates that the contents of the container will be expelled from the container and will be exposed to conditions, after being thus expelled, which are not necessarily similar to the conditions surrounding the container. . . .

Having thus determined that plaintiff's cause of action is cognizable under a breach of the implied warranty of merchantability as embodied in [UCC] 2-314 . . . , we must consider whether the warnings and instructions concerning the product and placed upon the label of the container are sufficient, as a matter of law, to give plaintiff adequate notice of any dangers and thus entitle defendant to judgment as a matter of law. We conclude that they were not so sufficient. The warnings and instructions, when read as a whole, may easily be construed as referring to the product and container as a unit, e.g. "Do not expose or store at temperature above 120° F," clearly contemplates both aerosol can and contents as a whole, since it is highly unlikely that a consumer will be storing the deodorant outside its container; the sentence preceding that one stating "Do not puncture or incinerate can" is reinforcement for the idea that the warnings are directed at the product and the can together. No suggestion is made that the contents might be flammable once they have reached their ultimate destination (i.e., armpits, etc.) and the fact that the contents are 92.77% alcohol by volume is not disclosed. The evidence is undisputed that plaintiff used the aerosol can in accordance with its directions and warnings, set the can down, walked across a room and then lit his cigarette, simultaneously igniting the alcohol in the deodorant he had applied to himself, causing it to burn with a blue flame. The instructions accompanying a product have been found to be "an integral part of the warranty."

If a manufacturer furnishes instructions as to the manner in which a product is to be used, the consumer is entitled to think that so used it will not injure him. There is an implied warranty that the goods are fit for that particular use.

. . . [W]e find that where the product was being used for its intended purposes in a normal way, the . . . expectation of the consumer may reasonably be found to lie within the warranty of fitness for ordinary purposes of [UCC] 2-314(2)(c). We further find that the labeling of the deodorant, when viewed in the light most favorable to plaintiff (who was the non-moving party) and in view of our interpretations of [UCC] 2-314(e) and (f), was not sufficient as a matter of law to entitle defendant to summary judgment. A question of fact as to the sufficiency of the packaging and labeling clearly exists and is one for the jury.

* * *

Reversed and remanded.

QUESTIONS FOR ANALYSIS

1. Why did the product breach the manufacturer's implied warranty of merchantability?
2. How could the company have avoided the liability in this case?

Implied Warranty of Fitness for a Particular Purpose

In some situations, a buyer purchases a good with a definite use in mind. Section 2-315 is more demanding about a seller who had reason to know the buyer's particular purpose for purchasing certain goods. If the buyer relies on the seller's skill or judgment to select the goods for that purpose, an implied warranty that the goods are suited for that purpose is created. The goods must be intended for something more specific than the general purpose for which they were made.

The buyer is required to demonstrate "actual reliance" on the seller's expertise. The buyer must also show that the seller had "reason to know"—not necessarily actual knowledge—of the buyer's purpose. Suppose that Flodden needs to paint rain gutters on her house. She tells the paint store salesperson what she needs. She is concerned about chipping and peeling and asks for a recommendation. The salesperson recommends Pittura Exterior. If Flodden buys Pittura based on the salesperson's recommendation and the paint chips and peels, there is a breach of implied warranty of fitness for a particular purpose.

Implied Warranties Arising under Trade Usage

Implied warranties may also arise, under §2-314, from course of dealing, course of performance, or *trade usage*. In some relationships, the parties are very knowledgeable about the goods, the practices used in selling the goods to their customers, and the uses to which those customers put the goods. In such cases, the courts infer that the buyer and seller intended for those customs to apply to their contract.

JURIS **prudence?**

Does It Come with a Warranty?

Quadro Tracker was introduced in 1995. Its Harleyville, South Carolina, inventor said that it could locate drugs, bombs, and just about anything else whether behind walls, inside cars, on persons, or out in fields. A brochure claimed that it could even detect drugs in a person's bloodstream just by being pointed at a person. An MIT physics professor said that the chances of the Quadro Tracker's working were slim to zero and that there are many hoaxes involving such incredible devices.

Nevertheless, dozens of law enforcement agencies and schools bought the device, also called the Positive Molecular Locator, for prices ranging from $400 to $8,000. Over 1,000 of the plastic boxes were sold, taking in more than $1 million, before a federal judge issued an injunction in 1996 banning the sale or distribution of the product. An FBI agent said, "The only thing this accurately detects is your checkbook."

Sources: *The Herald* (Rock Hill, S.C.) and *The Atlanta Journal and Constitution*

For example, it is customary for car dealers to check new cars prior to delivery to customers. Brown Ford fails to make those checks. If the checks had been done, the dealership would have discovered a problem that caused the engine's exhaust to leak into the passenger compartment. While driving the car, the buyer was overcome by carbon monoxide and hit a tree. The dealer may be liable to a buyer for the damages under a breach of an implied warranty arising from trade usage. If the dealership had performed according to trade custom, the problem would have been found and repaired before the buyer drove the car.

WARRANTY DISCLAIMERS

The warranty requirements imposed on sellers by the UCC is a form of strict liability under contract law. Because it is a tough standard, sellers may wish to limit or eliminate their liability by issuing *disclaimers*. If a seller has made an express warranty, the courts will not look with favor on disclaimers that are inconsistent with the promises made in the warranty. Under §2-316, boilerplate language that attempts to dismiss an express warranty is not allowed when the disclaimer denies or is inconsistent with the language of the warranty. The parol evidence rule generally prevents oral promises that are alleged to have been made from being a part of the warranty, when the oral statement contradicts the written warranty. The *Hoover* case gives an example of clear language in a sales contract that disclaimed various warranties.

Disclaimers of implied warranties are permitted if the disclaimer uses the word "merchantability" and the disclaimer is conspicuous. Under UCC §1-201, conspicuous means that it is written so that a reasonable person would have noticed it, such as is written in all capital letters, is in larger size type, or is in a different color than the rest of the text. Further, a seller is more likely held to have disclaimed warranties if there is a conspicuous notice that the goods are being sold "as is." However, this is one area of the UCC where there are many differences among the states in the kinds of disclaimers they allow. Some states severely restrict the ability of a seller to disclaim implied warranties in the sale of goods to consumers.

THIRD-PARTY BENEFICIARIES OF WARRANTIES

Section 2-318 extends any express warranty made by the seller to the buyer to designated third parties. It also extends the implied warranty of merchantability. Warranty disclaimers made to the buyer by the seller also apply to third parties. The seller may not give a warranty to the buyer but exclude or limit its application to third parties. This rule gives some third parties the benefit of the same warranties the buyer received in the contract for sale.

Remedies and Damages

When a buyer or seller breaches a contract for the sale of goods, the UCC provides the nonbreaching party with a number of remedies. Those remedies are designed to place the nonbreaching party in the same position as if the contract had been performed according to its terms. In applying its remedies, Section 1-106 of the UCC directs the courts to interpret the remedies liberally.

SELLER'S REMEDIES

The buyer may default on contractual obligations by rejecting a tender of goods that conforms to the contract, wrongfully revoking an acceptance, repudiating the contract, failing to make a payment, or failing to complete some other performance required by the contract. In each of these situations, the UCC provides the seller with remedies. As Exhibit 11.4 indicates, the seller is not restricted to any one remedy in particular. Rather, Section 2-703 states that the seller may use several remedies at the same time.

The remedies available to the seller depend on whether the buyer breached before or after receiving the goods (see Exhibit 11.4). When the buyer breaches

EXHIBIT 11.4	Status of the Goods	Seller's Rights and Remedies
Summary of Seller's Rights and Remedies	**Buyer breaches before receiving the goods.**	**The seller may** 1. Cancel the contract 2. Identify the goods; minimize losses if necessary by completing manufacture or by stopping production and salvaging the goods 3. Withhold delivery or, if needed, stop delivery 4. Resell the goods in a commercially reasonable manner 5. Sue the buyer to recover the price loss suffered by having to resell the goods and any resulting damages

	Buyer breaches after receiving the goods.	**The seller may**
		1. If the buyer does not pay, sue to recover the purchase price and resulting incidental damages
		2. If the buyer wrongfully rejects the goods or revokes an acceptance, the remedies depend on the following:
		  a. If the seller reclaims the goods, the remedies are the same as if the buyer had breached before receiving the goods.
		  b. If the seller does not reclaim the goods, the seller can sue to recover the purchase price and any resulting damages.

before receiving the goods, the seller may elect to cancel the contract, resell or salvage (recycle) the goods, or withhold or stop delivery. If the buyer breaches after having received the goods, the remedies available to the seller depend upon whether the seller reclaims the goods. If unable to reclaim the goods, the seller may sue the buyer to recover the purchase price and any resulting incidental damages. If the goods are reclaimed by the seller, the seller may use any of the same remedies available had the buyer's breach occurred before receiving the goods.

Seller's Damages

When reclaiming and reselling the goods does not fully compensate the seller for the buyer's breach, damages are the proper remedy. UCC's general damage measures are designed to put the seller in as good a position as if the buyer had performed contractual obligations. Furthermore, the seller is allowed to seek incidental damages for recovery of those costs resulting from the breach. Under §2-710, such costs may include expenses associated with stopping delivery, transporting and taking care of the goods after the breach, returning or reselling the goods, and taking any other necessary action.

BUYER'S REMEDIES

A seller usually breaches a sales contract in one of the following ways:

1. The seller repudiates the contract before tendering the goods.
2. The seller fails to make a scheduled delivery on time.
3. The seller delivers nonconforming goods.

The buyer's remedies vary somewhat depending on the type of breach by the seller. In any case, the buyer may respond by canceling the contract, arranging to obtain the goods from another supplier, and suing the nonperforming seller for damages. The buyer's rights and remedies are summarized in Exhibit 11.5.

EXHIBIT 11.5	Status of the Goods	Buyer's Rights and Remedies
Summary of Buyer's Rights and Remedies	**Seller repudiates the contract before delivery.**	**The buyer may** 1. Cancel the contract 2. Obtain goods from another supplier 3. Sue the seller for damages and to recover advance payments
	Seller fails to deliver.	**The buyer may** 1. Cancel the contract 2. Obtain goods from another supplier 3. Sue the seller for damages
	Seller delivers nonconforming goods; buyer rejects.	**The buyer may** 1. Cancel the contract 2. Obtain goods from another supplier if goods are rejected 3. Sue the seller for damages 4. Sell rejected goods to recover advance payments 5. If no advance payment, store or reship of goods
	Seller delivers nonconforming goods; buyer accepts.	**The buyer may** 1. Deduct damages from price of goods 2. Sue the seller for damages 3. Sue for breach of warranty

Buyer's Damages

Like the seller's damage provisions, the buyer's damage provisions under the UCC are designed to put the buyer in as good a position as if the seller had performed according to the contract. The terminology for damages is a bit different under the UCC than in the common law, so we consider the primary types of damages specified in the UCC.

Cover   When a seller fails to deliver goods, either by being too late to be useful or because the goods are nonconforming, the buyer is entitled to buy substitute goods and recover the price difference. This is referred to as *cover* in §2-712 of the UCC. The cover price is what is actually paid for the substitute goods; or the market price may be used to measure the damages. Of course, if similar goods are available at the same or a lower price, then the breaching seller does not have to provide cover. The UCC does not permit overcompensation for losses by requiring the seller to pay for the full cost of better-quality substitute goods.

Incidental Damages   When the buyer properly rejects a delivery, (or does not receive the goods) incidental damages, under §2-710, include the reasonable costs of inspecting, receiving, transporting, and taking care of the goods while they remain in her possession. If there was no delivery at all, or if delivery is late, Section 2-715 states that the buyer's incidental damages include all reasonable costs or direct expenses associated with the delay in receiving the goods or in tracking down substitute goods.

Consequential Damages   Consequential damages are foreseeable but not necessarily foreseen damages that result from the seller's breach. They differ from incidental damages in that consequential damages may result from the buyer's relations with parties other than the seller. That is, the breach may cause the buyer to lose sales and, most importantly, profits.

We end this section with the *Sons of Thunder* case, which has drawn considerable attention for the strong status the supreme court of New Jersey gives to the UCC requirement of good-faith dealings. The case also illustrates how parol evidence is used to help explain a contract and what damage award was regarded as appropriate in this particular circumstance.

Sons of Thunder, Inc. v. Borden, Inc.
Supreme Court of New Jersey
148 N.J. 396, 690 A.2d 575 (1997)

CASE BACKGROUND *Borden is the maker of Snow's Clam Chowder. Borden obtained clams from its own four-vessel fleet. DeMusz was captain of one of Borden's boats. After several years, Borden signed an agreement making DeMusz the manager of Borden's boats. DeMusz formed Sea Labor, Inc., to manage the boats. Sea Labor was paid five cents per bushel of clams harvested by the fleet; DeMusz was still paid as a boat captain.*

About the time Sea Labor was hired, Borden began to implement "Shuck-at-Sea," which involved putting equipment on board to shuck clams, allowing a larger haul of clams per voyage. Because the project would require *larger boats, DeMusz offered to buy a large boat, rig it to Borden's specifications, and use it for Shuck-at-Sea. Borden approved the idea. DeMusz and two partners then formed Sea Work, Inc., and bought a boat, the Jessica Lori, with a bank loan for $750,000, rigging it to the specifications needed for Borden's Shuck-at-Sea equipment.*

Booker, the Borden manager who signed the deal with DeMusz, explained to his manager in a company memo about why the contract was a good idea: "[W]e still have a significant mutual interest with DeMusz. His principal business will still be in chartering the Snow fleet . . . He needs a dependable customer for the clams that he catches, whether shell stock or meat. If we terminate our agreement with him, he would have a hard time making the payments on his boat." Sea Work and Borden signed a contract that Borden would put its clam-shucking equipment on Sea Work's boat in exchange for Sea Work offering to Borden all the clam meat shucked on the boat at fifty cents per pound. Sea Work was required to offer Borden a minimum of 15,000 pounds of clams each week.

The Shuck-at-Sea equipment caused difficulties, and it took two years to get it running properly, costing DeMusz a lot of money, some of which was covered by Borden. Booker and DeMusz discussed buying a second, larger boat for Sea Work that could be at sea during bad weather so that more clams could be provided to Borden. The parties entered into an oral agreement to give DeMusz a long-term supply contract for the second boat. An accountant for Borden helped DeMusz calculate how many bushels would have to be gathered and sold to finance the second boat. The parties signed a one-page contract to memorialize the oral agreement.

The contract stated:

"It is understood and agreed to by the parties hereto that [Borden] shall purchase [clams] from Sons of Thunder Corp. for a period of one (1) year at the market rate that is standardized throughout the industry. The term of this contract shall be for one (1) year, after which this contract shall automatically be renewed for a period up to five years. Either party may cancel this contract by giving prior notice of said cancellation in writing Ninety (90) days prior to the effective date."

DeMusz and two partners formed Sons of Thunder, Inc., to buy the second boat. Sons of Thunder needed $588,420 to buy and rig the boat. Booker provided DeMusz a letter of intent to help him get financing for the boat, and he told the bank that DeMusz had a solid relationship with Borden that he expected to last at least five years. A year later, after rigging, Sons of Thunder was put in operation.

About the time both boats went into operation, the Borden managers who had worked with DeMusz left the company or retired. The new managers, Gallant and Nicholson, were unaware of the history and had not seen the contracts. When Borden failed to buy the promised quantity, DeMusz showed the new managers the contract, but the relationship fell apart. Borden bought another boat and began to take most clams from it. Borden would not take the quantity from DeMusz or pay him the minimum price quoted in the contracts.

Borden decided the Shuck-at-Sea project was a failure and sent DeMusz a letter terminating agreements with both boats. The letter cited terms in the contracts that allowed the relationships to be ended on sixty- and ninety-days notice. DeMusz was financially ruined and had to sell his home. He sold one boat and tried to sell the second, but sales were difficult because the boats had been rigged to Borden's specifications, reducing their value to others.

Sons of Thunder sued Borden for failure to buy the contracted amount of clams and to pay the contract price. Both DeMusz and Booker testified at trial that they intended for the parties to be locked in for five years if the contract was successful at the end of the first year, which it was.

The trial judge found the meaning of the contract to be a matter for the jury to decide. It held that there had been a breach of contract and awarded damages of $412,000 for breach of good-faith obligations and $326,000 for failure to abide by the purchase requirements of clams. Borden appealed the damages for breach of good faith only. The appellate court reversed; Sons of Thunder appealed.

CASE DECISION Garibaldi, Justice.

* * *

Article 2 of the Uniform Commercial Code (UCC), adopted in New Jersey . . . governs the contract between Borden and Sons of Thunder because it is a contract for the sale of goods. Section 1-203 contains the general good faith requirement for every contract governed by the UCC. "Every contract or duty within this Act imposes an obligation of good faith in its performance or enforcement." §1-203. Good faith is defined as "honesty in fact in the conduct or transaction concerned." §1-201(19). . . .

The obligation to perform in good faith exists in every contract, including those contracts that contain express and unambiguous provisions permitting either party to terminate the contract without cause.

* * *

[A] party to a contract may breach the implied covenant of good faith and fair dealing in performing its obligations even when it exercises an express and unconditional right to terminate. Other courts have stated that a party can violate the implied covenant of good faith and fair dealing without violating an express term of a contract. As the Supreme Court of South Dakota noted Garrett v. BankWest Inc., "[t]he application of this implied covenant allows an aggrieved party to sue for breach of contract. . . . A breach of contract claim is allowed even though the conduct failed to violate any of the express terms of the contract agreed to by the parties."

* * *

[T]here is sufficient evidence for the jury's conclusion that Borden breached its duty to perform the contract in good faith. In reaching that conclusion, we consider only Borden's performance during the contractual period, including the conduct surrounding the termination of the contract. We do not consider Borden's dealings following the termination of the contract because they are irrelevant to whether Borden performed the contract in good faith.

Borden knew that Sons of Thunder depended on the income from its contract with Borden to pay back the loan. Yet, Borden continuously breached that contract by never buying the required amount of clams from the Sons of Thunder. Furthermore, after Gallant took Booker's place, he told DeMusz that he would not honor the contract with Sons of Thunder. Nicholson also told DeMusz that he did not plan to honor that contract. Borden's failure to honor the contract left Sons of Thunder with insufficient revenue to support its financing for the Sons of Thunder.

Borden was also aware that Sons of Thunder was guaranteeing every loan that Sea Work had taken to finance the rerigging and purchasing costs for the Jessica Lori. Thus, Borden knew that the corporations were dependent on each other, and that if one company failed, the other would most likely fail. Borden, however, fulfilled its obligations to Sea Work only for a short time. Eventually, Borden terminated its contract with Sea Work even though it knew that terminating the contract would leave Sea Work with no market to fish the Jessica Lori. . . .

Accepting those facts and the reasonable inferences therefrom offered as true, we determine that the jury had sufficient evidence to find that Borden was not "honest in fact," as required by the UCC.

* * *

The final issue is whether the jury's assessment of $412,000, approximately one year's worth of additional profits, for the breach of the implied covenant of good faith and fair dealing was a reasonable verdict. Specifically, can a plaintiff recover lost profits for a breach of the implied covenant of good faith and fair dealing? . . .

In general, the UCC's remedies are to be "liberally administered to the end that the aggrieved party may be put in as good a position as if the other party had fully performed." §1-106. Specifically, Section 2-708(2) of the UCC provides:

> If the measure of damages in subsection (1) is inadequate to put the seller in as good a position as performance would have done then the measure of damages is the profit (including reasonable overhead) which the seller would have made from full performance by the buyer, together with any incidental damages provided in this Chapter (§2-710), due allowance for costs reasonably incurred and due credit for payments or proceeds of resale.

* * *

The jury's award of $412,000, approximately one year's profit, for the breach of the implied covenant of good faith and fair dealing is reasonable and fair given the circumstances [and expert testimony that] Sons of Thunder's yearly profits would have been between $390,513 and $430,516 per year if the contract had run for the five-year term.

. . . The judgement of the trial court is reinstated.

QUESTIONS FOR ANALYSIS

1. This decision is considered important because the New Jersey high court is important on commercial law. Why do some observers think this case expands the general idea of fair dealing?
2. Suppose Borden had bought the required clams at the contracted price and then canceled the contract with proper notice. Would Sons of Thunder have had a case then?
3. Why should Sons of Thunder get one year's profit in damages if one believes the contract should have lasted for five years?

International Sales

As global commerce has expanded rapidly in recent decades, businesses have had to deal with the laws and customs of more countries. Litigation everywhere is costly, and people are often suspicious about the fairness of legal rules and procedures in other nations. So there are strong reasons to give business partners around the world reasons to believe that we will all play by the same "rules of the game" and that those who will serve as "referees" to disputes are qualified and impartial. Effective legal rules substantially reduce the cost of doing international business. While we discuss other aspects of international law in detail in Chapter 21, here we focus on how the law of the international sale of goods has been developing.

GENERAL PRINCIPLES

Parties who make contracts for the sale of goods that cross international boundaries are generally free, given limits set by various nations' domestic laws, to choose the law they want to apply to their contract. That is, if a company in Kansas is buying toys from Bangladesh, the two parties can specify the law that governs their contract. They can specify that the Uniform Commercial Code of California will govern the contract and that disputes will be resolved by the arbitration rules of the International Chamber of Commerce. If the parties do not specify how contract disputes are to be resolved, or if they are not clear, there are conflict-of-law rules that will determine what law will be used to resolve a dispute, and what court system or arbitrator will resolve the matter. Most people would prefer to control their legal destiny, so most contracts for the sale of goods specify what law governs. Alternatively, as we see next, many are now governed by a common set of rules.

U.N. CONVENTION ON CONTRACTS FOR THE INTERNATIONAL SALE OF GOODS

The *Convention on Contracts for the International Sale of Goods (CISG)* was adopted by the United Nations in an effort to have a commercial code that most parties would think unbiased to particular national interests. Since then, it has been ratified by most major nations, including the United States in 1988. Since CISG is a treaty adopted by Congress, it prevails over state laws such as the UCC. Contracts for the sale of goods that fall under the coverage of the CISG between a party in the United States and in another nation that adopted the CISG are resolved by the CISG. Hence, if an auto parts company in the United States buys parts from a German company, the contract is automatically governed by the CISG—unless the parties specify that they want to exclude application of the CISG, or some parts of it, and choose another law to govern.

Sales Covered by the CISG

The CISG applies to contracts for commercial sale of goods made by parties who have *places of business* in different countries that have ratified the CISG. It does not matter what the citizenship of the parties is; it is the location of the businesses that matters. Unlike the UCC, which applies to goods sold to the consuming public, contracts under the CISG only apply to commercial sales or sales between merchants. Even among merchants, certain kinds of sales are excluded from the CISG:

- Auction sales
- Consumer goods bought for personal or household use
- Contracts that are primarily for the supply of labor or of other services

Certain kinds of goods are excluded from the CISG:

- Electricity
- Ships and aircraft
- Securities such as stocks, negotiable instruments, and money

Again, parties to contracts that would normally be covered by the CISG can pick another law to govern their contract for the sale of goods, if they so desire.

Similarities to UCC

The CISG is not greatly different from the UCC or the commercial civil codes used in most nations. It is based on the business reality that many deals are not based on detailed contracts that account for all possibilities. It instructs judges to look at the plain meaning of words and to look for consistency.

Formality Contracts need not be formal; the CISG states that "A contract of sale need not be concluded in or evidenced by writing and is not subject to any other requirements as to form. It may be proved by any means, including witnesses." Judges are told to look at the circumstances of past dealings, such as the negotiations, the practices of the parties in dealing with each other, and "any practices which they have established between themselves." However, if parties to a contract made under the CISG so desire, they can insert a statement that judges are not to consider parol evidence and should not look beyond the words in the contract.

Offers Advertisements under the CISG are not offers that can be accepted to form a contract; they are only offers to enter into negotiations. However, offers made to "one or more specific persons" are valid offers to make a contract. Offers become effective when they reach the offeree, but can be revoked any time before acceptance is communicated.

Much like the UCC, the CISG holds that an offer "is sufficiently definite if it indicates the goods and expressly or implicitly fixes or makes provision for determining the quantity and price." When a contract does not expressly include the price, the parties are held "to have impliedly made reference to the price generally charged at the time of the conclusion of the contract for such goods sold under comparable circumstances in the trade concerned." Similarly, if there is uncertainty over a term, the courts will look to the practices "in the particular trade concerned." For example, in one case, the parties argued about what was meant by "chicken." One party claimed it meant young fryers, but the court found that industry practice meant any size cooking chicken.

Acceptance Acceptance of an offer must be made within the time stated in the offer, or, if not stated, within a reasonable time. Acceptance can be sent by any reasonable means. Any statement or conduct by the offeree to indicate acceptance that is communicated to the offeror is sufficient to form the contract. The acceptance is effective when it is received by the offeror, so an offer may be withdrawn up to the point the offeror receives acceptance. As with the UCC and common law, silence is normally not acceptance, but many contracts are formed by performance without stating that there will be performance. For example, if an offeror sends an order asking for 500 boxes of fried grasshoppers, the acceptance occurs when the requested act is performed.

Battle of the Forms It is common in business for orders (offers) to be sent that are accepted by the seller (offeree) returning a different standard form. When a dispute arises, the contract is based upon two forms with different terms. The CISG holds that if the differences are "material" then the second form is a counteroffer, not an acceptance, so there was no contract. Terms that are not "material" are a part of the contract unless specifically rejected by the offeror. In this sense, the CISG is less flexible than the UCC. Under the UCC, courts are more likely to fill in material terms than they are under the CISG.

Duties of the Parties The obligations that parties to a contract have under the CISG are very similar to those under the UCC. The seller must fulfill the obligation to deliver the goods with good title according to the terms specified, given reasonable commercial practices. If there is a problem, the buyer must notify the seller of defects "within as short a period as is practicable" after delivery. The seller may cure any defects in the delivered goods, so long as it is not costly to the buyer. If the goods are delivered properly, the buyer must take delivery and pay the price specified.

Remedies In the event of a breach of contract, parties are expected to behave in a reasonable manner and give the breaching party a notice of the alleged breach and an opportunity to cure the defect. In this sense, the CISG is like German commercial law, which requires a Nachfrist notice—a notice of the problem and a chance to perform properly—be given to the nonconforming party before suit for breach is filed. As under the common law and the UCC, if there is a failure to perform, there is an obligation to try to minimize the damages—make the best out of a bad situation so that the waste is minimized. If damages must be paid, they are usually the difference between the contract price and the value or cost incurred at the time of the breach.

RESOLVING INTERNATIONAL SALES DISPUTES: THE DOMINANCE OF ARBITRATION

There are very few cases in the courts ruling upon contract disputes that occur under the CISG because most commercial sales contracts specify arbitration as the required method of dispute resolution. The United Nations encourages the use of arbitration in commercial dealings through the *Convention on the Recognition and Enforcement of Foreign Arbitrable Awards*. If a country has adopted the Convention, as the United States has, then courts are bound to recognize and enforce arbitration decisions that have followed proper procedure unless it is in conflict with the law of the nation of one of the parties or has gone beyond the scope of the matter covered by arbitration. Hence, as with domestic contracts in the United States, the parties to a contract written under the CISG who mandate arbitration have little reason ever to be in court, as it is the duty of the arbitrators to resolve the dispute under the rules of the CISG. The *Quasem Group* case illustrates what happens when an unhappy party tries to go to court.

Quasem Group, Ltd. v. W.D. Mask Cotton Co.
United States District Court, W.D. Tennessee
967 F.Supp. 288 (1997)

CASE BACKGROUND *Quasem, a Bangladesh company, signed three contracts in 1991 and 1992 to buy a total of 26,000 bales of raw cotton from Mask, a cotton broker in Tennessee. The contracts stated:*

> *"If amicable settlement of quality difference is impossible, arbitration for quality to be governed by Liverpool Cotton Association, Ltd., Liverpool [England]. Any irreconcilable differences concerning contract terms, validity or alleged default to be referred to technical arbitration by Liverpool Cotton Association, Ltd., Liverpool."*

Liverpool Cotton Association (LCA) is an international association of cotton merchants, textile mills, and related businesses with members in fifty-eight countries. The LCA has trade rules to govern international commercial transactions in cotton and arbitration of disputes. The rules state that if a contract is made subject to LCA rules, then following its procedure for dispute resolution is "a condition precedent to the right of any party to such contract to commence legal proceedings against the other party" and that there is no right to litigation "except to enforce the award in any such arbitration."

Relations between Quasem and Mask fell apart, and in July, 1993, Quasem sued Mask in U.S. federal court for breach of contract, seeking to recover damages for Mask's shipping cotton alleged to be of inferior quality. Mask filed a motion to dismiss the suit, asserting that there was no subject matter jurisdiction. Quasem's only remedy under the contract was arbitration before the LCA. Quasem had failed to file a complaint with the LCA within the time required under its rules, so Quasem had lost its right to have the dispute arbitrated. [Under LCA rules, a party complaining about quality of a shipment must file a complaint and send cotton samples to the LCA within two months. Quasem did not do that.] The court dismissed the suit in 1994, ruling that "the contract contained an arbitration clause that was enforceable pursuant to the U.N. Convention on the Recognition and Enforcement of Foreign Arbitrable Awards" and that Quasem had to pursue its arbitration options.

In 1995, Quasem applied to the LCA for a time extension. The request was filed three years after the initial deadline for filing a complaint had passed. The LCA rejected the request, holding that there was no "unavoidable delay" that would have prevented Quasem from following LCA rules.

Quasem then again sued Mask in U.S. federal court for breach of contract and sought damages for specific performance.

CASE DECISION McCalla, District Judge.

* * *

Although the parties have not directly addressed the issue, this case presents a simple and straightforward question: What is the role of a court under the United Nations Convention on the Recognition and Enforcement of Foreign Arbitrable Awards ("Convention"), codified at 9 U.S.C. §§201–208 (1970), when a party seeks to enforce an arbitral award or where a party seeks to use the arbitral decision as a defense in an action brought by another party. A review of the Convention and codifying statute reveals that the role of the court is well defined.

Pursuant to 9 U.S.C. §207, a "court shall confirm the award unless it finds one of the grounds for refusal or deferral or recognition or enforcement of the award specified in the said Convention."

* * *

In this case, plaintiff makes two arguments against enforcement of arbitrator's decision. First plaintiff argues that no arbitration on the merits was undertaken and, therefore, arbitration failed to provide it with a forum for relief. Contrary to plaintiff's position, however, a decision not to hear a claim on the basis that the claim is time barred is, in itself, a decision of the arbitrator and, therefore, subject to the provisions of the Convention. If the Court were to accept plaintiff's argument, a claimant could avoid an arbitration agreement merely by waiting until the time for arbitration, under the relevant rules, expired. Because the rule argued by plaintiff would eviscerate the underlying purpose and rationale of the Convention, plaintiff's argument is unavailing.

Alternatively, plaintiff seeks to avoid enforcement and recognition of the LCA's decision on the grounds that the arbitration agreement is void or otherwise unenforceable.

* * *

Four questions [govern] the enforceability of arbitration clauses found in international commercial agreements:

1. Is there an agreement in writing to arbitrate the subject of the dispute?
2. Does the agreement provide for arbitration in the territory of a signatory country?
3. Does the agreement arise out of a legal relationship, whether contractual or not which is considered as commercial?
4. Is a party to the contract not an American citizen, or does the commercial relationship have some reasonable relation with one or more foreign states?

[If the court] answers these four questions affirmatively, it must enforce the arbitral agreement "unless it finds the agreement null and void, inoperative or incapable of being performed. Convention, Article II(3)." After considering each of the above factors, the Court [finds] that the arbitration agreement was enforceable. . . . In this case, the arbitrator found that plaintiff was barred by the applicable rules from pursuing its claims. Practically speaking, therefore, the arbitrator found in favor of defendant. Accordingly, defendant's motion to dismiss and/or for summary judgment is GRANTED, and this case is DISMISSED WITH PREJUDICE.

QUESTIONS FOR ANALYSIS

1. Why do most international sales contracts specify arbitration in the event of a dispute?
2. If a party to a contract misses the chance to go to arbitration, why should they not be allowed to go to court instead?

FULL CIRCLE

Centuries ago, when merchants could not rely upon public courts for resolution of disputes and commercial law was not well developed, the law merchant developed. It was a voluntary set of rules by which merchants across national boundaries could solve disputes under a common set of rules. It was based upon the way most business was done. Disputes were resolved by a process similar to arbitration—private dispute resolution.

Over many decades, nations adopted commercial law based upon business practices. Public courts were used to resolve some disputes. As international trade has grown, the basic rules of law under which most contracts are formed is much the same whether it is the law of a particular nation, such as the UCC, or the civil code of a nation such as France, or the CISG. The rules do not vary radically from country to country.

Increasingly, merchants have turned to private dispute resolution. As with contracts made in the United States, parties know that arbitration is quicker and cheaper than court litigation. In international dealings, parties worry that they may suffer discrimination, intentional or not, if they litigate disputes in the home courts of the other parties, so neutral arbitrators are again preferred. Courts around the world have come increasingly to enforce arbitration decisions, as in the *Quasem* case, so parties have confidence in the integrity of the international legal system.

Summary

- To make contract law more consistent with business practices, the Uniform Commercial Code was developed. Article 2 of the UCC governs contracts for the sale of goods. Goods are tangible things that are movable at the time of the identification of the contract. Real estate, fixtures attached permanently to real estate, services, stocks, bonds, bank accounts, patents, and copyrights are not goods under the UCC. Sales transactions involving those things are governed by the common law of contracts.

- Merchants involved in the sale of goods are often treated differently from non-merchants under the UCC. A higher standard of conduct is imposed on merchants than on nonmerchants. A person is a merchant if she deals, holds herself out as having special knowledge, or employs an agent, broker, or other intermediary who holds himself out as having special knowledge of the goods involved in the transaction. Merchants are required to conduct their activities in good faith like nonmerchants and must follow business practices common in the trade.

- The common law governs a transaction unless the UCC modifies or specifically changes the effect of the common law. Generally, when the UCC modifies the common law, the effect is usually to be less demanding than the common law. An acceptance under the UCC, for example, does not have to be unequivocal to form a contract. An indefinite offer can form the basis of a contract (even with open price, quantity, delivery, or payment terms) under the UCC but not under the common law.

- The basic obligation of the seller is to transfer and deliver the goods. The buyer is obligated to accept and pay for them. In performing their obligations, in contract performance and enforcement, the parties are required by the UCC to act in good faith.

- In delivering conforming goods to the buyer, the seller is concerned with the appropriate manner and timeliness of delivery, place of tender, and the quality of tender. The UCC instructs the courts to provide such terms according to the apparent intent of the parties or the trade custom.

- The common law's perfect tender rule requires that the seller's tender of delivery conform in detail to the terms of the contract. The UCC modifies the buyer's common-law right to reject the goods by providing the seller with the right to cure defects within the time frame of the contract.

- The UCC obligates the seller to warrant title to goods being sold. The seller warrants good title, the absence of any interests or liens on the goods, and that the goods are free of any patent, copyright, or trademark infringements.

- A seller may create an express warranty under the UCC by making a statement to the buyer about the goods or by providing the buyer with a description of the goods or a sample or model of the goods.

- The UCC provides an implied warranty of merchantability and an implied warranty of fitness for a particular purpose. To be merchantable, the good must conform to the contract description; be fit for the purposes for which it is intended; be of even kind, quality, and quantity; be adequately labeled; and conform to label descriptions. If a seller knows that a buyer has a particular purpose for purchasing a good and the buyer relies on the seller's skill or judgment in selecting a good, an implied warranty of fitness for a particular purpose may be created.

- The UCC extends to designated third parties any express warranty made by the seller to a buyer. To be consistent with other third-party beneficiary rules within a state, the UCC provides alternative rules.

- When a buyer or seller breaches a contract for the sale of goods, the UCC provides the nonbreaching party with remedies designed to place the nonbreaching party in the same position as if the contract had been performed according to its terms. The seller may recover for losses suffered due to buyer's failure to accept goods or to pay for goods. Buyer may recover the difference between what had to be paid to obtain substitute goods and the contract price. The seller and the buyer may seek incidental damages for recovery of costs resulting from the breach. The buyer is also allowed to recover consequential damages suffered, usually lost profits.

- The U.N. Convention on Contracts for the International Sale of Goods applies to contracts for commercial sale of goods by parties who have places of business in different countries that have ratified the CISG. Most major nations, including the United States, have ratified it. Such sales are covered by the CISG unless the parties specify that they want some other law to govern the contract.

- The CISG applies only to goods in commercial sales, that is, between merchants. Like the UCC, it does not require contracts to be formal writings, but gives priority to written terms in case of dispute. When terms are unclear, the courts are to look to the apparent intent of the parties and to usual business practices.

- In the event of a battle of the forms, under the CISG, when there are differences in material terms, no contract is formed; when changes are to minor terms, they may become incorporated into the contract unless objected to by a party.

- As with commercial contracts in the United States, most international commercial sale contracts include an arbitration clause. Many nations have adopted the Convention on the Recognition and Enforcement of Foreign Arbitrable Awards, so courts will uphold arbitration clauses and enforce arbitration results unless it conflicts with national policy or there was a serious problem with the arbitration process.

Issue

Will Y2K Be a Legal Catastrophe?

Between 1999 and early 2002, the extent of the Year 2000 problem will become known. Law firms have been gaining expertise in the problems of software and hardware that contain codes that cannot properly deal with 1999, 2000, 2001, or some other particular date. Among the legal problems that computer product vendors face is the possibility of breaches of implied or express warranties under the UCC. In this article, a lawyer who specializes in Y2K problems considers steps that managers can take to try to minimize potential legal problems.

Mr. Goldberg is with Cosgrove, Eisenberg & Kiley, P.C., a Boston law firm. Copyright © 1999 by Steven H. Goldberg. Reprinted by permission from www.2000legal.com.

Overview

The "Year 2000" problem refers to the inability of most computers to process date information later than December 31, 1999. Date codes in most programs are abbreviated to allow only two digits for the year, e.g., "97." Unless these programs are converted to handle the century date change, they will interpret the year "00," that is, 2000, as 1900. When that happens, some computers won't work at all and others will suffer critical calculation and other processing errors. Because of the unprecedented scope of the problem, long lead times of

YEAR 2000 COMPUTER FAILURES: MANAGING THE BUSINESS AND LEGAL RISKS

Steven H. Goldberg

several years are required to assess, correct and test automated systems to prevent computer failures and operational disruptions.

Although the problem is fundamentally a technical one, public and private enterprises should recognize the significant legal issues that will arise from Year 2000 failures and take appropriate measures now to protect themselves, their shareholders and their customers from liability exposure, financial losses and business interruptions. Indeed, directors and officers may have fiduciary duties to exercise due diligence to investigate and disclose potential Year 2000 problems. Avoiding foreseeable Year 2000 trouble spots also will help companies reduce their vulnerability to litigation and identify potential claims against non-compliant vendors.

The Technical Problem

A simple example of the Year 2000 problem is the calculation of someone's age, a vital piece of information for many business, government and professional computer applications. A person who was born in 1935 will turn 65 in 2000. But computers that cannot correctly process 21st century dates would subtract 1935 from 1900 and calculate the individual's age to be -35 (or possibly 35).

* * *

The problem is a serious one because computers use dates in many ways and for many purposes. Date information is critical to carrying out financial transactions, processing claims, establishing eligibility for various programs and services, and operating telecommunications, scheduling and process control systems. Possible consequences of Year 2000 failures include:

- Erroneous cancellation of customer accounts, orders and shipments of goods and supplies;
- Premature expiration of licenses, credit cards and drug prescriptions;
- Miscalculation (or non-payment) of employee compensation, pension and other fringe benefits, interest, and dividends;
- Inability to issue invoices, track accounts receivable and payable, execute stock and bond trades, and process tax, loan and lease payments;
- Malfunctioning of electronic data interchange systems, computerized assembly lines, power generating systems, waste treatment plants, and security and HVAC systems;

- Rejection of valid insurance claims and miscalculation of premiums; and
- Disruption of airline reservation systems, vehicle and equipment maintenance schedules, warehouse operations, and inventory control.

* * *

Responding Effectively to Year 2000 Business and Legal Risks

Widespread failures of computer systems around the world in all economic sectors are likely to give rise to significant business disruptions, financial losses and attendant legal exposure. Achieving internal Year 2000 compliance of one's own computers, although enormously difficult and expensive, is only half the challenge. In order to anticipate and respond to operational disruptions caused by *external* IT failures, organizations should undertake legal audits to identify outside business relationships that might be vulnerable to Year 2000 non-compliance. To do so, they must collect detailed information from those vendors and suppliers about their efforts to achieve compliance, and develop, implement and audit informed risk management strategies.

By undertaking such a comprehensive effort to prepare for Year 2000, organizations will be able to:

- Negotiate more secure contractual relationships and prepare contingency plans to insure that they can continue to meet their obligations to their customers;
- Incorporate Year 2000 information in due diligence reviews;
- Prepare for possible Year 2000-related litigation by and against the company; and
- Make legally-required disclosures of material Year 2000 contingencies.

A Year 2000 legal audit should include the following measures:

Contract Review and Negotiations. All contracts, insurance policies and procurements should be reviewed to evaluate the company's liability exposure and the legal responsibilities of third parties which could affect the company's ability to achieve Year 2000 compliance and conduct its business. The review should include representation, warranty, remedy, force majeure, and indemnification provisions in all contracts that are critical to the organization's mission, including both products and outsourced services such as data processing, facilities management, telecommunications, and distribution. New contracts should clearly assign responsibility for Year 2000 compliance and provide audit mechanisms to verify achievement of project milestones.

Requests for Compliance Information. Key suppliers and service providers should be contacted in writing for information about their ability to fulfill their responsibilities after 1999. This information is critical to identifying risky business dependencies and developing contingency plans. Detailed information about the scope of the problem, the use of qualified consultants, project schedules, and fallback options should be explored.

Required Disclosures. Accounting standards, auditing requirements, tax and securities laws, other regulatory requirements (e.g., banking, insurance, environmental), and financings, mergers and acquisitions may impose obligations on companies and institutions to exercise due diligence to investigate and disclose material information about potential adverse effects of internal or external Year 2000 failures.

Directors and Officers Liability. Board members and senior executives may face personal liability if they fail to exercise reasonable business judgment in connection with Year 2000 problems. Special care must be taken to act in accordance with fiduciary duties and comply with the requirements of indemnification provisions and D & O insurance policies.

Litigation Prevention and Control. The prospects of litigation by shareholders, customers, enforcement agencies, and private individuals arising from Year 2000 noncompliance are significant. SPR predicts that the costs and damage awards of Year 2000-related law suits "will probably far exceed the direct costs of repairing the problem itself. Appropriate steps should be taken to document the company's own compliance efforts, maintain the confidentiality of privileged communications and preserve claims against third parties whose failure to achieve Year 2000 compliance could interfere with the company's operations or expose it to losses or lawsuits. Insurance carriers should be notified of potential claims.

Conclusion

An ounce of prevention is the recommended strategy for mitigating the business and legal risks of Year 2000 computer failures. Companies that plan for external Year 2000 problems by working with their trading partners while there is still time to adjust contract terms and develop contingency plans will be in the best position to maintain operations and avoid or reduce liability exposure. Such enterprises may also secure an advantage in the marketplace against competitors that fail to do so.

ISSUE QUESTIONS

1. If it was believed at the time a computer product was produced that it would be obsolete and not used by 2000, should a warranty impose liability for possible losses due to Y2K problems when the product is still in use?
2. When novel legal issues arise, as will happen with Y2K problems, how should the courts resolve such matters—invent new rules or adapt old rules?

REVIEW AND DISCUSSION QUESTIONS

1. Define the following terms:

   sales contracts   perfect tender rule
   goods   warranty of title
   merchant   trade usage
   merchantability   statute of frauds

2. What is the advantage of the UCC compared to the common law of contracts? Are there disadvantages to the adoption of a statute such as the UCC?

CASE QUESTIONS

3. Cal-Cut had dealt with Idaho Pipe for years. In response to one of its ads, Idaho Pipe requested 30,000 feet of steel pipe from Cal-Cut. After phone conversations, Cal-Cut sent a written offer in August. Idaho Pipe accepted the offer by return mail, changed the delivery date from October 15 to December 15, and sent a check for $20,000 in partial payment, which Cal-Cut deposited. Cal-Cut returned confirmation of the order and did not change the October 15 delivery date, but wrote, "We will work it out" on the contract. Cal-Cut delivered 12,937 feet of pipe before October 5, which Idaho Pipe accepted. Then Cal-Cut refused to deliver any more pipe. The sale had become unprofitable, as the price of pipe had risen quickly. Was this deal enforced? Could Idaho Pipe recover any damages? [*Southern Idaho Pipe & Steel Co.* v. *Cal-Cut Pipe & Supply, Inc.*, 567 P.2d 1246 (Sup. Ct., Id., 1977)]

4. Polygram, a French company, makes records, tapes, and CDs. Defendant 32-03, a New York distributor, ordered goods from Polygram that were delivered in four shipments with written invoices. The invoices noted that payment was due in sixty days and that claims about problems with the goods must be made within three months after delivery. The companies had done business this way for years. 32-03's objections to the terms of sale arose for the first time in this incident. 32-03 refused to pay, claiming that there was no written contract in violation of the statute of frauds and that it was trade custom in the industry for distributors to be allowed to return any defective goods for credit. Polygram claims that the terms of the agreement were violated and sued for payment. Who was right? [*Polygram* v. *32-03 Enterprises*, 697 F.Supp. 132 (E.D.N.Y., 1988)]

5. Marquette agreed to provide all cement that Norcem would need for over two years. The quantity and sales price for the first two shipments were specified in the contract. The third shipment, according to the contract, was to be negotiated for a price "not to exceed $38 per short ton." At the time of the third shipment, Marquette told Norcem the price would be $38; Norcem responded that Marquette's insistence on the maximum price was not in good faith and refused to buy the cement. Marquette sued for breach of contract. Was Marquette right? [*Marquette Co.* v. *Norcem, Inc.*, 494 N.Y.S.2d 511 (Sup. Ct., App. Div., N.Y., 1985)]

6. In January, T.W. Oil purchased fuel oil at sea on the tanker *Khamsin.* After the purchase, T.W. Oil contracted to sell the oil to Consolidated Edison (ConEd). The contract called for delivery between January 24 and 30 and for the oil to have a sulfur content of 0.5 percent. During negotiations with ConEd, T.W. Oil learned that ConEd was authorized to use oils with sulfur contents up to 1.0 percent. The *Khamsin* arrived on time. However, the oil tested at 0.92 percent sulfur, 0.42 percent higher than specified in the contract. On February 14, ConEd rejected the shipment. T.W. Oil offered ConEd a reduced price. ConEd rejected the lower price offer. T.W. Oil offered to cure by providing a substitute due to arrive on February 28. ConEd rejected T.W. Oil's offer to cure. Was T.W. Oil's offer to cure properly rejected by ConEd? Was ConEd required to accept the substitute shipment tendered by T.W. Oil? [*T.W. Oil* v. *Consolidated Edison*, 443 N.E.2d 932 (Ct.App., N.Y., 1982)]

7. Community Television Services (CTS) contracted with Dresser Industries to design, construct, and install a 2,000-foot antenna tower in South Dakota for $385,000. The contract contained technical specifications warranting that the

tower would withstand winds of 120 mph. During negotiations, Dresser had given CTS a sales brochure that stated:

"Wind force creates the most critical loads to which a tower is normally subjected. When ice forms on the tower members, thereby increasing the surface area resisting the passage of wind, the load is increased. Properly designed towers will safely withstand the maximum wind velocities and ice loads to which they are likely to be subjected. Dresser . . . can make wind and ice load recommendations to you for your area based on U.S. Weather Bureau data. In the winter, loaded with ice and hammered repeatedly with gale force winds, these towers absorb some of the roughest punishment that towers take anywhere in the country . . . yet continue to give dependable, uninterrupted service."

The tower was built according to the contract's technical specifications. Six years later, the tower collapsed during an 80-mph blizzard. Is Dresser liable for breach of an express warranty? [*Community Television Services* v. *Dresser Ind.*, 586 F.2d 637 (8th Cir., 1978)]

8. Hartwig Farms bought seed potatoes from Pacific, which bought them from Tobiason. The seed potatoes were stated to be "blue tag certified," meaning they were certified by the North Dakota State Seed Department not to have more than one percent infection with a disease that ruins potatoes. Hartwig planted the seeds, but almost the entire crop turned out to be infected. Hartwig sued for damages from the loss of the crop. Tobiason defended, noting that when the seeds were shipped the invoice had a disclaimer: "Tobiason . . . gives no warranty, express or implied, as to description, variety, quality, or productiveness, and will not in any way be responsible for the crop. All claims must be reported immediately on receipt . . . or no claim will be allowed." Hartwig claimed that this was not a part of the contract, since nothing before the actual shipment of the seeds with the invoice said anything about a disclaimer. Is the disclaimer a part of the contract? [*Hartwig Farms* v. *Pacific Gamble Robinson* v. *Tobiason Potato*, 625 P.2d 171 (Ct. App., Wash., 1981)]

9. Caudle bought a house trailer from Sherrard. Caudle left the trailer with Sherrard for several days before he could transport it from Sherrard's property. Before Caudle returned, the trailer was stolen. Learning of the theft, Caudle stopped payment on his check. Sherrard sued Caudle on the contract of sale for the contract price. Who pays? That is, who bears the risk of loss? [*Caudle* v. *Sherrard Motor*, 525 S.W.2d 238 (Ct. Civ. App., Tex., 1975)]

10. Roth went to her hairstylist of seven years to have her hair bleached. The stylist proposed using a new product from Roux Laboratories. The stylist had used other Roux products with good results. However, the new product severely damaged Roth's hair, causing Roth embarrassment and distress until her hair grew back months later. The product's label stated that the product would not cause damage to hair. Roth sued the stylist and Roux, alleging negligence and breach of implied and express warranties. Did the product's performance breach a warranty? [*Roth* v. *Ray-Stel's Hair Stylists*, 470 N.E.2d 137 (App.Ct., Mass., 1984)]

11. ServBest Foods entered into a sales contract with Emessee. The contract called for Emessee to purchase 200,000 pounds of beef trimmings from ServBest at 52.5¢ per pound. ServBest delivered the warehouse receipts and the invoice for the beef trimmings to Emessee. The market price of beef trimmings then fell significantly, providing Emessee with the opportunity to buy the trimmings from another seller

at a lower price. Emessee returned the warehouse receipts and invoice to ServBest and canceled the contract. ServBest sold the trimmings for 20.25¢ per pound and sued Emessee for damages for breach of contract plus incidental damages. Should Emessee be required to pay damages in this case? [*ServBest Foods* v. *Emessee Ind.*, 403 N.E.2d 1 (App.Ct., Ill., 1980)]

12. In 1975, NDI contracted to manufacture 1,180 metric tons of ½-inch steel strand for Grand Pre-Stressed at a price of $675 per ton. The strand is used to reinforce concrete. NDI was to deliver the strand over a seven-month period, and Grand agreed to pay for each shipment. Grand accepted deliveries of 221.1 tons and still owed $57,960 for them when it repudiated the contract in May 1976. Of the 958.9 tons of strand that remained for delivery under the contract, NDI had already produced 317.9 tons and later sold them privately to other customers at prices averaging $608.47 per ton. At all times, NDI had sufficient capacity to produce 12,500 tons of strand annually at an average cost of $394.57 per ton. NDI sued Grand for breach of contract and won. Can you calculate the damages under the UCC? [*Nederlandse Draadindustrie NDI B.V.* v. *Grand Pre-Stressed Corp.*, 466 F.Supp. 846 (E.D.N.Y., 1979)]

13. "On August 20, 1983, Elmer and Martha Bosarge purchased from J&J Mobile Homes Sales in Pascagoula a furnished mobile home manufactured by North River Homes, an Alabama corporation. The Bosarges were extremely proud of their new home—described by a J&J salesman as the 'Cadillac of mobile homes.' This 'Cadillac,' which cost the Bosarges a whopping $23,900, turned out to be a jalopy. That is, upon moving into their new home, the Bosarges immediately discovered defect after defect after defect." After arguing with North River for a year, during which time only a few repairs were made, the Bosarges refused to make further monthly payments and sued North River for selling a mobile home of unmerchantable quality. North River countered that the Bosarges could not claim to reject the mobile home when they continued to live in it. Who was right? [*North River Homes* v. *Bosarge*, 594 So.2d 1153 (Sup. Ct., Miss., 1992)]

14. Anhui, a Chinese company, contracted to sell dyed yarn to Hart, an American company. The contract contained a clause requiring arbitration of disputes before the China Council for the Promotion of International Trade in Beijing. When a dispute arose and Hart refused to pay Anhui, it began arbitration proceedings. Hart did not respond but sued Anhui in federal court in the United States. Hart claimed the arbitration clause was not enforceable because arbitration in Beijing would be a hardship and, even if it were not, the dispute was over the validity of the contract itself, an issue of contract law, not a payment dispute. Since that was a legal matter, it could be litigated. What result in Federal court? [*Hart Enterprises Intl.* v. *Anhui Provincial Import & Export Corp.*, 888 F.Supp. 587 (S.D., NY, 1995)]

POLICY QUESTION

15. Consider the following two statements:

    This car has 10,000 miles on it, and we just mounted new radial tires on all four wheels.

    This is the best car for the money.

If made by a seller, does either statement create a warranty? Is there a difference?

ETHICS QUESTIONS

16. Joseph Steiner negotiated with representatives of Mobil Oil to operate a service station. During negotiations, Steiner made it clear that he would not operate the service station unless Mobil gave him a 1.4¢ per-gallon discount from the tank wagon price for ten years. However, Mobil's standard dealer contract provided that Mobil could revoke or modify the discount at any time. A Mobil representative sent Steiner a letter granting him a 1.4¢ discount for ten years. Shortly thereafter, Mobil gave Steiner a package of forms that described their agreement. Unknown to Steiner, one of the forms reduced the discount to 0.5¢ per gallon. Without looking at the agreements, Steiner signed the contract modification. What result?

17. Many U.S. retailers include in their contracts with suppliers, domestic and foreign, a requirement that the supplier agrees not to violate any local labor laws or the contract can be terminated. Yet the illegal use of child labor is common in many countries, especially in carpet making in Pakistan and in sewing operations in many countries. The retailers have been criticized as using the codes of conduct for publicity purposes, since enforcement is difficult and rare. Should such codes be used, and if so, how can they be enforced?

INTERNET ASSIGNMENT

Richard owned 170 shares of stock in Pecos Cantaloupe Company, Inc. ("Pecos"), which were reflected in a stock certificate dated August 1, 1977. In June 1978, Janie, then Richard's spouse, secured a loan from Ector Bank. As collateral, Janie delivered to Ector Bank the stock certificate representing Richard's 170 shares of stock, along with a hypothecation agreement and an irrevocable power of attorney for transfer of stock, both signed by Richard. Although he signed the hypothecation agreement, Richard did not realize that the agreement permitted Janie to use his 170 shares of stock as collateral. He apparently signed the hypothecation agreement in blank and did not read the document. In 1979, believing that his stock certificate for 170 shares was lost, Richard executed and tendered to Pecos a sworn affidavit affirming his belief. Pecos then issued a substitute stock certificate to Richard.

In early 1980, Permian Bank purchased Janie's note from Ector Bank for value. Later that year, Janie divorced Richard and promptly defaulted on the note. Permian sued Janie, and an agreed judgment was entered against her. According to the judgment, Permian's claims were to be satisfied in full upon transfer of the 170 shares of Pecos to Permian.

Permian then requested that Pecos register a transfer of the 170 shares. Pecos refused, arguing that it had issued a substitute stock certificate to Richard upon his representation that the original had been lost. Permian filed suit seeking an adjudication that it was the lawful owner of the 170 shares of stock and an injunction compelling its registration. Is Permian Bank the lawful owner of the stock? *See* UCC §8-301 et seq. (http://www.law.cornell.edu:80/ucc/ucc.table.html); *First United Financial Corporation* v. *Specialty Oil Company, Inc.*, United States Court of Appeals for the Fifth Circuit, No. 92-7379, November 2, 1993 (http://www.law.utexas.edu/us5th/us5th.html).

CHAPTER 12

Negotiable Instruments, Credit, and Bankruptcy

Money has been described as the lubrication that keeps the wheels of commerce spinning smoothly. No doubt, without money, transactions would be much more cumbersome—trading socks for CDs, books for pizzas, or toothpaste for gasoline is not realistic. Today only a small part of business is done on a "cash money" basis. We tend to rely on pieces of paper that create a claim to money now or in the future.

Global business would not be practicable without the use of *negotiable instruments* that allow the orderly creation and transfer of rights to the payment of money. Checks—pieces of paper (or electronic entries) that evidence a claim on money—are one of the most commonly used negotiable instruments; the Federal Reserve System processes about 70 billion checks a year.

Credit and its opposite, debt, are contractual relationships. Many such contracts are common-law contracts, but some fall under the UCC. Real property, such as an office building, is usually purchased by using debt. Most companies rely on debt to get operations going or to expand. When in business, most firms extend credit to their customers. Sometimes the promises to pay are negotiable instruments that can be traded, as happens to most mortgages on property.

The down side is that each year well over one million individuals and about 100,000 businesses file for bankruptcy. These are debtors with financial problems that overwhelm them. Their creditors—other individuals and businesses—share the pain by being forced to absorb more than $20 billion a year in unpaid debt.

Just as managing personal finances is important, balancing the cost of carrying debt and minimizing the losses from bad credit is critical. Most businesses operate on thin profit margins, so decisions about borrowing and issuing credit are important to survival. This chapter considers the legal aspects of debt obligations and the financial instruments often used to evidence the granting of credit; it ends with a look at the major parts of the federal bankruptcy code.

Negotiable Instruments

Like much law in the United States, the law of negotiable instruments had its origin in England. Five hundred years ago, the right to payment was a contract right; it could not be sold to another. This inhibited trade because of the difficulty it created for traders who worked on credit. Traders had to wait until they were paid by the buyer/debtor before they would have enough cash to acquire additional goods to sell.

To alleviate this problem, laws developed that allowed traders to *assign* the promise to pay to a third party. Typically, a trader would "sell" to a third party, at a discount, his right to the payment. The trader could then buy more goods without waiting for the debtor to pay. The third party made her profit by collecting the amount owed from the debtor. However, in taking the *assignment*, the third party took on any problems the trader may have had with the debtor. For example, if the debtor refused to pay because the goods were different than ordered, the third party was required to defend the shipment in the same way as if she were the trader. Thus, although the law provided the trader with another means of payment, at times it was difficult to find third parties willing to accept the assignment, because they feared such a dispute.

By the sixteenth century, the law recognized this weakness in assignments of promises to pay and moved to free third parties of responsibility for problems between the seller and the buyer/debtor through the use of negotiable instruments. In this way, the contractual promises to pay became much more readily and dependably tradable. In essence, negotiable instruments became another "good" that could be bought and sold in the marketplace. Over the years, the law of negotiable instruments became even more responsive to the needs of business, and they are now a part of the commercial law of every state in the United States through Article 3 of the UCC.

THE FUNCTIONS OF NEGOTIABLE INSTRUMENTS

The negotiable instrument began as a written promise or order to pay a certain sum of money. It functioned as a substitute for cash. Few wholesale or retail businesses today require cash in payment for customer purchases. Because the legal environment recognizes their validity, negotiable instruments such as checks are readily accepted as a substitute for cash by businesses for the payment of goods and services.

Negotiable instruments also provide a way for credit to be extended to debtors. Suppose Lynex wants to purchase new computers for its management information systems department but needs to borrow money to finance the purchase. The company may borrow the money from a financial institution by signing a negotiable instrument called a promissory note. In that note, Lynex promises to repay the money it borrows to make the purchase.

TYPES OF NEGOTIABLE INSTRUMENTS

UCC §3-104 identifies four types of negotiable instruments: drafts, checks, notes, and certificates of deposit. These instruments can be separated into two general categories: orders to pay and promises to pay. Orders to pay, which include drafts and checks, are three-party instruments used instead of cash and as credit devices. Promises to pay, which include notes and certificates of deposit, are two-party instruments used as credit devices.

Orders to Pay: Drafts

A *draft*, or bill of exchange, is an unconditional written order to pay that involves three parties in distinct capacities. It is created by one party (called the *drawer*) who orders another party (the *drawee*) to pay a certain sum of money to a third party (the *payee*). In most cases, the draft represents a debt the drawee owes to the payee. Generally speaking, a draft may be either a *time draft* or a *sight draft*. A time draft calls for a payment at a specified time in the future—for example, "60 days from date" of the draft. A common form of time draft is known as a *trade acceptance agreement*, an example of which is provided in Exhibit 12.1. A sight draft is payable upon presentation by the seller to the buyer of the goods. The buyer must pay the amount of the draft before receiving the goods.

A *sales draft*, which is a form of the trade acceptance agreement, is a draft used when a commercial transaction involves the sale of goods. It may be either a time or a sight draft, depending on the time specified for payment. The draft is drawn by the seller (the drawer). The purchaser of the goods accepts the responsibility of paying for the goods and becomes the drawee by signing and accepting the obligation to pay the payee—which in many cases is the seller/drawer. Normally, the draft states that payment is to be made within a specified time frame, such as "90 days after the date of the draft." In this way the instrument allows the buyer/drawee to use the draft as a credit device and delay payment to the seller/drawer for the

EXHIBIT 12.1

Sample Trade Acceptance Document

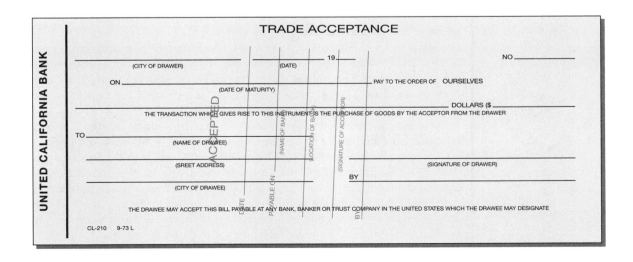

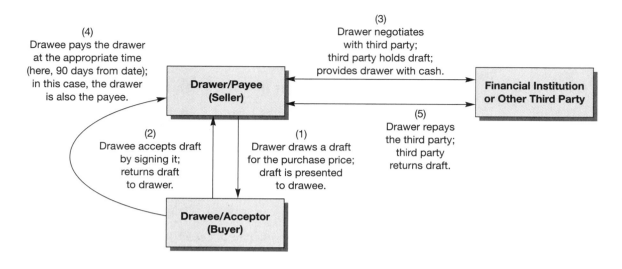

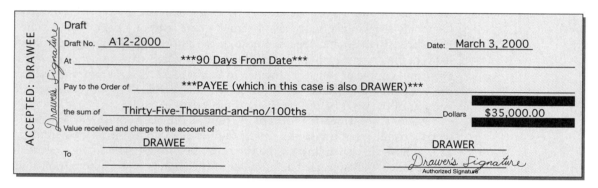

*Sales Draft
and Procedure*

period mentioned (here, 90 days). The seller/drawer may also use the document as a credit device. For instance, the seller may use the draft as collateral on a loan with third parties, since third parties have proof that the seller will be paid "90 days after the date of the draft." Exhibit 12.2 illustrates this process. Note that in the figure the seller/drawer is also the payee.

Orders to Pay: Checks

According to UCC §3-104(2), a *check* is a "draft drawn on a bank and payable on demand." The check is the most commonly used form of draft. However, unlike a draft—which may be payable at a later date and have a bank, an individual, or a corporation as a drawee—the check must be paid "on demand" and must have a bank as its drawee.

A *cashier's check* is a particular form of check in which the bank is both the drawer and the drawee. The customer gives money to the bank and designates a payee. The bank then writes a check on itself as drawee, with the check payable on demand to that payee. Cashier's checks are frequently used in transactions where the seller demands guaranteed payment. A common example is the purchase of real estate where the owner/seller of the property requires that a guarantee of payment occur when title to the property is to pass to the buyer. To meet the owner/seller's payment requirement, a buyer submits to the owner/seller a cashier's check.

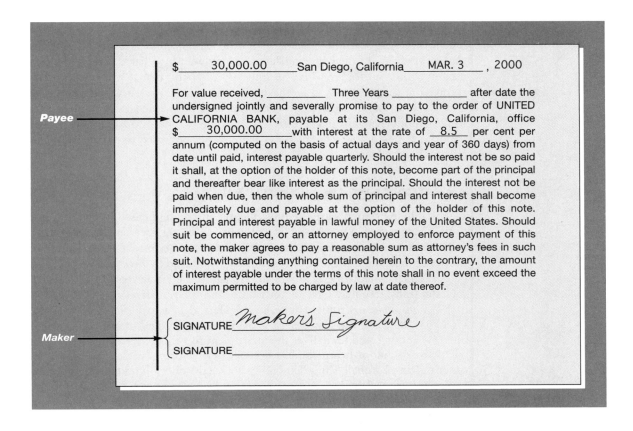

$_____30,000.00_____ San Diego, California ___MAR. 3___ , 2000

For value received, _____ Three Years _____ after date the undersigned jointly and severally promise to pay to the order of UNITED CALIFORNIA BANK, payable at its San Diego, California, office $_____30,000.00_____ with interest at the rate of _8.5_ per cent per annum (computed on the basis of actual days and year of 360 days) from date until paid, interest payable quarterly. Should the interest not be so paid it shall, at the option of the holder of this note, become part of the principal and thereafter bear like interest as the principal. Should the interest not be paid when due, then the whole sum of principal and interest shall become immediately due and payable at the option of the holder of this note. Principal and interest payable in lawful money of the United States. Should suit be commenced, or an attorney employed to enforce payment of this note, the maker agrees to pay a reasonable sum as attorney's fees in such suit. Notwithstanding anything contained herein to the contrary, the amount of interest payable under the terms of this note shall in no event exceed the maximum permitted to be charged by law at date thereof.

Payee

Maker

SIGNATURE *Maker's Signature*

SIGNATURE_____

EXHIBIT 12.3

A Sample Note

Because the check is drawn by the bank ordering itself to pay, the parties can be secure that the bank will honor the check when proper presentment is made.

Promises to Pay: Notes

The third classification of commercial paper is *notes*. A note is a promise (not an order) by one party (called the *maker*) to pay a certain sum of money to another party (the *payee*). Usually called *promissory notes*, these instruments involve two parties—the maker and the payee—rather than the three parties (a drawer, a drawee, and a payee) required for a draft or check. An example of a simple promissory note is provided in Exhibit 12.3.

Notes can have different names and forms, depending upon the business transactions in which they are used. Generally, the notes are still promissory notes—a promise by one person to pay money to another. For example, when personal property is used as collateral to back up a loan, the note created is called a *collateral note*. The party seeking the loan (the maker) promises to pay the party giving the loan (the payee) according to the loan agreement. If the loan repayment is not made, the payee has certain rights to the personal property to help repay the loan. When real estate is used in this way as collateral to secure the loan, the note is often called a *real estate mortgage note*. When the maker promises to repay the note in specified installments, the note is called an *installment note*. A *balloon note* is a note also providing for installment payments but with a required final payment more than double that of the installment payments, or for one final payment of all principal.

Promises to Pay: Certificates of Deposit

The fourth type of commercial paper is called a *certificate of deposit*. The UCC states that a certificate of deposit is an "acknowledgment by a bank" that it has received money from a customer with a promise by the bank that it will repay the money received at a date specified in the instrument or, in some instances, on demand. The bank as *maker* creates the certificate and acknowledges receipt of the customer's money, promising to repay the customer as *payee*. Most large certificates of deposit are negotiable, which allows them to be sold, used to pay debts, or used as collateral for a loan.

THE CONCEPT OF NEGOTIABILITY

Negotiable instruments are the most flexible instruments used in business transactions. Once issued, a negotiable instrument can be transferred to another party. If the instrument is *assigned*, the assignee has the same contract rights and responsibilities as the assignor. If the instrument is transferred by *negotiation*, the transferee takes the instrument free of any of the transferor's contract responsibilities. In this way, the transferee may have better rights than the transferor.

A negotiable instrument may be transferred in two basic ways according to UCC §3-202(1). If the instrument is made "to the order" of the payee, the payee must (1) endorse and (2) deliver the instrument to a third party. Endorsement without delivery cannot bring about a transfer. Therefore, if a check is made "To the order of John Kimball," and Kimball endorses the check but keeps it, there has not been a transfer of the instrument.

If an instrument is made "to bearer," the party in possession is required only to deliver the instrument to transfer it. Note that *bearer instruments* can be created in a number of ways. For example, the maker (drawer) may create a bearer instrument by stating: "to bearer," "to the order of bearer," "payable to bearer," "to cash," or "pay to the order of cash." Bearer instruments are, of course, more risky, since mere delivery creates a negotiation or transfer. Suppose a buyer of an automobile pays the seller by check. The check is made out "To the order of cash." Later, the seller loses the check. The check is found by Sam Jones, who uses it to purchase goods from April Smith Appliances. The check has been negotiated, since delivery is sufficient for the transfer of a bearer instrument.

GENERAL REQUIREMENTS FOR NEGOTIABLE INSTRUMENTS

To be negotiable, a commercial instrument must meet the general requirements of a negotiable instrument as provided by the UCC. Although commercial paper may be *negotiable* or *nonnegotiable*, only negotiable instruments fall within the scope of the UCC. A dispute could be resolved differently, depending on whether the instrument is categorized as negotiable or nonnegotiable under the UCC. If the instrument is determined to be nonnegotiable, the common law of contracts will apply. The assignee will be subject to any of the assignor's contract responsibilities under the instrument. If the commercial instrument is found to be negotiable, the UCC governs the resolution of the dispute.

The UCC Requirements for Negotiability

Whether an instrument is negotiable involves an examination of the instrument's form and its contents. According to UCC §3-104, a negotiable instrument falling within its scope of coverage must meet the following requirements:

1. It must be written.
2. It must be an unconditional order or promise to pay.
3. It must be signed by the maker or drawer.
4. It must be payable on demand or at a specified time.
5. It must be made out "to order" or "to bearer."
6. It must state a certain sum of money.

The UCC requires commercial instruments to be in writing for practical reasons. Oral promises would be nearly impossible to transfer to third parties. Under UCC §3-105, the writing must be signed and unconditional so that its terms of payment are easily determined and not subject to the occurrence of another event or agreement. It must contain a clear statement of an order or promise to pay and not merely be an acknowledgment of a debt. To allow its market value to be readily determined, UCC §3-106 requires that it must state a specific sum of money. If the instrument stated that payment was to be made in goods, for example, it would be too difficult for third parties to determine the market value of the instrument. The UCC also requires that the instrument be payable on demand or at a definite time. That is, the instrument must make it clear to the parties when payment is to be made and received. Finally, the instrument must be "payable to order" (called *order paper*, under UCC §3-110) or "to bearer" (called *bearer paper*, under UCC §3-111) to ensure that it is freely transferable. With this language (or its equivalent), the parties acknowledge that a third party who currently may be unknown may become the owner of the instrument.

Requirements for Holders in Due Course
If the instrument is negotiable under the UCC, it may be freely traded in the market without concern for existing contract responsibilities—if the instrument is in the possession of a holder in due course. The person in possession of a negotiable instrument may be either a *holder in due course* or an *ordinary holder*. The ordinary holder has the same contract responsibilities as an assignee under nonnegotiable instrument. UCC §3-302 states that to be a holder in due course, the transferee must

1. Give value for the negotiable instrument
2. Take the instrument without knowledge that it is overdue or otherwise defective
3. Take the instrument in good faith

Thus, a transferee may be defined as an ordinary holder who transforms her position to that of a holder in due course upon meeting these three requirements of the UCC. It is important to note that the courts will not allow the drawer or maker to assert any reasons for not paying the instrument once it is in the possession of a holder in due course. This is the case even when a hardship may be imposed.

Suppose Pamela Lee is negotiating with Tommy Lee to buy the rights to a J-Right Car Wash distributorship. Pamela Lee agrees to pay $50,000 by cashier's check to Tommy Lee for the distributorship. After sending the check, Pamela Lee is informed that Tommy Lee is going bankrupt. She then tries to stop payment on the check. However, Tommy Lee has already transferred the check to a third party, who meets the UCC's requirements for a holder in due course. Tommy Lee declares bankruptcy, so J-Right is probably worthless. The bank pays the third party upon proper presentation of the check. The court will find that the third party is a holder in due course and, despite the fact that Tommy Lee defrauded Pamela Lee, will not require the third party to repay Pamela Lee. To maintain the business community's confidence in negotiable instruments as a substitute for cash, the court will find for the third party.

Credit

Not all promises to pay are negotiable instruments. Other payment arrangements may have to be made. Whether a person or a business, a *creditor* is one who lends money to or allows goods or services to be purchased on credit by another party, the *debtor*. Businesses have credit policies that instruct employees about the factors to take into account in deciding whether credit should be granted and the terms that will be attached to the credit. Credit terms include when the bill is to be paid, such as in thirty days for materials or over thirty years for land. Credit terms must specify the interest rate, if any, that applies to the sum owed, the *principal* of the debt, and payment dates. As discussed following, creditors want evidence of debt, such as a signed loan agreement, and may attach terms to debt that increase the chance the debt will be repaid.

While large corporations raise much of their funding by *equity financing*, that is, the sale of stock in the company, which we discuss in Chapter 20 on securities regulation, smaller businesses tend to rely on *debt financing*, which usually means borrowing money evidenced by a contract. The debt incurred by business includes long-term debt (such as financing of a building) and short-term debt (for materials and inventory). Often, creditors will want to see debt backed by something more solid than a promise to repay the money plus interest, so discussion follows some of the devices used to strengthen the position of the parties to debt.

CREDIT POLICY

Some businesses, such as banks, are in the credit business. Other businesses give credit as a part of operations, whether the business provides accounting services or sells bricks. Since many businesses cannot demand cash at the time of the sale of their services or products, they have credit policies for establishing credit standards and terms as well as a collection policy. Credit policy focuses on such characteristics as the following:

EXHIBIT 12.4

Sources of Credit Information

Customer Financial Statements. It is normal practice to require a credit applicant to supply financial information. Individuals normally will be asked to provide financial statements, whereas business applicants may also be asked to provide audited balance sheets and income statements.

Banks. Banks may provide credit information about a customer. Credit departments of banks often share information about loan payment histories and related credit information about their customers.

Credit Reporting Agencies. Credit reporting agencies such as Dun & Bradstreet specialize in providing credit reports and credit ratings on companies. Credit histories of individuals can be purchased from reporting agencies such as TRW, Trans Union, and Equitax.

Trade Associations. A growing number of trade associations provide information about the credit experience of its members. The typical information provided deals with the credit obtained from suppliers and lists the amount of credit and the repayment history.

1. Capacity (the debtor's ability to pay)
2. Capital (the debtor's financial condition)
3. Character (the debtor's reputation)
4. Collateral (the debtor's assets to secure debt)
5. Conditions (the economic situation affecting debtor's business)

Since few lenders know all there is to know about a party seeking debt, sources are available to provide information about a potential borrower (see Exhibit 12.4). Most creditors use credit reporting agencies that sell reports about individuals and companies. Some consumers' rights with respect to credit reports are specified by the Fair Credit Reporting Act (discussed in Chapter 18). For our discussion here, which focuses on business debt, an important point is that credit reports are not always accurate. Mistakes are made, and information is difficult to collect. Reputations can suffer because of incorrect business and credit information. As the *Dun & Bradstreet* case indicates, it is possible for firms that have suffered reputational injuries to recover damages. However proof of damages in practice is not simple, so firms should be vigilant about the accuracy of their credit information.

Dun & Bradstreet, Inc. v. Greenmoss Builders, Inc.

United States Supreme Court
472 U.S. 749, 105 S.Ct. 2939 (1985)

CASE BACKGROUND *Dun & Bradstreet (D&B), a credit reporting agency, sold confidential reports to five business subscribers about the financial status of Greenmoss Builders (GB). The reports incorrectly stated that GB had filed for bankruptcy. Learning of the report from its bank, GB told D&B that the information was incorrect and asked who had been given the information. D&B would not reveal the names of the subscribers who had the information but issued a correction notice that GB was not bankrupt and that it "continued in business as usual." GB again demanded the names of the recipients of the information and was refused.*

GB sued D&B for defamation in Vermont state court, claiming that the false report had injured its reputation. At trial, it was shown that the mistake was made by a seventeen-year-old high school student working at D&B who mistakenly thought that the bankruptcy of a former employee of GB meant that GB was bankrupt. The report was not checked by anyone at D&B before the information was reported. The jury awarded GB $50,000 compensatory damages and $300,000 punitive damages. The trial judge overturned the jury verdict, ruling that D&B was protected by the First Amendment. The Vermont supreme court reversed, reinstating the jury verdict. D&B appealed. The Supreme Court accepted the case to clarify the law regarding liability for defamatory statements.

CASE DECISION Powell, Justice.

* * *

[S]peech on matters of purely private concern is of less First Amendment concern. . . . In such a case, "[t]here is no threat to the free and robust debate of public issues; there is no potential interference with a meaningful dialogue of ideas. . . ."

While such speech is not totally unprotected by the First Amendment, its protections are less stringent.

* * *

The only remaining issue is whether petitioner's credit report involved a matter of public concern. In a related context, we have held that "[w]hether . . . speech addresses a matter of public concern must be determined by [the expression's] content, form, and context . . . as revealed by the whole record." These factors indicate that petitioner's credit report concerns no public issue. It was speech solely in the individual interest of the speaker and its specific business audience. This particular interest warrants no special protection when—as in this case—the speech is wholly false and clearly damaging to the victim's business reputation. Moreover, since the credit report was made available to only five subscribers, who, under the terms of the subscription agreement, could not disseminate it further, it cannot be said that the report involves any "strong interest in the free flow of commercial information." There is simply no credible argument that this type of credit reporting requires special protection to ensure that "debate on public issues [will] be uninhibited, robust, and wide-open."

In addition, the speech here . . . is solely motivated by the desire for profit, which, we have noted, is a force less likely to be deterred than others. Arguably, the reporting here was also more objectively verifiable than speech deserving of greater protection. In any case, the market provides a powerful incentive to a credit reporting agency to be accurate, since false credit reporting is of no use to creditors. Thus, any incremental "chilling" effect of libel suits would be of decreased significance.

We conclude that permitting recovery of presumed and punitive damages in defamation cases absent a showing of "actual malice" does not violate the First Amendment when the defamatory statements do not involve matters of public concern. Accordingly, we affirm the judgment of the Vermont Supreme Court.

QUESTIONS FOR ANALYSIS

1. In practice, few suits brought against credit reporters such as D&B by companies that had incorrect reports issued about them are successful even when false information was reported. Why would that be?
2. Many states require that for there to be damages, false information must have been intentionally reported. Is this a sensible rule, or should damages be had anytime false information is reported?

Credit Accounts

When a company gives credit to its customers, it usually offers credit terms according to the size of the account and the importance of the customer to the company. Many accounts do not charge interest if the debt is paid within a certain time. Exhibit 12.5 lists the basic types of credit accounts offered by many companies.

In most cases, credit terms are determined by competitive conditions or industry standards. For credit under an *open account,* for example, the terms define the credit period available to the customer and any discounts offered for early payment. A typical industry standard is "net 60 days" from the date of invoice with a discount of 2 percent if paid within ten days of invoice. Consumer credit accounts—installment and revolving accounts—state the interest rate to be paid and the timing of the payments.

Collections Policy

Most bills are paid on time, making collections a routine task. However, a collections policy is needed for credit customers that fail to make timely payments. This usually begins with a follow-up letter to the initial invoice stating that the account

---

EXHIBIT 12.5

Common Types of Credit Accounts

Open Account. The most common form of credit. Goods and services are sold on an invoice that provides evidence of the transaction. Full payment is expected within a fixed time period.

Installment Account. Generally used by consumers for the purchase of durable goods such as automobiles and computers. Debtors repay through regular (generally monthly) payments.

Revolving Account. Similar to the installment account except that the debtor makes a minimum monthly payment, which is generally a fraction of the outstanding balance. More debt can be added to the account over time.

The Check Is in the (Foreign) Mail

 Your widget company, always looking for new markets, gets a large order for widgets from a company in Kabul, Afghanistan. Odds are the company cannot pay you until after it sells the goods. What if it defaults? Are you going to take it to court in Kabul?

How long it takes a business to pay for goods or services often depends on the state of the economy. When times are good, bills get paid faster. An electric motor company, Baldor, in Fort Smith, Arkansas, was doing well in Mexico until the economy took a nosedive. The Mexican sellers' market dried up, so the sellers were not getting the cash needed to pay Baldor. To compound problems, the peso fell in value. It took a year of effort, but most accounts were put back into business. Working with good customers to get their business going again paid off.

Payment also depends on where you are doing business and what the traditional practices are in various countries. For example, a European business survey by the accounting firm Grant Thornton showed that the average length of time for payment in the Netherlands was forty-seven days; in Italy it was almost twice as long, ninety days. The longer the time, the higher the costs of carrying the accounts.

is past due. A telephone call or a second letter may then follow. Depending on the business, letters may be followed by a personal visit.

At times, additional action is necessary to protect the creditor's rights. The alternatives depend on whether the business is an unsecured or a secured creditor. In most transactions, the business is an *unsecured (general) creditor:* it holds little more than the customer's promise to pay. If the customer proves to be *insolvent*— that is, unable to pay—the business receives nothing. If the customer simply will not pay, costly legal actions will have to be considered. Next we consider ways to make more formal credit agreements.

Credit with Security

In contrast to being an unsecured creditor, a business is a *secured creditor* when it has the ability to take the nonpaying customer's property to satisfy the debt. The law provides two avenues through which the creditor can obtain the customer's property (referred to as *security* or *collateral*):

1. By agreement with the debtor
2. By operation of law, and without an agreement between the lender and the borrower

BY AGREEMENT

The nature of the credit agreement depends upon whether the debtor's property is *real property* (real estate and other immovable property) or *personal property* (movable property or goods such as vehicles and supplies). The distinction between real and personal property is important for several reasons. The sale of goods is governed by the Uniform Commercial Code (discussed in Chapter 11). The sale of personal property can take place with relatively little or no formal documentation.

JURIS prudence?

So, Uh, Do We Write This Off as a Bad Loan?

Clancy and Ken Smith, newly married, bought a car. Since their credit was limited, Clancy's father co-signed the car loan from Trustmark Bank in Laurel, Mississippi. The couple fell behind on the loan, and the bank sent a tow truck to repossess the car. Clancy's parents made the needed payments to cover the loan to get the car back.

After five years, the loan was paid. But then the Smiths received a bill for $9,500. The bank had bought car insurance for them—at three times the normal price—when they let their insurance lapse in violation of the terms of the loan.

The Smiths and Clancy's father sued the bank. The jury awarded the Smiths and Clancy's father $19 million each. "We wanted to send a message to the insurance companies and financial institutions to straighten their act up," the jury foreman said.

Source: *The Wall Street Journal*

On the other hand, real property is governed by contract and property law and requires clear documentation before a sale can be finalized. The agreement providing security in real property is called a *mortgage* and is examined later.

Suretyship

Raising funds (working capital) to operate and to expand can be critical. Small businesses frequently are required to provide a *guaranty* or *suretyship* for major debts. In addition, if a business has a poor credit history, it may be required to provide a guaranty or suretyship for virtually any borrowing it would like to do.

For most small businesses, such a guaranty may be a pledge of personal assets by the owners. In addition, a third party may provide the guaranty or suretyship for a fee. In either case, a promise is made to pay a debt of a business in the event the business does not pay. In this way, a suretyship or guaranty is created, and the credit of the party providing it becomes the security for the debt owned.

Surety Defined A contract for *suretyship* is a promise by a third party (the *surety*) to be responsible for the borrower's payment (or *performance*) obligations to a creditor. The borrower or debtor is referred to as the *principal*. In addition to being a party providing a suretyship for a fee (or out of kindness), the surety could be an owner or shareholder in the business. A suretyship can be created only by an express contract between the surety and the creditor and, as such, is governed by the principles of contract law. The surety is obligated to pay the creditor until the principal has paid the debt (or provided the performance) to the creditor. A common form of suretyship is the cosignature on a bank loan.

A *guarantor* provides a guarantee of payment to another and therefore is the same as surety. That is, to guarantee is to assume the obligation of a surety. In some states, a distinction is drawn between a guaranty and a surety to the extent that a surety is primarily liable after the debtor, whereas the guarantor is secondarily liable. Generally, one contract binds both the surety and the borrower, and the creditor is not obligated to exhaust legal remedies before demanding payment by the surety. In states drawing a distinction between surety and guarantor, the guarantor can be obligated to pay only after the creditor has exhausted legal remedies against the borrower and any surety.

Defenses of Sureties Since suretyship is governed by contract law, the contract defenses available to the principal also are available to the surety. Depending upon whether the suretyship governs the borrower's performance or payment obligations, contract defenses available include impossibility, illegality, duress, and fraud—but not bankruptcy (because the surety is providing financial protection to the creditor for just such an event). More commonly, a surety will raise the defense that it is released when the creditor releases the borrower without its consent. Similarly, the surety will be released if material changes are made to the original contract between the creditor and the debtor without its consent.

When in a bind, small-business owners might take extraordinary financial risks, particularly when they believe in the company's product. When creditors push the business for payment and the future of the firm is in jeopardy, the owners may use personal assets to meet the demands of the creditors. To preserve the rights and interests of the business and the owners, care should be taken in the use of such personal assets. In the *Travis Pruitt* case, rather than enter into a surety agreement, the president of a company issued an unconditional promissory note and lost his right to all defenses available to a surety.

Travis Pruitt & Associates v. Smith
Court of Appeals of Georgia
192 Ga.App. 496, 385 S.E.2d 132 (1989)

CASE BACKGROUND *Roswell Properties, Inc., hired Travis Pruitt & Associates to do engineering and land-surveying work on a residential subdivision planned by Roswell. Smith was the president of Roswell. When Pruitt had completed about 75 percent of the work, it billed Roswell for work completed but received only a token sum. After sending several invoices, Pruitt stopped work. Smith proposed that he personally sign a note for $26,000. Pruitt insisted on a ninety-day unconditional promissory note for the full amount, plus a written agreement governing future work and payments. These documents were executed by Pruitt and Smith, but ninety days later, the promissory note went into default.*

Pruitt sued on the promissory note. In his counterclaim, Smith alleged negligent performance, breach of contract, and fraudulent inducement to sign the note by promising to complete the final engineering work while having no intent to fulfill the promise. The trial court granted Pruitt's motion for summary judgment against Smith. Smith appealed.

CASE DECISION Deen, Presiding Judge.

* * *

[T]he principal sum of the note represented an obligation that had already accrued. Pruitt's agreement to continue working and forbearance to sue on the overdue account would be sufficient consideration to Smith and his company. It appears from the record that Pruitt agreed to continue with the work contracted for, presumably to completion, the only condition being that his invoices for further work be paid in a timely manner, as they were rendered. This is a different matter altogether from the promissory note, which was a simple promise to pay an existing obligation; any "conditions" imposed by Pruitt referred to future work only, and were embodied in an agreement contemporaneous with but distinct from the promissory note. Moreover, Smith's and Roswell's contentions regarding alleged extra charges over and above the original contract price provide no defense, since all such defenses to the indebtedness were extinguished by the execution of the promissory note for a principal sum which was the total of the separate invoices. We find no failure of consideration and no indicia of fraud as regards Pruitt's relationship with either Smith or Roswell.

The contract underlying the action below was, of course, between Roswell and Pruitt; Smith was not a party but signed the contract only in his capacity as president of Roswell. Smith therefore actually has no standing as an individual to bring claims of negligent performance or breach of contract; and any claim of this sort should have been dismissed in the trial court.

* * *

Judgment affirmed.

QUESTIONS FOR ANALYSIS

1. What difference would it have made if Smith had signed as a surety on the obligation rather than sign an unconditional promissory note?
2. Assuming Smith does not pay the $26,000, what does Pruitt do next?

Surety's Rights against the Principal In the event the principal (borrower) does not meet its payment obligations to the creditor and the surety has to satisfy the debt, the principal is obligated to repay the surety. If the borrower could pay the creditor but refuses to do so, the surety is entitled to *exoneration*, a court order requiring the principal to perform. In addition, the surety is entitled to be *subrogated* to the rights of the creditor against the debtor. This generally occurs when the creditor is satisfied but part of that satisfaction came from the surety. In seeking reimbursement from the principal, the surety may assert any rights the creditor could have asserted against the principal had it not paid the creditor in the absence of the surety, including taking any security interests the creditor obtained from the borrower.

Secured Transactions

The law governing the financing of commercial sales of goods is *Article 9* of the UCC. When a good (not real estate) is sold to a customer (either a person or a business), the UCC provides that the product itself may secure the consumer's obligation to pay. Called a *secured transaction*, it occurs when a buyer wants a good and does not pay cash or have sufficient credit standing to obtain the good on open credit, which would be an unsecured debt. By meeting the requirements of the UCC, the seller obtains a *security interest* in the goods sold to the customer to secure payment of all or part of the sales price.

To make the security interest enforceable, the business must create the interest (or legal right) and make sure that the interest is *attached* and *perfected*. According to the UCC, for a security interest to attach, the security agreement must be signed by the customer, the seller must have provided value, and the customer must have legal, transferrable rights in the collateral. At this point, if the customer is unable to pay, the business has rights against the customer that are superior to unsecured creditors but not necessarily superior to other secured creditors and certain other creditors.

To establish superior rights—that is, to *perfect* the security interest—the business must give notice to others of the existence of the security interest. A primary way to perfect is to file the financing statement with the secretary of state or other relevant official so it is available for public inspection. This process must be followed unless the goods being sold are consumer goods. Under the UCC, a security interest for consumer goods is perfected without the necessity of a filing. Normally, the financing statement contains little more than the names and addresses of the firm and the customer, a description of the product, and the signature of the customer. The remaining details of the credit transaction, including the details of the amount actually financed, the payment schedule, interest rate, and other such matters, are left to the security agreement. A seller's retail installment contract is a typical security agreement. Consumer debt is covered in Chapter 18.

Interests in Inventory As collateral, supplies such as equipment, inventory, and raw materials can be classified as *tangible property*—goods that are movable at the time a security interest attaches (begins). To protect its interests, the lender extending credit to a business obtains a security interest, as we will see in the *HCC Credit* case. The procedure to be followed by the creditor is nearly the same as the procedure followed by the business when it extends credit to customers buying its product. As in that case, the security interest gives the lender rights against the borrower—rights that are superior to unsecured creditors and some other creditors in the event the borrower fails to meet its debt obligations.

A "Floating Lien" for Inventory Under the UCC, the term *inventory* includes goods held for sale as well as raw materials, work in process, or materials used or consumed by the organization. Inventory is constantly changing, being turned over, and renewed. This could create a problem for a creditor that provides financing to the business with specific inventory as collateral. To avoid the need to renew the financing contract every time something is sold or used in the production process, the UCC allows a perfected security interest in property acquired after the security agreement if the agreement between the borrower and the lender so provides. This permits a valid *floating lien*. The security interest in any specific item of inventory terminates upon the item's sale or use but attaches to new inventory that replaces or replenishes the stock.

Default by the Debtor

A security interest helps to protect the interests of the seller in the event the customer cannot or will not meet its repayment obligations (that is, when the customer *defaults*). Because the business has a security interest in the product, it has *priority* to the product over other, unsecured creditors. The lender must decide whether to sue the customer to recover the debt or simply to repossess the product and resell it.

The UCC provides that when repossessing a product, "a secured party may proceed without judicial process if this can be done without breach of peace." In taking possession of consumer goods, the seller is not obligated to notify other parties who also may have a security interest in the product. The creditor may either keep the product or resell it. If the product is resold, it must be sold in a "commercially reasonable manner." Any proceeds generated in excess of what is owed must be returned to the customer.

Default by a debtor usually affects more than one party. Repossession may or may not be possible, and in searching for funds to repay the debt, creditors commonly argue over who is eligible for whatever funds are available. The UCC, like the bankruptcy code, helps to determine who gets what when a debtor cannot satisfy all creditors. *HCC Credit* illustrates a not uncommon problem.

HCC Credit Corp. v. Springs Valley Bank & Trust Co.

Court of Appeals, Indiana
669 N.E.2d 1001 (1996)

CASE BACKGROUND *Lindsey Tractor sold farm equipment in French Lick, Indiana, until it filed for bankruptcy in 1991. Lindsey had bought equipment from its suppliers on credit provided by HCC, which had a perfected security interest in the equipment. That interest stated that proceeds from the sale of equipment would be paid immediately to HCC.*

Shortly before bankruptcy, Lindsey received $199,122 from a customer for equipment financed by HCC. Lindsey deposited the money in a checking account and then paid debts owed to Springs Valley Bank & Trust (SVB&T). SVB&T did not know the funds were from proceeds of a sale subject to HCC's security interest. After Lindsey declared bankruptcy, HCC sued SVB&T to recover the $199,122 it had received from Lindsey. Trial court granted SVB&T summary judgment. HCC appealed.

CASE DECISION Chezem, Judge.

* * *

HCC argues that it was entitled to judgment as a matter of law because it had a perfected security interest in the $199,122.00 proceeds from the tractor sale. HCC is correct that it had a valid perfected security interest in the proceeds. Indiana [UCC] 9-306(2) provides that "a security interest continues in collateral notwithstanding sale, exchange or other disposition thereof unless the disposition was authorized by the secured party in the security agreement or otherwise, and also continues in any identifiable proceeds including collections received by the debtor." In addition, Indiana UCC 9-201 provides: "Except as otherwise provided by IC 26-1, a security agreement is effective according to its terms between the parties, against purchasers of the collateral, and against creditors." This court has previously held "the Chapter 9 secured party, upon a debtor's default, [has] priority over 'anyone, anywhere, anyhow' except as otherwise provided by the remaining Code priority rules." Thus, absent a Code provision placing priority in the proceeds in SVB&T, HCC would have a superior claim to the proceeds.

Indiana has recognized that Comment 2(c) to UCC 9-306 is an exception to the Code's general priority rules. That comment provides:

> [w]here case proceeds are covered into the debtor's checking account and paid out in the operation of the debtor's business, recipients of the funds of course take free of any claim which the secured party may have in them as proceeds. What has been said relates to payments and transfers in the ordinary course. The law of fraudulent conveyances would no doubt in appropriate cases support recovery of proceeds by a secured party from the transferee out of ordinary course or otherwise in collusion with the debtor to defraud the secured party.

The operative question here, is what constitutes "payments and transfers in the ordinary course."

Recently, the Seventh Circuit Court of Appeals addressed this issue when it applied Indiana law to a factually similar case. . . .

In construing the language of Comment 2(c), the Seventh Circuit Court held that "where a debtor pays commingled funds in the operation of its business to a third party, the third party takes those funds in 'ordinary course' unless it knows the payment violates a superior secured interest in those funds." We agree with the Seventh Circuit's construction of the "ordinary course" language of Comment 2(c), and reiterate some of that Court's reasoning here.

The court reasoned that imposing liability too readily on payees from commingled accounts could impede the free flow of goods and services essential to business, as suppliers would take steps to insure that they will ultimately not have to return the money they receive. In addition, the court noted that it was reasonable to conclude that the drafters of the Code intended for the term "ordinary course" in Comment 2(c) to have a meaning similar to the same term as used in the statutory definition of "buyer in ordinary course of business." Indiana UCC 1-201 (9) defines a buyer in ordinary course of business as one "who [buys] in good faith and without knowledge that the sale to him is in violation of the ownership rights or security interest of a third party. . . ." The court reasoned that these factors, good faith and lack of knowledge, should be equally necessary to qualify a payment or transfer out of commingled funds as one in the ordinary course.

Having found this reasoning persuasive, we too hold that "under Comment 2(c), a payment is within the ordinary course if it was made in the operation of the debtor's business and if the payee did not know and was not reckless about whether the payment violated a third party's security interest."

Here, the . . . evidence does not support an inference that by accepting the $199,122.00 payment, SVB&T knew that Lindsey was not fulfilling his obligation to HCC. . . .

Neither does the . . . evidence support an inference that SVB&T accepted the $199.122.00 payment in reckless disregard of the fact that the payment violated HCC's security interest. We emphatically disagree with HCC's contention that the acceptance of an unprecedentedly large payment by a creditor is sufficient to support an inference of recklessness. Summary judgment was properly granted in favor of SVB&T.

Affirmed.

QUESTIONS FOR ANALYSIS

1. HCC argued that since SVB&T knew a security interest existed that it should have monitored Lindsey's account to make sure the interest was not being avoided. Is that possible?

2. What could HCC have done to help prevent the situation that occurred?

Property Exempt from Attachment

As discussed, it is not uncommon for business owners to pledge personal assets as security for the debts of the business (for example, as a surety). If the business is not able to pay, the creditor may have assets pledged as collateral seized and sold to repay the debt. If the debt is not fully paid after the sale, the creditor may sue the owners for the rest of the debt. To protect its interests, the creditor may ask the court for an attachment. After the judgment has been rendered and the owner is unable (or unwilling) to pay, the creditor may ask the court for a writ of execution.

In either instance, the creditor moves against the owner's *nonexempt property*. That is, most states provide that certain real and personal property are exempt from execution and attachment proceedings. In the interest of ensuring that a debtor has housing, for example, states provide a *homestead exemption*, which, depending on the state, allows the debtor to retain the family home entirely or up to a specified amount free from the claims of unsecured creditors. The same thing is true in bankruptcy. With regard to personal property, state statutes provide limited exemptions for, among other things, furniture, clothing, automobiles, and tools used in the debtor's trade or business. Most states have their own list of exemptions; Exhibit 12.6 provides the federal list of exemptions.

REAL ESTATE FINANCING

For most businesses, small or large, the purchase of real estate usually involves a large outlay of money. Normally, at least part, if not most, of the purchase price is borrowed. The real estate itself is used to secure the debt obligation and is evidenced by a *mortgage*. In most states, the mortgage is a lien (discussed following),

---

EXHIBIT 12.6

Federal List of Exempt Property

1. Up to $7,500 in equity in a residence
2. Up to $1,200 equity in one motor vehicle
3. Up to $200 for each item of household furnishings and clothing (including household goods, books, animals, musical instruments, and the like), the total value not to exceed $4,000
4. Up to $500 in jewelry
5. Up to $750 in books and tools used in the debtor's trade
6. Up to $400, plus up to $3,750 not used in (1) above, in any property owned by the debtor
7. Any unmatured life insurance contract owned by the debtor
8. Up to $4,000 cash surrender or loan value of an unmatured life insurance contract owned by the debtor and on the debtor's life
9. Alimony and child support payments
10. Certain rights in pension and profit-sharing plans, and other annuity plans, including Social Security and veterans and disability benefits
11. Up to $7,500 in payments from an award in a personal injury lawsuit

giving the holder the right to sell the property and repay the debt from sale proceeds in the event the borrower defaults. The debtor is referred to as the *mortgagor*, and the creditor as the *mortgagee*. Such transactions are governed by state common law and real estate statutes because the UCC does not apply to real estate mortgages.

The Mortgage

According to the Statute of Frauds, a mortgage must be in writing. In most states, a simple and concise form such as that shown in Exhibit 12.7 is recognized by statute. In meeting the necessary requirements of such documents, the mortgage normally contains a description of the property, sets forth any warranties relative to the property, states the debt, and states the mortgagor's duties concerning taxes, insurance, and repairs. To protect the mortgagee's rights against other creditors,

---

EXHIBIT 12.7

Sample Mortgage Agreement

Mortgage
(New York Statutory Form)

This mortgage, made the _____ day of _____, 20_____, between _____, [*insert residence*}, the mortgagor, and _____ [*insert residence*], the mortgagee.
Witnesseth, that to secure the payment of an indebtedness in the sum of _____ dollars, lawful money of the United States, to be paid on the _____ day of _____, 20 _____, with interest thereon to be computed from _____ at the rate of _____ per centum per annum, and to be paid _____, according to a certain bond or obligation bearing even date herewith, the mortgagor hereby mortgages to the mortgagee [*description*].
And the mortgagor covenants with the mortgagee as follows:

1. That the mortgagor will pay the indebtedness as hereinbefore provided.
2. That the mortgagor will keep the buildings on the premises insured against loss by fire for the benefit of the mortgagee; that he will assign and deliver the policies to the mortgagee; and that he will reimburse the mortgagee for any premiums paid for insurance made by the mortgagee on the mortgagor's default in so insuring the buildings or in so assigning and delivering the policies.
3. That no building on the premises shall be removed or demolished without the consent of the mortgagee.
4. That the whole or said principal sum and interest shall become due at the option of the mortgagee: after default in the payment of any installment of principal or of interests for _____ days; or after default in the payment of any tax, water rate or assessment for _____ days after notice and demand; or after default after notice and demand either in assigning and delivering the policies insuring the buildings against loss by fire or in reimbursing the mortgagee for premiums paid on such insurance, as hereinbefore provided; or afer default upon request in furnishing a statement of the amount due on the mortgage and whether any offsets or defenses exist against the mortgage debt, as hereinafter provided.
5. That the holder of this mortgage, in any action to foreclose it, shall be entitled to the appointment of a receiver.
6. That the mortgagor will pay all taxes, assessments or water rates, and in default thereof, the mortgagee may pay the same.
7. That the mortgagor within _____ days upon request in person or within _____ days upon request by mail will furnish a written statement duly acknowledged of the amount due on this mortgage and whether any offsets or defenses exist against the mortgage debt.
8. That notice and demand or request may be in writing and may be served in person or by mail.
9. That the mortgagor warrants the title to the premises. In Witness Whereof, this mortgage has been duly executed by the mortgagor.

the mortgage should be recorded. State statutes typically require that the mortgage be placed in a county office, often called the Recorder's Office or the Register of Deeds.

Default by the Mortgagor

If the borrower is unable to pay the mortgage, the mortgagee has the right to foreclose on the property. Foreclosure may be by judicial sale. If the proceeds of the sale are sufficient to cover the costs of the foreclosure and the debt, any surplus must be returned to the mortgage holder. If the proceeds are not sufficient, the mortgagee can seek to recover the remainder from the debtor by obtaining a deficiency judgment, obtained in a separate legal action after the foreclosure action. In about half the states, a mortgagor has the right to redeem the property by paying the debt within the *statutory redemption* period, normally within six months to a year after the default.

LIENS

Security obtained by a creditor though the operation of law is called a *lien*. Because it is obtained by the seller without the agreement of the customer, the security may be called a nonconsensual lien. The term *lien* is derived from the French language and means "tie" or "string." The legal meaning for lien is the legal right the seller has to the product or supplies now held by a customer. The lien helps to secure payment for goods or services, such as repairs to a product.

The procedures for using liens are generally determined by state common law and state statutes. The most common liens are the mechanic's lien (applicable to real property), the possessory lien (applicable to personal property), and court-decreed liens. In each case, a creditor may obtain the lien without the debtor's consent by following statutory procedures. An additional remedy, *garnishment*, is a statutory procedure under which a creditor gains the right to attach up to 25 percent of a customer's net wages to be applied to the outstanding debt.

Mechanic's Lien

A *mechanic's lien* is the most common lien on real property. The party that furnished material, labor, or services for the construction or repair of a building or other real property can place a lien on the property for unpaid bills. The primary obligation of the creditor is that all required legal steps be taken within the time specified in the statute. The requirements vary from state to state; some states require preliminary notice to the debtor before the lien is filed. Upon filing the lien, the creditor obtains security for the debt.

If the owner of the real property does not pay the lien, the creditor can move to force the sale of the property to satisfy the debt. Obviously, the debtor must be notified that the property is going to be sold. Normally, any sale proceeds beyond the amount required to satisfy the creditor's lien must be returned to the debtor. In some states, such a sale must take place within twelve months of the original filing. If no action is taken within twelve months, the lien expires and cannot be revived.

Possessory Lien

The *possessory lien* or *artisan's lien* is the most common lien on personal property. It provides a security interest for businesses that give credit for adding value to or caring for personal property. This lien offers the right to continue to hold goods on which work has been done, or for which materials have been supplied, until the customer pays. The business doing the work must have the property in its possession, and it must have agreed expressly or implicitly to provide the work on a cash, not a credit, basis. The lien stays in existence as long as the creditor retains possession, unless the lien is filed according to the requirements of a state's lien and recording statutes. In that way, the creditor gives notice of the existence of the lien to others and protects its interests upon the product's return to the customer.

If the customer does not pay for the work, the creditor can force the sale of the property to fulfill payment of the debt. Any sale proceeds beyond the amount needed to satisfy the creditor's lien must be returned to the debtor. As with the mechanic's lien, the debtor must have prior notice of the sale. Regardless of the kind of lien, an issue often arises with regard to which lien has priority when creditors compete for a debtor's property. As the *Holly Lake* decision discusses, liens obtain priority by proper recording.

Holly Lake Association v. Federal National Mortgage Association
Supreme Court of Florida
660 So.2d 266 (1995)

CASE BACKGROUND *Holly Lake Association is a homeowners' association for a mobile home development. When formed in 1974, the association recorded a declaration of covenants covering the real property within the development. The declaration required residents to pay a monthly assessment for maintenance of their mobile home sites and included this provision:*

> *In the event the monthly mobile type home site charge is not paid when due, Owner, or its designee, shall have the right to a lien against said site and the improvements contained thereon for any such unpaid charges; and shall have the right to enforce said lien in any manner provided by law for the enforcement of mechanic's or statutory liens, but Owner shall not be restricted to such procedure in the collection of said overdue charges.*

The McKessons bought a mobile home site in Holly Lake and executed a mortgage on the property to Federal National Mortgage Association (FNMA). The mortgage was recorded as a lien against the property in 1983. In 1991, when the McKessons failed to pay their monthly maintenance assessment, the association filed a lien against their property. In 1992, FNMA brought a foreclosure action against the McKessons for failing to make their mortgage payments. The association filed a claim against FNMA, asserting that it had a superior lien against the property because its declaration of covenants, which stated that it could file a lien in a case such as this one, dated back to 1974. FNMA claimed that its 1983 mortgage

lien should be compared against the 1991 lien filed by the association, which would put FNMA first in line against the McKessons. The trial court held that the association's lien had priority over FNMA's mortgage. The district court of appeals reversed, ruling in favor of FNMA. The court certified a question to the state supreme court, asking it for a statement of the law in this instance.

CASE DECISION Grimes, Chief Justice.

* * *

The Association and FNMA agree that the applicable rule governing priority of lien interests is "first in time is first in right." However, both parties assert that their respective lien was first in time and therefore had priority.

* * *

[T]he language in the declaration of covenants before us merely granted the Association the right to file a lien in the event of nonpayment.

The Association's declaration of covenants failed to put FNMA on notice that the Association claimed a continuing lien on the property securing the monthly maintenance assessments. When FNMA's mortgage was recorded in 1983, the Association had not yet filed a lien against the McKessons' property. Therefore, FNMA could not be charged with constructive notice of the existence of the Association's lien.

* * *

To hold that priority of such a debt relates back to the date the declaration is recorded or registered, would expose lenders to unknown risks, and would undercut the principle, embodied in the recordation and registration statutes, that persons who are about to acquire an interest in land are entitled to know the extent to which that interest is impaired.

We hold that in order for a claim of lien recorded pursuant to a declaration of covenants to have priority over an intervening recorded mortgage, the declaration must contain specific language indicating that the lien relates back to the date of the filing of the decla-ration or that it otherwise takes priority over interven-ing mortgages. We therefore approve the decision of the district court of appeal.

QUESTIONS FOR ANALYSIS

1. Could the association have worded its 1974 decla-ration differently to have given it priority over later liens, or must liens always be filed when non-payment occurs?
2. Since mortgages are more important than liens for maintenance, why would not mortgages always take priority over other liens?

Court-Decreed Liens After a debt has become past due, the creditor generally has the right to bring a lawsuit against the debtor. Creditors prefer alternatives to liti-gation for collections because of the time and expense involved. If it is necessary to use the court system, the creditor will find attachment and judgment liens at its dis-posal as judicial means for protecting its interests.

An *attachment lien* is a court-ordered seizure of the product from the customer to prevent the customer from disposing of it during the lawsuit. Under state statute, the requirements imposed on the creditor are specific and limited. To obtain an attachment lien, the business must show that the debtor is likely to dis-pose of the product. If the court concurs, it issues a *writ of attachment* directing the sheriff to seize the good. It is important for the creditor to follow state attachment procedures closely or it could be liable for damages for wrongful attachment.

If the creditor is successful in its legal action against the customer, the court awards a *judgment lien*. In general, no lien is created simply by the rendering of a court judgment. Rather, the creditor must obtain an *abstract of judgment*, which, when properly prepared, recorded, and indexed, creates a lien against the debtor's real property and provides notice to potential purchasers of the property of the existence of the judgment and lien. A judgment lien is not enforceable against exempt real property (discussed in the next section). Because judgment liens are creatures of statute, no lien attaches without substantial compliance with the rele-vant statutory terms. Normally, a lien holds for ten years.

If the customer does not pay the judgment, the creditor asks the court to issue a *writ of execution*. The writ is issued by the clerk of the court and directs the sher-iff to seize and sell any of the debtor's nonexempt real or personal property within the court's jurisdiction. Proceeds from the sale beyond the amount required to sat-isfy the creditor's lien and to pay for the costs of the sale are returned to the debtor.

Bankruptcy

Financial ruin comes to many in the marketplace. Some consumers and businesses engage in fraud, causing financial messes that others pay for, but most bankrupt-cies are due to bad luck or unintentional mismanagement. A study by Dun & Brad-street attributed 93 percent of business failures to "management incompetence."

Bankruptcy is not a new issue; the framers of the Constitution thought it such an important issue that they specifically made bankruptcy a matter of federal law.

The *Bankruptcy Reform Act* of 1978, called the *bankruptcy code*, has been amended several times, but it is the key statute that governs official bankruptcy procedure. That is, it states how matters are resolved when debts are greater than assets available. We review several major types of bankruptcy and then discuss the nonbankruptcy choices for distressed debtors.

CHAPTER 7

Chapter 7 of the bankruptcy code is the most commonly used alternative. It means liquidation and fair distribution of the debtor's assets for the creditors. Liquidating bankruptcy under Chapter 7 is available for corporations and other businesses, but, as we will see, only individuals can use Chapter 7 to obtain discharge.

Most Chapter 7 bankruptcies are filed voluntarily by the debtor. A petition is filed with the bankruptcy court, which may be the federal district court or a federal bankruptcy court. The filing is a statement of the financial affairs of the debtor, including a listing of all assets and liabilities, using specific forms. The petition provides the following:

- Statement of the financial affairs of the debtor
- List of all creditors and their addresses, with amounts owed
- List of properties owned by debtor
- Statement of current income and expenses of debtor

The filing of this petition means that an immediate freeze is made against all actions against the debtor or a debtor's property by any creditors. A temporary *trustee* is appointed to administer the debtor's estate. The trustee calls a meeting of the listed creditors within about a month to review the accuracy of the information provided by the debtor. The creditors usually approve formal appointment of the temporary trustee as the trustee. In an *involuntary bankruptcy*, creditors file a petition with the court, forcing the declaration of bankruptcy and the beginning of proceedings.

THE BANKRUPTCY PROCEEDING

A key feature of bankruptcy is the emphasis on creditors' receiving fair treatment. Under traditional state law, when it becomes clear that the debtor is unable to pay, the creditor who acts most quickly to gain control of the debtor's property is the creditor most likely to be paid. Under the federal system, once bankruptcy has been declared, a creditor cannot improve its position by getting to the debtor's property first. Nor can the debtor improve a favored creditor's position by transferring property to that creditor. It is the trustee's job to assure that no creditor has improved, by any means, its relative position. Some creditors may have learned of the debtor's financial plight and then gained control of some of the debtor's property. Hence, bankruptcy proceedings hold that such transfers of debtor's property made within ninety days of bankruptcy are void.

Role of the Trustee

The trustee's objective is to maximize the amount of the debtor's assets available for distribution to the creditors. However, as noted earlier, some of the debtor's property is exempt from bankruptcy. Normally, states exempt the debtor's house, house-

JURIS **prudence?**

Keep the Home Fires Burning for Me, Honey

Bonney, Bankruptcy Judge.

"When Godfrey Marks penned that rousing popular nautical chorus: 'Sailing, sailing over the bounding main; For many a stormy wind shall blow ere Jack comes home again,' he never considered that the stormy winds to which he referred might not be tempestuous billows or stormy blacks but bankruptcy. Alas!

"Jack is David Ernest Raymond of the United States Navy aboard the *USS America*. His wife is Susan Lucille known to the Court as debtor 81-00831-N. Interestingly, she also seeks to file Jack's bankruptcy petition by virtue of his power of attorney which she holds.

"There is an issue. May [or is it can?] one file bankruptcy for another under a power of attorney which one holds?

"There is an answer. No.

"Jack is out to sea and shall not return for several months. The couple's 'severe financial situation,' the application says, requires immediate relief. . . .

"Unfortunately, these fellows with 'severe financial situations' run into the lawyer's office just as the ship is leaving Pier 12 for an extended cruise rather than anticipating their needs. They expect miracles; we dispense few. We are not very good at it.

"[B]ankruptcy is not a right and it carries with it certain obligations. No pay, no go . . . no show, no go."

Source: *In Re Raymond, Debtor;* 12 B.R. 906.

hold furnishings, car, and tools of trade. The trustee is required to liquidate all the debtor's nonexempt property. The *liquidation* takes place through a sale at a public auction unless otherwise ordered by the court. After the property has been sold, the proceeds are disbursed among the creditors. All creditors holding a claim against the debtor are entitled to share in the distribution of the sales proceeds.

Priority Classes of Creditors

Bankruptcy law states that certain creditors take priority over other creditors in receiving shares of the debtor's assets to pay for the debts owed them. Standing first in line are *secured creditors*. As discussed previously, these creditors have a written security agreement that describes the property (collateral) that stands behind a particular debt. For a consumer, the most common would be a home mortgage or an automobile loan. In bankruptcy, the secured creditor may request that the court grant permission for it to take possession of the property covered by the debt. The *priority classes* in bankruptcy usually are as follows:

1. Secured creditors
2. Costs of preserving and administering the debtor's estate
3. Unpaid wage claims
4. Certain claims of farmers and fishermen
5. Refund of security deposits
6. Alimony and child support
7. Taxes
8. General (unsecured) creditors who can file a proof of claim

All the creditors of a particular class must be paid before the next-lower-priority creditors can be paid anything. Rarely is enough money received from the sale to pay general creditors what they are owed.

Discharge in Bankruptcy

The final stage of the bankruptcy proceeding for individuals is the *bankruptcy discharge*. However, the discharge may be denied if the debtor committed certain offenses listed in the Act, fraudulently conveyed property before the bankruptcy, refuses to answer material questions in the bankruptcy proceeding, unjustifiably fails to keep financial records, or fails to satisfactorily explain losses in assets. Discharge means that the nonexempt assets are liquidated and the proceeds distributed among the creditors, who may not ask for more. Again, the claimants are paid according to their priority, so unsecured credits are rarely paid and even secured creditors may get very little. The books have been cleared. The debtor gets a fresh start. However, a declaration of bankruptcy remains on a person's credit history for ten years and the debtor may not seek another discharge for six years.

Some debts are not discharged by bankruptcy proceedings. The reason for these exceptions is to discourage the use of bankruptcy to evade certain responsibilities. The following are among the debts not extinguished by bankruptcy:

* Alimony and child support payments
* Back taxes
* Some student loans
* Some debts incurred immediately before filing bankruptcy
* Debts incurred by fraud against the creditors
* Fines owed to the government

CHAPTER 11

A portion of the bankruptcy code with a very different intent is *Chapter 11*, which applies to businesses that wish to remain in operation and not be liquidated. Many businesses are worth more if they can be kept alive, generating revenue, than if they are liquidated when debts are greater than assets. The difference between the value of a business as a going concern compared with what is collected from selling the assets of the company is known as a "going concern surplus." It is that surplus that the creditors hope to capture by allowing the business to remain in operation so that they have a greater chance of full repayment. There is a risk, of course, that keeping the business in operation will only worsen things, in which case the creditors lose even more. It is a judgment call.

Although Chapter 11 has been used to restructure some multibillion-dollar businesses, most companies that file have assets worth less than $1 million. Well-planned Chapter 11 cases have much better track records and involve fewer legal fees than those done in haste. But many businesses are in dire straits before a reorganization plan is rushed to court to try to salvage operations as the creditors are pressing in.

Reorganization

As with Chapter 7, the filing under Chapter 11 automatically stays further action by any parties involved. An initial hearing with the trustee determines whether the plan should be allowed to proceed or whether some creditors are due immediate payment or return of property. In most cases, the debtor is allowed by the court to continue operating the "reorganized" business. Thus, the debtor acts as trustee of the operation, called a *debtor in possession*, running the business for the benefit of all parties. This means that the debtor now owes an extra duty of care because the debtor's duty is to act in the best interest of all, not just the owners of the business.

Watching over the debtor is the unsecured creditors' committee, composed of several creditors with the largest claims. These creditors are often the largest suppliers to the business. The committee supervises the management of the reorganized business, cooperating with the debtor to try to make a success of the operation. Any unusual actions by the debtor must be reviewed by the committee in advance; if the creditors object, the court will review the matter. As with Chapter 7, creditors must be satisfied by class in order of priority of claims. However, unlike Chapter 7, where discharge of debts is the goal, under Chapter 11, the purpose is to have the business survive and emerge as a profitable venture or to see it sold for its greatest value. The *Gaslight Club* case illustrates the failure of the debtor to fulfill his duty.

In the Matter of Gaslight Club, Inc.
United States Court of Appeals, Seventh Circuit
782 F.2d 767 (1986)

CASE BACKGROUND *Gaslight operated private dining clubs in cities around the country. It filed a voluntary petition in the bankruptcy court for reorganization under Chapter 11. Fredricks, president and majority shareholder of Gaslight, was designated by the court to be the debtor in possession, to keep the company operating to work its way out of financial distress. Gaslight then lost $1.6 million in eight months under Fredricks. The creditors' committee filed a motion with the bankruptcy court to force Gaslight to sell some property so that it could recover something. Fredricks failed to respond to a court order to put the property up for sale and to provide a new plan of action for the business. At the creditors' request and with Fredricks' consent, the court then appointed Brandt, an outsider, to become the debtor in possession.*

Under the bankruptcy code, the debtor in possession has "full and exclusive power . . . to employ [and] discharge . . . all managers, officers, directors, agents, employees and servants of the debtors, as he may deem necessary and advisable. . . ." Brandt fired Fredricks as president of Gaslight because Fredricks refused to recognize Brandt's authority and because Brandt was concerned about some of Fredricks's financial dealings. Fredricks got the board of directors of Gaslight, which he dominated, to hire a new attorney, who filed a request with the court that he replace Brandt as debtor in possession. The bankruptcy court and the district court refused, leaving Brandt in control of Gaslight. Fredricks appealed.

CASE DECISION Cudahy, Circuit Judge.

* * *

The Bankruptcy Code provides:

(a) At any time after the commencement of the case but before confirmation of a plan, on request of a party in interest or the United States trustee, and after notice and a hearing, the court shall order the appointment of a trustee—

(1) for cause, including fraud, dishonesty, incompetence, or gross mismanagement of the affairs of the debtor by current management, either before or after the commencement of the case, or similar cause, but not including the number of holders of securities of the debtor or the amount of assets or liabilities of the debtor; or

(2) if such appointment is in the interests of creditors, any equity security holders, and other interests of the estate, without regard to the number of holders of securities of the debtor or the amount of assets or liabilities of the debtor.

* * *

The Bankruptcy Code authorizes the bankruptcy court to "issue any order, process, or judgment that is necessary or appropriate to carry out the provisions of this title." Further, it states that the rights and powers of a debtor in possession are subject "to such limitations or conditions as the court prescribes." The case law demonstrates that the court has considerable authority to interfere with the management of a debtor corporation in order to protect the creditors' interests.

* * *

Fredricks continues to argue that designating someone, such as Brandt, as a person in control (virtually in lieu of a trustee) improperly avoids the statutory requirements for appointment of a trustee. We would certainly question recourse to the present procedure as a means generally to avoid appointment of a trustee. But we think the peculiar circumstances of the case before us as well as the consent on all sides to the procedure followed make this case different. The appointment of Brandt was appropriate to the circumstances and authorized by law.

* * *

Section 1107 [of the Bankruptcy Code] provides that "a debtor in possession shall have all the rights, other than the right to compensation under section 330 of this title, and powers, and shall perform all the functions and duties, except the duties specified in sections 1106(a)(2), (3), and (4) of this title, of a trustee serving in a case under this chapter." Hence Gaslight, the debtor in possession, had the power to retain counsel, subject to the court's approval. Brandt was the person designated to exercise the rights of the debtor in possession and hence he—not the board of directors—had the power to retain counsel. The order explicitly gave Brandt the full and exclusive power to employ all agents and employees of the debtors.

We therefore affirm the judgment of the district court.

QUESTIONS FOR ANALYSIS

1. Doesn't the decision in this case mean that the board of directors of the company in bankruptcy is largely irrelevant?
2. Why does the bankruptcy code give the bankruptcy court and debtor in possession (or trustee) such strong powers?

CHAPTER 13

Many personal bankruptcies are handled under *Chapter 13*. There is only a voluntary option under Chapter 13, which is filed like a Chapter 7 bankruptcy and is available only for individuals. Because a sole proprietorship is a small business owned by an individual, it may be handled under the Chapter 13 option.

In this bankruptcy proceeding, the debtor files a plan for payment of creditors over time. This installment repayment plan differs from that under which the existing payment of the legal debt obligations was due. Unlike in Chapter 7, where the debtor is relieved of all property except that protected by state statute, in Chapter 13, the debtor keeps the estate's property and shares administration of the bankrupt estate with a court-appointed trustee. The trustee collects income from the debtor and makes payments to creditors as called for by the *confirmation plan* that was approved. The trustee does not manage the affairs of the bankrupt; rather, the trustee is there to make sure that payments are made and to approve any changes in the debt and credit position of the debtor.

Unlike Chapter 7, the debts of the bankrupt are not discharged. Chapter 13 is a court-protected change of debt repayment that usually must be accomplished within three years but no more than five years. Long-term, secured debt, such as a house mortgage, is treated differently. If the plan fails to work, it is possible to shift to a Chapter 7 bankruptcy and have the financial decks cleared completely via discharge.

NONBANKRUPTCY ALTERNATIVES

Because bankruptcy is costly and affects how one is viewed in the business community, financial distress often is handled without going to bankruptcy even though it is available. All nonbankruptcy options are contractual, so they must be agreed to by the parties involved. We discuss here some of the most common alternatives, which can be quicker and cheaper than bankruptcy.

Japanese Business Reorganization Methods

Japan has several methods of handling bankruptcies, which are referred to as reorganization proceedings even if they involve liquidation. The most common method is *composition*, which allows a business to be liquidated or, more often, reorganized.

Composition proceedings may be requested only by the debtor, who files a reorganization plan when the petition is filed with the court. The plan may be revised after further negotiation with the creditors. A court-appointed examiner investigates the debtor's situation. The examiner recommends to the court that the case be allowed to proceed or that the debtor's request be rejected. If the case proceeds, the court appoints a composition trustee, who has fewer powers than the trustees appointed in Chapter 11 proceedings. The trustee supervises the negotiations between the debtor and creditors and watches to make sure business matters are handled properly before the matter is resolved.

If the trustee believes that most parties are satisfied with the plan, the plan is presented to the court for approval. If the trustee believes that no agreement can be reached, the court orders the business to be liquidated. When a plan is accepted, the debtor returns to full control of the business, which is run under the new debt obligations agreed to in the plan.

Although different from Chapter 11, many of the key features of composition are similar in practice. As in the United States, creditors in Japan claim that the process favors debtors, takes too long, and is unlikely to work. However, a study comparing the two systems indicates that more small and medium firms in Japan are likely to survive in reorganized form than are their liquidated counterparts in the United States.

Debt Composition or Extension

A business in difficulty may bargain with its creditors for relief in the form of *composition*, which is an agreement to repay some percentage of the total amount due to relieve the debt, or an *extension*, which allows more time to pay the debt than the original agreement provided. Because such agreements are reached by bargaining, they require good faith on the part of the parties and usually work only when there are a few creditors who can agree among themselves as to the terms being offered. Such agreements must be approved by all parties, and all terms must be known by all parties. Any unpaid portions of debts are *discharged*. Because this is a contractual agreement, not one governed by the bankruptcy code, the parties can include any debt in the discharge agreement. This is usually an option only for businesses, and not for individual consumers.

Bank Workout

If most of a company's debt is to a bank, it may be possible to rehabilitate the business with a *bank workout*. In a workout, the major creditor agrees to a new debt payment schedule. If the major creditor, which would lose the most in bankruptcy and incur bankruptcy proceedings expenses, thinks that the business may be saved or the losses minimized, it may help to deal with other creditors and even arrange new financing.

Assignment

Especially for small businesses facing bankruptcy, *assignment* may be a quicker and cheaper way to accomplish liquidation. It must be agreed to by all creditors. The debtor assigns all nonexempt assets (assets not tied to a specific creditor, such as a mortgage on a building) to an *assignee*, who acts as a fiduciary for the benefit of the creditors. The assignee liquidates the assets and distributes the proceeds among the creditors on an agreed share basis. The business is terminated; this is not a rehabilitation plan. Creditors voluntarily accept partial payment of the sums they are owed as satisfaction for their debts.

Summary

- Negotiable instruments function either as a substitute for cash or as a credit device. The UCC identifies four types of instruments as negotiable instruments: drafts, checks, notes, and certificates of deposit.

- Negotiable instruments are flexible commercial instruments because of their ability to be transferred. Once issued, a negotiable instrument can be transferred by assignment or by negotiation. If the instrument is assigned, the assignee has the same contract rights and responsibilities as the assignor. If the instrument is transferred by negotiation, the transferee takes the instrument free of the transferor's contract responsibilities.

- To be negotiable, a commercial instrument must meet the general requirements of a negotiable instrument as provided by the UCC. It must be written, be an unconditional order or promise to pay, be signed by the maker or drawer, be payable on demand or at a specified time, be made out "to order" or "to bearer," and state a certain sum of money.

- If an instrument is negotiable under the requirements of the UCC, the instrument may be freely traded in the marketplace without concern for existing contract responsibilities as long as the instrument is in the possession of a holder in due course.

- As a creditor, a business monitors its credit extension and debt collection policies. As a debtor, a business borrows to pay for equipment, inventory, and land and buildings. Creditors are interested in being protected in the event a debtor is unable or unwilling to pay.

- A secured creditor has the right to take specific property of an insolvent debtor to satisfy the debt. The law provides two ways the creditor can obtain a debtor's property (referred to as security or collateral): (1) by agreement with the debtor or (2) by operation of law, and without an agreement between the lender and the borrower.

- A lender may require that a financially strong third party guarantee a loan. Such a guaranty may be a pledge of personal assets by business owners or from a third party. A promise is made to pay a particular debt of the business in the event it does not pay. A suretyship or guaranty is created, and the credit of the party providing it is the security for the debt owed.

- When a product is sold to a customer, Article 9 of the UCC provides that the product itself may secure the customer's obligation to pay. When credit is extended this way, the sale is called a secured transaction. By meeting the requirements of the UCC, the creditor obtains a security interest in the product to secure payment.

- To make a security interest enforceable, the lender must create the interest and make sure the interest is attached and perfected. When a creditor has a security interest in the product, it has priority to the product over some other and unsecured creditors. The lender can sue the debtor to recover the debt or repossess the product and resell it.

- In most credit transactions except mortgages, creditors require that a security agreement and a financing statement be accepted and signed by the borrower. When money is borrowed for the purchase of real estate, the real estate itself secures the obligation and is evidenced by a mortgage. In most states, the mortgage is a lien, giving the holder the right to sell the property and repay the debt from proceeds in the event of default.
- Security obtained by a creditor through the operation of law is called a lien. The procedures for using liens are determined by state law. The most common liens are the mechanic's lien (applicable to real property), the possessory lien (applicable to personal property), and court-decreed liens. In each case, the lender may obtain the lien without the borrower's consent by following statutory procedures.
- The Bankruptcy Reform Act (the bankruptcy code) governs bankruptcy procedure. There are several approaches to bankruptcy, including Chapter 7 (providing for liquidation and fair distribution of the debtor's assets for creditors), Chapter 11 (allowing businesses to reorganize rather than being liquidated), and Chapter 13 (personal bankruptcy for individuals).
- The trustee (or debtor in possession) is the person in charge of the bankruptcy. It is the trustee's objective (under bankruptcy court supervision) to maximize the amount of the debtor's assets available for distribution to the creditors.
- Bankruptcy law states that certain creditors take priority over other creditors in receiving shares of the debtor's assets. Secured creditors take priority over unsecured creditors.
- Important alternatives to bankruptcy that can be quicker and cheaper include debt composition, debt extension, bank workouts, and assignments.

Issue

Will Creditors Work with Minorities?

 New businesses must have credit to get started and to survive. Some critics complain that because minorities and women have less experience in the credit market, they tend to be discriminated against, making it difficult for them to get going in business. This story illustrates how at least one bank is profiting by working with neglected groups.

HOW TINY METROBANK WINS BIG BY CATERING TO AN ETHNIC MARKET

Rick Wartzman

Reprinted by permission of *The Wall Street Journal* © 1996 Dow Jones & Company, Inc. All rights reserved worldwide. Wartzman is a staff reporter.

Gilbert Moreno figured it was $1 million he would never see.

Getting banks to do business in the barrio was hard enough, the Hispanic community leader knew. And the project at hand—buying a building to house an alternative high school for former dropouts—wasn't exactly risk-free. "There's no bank in town that's going to touch this," Mr. Moreno recalls a lending officer from Houston's biggest bank, Texas Commerce, telling him.

Well, almost none. MetroBank, founded by Taiwanese Americans in 1987, lent the $1 million without hesitation—and the school, whose finances have grown stronger over the years, hasn't missed a payment. "If this small Asian bank hadn't stepped up," Mr. Moreno says, "nobody would have."

* * *

But MetroBank . . . has eagerly looked for business beyond its own turf. In the process, it has become an emblem of multicultural cooperation in an age more commonly marked by racial discord. And its focus—catering to minority small-business owners and immigrants seeking home mortgages—has also proven lucrative. With assets of $320 million, the little bank is among the fastest growing in the Houston metropolitan area.

Whatever their ethnicity, says MetroBank Chairman Don Wang, "newcomers to this country have mutual problems—and mutual opportunities as well. It's a common way of life."

* * *

The pursuit of profits—as much as altruism—is what drives MetroBank. As the third Asian-American-owned bank to be established in Houston, it quickly realized that the city's ballooning Asian population still wasn't big enough to fuel the asset and earnings growth it wanted. So executives decided to reach out to others. "We had to learn to get outside the Asian pie," says Mr. Wang, 51, who came to America from Taiwan in 1969.

Their vision is by no means fully realized, however. Inroads into the African-American community, in particular, have been slow. Although it has begun to take steps to enlarge its black customer base, including bringing on several African-American consultants, MetroBank's relatively modest goal of making 25 loans to black-owned businesses last year fell short by five. Perhaps there are "some cultural barriers, in terms of Asians vs. blacks," says Larry Hawkins, chief executive officer of Houston's black-owned Unity National Bank.

Some rivals also question whether Metro-Bank may be expanding too fast for its own good. "I would be very concerned about . . . whether the loan quality is as high as you would like it to be," says Ning Weng, the president of Asian-American National Bank in Houston. MetroBank officials maintain that their loan portfolio is in solid shape, but they too acknowledge potential pitfalls.

For one thing, MetroBank executives openly wonder whether they'll have the same appeal to the sons and daughters of immigrants who, more immersed in the melting pot, may choose nonminority-owned banks.

Yet at least for now, MetroBank has succeeded in taking advantage of the swiftly changing demographics of the nation's fourth largest city. With some three million people, the Houston area is about 23% Hispanic, 19% black and, according to unofficial estimates from the mayor's office, as much as 8% Asian.

* * *

With just five branches around Houston, MetroBank is still tiny by major bank standards; its assets are a small fraction of Texas Commerce's $20 billion, for example, or Chemical's $188 billion. Still, its assets have exploded more than 100-fold, from a mere $3 million, in just eight years. And in 1995, MetroBank's net income rose 8% to $2.7 million from $2.5 million—its seventh consecutive earnings increase.

At best, profits are expected to be flat this year because of one-time costs associated with opening four new branches, including one in Dallas. With the new locations, "We're really becoming the McDonald's of multi-ethnic banking," says Mr. Tioseco, a native Filipino.

Unlike fast food, though, there is no cookie-cutter formula when it comes to banking. Although Asians are often lumped together as a single ethnic group, MetroBank must be especially attuned to cultural differences. The bank, for instance, purposefully placed an American-born manager of Chinese descent to run its downtown branch, which serves mainly Vietnamese customers. "If you were to bring in a native Taiwanese or some other type of Asian, it might not click" because of inherent suspicions held by some Vietnamese, explains Jairo "Jay" Cadena, MetroBank's Colombian-born executive vice president.

MetroBank literature is published in four languages: English, Spanish, Vietnamese and Chinese. And the bank's 200-member staff—37% Asian, 33% Hispanic and 9% black—reflects the diverse customer base it serves. "We even have a few gringos," jokes Mr. Cadena.

As MetroBank has crossed into new territory, barriers have fallen with surprising ease.

* * *

Much of MetroBank's product line is tailored to help small companies. For example, it offers a service that allows a business to sell to the bank at a discount its receivables—what it is owed by its own customers. The bank then uses its resources to collect the money, while the business gets an instant infusion of working capital.

While "factoring," as this practice is known, isn't unique to MetroBank, most lenders reserve such a service for big clients. MetroBank's operation, by contrast, strives to help struggling small businesses "when they're in that critical cash-flow crunch and wouldn't otherwise qualify for a line of credit," says Dennis David, a vice president.

MetroBank's strong Asian roots and links to the Latin community also have enabled it to build a thriving export-lending business to companies eyeing Mexico and the Far East. The U.S. Export-Import Bank has named MetroBank a "priority lender," a rare designation for an institution its size. And bank officials pride themselves on successful efforts at "playing the triangle"—acting as the middlemen for deals between Latin American companies looking to do business in Asia, and vice versa.

Meanwhile, MetroBank has begun focusing on making more home loans, formally establishing a mortgage department 10 months ago. Seeking to woo the same minority customers that it has won over in the business-loan market, the bank offers first-time mortgages to people who can make a large down payment but wouldn't

normally qualify for a loan because they lack a traditional credit history.

* * *

It is just such innovation—and willingness to take risks—that helped MetroBank score big in the Hispanic community in the first place. "This bank has helped us in so many ways," says Joe Gonzalez, a Houston restaurant owner who has used MetroBank to help secure two SBA-backed loans totaling more than $1 million.

* * *

ISSUE QUESTIONS

1. Would such expansion into minority markets occur without government pressure or subsidies?
2. Will minorities or women be better served by trying to have minority-owned and women-owned banks that specialize in lending to minorities and women?

REVIEW AND DISCUSSION QUESTIONS

1. Define the following terms:

negotiable instrument	mechanic's lien
draft	suretyship
secured creditor	trustee in bankruptcy
attachment	secured creditors
perfected security interest	composition

2. What are the basic differences between Chapters 7, 11, and 13 bankruptcy?

CASE QUESTIONS

3. Chrysler Credit Corporation (CCC) had a security interest in a Dodge pickup truck that had been purchased by Robert Keeling. After Keeling defaulted on his payments, CCC tried to repossess the vehicle but could not locate it for some time. The truck was found in the storage lot of Highway Tow Service. It had been towed there from an apartment complex at the request of the manager of the complex. CCC requested that Highway deliver the truck to it, but Highway refused, requesting payment of its towing and storage charges. CCC sued to gain possession. Is Highway entitled to an artisan's or possessory lien on the truck? [*Chrysler Credit Corp.* v. *Keeling*, 793 S.W. 2d 222 (Ct.App., Mo., 1990)]

4. Verbin Byrd bought a car from Basset Ford of Citronelle, Alabama, under a retail installment contract assigned to Ford Motor Credit. The agreement called for thirty-six monthly installments. Toward the end of the thirty-six-month period, Byrd was contacted by a professional "repo man," Sandy Craig, who asked if Byrd's payments were in arrears. The parties disagreed, with Craig asserting that the payments were in arrears and Byrd asserting that they were not. To resolve the dispute,

Byrd drove to Basset Ford. While Byrd was in the dealership disputing his payment records, the car was taken and put in storage. Byrd asserted that the repossession was undertaken through stealth and trickery. In that regard, was the repossession lawful? Did it breach the peace? [*Ford Motor* v. *Byrd*, 351 So.2d 557 (S.Ct., Ala., 1977)]

5. McDowell owned and operated Big River Harley Davidson in Wapello, Iowa. As required by law, McDowell took out a retail motor vehicle dealer's surety bond for $35,000 with United Fire & Casualty Insurance. The bond protects retail customers who get stuck when a motor vehicle dealer, because of fraud or some other reason, does not deliver a vehicle that has been paid for. The surety bond was in force when Big River went out of business and McDowell left the state. While in business, Big River sold two Harleys wholesale to Elworth Harley Davidson Sales and Service in Norfolk, Nebraska. Only one of the two Harleys was delivered; the second Harley, for which Elworth paid $12,000, was not delivered. Elworth sued United Fire as surety for the $12,000. Can Elworth recover? [*United Fire & Casualty Co.* v. *Acker*, 541 N.W.2d 517 (Sup. Ct., Iowa, 1995)]

6. Alice and Bobby Jordan formed a partnership called East Tennessee Foam Fabricators, which bought materials from Allied Foam, resulting in a debt of $60,000. The Jordans agreed to consolidate the payments due on the invoices in a note. A promissory note was executed in favor of Allied Foam for $60,000 at 14 percent interest, to be paid in thirty-six monthly installments. The note was signed by Bobby Jordan as president of East Tennessee Foam Fabricators and Alice Jordan as secretary/treasurer. The next day, another note was executed in favor of Allied Foam to replace the one just signed. It was a lengthy document that listed the number of invoices, the principal of $60,000, the interest rate of 14 percent, and thirty-six monthly installments of $2,055.65. On that note, Alice Jordan signed her name on the signature line provided for cosigners. She did not indicate whether she was signing in a personal or representative capacity. The words "COSIGNERS—SEE NOTICE ON REVERSE SIDE BEFORE SIGNING" appeared above the signature line. The reverse side of the note listed the terms, including a clause that Georgia law would govern the contract, and the following declaration:

> GUARANTEE—By signing below I unconditionally guarantee the payment of the note and any amounts agreed to be paid under the terms of the security agreement. I also agree that all of the terms of the note and, to the extent applicable, the security agreement will apply to me.

After making several payments, Bobby Jordan died and the note went into default. Is Alice Jordan personally liable for the note on the basis of her signature? [*Allied Foam Products* v. *Jordan*, 1995 WL 56361 (Ct.App., Tenn., 1995)]

7. Moody and three other people bought a business together and executed promissory notes for $8.17 million to be repaid on a certain schedule. For his contribution, Moody owned 20 percent of the business; the other three owned the other 80 percent of the business. Moody was unable to make several payments on schedule. The other owners covered the payments he was supposed to make so that the notes would not go into default. Moody was sued by the other three for his contribution. He asserted that he was the same as a surety. Since they made the payments that were due, he was no longer obligated on those payments. Is that correct? [*Krumme* v. *Moody*, 910 P.2d 993 (Sup. Ct., Ok., 1996)]

8. Mollinedo's home was damaged by fire. Her insurance company, Sentry, recommended ServiceMaster as a good repair company. An adjuster for Sentry visited the home with the home contractor from ServiceMaster and approved $30,000 worth of work, which ServiceMaster did with Mollinedo's approval. Sentry was suspicious about the origins of the fire and gave the payment of $30,000 to Mollinedo's mortgage company. Mollinedo filed for bankruptcy. ServiceMaster, which got nothing, sued Sentry for breach of contract and unjust enrichment. Did ServiceMaster, which never filed a lien, have a claim? [*ServiceMaster of St. Cloud* v. *GAB Business Services*, 544 N.W.2d 302 (Sup. Ct., Minn., 1996)]

9. The Boggses were declared bankrupt under Chapter 13. Shortly after their discharge, Somerville Bank & Trust contended that the Boggses did not pay off the interest on a loan secured by a mortgage on their principal residence. The bank had not raised the issue until after the bankruptcy court had issued its discharge order covering the indebtedness. The bank attempted to collect the debt as though there had been no discharge. Is the bank entitled to collect the interest? [*Boggs* v. *Somerville Bank & Trust Company*, 51 F.3d 271 (6th Cir., 1995)]

10. Noggle borrowed $1,005.72 from Beneficial Finance Company to finance a small business project. To obtain the loan, he gave Beneficial a security interest in certain specified household goods, a camera, some household appliances, and a Winchester rifle. Beneficial filed a financing statement to perfect its security interest in the property. Shortly thereafter, Noggle filed a voluntary petition in bankruptcy under Chapter 13. During the administration of the case, Noggle claimed the Winchester rifle as exempt household property. Using the federal list of exemptions, is the rifle exempt from the reach of the bankruptcy proceeding? [*Matter of Noggle*, 30 Bankr. 303 (E.D. Mich., 1983)]

11. Lazar was sued for wrongful interference with a contractual relationship. Three weeks after being notified of the lawsuit, he transferred a number of his assets to his daughters, including $180,000 in interest in a mortgage and $104,000 from his solely owned pension fund. The daughters then purchased a sixty-foot yacht upon which Lazar took residence. Shortly thereafter, Lazar lost the suit, resulting in a 2-million-dollar judgment against him. When the judgment creditors attempted to execute the judgment, Lazar filed a Chapter 7 bankruptcy petition, having stripped himself of his assets by the transfers to his daughters. Is Lazar entitled to protection under the Bankruptcy Code? [*In re Lazar*, 81 Bankr. 148 (S.D. Fla., 1988)]

12. Strumpf was in default on a loan with a balance of $5,069 owed to Citizens Bank. When Strumpf filed for bankruptcy under Chapter 13, the bank put a hold on his checking account at the bank so that he could not write checks and leave less than $5,069 in the account. Strumpf complained to the bankruptcy court that the bank's action was illegal because it gave the bank a setoff against the debt, rather than preserving the checking account on behalf of all creditors. Could the bank place a hold on the checking account? [*Citizens Bank of Maryland* v. *Strumpf*, 116 S.Ct. 286 (1995)]

13. Bussewitz borrowed money from Citibank and signed a promissory note. Pitassi also signed the promissory note as co-maker of the note. When Bussewitz failed to make payments and defaulted on the note, Citibank, under the terms of the note, declared the entire unpaid balance due and sued both makers. Pitassi

defended that he should not be liable because he signed the note only as a favor to Bussewitz and, furthermore, the note did not state when the first installment payment was due; that term had been left blank. Is Pitassi liable? [*Citibank* v. *Pitassi*, 432 N.Y.S.2d 389 (Sup. Ct., App. Div., N.Y., 1980)]

POLICY QUESTION

14. A million people a year and tens of thousands of businesses file for bankruptcy each year. Is this evidence that the bankruptcy law makes it too desirable to file for bankruptcy rather than try to pay off debts?

ETHICS QUESTIONS

15. Consider the following quote regarding the Texas Homestead Act attributed to Hugh Ray, managing partner of the Houston, Texas, firm of Andrew & Kirth: People should move here from out-of-state, buy up as much land as they could, then go bankrupt. It's a deadbeat's paradise. There are several anecdotes to back up Ray's statement. For example, Craig Hall was a wealthy real estate syndicator in Dallas, Texas, during the oil boom of the late 1970s and early 1980s. When the bottom dropped out of oil in the early 1980s, the bottom also dropped out of the real estate market. Just before filing for bankruptcy, Hall paid off a 1.5-million-dollar mortgage, giving him the homestead free and clear under Texas's liberal homestead law. Is this practice, although legal, also ethical? What about the impact on creditors?

16. Should a small business be allowed to seek discharge of debts through bankruptcy when those debts were incurred as a consequence of an automobile accident caused by one of its drivers who was legally drunk at the time of the accident? [See *Matter of Wooten*, 30 Bankr. 357 (N.D. Ala., 1983)]

Agency

The Levine Cancer Institute, like many health-care facilities, is concerned about cost control. One proposal recommends reducing the number of doctors and nurses employed directly by the hospital. It recommends that nurses and doctors be encouraged to form a company to provide professional medical services—their services—to the hospital. The hospital would contract with the company to obtain the services of the nurses and doctors it needed as independent contractors. While hospital administrators believe that the plan could reduce costs, they are concerned about several legal matters. Would the new company be an agent of the hospital? Would the hospital's liability change? By using the new company, is it possible to designate the doctors and nurses as independent contractors rather than as employees and thus reduce taxes?

Another proposal recommended is to have an outsider do all buying for the hospital, rather than have an employee do the supply purchasing. One manager thinks that, this way, if the buyer makes a mistake in product choice or if a patient is asserted to have been injured due to the use of an inappropriate product, then the buyer will be liable for the mistake instead of the hospital. Is that right?

These are among the subjects discussed in this chapter, which begins with a review of the nature of the agency relationship, how it is created, and the legal constraints on its formation and functions. The chapter then discusses the agent's authority to act for the principal, how that affects the principal's liability for the contracts and torts of the agent, and how an agency relationship can be terminated. The agency relationship is then compared to other legal relationships, including master-servant and employer–independent contractor. The issue article at the end of the chapter discusses the move by businesses to use more independent contractors.

The Agency Relationship

According to *Black's Law Dictionary*, an *agency relationship* is

> An employment [of an agent] for the purpose of representation in establishing relations between a principal and third parties.

An agency relationship is created whenever a person or company—the *agent*— agrees to act on behalf of and for, and to be subject to the control of, another person or company—the *principal*. Through this legal relationship, the agent becomes a representative of the principal. An agent may negotiate and legally bind a principal to contracts with third parties as long as he is acting within the scope of the authority granted by the principal. In dealing with third parties—normally the customers or suppliers of the principal—the agent is granted certain authority to act for and in the name of and in place of the principal. The typical agency relationship is compared with the typical two-party business transaction in Exhibit 13.1.

Since a principal can appoint an agent to conduct almost any business transaction, the principal's purpose for developing agency relationships is to expand business operations and opportunities. For example, Troy Aikman Auto Mall in Fort Worth employs managers and sales agents to make decisions about ordering and selling cars to customers. Troy Aikman and his customers enjoy business dealings that would not be possible without the ability to use agency relationships, since Aikman personally could sell very few cars.

Similarly, the board of directors of a corporation enters into agency relationships with officers of the corporation who are charged with the authority to manage the corporation. The managers represent the directors (the principals of the corporation) and have the authority to bind the principals to contracts. The agency relationship is essential to business.

CREATING AN AGENCY

No particular formal procedure exists through which an agency relationship is established. However, some affirmative indication must be made by the parties to enter into an agency. The principal must show a desire for the agent to act on behalf of the principal, and the agent must consent to do so. Most agency relationships are created without formal statements such as "I will represent you," but they can be based on a written contract. Within this framework, an agency can be established by

- Agreement of the parties
- Ratification of the agent's activities by the principal
- Application of the doctrine of estoppel
- Operation of law

EXHIBIT 13.1

A Contract and an Agency Relationship

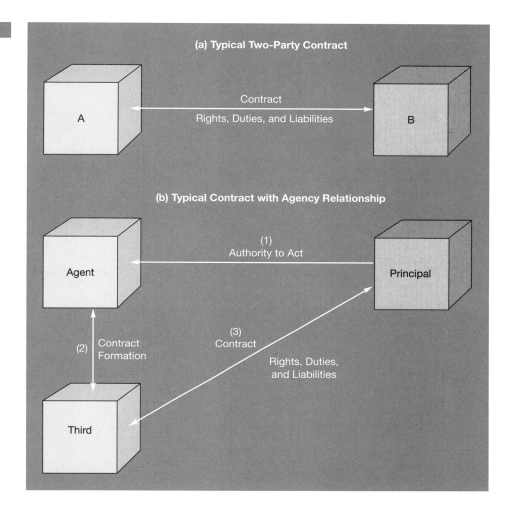

(a) Typical Two-Party Contract

A — Contract / Rights, Duties, and Liabilities → B

(b) Typical Contract with Agency Relationship

Agent ← (1) Authority to Act — Principal

(2) Contract Formation

(3) Contract / Rights, Duties, and Liabilities

Third

Agency by Agreement of the Parties

An agency is normally formed through agreement of the parties. The principal and agent establish their relationship through an oral or a written contract. A written contract is required by law in some instances. For example, many states require that the agency be established in writing when an agency relationship is to last longer than one year or is for the sale of land. However, most agencies are established by agreements that do not qualify as contracts. The fundamental basis of the agency relationship is that the agent acts for the benefit of the principal and is subject to the principal's control.

One legal document that establishes an agency is the *power of attorney*, a written document authorizing a person or a company to act as an agent for a principal (see Exhibit 13.2). The power of attorney can be general, or it can provide the agent with limited authority to act on behalf of the principal for a specific transaction. The term *power of attorney* describes the document itself and does not imply that the agent (who may be called an attorney-in-fact) is actually an attorney.

EXHIBIT 13.2

General Power
of Attorney

POWER OF ATTORNEY

KNOW ALL MEN BY THESE PRESENTS: That I, _____, of _____, have made, constituted and appointed, and by these presents do hereby make, constitute and appoint _____, of _____, by true and lawful attorney for me and in my name, place and stead and for my use and benefit:

(a) To ask, demand, sue for, collect, recover and receive all such sums of money, debts, dues, accounts, legacies, bequests, interests, dividends, annuities and demands whatsoever as are now or shall hereafter become due, owing, payable or belonging to me, and have, use and take all lawful ways and means in my name or otherwise for the recovery thereof, by actions at law or in equity, attachments, or otherwise, and to compromise and agree for the same, and acquittances, releases and other sufficient discharges for the same for me, and in my name to make, seal and deliver;

(b) To bargain, contract, agree for, purchase, receive and take lands, tenements and hereditaments and accept the seisin and possession of all lands and all deeds and other assurances in the law therefore;

(c) To lease, let, demise, bargain, sell, remise, release, convey, mortgage and hypothecate my lands or interests in lands, tenements and hereditaments, upon such terms and conditions, and under such covenants as he shall think fit;

(d) To vote at all meetings of any corporation or corporations and otherwise to act as my representative in respect of any shares now held or which may hereafter be acquired by me therein and for that purpose to sign and execute any proxies or other instruments in my name and on my behalf;

(e) To make deposits and withdrawals and otherwise engage in all banking transactions at any and all banking institution or institutions;

(f) To have access to such safety deposit box as may be leased by me;

(g) To borrow money on the security of the same or surrender the same and receive the surrender value thereof;

(h) To bargain and agree for, buy, sell, mortgage and hypothecate and in any and every way and manner deal in and with goods, wares and merchandise, shares of stock, bonds, choses in action, and other property, in possession or in action, and to make, do and transact all and every kind of business of what nature and kind soever; also for me and in my name and as my act and deed to sign, seal, execute, deliver and acknowledge such deeds, releases of dower, leases and assignments of leases, covenants, indentures, agreements, mortgages, hypothecations, bottomries, charter parties, bills of lading, bills, bonds, checks, notes, receipts, evidences of debt, releases and satisfaction of mortgages, judgments, and other debts, proofs of claims in receiverships and estates and such other instruments in writing of whatever kind or nature as may be necessary or proper in the premises.

GIVING AND GRANTING unto my said attorney, and his substitute or substitutes, full power and authority to do and perform all and every act and thing whatsoever requisite and necessary to be done in and about the premises, as fully to all intents and purposes as I might or could do if personally present, hereby ratifying and confirming all that my said attorney, or his substitute or substitutes, shall lawfully do or cause to be done in the premises.

In WITNESS whereof, I have hereunto set my hand this _____ day of _____, 20_____.

_____   _____

State of California   ⎫
County of _____ ⎬

On _____, before me, the undersigned, a Notary Public in and for said State personally appeared

_____

known to me to be the person _____ whose name _____ subscribed to the within instrument and

acknowledged that _____ executed the same.

(Seal) _____

Notary Public in and for said State

Witness my hand and official seal.

_____

Agency by Ratification by the Principal

An agency relationship may be created by the principal's ratification of the agent's activities. This arises when a person who is not an agent—or an agent who is acting beyond her authority—enters into a contract on behalf of a third party (the alleged principal). Under such circumstances, the alleged principal is ordinarily under no obligation to be bound by the person's actions. At his option, however, the alleged principal may accept being bound to the contract. Accepting responsibility is called a *ratification*. By ratifying the agreement, the alleged principal becomes the principal, who is then bound by the entire contract as if it had been negotiated by an agent with the authority to enter into the contract.

Suppose you advertised your car for sale for $9,000. A prospective buyer came to look at it while you were gone and offered $8,500, which your roommate accepted, thinking you would be happy to sell it for that. Since your roommate was not your agent, you would not be obligated to go through with the deal, but you could also ratify the deal by selling for that price.

Ratification can occur expressly or by implication. An *express ratification* involves the principal's clear and definite indication (to either the person or the third party) to be bound to the otherwise unauthorized agreement. *Implied ratification* takes place when the principal behaves as if he has the intention of ratifying an unauthorized agreement. In most cases, an implied ratification occurs when the principal in some way accepts the benefits of the agreement. As the *Watson v. Schmidt* case illustrates, ratification can also be implied if the principal fails to object to the unauthorized activities of the agent.

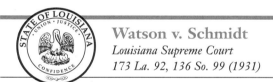

Watson v. Schmidt
Louisiana Supreme Court
173 La. 92, 136 So. 99 (1931)

CASE BACKGROUND *Needing money to pay bills due for her horses, on October 6, Watson, the plaintiff and principal, wired her agent, Holman (a defendant), informing him that he should sell a horse named Easter for $300. Instead, Holman sold another horse to Schmidt. On October 16, 1930, Holman wired the plaintiff to inform her: "We are lucky. Sold Kadiak for $2,000." On December 26, Watson sued, contending that Holman was without authority to sell the more valuable horse named Kadiak, and that Schmidt had to return it. The lower court found for Watson; Holman and Schmidt appealed.*

CASE DECISION Land, Justice.

* * *

Plaintiff admits that she received the telegram [of October 16 from her agent] the next day after it was sent, and that she actually knew of the sale at that time.

At no time, prior to the institution of this suit on December 26, 1930, did plaintiff notify defendant that

Holman was without authority to sell the horse, Kadiak; nor did plaintiff at any time before this suit tender to defendant the amount of the purchase price received by her, and demand the return to her of the horse.

. . . Kadiak ran but once from August 30, 1930, until October 15, 1930, the date of the sale by Holman to Schmidt, but, after the sale, he ran at the Jefferson Parish Fair in November and December, 1930, at least six times and won four races. During all of this time the horse was in the possession of the defendant. Under the above state of facts, it is clear that plaintiff has ratified the sale, for it is well settled that silence of a principal, after knowledge of an unauthorized or illegal act of his agent, is equivalent in law to an acquiescence in and ratification of the act or conduct of the agent.

It is also hornbook law that the owner who receives in whole or part the proceeds of a sale, made without his authority, ratifies it and cannot disturb the purchaser.

It is therefore ordered that the judgment appealed from be annulled and reversed. . . .

QUESTIONS FOR ANALYSIS

1. What factors swayed the court's decision to find that the principal had ratified the agent's sale of the horse?

2. What do you suppose may have caused the principal in this case to want the horse returned? Can you formulate a public policy argument for why silence would constitute a ratification in such a case?

Whether express or implied, a ratification has limits as to what can constitute it. A principal can ratify only agreements of which he has knowledge of the material (most important) facts. Further, an agreement can be ratified only if the agent purported to act on behalf of the principal. (If the agent was, in fact, acting only on her own behalf, the principal cannot later ratify the agreement and thereby bind himself to its terms.) The principal must ratify the entire agreement and must do so before the third party involved withdraws. Finally, if the original agreement between the agent and the third party was required by law to be in writing, such as a sale of real estate, the ratification must be in writing.

Agency by Estoppel

In an *agency by estoppel*, an agency is created by the words or actions of a "principal." Although no formal agency exists, the actions of the principal may lead one to reasonably believe that the presumed agent has the authority to act as an agent on behalf of the principal. When the agent then enters into a contract with a third party for the principal, the principal is bound to the contract and will be *estopped* to deny the existence of the agent's authority.

In one case, *Kanelles* v. *Locke*, 12 Ohio App. 210, a guest arrived at a hotel and was checked in at the front desk by a person "who appeared to be in charge." That person accepted jewelry and cash from the guest to put in the hotel safe. When the guest checked out the next day, the jewelry, cash, and the supposed receptionist were gone. The court held that an agency had been "created by estoppel." The hotel owner could not deny that a guest would have the right to presume that a person behind the lobby desk was an agent of the hotel even when he was not, and so was responsible for the loss suffered.

Agency by Operation of Law

The courts impose an agency relationship when a necessity or emergency exists and the actions of the "agent" are in the public interest. Suppose an emergency arises that requires the agent to act outside his delegated authority. The situation requires a decision, and the agent is unable to communicate with the principal. The courts allow the agent to act to avoid a substantial loss on the part of the principal. The agent, although acting beyond the authority granted by the principal, is provided the authority to do so in emergencies by *operation of law*.

CLASSIFICATION OF AGENTS

An agent's *authority* can be defined as the power to change the principal's legal status. That is, whenever an agent exercises authority, say, by making a contract with a third party, new legal rights and duties are created for the principal. The principal controls this by establishing the extent and the scope of the agent's authority to act on the principal's behalf.

Agents can be classified on the basis of the authority they are provided. The classifications of agents include universal, general, special, agency coupled with an interest, gratuitous, and subagents.

Universal Agents

A principal may designate someone to do all acts that can be legally delegated to an agent. Such an agent is called a *universal agent*. A universal agent is often designated by a principal who will be gone for some time period. The agent is usually provided a general power of attorney to legally undertake all business transactions on behalf of the principal.

General Agents

By authorizing a person to execute all transactions connected with a business, the principal designates a *general agent*. For example, the principal designates a general agent when appointing a manager to execute all business transactions to operate a hotel. The principal may limit the extent of the general agent's authority to a particular geographical area or some other aspect of the business.

Special Agents

The principal may provide an agent with authority to execute a specific transaction or series of transactions, but continuous service is not expected. Termed a *special agent*, the agent has authority to represent the principal only on the specified transaction or activity. An example of a special agent is an agent designated to buy or sell a piece of real estate.

Agency Coupled with an Interest

When an agent has paid for the right to exercise authority for a business, the agency created is called an *agency coupled with an interest*. Suppose a bank makes a loan to a company to buy some real estate, which is then rented. The loan agreement gives the bank the authority to collect monthly rent payments due to the borrower and to apply the proceeds to the loan repayment. The bank becomes the company's agent to collect the rent payments, with an interest in applying those payments to the repayment of the loan.

Gratuitous Agent

Although most agents receive compensation for their services, compensation is not a requirement for an agency relationship to exist. When a person volunteers with no expectation of being paid, she is a *gratuitous agent*. The principal and the gratuitous agent must consent to the relationship—one volunteers to assist with no compensation, and the other agrees to being assisted. The legal consequences are the same as in an agency relationship where the agent is paid.

Subagents

In some instances, a principal finds it advantageous to authorize an agent to delegate authority to other agents. The persons appointed by the agent are referred to as *subagents*. Subagents assist the agent in the performance of duties. Their acts bind the principal just as if they had been undertaken by the agent. Since subagents are agents of both the principal and the agent, they owe duties to both.

Agent's Authority to Act for the Principal

An agent's ability to transact business for the principal depends upon the scope of authority given to the agent. Such authority is determined from the oral or written expressions of the principal, the principal's conduct, or the trade customs in the business. An agent can have two general classes of authority: *actual authority* and *apparent authority*. Both may be present at the same time. If an agent claims to have authority but in fact has none, the principal is not responsible for the agent's dealings with third parties who would have no reason to think the agent has authority.

ACTUAL AUTHORITY

Actual authority, sometimes called real authority, is the authority given by the principal to the agent. Actual authority can come from express and implied authority. In either case, actual authority confers upon an agent the power and the right to change the principal's legal status.

Express Authority

Express authority consists of oral or written instructions given by the principal to an agent. Suppose the owner of an apartment complex hires a leasing agent and tells the agent to rent apartments at a certain price. The agent would have express authority to rent the apartments as instructed.

Implied Authority

Often, when an agent receives express authority, he also receives *implied authority* to do whatever is reasonable and customary to carry out the agency purpose. Suppose a landowner authorizes a real estate agent to find a buyer for some acreage. The landowner need not describe to the agent every step that could be taken to locate a buyer. Even though the parties may not discuss the matter, the agent would have the implied authority to post a "For Sale" sign on the property, advertise the offer for sale in a newspaper, and take prospective purchasers to the property. The agent would have implied authority to such customary things unless instructed not to by the principal.

APPARENT AUTHORITY

A principal can be bound by unauthorized acts of an agent who appears to have authority to act. *Apparent authority* arises when the principal creates an appearance of authority in an agent that leads a third party to conclude reasonably that the agent has authority to act for the principal. For example, in *Foley v. Allard*, 405 N.W.2d 503 (1987), Allard had an account at an investment company. Since he was a customer, the company let him use its facilities and take calls there. Allard convinced Foley to give him $10,000 to invest for her. He deposited the money into his account at the investment firm and spent it. Foley believed Allard was an employee of the investment firm because her calls to him there were accepted, giving the appearance that he worked there. Even though the firm did not know or approve of Allard's actions, allowing him "to take calls is a manifestation of authority by the principal." Since Allard had apparent authority to act for the investment firm, the firm could be held liable for Foley's losses.

Apparent authority commonly arises when a principal hires a business manager as an agent. As a rule, the general authority to manage a business confers upon the agent the implied authority to undertake activities that are customary in that business.

Duties of the Agency Parties

Once they have created an agency relationship, the parties have specific duties that govern their conduct and behavior toward each other. For example, each party is required to act in good faith toward the other and to share information having an important effect on the relationship. In addition, as Exhibit 13.3 summarizes, there are duties that each party specifically owes the other.

PRINCIPAL'S DUTIES TO AN AGENT

The law of agency emphasizes the duties an agent owes to his principal. This is understandable, since the acts central to the agency relationship are to be performed by the agent. Nevertheless, the principal owes the agent certain duties. Basically, unless the parties have agreed otherwise, the principal is required to

1. Cooperate with the agent so that the purpose of the agency can be fulfilled.
2. Pay the agent for services—either an agreed amount or an amount that is customary for such services.
3. Reimburse the agent for reasonable expenses.
4. Provide safe working conditions and meet any legal obligations, such as providing insurance, if required.
5. Indemnify the agent for legal liabilities incurred while performing the duties of the agency.

Duty to Cooperate with the Agent

The principal has a *duty to cooperate* with her agent by performing responsibilities defined in the contract or agreement forming the agency relationship. This duty generally includes the responsibility to compensate the agent, not to wrongfully

---

EXHIBIT 13.3

Duties in an Agency Relationship

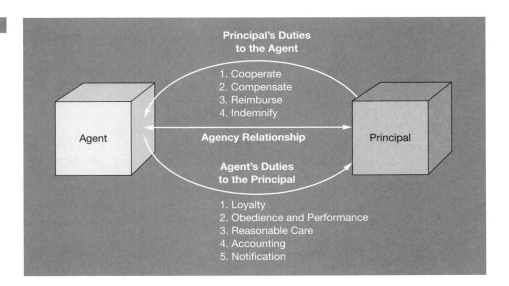

Principal's Duties to the Agent

1. Cooperate
2. Compensate
3. Reimburse
4. Indemnify

Agent

Agency Relationship

Principal

Agent's Duties to the Principal

1. Loyalty
2. Obedience and Performance
3. Reasonable Care
4. Accounting
5. Notification

terminate the agency relationship, and, in some circumstances, to furnish the agent with an opportunity to work. As to the latter, the principal must provide a safe working environment and warn the agent of any unreasonable risk associated with the agency. In addition, the principal must not furnish goods of inferior quality to the agent if the agency agreement calls for the sale of goods of a specific quality.

Duty to Compensate the Agent

Unless the agent has agreed to work for free, the principal is under a *duty to compensate* her agent. If the agency does not specify an amount or rate of compensation, the principal has a duty to pay for the reasonable value of the services provided by the agent. In such circumstances, the agent is paid the "customary" rate of compensation for the services provided.

Duty to Reimburse the Agent's Reasonable Expenses

A principal is under a duty to pay the reasonable expenses incurred by an agent. The principal would be expected, for example, to pay reasonable travel and lodging expenses. Hence, the principal is under a *duty to reimburse* any authorized payments the agent makes to third parties on behalf of the principal.

The agent cannot recover expenses incurred as a result of his misconduct or negligence. For example, an agent who sells property to the wrong person cannot recover from the principal expenses associated with correcting the error.

Duty to Indemnify the Agent for Losses

The principal is under a *duty to indemnify*—to pay for damages or, in effect, to insure the agent against losses suffered while undertaking authorized transactions on the principal's behalf. Suppose the principal has goods that belong to someone else and directs the agent to sell them. The agent sells the goods, believing they are the property of the principal. Later, if the agent is sued by the legal owner, the principal has a duty to indemnify the agent for losses incurred in the lawsuit, including attorney's fees. If, however, the agent knows the goods belong to another, the principal has no duty to indemnify the agent for losses from subsequent lawsuits.

AGENT'S DUTIES TO THE PRINCIPAL

The agent's duties to the principal arise from the fact that an agent is a *fiduciary* of the principal. That is, the agent occupies a position of trust, honesty, and confidence with respect to the principal. In addition to whatever specific responsibilities the principal and agent may agree upon in establishing the agency relationship, the law imposes certain duties, known as fiduciary duties, upon an agent. Those duties include (1) loyalty, (2) obedience and performance, (3) reasonable care, (4) accounting, and (5) notification.

Duty of Loyalty

An agent is required to meet a higher standard of conduct than that ordinarily imposed upon parties to business dealings. The *duty of loyalty* requires an agent to place the principal's interests before the agent's personal interests or those of any third party. Thus, it would be a violation of this duty if the agent also represented another party whose interests were in conflict with those of the principal.

Suppose a sales agent represents an electronics manufacturer and the agent's primary responsibility is to locate potential customers for that manufacturer's products and attempt to arrange sales. If the agent also represents a competing manufacturer, a violation of the duty of loyalty to the first manufacturer has taken place. Of course, the agent could legally represent both manufacturers with their consent.

It would also be a violation of the duty of loyalty if the agent were involved in self-dealing. That is, the agent must avoid acting on his own behalf while acting for the principal. Self-dealing would occur if an agent whose job was to buy particular goods for the principal bought the goods from himself with a profit added to the price. If an agent engages in self-dealing, the principal is entitled to void or rescind the transaction, as we see in the *Tarnowski* decision.

Tarnowski v. Resop
Minnesota Supreme Court
236 Minn. 33, 51 N.W.2d 801 (1952)

CASE BACKGROUND *Tarnowski hired Resop to investigate and negotiate the purchase of a jukebox route. Relying on Resop's advice, Tarnowski bought such a business from a third party. Later, Tarnowski discovered that Resop worked with the sellers to present false information about the value of the business. Tarnowski then demanded his money back, and, when the sellers refused, he successfully sued them.*

Tarnowski then sued Resop, alleging that he had collected a "secret commission" from the sellers for bringing about the sale. Tarnowski sought to recover that commission. The lower court found for Tarnowski, and Resop appealed. Resop argued that because Tarnowski collected from the sellers he was not also entitled to collect from him.

CASE DECISION Knutson, Justice.

* * *

[T]he principle that all profits made by an agent in the course of an agency belong to the principal, whether they are the fruits of performance or the violation of an agent's duty, is firmly established and universally recognized.

It matters not that the principal has suffered no damage or even that the transaction has been profitable to him.

The rule and the basis therefor [have been stated by this court]: "Actual injury is not the principle the law proceeds on, in holding such transactions void. Fidelity in the agent is what is aimed at, and, as a means of securing it, the law will not permit him to place himself in a position in which he may be tempted by his own private interests to disregard those of his principal." . . .

The right to recover profits made by the agent in the course of the agency is not affected by the fact that the principal, upon discovering a fraud, has rescinded the contract and recovered that with which he parted. *Restatement, Agency,* . . . reads: "If an agent has violated a duty of loyalty to the principal so that the principal is entitled to profits which the agent has thereby made, the fact that the principal has brought an action against a third person and has been made whole by such action does not prevent the principal from recovering from the agent the profits which the agent has made. Thus, if the other contracting party has given a bribe to the agent to make a contract with him on behalf of the principal, the principal can rescind the transaction, recovering from the other party anything received by him, or he can maintain an action for damages against him; in either event the principal may recover from the agent the amount of the bribe."

It follows that, insofar as the secret commission of $2,000 received by the agent is concerned, plaintiff had an absolute right thereto, irrespective of any recovery resulting from the action against the sellers for rescission.

* * *

Affirmed.

QUESTIONS FOR ANALYSIS

1. If the principal was fully compensated by his action against the sellers, why would the court also let him recover the commission from the agent?
2. What if the principal would make a profit as a consequence of collecting from the agent?

Duty of Obedience and Performance

An agent must perform instructions provided by the principal as closely as possible. The agent violates this *duty of obedience and performance* by ignoring the principal's instructions and is liable to the principal. However, an agent has no obligation to engage in illegal activity that could lead to personal liability. Nor is it a breach of this duty if the agent refuses to engage in unethical behavior. For example, a sales clerk in a sporting goods store who refuses to inform customers (as instructed by the principal) that sleeping bags are filled with goose down when in fact they are not would not be in violation of this duty.

In an emergency, it may be necessary for the agent to act contrary to instructions to protect the principal's interest. Suppose Klein appoints Martinez as her agent for the purpose of selling her sports car. Klein gives Martinez the keys to the car with instructions not to drive the car without her permission. If an emergency arose, such as a hailstorm that would damage the car, Martinez would not be in violation of his duty of obedience and performance if he drove the car to a safe place.

Duty of Reasonable Care

An agent is required to exercise *reasonable care* and skill in the performance of duties. Unless the agent has claimed to be an expert in the particular subject matter of the agency relationship or to possess a special skill, as in the case of an attorney or a broker, the duty is to perform responsibilities with the degree of care that a reasonable person would exercise under the circumstances. An accountant employed as an agent to prepare an income tax return who failed to take advantage of a legal tax deduction would violate this duty of reasonable care.

Duty to Account

An agent has a *duty to account* for the funds and property of his principal that have been entrusted to him or come into his possession. This does not mean that an agent must be an accountant, but the agent must keep a record of all money or property received during the agency. The agent must be able to show where money or property comes from and goes to. An agent must also avoid mixing personal funds with funds belonging to the principal. If funds are mixed without the principal's permission, a violation of the duty to account has occurred whether or not the principal is harmed in any way. A real estate broker, for example, who receives an earnest money deposit from a buyer of property must place the deposit in a separate bank account maintained for that purpose, not in a personal bank account.

The agent's duty to account extends to any personal profits the agent makes through any breach of a duty. If, for example, an agent was responsible for buying products for his principal and received a kickback from a seller, he would have a duty to account to the principal for that kickback, as the *Tarnowski* decision illustrated.

Duty to Notify

Finally, an agent is under a duty to keep his principal informed of all facts relevant to the agency purpose. Suppose Trapnell hires Amacher as her agent to sell 500 acres of farmland at a given price per acre. Amacher finds that in the next several months the farmland will likely increase dramatically in value because of a new highway to be built nearby. Amacher is under a duty to inform Trapnell of this information so that she can decide whether she still wants Amacher to sell according to her original instructions.

Liability for Contracts

The primary purpose of agency relationships is to help principals expand business activities. It is accomplished by authorizing agents to enter into contracts on behalf of the principal. In large part, the rights and liabilities of the principal and agent are determined by whether the principal is disclosed, partially disclosed, or undisclosed and by what authority the agent acted.

PRINCIPALS ARE DISCLOSED OR PARTIALLY DISCLOSED

According to the *Restatement (2d) Agency*, a *disclosed principal* is one whose identity is known by the third party at the time a contract is entered into with an agent. In contrast, although a *partially disclosed principal's* identity is unknown to the third party, the third party knows that the agent is acting for a principal at the time a contract is made.

Agents Have Actual Authority

As illustrated in Exhibit 13.4(a), a disclosed or partially disclosed principal is liable to a third party for a contract made by the agent if the agent has actual authority to act on behalf of the principal. Suppose Cook instructs Chan, her agent, to purchase a vehicle for her use. Chan contracts for a vehicle with a third party who knows that Chan is acting as an agent. Cook is bound by the contract and must honor it. The third-party seller of the vehicle is entitled to sue Cook if she fails to perform according to the agreement made on her behalf by Chan.

Agents Have Apparent Authority

As seen in Exhibit 13.4(b), the principal is contractually liable to a third party if the third party enters into a contract presented by an agent with the apparent authority to act for the principal. Under such circumstances, however, an agent who violates his duty of obedience to the principal is liable to the principal for any losses. To illustrate, suppose that Cook did not give Chan authority to buy a vehicle, but Cook's conduct in the past has led third parties to believe that Chan has such authority. If Chan contracts for a vehicle, Cook is bound by it. However, Chan must indemnify Cook for losses incurred as a consequence.

PRINCIPALS ARE UNDISCLOSED

An *undisclosed principal* is one whose identity is unknown by the third party. The third party also must have no knowledge that the agent is acting on behalf of another when the contract is made. Thus, the third party is unaware of both the identity of the principal and the existence of the agency relationship. In this situation, and as the *Rosen* decision illustrates, unless the agent reveals the agency or the identity of the principal, the agent is liable to the third party for the principal's nonperformance of the contract.

EXHIBIT 13.4

If Principal Is Disclosed or Partially Disclosed

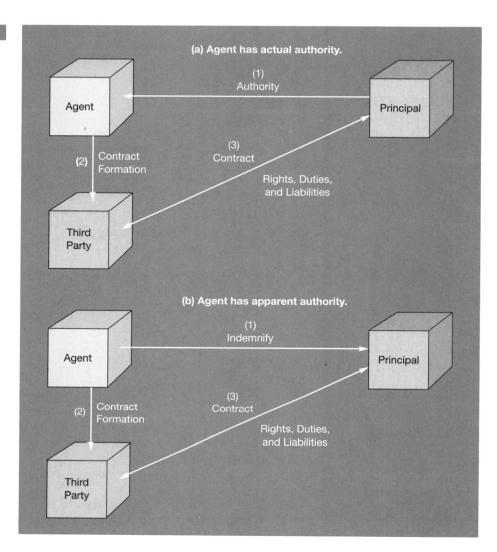

Rosen v. DePorter-Butterworth Tours, Inc.

Appellate Court of Illinois
62 Ill.App.3d 762, 379 N.E.2d 407 (1978)

CASE BACKGROUND *Rosen bought an African safari tour from DePorter-Butterworth Tours, Inc. DePorter did not disclose that it was an agent for the safari's sponsor, World Trek, the undisclosed principal.*

Rosen told DePorter that he would be in Europe before joining the safari group in Cairo. At DePorter's suggestion, Rosen agreed to contact the American Express office in Athens periodically in case DePorter made changes in the safari's schedule. However, DePorter failed *to contact Rosen through the American Express office as agreed when a change in the schedule was made. As a result, Rosen missed the tour and was stranded in Cairo for a week.*

Rosen sued to recover amounts paid to DePorter for the tour. DePorter responded that it was not liable to Rosen because it was merely an agent for World Trek. The lower court found for Rosen, and DePorter appealed.

CASE DECISION Barry, Presiding Justice.

* * *

The . . . issue presented for review is whether the trial court erred in finding DePorter liable to Rosen for the price of the tour. Inherent in a decision of this issue is a determination of the relationship between Rosen and DePorter and DePorter and the tour sponsor, World Trek. . . . [I]n the normal situation between a travel bureau and its traveler client a special agency relationship arises for the limited object of the one business transaction between the two parties. It is clear in the present case that Rosen employed the DePorter travel bureau as his special agent for the limited purpose of arranging the African Safari Tour sponsored by World Trek.

Although the sponsor of the tour, World Trek, . . . was not a party to this lawsuit, their relationship to DePorter is an important factor in deciding liability. The record contains a letter from DePorter to World Trek as plaintiff's Exhibit no. 4, which admits to DePorter's selling of World Trek's tour to Rosen and hints of a principal-agent relationship between World Trek and DePorter. The evidence also disclosed that DePorter received a 10% Commission from World Trek for selling its tour. The legal principle that an agent is liable as a principal to a third party in the case of an undisclosed agency relationship is well established and needs no citation for authority. In the instant case Rosen was aware that World Trek was sponsoring the tour but was without knowledge as to whether DePorter was truly representing him as his special agent for arranging the tour or whether DePorter was acting as an agent for World Trek in selling its tour to Rosen.

The traditional relationship between a travel bureau, such as DePorter, and the tour sponsors of the various tours sold has been categorized as one of agent and principal particularly in the field of tort liability of the travel bureau for injuries that occur to the traveler. . . . No sound reason exists for not finding the same principal-agent relationship between a tour sponsor and a travel bureau in the case of alleged liability for breach of an agreement involving the ultimate sale of the tour to an ordinary member of the traveling public, such as Rosen.

. . . [I]f an agent does not disclose the existence of an agency relationship and the identity of his principal, he binds himself to the third party with whom he acts as if he, himself, were the principal. . . . The fact that Rosen knew that World Trek and not DePorter was the tour sponsor does not satisfy the necessary disclosure to prevent DePorter from becoming liable as principal.

* * *

Affirmed.

QUESTIONS FOR ANALYSIS

1. What did Rosen know and not know about World Trek and DePorter that was important here?
2. Why was DePorter held liable in this case? How could it have avoided the lawsuit? Is World Trek responsible for any of the difficulties Rosen encountered here?

As Exhibit 13.4 illustrates, if the agent has authority, the undisclosed principal is bound to contracts formed with third parties by the agent just as if the identity had been disclosed at the time the contract was made. In fact, the principal may hold the third party to the contract except in the following cases:

1. The undisclosed principal is expressly excluded as a party to the contract between the agent and the third party.
2. The contract is a negotiable instrument. According to the UCC, if the identity of the principal or existence of the agency relationship is not shown in the instrument, only the agent is liable.
3. The agent's performance is personal to the contract.

In the event the agent is found liable to the third party and is forced to pay—say, in the event the principal failed to perform and the third party sues the agent—the agent is entitled to be indemnified by the principal. However, the agent must have been operating within the scope of his authority. If the agent has acted outside his authority or has no authority, the undisclosed principal is under no obligation to accept responsibility for the agent's actions.

Liability for Torts

Besides creating contractual liability on behalf of a principal, an agent can create tort liability. As Exhibit 13.5 illustrates, the principal is liable for the torts of an agent if the tort was authorized by the principal. The principal also is likely to be liable for an agent's unauthorized tort if the tort occurred within the scope of the agent's employment. If the agent commits an unauthorized tort outside the scope of employment, the agent is liable to the third party for damages incurred, and the principal is usually not liable.

PRINCIPAL'S LIABILITY

It is obvious that a principal is liable for torts committed by an agent that are ordered by the principal. If Mike the building contractor tells Marty the bricklayer to skimp on concrete and use low-quality bricks and that later causes a building to collapse, Mike the principal is liable in tort for injuries suffered as a result of the shoddy work done by his agent Marty.

Vicarious Liability

As we will see later in the *Santiago* decision, under *vicarious liability*, a principal can be liable for the unauthorized torts of an agent. A principal is likely to be liable for the unauthorized intentional or negligent torts of an agent if the agent was acting within the scope of employment. Courts consider many factors in determining whether an act was within the scope of employment. Some of the most important are whether

1. The act was of the same general nature as those authorized by the principal.
2. The agent was authorized to be where he was at the time the act occurred.
3. The agent was serving the principal's interests at the time of the act.

Respondeat Superior

A principal may be liable for the unauthorized intentional or negligent torts of an agent—if the agent was acting within the scope of employment. The rule of law imposing vicarious liability upon an innocent principal is known as *respondeat superior*. This doctrine has been justified on the grounds that the principal is in a better position to protect the public from such torts, by controlling the actions of its agents, and to compensate those injured. This rule also means that employers are liable for torts of employees that can be attributed to negligent hiring or supervision.

As Exhibit 13.5 illustrates, the agent is required to indemnify the principal for amounts the principal has to pay to the wronged party as a consequence of the agent's unauthorized torts. In most cases, however, the agent is unable to reimburse the principal, who must bear the full cost of the liability.

THE AGENT'S LIABILITY

As a rule, the principal is not liable for the torts of an agent when the tort is both unauthorized and outside the scope of employment. In such cases, the agent alone is liable to the wronged party. The most difficult situations are those in which the

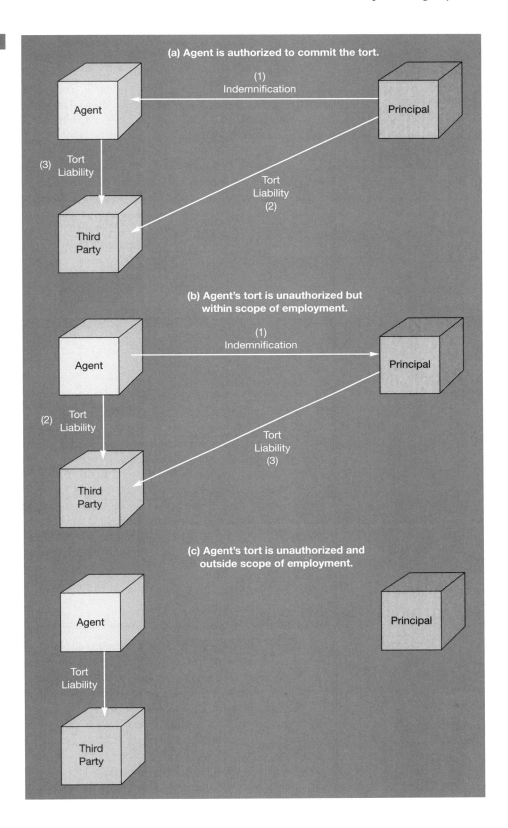

EXHIBIT 13.5

Tort Liability in an Agency Relationship

(a) Agent is authorized to commit the tort.

Agent

(1) Indemnification

Principal

(3) Tort Liability

Tort Liability (2)

Third Party

(b) Agent's tort is unauthorized but within scope of employment.

Agent

(1) Indemnification

Principal

(2) Tort Liability

Tort Liability (3)

Third Party

(c) Agent's tort is unauthorized and outside scope of employment.

Agent

Principal

Tort Liability

Third Party

Principals and Agents under a Civil-Law System

Comparing the common-law and civil-law traditions, it becomes apparent that agency relationships differ in important ways. For example, under the common law, an undisclosed principal is bound to contracts with third parties if the agent forming the contract has actual authority to enter into those contracts. The principal is able to hold the third party to the contract. In this situation, the common-law and the civil-law traditions can reach different conclusions. Under civil law, the "principle of lack of communication among parties that have no knowledge of each other's existence" prevails, and the principal is not bound. The principal is not able to hold the third party to the contract unless the third party had knowledge of the principal's existence.

Consider a situation where the principal and the agent have decided to establish their agency relationship on the basis of a written contract. With that contract, the agent has actual authority to act on behalf of the principal. The agent enters into a contract with a third party, and then the agency contract is found to have been invalid. Under the common-law tradition, the principal is not liable to the third party (unless through her actions she had created apparent authority in the agent). In most countries with a civil-law tradition, the agent's power to perform is independent of the validity of the agency contract. Thus, under civil law, the principal is liable to the third party.

agent was not doing his job at the time of the tort but may have been engaged in an authorized action.

Some cases involve agents who use company vehicles for unauthorized purposes. Suppose Burns is a sales representative for Reno's Pizza. She negligently injures a pedestrian while driving a company car between sales calls. She is clearly acting within the scope of her employment. Her principal would be liable for the pedestrian's injuries. However, if Burns has the accident while going to visit a friend, Reno's may or may not be liable, depending on the extent to which Burns has deviated from the principal's business. The point at which the principal gains or loses liability varies among jurisdictions. Traditionally, an agent who departs from his employment to the point of abandonment is not within the scope of employment.

Termination of an Agency

The agency relationship is largely consensual. Thus, when the principal withdraws or when the consent otherwise ends, the agency is *terminated*. Once an agency is ended, the agent's authority to act for the principal ceases. It may be necessary to give notice of the termination to third parties to end the agent's apparent authority.

An agency is usually established by agreement between the principal and the agent. The parties may set a specific time for an agency, which then ends automatically at a given date. If no time is set, the agency ends when its purpose, such as the sale of real estate, is fulfilled. The parties may agree to terminate the agency or to extend it beyond its original time and scope of duties. An agency can be ended unilaterally upon reasonable notice by either the agent or the principal. A unilateral termination is effective even if it is in breach of a contract between the parties, but the breaching party may be liable for contract damages.

Certain events will automatically terminate an agent's ability to act on behalf of the principal. Termed *termination by operation of law*, an agency is terminated without any action by the principal or the agent. For example, if either the principal or the agent dies, the agency ends. It also ends automatically if the subject matter of the agreement is lost or destroyed (a house for sale burns down). Similarly, if economic conditions change and the subject matter of the agency is unusually affected, the agent can reasonably expect that the principal will want to terminate the agency. Finally, bankruptcy of either party terminates an agency if it makes the agent unable to perform necessary duties.

Agents Compared to Employees and Contractors

An agency creates certain unique rights and duties. Two important relationships that are similar to but legally distinct from agency relationships are the *master-servant* (*employer-employee*) and *employer–independent contractor* relationships. As Exhibit 13.6 illustrates, while they share similarities with agency, each differs in important ways.

MASTER-SERVANT RELATIONSHIP

Master-servant is an old term still often used in law that describes the employment relationship. The servant (employee) is hired by a master (employer). Traditionally, servants or employees performed manual labor; they were not in a position to act on behalf of the master or employer when dealing with third parties. The master-servant rules still apply when an employee is under the direct control of an employer, such as a food service or road maintenance worker. When the employee does not have authority to represent the employer in business dealings, no agency exists, and a master-servant relationship exists. Since employers are presumed to be in control of their employees, employers are liable for the torts committed by employees in the course of employment. As we will see, this may not be the case when an agency relationship exists.

Employees as Servants and Agents

Many employees now are agents and servants. Some of their work is under the direct control of their employer or master, but, in other capacities, they are empowered to act as agents, in which case their employers are also principals. Employees often make business decisions that affect their employer and do so

EXHIBIT 13.6	Types of Relationships	Characteristics
Distinguishing Legal Relationships	**Principal-Agent**	Agent acts on behalf of or for the principal, with a degree of personal discretion.
	Master-Servant (Employer-Employee)	The servant is an employee whose conduct is controlled by the employer. A servant can also be an agent.
	Employer–Independent Contractor	An independent contractor is not an employee, and the employer does not control the details of the independent contractor's performance. The contractor is usually not an agent.

without consulting the employer on each matter. In this sense, they are agents and employees. Sales representatives at Troy Aikman Auto Mall who are authorized to sell cars within certain price ranges without permission of a supervisor are employees with certain agency powers to act on behalf of their employer.

The distinction between agent-principal and master-servant is often blurred. Most employers do not specify to their employees that they are agents in certain matters and employees in others. What matters is what legal authority or responsibility exists when questions arise about the validity of a contract or the responsibility for a tort.

EMPLOYER-INDEPENDENT CONTRACTOR RELATIONSHIP

The employer–independent contractor relationship differs from the agency and master-servant relationships in several ways. Consider how *independent contractor* is defined by the *Restatement (2d) Agency*:

> An independent contractor is a person who contracts with another to do something for him but who is not controlled by the other nor subject to the other's right to control with respect to his physical conduct in the performance of the undertaking.

As this definition implies, the independent contractor is distinguished by the extent of control the employer retains over work performance. In the *Santiago* case, the court expands upon the factors listed in the *Restatement*. The more control the employee retains, the more likely the employee will be characterized as an independent contractor. As a rule, the employer is not liable for the torts of an independent contractor.

Contractors as Agents

Some independent contractors are also agents. Contractors authorized to enter into contracts for the principal are agents. This often includes attorneys, auctioneers, and other such persons who conduct business on behalf of the principal. Some contractors do not have authority to enter into contracts for the principal and so are not agents. This would usually include building contractors and others hired to perform certain tasks for an employer.

JURIS prudence?

Who, Him? Must Be an Independent Contractor

Armando Martinez worked for Harjeet Singh at Singh's Donuts R' More shop in Sacramento. If Martinez is recognized as Singh's employee, Singh would be required to pay payroll taxes, such as for workers' compensation and social security. Martinez was an employee of Singh, but Singh was not paying these taxes.

After Martinez was shot by gunmen who robbed Singh's store, Singh dragged him outside and told police Martinez was a customer. Singh then told an insurance agent that Martinez was a friend who had dropped by to watch him make doughnuts. Singh was fined $1,000 for falsifying information at a crime scene but was also sued by Martinez, who was, in fact, his employee.

Source: *Sacramento Bee*

Determining Liability

Whether a person acts as an agent or as an independent contractor can be important in determining tort or contract liability. An employer-principal is liable for contracts made on her behalf by a person acting as her agent but is not likely to be liable for torts involving the same person when acting as an independent contractor.

Suppose Cristina hires Jaime, an attorney, to make a deal on her behalf. Jaime makes a deal with Ahmad on Cristina's behalf. Cristina is responsible for that contract. If Jaime later gets angry at Ahmad and hits him on the head with a brick, Cristina is not liable for the tort committed by Jaime against Ahmad because Jaime is an independent contractor. However, if Jaime worked for Cristina as an in-house attorney at Cristina's offices, Cristina could well be liable for the tort because Jaime would be an employee, not an independent contractor. Cristina could be liable for Jaime's tort because principals or employers may be responsible for the actions of their agents or employees even if the actions were obviously against the employer's wishes. (The notion of vicarious liability arises in the *Santiago* decision.)

Suppose Cristina pays Anthony $40,000 to build an addition to her office. Anthony is an independent contractor, not an agent, so Cristina is unlikely to be liable for any contracts he signs related to the construction work and is not liable if he hits Jaime on the head with a brick at the construction site.

When such cases arise, the courts have certain guidelines they look to rather than the words the parties themselves may attach to their relationship. The *Santiago* decision outlines the major issues that courts consider in such cases.

Santiago v. Phoenix Newspapers, Inc.
Supreme Court of Arizona
794 P.2d 138 (1990)

CASE BACKGROUND *Frausto delivered the Arizona Republic for Phoenix Newspapers (PNI). He worked under a "Delivery Agent Agreement" that stated that he was an independent contractor. He could work as he pleased, but he had to deliver the papers himself at least 75 percent of the time, and if the papers were not delivered properly and on time, he could be dismissed. He picked up the papers at a distribution point each morning and delivered them to a list of addresses provided by PNI. The number of people on his route varied over time, but he was paid a set amount. Frausto was delivering papers when his car hit a motorcycle driven by Santiago, who sued PNI for negligence, claiming that Frausto was PNI's agent. The trial court and appeals court held that Frausto was an independent contractor and not an agent and, thus, that Santiago could sue only Frausto and not PNI. Santiago appealed, contending that Frausto was an employee or agent of PNI and that vicarious liability in tort could be imposed on PNI for Frausto's alleged negligence.*

CASE DECISION Grant, Chief Judge, Court of Appeals.

* * *

[W]e reject PNI's argument that the language of the employment contract is determinative. Contract language does not determine the relationship of the parties, rather the "objective nature of the relationship [is] determined upon an analysis of the totality of the facts and circumstances of each case." . . .

The fundamental criterion is the extent of control the principal exercises or may exercise over the agent. . . .

In determining whether an employer-employee relationship exists, the fact finder must evaluate a number of criteria. They include:

1. The extent of control exercised by the master over details of the work and the degree of supervision;
2. The distinct nature of the worker's business;
3. Specialization or skilled occupation;

4. Materials and place of work;
5. Duration of employment;
6. Method of payment;
7. Relationship of work done to the regular business of the employer;
8. Belief of the parties.

Analysis of Relationship between Frausto and PNI

1. The extent of control exercised by the master over the details of the work

Such control may be manifested in a variety of ways. A worker who must comply with another's instructions about when, where, and how to work is an employee. . . . In deciding whether a worker is an employee we look to the totality of the circumstances and the indicia of control. In this case, PNI designated the time for pick-up and delivery, the area covered, the manner in which the papers were delivered, i.e., bagged and banded, and the persons to whom delivery was made. Although PNI did little actual supervising, it had the authority under the contract to send a supervisor with Frausto on his route. Frausto claimed he did the job as he was told, without renegotiating the contract terms, adding customers and following specific customer requests relayed by PNI.

2. The distinct nature of the worker's business

Whether the worker's tasks are efforts to promote his own independent enterprise or to further his employer's business will aid the fact finder in ascertaining the existence of an employer-employee relationship. . . . As far as the nature of the worker's business, Frausto had no delivery business distinct from that of his responsibilities to PNI. Unlike the drivers in [another case], Frausto had an individual relationship and contract with the newspaper company. Furthermore, he did not purchase the papers and then sell them at a profit or loss. Payments were made directly to PNI and any complaints or requests for delivery changes went through PNI. If Frausto missed a customer, a PNI employee would deliver a paper.

3. Specialization or skilled occupation

The jury is more likely to find a master-servant relationship where the work does not require the services of one highly educated or skilled. PNI argues that its agents must drive, follow directions, and be diligent in order to perform the job for which they are paid. However, these skills are required in differing degrees for virtually any job. Frausto's services were not specialized and required no particular training. In addition, an agreement that work cannot be delegated indicates a master-servant relationship. In this case, Frausto could delegate work but only up to twenty-five percent of the days.

4. Materials and place of work

If an employer supplies tools, and employment is over a specific area or over a fixed route, a master-servant relationship is indicated. In this case, PNI supplied the product but did not supply the bags, rubber bands, or transportation necessary to complete the deliveries satisfactorily. However, PNI did designate the route to be covered.

5. Duration of employment

Whether the employer seeks a worker's services as a one-time, discrete job or as part of a continuous working relationship may indicate that the employer-employee relationship exists. The shorter in time the relationship, the less likely the worker will subject himself to control over job details. In addition, the employer's right to terminate may indicate control and therefore an employer-employee relationship. The "right to fire" is considered one of the most effective methods of control. In this case, the contract provided for a six-month term, renewable as long as the carrier performed satisfactorily. Frausto could be terminated without cause in 28 days and with cause immediately. The definition of cause in the contract was defined only as a failure to provide "satisfactory" service. A jury could reasonably infer that an employer-employee relationship existed since PNI retained significant latitude to fire Frausto inasmuch as the "satisfactory service" provision provides no effective standards. In addition, the jury could also infer that PNI provided health insurance to encourage a long-term relationship and disability insurance to protect itself in case of injury to the carrier, both of which support the existence of an employer-employee relationship.

6. Method of payment

PNI paid Frausto each week, but argues that because Frausto was not paid by the hour, he was an independent contractor. Santiago responds that payment was not made by the "job" because Frausto's responsibilities changed without any adjustment to his pay or contract. . . .

7. Relation of work done to the employer's regular business

A court is more likely to find a worker an employee if the work is part of the employer's regular business. . . . PNI is hard-pressed to detach the business of delivering news from that of reporting and printing it, especially when it retains an individual relationship with each carrier.

8. Belief of the parties

As stated above, Frausto believed that he was an employee, despite contract language to the contrary. Even if he believed he was an independent contractor, that would not preclude a finding of vicarious liability. As the *Restatement* explains: "It is not determinative that the parties believe or disbelieve that the relation of master and servant exists, except insofar as such belief indicates an assumption of control by the one and submission of control by the other." . . .

Conclusion and Disposition

Whether an employer-employee relationship exists may not be determined as a matter of law in either side's favor, because reasonable minds may disagree on the nature of the employment relationship. A jury could infer from these facts that Frausto was an employee because PNI involved itself with the details of delivery, received directly all customer complaints and changes so as to remove much of Frausto's independence, retained broad discretion to terminate, and relied heavily on Frausto's services for the survival of its business. The jury could also infer that Frausto was an independent contractor because he used his own car, was subject to little supervision, provided some of his own supplies, and could have someone else deliver from him within limits. Therefore, the trial court erred in finding as a matter of law that Frausto was an independent contractor. Summary judgment on the vicarious liability claim was inappropriate. The opinion of the court of appeals is vacated and the case is remanded to the superior court for proceedings consistent with this opinion.

QUESTIONS FOR ANALYSIS

1. Why should employers not be liable for the torts of independent contractors they hire when they may be liable for people they hire who are classified as employees?
2. Suppose PNI sold Frausto papers that Frausto then sold to customers on delivery routes run by his employees. Would Frausto and his employees be employees or agents of PNI?

JURIS prudence?

My Tenants Are Doing WHAT?

Show World, an "adult entertainment" enterprise in New York, provides "booths, known as one-on-one fantasy booths, where customers can communicate with performers, known as 'visual telephonic communicators'. . . . What happens inside the booths is private, determined by the number of coins the customer deposits and conversation with the performer."

"At the end of the day (or night), when the performer has finished her shift, the tokens are collected and the visual telephonic communicator is paid 40% of the coins deposited; Show World keeps the additional 60%. The performers are then asked to sign a purported lease agreement. . . . Show World argues that as a result of this lease, the visual telephonic communicators are tenants."

The IRS argued that the performers are employees, not tenants. Show World argued that if they are not tenants, they are independent contractors. Not so, held Judge Sand, who says that the IRS is right: the visual telephonic communicators are employees, not tenants or independent contractors. Show World had to pay $290,000 in back taxes.

Source: *303 West 42nd Street Enterprises* v. *IRS*, 916 F.Supp. 349

For many businesses, whether workers are classified as employees or as independent contractors can have significant tax consequences. Under both state and federal tax laws, an employer must pay employment and insurance taxes on employees—but not on independent contractors. By hiring independent contractors, businesses can avoid thousands of dollars in taxes and paperwork each year for each employee so classified. Both the Internal Revenue Service (IRS) and state tax agencies have begun looking more closely at such practices. The Issue at the end of the chapter discusses IRS efforts to reclassify businesses as employers.

Summary

- An agency relationship is created when an agent agrees to act on behalf of and to be subject to the control of the principal. As the principal's representative, the agent may bind the principal to contracts with third parties. By using agents, a principal can expand business activities.
- No formal procedure exists for the creation of an agency relationship. There must, however, be an affirmative response on the part of the parties, with the principal manifesting a desire that the agent act on her behalf.
- Agency relationships can be established by agreement of the parties, ratification of the agent's activities by the principal, application of the doctrine of estoppel, or operation of law.
- Agents' authority can range from the extensive powers of a universal agent, the broad business powers of a general agent, to the more limited powers of a special agent, a gratuitous agent or a subagent.
- The agent's ability to act on behalf of the principal depends on the scope of authority granted by the principal. An agent can have actual authority and apparent authority.
- The agent has actual authority if the principal has given the agent authority to act. For such actions, the principal is generally liable for the contracts entered into on her behalf and for the torts the agent may commit in the process.
- Once an agency is created, the parties have the duty to share information and to act in good faith. The principal owes the agent the duties to cooperate, compensate, reimburse, and indemnify. The agent owes the principal the duties of loyalty, obedience and performance, reasonable care, accounting, and notification.
- The agent has apparent authority if the principal created the appearance of authority in the agent. While the principal is generally liable for the torts and the contracts of an agent with apparent authority, the agent may be obliged to indemnify the principal for losses incurred.
- Agency relationships may terminate through the activities of the parties or by operation of the law. Once an agency relationship is terminated, the agent's authority to act for the principal ceases. It may be necessary to notify third parties to end the agent's apparent authority.
- Agency is distinguishable from master-servant (employer-employee) and employer–independent contractor relationships. Servants and independent contractors do not have authority to represent the employer in business dealings unless they are also authorized to be agents. An employer is liable for the torts of a servant and an agent in the course of business, but not of the independent contractor.

Why Are Businesses Hiring Independent Contractors?

 More and more businesses hire temporary rather than permanent personnel. By hiring workers from a service or as self-employed consultants, the business can call such workers independent contractors and avoid state and federal employment taxes.

The Internal Revenue Service (IRS) has been looking into the practice. In 1992, the IRS forced employers to reclassify 90,000 independent contractors as employees. The businesses were forced to pay $131 million in additional taxes and penalties. In this article, the author examines the problem and discusses the strategies the IRS is employing to control the practice.

REGULATORY CHOKEHOLD: THE IRS VS. THE SELF-EMPLOYED

James Bovard

The Internal Revenue Service is carrying out a sweeping campaign to slash the number of Americans permitted to be self-employed—and to punish the companies that contract with them. The IRS's attack has devastated thousands of small businesses and is under-mining high-tech industries, the health-care industry, and even freedom of religion. IRS officials indicate that more than half the nation's self-employed should no longer be allowed to work for themselves.

This controversy originates in arcane federal regulations on the proper classification of workers. If a person is an employee, the employer must withhold all of that person's payroll taxes and remit them to the IRS, pay half of the employee's Social Security taxes and all of the unemployment insurance tax. But if an individual is an independent contractor, a business need only file a Form 1099 with the IRS reporting how much it paid that person, and the contractor pays his taxes directly to the IRS.

The IRS has long sought to forcibly reduce the number of self-employed Americans and maximize the number subject to tax withholding. The IRS enforcement campaign is targeting businesses with less than

$3 million in assets—in most cases, businesses without in-house counsel that cannot afford a lengthy court fight. The House Government Operations Committee concluded in a report . . . that "IRS enforcement activities on independent contractors present small business taxpayers with a veritable nightmare of problems and policies that defy common sense."

The IRS bases its classification decisions primarily on a list of 20 questions on the relationship between the employer and the contractor/employee. . . .

Once an IRS agent announces that a company has misclassified its employees (as happens in nine of 10 audits), the company often faces a staggering tax bill—largely because the IRS intentionally forces businesses to double-pay taxes already paid by independent contractors. The House Government Operations Committee noted: "The assessments are based on the use of preset mandatory formulas which even the IRS admits result in double tax collections. These back tax assessments have been responsible for putting a number of those businesses out of business." IRS agents have assessed more than $500 million in penalties and back taxes since 1988 (averaging $68,000 per company) and forced businesses to reclassify over 400,000 independent contractors as employees. (The IRS is now "converting" almost 2,000 independent contractors into employees each week.)

These businesses, in most cases, have not broken any clear law or manifested any intent to dodge taxes. Harvey Shulman, counsel for the National Association of Computer Consultant Businesses, observed: "I have had grown men and women—40 or 50 years old—cry on the phone to me, telling me that their marriage is threatened, they are seeking counseling, all because the business that they built up in the last 15 years of their lives—the house and other things they've earned from the fruits of their labor—is all threatened by this IRS employment classification audit. They ask me, 'What did I do wrong? Why am I being persecuted?'"

Many IRS officials threaten harsh penalties to coerce businesses to sign agreements promising not to use independent contractors in return for a reduction or waiver of the taxes and penalties. Such perpetual cease-and-desist orders may be appropriate when the government is dealing with wife-beaters or child molesters, but they are bizarre when it is seeking a pretext to permanently control the day-to-day operation of small businesses.

One industry that is especially hurt by the IRS crackdown is health care. Marc Catalano, president of the Private Care Association, an association of health-care agencies, accused the IRS of following a "search and destroy posture with respect to businesses that use independent contractors." Comprehensive Care Corp. was hit in 1991 with an IRS demand for $19.4 million in back taxes and penalties for treating psychologists and physicians as independent contractors.

John Bailey, a psychologist at the Family Therapy Center of Madison, Wis., complained to a congressional committee . . . that his clinic had "come under attack. . . . The IRS methods are too subjective, applied with ferocity and arbitrariness, and have caused untold grief for us and other well-meaning small businesses." Mr. Bailey reported that the IRS "attack has threatened the very survival" of several Wisconsin clinics.

The IRS tried to penalize several Pennsylvania corporations for paying dentists as independent contractors instead of employees. But the Pennsylvania Dental Board had warned the corporations that it would be illegal under state law for the corporations to hire dentists as employees, since the corporations themselves were not licensed to practice dentistry. A federal judge threw out the IRS's case in 1991.

* * *

High-tech industries have probably been hit hardest by the IRS's crackdown. In 1978, Congress enacted a provision to prevent the IRS from penalizing companies that had a "reasonable basis" for classifying people as independent contractors. But in the 1986 tax act, Sen. Daniel Patrick Moynihan (D., N.Y.) slipped in an amendment—Section 1706—that revoked the "reasonable basis" protection for engineers, computer programmers and other technical service professionals.

A 1987 Data Processing Managers Association survey found that 74% of firms decreased their contracts made directly with independent technical service consul-

tants as a result of Section 1706. Rep. Major Owens (D., N.Y.) said last year that "many African-American computer programmers and analysts have had the door to self-employment slammed in their faces because of Section 1706."

IRS agents are often heavy-handed in how they carry out employment tax audits. IRS officials have encouraged private companies to secretly betray their competitors. At a 1990 meeting in California, an IRS agent distributed "snitch sheets" to business people and asked them to make allegations of illegal independent contractor use by other companies. The IRS agent told attendees to mail the completed snitch sheets to him in unmarked plain envelopes and promised to follow up all leads.

The IRS estimates that 3.4 million Americans now working as independent contractors should be reclassified as employees. The Small Business Administration says that there are roughly five million independent contractors. Thus, more than half of all the independent contractors in the United States could be forced to find a boss.

The IRS justifies its crackdown because some of the self-employed dodge taxes. But the Treasury Department concluded in a 1991 report on technical service workers: "Misclassification of employees as independent contractors increases tax revenues . . . and tends to offset the revenue loss from undercompliance by such individuals, because direct compensation to independent contractors is substituted for tax-favored employee fringe benefits."

The IRS apparently believes that payroll tax withholding is more important than Americans' freedom of contract. Being self-employed and starting one's own business have long been part of the American Dream. But the IRS has apparently decided that it can no longer afford to permit others to pursue their dreams.

ISSUE QUESTIONS

1. Are IRS efforts interfering with freedom of contract rights as the author suggests?
2. Should the IRS encourage companies to secretly betray their competitors?

REVIEW AND DISCUSSION QUESTIONS

1. Define the following terms:

agency relationship	principal
agent	power of attorney
gratuitous agent	independent contractor
special agent	servant
general agent	fiduciary
subagent	vicarious liability
apparent authority	respondeat superior
actual authority	undisclosed principal

2. An agent embezzles funds from his principal and uses the funds to buy a car. What duties has the agent violated? Who is entitled to ownership of the car?

CASE QUESTIONS

3. Barbara Patridge was sued by a lender for failure to pay a loan that was due. Her husband had obtained the loan and admitted his liability, but he signed her name to the loan without her knowledge. Later, when one payment had been sent to the lender, Barbara attached a letter that said, "Enclosed is a check for $100 as payment toward the outstanding balance on our account. We apologize for the delay as Bill has been in the hospital. I think we've been delinquent in providing you with a plan for repayment. . . . we will make payments to you to show good faith that we wish to satisfy our debt with you. . . ." Was she a principal who could be held liable for the debt? [*Southern Oregon Production Credit* v. *Patridge*, 691 P.2d 135 (Ct. App., Ore., 1984)]

4. Linda Steele, dba (doing business as) The Travel Haus, sold Ben Douglas a vacation package to Hawaii. She had heard that the company she was buying the trip from, Total Hawaii, was having some problems, but she sold Douglas a Total Hawaii package anyway. She sent Douglas's check to Total Hawaii, which went bankrupt, taking Douglas's money with it. Douglas sued Steele for the amount paid; Steele countered that she was only an agent for Total Hawaii and was not liable. Legally, what kind of agent was she? Was she liable? [*Douglas* v. *Steele*, 816 P.2d 586 (Ct. App., Okla., 1991)]

5. Hunter Mining hired Hubco Data to install and customize computer equipment peculiar to Hunter's needs. Before the job was done, Hubco went out of business. Hunter sued MAI, the company that made the computer products that Hubco sold to Hunter, for breach of contract. Hubco was a licensed distributor of MAI when it sold Hunter the computer package. Was MAI liable for Hubco's failure? [*Hunter Mining* v. *Management Assistance, Inc.*, 763 P.2d 350 (Sup. Ct., Nev., 1988)]

6. Zimmerman, a real estate salesman, asked Robertson whether she was interested in selling her property. Robertson said she might be. Zimmerman came to Robertson's with an offer by Velten to buy the property. After some negotiations, both sides signed a contract for sale. Zimmerman told Robertson he was being paid a commission by Velten. Before the deal on the property was to close, Robertson asked for a copy of the agreement between Zimmerman and Velten, but they refused. Robertson refused to go through with the deal. Velten sued, claiming there was a valid contract. Robertson said that Zimmerman violated his fiduciary duty to her to disclose his interests. Is the deal valid? [*Velten* v. *Robertson*, 671 P.2d 1011 (Ct. App., Colo., 1983)]

7. A Pittsburgh real estate firm, George Brothers, managed some theaters owned by Peoples-Pittsburgh Trust Co. George hired McKnight to manage the theaters for it, which McKnight did for over ten years. McKnight received a salary plus one-third of the commissions received from George from Peoples-Pittsburgh Trust. When the theaters were sold, McKnight claimed that he was due one-third of the final sale commission that George received. Was he? [*McKnight* v. *Peoples-Pittsburgh Trust Co.*, 61 A.2d 820 (Sup. Ct., Pa., 1948)]

8. Dr. Leonard, head of the Department of Otolaryngology at Jefferson Medical College, negotiated a contract to hire Jacobson as a professor at a specified salary. After Jacobson accepted the position, put his house up for sale, and resigned his current employment, Leonard withdrew the job offer, stating that some other faculty opposed the appointment and that any job offer had to be approved by the dean of the medical school; that is, Leonard did not have authority to offer an employment contract. Jacobson sued for breach of contract. Could he prevail? [*Jacobson* v. *Leonard*, 406 F. Supp. 515 (E.D., Pa., 1976)]

9. Mary Kidd sued Thomas A. Edison, Inc. (Edison), alleging that a Mr. Fuller, acting for Edison, contracted with her to sing at a series of recitals for record dealers. At the recitals, Kidd was to sing so that the dealers could compare her recorded voice with her actual voice. Kidd was not paid and brought suit against Edison. According to Edison, Fuller never agreed that Edison would pay Kidd, because Fuller's only authority was to hire Kidd for those recitals for which he could persuade record dealers to pay. Is Edison liable to Kidd? Why or why not? [*Kidd* v. *Thomas A. Edison, Inc.*, 239 Fed. 405 (S.D.N.Y., 1917)]

10. Finlay worked as a hearing aid salesman for Robbins (dba Beltone Utah). Finlay did not like the terms of his employment, quit, and went into competition, selling another brand of hearing aids. Some of his customers had been customers of his while he had worked for Robbins. Robbins sued Finlay, claiming that he breached his duty as an agent not to take customers away from his principal. Was Robbins correct? [*Robbins* v. *Finlay*, 645 P.2d 623 (S. Ct., Utah, 1982)]

11. Two stockbrokers, in clear violation of the rules of their employer, sold worthless stocks to unsuspecting customers. There was no question that the brokers did not have actual or implied authority to sell the stock. The customers who lost money sued the brokerage firm, contending it was liable for their losses because the brokers had apparent authority. Did they? [*Badger* v. *Paulson Investment Co.*, 803 P.2d 1178 (Sup. Ct., Ore., 1991)]

12. Betty Hall had a VISA card account. At her request, a card was issued to her and one was issued to her husband, who was authorized to use the card. Soon after, Hall informed the bank that she would not be responsible for charges her husband made to her account. The bank requested the return of the credit cards numerous times, but it took four months for them to be returned. In the meantime, Hall's husband charged over $2,500 to the card, which Hall refused to pay. Is Hall responsible for her husband's charges because he had authority to use the card? [*Walker Bank & Trust* v. *Jones*, 672 P.2d 73 (S.Ct., Utah, 1983)]

13. Picard was a security guard for National Detective Agency. In violation of company rules, he had his own trained German shepherd dog with him while on duty. Meyers stopped to talk to Picard about the dog, which was in the back of a marked company car. Picard said he could show Meyers how well the dog was trained. When he took the dog from the car, it attacked and injured Meyers. Mey-

ers sued National Detective, which argued that Picard's actions were outside the scope of his employment because he was clearly violating company policy. Could the employer be liable? [*Meyers* v. *National Detective Agency*, 281 A.2d 435 (Ct. App., D.C., 1971)]

14. Schropp bought a new Mercedes Benz from Crown Eurocars. After the sale, he complained repeatedly to Cohen, Crown's sales manager, about spots on the finish of the car. After leaving the car at the dealership several times to have the problem fixed, it appeared that nothing had been done. Schropp sued Cohen and Crown for fraud for lying to him about supposed efforts to fix the car. The jury found both Cohen and Crown liable and awarded Schropp $500 in compensatory damages. The jury also found that Crown, but not Cohen, acted with malice and awarded Schropp $200,000 in punitive damages from Crown. Could the principal, Crown, be found to have acted with malice if Cohen, its agent who dealt with Schropp, did not act with malice? [*Schropp* v. *Crown Eurocars*, 654 So.2d 1158 (S.Ct., Fla., 1995)]

15. Heard was responsible for an injury accident while he was delivering pizzas for a pizza franchise owned by Lee. Lee's liability was determined by Heard's employment status. Heard's agreement with Lee stated that Heard was an independent contractor and required Heard to provide his own car and insurance. Heard was paid a 10 percent commission for each pizza delivered. He was to pay his own taxes and provide his own workers' compensation coverage. He delivered pizzas to customers as directed by Lee and returned all monies collected. He could be terminated for any reason on one-day notice. Was he an employee or an independent contractor? [*Toyota* v. *Superior Court*, 220 Cal.App.3d 864 (Ct. App., Cal., 1990)]

POLICY QUESTION

16. Should the law be more or less flexible about allowing employers to declare the people they work with to be employees or independent contractors, especially if the person agrees to the designation? Some people would prefer, in their work, to be classified as independent contractors rather than employees, because they would rather be paid more cash rather than have the employer pay various taxes on their behalf as employees. If the employer and the employee/independent contractor agree on the relationship, should their choice control?

ETHICS QUESTIONS

17. Agents are in a position to be privy to information of significant value. Should they be prohibited from using it? What if the purpose for which the agent uses such information would not in any way injure the principal?

18. Clarence has been released from prison after a six-year term for armed robbery and assault. Having "paid his debt to society" for his crimes, he is now looking for work. You are advertising to hire workers for furniture-moving crews. Normally two people work together all the time, so you know Clarence would be accompanied by another employee when on the job. However, you know of recent cases in which employers have been held liable for employees having gone astray during the job and committed crimes. Since Clarence would be in people's homes, it is not impossible that this could happen. Should you not hire Clarence because of this worry?

INTERNET ASSIGNMENT

Suppose Edith and Bill make an oral agreement for the sale of an oil well: Edith will sell Bill her oil well for $250,000. Bill draws up a deed of sale that seems to Edith to accurately reflect their oral agreement. However, before signing the contract, Edith wants her grandson, Derek, a partner with the law firm of Derek & Dustin, a Texas partnership, to review the contract to ensure that it means what it says. After reviewing the contract, Derek advises Edith that the document seems to be in good order. However, Derek also advises Edith that she should verify that she actually has clear legal title to the oil well before signing a contract to sell it. Edith asks Derek to conduct the title search, and all agree to meet the following afternoon to close the deal.

That evening, after conducting the title search, Derek contacts his mother, Janie Ann, who is an attorney and shrewd oil and gas speculator from west Texas, and asks her if she has any thoughts regarding the prospects for Edith's well. Janie Ann informs Derek that, using new recovery methods, Edith's well will yield significantly more oil than previously estimated and that a fair price for Edith's well would be $500,000—a fact, she adds, that Bill knows darn well. Based on his mother's advice, Derek contacts Edith and offers her $500,000 for the well. The next morning Derek buys Edith's well himself for $500,000.

Bill sues the Derek & Dustin law firm, seeking compensatory and punitive damages claiming tortious interference with business and fraud. Bill's fraud claim is based on Derek's representation as an attorney that he would review the original contract to ensure that it reflected his deal with Edith, while, in fact, Bill alleges, Derek was looking for an opportunity to misappropriate an economic benefit. Bill alleges that the Derek & Dustin law firm is vicariously liable for damages under the doctrine of *respondeat superior* because Derek was at all relevant times acting as an agent of the law firm. Can Bill recover against the Derek & Dustin law firm on his fraud claim? See *Entente* v. *Parker,* United States Court of Appeals for the Fifth Circuit, No. 91-1290, March 31, 1992 (http://www.law.utexas.edu/us5th/us5th.html). What result if, instead of buying Edith's well, Derek sold a well of his own to Bill? What result if Derek had used Derek & Dustin's money to buy Edith's well? Hint: For the elements of fraud, see *Jackson* v. *Speer,* United States Court of Appeals for the Fifth Circuit, No. 92-1419, October 14, 1992 (http://www.law.utexas.edu/us5th/us5th.html).

CHAPTER 14

Business Organizations

A couple of thousand years ago, merchants in inland China shipped their wares, such as pottery, down the Chang (Yangtze) River to cities such as Nanjing and Shanghai. Since the voyage was long and the river could be wild, the loss of boats and cargo was high. The merchants joined together to spread their merchandise on different boats. This minimized the financial consequences from the loss of boats that was suffered by any one merchant. This is one of the first recorded business arrangements known; it was a joint venture.

There are over 20 million businesses in the United States. Sole proprietorships, often small businesses such as computer repair stores, dry cleaners, and restaurants, account for about three-quarters of the total. Proprietorships take in about 5 percent of all business revenues but over 25 percent of all business profits. Corporations are fewer in number—less than 19 percent of the total—but account for 90 percent of all revenues. Partnerships take in 4 percent of business receipts while making up 7 percent of all businesses.

This chapter begins with a discussion of the major forms of business organization, including sole proprietorships, partnerships, corporations, and limited liability companies. Every state has laws concerning some aspects of corporation and partnership formation, operation, and dissolution, but business organizations are primarily created by actions and contracts. The statutory requirements regarding business formation are not burdensome. Each form has advantages and disadvantages. The chapter considers several factors that may significantly influence a business's choice of business organization. Finally, the chapter examines alternative forms that may have applications in various circumstances, such as joint ventures, joint stock companies, cooperatives, syndicates, and, increasingly, franchises.

Sole Proprietorships

A person doing business for himself or herself is a *sole proprietor;* the business organization is a *sole proprietorship.* The sole proprietorship is the oldest and simplest form of business organization. As a proprietor, a person may simply begin to do business without formality in enterprises that do not require a government license or permit (although most states require business names to be registered if a fictitious business name is used). The proprietor generally owns all or most of the business property and is responsible for the control, liabilities, and management of the business.

In a sole proprietorship, legally and practically, *the owner is the business;* capital must come from the owner's own resources or be borrowed. Perhaps the greatest disadvantage of the sole proprietorship is the fact that limited alternatives exist for raising capital. Because the profits of the business are taxed to the owner personally, a tax return in the business's name is not required so long as records of income and expenses are kept. The operational and record-keeping formalities of the business are at the owner's discretion as long as the various taxing authorities are satisfied.

Partnerships

A *general partnership* is defined as an association of two or more persons to carry on a business as co-owners for a profit. The *partners* or *general partners* share control over the business's operations and profits. Many attorneys, doctors, accountants, and retail stores are organized as partnerships. A "person" in a partnership may be another partnership or a corporation.

At common law, a partnership was not treated as an independent legal entity. As a consequence, a case could not be brought by or against the business. The partners had to sue or be sued individually. State law now provides that for many purposes, a partnership may be treated as an independent entity. Thus, a partnership may sue or be sued and collect judgments in its own name. The federal courts also provide that, in most circumstances, a partnership is treated as a legal entity.

Partnership law originated in the common law but is now codified in the *Uniform Partnership Act (UPA).* The UPA has been adopted in every state except Louisiana and governs partnerships and partnership relations. The UPA determines the operation of partnerships when the partnership agreement is silent or where there is no formal agreement among the partners.

FORMATION OF A PARTNERSHIP

A partnership can begin with an oral agreement between two or more persons to do business as partners or with an implied agreement that may be inferred from the

Small Is Not So Beautiful in Japan

Each year about 700,000 new businesses are started in the United States. In Japan, adjusting for population, the number of new businesses would run about 190,000 per year, less than one-third of those in the United States. Attitudes seem very different in the two countries; in the United States, small businesses are looked on with favor; in Japan, they are discriminated against by government policy and are considered less desirable places to work.

Tetsu Anzai is head of a chain of stores selling CD-ROMs with revenues of $12 million a year. He reports that qualified people do not answer his job ads even though unemployment is at the highest level in decades. Worker wariness of small firms reflects government policy.

Government banking regulations favor big businesses. Small firms without large sums of cash to bankroll operations, including paying large deposits to be able to rent office space, are usually out of luck. Since tax rates run as high as 65 percent, it is hard for entrepreneurs to reinvest their earnings. The stock market is of limited help, as regulations make it difficult for newer firms to be able to offer stock.

As the Japanese economy has hit hard times, consideration is being given to rules that would help small businesses stimulate the growth that was for so many years generated by the big firms smiled upon by public policy.

---

conduct of the partners as they do business together. Typically, the parties formalize their relationship by a written agreement. The partnership agreement usually specifies such matters as the business name, ownership interests of the partners, partners' responsibilities, method of accounting, duration of the partnership, and procedures for the partnership's dissolution. Exhibit 14.1 is an example of a partnership agreement. In the absence of a specific agreement, the UPA specifies and governs the relationship of the parties. Since the law does not require that a partnership have a name or that it be registered, outsiders might not know of its existence or who is involved.

Duty of Partners

A partnership is a relationship based on extraordinary trust and loyalty. Partners owe a fiduciary duty to one another. A fiduciary relationship requires that each partner act in good faith for the benefit of the partnership. As in the fiduciary relationship between a principal and agents, the partners must place their personal interests below those of the partnership. The Supreme Court stated the duty of partners as follows in *Latta* v. *Kilbourn*, 150 U.S. 524 (1893):

> [It is] well settled that one partner cannot, directly or indirectly, use partnership assets for his own benefit; that he cannot, in conducting the business of a partnership, take any profit clandestinely for himself; that he cannot carry on the business of the partnership for his private advantage; that he cannot carry on another business in competition or rivalry with that of the firm, thereby depriving it of the benefit of his time, skill, and fidelity without being accountable to his copartners for any profit that may accrue to him therefrom; that he cannot be permitted to secure for himself that which it is his duty to obtain, if at all, for the firm of which he is a member. . . .

EXHIBIT 14.1

Example of a Basic Partnership Agreement

[Name]
PARTNERSHIP AGREEMENT

This agreement, made and entered into as of the [Date], by and among [Names] (hereinafter collectively sometimes referred to as "Partners").

WITNESSETH:

Whereas, the Parties hereto desire to form a General Partnership (hereinafter referred to as the "Partnership"), for the term and upon the conditions hereinafter set forth;

Now, therefore, in consideration of the mutual covenants hereinafter contained, it is agreed by and among the Parties hereto as follows:

Article I
BASIC STRUCTURE

1.1 Form. The Parties hereby form a General Partnership pursuant to the Laws of [Name of State].

1.2 Name. The business of the Partnership shall be conducted under the name of [Name].

1.3 Place of Business. The principal office and place of business of the Partnership shall be located at [Describe], or such other place as the Partners may from time to time designate.

1.4 Term. The Partnership shall commence on [Date], and shall continue for [Number] years, unless earlier terminated in the following manner:

(a) By the completion of the purpose intended, or

(b) Pursuant to this Agreement, or

(c) By applicable [State] law, or

(d) By death, insanity, bankruptcy, retirement, withdrawal, resignation, expulsion, or disability of all of the Partners.

1.5 Purpose—General. The purpose for which the Partnership is organized is _____ .

Article II
FINANCIAL ARRANGEMENTS

2.1 Initial Contribution of Partners. Each Partner has contributed to the initial capital of the Partnership property in the amount and form indicated on Schedule A attached hereto and made a part hereof. Capital contributions to the Partnership shall not earn interest. An individual capital account shall be maintained for each Partner.

2.2 Additional Capital Contribution. If at any time during the existence of the Partnership it shall become necessary to increase the capital with which the said Partnership is doing business, then (upon the vote of the Managing Partner(s) each party to this Agreement shall contribute to the capital of this Partnership within ____ days notice of such need in an amount according to his then Percentage Share of Capital as called for by the Managing Partner(s).

2.3 Percentage Share of Profits and Capital. (a) The Percentage Share of Profits and Capital of each Partner shall be (unless otherwise modified by the terms of this Agreement) as follows:

Names	Initial Percentage Share of Profits and Capital

2.4 Interest. No interest shall be paid on any contribution to the capital of the Partnership.

2.5 Return of Capital Contributions. No Partner shall have the right to demand the return of his capital contributions except as herein provided.

2.6 Rights of Priority. Except as herein provided, the individual Partners shall have no right to any priority over each other as to the return of capital contributions except as herein provided.

EXHIBIT 14.1

Continued

2.7 Distributions. Distributions to the Partners of net operating profits of the Partnership, as hereinafter defined, shall be made at (least monthly/at such times as the Managing Partner(s) shall reasonably agree). Such distributions shall be made to the Partners simultaneously.

2.8 Compensation. No Partner shall be entitled to receive any compensation from the Partnership, nor shall any Partner receive any drawing account from the Partnership.

Article III
MANAGEMENT

3.1 Managing Partners. The Managing Partner(s) shall be [Names] [or "all partners"].

3.2 Voting. All Managing Partner(s) shall have the right to vote as to the management and conduct of the business of the Partnership according to their then Percentage Share of [Capital/Income]. Except as otherwise herein set forth a majority of such [Capital/Income] shall control.

Article IV
DISSOLUTION

4.1 Dissolutions. In the event that the Partnership shall hereafter be dissolved for any reason whatsoever, a full and general account of its assets, liabilities, and transactions shall at once be taken. Such assets may be sold and turned into cash as soon as possible and all debts and other amounts due the Partnership collected. The proceeds thereof shall thereupon be applied as follows:

(a) To discharge the debts and liabilities of the Partnership and the expenses of liquidation.

(b) To pay each Partner or his legal representative any unpaid salary, drawing account, interest or profits to which he shall then be entitled and in addition, to repay to any Partner his capital contributions in excess of his original capital contribution.

(c) To divide the surplus, if any, among the Partners or their representatives as follows: (1) First (to the extent of each Partner's then capital account) in proportion to their then capital accounts. (2) Then according to each Partner's then Percentage Share of Capital/Income.

4.2 Right To Demand Property. No partner shall have the right to demand and receive property in kind for his distribution.

Article V
MISCELLANEOUS

5.1 Accounting Year, Books, Statements. The Partnership's fiscal year shall commence on January 1st of each year and shall end on December 31st of each year. Full and accurate books of account shall be kept at such place as the Managing Partner(s) may from time to time designate, showing the condition of the business and finances of the Partnership; and each Partner shall have access to such books of account and shall be entitled to examine them at any time during ordinary business hours.

5.2 Arbitration. Any controversy or claim arising out of or relating to this Agreement shall be settled only by arbitration in accordance with the rules of the American Arbitration, one Arbitrator, and shall be enforceable in any court having competent jurisdiction.

Witnesses	Partners
_____	_____
_____	_____

Control of Partners

Unless otherwise specified in the partnership agreement, which can allocate control any way that the partners want, the basic rule is that each partner has an equal voice in partnership management. Regardless of the size of the interest in the partnership, each partner has one vote in managerial decisions. Except in the case of major decisions that require consent of all partners—such as decisions to change the nature of the partnership's business, to admit new partners, or to sell the business—a majority vote is controlling. In most large partnerships, the partners usually delegate most management responsibilities to one person or group, often referred to as the managing partner or partners.

Regardless of who runs a partnership, the partners have a duty to one another to disclose all financial aspects of the business and to be completely honest, regardless of personal differences. As the *Lubritz* case discusses, the courts, when resolving disputes, look to the reality of a business arrangement and the promises parties made to each other.

Clark v. Lubritz
Supreme Court of Nevada
113 Nev. 1089, 944 P.2d 861 (1997)

CASE BACKGROUND *Lubritz and four other physicians orally agreed to form a preferred provider organization called NPP in 1983. Each invested $15,000 initially, and they agreed to share any profits or losses equally. The partnership was soon incorporated, but the doctors continued to refer to each other as partners. When NPP hired a manager, he "learned that the physicians [were] all equal partners, put the same amount in, and were going to be paid or receive the same benefits."*

In 1986, after arguments about policy with some of the other doctors, Lubritz resigned as president and from the board of directors, but he continued to perform his professional services. Starting in 1990, the other doctors cut Lubritz's share of the annual profits and paid themselves more. Lubritz discovered this in 1993. The other doctors told him they paid him less because he contributed less to the work of NPP. Lubritz sued.

At trial it was noted that NPP ignored the bylaws of the corporation. "Stocks were not issued, annual shareholders meetings were not held, and the officers and directors were not elected." From 1991 to 1993, the Secretary of State of Nevada revoked NPP's corporate charter for failure to file its annual list of officers and directors as required by state law.

The jury awarded Lubritz $195,942 for breach of contract and breach of fiduciary duty, $200,000 in puni-

tive damages, and $75,000 in attorney's fees. The other doctors appealed.

CASE DECISION Per Curiam.

* * *

Breach of Contract

The appellants argue that the district court judge erroneously allowed the jury to find a breach of the oral agreement because it is legally impermissible for a business to be conducted as a corporation and a partnership at the same time. They claim that the incorporation of NPP necessarily precludes Lubritz from recovering for breach of contract. We disagree.

. . . Although this court has not yet addressed this issue, courts in other states are of the opinion that "when joint adventurers use the corporate form for convenience in carrying out their project, their mutual rights and liabilities will be determined in furtherance and in harmony with their joint purpose rather than with the form of their operation, and the corporate entity will be recognized or ignored accordingly." . . .

Additionally . . . Nevada [corporation] law . . . states [that when an agreement of the shareholders] treats the corporation as a partnership [that the business arrangement is still legal and the law will] treat the corporation as if it were a partnership. . . .

Based on the foregoing, we hold that the oral agreement was not invalid per se when the parties formed the corporation. Thus, the district court properly allowed the jury to determine whether the parties breached the oral agreement.

* * *

Therefore, because there is ample evidence in the record to support a finding that the parties intended the oral agreement to control the manner in which the five physicians were paid by the corporation, this court will not disturb the jury's finding that the appellants breached that agreement when they reduced Lubritz's payments to less than one-fifth.

Breach of Fiduciary Duty

The appellants also argue that there was no evidence that they breached a fiduciary duty in not disclosing the unequal distributions to Lubritz.

The fiduciary duty that partners owe one another has been described as follows:

> The fiduciary duty among partners is generally one of full and frank disclosure of all relevant information for just, equitable and open dealings at full value and consideration. Each partner has a right to know all that the others know, and each is required to make full disclosure of all material facts within his knowledge in anything relating to the partnership affairs. The requirement of full disclosure among partners in partnership business cannot be escaped. . . . Each partner must . . . not deceive another partner by concealment of material facts.

59(A) Am.Jur.2d Partnership §425 (1987). In addition, a partner's motives or intent do not determine whether his actions violate his fiduciary duty. Therefore, the appellants owed Lubritz a fiduciary duty of full disclosure of material facts relating to the partnership affairs.

In this case, there was sufficient evidence to show that the appellants breached that duty. The evidence clearly indicated that the appellants did not disclose the unequal distribution. Moreover, as discussed more fully above, there is sufficient evidence upon which a jury could determine that the appellants desired to conceal the unequal distribution from Lubritz. Therefore, this court will not disturb the jury's award for breach of fiduciary duty.

* * *

[Further] we conclude that the breach of fiduciary duty arising from the partnership agreement is a separate tort upon which punitive damages may be based.

* * *

The district court's judgment in favor of Lubritz is hereby affirmed.

QUESTIONS FOR ANALYSIS

1. Suppose Lubritz was contributing less work than the other partners. Why should he share equally in profits?
2. Since the original agreement called for equal shares, if the other doctors wanted Lubritz out, how could they have gotten rid of him?

TERMINATION OF THE PARTNERSHIP

A change in the relationship of the partners that shows an unwillingness or an inability to continue with business will bring about *termination* of the partnership. A complete termination comes about only after the partnership has been dissolved and its affairs have been wound up. The *dissolution* of the partnership occurs when an event takes place that precludes the partners from engaging in any new business. The *winding up* of partnership affairs involves completing any unfinished business and then collecting and distributing the partnership's assets.

Dissolution can come about in several ways. Change in the composition of the partners results in a new partnership and dissolution of the old one. Thus, the withdrawal or death of a partner causes the partnership to be dissolved. Similarly, the partnership is dissolved if a partner is bankrupt. Since it would be expensive and disruptive for partnerships to be terminated and re-formed because of the withdrawal, death, or bankruptcy of one partner, many agreements have provisions to allow the partnership to continue despite such events.

Limited Partnership

A limited partnership is a special form of a general partnership. Like a general partnership, a *limited partnership* is a business organization made up of two or more persons (*partners*) who have entered into an agreement to carry on a business venture for a profit. Unlike in a general partnership, however, not all partners in a limited partnership have the right to participate in the management of the enterprise.

FORMATION OF A LIMITED PARTNERSHIP

All states except Louisiana use some form of the *Uniform Limited Partnership Act* or the *Revised Uniform Limited Partnership Act.* Partners must execute a written agreement, called a *certificate of limited partnership*, and file it with the appropriate state official, often the secretary of state. The Uniform Act requires that certificates contain the following information:

1. Name of the business
2. Type or character of the business
3. Address of an agent who is designated to receive legal process
4. Names and addresses of each general and limited partner
5. Contributions (cash, work, and property) of each partner
6. Duration of the limited partnership
7. The rights for personnel changes in the partnership and the continuance of the partnership upon those changes
8. The proportion of the profits or other compensation that each partner is entitled to receive

In addition, the parties to the limited partnership agreement may agree to bind themselves in ways not required by the certificate.

RELATIONSHIP OF THE PARTIES

A limited partnership has at least one *general partner* and one or more *limited partners.* The general partners are treated in the same manner as partners in a general partnership. They have responsibility for managing the business and are personally liable to the partnership's creditors.

Limited partners are investors who may not participate in managing the business. Although they have the right to see the partnership books and to participate in the dissolution of the business, limited partners are not liable for the debts or torts of the limited partnership beyond their capital contributions. Limited partners lose their limited liability and become general partners if they take an active role in managing the business. To avoid an inference of managerial control, limited partners may not take control of the firm, contribute services to the business, or allow their names to appear in the name of the business. As the *Northampton Valley* decision illustrates, creditors of the business may want to assert that the limited partners have conducted their affairs so as to become general partners.

Northampton Valley Constructors, Inc. v. Horne-Lang Associates

Superior Court of Pennsylvania
310 Pa.Super. 559, 456 A.2d 1077 (1983)

CASE BACKGROUND *Northampton Valley Constructors sued Horne-Lang Associates for breach of contract for nonpayment. Under contract, Northampton installed a sewer system on land owned by Horne-Lang. Upon completion of the work, Horne-Lang was unable to pay.*

Horne-Lang was a Pennsylvania limited partnership with a general partner and eighteen limited partners. Northampton alleged that the limited partners were actually general partners and thus were personally liable under the contract. The lower court dismissed Northampton's suit, and Northampton appealed.

CASE DECISION McEwen, Judge.

* * *

A limited partnership is a creation of our legislature and "(i)t permits a manner of doing business whereby individuals may invest their money free of the fear of unlimited liability and of the responsibilities of management." The pertinent statute, the Uniform Limited Partnership Act, provides:

> Sec. 511. Limited partnership defined
>
> A limited partnership is a partnership formed by two or more persons under the provisions of section 512 (relating to formation), having as members one or more general partners and one or more limited partners. The limited partners as such shall not be bound by the obligations of the partnership. . . .

The certificate of the limited partnership we here study contains . . . the following provision concerning additional contributions:

> No additional contributions have been agreed to be made. However, additional contributions are required if the General Partner determines that the partnership requires additional funds to meet the obligations of the partnership.

It must be emphasized that this claim against the limited partners is exerted by a creditor of the partnership and not by the partnership. A creditor may pursue a claim against a limited partner as a general partner only in the limited circumstances prescribed by the Act, namely, when the limited partner "takes part in the control of the business." Northampton did not,

however, allege and does not now argue that the limited partners took part in the control of the business.

This claim against the limited partners . . . is based upon the aforementioned provision of the partnership certificate concerning additional contributions. Northampton contends that, as a result of this provision, the limited partners were *de facto* general partners and argues that, since the general partner could have and should have called upon the limited partners to provide additional capital to the partnership in order to pay the creditors of the partnership, the limited partners are liable to creditors for the debts of the partnership over and beyond their investment. Northampton asserts that since "the limited partners have committed to make their investment equal to the obligations, they are bound for that sum not because they are bound beyond the limit of their commitment but because their commitments equal those obligations." The premise for this assertion is, however, simply not correct since the limited partners did not commit to make their investments in the partnership equal to the obligations of the partnership; nor does the clear meaning of the plain language concerning additional contributions permit interpretation, let alone allow the inference urged by Northampton.

Northampton does allege in the complaint that "the General Partner determined that the partnership required additional funds to meet the obligations of the partnership" and, as we have earlier noted, we are obliged to accept that averment as a fact. Nonetheless, whatever liability such a determination by the general partner may have imposed upon the limited partners in favor of the partnership, we are not persuaded that the limited partners thereby became as equally liable to creditors as were the general partner and the partnership.

Order affirmed.

QUESTIONS FOR ANALYSIS

1. Why were the limited partners not liable personally to Northampton?
2. Can you alter the facts so that the limited partners would be liable to Northampton?

TERMINATION OF A LIMITED PARTNERSHIP

A limited partnership is terminated in much the same way as a general partnership. Events that affect a general partner and would bring about the dissolution of a general partnership also dissolve a limited partnership. While the bankruptcy of a general partner dissolves a limited partnership, the bankruptcy of a limited partner usually does not.

The business continues to operate while it is winding up, but it may not enter into any new commitments. In the final dispersal of the assets of the limited partnership, creditors' rights precede partners' rights. The limited partners receive their share of the profits and their capital contributions before general partners receive anything, unless the limited partnership agreement holds otherwise.

Corporations

When most people think of a business, they think of a *corporation*. Most large, well-known businesses—such as Exxon, Coca-Cola, General Motors, and Microsoft—are corporations. Although businesses have produced and traded goods for thousands of years, the modern corporation was first developed in the United States during the late 1700s. State governments issued *corporate charters* to selected businesses. Because the charter often granted some special privilege, there was intense competition to decide who received charters. A charter might, for example, give a business the exclusive privilege of operating a toll bridge over a river or having the only bank in a town. In this way, monopoly power was often associated with early corporate charters.

In the late 1800s, the first "liberal" *general incorporation statutes* were enacted. Those statutes established a simple procedure for incorporating a business. Incorporation was thereby made available to most businesses regardless of their field of operation, size, or political influence.

CREATING A CORPORATION

Every state has a general incorporation statute that sets forth the procedure for incorporation. Although the procedures vary across the states, the basic requirements are similar. In general, a corporation's *articles of incorporation* along with an application must be filed with the appropriate state office. As Exhibit 14.2 shows, the articles of incorporation usually provide the following:

1. Name and address of the corporation
2. Name and address of the corporation's registered agent
3. Purpose of the business
4. The class(es) of stock to be issued and their par value
5. Names and addresses of the incorporators

After reviewing the corporation's application for completeness, the state issues a *certificate of incorporation*. As a rule, the incorporators wait until the state has issued the certificate before holding their first formal organizational meeting. At that meeting, the incorporators elect a board of directors, enact the corporation's bylaws, and issue the corporation's stock. The *bylaws* are the "rules" that regulate and govern the internal operations of the corporation. The shareholders, directors, and officers of the corporation must follow the bylaws in conducting corporate activities.

EXHIBIT 14.2

Example of Certificate of Incorporation

Certificate of Incorporation
Of
_____ Corporation

1. Name. The name of the Corporation is _____ Corporation.

2. Registered Office and Registered Agent. The address of the Corporation's registered office in Delaware is ____ Street in the City of ____ and County of ____, and the name of its registered agent at such address ____.

3. Purposes. The purpose of the Corporation is to engage in any lawful act or activity for which Corporations may be now or hereafter organized under the General Corporation Law of Delaware.

4. Capital Stock (Providing for Two Classes of Stock, One Voting and One Nonvoting). The total number of shares for all classes of stock the Corporation shall have authority to issue is _____, all of which are to be without par value. ____of such shares shall be Class A voting shares and _____ of such shares shall be Class B nonvoting shares. The Class A shares and the Class B shares shall have identical rights except that the Class B shares shall not entitle the holder thereof to vote on any matter unless specifically required by law.

5. Incorporators. The names and mailing addresses of the incorporators are

Name	Mailing Address
_____	_____
_____	_____

6. Regulatory Provisions. [The Corporations may insert additional provisions for the management of the business and for the conduct of the affairs of the Corporation, and creating, defining, limiting, and regulating the powers of the Corporation, the Directors and the Stockholders, or any class of Stockholders.]

7. Personal Liability. The Stockholders shall be liable for the debts of the Corporation in the proportion that their stock bears to the total outstanding stock of the Corporation.

8. Amendment. The Corporation reserves the right to amend, alter, change or repeal any provision contained in the Certificate of INCORPORATION, in the manner now or hereafter prescribed by statute, and all rights conferred upon Stockholders herein are granted subject to this reservation.

We, the undersigned, being all of the incorporators above named, for the purpose of forming a Corporation pursuant to the General Corporation Law of Delaware, sign and acknowledge this Certificate of Incorporation this _____ day of ____, 20 ____.

Acknowledgment

State of _____
County of _____
On this _____ day of _____, 20 ____, before me personally came _____, one of the persons who signed the foregoing certificate of incorporation, known to me personally to be such, and acknowledged that the said certificate is his act and deed and that the facts stated therein are true.

_____
Notary Public

[seal]

Legal Entity Status

Unlike sole proprietorships, the corporation is a *legal entity*. It is recognized under both federal and state law as a "person" and enjoys some of the same rights and privileges accorded U.S. citizens. Corporations are thus entitled to many constitutional protections, including free speech, equal protection under the law, and protections against unreasonable searches and seizures. As a person, a corporation has the right of access to the courts as an entity that may sue and be sued. However, although the officers and employees of a corporation enjoy the privilege against self-incrimination under the Fifth Amendment, the corporation itself does not.

Close and Public Corporations

Corporations are often referred to as being a *close corporation* or a *closely held corporation* as compared to a *public corporation* or a *publicly held corporation*. Numerically, most corporations are closely held; that is, they have a limited number of stockholders and the stock is not traded on a stock exchange. The rules of the Securities and Exchange Commission, as we will see in Chapter 20, help determine such status. Some closely held corporations, such as Cargill and Koch, would be among the largest firms in the nation if their stocks were public, so there is no size limit. Publicly held corporations are those with stock trades on a stock exchange and, therefore, are likely to have many shareholders. Some corporations "go public" at the start of operations, which may be quite small, so that outside investors can help bankroll the new business. Whether a corporation is close or public, the basic rules are much the same.

RELATIONSHIP OF THE PARTIES

A corporation consists of three distinct groups: the shareholders, the board of directors, and the managers. Each shares specific duties and responsibilities to the other groups, to the corporation, and to third parties.

Shareholders

The *shareholders* own the corporation. Ownership shares may be shown on a *stock certificate*, but, as a practical matter, most parties just keep records of who owns how many shares. Shareholders have the right to buy any additional stock issued by the corporation before it is offered to the public. Shareholders have a limited right to inspect the corporation's books and records. As a rule, inspection is provided to shareholders if it is for a proper purpose and a request is made in advance. Finally, unless stated to the contrary on the stock certificate or the bylaws, shareholders are not restricted from selling or giving the stock to someone else.

The shareholders are not responsible for managing the corporation. That is the duty of the board of directors, which generally delegates most responsibility to hired managers. Shareholders elect the board of directors and vote on matters that change the corporation's structure or existence (such as a merger with another firm or an amendment to the corporation's articles of incorporation).

Elections take place at shareholder meetings, which are usually held annually. Notice of shareholder meetings must be provided in advance, and a quorum—usually more than half of the total shares—must be represented at the meeting. Most shareholders give third parties their *proxy*—a written authorization to cast their vote so that they do not have to attend the meeting. The proxy is often solicited by the corporation's management.

At the meeting, important corporate business is presented to the shareholders in the form of *resolutions*, which shareholders vote to approve or disapprove. The articles of incorporation establish voting rules. They usually require more than a simple majority for resolutions for actions such as amendments to the articles of incorporation and the bylaws or the dissolution or merger of the corporation.

The shareholder has no legal relationship with creditors of the corporation. A shareholder's obligation to creditors is limited to capital contributions (usually the amount paid to buy stock). A shareholder, however, may become a creditor of the cor-

JURIS **prudence?**

Your Honor, I'll Turn Rocks into Gold

Marinov, a Russian immigrant, formed Amrox Corporation. He gave himself one-half of the stock for his secret knowledge and equipment. Four investors bought the rest of the stock for $330,000.

Marinov claimed to have a Ph.D. in solid-state physics from a Moscow university and medical degrees from Bulgaria, Sweden, and Germany. He told the investors that this supposed education had taught him how to turn corundum, which is cheap, into high-quality rubies and sapphires that would be certified by the American Gemological Institute.

Nothing was ever produced, and the investors sued Marinov. The district court ruled for the investors; Marinov appealed. The appeals court upheld the verdict. Marinov told the court that "he is developing a linear accelerator which he wishes to sell to the United Nations." The court found that claim and others "absolutely incredible." Marinov was held to have breached his fiduciary duty to the investors.

Source: *Gizzi* v. *Marinov*, 79 F.3d 1148

poration (for example, by supplying needed material or by working for the business) and enjoy the same rights of recovery against the corporation as any other creditor.

Board of Directors

The initial *board of directors* is specified in the articles of incorporation or designated by the incorporators at the first corporate meeting. Thereafter, the selection of directors is a shareholder responsibility. Once elected, directors serve terms for a time specified in the articles, although the shareholders can remove a director from office *for cause* (generally for a *breach of duty* or *misconduct*).

Legally, the board is the principal of a corporation. Its functions include making corporate policy, such as the sale of corporate assets, entrance into new product lines, major financing decisions, appointment and compensation of corporate officers, and oversight of labor-management agreements. The directors act, usually by majority vote, to exert managerial authority. Directors are under a *duty of care* to conduct themselves on behalf of the corporation as a reasonably prudent person in the conduct of personal business affairs. Honest mistakes in judgment not resulting from negligence do not result in personal liability to the directors. The *business judgment rule* protects directors and managers who make honest mistakes in judgment.

Directors are subject to a *fiduciary duty of loyalty*. This fiduciary duty requires that directors place the interests of the corporation before their own interests. As a rule, the board has the duty to undertake actions to preserve the corporate entity. That duty would be different, for example, if the corporation became the target of a takeover attempt by another corporation. Then the fiduciary duty of the directors might change from preserving the corporation to maximizing its sales price in the interest of the shareholders.

While we ordinarily think that the duty of a board of directors is to ensure that profits are maximized, in the *Wrigley* decision the court notes that such is not the only factor that directors must take into account. The business judgment rule gives directors leeway to consider factors that, in their judgment, are important to the corporation as a going concern.

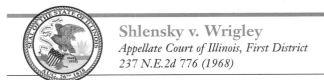

Shlensky v. Wrigley
Appellate Court of Illinois, First District
237 N.E.2d 776 (1968)

CASE BACKGROUND AND DECISION Sullivan, Justice.

* * *

This is an appeal from a dismissal of plaintiff's amended complaint on motion of the defendants. The action was a stockholders' derivative suit against the directors for negligence and mismanagement. The corporation was also made a defendant. Plaintiff sought damages and an order that defendants cause the installation of lights in Wrigley Field and the scheduling of night baseball games.

Plaintiff is a minority stockholder of defendant corporation, Chicago National League Ball Club (Inc.), a Delaware corporation with its principal place of business in Chicago, Illinois. Defendant corporation owns and operates the major league professional baseball team known as the Chicago Cubs. The corporation also engages in the operation of Wrigley Field, the Cubs' home park, the concessionaire sales during Cubs' home games, television and radio broadcasts of Cubs' home games, the leasing of the field for football games and other events and receives its share, as visiting team, of admission moneys from games played in other National League stadia. The individual defendants are directors of the Cubs and have served for varying periods of years. Defendant Philip K. Wrigley is also president of the corporation and owner of approximately 80% of the stock therein.

Plaintiff alleges that since night baseball was first played in 1935 nineteen of the twenty major league teams have scheduled night games. In 1966, out of a total of 1620 games in the major leagues, 932 were played at night. Plaintiff alleges that every member of the major leagues, other than the Cubs, scheduled substantially all of its home games in 1966 at night, exclusive of opening days, Saturdays, Sundays, holidays and days prohibited by league rules. Allegedly this has been done for the specific purpose of maximizing attendance and thereby maximizing revenue and income.

The Cubs, in the years 1961–65, sustained operating losses from its direct baseball operations. Plaintiff attributes those losses to inadequate attendance at Cubs' home games. He concludes that if the directors continue to refuse to install lights at Wrigley Field and schedule night baseball games, the Cubs will continue to sustain comparable losses and its financial condition will continue to deteriorate.

* * *

Plaintiff further alleges that defendant Wrigley has refused to install lights, not because of interest in the welfare of the corporation but because of his personal opinions "that baseball is a 'daytime sport' and that the installation of lights and night baseball games will have a deteriorating effect upon the surrounding neighborhood." It is alleged that he has admitted that he is not interested in whether the Cubs would benefit financially from such action because of his concern for the neighborhood, and that he would be willing for the team to play night games if a new stadium were built in Chicago.

Plaintiff alleges that the other defendant directors, with full knowledge of the foregoing matters, have acquiesced in the policy laid down by Wrigley and have permitted him to dominate the board of directors in matters involving the installation of lights and scheduling of night games, even though they knew he was not motivated by a good faith concern as to the best interests of defendant corporation, but solely by his personal views set forth above. It is charged that the directors are acting for a reason or reasons contrary and wholly unrelated to the business interests of the corporation; that such arbitrary and capricious acts constitute mismanagement and waste of corporate assets, and that the directors have been negligent in failing to exercise reasonable care and prudence in the management of the corporate affairs.

The question on appeal is whether plaintiff's amended complaint states a cause of action. It is plaintiff's position that fraud, illegality and conflict of interest are not the only bases for a stockholder's derivative action against the directors. Contrariwise, defendants argue that the courts will not step in and interfere with honest business judgment of the directors unless there is a showing of fraud, illegality or conflict of interest.

The cases in this area are numerous and each differs from the others on a factual basis. However, the courts have pronounced certain ground rules which appear in all cases and which are then applied to the given factual situation. The court in Wheeler v. Pullman Iron and Steel Company, 143 Ill. 197, 207, 32 N.E. 420, 423, said:

> It is, however, fundamental in the law of corporations, that the majority of its stockholders shall control the policy of the corporation, and regulate and govern the lawful exercise of its franchise and business. . . . Every one purchasing or subscribing for stock in a corporation impliedly agrees that he will be bound by the acts and proceedings done or sanctioned by a majority of the shareholders, or by the agents of the corporation duly chosen by such majority, within the scope of the powers conferred by the charter, and courts of equity will not undertake to control the policy or business methods of a corporation, although it may be seen that a wiser policy might be adopted and the business more successful if other methods were pursued. The majority of shares of its stock, or the agents by the holders thereof lawfully chosen, must be permitted to control the business of the corporation in their discretion, when not in violation of its charter or some public law, or corruptly and fraudulently subversive of the rights and interests of the corporation or of a shareholder.

* * *

In a New Jersey case the Court stated the law as follows: "In a purely business corporation . . . the authority of the directors in the conduct of the business of the corporation must be regarded as absolute when they act within the law, and the court is without authority to substitute its judgment for that of the directors."

* * *

There must be fraud or a breach of that good faith which directors are bound to exercise toward the stockholders in order to justify the courts entering into the internal affairs of corporations.

* * *

Plaintiff in the instant case argues that the directors are acting for reasons unrelated to the financial interest and welfare of the Cubs. However, we are not satisfied that the motives assigned to Philip K. Wrigley, and through him to the other directors, are contrary to the best interests of the corporation and the stockholders. For example, it appears to us that the effect on the surrounding neighborhood might well be considered by a director who was considering the patrons who would or would not attend the games if the park were in a poor neighborhood. Furthermore, the long run interest of the corporation in its property value at Wrigley Field might demand all efforts to keep the neighborhood from deteriorating. By these thoughts we do not mean to say that we have decided that the decision of the directors was a correct one. That is beyond our jurisdiction and ability. We are merely saying that the decision is one properly before directors and the motives alleged in the amended complaint showed no fraud, illegality or conflict of interest in their making of that decision.

* * *

Directors are elected for their business capabilities and judgment and the courts cannot require them to forego their judgment because of the decisions of directors of other companies. Courts may not decide these questions in the absence of a clear showing of dereliction of duty on the part of the specific directors and mere failure to 'follow the crowd' is not such a dereliction.

For the foregoing reasons the order of dismissal entered by the trial court is affirmed.

QUESTIONS FOR ANALYSIS

1. Investors buy stock to make money. If directors fail to maximize profits because of such things as "concern for the neighborhood," would they not be able to make vague claims about community or worker concern as a cover for poor decisions that reduce profitability?
2. Several years after this case, the Cubs installed lights and began to play night baseball. They simply lost too much revenue by playing only day games. Is this not further evidence that the minority shareholder was right in his claims in this suit?

Managers

The corporation's board of directors hires *managers* to operate the corporation on a day-to-day basis. The extent of managerial control and the compensation enjoyed by managers are matters of contract and agency between the board and the managers. Once hired, managers have the same broad duties of care and loyalty as the directors.

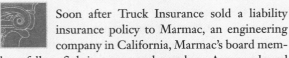

Mad at Each Other? Everybody Sue the Insurance Company

Soon after Truck Insurance sold a liability insurance policy to Marmac, an engineering company in California, Marmac's board members fell to fighting among themselves. Amey, a board member, 40 percent stockholder, and executive vice president, was demoted by the other board members. He sued Marmac and its officers for breach of fiduciary duty, breach of duty of good faith, intentional infliction of emotional distress, and seven other complaints.

Marmac insisted that Truck Insurance pay for the company and its officers' defense against Amey. Truck refused. The insurance policy covered torts inflicted by Marmac on outsiders; it did not provide coverage for torts board members commit against each other. The jury did not agree, awarding Marmac and its board members over $61 million in damages from the insurance company.

The Supreme Court of California noted that "the Amey lawsuit sets forth nothing more than a business dispute." The court tossed out the damage award; the board members would have to carry on their fight without the help of their insurer.

Source: *Waller* v. *Truck Insurance Exchange*, 44 Cal.Rptr.2d 370

The use of hired management is an advantage of the corporate form of business organization where management by the owners of the business is impractical.

TERMINATION OF THE CORPORATION

The termination of a corporation, like the termination of a partnership, is essentially conducted in two phases: the dissolution phase and the winding-up phase. *Dissolution* may be voluntary or involuntary and effectively marks the end of the corporation. Upon dissolution, the corporation may not take on any new business. A *voluntary dissolution* involves approval of the shareholders and the board of directors. *Involuntary dissolution* usually occurs because of bankruptcy, but it can also occur as a result of fraud in the establishment of the corporation.

When a corporation is dissolved voluntarily, the board of directors (acting as trustee) is responsible for *winding up* the affairs of the corporation. If the board refuses to act as trustee or if shareholders or creditors object, the court appoints a trustee (just as it would if the dissolution were involuntary). After the corporation's affairs have been completed, the assets are liquidated. The proceeds of the liquidation are first used to satisfy creditors, with any remainder going to the shareholders.

PROFESSIONAL CORPORATIONS

Many professional associations, such as groups of doctors in practice together, used to be partnerships. In recent decades, all states have enacted statutes to allow *professional corporations* (*PCs*) to be formed. One reason for this is so that the liability of the members of the group, such as the doctors, would be limited to what is invested in the PC. Each doctor is not personally liable for the debts of all others, which would be most likely to arise from a costly malpractice judgment against one doctor in the group. The doctor who loses such a case does not have limited liability due to the fact that the practice is a PC.

In most states, the owners of PC can only be the professionals involved in the firm itself, that is, the doctors whose practices are tied together to some extent. Stock cannot be sold to outside investors. The tax treatment of PCs is complicated, but tax considerations are why many professionals choose this form of organization.

Limited Liability Companies

Compared with partnerships and proprietorships, the corporate form of organization presents entrepreneurs with a disadvantage—double taxation of profits—and an advantage—limited personal liability. Although the corporate form might encourage entrepreneurs to undertake risky business ventures because of limited liability, the double taxation is discouraging.

These concerns have not escaped the attention of state legislatures. To encourage small business ventures by overcoming the difficulties found in some forms of business organization in the early 1990s, almost all states enacted statutes authorizing limited liability companies. A *limited liability company (LLC)* is a business organization that is treated like a corporation for liability purposes but like a partnership for federal tax purposes.

BACKGROUND

Although limited liability companies have been common in Latin America, Asia, and Europe for some time (for example, the GmbH in Germany), they were not of great interest to U.S. entrepreneurs until the Internal Revenue Service ruled that it would treat LLCs like partnerships for federal tax purposes. As a result, LLC activity increased markedly, and almost all states enacted statutes allowing the formation of limited liability companies. Most states adopted at least parts of the *Uniform Limited Liability Company Act.*

The IRS regulations state that businesses operating as LLCs will be taxed as partnerships—as long as the company structure is more like a partnership than a corporation. In making this assessment, the IRS considers four factors:

1. Limited liability
2. Management centralization
3. Transferability of member interests
4. Continuity of life

If the LLC has more than two of these characteristics, the IRS considers it a corporation—and not a partnership—for tax purposes. To help ensure federal taxation as a partnership, state LLC statutes focus on placing restrictions on the transferability of member interests and on the length of the time the company is expected to be in existence.

METHOD OF CREATION

As in the case of corporations, state laws provide the procedure to be followed in the creation of an LLC. The organizers file a document referred to as *articles of organization*, which are similar to a corporation's articles of incorporation and contain basic information:

1. Company name (must include "Limited Liability Company" or "LLC")
2. Address of the company or its registered agent

3. Whether the LLC is to be managed by its members or by a manager
4. Names and addresses of company members
5. Date (or event) upon which the company will be dissolved, if any
6. Whether any members are to be liable for company debts

LIMITED LIABILITY

After reviewing the application, the state issues a certificate allowing the business to operate as an LLC. Most LLC statutes state that no member or manager will be personally liable for the debts of an LLC. However, members may agree by contract to be personally liable for the company's debts.

RELATIONSHIP OF THE PARTIES

An LLC usually is formed by two or more *members* having equal status. (In Texas and Florida, it is possible to form an LLC with just one member.) The members have a *membership interest* in the company, somewhat like owning stock in a corporation or being a limited partner in a limited partnership. There are generally no restrictions on the number of members. Individuals, corporations, partnerships, and other LLCs may be members.

Unless the agreement says otherwise, members may not transfer membership interests without the consent of the other members. Thus, in contrast to stock in many corporations, membership interests may not be freely sold or given to third parties.

In most cases, the members enter into an agreement, usually referred to as an *operating agreement.* Similar to the bylaws of a corporation, the operating agreement provides rules about the operation of the company and the relationships of the members. It establishes the company's method of management allocation of profits and losses among members, restrictions on the transfer of membership interests, and the process to be followed in dissolving the company. State statutes provide default provisions to cover issues not stated in the agreement.

Certain management issues are covered in the articles of organization. The LLC agreement may give each member an equal voice in management regardless of ownership percentage. More typically, the agreement provides that members may hire a manager to run the LLC. The manager need not be a member. The right to set management policy can be delegated to a group of members based on the members' percentage ownership or on any other basis to which the members agree.

THE CONTINUITY-OF-LIFE FACTOR

To enjoy federal taxation as a partnership, an LLC usually is not allowed "perpetual" life. IRS regulations state that, as with a partnership, continuity of life does not exist if the death, bankruptcy, retirement, resignation, or expulsion of any member causes dissolution of the company. This means that a change in the relationship of the LLC members is determined under state law. Although death, bankruptcy, retirement, resignation, or expulsion of any member terminates the membership of a member, the LLC itself can continue if all remaining members give their consent. In this way, although the company continues to exist, the relationship of the members has changed—satisfying the IRS regulations regarding continuity of life and the application of partnership taxation. The ability of the members to consent to the continuation of the LLC must be set forth in the articles of organization.

TERMINATION

A limited liability company will be dissolved and its affairs need to be wound up under any of the following conditions:

1. Upon the expiration of a period fixed for the duration of the company (if any) in the articles of organization
2. By the occurrence of an event specified in the articles of organization to bring about the dissolution of the company
3. By the consent of all the members
4. By death, retirement, resignation, expulsion, or bankruptcy of a member or dissolution of a member company or occurrence of any other event that terminates the continued membership of a member, and the remaining members vote not to continue the business

In some states, if there is no event or time specified in the articles of organization, the LLC is dissolved by statute thirty years after its formation. When dissolved, the LLC must wind up its affairs, defend itself against legal actions, and dispose of its property. The company may not take on any additional business. After the LLC has wound up its affairs, its assets are liquidated, first to satisfy creditors and then to the members. In some states, the company must file a certificate of cancellation of articles of organization with the appropriate state office.

Key Organizational Features

Most businesses begin and stay as sole proprietorships, but some businesses find it advantageous to incorporate or take some other business form. Several factors influence the choice of business organization, including the potential liabilities imposed on the owners, the transferability of ownership interests, the ability of the business organization to continue in the event of the death or withdrawal of one or more of the owners, the capital requirements of the business, and the tax rate applicable to the business organization selected. Exhibit 14.3 summarizes the differences between the major forms of business discussed so far. The following subsections review some of these factors in more detail.

LIMITED LIABILITY

Limited liability allows persons to invest in a business without placing their personal wealth at risk. Limited liability can also allow investors to be passive toward the internal management of the business.

Entities with Unlimited Liability

Sole proprietors and general partners have unlimited personal liability for the debts of the business, including its torts. Some states require that creditors exhaust the business partnership property before moving against the personal property of the partners. After those assets are exhausted, however, the creditor may require any of the partners to pay the entire remaining debt. Partners forced to pay more than

	Proprietorship	Partnership	Corporation	Limited Liability Company
Method of Creation	Owner begins business operations	Created by agreement of parties; statutes may apply	Chartered under state statute	Created under statute by agreement of members
Entity Status	Not separate from owner	Separate from owners for some purposes	Legal entity distinct from owners	Separate from owners for some purpose
Liability of Owners	Owner personally liable for debts	Unlimited liability except for limited partner in a limited partnership	Shareholders liable only to the extent of paid-in capital	Members liable to the extent of paid-in capital
Duration	Same as owner	Ended by agreement or by death or withdrawal of a partner, but easily recreated	May have perpetual existence	Company dissolves after fixed time or the occurrence of a specific event
Transferability of Ownership Interests	May be sold at any time; new proprietorship formed	Generally, sale of partnership interest terminates partnership	Shares of stock can be transferred unless restricted by contract	Other members must consent to transfers
Control	Determined by owner	Partners have equal control unless otherwise stated by partnership agreement; limited partners have no management rights	Shareholders elect board of directors who set policy and appoint officers to manage	Operating agreement specifies management control
Capital	Limited to what owner can raise	Limited to what partners contribute or can borrow	Sale of more shares increases capital; may also borrow	Limited to what members contribute; may also borrow
Taxation	Profits taxed to owner as individual	Profits taxed to each owner as agreed upon or all share equally	Double taxation; profits of corporation are taxed, and shareholders pay income tax on their share of profits	If IRS conditions are met, same as a partnership

EXHIBIT 14.3

Comparing Characteristics of Major Forms of Business Organization

their proportionate share of a debt may be entitled to reimbursement from other partners unless the original agreement provides otherwise.

Entities with Limited Liability

The liability of a limited partner is limited to the capital the partner has contributed to the limited partnership. Like the limited partner, the shareholders of a corporation and the members of a limited liability company risk only their capital investment if the corporation fails. They are not personally liable for the business debts or torts of the firm unless they contract to make themselves personally liable.

In certain circumstances, the court will "pierce the corporate veil" and hold shareholders personally liable. That is, the court disregards the corporate entity by finding that the corporation is a sham and that the owners actually intend to operate the business as a proprietorship or partnership. Although not common, and usually only involving close corporations, the court can impose liability on shareholders in instances of fraud, undercapitalization, or failure to follow corporate formalities. As the following case illustrates, the corporate form of business organization may not be used merely to avoid business obligations.

Tigrett v. Pointer
Court of Civil Appeals of Texas
580 S.W.2d 375 (1978)

CASE BACKGROUND *Pointer was sole shareholder and president of Heritage Building Company, which was sued in April 1974 by Tigrett. Pointer transferred all of Heritage's assets to himself to repay a loan he had made to the company. The same day, Pointer transferred those assets to Heritage Corporation (a new corporation) as a loan. In 1976, the trial court ordered Heritage to pay Tigrett $49 per week for 401 weeks. However, Heritage was insolvent according to Pointer's testimony.*

Tigrett brought this suit in the form of an application for a writ of garnishment against Pointer, Heritage Corporation, and other corporations owned and controlled by Pointer, alleging that they were indebted to Heritage Building Company as a result of the fraudulent transfer of its assets. She further alleged that Heritage Building Company, Heritage Corporation, and the other corporations were merely the alter egos of Pointer and that all were jointly and severally liable for the previous judgment. The trial court found for Pointer, and Tigrett appealed.

CASE DECISION Guittard, Judge.

* * *

In this garnishment proceeding the holder of a judgment against a corporation seeks to pierce the corporate veil and hold its sole stockholder, and also other corporations owned by him, personally liable for the judgment. . . .

Heritage Building Company was chartered in 1955. . . . It was capitalized for $1,000 in cash. . . . Pointer has since become sole stockholder, and he has always served as president and as chairman of the board of directors. . . .

The corporation's ledger contains a "loan account" showing its indebtedness to Pointer. On April 30, 1974, the ledger showed this indebtedness to be $484,218.00. No notes were signed, no security

taken, and no interest paid. The only written evidence of the indebtedness in the present record is the notation in the corporate books. Pointer testified that he considered this a loan rather than a capital investment. The corporate financial statement, however, designates it as "capital."

On April 30, 1974, at a special meeting of the board of directors of Heritage Building Company, six days after service of process in plaintiff's suit, a resolution was adopted authorizing transfer of substantially all its assets to its president and sole stockholder, Gerald M. Pointer, in consideration of a reduction of the company's debt to him. On the next day entries were made on the books of the company, showing the transfer and listing in detail both real and personal property. Corresponding entries were made in Pointer's personal books showing this purchase of these assets. At the same time entries were made on the books of Heritage Corporation, also solely owned by Pointer, showing a transfer of the same assets from Pointer to it. No money changed hands. The books of Heritage Building Company showed a reduction of $389,967.00 in its debt to Pointer. This figure was determined by the book value of the assets, less the debts against them. The books of Heritage Corporation showed a loan of the same amount to it by Pointer. . . . Operation of the business continued without change. The same employees continued to perform the same duties in the same suite offices. New stationery was printed, but "Heritage Building Company" remained on the office door and was still there at time of this trial.

* * *

With these facts in mind, we turn to the . . . alter ego question. It has been said that each case involving disregard of the corporate entity must rest on its own special facts. . . . When all the material facts are undisputed, however, application of the alter ego doctrine is a question of law. . . .

Of course, domination of corporate affairs by the sole stockholder does not in itself justify imposition of personal liability. . . . Personal liability may be imposed on the sole stockholder only in extraordinary circumstances. Various statements of the circumstances justifying personal liability are found in judicial opinions, but common to all is the concept that the corporate form may be disregarded when it is used to perpetrate a fraud or is relied on to justify wrong or injustice.

* * *

Inadequate capitalization by itself may not be a sufficient ground to pierce the corporate veil. . . . Thus, a party who has contracted with a financially weak corporation and is disappointed in obtaining satisfaction of his claim cannot look to the dominant stockholder or parent corporation in the absence of additional compelling facts. . . . Grossly inadequate capitalization, however, as measured by the nature and magnitude of the corporate undertaking, is an important factor in determining whether personal liability should be imposed.

* * *

Pointer organized Heritage Building Company with a minimum of capital stock and advanced the necessary working funds from time to time in the form of loans. When the corporation ran into financial diffi-

culty, he used his dominant position as president, director, and sole stockholder to withdraw substantially all assets from the corporation without making any provision for payment of plaintiff and other creditors. . . . This maneuver was a violation of his fiduciary duty as officer and director of an insolvent corporation to preserve the assets for the benefit of all the creditors. It was particularly inequitable and unfair in that he preferred himself as a creditor, although in view of the inadequate capitalization, his loan to the corporation must be treated as an advance of capital, or, at most, as a claim subordinate to those of other creditors. Although not one of these circumstances, standing alone, would justify piercing the corporate veil, when taken together, they demonstrate conclusively that while Pointer observed the form of the corporate enterprise, he ignored his substantive duties as a corporate officer and director and acted solely in his own interest.

* * *

[P]laintiff is entitled . . . under this evidence . . . to pierce the corporate veil with respect to Heritage Building Company and Heritage Corporation.

QUESTIONS FOR ANALYSIS

1. Why did Pointer transfer the assets of Heritage Building Company to Heritage Corporation? Is such a transfer legal?
2. Does this decision defeat one of the basic advantages of the corporate form of business organization?

TRANSFERABILITY OF OWNERSHIP INTERESTS

The *transferability of ownership interests* refers to the ability of an owner in a business venture to sell or pass that interest to others. The ability of owners to transfer ownership interests differs among the various forms of business organizations.

Nontraded Entities

The proprietor of a sole proprietorship is, in essence, the business. A decision to sell the business ends the existing proprietorship and means the creation of a new one. Selling proprietorships, partnerships, and other small businesses can be expensive (relative to the value of the business) because such businesses can be hard to price. Often, specialists are required to help determine the market value of the business.

If a partner sells or assigns his interest in a partnership, the partnership continues but the new person does not automatically become a partner. The person is entitled to receive the share of profits the partner would have received, but she gains neither the right to participate in the management of partnership affairs nor continuous access to partnership information as would the partner. As with sole proprietorships, the sale of partnerships or partnership shares often requires specialists to assist in determining the value of the business.

The sale of shares in a *close corporation* is similar to the sale of a sole proprietorship or an interest in a partnership or an LLC. Because the price of the share is not determined on a stock exchange, the parties themselves, perhaps with the help of a specialist, must determine the market value of the corporation.

Publicly Traded Corporations

The stock of public corporations may be traded on a stock exchange such as the New York Stock Exchange; the transfer of ownership of shares is very simple and can be done at very low cost. Since the price of the shares is determined by the many buyers and sellers of the stock, no specialists are needed to determine their market value. The transfer itself is managed by a stockbroker for a modest commission. Thus, the transfer of ownership shares in complex corporations such as IBM is far easier than the transfer of ownership in sole proprietorships and partnerships.

DURATION

A business's *duration* refers to its ability to continue to operate in the event of the death, retirement, or other incapacity of an owner of the business. The ability of a business to continue under such circumstances can depend on the form of business organization.

Limited Life

A sole proprietorship terminates with the death or incapacity of the proprietor. Similarly, at common law, a partnership is dissolved by the death, retirement, or other incapacity of a partner, but it is not necessarily terminated. To avoid liquidation, partners usually agree in advance to a continuation agreement. The same is true of LLCs. The agreement allows the remaining partners or members to continue to operate the business until a settlement is reached with the departed partner or his heirs.

Perpetual Existence

Unless its articles of incorporation provide for a specified period of duration, a corporation has *perpetual existence*. With perpetual existence, the death or retirement of a shareholder does not bring about the termination of the corporation. In most corporations, the death of a shareholder has no impact on the operations of the business.

On the other hand, in a close corporation or an LLC with few members, the death of a shareholder can have an impact on the business. Although the business need not terminate with the shareholder's death, if the shareholder is also a key officer in the company, it may be difficult for the business to continue. Suppose Midstates Construction is a close corporation with five shareholders and fifty employees, including Mertz, the president. If Mertz dies, the company will not legally be terminated, but it may be "forced" to liquidate because Mertz was the key employee.

Other Forms of Business Organization

In addition to the most common forms of business organization reviewed to this point, other forms are available, including joint ventures, joint stock companies, cooperatives, and syndicates. These alternative business organizations are generally used as vehicles to manage a specific project or business concept.

JOINT VENTURES

The Supreme Court has defined a *joint venture* as a general partnership for a limited time and purpose. Generally, a joint venture has several characteristics of a general partnership, including the same rights of control, risks of loss, and manner in which profits are taxed. It usually involves two or more persons who agree to join in a specific project and to share in the losses or profits.

A joint venture is not usually considered a legal entity and therefore may not sue or be sued in its own name. In addition, the members of a joint venture usually have limited authority to bind each other to matters not directly related to the project. Joint ventures vary in size and are most popular as an international business organization.

JOINT STOCK COMPANIES

A *joint stock company* is an organization involving a unique mixture of partnership and corporation characteristics. The joint stock company resembles the corporate form in that ownership is represented by shares of stock and the company is usually managed by directors and officers and can have perpetual life.

Despite these characteristics, joint stock companies are generally treated like partnerships. They are usually created through an agreement. Their form does not follow the terms of state law. In addition, joint stock company property is held in the names of the shareholders/members who have personal liability for company actions. The company is generally not considered a legal entity and therefore may not sue or be sued in its own name.

COOPERATIVES

A *cooperative* is an association (that may or may not be incorporated) organized to provide an economic service without profit to its members. Cooperatives are usually formed by persons who want to pool their purchasing power to gain some advantage in the marketplace. They may obtain lower product prices for their members by buying products in large quantities at a discount.

Cooperatives that are not incorporated are usually treated as partnerships; the members are jointly liable for the acts of the cooperative. If the cooperative is formed as a corporation, it must follow state laws governing nonprofit corporations. In contrast to corporate dividends, however, cooperative dividends are provided on the basis of a member's (shareholder's) transactions with (purchases from) the cooperative rather than on the basis of capital contributed.

SYNDICATES

A *syndicate* is the name given to a group of persons who join together to finance a specific project. Syndicates are commonly used in financing real estate develop-

Avoiding Joint Venture Pitfalls in China

Anxious to get into the booming market in China, many U.S. firms have established over $20 billion worth of joint ventures with Chinese partners. Unlike in the United States, where parties are largely free to form a joint venture of any structure, in China the process is bureaucratic. If proper procedure is not followed, the failure rate will be high and there is unlikely to be legal recourse.

Before a contract is signed, the parties to the potential joint venture must send the proper government agency a letter of intent to form a joint venture called a "project establishment report." Without the agency's blessing, the deal will not be valid. The larger the proposed venture, the higher the level of approval required. Once approved, the contract to form the joint venture can go forward, but the agency involved will want to oversee certain details of the project. How a deal works in practice is likely to be different from what was origi-

nally planned, but change in plans means reporting back to the agency involved about the changes.

When an established company does business in China, often its major contribution is advanced technology, such as a patented production process. But the Chinese government often aserts that technology transfer can have only a small value and the foreign company must contribute other assets.

Deals in China are also complicated because the government insists on strict timetables for capital payments, which may make little sense, given a project's progress. The Chinese government also requires the venture's books to be kept according to Chinese accounting practices, which conflict with international standards, making it difficult for a venture partner to know where it stands. Without experienced counsel on both sides of the venture, these and other peculiarities are likely to sink an otherwise profitable joint venture.

ments, such as a shopping center or office buildings. Although their specific structure varies considerably, such organizations may exist as general partnerships, limited partnerships, or corporations. It is not uncommon for the members of a syndicate simply to own property together with no other formal business organization.

Franchises

Over one-third of retail sales—about $1 trillion per year—take place in franchise outlets. Hence, franchises are a major form of business enterprise. Nationwide, there are about 3,000 franchises and more than half a million franchise outlets. Before the 1950s, only automobile manufacturers, soft-drink companies, and oil companies used franchising to market and distribute their goods. In the 1950s and 1960s, however, many of today's most recognized companies began franchising. Among others, they include Holiday Inn, TGI Friday's, The Gap, H&R Block, Baskin-Robbins, and McDonald's.

Generally a *franchise* exists whenever a *franchisee*, in return for payment of a "franchise fee," is granted the right to sell goods or services by a *franchisor* according to a marketing plan. The plan must be substantially associated with the franchisor's trademark, trade name, or trade dress. As a rule, a franchisee operates as an independent business (usually as a corporation) subject to the standards specified by the franchisor. Successful franchises have two characteristics in common: a trademark (conveying authenticity and exclusivity) and a uniform product or service. For example, as consumers travel throughout the country, they recognize the Burger King name and expect the product to taste the same in California as it does in South Carolina.

TYPES OF FRANCHISES

Franchises may be separated into two basic categories: (1) product and trade-name franchising and (2) business format franchising. In terms of sales, product and trade-name franchising is the largest, accounting for more than 70 percent of franchise sales. Businesses in this category include distributorships (such as auto dealerships and gasoline stations) and manufacturing plants (such as soft-drink bottlers). These franchises are licensed either to distribute the product as it comes from the franchisor or to take essential ingredients (for example, Coca-Cola syrup) and manufacture and distribute the product.

In business format franchising, the franchisor provides the franchisee with everything needed to begin the business, demanding that the franchisee operate the business according to fixed standards and procedures. Business format franchises have been responsible for franchising growth in recent years. Included in this category are franchised restaurants, nonfood retailers, business services, rental companies, and motels.

THE LAW OF FRANCHISING

Because franchising was not pursued aggressively until the 1960s, franchise law is still developing. Federal and state laws are intended to protect investors from crooked or unethical operators. Franchise scams have defrauded investors of hundreds of millions of dollars over the years. In response, federal and state regulations require franchisors to register the franchise and to disclose all relevant information necessary for franchisees to make informed investment decisions.

The FTC Franchise Rule

Federal statutory protections can be found in the Federal Trade Commission's *franchise rule*, which requires the franchisor to give prospective franchisees an *offering circular*, that is, a detailed disclosure document, at least ten days before any money changes hands or before a franchisee is committed to a purchase. The franchise rule's disclosure document must provide the following important information about the business:

- Names, addresses, and telephone numbers of other franchisees
- An audited financial statement of the franchisor and its financial history
- The background and experience of the business's key executives
- The responsibilities that the franchisor and the franchisee will have to each other once the contract is signed
- The number of franchisees and how many have gone out of business

This document enables prospective investors to know about the background of the business. If the information provided is not true, it provides a legal basis for the franchisee to attempt recovery directly from or for the FTC to bring an action against the franchisor. See http://www.ftc.gov for more details about franchises and the franchise rule.

State Regulation

State regulation of franchises began in 1971 with the enactment of the California Franchise Investment Law. The California act requires franchisors to register franchises with the state and to provide prospective franchisees with a prospectus-disclosure document before selling any franchises. The document must detail all important facts about the franchise transaction. California's registration and disclosure law seeks to prevent misrepresentation in the offering of franchises to prospective franchisees and to force the disclosure of information important for making investment decisions. Fourteen other states have enacted similar laws. Another eight states have more limited business opportunity disclosure laws. In each case, the requirements imposed go beyond those imposed by the FTC franchise rule (see the FTC web site for a list of the states).

Most states have agencies, such as the attorney general, that have the authority to monitor franchises. The power to investigate franchise fraud is usually very broad. If franchise administrators find fraud, they can institute a civil lawsuit seeking damages, injunctions, and fines. In some cases, criminal liability may be imposed.

THE FRANCHISE AGREEMENT

The *franchise agreement* sets forth the rights and obligations of the franchisor and franchisee. Key elements that might be included in a business format franchise are shown in Exhibit 14.4. They include, among other things, the rights and limits associated with the use of the franchise trademarks or trade names, the use of the franchise operating manual, the location and designated territory of operation, fee and royalty payments, the advertising commitment, and termination.

Trade Name and Procedure

The agreement grants the franchisee the right to use the franchisor's name and identifying trademarks and trade dress. The franchisee normally must undergo training and will be given the use of the franchisor's confidential operating manual. The franchisor may specify requirements regarding record keeping, advertising, hours of operation, hiring and training practices, and other details of the franchise's operations.

CYBERLAW

Offering Franchises on the Internet

 The FTC, recognizing the reality of Internet transactions, has ruled that franchises can be marketed through the Internet. So long as a franchisor satisfies the disclosure requirements of the Franchise Rule (16 Code of Federal Regulations 436), such as spelled out in the Uniform Franchise Offering Circular (58 Federal Register 69,224), it does not matter if a prospective franchisee gets the offering in paper or on the Internet. The entire transaction can be carried out on the Internet. The FTC and the National Fraud Information Center's Internet Fraud Watch (see www.fraud.org) will look for evidence of investment scams run on the Internet.

Franchisor's Duties and Responsibilities	Franchisee's Duties and Responsibilities
Grants franchisee the right to • Operate a franchised unit • Use all of the franchisor's know-how related to the product • Use trademarks or trade dress of the franchise • Use franchise for a fixed period of time, perhaps with options for renewal **Furnishes franchisee with** • Manual setting forth the franchise's operating procedures, including employee training • Specifications regarding the building, accounting, advertising, and other procedures • Training for how franchisee is to operate the business • Company image **May provide franchisee with** • Territorial exclusivity • Source of product supply • A regional or national advertising program • Quality control inspections • Group purchasing power	**Pays the franchisor a franchise fee** **Is obligated to use the franchisor's name** **As required, build the franchise unit's facility** **Promises to the franchisor to** • Pay a continuing royalty • Conduct the business according to the franchisor's standards • Take the franchisor's training program • Keep franchise information confidential • Prepare franchise's books and records as franchisor requires • Purchase certain products from franchisor • Comply with employee hiring and training requirements • Follow certain procedures upon termination of the franchise **May promise the franchisor to** • Sell only the products of the franchisor • Pay for national advertising • Purchase supplies only from approved suppliers • Exercise personal supervision of franchise operations • Maintain facilities according to franchisor's requirements • Maintain specified hours of operation • Consent to periodic inspections

EXHIBIT 14.4

The Franchise Agreement between Franchisor and Franchisee

Territorial Rights

The agreement may impose limits on the territorial rights of the franchisee and the franchisor. For example, the franchisor may not be allowed to operate additional outlets in the territory unless the franchisee does not live up to certain performance standards. The franchisee may be limited to operating only one unit within the territory. The agreement also states which party has the responsibility to select the site and to construct the facility.

Franchise Fees and Royalties

Naturally, the initial franchise fee or up-front payment is specified. Once the business is operating, the franchisor may require a continuing royalty—generally a percentage of annual sales. The franchisor may also require payments for advertising. The advertising fees depend on whether the franchisor does local or national advertising on behalf of its franchises. To protect the trade name, most franchise agreements prohibit franchisees from engaging in any advertising or promotional programs not approved by the franchisor.

Despite the various federal and state regulations, most cases of conflict between franchisors and franchisees involve civil litigation over violations of the terms of the agreement. The largest such case was a suit brought against Meineke muffler chain by 2,500 franchisees who claimed that over a decade Meineke kept $31 million from a common advertising fund the franchisees contributed to that should have been spent on advertising. In 1997, a federal judge in North Carolina ordered Meineke to pay the franchisees $600 million (damages were tripled under the North Carolina unfair business practices act) for breach of fiduciary duty.

Termination

Franchise agreements are usually explicit about the conduct or events that can bring about the franchise's termination. Typical provisions give the franchisor the right to terminate upon the occurrence of events ranging from the bankruptcy of a franchisee to the failure of a franchisee to submit to inspection by the franchisor. Notice of termination must be given to the franchisee. In some states, franchisors must give the franchisees reasonable time to correct problems. In addition, several states have laws that restrict a franchisor's ability to terminate a franchise unless there is "good cause." Upon termination, the franchisee loses all rights to the franchisor's trade name.

Summary

- The most prominent forms of business organization are the sole proprietorship, partnership, limited partnership, corporation, and limited liability company. Less frequently employed forms include joint ventures, joint stock companies, cooperatives, and syndicates.
- Sole proprietorships automatically come into existence whenever people begin to do business for themselves. Legally, the sole proprietor is the business, responsible for business's debts and torts, liable for its taxes, and in control of its operation and its transfer.
- General partnerships are composed of two or more persons, general partners, who agree to carry on a business for profit. Partnerships may be structured in almost any manner desired by the partners. When an agreement does not specify what happens in some instance, such as death of a partner, the law of partnership, codified in the Uniform Partnership Act, determines the result. In general, partners share in the managerial control, debts, tort liability, and profits of the business. They are taxed personally on the gains from the partnership.
- Limited partnerships are governed by state law. They must have at least one general partner. The limited partners are investors who may not share in managerial control of the business. Their liability is limited to the amount they invest unless they try to exercise managerial control and become general partners, who are fully liable.
- Corporations are created under state law and are recognized as legal entities. They have their own legal life, which is potentially perpetual. They are responsible for their own debts and tort liabilities. Shareholders (investors in corporations) are liable only to the amount they invest in the corporation.
- Shareholders vote to elect the board of directors and must vote on major issues such as selling the corporation. The board of directors is the principal of a corporation. It has responsibility for determining how the company is to be operated and for hiring and instructing the management. Managers are agents of the board and respond to the board's instructions.

- A limited liability company (LLC) provides limited liability for its members (investors) and is taxed as a partnership. Members are thus taxed on the income rather than being subject to the double taxation of a corporation and its shareholders. An LLC must restrict the transfer of member interests and is intended to operate for a fixed or definite time period rather than have perpetual life.
- A key factor in the choice of business form is limited liability, which investors in corporations, limited partnerships, and limited liability companies have but proprietors and general partners do not have. Transfer of ownership interests is easiest in corporations with publicly traded stock. In other organizations, the value of interests is often not known, and often restrictions are placed on transfers. A corporation may have perpetual existence as a legal entity, but in practice, other organizations can last for very long times under contracts that control what happens in case of death or retirement of an investor or partner.
- A franchise exists when a franchisee pays a fee and is granted the right to sell a franchisor's goods or services. Marketing is associated with the franchisor's trade name or trademark. The relationship is defined by a franchise agreement that sets forth the rights and duties associated with the use of the franchise marks or names, the use of the franchise operating manual, designated territory of operation, royalty payments, the advertising commitment, and termination.

Issue

Should Boards of Corporations Be More Diverse and Force More Diversity?

Large corporations are often accused of having a "glass ceiling" that women and minorities find hard to penetrate. The high-level executive positions are dominated by white males. Many companies have mentor programs or take other steps to help women and minorities be more likely to climb the ranks. Some critics assert that these steps are not enough, or are merely cosmetic. A blowup at one large corporation raised a number of issues in this regard.

CIGNA DIRECTOR'S DIVERSITY CHALLENGE HITS A DEAD END

Joann S. Lublin

Lublin is a reporter for *The Wall Street Journal*. Reprinted by permission of *The Wall Street Journal* © 1998 Dow Jones & Company, Inc. All rights reserved worldwide.

Frank S. Jones shook the clubby world of corporate directors last year when he stepped down from his seat on the board of Cigna Corp. to protest its pace in hiring and promoting from minority groups.

There are "people of color in the ranks of our company who feel a severe estrangement and devaluation in their working lives—lives which should otherwise be filled with promise, pride and hope," the black director said in a blunt letter to Cigna's chairman and chief executive, Wilson H. Taylor. Mr. Jones, a 21-year Cigna board veteran, urged the company to create a new board panel, name a special internal auditor and pick an independent outsider to monitor diversity efforts. He went on to accuse Mr. Taylor of treating his concerns with "indifference, bordering sometimes on disdain."

It is rare for a corporate director to press a company on any issue in a public forum. It is all but unheard of for a black director to crusade publicly about a major corporation's diversity shortcomings. Minority directors hold just 6.3% of board seats at the largest U.S. companies. Many don't raise a fuss about the issue of workforce diversity "because they don't want to be pigeonholed," says Robert J. Brown, a black management consultant on the board of Sonoco Products Inc. and three other big companies. "They want to be part of the whole."

Mr. Jones's short-lived campaign raised a thicket of questions about how big companies should manage diversity—and how they can be most effectively pressured on the issue. His abrupt abandonment of the fight, amid acrimony and frustration on both sides, left most of the questions unanswered.

The Jones resignation triggered controversy inside the Philadelphia insurance and financial-services giant—as did Cigna's response to it. Shortly after Mr. Jones stepped down, Cigna disclosed in an April 1997 SEC filing that it had hired a prominent black Washington attorney, William T. Coleman Jr., to conduct a "prudence review" of Cigna's diversity policies and address the issues Mr. Jones had raised.

* * *

A self described "maverick," Mr. Jones is the son of the president of Bennett College, a historically black women's college in Greensboro, N.C., and the great-grandson of a slave. He became the first black manager of the Harvard University football team in 1949. He went on to become the first black tenured professor at Massachusetts Institute of Technology, taking early retirement in 1992 after a long, fruitless fight over how to reduce high attrition among black students there.

Mr. Jones has been a director at Polaroid Corp. since 1973. He acts like "a spiritual coach on diversity" because he brings it up at almost every board meeting, says Carole Ulrich, executive vice president and head of Polaroid's commercial-imaging group. "His presence on the board has made a difference" in advancing women and minorities, she says. Five of Polaroid's 25 corporate officers are female or black.

On Cigna's board, Mr. Jones wasn't always outspoken. He says in 1986 he "got kicked off" the People Resources Committee, which monitors diversity efforts, because his fellow members tired of listening to him complain about Cigna's executive pay and diversity record at committee meetings. Mr. Jones says he didn't raise the issues at full board meetings, though.

Hicks Waldron, retired CEO at Avon Products Inc. and chairman of the panel at the time, recalls Mr. Jones as "abrasive at times" and an unpopular loner. "Were the people on the committee sorry to see him go?" Mr. Waldron says. "I don't think so."

Mr. Jones says his concern over the scarcity of senior minority executives at Cigna grew over the years. Still, he rarely challenged top brass about improving the workforce make-up. "I was a coward," Mr. Jones admits. "I knew I wouldn't get support" because there was just one other minority director on the board, he says. "It's a very lonely proposition."

He eventually grew bolder. In August 1994, at the request of disgruntled black staffers and with Mr. Taylor's consent, Mr. Jones held two gripe sessions with Cigna's highest-ranking minority employees, most of them middle managers. He prepared a report for Mr. Taylor that documented their opinions anonymously, although it listed their names.

Cigna management views minority employees "as being incapable of consistent high-level responsibility" and so they're generally denied fast-track jobs, Mr. Jones's report concluded. "Minorities are not consulted or even considered in key people moves." Among other recommendations, Mr. Jones proposed evaluating and rewarding managers on their affirmative-action gains.

Cigna's Mr. Taylor says he rejected Mr. Jones's suggestions as "things we were already doing." Disgusted by the brush-off, Mr. Jones says he "went home and took a long bath." He says he never released his report to the full board in order to avoid embarrassing the CEO.

The unexpected dead end did, however, spur Mr. Jones to raise the diversity issue more often during full board sessions. "He chose a somewhat confrontational approach," recollects a former executive who attended some of the meetings and watched him rankle the CEO. "It was like a mosquito at a picnic," the former executive says.

By December 1996, Mr. Jones was no longer content to play gadfly. Texaco Inc. had just settled a race-bias suit in November for a record $176.1 million. Its recently retired leader, Alfred C. DeCrane, was now presiding over Cigna's People Resources Committee. (He succeeded Mr. Waldron in 1989.) With Texaco and diversity suddenly making headlines, Mr. Jones asked Mr. Taylor, through an aide, to re-examine Cigna's diversity efforts with the full board.

Mr. Jones contends Mr. Taylor ignored the request. Mr. Taylor says he was unaware of any specific agenda items Mr. Jones wanted aired during the December board meeting. Though seething inside, Mr. Jones says he kept mum about Texaco and diversity: "I wasn't out to embarrass Taylor," he says.

But two days later, Mr. Jones stunned the CEO by phoning him to announce that he planned to quit over the issue. "I felt we were already making good [diversity] efforts," Mr. Taylor remembers telling Mr. Jones. "I felt he should stay and make his points on the board."

* * *

Mr. Coleman completed his prudence review in the summer of 1997. "In my judgment, Cigna has done the diversity job as well as any company I've seen," he concluded. "There wasn't any instance in which anybody violated state or federal job-bias laws." Still, some Cigna employees perceived the report as a whitewash. "Inequitable treatment of minorities still persists as it relates to pay, promotions, hiring, evaluation of performance, etc.," one female black employee wrote in People of Color Newsletter, an underground electronic newsletter circulated among employees.

Almost a dozen current and former officials say they haven't noticed much upward mobility among Cigna's minority employees since the prudence review was completed. "People don't see increasing numbers of women and minorities at the higher levels of the corporation," gripes Mary Hewlett, a black vice president. None of Cigna's 11 highest officers is from a minority group. One is female. Since Mr. Jones's departure, Cigna has had one minority director.

* * *

ISSUE QUESTIONS

1. Can boards of directors effectively address diversity issues if the board composition is not, itself, diverse?
2. When women and minorities are elected to boards of directors, do they have a special duty to work on diversity issues, or should their concern be the long-run performance of the company as a business, whether or not that includes diversity issues?

REVIEW AND DISCUSSION QUESTIONS

1. Define the following terms:

sole proprietorship	limited liability
partnership	joint venture
limited partnership	cooperative
corporation	syndicate
limited liability company	franchise

2. Four people jointly own a summer cottage and use it solely for their personal enjoyment. Is this a partnership? What if they rent the cottage to other people for part of the year? Suppose a renter dies in the cottage due to a gas leak. Could all owners be liable?

CASE QUESTIONS

3. Dr. Citrin had an agreement that had Dr. Mehta work in Citrin's medical offices to see his patients when he was on vacation. When Citrin was on vacation, Mehta saw a patient and misdiagnosed the problem; the patient died. The heirs of the patient sued Citrin, claiming that Citrin and Mehta were partners. Were they? [*Impastato* v. *De Girolamo*, 459 N.Y.S.2d 512 (NY Sup.Ct., Special Term, 1983)]

4. Pena and Antennucci were partners in a medical practice. Both were sued by a patient for malpractice committed by Pena. The jury found that Pena had com-

mitted malpractice and imposed a judgment of $4 million against Pena and Antennucci. Antennucci contended he should not be liable because he was not involved in the malpractice. Was he right? [*Zuckerman* v. *Antennucci*, 478 N.Y.S.2d 578 (Sup. Ct., NY, 1984)]

5. Covalt owned 25 percent and High owned 75 percent of CSI, a corporation that they operated together. They also entered into a partnership to build an office building that they leased to CSI. Covalt resigned from CSI and went to work for a competitor. When the lease on the office building expired, Covalt demanded that High raise CSI's rent in a new lease, from $1,850 to $2,850 per month. High signed CSI to a new lease in the building at the old rent. Covalt sued High for breach of fiduciary duty to the partnership. Who was right? [*Covalt* v. *High*, 675 P.2d 999 (Ct. App., N.M., 1983)]

6. Bane was a partner in a Chicago law firm before he retired in 1985. The law firm had a retirement plan funded by current income, not by partners' contribution during their working lives. Retired partners were to be given a pension based on their income before retirement. The law firm merged with another law firm. The merger did not work, and the new firm was dissolved in 1988, which left no retirement funds for Bane. Bane sued the managing partners of the law firm, claiming that their mismanagement was responsible for the loss of his pension. Did he win? [*Bane* v. *Ferguson*, 890 F.2d 11 (7th Cir., 1989)]

7. When Dr. Witlin died, his wife inherited his 2.654 percent share of a partnership that owned a hospital. As the partnership agreement called for, the dead partner's share was paid off. The amount paid was based on the financial records of the time of the payment. The other partners did not reveal that they were in the process of selling the hospital, which soon happened and more than tripled the value of the partners' shares. Was Mrs. Witlin due the sale price of the hospital or its book value at the time of her husband's death? [*Estate of Witlin*, 83 Cal.App.3d 167 (Ct. App., Calif., 1978)]

8. The Fabry Partnership sold the Silver Queen Motel to the Silver Queen Limited Partnership for $3.2 million, which included $500,000 cash and a note for $2.7 million. Four limited partners contributed to the Silver Queen Limited Partnership, which was recorded with the county recorder's office. After two years, the motel partnership went into default on the note. Fabry then reclaimed the motel and sued the limited partners individually for the amount owed. Fabry contended that a limited partnership had not been properly formed because it was not registered until after the sale of the motel took place, a violation of the limited partnership law that requires recording notice of the partnership when it is first formed. Do the limited partners lose their protection? [*Fabry Partnership* v. *Christensen*, 794 P.2d 719 (Sup. Ct., Nev., 1990)]

9. Citicorp owned two credit card operations, Diners Club and Carte Blanche International (CBI). CBI provided various services for other Carte Blanche operations, such as Carte Blanche Singapore (CBS). Citicorp merged Diners Club and Carte Blanche into one operation dominated by Diners Club. Diners Club quit offering various services to other Carte Blanche companies, such as CBS. CBS sued, claiming that CBI violated its duty to provide CBS various services. The inability to provide such services had ruined the value of CBS. CBS asked the court to pierce the corporate veil and hold that CBI and Diners Club were really one

operation. Keeping the two names separate was a fiction, given that Diners Club really ran everything. Hence, Diners Club could be liable to CBS for the losses it claimed to have suffered. Can CBS pierce the veil and make Diners Club a defendant? [*Carte Blanche (Singapore) v. Diners Club International*, 2 F.3d 24 (2nd Cir., 1993)]

10. A board of directors amended its company's bylaws to state that the bylaws could be amended only by a two-thirds vote of the shareholders (up from a simple majority) and that company directors could be removed from office only for cause and by a vote of three-fourths of the shareholders. This action had the desired effect of scaring off a company that had previously appeared interested in buying half the company's stock so that it could get control by changing the bylaws and voting out existing directors. Some shareholders sued the board, claiming that to change the rules in such a way that helped to protect them in office was a breach of their fiduciary duty to the shareholders. Is that right? [*Treco, Inc.* v. *Land of Lincoln Savings and Loan*, 749 F.2d 374 (7th Cir., 1984)]

11. Cloney was president of the Boston Athletic Association (BAA), a nonprofit corporation that sponsors the Boston marathon. The board of directors authorized Cloney to negotiate the best deal he could get for sponsorship of the marathon. Cloney signed a contract with a company that turned the marathon over to it in exchange for a certain payment, and this deal would last forever if the new company wanted it to. Hence, BAA no longer controlled the marathon. The board sued Cloney and the other company, claiming that Cloney had exceeded his authority. Any such long-term, binding deal would have to have been approved by the board of directors. Was the board right? [*BAA* v. *International Marathons, Inc.*, 467 N.E.2d 58 (Sup.Jud.Ct., Mass., 1984)]

12. Morales owned 20.4 percent of the stock in TV Answer, Inc. After a dispute with other director-shareholders who owned 75 percent of the stock, Morales left the board of the company. The directors made a new stock offering to all shareholders except Morales. When Morales contested the legality of being excluded from the offering, he was given three days to pay a 5-million-dollar purchase price. He then sued the directors, contending that he was being treated in a discriminatory fashion, which was a breach of the fiduciary duty of the directors to treat all shareholders equally. Was he right? [*Morales* v. *TV Answer*, 19 Del.J.Corp.L. 290 (Ct. Chan., Del., 1993)]

13. Rust and Kelly each contributed half the price of a plot of land they intended to subdivide and sell. Rust gave Kelly his share of the purchase price. When Kelly bought the land, he put the title to it in his name only. Several years later, Rust found out that Kelly had left him off the deed on the property and sued for his share of the purchase price plus interest. Kelly claimed that Rust had abandoned the property, and so he did not owe him anything. Rust claimed they had a joint venture. Was there a joint venture? [*Rust* v. *Kelly*, 741 P.2d 786 (Sup. Ct., Mont., 1987)]

14. For thirty years, Cooper distributed Amana appliances to retailers in New Jersey. Amana, like other manufacturers, decided to sell directly to retailers rather than through distributors. As stated in the distribution agreement, Amana gave Cooper ten days' notice that it was canceling the distribution agreement. Cooper sued, claiming that it was a franchisee under the New Jersey Franchise Practices

Act. That law requires that franchisees may be terminated only "for good cause." A jury agreed and awarded Cooper millions of dollars in damages. Amana appealed, claiming that Cooper was not a franchisee but was a distributor. What is Cooper? [*Cooper Distribution* v. *Amana Refrigeration*, 63 F.3d 262 (3rd Cir., 1995)]

15. Domino's Pizza sold two franchises to experienced Domino's managers. The agreement stated that the franchisees agreed to "operate the Store in full compliance with all applicable laws, ordinances and regulations." If not, Domino's had the right to terminate the franchise if problems were not corrected within thirty days of notification. Later, the franchisees' books were a mess, reports were not filed on time, and the franchisees failed to pay city, state, or federal payroll, income, and sales taxes. After six months of the franchisees' not correcting the problems, Domino's gave the franchisees thirty days' termination notice. The franchisees put the stores up for sale. When prospective buyers asked Domino's about the history of the stores, Domino's told the truth, which led to the sale price falling below what would have been offered if Domino's had not said anything and let the franchisees sell on their own. The franchisees sued Domino's; a jury awarded the franchisees over $2 million damages. Did this decision stand? [*Bennett Enterprises* v. *Domino's Pizza*, 45 F.3d 493 (D.C. Cir., 1995)]

16. Several investors, organized through corporations, owned several Burger Kings in Wisconsin. The franchise agreement stated that franchise owners could not own competitor franchises. The investors formed other corporations and then obtained Hardee's franchises. Burger King terminated its franchise agreements with the owners for violating the franchise agreements. The owners argued that since the Burger King and Hardee's franchises were owned by different corporations the agreement had not been breached. Is that correct? [*Deutchland Enterprises* v. *Burger King*, 957 F.2d 449 (7th Cir., 1992)]

POLICY QUESTION

17. In selecting a state in which to incorporate, businesses often look for a state that offers the most advantageous tax or incorporation provisions in their incorporation statutes. Historically, Delaware has had among the least restrictive incorporation statutes. Should states be able to compete on the basis of incorporation statutes? Are there advantages to consumers in allowing states to compete? Are there disadvantages?

ETHICS QUESTIONS

18. Jensen and Cross had a partnership selling insulation to contractors. The business was successful, and the two became wealthy. As the business grew, they discussed the advantages of the corporate form of business. Since their partnership agreement served them well, the change to a corporation was not undertaken. The partners came to fear that some of the workers for the contractors to whom they sold insulation were developing illnesses that may have been caused by long-term exposure to the insulation. By incorporating now, Jensen and Cross hoped to avoid personal liability for the possible injuries to those workers. Was the move to incorporate ethically justifiable even if it was a good business practice?

19. Cook and Smith formed a limited partnership called Trinty Development to develop a shopping center. Adjacent to the shopping center was a ten-acre tract of undeveloped land that came up for sale after the limited partnership had begun its operations. Cook, the general partner, purchased the property from McCade, but only after McCade had refused to sell the property to Trinty. McCade stated that he did not want to do business with Smith. Cook then sold the property to another developer for a $60,000 profit. If Cook had sold the property to Trinty, Trinty could have profited. Smith has objected to the sale and purchase by Cook. What alternatives did Cook have? With regard to his employment with Trinty, what was the ethical choice? How was Trinty damaged? With regard to Cook's relationship with McCade, what were Cook's alternatives?

INTERNET ASSIGNMENT

Under the Uniform Partnership Act ("UPA"), which has been adopted by all the states, except Louisiana, *see, e.g.,* Indiana Code, Title 23, Article 4, Chapter 1 (http://www.law.indiana.edu:80/codes/in/23/art-23-4.html), a partner in a partnership has certain property rights: (1) rights in specific partnership property, (2) interest in the partnership, and (3) right to participate in management of the partnership. *See, e.g.,* 23 I.C. §4-1-24 (/codes/in/23-4-1-24.html). A partner's interest in a partnership is defined by the UPA as a share of the profits and surplus. *See, e.g.,* 23 I.C. §4-1-26 (/codes/in/23-4-1-26.html). One risk from choosing the partnership form is that a partnership can be held liable for the acts of its partners. *See, e.g.,* 23 I.C. §4-1-13 (/codes/in/23-4-1-13.html) and 23 I.C. §4-1-14 (/codes/in/23-4-1-14.html). Moreover, partners become personally liable for their partnership's liabilities. *See, e.g.,* 23 I.C. §4-1-15 (/codes/in/23-4-1-15.html).

Assume Derek is an equal partner with his brother Dustin in the partnership of Derek & Dustin, a real estate holding company owning undeveloped land in the Permian Basin of west Texas. Many of Derek & Dustin's tracts are known to have good oil and gas reserves, while others are considered to be nearly worthless. In early 1999, with Dustin's knowledge, Derek formed a new corporation, Haymeadow Oil Company, for the purpose of acquiring mineral leases and conducting explorations and gathering operations on the partnership's least promising tracts. To fund operations, Haymeadow borrowed money from Shain. As collateral for the loan, Haymeadow gave Shain a 100 percent security interest in all of its present and future mineral leases. *See generally* UCC Article 9 (http://www.law.cornell.edu:80/ucc/ucc.table.html). Derek also executed a personal guaranty giving Shain a 100 percent security interest in his Derek & Dustin partnership interest. *Id.*

In late 1999, Haymeadow struck oil on its first well and turned a large profit. In 2000, however, due to falling oil prices on the world market, Haymeadow became unprofitable and, in early 2001, defaulted on its loan. Haymeadow's mineral leases were sold and the proceeds applied against its loan, leaving Shain with a substantial deficiency.

To recover his losses, Shain filed suit asserting his rights under Derek's guaranty. Shain argues that the security interest given to him by Derek entitles him to look directly to Derek & Dustin's properties for satisfaction. Alternatively, Shain argues that he is entitled to Derek's rights as a partner in Derek & Dustin, thus entitling him to oust Derek from the partnership, install himself as a partner, and then to take the partnership into dissolution so that its properties can be sold. Derek & Dustin defends, arguing that Shain's claim is limited to Derek's future distributions from the partnership, if any, and that Shain may not oust Derek and become a partner or otherwise look to Derek & Dustin's properties. What result? *See generally* UPA (http://www.law.indiana.edu:80/codes/ in /23/art-23-4.html).

PART 3

The Regulatory Environment of Business

Decades ago, business was almost entirely governed by private relationships based upon common-law principles. However, now the legal environment is much more complex. Federal regulation has expanded, often in bursts, over the past century. Regulation is now so common that businesses actively participate in the political process that determines the extent of regulations and how they are enforced.

Why did these laws come about? A century ago, there was concern about the power of large corporations and trusts. After much political agitation, antitrust laws were passed. During the Great Depression, workers believed that they were denied the right to band together to protect their interests. Labor violence became common, and the National Labor Relations Act emerged. The 1960s saw social problems, such as discrimination, that were not being resolved. The civil rights movement helped to produce a consensus that restrictions on employment discrimination must be put in place. Pollution became a major issue in the 1970s, when most of the environmental statutes emerged. Today, as international trade expands, businesses must manage complexities in the law that were not imagined in times past.

CHAPTER 15

Labor and Employment Law Major laws regarding labor unions were passed in the 1930s and have been important since then. Over time, other statutes—such as substance abuse controls, workplace safety, and family leave policies—have come to change traditional employment relationships.

CHAPTER 16

Employment Discrimination Specific legal protections for persons based on race, sex, religion, national origin, age, and disability were first passed in the 1960s. This now constitutes a major legal consideration for business managers.

CHAPTER 17

Environmental Law Before the 1970s, there were common-law restraints on abuse of air, water, and land. Passage of major environmental statutes has resulted in pervasive regulation of most parts of the environment, and, recently, global environmental issues have come to be of concern to many business operations.

CHAPTER 18

Consumer Protection Food and drug regulations were the first major area of federal consumer safety protection to develop. Over the years, the Federal Trade Commission and other agencies have been given expanded control over other areas of consumer concern, including consumer credit.

CHAPTER 19

Antitrust Law Federal antitrust law is over a century old. First established to burst the big trusts that dominated some areas of industry, antitrust law has evolved under Supreme Court direction to limit price-fixing, market sharing, boycotts, and other business practices believed harmful to competition and consumers.

CHAPTER 20

Securities Regulation Federal supervision of the securities markets began in the 1930s. Trillions of dollars of wealth are held in securities, and billions of dollars in securities are traded daily on securities markets. The markets and the professionals who work in the securities industry are subject to federal oversight.

CHAPTER 21

The International Legal Environment of Business The globalization of business means that managers face an ever-greater range of legal issues. This chapter focuses on domestic controls on international trade and on some of the major international legal rules that often come into play in international business.

CHAPTER 15

Labor and Employment Law

Twenty years ago, anyone hired by IBM believed they had a job for life. The company had grown for years and found ways even to care for employees who were not quality performers. But "Big Blue," once the dominant firm in the computer world, was humbled by tough upstarts. Job security went out the window as the company tightened operations and retrenched for the world of global competition that arose from firms that did not even exist twenty years ago.

Like other firms in the rapidly changing economy of today, IBM must deal with drug problems, family leave issues, and a generation of workers that, while accepting of the lack of permanence, are more likely to challenge decisions to fire employees. The strict hierarchy that existed in most firms in years past is being replaced by a more fluid labor market that is far more diverse, not only in terms of race, sex, and ethnicity, but also in terms of employee expectations that employers learn to live with. Changes in the law reflect the changes in societal composition and attitudes. Managing human resources is far more complex than in the days when most workers had "routine" assembly line jobs that changed slowly.

In this chapter, we first look at labor law, that is, the law that generally concerns labor unions. As unions—once the dominant part of employment law—have shrunk in the private sector over the years, most managers have come to know more about the other areas of employment law that make up the modern legal environment. The second half of this chapter reviews those issues, starting with employment at will and moving to drug policy and other parts of modern employment law that make managing personnel an increasingly complex legal challenge.

National Labor Relations Act

The federal labor code, generally referred to as the *National Labor Relations Act (NLRA)*, was enacted in three major phases: the Wagner Act in 1935, the Taft-Hartley Act in 1947, and the Landrum-Griffin Act in 1959. Before passage of those acts, the public policy of the United States with regard to unions and union activities was first developed in the Norris–La Guardia Act of 1932. We first review the major acts and then discuss the key aspects of labor law in practice.

NORRIS–LA GUARDIA ACT

Before passage of the *Norris–La Guardia Act* in 1932 the courts showed little consistency in their labor law decisions. There was little federal legislation that specifically addressed labor issues, so courts applied various common-law rules and the antitrust laws. Some courts held union activities to be criminal conspiracies, while others upheld similar activities as legal. The most common tactic of employers was to plead for an injunction to stop strikes, boycotts, and other union activities. The Norris–La Guardia Act ended such court intervention. The Act declared that every worker should "have full freedom of association, self-organization, and designation of representatives of his own choosing, to negotiate terms and conditions of his employment."

Injunctions Prohibited

Norris–La Guardia prohibits federal courts from issuing injunctions in nonviolent *labor disputes*, increasing the ability of unions to use economic leverage to force employers to bargain about employment terms and conditions. Specific acts that are not subject to court injunctions include *striking* or quitting work, belonging to a union, paying strike or unemployment benefits to labor dispute participants, publicizing a labor dispute, picketing, peacefully assembling, and advising others to do any of these acts without violence or fraud. The Act also prohibits employers from requiring employees to sign *yellow-dog contracts*. Under such contracts, employees agreed not to join a union; if they did, they were fired.

The 1982 Supreme Court case *Jacksonville Bulk Terminals*, 102 S.Ct. 2672, indicates how far-reaching the Norris–La Guardia Act is in keeping courts out of labor disputes. In that case, to protest the Russian invasion of Afghanistan, the union at the port of Jacksonville (Florida) told the workers to refuse to load goods onto ships that were bound for the Soviet Union; the goods sat on the dock. The shippers said that the issue was a political dispute concerning Russian foreign policy, not a labor dispute, and wanted a court order to force the workers to go back to work. The Supreme Court said that since the Act prohibits court involvement in "any labor dispute," the courts could not intervene in this dispute even though the motive was political. Hence, management must deal with the union or begin administrative proceedings involving the National Labor Relations Board (discussed later in the chapter).

WAGNER ACT OF 1935

The basic goal of the *Wagner Act* of 1935 (the first phase of the *National Labor Relations Act*, or *NLRA*) was to ensure workers the right to "self-organization, to form, join, or assist labor organizations, to bargain collectively through representatives of their own choosing, and to engage in other concerted activities for the purpose of collective bargaining or other mutual aid or protection. . . ." The *National Labor Relations Board (NLRB)* was created to monitor unfair labor practices and assure that union representation elections are fair. The NLRB does not regulate the substance of bargaining—the actual terms and conditions of employment—between employers and employees; its concern is mostly about proper procedure and review of claims that the NLRA has been violated.

THE TAFT-HARTLEY ACT OF 1947

The *Taft-Hartley Act* of 1947 (the Labor-Management Relations Act), which amended the NLRA, marked a change in federal policy from one of actively encouraging labor union formation to one of a more balanced approach. Employers could now file charges with the NLRB for unfair labor practices. The Act prohibits unions from the following activities:

1. Coercing employees to support the union
2. Refusing to bargain in good faith with employers about wages and working conditions
3. Carrying out certain kinds of strikes, such as secondary boycotts, charging "excessive" union initiation fees or dues, or engaging in *featherbedding* (making employers pay for work not performed)

THE LANDRUM-GRIFFIN ACT OF 1959

The *Landrum-Griffin Act* of 1959 (Labor-Management Reporting and Disclosure Act), which amended the NLRA, increased regulation of internal union affairs. Senate investigations revealed the improper use of union funds and other problems. The Act is intended to assure that union members are protected from improper actions by union leaders.

Monitoring Leadership

The financial status of unions is subject to federal review, and a report is supposed to be available to union members so that they know how their dues are used. Union officials who betray the trust of their office are subject to prosecution. Penalties were established also to reduce employer wrongdoing, such as bribing union officials or attempting to hold off union activities by other illegal means. Employers report annually to the Secretary of Labor about company expenditures to attempt to influence collective bargaining activities.

Union Member Bill of Rights

A "bill of rights" for union members is included in the Landrum-Griffin Act that provides certain rights in nominating candidates for union offices, maintaining fair election procedures, and participating in union business, subject to "reasonable" union rules. Union dues and fees are to be set by majority vote of the members. If a union member is to be disciplined by the union, procedural safeguards protect the member's rights, and punishment may not be inflicted on members who challenge union leadership or its actions. Members must be given copies of their collective bargaining agreement and be made aware of their rights under the Act.

The Supreme Court applied this law in the 1989 decision *Sheet Metal Workers'* v. *Lynn*, 109 S.Ct. 639. In that case, the head of a local union was removed from his position by union leadership after he spoke out against proposals recommended by the leadership. The Court held that removal from office in retaliation for the statements made violated the free speech rights about union policy guaranteed by the Landrum-Griffin Act.

The National Labor Relations Board

The NLRB administers the National Labor Relations Act. NLRB leadership includes five board members, a general counsel, regional directors, and administrative law judges. Board members are appointed by the President with the consent of the Senate for five-year terms. The board acts as a quasi-judicial body to review unfair labor practice case decisions by regional directors or administrative law judges. The general counsel oversees the investigation and prosecution of unfair labor practice charges and represents the NLRB in court. The NLRB has regional and field offices throughout the country. See http://www.nlrb.gov for more information.

The NLRB has jurisdiction over all employers and all employees where a labor dispute affects interstate commerce. Certain classes of employees are not covered by the NLRA—federal, state, and municipal employees (the public sector), supervisors, managers, independent contractors, domestic servants, and agricultural laborers. Airline and railroad employees are covered by the Railway Labor Act, which is similar to the NLRA.

UNFAIR LABOR PRACTICE COMPLAINTS

In general, *unfair labor practices* are actions that impair the goals of the NLRA. Such practices include employer interference with employee rights guaranteed by the Act; employer-formed or -dominated "company unions"; discrimination by employers on account of union activity in hiring, firing, or other matters of employment; discrimination by employers against employees who testify or file charges before the NLRB; and failure by employers to bargain collectively with the union selected by employees.

More than 50,000 cases a year are filed with the NLRB. Most are charges of unfair labor practice. Charges filed against employers outnumber charges filed against unions about two to one. Each case must be filed by a private party, such as a worker, a union, or an employer.

Most casework is done in the field through the regional offices and involves the following process. Charges of unfair labor practices are filed at field offices that do investigations. If the investigation shows the case has merit, the regional director files a *complaint*. About two-thirds of the charges filed do not lead to a complaint being filed; they are either dismissed by the regional director or withdrawn by the complaining party when informed of their likely lack of success. Of the charges that do lead to a complaint, most are settled before a hearing takes place.

Hearing Complaints

An administrative law judge (ALJ), an employee of the NLRB, presides over complaints that are heard. After taking evidence and receiving briefs, the ALJ issues a decision and order. The order either sets out the appropriate remedy or recommends that the complaint be dismissed. Unless one of the parties involved files an *exception*, the decision is final.

If an exception to the decision is filed, the case is heard in Washington by a panel of three NLRB members if the case is routine, or by the entire board if the case is considered important. Board members hear no evidence and see no witnesses; in that sense they are similar to an appellate court. The board issues decisions in about 1,600 cases a year.

If one of the parties refuses to accept the board's decision, the case will be referred to the U.S. Court of Appeals for enforcement or review of the order. Most decisions of the board that are referred to the Court of Appeals are upheld. In rare instances, the case may be taken for final review by the U.S. Supreme Court.

PIVOTAL ROLE OF NLRB

The NLRA gives the NLRB great leeway to make policy and remedies regarding unfair labor practices. For example, in *ABF Freight System* v. *NLRB*, 114 S.Ct. 835 (1994), an employee contested his dismissal as a violation of a collective bargaining agreement. The worker lied to his employer about the incident for which he was fired; he also lied under oath to the ALJ, which was perjury. The ALJ upheld his dismissal. The NLRB reinstated the worker with back pay, declaring that the lies were less important than other issues in the case. The Court upheld the decision of the NLRB because Congress gave it broad authority in labor disputes. Its determinations are not to be reversed unless they are arbitrary, capricious, or manifestly contrary to the NLRA.

Because of the board's powers to determine much of the substance of labor law in practice, appointment to the NLRB is politically sensitive. Presidents who are sympathetic to labor unions, especially because of political support, appoint "pro-labor" members; presidents who are more sympathetic to the interests and financial support of employers appoint "pro-management" members. As the composition of the NLRB changes, its rulings tend to swing in one direction or another.

REMEDIES

If the NLRB finds that an employer has committed an unfair labor practice, the remedies it may impose include

- Posting a notice in the workplace
- Issuing a cease and desist order
- Providing back pay for lost wages
- Reinstating dismissed workers
- Issuing an order to bargain with the union

Unionization

A major responsibility of the NLRB is to determine whether employees want to be represented by a union. The NLRA focuses on the right of employees to "self-organization, to form, join, or assist labor organizations." To ensure that the employees' right of self-organization can be exercised effectively, the NLRB has rules governing employer and union conduct.

German Workers and Employers Belong to Unions

 The competitive U.S economy has always limited the strength of employee unions. If a union representing workers at one firm gets a generous package that makes the firm less cost competitive than other firms in the industry, the firm and its employees both lose. In Germany, competition among firms has been limited because most workers belong to trade unions and most employers belong to industry associations.

Since all autoworkers belong to the same union and all automakers belong to the same industry association, one collective bargaining agreement has traditionally covered all employees and all firms, so that wages and conditions are the same at all firms. Over the years, German workers have enjoyed higher wages and shorter work hours than in any major nation in the world. But the high costs have made German products less price competitive in the international market, putting pressure on the entire system. For example, in the first half of the 1990s, labor costs rose 22 percent in Germany, while they fell 10 percent in the United States.

Pressure on the Mitbestimmung system is showing up in the growth of small, nonunion firms that can offer employees flexible wage and working conditions compared to the one-size-fits-all industry agreements. Volkswagen, which has long been in trouble, broke away from the industry agreement and signed its own deal with the employee union.

German companies have begun to build more plants in lower-cost countries, including the United States. Persistent high unemployment in Germany also put pressure on the system to become more flexible and allow more workers to find employment. The merger of Chrysler and Mercedes-Benz may mean increased flexibility in German auto production, or more jobs may leave the country.

UNIONIZATION PROCESS

If employees are not represented by a union, a move to unionize might come about by some interested employees who contact a union for assistance or by a union organizer who contacts employees to determine whether interest exists. The union starts an organization drive. An employee committee is formed and with the help of the organizer calls informational meetings and distributes information.

Representation Elections

If a union organizer collects *authorization cards* signed by 30 percent or more of the employees asking for an election to be held to determine whether the union should be their agent in collective bargaining (the cards are kept secret from the employer), the organizer turns the cards over to the NLRB and requests a *representation election*. The election determines whether a majority of employees in a *bargaining unit* want the union as their agent. A bargaining unit may be all workers at a company, the workers at one plant, or workers in certain skills at one or more work sites, such as nurses at a hospital or at several hospitals. Managers may not be in the bargaining unit. Unions win less than half of the representation elections. As employers have become more sophisticated in responding to union challenges, the trend has been against unions.

Before the NLRB-monitored election, a campaign is held in which the union tells the workers of the benefits of unionization and management tells the workers the benefits the company provides without a union. The company is prohibited from threatening those who favor unionization, nor may it promise, say, a 10 percent pay raise if the workers defeat the union. The company must argue in general terms about real problems it sees from unionization.

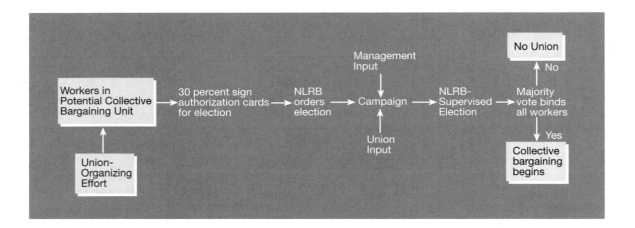

EXHIBIT 15.1

Unionization Process

Union Certification

NLRB agents supervise the election, which is often held at the workplace. After the election, the NLRB certifies the results. If more than 50 percent of the employees vote for the union, the union will be *certified* by the NLRB as the *exclusive bargaining agent* for all employees in the bargaining unit and must be recognized as such by the company. All employees in the bargaining unit, even those who do not want the union, are bound by the recognition of the union as the exclusive bargaining agent. (Exhibit 15.1 illustrates the unionization process.)

On the other side of the coin, 30 percent of the workers can call for an election to attempt to *decertify* unions, that is, to get a majority of employees to vote to remove the union as bargaining agent. The number of such elections has increased over the years.

EMPLOYER RESPONSES TO UNION ORGANIZING

It is illegal for an employer to interfere with, restrain, or coerce employees in the exercise of the rights to organize and bargain collectively. However, employer conduct is lawful if it advances a substantial and legitimate employer interest in plant safety, efficiency, or discipline.

The NLRB and the courts accommodate the interests of both the employees in gaining access to union communications and the employers in controlling business interests without interference. As a general rule, the NLRB and the courts do not permit access to company property by outside organizers. The Supreme Court addressed this issue in the *Lechmere* decision.

Lechmere, Inc. v. National Labor Relations Board
United States Supreme Court
502 U.S. 527, 112 S.Ct. 841 (1992)

CASE BACKGROUND *The AFL–CIO wanted to organize the 200 employees of Lechmere's retail store in Newington, Connecticut. Union organizers entered Lechmere's property and put flyers on the windshields of cars in* *the employee parking lot. The store manager told the organizers that Lechmere prohibited any solicitations on its property, told them to leave, and removed the flyers. Organizers then stood at a public entrance to the parking* *lot, passed out flyers to cars entering and leaving the parking lot at peak times for employee traffic, and picketed the store for months. They copied license plate numbers of cars parked in the employee lot, got names and addresses from the Department of Motor Vehicles, and sent mailings to these employees. Their efforts were not successful.*

The union filed an unfair labor practice charge with the NLRB, which held that union organizers could go into the parking lot to distribute flyers to make contact with employees. The Court of Appeals upheld the board's order against Lechmere, which appealed to the Supreme Court.

CASE DECISION Thomas, Justice.

* * *

As a rule . . . an employer cannot be compelled to allow distribution of union literature by nonemployee organizers on his property. As with many other rules, however, we recognized an exception.

* * *

[This exception—when employers must allow union organizers to enter their property—is to protect the] rights of those employees who, by virtue of their employment, are isolated from the ordinary flow of information that characterizes our society. . . .

The Board's conclusion in this case that the union had no reasonable means short of trespass to make Lechmere's employees aware of its organizational efforts is based on a misunderstanding of the limited scope of this exception. Because the employees do not reside on Lechmere's property, they are presumptively not "beyond the reach" of the union's message. Although the employees live in a large metropolitan area (Greater Hartford), that fact does not in itself render them "inaccessible". . . . Their accessibility is

suggested by the union's success in contacting a substantial percentage of them directly, via mailings, phone calls, and home visits. Such direct contact, of course, is not a necessary element of "reasonably effective" communication; signs or advertising also may suffice. In this case, the union tried advertising in local newspapers; the Board said that this was not reasonably effective because it was expensive and might not reach the employees. Whatever the merits of that conclusion, other alternative means of communication were readily available. Thus, signs (displayed, for example, from the public grassy strip adjoining Lechmere's parking lot) would have informed the employees about the union's organizational efforts. (Indeed, union organizers picketed the shopping center's main entrance for months as employees came and went every day.) Access to employees, not success in winning them over, is the critical issue—although success, or lack thereof, may be relevant in determining whether reasonable access exists. Because the union in this case failed to establish the existence of any "unique obstacles" that frustrated access to Lechmere's employees, the Board erred in concluding that Lechmere committed an unfair labor practice by barring the nonemployee organizers from its property.

The judgment of the First Circuit is therefore reversed, and enforcement of the Board's order is denied.

QUESTIONS FOR ANALYSIS

1. Can employers prohibit employees from acting as union organizers while on the job?
2. Can employers prevent employees from having union materials distributed to them at work, such as in their mailboxes?

Employer Communications

One of the most controversial aspects of union organizing involves what employers may say during union election campaigns. Section 8(c) of the NLRA provides the following:

> The expressing of any views, argument, or opinion or the dissemination thereof, whether in written, printed, graphic, or visual form, shall not constitute or be evidence of an unfair labor practice under any of the provisions of this Act, if such expression contains no threat of reprisal or force or promise of benefit.

Although an employer cannot make threats, some employers have told employees that if they vote to unionize, and if the union gets the demands it is making, the operation would be unprofitable and all jobs could therefore be eliminated. The courts have said that such statements, when based on credible estimates of the economic consequences of unionization, are not unfair labor practices. On the other hand, closing a plant in retaliation for a vote to unionize the plant to scare workers at other plants into thinking that they will lose their jobs if they vote to unionize is an unfair labor practice. In general, employers have the right to close a plant for economic reasons and open a new operation in a lower labor-cost location.

AGENCY SHOPS

When a union is selected to be the collective bargaining agent for the workers at a worksite, the workers who join the union must pay union dues. What about the workers who do not want to be union members?

The NLRA prohibits *closed shops*, where an employee must be a union member before going to work at a unionized worksite. It also prohibits *union shops*—worksites where being a member of the union is a condition of employment. *Agency shops*—places of employment where a majority of employees have voted to be represented by a union in a collective bargaining agreement—are legal. In an agency shop, employees who belong to the union pay union dues, while employees who do not want to join the union pay *agency fees*. That is, nonunion employees are represented by the union and have fees deducted from their paychecks that are given to the union to cover the costs of union services. Agency fees are a little lower than union dues.

Political Action

The use of agency fees paid by nonunion employees to support union political activities unrelated to the union's duties as a bargaining representative raises concerns about the constitutional rights of employees who are forced to provide financial support for union political action. A number of Supreme Court cases have been heard on this issue. In a 1986 decision—*Chicago Teachers Union*, 106 S.Ct. 1066—the Court listed four requirements regarding agency fees paid by nonunion workers to unions at unionized workplaces. There must be

1. An adequate explanation of the basis for the fee
2. A reasonably prompt explanation of the basis for the fee
3. A reasonably prompt opportunity to challenge the amount of the fee before an impartial decision maker
4. An escrow account for the amounts reasonably in dispute while such challenges are pending

This was followed by the *Beck* decision in 1988, 108 S.Ct. 2641. The Supreme Court found that 79 percent of the agency fees paid by Beck and other AT&T employees represented by the Communications Workers of America went to purposes other than collective bargaining, primarily political action. The Court ordered the union to cut its agency fees, refund the excess fees collected from nonunion workers, and keep clear records about union expenditures by category. Justice Brennan noted that unions are not "free to exact dues equivalents from nonmembers in any amount they please, no matter how unrelated those fees may be to collective-bargaining activities."

In practice, the Supreme Court decisions have been difficult to enforce. About two million workers are represented by unions but do not belong to the unions, and so pay agency fees. Most agency fees, like union dues, go to support political action and other union activities not related to the expenses of collective bargaining at a workplace. Unions generally ignore the *Beck* ruling, forcing employees to go to the expense of litigation, as has happened in several cases. In 1992, President Bush issued an Executive Order requiring employers to post notices informing union-represented workers of their rights as determined by the Supreme Court. President Clinton rescinded the order in 1993. Hence, as in other situations, just because the Supreme Court makes a pronouncement about rights does not mean that other branches of government always help enforce the law.

Right-to-Work Laws

A hotly contested feature of the Taft-Hartley Act is the provision that allows states to pass *right-to-work laws* that prohibit agency shops. In right-to-work states, if a majority of the employees vote for union representation and pay union initiation fees and dues, the union is the collective bargaining agent for all employees. However, no employees can be required to pay agency fees even though their wages and working conditions are determined by the collective bargaining agreement. Since some employees receive the benefits of the union without paying union dues or agency fees, unions claim they are free riders. Right-to-work laws, in effect in twenty-one Southern and Western states, clearly retard the effectiveness of unions in such states.

Collective Bargaining

Once employees choose a bargaining representative, that representative—the union—becomes the legal representative of the employees. The employer must bargain with the union. *Collective bargaining* refers to the process by which the employer and the union, on behalf of all employees in a collective bargaining unit, negotiate a contract, setting forth the terms and conditions of employment for a given time period. Collective bargaining is more than the initial contract negotiation; it is the entire process of contract administration resulting in a continuous relationship between an employer and the employee representative.

GOOD-FAITH BARGAINING

The NLRA defines the duty to bargain in good faith as follows:

> [T]o bargain collectively is the performance of the mutual obligation of the employer and the representative of the employees to meet at reasonable times and confer in good faith with respect to wages, hours, and other terms and conditions of employment, or the negotiation of an agreement, or any question arising thereunder, and the execution of a written contract incorporating any agreement reached if requested by either party, but such obligation does not compel either party to agree to a proposal or require the making of a concession. . . .

The main problem is defining good faith, since it can involve trying to interpret another's state of mind. Essentially, *good faith* means an obligation to meet and be willing to present proposals and explain reasons, to listen to and consider the proposals of the other party, and to search for some common ground that can serve as the basis for an agreement—but with no legal requirement that agreement be reached.

So long as no unfair labor practices are used by the employer or the union, even if there is bitterness, the use of legal labor practices is not a failure to bargain in good faith. The Supreme Court has indicated that the NLRB and the courts should not become too involved in the details of the bargaining process, since Congress did not intend for direct intervention in the substance of labor bargains. Rather, Congress took the position that the parties should be free to reach an agreement of their own making.

Actions Not in Good Faith

Certain actions are recognized as a failure to bargain in good faith. For example, in *NLRB* v. *Katz*, 82 S.Ct. 1107 (1962), the Supreme Court said that an employer cannot unilaterally change the terms of an existing agreement with a union. To increase or decrease employment terms—wages or benefits—without consulting the union may be held to be a bad-faith attempt to convince the workers that they do not need the union or to create confusion in bargaining. In remedying bad-faith bargaining, the NLRB is limited to issuing a cease and desist order; it cannot insert a clause into a collective bargaining agreement.

MANDATORY SUBJECTS OF BARGAINING

The NLRA states that bargaining in good faith must occur with respect to "wages, hours, and other terms and conditions of employment." These are *mandatory subjects* about which employers and unions must bargain in good faith but about which either party may insist on its position and back its insistence with a strike or a lockout.

Employers and unions are free to bargain over any topics they agree to discuss. Among the topics that may be placed on the bargaining table because they have been determined by the NLRB or the courts to be subject to mandatory bargaining are the following:

- Pay rate
- Insurance plans
- Holidays
- Overtime pay
- Vacations
- Retirement plans
- Work hours
- Individual merit raises
- Breaks and lunch periods
- Safety practices
- Seniority rights
- Discipline procedures
- Termination procedures
- Layoff procedures
- Recall rights
- Union dues collection
- Grievance procedures
- Arbitration procedures
- No-strike clauses
- Drug testing

There is no requirement that every such issue be covered in a collective bargaining contract, only that the employer must consider demands about such issues raised by the union. In the event of a stalemate between the employer and the union, a private arbitrator may be called in to help get the talks going, or either party may request the assistance of the Federal Mediation and Conciliation Service. These mediators have no authority to impose a settlement but often help the parties reach a settlement.

Arbitration Clauses

Under *grievance arbitration* clauses and arbitration procedures defined in collective bargaining agreements, disputes between employers and unions are to be resolved by an internal grievance procedure. If the results are not satisfactory, disputes are

JURIS **prudence?**

We Want Higher Wages, Less Work, and Mauve Carpeting

Collective bargaining agreements can include any subject relevant to the workplace that the parties agree upon or that federal labor regulators say must be included in negotiations. Unions representing federal government workers have convinced labor regulators to declare that the interior design schemes are subject to negotiation.

A fight between the Federal Aviation Administration and the National Air Traffic Controllers Association over the interior colors of the control towers at Denver International Airport lasted six years. Hundreds of hours of testimony were taken, and numerous hearings were held. The Federal Labor Relations Authority finally ruled that if the controllers do not like the paint, wallpaper, and tiles used in the newly opened airport, the FAA would have to have the control towers repainted, repapered, and retiled because the FAA failed to consult sufficiently with the union about the choices made during construction.

Source: *The Washington Post*

heard by an outside labor arbitrator. If an arbitration decision is violated, the aggrieved party may then go to federal court for enforcement.

More than 90 percent of existing collective bargaining agreements contain such dispute-resolution clauses. The federal courts encourage the use of the grievance arbitration process. This helps prevent the federal court system from being clogged with thousands of disputes.

CONCERTED ACTIVITIES

For productive collective bargaining, an employer and a union must be able to back up their positions. A union can do so with a strike, an employer can lock out the workers, or each side may use some other activity that puts pressure on the other party to settle. To promote productive collective bargaining, Congress provided that certain activities would be protected so that the parties could effectively support bargaining demands.

Protected Activities

The NLRA protects the rights of employees, individually or in groups, to engage in *concerted activities* for mutual aid or protection. Protected concerted activity includes most union organizing efforts. It also involves actions by employees, unionized or not, such as a refusal to work because of unreasonable hazards or other working conditions that endanger health or safety.

That concerted activity by employees is protected whether or not a union is involved was made clear by the Supreme Court in *NLRB* v. *Washington Aluminum Co.*, 82 S.Ct. 1099 (1962). Seven employees who did not belong to a union left work without permission because the furnace at their plant was broken; it was eleven degrees outside and freezing in the plant. The company fired the workers, claiming they had to make specific demands to which the company could respond rather than just walk out. The Court held that action taken by the employees to protect themselves from intolerable working conditions is a concerted activity protected by the NLRA. Because the decision to walk out was reasonable given the conditions, the workers could not be fired.

Unprotected Activities

If workers engage in threats or acts of violence, they will not be protected by the law and the employer may discipline or fire them. The Supreme Court has held that employers may fire employees for insubordination, disobedience, or disloyalty unless the reason for such activity involves protected concerted activity. That is, a worker may not be fired for engaging in a union organizing activity that the employer thinks is disloyal.

Strikes and Boycotts

A *primary boycott*—a strike by a union against an employer whose collective bargaining agreement is in question—is clearly legal. The law restricts *secondary boycotts*, which occur when a union uses economic pressure to try to force others to stop doing business with an employer not directly involved in a primary labor dispute. The following secondary boycotts are illegal:

- A strike against an employer other than the one involved in the primary labor dispute, such as a strike against the steel companies that sell steel to the automakers if a strike is going on against the automakers.
- Refusal to handle goods or perform services for a secondary employer, such as refusing to carry steel from the steel companies to the automakers during a strike against the automakers.
- Threats, coercion, or restraints against any person engaging in commerce—usually an employee—in an effort to spread the dispute beyond the primary employer. For example, in a strike against the food manufacturer Hormel, the union picketed local banks, some of which did business with Hormel, others of which did not. The NLRB ruled that the union could not picket any of the banks, since none were involved in the distribution of Hormel products. The picketing was an unfair labor practice, an illegal secondary boycott.

Public Support

One way to make a strike more effective is to get cooperation from the customers of the employer. A union may make a peaceful request to other firms or the public not to buy certain products. That is a right of free speech, just as is the right to picket a store peacefully to give customers information about certain products sold at the store that the union would like to see the public stop buying. For example, the 1988 Supreme Court decision *Edward J. DeBartolo Corp.* v. *Florida Gulf Coast Building & Construction Trades Council*, 485 U.S. 568, held that it was legal for the union to distribute leaflets at a shopping mall urging customers not to shop there because of a labor dispute between the union and a construction company building a store at the mall.

EMPLOYER ECONOMIC RESPONSES

Although employers may not retaliate against employees for engaging in protected activities, they have the right to use economic pressure. As previously noted, an employer may lock out the employees, that is, refuse to let employees work until the dispute with the union is settled.

Lockouts are legal if evidence of bad intent is not shown, such as trying to break the union. A lockout is usually defensive—in response to a strike, to prevent a sitdown strike in the plant, or to prevent some other activity that would be destructive to the plant or its materials. So long as the lockout is seen as promoting the settlement of the collective bargaining process, it should be upheld as legal.

Replacement Workers

A tactic successfully used by companies in recent years is the hiring of nonunion workers to replace striking workers. Once a collective bargaining agreement expires, if the union and the employer have not agreed to a new contract and the union calls for a strike, the employer is free to hire new workers and to keep using existing workers who will cross the picket line ("crossovers"). In some cases, a strike has gone on so long and there were enough replacement workers and crossovers that the union disappeared or lost substantial strength by the time a new agreement was signed. This is illustrated by the *TWA* case, where deregulation of airlines has forced firms to be much more cost-conscious than they previously had been.

Trans World Airlines v. Independent Federation of Flight Attendants
United States Supreme Court
489 U.S. 426, 109 S.Ct. 1225 (1989)

CASE BACKGROUND *TWA and the flight attendants union began bargaining in March 1984 on a new collective bargaining agreement to replace the contract that expired in July 1984. By March 1986 a new agreement had not been reached. The attendants were working under the terms of the old contract, and a strike was called. TWA announced that it would stay in operation and would hire permanent replacements for striking attendants but that it welcomed attendants who crossed the picket line to continue working. One-quarter of the 5,000 attendants continued to work, and TWA hired 2,350 new attendants. When the strike was settled after seventy-two days with a new contract, TWA recalled only 197 of the striking attendants. By May 1988, only 1,100 strikers had been recalled—all with full seniority.*

The union sued, claiming that (1) it was an unfair labor practice to hire new attendants and (2) even if hiring the new attendants was legal, the striking attendants had to be hired back because they had more seniority than the newly hired attendants. The District Court upheld TWA's policy; the Court of Appeals reversed in favor of the union. The Supreme Court reviewed the matter.

CASE DECISION O'Connor, Justice.

* * *

[I]n virtually every strike situation there will be some employees who disagree with their union's decision to strike and who cannot be required to abide by

that decision. It is the inevitable effect of an employer's use of the economic weapons available during a period of self-help that these differences will be exacerbated and that poststrike resentments may be created. Thus, for example, the employer's right to hire permanent replacements in order to continue operations will inevitably also have the effect of dividing striking employees between those who, fearful of permanently losing their jobs, return to work and those who remain stalwart in the strike.

While the employer and union in many circumstances may reach a back-to-work agreement that would displace crossovers and new hires or an employer may unilaterally decide to permit such displacement, nothing in the NLRA or the federal common law we have developed under that statute requires such a result. That such agreements are typically one mark of a successful strike is yet another indication that crossovers opted not to gamble; if the strike was successful the advantage gained by declining to strike disappears.

* * *

[T]he decision to guarantee to crossovers the same protections lawfully applied to new hires was a simple decision to apply the preexisting seniority terms of the collective bargaining agreement uniformly to all working employees. That this decision had the effect of encouraging prestrike workers to remain on the job during the strike or to abandon the strike and return to work before all vacancies were filled was an effect of the exercise of TWA's peaceful economic power, a power that the company was legally free to deploy once the parties had exhausted the private dispute resolution mechanisms. . . . Accordingly, the judgment of the Court of Appeals is Reversed.

QUESTIONS FOR ANALYSIS

1. If the collective bargaining agreement provides for preference based on seniority, as was the case here, why would the senior attendants who had been on strike not have preference in hiring?
2. Can employers use this tactic to "break" a union?

As companies have become more adept at hiring replacement workers during strikes, the economic power of unions has declined, and the unions often settle for about what the company initially offered. In an effort to help the unions, President Clinton issued an Executive Order in 1995 prohibiting the government from doing business with firms that use replacement workers during a strike. Since the federal government buys about $400 billion worth of goods and services annually, the impact of the rule could have been significant. But since the order was held in violation of the NLRA by the Court of Appeals in *Chamber of Commerce* v. *Reich,* 74 F.3d 1322 (1996), replacement of striking workers continues to be a primary employer tactic.

Employment at Will

Most employees are not represented by unions. At common law, employees are presumed to work at will. That is, employers are free to discharge employees for any reason at any time, and employees are free to quit their jobs for any reason at any time. The *employment-at-will* doctrine is limited by contract, statutes, and court-imposed restrictions. The *Geary* decision shows that the employment-at-will rule can produce harsh results.

Geary v. United States Steel Corp.
Supreme Court of Pennsylvania
319 A.2d 174 (1974)

CASE BACKGROUND *George Geary sold oil and gas pipe for U.S. Steel for fourteen years. He determined that a new pipe for high-pressure use "constituted a serious danger to anyone who used it." He told his superiors about the problem and was told to "follow directions." He finally revealed the problem to a vice president, who had the product evaluated and then pulled it from the market. Geary was fired by his supervisor. He sued, requesting damages for loss of reputation, mental anguish, and financial harm. The trial court dismissed Geary's suit. Geary appealed.*

CASE DECISION Pomeroy, Justice.

* * *

The Pennsylvania law is in accordance with the weight of authority elsewhere. Absent a statutory or contractual provision to the contrary, the law has taken for granted the power of either party to terminate an employment relationship for any or no reason.

* * *

The most natural inference from the chain of events recited in the complaint is that Geary had made a nuisance of himself, and the company discharged him to preserve administrative order in its own house.

* * *

In essence, Geary argues that his conduct should be protected because his intentions were good. No doubt most employees who are dismissed from their posts can make the same claim. We doubt that establishing a right to litigate every such case as it arises would operate either in the best interest of the parties or of the public.

* * *

Of [great] concern is the possible impact of such suits on the legitimate interest of employers in hiring and retaining the best personnel available. The ever-present threat of suit might well inhibit the making of critical judgments by employers concerning employee qualifications.

The problem extends beyond the question of individual competence, for even an unusually gifted person may be of no use to his employer if he cannot work effectively with fellow employees. Here, for example, Geary's complaint shows that he by-passed his immediate superiors and pressed his views on higher officers, utilizing his close contacts with a company vice president.

The praiseworthiness of Geary's motives does not detract from the company's legitimate interest in pre-serving its normal operational procedures from disruption. In sum, while we agree that employees should be encouraged to express their educated views on the quality of their employer's products, we are not persuaded that creating a new non-statutory cause of action of the sort proposed by appellant is the best way to achieve this result. On balance, whatever public policy imperatives can be discerning here seem to militate against such a course.

Order Affirmed.

QUESTIONS FOR ANALYSIS

1. Is the court correct that, even if employers use poor judgment in cases such as this, to allow litigation about who was right about internal company matters would open the door to endless litigation?
2. Should there be an exception to the at-will rule in a case involving public safety where the employee kept all information confidential, compared to a case in which the employee goes public with negative information?

PUBLIC POLICY EXCEPTIONS

Over time, state supreme courts and legislatures have chipped away at the employment-at-will doctrine. There are *public policy exceptions* to at-will discharges for acts that public policy encourages or for refusal to do an act that public policy condemns. In most states, employees may not be terminated for the following:

1. Refusing to commit an illegal act (such as falsifying reports required by a government agency)
2. Performing an important public duty (such as reporting for jury duty when called)
3. Exercising a public right (such as filing a claim for workers' compensation)

Some states allow a fourth public policy exception—the *whistle-blower* exception. This occurs when an employee reports an employer's illegal act. The general test of when the exception applies is that the whistle blowing is primarily for the public good—to enhance law enforcement and to expose unsafe conditions—rather than for private gain.

When a firm dismisses an employee in violation of the public policy exceptions to the presumption of the right of at-will discharge, the employee may sue for *wrongful discharge* or *retaliatory discharge*, which are torts. Most courts restrict the public policy exceptions to cases in which there is a clear constitutional or statutory basis. That is, the wrongful discharge suits exist because the state wants to enforce and protect certain public goals, such as reporting for jury duty and reporting health violations, not because there is a desire to control the employment relationship.

For example, in the 1997 case *Fox* v. *MCI Communications*, 931 P.2d 857, the supreme court of Utah held that firing an employee in retaliation for good-faith reporting by the employee to company management of alleged violations of the law (churning long-distance phone accounts) by co-workers was not in violation of public policy. On the other hand, the Washington supreme court, in *Gardner* v. *Loomis Armored*, 913 P.2d 377 (1996), held that it violated public policy for an armored car company to fire an employee who, in violation of company policy, abandoned his vehicle in order to save a person from a life-threatening hostage situation during a bank robbery. Such cases are, however, uncommon. The at-will doctrine dominates.

CONTRACTUAL LIMITS TO AT WILL

By definition, an *employment contract* exists when a worker is paid for work by an employer. Employment at will presumes that the contract may be terminated by either party at any time unless the contract includes terms that would indicate otherwise. Numerous cases have been brought claiming breach of employment contract; they generally can be summarized under three categories:

1. If an *express contract* exists in which the employer and employee agree on employment for a certain time or that job security is provided, the presumption of at-will employment does not apply. The terms of the contract must be considered. If a company sends an employee to Mexico City on a three-year assignment, an express contract is likely to exist. Dismissing the employee without just cause—e.g., evidence of incompetence or proof of financial crisis—and without evidence that termination is justified could be a breach of contract.

2. An *implied contract*, based on written or oral statements, may be found to restrict the grounds for termination or to require specific procedures to be followed in a dismissal. Evidence includes the policies and past practices of the employer. More and more, courts expect employers to behave consistently in such matters, not just follow procedure when the mood strikes.

   For example, the supreme court of Connecticut found an implied contract to have been breached in *Coelho* v. *Posi-Seal International*, 544 A.2d 170 (1988), when an employee was fired without good cause despite explicit statements by the company president that he had job security and that the president supported him in several conflicts with other employees. The court stated that "there was sufficient evidence to permit the jury to find that the parties had an implied agreement that, so long as he performed his job properly, the plaintiff would not be terminated. . . ."

3. Similarly, because contracts contain an *implied covenant of good faith and fair dealing*, some states have extended this to employment contracts. The Montana supreme court took that position in the 1986 case *Flanigan* v. *Prudential Federal Savings & Loan*, 720 P.2d 257, when it upheld a jury verdict of $1.5 million for a bank employee dismissed after twenty-eight years of service. No good cause for the discharge was provided; it was found to be a breach of the implied covenant of good faith in employment dealings. Similarly, some successful suits have been brought against employers who misrepresented employment conditions in order to attract an employee.

EMPLOYEE HANDBOOKS

Many employers issue *employee handbooks* or *manuals* to explain company policies, benefits, and procedures. The handbooks often discuss grounds for discipline and dismissal. Some explain policy about how such matters will be handled; some assert that employees will be dismissed only for "good cause" and that certain dismissal safeguards exist, such as review by a committee or managerial supervisor. Many courts hold that such handbooks create express or implied contracts that limit the ordinary presumption of employment at will.

As the California supreme court noted in *Foley* v. *Interactive Data*, 765 P.2d 373 (1988), "breach of written 'termination guidelines' implying self-imposed limitations on employer's power to discharge at will may be sufficient to state a cause of action for breach of employment contract." That is, in California and most other states, the courts will look to employment practices, as expressed in a handbook, or as matters were handled in fact, as possible limits on dismissal at will. Even if the handbook states that employment is at will, if other provisions of the handbook or actual company practice indicate otherwise, the employer may have to show that dismissal was for good cause and that proper procedure was followed. Hence, managers should be sure that handbooks and policies, including oral statements to employees about employment safeguards, are procedures the company will follow, or suits for damages for wrongful dismissal may be filed. The supreme court of Idaho discussed some of these issues in the *Metcalf* decision, by which Idaho joined a growing number of states in specifying contractual limits on employment at will.

Metcalf v. Intermountain Gas Co.

Supreme Court of Idaho
778 P.2d 744 (1989)

CASE BACKGROUND *Armida Metcalf began work as a clerk at Intermountain's Hailey, Idaho, seven-employee office in 1979. Intermountain's policy was that an employee could accumulate sick leave at a rate of one day per month. From 1984 to 1985, Metcalf missed eight weeks of work for two operations. She did not use all her sick leave, but her absence was more than the company average, and it caused work problems for the rest of the staff. Another clerk was hired. In September 1986, Metcalf was reduced to part-time status. She resigned to find another job and sued Intermountain for breach of employment contract and for breach of covenant of good faith and fair dealing. The trial court ruled in favor of the employer. Metcalf appealed.*

CASE DECISION Bakes, Justice.

* * *

As the result of numerous decisions of this Court in recent years, it is now settled law in this state that:

Unless an employee is hired pursuant to a contract which specifies the duration of the employment or limits the reasons for which an employee may be discharged, the employment is at the will of either party

and the employer may terminate the relationship at any time for any reason without incurring liability.

Thus, in the absence of an agreement between the employer and the employee limiting the employer's (or the employee's) right to terminate the contract at will, either party to the employment agreement may terminate the relationship at any time or for any reason without incurring liability. However, such a limitation on the right of the employer (or the employee) to terminate the employment relationship "can be express or implied." A limitation may be implied if, from all the circumstances surrounding the employment relationship, a reasonable person could conclude that both parties intended that the employer's (or the employee's) right to terminate the employment relationship-at-will had been limited by the implied-in-fact agreement of the parties.

This Court has recognized that "[a]n employee's handbook can constitute an element of the contract." Unless an employee handbook specifically negates any intention on the part of the employer to have it become a part of the employment contract, a court may conclude from a review of the employee handbook that a question of fact is created regarding whether the handbook was intended by the parties to impliedly express a term of the employment agreement.

In the present case the employee handbook was silent on the question of whether the terms and employee benefits set out in the handbook affected or otherwise modified the employer's right to terminate the employment relationship at will. Accordingly, we conclude, after considering all the circumstances of this case, that a material issue of fact exists regarding whether, by providing for accumulated sick leave benefits, the employer impliedly agreed with the employee that the employment relationship would not be terminated or the employee penalized for using the sick leave benefits which the employee had accrued. . . .

Accordingly, the partial summary judgment on Metcalf's breach of contract cause of action is reversed, and that cause remanded for trial.

* * *

Until today, this Court has not recognized an implied-in-law covenant of good faith and fair dealing in employment contracts. . . .

Nevertheless, it is the opinion of this Court today that in employer-employee relationships we should adopt an implied-in-law covenant of good faith and fair dealing (the covenant) as hereinafter outlined. In changing this Court's prior course, it is important to explain what the covenant which we adopt is. For guidance we turn to the rationale of some of our adopting sister states. Recognizing that we are joining the minority view in this country, we further acknowledge the concerns expressed by courts which have rejected the covenant out of concern that it would place undue restrictions on management and would infringe on the employer's legitimate exercise of management discretion.

First, the covenant is implied in contracts. A breach of the covenant is a breach of the employment contract, and is not a tort. The potential recovery results in contract damages, not tort damages.

* * *

Second, we hold that the covenant protects the parties' benefits in their employment contract or relationship, and that any action which violates, nullifies or significantly impairs any benefit or right which either party has in the employment contract, whether express or implied, is a violation of the covenant which we adopt today.

* * *

We recognize that our decision today is a departure from long established principles of contract law. . . .

Accordingly, it will only be applied prospectively to breaches or violations of the covenant occurring after the effective date of this opinion, and to the claims in this case. The summary judgment of the trial court is reversed, and the case is remanded to the trial court for further proceedings consistent with this opinion.

QUESTIONS FOR ANALYSIS

1. While the court discusses the employment contract as a two-way street, is not the burden on the employer to meet the good faith requirement? The employee can sue if the employer does not meet the standard, but can the employer sue an employee who fails to meet the standard?
2. Is there an incentive created by this rule for employers to make it very clear to employees that they are strictly at will and that there are no assurances as to the future?

MODEL TERMINATION ACT

The volume of wrongful dismissal litigation that arose since the 1980s and the variety of grounds for suits in the states led the Uniform Law Commissioners to accept a Model Employment Termination Act in 1991 that state legislatures are encouraged to adopt. The Model Act provides expanded substantive "good cause" protections for employees against discharges. The remedies available to employees would be limited to reinstatement and back pay or severance pay. Compensatory and punitive damages would be eliminated; a prevailing employee also would be granted attorney's fees. Arbitration is recommended as the preferred method of enforcement. Montana is the only state that has adopted a statute similar to the Model Employment Termination Act, replacing employment-at-will common law.

But states are, by statute and by common law, gradually imposing standards that must be met to justify employee dismissal.

Substance Abuse

Some abused substances, such as cocaine, are illegal; others, like Valium, are legal but can be dispensed illegally. Because of the many sources of abused substances, the full extent of the problem is unknown. The most common abused substance is alcohol. The National Institute of Mental Health reports that 13.6 percent of all adults have experienced alcohol addiction or abuse at one time or another. About 8 percent of the working population are alcoholics, that is, abusers of a legal drug. Add to this the estimated 5 percent to 10 percent of the adult population who abuse or are addicted to illegal drugs or improperly dispensed drugs, and it means that as many as one in six working-age people has a substance abuse problem.

PRACTICAL PROBLEMS FOR BUSINESS

Tragic stories about lives ruined by substance abuse are common. Substance abuse directly affects employers because it means reduced productivity and higher medical insurance costs, which cost employers well over $100 billion per year. The National Institute on Alcoholism and Alcohol Abuse estimates that the average health-care (insurance) costs for families with an alcoholic are double the costs incurred by families with no alcoholics. The huge cost of substance abuse obscures the costs imposed by another widely used, highly addictive legal drug, nicotine, which also reduces productivity and increases medical expenses.

Expensive Consequences

The oil spill caused by the wreck of the Exxon *Valdez* off the Alaska coast in 1989 raised issues beyond environmental liability, because it appears to have been a problem directly related to substance abuse. The captain of the ship had a history of alcohol abuse. He was found guilty of operating the ship under the influence of alcohol, which was, of course, in violation of company policy. While he suffered a small legal penalty for his action, Exxon suffered over $4 billion in costs. The company subsequently announced that all known alcohol and other drug abusers, even after treatment, would not be allowed to return to critical duties such as piloting a ship or operating a refinery. Such workers would be given less sensitive—and less productive—assignments.

The problem is not unique to that incident. The U.S. Chamber of Commerce reports that workers under the influence of alcohol or other drugs are 3.6 times more likely to suffer an injury or cause one to someone else. The Federal Railroad Administration found that over ten years, forty-eight railroad accidents that killed thirty-seven people and caused millions of dollars in damages were caused by alcohol or other drug-impaired workers. The National Transportation Safety Board found alcohol or other drugs a factor in one-third of accidents involving truck drivers killed in highway accidents.

Testing and Treatment

While some drugs are new to the market, substance abuse is not new; it is a problem that only recently has been brought into the open. In 1983, only 3 percent of the *Fortune 500* firms had drug-testing programs of any sort. Today, testing and treatment programs are common among larger firms.

Most companies provide employee assistance programs to help deal with alcohol and other drug problems. Treatment is expensive, costing as much as $10,000 per month. Even if employers do not offer assistance with such expensive programs as a part of employees' health benefits, the costs of dealing with substance abuse show up in various ways. Companies must balance the costs of treatment against the costs of lower productivity, higher medical bills, and the prospect of liability from accidents caused by employee substance abuse.

LEGAL ISSUES IN DRUG TESTING

Companies that are unionized cannot implement a drug-testing program for their workers unless approved by the union in collective bargaining. Since a testing program is a condition affecting work, the NLRA requires that the employer negotiate with the union for a program that is spelled out in the collective bargaining agreement. Hence, the discussion here largely concerns nonunionized places of employment. Further, a substance abuser may have certain rights under the Rehabilitation Act of 1973 and the Disabilities Act of 1990, an issue that is discussed in the next chapter.

Drug-Free Workplace Act

The *Drug-Free Workplace Act* of 1988 requires all companies with more than $25,000 worth of business with the federal government (which includes all companies of any size) to certify that they will provide a "drug-free" workplace. The primary requirements are that the employer

1. Publish and distribute a statement notifying employees that the use, distribution, or possession of drugs in the workplace is prohibited.
2. Specify what action will be taken against employees who violate the policy, which may range from completion of a rehabilitation program to dismissal.
3. Establish a drug-free awareness program and make a serious effort to make it work.
4. Notify employees that as a condition of employment, the employer must be notified of any drug-related convictions that occur in the workplace; the employer must notify the federal government.

Employers failing to comply may lose their business with the federal government. In practice, this statute has been simple to deal with and is not regarded as having a significant effect in fighting substance abuse.

Federal Requirements

Federal employees in certain positions, such as narcotics agents, are required to participate in drug-testing programs. The Omnibus Transportation Employee Testing Act of 1992 requires employers who operate aircraft, public transportation, or commercial motor vehicles to test their employees for use of alcohol and illegal drugs. The tests include preemployment testing, random testing during employment, and testing after any accident. Confidentiality of test results is maintained, and the laboratory procedures used are highly accurate.

State Statutory Standards

Some state legislatures have enacted statutes concerning drug testing, so one must be aware of local requirements. Iowa allows employees to be tested if:

1. The employer has "probable cause" to believe that the employee's job performance is impaired by drug use.
2. The employee poses a safety danger to persons or property.
3. The drug test is sent to a state-approved laboratory.

There may be no disciplinary action for a first drug offense if the employee completes the treatment that is recommended upon evaluation.

Minnesota allows testing of job applicants if a job offer is extended, if all applicants in the same job classes are required to be tested, and if those who fail the test are notified. Like Connecticut, Minnesota allows random drug testing of current employees only for those in safety-sensitive positions. Vermont, Montana, and Rhode Island, among others, allow testing of employees only if there is "reasonable suspicion" or "probable cause" to believe that alcohol or other drug use is impairing job performance.

Maryland and Nebraska do not restrict the conditions under which drug tests may be required. However, they do provide quality and procedural safeguards for the tests to ensure that records are kept properly and that there is a chance for independent verification of test results.

Utah holds employers immune from liability for action taken by employees dismissed for drug usage or by applicants rejected because they failed a drug test, so long as the employer has a written policy, informs employees of positive tests, and maintains proper documentation of tests.

On the other hand, an employee won a wrongful discharge suit against his employers, in *Garner* v. *Rentenbach Constructors*, 501 S.E.2d 83 (1988), when he was fired for failing a drug test that was improperly processed at a laboratory not on the list of labs approved by the state of North Carolina. Again, following proper procedure is critical.

Court Rulings

As the different statutory standards indicate, the law in this area is not settled. Since the law of contract and agency is the basis of most of the employment relationship, employers are presumed to have wide latitude to adopt drug policies. A variety of conflicting cases have arisen, but the Supreme Court has indicated that drug-testing requirements will be upheld if there are reasons, such as safety, for the testing and if the procedures are no more than are reasonably required under the circumstances.

EMPLOYER SUBSTANCE ABUSE POLICY

Numerous court cases give general guidance as to what private employers can do in the area of substance abuse testing. Because the elements listed here may not be treated the same in all states, managers are advised to seek counsel or employ an experienced drug-testing firm.

1. Preemployment screening of job applicants for substance abuse is usually legal.
2. Routine testing of employees on an annual basis or as a part of occasional physical examinations is generally legal. However, physical examinations must be voluntary or directly related to the ability to perform the job. These tests are upheld when the job in question is safety sensitive, when the policy is announced, and when it is applied consistently.
3. Random drug tests, when announced in advance as a condition of employment, are upheld for job classifications where safety is an issue, such as for

truck drivers and pipeline welders. Drug tests for employees not in sensitive positions, such as a vegetable stocker at a grocery store, are more likely to be subject to challenge.

4. Drug tests after accidents have been upheld, again because the public safety issues generally outweigh the employee's right to privacy.

5. Substance tests given because of "reasonable suspicion" of improper usage are most likely to be upheld when there is an announced policy of such tests and when safety is an issue. Testing an employee because someone reported that the employee was seen in the company of drug users is less likely to be upheld unless the person is in a position of sensitivity or safety.

In all cases, a substance abuse policy should be clear and should indicate that the testing is not discriminatory or done carelessly. The policy should state why the tests are done, what is being tested for, what will be done with the results, and what will be the consequences of the test results. To eliminate the chance of a false test result, employees should be given an opportunity to have a second, high-quality test if they challenge the results of a positive test result. Exhibit 15.2 shows some of the primary features of one major company's policy.

EXHIBIT 15.2

Substance Abuse Prevention and Chemical Screening Program

[Company X] is committed to provide safe workplaces for its employees and to maintain programs promoting high standards of conduct to ensure safety and productivity. Consistent with the intent and spirit of its commitment, the company prohibits the possession, use, manufacture, distribution, or dispensation of any controlled substance in the workplace. In addition, company employees are required to report to work in proper condition to perform their duties. Violation of this prohibition or requirement may result in unpaid suspension, termination of employment and/or mandatory enrollment in a company-approved substance abuse rehabilitation program.

V. CHEMICAL SCREENING PROCEDURES

Specific procedures concerning chemical screening and conducting investigations under this section are outlined in the Supervisory Drug Awareness Manual.

A. Preemployment
   All candidates for hire are required to submit to the chemical screening process as a condition of employment. Failure to submit to the chemical screening process or a confirmed positive test will result in denial of employment.

B. Testing Current Employees for Substance Abuse
   The specific procedures for conducting investigations under this section are outlined in the Supervisory Drug Awareness Manual.

   1. Aberrant behavior
      Employees reasonably suspected of using or being under the influence of controlled substances as manifested through deteriorating job performance and/or uncharacteristic behavior may, upon proper investigation, documentation and review, be required to submit to chemical screening.

   2. Post-Accident
      Any employee in an accident that upon proper investigation, documentation and review by appropriate management is deemed to be of a suspicious nature will be asked to submit to chemical screening.

EXHIBIT 15.2

Continued

3. Workplace Criminal Drug Statute Conviction

Upon receipt of verified information that an employee has been convicted of any criminal drug statute for a violation occurring in the workplace, the company, upon investigation and review, will take appropriate personnel action against such employee up to and including termination.

C. Sensitive Position

1. No employee shall be assigned to a designated "sensitive position" unless they have submitted to a chemical screening process immediately prior to the assignment and the results are negative.

2. Employees assigned to "sensitive positions" may be subject to periodic unannounced chemical screening. Positive test results shall result in immediate removal of the employee from the sensitive position and imposition of the sanctions noted in VI.B.

VI. POST-INVESTIGATIVE OPTIONS

Once an investigation is complete, one of the following actions will be taken:

A. The employee will receive full pay for the length of the suspension up to five working days if the chemical screening results are negative.

B. The employee whose chemical screening test result is positive will be required to enroll in rehabilitation recommended through the Employee and Family Assistance Program as a condition of employment and be subject to periodic unannounced chemical screening for up to one year. A subsequent positive test will result in immediate termination.

C. An employee who refuses to submit to chemical screening once reasonable cause has been established will be subject to immediate termination.

D. The employee having a confirmed positive test result who refuses to seek and accept rehabilitation assistance will be subject to immediate termination.

E. An employee who is not terminated as a result of an investigation conducted for a workplace criminal drug statute conviction may be required to submit to chemical screening. Said employee may also be required to enroll in rehabilitation recommended through the Employee and Family Assistance Program and be subject to periodic, unannounced chemical screening for up to a year. A positive test during that period will result in immediate termination.

VII. REQUIRED NOTIFICATION PROCEDURES

A. Candidates for Hire

As a condition of employment, candidates for hire shall be required to sign a statement of understanding acknowledging their agreement to abide by the terms and conditions of this policy.

B. Employees

As a condition of employment, employees shall notify the company of any criminal drug statute conviction for a violation occurring in the workplace no later than five days after such conviction.

C. Company

1. The company, by law, regulations or contract may be required to report drug statute convictions or provide other data related to drug abuse statistics. The company will fulfill such requirements with maximum respect for individual confidentiality.

Worker Safety and Health

Concern about worker safety and health dates to the 1800s and state regulation of coal-mine safety. Federal regulations of job safety in coal mines were first enacted in the late 1800s. Early legislative efforts concentrated on issues of job safety—accidents, injuries, and deaths. Between 1890 and 1920, most states enacted job safety laws, although many of the laws were weak and poorly enforced. Over the years, various laws have imposed requirements on employers to provide certain levels of safety and health protection on the job.

OCCUPATIONAL SAFETY AND HEALTH ACT

In 1970, the National Safety Council reported that 14,000 workers died and two million workers suffered serious injuries on the job every year. Other studies estimated that occupational illnesses, such as exposure to toxic substances, cause additional deaths each year. Congress enacted the Occupational Safety and Health Act of 1970 (OSHAct), which created the *Occupational Safety and Health Administration (OSHA)*. The Act states that employers have an obligation to provide employees a workplace "free from recognized hazards that are causing or are likely to cause death or serious physical harm" and that employers must "comply with occupational safety and health standards" issued by OSHA under the statute. See http://www.osha.gov for detailed information.

Inspections

To help ensure compliance, OSHA inspectors routinely visit workplaces as well as respond to workers' calls of concern. The Supreme Court reviewed the issue of workplace inspection by government agents in a case involving OSHA in *Marshall v. Barlow's, Inc.*, 436 U.S. 307 (1978). The Court held that the Fourth Amendment prohibits warrantless searches. But because OSHA inspectors routinely obtain administrative warrants that do not require a showing of probable cause, unlike such a requirement for obtaining a criminal search warrant, the warrant requirement is not cumbersome.

Most workplace inspections include an examination of health and safety records, interviews with employers, and a walk-around inspection of the plant itself. Representatives of the company and the employees have the right to accompany the inspector. OSHA concentrates inspection efforts in industries where health and safety problems are perceived to be the worst—such as construction, petrochemicals, and heavy manufacturing. The Occupational Safety and Health Review Commission reviews challenges to citations issued for safety and health violations. Appeals from Commission decisions go to the federal courts of appeals.

Employee Rights

It is unlawful for an employer to punish an employee for participating in an OSHA inspection or exercising any right guaranteed by the OSHAct. In particular, employees have the right to refuse work assignments they believe might pose a serious threat to their safety or health.

The Supreme Court reviewed such an incident in *Whirlpool Corp. v. Marshall*, 100 S.Ct. 883 (1980). Two employees refused to work on a screen twenty feet above the plant floor. The safety of the screen was at issue, since one employee had fallen through it and been killed and there had been several other close calls. When the employees refused to go on the screen, they were sent home, lost pay, and had a reprimand placed in their file. OSHA sued the employer on behalf of the workers, asking that the workers' records be cleared and that the workers be paid the lost wages. The Supreme Court supported the workers, holding that the OSHA rule that allows employees to refuse to obey orders that pose a risk of death or serious injury was within the intent of Congress when the law was passed.

Penalties

Based on inspections by compliance officers, citations may be issued for violations of OSHA rules or for failure to meet the general standard of a workplace free of preventable hazards that could cause injury or death. Monetary penalties may be imposed under Section 17 of OSHAct for the following:

- A willful or repeated violation—up to $70,000 per violation
- A serious violation—up to $7,000 per violation
- A nonserious violation—up to $7,000 per violation
- Failure to correct a violation—up to $7,000 per day—or for knowingly making false statements in OSHA records
- A willful violation resulting in the death of an employee may result in criminal penalties being imposed: first conviction—up to $10,000 and six months in jail; subsequent convictions—up to $20,000 and one year in jail

Since fines are often multiplied because of numerous violations that continue over time, the total fine against an employer can be quite high. For example, Bridgestone/Firestone was fined $7.5 million for willful safety violations that resulted in the death of a worker at an Oklahoma City plant.

WORKERS AND TOXIC SUBSTANCES

Most OSHA standards concern safety and include specifications for machine design and placement, stairway design, and height of fire extinguishers. A few health standards have been issued, most of which have had a major impact. Protection from exposure to asbestos was one of the first health standards developed; compliance costs billions of dollars. Other standards have been issued for exposure to vinyl chloride, coke-oven emissions, and other industrial carcinogens.

OSHA must issue standards that "most adequately assure, to the extent feasible, . . . that no employee will suffer material impairment of health or functional capacity even if such employee has regular exposure to the hazard . . . for the period of his working life." Every health standard that OSHA has issued has been attacked by industry and labor. Supreme Court decisions that resulted from those attacks significantly influence OSHA's health standard-setting process.

Risks and Benefits

In the "benzene case"—*Industrial Union* v. *American Petroleum Institute*, 100 S.Ct. 2844 (1980)—the Supreme Court held that before OSHA sets a standard for worker exposure to a toxic substance it must have scientific evidence that current exposure levels "pose a significant health risk in the workplace" and that the proposed standard is "reasonably necessary or appropriate to provide safe or healthful employment." In the "cotton dust" case—*American Textile Manufacturers* v. *Donovan*, 101 S.Ct. 2478 (1981)—the Court held that cost-benefit analysis is not required to justify a standard; standards need only be technologically feasible. Thus, costs of complying with a health or safety standard may outweigh the estimated benefits.

Hazard Communication Standard

Besides imposing exposure limits for some specific toxic substances, the *hazard communication standard (HazCom)* covers all employees exposed to hazardous chemicals. Chemical producers and users must conduct a "hazard determination" of each chemical they produce or use in which they identify scientific evidence about the hazards of each chemical. Information about chemical hazards must be updated as new evidence becomes available. Where hazardous chemicals are used, employers must have

1. A written hazard communication program that includes
   - A list of hazardous chemicals in the workplace.
   - The manner in which safety data sheets, chemical labels, and worker training about chemical safety will be handled.
   - A description of how employees will be trained for nonroutine tasks, such as chemical spills or explosions.
2. Labels for all hazardous chemical containers that identify the chemical, appropriate hazard warnings, and the name and address of the producer or seller of the chemical.
3. Material safety data sheets provided by every chemical distributor with every container. The data sheets must identify the chemical, its characteristics, its physical (such as fire) and health hazards, its primary route of entry (such as skin contact), safe exposure limits, cancer dangers, precautions for safe handling and use, proper control measures in the workplace, emergency procedures, date of issue, and identity of producer who can provide more information.
4. Programs to inform employees of the HazCom requirements and to train employees to detect hazards, to know the consequences of the chemicals, to protect themselves, and to take certain actions in an emergency.

VOLUNTARY PROTECTION PROGRAMS

OSHA has been encouraging firms to join its *Voluntary Protection Programs (VPP)*. About 500 worksites around the country have been qualified by a visiting OSHA team to have excellent safety and health management, employee training and involvement, and appropriate resources to stay in compliance with OSHA standards. Firms that meet the OSHA standards are recognized as in compliance and are not subject to routine inspections. OSHA asserts that sites in compliance have 60 to 80 percent fewer lost-workday injuries than would be expected according to industry averages. While OSHA will inspect a VPP site if there are formal complaints by workers, a major accident, or a chemical spill, ordinarily inspections will occur no more than once a year or once every three years, depending on the VPP criteria met by an applying worksite.

Workers' Compensation

In 1910, states first enacted *workers' compensation laws* to require employers to pay insurance premiums for injury and death benefits for employees. The benefits are paid regardless of the cause of a work-related injury; that is, workers' comp is no-fault insurance. Workers' compensation benefits are set by state law. In exchange for paying premiums, employers become immune from employee damage suits (torts) arising from on-the-job accidents. The following objectives underlie the compensation laws:

1. Provide sure, prompt, and reasonable income and medical benefits to work-accident victims or income benefits to their dependents, regardless of fault.
2. Provide a certain remedy and reduce court costs and time delays associated with tort litigation.
3. Prevent public and private charities from incurring the financial strains that would accompany uncompensated accidents.
4. Reduce payment of fees to lawyers and expert witnesses.
5. Encourage employer interest in safety and rehabilitation of workers through an insurance scheme that bases rates on the accident rating of the employer.
6. Promote open discussion of the causes of accidents rather than encourage concealment of fault, thus helping to reduce accidents and health hazards.

COMPENSATION CLAIMS

About 90 percent of all workers are covered by workers' compensation laws. Many who are not covered are protected by other laws, such as the Federal Employer's Liability Act. To have a claim, workers must generally be able to show that they have (1) a personal injury, (2) as a result of an accident or occupational disease, (3) that arose out of and in the course of employment. The negligence or fault of the employer in causing the injury is not an issue. The application of the law is broad. Compensable injuries can include mental and nervous disorders and heart attacks that occur on the job.

Most courts are strict in interpreting state statutes that clearly state that the liability coverage of workers' compensation "shall be exclusive in place of any and all other liability to such employees . . . entitled to damages in any action at law or otherwise on account of any injury or death . . . ." The actions of the employer, employee, or third person become relevant only if there was intentional infliction of harm, that is, an intentional tort. The employee may then file a civil action for damages outside the workers' compensation system. Attempts to evade this by claims of mental distress imposed by supervisory harassment are not allowed except in cases of intentional harm. Employers are forbidden by statute or by public policy from punishing employees who seek compensation by filing claims.

BENEFITS AND INCENTIVES

Workers' compensation usually has five benefit categories: death, total disability, permanent partial disability, temporary partial disability, and medical expenses. Most states do not restrict the amount or duration of medical benefits. While some injuries require only medical assistance, others take the worker out of the workplace for some recovery period, sometimes forever. Workers usually receive about two-thirds of their gross wages as disability income up to a state-imposed weekly maximum, as low as $200 in some states to over $700. In some states, the benefits run for more than ten years for temporary disability. For permanent disability, the benefits last a lifetime but may be offset by Social Security disability payments.

Premiums Tied to Safety

Generally, workers' compensation provides employers with financial incentives to invest in safety at the worksite. Insurance premiums are based on injury claims records. Hence, firms with the lowest number of injuries, and therefore the fewest claims, will have the lowest premiums. For example, in North Carolina, the average workers' compensation premium is $2 per $100 of wages paid, but the rate falls

JURIS **prudence?**

Watch Out for the Glazed Ones!

 David Howard was snacking on donuts and coffee while driving a truck in Oklahoma. He stated that he choked on a donut bite, which caused him to sneeze, which caused pain in his lower back. After chiropractors could not solve the problem, Howard had surgery to remove a herniated disk.

Howard applied for disability benefits, testifying that eating donuts and drinking coffee is customary in the truck-driving business. The trucking company argued that sneezing is a "personal internal weakness not related to his employment."

A Missouri workers' compensation administrative law judge sided with Howard and awarded him $18,542 in permanent partial disability benefits. The award was upheld by the Missouri Labor and Industrial Relations Commission, although a dissenting commissioner said that he had "serious doubts" about a "donut disability."

Source: *National Law Journal*

to as low as 23¢ per $100 for lawyers and rises to as high as $52 per $100 for painters who work on high metal structures.

A Flawed System?

Employers complain that workers' compensation insurance is too expensive. Employers pay premiums of $60 billion per year, or more than $600 per employee. Despite rising premiums, many compensation systems have run in the red. One reason for the expense appears to be that too many awards are given for permanent partial disability, which results in lifetime payment awards, when the worker is in fact not permanently disabled.

On the other side, consider the amounts paid for losses suffered from injuries that are usually fixed by a schedule. Suppose a worker loses a foot but is able to return to work. Medical expenses and lost work time aside, how much is a foot worth? The state of Georgia says it is worth about $25,000. On the higher side, the state of North Carolina says over $50,000. It is likely that if a jury were allowed to determine the worth of the loss of a foot for a lifetime where an employer was negligent, the award would be much larger. It is unlikely that employers would prefer to operate under the tort system rather than under this system of awards determined by statute.

General Regulation of Labor Markets

Besides the major laws already discussed, a variety of other laws restrict the labor market. Immigration laws restrict who is allowed to work in the country. The minimum wage law sets a low limit on what employees may be paid. Many states restrict entry into occupations by a series of licensing requirements. Employers must warn employees of pending plant closings and must provide family-leave opportunities. Employee pensions are also subject to federal regulation.

RESTRICTIONS ON IMMIGRATION

The United States is a nation of immigrants and is the most popular destination for peoples from many countries that have fewer work opportunities. Millions of undocumented immigrants work in the country, most of whom are concentrated in California, Arizona, New Mexico, Texas, and Florida. The *Immigration Reform and Control Act* of 1986 sets standards for employees and employers. To be hired legally in the United States, a person must be able to present certain documents to show his or her identity and authorization to work. Such documentary proof is required even if a person is a U.S. citizen. For more details, see http://www.ins.usdoj.gov.

Since violations of the law can mean criminal penalties, employers must be sure to meet the basic requirements. Employers must collect evidence of citizenship or of legal work status for all new employees. The following documents are proof of personal identity and of employment eligibility:

- U.S. passport
- Unexpired employment authorization card
- Unexpired temporary resident card
- Foreign passport with employment authorization
- Alien registration card with photograph

Combinations of other documents, such as driver's license, school ID card, original Social Security card, or birth certificate, may provide proof to satisfy Immigration and Naturalization Service of identity and employment eligibility requirements.

FEDERAL MINIMUM WAGE REQUIREMENTS

Federal *minimum wage* requirements were initiated in 1938 as a part of the Fair Labor Standards Act. Over the years, the minimum wage has averaged about 50 percent of the average manufacturing wage. The minimum wage was set at $5.15 an hour as of 1997. Employers must also pay Social Security tax (7.65 percent), workers' compensation insurance, and unemployment insurance. These rules apply to almost all nonsupervisory employees in the private sector.

Supporters of the minimum wage contend that the law requires employers to pay a fair wage to employees and will not allow workers to be paid so little that they have trouble buying the necessities of life. Critics argue that the law results in lower demand for workers in the minimum wage category—usually young persons, often minorities, with little education or job experience. The result is relatively high unemployment among persons in those groups who never get the opportunity to work to develop labor skills that will command higher wages.

OCCUPATIONAL LICENSURE AND REGULATION

Entry into many occupations is controlled by various regulations or *licensing requirements*. In such occupations, a person cannot simply set up and begin to operate a business. Rather, permission from the regulating agency is required. Such permission usually requires some demonstration of competency or payment of a high entry fee. The expressed purpose of these labor restrictions is to protect the consumer. The restrictions are supposed to help guarantee that businesses will provide service of a certain quality and that fewer unscrupulous people will operate in the professions.

JURIS **prudence?**

You Want Me to Feed Him, Too???

 The New York City Transit Authority Police Department has a canine unit. Officers volunteer to be canine handlers. Each officer receives a male German shepherd dog that lives at the officer's home and is used to patrol the subway system.

The Department of Labor sued the Transit Authority, claiming that the officers should be paid for the time they spend going to and from their homes to work because they had their dogs with them. The Authority responded that the officers had to get to and from work anyway, that the dogs did not add to the commute time, and that this was a part of the arrangement that the officers knew about when they volunteered.

The court noted that the logic of the Labor Department would mean that the handlers should be paid for working twenty-four hours a day, since the dogs live at their homes and the officers are required "to maintain a suitable relationship with the dog at all times." The court rejected Labor's position by noting that "the vast majority of the time, while the handler is driving. . . . the dog is quietly occupying the back of the car."

Source: *Reich* v. *NYC Transit Auth.*, 45 F.3d 646

Regulation Set by State Law

Although entry controls for a few occupations are set at the federal level, most restrictions are set at the state level. In most states, a person must receive a license or certificate from the state to practice as a lawyer, doctor, dentist, nurse, veterinarian, optometrist, optician, barber, cosmetologist, or architect. In various states, an individual must be licensed to be a dog groomer, beekeeper, industrial psychologist, building contractor, electrician, plumber, or massage parlor operator. Usually, a state commission determines the entry criteria for a person to be licensed to practice. In most cases, there is a formal education requirement; in some cases, an apprenticeship period is required or a standardized test of knowledge about the profession must be passed.

FAMILY AND MEDICAL LEAVE

The *Family and Medical Leave Act* of 1993 applies to private employers with fifty or more employees and applies to all governmental units. Employers must offer workers up to twelve weeks of unpaid leave after childbirth or adoption; to care for a seriously ill child, spouse, or parent; or in case of an employee's own serious illness. While on leave, the employees' health-care benefits must remain in force. When the employees return from such leave, they must be returned to the same job or given a comparable position. Employers in violation of the law are subject to suit by the employee whose rights are denied or by the U.S. Department of Labor.

Coverage may be denied, on a case-by-case basis, to "key" employees. This may only include employees among the 10 percent highest paid whose leave would cause "substantial and grievous economic injury to the operations of the employer." Also not covered are employees who have not worked for at least one year and who have not worked at least 1,250 hours in the past year. Employees are required to notify employers at least thirty days in advance for foreseeable leave, such as for birth, adoption, or planned medical treatment.

Laws in Europe Restrict Employment at Will

The notion of employment at will is foreign to Europeans. Not only is unionization more common in Europe, which takes workers out of the employment-at-will sector, but nonunion workers are protected by employment laws that restrict management options. American firms that open operations in Europe are often shocked by the rules they find.

When companies cut back their workforce in the United States, the average severance pay is one week's pay for each year of service. In Germany, workers get at least one month's pay for each year of service. In some countries in Europe, dismissed workers must be paid up to 90 percent of their regular wage for up to two years. In the United States, workers are usually notified of layoffs about one month in advance; in Germany, layoffs must be announced up to seven months in advance.

The Family and Medical Leave Act in the United States allows most workers to take up to twelve weeks of unpaid medical leave. In Germany, workers are guaranteed up to six weeks of paid medical leave annually plus substantially more paid vacation time than workers have in the United States.

WARNING EMPLOYEES OF PLANT CLOSINGS

The *Worker Adjustment and Retraining Notification Act (WARN)* requires employers with one hundred or more full-time employees to give advance notice of a plant closing or mass layoff if fifty or more employees will be affected. The notice must be given directly to each affected employee sixty days in advance of the closing or layoff. Notices must also be sent to collective bargaining agents, local elected officials, and state labor department officials. Such notices must be given for permanent terminations, layoffs of six months or longer, and reduction in work time of 50 percent or more for six months or longer.

Employees who do not receive proper notice of plant closing or mass layoff may sue for up to sixty days' back pay and fringe benefits, interest, and attorney's fees. If the local government has not been properly notified, it may sue the company for up to $500 per day for each day there was no notice. If a firm fails to comply with WARN, it may not be ordered to not cut its labor force, but the court may move to secure money to pay prospective damages. In several states—including Connecticut, Maine, Massachusetts, and Wisconsin—state plant closing requirements go beyond the federal requirements.

EMPLOYEE RETIREMENT PLANS

The most important legislation regulating private employee retirement plans is the *Employee Retirement Income Security Act* of 1974 (ERISA). The main objective of ERISA is to guarantee the expectations of retirement plan participants and to promote the growth of private pension plans. ERISA was prompted by horror stories about employees who made years of contributions to retirement funds only to receive nothing. For example, the closing of Studebaker in 1963 left more than 8,500 employees without retirement benefits.

ERISA is directed at most employee benefit plans, including medical, surgical, or hospital benefits; sickness, accident, or disability benefits; death benefits; unemployment benefits; vacation benefits; apprenticeship or training benefits; day-care centers; scholarship funds; prepaid legal services; retirement income programs; and deferred income programs.

Vesting Requirements

The law establishes *vesting* requirements; that is, it guarantees that plan participants will receive some retirement benefits after a reasonable length of employment. All plans must be adequately funded to meet their expected liabilities. A termination insurance program is to be provided in case of the failure of a plan. The law provides standards of conduct for trustees and fiduciaries of employee benefit plans.

The major problem addressed by ERISA was that of the loss of all benefits by employees who had many years of service with a company and then either quit or were fired. The law makes all full-time employees over the age of twenty-five with one year of service eligible for participation in employee benefit plans.

Mandatory vesting (when the employee becomes the owner of the retirement proceeds) was established by ERISA. It provides the employee with three options: (1) to have 100 percent vesting after ten years of employment; (2) to have 25 percent vesting after five years, then 5 percent vesting a year for five years, then 10 percent vesting a year for five years, to achieve 100 percent vesting in fifteen years; and (3) vesting under the rule of forty-five vesting. Under the rule of forty-five, if the age and years of service of an employee total forty-five or if an employee has ten years' service, there must be at least 50 percent vesting. Each added year of employment provides 10 percent more vesting so that an employee will be fully vested within fifteen years.

Summary

- Under the Norris–La Guardia Act, federal courts may not issue injunctions against unions in labor disputes. Employers must bargain with unions according to the terms of the collective bargaining agreement rather than seek relief in federal court.
- The National Labor Relations Act (NLRA) originated with the Wagner Act in 1935. It gives employees the right to organize unions and to bargain collectively through representatives of their choosing. It is illegal for an employer to interfere with employees in the exercise of those rights, and employee actions may not interfere with the employer's interest in plant safety, efficiency, and discipline. The Act created the National Labor Relations Board (NLRB), which is responsible for resolving unfair labor practice complaints and supervising matters of union representation.
- The Landrum-Griffin Act, a part of the NLRA, regulates internal union affairs. The law is intended to make union procedures and elections democratic. It covers the election of union leadership, protects the right of union members to speak out about union matters, and assures union members the right to see the books of the union, which are audited by the Department of Labor.

- If more than 30 percent of the workers at a workplace petition for a union representation election, the NLRB holds an election to determine whether a majority of the workers want union representation. Workers can also vote to end union representation. The employer and the union debate the pros and cons of union representation before workers vote.

- When a majority of the workers at a workplace vote for union representation, all workers are covered by the collective bargaining agreement settled by management and the union, and all workers must follow the procedures established for handling complaints. Workers who are not union members must follow the rules set by the collective bargaining contract.

- Workers who work at a unionized workplace must either join the union and pay dues or, if they do not want to join the union, pay agency fees to the union. Agency fees should not include money used for union political purposes; they are to cover the cost of union representation. In the twenty-one right-to-work states (which are allowed under the Taft-Hartley Act), workers at unionized workplaces cannot be forced to pay agency fees, making unions less effective in such states.

- Most workers are employed at will. There are public policy and statutory exceptions to the rule of employment at will, but most aspects of job rights are determined by written, verbal, or implied contracts, which can include the terms established in a firm's employee handbook. Companies can be open to charges of unjust dismissal if they do not follow promised procedures.

- Most companies have policies regarding testing for substance abuse and steps that must be taken by an employee if abuse is detected. Generally, companies are free to require drug tests of job applicants and of employees in positions that impact health, safety, or large sums of money. Companies may wish to control substance abuse to reduce medical expenses, improve worker productivity, and reduce accidents.

- OSHA may impose work safety and health regulations. If a company fails to meet minimal safety standards, workers have the right to walk off the job to protect their health. OSHA regulations must be justified by documented health or safety needs, but there is no requirement that they be cost effective. OSHA HazMat rules regard worker handling of hazardous chemicals.

- Most employers must pay for workers' compensation insurance to ensure that injured employees, regardless of fault, have medical expenses covered and receive partial compensation for lost wages. Workers' compensation prohibits tort suits except in cases of intentional infliction of injury.

- Labor regulations require employers to collect evidence that all new employees are U.S. citizens or are noncitizens with a legal work status. Employers must also comply with federal minimum wage requirements. Employers of more than one hundred employees must notify employees at least sixty days in advance of any plant closings or layoffs that will affect fifty or more employees. Employers with fifty or more employees must allow employees to take up to twelve weeks unpaid leave for family or medical reasons.

- The Employee Retirement Income Security Act gives employees the right to their pension benefits after a certain time of service and provides federal inspection and guarantee of the solvency of pension funds.

Does Labor Law Need Modernization?

 The NLRA was written more than a half century ago when most workers were in factories, authority was very authoritarian, and labor-management relations were poor. In recent decades, even in production factories, but even more so in service industries, management has learned the value of integrating workers into the decision process. But efforts to give workers more authority have run afoul of the NLRA. If management allows workers to have a committee to determine smoking policy, that can be held to be an effort by management to dominate labor organizations. The reading discusses legislation to revise labor law to allow greater cooperation at the workplace.

CONGRESS SHOULD STRENGTHEN THE CORPORATE TEAM

William C. Byham

Byham is president and CEO of Development Dimensions International, a Pittsburgh-based human resource consulting firm. Reprinted by permission of *The Wall Street Journal* © 1996 Dow Jones & Company, Inc. All rights reserved.

In his State of the Union address, President Clinton said: "When companies and workers work as a team, they do better—and so does America." Indeed, today's most successful companies delegate authority and responsibility to the people who are closest to the product and the customer. But unless Congress acts quickly to amend an antiquated section of the National Labor Relations Act, the worker-management teams that are increasing our ability to compete in the global marketplace may soon become only a fond memory.

On manufacturing plant floors and in corporate offices across the country, these teams are making their companies more efficient and productive: Over the course of just a few years, food retailer Hannaford Brothers experienced fewer on-the-job injuries, resulting in a savings of more than $500,000 in worker compensation costs; Miller Brewing saw a 30% reduction in labor costs and requirements and a corresponding increase in productivity; Texas Instruments' customer return rates fell to 0.03% from 3%.

A recent survey found that 96% of large employers have incorporated employee involvement to some extent in their operations. Nearly 60% of smaller companies have implemented it in the past three years. Other studies show that employees in high-involvement organizations like their jobs better, are less likely to change jobs, and take more pride in the results they produce.

Unfortunately, chilled by recent National Labor Relations Board rulings, nervous American leaders are putting involvement initiatives in the deep freeze. To take just one example, a large distribution company of my acquaintance planned to train its drivers in team and problem-solving skills but gave up on its plans to increase the drivers' authority and responsibility out of fear of legal reprisals. To date, about 20 such cases are pending or have been decided by the National Labor Relations Board.

Section 8(a)(2) of the National Labor Relations Act forbids nonunion employees from sharing decision making power with management over important workplace issues—health and safety, efficiency and productivity rewards, work schedules and job descriptions are all off limits. This section was included in the NLRA decades ago to prevent "sham" employer-run unions. Unfortunately, recent interpretations by the National Labor Relations Board have branded almost all employee involvement initiatives as illegal employer-dominated "labor organizations." Even a worker-management committee established at the employees' insistence to discuss workplace issues was forced to disband.

The Teamwork for Employers and Managers Act [TEAM]—an amendment to Section 8(a)(2)—would enable employers and employees to seize improvement opportunities through team-based employee involvement while preserving the prohibition against "sham" company unions.

* * *

Some unions have recognized the advantage of an empowered, involved workforce. For example, the United Auto Workers has developed a "modern operating agreement" with the major auto makers to encourage a high degree of worker participation in a wide range of decision making. But the AFL–CIO is pulling out all the stops to oppose this legislation. It fears that if employees have a greater voice in the workplace, they may be less likely to seek formal union representation.

Without the TEAM Act, the only legal mechanism for employers and employees to discuss workplace issues will be traditional collective bargaining. Thus, for the 85% of the private sector work force not formally represented by a labor union, the only legally safe course for an employer is to return to a traditional top-down way of managing.

The TEAM Act is our only hope in thawing what could be a very big freeze in America's global competitiveness.

ISSUE QUESTIONS

1. Could union resistance to such changes be a reason that they now represent only one of nine employees in the private sector?
2. Could managers use team problem solving in firms as a way to trick employees into quitting unions?

REVIEW AND DISCUSSION QUESTIONS

1. Define the following terms and phrases:

   yellow-dog contract
   authorization card
   union certification
   agency shop
   agency fees
   right-to-work law
   collective bargaining
   mandatory subjects of bargaining
   concerted activity

   secondary boycott
   lockout
   employment at will
   whistle-blower
   employee handbooks
   substance abuse policy
   workers' compensation
   licensing requirements
   vesting

2. Do firms have the right to test all job applicants and refuse to hire applicants who test positive for drug use even if the job in question has no safety or sensitivity concerns?

CASE QUESTIONS

3. Nastasi drove a propane gas delivery truck for Synergy Gas. He had been very active in getting a union certified as the bargaining agent for fellow employees. The unionization fight was bitter, and the company was cited by the NLRB for five unfair labor practices. Soon after the unionization fight, Nastasi was in a serious accident in his truck. Synergy fired him, claiming that it fired all drivers in serious accidents because of the danger involved in driving such trucks. The union protested that the firing was because of Nastasi's union leadership. The NLRB ordered Nastasi reinstated to his job; Synergy appealed. What was the result? [*Synergy Gas* v. *NLRB*, 19 F.3d 649 (D.C. Cir., 1994)]

4. During a campaign for a company's production facility to become unionized, the management showed a movie to employees that dramatized some supposed risks of unionization. The union complained this was an unfair labor practice, and the NLRB agreed. The company claimed this was protected by freedom of speech and was not an unfair labor practice. What was the result when the case was appealed to the federal court of appeals? [*Luxuray of New York* v. *NLRB*, 447 F.2d 112 (2d Cir., 1971)]

5. During a campaign to get the printing department workers at a large company to become represented by the same union that represented most workers at the company, the printing department's manager told the workers that if they unionized they could end up getting paid less because they would be paid by the hour instead of by the month and that their work could be organized such that they would be needed for fewer hours. The manager also said the workers could lose the flexible arrangements they enjoyed for breaks and lunch. The union lost a close vote and filed a claim of unfair labor practice by the employer. Was the employer engaging in unfair practices? [*NLRB* v. *Lenkurt Electric Co.*, 438 F.2d 1102 (9th Cir., 1971)]

6. During a unionization campaign, a company told workers that no materials related to the union effort could be posted on employee bulletin boards. A supervisor told a union supporter that "if we got a union in there, we'd be in the unemployment line." The union claimed these were unfair labor practices. The NLRB agreed; did the court? [*Guardian Industries* v. *NLRB*, 49 F.3d 317 (7th Cir., 1995)]

7. Mead operates a large paper mill where most workers are represented by a union. When Mead and the union negotiated a new agreement, they fought over the company's "flex" plans that gave all personnel broader responsibilities and a wage increase. The new agreement included the flex plans, but the union was not happy. Workers wore T-shirts, buttons, and decals that said "Hey Mead—Flex This," "Just Say No—Mead," and other sayings in reference to the fight. After a year, Mead issued an order banning such shirts, buttons, and decals from company property. Mead said this was needed to maintain discipline and to not send negative messages to the public. The union protested that this violated their right to come together for mutual aid and protection. The NLRB sided with the union; did the court? [*NLRB* v. *Mead Corp.*, 73 F.3d 74 (6th Cir., 1996)]

8. When bargaining for a new agreement, the company wanted a pay cut and the union wanted a raise. The company said that it was in poor financial shape but refused to provide financial statements the union requested. After four months of negotiations, the company declared an impasse, laid off forty employees, hired replacement workers, and continued operations without a bargaining agreement. The union claimed all of these were unfair labor practices. The NLRB and federal district court judge agreed, ordering the company to produce its financial statements, continue negotiations, and rehire the laid-off employees. Did the appeals court agree? [*Rivera-Vega* v. *ConAgra*, 70 F.3d 153 (1st Cir., 1995)]

9. The employees of a Cleveland television station were on strike. Union members distributed handbills at the entrances to various businesses that advertised on the station. They also contacted the businesses directly, asking them not to advertise on the station or the union would ask the public to boycott their businesses. The station owner sued the union, claiming it was involved in an illegal secondary boycott, but the NLRB ruled for the union. What was the result on appeal? [*Storer Comm.* v. *Natl. Assn. of Broadcast Employees and Technicians*, 854 F.2d 144 (6th Cir., 1988)]

10. Barbara Reynolds and Jason Stephens were at-will truck driver employees of Ozark Motor Lines. They were fired when they refused to begin a trip from Memphis to Chicago without having adequate time to inspect the truck as required by safety provisions of the Tennessee Motor Carriers Act. The jury found this to be wrongful dismissal because Ozark violated statutory public policy. Was this upheld on appeal? [*Reynolds* v. *Ozark Motor Lines*, 887 S.W.2d 822 (Tenn. Sup.Ct., 1994)]

11. Diane Ostrander was an insurance agent for Farm Bureau Mutual Insurance for fourteen years before she was fired. Her agreement stated that she was an independent contractor and that either party could cancel the agreement at any time, with or without cause. Ostrander sued, claiming that the termination of the agreement, without cause, violated the covenant of good faith and fair dealing. Could she have a case? [*Ostrander* v. *Farm Bureau Mutual Insurance Co.*, 851 P.2d 946 (Sup. Ct., Id., 1993)]

12. When Norton was hired in 1978, he signed an "Employment Agreement" that stated that his employment could be terminated at any time. Several years later, his employer issued a "Work Rule Policy & Handbook" that established policy for discipline and dismissal. Steps for notifying an employee about unsatisfactory performance were described. Norton was fired in 1989 because his boss was unhappy with sales in the office that Norton ran. Norton sued for violation of his employment contract because the company did not follow the steps in the handbook. A jury awarded him $305,000 in back pay for breach of contract. Was the award upheld on appeal, or was Norton an at-will employee? [*Norton* v. *Caremark, Inc.*, 20 F.3d 330 (8th Cir., 1994)]

13. Scholz began working for Montgomery Ward in 1970. She told the manager she did not want to work on Sunday and was told that that was fine. Over the years, when she was asked to work on Sunday, she refused, and the matter was dropped. In 1982, Scholz and other employees signed a sheet agreeing to the terms of a new employee manual that stated that all were employees at will and that the company could change the terms and conditions of employment at any time. In 1983, Scholz was told to work Sunday or be fired; she refused and was fired. Her work record was excellent otherwise. She sued for breach of contract, contending she had been told by the manager she did not have to work on Sunday. Was that correct? [*Scholz* v. *Montgomery Ward*, 468 N.W.2d 845 (Mich. Sup. Ct., 1991)]

14. An engineer worked for a company for ten years with no written employment contract. The personnel manual said employees could be fired only for good cause. Soon after the engineer wrote a memo about a structural problem with one of the company's buildings, he was fired. He sued, claiming he was fired without good cause and that an implied contract existed because of the policy manual. The lower courts ruled that he did not have a claim. What was the result of the appeal? [*Woolley* v. *Hoffmann–La Roche*, 491 A.2d 1257 (N.J. Sup. Ct., 1985)]

15. Tanks was a bus driver for the Greater Cleveland Rapid Transit Authority (GCRTA). The GCRTA had a published substance abuse policy to protect public safety that required drivers to be tested after accidents. Tanks ran into a pole. As required, she submitted blood, saliva, and urine samples, which tested positive for cocaine. Under the terms of the policy, Tanks was fired. She sued, claiming that the drug test was an unreasonable search in violation of the Fourth Amendment to the Constitution. Did she have a case? [*Tanks* v. *GCRTA*, 930 F.2d 475 (6th Cir., 1991)]

16. A group of Boeing workers sued for injuries and disabilities from their four-year exposure to toxic chemicals. There was evidence that Boeing had known of the problem but did nothing about it. Boeing asserted that the employees could collect, if anything, under workers' compensation; the employees sued for intentional tort. Could they bring such an action? [*Birklid* v. *Boeing*, 904 P.2d 278 (Wash. Sup. Ct., 1995)]

17. Fifteen-year-old Joshua Zimmerman was on his third day on the job at a car wash run by Valdak in North Dakota. Valdak used an industrial centrifuge extractor to spin dry towels for use at the car wash. The extractor had a warning: "NEVER INSERT HANDS IN BASKET IF IT IS SPINNING EVEN SLIGHTLY." It had an interlocking device to prevent the lid from being opened while it was spinning, but the interlock did not work all the time and was not working when Joshua reached inside for towels and had his arm severed at the elbow (the arm was reattached by surgeons). OSHA cited Valdak for a willful violation and fined it $28,000. Valdak appealed. Did the finding of willfulness stand? [*Valdak v. OSHA*, 73 F.3d 1466 (8th Cir., 1996)]

18. A Dallas nightclub signed independent contracting agreements with topless dancers providing that the dancers could work when they wanted and were responsible for their own costumes, and stating that they are not employees of the club. To be allowed to dance, each dancer agreed to pay the club a $35 administrative fee every time she worked. The dancers' sole source of income is tips for performing on stage or at private tables. Are the dancers employees covered by the Fair Labor Standard Act's minimum wage requirement, or are they independent contractors not covered by the law? [*Martin* v. *Priba Corp.*, 1992 WL 486911, 61 USLW 2307 (N.Dist.Texas, 1992)]

POLICY QUESTION

19. In recent years, some states have used their state employee pension funds to invest in new businesses built in the state. In many cases, this means loans are being made to firms that could not get such favorable terms from private lenders because those lenders believe the businesses to be too risky. Is it good policy to put employees' pension funds in projects that have high risk? Is it good policy for a company to have its employees' pensions tied up in company stock?

ETHICS QUESTIONS

20. Contemplating the opening of a factory, you discover that it appears to be a toss-up between building a plant that uses cheaper machinery and 200 workers who will earn an average of $6 an hour and building a plant that uses more expensive, sophisticated machinery and 70 workers likely to earn about $15 an hour. Is it more responsible to build one kind of factory than another? What if you know that the first kind of factory will probably never be unionized but the second kind of factory is more likely to be unionized?

21. You are manager of a company. The employees' handbook for your company is rather poorly written and says things to the effect that "so long as your work record is good you have no reason to expect to be fired." You realize that although the handbook has never been used, it could be used as evidence of a contractual standard in a court case by a terminated employee. You are pretty sure that if you revise the manual so that it conforms to the employment-at-will standard, employees will probably not realize that they may have lost some valuable employment rights. Is there anything wrong with making the change, given that the original was not taken seriously?

INTERNET ASSIGNMENT

Provide a brief (one or two sentence) summary of the mandate of each of the following labor-related statutes or rules. Hint: these statutes and rules are summarized at a single site on the World Wide Web. Browse the "Publications, News Services and Print Materials" hyperlinks within the LaborNet Web site (http://www. igc.apc.org/labornet/) to find the Labor Policy Association's Web pages.

- a. The National Labor Relations Act (Wagner Act) (1935), 29 U.S.C. §151 *et seq.*
- b. Davis-Bacon Act (1931), 40 U.S.C. §276 *et seq.*
- c. Fair Labor Standards Act (1938), 29 U.S.C. §201 *et seq.*
- d. Labor Management Relations Act of 1947 (Taft-Hartley Act), 29 U.S.C. §141 *et seq.*
- e. Labor-Management Reporting and Disclosure Act (1959), 29 U.S.C. §401 *et seq.*
- f. Contract Work Hours Safety Standards Act (1962), 40 U.S.C. §327 *et seq.*
- g. Executive Order 11246 (1965), 42 U.S.C.A. §2000e
- h. Service Contracts Act (1965), 41 U.S.C. §351 *et seq.*
- i. Federal Coal Mine Health and Safety Act (1969), 30 U.S.C. §801 *et seq.*
- j. Occupational Safety and Health Act (OSHA)(1970), 29 U.S.C. §§553, 651 *et seq.*
- k. Rehabilitation Act (1973), 29 U.S.C. §701 *et seq.*
- l. Employee Retirement Income Security Act (ERISA) (1974), 29 U.S.C. §§301, 1001 *et seq.*
- m. Black Lung Benefits Reform Act (1977), 30 U.S.C. §901 *et seq.*
- n. Labor-Management Cooperation Act (1978), 20 U.S.C.A. §141 notes, 173, 175a.
- o. Multi-employer Pension Plan Amendments Act (1980), 29 U.S.C. §1001a *et seq.*
- p. Job Training Partnership Act (1982), 29 U.S.C. §1501 *et seq.*
- q. Migrant and Seasonal Agricultural Worker Protection Act (1983), 29 U.S.C. §1801 *et seq.*
- r. Economic Dislocation and Worker Adjustment Assistance Act (1988), 29 U.S.C. §§1651–53
- s. Employee Polygraph Protection Act (1988), 29 U.S.C. §2001 *et seq.*
- t. Worker Adjustment and Retraining Notification Act (WARN)(1988), 29 U.S.C. §2101 *et seq.*
- u. Whistleblower Protection Statutes (1989), 10 U.S.C. §2409; 12 U.S.C. §1831j; 31 U.S.C. §5328; 41 U.S.C. §265

CHAPTER 16

Employment Discrimination

The owner of an Iowa electronics company made sexual advances to an employee after she posed nude in a nationally distributed magazine. Was he guilty of sex discrimination? "John Doe" worked as an engineer at Boeing aircraft. After six years, he, under physician supervision, decided to become "Jane Doe." Prior to sex-transformation surgery, he began to live the social role of a woman. Boeing fired "John/Jane Doe" for using the women's restroom and dressing as a woman despite company orders not to do so prior to sex-change surgery. Was Boeing guilty of disability discrimination?

These cases illustrate the wide range of employment issues that arise today. Years ago, neither of these cases would have emerged, but now the law restricts employment practices with respect to discrimination based on personal characteristics. In this chapter, we focus on the Civil Rights Act of 1964—the primary basis of modern employment discrimination law; the statutes that have been added over the years; and the cases that have helped to define the rights and duties of employees and employers in dealing with race, sex, color, religion, national origin, age, and disability. (The answer to the first question—Was he guilty of sex discrimination?—is yes; the answer to the second question—Was Boeing guilty of disability discrimination—is no.)

Origins of Discrimination Law

Discrimination in employment based on personal characteristics such as sex, race, religion, national origin, or disability is not unique to America. All countries witness various forms of employment discrimination. For example, in Asian nations, female executives are much more uncommon than in the United States.

There are considerable statistical differences in employment based on sex and race. For example, the unemployment rate for African-Americans is regularly twice the unemployment rate for whites. Of those working, about one in four African-Americans has a white-collar job, compared to one in two working whites. White male wageworkers earn an average of 35 percent more than African-American and Hispanic male wageworkers. Men predominate many higher-paying professions, such as medicine, law, and management, while women are traditionally concentrated in lower-paying professions such as nursing, paralegal, and clerical. White male wageworkers earn an average of 30 percent more than female wageworkers.

Much of the difference between men and women and between racial and ethnic groups may be unintentional and attributable to employment patterns. Much of the "wage gap" is attributed to differences in education, training, family demands, and years of experience in the workforce. Professor June O'Neill and other scholars have estimated that the wage gap for younger men and women with similar experience and life situations has nearly disappeared. Still, some disparity is probably due to stereotyped assumptions about productivity and to preferences for associating in the workplace with "one's own kind." It is this kind of employment discrimination that has produced a legal response.

THE CIVIL RIGHTS MOVEMENTS

Historically, employers could hire and fire, within contractual limits, at will. Employers could discriminate or not based on race, sex, or any other personal characteristics. Similarly, labor unions could impose discriminatory membership policies. Although some states enacted laws limiting discriminatory practices, employers and unions were largely free to conduct their affairs without judicial or administrative interference. The situation was worsened by federal and state laws (Jim Crow laws) that directly or indirectly supported segregation and labor market discrimination.

The drive for civil rights in employment and other aspects of life that arose in the South in the 1950s became a national movement in the early 1960s. Thus, there was an emerging but incomplete patchwork of remedies for employment discrimination coupled with rising public concern. In partial response, Congress enacted the first federal employment discrimination statute in 1963, the Equal Pay Act, followed by the Civil Rights Act of 1964, the cornerstone of federal employment discrimination law.

EQUAL PAY ACT OF 1963

The *Equal Pay Act of 1963* was the first federal law that specifically addressed employment discrimination. It prohibits pay discrimination on the basis of sex. The Act holds it illegal to pay men and women employees different wages when a job requires equal skill, effort, responsibility, and the same working conditions. Job titles are not relevant; job content is reviewed. The Equal Pay Act allows differences in wages if they are due to "(i) a seniority system; (ii) a merit system; (iii) a system which measures earnings by quantity or quality of production; or (iv) a differential based on any factor other than sex." Pay differentials on the basis of sex are to be eliminated by raising the pay of the female employees, not by lowering the pay of the male employees.

To help enforce the Act, employers are required to keep records of each employee's hours, wages, and other relevant information. Government investigators may enter a business to examine the records, which must be kept for several years. If a firm is found in violation, the most likely result will be an order to pay employees who have suffered discrimination an amount equal to the wages they should have received. The employees may also receive an additional amount to serve as a penalty to the employer. If employees hire an attorney to bring the suit and they win, they will be awarded reasonable attorney's fees and court costs. Some discrimination suits are still brought based on this statute, but most potential suits are also covered by the next statute.

Title VII of the 1964 Civil Rights Act

The most important source of antidiscrimination in employment law is *Title VII of the Civil Rights Act of 1964*. The Act was amended in 1972 by the *Equal Employment Opportunity Act* to give the *Equal Employment Opportunity Commission (EEOC)* the power to enforce the Act, by the *Pregnancy Discrimination Act* in 1978, and by the *Civil Rights Act of 1991*. Title VII makes it unlawful for an employer

(1) to fail or refuse to hire or to discharge any individual, or otherwise to discriminate against any individual with respect to his compensation, terms, conditions, or privileges of employment; or

(2) to limit, segregate, or classify his employees or applicants for employment in any way which would deprive or tend to deprive any individual of employment opportunities or otherwise adversely affect his status as an employee because of such individual's race, color, religion, sex, or national origin.

PROTECTED CLASSES

Title VII applies to employers, employment agencies, and labor unions in the private and public sectors. In general, it forbids *discrimination* in all aspects of employment on the basis of *race, color, religion, sex, or national origin*. Employers with fifteen or more employees and unions with fifteen or more members are subject to the law. The Supreme Court has stated that law firms and other partnership organizations are covered by the law, but the law does not apply to business relationships or to the selection of independent contractors.

Title VII requires *equal employment opportunity* regardless of race, color, religion, sex, or national origin. Congress sought to protect certain classes of people who had a history of discriminatory treatment in employment relationships. Race, color, national origin, religion, and sex are the characteristics that determine *protected classes* for purposes of Title VII coverage.

Race

The courts have had little difficulty in determining racial class. Congress stated that its primary purpose in enacting Title VII was "to open employment opportunities for Negroes in occupations which have been traditionally closed to them." In addition to black, the law officially recognized four other major racial groupings: white, Native American, Hispanic, and Asian.

Congress's emphasis on eliminating discrimination against minorities does not mean that whites are not protected under Title VII. That interpretation was rejected by the Supreme Court in *McDonald* v. *Santa Fe Trail Transportation Company*, 96 S.Ct. 2574 (1976). In *McDonald*, an African-American employee and a white employee had stolen property from their employer. The African-American employee was reprimanded but allowed to keep his job, while the white employee was fired. In declaring that Title VII protected whites against racial discrimination, the Court stated:

> Title VII prohibits racial discrimination against the white petitioners upon the same standards as would be applicable were they Negroes. . . . While Santa Fe may decide that participation in a theft of cargo may render an employee unqualified for employment, this criteria must be applied alike to members of all races.

Reverse discrimination—preferential treatment to members of protected classes—is illegal, but if minorities or women are *underrepresented* in a particular job classification, it is legal for an employer to take steps to see that more minorities or women are hired to increase their share of the jobs. Affirmative action programs (discussed later) designed to remedy discrimination against minorities or women may be adopted and not violate the rule against reverse discrimination.

Color

In practice, the term *color* means little, since very few cases have been brought claiming discrimination on that basis alone. Usually, color is added in cases of discrimination based on race or national origin.

National Origin

According to the Supreme Court in *Espinoza* v. *Farah Manufacturing*, 94 S.Ct. 334 (1973), the term *national origin* is to be given the same meaning it has in ordinary communications:

> [The term national origin] refers to the country where a person is born or . . . the country from which his or her ancestors came.

Discrimination has been held to exist in situations where a person has a physical, cultural, or speech characteristic of a national origin group. It is also discrimination to require that English be spoken at all times in the workplace. However, if business necessity requires that English be spoken, such as for reasons of safety or productivity, it may be a legitimate job requirement. Employment discrimination can take place when an employer allows ethnic slurs to occur and does not take steps to prevent such actions.

This protection is not provided to noncitizens employed or seeking employment in this country. However, while an employer may discriminate against aliens, the employer may not discriminate on the basis of different origins of citizenship. For example, an employer may not accept aliens from Italy but reject aliens from Mexico.

Religion

Title VII does not define the term *religion* but states that "religion includes all aspects of religious observances and practice." The courts have defined the term broadly to resolve constitutional issues. According to the Court in *United States* v. *Seeger,* 380 U.S. 163 (1965):

> [All that is required is a] sincere and meaningful belief occupying in the life of its possessor a place parallel to that filled by the God of those [religions generally recognized].

The employer is required to reasonably accommodate an employee's religious practices. The employer may discriminate, however, if the accommodation will impose an *undue hardship* on the conduct of business. The Court has stated that undue hardship is created by accommodations that would cost an employer more than a minimal amount. A religious institution, such as a seminary training ministers or rabbis, may legally hire only members of a particular religion for jobs in which that is critical.

Sex

The prohibition against sex discrimination was included with little legislative history to provide insights into how Congress intended to define sex discrimination. Thus, the courts have had to take an active role in defining the limits of the term.

The courts have taken the position that the term *sex* should be given the meaning it has in ordinary language. Thus, Title VII prohibits sex discrimination simply on the basis of whether a person is male or female. In that light, the courts have held that discrimination on the basis of sexual preference or sexual identity is not protected by Title VII, although several states prohibit discrimination on the basis of sexual orientation. Title VII does not prohibit discrimination on the basis of marital status, as long as an employer applies employment rules evenly to employees of both sexes. However, many states prohibit discrimination against employees on the basis of marital status.

Pregnancy Discrimination   Title VII was amended in 1978 by the *Pregnancy Discrimination Act,* which states that an employer may not discriminate against women because of pregnancy, childbirth, and related medical conditions. Women affected by these conditions "shall be treated the same for all employment-related purposes, including receipt of benefits under fringe benefit programs." Examples of pregnancy discrimination include the following:

- Denying a woman a job, assignment, or promotion because she is pregnant or has children
- Requiring a pregnant woman to go on leave when she is able to do her job
- Treating maternity leave from work different from other leaves for temporary disabilities
- Discriminating in fringe benefits, such as health insurance, to discourage women of childbearing age from working

Sexual Harassment   A sexually hostile work environment is a form of sex discrimination that violates Title VII. *Sexual harassment* is defined by the EEOC in the *Code of Federal Regulations* as

> "unwelcome sexual advances, requests for sexual favors, and other verbal or physical conduct of a sexual nature . . . when
>
>> 1) submission to such conduct is made either explicitly or implicitly a term or condition of an individual's employment,

JURIS **prudence?**

Hand Me a Lawsuit on a Silver Platter, Please

La Petite Academy, a day-care center, employed Cynthia Thompson as a cook and van driver. Her work was rated fine for several months, but a new director, Joanne Berns, criticized her for several problems. The two did not get along. About the same time, Thompson became pregnant.

Soon after, Berns called Thompson into her office and told her she was fired. Thompson asked why. Berns said, "Because your attitude has changed since you have become pregnant." Berns explained the same thing to other employees, saying that Thompson needed to be more perky. On the company form reporting the firing, Berns wrote that Thompson was "Not happy on the job—low energy."

The court rejected La Petite's request to dismiss the suit: "plaintiff has presented direct evidence that she was discharged because of her pregnant condition."

Source: *Thompson* v. *La Petite Academy*, 838 F.Supp. 1474

2) submission to or rejection of such conduct by an individual is used as a basis for employment decisions affecting such individual, or
3) such conduct has the purpose or effect of unreasonably interfering with an individual's work performance or creating an intimidating, hostile, or offensive working environment."

In practice, there are two basic forms of sexual harassment. The first is *quid pro quo* or "this for that," where there is a promise of reward, such as promotion or pay raise, for providing sexual favors being demanded or there is a threat of punishment, such as being fired or demoted, for not going along with sexual requests. The second form is a *hostile environment* created at work by others. An abusive work environment is created by words or acts related to a person's sex. Examples are

- Discussing sexual activities
- Commenting on physical attributes
- Unnecessary touching or gestures
- Using crude, demeaning, or offensive language
- Displaying sexually suggestive pictures

Trivial and isolated incidents usually are not sufficient grounds for a sexual harassment suit. The courts look to factors such as how often such conduct occurred, whether the harassment was by a supervisor who could control progress, pay, and working conditions, or a co-worker, whether there was talk or actual touching, and whether more than one person was involved. The courts are also recognizing that men and women, on average, have different sensitivities. That is, language and physical contact that many men think unobjectionable are offensive to many women. The standard for women employees is thus becoming what some courts have called a "reasonable woman" under the circumstances.

Many employers have announced policies and procedures regarding sexual harassment and train supervisors to be sensitive to such matters. Although the boundaries of sexual harassment under Title VII are still being determined, the Supreme Court offered guidance in the *Harris* decision.

CYBERLAW

Your E-Mail Is Your Boss's E-Mail

In general, E-mail that is sent at work on company computers is available for company inspection. Whether the employee is told or not, employers have the right to monitor employee E-mail. A class-action suit by Epson employees against their employer for routinely reading employee E-mail was dismissed by the court because there was no right-of-privacy issue.

A sports writer for a Chicago newspaper was told by his employer to quit sending unwanted E-mails to a female coworker. When he did not quit sending her E-mail, the employer transferred the writer to another department. A federal court held that the paper was within its rights to do so; he could not complain about the interference with his E-mail, nor could he claim sex discrimination. The employer "was obviously trying to make the best of a difficult situation." See *Greenslade v. Chicago Sun-Times, Inc.,*. 112F.3d 853.

Why do employers care so much about E-mail transmissions at work? Chevron paid $2.2 million to settle sexual harassment claims of women employees for dirty jokes that were transmitted around the office on the E-mail system.

Harris v. Forklift Systems, Inc.
United States Supreme Court
510 U.S. 17, 114 S.Ct. 367 (1993)

CASE BACKGROUND *Teresa Harris worked as a rental manager for two years for Forklift Systems, a company that sells, rents, and repairs forklifts. Her boss, Charles Hardy, often insulted her in front of others because of her sex and made her the target of sexual suggestions. He would say, "We need a man as the rental manager," and "You're a woman, what do you know?" He told her she was "a dumb-ass woman," and that they should "go to the Holiday Inn to negotiate [her] raise." Hardy would ask Harris and other women employees to get coins from his front pants pocket, throw things on the ground and ask women to pick them up, and make sexual comments about the women's clothing. Harris finally complained to Hardy about his comments. Hardy said that he was sorry but that he was only kidding. Soon after, while Harris was arranging a deal with a customer, Hardy asked her, "What did you do, promise the guy [sex] Saturday night?" Harris quit and sued, claiming that Hardy's conduct created a hostile work environment for her because of her gender. The district and appeals courts ruled against her. She appealed.*

CASE DECISION O'Connor, Justice.

* * *

When the workplace is permeated with "discriminatory intimidation, ridicule, and insult" that is "sufficiently severe or pervasive to alter the conditions of the victim's employment and create an abusive working environment," Title VII is violated.

This standard . . . takes a middle path between making actionable any conduct that is merely offensive and requiring the conduct to cause a tangible psychological injury. As we pointed out [before] "mere utterance of an . . . epithet which engenders offensive feelings in an employee," does not sufficiently affect the conditions of employment to implicate Title VII. Conduct that is not severe or pervasive enough to create an objectively hostile or abuse work environment—an environment that a reasonable person would find hostile or abusive—is beyond Title VII's purview. Likewise, if the victim does not subjectively perceive the environment to be abusive, the conduct has not actually altered the conditions of the victim's employment, and there is no Title VII violation.

But Title VII comes into play before the harassing conduct leads to a nervous breakdown. A discriminatorily abusive work environment, even one that does not seriously affect employees' psychological well-being, can and often will detract from employees' job performance, discourage employees from remaining on the job, or keep them from advancing in their careers. Moreover, even without regard to these tangible effects, the very fact that the discriminatory conduct was so severe or pervasive that it created a work environment abusive to employees because of their race, gender, religion, or national origin offends Title VII's broad rule of workplace equality. . . .

This is not, and by its nature cannot be, a mathematically precise test. We need not answer today all the potential questions it raises. . . . But we can say that whether an environment is "hostile" or "abusive" can be determined only by looking at all the circumstances. These may include the frequency of the discriminatory conduct; its severity; whether it is physically threatening or humiliating, or a mere offensive utterance; and whether it unreasonably interferes with an employee's work performance. The effect on the employee's psychological well-being is, of course, relevant to determining whether the plaintiff actually found the environment abusive. But while psychological harm, like any other relevant factor, may be taken into account, no single factor is required.

* * *

We therefore reverse the judgment of the Court of Appeals, and remand the case for further proceedings consistent with this opinion.

QUESTIONS FOR ANALYSIS

1. The Court held that the actions must be severe enough to create a hostile work environment to a reasonable person. The boss said that his comments were only meant to be funny and that he did not intend to be mean. If this issue were left to a jury, might not some people on the jury, especially men, be likely to think that Harris overreacted?
2. Two concurring opinions indicated that another standard that might be focused on is whether the abusive actions are sufficient to affect work performance. Would that provide better guidance?

The Supreme Court further clarified the law of sexual harassment in 1998. In *Oncale* v. *Sundowner Offshore Services, Inc.*, 118 S.Ct. 998, a case concerning male-on-male sexual harassment, the Court held that same-sex harassment is prohibited by Title VII. The law "does not reach genuine but innocuous differences in the ways men and women routinely interact with members of the same sex and of the opposite sex. The prohibition of harassment on the basis of sex requires neither asexuality nor androgyny in the workplace; it forbids only behavior so objectively offensive as to alter the 'conditions' of the victim's employment." Further, the Court held "that the objective severity of harassment should be judged from the perspective of a reasonable person in the plaintiff's position, considering 'all the circumstances.'. . . Common sense, and an appropriate sensitivity to social context, will enable courts and juries to distinguish between simple teasing or roughhousing among members of the same sex, and conduct which a reasonable person in the plaintiff's position would find severely hostile or abusive."

AGE DISCRIMINATION

Enacted in 1967 and amended several times, the *Age Discrimination in Employment Act (ADEA)* prohibits discrimination in employment against persons over age 40. All employers, private and public, who have twenty or more employees must comply with this statute. The ADEA generally parallels Title VII in its prohibitions, exceptions, remedies, and enforcement. So, while the ADEA is a separate statute, we presume it acts the same way as Title VII unless specifically noted. The law prohibits employment discrimination, such as failing or refusing to hire or promote because of age, terminating employees because of age, or other discrimination in the terms and conditions of employment.

JURIS prudence?

It Works Both Ways, Ladies

David Papa was manager of a Domino's Pizza in Port Richey, Florida. He claimed he was repeatedly harassed by his supervisor, Beth Carrier. Several times Carrier squeezed his buttocks and made comments about his body. She told him she loved him and wanted to live with him. After he told her to quit bothering him, she fired him.

This was the first case the EEOC litigated involving a man harassed by a woman. A federal judge ordered Domino's to pay Papa $237,257 and told the company to post a sexual harassment policy at its stores and to hold programs for its managers about how to properly deal with such matters.

Source: *Associated Press*

Often the courts must, as in cases of race or sex discrimination, look to see whether age discrimination can be inferred by studying practices at the place of employment. The following are examples of age discrimination:

- Forcing retirement because of age
- Assigning older workers to duties that restrict their ability to compete for higher-level jobs in the organization
- Requiring older workers to pass physical examinations as a condition of continued employment
- Indicating an age preference in advertisements for employees, such as "young, dynamic person wanted"
- Choosing to promote a younger worker rather than an older worker because the older worker may be retiring in several years
- Cutting health-care benefits for workers over age 65 because they are eligible for Medicare

The *Minnesota Historical Society* decision is an example of how courts review the relevant evidence.

Johnson v. Minnesota Historical Society
United States Court of Appeals, Eighth Circuit
931 F.2d 1239 (1991)

CASE BACKGROUND *Loren Johnson was employed for twenty-three years by the Minnesota Historical Society to help in the restoration of historical sites. He was fired in 1986 at age fifty-four. At the time, he had a permanent back injury from a car accident, was nearly blind in one eye, and had a cataract in the other eye.*

After funding fell, the Society had reorganized the work of twenty employees and fired two, including Johnson. The Society claimed that because of the decline in

funds, it eliminated most restoration work and therefore no longer needed Johnson. Johnson offered to continue to work at half salary, but the Society refused because Johnson's expertise in restoration was not needed.

Johnson filed an age discrimination suit. The district court dismissed the suit, ruling that there was no evidence of age discrimination and that in any event, the Society gave a legitimate reason for his dismissal. Johnson appealed.

CASE DECISION Strom, District Judge.

* * *

In this case, conflicting evidence exists as to whether Johnson's job in its various parts continued in existence after his termination. The district court noted that the Society argued "most of Johnson's responsibilities were not performed after he was discharged because the funding for restoration and reconstruction projects declined sharply. . . . [T]he responsibilities which remained were reassigned to Johnson's supervisor and to a second employee, Charles Nelson, or performed by outside agencies." Johnson argued that after his dismissal, the Society continued to conduct significant amounts of reconstruction and rehabilitation work which he could have performed and that his responsibilities had been reassigned to younger employees. However, the district court concluded that the evidence showed only a minimal amount of work was reassigned to a younger employee, Charles Nelson, and therefore Johnson failed to establish a . . . case because the evidence was insufficient to support a finding that his job in its various parts continued in existence.

Johnson refers to various disparaging remarks made by employees of the Society to him such as that he was a "blind old bat," "old coot," "blind old coot," and "dirty old man." Johnson alleges that his supervisor mocked his back problems by mimicking his posture and walk.

* * *

Further, it is a question of fact whether Johnson's age was a determining factor in the Society's actions. The factually oriented, case-by-case nature of discrimination claims requires the court not be overly rigid in considering evidence of discrimination offered by a plaintiff. It is for the trier of fact to decide the issue . . . by reviewing all the direct or circumstantial evidence presented and giving it whatever weight and credence it deserves. The Court cannot say as a matter of law that all the evidence thus presented points only one way and is not susceptible of a reasonable inference in favor of Johnson. Therefore, the district court erred in granting summary judgment in favor of the Society and dismissing Johnson's discrimination claims.

* * *

Accordingly, we vacate the dismissal . . . and remand the case to the district court for further proceedings consistent with this opinion.

QUESTIONS FOR ANALYSIS

1. Do unkind comments about one's age create a hostile environment that may be, by itself, a violation of the age discrimination law?
2. What difference does it make if the Society assigned some of Johnson's duties to another worker?

PROCEDURE

The first step for a person claiming to be the victim of a discriminatory act (under Title VII or the ADEA) is to file a charge with a federal, state, or local equal employment opportunity (EEO) office (see http://www.eeoc.gov). For example, a person in Illinois who believes he or she has a Title VII claim would file a complaint with the Illinois Department of Human Rights or the federal EEOC office; all states, and many cities, have offices that handle EEO matters. Charges must be filed with the EEOC within 180 days of the alleged discriminatory act. In states or localities with an antidiscrimination law, the complaint must be filed at the state or local office within 300 days of the discriminatory act, or at a federal EEOC office. We discuss only EEOC procedure here, but state EEO procedures are much the same.

When a charge is filed, the EEOC notifies the employer, and the EEOC investigates the complaint to determine whether there is reasonable cause to believe the complaint. The employer is asked to come to the EEOC office for a fact-finding conference. The EEOC agent hears statements from both parties; many complaints are settled at this stage by a conciliation agreement. If there is no settlement, the EEOC finishes the investigation and informs both parties of the result. As Exhibit 16.1 shows, the EEOC may find no merit to the complaint; if it does

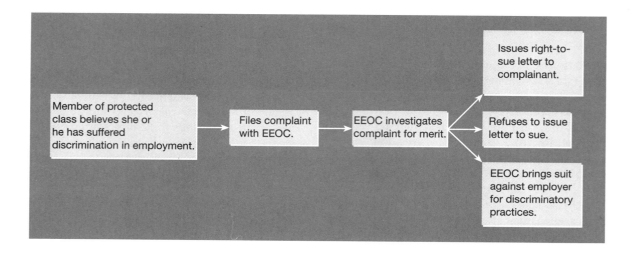

EXHIBIT 16.1

Usual Steps in a Discrimination Complaint to EEOC

find merit, it issues a right-to-sue letter to the employee, giving her or him the right to bring an action against the employer in federal court, or, in a few cases, the EEOC sues the employer.

The average response time on the more than 100,000 complaints filed each year is about a year. EEOC offices categorize complaints by priority, based on their initial evaluation. Top priority cases, when discrimination appears likely, get the most attention. Second-category cases include complaints that may have merit that require added investigation for a determination. Complaints that appear to lack a legitimate claim may be dismissed immediately.

TYPES OF DISCRIMINATION CLAIMS

The courts have struck down employment practices that impose *differential standards* on employees on the basis of race, sex, or age. For example, it would be illegal to give men positions as traveling sales representatives but not give such positions to women, even though the employer's reason may be concern about the possible dangers that traveling women face.

While it is obvious that it is illegal to pay women or minorities lower salaries for the same work as performed by white men, when the assignments and the years of service are the same, illegal *compensation differentials* also take into account differences in fringe benefits. That is, it is illegal to base health or retirement benefits on race, sex, or age.

Everyone understands that the most obvious forms of *segregation* in the workplace are illegal. Segregation today tends to be subtle and cases are not common. It is illegal to assign employees to customers based on race. That is, it is illegal to send Hispanic employees to serve only Hispanic customers and Asian-American employees to serve Asian-American customers.

Title VII cases have concerned unequal treatment in hiring, promotion, compensation, and discharge decisions. It is also illegal to make life so miserable on the job for an employee in a protected class that the employee is "forced" to quit, as we saw in the *Harris* case. To make the working conditions intolerable is illegal *harassment*. If the employee quits because of harassment, it is a *constructive discharge*, which is treated the same as if the employee had been fired illegally.

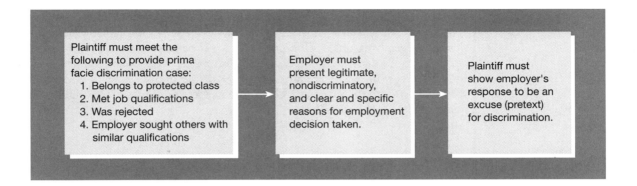

EXHIBIT 16.2

Initial Steps in Disparate Treatment Cases

Employers can legally differentiate among current or potential employees, but the laws against discrimination restrict the grounds for treating employees differently and restrict the ways that employees may be treated. Although there are many different ways that discrimination may appear, when the line has been crossed, there are two primary types of discrimination claims under Title VII. In general, a plaintiff can make a case by proving either disparate treatment or disparate impact by the employer. These two major categories cover cases of intentional discrimination and unintentional discrimination.

Disparate Treatment

To recover for discrimination prohibited under Title VII, whether for race, color, religion, sex, or national origin, or under the ADEA, in a claim of *disparate treatment* or illegally motivated employment decision, the plaintiff must prove that the employer *intentionally* discriminated against her or him.

Plaintiff Must Establish a Prima Facie Case The Supreme Court established a four-part test in 1973 in the *McDonnell-Douglas* v. *Green* decision, 93 S.Ct. 1817, that the plaintiff in a disparate treatment case must meet to provide a *prima facie discrimination case*. Exhibit 16.2 lists the four steps that must be met for a case to go forward. This test holds for all aspects of employment—hiring, promotion, compensation, conditions, discipline, and termination. If the plaintiff satisfies the McDonnell-Douglas test, the burden shifts to the defendant to overcome the presumption of discrimination.

Burden Shifts to Defendant After a plaintiff shows a prima facie case of employment discrimination, the burden shifts to the defendant to present evidence that the claim is untrue or that there was a legal reason for its employment decision. The employer must show legitimate, nondiscriminatory, and a clear and reasonably specific reason(s) for its decision to overcome the presumption of discrimination. The courts prefer objective standards for employment decisions rather than vague rationales that amount to "I felt like it." Legitimate reasons include, as we will see following, such factors as seniority, education, and experience.

Burden Shifts Back to Plaintiff After the employer offers legitimate, nondiscriminatory, and clear and specific reasons for the employment decision in question, the burden shifts back to the plaintiff to show that the defendant had an illegal motive. The plaintiff must show that the rationales offered by the employer are just *pretexts* or unacceptable, impermissible excuses for disparate treatment. Such evidence can take many forms, such as showing inconsistency in decisions made by the employer, giving different reasons at different times for the decision, and presenting statistical evidence of discrimination based on sex or race. While discrimination is clear in some cases, in most it requires a review of the entire situation and testimony from witnesses to the situation. The Supreme Court discussed the weighing of evidence in the *Hopkins* decision.

Price Waterhouse v. Hopkins

United States Supreme Court
490 U.S. 228, 109 S.Ct. 1775 (1989)

CASE BACKGROUND *Ann Hopkins worked at Price Waterhouse, a nationwide accounting partnership, as a senior manager. She was the only woman proposed for promotion to partner (along with eighty-seven men candidates). Her candidacy for partnership was put on hold for a year, at which time she was not renominated. She sued under Title VII, charging that her employer had discriminated against her on the basis of sex. She won at District Court (Judge Gesell) and Court of Appeals. Price Waterhouse appealed.*

CASE DECISION Brennan, Justice.

* * *

In a jointly prepared statement supporting her candidacy, the partners in Hopkins' office showcased her successful 2-year effort to secure a $25 million contract with the Department of State, labeling it "an outstanding performance" and one that Hopkins carried out "virtually at the partner level.". . .

The partners in Hopkins' office praised her character as well as her accomplishments, describing her in their joint statement as "an outstanding professional" who had a "deft touch," a "strong character, independence and integrity.". . .

On too many occasions, however, Hopkins' aggressiveness apparently spilled over into abrasiveness. Staff members seem to have borne the brunt of Hopkins' brusqueness. Long before her bid for partnership, partners evaluating her work had counseled her to improve her relations with staff members. . . . Virtually all of the partners' negative remarks about Hopkins—even those of partners supporting her—had to do with her "interpersonal skills." Both "[s]upporters and opponents of her candidacy," stressed Judge Gesell, "indicated that she was some-

times overly aggressive, unduly harsh, difficult to work with and impatient with staff."

There were clear signs, though, that some of the partners reacted negatively to Hopkins' personality because she was a woman. One partner described her as "macho"; another suggested that she "overcompensated for being a woman"; a third advised her to take "a course at charm school." Several partners criticized her use of profanity; in response, one partner suggested that those partners objected to her swearing only "because it's a lady using foul language." Another supporter explained that Hopkins "ha[d] matured from a tough-talking somewhat masculine hardnosed mgr to an authoritative, formidable, but much more appealing lady ptr candidate." But it was the man who, as Judge Gesell found, bore responsibility for explaining to Hopkins the reasons for the Policy Board's decision to place her candidacy on hold who delivered the *coup de grace:* in order to improve her chances for partnership, Thomas Beyer advised, Hopkins should "walk more femininely, talk more femininely, dress more femininely, wear make-up, have her hair styled, and wear jewelry."

* * *

Judge Gesell found that Price Waterhouse legitimately emphasized interpersonal skills in its partnership decisions, and also found that the firm had not fabricated its complaints about Hopkins' interpersonal skills as a pretext for discrimination. Moreover, he concluded, the firm did not give decisive emphasis to such traits only because Hopkins was a woman; although there were male candidates who lacked these skills but who were admitted to partnership, the judge found that these candidates possessed other, positive traits that Hopkins lacked.

The judge went on to decide, however, that some of the partners' remarks about Hopkins stemmed from an impermissibly cabined view of the proper behavior of women, and that Price Waterhouse had done nothing to disavow reliance on such comments. He held that Price Waterhouse had unlawfully discriminated against Hopkins on the basis of sex by consciously giving credence and effect to partners' comments that resulted from sex stereotyping.

* * *

[O]ur assumption always has been that if an employer allows gender to affect its decisionmaking process, then it must carry the burden of justifying its ultimate decision. . . .

In saying that gender played a motivating part in an employment decision, we mean that, if we asked the employer at the moment of the decision what its reasons were and if we received a truthful response, one of those reasons would be that the applicant or employee was a woman. In the specific context of sex stereotyping, an employer who acts on the basis of a belief that a woman cannot be aggressive, or that she must not be, has acted on the basis of gender. . . .

Remarks at work that are based on sex stereotypes do not inevitably prove that gender played a part in a particular employment decision. The plaintiff must show that the employer actually relied on her gender in making its decision. In making this showing, stereotyped remarks can certainly be evidence that gender played a part. In any event, the stereotyping in this case did not simply consist of stray remarks. On the contrary, Hopkins proved that Price Waterhouse invited partners to submit comments; that some of the comments stemmed from sex stereotypes; that an important part of the Policy Board's decision on Hopkins was an assessment of the submitted comments; and that Price Waterhouse in no way disclaimed reliance on the sex-linked evaluations. This is not, as Price Waterhouse suggests, "discrimination in the air"; rather, it is, as Hopkins puts it, "discrimination brought to ground and visited upon" an employee.

* * *

As to the employer's proof, in most cases, the employer should be able to present some objective evidence as to its probable decision in the absence of an impermissible motive. . . . An employer may not, in other words, prevail in a mixed-motives case by offering a legitimate and sufficient reason for its decision if that reason did not motivate it at the time of the decision. Finally, an employer may not meet its burden in such a case by merely showing that at the time of the decision it was motivated only in part by a legitimate reason. The very premise of a mixed-motives case is that a legitimate reason was present, and indeed, in this case, Price Waterhouse already has made this showing by convincing Judge Gesell that Hopkins' interpersonal problems were a legitimate concern. The employer instead must show that its legitimate reason, standing alone, would have induced it to make the same decision.

. . . the employer must make this showing by a preponderance of the evidence.

* * *

[Case remanded for further proceedings.]

CASE NOTE On remand to the District Court, Hopkins was granted partnership and $371,000 in back pay.

QUESTIONS FOR ANALYSIS

1. The dissent argued that Price Waterhouse should win unless it could be shown that Hopkins was not granted a partnership because of gender. Does mix of motives make it hard to tell whether sex really was the bar to promotion?
2. Will decisions like this cause firms to persuade managers to keep their mouths shut so as to avoid possible negative evidence?

A decision by the Supreme Court in 1998 further clarified the liability of employers for discrimination that occurs in the workplace and noted the importance of proper procedure to help reduce liability. In *Burlington Industries, Inc. v. Ellerth,* 118 S.Ct. 2257, the Court held that an employer is subject to vicarious liability for a hostile environment created by a supervisor with higher authority over the employee. This may be so even if the employee suffers no adverse, tangible job consequences. An affirmative defense that an employer may present in such cases, when a supervisor has discriminated against (or sexually harassed) an employee in violation of company policy, is that the employer took reasonable care to prevent and correct promptly any discriminatory behavior (sexual harassment) and that the employee unreasonably failed to take advantage of any preventive or corrective opportunities provided.

Disparate Impact

Liability for employment discrimination may be based on a claim of *disparate impact* or adverse impact, which means that the employer used a decision rule that caused discrimination in some aspect of employment based on protected class status. The discrimination may have been *unintentional*, but the effect of the employer's action was to limit employment opportunities for a person or group of persons based on race, color, religion, sex, or national origin. In practice, few age discrimination suits fall into the disparate impact category. These cases involve employment practices that appear to be neutral but in fact have a disproportionately adverse impact on an employee or group of employees who are members of a protected class. Proof of intent to discriminate is not required, but the plaintiff must prove that the employment practice adversely impacts employment opportunities for members of a protected class. Hence, the key issues are:

1. Does an employer have rules or practices that affect members of a protected group differently than other workers?
2. Are the rules or practices justified by business necessity or because they relate to valid job requirements?

For example, employment procedure often requires that applicants have a high school diploma, achieve a minimum score on a specified test, or meet some other specified selection device. If it is asserted that the employer's hiring or promotion practices have a discriminatory impact on an applicant, the employer must show that the applicant was rejected not because of race, color, religion, sex, or national origin but because the qualification requirements of the job were not met. The impact of employment rules must be neutral—that is, the rules must not have a disparate impact on a protected class. Congress reemphasized this point in the 1991 Civil Rights Act.

The relationship between the use of such rules and Title VII was established in *Griggs* v. *Duke Power*, which determined that neutral employment criteria will be judged by their impact, not by the good or bad faith involved in their implementation.

Griggs v. Duke Power Company
United States Supreme Court
401 U.S. 424, 91 S.Ct. 849 (1971)

CASE BACKGROUND *Duke Power was a segregated company before the 1964 Civil Rights Act. African-Americans were hired only to work in certain low-level jobs; all higher-level jobs were held by whites. When Title VII took effect, Duke Power allowed all persons to compete for all jobs. Except for jobs already held by African-Americans, the company required a high school diploma and certain scores on two aptitude tests. These job requirements, while neutral on their face, were claimed to have a discriminatory impact against African-American* *applicants. At that time, 34 percent of the white men in North Carolina had high school diplomas, while only 12 percent of African-American men had them; and 58 percent of the whites passed the aptitude tests, but only 6 percent of the African-Americans passed.*

The district court ruled in favor of Duke Power, saying that the purpose of the standards was not to discriminate but to achieve a work force of a certain quality. The court of appeals agreed, saying that there was no discriminatory motive. Griggs appealed to the Supreme Court.

CASE DECISION Burger, Chief Justice.

* * *

The objective of Congress in the enactment of Title VII . . . was to achieve equality of employment opportunities and remove barriers that have operated in the past to favor an identifiable group of white employees over other employees. Under the Act, practices, procedures, or tests neutral on their face, and even neutral in terms of intent, cannot be maintained if they operate to "freeze" the status quo of prior discriminatory employment practices.

* * *

On the record before us, neither the high school completion requirement nor the general intelligence test is shown to bear a demonstrable relationship to successful performance of the jobs for which it was used. Both were adopted . . . without meaningful study of their relationship to job-performance ability. Rather, a vice president of the Company testified, the requirements were instituted on the Company's judgment that they generally would improve the overall quality of the work force.

The evidence, however, shows that employees who have not completed high school or taken the tests have continued to perform satisfactorily and make progress in departments for which the high school and test criteria are now used. The promotion record of present employees who would not be able to meet the new criteria thus suggests the possibility that the requirements may not be needed even for the limited purpose of preserving the avowed policy of advancement within the Company. . . .

. . . Congress directed the thrust of the Act to the consequences of employment practices, not simply the motivation. More than that, Congress has placed on the employer the burden of showing that any given requirement must have a manifest relationship to the employment in question.

* * *

Nothing in the Act precludes the use of testing or measuring procedures; obviously they are useful. What Congress has forbidden is giving these devices and mechanisms controlling force unless they are demonstrably a reasonable measure of job performance. Congress has not commanded that the less qualified be preferred over the better qualified simply because of minority origins. Far from disparaging job qualifications as such, Congress has made such qualifications the controlling factor, so that race, religion, nationality, and sex become irrelevant. What Congress has commanded is that any test used must measure the person for the job and not the person in the abstract.

The judgment of the Court of Appeals is . . . reversed.

QUESTIONS FOR ANALYSIS

1. Does this decision reduce the incentives for people to obtain high school diplomas and college degrees?
2. Suppose an employer knows of a valid aptitude test that is related to job performance but is one on which African-Americans do less well than they do on another, similar test. May the employer use the valid test that discriminates more against African-Americans than would an alternative test?

DEFENSES UNDER TITLE VII

As we saw in cases of disparate treatment, the employer must present a legitimate, nondiscriminatory, and clear and specific reason for the employment action taken. Certain business practices are specifically protected by Title VII. Other defenses are more general and have been determined by the courts as they have evaluated cases and considered the evidence presented.

Business Necessity

If employment practices can be shown to have a discriminatory impact on some employees, the 1991 Civil Rights Act clarified that the burden is on the employer to establish that the challenged practices must be justified as a *business necessity* and are *job related*. Business necessity is evaluated with reference to the ability of the employee to perform a certain job. Written tests, no matter how objective, must meet this business necessity test.

Experience and skill requirements, frequently measured by seniority, are often accepted as necessary. For example, to be a skilled bricklayer generally requires experience gained only by performance over a period of time. To require such experience for certain positions is not a violation of Title VII. Similarly, if a job requires certain abilities with respect to strength and agility, tests for such ability are legitimate.

Selection criteria for professional, managerial, and other "white-collar" positions must also meet the business necessity test. Insofar as objective criteria often cannot be used in such instances, subjective evaluations such as impressions made by job interviews, references, and some aspect of job performance evaluation are common and generally recognized as necessary in hiring and promoting professional personnel. Similarly, positions may have an education requirement. As in *Griggs*, educational requirements for manual or semiskilled jobs are less likely to be held necessary. However, for jobs such as teachers, police officers, laboratory technicians, airline pilots, and engineers, education requirements are usually valid.

Professionally Developed Ability Tests

Tests are often used by employers to determine whether applicants for a job possess the necessary skills and attributes. According to Title VII:

> [It] shall [not] be an unlawful employment practice for an employer to give and to act upon the results of any professionally developed ability test provided that such test, its administration, or action upon the results is not designed, intended, or used to discriminate because of race, color, religion, sex, or national origin.

In general, as stated by the Supreme Court in *Griggs*, such tests must be shown to predict the work ability required for the job. Employers are usually required to supply statistical validation of the tests. Expert testimony from educational and industrial psychologists is often used to interpret the results.

Bona Fide Seniority or Merit Systems

It is common for employers to provide employees with differential treatment based on seniority or merit. Title VII requires the courts to uphold *bona fide seniority* or *merit systems*. Seniority is usually the length of time an employee has been with an employer and can be used to determine such things as eligibility for pension plans, length of vacations, security from layoffs, preference for rehire and promotion, and amount of sick leave. According to Title VII:

> [I]t shall not be an unlawful employment practice for an employer to apply different . . . terms, conditions, or privileges of employment pursuant to a bona fide seniority or merit system . . . provided that such differences are not the result of an intention to discriminate because of race, color, religion, sex, or national origin. . . .

The effects of seniority systems come under attack most often in cases involving layoffs on the basis of seniority. Many employers hold that in the event of a cutback in the workforce, workers with the most seniority have the most job protection—last hired, first fired. This means that minorities may suffer a greater relative share of the layoffs in a workforce cutback because they have less seniority than white workers who were hired when discrimination was practiced. The Supreme Court recognizes this unfortunate fact but holds that seniority rights are protected by statute.

The Bona Fide Occupational Qualification (BFOQ)

Another defense is that of a *bona fide occupational qualification (BFOQ)*. Title VII states that discrimination is permitted in instances in which sex, religion, or national origin (but not race) is a BFOQ "reasonably necessary to the normal operation of that particular business."

The EEOC has given this defense a narrow interpretation. Just because certain jobs have been traditionally filled by men does not mean that a legitimate defense exists for not hiring women for such positions. Simply because people were used to seeing and may have preferred female flight attendants does not mean that airlines can refuse to hire male flight attendants. No BFOQ on the basis of race is allowed. For example, an employer cannot assert that the business must have a white person for a particular job.

Generally, the increased cost of hiring members of the opposite sex may not be used to justify discrimination. The fact that separate bathroom facilities will have to be constructed is not a BFOQ.

A BFOQ exists where hiring on the basis of a personal characteristic is needed to maintain the "authenticity" of a position. For example, a topless bar can argue that the cocktail servers should be female, since customers expect that as a part of

JURIS **prudence?**

We're Spreading Love All Over Texas

 When Southwest Airlines started operations in Texas in the 1970s, it would hire only women flight attendants and ticket agents. When sued by some men for sex discrimination in violation of Title VII, Southwest defended that its decision was based on business necessity.

A Dallas advertising agency described the image Southwest would develop this way:

> This lady is young and vital . . . she is charming and goes through life with great flair and exuberance . . . you notice first her exciting smile, friendly air, her wit . . . yet she is quite efficient and approaches all her tasks with care and attention. . . .

Southwest's ads promised "in-flight love," flight attendants wore hot-pants, served "love bites" (toasted almonds), and distributed "love potions" (cocktails). Its ticketing system featured a "quickie machine" that provided "instant gratification."

The court struck down Southwest's employment policy: "Southwest is not a business where vicarious sex entertainment is the primary service provided. Accordingly, the ability of the airline to perform its primary business function, the transportation of passengers, would not be jeopardized by hiring males."

Source: *Wilson v. Southwest Airlines*, 517 F.Supp. 292

the service. Male clothing is expected to be modeled by a male model. In some medical care situations, hospitals may restrict the sex of attendants for the comfort of patients or to protect sexual privacy.

Age Discrimination Defenses

Almost all age discrimination suits are disparate treatment (intentional discrimination) cases in which the plaintiff must establish a prima facie case that the employer must rebut with an acceptable business reason for the action taken. The ADEA specifies defenses that employers rely on when defending age discrimination suits. These are much like the defenses in Title VII cases, but some are more specific to issues that arise because of age:

1. Good cause. Employers may discharge or discipline an employee for unsatisfactory performance or for violating work rules. That is, ordinary good-faith business decisions are not prohibited; protected class status—in this case, age—is not a protection.

2. Bona fide occupational qualification. Employers may discriminate on the basis of age "where age is a bona fide occupational qualification reasonably necessary to the normal operation of the particular business." The EEOC and courts are skeptical of this justification. Mandatory retirement for public safety employees, such as police officers, prison guards, and firefighters, has been allowed.

3. Reasonable factors other than age. The ADEA states that employers may use criteria that happen to discriminate against older employees "where the differentiation is based on reasonable factors other than age." Employers may not discharge older workers in favor of hiring new entrants in their place at lower wages. Rather, replacements must be made because the employee's performance has deteriorated. Age should be irrelevant to performance evaluations.

4. Seniority. As with Title VII, the ADEA states that employers may "observe the terms of a bona fide seniority system that is not intended to evade the purposes of" the ADEA. Hence, if a company has a reduction in force (RIF) and a protected worker loses a job instead of a younger worker who happens to have more seniority, there is no violation. An announced rule in a RIF, such as a rule that seniority (last-in, first-out) decides who will be terminated, means less likelihood of violating the law.

5. Bona fide employee benefit plans. The ADEA was amended in 1990 by the *Older Workers Benefit Protection Act*, which states that an employer may "observe the terms of a bona fide employee benefit plan . . . that is a voluntary early retirement incentive plan consistent with the relevant purpose . . . of this Act." That is, employers are not supposed to force "involuntary retirement," but if early retirement incentive plan (ERIP) benefits are so generous that an employee chooses to retire, the employee cannot claim to have been forced to retire. Employers may ask employees to sign "knowing and voluntary waivers" of age discrimination claims when they agree to retire early in response to an ERIP. The ADEA also exempts senior executives in high-level policy positions who are at least age 65 and are entitled to a company pension of at least $44,000 per year.

REMEDIES

Title VII states that when an employer has been found to have engaged in an unlawful discriminatory employment practice:

the court may enjoin the . . . practice, and order such affirmative action as may be appropriate, which may include, but is not limited to, reinstatement or hiring of employees, with or without back pay . . . or any other equitable relief as the court deems appropriate.

Courts have used their statutory powers to order offending employers to reinstate employees with back pay, promote employees, give artificial seniority to existing or new employees, and implement an affirmative action program. Relying on the Act's reference to "equitable relief," the courts have broad and flexible powers to provide the most appropriate relief.

The 1991 Civil Rights Act amended Title VII so that the kinds of damages that may be sought by a plaintiff are the same in most discrimination suits. Compensation may go beyond back wages, such as payment for therapy or medical treatment related to the discrimination or for pain and suffering.

Punitive damages as a remedy are also authorized by the 1991 Act if the employer acted "with malice or with reckless indifference" to plaintiff's rights. When punitive damages are requested, companies with fewer than 15 employees are exempt; companies with 15 to 100 employees may be sued for up to $50,000; between 101 and 200 employees, $100,000; between 201 and 500 employees, $200,000; and more than 500 employees, $300,000.

In addition, the court is empowered "in such circumstances as [it] may deem just" to appoint an attorney for an impoverished plaintiff. Ordinarily, the prevailing plaintiff is awarded attorney's fees. A prevailing employer may be awarded attorney's fees only if the court determines that the plaintiff's action was frivolous, unreasonable, or without foundation.

Affirmative Action Programs

An *affirmative action program* is a deliberate effort by an employer to remedy discriminatory practices in the hiring, training, and promotion of protected class members when a particular class is underrepresented in the employer's workforce. Such programs have been adopted based only on race or sex—not on color, religion, national origin, or age.

After finding that members of a protected class are underrepresented in the company's workforce, an employer may voluntarily implement an affirmative action program to ensure that the company provides more opportunities for women or minorities in certain job categories. An involuntary program may be imposed by the courts as a remedy to correct past discriminatory employment practices by the company or, in the special case of government contractors, by the federal government as a prerequisite to entering into a government contract. This is probably the most controversial part of employment discrimination law and is now subject to legislative and judicial scrutiny.

EXECUTIVE ORDER 11246

As the chief executive officer of the United States, the president has the authority to determine certain conditions for government business that are specified in *executive orders* issued by the president. Referred to as *government contractors*, businesses must abide by the executive orders when they contract with the government. In 1965, President Johnson issued Executive Order 11246, which has developed into a requirement that government contractors adopt *affirmative action*.

Employment Discrimination in Europe and Japan

 Europeans often are portrayed as more sophisticated than Americans with regard to social legislation. However, in many respects they are years behind the United States in their treatment of minorities and women in the labor force. Most European countries and Japan have antidiscrimination statutes on the books, but the laws are not nearly as strict as the U.S. laws.

Employees in Europe can be forced to retire between ages fifty-five and sixty-five, depending on the country. Europeans over age forty-five who lose their jobs have a harder time finding employment again than do their counterparts in the United States.

The first sexual harassment case in Japan was not decided until 1992. A woman who was harassed by her boss for two years was fired for complaining. She was awarded $12,500 in damages. While trivial by American standards, the case was a landmark in Japan.

Minority immigrants are treated as second-class citizens in most countries. In general, it is much harder for a noncitizen, especially a member of a racial minority, to obtain work and citizenship in Japan and most of Europe than it is in the United States.

Where affirmative action exists, it tends to be trivial or even overtly discriminatory in favor of male-citizen workers who already dominate the labor force. Women are kept out of many higher-level jobs and are not paid as much as men for equal work—especially in Japan.

European countries and Japan appear to treat women better in certain respects, such as by mandating generous maternity benefits, but one effect of those laws is to encourage employers not to hire women because of the high cost of the benefits to which women are entitled if they have children.

Monitored and enforced by the Office of Federal Contract Compliance Programs (OFCCP), the order requires companies with federal contracts totaling $10,000 per year to take affirmative action. Those with $50,000 in contracts and fifty or more employees must have a written affirmative action plan, which requires a contractor to conduct a *workforce analysis* for each job within the organization. Jobs are identified and analyzed according to rank, salary, and the percentage of those employed in the job on the basis of race and sex.

The contractor must undertake an *underutilization analysis*, comparing the percentage of minorities and women in the community in each job category with that percentage employed by the contractor. If underutilization is found—say because 19 percent of the lab technicians are women compared with 41 percent of the lab technicians available in the community—the contractor must establish an affirmative action plan to increase the number of women in these positions.

The program may require that efforts be made to hire more women or to invest in training women to enhance their qualifications for certain jobs. If these efforts fail because it appears the employer was not serious, a numerical goal may be set, such as to double the number of female lab technicians in three years. In recent years, this has not been common. Hiring and promotion quotas that are set are reviewed periodically to determine whether adequate progress is being made. In the event that progress is not being made, federal contracts may be canceled.

AFFIRMATIVE ACTION AS A REMEDY

Title VII provides that in the event an employer is found to have engaged in illegal discrimination, "the court may . . . order such affirmative action as may be appropriate. . . ." Courts may require an offending employer to implement an affirmative action program. The court could require the employer to reinstate or hire qualified employees in the protected class to make up for past discriminatory activities. The action may be oriented at new employee recruitment, or it could be devotion of more resources to training current minority or women employees to become qualified candidates for promotion into positions in which they are under-represented.

In recent years, as the worst vestiges of overt discrimination have been reduced, court-ordered affirmative action programs have become less common than voluntary affirmative action programs. Most employers adopt a program before one is forced upon them. The Supreme Court has approved mandated programs where a pattern of intentional discrimination makes it clear that a strong remedy is required under the flexible powers granted courts by the Civil Rights Act. In *U.S. v. Paradise*, 107 S.Ct. 1053, (1987), the Court upheld a court-ordered hiring and promotion goal program for the Alabama Department of Public Safety, which had failed to hire African-American troopers for years after passage of Title VII. Consistent with the state population, the Court upheld an ordered goal that 25 percent of all employees at all ranks should be qualified African-Americans.

VOLUNTARY AFFIRMATIVE ACTION PROGRAMS

Employers may voluntarily implement an affirmative action program. They may do so to be sure they are in compliance with Executive Order 11246. Employers often implement a program after determining that a protected class is underrepresented in its workforce in certain job categories. An affirmative action program allows an employer to correct for underrepresentation. The Supreme Court examined a voluntary affirmative action program in the *Johnson* decision.

Johnson v. Transportation Agency, Santa Clara Co., Calif.
United States Supreme Court
480 U.S. 616, 107 S.Ct. 1442 (1987)

CASE BACKGROUND *The Transportation Agency voluntarily adopted an affirmative action plan for hiring and promoting employees. Women were significantly underrepresented in some job categories. To achieve a better balance in the workforce, the sex of qualified applicants would be given consideration. No specific goals were set for the number of positions to be occupied by women, but annual goals were adjusted each year based on experience.*

The agency announced a vacancy for the position of road dispatcher in the skilled craft job category. Johnson, a man, and Diane Joyce applied and were rated the top two applicants for the position. Johnson scored a 75 on the interview test, Joyce a 73. After taking into account Joyce's sex, she was picked over Johnson, who then sued, claiming that he had been discriminated against on the basis of sex.

The district court held the affirmative action plan illegal because it had no ending point or clear goals. The Court of Appeals reversed, finding that the plan was legal. Johnson appealed.

CASE DECISION Brennan, Justice.

* * *

As the Agency Plan recognized, women were most egregiously underrepresented in the Skilled Craft job category, since none of the 238 positions was occupied by a woman. In mid-1980, when Joyce was selected for the road dispatcher position, the Agency was still in the process of refining its short-term goals for Skilled Craft Workers in accordance with the directive of the Plan. This process did not reach fruition until 1982, when the Agency established a short-term goal for that year of three women for the 55 expected openings in that job category—a modest goal of about 6% for that category.

We reject petitioner's argument that . . . it was inappropriate for the Director to take into account affirmative action considerations in filling the road dispatcher position. The Agency's Plan emphasized that the long-term goals were not to be taken as guides for actual hiring decisions, but that supervisors were to consider a host of practical factors in seeking to meet affirmative action objectives, including the fact that in some job categories women were not qualified in numbers comparable to their representation in the labor force.

By contrast, had the Plan simply calculated imbalances in all categories according to the proportion of women in the area labor pool, and then directed that hiring be governed solely by those figures, its validity fairly could be called into question. This is because analysis of a more specialized labor pool normally is necessary in determining underrepresentation in some positions. If a plan failed to take distinctions in qualifications into account in providing guidance for actual employment decisions, it would dictate mere blind hiring by the numbers, for it would hold supervisors to "achievement of a particular percentage of minority employment or membership . . . regardless of circumstances such as economic conditions or the number of qualified minority applicants . . ."

* * *

Affirmed.

QUESTIONS FOR ANALYSIS

1. Why might a company or organization undertake a voluntary affirmative action program?
2. In the absence of its affirmative action program, could the agency have hired Joyce over Johnson?

Discrimination on the Basis of Disability

The *Rehabilitation Act* of 1973 provides protection for disabled persons seeking employment with or currently employed by employers that receive federal funds. The Act tends to follow the steps in Title VII employment discrimination suits. Section 503 of the Act is most important. It holds that all companies with federal contracts of $2,500 or more have a duty to ensure the disabled an opportunity in the workplace by providing reasonable accommodations.

The *Americans with Disabilities Act (ADA)* of 1990 expands the rights of persons with disabilities in employment and supplements access rights to public accommodations, such as hotels, restaurants, theaters, public transportation, telecommunications, and retail stores. The ADA expands the rights of people with mental and physical disabilities beyond those provided by the Rehabilitation Act. Besides encompassing the Rehabilitation Act, the ADA incorporates most remedies and procedures set out in Title VII. The ADA applies to all employers with fifteen or more employees.

DEFINITION OF DISABLED

The Rehabilitation Act and the ADA define *a person with disabilities* as

any person who (i) has a physical or mental impairment which substantially limits one or more of such person's major life activities, (ii) has a record of such an impairment, or (iii) is regarded as having such an impairment.

The Supreme Court has recognized regulations by the Department of Health and Human Services as a guide to determining what is a disability. The regulations define "major life activities" as "functions such as caring for one's self, performing manual tasks, walking, seeing, hearing, speaking, breathing, learning, and working." Examples of disabilities covered by the statutes include people:

- With a history of alcohol or other drug abuse
- With a severe disfigurement
- Who have had a heart attack
- Who must use a wheelchair
- Who are hearing- or vision-impaired

Even if a person is not actually impaired, if other people think the person is impaired, the person is considered disabled. For example, former cancer patients have found that some people are afraid to hire them because they believe cancer is contagious. As a result, even though no impairment exists and even though doctors may say there is no disease present, bias against the person who had the disease makes the person disabled for purposes of this law.

Lesser impairments do not constitute a disability. For example, in a decision by the Fourth Circuit Court of Appeals, a newly hired utility repairman was fired because he had a fear of heights and would not climb ladders to make repairs expected in his position. He sued, alleging that fear of heights caused him to be disabled. The court upheld dismissal of his suit because there was no "*substantial* limitation of a *major* life activity." Also, in dismissing claims of discrimination against people who are left-handed, the courts note they have no desire to trivialize the statute by allowing it to apply to inconveniences and personal oddities.

COMPLIANCE WITH THE STATUTES

The Rehabilitation Act is enforced primarily by complaints to the Department of Labor, which may bring suit on behalf of people with disabilities. Only a small number of suits have been filed. Suits under the ADA arise the same way that discrimination suits brought under Title VII come about—by filing complaints with the EEOC. The suits proceed much the same way as do Title VII suits.

Reasonable Accommodation

Employers are obliged to make *reasonable accommodations* for persons with disabilities. Employers are expected to incur expenses in making a position or workstation available to qualified disabled applicants and employees. Exactly where the line is drawn is not clear. Ford does not have to redesign its assembly line at high cost so that a worker in a wheelchair could work on the assembly line, because that would impose an *undue hardship* on business operations. However, when a workstation can be redesigned for several thousand dollars to accommodate a person with a disability, that must be done. The Department of Labor estimates that in most cases, the cost of accommodation is under $500. However, firms are also expected to provide special equipment and training for the disabled and allow modified work schedules. The *Arline* decision is the Supreme Court's most important holding in this area. Although it concerned a claim under the Rehabilitation Act, the analysis is the same for the ADA.

School Board of Nassau County, Florida v. Arline
United States Supreme Court
480 U.S. 273, 107 S.Ct. 1123 (1987)

CASE BACKGROUND *Gene Arline was hospitalized for tuberculosis in 1957. The disease was in remission for the next twenty years, during which time she taught* *school. In 1977 and 1978, tests showed the disease was again active. Because the disease had a (small) chance of being spread to the schoolchildren, the school board* *suspended Arline with pay for parts of two school years. Arline was dismissed after the 1978–79 school year because of her illness. She claimed protection under the Rehabilitation Act.*

The district court held against Arline, saying that she was not disabled under the statute because contagious diseases are not covered. That is, she was no longer qualified for her position as a schoolteacher because of the danger she posed to the children. The Court of Appeals reversed, holding that persons with contagious diseases are covered. The court ruled that the school board should consider the risk of infection that Arline posed. If the risk were deemed to be unsatisfactory, the board should consider other assignments within the school system for Arline where there would be less exposure to children, such as in an administrative position. The school appealed.

CASE DECISION Brennan, Justice.

* * *

We do not agree with petitioners that, in defining a handicapped individual under [the Act], the contagious effects of a disease can be meaningfully distinguished from the disease's physical effects on a claimant in a case such as this. Arline's contagiousness and her physical impairment each resulted from the same underlying condition, tuberculosis. It would be unfair to allow an employer to seize upon the distinction between the effects of a disease on others and the effects of a disease on a patient and use that distinction to justify discriminatory treatment.

* * *

The fact that some persons who have contagious diseases may pose a serious health threat to others under certain circumstances does not justify excluding from the coverage of the Act all persons with actual or perceived contagious diseases. Such exclusion would mean that those accused of being contagious would never have the opportunity to have their condition evaluated in light of medical evidence and a determination made as to whether they were "otherwise qualified." Rather, they would be vulnerable to discrimination on the basis of mythology—precisely

the type of injury Congress sought to prevent. We conclude that the fact that a person with a record of a physical impairment is also contagious does not suffice to remove that person from coverage under [the Act].

* * *

The remaining question is whether Arline is otherwise qualified for the job of elementary schoolteacher. To answer this question in most cases, the district court will need to conduct an individualized inquiry and make appropriate findings of fact. Such an inquiry is essential if [the Act] is to achieve its goal of protecting handicapped individuals from deprivations based on prejudice, stereotypes, or unfounded fear, while giving appropriate weight to such legitimate concerns . . . as avoiding exposing others to significant health and safety risks. . . .

In making these findings, courts normally should defer to the reasonable medical judgments of public health officials. The next step in the "otherwise-qualified" inquiry is for the court to evaluate, in light of these medical findings, whether the employer could reasonably accommodate the employee under the established standards for that inquiry.

* * *

We remand the case to the District Court to determine whether Arline is otherwise qualified for her position. The judgment of the Court of Appeals is Affirmed.

QUESTIONS FOR ANALYSIS

1. Suppose the school board decides that the risk of infection is small, but a year later one of Arline's students develops tuberculosis. Could the parents of the student sue the administrators and school board?

2. Suppose the school board decided that the safest bet was to put Arline in an administrative position, but none were open. Ignoring the possibility of a collective bargaining agreement, could the board fire the person currently in the position it wants for Arline?

EEOC Guidance

In the *Arline* case, the employer did not attempt to make reasonable accommodations, such as place Arline in an administrative position in which exposure to children would not be a problem but her experience would be utilized. Discrimination cases are evaluated one by one. The EEOC has issued *ADA Enforcement Guidance:*

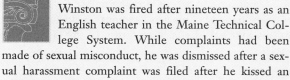

Get the Women Out of My Classes

Winston was fired after nineteen years as an English teacher in the Maine Technical College System. While complaints had been made of sexual misconduct, he was dismissed after a sexual harassment complaint was filed after he kissed an eighteen-year-old female student "after a sexually suggestive conversation."

Winston sued, "claiming that he was terminated because of his 'mental handicap of sexual addiction.'" His expert witness testified that this disorder, which had led to his seeking the services of prostitutes, was a permanent condition but that Winston could perform his job as a teacher.

The supreme court of Maine tossed out the complaint, noting that the ADA specifically excludes "sexual behavior disorders" from the term *disability*.

Source: *Winston* v. *Maine Tech. College Sys.*, 631 A.2d 70

Preemployment Disability-Related Questions and Medical Examinations (1995). The guidelines note that the ADA prohibits employers from asking disability-related questions or requiring medical exams before a job is offered. Hence, employers cannot ask questions about the nature or severity of a disability. The following are examples of questions that are illegal to ask during a job interview:

- Do you have AIDS?
- Have you ever been treated for mental health problems?
- Have you ever filed for workers' compensation benefits?
- Do you have a disability that would interfere with your ability to perform the job?
- How many sick days were you out last year?
- Have you ever been unable to handle work-related stress?
- Have you ever been treated for drug addiction or drug abuse?

In the case of drugs, past addiction is treated as a disability, but current use of illegal drugs is not, so applicants may be asked about current use and may be given a drug test. However, current alcoholism is a protected disability, and applicants may not be asked questions about drinking habits, although it is permissible to ask whether an applicant has been arrested for driving under the influence of alcohol.

If a disability is obvious or if an applicant volunteers a disability, some questions may be asked about the need for reasonable accommodation. For example, if an applicant discloses that she needs to take breaks to take diabetes medication, the employer may ask how often such breaks are needed and how long they would be. Employers may make clear the requirements needed to perform a job, and if it is dubious that someone could perform a job function, an applicant may be asked to demonstrate how he or she could accomplish the task.

Once a job offer has been made, an employer may ask for documentation of a disability and may ask more questions about the reasonable accommodation needed for the employee. If a physical exam is given to new employees, similar exams must be given to all employees in the same job categories and the results must be kept confidential. Such exams can be given so long as they are related to the ability to do the job, and not because an employer is trying to screen out employees with potential health problems.

Violations by Employers

As in the case of discrimination based on race, sex, or age, the law is broken if a person is denied an opportunity, for which he or she is qualified, primarily because of disability. However, in the case of disabilities, besides not discriminating, an employer must also make reasonable accommodations— go the extra step to make adjustments for the disability. In this sense, there is an affirmative action requirement, but it is not one tied to specific goals. This requirement works on a case-by-case basis. Employment situations that have been in violation of the law include

- Using standardized employment tests that tend to screen out people with disabilities
- Refusing to hire applicants because they have a history of alcohol abuse rather than because they are currently alcohol abusers
- Rejecting a job applicant because he or she is HIV-positive
- Asking job applicants if they have disabilities rather than asking if they have the ability to perform the job
- Limiting advancement opportunities for employees because of their disabilities
- Not hiring a person with a disability because the workplace does not have a bathroom that can accommodate wheelchairs

The first judgment under the ADA occurred in 1993. AIC Security Investigation fired an executive who was suffering from terminal brain cancer but was still able to work. The EEOC pursued the case on the executive's behalf, and the jury awarded the man more than $500,000 in damages plus back pay. Since the 1991 Civil Rights Act restricts damages in employment discrimination cases such as this one to $200,000 plus back pay, the jury verdict had to be reduced. The case delivered a clear message that as employment rights of persons with disabilities expand, employers must adjust. Now, about 25,000 complaints are filed with the EEOC annually.

Summary

- Title VII of the Civil Rights Act and the Age Discrimination in Employment Act require employers not to discriminate on the basis of sex, race, color, religion, national origin, or age. This applies to all aspects of the employment process—hiring, promotion, discipline, benefits, and firing. The laws are enforced by the EEOC and private party suits.
- Sex discrimination specifically includes discrimination with respect to childbearing plans, pregnancy, and related medical conditions. Sexual harassment now poses a legal challenge for managers, who must take steps to inform employees of the seriousness and the consequences of harassment and establish internal procedures to allow claims to be investigated with an assurance of confidentiality.
- Key tests that the courts use to look for discrimination are *disparate treatment*, where, everything else being equal, employment decisions are illegally motivated by discrimination based on race, sex, national origin, religion, or age; and *disparate impact*, where the effect of hiring or promotion standards is to discriminate, even if unintentionally, on the basis of protected class status.
- When employers are sued under the discrimination laws, they must present a preponderance of evidence that the practices they engage in are not discriminatory. The practices must be related to legitimate business necessity. Practices that when properly designed are allowed to stand include professionally developed ability tests, bona fide seniority and merit systems, and bona fide occupational qualifications that provide a rationale for personnel decisions.

- An affirmative action plan may be adopted by an employer and a union in a collective bargaining agreement, or it may be adopted voluntarily by an employer. Strategically, adopting such a plan voluntarily might reduce the likelihood of a more rigid program being imposed on the company in the event of a lawsuit or government investigation of discrimination charges.

- Employers may have affirmative action plans imposed on them by court order as a remedy for discrimination. Federal contractors must have affirmative action plans in place. These plans are designed to increase minority or female representation in certain job categories. This may be done by setting goals to be met within certain time frames.

- The Rehabilitation Act of 1973 and the Americans with Disabilities Act of 1990 require employers to take positive steps to make accommodations for disabled workers. Court decisions have broadened the definition of a disabled person to include alcohol and other drug addicts as well as persons with serious diseases such as AIDS. Employers must balance the interests and safety of other employees and customers against the rights of the disabled employees to gain or retain meaningful employment.

Issue

Can Race Discrimination Be Justified to Help Minority Businesses?

 Title VII prohibits race discrimination in employment. As the text has discussed, even if the customers of a business prefer to deal with employees of a certain race, that is not an excuse for employment discrimination by the business. But, as this article discusses, the fact of race discrimination means that some minority business owners believe that they must use employees of particular races to be able to compete effectively.

COLOR CODE: BLACK ENTREPRENEURS FACE A PERPLEXING ISSUE: HOW TO PITCH TO WHITES

Angelo B. Henderson

Reprinted by permission of *The Wall Street Journal* © 1999 Dow Jones & Company, Inc. All rights reserved worldwide. Henderson is a reporter for *The Wall Street Journal*.

DETROIT—When suburban clients close a deal with First Impressions Inc., they will probably shake hands with William Ashley or someone else who is white, although Eric Giles, who is African-American, did the

client research, helped develop the sales strategy and made initial telephone contact for this restaurant and food-service employment agency.

"Unfortunately, in the end I can't send him out as the person who does the face-to-face and gets the deal signed," says Judy Y. Wiles, owner of Detroit-based First Impressions.

This might raise eyebrows about Ms. Wiles's own racial attitudes—except she is black herself. She says she has "unwavering confidence" in Mr. Giles. Ultimately, though, both worry that their success and even survival is based on what their company name suggests: first impressions. And in a business where restaurants, hotels and party givers can choose any number of white companies to supply bartenders, waiters, chefs and other restaurant personnel, First Impressions can't afford to lose a contract because some clients may hole preconceived notions about blacks.

Says Ms. Wiles, who is convinced that, over the years, she has lost as many as 20 jobs because of this very issue: "It's that fear that encourages me to use Bill or [another] front person."

The fear of this black entrepreneur, though some argue it is overblown, is one nonetheless often shared by other African-American businesspeople who cater to a largely white clientele. Whether at a Detroit car dealer, a regional fast-food franchiser or an employment agency like First Impressions, blacks find they face an array of tricky marketing issues, the most wrenching perhaps is whether to show their faces.

* * *

Mel Farr, a Detroit resident and former professional football star whose 15 automobile franchises make him among America's most successful African-American car dealers, agrees. Mr. Farr is happy to mug for the camera in a Superman cape for commercials that are broadcast in racially mixed Detroit. But for most of the past seven years, he has used a white stand-in for TV spots that are broadcast in predominantly white areas downstate.

This, even though he commands the kind of sports celebrity that has often paved the way for black athletes in the white business world. "I don't want to offend someone and give them a reason not to come and do business with me because of my color. I want everybody to buy a car from me," Mr. Farr says.

This is hardly a new dilemma, of course. In this same city 40 years before, music baron Berry Gordy of legendary Motown Records made a conscious decision to hire a white Italian-American to promote records by black artists on white radio stations. It was the same notion that explained why album covers of many Motown stars, such as the Isley Brothers and Mary Wells, depicted white couples dancing or beach scenes—anything but a black face.

Recalls Mr. Gordy's sister, Esther Gordy Edwards: "There were places, especially in the South, where a black face wouldn't sell."

That said, some think the times are changing, pointing to the phenomenal marketing success of basketball superstar Michael Jordan, who moves huge amounts of goods and services for white-owned companies, and, tangentially, the crossover appeal of black celebrities such as Will Smith and Denzel Washington with white audiences.

Indeed, even some blacks in business find these racial concerns overwrought; beyond that, some think successful black entrepreneurs, out of pride, ought not to make concessions in their marketing. "I think it's terrible. As far as I'm concerned, I'd rather lose the business than have to front as some white company," says Ray Jenkins,

65, who has operated a real-estate company in Detroit since 1962.

Ken Smikle, president of Target Market News, a Chicago-based research firm that monitors African-American consumers, disagrees. "These black business owners are not paranoid, they are being realistic," says Mr. Smikle.

In fact, for many black business owners, the reluctance to reveal their race in marketing is sometimes rooted in unpleasant personal experiences. They also point to disturbing studies, like one not long ago by the Employment Discrimination Project of Chicago, that demonstrated a reluctance of white managers to hire blacks for sales jobs in suburban home-improvement stores because they feared white customers wouldn't buy from them. "Our tests show that the employer was clearly seeking to hire sales people whose race reflected their customer base," says the council's LeeAnn Lodder, who helped conduct the studies.

This comes as no surprise to Ms. Wiles, 42 years old, and Mr. Giles, 33, who recall early in their business relationship that a white-owned company that seemed very eager to do business with them over the phone never phoned back after they met Mr. Giles, a 6-foot-5-inch black man, in person. While not ruling out other factors, they decided from then on that it would be better to be safe than sorry. So they often go to extraordinary lengths to play down or disguise their race, while minimizing person-to-person contact with new white clients. Sending out Mr. Ashley, a well-dressed 50-something white as a front man, is but one example.

When Ms. Wiles started the business 11 years ago, she sometimes pinched her nose and spoke nasally to make her voice more "white" on the phone; she has also removed the words "owner" from her business card so that should she meet a prospective white customer, they will think she is simply an employee.

Ms. Wiles and Mr. Giles have also crafted a slick portfolio of past functions staffed by First Impressions that Mr. Ashley shows on sales calls. Its opening pages picture two white women standing by the door in bow ties, tuxedo shirts and black pants. A white man in a chef's hat carves a roast. Page after page features smiling Caucasians.

Quite a statement for a black-owned business whose roster of about 300 temporary workers is actually 98%

African-American. "It's lily white, isn't it?" says Mr. Giles of the sales portfolio. Adds Ms. Wiles: "From the pictures, it gives the customer the impression—though these people do, and have, worked for us—that you are dealing with a white firm."

If this seems excessive, Ms. Wiles reluctantly trots out the story of what happened two years ago when a wealthy white suburban woman phoned First Impressions to get them to staff a private party because a wealthy white friend had recommended the firm. The woman became agitated with a First Impressions receptionist and said, "You sound black."

When the receptionist said she was black, the woman demanded to speak to someone else. She got Mr. Giles and, unaware that he was also black, proceeded to discuss her party needs while telling him not to send blacks whom she feared would "steal my furs" or other things. Ms. Wiles reluctantly booked the party but, alarmed by other acts of overt racism, declined at the last minute to send her staff.

"I did the right thing because I was standing on principle," Ms. Wiles says, but the decision cost her. The referring client also stopped using her company because of the conflict, she says.

* * *

ISSUE QUESTIONS

1. The hiring practices discussed in the article are illegal. As is the case with many instances of illegal discrimination, the employer simply has not been challenged. Should minority-owned businesses be allowed to discriminate on the basis of race, so long as they can demonstrate that it is for the purpose of helping them compete? Similarly, should white-owned businesses be allowed to discriminate on the basis of race for the same reason?

2. Should customers who discriminate against firms on the basis of race, such as the lady who did not want African-American workers in her home, be subject to prosecution for discrimination?

REVIEW AND DISCUSSION QUESTIONS

1. Define the following terms and phrases:

discrimination	disparate treatment
protected class	disparate impact
constructive discharge	prima facie discrimination case
equal employment opportunity	bona fide occupational qualification
color	artificial seniority
national origin	affirmative action
hostile environment	reasonable accommodation

2. Would a dress code that required men to wear three-piece suits but stated only that women had to "look professional" be discriminatory against the male employees? What differences would be considered discriminatory?

CASE QUESTIONS

3. Wise was fired for getting into a fight with another employee during lunch at the company lunchroom. She kicked and scratched the other employee and used abusive language. She claimed sex discrimination under Title VII because male employees who had been in fights had not been fired. Was this sex discrimination? [*Wise* v. *Mead Corp.*, 614 F.Supp. 1131 (1985)]

4. Michele Vinson worked for Sidney Taylor at Meritor Savings for four years. During that time, they had sexual relations. Vinson was promoted three times and

received good evaluations. When she was fired, she claimed that it was because she started going with a new boyfriend. She said that her relations with Taylor had been involuntary; she had relations to keep her job. Other employees testified that Taylor was very aggressive with Vinson. Taylor said Vinson was fired for taking too much sick leave. Vinson sued for sexual harassment. The district court ruled against Vinson, holding that the relations were voluntary and were irrelevant to her bank employment. The appeals court ruled in her favor. What did the Supreme Court say? [*Meritor Savings Bank* v. *Vinson*, 106 S.Ct. 2399 (1986)]

5. Parr applied for a position as an insurance representative for which he was well qualified and had experience. The manager who interviewed Parr told him he would probably be hired and also told him the company did not sell insurance to African-Americans. Parr told the employment service that set up the interview of the manager's remarks and told the service that he was married to an African-American woman. The employment service told the insurance company of Parr's interracial marriage, at which point they declined to hire him. Was that a violation of Title VII? [*Parr* v. *Woodmen of the World Life Insurance Co.*, 791 F.2d 888 (11th Cir., 1986)]

6. Calvin Roach, "a native born American of Acadian descent" (that is, a Louisiana Cajun) claimed that he was fired from his job because of discrimination of his national origin. His employer moved to have the case dismissed because Acadia (the French name for Nova Scotia, Canada, when occupied by French settlers in the 1600s who moved to Louisiana in the late 1700s) never was a country. Could Roach claim national origin discrimination protection under Title VII? [*Roach* v. *Dresser Ind.*, 494 F.Supp 215 (W.D., La., 1980)]

7. Talley was a chef at Bravo Pitino Restaurant in Lexington, Kentucky, owned by Rick Pitino and Jodi DiRaimo, who was also the general manager. One night after closing, DiRaimo's wife, who had no formal role at the restaurant but was treated by employees as if she were a manager, told Talley to reopen the restaurant for her and some friends and for the employees who were still there. Talley said he did not think it was a good idea, but DiRaimo's wife told him she would be "responsible for it." The group stayed for two hours, drinking without paying, then left. Pitino heard about the incident and fired all employees involved, including Talley. He soon rehired all employees except Talley, the only black in the group. A white was hired to replace Talley. Talley sued for racial discrimination in employment. Pitino defended that Talley, as the only chef in the group, was not in a comparable employment category to the other employees and that he violated his management responsibility by opening the restaurant. Did Talley have a case? [*Talley* v. *Bravo Pitino Restaurant*, 61 F.3d 1241 (6th Cir., 1995)]

8. Rawlinson was a twenty-two-year-old college graduate who had majored in correctional psychology. She applied for a position as a correctional counselor—a prison guard—with the Alabama prison system. The primary duty was to maintain security and control the inmates by supervising their activities. The Alabama Board of Corrections rejected her application because she failed to meet the minimum 120-pound weight requirement set by Alabama statute. The statute also imposed a minimum five-foot, two-inch height requirement on applicants. Did the Alabama statute violate Title VII? What if the requirements were imposed for the protection of prison guards? [*Dothard* v. *Rawlinson*, 97 S.Ct. 2720 (1977)]

9. The Jackson, Michigan, Board of Education had a rule that in the event of a cutback in teachers, the layoffs would be proportional on the basis of race. That way,

students would be guaranteed more minority teachers as role models. This was done because more of the older teachers were white; if the layoff was based on seniority only, more minority teachers would be laid off proportional to the white teachers. The district court and court of appeals agreed with the school board, saying the rule helped to remedy past discrimination. What did the Supreme Court say? [*Wygant* v. *Jackson Board of Education*, 106 S.Ct. 1842 (1986)]

10. Two male prison guards sued for sex discrimination when the Iowa Department of Corrections decided that only female guards could staff the women's section at a minimum security prison. The men argued that this violated their rights as senior employees to have first choice of assignments and that it conflicted with a previous holding that allowed women guards to work in men's prisons, which included pat-down searches and watching prisoners in the showers. Was this sex discrimination? [*Tharp* v. *Iowa Dept. Corr.*, 68 F.3d 223 (8th Cir., 1995)]

11. Two applicants over age forty who could not meet the maximum weight limits for their height set for flight attendants, and so were rejected for consideration, sued United Airlines for age discrimination. They claimed the weight limits discriminated against persons over age forty and so were intentional discrimination. They claimed that even if the discrimination was not intentional, the weight rule has a disparate impact and so also violated the ADEA. Did they have a case? [*Ellis* v. *United Airlines*, 73 F.3d 999 (10th Cir., 1996)]

12. Weber, a white male, worked at a unionized plant. The union and the employer agreed on an affirmative action program, which resulted in Weber's being passed over for a training and promotion opportunity in favor of a less-qualified minority applicant who had less seniority. Weber sued the union and the employer, claiming illegal discrimination based on race. Is he right? [*United Steelworkers of America* v. *Weber*, 99 S.Ct. 2721 (1979)]

13. The New York City Transit Authority had a policy against hiring people who use narcotics. This included people using methadone, a narcotic given to addicts to break their dependency on heroin. Several people on methadone were refused jobs by the Transit Authority. They sued, claiming the policy was racially discriminatory under Title VII because 80 percent of the methadone users were African-American or Hispanic. The district court and court of appeals ruled for the plaintiffs, saying that while they could be excluded from safety-sensitive jobs such as subway car driver, the narcotics users could not be excluded from other jobs. What was the result of the appeal to the Supreme Court? [*New York City Transit Authority* v. *Beazer*, 99 S.Ct. 1355 (1979)]

14. A Vermont ski resort hired a cleaning woman who wore dentures. The woman had a good work record, and she had a neat and clean appearance, but she quit wearing her dentures because they hurt. The resort manager told her she had to wear her dentures or she would be dismissed, which she was because her appearance hurt their high-class image. She sued for disability discrimination under Vermont's Fair Employment Practices Act, which contains language nearly identical to that in the ADA. Is she protected? [*Hodgdon* v. *Mt. Mansfield Co.*, 624 A.2d 1122 (Sup. Ct., Vt., 1992)]

15. Bolton worked in a grocery warehouse for two years when he suffered a work-related injury that required medical leave. Under company policy, an employee on medical leave could not return until the company doctor certified that the employee was fit to resume work. When Bolton wanted to return, the doctor

declared him unable to perform his work in the warehouse, which refused to rehire him. Bolton sued, claiming disability discrimination. Did he have a case? [*Bolton v. Scrivner, Inc.*, 36 F.3d 939, (10th Cir., 1994)]

16. Daugherty was a bus driver for the City of El Paso when he was diagnosed as an insulin-dependent diabetic. Under Department of Transportation rules, for safety reasons, an insulin-dependent diabetic may not be a bus driver, so Daugherty was terminated, although the city did help him with retraining and with job search. Daugherty sued, contending ADA violation because the city did not seek a waiver of the safety rule to get him reinstated as a bus driver or, in the alternate, assign him to other duties for the city. A jury awarded him $5,000 damages. Did this hold on appeal? [*Daugherty* v. *City of El Paso*, 56 F.3d 695 (5th Cir., 1995)]

POLICY QUESTION

17. The Age Discrimination in Employment Act now holds that since 1994, colleges cannot force professors to retire at any age. Colleges are concerned that they will eventually be filled with a large number of very old faculty and few young faculty, so that students will not be able to relate well to the faculty and mental lethargy will set in. Should colleges be allowed to adopt contracts for, say, periods of five or ten years rather than indefinite tenure so they can get rid of older faculty?

ETHICS QUESTION

18. You are a supervisor at a company that does not have an affirmative action program. In looking to hire a new person for a certain position, the person who best fits the job criteria is a white male age thirty. Two other candidates are also well qualified for the position but just slightly less so than the top candidate. One of the other candidates is African-American; the third is a white woman age sixty-three. You believe that, in general, there is societal discrimination against minorities and older people. Should you give a little extra credit to the candidates who are in protected classes, given that you can justify whatever choice you make? How would you decide between the African-American man and the older white woman? Should you take into account that the man supports a wife and three children, whereas the woman has an employed husband and no children?

INTERNET ASSIGNMENT

Provide a brief (one or two sentence) summary of the mandate of each of the following discrimination-related statutes or rules. Hint: these statutes and rules are summarized at a single site on the World Wide Web. Browse the "Publications, News Services and Print Materials" hyperlinks within the LaborNet Web site (http://www.igc.apc.org/labornet/) to find the Labor Policy Association's Web pages.

   a. Equal Pay Act (1963), 29 U.S.C. §201 *et seq.*
   b. Civil Rights Act of 1964, 42 U.S.C. §2000 *et seq.*
   c. Age Discrimination in Employment Act of 1967 (ADEA), 29 U.S.C. §621 *et seq.*
   d. Vietnam Era Veterans' Readjustment Assistance Act (1974), 38 U.S.C. §4301
   e. Pregnancy Discrimination Amendment (1978), 42 U.S.C. §2000 *et seq.*
   f. Immigration Reform and Control Act (IRCA)(1986), 29 U.S.C. §1802 *et seq.*
   g. Americans with Disabilities Act (ADA)(1990), 42 U.S.C. §12101 *et seq.*
   h. Older Workers Benefit Protection Act (1990), 29 U.S.C. §623 *et seq.*
   i. Family and Medical Leave Act (1991), 29 U.S.C. §2601 *et seq.*

CHAPTER 17

Environmental Law

The Environmental Protection Agency (EPA) and Amoco Corporation cooperated on a four-year project to study pollution control effectiveness. The EPA listened to company experts; the company revealed operation details to EPA officials. The study revealed, among other things, that EPA regulations required Amoco to spend $41 million to trap air pollution from a refinery wastewater system, when the same control could be achieved for $11 million; the regulations did not allow the cheaper control methods. The study also showed that no controls were required on another part of the refinery that emitted five times as much pollution as the pollution being controlled at a cost of $41 million.

More than $100 billion per year is spent on pollution controls in the United States, which is the largest share of any major nation's income. Because pollution controls are so costly, there has been a fight between industry and regulators. Some expensive pollution controls achieve little, while some major sources of pollution go largely uncontrolled. Carol Browner, head of the EPA in the Clinton administration, says, "The adversarial relationship that now exists ignores the real complexities of environmental and business problems." Whether this recognition will translate into more cost-effective pollution controls that deliver better environmental quality at a lower price remains to be seen.

This chapter reviews the major federal laws providing environmental protection, but it begins with a discussion of common-law rules that regulate environmental quality, such as the application of nuisance law. The chapter then discusses the creation of the EPA and the most important environmental statutes, including the Clean Air Act, the Clean Water Act, the Resource Conservation and Recovery Act, Superfund, and the Endangered Species Act.

Pollution and the Common Law

Environmental pollution was not subject to serious federal regulation until after 1970. Before then, pollution was a problem best controlled by state and local laws. State laws were developed to control pollution in the areas with some of the worst problems, but often citizens relied on the common law for relief from environmental damage.

To resolve disputes involving pollution, judges relied on the law of nuisance, trespass, negligence, and strict liability for abnormally dangerous activities. Citizens relied most heavily on the law of nuisance in bringing actions against business, whether the pollutant affected water, air, or land. According to William Rodgers, a prominent environmental law professor:

> Nuisance actions . . . challenged virtually every major industrial and municipal activity which is today the subject of comprehensive environmental regulation—the operation of land fills, incinerators, sewage treatment facilities, activities at chemical plants, aluminum, lead and copper smelters, oil refineries, pulp mills, rendering plants, quarries and mines, textile mills and a host of other manufacturing activities.

NUISANCE LAW AND POLLUTION

As we saw in the torts chapter, nuisances may be public or private. A *public nuisance* is an unreasonable interference with a right held in common by the general public. In a pollution case, the right held in common is a community's right to a reasonably clean and safe environment. As a rule, a public nuisance case will be brought against the polluter in a community's name by a city or state attorney. A *private nuisance* is a substantial and unreasonable interference with the use and enjoyment of the land of another. It generally involves a polluter who is injuring one person or a group of people.

Pollution cases often involve a production process that is offensive or harmful to a polluter's neighbors. A plaintiff must be able to show that there is an unreasonable interference—that is, the pollution is harmful. Air and water pollution cases dating back into the 1800s show a variety of approaches. In some cases, the courts weighed the costs to society from the pollution that occurred against the benefits from the jobs and products that came from the polluter. The benefits may be so large as to eliminate any request for relief from pollution. In many cases, the polluter was ordered to pay damages to the parties suffering pollution damage; in some cases, if the pollution could not be controlled, the polluter was ordered to shut down. For example, in the 1907 case *Georgia* v. *Tennessee Copper Company*, 206 U.S. 230, the Supreme Court reviewed a complaint by the state of Georgia that a copper smelter in Tennessee was discharging gases that killed vegetation in Georgia and threatened human health. The Court held that an injunction against the smelter to shut it down could be issued if the smelter could not control the pollution enough to stop the damage.

TRESPASS AND POLLUTION

Recall that a *trespass* is an unauthorized and direct breach of the boundaries of another's land. The main difference between trespass and nuisance is that a trespass occurs whenever there is physical invasion of a plaintiff's property. A nuisance requires proof that interference with property is substantial and unreasonable. In practice, nuisance and trespass are difficult to distinguish in many pollution cases. For example, when toxic gases float onto the property of another person, there may be both a nuisance and a trespass. The Supreme Court of Washington reviewed these issues in the *Bradley* case.

Bradley v. American Smelting and Refining Company
Supreme Court of Washington
104 Wash.2d 677, 709 P.2d 782 (1985)

CASE BACKGROUND *Michael and Marie Bradley lived on Vashon Island, Washington, four miles from a copper smelter run by American Smelting and Refining Company (ASARCO). The Bradleys sued ASARCO, a New Jersey corporation, in federal court for damages in trespass and nuisance from the deposit on their property of airborne particles of heavy metals from ASARCO's smelter. The smelter had operated since 1905; it was regulated by state and federal air pollution laws and was in compliance with all regulations. The gases that passed over and landed on the Bradleys' land could not be seen or smelled by humans; they required microscopic detection.*

The federal district court certified several issues to the Washington state supreme court; that is, the district court, which would use common law to resolve the matter, asked the Washington supreme court to tell it the status of Washington common law of nuisance and trespass as applied to air pollution.

CASE DECISION Callow, Justice.

* * *

1. Did the defendant have the requisite intent to commit intentional trespass as a matter of law?

The parties stipulated that as a part of the smelting process, particulate matter including arsenic and cadmium was emitted, that some of the emissions had been deposited on the plaintiffs' land. . . . The defendant cannot and does not deny that whenever the smelter was in operation the whim of the winds could bring these deleterious substances to the plain-

tiffs' premises. We are asked if the defendant, knowing what it had to know from the facts it admits, had the legal intent to commit trespass. . . .

Intent is not . . . limited to consequences which are desired. If the actor knows that the consequences are certain, or substantially certain, to result from his act, and still goes ahead, he is treated by the law as if he had in fact desired to produce the result.

The defendant has known for decades that sulfur dioxide and particulates of arsenic, cadmium and other metals were being emitted from the tall smokestack. It had to know that the solids propelled into the air by the warm gases would settle back to earth somewhere. It had to know that a purpose of the tall stack was to disperse the gas, smoke and minute solids over as large an area as possible and as far away as possible, but that while any resulting contamination would be diminished as to any one area or landowner, that nonetheless contamination, though slight, would follow.

* * *

2. Does an intentional deposit of microscopic particulates, undetectable by the human senses, upon a person's property give rise to a cause of action for trespassory invasion of the person's right to exclusive possession of property as well as a claim of nuisance? . . .

Today, the line between trespass and nuisance has become "wavering and uncertain." The basic distinction is that trespass can be defined as any intentional invasion of the plaintiff's interest in the exclusive possession of property, whereas a nuisance requires a substantial and unreasonable interference with his use and enjoyment of it. That is to say, in trespass cases defendant's conduct typically results in an encroachment by "something" upon plaintiff's exclusive rights of possession. . . .

We hold that the defendant's conduct in causing chemical substances to be deposited upon the plaintiffs' land fulfilled all of the requirements under the law of trespass.

We hold that theories of trespass and nuisance are not inconsistent, that the theories may apply concurrently, and that the injured party may proceed under both theories when the elements of both actions are present. The *Restatement (Second) of Torts* §821D . . . states:

> For an intentional trespass, there is liability without harm; for a private nuisance, there is no liability without significant harm. In trespass an intentional invasion of the plaintiff's possession is of itself a tort, and liability follows unless the defendant can show a privilege. In private nuisance an intentional interference with the plaintiff's use or enjoyment is not of itself a tort, and unreasonableness of the interference is necessary for liability. . . .

The two actions, trespass and private nuisance, are thus not entirely exclusive or inconsistent, and in a proper case in which the elements of both actions are fully present, the plaintiff may have his choice of one or the other, or may proceed upon both.

* * *

3. Does the cause of action for trespassory invasion require proof of actual damages? . . .

The elements that we have adopted for an action in trespass . . . require that a plaintiff has suffered actual and substantial damages. Since this is an element of the action, the plaintiff who cannot show that actual and substantial damages have been suffered should be subject to dismissal of his cause upon a motion for summary judgment.

* * *

[4. Is this action precluded by time limitations or by state statutes that regulate ASARCO's smelter?] . . .

In conclusion, we answer the certified questions as follows:

1. The defendant had the requisite intent to commit intentional trespass.
2. An intentional deposit of microscopic particulates, undetectable by the human senses, gives rise to a cause of action for trespass as well as a claim of nuisance.
3. A cause of action under such circumstances requires proof of actual and substantial damages.
4. The appropriate limitations period for such a trespass is three years, but if the trespass continues, suit for damages may be brought for any damages not recovered previously and occurring within the three-year period preceding suit. The period of limitations runs from the date the cause of action accrues. . . . The cause of action for trespass is not preempted by the Washington Clean Air Act.

The United States District Court for the Western District of Washington shall be notified for such further action as it deems appropriate.

CASE NOTE The case was returned to the federal district court, which dismissed the case because there was no evidence of damage to plaintiffs from the air pollution.

QUESTIONS FOR ANALYSIS

1. Common-law actions in pollution cases are quite rare these days. Why might that be?
2. What would be required for the Bradleys to win their case given the holding here?

NEGLIGENCE, STRICT LIABILITY, AND POLLUTION

Both *negligence* and *strict liability for abnormally dangerous activities* may apply in pollution cases. Tort liability may be due to negligence—failure to use reasonable care to prevent pollution from causing a foreseeable injury. Strict liability for abnormally dangerous activities applies to businesses that produce toxic chemicals or emit toxic pollutants. In imposing strict liability, the courts emphasize the risks created by the toxic pollutant and the location of the business relative to population centers. The doctrine is simple; it requires proof that the discharge of the pollutant was abnormally dangerous and that the pollutant was the cause of the plaintiff's injury. Courts have found crop dusting, the storing of flammable liquids in quantity in a populated area, and the emitting of noxious gases by factories all to be abnormally dangerous. The following case illustrates the application of strict liability to the contamination of groundwater.

Branch v. Western Petroleum, Inc.
Supreme Court of Utah
657 P.2d 267 (1982)

CASE BACKGROUND *Branch owned property next to the property of Western Petroleum. Western built a pond into which it dumped wastewater from oil wells. The wastewater contained toxic chemicals. Western knew that the water in the pond would dissipate by evaporating into the air and percolating into the ground. The wastewater did percolate, contaminating the groundwater and Branch's water wells. Water from the wells killed one hundred chickens.*

Branch sued, alleging that since Western's activities created an abnormally dangerous condition, strict liability should apply. The trial court agreed with Branch, holding Western strictly liable for the damages caused by the pollution of the wells. Western appealed.

CASE DECISION Stewart, Justice.

* * *

[A]ccording to Western, the trial court erred in entering judgment on the basis of strict liability. . . . The Branches, on the other hand, take the position that Western created an abnormally dangerous condition by collecting contaminated water on its land for the purpose of having it seep or percolate into the groundwater and that, therefore, the law of strict liability controls. . . .

This Court has not heretofore had occasion to consider the legal principles which govern liability for the pollution of subterranean waters by industrial wastes. Our survey of cases from other states and of legal scholars indicates that a variety of legal theories have been relied on. The theories that have been employed include negligence, private nuisance, public nuisance, negligent trespass, and strict liability. The variety of approaches reflects numerous considerations, such as the general hydrological conditions in the state; the relative significance of promoting industrialization compared with the importance of promoting conservation of water; the nature of the particular state's water law; and, in particular, whether the doctrine of correlative rights applies to the use of water resources. . . . In American law it is generally recognized that a landowner has no absolute right to pollute percolating waters. In this state, a landowner has no such absolute right because percolating waters belong to the people of the state. For that reason, and because percolating waters are migratory and the rights of the landowners to those waters are correlative, such waters are subject to the maxim that one may not use his land so as to pollute percolating waters to the injury of another.

* * *

There are grounds for holding Western strictly liable for the pollution of the Branches' wells. First, the facts of the case support application of the rule of strict liability because the ponding of the toxic formation water in an area adjacent to the Branches' wells constituted an abnormally dangerous and inappropriate use of the land in light of its proximity to the Branches' property and was unduly dangerous to the Branches' use of their well water. . . .

The court also found support for the rule of strict liability in the policy consideration that an industry should not be able to use its property in such a way as to inflict injury on the property of its neighbors because to do so would result in effect in appropriating the neighbor's property to one's own use. An industrial polluter can and should assume the costs of pollution as a cost of doing business rather than charge the loss to a wholly innocent party.

We know of no acceptable rule of jurisprudence which permits those engaged in important and desirable enterprises to injure with impunity those who are engaged in enterprises of lesser economic significance. The costs of injuries resulting from pollution must be internalized by industry as a cost of production and borne by consumers or shareholders, or both, and not by the injured individual.

* * *

[Affirmed.]

QUESTIONS FOR ANALYSIS

1. On what basis was the court able to make the argument for applying strict liability for abnormally dangerous activities to the facts of this case?
2. Suppose groundwater contamination was from drums of chemicals buried on the property twenty years ago. Would that make the case more difficult? What if the defendant cannot be found?

WATER RIGHTS AND POLLUTION

As the court in the *Branch* decision noted, there is no common-law right to pollute water. Most states rely on *riparian water law*, although the Western states have a variety of other water rights. Riparian water law essentially says that people who live along rivers and other bodies of water have the right to use the water in reasonable amounts but must allow the water to flow downstream in usable form. That is, people have no right to pollute the water so that it is not usable downstream. Hence, along with nuisance and other common-law rights, enforcement of riparian water rights has long been a basis for suing polluters. The *Whalen* decision illustrates how the law works to protect water quality.

Whalen v. Union Bag & Paper Co.
Court of Appeals of New York
208 N.Y. 1, 101 N.E. 805 (1913)

CASE BACKGROUND *Whalen owned a farm on Brandywine Creek in New York. He used water from the creek to water plants and livestock. Union Bag built a pulp mill upstream, employing about 500 people. The mill polluted the creek so that Whalen could not use the water.*

Whalen sued Union Bag for damages and requested that the court issue an injunction to stop the pollution. The trial court [special term] awarded damages of $312 per year and issued an injunction to take effect in one year. Either the pollution stopped, or the mill was to be shut down. The appellate court eliminated the injunction and reduced damages to $100 per year. Whalen appealed to the highest court in New York.

CASE DECISION Werner, Justice.

* * *

The setting aside of the injunction was apparently induced by a consideration of the great loss likely to be inflicted on the defendant by the granting of the injunction as compared with the small injury done to the plaintiff's land by that portion of the pollution

which was regarded as attributable to the defendant. Such a balancing of injuries cannot be justified by the circumstances of this case.

. . . Although the damage to the plaintiff may be slight as compared with the defendant's expense of abating the condition, that is not a good reason for refusing an injunction. Neither courts of equity nor law can be guided by such a rule, for if followed to its logical conclusion it would deprive the poor litigant of his little property by giving it to those already rich. It is always to be remembered in such cases that "denying the injunction puts the hardship on the party in whose favor the legal right exists, instead of on the wrongdoer." . . .

The fact that the appellant has expended a large sum of money in the construction of its plant, and that it conducts its business in a careful manner and without malice, can make no difference in its rights to the stream. Before locating the plant the owners were bound to know that every riparian proprietor is entitled to have the waters of the stream that washes his land come to it without obstruction, diversion, or corruption, subject only to the reasonable use of the water, by those similarly entitled, for such domestic purposes as are inseparable from and necessary for the free use of their land; they were bound also to know the character of their proposed business, and to take notice of the size, course, and capacity of the stream, and to determine for themselves at their own peril whether they should be able to conduct their business upon a stream of the size and character of Brandywine creek without injury to their neighbors; and the magnitude of their investment and their freedom from malice furnish no reason why they should escape the consequences of their own folly. . . .

The judgment of the Appellate Division, insofar as it denied the injunction, should be reversed and the judgment of the special term in that respect reinstated, with costs to the appellant.

QUESTIONS FOR ANALYSIS

1. If the common law was this tough, why would we need federal regulation of water pollution?
2. Should damages be the only resort in such cases? Assuming that the real loss to Whalen was $312 per year, why should he be able to get an injunction that would put hundreds of people out of work?

This decision contrasts sharply with a famous decision years later by the same court, *Boomer* v. *Atlantic Cement Company*, 257 N.E.2d 870 (1970). The air pollution, noise, and vibration from a cement plant created a nuisance for nearby homeowners. The court refused to issue an injunction, instead only awarding damages to the homeowners. The court reasoned that the value of the cement plant was higher than the cost suffered by the homeowners, so no injunction should be issued. Unlike in the *Whalen* case, where no price tag was put on rights and where costs and benefits were not compared, the *Boomer* court compared costs and benefits and made the economically "efficient" decision rather than simply order the nuisance to be stopped. This kind of decision played a large role in the push for federal regulation of pollution.

Federal Environmental Protection

During the 1960s, the environment became a major issue. Books such as Rachel Carson's *Silent Spring*, which discussed problems such as the effects of heavy pesticide use on birds, brought national attention to environmental concerns. Since that time there has been broad political support for federal legislation to enhance environmental quality. Whether the legislation has been effective in reducing pollution or is cost-effective in getting the most protection for the money spent is another issue. While that is beyond the scope of what we study here, when revisions to environmental laws are considered, such issues arise.

Federal control of the environment essentially began in 1970. Before then, pollution laws were on the books, but they meant little in practice. Since 1970, an explosion of federal legislation has affected most aspects of the environment. Exhibit 17.1 lists only a fraction of the environmental statutes on the books now, but those statutes are the ones that have the greatest effects.

To implement and enforce federal environmental mandates, Congress created the EPA in 1970. Today, the EPA is one of the largest federal agencies, with more than 17,000 employees and a budget of about $8 billion. Add to that the state environmental agencies that are required to help enforce the federal laws and state laws that complement the federal requirements. The EPA has primary responsibility for four major external environmental problems: air pollution, water pollution, land pollution, and pollution associated with certain products (see www.epa.gov). The rest of the chapter reviews the key features of the major federal mandates.

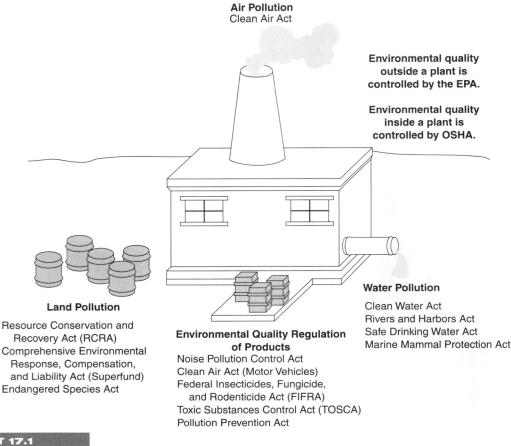

Air Pollution
Clean Air Act

Environmental quality
outside a plant is
controlled by the EPA.

Environmental quality
inside a plant is
controlled by OSHA.

Land Pollution

Resource Conservation and
Recovery Act (RCRA)
Comprehensive Environmental
Response, Compensation,
and Liability Act (Superfund)
Endangered Species Act

**Environmental Quality Regulation
of Products**
Noise Pollution Control Act
Clean Air Act (Motor Vehicles)
Federal Insecticides, Fungicide,
and Rodenticide Act (FIFRA)
Toxic Substances Control Act (TOSCA)
Pollution Prevention Act

Water Pollution

Clean Water Act
Rivers and Harbors Act
Safe Drinking Water Act
Marine Mammal Protection Act

EXHIBIT 17.1

*Federal Regulation
of Environmental
Pollution*

Clean Air Act

The *Clean Air Act of 1970*, which had major amendments in 1977 and 1990, sharply increased federal authority to control pollution. In the words of the Supreme Court, Congress intended to "take a stick to the states" with this law. The Act requires the EPA to set pollution standards and, through forced cooperation of the states, to implement the standards across the country.

NATIONAL AMBIENT AIR QUALITY STANDARDS

The basis of the regulatory program to achieve air quality is the *National Ambient Air Quality Standards* (*NAAQS*). The EPA determines NAAQS for air pollutants that, in its judgment, "arise or contribute to air pollution which may reasonably be anticipated to endanger public health and welfare." The NAAQS set limits for how many of the pollutants are allowed to be found in the air outside (ambient air) as its quality is measured at hundreds of sites around the country. The primary fac-

Pollutant	Characteristics	Sources	Health Effects
Sulfur Dioxide (SO₂)	Colorless gas with pungent odor; oxidizes to form sulfur trioxide, which forms acid rain	Power and industrial plants that burn sulfur-containing fossil fuels; smelting of sulfur-bearing ores	Causes and aggravates respiratory ailments, inducing asthma, chronic bronchitis, emphysema
Particulates (PM)	Any particle dispersed in the atmosphere, such as dust, ash, and various chemicals	Wind erosion; stationary sources that burn solid fuels; agricultural operations	Chest discomfort; throat and eye irritation
Ozone (O₃)	A gas formed from hydrocarbon vapors and nitrogen oxides in sunlight; smog	Mostly from vehicle exhaust, refineries, and chemical plants	Aggravates respiratory ailments; causes eye irritation
Carbon Monoxide (CO)	Colorless, odorless gas	Motor vehicle exhaust and other carbon-containing materials; natural sources	Reduces oxygen-carrying capacity of blood; impairs heart function, visual perception, and alertness
Nitrogen Oxide (NOₓ)	Brownish gas with pungent odor; component in photochemical oxidants	Motor vehicle exhaust; power plants	Aggravates respiratory ailments
Lead (Pb)	Heavy metallic chemical element; often occurs as lead oxide or dust	Nonferrous metal smelters; motor vehicle exhaust	Can cause mental and physical disabilities (lead poisoning)

EXHIBIT 17.2

Major Air Pollutants Subject to NAAQS

tors for a pollutant's NAAQS are the public health effects. Secondary factors are its considerations of public welfare effects (impact on plants, animals, soil, and constructed surfaces). The EPA has national standards for sulfur dioxide, particulates, ozone, carbon monoxide, nitrogen oxide, and lead. Exhibit 17.2 summarizes the principal characteristics, health effects, and sources of those major air pollutants.

STATE IMPLEMENTATION PLANS

Following the EPA's establishment of NAAQS, each state develops a *State Implementation Plan* (*SIP*). The SIPs define the specific control efforts to be implemented in each state to achieve the national standards. In theory, if each emission source in a state met its pollution control requirements as dictated by the SIP, the state's air quality would meet the national standards. The Act requires that regulated emission sources are to meet pollution control requirements as specified by the SIP by a specified date.

The Clean Air Act, like some of the other major pollution statutes, places the primary enforcement burden on the states. The EPA is the oversight agency that sets the limits of what the states may do and sets the minimum regulations they must impose. Whenever the EPA changes air pollution standards, states must revise their SIPs, which are then reviewed by the EPA. If a state does not submit an adequate plan, the EPA writes one for it. All SIPs must include

- Enforceable emission limits
- Schedules and timetables for compliance
- Measures for monitoring air quality and emissions from pollution sources
- Adequate funding, personnel, and authority for implementing and enforcing the SIP

THE PERMIT SYSTEM

The Clean Air Act sets specific procedures for the construction of new industrial plants or major reconstruction of existing facilities. The requirements imposed on plant owners depend on the air quality of the area in which a plant is built. One set of requirements applies if the plant is built in a "clean air area," and another set applies if it is built in a "dirty air area." In either case, the plant owner is required to obtain a preconstruction permit from the EPA or the state agency that enforces the Act.

Clean Air Areas

Areas with clean air—air of better quality than required by the NAAQS—are called *attainment areas* or *prevention of significant deterioration (PSD)* areas. PSD areas include national parks, wilderness areas, and other areas where the air quality is better than the national standards. Because of the sensitive nature of those areas, only a slight increase in pollution is allowed. That slight increase is called the *maximum allowable increase.* Any activity, including the construction or expansion of a plant, that will cause the maximum allowable increase to be exceeded is prohibited in a PSD area.

New construction is allowed in PSD areas if two basic requirements are met. First, the owner must agree to install the *best available control technology (BACT)*—as determined by the EPA—on the new plant to control its pollution. Second, the owner must demonstrate that the pollution from its plant will not cause the maximum allowable increase in the area to be exceeded. The maximum allowable increase in the various forms of air pollution depends upon the classification of an area and the effect a particular pollutant would have on the air there. Some PSD classes, such as wilderness areas, are subject to much stricter controls than are less sensitive PSD areas.

Dirty Air Areas

Dirty air areas are called *nonattainment areas,* signifying that they have not met the NAAQS. Businesses wanting to build in nonattainment areas are required to meet even more restrictive and expensive requirements than those imposed in PSD areas. The *emissions offset policy* imposes three requirements on owners of new or expanded plants:

1. A new plant's pollution must be controlled to the maximum degree possible. The plant must use the *lowest achievable emissions rate (LAER) technology.* LAER is a more stringent (and more expensive) technology than the BACT requirement in PSD areas. Generally, the EPA designates the LAER as the most stringent technology in use by any similar plant in the country.
2. New plant owners must certify that any other plants they have in the area meet SIP requirements. If a business cannot verify compliance, the EPA will not allow the new plant to be built.
3. A new plant can be built in a nonattainment area only if the air pollution from the new plant is *offset* by reductions in the same pollutants from other plants in the area. The offset from other plants must match the air pollution from the new plant more than one for one. That is, when the new plant is operating, the area must enjoy a net air quality improvement.

To illustrate, suppose Polo Automotive decides to build a new plant in Detroit, a nonattainment area for sulfur dioxide. Polo must obtain a preconstruction permit from the EPA. The EPA will require Polo to show that it will apply the LAER technology and that any other plants it owns in the area are in compliance with Michigan's SIP. Polo must also obtain an emissions offset by reducing pollution in other plants by buying them and closing them or by paying for their pollution controls. That is, if Polo's new plant will add ten units of pollution to the air, Polo must reduce pollution elsewhere in the area by more than ten units. When the plant begins operation, air quality in the area should improve.

The Bubble Concept

The EPA has a strategy similar to the emissions offset policy called the *bubble concept*, which treats all emission sources in one company's complex as a single pollution source. A complex, such as an oil refinery, is under an imaginary glass bubble that has one "smokestack" at its top. All emissions from the complex are measured from that smokestack rather than from each smokestack in the complex. The net effect of new construction in the complex—as measured from the smokestack on the bubble—must be a decrease in emissions.

Suppose Bowden Smelting adds a fourth unit to a three-plant complex. Bowden must certify that its plants are in compliance with the SIP. Under the offset policy, Bowden must apply the LAER technology to the new plant and obtain an offset. Under the bubble concept, when Bowden adds the new unit, it may choose any control devices it wants at any of the plants in the complex. The net result must be a decrease in total pollution. How much emissions must be reduced depends on the air quality in the area for various pollutants.

The bubble concept and the offset policy both produce air quality improvement. The bubble concept tends to be less expensive because companies have greater discretion in selecting pollution control devices. Despite its cost savings in achieving emission reductions, the bubble concept was challenged. In *Chevron*, the Supreme Court considered its validity.

Chevron, U.S.A., Inc. v. Natural Resources Defense Council, Inc.

United States Supreme Court
467 U.S. 837, 104 S.Ct. 2778 (1984)

CASE BACKGROUND *To help implement the Clean Air Act, the EPA developed the bubble concept, which allows a company to treat all pollution-emitting devices in one industrial complex as if they were under a bubble with a single smokestack. The owner of the complex can regulate the different pollution sources under the bubble so that the emissions from the single imaginary smokestack meet the net air quality improvement requirements of the law. The EPA allowed Chevron to use the bubble concept to meet its air pollution control requirements at a refinery complex.*

The Natural Resources Defense Council (NRDC) opposed the bubble concept regulations, contending that the Act's treatment of stationary sources requires that each pollution-emitting device be measured separately.

Although the Act does not define "stationary source," the court of appeals agreed with the NRDC and set aside the regulations. Chevron and the EPA appealed to the Supreme Court.

CASE DECISION Stevens, Justice.

* * *

[T]he EPA . . . noted that the [definition of "stationary source"] was not squarely addressed in either the statute or its legislative history and therefore that the issue involved an agency "judgment as how to best carry out the Act." It then set forth several reasons for concluding that the plantwide definition [for the bubble concept] was more appropriate. It pointed out that the [NRDC's interpretation of stationary source] "can act as a disincentive to new investment and modernization by discouraging modifications to existing facilities" and "can actually retard progress in air pollution control by discouraging replacement of older, dirtier processes or pieces of equipment with new, cleaner ones." . . . The agency explained that [the bubble concept] would accomplish the fundamental purposes of achieving attainment with NAAQS's as expeditiously as possible.

* * *

[T]he plantwide definition [used in the bubble concept] is fully consistent with . . . the allowance of reasonable economic growth and [meeting] the environmental objectives as well. Indeed, its reasoning is supported by the public record developed in the rulemaking process, as well as by certain private studies.

When a challenge to an agency construction of a statutory provision, fairly conceptualized, really centers on the wisdom of the agency's policy, rather than whether it is a reasonable choice within a gap left open by Congress, the challenge must fail. In such a case, federal judges . . . have a duty to respect legitimate policy choices. . . .

The judgment of the Court of Appeals is reversed.

QUESTIONS FOR ANALYSIS

1. Why did the Court defer to the expertise of the agency in this matter?
2. If our goals are to obtain a clean environment, should the EPA be able to take costs into account in determining the applicability of a particular technology?

MOBILE SOURCES OF POLLUTION

Since the Clean Air Act was passed, some major air pollutants, such as lead, have nearly disappeared from the atmosphere. Substantial reductions have occurred in particulates and carbon monoxide. But ozone (at lower levels of the atmosphere) has changed little. It is mostly produced by the imperfect burning of petroleum products. Since motor vehicles are the primary source, the law has consistently tightened controls on vehicles. While vehicles produce fewer hydrocarbons that help form ozone than they did when the Clean Air Act was passed, many more miles are driven by more vehicles today, keeping ozone emissions up.

The level of ozone allowed is determined by the NAAQS, but the law also imposes direct controls on certain emissions. Tailpipe exhaust standards for cars, trucks, and buses constantly become tougher. Where ozone pollution is especially bad, which is in most major cities, SIPs impose tougher vehicle emission inspections, vapor recovery systems at gas stations, reformulated gasoline, and alternative fuel sources. Forced carpooling was to have become common in some cities by 1995, but the potential political backlash caused Congress and the EPA to back away from that strategy to reduce ozone emissions.

The law allows states to impose emissions standards that go beyond the federal requirements. California has set tougher auto emissions standards and requirements for cleaner burning gasoline and has forced use of alternative-fuel and electric-powered cars. The regulations are supposed to cut auto pollution 50 percent more than do the federal standards. New York, New Jersey, Pennsylvania, Massachusetts, Virginia, Maryland, Delaware, New Hampshire, Maine, Rhode Island, and Vermont have adopted the California standards, which means that some California standards could become the national standard.

TOXIC POLLUTANTS

As amended in 1990, the Clean Air Act lists 191 substances declared to be hazardous air pollutants. The EPA must set *minimum emission rates (MERs)* for each

Auto Emission Controls in Europe

The European car market, the largest in the world, is working to achieve uniform pollution controls on auto emissions. In contrast to the United States, where automakers have been required to control automobile pollution for over thirty years, Europe does not uniformly regulate auto pollution. Cars sold in countries within the European Union (EU) can legally spew exhaust that contains more hydrocarbon and nitrogen oxide than the United States permits. Germany has pushed hardest for pollution controls, and while lead-free gasoline—*bleifrei*—is available everywhere in Germany, it is available at only certain stations in some parts of Europe.

As a consequence of lax standards and dense population, Europe has a serious air pollution problem. To curb the problem, several European countries outside the EU have imposed emission controls. Automobiles sold in Switzerland, for example, must meet U.S. standards.

After years of talks, the EU is moving toward uniform auto emissions. Germany, Denmark, and the Netherlands support stricter standards. The cost of this (about 15 percent of the sticker price) causes France, Spain, and Italy to support less stringent standards. European officials fear that different standards will force carmakers to produce variations of each model and make European cars less competitive in the United States and Japan.

The stricter pollution standards in Switzerland improved sales for General Motors Europe. While U.S. manufacturers have no competitive advantage in countries that have minimal pollution standards, years of experience in meeting U.S. standards gives them a considerable edge in the countries imposing standards.

pollutant. The general goal is a 90-percent reduction in emissions for the pollutants that had been uncontrolled and a 75-percent reduction in cancer caused by air pollution. If the EPA determines that a pollutant is a threat to public health or the environment, tighter control standards are to be imposed without regard to such economic factors as cost or technological feasibility. Tough standards for many pollutants, such as emissions from dry-cleaning establishments, are gradually being issued by the EPA.

ACID RAIN

The main sources of *acid rain* are sulfur dioxide and nitrous oxides, which mostly come from burning coal or oil to produce electricity. These chemicals become sulfuric and nitric acid, returning to earth in rain or other precipitation. While the extent of the problem caused by acid rain is not established, it is clear that much of it occurs in the northeast, as winds carry acids from electricity plants, mostly in the Midwest and the Appalachian region, especially from those burning soft coal. The 1990 amendments to the Clean Air Act require that about half of the sulfur dioxide and nitrous oxide emissions that were produced in 1990 be eliminated.

ENFORCEMENT

The EPA has primary authority to enforce the Clean Air Act and other environmental statutes, but state environmental agencies also are involved because they carry out a large part of the regulatory mission. Citizens, including environmental groups, have certain rights to bring *citizen suits* to enforce the environmental statutes when government agencies fail to do so. Like most regulations, the environmental statutes list the penalties that may be imposed on violators. Enforcement powers have been greatly expanded in the last decade, and a wide range of remedies is now available. Many are much more costly than normal federal regulatory fines.

In recent years, more environmental offenses have been prosecuted as criminal matters, which has meant more than 100 criminal indictments per year. Business facilities may be banned from receiving any type of federal contract because of environmental crime convictions. The size of fines that can be imposed also has risen. EPA and state environmental agencies collect hundreds of millions of dollars per year.

The amounts collected in environmental fines are growing because enforcement agencies are allowed to sue to recover the costs involved in cleaning contaminated sites and for the damages suffered by the public from environmental damage. When companies settle suits, the bargain often includes a commitment to spend substantial sums on new pollution-control equipment.

Carrot-and-Stick Approach

Enforcement has used a carrot-and-stick approach in the past, and it appears to be heading even further in that direction. The U.S. Sentencing Guidelines punishment for environmental crimes holds that the penalties imposed on a company and its executives should take into account several factors. Punishment would be lessened, in the hundreds of criminal suits brought each year by EPA, for companies that

- Cooperate with the government in investigations
- Voluntarily report illegal actions
- Educate their workforce about environmental standards
- Assist those who suffer from environmental wrongdoing
- Have a strong internal environmental compliance program

Clean Water Act

Federal statutory control over water pollution traces at least as far back as the Rivers and Harbors Act of 1886 and 1899. But like the Federal Water Pollution Control Act of 1948, there was little effective federal control over water pollution. Primary responsibility was left with the states. By 1970, marine life in Lake Erie was almost gone, and many rivers were unfit for drinking water or recreation.

The *Clean Water Act* was passed in 1972 and was substantially amended in 1977 and 1986. The objective of the Clean Water Act is to "restore and maintain the chemical, physical, and biological integrity of the Nation's waters." The Act has five main elements:

1. National *effluent* (pollution) standards set by the EPA for each industry
2. Water quality standards set by the states under EPA approval
3. A *discharge permit* program that translates water quality standards into enforceable pollution limits
4. Special provisions for toxic chemicals and oil spills
5. Construction grants and loans from the federal government for *publicly owned treatment works (POTWs)*

The Act makes it unlawful for any person—defined as an individual, business, or governmental body—to discharge pollutants into navigable waters without a *permit*. Although the Act does not define the phrase "navigable waters," the *Quivira* decision illustrates that it is broadly interpreted.

Quivira Mining Co. v. U.S.E.P.A.
United States Court of Appeals, Tenth Circuit
765 F.2d 126 (1985)

CASE BACKGROUND *Quivira Mining challenged the EPA's authority to regulate the discharge of pollutants from uranium mining facilities into gullies or arroyos. Quivira discharged wastes into Arroyo del Puerto and San Mateo Creek. The company contended that Arroyo del Puerto and San Mateo Creek were not "navigable waters of the United States" because they were dry most of the year and therefore were beyond the EPA's jurisdiction. The EPA denied Quivira's request to review its claims, so Quivira appealed.*

CASE DECISION Saffels, Judge.

* * *

It is the national goal of the Clean Water Act to eliminate the discharge of pollutants into navigable waters. The term "navigable waters" means "the waters of the United States, including the territorial seas." In [an earlier case], this court noted that the Clean Water Act is designed to regulate to the fullest extent possible sources emitting pollution into rivers, streams and lakes. "The touchstone of the regulatory scheme is that those needing to use the waters for waste distribution must seek and obtain a permit to discharge that waste, with the quantity and quality of the discharge regulated."

* * *

In [another case] the court found [a small creek] to be a "water of the United States," although it is not navigable in fact nor does it transport any goods or materials and although it is located entirely in Costilla County, Colorado. Although the [creek] did not provide a very significant link in the chain of interstate commerce, the court found . . . at least some interstate impact from the stream and that was all that was necessary under the act. There, the facts were that the stream supported trout and some beaver, the water

collected in the reservoirs was used for agricultural irrigation, and the resulting products were sold into interstate commerce. The court stated, "It seems clear Congress intended to regulate discharges made into every creek, stream, river or body of water that in any way may affect interstate commerce." . . .

This court's findings in [other cases] compel a finding herein affirming the decision of the EPA. Substantial evidence here supports the Administrator's findings that both the Arroyo del Puerto and San Mateo Creek are waters of the United States. Substantial evidence before the Administrator supports his finding that during times of intense rainfall, there can be a surface connection between the Arroyo del Puerto, San Mateo Creek and navigable-in-fact streams. Further, the record supports the finding that both the Arroyo del Puerto and San Mateo Creek flow for a period after the time of discharge of pollutants into the waters. Further, the flow continues regularly through underground aquifers fed by the surface flow of the San Mateo Creek and Arroyo del Puerto into navigable-in-fact streams. The court finds that the impact on interstate commerce is sufficient to satisfy the commerce clause. . . . it was the clear intent of Congress to regulate waters of the United States to the fullest extent possible under the commerce clause.

The decision of the Administrator is affirmed.

QUESTIONS FOR ANALYSIS

1. How does the definition of navigable waterway differ between what is navigable to a sailor and what is navigable under the Clean Water Act?
2. Should Quivira be subject to regulation in this case? Can you make an argument without referring to the "navigable waters" criterion employed in this case?

As *Quivira* makes clear, Congress has the authority to control water pollution in all forms and places. Getting the job done has been much more expensive and has taken longer than was anticipated when the Clean Water Act was passed in 1972. At that time, Congress said that the discharge of pollutants into any waters would be eliminated by 1985. That was an impossible goal. As it stands, discharges have probably dropped to about half of what they were when the Act was passed.

But since pollutants that are easiest to eliminate have been attacked first, the cost of removing more pollutants will be much higher.

POINT SOURCE POLLUTION

Water pollution easiest to identify comes out of a pipe. We can see it, measure it, and, given technical knowledge, treat the discharge. Control of such *point source* water pollution has been the primary focus of federal law since 1972. Sewage from homes and from some industrial sources (point sources) is often treated at publicly owned treatment works (POTWs). Billions are spent every year to improve existing POTWs (sewage treatment plants) and to put new ones in place in small towns that have minimal systems. Since most of the effluents treated at POTWs are not toxic, the *sludge*—the glop that is removed during sewage treatment—is often used for fertilizer. The treated water is pumped back into rivers or lakes. Exhibit 17.3 illustrates primary water effluent sources.

Under the Clean Water Act, states must designate all surface water as to intended use. If the use is drinking water, treated water dumped into a bay, lake, or river must be quite pure; if the body of water is designated for recreation, the treated water must be clean enough not to contaminate swimmers or fish.

Industrial Permits

Industrial wastewater discharges from production processes are subject to a permit process. The EPA and state environmental agencies, under the *National Pollutant Discharge Elimination System (NPDES)*, require industrial polluters to list the amount and type of their discharges. The polluters are issued permits to release certain pollutants in certain quantities.

EXHIBIT 17.3

Primary Sources of Water Effluents

Control Technology Each firm in an industry must meet the effluent limits set by the EPA for each chemical discharged in its wastewater. The list of controlled sub-

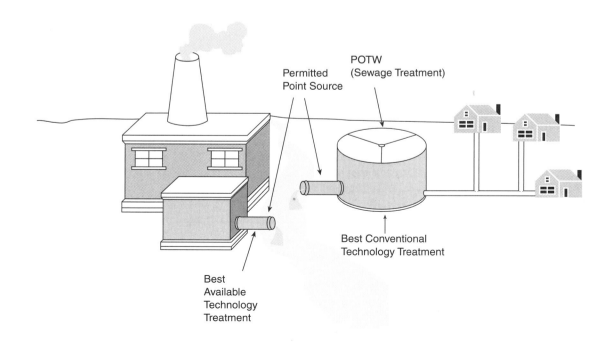

POTW
(Sewage Treatment)

Permitted
Point Source

Best Conventional
Technology Treatment

Best
Available
Technology
Treatment

stances is expanding, and the degree to which the substances must be controlled grows gradually tighter. Conventional pollutants, like human waste, must be controlled by the *best conventional technology (BCT)*. Congress ordered the EPA to consider cost-effectiveness when setting such standards.

Cost considerations are not as important for toxic or unconventional pollutants, which are subject to tighter control, called *best available technology (BAT)*— defined by the EPA as the "very best control and treatment measures that have been or are capable of being achieved." Hence, as better technology is invented to control pollutants, polluters must use it to reduce their pollution. Regardless of the kind of pollutants, if a polluter is located on a particularly sensitive waterway, even more stringent controls may be ordered, including controls that could force a producer to move operations.

When a new plant is built or a new source of pollution is created by a producer, it is subject to even tighter controls—called *new source performance standards (NSPS)*. The law says that the standard is "the greatest degree of effluent reduction . . . achievable through application of the best available demonstrated control technology, processes, operating methods, and other alternatives, including, where practicable, standards permitting no discharge of pollutants." Using BAT controls for the pollution produced is not enough; the entire production process must use the best technology that exists to minimize pollution output in the entire production process.

ENFORCEMENT

Since point source water pollution control is based on a permit system, it is the key to enforcement. Under the NPDES, the states have primary responsibility for enforcing the permit system, subject to EPA monitoring and approval. As the *Arkansas* v. *Oklahoma* decision explains, when there is a conflict about the appropriate pollution standard, the EPA is likely to prevail.

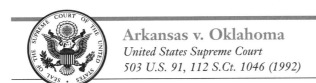

Arkansas v. Oklahoma
United States Supreme Court
503 U.S. 91, 112 S.Ct. 1046 (1992)

CASE BACKGROUND *In compliance with NPDES, Fayetteville, Arkansas, received a permit from the EPA for its sewage treatment plant. The permit authorized the city to discharge certain levels of effluents into waters that flow into the upper Illinois River, which flows into Oklahoma. The State of Oklahoma protested that the water discharged from the plant violated Oklahoma water quality standards for the Illinois River. Under Oklahoma law, no discharges may be made into the river that degrade the river's quality. The EPA reviewed the matter and allowed the Arkansas discharge permit to stand.*

The Court of Appeals reversed the EPA, ruling that the Clean Water Act does not allow a permit to be issued

where a source would discharge effluents that would contribute to conditions that violate water quality standards. Since the Arkansas effluents would contribute to the deterioration of the Illinois River in Oklahoma, the permit would have to be revised to require less pollution to be discharged. Arkansas and the EPA appealed.

CASE DECISION Stevens, Justice.

* * *

The EPA provides States with substantial guidance in the drafting of water quality standards. Moreover, §303 of the [Clean Water] Act requires that state authorities periodically review water quality standards and secure the EPA's approval of any revisions in the standards. If the EPA recommends changes to the standards and the State fails to comply with that recommendation, the Act authorizes the EPA to promulgate water quality standards for the State.

The primary means for enforcing these limitations and standards is the National Pollution Discharge Elimination System (NPDES), enacted in 1972 as a critical part of Congress' "complete rewriting" of federal water pollution law.

* * *

In issuing the Fayetteville permit, the EPA assumed it was obligated by both the Act and its own regulations to ensure that the Fayetteville discharge would not violate Oklahoma's standards.

. . . The Court of Appeals construed the Clean Water Act to prohibit any discharge of effluent that would reach waters already in violation of existing water quality standards. We find nothing in the Act to support this reading. . . .

Although the Act contains several provisions directing compliance with state water quality standards, the parties have pointed to nothing that mandates a complete ban on discharges into a waterway that is in violation of those standards.

The Court of Appeals also concluded that the EPA's issuance of the Fayetteville permit was arbitrary and capricious because the Agency misinterpreted Oklahoma's water quality standards. . . .

In such a situation then, state water quality standards—promulgated by the States with substantial guidance from the EPA and approved by the Agency—are part of the federal law of water pollution control. . . .

Because we recognize that, at least insofar as they affect the issuance of a permit in another State, the Oklahoma standards have a federal character, the EPA's reasonable, consistently held interpretation of those standards is entitled to substantial deference. . . .

In sum, the Court of Appeals made a policy choice that it was not authorized to make. Arguably, as that court suggested, it might be wise to prohibit any discharge into the Illinois River, even if that discharge would have no adverse impact on water quality. But it was surely not arbitrary for the EPA to conclude—given the benefits to the River from the increased flow of relatively clean water and the benefits achieved in Arkansas by allowing the new plant to operate as designed—that allowing the discharge would be even wiser. It is not our role, or that of the Court of Appeals, to decide which policy choice is the better one, for it is clear that Congress has entrusted such decisions to the Environmental Protection Agency.

Accordingly, the judgment of the Court of Appeals is reversed.

QUESTIONS FOR ANALYSIS

1. If Arkansas is polluting Oklahoma waters and the EPA approves, does Oklahoma have any other recourse?
2. Why would the EPA allow one state to pollute the waters of another state?

Operating without a permit or discharging more pollution than is allowed under a permit is a violation of the law. Firms that have pollution permits must monitor their own performance and file *discharge monitoring reports (DMRs)*, available for public inspection. Hence, firms must report violations of the amount they are allowed to pollute under their permits. Lying about violations is more serious than admitting to violations. Serious violations can lead to criminal prosecution. Every year, prison sentences are handed down for violators who dump toxic wastes.

Citizen suits against polluters are quite common under the Clean Water Act, running at least 200 per year. The citizen, which is usually an environmental organization, must notify the EPA and the alleged permit violator of the "intent to sue." If the EPA takes charge of the situation, the citizen suit is blocked. However, if the EPA does not act diligently and the violations continue, the private suit to force enforcement of the law may proceed. If the plaintiff wins a citizen suit, the loser pays for attorneys' fees.

NONPOINT SOURCE POLLUTION

About half of all waterborne pollution is from *nonpoint sources*—construction sites, logging and mining operations, runoff from streets, and runoff from agriculture. Various pollutants are washed by rain into streams and lakes and seep into ground-water. Much of this pollution has only recently come under federal control efforts. The complexity of the problem requires the problem to be approached from various directions.

Because runoff from streets usually occurs during rainstorms, when sewage treatment plants do not have the capacity to treat all runoff water, holding tanks may have to be built, allowing the water to be treated later. The City of Chicago spent $4 billion to dig enormous caverns below the city to contain runoff. Since a lot of runoff pollution is due to air pollution that settles on the ground or is washed from the atmosphere by rain, tighter air pollution rules result in less nonpoint source water pollution.

The consequences of groundwater pollution that comes from agricultural fertilizers and sprays are considered by various agencies under statutes in addition to the Clean Water Act. These include the Safe Drinking Water Act; the Federal Insecticide, Fungicide, and Rodenticide Act; the Toxic Substances Control Act; and other laws that deal one way or another with pollution that shows up in water from nonpoint sources. Although regulations to reduce runoff from construction sites, mining and logging operations, and agriculture have been gradually tightened, runoff pollution remains a problem that is difficult to resolve technologically or politically.

WETLANDS

Until a few years ago, *wetlands* were nuisances to be drained and filled. Wetlands destruction was subsidized by such agencies as the Department of Agriculture and the Army Corps of Engineers. Now that the environmental value of wetlands is better known, there have been moves to protect them. Developers and others are now forced to protect wetlands instead of being encouraged to destroy them. The EPA defines wetlands as

> Those areas that are inundated or saturated by surface or groundwater at a frequency and duration sufficient to support, and that under normal circumstances do support, a prevalence of vegetation typically adapted for life in saturated soil conditions. Wetlands generally include swamps, marshes, bogs, and similar areas.

This definition includes mangrove swamps of coastal saltwater shrubs in the South; prairie potholes in the Dakotas and Minnesota, where shallow depressions that hold water during part of the year are visited by migrating birds; and playa lakes in the Southwest that are rarely flooded basins. Wetlands can be small holes or large areas and may contain one plant or dozens of important species. What is covered by the law is not yet fixed. The EPA asserts that wetlands cover an area in the lower forty-eight states that is larger than the state of California and that over half of the wetlands that existed originally have disappeared.

Permit System

Anyone wanting to change a wetland must receive a permit from the Army Corps of Engineers. The EPA may block an Army Corps permit, under *Section 404* of the

Clean Water Act, to prevent environmental damage. About 10,000 permits are issued each year to allow dredging or filling of wetlands. Another 75,000 permits are issued each year for activities that "cause only minimal adverse environmental effects" to wetlands. Hence, businesses involved in construction or other activities that disturb earth must make sure that wetlands requirements have been met.

Wetlands Takings

The wetlands permit system can result in prohibitions on building or modifying land that was purchased with the expectation that certain uses were allowed. Some landowners have been imprisoned for unknowing wetlands violations, and others have discovered their land to be worthless because they cannot get a permit for the land to be modified. Several cases, such as *Loveladies Harbor* v. *U.S.*, 28 F.3d 1171 (1994), have resulted in decisions that the government must pay for land it forces out of circulation for wetlands protection.

In *Loveladies*, a New Jersey coastal development that had been under construction for thirty years was halted when the Army Corps prohibited any further construction. Fifty acres of wetlands fell from $2.66 million in value to nearly nothing. The Federal Circuit Court of Appeals ordered the government to pay the developer for the land as a taking for public benefit. If such compensation requirements increase, controls on wetlands may be slowed.

Land Pollution

Millions of tons of hazardous waste are disposed of each year. Much of that waste is not destroyed but is stored in drums and deposited in clay-lined dumps, injected deep underground between layers of rock, or merely abandoned in vacant lots, lagoons, and landfills. Some storage methods fail as storage containers corrode and rain washes the wastes from storage sites. Hazardous waste can make its way into lakes, streams, and groundwater.

To reduce the amount of toxic substances that are dumped into the environment and to limit exposure to chemicals that are extremely toxic to people or animals, controls are imposed on the production, distribution, use, and disposal of toxic chemicals. Careless disposal of chemicals in the past means that billions are now being spent to clean up waste sites. As Exhibit 17.4 indicates, managers must be aware of the liability that can arise from use of chemicals today and from ownership of property that may contain toxic wastes.

TOXIC SUBSTANCES CONTROL ACT

More than 70,000 chemicals are in commercial use. Under the *Toxic Substances Control Act (TOSCA)* passed in 1976, the EPA controls and keeps track of chemicals. Because chemicals can cause health hazards, accurate information about their possible effects is vital.

When a producer wants to sell a new chemical, it must notify the EPA, which studies the substance and its proposed uses to determine environmental hazards. The EPA will not reveal trade secret information in new chemical developments. Producers may be required to run tests for toxicity and other effects so that the EPA can determine whether any restrictions should be placed on the chemical. Restrictions may be nothing more than labeling requirements; some chemicals are allowed only in restricted cases; and some are banned.

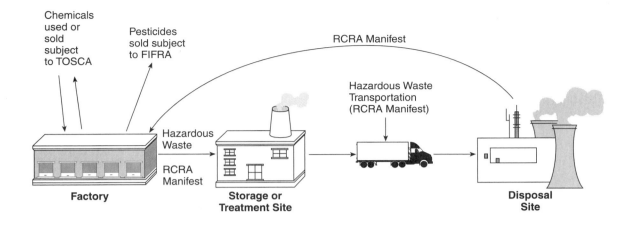

Regulation of Hazardous Substances

Biotechnology—the manipulation of biological processes to produce chemicals or living organisms for commercial use—is subject to TOSCA. Since the results may be eligible for patents, this is a field with valuable products worth tens of billions of dollars. Genetic engineering produces such things as enzymes that can purify water and consume the oil in oil spills. The EPA monitors efforts to use natural organisms in new ways and to use genetically altered microorganisms.

PESTICIDES

Pesticides are used to prevent, kill, or disable pests, including undesirable plants, insects, rodents, fungi, and molds. Most pesticides are toxic, and some are extremely toxic to people and the environment. Congress originally passed the *Federal Insecticide, Fungicide, and Rodenticide Act (FIFRA)* in 1947 and has amended it several times since.

The EPA has registered more than 20,000 products under FIFRA. Registration means that before a pesticide is sold, the EPA has examined scientific data about the product's effects and the label on the product is accurate as to proper usage and precautions. Registration is approved for five years at a time for pesticides that meet these conditions:

1. The product does what the producers claim it will do.
2. The registration materials are accurate, and the label is accurate as to proper usage of the product.
3. The product will do what it is supposed to when used properly without "unreasonable adverse effects on the environment."

FIFRA requires that the economic and environmental costs and benefits of each product be considered. The EPA tries to determine what risk might be posed by a pesticide, such as groundwater contamination or skin irritation, so that it can limit how the product is used and who may use it. Since some products pose a danger to certain species, the EPA may restrict use to locations that minimize exposure for those who could be harmed. Working with the Food and Drug Administration, the EPA sets usage requirements to take into account the residues that remain in food products to ensure that consumers are not exposed to unsafe levels of pesticides.

RESOURCE CONSERVATION AND RECOVERY ACT

TOSCA and FIFRA are primarily concerned with controlling toxic substances before they get to the market. How toxic substances are handled once they are in the market or when they are being disposed of is the concern of the *Resource Conservation and Recovery Act (RCRA)* passed in 1976 and amended in 1984.

"Out of sight, out of mind" was the "procedure" for the disposal of most hazardous wastes before we came to know about the environmental consequences of improper disposal. RCRA requires that the one-half million generators of about 200 million tons of hazardous waste each year comply with an EPA regulatory program—over the transportation, storage, treatment, and disposal of hazardous waste—that reduces dangers to health and the environment.

Hazardous Waste

RCRA requires the EPA to identify and maintain a list of hazardous wastes. The Act defines *hazardous waste* as follows:

> . . . [a] solid waste . . . which because of its quantity, concentration, or physical, chemical, or infectious characteristics may—
> (a) cause, or significantly contribute to an increase in mortality or an increase in serious irreversible, or incapacitating reversible, illness; or,
> (b) pose a substantial present or potential hazard to human health or the environment when improperly treated, stored, transported, or disposed of, or otherwise managed.

Wastes so identified may be stored or disposed of only at sites whose owners or operators have obtained a permit from the EPA. To get the permit, the owners of the *treatment, storage, and disposal (TSD) sites* agree to meet all regulations regarding the handling of hazardous wastes.

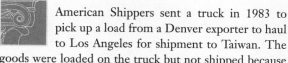

JURIS prudence?

Hot Cargo!

American Shippers sent a truck in 1983 to pick up a load from a Denver exporter to haul to Los Angeles for shipment to Taiwan. The goods were loaded on the truck but not shipped because the export paperwork was not in order and the Taiwanese company could not be located. The Denver exporter went bankrupt.

The trucking company wanted to get rid of its load, which contained radioactive smoke-detector circuit boards. It called the EPA, which said the problem was the responsibility of the Colorado Health Department. The Health Department wanted $40,000 to properly dispose of the load. So the trucking company let the goods sit in a truck until it went bankrupt in 1990.

A couple years later, the new owner of the trucking company looked for help. The Department of Energy took two years to respond to a request for help from the governor of Colorado and said it could do nothing. The Nuclear Regulatory Commission then said that it could not help but suggested that the EPA be contacted.

Source: *Denver Post*

Regulation of TSD Sites

RCRA requires the EPA to regulate TSD sites. Over time, fewer hazardous wastes may be legally disposed of before being treated. A treatment facility is where any method is used to change the physical, chemical, or biological character of any hazardous waste to make it less hazardous, to recover energy or materials from it, or to otherwise process it. A storage facility is where waste is held, such as in storage tanks, until it can be disposed of or treated. A disposal facility is where hazardous wastes are placed into water or land, such as sealed landfills. The EPA and designated state agencies regulate every aspect of TSD operations.

The Manifest System

RCRA forces compliance by generators, transporters, and TSD-site owners by a *manifest system*. The generator of a hazardous waste must complete a *manifest*—a detailed form that states the nature of the hazardous waste and identifies its origin, routing, and final destination. In addition, the generator must assure that the waste is packaged in appropriate and properly labeled containers.

Generators must give transporters of hazardous waste a copy of the manifest. Transporters must sign the manifest and, upon delivery, provide a copy to the owner of the TSD site who must return a copy of the manifest to the generator, thereby closing the circle. If a generator is not informed of the safe deposit of the waste, it is to notify the EPA. This reporting system provides regulatory authorities with the ability to track hazardous waste through its generation, transportation, and disposal phases. That is, the manifest system provides the EPA with cradle-to-grave control over hazardous waste.

SUPERFUND

RCRA helps prevent improper disposal of hazardous wastes today, but improper dumping practices in the past have left many ground and water sites contaminated with toxic waters. Cleaning up these dump sites is costing tens of billions of dollars and taking decades to accomplish. The EPA has evaluated thousands of waste sites and identified 1,327 that need action (as of 1998); these sites are placed on the *National Priority List*, as Exhibit 17.5 shows. The listing process takes about a decade. As Exhibit 17.6 shows, sites on the National Priority List are scattered throughout the country. Over 200 sites have been completed since 1980; most are still in process. Most cleanups involve digging up and removing contaminated soil for treatment, such as burning, and restoration of the land to something like its natural state. This takes an average of ten years.

Congress enacted the *Comprehensive Environmental Response, Compensation, and Liability Act (CERCLA)* in 1980. Called the *Superfund*, the Act provides the president with the authority to clean up abandoned hazardous sites and to provide necessary remedial actions in the case of spills. Congress amended the Superfund program in 1986 with the *Superfund Amendments and Reauthorization Act (SARA)*, which increased federal funding of the hazardous waste cleanup program. SARA imposes a tax on the petroleum and chemical industries. The $1 billion to $2 billion per year in revenues are specifically earmarked for Superfund cleanup efforts and cannot be used by the government for other purposes. However, many private parties are incurring substantial costs. The Congressional Budget office estimated cleanup costs could total $500 billion over eighty years, not counting the cost of cleaning up contaminated federal lands, which could be even more costly.

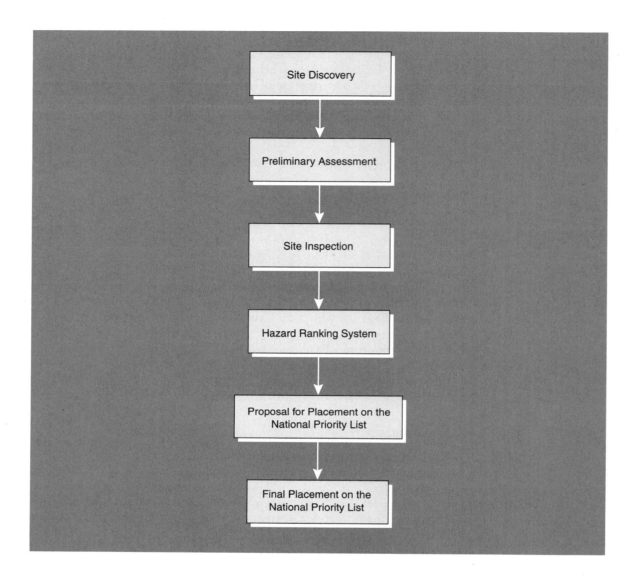

How a Site Gets on the
Superfund National
Priority List

Responsible Parties

An abandoned dump site might contain many hazardous wastes disposed of by
many waste generators. In addition, the dump site may have been operated by different parties over the years. Thus, it may be impossible to determine one *respon-*
sible party. CERCLA defines who can be held liable for both cleanup costs and
damages to natural resources:

1. Current owners of a hazardous waste site
2. Prior owners of a site at the time of hazardous waste disposal
3. Any hazardous waste generator who arranged for disposal at the site
4. Any transporter of hazardous waste who selected the site for disposal

The parties may be held *strictly and jointly and severally liable* for these costs; that is,
each of the parties can be liable for the entire cleanup cost regardless of the size of
its contribution to the hazardous waste at the site.

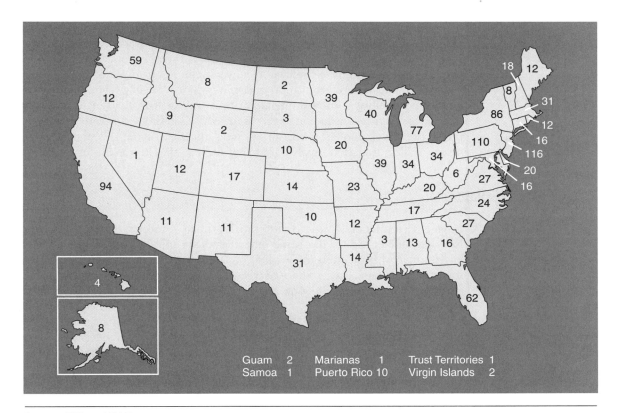

The map shows numbers for each state. Territory figures below:

Guam	2	Marianas	1	Trust Territories	1
Samoa	1	Puerto Rico	10	Virgin Islands	2

Source: EPA and GAO

EXHIBIT 17.6

Hazardous Waste Sites on the Superfund National Priority List (1998)

Practical Problems

The EPA may begin a cleanup if there is a threat to public health or the environment if cleanup is delayed. Later, the government can try to recover expenses by suing responsible parties if the parties can be located. More commonly, the EPA can order private parties to pay to clean up the site under EPA supervision. This generates a lot of expensive litigation. A study by the Rand Institute for Civil Justice found that of the $1.3 billion spent on Superfund claims in the late 1980s, 80 percent of the money went for legal bills. Later studies have shown that most Superfund money goes to legal background and engineering studies, not actual cleanup.

A problem that now exists when purchasing property is whether the property contains toxic wastes that may have been buried years ago or, when buying a business, whether the business was involved in handling toxic materials. In such cases, the new owner may be held responsible for cleanup costs. Some new owners have been handed cleanup bills for far more than the property is worth, even though the new owners were not responsible for the waste. If they cannot find other responsible parties capable of paying the bill, the new owners are stuck. As a result, many firms have an *environmental audit* performed for property they intend to purchase.

Because of the nearly unlimited liability for unknown cleanup costs, useful property sits abandoned. The Cleveland *Plain Dealer* built a new production plant for the newspaper. It built in the suburbs when the abandoned urban site it had chosen was found to have chemical residues in the soil from years before. Such old abandoned sites are referred to as *brownfields*. Since the newspaper could not risk Superfund liability, it moved outside of town rather than help restore downtown Cleveland. Congress is looking at ways to reduce liability to encourage abandoned property to be developed so that urban areas might be revitalized, and to lessen the nearly endless litigation involved in many sites, so that more cleanups get done.

Species Protection

Most environmental laws are written with primary concern for the effect of pollutants on human health. But some federal laws specifically address the problem of environmental protection for wildlife or, more broadly, for all species. The most important of these laws is the *Endangered Species Act (ESA)*, enacted in 1973 and amended several times. In some respects, the ESA is the toughest environmental statute of all.

The Act recognizes the value of habitat and the need to manage on an ecosystem scale. It authorizes designation of critical habitat—areas needed to preserve endangered species—and calls for preparation of recovery plans for listed species. The Department of the Interior has estimated that a recovery program for the 1,400 recognized threatened and endangered species would cost about $5 billion, but funding from the federal government is only a few million dollars per year.

HABITAT PROTECTION

The ESA authorizes the Secretary of the Interior to declare species of animal or plant life "endangered" and to establish the "critical habitat" of such species. An *endangered species* is defined by the ESA as "any species which is in danger of extinction throughout all or a significant portion of its range. . . ." When a species is listed as endangered, the Act imposes obligations on both private and public parties. Under the ESA, no person may "take, import, or conduct commercial activity with respect to any endangered species." In most disputes involving an endangered species, both parties will generally agree that the species is deserving of protection; the conflict usually centers on the degree of protection to be afforded.

Since little federal money is available to accomplish the goals of the ESA, the Act's primary use is to block or alter development when an endangered species is present. This first came to attention in the 1978 Supreme Court decision *Tennessee Valley Authority* v. *Hill*, 437 U.S. 153. The Court prohibited completion of the Tellico Dam on the Little Tennessee River. Even though the federal government had spent $100 million on the dam, the Court ordered work on the dam stopped because the dam would destroy the habitat of a tiny fish, the snail darter. The Act says that no project may "result in the destruction or modification of habitat of such [endangered] species."

The northern spotted owl, which is on the threatened species list, has brought the most attention to the ESA. In 1991, a federal court ordered logging stopped on most federal lands in Washington, Oregon, and Northern California until the Forest Service could devise a plan to protect the forest habitat of the northern spotted owl. The cost of the logging ban has been estimated to be as much as $20 billion. There were conflicting cases regarding the extent of the application of the ESA to species of animals on private land. The Supreme Court addressed that issue in the *Sweet Home* decision.

Babbitt v. Sweet Home Chapter of Communities for a Great Oregon
United States Supreme Court
515 U.S. 2407, 115 S.Ct. 2407 (1995)

CASE BACKGROUND *Private landowners, logging companies, and families dependent on forest products for a living sued the Secretary of the Interior and the Fish and Wildlife Service (FWS). They challenged the Secretary's definition of the word "harm" in regulations issued to enforce the protection of species protected by the Endangered Species Act (ESA).*

> *"Harm . . . means an act which actually kills or injures wildlife. Such act may include significant habitat modification or degradation where it actually kills or injures the wildlife by significantly impairing essential behavioral patterns, including breeding, feeding, or sheltering."*

Under this regulation, the FWS controls interference with the habitat of the northern spotted owl (a threatened species) in the Pacific Northwest and of the red-cockaded woodpecker (an endangered species) in the Southeast. The plaintiffs contended that the "harm" regulation went beyond what Congress intended in the ESA and injured them economically by limiting their right to log timber. The court of appeals agreed, holding that the statute did not intend to give such broad meaning to the word "harm." The Secretary and FWS appealed.

CASE DECISION Stevens, Justice.

* * *

[W]e assume respondents have no desire to harm either the red-cockaded woodpecker or the spotted owl; they merely wish to continue logging activities that would be entirely proper if not prohibited by the ESA. On the other hand, we must assume arguendo that those activities will have the effect, even though unintended, of detrimentally changing the natural habitat of both listed species or that, as a consequence, members of those species will be killed or injured. . . . The Secretary . . . submits that the . . . prohibition on takings, which Congress defined to include "harm," places on respondents a duty to avoid harm that habitat alteration will cause the birds unless respondents first obtain a permit. . . .

The text of the Act provides three reasons for concluding that the Secretary's interpretation is reasonable. First, an ordinary understanding of the word "harm" supports it. . . .

Second, the broad purpose of the ESA supports the Secretary's decision to extend protection against activities that cause the precise harms Congress enacted the statute to avoid. . . .

Third, the fact that Congress in 1982 authorized the Secretary to issue permits for takings that [the ESA] would otherwise prohibit, "if such taking is incidental to, and not the purpose of, the carrying out of an otherwise lawful activity," strongly suggests that Congress understood [the ESA] to prohibit indirect as well as deliberate takings. The permit process requires the applicant to prepare a "conservation plan" that specifies how he intends to "minimize and mitigate" the "impact" of his activity on endangered and threatened species, making clear that Congress had in mind foreseeable rather than merely accidental effects on listed species.

* * *

When it enacted the ESA, Congress delegated broad administrative and interpretive power to the Secretary. . . . When Congress has entrusted the Secretary with broad discretion, we are especially reluctant to substitute our views of wise policy for his, . . . the Secretary reasonably construed the intent of Congress when he defined "harm" to include "significant habitat modification or degradation that actually kills or injures wildlife."

* * *

The judgment of the Court of Appeals is reversed.

QUESTIONS FOR ANALYSIS

1. If the habitat of a bird is modified because it must move its nest from one tree to another, can that be considered "significant habitat modification" that "injures wildlife"?

2. The plaintiffs argued that the ESA provided the Secretary with the authority to buy habitat for endangered species and that that should be required rather than force private lands to be taken out of production, thereby imposing the cost on the landowner rather than on taxpayers. Is that a legitimate alternative?

Controversy and Uncertainty

Endangered species protection joins wetlands in being one of the most controversial environmental issues in recent years. There is no clear legal definition of species or habitat, nor is it clear when something should be declared endangered. The legal requirements for adding a species to the list are minimal. Because listing a species can lead to very tight controls on private property use, landowners fear having their land removed from any use other than uncompensated habitat protection. In response, in 1995, Congress essentially froze ESA listings while pondering alternatives. Of all species listed, habitats have been defined for only about 10 percent. Although hundreds of species are endangered, the Fish and Wildlife Service (www.fws.gov) devotes most of its resources to protecting the most "popular" species, such as the bald eagle, the manatee, and the grizzly bear. Creatures like the Alabama cave fish and the red hills salamander are largely ignored. When resources are limited, how does one decide which species are most deserving of protection?

Global Environmental Issues

Some of the biggest environmental issues—the ozone layer, global climate change, habitat destruction, and the marine environment—must be dealt with on an international scale. Even if the United States did not contribute to global environmental problems, the consequences would still be borne here, so the United States must work with other countries to decide what to do about such issues. The ozone issue provides a good example of an international legal solution to a potentially serious environmental problem.

THE OZONE

While too much ozone (O_3) in the air we breathe is a problem caused largely by vehicle exhaust, ozone depletion at high levels in the atmosphere is caused by chemicals called chlorofluorocarbons (CFCs), known popularly by such brands as Freon. CFCs were widely used as refrigerants in air-conditioning systems, in making computer chips, and in some plastics products. In the stratosphere, CFCs are presumed to eat away at the ozone layer, which protects life on earth from ultraviolet radiation. The effect on humans would be an increase in skin cancer, more cataracts, and suppression of the immune system.

Evidence of a "hole" in the ozone layer over Antarctica by 1985 convinced industry and the government that CFCs could pose a serious problem. Since there were estimates that the ozone loss could cause tens of thousands of additional deaths per year from skin cancers, the possibility of tort liability existed. In the United States, the makers of CFCs—DuPont, Allied Chemical, Pennwalt, Kaiser,

JURIS prudence?

From the People Who Produced Chernobyl . . .

Oleg Khabarov, a Russian scientist and member of the Russian Academy for Life Sustenance Problems, proposed to the Russian parliament, the Duma, that thirty to fifty satellites should be put in orbit to bombard the atmosphere with lasers. The effect would be, Khabarov claimed, to restore the upper atmosphere's ozone.

The Russian parliament was interested because Russia is in violation of the Montreal Protocol. The country needs to spend huge sums to comply with the Protocol and claims it cannot afford the measures called for by the Protocol. Of course, Khabarov's program, which he estimates would cost $100 billion, would cost a tad more.

Source: *International Industrial Information Ltd.*

and Racon—which produced one-third of the world supply, agreed with the EPA that CFC production had to be eliminated.

The producers agreed to support the *Montreal Protocol* of 1987, which the United States signed. Under the protocol, an international treaty, most nations that produce CFCs agreed to cut production by 50 percent by 1998. The protocol was revised by the London treaty of 1990, requiring CFCs and halon (the best fire-fighting chemical) production to be eliminated by 2000.

A solution was achieved that resulted in producers giving up a multibillion-dollar-per-year market. Producers' cooperation was hastened by the promise from the government that the existing producers would have a monopoly over the product during its remaining years. The total cost to the world's economy of the CFC phaseout is estimated to be $200 billion.

INTERNATIONAL COOPERATION

CFC production was largely in the United States, Japan, and European nations, countries that could essentially force the decision on this issue. However, other international environmental issues require more cooperation from less-developed nations, since those nations will bear more of the effects of changes in policies that would eliminate environmental problems.

The Montreal Protocol provided a fund, set up by wealthier nations, to pay poorer nations to sign the agreement to ban CFCs. That is, the United States bought environmental cooperation from other nations. Similarly, the United States helps to pay the cost of water treatment plants in Mexico located near the U.S. border to reduce pollution of the Rio Grande and the Pacific Ocean.

As we have seen in this chapter, the environmental challenge is large in the United States. Most of the rest of the world is in far worse condition and does not have the resources necessary to deal with the problem. The German government had to spend perhaps $100 billion to begin to bring the environment of former East Germany up to the standards expected in West Germany. Yet East Germany was the wealthiest communist nation, with a population of only twenty million. The cost of environmental cleanup in the former communist nations and in the third world is staggering, and its resolution is unclear.

Take Back Your Trash

 Since the early 1990s, Germany has phased in a packaging law that forces manufacturers to be responsible for product packing. It is also one of several countries requiring producers to take back certain products when consumers are finished with them. Environmental officials from other countries are watching these programs to see how they work.

German manufacturers or importers who use packing materials such as drums, crates, foam containers, boxes, and shrink wrap must take back the materials and may not dispose of them in the public waste disposal system. Retailers must take back packaging materials such as cartons, blister packs, and antitheft devices placed on compact discs and other products. Retailers must either remove these materials at the store or allow consumers to return them. Finally, retailers must accept sales packaging used to transport and protect products up to the time of use, such as sacks, wrappers, bottles, and cartons. Retailers give the materials back to the manufacturer, importer, or distributor. The materials must be reused or recycled outside of the public disposal system.

Having watched the German experiment, the European Union is devising rules that would apply to most of Europe. Germany has considered forcing manufacturers of electronic equipment to take back their products for recycling or disposal when consumers are finished with them. Automobile take-backs are under consideration, too. Japanese and U.S. firms are concerned that rules requiring manufacturers to take back their products for recycling could make it more difficult for them to compete in the European market.

There is little doubt that if the United States and other nations are concerned about species preservation and other environmental issues, they must pay less-developed nations to protect species and to cover the costs of some pollution controls.

GLOBAL WARMING

Greenhouse gases that many scientists link to global warming are the basis of the current major environmental issue. A treaty drafted in Kyoto, Japan, in 1997 contains assertions by most developed nations that they will take steps to substantially reduce gas (such as carbon dioxide) emissions by 2008–2012. The Clinton administration signed the treaty in 1998 but did not submit it to Congress for ratification because it would not pass. Hence, the treaty is not law in the Untied States. A meeting in Buenos Aires in 1998 of 160 nations reaffirmed the international commitment to greenhouse gas reduction, but, as yet, has generated minor substantive domestic changes as politicians around the world try to determine how to make such a high-cost policy politically acceptable.

Pollution Prevention

Most environmental legislation has been concerned with cleaning up pollution and setting limits on how much pollution can be dumped into the air, water, and land. The *Pollution Prevention Act* of 1990 provides a framework for thinking about the environment as we plan for the future. It focuses on waste management and says that priority should be given to reducing sources of pollution.

The Act emphasizes the reduction of industrial hazardous wastes and encourages making changes in equipment and technology; redesigning products to minimize environmental damages that arise from the production process and the consequences of the product; substituting raw materials; and improving maintenance, training, and inventory control. The EPA is required to address industrial pollution prevention by the following measures:

- Identify measurable goals.
- Improve measurement, data collection, and access to data.
- Assess existing and proposed programs and identify barriers.
- Offer grants to states for technical assistance programs.
- Require companies to disclose amounts of toxic chemicals they release.
- Use federal procurement to encourage source reduction.

Businesses can integrate pollution prevention into all aspects of operations. Companies make environmental management a part of routine goals when they encourage a companywide commitment to managing pollution control rather than just responding to specific rules on a case-by-case basis.

Summary

- Before passage of federal environmental laws, environmental protection relied on common-law remedies, including private and public nuisance actions, trespass, negligence, strict liability for hazardous activities, and riparian water rights. Actions could result in a verdict for damages or an injunction ordering the offender to cease damaging activities. The EPA is now the key regulator of the environment. It works with environmental agencies in all states to enforce federal requirements.
- The Clean Air Act sets air quality standards for several major pollutants: sulfur dioxide, particulates, ozone, carbon monoxide, nitrogen oxide, and lead. These standards are constantly tightened. New polluters must use the best pollution control technology available. In some areas, if a business is to produce any new air pollution, it must buy pollution rights from existing polluters, who either are paid to quit polluting or install better pollution control equipment.
- The Clean Water Act focuses on point source pollution, which comes out of pipes from factories or sewer systems. Point sources must have permits that allow them to discharge certain amounts of pollution into water bodies. States must declare what standards according to the use—drinking versus swimming quality—all bodies of water in the state will meet. Nonpoint source pollution—runoff from farms, streets, construction sites, mining, and logging—is just beginning to be addressed.
- Wetlands are lands saturated with water at least part of the year. Prior to building on or disturbing a wetland, a permit from the Army Corps of Engineers must be obtained. The EPA has final say on wetlands use.
- The Toxic Substances Control Act and the Federal Insecticide, Fungicide, and Rodenticide Act require EPA review and approval of toxic substances before they are sold. The EPA may restrict product usage and keep track of evidence of harm from such products.
- The Resource Conservation and Recovery Act requires comprehensive paperwork (manifests) to follow the production, distribution, and disposal of

hazardous substances. Hazardous waste treatment, storage, and disposal facilities are subject to strict licensing and regulatory control.

- The Superfund program provides federal support to clean up abandoned hazardous waste sites. Any parties who contribute to the disposal of the wastes, even if legal at the time, may be held liable for part or all of the cleanup costs. Land purchasers should consider an environmental audit to check for possibilities of hazardous wastes, wetlands, or endangered species.

- The Endangered Species Act can block any economic activity, without compromise, if the activity can harm the habitat of an endangered species. Compromises that demonstrate habitat protection may allow a project to go forward as approved by the Fish and Wildlife Service.

- Some environmental controls are imposed by international agreements. The Montreal Protocol requires the production of chlorofluorocarbons (CFCs) and halon—chemicals used in refrigeration systems, plastics production, and firefighting chemicals—to be eliminated. Protection of biological diversity and reduction of greenhouse gases are other international issues that will require the United States and other advanced nations to pay for environmental protection in poor nations.

- The Pollution Prevention Act of 1990 encourages businesses and government agencies to think about environmental issues in all phases of operations. Integration of environmental concerns into regular managerial controls is becoming a necessity.

Issue

Is Species Preservation in Poor Countries Possible?

The Endangered Species Act means that, in some cases, huge sums are dedicated to habitat preservation for individual species in the United States. But, in most nations, there is no such law, and, even if there were, economic conditions do not favor preservation. The sudden collapse of the economy in Indonesia indicates how fragile environmental assets can be.

TASTE OF DEATH: DESPERATE INDONESIANS DEVOUR COUNTRY'S TROVE OF ENDANGERED SPECIES

Peter Waldman

Waldman is a Staff Reporter. Reprinted by permission of *The Wall Street Journal* © 1998 Dow Jones & Company, Inc. All rights reserved worldwide.

BITUNG, Indonesia—The Indonesian crisis is jumping species. It's well known that people are hungry, hurting and scared. Now, down the food chain, elephants, monkeys, and other wildlife are dying.

Along the docks of this remote port 1,500 miles northeast of Jakarta, Taiwanese fishermen feast on fruit-bat curry, fried forest rat and barbecued snake. For the foreigners on shore leave, the exotic delicacies are a steal in Indonesian currency. Takeout orders sail up by dinghy: One captain of a big tuna trawler orders a dozen young crested black macaques—an endangered species of primate—delivered to his boat, alive.

The request is relayed over palm-studded hills to the village of Bingaguminan, on the edge of Tangkoko Nature Reserve. Trappers there trek days in the jungle refuge to bag the rare animals. To take baby macaques alive, mothers are shot.

Aboard the trawler, galley hands bind the monkeys' hands and feet. Then, using sharp bamboo sticks, the Taiwanese puncture the babies' soft skulls. As the convulsions ebb, brains are served raw.

"Prices have tripled for monkey, but foreigners can't get enough," says a dock-side chef here who deals in the legally protected macaques. "Koreans ask for snake and monkey stew. Taiwanese like brains."

Foreigners aren't the only monkey eaters in this majority-Christian province called North Sulawesi, where the playful macaques have been hunted nearly to extinction for local palates as well. But throughout Indonesia, the unsustainable is becoming the unfathomable: Nature is being pillaged, as a nation hit by economic calamity falls back on land and sea to survive.

"We're about to lose a lot more species, no doubt about it," says Tony Sumampau, a leading Indonesian conservationist. "It's worse than losing money; animals we can't get back."

Indonesia's economic crisis is breeding an ecological one. Even in good times, this huge archipelago, ever-pressed to feed its 200 million people—the world's fourth-largest population—paid little mind to environmental protection. But there was progress in recent years, environmentalists say, as a growing middle class learned about Indonesia's wondrous biodiversity and took steps to save it.

"Now, it's back to every species for itself," says Emil Salim, a former Indonesian environment minister.

Unique ecosystems are under threat. Indonesia is home to more plant and animal species than any country in the world, except Brazil. But what matters most to conservationists is the extraordinary number of these species that are endemic to Indonesia, meaning that they live nowhere else. Of Indonesia's 515 mammal species, 36% are endemic. Of its 1,519 bird species, 28% are endemic. Some scientists say the threat to Indonesia's biodiversity is a threat to the globe's as well.

"The destruction of Indonesia's ecosystems is a biological tragedy without parallel in human history," says Timothy Jessup, a scientist with the World Wide Fund for Nature in Jakarta. "In terms of species extinction, nothing on this scale has happened since an asteroid impact wiped out the dinosaurs 60 million years ago."

Though some Indonesian forests are getting a reprieve from weaker timber demand in Asian markets, many others are coming down. In many places, hungry Indonesians are overrunning government-protected forests, decimating the wildlife, clear-cutting ancient hardwoods and other native plants, and replanting rain forests with ecologically damaging food and cash crops. Long term, government reforms in Jakarta, particularly

efforts to root out corruption, are critical to better resource management. For now, however, chaos rules.

* * *

At sea, fishermen are ravaging coral reefs that encircle Indonesia's 17,000 islands—the richest marine resource in the world, scientists say. Dynamite fishing is becoming rampant, a practice that destroys whole coral colonies to yield nets full of fish. Also on the rise is the use of cyanide by divers to capture groupers and other big reef fish for the live-fish trade. One squirt stuns the larger fish, who wind up in display tanks in restaurants in Hong Kong and Singapore. But the toxin wipes out smaller fish and coral in its wake.

"This is a crisis for coral reefs like never before," says Australian marine biologist John Veron, who, on a recent diving expedition in Indonesia, recorded dynamite blasts every 15 to 30 minutes. "I mostly saw reefs that were trashed beyond hope of recovery."

* * *

The depletion of North Sulawesi's forests is particularly alarming to biologists because of the area's extraordinary range of unique species, even for Indonesia. Of this region's 127 mammal species, 62% live nowhere else. Take out 47 bat species, and the mammal rate soars to an unheard-of 98%.

* * *

But as the rain forest comes crashing down, so do incomes. Since the crisis began, the poverty rate among Temboan's 235 families has tripled, to 65%. Fanci Batas, 25, used to work three days a week in his small garden to feed his wife and child. Now he works double time, felling trees in the nature reserve, but comes up short. After renting a chain saw and a cow, he clears a tiny profit logging the low-grade trees available near town.

In Sumatra, troops based at a huge Suharto-family shrimp farm still hunt in neighboring Way Kambas National Park, according to rangers who say they have been fired on by the soldiers. Way Kambas is home to significant populations of elephants, tigers and rhinos, generally well-guarded by an internationally funded protection program. But for the first time in years, poachers, eyeing the lucrative Chinese-medicine market, recently killed three of the park's 37 known tigers. A local police chief was arrested, with a tiger slaughtering house in his backyard. But after being held the maximum 21 days without charges, he was released.

1. Would an Endangered Species Act in Indonesia make any difference?

2. What can wealthy Western nations do to assist with species preservation?

3. What difference does lack of private ownership of forest lands make?

REVIEW AND DISCUSSION QUESTIONS

1. Define the following terms:

riparian rights	nonpoint source pollution
national ambient air quality standards	manifest system
prevention of significant deterioration area	wetlands
bubble concept	citizen suit
acid rain	Superfund
point source pollution	endangered species

2. Were common-law actions—such as nuisance, trespass, and strict liability—against pollution too weak? That is, was federal statutory intervention needed to prevent serious environmental damage?

3. Under the Endangered Species Act, what happens if an endangered animal eats an endangered plant?

CASE QUESTIONS

4. A land developer started a retirement village in an area known for its large cattle feedlots. Later, after much of the village is built and sold, the developer brings an environmental nuisance action against the largest feedlot owner in the area. The developer claims that the feedlot is polluting the air with terrible odors, causing discomfort to the residents of the village, and reducing the sale value of the remaining lots. What factors will the court consider in determining whether the feedlot is a nuisance? Assume the court finds the feedlot to be a nuisance. What should be the remedy? Could the feedlot be a nuisance in one location and entirely acceptable in another? [*Spur Industries v. Del Webb Development Co.*, 108 Ariz. 178, 494 P.2d 700 (Sup. Ct., Ariz., 1972)]

 5. For ten years, a company dumped millions of gallons of chemical wastes on its property in Tennessee. The state shut down the site. Residents around the property sued the company, claiming that their drinking water was contaminated. What basis for suit did they have, and could they win? [*Sterling* v. *Velsicol Chemical Corp.*, 647 F. Supp. 303 (W.D. Tenn., 1986)]

6. The EPA set emission standards for vinyl chloride, a toxic substance that is carcinogenic to humans. The Clean Air Act says such standards must be "at the level which . . . provides an ample margin of safety to protect the public health." The exact threat from vinyl chloride was not known. The EPA said that the proper emissions requirement is the lowest level attainable by best available control technology. The Natural Resources Defense Council sued, contending that since there was uncertainty about the danger, the EPA had to prohibit all emissions. Which position was held correct? [*NRDC* v. *EPA*, 824 F.2d 1146 (D.C. Cir., 1987)]

7. As required by the Clean Water Act, the EPA issued standards for discharges from hundreds of sources. Despite the standards, the EPA issues on a case-by-case basis variances to some water polluters, allowing them to exceed the discharge standards. The Natural Resource Defense Council sued to oppose such variances; the Chemical Manufacturers Association defended the variances. Who won? [*Chemical Manufacturers Assn.* v. *NRDC*, 470 U.S. 116, 105 S.Ct. 1102 (1985)]

8. The Sierra Club filed a citizen suit under the Clean Water Act against an oil company. The club asked the court to penalize the company and issue an injunction against further violations of the CWA by discharging waste into the water without a permit issued under the National Pollution Discharge Elimination System. The company responded that the EPA had not yet established effluent limitations for the waste it was discharging. Was the Sierra Club suit valid? [*Sierra Club* v. *Cedar Point Oil Co.*, 73 F.3d 546 (5th Cir., 1996)]

9. Leslie Salt Company owned a piece of land near San Francisco Bay that it used for making salt. The land is dry except during part of the winter and spring, when rain creates temporary ponds that migratory birds use. The "ponds" are not natural; they are created by the salt-making operation. The Army Corps of Engineers fined Leslie for dumping fill dirt on some of its land without a permit. Leslie contended that the land was not subject to Army Corps control as a wetland because it was not "navigable waters." Could the Army Corps control the use of the land? [*Leslie Salt Co.* v. *U.S.*, 55 F.3d 1388 (9th Cir., 1995)]

10. James City County, Virginia, planned to build a dam and reservoir across a creek in the county to improve the local water supply. The Army Corps of Engineers granted the building permit, but the EPA rejected it. The county appealed to federal district court, claiming that the project was the most practical method for improving water for county residents. The court ordered the building permit to be issued. The EPA said that it could reject the permit solely on environmental grounds; it did not have to consider the community's need for water. What did the court of appeals say? [*James City County, Virginia,* v. *EPA*, 12 F.3d 1330 (4th Cir., 1993)]

11. The Army Corps of Engineers noticed that Child filled about 4/100 of an acre in a 400-acre parcel he owned in Kane County, Utah. The Corps told Child to remove the fill dirt or face prosecution for violation of the wetlands provisions of the Clean Water Act. The Corps said that because the land is a wetlands, it is in the "waters of the United States" and is therefore subject to Corps jurisdiction. Child removed the fill but sued, claiming that the Corps did not have jurisdiction over such an isolated bit of land. Was the Corps upheld? [*Child* v. *U.S.*, 851 F.Supp. 1527 (D. Utah, 1994)]

12. Congress gave the EPA the power in RCRA to regulate "solid wastes." The EPA declared that this includes materials that are being recycled. This was challenged as incorrect, that Congress meant the regulation of materials being discarded or disposed of, not materials being reused. Which position is correct? [*American Mining Congress* v. *EPA*, 824 F.2d 1177 (D.C. Cir., 1987)]

13. The city of Chicago dumped ash from a solid waste incinerator in a waste disposal facility that did not meet RCRA standards for treatment and disposal of hazardous waste. The EPA approved Chicago's action, but an environmental group objected that failure to meet RCRA standards violated the statute. Could EPA

exempt Chicago from RCRA? [*Chicago* v. *Environmental Defense Fund*, 114 S.Ct. 1588 (1994)]

14. A South Carolina company ran a hazardous waste disposal and recycling operation. Several companies sent their hazardous wastes to the site. The facility was improperly managed: waste was dumped on the ground, chemicals were mixed, and records were not kept about what was there. The EPA cleaned up the site under Superfund and sued the companies that sent their waste to the site (since the owners of the site could not pay the bill). The companies responded that they were not liable under CERCLA because there was no evidence that the particular waste they sent had been improperly disposed of. Were they right? [*U.S.* v. *S.C. Recycling and Disposal*, 653 F.Supp. 984 (Dist. S.C., 1984)]

15. Georgoulis was sole shareholder and president of TICI, which owned White Farm Equipment (WFE) from 1980 to 1985. During those years, WFE dumped its hazardous waste in a dump in Iowa owned by another company. The EPA declared the dump to be a Superfund site. It claimed Georgoulis was a responsible party and should have to contribute personally to the cleanup costs. The court found that Georgoulis did not "have any personal knowledge of the disposal practices at the dumpsite, or was in any way directly involved in waste disposal matters. However . . . Georgoulis had authority to control, and did in fact exert direct control over many significant aspects of the ongoing operations and management of WFE." Could Georgoulis be liable? [*U.S.* v. *TIC Investment Corp.*, 68 F.3d 1082 (8th Cir., 1995)]

16. Rankin contracted to buy some land in Hammond, Indiana, from SCM Corporation for $500,000. SCM delivered good title but gave no warranty as to the quality of the land. Rankin discovered hazardous waste on the land which could lead to a costly cleanup. Could Rankin rely on CERCLA to get out of the contract to buy? [*HM Holdings* v. *Rankin*, 70 F.3d 933 (7th Cir., 1995)]

POLICY QUESTIONS

17. Should pollution control requirements be more or less stringent on pollutants thought to be hazardous but for which little scientific knowledge exists about their actual health effects? Or should the requirements be set according to the existing level of knowledge and then be increased as knowledge of the pollutant's health effects becomes available?

18. Consider the following statement: "Like other environmental laws, the Toxic Substances Control Act's requirements are too strict. They will drive small firms out of business." Should the EPA consider the impacts on small companies when they implement the environmental laws? What if environmental laws cause severe unemployment?

ETHICS QUESTIONS

19. You are an executive with a leading manufacturing company, and one aspect of your business pollutes heavily. You know that you can build a plant in a third world country to handle that aspect without pollution control. This would mean that for the same amount of production, you would add ten times as much pollution to the world's environment as you do now, but it would be more profitable for the company. Can you legally move the plant? Should you?

20. A chemical company is owned by a family that is concerned about the impact of pollution. Recently the family has become concerned about the company's hazardous waste disposal site. Investigators have determined that the site is located over the town's underground water supply. Fortunately, they also determined that the site poses no current threat to the water supply. To be safe, the family would like to move the site. However, because the move would be very expensive, they would like to share the cost with the town's residents. Should this expense be shared by the community?

CHAPTER 18

Consumer Protection

People suffering from AIDS and other deadly diseases are willing to try new drugs before the drugs are fully tested because they see no advantage in waiting. However, the Food and Drug Administration and drug manufacturers engage in years of tests on animals and limited tests on humans before marketing drugs so that the public is protected from defective drugs and manufacturers can possibly avoid expensive liability suits for selling drugs with undesirable side effects.

Abbott Laboratories was working on a drug (HIVIG) for HIV-infected people. The National Institutes of Health and various private groups wanted Abbott to begin tests on people in 1992. Abbott was concerned that the drug could increase the risk that a baby born to a parent who used the drug would be more likely to become AIDS-infected. Abbott refused to go ahead with human tests unless it was granted immunity from liability for side effects. The American Civil Liberties Union sued, claiming Abbott had a duty to test the drug. Abbott walked away from all rights to the drug, giving up its investment. The government ordered the drug turned over to a small company that had little to lose if liability problems arose.

Drug regulation, like other forms of consumer protection covered in this chapter, such as credit regulation, affects liability and the decisions made by consumers and producers. Regulations can protect consumers but can also prevent parties from entering into contracts to which they might otherwise agree. Should the government prohibit voluntary agreements among informed, consenting parties? As we discuss various regulations, consider whether producers such as AIDS drug makers should be allowed to avoid government regulation and deal directly with consumers, such as AIDS victims.

The FDA: Food and Drug Regulation

The Food and Drug Administration (FDA) is charged with monitoring food and drug safety (see www.fda.gov). About one-third of its annual billion-dollar budget is devoted to foods. Food additives, food sanitation and processing, and food contaminants are the primary areas of concern. One-quarter of the budget is devoted to the study of the quality of marketed drugs and new-drug evaluations. Smaller portions of the budget support the study of biological products, veterinary products, medical devices, radiological products, cosmetics, and the National Center for Toxicological Research. Every year, more than 1,000 FDA inspectors from over 150 offices inspect tens of thousands of establishments and their products that have annual sales of $1 trillion per year.

FOOD SAFETY

The control of safety in commercial food, drink, drugs, and cosmetics affects a large sector of the economy. Regulations concerning these products have a longer history than do most product controls. The Pure Food and Drug Act of 1906 was the first major step in developing comprehensive regulations. For years the primary concern was food safety. This was triggered by several events:

- More soldiers in the American army during the Spanish-American War were reputed to have died from impure food than from enemy bullets.
- Upton Sinclair's *The Jungle*, while failing to stir the public to support socialism as Sinclair had hoped, caused much controversy about food safety with its graphic description of food processing.
- The chief chemist of the U.S. Department of Agriculture studied the safety of some food preservatives on human subjects and determined that some were harmful to human health.

The 1906 Act concerned sanitation and misbranding of food and drug products. The Bureau of Chemistry of the Department of Agriculture performed food analyses for identification of misbranded or impure foods. When warranted, the Secretary of Agriculture could ask a U.S. attorney for criminal prosecution of a violator of the law and could ask to have the goods seized and destroyed. The Bureau of Chemistry of the Department of Agriculture administered the Food and Drug Act until the FDA was created as a separate unit in 1927.

FDA Powers Expanded in the 1930s

Following a drug disaster in which many people were poisoned by a nonprescription medicine, Congress passed the *Food, Drug, and Cosmetic Act* in 1938. The Act greatly expanded the regulatory reach of the FDA by providing the agency with the power not only to extend the standards for foods beyond canned goods but also to prohibit false advertising of drugs, classify unsafe food as adulterated, add new enforcement powers, form inspection systems, and set the safe levels of additives in foods.

The burden of responsibility was placed on manufacturers to assure that no damage to health was possible from the substances present in their food. This responsibility was emphasized by the Supreme Court in the *Park* decision, which addresses the issue of the responsibilities of corporate executives for compliance with the Food, Drug, and Cosmetic Act.

United States v. Park
Supreme Court of the United States
421 U.S. 658, 95 S.Ct. 1903 (1975)

CASE BACKGROUND *Park was chief executive officer of Acme Markets, a grocery store chain with 874 retail outlets. Acme and Park were charged with violations of the Food, Drug, and Cosmetic Act, because food in Acme warehouses was found on several inspections to be contaminated by rodents.*

Acme and Park were convicted in district court of violating the law. Park appealed, and his conviction was overturned. The court of appeals held that Park could not be held responsible. The government appealed.

CASE DECISION Burger, Chief Justice.

* * *

The rationale of interpretation given the Act . . . as holding criminally accountable the persons whose failure to exercise the authority and supervisory responsibility reposed in them by the business organization resulted in the violation complained of, has been confirmed in our . . . cases. Thus, the Court has reaffirmed the proposition that "the public interest in the purity of its food is so great as to warrant the imposition of the highest standard of care on distributors." In order to make "distributors of food the strictest censors of their merchandise," the Act punishes "neglect where the law requires care, or inaction where it imposes a duty. The accused, if he does not will the violation, usually is in a position to prevent it with no more care than society might reasonably expect and

no more exertion than it might reasonably exact from one who assumed his responsibilities.". . .

Thus . . . in providing sanctions which reach and touch the individuals who execute the corporate mission—and this is by no means necessarily confined to a single corporate agent or employee—the Act imposes not only a positive duty to seek out and remedy violations when they occur but also, and primarily, a duty to implement measures that will insure that violations will not occur. The requirements of foresight and vigilance imposed on responsible corporate agents are beyond question demanding, and perhaps onerous, but they are no more stringent than the public has a right to expect of those who voluntarily assume positions of authority in business enterprises whose services and products affect the health and well-being of the public that supports them.

* * *

Reversed.

QUESTIONS FOR ANALYSIS

1. Suppose Park did not know of the inspection reports issued by the FDA inspectors because his subordinates did not pass them along to him. Should he still be responsible?
2. Who in corporate leadership could be held responsible under this Supreme Court interpretation of leadership responsibility?

Food Quality Protection

The Food Additives Amendment, known as the *Delaney Clause*, was added to the Food, Drug, and Cosmetic Act in 1958. It gave the FDA authority to set the safe-use level of food additives. It was so strict in practice (a "zero risk" standard) that it was replaced by the more flexible Food Quality Protection Act of 1996. The FDA is to insure that there is a "reasonable certainty of no harm" (meaning no more than a one-in-a-million lifetime chance of cancer) from any source that affects foods, raw or processed, whether added directly, such as food coloring, or indirectly, such as pesticide residues. The Food Quality Protection Act expands FDA jurisdiction over thousands of pesticides used in food production.

NUTRITION LABELING

The FDA began issuing regulations for *nutrition labeling* in 1973. The *Nutrition Labeling and Education Act* of 1990 required the FDA to issue new nutrition labeling regulations in 1994. These requirements apply to hundreds of billions of dollars worth of food sold annually in more than 250,000 products. The Department of Agriculture, which regulates meat and poultry, works with the FDA to have regulations for those foods that are consistent with the FDA rules. The intent is to prevent misleading product claims and to help consumers make informed purchases.

Nutrients by Serving Size

FDA regulations list 139 categories of food, from soup to nuts, whose nutrients must be listed by standard serving size. Such listing gives nutrients in realistic serving sizes rather than by, say, one ounce, which may not be related to a normal eating portion. The following components must be listed per serving portion on nutrition labels:

- Total calories and calories from fat
- Total fat and saturated fat
- Carbohydrates (sugar and starch separately)
- Cholesterol
- Calcium
- Fiber
- Iron
- Sodium
- Protein
- Vitamins A and C

Producers may list other nutrients, such as potassium, other essential vitamins and minerals, and polyunsaturated fat. Vitamins that are so common—thiamin, riboflavin, and niacin—that there is no shortage in American diets do not have to be listed.

Standards for Health Claims

Since many consumers know little about nutrition but express concern about it, labels must conform to standards for words commonly used so that consumers can learn more about what they are buying. For example, "fresh" can refer only to raw food that has not been processed, frozen, or preserved; "low fat" means 3 or fewer grams of fat per serving and per 100 grams of the food; "low calorie" means fewer than 40 calories per serving and per 100 grams of food; and "light" or "lite" may be used on foods that have one-third fewer calories than a comparable product.

Further, health claims that are not sufficiently established, such as the claim that fiber reduces heart disease and cancer, may not be made unless sufficiently documented by the seller. The food/health claims that may be noted on labels involve the health connection between calcium and osteoporosis, sodium and high blood pressure, fat and heart disease, and fat and cancer.

Exporting Drug Regulation

The FDA has a major effect on drug production around the world. Many nations adopt FDA regulations as a part of their drug standards. In many countries, the domestic market is not regulated—many drugs sold would be illegal in the United States—but the export market is regulated to FDA standards. This is intended to make pharmaceutical producers competitive in world markets. Since countries do not want a reputation for producing low-quality drugs, they require their exporters to meet U.S. standards.

Another reason countries adopt FDA standards is that foreign drug producers must be licensed and inspected by the FDA to be eligible to export drugs to the United States. FDA inspectors visit foreign plants to assure that U.S. standards are met.

European nations do not have as stringent drug regulations as those of the FDA. Introducing a new drug to the market often happens years sooner in Europe, where the long testing period prescribed by the FDA may not be required. Many drugs that require prescriptions in the United States may be bought over the counter in Europe. Similarly, foreign producers who want to sell drugs in most of Europe do not need to be licensed by each country, since the European Union recognizes the inspections conducted by each member country. That is, a Ministry of Health inspection and approval in the United Kingdom qualifies a British producer to export to Germany, France, and the other EU countries.

The American system probably better reduces risk from defective drugs, but it also keeps lifesaving, pain-reducing, and disease-curing drugs off the market for a longer time than does Europe's system. The result of differences in regulatory standards is that drug research and development has grown more rapidly in Europe (and Japan) than in the United States.

DRUG SAFETY

Until 1938, drug control was intended to protect the public against quacks, fraudulent claims, mislabeling, and the sale of dangerous drugs. After the death of about a hundred people poisoned by a drug, the Food, Drug, and Cosmetic Act provided federal regulators with new powers in 1938. The law has been amended numerous times, including the Food and Drug Administration Modernization Act of 1977, which streamlined regulatory procedures. The law prohibits the sale of any drug until the FDA approves the application submitted by the manufacturer. The applicant must submit evidence that the drug is *safe* for its intended use. This prevents the sale of untested, potentially harmful drugs in a market that now generates over $100 billion per year in sales.

Designation of Prescription Drugs

Before the 1938 Act, no drugs were designated as *prescription drugs*—that is, drugs that may be used only with the permission of a physician. Drugs were either legal or illegal. Since 1938, the FDA has determined which drugs will be prescription drugs—that is, sold by pharmacies only with a physician's permission.

Drug Effectiveness

The *Kefauver Amendment* of 1962 requires the FDA to approve drugs based on their proven effectiveness—not just on their safety, as required before. The FDA must approve testing of drugs on humans and may specify the details of the testing. Interpretation of the legislation by the FDA has produced strict regulations concerning testing and adoption of new drugs. It now costs an average of over $250 million and takes twelve years to develop a new drug and to clear all FDA rules before marketing the product.

The requirements for testing of drugs and for certification by the FDA have led to questions about the liability of drug manufacturers for injuries from FDA-approved drugs. That is, if a drug is FDA-approved, should tort liability be reduced? The questions the courts face in such cases are illustrated in the *Tobin* decision.

Tobin v. Astra Pharmaceutical Products

United States Court of Appeals, Sixth Circuit
993 F.2d 528 (1993)

CASE BACKGROUND *Kathy Tobin was pregnant with twins at age nineteen. Her due date was early April. In January she went into early labor and was put on the drug ritodrine to suppress contractions. She reported various side effects of the medicine—racing heart and swelling—but was told they were normal reactions. On March 17 she was admitted to the hospital for a variety of problems, including fluid in the lungs and enlarged heart caused by congestive heart failure. She was taken off the medicine and delivered healthy twins.*

In and out of the hospital after that, within a month she had a heart transplant. She sued the Dutch maker of ritodrine and its American distributor, Astra. The companies moved to have the case dismissed because the drug has been approved by the FDA as effective. They claimed that Tobin "should not have been permitted to litigate this issue, because it is a mockery of the scientific analysis employed by the FDA and the Advisory Committee which conclusively found that ritodrine was efficacious." The judge rejected the motion; the drug companies appealed.

CASE DECISION Guy, Circuit Judge.

* * *

We reject the argument that FDA approval preempts state product liability claims based on design defect. While this circuit has not directly ruled on whether a plaintiff in a product liability action may litigate an FDA finding that a drug is efficacious, the Fifth Circuit has ruled that the Food, Drug and Cosmetic Act does not preempt state law claims based on defective design. In so holding, the Fifth Circuit reversed the district court's finding of preemption, noting that "the great majority of United States dis-

trict courts which have addressed this issue have ruled against preemption."

FDA approval is evidence which the jury may consider in reaching its verdict. The jury may weigh FDA approval as it sees fit, especially in a case where the plaintiff has presented evidence to support an articulable basis for disregarding an FDA finding—in this case the finding that ritodrine was effective. Tobin presented an articulable basis for disregarding the FDA's finding that ritodrine was effective in improving neonatal outcome: the individual studies relied on by the FDA were insufficient to support a finding of efficacy as found by the FDA Advisory Committee, and the pooled data requested by the Advisory Committee was statistically invalid.

We do not sit to review the findings of the FDA; our only role in this appeal is to decide if there was sufficient evidence on which the jury could base its verdict. Plaintiff introduced evidence, through the cross-examination of Astra officials, that a reasonably prudent manufacturer would not market ritodrine if the evidence of its efficacy was inconclusive. Plaintiff also introduced sufficient evidence regarding the various clinical studies concerning the efficacy of ritodrine. The jury found that ritodrine, as manufactured and marketed by Astra, was in a defective condition and unreasonably dangerous to plaintiff. We find that there was sufficient evidence before the jury to conclude that a prudent manufacturer knowing all the risks would not market ritodrine.

Defendant argues that if the warning accompanying ritodrine was adequate then it cannot be held strictly liable. The cases cited by defendant to support its position, that a drug manufacturer should be shielded from liability [are] based on comment k of the

Restatement (Second) of Torts §402A. Comment k provides that the seller of "unavoidably unsafe products" "is not to be held to strict liability for unfortunate consequences attending their use." For comment k to apply, however, the product must be "an apparently useful and desirable product." It is the useful or effective nature of ritodrine which plaintiff has called into question. Kentucky has ruled that comment k shields manufacturers from liability for "highly useful and desirable product[s] attended with a known but reasonable risk." A drug that prolongs pregnancy in order to reduce infant morbidity and mortality, if effective, is a highly useful and desirable product. Plaintiff, however, has attacked the linchpin of this theory—effectiveness—with various evidence. The jury was instructed:

A product such as ritodrine is not in a defective condition unreasonably dangerous if it cannot be made completely safe for all users, but is nevertheless a useful and desirable product which is accompanied by proper directions and warnings.

The jury verdict rejecting this argument is supported by the evidence that was presented.

* * *

Affirmed.

QUESTIONS FOR ANALYSIS

1. Does it make sense that a jury of nonexperts can listen to plaintiff's expert witness, who asserts that the studies relied upon by the drug manufacturer and FDA experts were not valid, and thereby ignore FDA findings regarding drug effectiveness?
2. Many drugs are dangerous to some users but, in net, are helpful. If the drug is the best that medical science can produce, should liability be imposed in cases where there are known side effects but it cannot be predicted who will suffer?

The courts, as in the *Tobin* decision, give weight to the protection offered consumers by the regulatory process. The number of liability suits from consumers injured by side effects of a drug is reduced because some effects are not preventable given the state of technology. But FDA approval is only evidence of safety, not a shield against liability, except in certain medical device cases. Similarly, most medical devices that have FDA approval, such as heart valves, are not immune from tort liability under the Medical Device Amendments, the Supreme Court held in 1996 in *Medtronic* v. *Lohr*, 116 S.Ct. 2240.

What if a drug was improperly administered? The drug companies are not likely to be liable, assuming they have given proper dosage instructions. If a physician ignores the instructions and changes the recommended dosage, resulting in an injury, the drug manufacturer is shielded from liability by the *learned intermediary doctrine*. That is, the learned intermediary—the doctor—would be liable for misuse of the product.

ENFORCEMENT ACTIVITIES

Besides deciding when drugs will be allowed to be marketed, the FDA can force existing products, including food, cosmetics, and medical devices, to be removed from the market if their claims appear to be misleading or if new information becomes available that indicates the product was not as safe as previously thought. The FDA forces over 3,000 products a year off the market and seizes 30,000 import shipments each year.

Most silicone breast implants were ordered off the market by the FDA when questions were raised about the long-term health consequences of the product. The FDA seized shipments of Citrus Hill Fresh Choice orange juice because the juice was made from concentrate and not "fresh" from oranges. The agency ordered vegetable oil manufacturers to remove "no cholesterol" from the labels of their product. The no-cholesterol claim was not false, but the FDA said it was misleading, since many consumers think cholesterol is the same as fat, which is not the case.

While enforcement has become tougher, for the first time the FDA has been allowing quick approval for use of drugs that show some promise in life-threatening diseases such as AIDS. Rather than require the full, lengthy review process before the drugs are allowed to be sold to informed patients, the FDA is allowing the drugs to be carefully distributed.

The FTC and Consumer Protection

The Federal Trade Commission (FTC) was established in 1915 to help enforce the antitrust laws, but the FTC also devotes substantial resources to its Bureau of Consumer Protection, which handles a wide range of matters such as deceptive advertising and marketing practices (see www.ftc.gov). Some responsibilities are specifically granted by Congress, such as enforcement of the Magnuson-Moss Warranty Act and the various consumer credit statutes. But most consumer protection efforts evolve as the FTC decides what Congress meant when it amended the FTC Act in the 1930s and said, in Section 5, that "unfair and deceptive acts or practices in or affecting commerce are hereby declared unlawful."

Based on its experience, and in response to concerns expressed by Congress, the FTC investigates a wide range of practices suspected to be *unfair and deceptive*. The FTC staff proposes complaints to the five commissioners, who decide by majority vote whether to issue a complaint. The complaint begins formal legal proceedings against a business engaged in practices the commission would like to see ended or modified.

Many complaints are settled by a *consent decree* agreed upon by the parties charged in an FTC complaint. Consent decrees contain the terms of a settlement and frequently include prohibition of certain practices, redress for consumers, and payment of civil penalties. A few cases result in administrative trials at the FTC. If the accused party or the FTC attorneys are not satisfied with the decision of the administrative law judge, they may appeal to the commissioners for review. An accused party who is not satisfied with the decision of the commissioners may appeal to a federal court of appeals.

UNFAIR AND DECEPTIVE ACTS OR PRACTICES

Congress ordered the FTC to fight "unfair and deceptive acts or practices." The lack of a clear legal definition for those terms means that the FTC has considerable leeway in deciding what cases to bring—what advertising is deceptive and what sales practices are unfair. The key term has always been *deceptive*. Essentially, things held to be deceptive are also unfair.

Policy Statement on Deception

To give the FTC staff guidance, the commissioners adopted a *deception policy statement* that summarizes a three-part test for deciding whether a particular act or practice is *deceptive*. There is deception if the following are true:

1. There is a misrepresentation or omission of information in a communication to consumers.

Who's Dumb and Dumber?

Each year the Center for Science in the Public Interest gives Lemon Awards for the ten most deceptive advertisements. Malibu rum was cited for its tropical ad scene in which a woman says, "You're going to call your boyfriend back home. As soon as you can remember his name." This ad was attacked for promoting reckless drinking.

Hasbro was cited for its Play-Doh Cookie Lovin' Oven. A consumer group charged that the ads could make children think that they could bake real cookies in the oven out of Play-Doh. Hasbro said nonsense, it's just a toy. There is no heating element in the little oven, as any consumer could see, "It simply molds dough into cookie forms." The company had received no complaints from unhappy consumers, a company vice president said. "Even if, God forbid, somebody did try to eat the cookies, nothing would happen to them. Everybody's tried Play-Doh at some point in their life."

Source: *The Wall Street Journal*

2. The deception is likely to mislead a reasonable consumer.
3. The deception is material; that is, it is likely to be misleading to the detriment of consumers.

Some points help clarify the elements of deception. First, not all omissions are deceptive. Omissions (failure to reveal information) are not deceptive if there is no affirmative misrepresentation or practice that takes advantage of consumer misimpression. Second, to decide whether a representation or omission is deceptive, the FTC looks at the entire context. The words in an advertisement are examined in the context of the entire ad, and consideration is given to evidence about what consumers think the ad means. Third, a reasonable consumer is an "ordinary person." Consideration is given to the target audience of a questionable practice. For example, ads directed at children or ill people are held to a tougher standard. Fourth, the representation or omission must be likely to affect a consumer's product choice. Fifth, no proof of injury to consumers (usually financial loss—money wasted) is needed if evidence exists that an injury is likely to occur, given the practice in question. Here are some examples.

Telemarketing Fraud The FTC obtained an injunction against five telemarketing firms for making misrepresentations in the sale of water purifiers and home security systems. The FTC charged that the companies mailed postcards telling consumers they had won valuable awards, including $5,000 in retail merchandise checks. In fact, the awards consisted only of certificates that required payment of substantial sums of money to obtain the merchandise. The telemarketers also made charges against consumers' credit cards without authorization and billed customers for merchandise never sent.

Oil- and Gas-Well "Investments" Several companies were involved in oil- and gas-well lease scams. They persuaded more than 8,000 people to invest $5,000 to $10,000 each in application fees to participate in a lottery for mineral (oil and gas) rights on federal lands. The FTC obtained $47 million in refunds, which was about 90 cents on the dollar lost. Not only were the promoters sued, so were all the companies that worked with them in the scheme, such as insurance companies, banks, and accounting firms.

Work-at-Home Opportunities A federal appeals court upheld a $16-million judgment against a company and its officers in *FTC* v. *Febre*, 128 F.3d 530, for deceptive practices in four work-at-home "opportunities." This included mailing postcards, which supposedly could earn up to $15,000 per day. Almost 200,000 consumers had paid the promoters over $13 million, which was ordered rebated to the consumers, plus $3 million in damages.

Invention-Promotion Scams The FTC sued twelve companies that raked in $90 million by claiming that they were consultants who help people make deals for valuable new inventions. "Project Mousetrap" discovered that people paid between $10,000 and $20,000 each to get "expert advice" in licensing and marketing such things as a toothbrush with bristles at both ends and a device that collects the shavings scratched off lottery tickets. While the operations were closed, only $250,000 remained for consumer redress.

Art Fraud The FTC obtained a consent decree against Austin Galleries, which has art galleries in Chicago, San Francisco, Carmel, and Laguna Beach. Austin bilked consumers by selling fake Salvador Dali, Marc Chagall, Pablo Picasso, and Juan Miro prints as good investments. The company paid $635,000 in consumer refunds and agreed to stop falsely representing the art it sells.

Unfairness

Section 5 of the FTC Act says ". . . unfair or deceptive acts or practices in or affecting commerce, are declared unlawful. . . ." The word *unfair* is usually tagged on to a charge of deception. The FTC has given operational meaning to unfair acts or practices in business by issuing a policy statement that gives a consumer injury standard:

1. It causes substantial harm to consumers.
2. Consumers cannot reasonably avoid injury.
3. The injury is harmful in its net effects.

The first major consumer unfairness case that did not involve a claim of deception was the *Orkin* case (which was supervised by one of the authors of this text while working for the FTC). The decision to bring the case was based on the belief that the unfairness seemed much like fraud or breach of contract, both of which are common-law standards the courts have long enforced.

Orkin Exterminating Company v. Federal Trade Commission
United States Court of Appeals, Eleventh Circuit
849 F.2d 1354 (1988)

CASE BACKGROUND *Beginning in 1966, Orkin Exterminating offered customers a "continuous protection guarantee" if they had their houses treated for termites. The contract said that by paying a small annual fee,* customers were guaranteed free retreatment if termites reappeared for as long as they owned their house.

By 1975, Orkin realized that the promise was a mistake. The annual fee was too low to cover the costs. Orkin *then notified over 200,000 customers that the fee was being raised $25 or 40 percent, whichever was greater. If the customers did not pay the fee, the guarantee was lost. The new fee was consistent with market prices but differed from what the contract stated. Most customers paid the higher fees. The FTC found the fee increase to be unfair and ordered Orkin to roll back its prices to the original levels. Orkin appealed to the U.S. Court of Appeals.*

CASE DECISION Clark, Circuit Judge.

* * *

The Commission's conclusion was simply that it was an "unfair" practice to breach over 200,000 contracts. We think this was a reasonable application of the Commission's unfairness standard.

There remains . . . the question whether this case represents a significant departure from prior Commission precedent. We note what has been written in a recent law review article:

> Some of the oldest "unfairness" decisions involve sellers' refusals to live up to the terms of their contract. The Commission has often challenged sellers for traditional breaches of contract: failure to fill orders, delivery of inferior merchandise, refusal to return goods taken for repair, or refusal to return promised deposits. Recent trade regulation rules have focused on similar issues. These actions have attracted little controversy. Breach of contract has long been condemned as a matter of law, economics, and public policy.

Orkin claims the statements in this article are erroneous, for each of the cases cited therein involved some sort of deceptive practice. We think it important to remember, however, that section 5 by its very terms makes deceptive and unfair practices distinct lines of inquiry which the Commission may pursue. As is suggested above, while a practice may be both deceptive and unfair, it may be unfair without being deceptive. . . .

An adoption of Orkin's position would mean that the Commission could never proscribe widespread breaches of retail consumer contracts unless there was evidence of deception or fraud. The Supreme Court has, on more than one occasion, recognized that the standard of unfairness is "by necessity, an elusive one," which defies such a limitation. The statutory scheme at issue here "necessarily gives the Commission an influential role in interpreting section 5 and in applying it to facts of particular cases arising out of unprecedented situations."

* * *

This case may be "unprecedented" to the extent it concerns non-deceptive contract breaches. But given the extraordinary level of consumer injury which Orkin has caused and the fact that deceptiveness is often not a component of the unfairness inquiry, we think the limitation of the Commission's section 5 authority urged by Orkin would be inconsistent with the broad mandate conferred upon the Commission by Congress. Thus, because the Commission's decision fully and clearly comports with the standard set forth in its Policy Statement, we conclude that the Commission acted within its section 5 authority.

* * *

Affirmed.

QUESTIONS FOR ANALYSIS

1. Assuming that other courts would have found that Orkin had breached its contracts with 200,000 consumers, why not let the consumers sue Orkin rather than have the FTC get involved?
2. Does the ability to bring suits for a practice being "unfair" open the door to almost everything being challenged as such, since we all have different ideas of what is unfair?

REGULATING ADVERTISING CLAIMS

More than $125 billion is spent on advertising each year. The *advertising substantiation program* requires advertisers and advertising agencies to have a reasonable basis before they disseminate claims. When advertisers claim that "studies show" or "tests prove," they must actually possess evidence that provides a reasonable basis for the claims. The FTC considers the following items to determine what is a reasonable basis:

- The product
- The type of claim

JURIS prudence?

You Mean Bruce Didn't Squeeze My Juice?

Tropicana had a commercial that showed Olympic gold medalist Bruce Jenner squeezing an orange into a Tropicana orange juice container and saying, "It's pure, pasteurized juice as it comes from the orange."

Minute Maid Orange Juice sued, claiming the ad was false because the juice was, in fact, sometimes frozen before packaging. At trial, consumer perceptions tests showed that 85 percent of consumers understood the ad was not literally true. The court issued an injunction against the ad, ruling that consumer perceptions did not matter, because the ad was false on its face.

Source: *Brandweek*

- The consequences of a false claim and the benefits of a truthful claim
- The cost of developing substantiation for the claim
- The amount of substantiation that experts believe is reasonable

What Advertising Is Deceptive?

A number of years ago, the FTC noted in a decision: "Perhaps a few misguided souls believe . . . that all 'Danish pastry' is made in Denmark. Is it therefore an actionable deception to advertise 'Danish pastry' when it is made in this country? Of course not." The point is that some people may misunderstand certain advertisements, but that does not mean that the FTC will be concerned. For example, if a hair dye is advertised as "permanent" and someone thinks it means that their hair will be the color of the dye forever rather than that only existing hair will be the color of the dye, no deception is involved. Most consumers know what is meant, and those who do not understand do not incur significant injury.

The number of people deceived by an ad does not necessarily determine whether there is an ad deception case. For instance, a car ad may say that the Fireball model got thirty miles per gallon in tests. The ad may be seen by tens of millions, of whom several hundred thousand may incorrectly think that all Fireball models always get thirty miles per gallon. So long as the claim made was true—and since most consumers know that miles-per-gallon tests do not mean that all cars always get exactly the test results—there is no deception that would lead one to believe that the effect injures consumers such that the ad should be changed.

On the other hand, some ads that reach a small number of people, such as pamphlets handed out door-to-door, may deceive many who read it because the claims are false and likely to deceive. Other ads may reach a large number of people, deceive very few, yet be held to be deceptive. For instance, if a small number of consumers lose a lot of money because they believe a deceptive claim, the FTC may act because of the seriousness of the injury. Note that most states have laws similar to the FTC Act that allow state attorneys general to file suit in deceptive advertising cases.

Examples of Deceptive Ad Cases

Gateway Educational Products settled FTC charges that the claims about the ability of its "Hooked on Phonics" program to teach users, including those with learning disabilities, to read were unsubstantiated. The FTC contended that consumer

Foreign Advertising Regulation

Advertising is subject to very different controls around the world. Except for prohibitions on the advertising of certain products, most countries impose fewer regulations on ads than is the case in the United States. In Europe, ad regulations tend to be tightest in northern Europe and loosest in the Mediterranean countries.

Britain has an Office of Fair Trading that operates somewhat like the FTC with respect to ad regulation. The general standard is that an ad is illegal if it misrepresents a product, whereas in the United States it may be illegal if it simply misleads. For an ad to misrepresent a product, there must be an estimation that consumers suffer damages because they have not been told the truth in the ad. For example, a soup ad in the United States was held illegal by the FTC because the soup was photographed to look as though it had more chunky bits in it than a random bowl of the soup really would have. In most of Europe and Japan, that ad would not be illegal because, while it misleads, it does not injure consumers.

Beer ads in Japan promote the "extra strong" alcohol content, a practice that would be illegal in the United States under the alcoholic-beverage advertising rules of the Bureau of Alcohol, Tobacco, and Firearms. As the chairman of a Japanese advertising firm explained, "When you come to Japan, you have to do as the Japanese do, especially in advertising.

testimonials did not represent typical experiences and that experts on reading disability assert that phonics instruction may not help many people with dyslexia or other reading disabilities. The producer promised to stop the challenged claims and make no other claims without substantiation.

Enforcing FDA definitions of food claims, the FTC settled a case with Häagen-Dazs about the fat and calorie claims on its frozen yogurt products: "And each with just 1 gram of fat and 100 calories." In fact the products contained up to twelve grams of fat per serving (compared to the FDA definition of low fat as three grams or less) and up to 230 calories per serving. The company agreed to meet FDA standards for labeling food products and not to misrepresent the amount of fat or calories.

The FTC sued Bee-Sweet for its medical claims about its bee-pollen products: "Studies performed by doctors around the world have shown bee pollen to be effective in treating illnesses from allergies to arthritis, anorexia to overweight, fatigue to arteriosclerosis." Because there was no scientific evidence to back up the claims, the company agreed to stop making such claims and to inform all product distributors about the settlement with the FTC.

Quaker State agreed to stop running unsubstantiated ads for Slick 50, the nation's top-selling engine treatment. Ashland, while denying any wrongdoing, agreed to end a major ad campaign that touted Valvoline TM8 Engine Treatment. The ads claimed the additive would reduce wear on some engine parts by as much as 75 percent and that the product provides twice as much engine protection as untreated oil under high-temperature conditions.

Most deceptive advertising cases are settled in a similar manner—the advertiser promises to stop making false claims. In some cases, a civil penalty is imposed, but large sums are not common. In rare instances, the FTC will order a company to engage in corrective advertising to make up for past false claims.

Regulating Cyberspace Advertising

 The FTC has prosecuted dozens of cases involving alleged on-line scams and false advertising. Zygon International paid $195,000 in consumer redress in response to an FTC challenge to its claims for "self-improvement" products. In another case, involving Fortuna Alliance, the FTC charged that the company collected more than $6 million based on false claims that "investors" could easily earn large sums in what amounted to a pyramid scheme. The FTC seized Fortuna's assets and obtained a court order that a notice of the FTC's action had to be placed on Fortuna's web site.

The FTC pushed for, and got, Congress to pass the Children's On-line Privacy Protection Act of 1998, which requires the FTC to adopt rules requiring web sites that appeal to children (under age thirteen) to provide parents with notice of information that is being collected and how the web site uses the information. Such sites must obtain "verifiable parental consent" regarding the collection, distribution, and use of their children's information, and parents must be able to withdraw consent.

FALSE ADVERTISING AND THE LANHAM ACT

Another way that false advertising claims may be struck down, and one that can yield far more expensive results than most FTC advertising cases, is when a private party initiates civil action under the *Lanham Act*. Section 43 of the Act states:

> Any person who, or in connection with any goods or services, or any container for goods, uses in commerce any word, term, name, symbol, or device . . . or any false designation "of origin, false or misleading description of fact, or any false or misleading representation" of fact, which (1) is likely to cause confusion, or to cause mistake, or to deceive as to the affiliation, connection, or association of such person with another person, or as to the origin, sponsorship, or approval of his or her goods, services, or commercial activities by another person, or (2) in commercial advertising or promotion, misrepresents the nature, characteristics, qualities, or geographic origin of his or her or another person's goods, services, or commercial activities, shall be liable in a civil action by any person who believes that he or she is or is likely to be damaged by such act.

When cases claiming misleading advertising are brought under the Lanham Act, the courts generally consider the meaning of "deceptive" as it has evolved in FTC advertising cases. Most cases result in injunctions against further false advertising claims, much like most FTC deceptive advertising cases. But under the Lanham Act, plaintiffs also may recover damages, as in the 1986 case *U-Haul International* v. *Jartran*, 793 F.2d 1034, where the appeals court upheld an award of $40 million. The Act allows injured parties (the defendant's competitors) to collect double the value of the profits that the defendant earned from false advertising.

Similarly, many states have laws, such as the Business and Professions Code of California, that prohibit false and misleading advertising. Competitors or consumers injured by such advertising may sue. For example, in *Consumers Union of*

Born in the USA . . .

 New Balance Athletic Shoe was sued in 1994 for "making false and misleading advertising and labeling claims that its athletic shoes are 'Made in the USA.'" The FTC wanted a court order that would prohibit New Balance from making "Made in the USA" claims "unless all, or virtually all, of the components and labor are of U.S. origin."

The Boston-based company responded that its shoes are assembled in the United States and about 70 percent of the shoes' components are from the United States. Since rubber is not grown in the United States, it has to be imported, thereby, according to the FTC, preventing New Balance from saying that its shoes are "Made in the USA."

New Balance pressed the issue. Different agencies use different rules for what constitutes "Made in the USA." NAFTA holds that 55 percent of the labor and components must be from Canada, Mexico, or the United States. The Department of Transportation says that 75 percent of an automobile must be from the United States. Customs says that only 50 percent must be from the United States.

The FTC dropped the case against New Balance and reviewed the matter. In 1997, the agency floated a rule of 75 percent parts and labor to mean "Made in the USA." That resulted in protests from unions and domestic producers. The FTC then said 90 percent.

Source: *Federal Trade Commission* and *Wall Street Journal*

U.S. v. *Alta-Dena Certified Dairy*, 6 Cal.Rptr.2d 193 (1992), a California appeals court upheld an order for a large milk producer to place safety warnings on its commercial food products to remedy the past effects of false advertising.

TRADE REGULATION RULES

Under Section 18 of the FTC Act, the FTC has the authority to issue *trade regulation rules* that set boundaries for practices thought to be ripe for deception. Such rules tend to be based on FTC experience of problems in certain areas, although critics charge that the rules can be used to protect existing competitors from innovative entrants by making certain practices the industry standard. Because numerous trade regulation rules are on the books—most dealing with very narrow areas—here we consider only a few major rules.

When the FTC proposes a rule, the rule must be published in the *Federal Register* so that interested parties may comment on it before it is finalized. When the rule is put in place, it gives the FTC solid grounds for charging that violators of the rule are committing an unfair and deceptive act, since firms in an industry are required to know about rules that apply to them. Further, as we noted in Chapter 10, such rules may limit certain contracts, as in the case of the rule that allows buyers to cancel contracts they agreed to in case of certain door-to-door sales.

The Insulation R-Value Rule

The FTC's Trade Regulation Rule concerning the Labeling and Advertising of Home Insulation (the *R-value rule*) was written because of the problems consumers have understanding various insulation claims. By standardizing R-values, the FTC requires insulation manufacturers and installers to use the same terminology and to measure the R-value of their products using specified tests and to disclose the results.

The rule provides a uniform standard to evaluate home insulation products. If a company claims that it provides R-19-value insulation and it has not, there is a standard to measure the R-value that makes the company subject to suit by the FTC in a straightforward manner, rather than trying to establish case by case the proper measure of insulation. For example, the FTC settled a consent decree with Sears for violating the R-value rule. Sears advertised the thickness and price of an insulation product but failed to disclose the R-value. In the decree, Sears agreed to pay a $100,000 civil penalty, to comply with the rule in the future, and to pay for advertisements to educate consumers about home insulation and R-values.

The Mail-Order Rule

One of the best-known trade regulation rules is the *Mail-Order Rule*. If a company sells merchandise by mail, it must have a reasonable basis for expecting to ship merchandise within the time stated in its ads. Shipping dates must be stated on the offers (such as "Allow five weeks for shipment") or the merchandise must be shipped within thirty days of receipt of an order. If the goods cannot be shipped on time, customers must be sent an option notice allowing them to cancel the order and receive a refund or to agree to a new shipping date—which must be reasonable and must be met. The rule gives the FTC a simple basis for issuing complaints against companies that fail to live up to the terms of their offers.

The Used Car Rule

The FTC *Used Car Rule* requires dealers to give consumers clear information on who pays for repairs after a sale. A Buyer's Guide must be placed in the side window of each used car offered for sale. The guide must contain the following:

1. A statement of the terms of any warranty offered with the car
2. A prominent statement of whether the dealer is selling the car "as is" and, if so, that the consumer must pay for any repairs needed after buying the car
3. A warning that oral promises are difficult to enforce, with a suggestion to get all promises in writing
4. A suggestion that the consumer ask for an independent inspection of the car

The FTC sued a San Francisco car dealer for violating the rule by failing to display window stickers on used cars offered for sale. The dealer also failed to give consumers copies of the Buyer's Guide or disclosures concerning warranty. The dealer agreed to comply with the law and paid a civil penalty of $20,000.

MAGNUSON-MOSS WARRANTY ACT

An amendment to the FTC Act gave the FTC power to set guidelines for consumer products warranties. Compliance with the *Magnuson-Moss Warranty Act* does not appear to have been very costly. Few cases have been brought under the law.

Required Written Warranty Information

The law requires *written warranties* to include information about the following:

- The parts of the product or the types of problems the warranty covers and, if necessary for clarity, the parts or problems it does not cover
- The time period of coverage

- What will be done to correct problems and, if necessary for clarity, what will not be done
- How the customer can get warranty service
- How state law may affect warranty

Full or Limited Warranty

Products that cost more than ten dollars and have warranties must state clearly and conspicuously whether the warranty is full or limited. A *full warranty* meets the following five standards:

1. Warranty service is provided to anyone who owns the product during the warranty period.
2. Warranty service is provided free of charge, including such costs as returning or removing and reinstalling the product when necessary.
3. At the consumer's choice, a replacement or a full refund will be provided if the product cannot be repaired after reasonable efforts.
4. Warranty service is provided without requiring that consumers return a warranty registration card.
5. The implied warranties are not limited.

If any of these conditions are not met, the warranty is a *limited warranty* and must be so stated. A product has a multiple warranty when part of the product is covered by a full warranty and part is covered by a limited warranty. In all events, to comply with the FTC's Rule of Disclosure of Written Consumer Product Warranty Terms and Conditions, warranties must be clear, simple, and useful. If a company writes an unclear warranty in fine print to discourage or confuse consumers, it will be subject to FTC attack, especially if consumers have difficulties enforcing the warranty. State courts have made similar determinations in cases brought under contract law. Fine print is not held in favor.

Consumer Credit Protection

Congress first involved the federal government in the direct regulation of consumer credit with the *Consumer Credit Protection Act* (*CCPA*) of 1968. At that time there was about $100 billion worth of consumer credit outstanding; now the figure is over $1 trillion. Credit cards, which were somewhat rare thirty years ago, now carry a huge volume of transactions. CCPA has become an umbrella law containing several credit-related laws. The laws provide certain rights for consumers in credit transactions and place certain requirements on creditors, including the following:

- Creditors are required to disclose all relevant terms in credit transactions (truth in lending).
- Procedures for correcting inaccurate and disputed bills and charges must be provided (fair credit billing).
- Credit-reporting agencies are required to provide accurate information in consumer reports (fair credit reporting).
- Creditors are prohibited from using certain personal characteristics of consumers (such as sex or race) in determining a person's creditworthiness (equal credit opportunity).
- Abusive debt collection techniques are prohibited (fair debt collection practices).

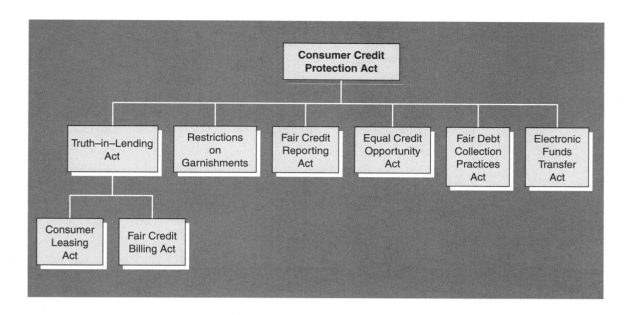

EXHIBIT 18.1

*The Major Elements
of Consumer Credit
Legislation*

TRUTH-IN-LENDING ACT

As Exhibit 18.1 shows, the first law to come under the CCPA was the *Truth-in-Lending Act* (*TILA*), which requires creditors in consumer transactions to disclose basic information about the cost and terms of credit to the consumer-borrower. By making borrowers aware of specific charges and other relevant information, and by standardizing credit terms and methods of calculation, it encourages people to shop for the most favorable credit terms much as they would shop for the best price for a car.

Finance Charge Disclosures

Until TILA was passed, creditors quoted interest in many ways, which could cause confusion. For example, an 8 percent "add-on interest rate" is approximately the same as a 15 percent "simple interest rate." This is because an add-on rate calculates interest on the initial amount of the loan regardless of the outstanding principal, whereas the simple interest rate calculates interest only on the outstanding principal. Both methods are legitimate, but standardized terms under TILA let consumers make better comparisons among competing lenders.

TILA does not control interest rates; it requires that consumers be given standardized loan terms before they commit to a credit transaction. TILA covers only consumer credit transactions, since the debtor must be a "natural person," not a business organization. Since the creditor must be in the credit business, TILA does not apply to transactions such as loans to friends. The law does not apply if the credit transaction does not include a finance charge, unless the consumer repays the creditor in more than four installments. Finally, the Act does not apply to consumer credit transactions for more than $25,000, except real estate purchases.

Credit Cost Disclosure

Transactions covered by TILA must disclose the credit costs in dollars (the *finance charge*) and the interest rate of that finance charge (the *annual percentage rate*, or *APR*). These items must be disclosed more conspicuously than other items in the agreement. *Regulation Z*, written by the Federal Reserve Board to implement the Truth-in-Lending Act, specifies items that must be listed if part of the finance charge. These items include the following:

1. Service, activity, carrying, and transaction charges
2. Loan fees and points
3. Charges for credit life and credit accident and health insurance
4. In non–real-estate transactions, the fees for credit reports and appraisals

Certain other items, such as licenses and fees imposed by law, are not part of the finance charge if they are itemized and disclosed to the consumer in the transaction. In all, twelve items related to credit transactions must be disclosed to the borrower. Exhibit 18.2 shows the disclosure required in the sale of a car on credit.

Enforcement and Penalties

TILA provides for both civil and criminal penalties. The creditor can avoid liability for a violation, such as a failure to specify all finance charges, if the violation is corrected within fifteen days from the time it is discovered by the creditor and before the consumer gives written notification of error. In addition, good-faith reliance on official Federal Reserve Board comments about how to follow the law protects creditors from civil liability.

Consumers may sue creditors who violate TILA disclosure rules for twice the amount of the finance charge—up to $1,000—court costs, and attorney's fees. A creditor who willfully or knowingly gives inaccurate information or fails to make proper disclosures is subject to criminal liability, including a fine of up to $5,000, imprisonment of not more than one year, or both, for each violation of the Act.

CONSUMER LEASING ACT

The *Consumer Leasing Act* does for consumer leases, such as for automobiles, what the Truth-in-Lending Act does for consumer credit. That is, it provides standard terms to help consumers shop for leases. The Act applies to leases of personal property to be used for personal, family, or household purposes, not for business purposes. The lease must be longer than four months and have an obligation of less than $25,000. Apartment leases are not covered by the Act because the property leased is real, not personal, property. Most car rentals are not covered because the term of the agreement is not long enough.

Disclosure Requirements

The Consumer Leasing Act specifies information that must be given before the consumer becomes obligated for the lease. The required disclosures include the following items:

- Number, amount, and period of the payments and the payment total
- Any express warranties offered by the leasing party or the manufacturer of the leased property
- Identification of the party responsible for maintaining or servicing the leased property
- Whether the consumer has an option to buy the leased property and, if so, the terms of that option
- What happens if the consumer terminates the lease before the lease expires

Big Wheel Auto				**Alice Green**
ANNUAL PERCENTAGE RATE The cost of your credit as a yearly rate.	FINANCE CHARGE The dollar amount the credit will cost you.	Amount Financed The amount of credit provided to you or on your behalf.	Total of Payments The amount you will have paid after you have made all payments as scheduled.	Total Sale Price The total cost of your purchase on credit, including your down-payment of $ 1500—
14.84%	$ 1496.80	$ 6107.50	$ 7604.30	$ 9129.30

You have the right to receive at this time an itemization of the Amount Financed.
☐ I want an itemization.   ☒ I do not want an itemization.

Your payment schedule will be:

Number of payments	Amount of Payments	When Payments Are Due
36	$211.23	Monthly, beginning 6-1-99

Insurance:
Credit life insurance and credit disability insurance are not required to obtain credit, and will not be provided unless you sign and agree to pay the additional cost.

Type	Premium	Signature	
Credit Life	$120—	I want credit life insurance.	*Alice Green* Signature
Credit Disability		I want credit disability insurance.	Signature
Credit Life and Disability		I want credit life and disability insurance.	Signature

Security: You are giving a security interest in:
☒ the goods being purchased.
☐ _____.

Filing Fees $_____   Non-filing insurance $_____

Late Charge: If a payment is late, you will be charged $10.

Prepayment: If you pay off early, you
☐ may   ☐ will not   ☐ have to pay a penalty.
☒ may   ☐ will not   ☐ be entitled to a refund of part of the finance charge.

See your contract documents for any additional information about nonpayment, default, any required repayment in full before the scheduled date, and prepayment refunds and penalties.

I have received a copy of this statement.

Alice Green _____   5-1-99
Signature   Date

_____
e means an estimate

EXHIBIT 18.2

Sample Credit Sale
Disclosure Form

FAIR CREDIT BILLING ACT

TILA includes the *Fair Credit Billing Act* (*FCBA*). Before the Act, some consumers complained they were unable to get creditors to correct inaccurate charges or remove unauthorized charges that appeared on billing statements. Consumers who believed they did not owe the disputed charge would not pay the bill. The non-payment was reported to credit bureaus, and consumers' credit histories were damaged. Another problem was that credit cards were sent to people who did not request them. Some unsolicited cards were lost or stolen, and consumers who never requested the cards were billed for unauthorized purchases. The FCBA addresses these problems in three ways:

1. It has a procedure to dispute *billing errors*. A consumer must notify the creditor in writing within sixty days of the first billing of a disputed charge. The creditor must acknowledge the complaint within thirty days of receipt and has ninety days to resolve the problem and notify the consumer. If the creditor fails to follow required procedures, it cannot collect the first fifty dollars of the questioned amount.
2. It prohibits the mailing of unsolicited credit cards.
3. It establishes procedures to report lost or stolen credit cards. Liability for unauthorized charges is fifty dollars.

Enforcement

Most billing disputes are resolved through the procedures established by the FCBA. Dissatisfied consumers can also sue for civil penalties for FCBA violations. In successful actions, creditors are liable for twice the amount of the finance charge, plus attorney's fees and court costs.

The FTC is the principal FCBA enforcement agency, with jurisdiction over department stores, gasoline retailers, and non–bank-card issuers, such as American Express. Other federal agencies enforce the credit statutes for other credit-granting institutions. Most banks are regulated by the Federal Reserve Board.

FAIR CREDIT REPORTING ACT

The *Fair Credit Reporting Act* (*FCRA*) regulates *credit bureaus* (consumer reporting agencies). It focuses on confidentiality and accuracy in compiling and distributing *consumer credit reports*. No limit is placed on the kinds of information that consumer reporting agencies may include in their files (such as information on political beliefs or sexual practices), so long as the information is accurate.

Agencies may sell consumer reports only if the reports are used for the purposes stated in the Act. A report may be issued if a business needs to evaluate an applicant for credit, insurance, employment, or other legitimate business needs. Any other use requires a court order or the consumer's permission.

Consumer Rights

The FCRA gives consumers the right to see information reported about them to a creditor that results in credit being denied. Further, since 1997, credit bureaus must

- Respond to consumer complaints about inaccurate information within thirty days.
- Tell consumers, on request, who has asked for copies of their credit history in the past year.

- Provide a toll-free consumer service number.
- Get the consumer's permission before giving a report to an employer or before releasing a report containing medical information.

When a consumer tells a reporting agency about incorrect information, the information must be deleted or changed or a statement from the consumer about the problem must be placed in the file.

To settle a lawsuit with the FTC and various states, the big three consumer credit reporting agencies—TRW, Equifax, and Trans Union—agreed to allow consumers to have copies of their credit report so that they can check them for accuracy.

Enforcement and Penalties

The FTC has responsibility for enforcing the FCRA. The Act provides civil remedies to injured consumers, who may recover actual damages when noncompliance is negligent. When the credit agency or the user is in willful noncompliance, the consumer may recover actual damages and a punitive penalty. In a 1991 Wyoming suit, TRW was ordered to pay $290,000 in damages—of which $275,000 was punitive damages—for willfully ignoring a consumer's attempt to correct errors in his credit report.

EQUAL CREDIT OPPORTUNITY ACT

The *Equal Credit Opportunity Act* (*ECOA*) was added to the CCPA in 1974 to prohibit discrimination against applicants for credit. The ECOA prohibits *credit discrimination* on the basis of race, sex, color, religion, national origin, marital status, receipt of public benefits, the good-faith exercise of the applicant's rights under any part of the CCPA, or age (provided the applicant is old enough to sign a contract). Creditors are prohibited from using such criteria (known as *prohibited bases*) in determining creditworthiness.

The ECOA requires a creditor to notify a consumer of its decision to accept, reject, or modify a credit request within thirty days of the completed application. If the credit request is denied or accepted but the terms are unfavorably changed, the creditor must give specific notice of the reasons for the decision and the name and address of the federal agency regulating that creditor.

Unlawful Credit Discrimination

The guiding law for ECOA compliance is simple:

> A creditor shall not discriminate against an applicant on a prohibited basis regarding any aspect of a credit transaction.

Because this provision is broad, *Regulation B*, issued by the Federal Reserve Board, provides specific rules explaining what constitutes unlawful discrimination. Some of the rules are as follows:

- A creditor may not make any written or oral statements related to a prohibited basis to discourage a person from applying for credit.
- A creditor may not use information concerning the likelihood that the applicant may have children or that the applicant is likely, for that reason, to have reduced or irregular income. Before ECOA, many creditors discounted or considered only a portion of a married woman's income, and in some cases, required the husband and wife to sign a statement that they would not have children.

JURIS prudence?

Don't Give This Bum Credit!

Lawrence Lindsey was rejected for a Toys "R" Us credit card, issued by the Bank of New York. The reason for the rejection was that Lindsey's credit history caused him to fail the computer model used for such credit requests. Lindsey does not have a savings account. Even more importantly, "Multiple companies requested your credit report in the past six months."

The bank was a bit embarrassed when Lindsey, a member of the Board of Governors of the Federal Reserve System, used this rejection in a speech to the Boston Bar Association as an example of problems with the credit scoring system. Lindsey, whose income is well above average and who has a spotless credit record, was immediately offered a credit card with a $15,000 limit. He declined.

Source: *The Wall Street Journal*

- If a creditor considers credit history in evaluating creditworthiness, it must, at the applicant's request, consider not only the applicant's direct credit history but also the applicant's indirect credit history (for example, accounts that the applicant was liable for and accounts listed in the name of a spouse or former spouse that the applicant can show reflects his or her credit history).
- A creditor may not request information about a spouse or former spouse of the applicant unless (a) the spouse will use the account or will be contractually liable for the debt; (b) the applicant is relying on the spouse's income or on alimony, child support, or maintenance payments from the former spouse; or (c) the applicant lives in a community property state or community property is involved.

A violation of ECOA exists if it is determined that a creditor used a factor specifically prohibited by the Act. The consumer can sue the creditor for ECOA violations. If the consumer is successful, the creditor is liable to the consumer for actual damages, punitive damages up to $10,000, attorney's fees, and court costs, whether the discrimination was intentional or not.

ECOA Notification Requirements

When a consumer's credit application is denied or accepted at less-favorable terms, the creditor must provide *written notification* containing the following information:

1. The basic provisions of ECOA
2. Name and address of the federal agency regulating compliance by the creditor issuing the notice
3. Either (a) a statement of the specific reasons for the action taken or (b) a disclosure of the applicant's right to receive a statement of reasons

The first and second notification requirements tell rejected applicants that it is against the law to discriminate on a prohibited basis and point them to the federal agencies that enforce the Act. Applicants thus know where to report suspected acts of discrimination and to ask questions about ECOA. The third requirement is the most significant. By knowing why they were rejected, applicants can reapply when

Consumer Credit Protection Abroad

The consumer credit regulatory scheme discussed here would make little sense to most lenders in other countries, because few of the rules that exist in the United States under the CCPA are mandated by legislation in most developed nations.

Most nations do not have statutes that prevent discrimination in credit markets based on sex, race, or other personal characteristics. The Race Relations Act in the United Kingdom limits some discrimination based on race or color, but in most countries, minorities have little political clout. Further, women do not have the statutory protection in most countries that is provided by the CCPA in the United States.

Most nations have general laws against misrepresentation and fraud that apply to credit markets. However, the kind of standardization that has come about in the United States under the CCPA is not as common in other nations, nor are there as many regulators like the FTC or the various banking authorities who write and enforce credit regulations.

their situation changes, or they can correct any misinformation used by the creditor. By knowing the reasons for the credit denial, applicants can better understand how credit decisions are made.

FAIR DEBT COLLECTION PRACTICES ACT

Creditors have the right to take steps to collect debts they are owed. If unable to collect, under state law they may go to court and ask for an order to *garnish* (set aside a portion of) the wages of the debtor to pay the debt, but that is a costly process. If unsuccessful in trying to collect a debt, a creditor can sell the debt to a company that specializes in collecting debts—*a debt collection agency*—or pay the agency a commission for the funds it collects. The commissions often are about one-third of the debt collected. Agencies handle about $100 billion in claims each year.

To collect delinquent accounts, debt collectors advise consumers by telephone or letter of the outstanding debt and urge them to pay. Sometimes, however, delinquent consumers are subjected to phone calls in the middle of the night, obscene language, threats of debtor's prison, and other forms of harassment and abusive tactics. The *Fair Debt Collection Practices Act (FDCPA)* is designed to eliminate unfair, deceptive, and abusive collection techniques used by some debt collectors but permits reasonable collection practices.

Restrictions Imposed

The FDCPA regulates the conduct of about 5,000 independent debt collection agencies that collect billions of dollars each year from millions of consumers. In *Heintz* v. *Jenkins*, 115 S.Ct. 1489 (1995), the Supreme Court held that the FDCPA "applies to attorneys who regularly engage in consumer-debt collection activity." The law does not apply to creditors attempting to collect their own debts, such as a department store trying to collect from a customer. The Act makes abusive debt collection practices illegal and contains a list of required actions and prohibited conduct by collection agencies.

Harassing, deceptive, and unfair debt collection practices—including threats of violence or arrest, obscene language, the publication of a list of delinquent consumers, and harassing or anonymous phone calls—are prohibited. Debt collectors may not discuss the debts with other people, including the debtor's employer. The Act prohibits the use of false or misleading representations in collecting a debt. For example, the collector cannot impersonate an attorney in attempting to collect a debt and cannot misrepresent that papers being sent to the debtor are legal forms. To illustrate the kinds of collection practices the law is intended to prohibit, consider the tactics used in the *Gammon* case.

Gammon v. GC Services
United States Court of Appeals, Seventh Circuit
27 F.3d 1254 (1994)

CASE BACKGROUND *GC Services, a debt collection agency, was trying to collect a debt Gammon owed to American Express. GC sent him a collection form letter that said the following:*

> *You should know that we are an experienced collection agency. We provided the systems used by a major branch of the federal government and various state governments to collect delinquent taxes. We have collected millions of accounts from people in similar circumstances. Now we intend to collect your debt. We know what we are doing, and we are very efficient. We have handled every kind of account—and dealt with every kind of excuse.*
>
> *You must surely know the problems you will face later if you do not pay. Send us your payment in full in the enclosed envelope, which is directed to the post office box we maintain for American Express accounts.*

Gammon sued, claiming GC violated the section of the Fair Debt Collection Practices Act (FDCPA) that holds illegal "the false representation or implication that the debt collector is vouched for . . . or affiliated with the United States or any State. . . ." The district court dismissed the case, claiming that GC's statements could not be read to mean that the company was somehow linked to any government. Gammon appealed.

CASE DECISION Kanne, Circuit Judge.

* * *

The district court viewed Gammon's claim "through the lens of the 'least sophisticated debtor' or 'least sophisticated consumer' " standard. . . . [T]he widely-adopted least sophisticated consumer standard was grounded in an effort to effectuate the goal of consumer protection laws by protecting "consumers of below-average sophistication or intelligence" who are "especially vulnerable to fraudulent schemes."

* * *

In maintaining the principles behind the enactment of the FDCPA, we believe a simpler and less confusing formulation of a standard designed to protect those consumers of below-average sophistication or intelligence should be adopted. Thus, we will use the term, "unsophisticated," instead of the phrase, "least sophisticated," to describe the hypothetical consumer whose reasonable perceptions will be used to determine if collection messages are deceptive or misleading. We reiterate that an unsophisticated consumer standard protects the consumer who is uninformed, naive, or trusting, yet it admits an objective element of reasonableness. The reasonableness element in turn shields complying debt collectors from liability for unrealistic or peculiar interpretations of collection letters.

Application of Standard

Applying the standard to this case, we conclude that an unsophisticated consumer reasonably could interpret the statement, "We provided the systems used by a major branch of the federal government and various state governments to collect delinquent taxes," to imply that those governmental bodies vouch for or are affiliated with GC Services. Thus, Gammon has sufficiently stated a claim upon which relief can be granted. By prohibiting representations by debt collectors that they are "affiliated with" or "vouched for" by a governmental entity, the FDCPA forbids a range of implications wider than merely the direct representation that the debt collector is or is a part of state or federal government. "Affiliate" is defined as "signify[ing] a condition of being united; being in close connection, allied, associated, or attached as a member or branch." Black's Law Dictionary 58 (6th ed. 1990). To "vouch" is defined as "[t]o give personal assurance or serve as a guarantee."

The language in the collection letter appears to be cleverly drafted in order to insinuate what obviously cannot be stated directly. It is difficult to image what end GC Services intended to accomplish with its statement other than the intimidation of unsophisticated consumers with the power of having the tax collecting units of the federal and state governments in its corner, or at least at its disposal.

* * *

GC Services appears to have implied that its development of governmental "systems" for the collection of delinquent taxes would enable it to cause "problems" for the delinquent debtor. An unsophisticated consumer could reasonably believe that his future "problems" would be with "a major branch of the federal government" because of GC Services'

development of the government's "systems." GC Services' letter, by which it sought to collect a delinquent account of Jeffrey Gammon may have violated the provisions of [the FDCPA] by falsely implying that it had an affiliation with the United States or various states.

Because Gammon has stated a claim upon which relief can be granted, we vacate the district court's dismissal for lack of subject matter jurisdiction. The case is reinstated and we remand for further proceedings.

QUESTIONS FOR ANALYSIS

1. Why are the courts concerned about applying the law with a standard of the "unsophisticated consumer" instead of the ordinary consumer?
2. The tactics prohibited by the FDCPA may be nasty, but if they result in more legal debts being collected, does that not benefit all debtors? That is, the lower the collection rate on debts, the higher the interest rate and the harder it will be to get credit.

The FDCPA requires the debt collector to send certain information to the consumer within five days of the initial communication:

- Amount of debt
- Name of the creditor to whom the debt is owed
- A statement that unless the consumer disputes the validity of the debt within thirty days, the debt collector will assume the debt is valid
- A statement that the debt collector must show proof of the debt if the consumer advises the debt collector within thirty days of the notification that the consumer disputes the debt

Contact with the consumer must end when the collector learns that the consumer is represented by an attorney or when the consumer requests in writing that contact end. The debt collector can wait for payment or sue to collect the debt.

Enforcement
Consumers subjected to collection abuses enforce compliance by bringing lawsuits. A collector who violates the FDCPA is liable for actual damages caused as well as any additional damages (not over $1,000) deemed appropriate by the courts. Consumers bringing action in good faith will have their attorney's fees and court costs paid by the collector. The FTC can sue collectors that violate the act, as can state attorneys general in states with similar laws.

When debt collection practices go overboard, the debtor may, of course, sue in tort, as well as for violations of the FDCPA. In a case in 1996, an El Paso, Texas, jury awarded debtors $11 million in damages against Household Credit Services, their creditor, and Allied Adjustment Bureau, a collection agency used by Household

Credit. Attempting to collect a $2,000 debt, bomb and death threats and numerous other violations of the debtor's rights were made. Damages under the Texas Debt Collection Act were a tiny fraction of the jury verdict.

ELECTRONIC FUND TRANSFER ACT

Various *electronic fund transfer* services are available to consumers:

- Automated teller machines (ATMs), also known as 24-hour tellers, that let consumers perform a variety of banking transactions at any time
- Pay-by-phone systems, permitting consumers to telephone the bank and order payments to third parties or a transfer of funds between accounts
- Direct deposits of wages and other funds into a consumer's bank account or automatic payments that deduct funds from the consumer's account to make regular payments, such as automobile loan payments
- Point-of-sale transfers (debit cards), which allow consumers, through computer terminals at retail establishments, to transfer money from their bank account to a merchant.

As these electronic innovations developed, Congress became concerned about the rights and liabilities of the consumers, financial institutions, and retailers who use an electronic fund transfer system. The *Electronic Fund Transfer Act* was passed in 1979 and required the Federal Reserve Board to write *Regulation E* to implement the Act.

Liability for Stolen Cards

One important protection provided by the Act is the liability limit when a consumer's ATM card is stolen and an unauthorized user drains the account. Unlike the Fair Credit Billing Act's fifty-dollar limit on liability for lost or stolen credit cards, the Electronic Fund Transfer Act's limit on liability is much greater. In some circumstances, the consumer may be liable for an amount equal to all the money in the bank account.

Regulation E provides that the consumer's liability is no more than fifty dollars if the financial institution is notified within two days after the consumer learns of the theft. The consumer's maximum liability becomes $500 as long as the financial institution is notified within sixty days. If the consumer does not report the theft within sixty days after receiving the first statement containing unauthorized transfers, the consumer is liable for all amounts after that.

Liability for Mistakes

The Act makes financial institutions liable to consumers for damages caused by failure to make electronic transfers of funds. However, liability is limited to actual damages proved, such as costs incurred by a consumer when goods are repossessed for failure to make a required payment.

Consumers are to receive a monthly statement from financial institutions. Consumers have sixty days to report any errors. When a consumer reports an error, the institution is required to investigate and resolve the dispute within forty-five days. If an investigation takes more than ten business days to complete, the institution must recredit the disputed amount to the consumer's account; the consumer has use of the funds until the complaint is resolved. Failure to undertake a good-faith investigation of an alleged error makes the institution liable for triple the consumer's actual damages.

Summary

- The Food, Drug, and Cosmetic Act, enforced by the FDA, imposes liability on companies and persons involved in the production and distribution of food and drug products. The primary concern for food is safety. The FDA is helped by the U.S. Department of Agriculture and various state agencies in food inspection to ensure sanitation.

- Food additives must be approved by the FDA before being sold to the public. The Delaney Clause holds that no food additives may allow any risk of cancer. Nutrition labels on processed foods must list by standard consumer portions fat, carbohydrates, cholesterol, and other nutrients, as well as certain vitamins and minerals and total calories.

- The FDA determines when drugs are safe and effective for sale and whether drugs will be sold by prescription only or over the counter. Food, drugs, cosmetics, and medical devices that the FDA determines to be unsafe may be ordered off the market or seized.

- The FTC has broad authority to attack unfair or deceptive business practices. The consumer protection mission includes the advertising substantiation program, which requires advertisers to be able to demonstrate the truth of product claims.

- The FTC issues trade regulation rules to govern business practices that have raised problems. The rules fix standards that businesses must meet, which makes prosecution for rule violations quite simple.

- The Truth-in-Lending Act, which applies to most consumer loans, requires that lenders meet requirements on how the details of loan amounts, interest charges, and other items are calculated and stated to the borrower. There is no defense for certain violations of this statute. The Consumer Leasing Act sets similar standards for consumer leases.

- The Fair Credit Billing Act details the rights of consumers to resolve billing errors. Creditors must follow requirements on how long they have to respond to the consumer and what they must do to resolve the dispute. As under other parts of the credit statutes, violations mean double damages, plus attorney's fees, for the plaintiff.

- Credit bureaus sell lenders the credit history about consumers seeking credit. The Fair Credit Reporting Act specifies consumers' rights to challenge the accuracy of reports issued by these bureaus. Credit bureaus must respond to inquiries from consumers about errors in credit reports.

- Under the Equal Credit Opportunity Act, creditors may not consider the following factors in determining who will be granted credit: race, sex, age, color, religion, national origin, marital status, receipt of public benefits, or the exercise of legal rights. Specific regulations govern how lenders must comply with this statute.

- Debt collectors may not abuse the rights of debtors granted by the Fair Debt Collection Practices Act. They may not make abusive phone calls, threats, or claims of legal action not actually under way or use other forms of harassment. A debt collector informed by any debtor that no further contact is desired may not contact the debtor except for notice of legal action.

- Consumer rights and responsibilities for credit cards and ATM cards that have been stolen are spelled out in the law. To limit liability for unauthorized charges, the consumer must notify the card issuer of the theft of the card.

Can Consumer "Protection" Go Overboard?

 The FDA keeps many drugs off the market that are legal in Europe and elsewhere. The agency has been accused of being too conservative, keeping effective drugs and nontraditional medical products from consumers that may be beneficial or that informed consumers should have the right to purchase. One example is discussed by a consumer who suffers the consequences of the FDA's "protection."

MY BLINDNESS—AND THE FDA'S

Woodrow Wirsig

Mr. Wirsig lives in Palm City, Florida. Reprinted by permission of *The Wall Street Journal* © Dow Jones & Company, Inc. 1996. All rights reserved worldwide.

I am going blind.

The Food and Drug Administration could save my sight—safely and effectively—if it wanted to. But it doesn't want to. The FDA is more interested in power, in controls, in procedures it devises than in the health of millions of Americans who suffer problems similar to mine.

My story is short—and desperate. I suffer wet macular degeneration. Already, in just the past six months, I've lost the sight in my left eye from the little blood vessels whose growth wrenches the retina out of sync. And my right eye already contains drusions, the little specks that indicate future damage—unless the damage is stopped now.

I know what to do, where to go. A procedure at the Scheie Eye Institute in Philadelphia uses the angiogenesis inhibitor Thalidomide to stop the growth of these unwanted blood vessels. I was there for a thorough eye examination just a few weeks ago. I admire everything about this institute. I praise it for its creative efforts to prevent damage to eyes. This clinic is following, strictly and honestly, all the FDA rules controlling its procedures. It does not complain; in fact, it may not agree with my complaint.

As long as I'm not pregnant, I'm told, using Thalidomide is safe for me. Even my body is supportive, normally resisting the growth of unwanted blood vessels as a natural condition.

But—according to the FDA rules—my left eye is too *bad* to qualify for the Scheie, and my right eye is too *good*. In other words, nothing can be done for me.

My anger at the FDA's irrational position is not new. I have been trying to cope with FDA rules and procedures for almost 10 years, ever since I had to fight the FDA to get my Alzheimer's-ailing wife into an FDA-controlled test program for Cognex. I testified at the three FDA advisory committee hearings on that drug. In the first two, March 1991 and July 1991, Cognex was rejected for reasons that are still a mystery. Then, seven years late, in March 1994, Cognex was approved unanimously. But have five million victims benefited?

The FDA, in its usual spirit of retaliation against those who don't kowtow to its regulations, continues to put roadblocks in the way of physicians' information. Thus, most of them do not know how to use the right doses of this drug.

Sadly, my two situations reflect a universe of FDA flimflam. Here's how the FDA and its political friends basically fool the public, the media and many legislators: Everybody supports the FDA's power and control over the safety of food and drugs. In fact, most of us would like to see the FDA's control over safety widened and strengthened. But the FDA also controls "effectiveness," and this is where the confusion exists and where, in fact, lie most of the complaints of "late approval" of desperately needed drugs.

Millions of cancer patients, Alzheimer's patients and many others must wait while the FDA dithers over drugs already deemed safe but whose effectiveness has not yet reached the 100% rate it insists upon. Since 1962, the FDA has controlled drug approval on the basis of safety *and* effectiveness. And in almost every instance since then, new drug approval has taken anywhere from eight to 10 years because of effectiveness considerations. Safety, in just about every case, has easily been established.

FDA Commissioner David Kessler and such supporters as Derek Link, spokesman for the so-called Patients Coalition and an assistant director at the Gay Men's Health Crisis, frighten less knowledgeable people. They falsely claim that new bills now being considered by Congress, by shortening approval times, will weaken the standards that ensure that drugs be both safe and effective.

But safe they still will be. And effectiveness should be none of the FDA's business. It should be the business of physicians and their patients, who should have the right to make their own decisions about using drugs already ruled safe.

I continue to go blind, in the meantime. If the FDA wanted to, without any problem at all, it could let me try the angiogenesis inhibitor procedure and stop the growth of those insidious blood vessels behind my retinas. But the FDA won't relent. So I'll be forced to search out clinics overseas that will perform this therapy or resort to underground suppliers and providers. How safe could they be?

Someday, for the sake of Americans' health, Congress and private organizations will successfully separate "safety" and "effectiveness" in drug questions. Let's hope they will also cope with those politicians in and out of government who slyly raise false fears.

Until now, though, nothing is saving my eyes.

ISSUE QUESTIONS

1. Should the FDA keep drugs off the market that have harmful side effects if the drug might help people who would probably die otherwise?
2. Should informed citizens have the right to purchase whatever medical drugs they want?

REVIEW AND DISCUSSION QUESTIONS

1. Define the following terms:
   Delaney Clause
   learned intermediary doctrine
   consent decree
   deception
   unfairness
   advertising substantiation
   trade regulation rules
   full warranty
   limited warranty
   consumer credit reports
   debt collection agency
2. What incentives do FDA administrators have to approve new drugs for sale? Do they have an incentive to hurry the process or to be very careful?
3. If consumers think agencies such as the FTC prevent unfair and deceptive practices, will they become less careful in watching out for themselves, thereby encouraging more bad business practices?

CASE QUESTIONS

4. Laetrile is a drug not approved by the FDA for sale. Some people believe it helps fight certain types of cancer. People who had cancer would travel to Mexico to be treated with Laetrile. Some people with cancer sued the FDA, saying they had a constitutional right to privacy that was being denied by the FDA's refusal to let them have access to Laetrile. A court of appeals held that it is not reasonable to apply the FDA's drug safety and effectiveness standards to dying cancer patients. The Supreme Court reviewed the case. What was the result? [*U.S. v. Rutherford*, 99 S.Ct. 2470 (1979)]

5. Jo Ellen Heath took Ortho-Novum oral contraceptive from 1967 to 1970 and from 1972 to 1974, when, at age 28, she suffered kidney failure that eventually required a kidney transplant. She sued Ortho, claiming the kidney failure was caused by Ortho-Novum, which did not adequately warn physicians to monitor blood pressure or watch for signs of kidney problems. Ortho defended itself, noting that it was in complete compliance with FDA regulations in marketing the product and in the literature that accompanied the drug; hence, it claimed that it

should not be subject to common-law strict liability or negligence. Could the case go to the jury, or did federal regulation of the drug remove common-law liability? [*Ortho Pharmaceutical* v. *Heath*, 722 P.2d 410 (Colo. Sup. Ct., 1986)]

6. Buckingham Productions sold various diet plans, such as the Rotation Diet and the Freedom Diet. It claimed that dieters could eat almost anything they wanted for four days each week and lose weight if during the other three days they followed a low-calorie diet and took the company's vitamin supplements and other products. The company reported that the average monthly weight loss was eight to twenty pounds for women and twelve to twenty-five pounds for men. What government agency would likely sue the company and on what grounds, and what would be the likely result?

 7. A store constantly has big signs in its windows and puts ads in the newspapers that take different approaches. For a month the store will advertise "Gigantic Savings of 75%" and similar claims. The next month it will advertise "Going-Out-of-Business Clearance Sale." The next month it will advertise "Distress Sale Prices—Everything Must Go." In fact, the store is not going out of business, and most of its prices are always the same. The prices are competitive, but not 75 percent off normal retail. Is this deceptive advertising?

8. BASF and Old World Trading compete in the private-label antifreeze market. Old World advertised that its antifreeze met various industry specifications, such as those of GM and Ford. BASF sued under the Lanham Act for false advertising and showed in court that Old World had not tested its antifreeze to see whether it met industry standards, which it did not. During the years in question, Old World's market share rose from 4 percent to 15 percent. The district court awarded BASF $2.5 million for lost profits it would have earned if Old World had not taken so much of the market. Old World appealed, claiming that there is no way the trial court could estimate such damages. Was the trial court right? [*BASF* v. *Old World Trading*, 41 F.3d 1081 (7th Cir., 1994)]

9. Martha Rodash borrowed $102,000 in a home equity mortgage. At closing, the lender gave her (1) the Truth-in-Lending Disclosure Statement, (2) the Mortgage Settlement Statement, (3) a Notice of Right to Cancel (which gave her three days to cancel the deal), and (4) an Acknowledgement of Receipt of Notice of Right to Cancel and Election Not to Cancel (which she signed). The Settlement Statement itemized charges of $22 for Federal Express, $204 for Florida taxes, and $6 for mortgage assignment fees. Six months later, Rodash stopped making payments on the loan and then sued to rescind the deal, claiming that the Truth-in-Lending Act had been violated. The violation was that the lender did not clearly disclose her right to rescind the deal within three days. The lender claimed the forms explained that right and that she had signed the "Election Not to Cancel" on the spot. She claimed she thought if she did not sign on the spot the deal might not go through, so she had been misled. Could she rescind? [*Rodash* v. *AIB Mortgage Co.*, 16 F.3d 1142 (11th Cir., 1994)]

10. A requirement of the Truth-in-Lending Act and Regulation Z is that each borrower receive two copies of the Notice of Right to Cancel. The lender gave Jacquelyn Elsner and her husband Max each one copy of the notice, along with other materials on the loan document they both signed. The Elsners later moved to cancel the loan agreement because they did not *each* receive two copies of the notice, which was a simple oversight by the lender. Is the loan good, or can the Elsners

walk away because of a technical violation of the Act? [*Elsner* v. *Albrecht*, 460 N.W.2d 232 (Ct.App., Mich., 1990)]

11. Joseph Ricci (an Italian-American) and his partner (Davidson) were turned down by a bank for a loan for their business. They sued, claiming that the bank discriminated against Ricci, based on his national origin, in violation of the Equal Credit Opportunity Act and that it failed to give a written statement of reasons for the rejection as required by the law. They claimed this violation of the law was willful, wanton, and malicious in reckless disregard of the law. The jury awarded the maximum $10,000 punitive damages allowed by the Act but tacked on $15 million more in damages, including $1 million for Davidson because he was not given a written statement of reasons for the rejection and $6 million for Ricci for intentional infliction of emotional distress related to the loan rejection. Can such claims go together? [*Ricci* v. *Key Bancshares of Maine*, 662 F.Supp. 1132 (D. Maine, 1987)]

12. Virginia Miller's husband had an American Express card, and Virginia Miller had a supplementary card on that account, which had a different number on the card and her name on it. The supplementary card carried an annual fee, and Miller was liable for all charges. Upon her husband's death, American Express canceled Miller's card, saying that Miller could apply for a new card. Miller did and was given a new American Express card and account. She sued American Express for violation of the Equal Credit Opportunity Act based on marital status. Did she have a case? [*Miller* v. *American Express*, 688 F.2d 1235 (9th Cir., 1982)]

13. Seymour Roseman quit his job as an insurance agent after a company investigation found money missing from his account. The credit bureau report on him had this statement in it: "We have handled [the investigation] at the home office in Boston and find that Roseman was employed as a debit agent [for the insurance company]. He resigned due to discovery of discrepancies in his accounts amounting to $314.84. This was all repaid by Roseman. His production in 1970, 1971, and 1972 was above average, and in 1973 and 1974, it was below average. This was the extent of the information available from [the insurance company] due to strict company policy." Roseman asked the credit company to check the accuracy of this information. The credit company did, confirmed its accuracy, and refused to remove the information from his credit history. He sued under the Fair Credit Reporting Act, claiming his rights had been violated. What was the result? [*Roseman* v. *Retail Credit Co.*, 428 F.Supp. 643 (E.D.Pa., 1977)]

POLICY QUESTION

14. Trade regulation rules exist primarily to make it easier for the FTC to sue companies that are engaging in practices the FTC does not like. Once a rule is implemented, all firms covered by it are "on notice" of the standard. Some have claimed that such rules are bad because they tend to set the industry practices to protect existing firms, discouraging innovation by would-be competitors. Does this make sense?

ETHICS QUESTIONS

15. The FDA, FTC, or some other agency is proposing a regulation that would hurt the sales of one of the products your company produces. The agency believes that there is a long-run consumer health issue that it should address. You estimate

the regulation will cost your company $20 million a year in sales and $2 million a year in profits. The three other firms in the industry that make a similar product will likewise be hurt. Your Washington representative tells you that if all four firms are willing to spend $5 million in lobbying efforts and campaign contributions, you will probably get a rider put on the agency's annual appropriation bill that will kill the proposed regulation. All other firms agree to help foot the bill. This method of killing proposed regulations has been used by other firms and industries numerous times in the past. Should you pay to help get the regulation killed?

16. You own a large furniture and appliance store that sells primarily to low-income people. Your store offers credit to customers, including many who have trouble getting credit elsewhere. The prices you charge, credit rates you charge, and profits you earn are determined largely by the default rate of your credit customers. You have a debt collection department in your store rather than using a debt collection agency. You comply with all federal and state credit statutes. However, you have found that by being *very* aggressive in collecting on delinquent debts, your losses are lowered. You use tactics that would violate the Fair Debt Collection Practices Act if it applied to your store. Should you use these tactics?

CHAPTER 19

Antitrust Law

As far back as the 1500s, the courts in England refused to enforce contracts designed to eliminate competitors. This common-law tradition has been maintained in the United States. As we saw in the chapter on contract law, the courts do not enforce contracts that are contrary to public policy. The courts held contracts in restraint of trade to be against public policy long before Congress enacted the antitrust statutes. However, before the statutes were enacted, there were no formal prohibitions on attempts by competitors to work together to *restrain competition* and *injure competitors.* As we will see, the general language of the antitrust statutes requires the courts to determine what really constitutes antitrust law.

Suppose Toyota wanted to buy Ford Motor Company. The antitrust statutes written by Congress do not tell us whether that would be legal. Instead, the courts must interpret the very general language in the statutes to determine what activities are prohibited and what activities are allowed to occur. Antitrust law, therefore, refers to the antitrust statutes, the interpretation of the statutes by the courts, and the enforcement policies of administrative agencies, especially the Department of Justice and the Federal Trade Commission. This chapter reviews the antitrust statutes and looks at how antitrust law is applied to both horizontal and vertical business arrangements.

Antitrust Common Law

Before the antitrust statutes were enacted, U.S. courts relied on the common law to restrict anticompetitive behavior. The principles applied by the courts were derived from our English legal origins. The American common law disapproved of business practices or agreements that were believed to restrain trade. A practice or agreement restrains trade when it prevents competition.

Nineteenth-century common-law cases did not hold *restraints of trade* to be illegal. Rather, when a court found a restraint of trade to be unreasonable, it refused to enforce the restraint, although the parties to the restraint were not liable for civil or criminal wrongdoing. For example, in the 1875 case *Craft v. McConoughy*, 79 Ill. 346, three grain merchants sued to force a fourth grain merchant to abide by a price-fixing agreement to which all four merchants had earlier agreed. The Illinois Supreme Court, finding price fixing to be an unreasonable restraint of trade, refused to enforce the agreement. None of the merchants, however, violated any civil or criminal law. Courts could not stop businesses from agreeing to fix prices or to divide their markets; they could only refuse to help them enforce such deals.

The Antitrust Statutes

The growth of large nationwide corporations in the late nineteenth century led to calls for more constraints on business behavior than existed under the common law. The result was the passage of federal antitrust legislation: the Sherman Act, the Clayton Act, and the Federal Trade Commission (FTC) Act. The key parts of these broadly written statutes are excerpted in Appendix H. Except for some actions that are clearly illegal under the statutes, it has been left largely to the federal courts to determine how the laws will be applied in practice.

THE SHERMAN ACT

The *Sherman Antitrust Act* was passed by Congress in 1890 in response to the general unpopularity of the large business organizations that arose after the Civil War. The most famous was the Standard Oil Trust, in reference to which the word *antitrust* was coined. The sponsors of the Act regarded it largely as a way to reduce concerns that Congress was dominated by large business interests. The major sections of the Sherman Act are so broad that one could find almost any business activity to be illegal:

> Sec. 1: Every contract, combination in the form of trust or otherwise, or conspiracy, in restraint of trade or commerce among the several States, or with foreign nations, is hereby declared to be illegal.
> Sec. 2: Every person who shall monopolize, or attempt to monopolize, or combine or conspire with any other person or persons, to monopolize any part of the trade or commerce among the several States, or with foreign nations, shall be deemed guilty of a felony.

THE CLAYTON ACT

Enacted in 1914, the *Clayton Act* was meant to supplement the coverage of the Sherman Act. In large measure, the Clayton Act was enacted in response to the

Supreme Court's early interpretations of the Sherman Act, which had limited its application.

Supporters of the Clayton Act wanted government to have the ability to attack a business practice early in its use to prevent a firm from becoming a monopoly (in addition to having the ability to attack the monopoly after it had been formed). Thus, the Clayton Act gave government the ability to attack business activities when the effect of the activity was "to substantially lessen competition or tend to create a monopoly." The following are the most important sections of the Clayton Act:

Sec. 2: It shall be unlawful for any person engaged in commerce, in the course of such commerce . . . to discriminate in price between different purchasers of commodities of like grade and quality . . . and where the effect of such discrimination may be substantially to lessen competition or tend to create a monopoly in any line of commerce, or to injure, destroy, or prevent competition . . . [*This section was added by the Robinson-Patman Act of 1936, and restricts price discrimination.*]

Sec. 3: It shall be unlawful for any person engaged in commerce, in the course of such commerce, to lease or make a sale . . . or fix a price charged therefore, or discount from, or rebate upon, such price, on the condition . . . that the lessee or purchaser thereof shall not use or deal in the goods . . . or other commodities of a competitor or competitors of the lessor or seller, where the effect . . . may be to substantially lessen competition or tend to create a monopoly in any line of commerce. [*This is the restriction on tying sales and exclusive dealing.*]

Sec. 7: No corporation engaged in commerce shall acquire, directly or indirectly, the whole or any part of the stock or other share capital and no corporation . . . shall acquire the whole or any part of the assets of another corporation engaged also in commerce, where . . . the effect of such acquisition may be substantially to lessen competition, or to tend to create a monopoly. [*This prevents mergers with or acquisitions of competitors.*]

Sec. 8: No person at the same time shall be a director in any two or more corporations . . . if such corporations are or shall have been . . . competitors, so that the elimination of competition by agreement between them would constitute a violation of . . . the antitrust laws. [*This restricts interlocking directorates.*]

THE FEDERAL TRADE COMMISSION ACT

In addition to enacting the Clayton Act, Congress enacted the *Federal Trade Commission Act* in 1914. The Act established the FTC as an agency empowered to investigate and enforce violations of the antitrust laws. Although most of the Act provides for the structure, powers, and procedures of the FTC, it also provides a major addition to antitrust law:

Sec. 5: Unfair methods of competition in or affecting commerce, and unfair or deceptive acts or practices in commerce, are hereby declared unlawful.

The *unfair methods of competition* referred to in the FTC Act have been interpreted by the courts as any business activity that may tend to create a monopoly by unfairly eliminating or excluding competitors from the marketplace.

Exemptions from and Enforcement of the Antitrust Laws

Not all businesses or business activities are subject to the antitrust laws. In many cases, successful lobbying of Congress resulted in statutory exemptions from antitrust scrutiny.

EXEMPTIONS

The justifications typically provided for exemptions are that the business is regulated by some other government agency or that the business requires protection from competition based on some other public policy rationale. The following activities and businesses are provided exemptions:

- The Clayton Act exempts nonprofit and certain agricultural or horticultural organizations. Extensions have been made to cover agricultural, fishing, and some other cooperatives.
- The Interstate Commerce Act regulates motor, rail, and ship common carriers (means of public transport). Generally, if the Interstate Commerce Commission (ICC) approves the actions of these businesses, the businesses are exempt from the antitrust laws. However, when the activities involved are not or would not be approved by the ICC, the government can take action. One example would be a conspiracy among truck freight carriers to set rates. Similarly, the Shipping Act defers to the Federal Maritime Commission in regulating water carriers of freight. Certain aspects of air transportation are regulated by the Federal Aviation Administration (FAA) and by the Department of Transportation (DOT).
- The Export Trading Company Act allows a seller or group of sellers to receive a certificate from the Department of Commerce and the Department of Justice allowing limited antitrust immunity for the purpose of export trade. For example, a group of domestic producers may be allowed to join together to enhance their ability to sell their products in other countries.
- The Parker doctrine allows state governments to restrict competition in such industries as public utilities (e.g., cable television), professional services (e.g., nursing or dog grooming), and public transportation (e.g., taxicabs). However, in 1992 (*FTC* v. *Ticor Title Insurance*, 112 S.Ct. 2169), the Supreme Court held that for the *state action doctrine* to protect private parties from antitrust actions, the state must play "a substantial role in determining the specifics of the economic policy." That is, the state must have intended to fix prices.
- The McCarran-Ferguson Act exempts the business of insurance from federal antitrust laws so long as the states adequately regulate insurance.
- Under the Noerr-Pennington doctrine, lobbying to influence a legislature is not illegal. This is because the First Amendment gives persons the right to petition their government even if the purpose is anticompetitive.
- Certain activities of labor unions are exempt because the National Labor Relations Act protects collective bargaining to set conditions of employment.

ENFORCEMENT

The antitrust laws we will review in detail may be enforced by various parties. Private parties—individuals and businesses—have the right to sue alleged violators and may seek damages and other remedies (discussed next). The majority of antitrust suits are such private actions. The Antitrust Division of the Justice

Department brings criminal antitrust prosecutions. For a civil lawsuit under the Sherman Act or Clayton Act, a choice must be made as to whether the Justice Department or the FTC will bring the case. The agencies have agreed to divide jurisdiction by industry but may consult on individual matters to decide which agency will handle a particular case.

Sherman Act

Violations of the Sherman Act carry the most severe penalties of the antitrust statutes:

- Violations of Sections 1 and 2 of the Sherman Act are *criminal felonies*. Individuals found guilty of violating the Act face up to three years in prison, a fine of $350,000, or both. Corporations found guilty can be fined up to $10 million. Criminal cases are brought by the Antitrust Division of the U.S. Department of Justice.
- Private parties or the government can seek injunctive relief under the Act in a civil proceeding. An *injunction* is an order preventing the defendant (the party who may have violated the Act) from continuing the challenged behavior.
- Private parties who have been harmed by a violation of the Sherman Act can sue for *treble damages;* if they win, they get three times their actual money damages, plus court costs and attorney's fees.

Clayton Act

Individuals and corporations violating the Clayton Act face penalties different from those provided by the Sherman Act. While the Department of Justice and private parties may initiate civil proceedings, the normal procedure has been for the FTC, which shares jurisdiction with the Justice Department in Clayton Act matters, to issue cease and desist orders, prohibiting further violation by a party. The FTC has the authority to investigate suspect business dealings, hold hearings (rather than trials), and issue an administrative order approved in federal court that requires a party to discontinue or modify certain business acts. Only when these orders are ignored may there be criminal sanctions.

FTC Act

Violation of this statute carries a variety of penalties, ranging from an order preventing a planned merger to substantial civil penalties. The Sherman Act's prohibition of attempts to monopolize can overlap the FTC Act's unfair competition ban. Since, unlike the Justice Department, the FTC is not required to initiate the prosecution of alleged violators through the federal court system, the effect of this overlap is to give the government administrative jurisdiction to proceed against potential Sherman Act violations without the more difficult task of having to prove a criminal violation.

REMEDIES AVAILABLE

An action to halt conduct that appears to be an antitrust violation can be brought either by a private plaintiff or by the government. The federal courts can provide a number of remedies, including the following:

- Restrain a company or individuals from certain conduct.
- Force a company to divest a subsidiary.
- Use company assets to form another company to compete with the original company.

Extraterritorial Antitrust Enforcement

All companies are subject to the antitrust laws of the country in which they are located regardless of where the firm has its headquarters. That is, an American firm with an office in Japan is subject to the rules of the Japan Fair Trade Commission even if all of the company's employees in Japan are U.S. citizens.

Controversy has occurred over the claim by the U.S. Department of Justice and the FTC that they have jurisdiction over antitrust violations that occur overseas and affect U.S. markets even if the violations do not break the antitrust law of the nation in which they occur.

An American company with operations in Germany may be accused of conspiring with German companies, in Germany, to monopolize some aspect of the U.S. market in which the companies operate. The activity does not violate German antitrust laws but may violate U.S. antitrust laws. The American antitrust authorities claim that they can gather documents overseas (enforce subpoenas) and prosecute the American company in U.S court for the actions that occurred in Germany. European nations do not claim that their antitrust authorities have such an international reach over potential defendants. Hence, managers must be consistently aware not only of the differences in laws in various countries but also of the differences in the laws' enforcement.

- Force a company to let others use its patents or facilities (licensing).
- Cancel or modify existing business contracts.

For a firm to recover damages under the antitrust laws, the harm suffered by the plaintiff must be the kind of harm that the antitrust laws are meant to avoid. For example, a firm buying inputs from suppliers involved in a price-fixing scheme can sue these suppliers for damages. Price-fixing is an activity that the antitrust laws aim to prevent. In contrast, a firm that loses profits because a new competitor enters its market cannot sue for damages, because increased competition is favored by antitrust law.

What Is Not Allowed

In *Brunswick Corp.* v. *Pueblo Bowl-O-Mat*, 429 U.S. 477 (1977), bowling-alley operators sued Brunswick Corporation for buying out and continuing to operate bowling alleys that were on the verge of bankruptcy. The plaintiffs argued that if Brunswick had not acquired the bowling alleys, the plaintiff's market share and profits would have increased when the alleys went out of business. The Court ruled that the injury suffered by the plaintiffs in *Brunswick* is not the kind of injury the antitrust laws guard against. According to the Court, "it is inimical to the purposes of these laws to award damages for the type of injury claimed here." Only plaintiffs suffering injuries caused by *anti*competitive behaviors of defendants can recover damages under antitrust law.

The Courts and Antitrust Analysis

The Supreme Court has stated that antitrust law is dynamic—it changes as business and society change and as more is learned about the costs and benefits to society from different business agreements, arrangements, and activities. One question the courts must address is whether, as a matter of policy, a certain business practice will be held to be per se illegal or whether a rule of reason is appropriate.

PER SE RULE AND THE RULE OF REASON

A *per se rule* means that a certain business agreement, arrangement, or activity will automatically be held to be illegal by the courts. The classic example of per se violation is a group of competitors sitting in a hotel room agreeing on the prices they will charge for their goods or on the sales territories that each will serve without competition. The agreement, arrangement, or activity is per se illegal because the courts believe that its use by a business will almost always result in a substantial restraint of trade. In discussing the notion of per se illegality, the Supreme Court in *Northern Pacific Railway Co. v. United States*, 356 U.S. 1 (1958), stated that there are certain activities that

> because of their pernicious effect on competition and lack of any redeeming virtue are conclusively presumed to be unreasonable and therefore illegal without elaborate inquiry as to the precise harm they have caused or business excuse for their use.

A *rule of reason*, in contrast, means that the court will look at the facts surrounding an agreement, arrangement, or other restraint before deciding whether it helps or hurts competition. In reaching its decision, the court will consider such factors as the history of the restraint, the business reasons behind the restraint, the restraining business's position in its industry, and the structure of the industry.

If, after such an investigation, the court concludes that the challenged business practice on net promotes competition, the court will dismiss the plaintiff's case. But, if the court finds that the practice on net reduces competition, the court will rule that in the present case the practice violates the antitrust laws.

Horizontal Restraints of Trade

When businesses at the same level of operation (such as retailers of a common product or producers of a raw material) come together (integrate) in some manner—through contract, merger, or conspiracy—they risk being accused of restraining trade. A *horizontal restraint of trade* occurs when the businesses involved operate at the same level of the market and generally in the same market. It is easy to visualize a horizontal arrangement among competitors by examining the diagram in Exhibit 19.1. For example, envision three manufacturers of lightbulbs who agree to charge the same price for bulbs or to split the market on a geographical basis.

EXHIBIT 19.1

Horizontal Business Relationships

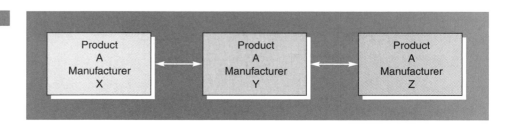

The diagram could also show an arrangement among wholesalers or among retailers of a certain product. A collection of rival firms that come together by some form of agreement in an attempt to restrain trade by restricting output and raising prices is called a *cartel*. The most famous cartel of our day is the Organization of Petroleum Exporting Countries (*OPEC*), the group of oil-producing nations that banded together for the express purpose of controlling the output and raising the price of crude oil. Since that cartel consists of sovereign nations, American antitrust laws do not affect it. When private firms in the United States attempt to cartelize an industry, however, they are subject to antitrust law.

Mergers

A *merger* involves two or more firms coming together to form a new firm. The combination can be created by one firm's acquiring all or part of the stock or the assets of another firm. A merger is termed a *horizontal merger* when the two firms were competitors before they merged (e.g., Texaco and Getty Oil). Largely because mergers frequently involve well-known businesses and thus attract public attention, the general public most often associates the term *antitrust* with merger cases. Each year the Justice Department and the FTC challenge about twenty to thirty mergers. One of the most famous merger decisions, *Standard Oil*, established the rule of reason as the approach the courts use in judging merger activities.

Standard Oil Co. of New Jersey v. United States
United States Supreme Court
221 U.S. 1, 31 S.Ct. 502 (1911)

CASE BACKGROUND *Claiming violations of Sections 1 and 2 of the Sherman Act, the Department of Justice sued seventy-one corporations and partnerships and seven individuals, including John D. Rockefeller, for conspiring "to restrain the trade and commerce in petroleum [in the United States] and to monopolize the said commerce." The conspiracy was traced back to 1870, when Rockefeller began to merge his company, Standard Oil of Ohio, with other oil companies and formed agreements with others to control all aspects of the petroleum business. Over the years, the companies were joined together in the Standard Oil Trust, which controlled as much as 90 percent of the production, shipping, refining, and selling of petroleum products. This allowed the trust to fix the price of oil and to monopolize interstate commerce in these products.*

The government requested, and the lower court ordered, that the trust be broken up so that companies would operate independently and compete with each other. After reviewing the complex background of this case, the Court explained the application of Sections 1 and 2 of the Sherman Act.

CASE DECISION White, Chief Justice.

* * *

[H]aving by the 1st section forbidden all means of monopolizing trade, that is, unduly restraining it by means of every contract, combination, etc., the 2d section seeks, if possible, to make the prohibitions of the act all the more complete and perfect by embracing all attempts to reach the end prohibited by the 1st section, that is, restraints of trade, by any attempt to monopolize, or monopolization thereof. . . . And, of course, when the 2d section is thus harmonized with and made . . . the complement of the 1st, it becomes obvious that the criteria to be resorted to in any given case for the purpose of ascertaining whether violations of the section have been committed is the rule of reason guided by the established law and by the plain duty to enforce the prohibitions of the act, and thus the public policy which its restrictions were obviously enacted to subserve.

* * *

a. Because the unification of power and control over petroleum and its products which was the inevitable result of the combining in the [Trust] . . .

of the stocks of so many other corporations, aggregating so vast a capital, gives rise, in and of itself, in the absence of countervailing circumstances, to say the least, to the prima facie presumption of intent and purpose to maintain the dominancy over the oil industry, not as a result of normal methods of industrial development, but by new means of combination which were resorted to in order that greater power might be added than would otherwise have arisen had normal methods been followed, the whole with the purpose of excluding others from the trade, and thus centralizing in the combination a perpetual control of the movements of petroleum and its products in the channels of interstate commerce.

b. Because the prima facie presumption of intent to restrain trade, to monopolize and to bring about monopolization, resulting from the act of expanding the [Trust] . . . and vesting it with such vast control of the oil industry, is made conclusive by considering (1) the conduct of the persons or corporations who were mainly instrumental in bringing about the extension of power in the [Trust] . . . before the consummation of that result and prior to the formation of the trust agreements of 1879 and 1882; (2) by considering the proof as to what was done under those agreements and the acts which immediately preceded the vesting of power in the [Trust] . . . as well as by weighing the modes in which the power vested in that corporation has been exerted and the results which have arisen from it.

* * *

The Remedy to Be Administered

It may be conceded that ordinarily where it was found that acts had been done in violation of the statute, adequate measure of relief would result from restraining the doing of such acts in the future. But in a case like this, where the condition which has been brought about in violation of the statute, in and of itself is not only a continued attempt to monopolize, but also a monopolization, the duty to enforce the statute requires the application of broader and more controlling remedies. As penalties which are not authorized by law may not be inflicted by judicial authority, it follows that to meet the situation with which we are confronted the application of remedies two-fold in character becomes essential: 1st. To forbid the doing in the future of acts like those which we have found to have been done in the past which would be violative of the statute. 2d. The exertion of such measure of relief as will effectually dissolve the combination found to exist in violation of the statute, and thus neutralize the extension and continually operating force which the possession of the power unlawfully obtained has brought and will continue to bring about.

Our conclusion is that the decree below was right and should be affirmed. . . .

QUESTIONS FOR ANALYSIS

1. Justice Harlan, who dissented in part, said the court should not use a rule of reason; all contracts in restraint of trade should be per se illegal. Is that practical?
2. Standard Oil controlled about 90 percent of the market, yet during the decades of the trust, the price of oil dropped consistently, thereby benefiting consumers. Should the court have taken this fact into account?

DETERMINING MARKET POWER

To help businesses and regulators assess the antitrust implications of a merger, over the years the Department of Justice has issued *merger guidelines*. Revised by Justice and the FTC in 1982, and again in 1992, the guidelines discuss factors that will be considered in determining whether a merger will likely be challenged. Many of the factors considered important by the Supreme Court in merger cases over the years have been incorporated into the guidelines, which place particular importance on the notion of *market power:*

> The unifying theme of the Guidelines is that mergers should not be permitted to create or enhance *market power* or to facilitate its exercise. . . . [T]he ability of one or more firms profitably to maintain prices above competitive levels for a significant period of time is termed *market power*.

Market Share

To assess a firm's market power, the courts begin by determining the *market share* held by each of the firms involved in the merger. A firm's market share refers to the percentage of the relevant market controlled by the firm. Defining the relevant market as the Internet browser industry in the nation as a whole, for example, Microsoft enjoyed a 28-percent market share as of 1999. That is, about three out of ten Internet browser programs in the United States are Microsoft products.

Recall that the Clayton Act states that the legality of a merger between two firms rests on whether "in any line of commerce in any section of the country, the effect of such acquisition may be substantially to lessen competition, or tend to create a monopoly." The phrase "in any line of commerce" refers to the particular *product market* in which the firms operate. In the *Philadelphia National Bank* case, the product market was "the cluster of products (various kinds of credit) and services (such as checking accounts) denoted by the term 'commercial banking.' " The phrase "in any section of the country" has reference to a *geographic market*. In *Philadelphia National Bank*, the geographic market was "the four-county Philadelphia metropolitan area." Therefore, in determining the *relevant market* from which to calculate a firm's market share, the courts take into account the appropriate product and geographic markets.

After determining the relevant market, a firm's market share can be determined by dividing the firm's sales by total sales within that market. In a merger case, the court will often consider whether the combined market share of the merging firms will exceed some maximum market share and will, therefore, "substantially . . . lessen competition" within the relevant market. The determination of the product and geographic markets, however, is rarely straightforward. It may even include estimates of the likelihood of future or potential competitors.

Product Market

In a competitive industry, there are enough producers so that one firm cannot affect the market for the products. One firm will not have sufficient market power

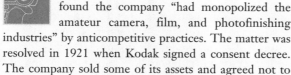

JURIS **prudence?**

Didn't We Just Sue Them 80 Years Ago?

Kodak lost an antitrust case in 1915 that found the company "had monopolized the amateur camera, film, and photofinishing industries" by anticompetitive practices. The matter was resolved in 1921 when Kodak signed a consent decree. The company sold some of its assets and agreed not to sell "private-label" film, that is, film under any name besides Kodak.

Years later, in 1995, Kodak was arguing to a federal appeals court that it should be freed from the 1921 decree and allowed to sell private-label film. The government opposed releasing Kodak from the decree, arguing that Kodak may still be benefiting from "its illegal monopoly ninety years ago." The court found, however, that the film market is competitive. Kodak has 36 percent of world sales, followed by Fuji at 34 percent, Konica at 16 percent, Agfa at 10 percent, and 3M at 4 percent. Since Kodak "lacks market power" in the film market, it was released from the 1921 decree.

Source: *U.S. v. Kodak*, 63 F.3d 95 (1995)

to raise the price of its product without having its customers purchase the lower-priced products of its competitors. That is, in a competitive industry, each firm effectively provides a substitute product for the other firms in the industry. A monopoly exists when there is only one firm producing a product for which there is no good substitute. The monopolist can raise prices above competitive levels because lower-priced substitute products are not available.

Geographic Market

Depending upon the nature of the product, the geographic market could be local, regional, national, or international. It is influenced by several factors. For sellers of products, the geographic area is most significantly influenced by transportation costs. Heavy, bulky products such as cement tend to compete in local markets; lighter, high-value products such as computer software are shipped nationwide and internationally. In the *Brown Shoe* case, 82 S.Ct. 1502, in 1962, while it examined some local markets, the Supreme Court found that the geographic market for shoes was nationwide because of the low shipping costs involved in transporting shoes to the marketplace:

> The relationship of product value, bulk, weight, and consumer demand enables manufacturers to distribute their shoes on a nation-wide basis, as Brown and Kinney, in fact, do.

Product buyers also influence the determination of the geographic market. The geographic market is generally limited to the area where consumers can reasonably be expected to make purchases. Consumers are generally more willing to search a larger market if the product being purchased is expensive and purchased infrequently. Personal computers likely will be judged as being sold in a nationwide geographic market, while paper for office copiers will be sold in local markets.

SUPREME COURT'S APPROACH TO MERGERS

Congress provided no guidance on what constitutes monopolistic behavior. Thus, in using the Sherman and Clayton Acts to control monopolies, the courts must appraise market structures and monopolistic behavior. Measuring monopoly power, however, is not an easy task. An ideal measure would involve a comparison of prices, outputs, and profits of firms in an industry under competition with those under monopoly control. But such a comparison does not lend itself to measurement.

The Supreme Court's *Philadelphia National Bank* decision provides many of the points to be considered when reviewing mergers. Although this case might not produce the same result if it were brought today, the issues raised by the Court in its analysis reflect the Court's modern approach to horizontal mergers.

United States v. Philadelphia National Bank
United States Supreme Court
374 U.S. 321 (1963)

CASE BACKGROUND *Philadelphia National Bank (PNB) sought to merge with Girard Trust Corn Exchange Bank. The banks were the second and third* *largest commercial banks in the Philadelphia vicinity. If the merger was allowed, the merged bank would be the largest bank in the region, doing about one-third of the* *region's banking business. Concerned about a trend toward concentration in the banking industry, the government filed a civil suit under Section 7 of the Clayton Act and Section 1 of the Sherman Act to enjoin the merger. After losing in the lower court, the government appealed to the Supreme Court, which regarded appropriate market definition to be crucial to the outcome of the case.*

CASE DECISION Brennan, Justice.

* * *

We have no difficulty in determining the "line of commerce" (relevant product or services market) and "section of the country" (relevant geographical market) in which to appraise the probable competitive effects of appellees' proposed merger. We agree with the District Court that the cluster of products (various kinds of credit) and services (such as checking accounts and trust administration) denoted by the term "commercial banking," composes a distinct line of commerce. Some commercial banking products or services are so distinctive that they are entirely free of effective competition from products or services of other financial institutions; the checking account is in this category. Others enjoy such cost advantages as to be insulated within a broad range from substitutes furnished by other institutions. Finally, there are banking facilities which, although in terms of cost and price they are freely competitive with the facilities provided by other financial institutions, nevertheless enjoy a settled consumer preference, insulating them, to a marked degree, from competition; this seems to be the case with savings deposits. In sum, it is clear that commercial banking is a market "sufficiently inclusive to be meaningful in terms of trade realities."

We part company with the District Court on the determination of the appropriate "section of the country." The proper question to be asked in this case is not where the parties to the merger do business or even where they compete, but where, within the area of competitive overlap, the effect of the merger on competition will be direct and immediate. This depends upon "the geographic structure of supplier-customer relations." . . .

We recognize that the area in which appellees have their offices does not delineate with perfect accuracy an appropriate "section of the country" in which to appraise the effect of the merger upon competition. Large borrowers and large depositors, the record shows, may find it practical to do a large part of their banking business outside their home community; very small borrowers and depositors may, as a practical matter, be confined to bank offices in their immediate neighborhood; and customers of intermediate size, it would appear, deal with banks within an area intermediate between these extremes. So also, some banking services are evidently more local in nature than others. But that in banking the relevant geographical market is a function of each separate customer's economic scale means imply that a workable compromise must be found: some fair intermediate delineation which avoids the indefensible extremes of drawing the market either so expansively as to make the effect of the merger upon competition seem insignificant, because only the very largest bank customers are taken into account in defining the market, or so narrowly as to place appellees in different markets, because only the smallest customers are considered. We think that the four-county Philadelphia metropolitan area, which state law apparently recognizes as a meaningful banking community in allowing Philadelphia banks to branch within it, and which would seem roughly to delineate the area in which bank customers that are neither very large nor very small find it practical to do their banking business, is a more appropriate "section of the country" in which to appraise the instant merger than any larger or smaller or different area. . . .

The merger of appellees will result in a single bank's controlling at least 30% of the commercial banking business in the four-county Philadelphia metropolitan area. Without attempting to specify the smallest market share which would still be considered to threaten undue concentration, we are clear that 30% presents that threat. Further, whereas presently the two largest banks in the area (First Pennsylvania and PNB) control between them approximately 44% of the area's commercial banking business, the two largest after the merger (PNB-Girard and First Pennsylvania) will control 59%. Plainly, we think, this increase of more than 33% in concentration must be regarded as significant.

* * *

The judgment of the District Court is reversed and the case remanded with direction to enter judgment enjoining the proposed merger.

QUESTIONS FOR ANALYSIS

1. Would a 30 percent share of the market enjoyed by the merged banks really "threaten undue concentration" as the Court held?
2. Why did the Court bother to list the share of the market that would be held, if the merger went through, by the two largest banks in the Philadelphia area?
3. Why did the Court find the Philadelphia metropolitan area to be the appropriate geographic market?

POTENTIAL COMPETITION

Ordinarily one thinks of competitors as offering similar products in the same market area. If the companies do not compete in this sense, should the courts be concerned about a merger? The Supreme Court has stated that the possibility that the two companies are *potential competitors* may be enough to stop a merger.

For example, in *United States* v. *El Paso Natural Gas,* 376 U.S. 651 (1964), a gas pipeline company with a large share of the natural gas market in California wanted to merge with a pipeline company that operated in the northwest. The Court blocked the merger because the possibility that the northwest company could move into California served as a check on El Paso's operations in California. The Court wanted El Paso to have the threat of strong potential competition that would be eliminated by the merger.

The rationale of potential competition was also used in the Court's 1967 decision, *FTC* v. *Procter & Gamble Co.,* 386 U.S. 568, in which the merger of Procter & Gamble, a large household products maker, with Clorox, the leading manufacturer of liquid bleach, was prohibited. After finding that bleach was the relevant product market, the Court held that even though Procter & Gamble did not make bleach or any close substitute, it could not merge with Clorox, because Procter & Gamble could make bleach in the future. Since Clorox had 49 percent of the liquid bleach sales, the Court thought it important that Clorox not be given a further dominant position by merging with a large company like Procter & Gamble. The Court wanted Clorox to be faced with the *threat* of strong potential competition by a company like Procter & Gamble.

DEFENSES: WHEN MERGERS ARE ALLOWED

The Court has noted in several cases that if one of the firms involved in a merger has been facing bankruptcy or other serious financial circumstances that threaten the firm, the Court will look more favorably upon the merger. The Court was referring to the *failing firm defense.* According to the Court in *International Shoe* v. *Federal Trade Commission,* 280 U.S. 291 (1930):

> [If] a corporation with resources so depleted and the prospect of rehabilitation so remote that it face[s] the grave probability of a business failure with resulting loss to its shareholders and injury to the communities where its plants were operated, . . . the purchase of its stock by a competitor (there being no other prospective purchaser), not with a purpose to lessen competition, but to facilitate the accumulated business of the purchaser and with the effect of mitigating seriously injurious consequences otherwise probable, is not in contemplation of law prejudicial to the public and does not

substantially lessen competition or restrain commerce within the intent of the Clayton Act.

The failing firm defense was created by the courts and not provided by statute. To use the defense to avoid violating Section 7 of the Clayton Act, the merging firms must establish that

1. The firm being acquired is not likely to survive without the merger.
2. Either the firm has no other prospective buyers or, if there are other buyers, the acquiring firm will affect competition the least.
3. All other alternatives for saving the firm have been tried and have not succeeded.

The merger guidelines note that the major defense to a merger is the demonstration that it will enhance efficiency in the market, benefiting consumers by the more efficient allocation of resources.

Considering Business Realities

The Court weighs economic evidence and, as a result, has decided that some mergers are not harmful to consumers. One defense used recently by some federal courts is the *power-buyer defense*. Under this defense, a merger that increases concentration to high levels can be defended by showing that the firm's customers are sophisticated and powerful buyers. If the court finds that powerful buyers have sufficient bargaining power to ensure that the merged firm will be unable to charge monopoly prices, the merger might be allowed. For example, in the 1990 case *United States* v. *Baker Hughes*, 908 F.2d 981, the D.C. Circuit Court of Appeals denied the government's attempt to stop a merger of manufacturers of hardrock hydraulic underground drilling rigs. Even though this industry was heavily concentrated, the court found that the sophisticated and powerful buyers of such drilling rigs—oil companies—had sufficient bargaining power to ensure that the merged firm would be unable to charge monopoly prices for its rigs.

The Supreme Court has yet to rule on the power-buyer defense. A more traditional defense to a merger challenge was the object of the *General Dynamics* decision, in which the Court allowed a merger of two coal-producing companies, one of which was a subsidiary of General Dynamics, a large diversified corporation. The fact that one of the merging companies was very large was not decisive, since the company did not have monopoly power in the coal industry.

United States v. General Dynamics Corporation

United States Supreme Court
415 U.S. 486, 94 S.Ct. 1186 (1974)

CASE BACKGROUND *The government challenged the acquisition of a strip-mining coal-producing company by General Dynamics, a large, diversified firm that owned a company engaged in deep-mining coal production. The acquisition was claimed to be a violation of Section 7 of the Clayton Act because it lessened competition in the production and sale of coal in Illinois and another geographic region comprising several states. The government noted that in the previous decade the demand for coal had fallen and the number of producers had dropped from 114 to 39 in the geographic market area. The government noted that when the two firms combined, they would have 22 percent of the Illinois coal market and 11 percent of the regional market.*

The district court ruled against the government, allowing the acquisition. The lower court noted that because coal was consistently losing market share in energy production, it was a declining industry. It also noted that most coal was being sold on long-term contracts to utilities for electrical power production. The Department of Justice appealed.

CASE DECISION Stewart, Justice.

* * *

Because of these fundamental changes in the structure of the market for coal, the District Court was justified in viewing the statistics relied on by the Government as insufficient to sustain its case. Evidence of past production does not, as a matter of logic, necessarily give a proper picture of a company's future ability to compete. In most situations, of course, the unstated assumption is that a company that has maintained a certain share of a market in the recent past will be in a position to do so in the immediate future. Thus, companies that have controlled sufficiently large shares of a concentrated market are barred from merger by §7 not because of their past acts, but because their past performances imply an ability to continue to dominate with at least equal vigor. . . . Evidence of the amount of annual sales is relevant as a prediction of future competitive strength, since in most markets distribution systems and brand recognition are such significant factors that one may reasonably suppose that a company which has attracted a given number of sales will retain that competitive strength.

In the coal market, as analyzed by the District Court, however, statistical evidence of coal *production* was of considerably less significance. The bulk of the coal produced is delivered under long-term requirements contracts, and such sales thus do not represent the exercise of competitive power but rather the oblig-

ation to fulfill previously negotiated contracts at a previously fixed price. The focus of competition in a given time-frame is not on the disposition of coal already produced but on the procurement of new long-term supply contracts. In this situation, a company's past ability to produce is of limited significance, since it is in a position to offer for sale neither its past production nor the bulk of the coal it is presently capable of producing, which is typically already committed under a long-term supply contract. A more significant indicator of a company's power effectively to compete with other companies lies in the state of a company's uncommitted reserves of recoverable coal. A company with relatively large supplies of coal which are not already under contract to a consumer will have a more important influence upon competition in the contemporaneous negotiation of supply contracts than a firm with small reserves, even though the latter may presently produce a greater tonnage of coal. In a market where the availability and price for coal are set by long-term contracts rather than immediate or short-term purchases and sales, reserves rather than past production are the best measure of a company's ability to compete.

* * *

Since we agree with the District Court . . . it follows that the judgment before us [is] affirmed.

QUESTIONS FOR ANALYSIS

1. Why was the Court impressed with the fact that most of the customers of coal production were large utilities? Might things have been different had the customers been individuals?
2. The Court noted in its decision that the coal industry is relatively easy to get into compared with other industries. What difference should that make in determinations about competition?

Horizontal Price-Fixing

The Sherman Act prohibits "every contract, combination or conspiracy, in restraint of trade or commerce among the several states, or with foreign nations." Thus, when firms selling the same product agree to fix prices, the agreement will almost certainly violate the Sherman Act. One question the Supreme Court must decide as a matter of policy is whether price-fixing is *per se illegal* or whether a *rule of reason* may be applied.

THE PER SE RULE IN PRICE-FIXING CASES

The Supreme Court has ruled that *horizontal price-fixing* is per se illegal. One of the classic antitrust cases condemning direct price-fixing as an unreasonable per se restraint of trade under the Sherman Act is the *Trenton Potteries Company* case. As the decision illustrates, the Court reasoned that the ability of a firm or a group of firms to fix prices involved the power to control the market. Firms with the power to fix even reasonable prices could use that power to fix unreasonable prices.

United States v. Trenton Potteries Company
United States Supreme Court
273 U.S. 392, 47 S.Ct. 377 (1927)

CASE BACKGROUND *The defendants, twenty-three corporations and twenty individuals, were convicted in federal district court of violating the Sherman Act. The appeals court reversed and dismissed the complaint. All defendants were members of the Sanitary Potters' Association and produced or distributed 82 percent of the sanitary pottery in the United States. They were found guilty of combining to fix and maintain uniform prices for the sale of bathroom fixtures and to restrain sales at the wholesale level to a special group of "legitimate jobbers." The evidence of the combination to restrain trade and fix prices was clear. The defendants did not object to the claims that they fixed prices, limited sales, and possessed the power to fix prices and to control the market. Rather, they argued that the trial court should have submitted to the jury the question of whether the price-fixing agreements were unreasonable restraints of trade.*

CASE DECISION Stone, Justice.

* * *

The aim and result of every price-fixing agreement, if effective, is the elimination of one form of competition. The power to fix prices, whether reasonably exercised or not, involves power to control the market and to fix arbitrary and unreasonable prices. The reasonable price fixed today may through economic and business changes become the unreasonable price of tomorrow. Once established, it may be maintained unchanged because of the absence of competition secured by the agreement for a price reasonable when fixed. Agreements which create such potential power may well be held to be in themselves unreasonable or unlawful restraints, without the necessity of minute inquiry whether a particular price is reasonable or unreasonable as fixed and without placing on the government in enforcing the Sherman Law the burden of ascertaining from day to day whether it has become unreasonable through the mere variation of economic conditions. Moreover, in the absence of express legislation requiring it, we should hesitate to adopt a construction making the difference between legal and illegal conduct in the field of business relations depend upon so uncertain a test as whether prices are reasonable.

* * *

It follows that the judgment of the circuit court of appeals must be reversed and the judgment of the district court reinstated.

QUESTIONS FOR ANALYSIS

1. What would be the practical problems with using a rule of reason approach to price-fixing cases?
2. Suppose the firms involved in this case could show that after they began fixing prices the prices of their products fell. Would (or should) that change the result?

The Supreme Court again discussed price-fixing in 1982, in *Arizona v. Maricopa County Medical Society*, 457 U.S. 332. Two medical societies formed two foundations for medical care for the purpose of promoting fee-for-service medicine and to provide the community with a competitive alternative to existing health insurance plans. Doctors joining the foundations agreed not to charge more than the

JURIS **prudence?**

We're Lawyers, and We're Here to Help You

Nineteen lawyers teamed together to bring a class-action antitrust suit on behalf of consumers against three gasoline retailers in Dothan, Alabama. In a trial that lasted six weeks in federal court, the jury found that there was a conspiracy to fix gasoline prices. Damages were found to be $1. However, under the law, the guilty party is also responsible for attorney's fees. The judge granted the attorneys $2 million in legal fees for their diligent efforts.

Source: *Associated Press*

maximum fees for medical services set by the foundations. The state of Arizona sued, claiming that the arrangement violated Section 1 of the Sherman Act. The Supreme Court held that the maximum-fee arrangements are price-fixing agreements and are per se illegal.

THE RULE OF REASON IN PRICE-FIXING CASES

While the Supreme Court takes a hard line against collusion for the purpose of rigging prices, it has always said that any one company has the right to charge whatever price it wishes for its products or services. In some cases, the Court has recognized that certain organizations, such as joint ventures, may help markets to work better. In some cases, a joint venture helps to set market prices, and if the Court finds that a beneficial reason exists for this, it will allow the practice to stand.

Consider the problem faced by the thousands of artists and owners of performance rights who are to earn royalties from having their music played by thousands of radio stations and other commercial users of their music. Because the artists could not possibly contract with every user of their music, they join organizations such as Broadcast Music, Inc. (BMI), or the American Society of Composers, Authors and Publishers (ASCAP), which issue "blanket licenses" that set the fees to be paid by any commercial users of the music. In *Broadcast Music, Inc.* v. *CBS*, 441 U.S. 1 (1979), the Court held that blanket licensing in such situations are not illegal price-fixing because there is no other way for this market to work. Since the market works better than it would if BMI and ASCAP did not exist, the "price-fixing" is not illegal.

The Supreme Court made the sports pages when it announced that under a rule of reason analysis, the National Collegiate Athletic Association (NCAA) could not fix prices that colleges receive for appearances their football teams make on television.

NCAA v. Board of Regents of University of Oklahoma
United States Supreme Court
468 U.S. 85, 104 S.Ct. 2948 (1984)

CASE BACKGROUND *Since its creation in 1905, the NCAA has regulated playing rules, academic eligibility, recruitment of athletes, and the size of athletic squads and coaching staffs for college athletics. Since 1951, the* *television committee of the NCAA regulated the televising of football games, something the NCAA did not do for any other sport. The NCAA signed an agreement in 1981 with ABC and CBS to telecast a certain number of games for a certain sum of money (TBS had a contract for cablecast of NCAA football games). Fees were paid to the participating universities according to the type of telecast (a Division I national game got a higher fee than a Division II regional game). However, the amount paid to the universities did not vary with the size of the viewing audience or the number of markets in which the game was to be telecast or according to the popularity of a particular team. There was also a limit on the number of times any one team could be on television, and universities were prohibited from making other arrangements for telecasts. Universities with the most popular football teams realized that they were subsidizing universities with less popular football teams.*

The district court agreed with the Universities of Oklahoma and Georgia that the NCAA was a cartel that fixed prices, limited output, and boycotted potential telecasters. The court of appeals agreed, holding that the NCAA television plan was per se illegal price-fixing. The NCAA appealed to the Supreme Court.

CASE DECISION Stevens, Justice.

* * *

There can be no doubt that the challenged practices of the NCAA constitute a "restraint of trade" in the sense that they limit members' freedom to negotiate and enter into their own television contracts. In that sense, however, every contract is a restraint of trade, and as we have repeatedly recognized, the Sherman Act was intended to prohibit only unreasonable restraints of trade.

* * *

Because it places a ceiling on the number of games member institutions may televise, the horizontal agreement places an artificial limit on the quantity of televised football that is available to broadcasters and consumers. By restraining the quantity of television rights available for sale, the challenged practices create a limitation on output; our cases have held that such limitations are unreasonable restraints of trade. Moreover, the District Court found that the minimum aggregate price in fact operates to preclude any price negotiation between broadcasters and institutions, thereby constituting horizontal price-fixing, perhaps the paradigm of an unreasonable restraint of trade.

Horizontal price-fixing and output limitation are ordinarily condemned as a matter of law under an "illegal *per se*" approach because the probability that these practices are anticompetitive is so high; a *per se* rule is applied when "the practice facially appears to be one that would always or almost always tend to restrict competition and decrease output." In such circumstances a restraint is presumed unreasonable without inquiry into the particular market context in which it is found. Nevertheless, we have decided that it would be inappropriate to apply a *per se* rule to this case. This decision is not based on a lack of judicial experience with this type of arrangement, on the fact that the NCAA is organized as a nonprofit entity, or on our respect for the NCAA's historic role in the preservation and encouragement of intercollegiate amateur athletics. Rather, what is critical is that this case involves an industry in which horizontal restraints on competition are essential if the product is to be available at all.

. . . What the NCAA and its member institutions market in this case is competition itself—contests between competing institutions. Of course, this would be completely ineffective if there were no rules on which the competitors agreed to create and define the competition to be marketed. A myriad of rules affecting such matters as the size of the field, the number of players on a team, and the extent to which physical violence is to be encouraged or proscribed, all must be agreed upon, and all restrain the manner in which institutions compete.

* * *

Per se rules are invoked when surrounding circumstances make the likelihood of anticompetitive conduct so great as to render unjustified further examination of the challenged conduct. But whether the ultimate finding is the product of a presumption or actual market analysis, the essential inquiry remains the same—whether or not the challenged restraint enhances competition. Under the Sherman Act the criterion to be used in judging the validity of a restraint on trade is its impact on competition.

* * *

Because it restrains price and output, the NCAA's television plan has a significant potential for anticompetitive effects. The findings of the District Court indicate that this potential has been realized. The District Court found that if member institutions were free to sell television rights, many more games would be shown on television, and that the NCAA's output restriction has the effect of raising the price the networks pay for television rights. Moreover, the court found that by fixing a price for television rights to all games, the NCAA creates a price structure that is unresponsive to viewer demand and unrelated to the prices that would prevail in a competitive market. And, of course, since as a practical matter all member institutions need NCAA approval, members have no real choice but to adhere to the NCAA's television controls.

The anticompetitive consequences of this arrangement are apparent. Individual competitors lose their freedom to compete. Price is higher and output lower than they would otherwise be, and both are unresponsive to consumer preference.

* * *

Our decision not to apply a *per se* rule to this case rests in large part on our recognition that a certain degree of cooperation is necessary if the type of competition that petitioner and its member institutions seek to market is to be preserved. It is reasonable to assume that most of the regulatory controls of the NCAA are justifiable means of fostering competition among amateur athletic teams and therefore procompetitive because they enhance public interest in intercollegiate athletics.

* * *

Accordingly, the judgment of the Court of Appeals is Affirmed.

QUESTIONS FOR ANALYSIS

1. Is the Court saying in this decision that, since a rule of reason is to be used, some forms of price-fixing may be legal?
2. After this case, the number of football games televised increased substantially, but the total revenues paid for telecasts fell. What does that tell you?

Exchanges of Information

One problem in antitrust law is deciding whether the trading of information among businesses helps or restrains the competitive process. Some business information is collected and disseminated by the government, but many exchanges are performed by private organizations, such as trade associations composed of firms in the same industry. If each business knows its competitors' sales, production, planned or actual capacities, cost accounting, quality standards, innovations, and research developments, is competition enhanced or is the information likely to be used to restrain trade? Does such information encourage better products and reduce waste and inefficiency?

INFORMATION SHARING

The Supreme Court considered the issue of the sharing of information by competitors in a 1978 decision, *U.S.* v. *United States Gypsum Co.*, 438 U.S. 422. Six major producers of gypsum were charged with conspiracy to fix prices. Manufacturers called each other to determine the price being offered on gypsum products to a certain customer. That is, a buyer would tell Company B that Company A had offered to sell a certain quantity of gypsum board at a certain price. Company B would have to beat that price to obtain the buyer's business. Company B would call Company A to confirm the offer to make sure the buyer was telling the truth. The gypsum companies defended the practice as a good-faith effort to meet competition.

On this aspect of the case, the Court said that a rule of reason may be applied, but in general, the practice was not defensible. "As an abstract proposition, resort to interseller verification as a means of checking the buyer's reliability seems a possible solution to the seller's plight [of dealing with inaccurate information from buyers], but careful examination reveals serious problems with the practice." The Court said that in a concentrated industry, an exchange of price information by competitors would most likely help to stabilize prices and so could not be justified. However, the Court did not apply a per se rule against such price information exchanges. Instead, it warned that such exchanges would be examined closely and would be allowed in limited circumstances.

CONSPIRACY TO RESTRAIN INFORMATION

Although the courts have indicated that it is legal to share price information in an open manner and it is illegal to share information secretly among competitors or for the purpose of constructing a common price list for competitors, it may also be illegal to band together to restrain certain nonprice information.

In the 1986 Supreme Court decision *FTC* v. *Indiana Federation of Dentists*, 476 U.S. 447, the Court held that the FTC justifiably attacked the policy of an Indiana dentists' organization requiring members to withhold X rays from dental insurance companies. Insurance companies sometimes required dentists to submit patient X rays to help evaluate patients' claims for insurance benefits. The X rays were intended to help eliminate insurance fraud and to make sure that dentists did not prescribe dental work not required. The FTC attack on this policy was upheld under a rule of reason analysis that showed the dentists' policy to be a conspiracy in restraint of trade. The Court noted that no procompetitive reason for the anti–X-ray-sharing rule was found.

Horizontal Market Divisions

A horizontal market division occurs when firms competing at the same level of business reach an agreement to divide the market on geographic or other terms. The effect of the agreement is to eliminate competition among those firms. Firms competing in a national market, for example, may reach an agreement to divide the market into regional markets, with each firm being assigned one region. Each firm can then exercise monopoly power within its region.

Agreements intended to provide horizontal customer or *territorial allocations* are often held to violate antitrust law. When the agreement does not involve price-fixing by the firms party to the agreement, the case may be considered under a rule of reason; that is, each challenged agreement will be evaluated in light of its effect on consumer welfare. However, as its decision in *Sealy* reflects, the Supreme Court is more stringent in cases involving common *pricing* by the firms to the agreement.

United States v. Sealy, Inc.
United States Supreme Court
388 U.S. 350, 87 S.Ct. 1847 (1967)

CASE BACKGROUND *Sealy licensed independently owned and operated manufacturers to make (according to specifications) and sell mattresses under the Sealy name and trademark. Sealy worked around the country to ensure the quality of Sealy-brand products and to fix minimum retail prices for Sealy products. Territorial restrictions were imposed by Sealy—each manufacturer had a separate territory. Sealy was controlled by about thirty* *manufacturer-licensees who set company policy. The government sued Sealy for conspiring with its licensees to fix prices and to allocate exclusive territories among the licensees. The district court held that the common pricing practices were per se illegal. However, the court found that Sealy's territorial divisions were not an unreasonable restraint of trade. The government appealed to the Supreme Court.*

CASE DECISION Fortas, Justice.

* * *

There is no dispute that exclusive territories were allotted to the manufacturer-licensees. Sealy agreed with each licensee not to license any other person to manufacture or sell in the designated area, and the licensee agreed not to manufacture or sell "Sealy products" outside the designated area. A manufacturer could make and sell his private label products anywhere he might choose.

* * *

If we look at substance rather than form, there is little room for debate. These must be classified as horizontal restraints. . . .

There are about 30 Sealy "licensees." They own substantially all of its stock. Sealy's bylaws provide that each director must be a stockholder or a stockholder-licensee's nominee. Sealy's business is managed and controlled by its board of directors. Between board meetings, the executive committee acts. It is composed of Sealy's president and five board members, all licensee-stockholders. Control does not reside in the licensees only as a matter of form. It is exercised by them in the day-to-day business of the company, including the grant, assignment, reassignment, and termination of exclusive territorial licenses. Action of this sort is taken either by the board of directors or the executive committee of Sealy, both of which, as we have said, are manned, wholly or almost entirely, by licensee-stockholders. . . .

Since the early days of the company in 1925 and continuously thereafter, the prices to be charged by retailers to whom the licensee-stockholders of Sealy sold their products have been fixed and policed by the licensee-stockholders directly, by Sealy itself, and by collaboration between them. . . . These activities, as the District Court held, constitute a violation of the Sherman Act. Their anticompetitive nature and effect are so apparent and so serious that the courts will not pause to assess them in the light of the rule of reason. . . .

Appellee has not appealed the order of the District Court enjoining continuation of this price-fixing, but the existence and impact of the practice cannot be ignored in our appraisal of the territorial limitations. In the first place, this flagrant and pervasive price-fixing, in obvious violation of the law, was, as the trial court found, the activity of the "stockholder representatives" acting through and in collaboration with Sealy mechanisms. This underlines the horizontal nature of the enterprise, and the use of Sealy, not as a separate entity, but as an instrumentality of the individual manufacturers. In the second place, this unlawful resale price-fixing activity refutes appellee's claim that the territorial restraints were mere incidents of a lawful program of trademark licensing. . . . The territorial restraints were a part of the unlawful price-fixing and policing. As specific findings of the District Court show, they gave to each licensee an enclave in which it could and did zealously and effectively maintain resale prices, free from the danger of outside incursions. . . .

It is urged upon us that we should condone this territorial limitation among manufacturers of Sealy products because of the absence of any showing that it is unreasonable. . . . [But] here, the arrangements for territorial limitations are part of "an aggregation of trade restraints" including unlawful price-fixing and policing. . . . Within settled doctrine, they are unlawful under §1 of the Sherman Act without the necessity for an inquiry in each particular case as to their business or economic justification, their impact in the marketplace, or their reasonableness.

* * *

Accordingly, the judgment of the District Court is reversed. . . .

QUESTIONS FOR ANALYSIS

1. Do you think the Court's decision might have been different if there had been no pricing agreement? That is, what if Sealy only existed to cooperate on joint advertising and territorial restrictions?
2. Can it be argued that this was really a vertical business arrangement, not a horizontal one?
3. Should the Court have considered the effect of Sealy on competition between brands rather than focus on competition among the producers of Sealy products (intrabrand competition)?

Sealy has been criticized by several observers. *Sealy* involves a form of business integration—numerous smaller firms banding together to produce a similar product with national recognition. The price-fixing condemned by the Court as detrimental to consumers would not have been illegal had Sealy simply built its own factories around the country or, over time, merged with many smaller mattress makers. That would have resulted in one very large corporation making mattresses nationwide—and selling them at prices fixed by the executives of Sealy. Under the arrangement that existed, the small independent mattress makers could stop working with Sealy to sell as an independent or sell under another brand name.

As the Court stated in its 1984 *Copperweld Corp.* v. *Independence Tube Corp.*, 467 U.S. 752, decision, a company and its subsidiaries—because they are a single legal entity—are incapable of conspiring to violate the antitrust laws. Since there must be a contract, conspiracy, or other such agreement by two or more parties before a particular activity can violate the antitrust laws, an activity that is legal if undertaken by a single firm may be illegal if undertaken by a group of firms.

Vertical Business Relationships

Until now, we have considered antitrust law as it applies to business *horizontal restraints of trade*. We now turn to antitrust issues such as vertical restraints of trade, exclusionary practices, and price discrimination. *Vertical restraints of trade* concern relationships between buyers and sellers, such as between the manufacturer and its wholesalers or the wholesalers and retailers. A key subject of this part of the chapter is how firms deal with each other along the business chain. We look at how producers', distributors', and retailers' dealings are controlled by antitrust law.

Vertical business arrangements govern relationships in the different stages of the production, distribution, and sale of the same product. It is easy to visualize a vertical restraint of trade by examining Exhibit 19.2. For example, envision a manufacturer who imposes resale restrictions on the retailers, thereby controlling the retailers' resale price, the area of resale, or the retailers' customers. Since these

EXHIBIT 19.2

Vertical Business Relationships

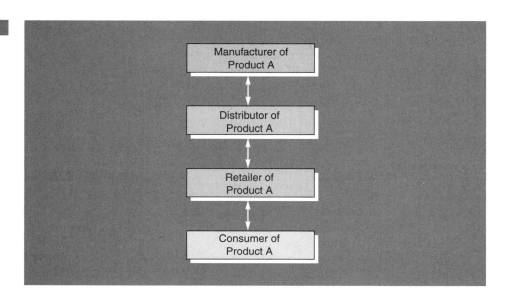

arrangements may restrain competition, they may be challenged as being contrary to the goals of antitrust law.

A company that does more than one function internally, such as manufacturing and distribution, is not constrained by the antitrust laws. However, a group of firms doing business at different levels in a given product are prohibited from engaging in certain practices. Vertical restraints of trade often pose very subtle questions concerning their effects on consumer welfare and are the subject of vigorous debate.

Vertical Price-Fixing

Vertical price-fixing arrangements generally involve an agreement between a manufacturer, its wholesalers, its distributors, or other suppliers, and the retailers who sell the product to consumers. As a rule, these arrangements are intended to control the price at which the product is sold to consumers. In many instances, it is the retailer who approaches the manufacturer and requests a price agreement. In other instances, the manufacturer requires the wholesaler (supplier) to control the price being charged by the retailer. Agreements can call for the retailer to fix minimum prices or maximum prices.

RESALE PRICE MAINTENANCE

Resale price maintenance (RPM) is an agreement between a manufacturer, supplier, and retailers of a product under which the retailers agree to sell the product at not less than a minimum price. One purpose of these arrangements is to prevent retailers from cutting the price of a brand-name product. Although manufacturers contend that such arrangements make product distribution more efficient, some antitrust authorities argue that in most instances, such arrangements are an illegal restraint of trade.

Dr. Miles Case

In 1911 the Supreme Court pronounced a basic rule about RPM. It stated that once a producer or supplier sells a product to a retailer, it cannot fix or otherwise dictate the price the retailer will charge consumers. In *Dr. Miles Medical Co.* v. *John D. Park & Sons Co.*, 220 U.S. 373, a producer of patented medicines sold its products to wholesalers and told them the price they must charge to retailers and, then, the price retailers must charge customers. Any wholesaler or retailer who would not follow the pricing scheme set by Dr. Miles would be cut off from further sales. The court held that a manufacturer can, of course, sell its product for whatever it wants, but it cannot "fix prices for future sales." That is, it cannot set prices further down the sales chain.

Pros and Cons of Resale Price Maintenance

RPM has been the subject of political wrangling in Congress and of scholarly debate by lawyers and economists since the time of *Dr. Miles*. The arguments have not changed much over the years. The groups favoring the ability to control resale prices have been the producers of quality, well-known products and small retailers. Opponents have been mass retailers and producers of lesser-known products.

Because small retailers favor RPM, they are more likely to have the same prices as the mass merchandisers. That is, most small retail stores cannot match Wal-Mart prices, so they would like to see all retailers forced to offer goods at the same prices. As we will see later in the chapter, this was one reason for passage of the Robinson-Patman Act. Even in the absence of competition from discount retailers, if the retailers are strong enough, they band together to demand that the producer impose RPM so that retailers will not compete with each other by price-cutting. RPM thus prevents cheating by members of the retail cartel.

Producers of well-known, established products (such as Sony televisions) often favor RPM because it allows retailers to earn higher profits from the sale of their products. These higher retail profits, in turn, encourage retailers to advertise the products to customers, to give good service to customers, and to compete at the retail level on the basis of service.

Mass retailers oppose RPM because they have grown large by slashing retail prices and taking customers away from smaller stores. The mass retailers often offer little point-of-sale service; their concern is selling a large volume of products at lower markup. Similarly, the producers of lesser-known brands want to compete on the basis of price, so they like the chance to be on the mass retailers' shelves with the best-known products. They have not incurred the high costs of establishing a good reputation, so their prices are lower even if the quality is good.

Consider how most people buy television sets. In the absence of an RPM arrangement between manufacturers and retailers, consumers may *shop* for the television sets at stores providing point-of-sale promotions because of the product information those stores provide, but they may *buy* the television at discount stores that sell for less but do not provide services or product information. If the result is that fewer full-service stores can afford to stay in business, RPM advocates claim that consumers and well-established brands may be worse off by the disappearance of the information and service that would be provided under an RPM arrangement.

VERTICAL MAXIMUM PRICE-FIXING

As we will see in the *Sharp* case, it is not clear that there are many restrictions left on vertical controls by producers. While *Dr. Miles* is still good law in that producers may not completely control prices down the distribution chain, in 1997 the Supreme Court overruled a thirty-year-old case (*Albrecht*) that prohibited maximum price-fixing in vertical relationships.

In *State Oil Co.* v. *Khan*, 118 S.Ct. 275 (1997), a gasoline distributor controlled the maximum gasoline sales markup that its gasoline station dealers could charge customers. One gas station owner wanted to charge more for retail gasoline that the distributor would allow and sued, claiming this was illegal price-fixing. The Supreme Court upheld the practice, noting that low prices benefit consumers regardless of how the prices are set. A rule of reason will be applied in such cases.

Vertical Nonprice Restraints

Manufacturers frequently impose nonprice restraints on their distributors and retailers. Such vertical arrangements often take the form of territorial or customer restrictions on the sale of the manufacturer's products. Coca-Cola, Pepsico, and other soft-drink companies, for example, set *territorial restrictions* on their bottlers. Each bottler is permitted to sell and deliver the product within its designated territory. Delivery outside that territory—that is, delivery in competition with another bottler—is grounds for revocation of the franchise agreement.

Customer restrictions may be imposed on suppliers by manufacturers when the manufacturer elects to sell directly to a certain customer category. A construction materials manufacturer, for example, may elect to deal directly with large commercial accounts but allow suppliers to deal with smaller and more numerous residential accounts.

Since its first decision on a vertical nonprice restraint in *White Motor Company* v. *United States*, 372 U.S. 253 (1963), the Supreme Court generally applied the rule of reason. In *White Motor*, the Court was faced with a vertical territorial limitation on sales. The truck company required its dealers to sell trucks only in an exclusive territory around their dealerships. In addition, White Motor sold trucks directly to certain customers—such as governments—and prevented its dealers from selling to those customers. Justice Douglas, writing for the majority, said that while horizontal territorial restrictions are illegal, vertical territorial restrictions would be weighed on their merits; that is, a rule of reason would be applied to each vertical restriction. After analyzing the territorial restriction under the rule of reason, the Court did not strike down the White Motor arrangement.

TERRITORIAL RESTRAINTS AND THE RULE OF REASON

In most territorial restraint cases, the plaintiff is a retailer or distributor that has been terminated by a manufacturer in the process of implementing a vertical territorial restraint strategy. To implement the strategy, the manufacturer often eliminates some distributors so that the remaining distributors have the necessary territorial or customer exclusivity.

In retaliation, distributors hurt by the manufacturer's strategy often sue, asserting that the manufacturer is attempting to monopolize the market. For example, in *Continental T.V.* v. *GTE Sylvania*, 433 U.S. 36 (1977), Sylvania implemented a vertical territorial restraint strategy with the intent to increase its share of the new television set market. Sylvania's share had fallen to less than 2 percent of the new television market. Sylvania decided to sell its television sets directly to franchised retailers. Although these retailers could sell other televisions, by agreeing to sell Sylvanias, they knew that no other Sylvania dealer would be in close physical competition. Sylvania's intent was to attract more aggressive retailers, who would have an added incentive to push Sylvania's products. Within three years, Sylvania's market share rose to about 5 percent. Sylvania's territorial-based franchise dealers appeared to work well for most parties involved, but one unhappy dealer that had been terminated—Continental T.V.—sued Sylvania.

The Supreme Court upheld Sylvania's location restriction under a rule of reason analysis. The Court noted that interbrand competition—competition among the same kinds of products (televisions) produced by different manufacturers—was more important in this market than intrabrand competition—competition among dealers of the same product. "Vertical restrictions promote interbrand competition by allowing the manufacturer to achieve certain efficiencies in the distribution of his product." The nonprice restriction imposed by Sylvania made the company a real competitor in the television market, which benefited consumers.

Greater Flexibility

Sharp Electronics is the Court's most recent major holding on this issue. Commentators believe that *Sharp* reduces the likely success rate of distributors bringing suit against manufacturers who terminate them. The decision has already encouraged some manufacturers—such as Sony—to limit the distribution of their products to wholesalers and retailers that they believe will follow the marketing strategies of the parent company. The general reading of this case is that unless a conspiracy can be shown to exist or unless direct price-fixing is involved, manufacturers have wide latitude in selecting dealers to distribute their products.

Business Electronics Corp. v. Sharp Electronics Corp.

United States Supreme Court
485 U.S. 717, 108 S.Ct. 1515 (1988)

CASE BACKGROUND *Sharp appointed Business Electronics in 1968 to be its exclusive retailer in Houston. It appointed Hartwell as a second retailer in Houston in 1972. Sharp published a list of suggested retail prices, but dealers were not contractually bound to follow those prices. Business Electronics sold Sharp calculators below Sharp's suggested minimum prices and below Hartwell's prices. Hartwell complained to Sharp that it would quit selling Sharp products unless Business Electronics was terminated as a Sharp dealer. Sharp terminated Business Electronics, which then sued Sharp for conspiracy under Section 1 of the Sherman Act. The district court held Sharp to be guilty of a per se violation of the Sherman Act. The court of appeals reversed, applying the rule of reason. Business Electronics appealed to the Supreme Court.*

CASE DECISION Scalia, Justice.

* * *

Our approach to the question presented in the present case is guided by the premises of *GTE Sylvania* . . . : that there is a presumption in favor of a rule-of-reason standard; that departure from that standard must be justified by demonstrable economic effect, such as the facilitation of cartelizing, rather than formalistic distinctions; that interbrand competition is the primary concern of the antitrust laws; and that rules in this area should be formulated with a view towards protecting the doctrine of *GTE Sylvania.* . . .

There has been no showing here that an agreement between a manufacturer and a dealer to terminate a "price cutter," without a further agreement on the price or price levels to be charged by the remaining dealer, almost always tends to restrict competition and reduce output. Any assistance to cartelizing that such an agreement might provide cannot be distinguished from the sort of minimal assistance that might be provided by vertical nonprice agreements like the exclusive territory agreement in *GTE Sylvania*, and is insufficient to justify a *per se* rule. Cartels are neither easy to form nor easy to maintain. Uncertainty over the terms of the cartel, particularly the prices to be charged in the future, obstructs both formation and adherence by making cheating easier. . . .

Without an agreement with the remaining dealer on price, the manufacturer both retains its incentive to cheat on any manufacturer-level cartel (since lower prices can still be passed on to consumers) and cannot as easily be used to organize and hold together a retailer-level cartel. . . .

Any agreement between a manufacturer and a dealer to terminate another dealer who happens to have charged lower prices can be alleged to have been directed against the terminated dealer's "price cutting." In the vast majority of cases, it will be extremely difficult for the manufacturer to convince a jury that its motivation was to ensure adequate services, since price cutting and some measure of service cutting usually go hand in hand. Accordingly, a manufacturer that agrees to give one dealer an exclusive territory and terminates another dealer pursuant to that agreement, or even a manufacturer that agrees with one dealer to terminate another for failure to provide contractually-obligated services, exposes itself to the highly plausible claim that its real motivation was to terminate a price cutter. Moreover, even vertical restraints that do not result in dealer termination, such as the initial granting of an exclusive territory or the requirement that certain services be provided, can be attacked as designed to allow existing dealers to charge higher prices. Manufacturers would be likely to forgo legitimate and competitively useful conduct rather than risk treble damages and perhaps even criminal penalties. . . .

As the above discussion indicates, all vertical restraints, including the exclusive territory agreement held not to be *per se* illegal in *GTE Sylvania*, have the potential to allow dealers to increase "prices" and can be characterized as intended to achieve just that. In fact, vertical nonprice restraints only accomplish the benefits identified in *GTE Sylvania* because they reduce intrabrand price competition to the point where the dealer's profit margin permits provision of the desired services. . . . "The manufacturer often will want to ensure that its distributors earn sufficient profit to pay for programs such as hiring and training additional salesmen or demonstrating the technical features of the product, and will want to see that 'free-riders' do not interfere."

* * *

In sum, economic analysis supports the view, and no precedent opposes it, that a vertical restraint is not illegal *per se* unless it includes some agreement on price or price levels. Accordingly, the judgment of the [appeals court] is Affirmed.

QUESTIONS FOR ANALYSIS

1. Why was this case not treated as an RPM? In what way(s) was this case different from an RPM case?
2. Does this decision mean that producers will have more control over retailers, or does it mean that more terms of trade will be settled by contract than was the case before?

Sharp clearly indicates that retail dealers and manufacturers are free to discuss ways in which the profitability of both parties will be enhanced by various business practices so long as there is no clear evidence of collusion in determining retail prices. If several retailers sell the same brand of product in an area, the manufacturer may work with the retailers to encourage practices that strengthen consumer satisfaction with its brand. If a manufacturer wants retailers to invest in service departments and other extras, discount dealers, who will not incur the costs of such extras, will likely be dropped from the list of retailers as a consequence. The Court is more concerned with interbrand competition than intrabrand competition.

Exclusionary Practices

A principal concern of the antitrust laws is the extent to which firms with market power can exercise that power and control the markets in which they do business. Various business practices, some undertaken by formal contract, are designed to indirectly exclude competitors from a particular market. Those practices are intended to make it more difficult for competitors to challenge the market dominance of the firm using such tactics. Such practices, which include tying arrangements, exclusive-dealing agreements, and boycotts, can come under antitrust attack if the courts find them to be anticompetitive. Section 3 of the Clayton Act applies to tying arrangements and exclusive-dealing agreements, while Section 1 of the Sherman Act governs the antitrust aspects of group boycotts.

TYING ARRANGEMENTS

In *Northern Pacific Railway Company* v. *United States*, 356 U.S. 1 (1958), the Supreme Court defined a *tying arrangement* or *tie-in sale* as

> an agreement by a party to sell one product [the tying product] but only on the condition that the buyer also purchases a different [complementary or tied] product, or at least agrees that he will not purchase that product from any other supplier.

International Distributorships

 Managers must be careful in international operations to be sure that a business practice legal in the United States is not a violation of antitrust laws elsewhere. The past decade's cases in the United States involving vertical restrictions in the distribution of products have encouraged firms to establish distributorships with exclusive territories. So long as prices are not controlled by the distributor, there seem to be few limits on vertical restraints.

In Europe, on the other hand, and specifically in the fifteen nations that the European Union (EU) comprises, the European Economic Treaty prohibits exclusive distributorships by territory, since they create intra-EU barriers. Hence, restrictions on the distribution of products that may be legal in the United States may cause legal action in EU nations and elsewhere.

The EU prohibition is not absolute, and a large number of goods and services have been exempted. At the same time, consideration is being given to exempting certain product classes that are subject to the current rule. In any event, legal counsel is needed in each country in which a business operates to ensure antitrust compliance.

The Supreme Court consistently holds that where monopoly power exists, tying arrangements violate the antitrust laws; the arrangements extend the firm's market power over the tying product into the market for the tied product. The courts apply either Section 1 of the Sherman Act—viewing tying arrangements as an unreasonable restraint of trade—or Section 3 of the Clayton Act—viewing tying arrangements as a conditional sales contract that may substantially lessen competition or tend to create a monopoly. The Sherman Act applies to both products and services, while the Clayton Act applies only to products.

The practice of tying products together is found in other, generally legal, business practices. A grocery store, for example, that offers a bag of Brand A flour at half price when a buyer purchases a bag of Brand A sugar is conducting a tie-in sale that is legal. It is legal because Brand A has no monopoly power over either product. Since you can buy many different brands of flour and sugar, Brand A sugar has no monopoly power over consumers. Also, a tie-in sale may be justified if the seller can demonstrate that a technology in a highly sensitive machine operates properly only when the seller's replacement parts and service are used.

Rule of Reason Applied to Tie-In Cases

In recent years, the Supreme Court has held that tie-ins meet a rule of reason test so long as competitive alternatives exist. That is, if a tie-in creates a monopoly when there are no or few good alternatives, it is likely illegal; but if products or services are tied together when there are competitors, the tie-in will likely pass the rule of reason test, as the Court held in the 1977 case *U.S. Steel Corp.* v. *Fortner Enterprises*, 429 U.S. 610.

U.S. Steel produced, among other things, prefabricated housing. Fortner needed $2 million to develop land on which to place mobile homes that he promised to buy from U.S. Steel if it would loan him the money. The credit division of U.S. Steel made the loan. Later, Fortner's venture failed, and Fortner claimed the contract with U.S. Steel violated antitrust law because there was a tie-in between the purchase of homes and the financing. The mobile homes were the product tied to U.S. Steel's alleged power over the credit market. The Court rejected that argument, holding that U.S. Steel, while large, had no monopoly power over credit or over mobile homes, both of which are highly competitive markets. Since the tie-in did not exploit any monopoly power, the actions of U.S. Steel did not violate the antitrust law under a rule of reason analysis.

The Court continued its rule of reason approach in the 1984 decision *Jefferson Parish Hospital District No. 2* v. *Hyde*, 466 U.S. 2. There the Court considered a suit filed by Hyde, a board-certified anesthesiologist, who applied for admission to the medical staff of East Jefferson Hospital. Hyde was denied admission because the hospital had a contract with a professional medical corporation requiring all anesthesiological services for the hospital's patients to be performed by that firm. Hyde claimed the exclusive contract violated Section 1 of the Sherman Act. The Supreme Court held that the contract was not illegal.

The Court noted that in such an inquiry, one must look at the markets involved and the amount of market power possessed by the providers of the services. Justice Stevens noted for the majority that since patients are generally free to choose hospitals other than East Jefferson, they could obtain other anesthesiological services if they wished. Simply because the two services (e.g., surgery and anesthesia) go together does not make the contract illegal. Tying arrangements will be condemned if they restrain competition on the merits by forcing purchases that would not otherwise be made. Here there was no evidence that price, quality, or supply or demand for either the tying or the tied product was adversely affected by the exclusive contract.

Vertical Restraint Guidelines

The Department of Justice issued *Vertical Restraint Guidelines* in 1985. Citing the *Jefferson Parish* decision, the guidelines claim that the Supreme Court is likely to impose a per se rule of illegality only when three conditions are met:

1. The seller has market power in the tying product.
2. Tied and tying products are separate.
3. There is evidence of substantial adverse effect in the tied product market.

In other situations, the rule of reason approach is to be employed. The Justice Department said that in such cases, the following test would hold:

> The use of tying will not be challenged if the party imposing the tie has a market share of thirty percent or less in the market for the tying product. This presumption can be overcome only by a showing that the tying agreement unreasonably restrained competition in the market for the tied product.

The Supreme Court's most recent decision on tie-ins (*Eastman Kodak*) indicates that rule of reason does not mean that all tie-in arrangements will be upheld.

Eastman Kodak Co. v. Image Technical Services, Inc.

United States Supreme Court
504 U.S. 451, 112 S.Ct. 2072 (1992)

CASE BACKGROUND *Kodak makes and sells high-volume photocopiers and micrographics equipment (which capture and replay images, including computer informa-* *tion, on microfilm). Some of this complex equipment is unique to Kodak. Kodak makes replacement parts for its machines or has the parts made for Kodak by independent* *manufacturers. Kodak also provides service for its machines after the initial warranty period. The prices it charges for machines, parts, and service differ according to the deal struck with each customer.*

In the early 1980s, independent service organizations (ISOs) began repairing and servicing Kodak equipment at lower prices. The ISOs also sold Kodak parts and reconditioned and sold used Kodak equipment. In 1985, Kodak said that it would sell replacement parts only to buyers of Kodak equipment who use Kodak service or who repair their own machines. Kodak made it very difficult for ISOs to obtain its parts. Most ISOs lost service and parts business to Kodak; some went out of business.

Eighteen ISOs sued Kodak, charging that it unlawfully tied the sale of service for Kodak machines to the sale of parts. District court granted summary judgment in favor of Kodak. The court of appeals reversed, ordering a trial on the issue of whether an illegal tying arrangement existed. Kodak appealed, asking the Supreme Court to uphold the judgment in its favor.

CASE DECISION Blackmun, Justice.

* * *

Kodak did not dispute that its arrangement affects a substantial volume of interstate commerce. It, however, did challenge whether its activities constituted a "tying arrangement" and whether Kodak exercised "appreciable economic power" in the tying market. We consider these issues in turn.

* * *

For service and parts to be considered two distinct products, there must be sufficient consumer demand so that it is efficient for a firm to provide service separately from parts. Evidence in the record indicates that service and parts have been sold separately in the past and still are sold separately to self-service equipment owners. Indeed, the development of the entire high-technology service industry is evidence of the efficiency of a separate market for service.

Kodak insists that because there is no demand for parts separate from service, there cannot be separate markets for service and parts. By that logic, we would be forced to conclude that there can never be separate markets, for example, for cameras and film, computers and software, or automobiles and tires. That is an assumption we are unwilling to make. . . .

Kodak's assertion also appears to be incorrect as a factual matter. At least some consumers would purchase service without parts, because some service does not require parts, and some consumers, those who self-service for example, would purchase parts without service. Enough doubt is cast on Kodak's claim of a unified market that it should be resolved by the trier of fact.

* * *

Having found sufficient evidence of a tying arrangement, we consider the other necessary feature of an illegal tying arrangement: appreciable economic power in the tying market. Market power is the power "to force a purchaser to do something that he would not do in a competitive market.". . .

Kodak counters that even if it concedes monopoly *share* of the relevant parts market, it cannot actually exercise the necessary market *power* for a Sherman Act violation. This is so, according to Kodak, because competition exists in the equipment market. Kodak argues that it could not have the ability to raise prices of service and parts above the level that would be charged in a competitive market because any increase in profits from a higher price in the aftermarkets at least would be offset by a corresponding loss in profits from lower equipment sales as consumers began purchasing equipment with more attractive service costs. . . .

Legal presumptions that rest on formalistic distinctions rather than actual market realities are generally disfavored in antitrust law. This Court has preferred to resolve antitrust claims on a case-by-case basis, focusing on the "particular facts disclosed by the record." . . .

Kodak, then, bears a substantial burden in showing that it is entitled to summary judgment. It must show that despite evidence of increased prices and excluded competition, an inference of market power is unreasonable. To determine whether Kodak has met that burden, we must unravel the factual assumptions underlying its proposed rule that lack of power in the equipment market necessarily precludes power in the aftermarkets. . . .

It is clearly reasonable to infer that Kodak has market power to raise prices and drive out competition in the aftermarkets, since respondents offer direct evidence that Kodak did so. It is also plausible, as discussed above, to infer that Kodak chose to gain immediate profits by exerting that market power where locked-in customers, high information costs, and discriminatory pricing limited and perhaps eliminated any long-term loss. Viewing the evidence in the light most favorable to respondents, their allegations of market power "mak[e] . . . economic sense."

* * *

As recounted at length above, respondents have presented evidence that Kodak took exclusionary action to maintain its parts monopoly and used its control over parts to strengthen its monopoly share of the Kodak service market. Liability turns, then, on whether "valid business reasons" can explain Kodak's actions. Kodak contends that it has three valid business justifications for its actions: "(1) to promote interbrand equipment competition by allowing Kodak to stress the quality of its service; (2) to improve asset management by reducing Kodak's inventory costs; and (3) to prevent ISOs from free riding on Kodak's capital investment in equipment, parts and service." Factual questions exist, however, about the validity and sufficiency of each claimed justification, making summary judgment inappropriate.

* * *

Accordingly, the judgment of the Court of Appeals denying summary judgment is affirmed.

QUESTIONS FOR ANALYSIS

1. Kodak claimed that it was selling one product—the machine, parts, and service—that required "life-cycle" pricing of the whole bundle. To allow ISOs to demand their parts and cut into their service is allowing them to free ride on the sophisticated machinery Kodak invented. Why did the Court seem not to like that argument?
2. Many manufacturers are the only producers of parts used in their machines. Does this opinion indicate that such producers may be required to sell their parts to anyone requesting them?

BOYCOTTS

A *boycott* occurs when a group conspires to prevent the carrying on of business or to harm a business. It can be executed by any organized group—consumers, union members, retailers, wholesalers, or suppliers—who, when acting together, can inflict economic damage on a business. The boycott is often used to force compliance with a price-fixing scheme or some other restraint of trade. Boycott cases usually fall under the per se rule against price-fixing.

In an early leading decision, *Eastern States Retail Lumber Dealers' Assn.* v. *United States*, 234 U.S. 600 (1914), the Court struck down a boycott designed to punish lumber wholesalers who sold directly to the public. Lumber retailers would turn in

---

Flash! Zap That Market!

Flash and Zap are special-events photographers who compete for business taking pictures at fraternity and sorority parties at the University of Alabama. Their photographers attend parties, take pictures, then display the results later and take orders. Flash sued Zap for monopolizing "the event photography industry in Tuscaloosa."

The Alabama supreme court found that Zap had monopoly power in that market "and that it acquired the power through business acumen and through having a superior product, which are legally permissible." How-

ever, Zap got some Greek houses to sign exclusive contracts giving it the sole right to take photographs at parties for two years.

The court struck down this monopolistic practice in the "Tuscaloosa event photography market" by holding that Zap could sign only one-year exclusive contracts, thereby allowing Flash the chance to obtain more contracts.

Source: *McCluney, d/b/a Flash* v. *Zap*, 663 So.2d 922 (1995)

to their association the names of wholesalers who sold to the public. The retailers were trying to limit competition in lumber sales to the public. The association would then send to retailers the names of wholesalers who sold directly to the public in hopes that the retailers would boycott those wholesalers. Even though there was no enforcement mechanism—retailers were free to deal with such wholesalers—and there was no evidence that the boycott of the lumber wholesalers who sold to the public caused any loss of business, the Court said the Sherman Act prohibits such boycotts.

Unlike other vertical restrictions where one manufacturer negotiates with individual dealers about terms of trade, boycotts involve either all manufacturers getting together to tell dealers what they must do, or all dealers getting together to tell manufacturers what they must do. In 1990, the Supreme Court reiterated that when horizontal competitors use a boycott to force a change in the nature of a vertical relationship, there is a per se violation of the law.

FTC v. Superior Court Trial Lawyers Association
United States Supreme Court
493 U.S. 411, 110 S.Ct. 768 (1990)

CASE BACKGROUND *Operating under the Criminal Justice Act (CJA), a group of about 100 lawyers in private practice regularly acted as court-appointed attorneys for indigent criminal defendants charged in the District of Columbia. The attorneys belonged to the Superior Court Trial Lawyers Association (SCTLA), a private organization. Their fees for legal work ($30 per hour for court time, $20 per hour for out-of-court time) were paid by the District of Columbia on behalf of their clients. The average annual income for the attorneys from this work was $45,000 in 1982 (about $75,000 in 2000 dollars). The SCTLA demanded that the government of the District of Columbia double its fees. When this did not happen, the SCTLA organized a boycott. About 90 of the 100 attorneys boycotted the criminal courts of the District, which nearly brought the system to a stop. After two weeks, the District raised attorney fees to $35 per hour for all work and promised to double the original fees as demanded as soon as possible.*

The FTC charged the SCTLA with a conspiracy to fix prices and to conduct a boycott that constituted unfair methods of competition under Section 5 of the FTC Act. Although the administrative law judge (ALJ) of the FTC concluded that the complaint should be dismissed, the Commission ruled that the boycott was illegal per se. The court of appeals reversed the FTC, holding that the boycott was a political expression protected by the First Amendment. The Supreme Court reviewed the decision.

CASE DECISION Stevens, Justice.

* * *

Prior to the boycott CJA lawyers were in competition with one another, each deciding independently whether and how often to offer to provide services to the District at CJA rates. The agreement among the CJA lawyers was designed to obtain higher prices for their services and was implemented by a concerted refusal to serve an important customer in the market for legal services and, indeed, the only customer in the market for the particular services that CJA regulars offered. "This constriction of supply is the essence of 'price-fixing,' whether it be accomplished by agreeing upon a price, which will decrease the quantity demanded, or by agreeing upon an output, which will increase the price offered." The horizontal arrangement among these competitors was unquestionably a "naked restraint" on price and output. . . .

The social justifications proffered for [the SCLTA's] restraint of trade thus do not make it any less unlawful. The statutory policy underlying the Sherman Act "precludes inquiry into the question whether competition is good or bad." [the SCLTA's] argument . . . asks us to find that their boycott is permissible because the price it seeks to set is reasonable. But it was settled shortly after the Sherman Act was passed that it "is no excuse that the prices fixed are themselves reasonable." [the SCLTA's] agreement is not outside the coverage of the Sherman Act simply because its objective was the enactment of favorable legislation.

* * *

The *per se* rules in antitrust law serve purposes analogous to *per se* restrictions upon, for example, stunt flying in congested areas or speeding. Laws prohibiting stunt flying or setting speed limits are justified by the State's interest in protecting human life and property. . . .

So it is with boycotts and price-fixing. Every such horizontal arrangement among competitors poses some threat to the free market. . . .

Of course, some boycotts and some price-fixing agreements are more pernicious than others; some are only partly successful, and some may not succeed when they are buttressed by other causative factors, such as political influence. But an assumption that, absent proof of market power, the boycott disclosed by this record was totally harmless—when overwhelming testimony demonstrated that it almost produced a crisis in the administration of criminal justice

in the District and when it achieved its economic goal—is flatly inconsistent with the clear course of our antitrust jurisprudence. Conspirators need not achieve the dimensions of a monopoly, or even a degree of market power any greater than that already disclosed by this record, to warrant condemnation under the antitrust laws.

* * *

The judgment of the Court of Appeals is accordingly reversed insofar as that court held the *per se* rules inapplicable to the lawyers' boycott.

QUESTIONS FOR ANALYSIS

1. The lawyers claimed that their freedom of speech was repressed by the antitrust laws—that is, that their First Amendment rights to gather for political expression were curtailed by seeing this as an economic boycott issue. Is there merit to this argument?
2. Is there a difference between horizontal and vertical price-fixing?

The Robinson-Patman Act

The Robinson-Patman Act, enacted in 1936, amends the Clayton Act. Section 2(a) states that "it shall be unlawful for any person engaged in commerce . . . to discriminate in price between different purchasers of commodities of like grade and quality . . . where the effect of such discrimination may be substantially to lessen competition or tend to create a monopoly in any line of commerce." Thus, a seller is said to engage in *price discrimination* when the same product is sold to different buyers at different prices.

Section 2(a) is perhaps the most controversial part of antitrust law, as the initial reason for its passage was to limit the ability of chain stores to offer merchandise at a price lower than their single-store competitors. The intent of the Act is to deny consumers the benefits from lower prices that result from mass merchandising. As a consequence, the Department of Justice and the FTC have been reluctant to enforce the Act. The majority of cases brought under the Robinson-Patman Act are private actions.

PRICE DISCRIMINATION

Many of the cases brought under the Robinson-Patman Act concern alleged economic injuries either from a firm charging different prices in different markets or from bulk sale discounts given to larger volume retailers. To illustrate the first type of injury, suppose that two sellers—Allen's Wholesale and Ceplo Distributors—sell the same products in competition with each other in San Francisco. Allen's also sells the product in Oakland, but Ceplo does not. If Allen's reduces its price levels in San Francisco but not in Oakland, that price cut may violate the Robinson-Patman Act. Allen's is engaging in price discrimination—charging different prices in different markets to the detriment of its competitors, which in this case is Ceplo.

Predatory Pricing

The type of business practice just described is sometimes called *predatory pricing*. That is, Allen's attempts to undercut Ceplo in San Francisco in an effort to drive Ceplo from the market. Allen's, however, continues to sell the product for a higher price in other markets in which it does not compete with Ceplo. Presumably, Allen's intends to drive Ceplo from the San Francisco market and then raise prices there when Ceplo goes out of business.

Firms can file suits alleging predatory pricing under both the Robinson-Patman Act and Section 2 of the Sherman Act. However, because it is difficult to distinguish predatory prices from prices driven low by competition, the Court today is reluctant to rule in favor of plaintiffs alleging predation. In *Matsushita Electric Industrial Co., Ltd.* v. *Zenith Radio Corp.*, 106 S.Ct. 1348 (1986), and in *Brooke Group, Ltd.* v. *Brown & Williamson Tobacco Corp.*, 113 S.Ct. 2578 (1993), the Court increased the evidentiary burden on plaintiffs in predatory-pricing cases.

To win, a plaintiff must present strong evidence showing that

1. The defendant priced below cost.
2. The defendant's below-cost prices created a genuine prospect that the defendant would monopolize the market.
3. The defendant would enjoy its monopoly at least long enough to recoup the losses it suffered during the price war.

The Court puts this heavy burden on predatory-pricing plaintiffs because it understands that firms might otherwise sue their price-cutting rivals for no reason other than to keep these rivals from lowering prices to competitive levels. As the Court said in *Brooke Group*, "It would be ironic indeed if the standards for predatory pricing liability were so low that antitrust suits themselves became a tool for keeping prices high."

Volume Discounts Legal?

The Robinson-Patman Act is also concerned with sales discounts given to large-volume retailers. To illustrate, suppose Allen's and Ceplo both buy the same product from Central Distributors for the purpose of selling it retail. Because Allen's is a larger-volume retailer, Central gives Allen's a price discount on its larger bulk purchases. The price discount gives Allen's a competitive advantage over Ceplo in the sale of the product to customers in the area. The alleged injury to competition is the price discount given to Allen's, the larger purchaser. This type of action generates numerous private actions against producers who discriminate in pricing to wholesalers or retailers.

DEFENSES

A key defense for firms charged with violating the Robinson-Patman Act is to show a *cost justification* for different prices charged in different markets or to different buyers. An obvious cost-justification defense is a difference in transportation costs—it usually costs more to deliver a refrigerator three hundred miles than fifty miles. Similarly, on a per unit basis, it is cheaper to deliver one thousand refrigerators than it is to deliver five refrigerators. The major problem with using the cost-justification defense is that it is virtually an accounting and economic impossibility to assign specific costs of production to individual products. As a consequence, the cost-justification defense is rarely successful by itself.

The other defense that may be used is that of *meeting competition*. That is, a firm cuts its price in response to a competitor's cutting its price first. The problem with this defense can be that the original price cut will be held illegal under Robinson-Patman, which will mean that subsequent price cuts may also be illegal, at least at some point. Competitors must show that the meeting-competition price cut was done in good faith, not in an effort to injure competitors but to stay competitive. In the *Texaco* decision, the Supreme Court considers a defense of price discrimination.

Texaco v. Hasbrouck
United States Supreme Court
496 U.S. 543 110 S.Ct. 2535 (1990)

CASE BACKGROUND *Texaco sold gasoline to Hasbrouck (Rick's Texaco) and other independent Texaco gas stations in Spokane, Washington. Texaco also sold its gasoline to Gull and Dompier—but at lower prices. Gull sold the gasoline under the Gull name. Dompier sold the gasoline under the Texaco brand name. Because Gull and Dompier paid less for their gasoline, they sold it for less at retail and grew rapidly. Sales at Rick's Texaco and the other independent Texaco stations dropped from 76 percent to 49 percent of Texaco retail sales in the area.*

The only difference in operations between Dompier's Texaco stations and the independent Texaco stations was that Dompier used his own tanker trucks to pick up gasoline from Texaco's plant. The independent dealers asked Texaco if they could hire their own tanker trucks to pick up the gasoline and pay the same price as Dompier and Gull. Texaco said no.

Hasbrouck and other independent Texaco station owners sued Texaco for violating Section 2(a) of the Robinson-Patman Act, alleging that Texaco's discounts to Dompier and Gull were illegal. The trial court awarded treble damages to Hasbrouck, and the court of appeals affirmed. Texaco appealed, claiming that the lower price charged to Dompier and Gull were legal functional discounts, that is, "discounts given to a purchaser based on its role in the supplier's distribution system [that] reflect the cost of the services performed by the purchaser for the supplier."

CASE DECISION Stevens, Justice.

* * *

The Robinson-Patman Act contains no express reference to functional discounts. It does contain two affirmative decisions that provide protection for two categories of discounts—those that are justified by savings in the seller's cost of manufacture, delivery or sale, and those that represent a good faith response to the equally low prices of a competitor. As the case comes to us, neither of those defenses is available to Texaco.

In order to establish a violation of the Act, respondents had the burden of proving four facts: (1) that Texaco's sales to Gull and Dompier were made in interstate commerce; (2) that the gasoline sold to them was of the same grade and quality as that sold to respondents; (3) that Texaco discriminated in price as between Gull and Dompier on the one hand and Hasbrouck on the other; and (4) that the discrimination had a prohibited effect on competition. Moreover, for Hasbrouck to recover damages, he had the burden of proving the extent of his actual injuries.

The first two elements of Hasbrouck's case are not disputed in this Court, and we do not understand Texaco to be challenging the sufficiency of Hasbrouck's proof of damages. Texaco does argue, however, (1) that although it charged different prices, it did not "discriminate in price" within the meaning of the Act, and (2) that, at least to the extent that Gull and Dompier acted as wholesalers, the price differentials did not injure competition. We consider the two arguments separately.

Texaco's first argument would create a blanket exemption for all functional discounts. Indeed, carried to its logical conclusion, it would exempt all price differentials except those given to competing purchasers. . . . [W]e remain persuaded that the argument is foreclosed by the text of the Act itself. In the context of a statute that plainly reveals a concern with competitive consequences at different levels of distribution, and carefully defines specific affirmative defenses, it would be anomalous to assume that the Congress intended the term "discriminate" to have such a limited meaning. . . .

Since we have already decided that a price discrimination within the meaning of §2(a) "is merely a price difference," we must reject Texaco's first argument.

* * *

[In its second argument, Texaco asserts that the price differentials did not injure competition.] A supplier need not satisfy the rigorous requirements of the cost justification defense in order to prove that a particular functional discount is reasonable and accordingly did not cause any substantial lessening of competition between a wholesaler's customers and the supplier's direct customers. The record in this case, however, adequately supports the finding that Texaco violated the Act.

. . . A price differential "that merely accords due recognition and reimbursement for actual marketing functions" is not illegal. In this case, however, both the District Court and the Court of Appeals concluded that even without viewing the evidence in the light most favorable to Hasbrouck, there was no substantial evidence indicating that the discounts to Gull and Dompier constituted a reasonable reimbursement for the value to Texaco of their actual marketing func-

tions. Indeed, Dompier was separately compensated for its hauling function, and neither Gull nor Dompier maintained any significant storage facilities.

* * *

One would expect that most functional discounts will be legitimate discounts which do not cause harm to competition. At the least, a functional discount that constitutes a reasonable reimbursement for the purchasers' actual marketing functions will not violate the Act. When a functional discount is legitimate, the inference of injury to competition . . . will simply not arise. Yet it is also true that not every functional discount is entitled to a judgment of legitimacy, and that it will sometimes be possible to produce evidence showing that a particular functional discount caused a price discrimination of the sort the Act prohibits. When such anticompetitive effects are proved—as we believe they were in this case—they are covered by the Act.

* * *

The judgment is Affirmed.

QUESTIONS FOR ANALYSIS

1. Suppose Texaco could show that the result of its pricing decision was to make the retail gasoline market more competitive in Spokane, thereby helping consumers. Would that be a defense?
2. Texaco claimed that Dompier and Gull were wholesale distributors, while Hasbrouck was a retailer. Texaco justified the price difference because it was selling to wholesalers versus selling to retailers. Is this a plausible defense?

Summary

- The three most important antitrust statutes—the Sherman Act of 1890, the Clayton Act of 1914, and the FTC Act of 1914—were enacted in response to concern about the economic power of the large industrial corporations and trusts that emerged during the late nineteenth century. Before the enactment of the statutes, common-law precedent was relied on to combat certain restraints of trade, but the government had little authority to intervene.
- Congress exempts agricultural cooperatives, the insurance industry, labor unions, and others from the antitrust laws. The state action doctrine allows states to regulate business in such a way as to fix prices or otherwise monopolize a market.
- Violations of the antitrust laws can expose defendants to criminal penalties, which can include prison sentences, as well as civil penalties. Defendants who

lose antitrust suits in which damages are found must automatically pay treble damages. The antitrust laws are enforced by the Antitrust Division of the Justice Department, the Federal Trade Commission, and private parties. Only the Justice Department can bring criminal charges for alleged antitrust violations.

- Most antitrust matters are determined by a rule of reason analysis, where the courts weigh the pros and cons of business practices alleged to be anticompetitive. Some practices, such as price-fixing by competitors, are so clearly anticompetitive that they are declared to be per se illegal.

- Horizontal restraints of trade occur when business competitors at the same level of business, such as producers of similar products, agree to act together.

- Mergers of competitor companies are likely to be challenged only if the merger would significantly reduce competition in a market. The market is defined along both territory and product lines.

- Independent companies in the same industry are usually not allowed to agree to segregate the market geographically, by type of customer, or in any other arrangement that reduces competition.

- Horizontal price-fixing occurs when competitors agree to act together to set prices for their products or services. This can happen at any level of operation and is usually per se illegal.

- There is no defense for companies in the same industry that get together, by any means, to agree on product prices in the markets in which they operate. Prices may not be fixed at any level by competitors unless there are special circumstances that make the arrangement procompetitive, which is rare.

- Companies in an industry may share price and other market information through a trade association so long as the information is not used to control the market and the information is available to the public.

- Vertical relationships are between sellers and buyers at different levels of business, such as between manufacturer and distributor. Vertical restraints of trade occur when a firm at one level of business controls the practices of a firm at another level, such as a distributor telling a retailer what price to charge its customers for its products.

- Vertical price-fixing, or resale price maintenance, where the producer or distributor tells the retailers of its products the minimum or maximum prices at which to sell the products, is per se illegal. Suggested retail prices are legal but may not be enforced by a threat to cut off a retailer who will not adhere to them.

- Vertical nonprice restraints, such as granting exclusive territory to dealers, are viewed under a rule of reason. Recent cases indicate that manufacturers are given wide latitude in picking dealers and deciding the terms under which they will retain them. The producer may not conspire with a dealer against another dealer.

- Tie-in sales, where the sale of one product is tied to the sale of another, are judged under a rule of reason. For such a sale to be illegal, it must be shown that monopoly power in one product existed and was extended to the other product.

- When any organized group at one level of business (such as hardware store owners) gets together to agree to a joint action (such as refusal to deal) against one or more businesses at another level of business (such as a particular hardware supplier), such action is a boycott, which is usually per se illegal.

- The Robinson-Patman Act holds that price discrimination—selling the same product to different buyers at different prices—must be justified by differences in the cost of selling to the different buyers or because the price difference was required to meet competition. This is one of the most troublesome areas of law for producers, since hundreds of private lawsuits are filed each year by unhappy buyers (usually retailers) claiming they were discriminated against. The courts are not sympathetic to such cases, but the cases pose expensive problems that can be avoided by careful planning with legal counsel.

How Stable Are Japan's Cartels?

For years, critics have complained of the Japanese economy's domination by cartels. In addition to harming Japanese consumers, these cartels allegedly give Japanese firms an unfair advantage in world trade. In 1990, American corporate raider T. Boone Pickens recommended in The Wall Street Journal *that the U.S. government take steps to dismantle Japanese cartels. As the following article shows, however, the Japanese themselves are beginning to eliminate these cartels.*

JAPAN'S BUSINESS CARTELS ARE STARTING TO ERODE, BUT CHANGE IS SLOW

David P. Hamilton and Norihiko Shirouzu

Reprinted by permission of *The Wall Street Journal* © 1995 Dow Jones & Company, Inc. All rights reserved worldwide. Hamilton and Shirouzu are staff reporters for *The Wall Street Journal.*

TOKYO—Japan's entrenched cartels and other cozy business arrangements that prop up prices and impede imports are slowly starting to unravel.

After decades of quasilegal price-fixing, the cartels are under pressure from four years of near-zero economic growth, from tougher antitrust enforcement and from aggressive foreign competitors, whose products are made cheaper by the strong yen.

Also eroding are the close relationships between manufacturers and suppliers as buyers push for bargains: Auto makers such as Nissan Motor Co. are importing South Korean steel to pressure Japanese suppliers to cut prices.

Even the government claims that it is serious about eliminating cartels. Politicians such as Ryutaro Hashimoto, the minister of International Trade and Industry and president of Japan's largest political party, talk about attacking monopolistic practices to spur economic growth.

A Difficult Process

To be sure, cartel-busters face a long slog against business collusion. But companies in endangered cartels face plenty of turmoil, too.

A case in point: the once-fearsome cement cartel. In response to overcapacity and low demand in the 1980s, Japan had let cement makers limit production to stabilize prices. What's more, the companies agreed to punish builders that bought imports, says Ichiro Nakayasu, a general manager for cement sales at Ube Industries Ltd. "We would tell them, 'If you want to buy imports, that's fine, but you may have supply trouble in the future'" with domestic makers, he says.

Then, in 1991, Japan's Fair Trade Commission fined the industry $110 million for price-fixing. Stunned, cement makers turned on one another in a vicious price war that cut prices 20% during the next four years. The result: Major producers' profits are only 10% of 1991 levels. "Once, our industry engaged in cartel-like activities, and we could keep prices at a high level," Mr. Nakayasu laments. "Now, we must fight to the death."

So must many other companies. But cartel-busting is exactly the kind of bold reform the economy needs, many economists say, to pull itself out of its slump. Cartels and collusion cost Japanese consumers up to $140 billion a year, by one estimate.

* * *

The government's recent economic-stimulus plans include money to increase the [Japanese] FTC staff, which has grown to 220 investigators from 165 in 1991.

In the past year, the FTC has cracked down on illegal price-fixing in a half-dozen industries, from cosmetics to warehousing. And despite the recession, the government hasn't tried to form any new cartels to bolster depressed industries in nearly a decade; the FTC, meanwhile, promises to eliminate those that remain by April 1999.

* * *

But while economic and political forces are undermining cartels, business collusion remains deeply woven into Japan's economic fabric. Roughly half of its manufacturing industry still engages in some sort of price-fixing. . . . Such practices pervade agriculture, basic materials, cosmetics and many other industries. Consumers even get clipped by a barbershop cartel that keeps haircut prices in Tokyo at about $35.

"Cartels are a cultural tradition" dating back to the 1600s, says Ushio Chujo, a Keio University economist. Most Japanese don't disapprove, he says, so "there is a lingering tendency to tolerate or even encourage anti-competitive behavior."

* * *

Nevertheless, the FTC has started to open even seemingly unassailable cartels to market forces. Since the 1970s, three Japanese flat-glass makers exhibited what regulators consider evidence of cartel behavior; they held unchanging market shares: Asahi Glass Co. had 50%, Nippon Sheet Glass Co. 30% and Central Glass Co. 20%.

Glassmakers discouraged imports by first shipping glass to distributors and *then* setting a price on it—preventing distributors from shopping around. But in 1993, the FTC "advised" glassmakers to halt the practice, and now distributors are more willing to import: Flat-glass imports soared 35% in the first nine months of 1995. Imported glass is expected to win a 6% market share this year, up from zero three years ago.

Restive customers also are starting to force cartels open. Until recently, Japan's car makers bought all their steel for domestic vehicles from Japanese producers. But Japan's five big steelmakers have long kept domestic prices above world levels by fixing prices and shipment quantities at weekly meetings, says Morio Yokoyama, a former Kawasaki Steel Corp. official who now runs a steel import business. Steelmakers deny they fix prices.

Now, in a trial program, Nissan's Kyushu-island plant uses South Korean steel in inner panels on cars and sport-utility vehicles. Nissan officials say they are pleased with the quality of the metal, which is 10% to 15% cheaper. Honda Motor Co. also is testing Korean steel, and Mitsubishi Motors Corp. regularly uses it in some vehicles.

* * *

Another challenge to cartels comes from foreign competitors. For 25 years, a triumvirate of Japanese movie-theater operators raised "ticket prices" to uniformly high levels—now $17 to $18—to compensate for shrinking audiences, industry officials say. But U.S. distribution giants such as Time Warner Inc. and AMC Entertainment Inc. are breaking up that cozy system.

Time Warner's first brush with the cartel was 15 months ago in Hirosaki. Fearing price differentials "would jeopardize our chance for coexistence," the city's theater-owner association asked Time Warner to keep ticket prices high, says Hitoshi Yamazaki, a member of the group. Time Warner refused and opened a six-screen theater with big discounts for matinees and special showings. Three of the five local theaters have closed; only an art-film house and a porn joint remain.

Yet Japanese theater operators say such shake-ups may reinvigorate the industry. The Warner theaters "are seeing people who have never been to a theater before," marvels Shoji Yakigaya, a director at Shochiku Co., which plans to spend $80 million on its own multiplex chain. Almost apologetically, he adds: "It's not that we're being highly competitive; it's that if we don't do it, foreign companies will come in and do it themselves."

ISSUE QUESTIONS

1. The stronger the yen, the greater the number of dollars that Japanese consumers can purchase with a given amount of yen. Thus, a strong yen means that foreign goods are less expensive for Japanese buyers. What do the authors mean when they suggest that a strong yen helps to undermine the stability of Japan's cartels?

2. The story presents evidence—for example, in the Japanese movie theater industry—that high cartel prices attract additional competitors, who force prices lower. Can an economy remain competitive without antitrust laws by relying exclusively upon new competition to challenge monopolistic practices?

REVIEW AND DISCUSSION QUESTIONS

1. Define the following terms:

   per se rule   territorial allocation
   rule of reason   vertical restraint of trade
   horizontal business arrangements   resale price maintenance
   market share   tie-in share
   potential competition   boycott
   failing firm defense   price discrimination
   horizontal price-fixing

2. Why was the Sherman Act written in such broad language? Is it possible that Congress wrote the legislation in an unclear manner to give the courts broad leeway in attacking monopolistic business practices? Would it have been better for Congress to have specified more of the terms of antitrust violations?

3. The courts use a rule of reason in looking at territorial restrictions. Why should there be any concern about territorial restrictions? So long as there is competition between brands, is not that more important than intrabrand competition by the sellers of a product in a given geographic market? That is, can you think of cases in which intrabrand competition might be more important than interbrand competition?

CASE QUESTIONS

4. Many professional engineers belong to a trade association called the National Society of Professional Engineers that governs the nontechnical aspects of the practice of engineering. The canon of ethics adopted by the society held that engineers could not bid against one another for a particular job. The society claimed that this rule was to prevent engineers from engaging in price-cutting to get engineering jobs, which could then give them incentives to cut corners on the quality of work to save time and resources. Such a practice could lead to inferior work that could endanger the public. The Justice Department sued, claiming that this was a violation of Section 1 of the Sherman Act. The government claimed that the ethical rule reduced price competition and gave an unfair advantage to engineers with well-established reputations. Who wins? [*National Society of Professional Engineers* v. *United States*, 98 S.Ct. 1355 (1978)]

5. Professional basketball players and their union sued the National Basketball Association (NBA) for various practices, such as the draft of college players and its salary-cap system. They claimed that this violated the antitrust law by restricting opportunities for professional basketball players. Could such practices survive a rule of reason analysis? [*NBA* v. *Williams*, 45 F.3d 684 (2nd Cir., 1995)]

6. Certified registered nurse anesthetists (CRNAs) sued a hospital and its doctors, claiming a violation of Section 1 of the Sherman Act, based on the hospital's staffing decision to terminate its contract with the CRNAs and instead use a group of physician anesthesiologists, a competitor, that would provide anesthesia services for the hospital at lower cost. The district court dismissed the case. Was that the correct decision? [*BCB Anesthesia Care* v. *Passavant Memorial Area Hospital*, 36 F.3d 664 (7th Cir., 1994)]

7. Several companies operated downhill ski facilities in Aspen, Colorado. They all sold a joint ticket that allowed skiers to ski at all facilities; the receipts were later divided according to various use rates. Eventually, one firm owned all the ski areas but one. This firm stopped issuing the joint ticket and instead issued a ticket good

for all of its ski areas. The firm that owned only one ski facility saw its market share fall from 20 percent to 11 percent over a four-year period. It sued, claiming that the larger firm violated Section 2 of the Sherman Act by attempting to monopolize skiing by ending the joint ticket arrangement. Is the sale of the joint ticket a violation of the antitrust law? [*Aspen Skiing Company* v. *Aspen Highlands Skiing Corporation*, 472 U.S. 585, 105 S.Ct. 2847 (1985)]

8. For years the American Medical Association (AMA) stated that chiropractors were unscientific cult members. The Principles of Medical Ethics of the AMA said that a "physician should practice a method of healing founded on a scientific basis; and she should not voluntarily associate with anyone who violates this principle." This was the basis of medical discrimination against chiropractic until the AMA dropped these statements in 1980. Five chiropractors sued the AMA after 1980, claiming that the effect of the past actions had "lingering effects" that injured their business in the medical market and that this was an illegal boycott. What result? [*Wilk* v. *AMA*, 895 F.2d 352 (7th Cir., 1990)]

9. Raymond Syufy eventually bought all of Las Vegas's first-run movie theaters. The government sues Syufy for monopolization. While admitting that he controls a substantial share of the market, Syufy defends his mergers by pointing out the following facts: first, movie prices in Las Vegas are no higher than movie prices in comparable cities; second, no sooner did Syufy acquire all of Las Vegas's first-run theaters than other competitors successfully entered the market; and third, movie studios (for example, Paramount Pictures) are such powerful firms with an interest in avoiding theater monopolization that they can be relied upon to ensure that Syufy does not abuse his market dominance. Evaluate Syufy's argument in light of antitrust law. [*United States* v. *Syufy*, 903 F.2d 659 (9th Cir., 1990)]

10. Compcare, an HMO (health maintenance organization), sues Marshfield Clinic for monopolizing the HMO market. HMOs charge their members fixed annual fees. The HMO negotiates with each physician it has under contract the amount it will pay for each medical procedure performed. The idea is that HMOs can bargain with physicians for lower fees and then pass the savings on to HMO members. Compcare objects that Marshfield Clinic signed up so many physicians that there were too few physicians left in the region for Compcare to use. Marshfield defended by pointing out that all of its HMO physicians remain free to treat patients from other HMOs. What result? [*Blue Cross & Blue Shield United of Wisconsin* v. *Marshfield Clinic*, 65 F.3d 1406 (7th Cir., 1995)]

11. The publisher of the St. Louis morning newspaper sold its papers to wholesalers who distributed them to subscribers through the wholesaler's carriers. Some wholesalers raised subscription prices for home delivery above the price set by the newspaper. The publisher sent its own carriers around to offer the paper for the lower price it wanted to charge. Did the newspaper violate the antitrust law? [*Albrecht* v. *Herald Co.*, 88 S.Ct. 869 (1968)]

12. A maker of hamburger patty machines requires its dealers to also purchase its hamburger patty paper. A dealer that did not like this requirement was cut off by the manufacturer. The dealer sued, claiming that his was an illegal tie-in sale. The dealer was awarded $300,000 damages for the value of its lost sales, which were trebled. Was this the correct decision? [*Roy B. Taylor Salves* v. *Hollymatic Corp.*, 28 F.3d 1379 (5th Cir., 1994)]

13. The Utah Pie Company made and sold frozen pies in the Salt Lake City area. It was very successful and soon had two-thirds of the frozen-pie market in that area.

In response to the loss of their market shares, three large pie makers—Carnation, Pet, and Continental—cut their prices in the Salt Lake area but not elsewhere. As a result, their sales picked back up and Utah Pie's fell to 45 percent of the market. The result was lower frozen-pie prices for consumers in that market. Utah Pie sued the other three companies for violating what part of the antitrust law? Did it win? [*Utah Pie Co.* v. *Continental Baking Co.*, 87 S.Ct. 1326 (1967)]

POLICY QUESTIONS

14. Should the antitrust laws be concerned about a merger that would give the merging firms a large share of a market in a small geographical area? Are nearby competitors enough competition to prevent consumers from being hurt?

15. The Robinson-Patman Act was called the Anti-Chain Store Discrimination Act. Can you see why? The backers of the act were small-store owners who were being hurt by competition from the growing chain stores in the 1920s and 1930s, which by now dominate retailing. Is this legislation procompetitive, or does it hurt consumers?

ETHICS QUESTIONS

16. The largest American filmmakers—Paramount, MCA, Metro-Goldwyn, and United Artists—formed a joint venture called United International Pictures to distribute films in Europe and other parts of the world. This venture would clearly be an illegal horizontal restraint of trade in the United States but was sanctioned in Europe by the EU despite complaints by European filmmakers who had seen the American company grab a quarter of the market since 1989. Should American companies engage in business practices outside the United States that are legal in other countries but would be illegal at home?

17. Your firm produces electric blenders. A certain popular model has a suggested retail price of $30. Your firm sells it wholesale for $18. Smaller stores tend to sell the blender at the suggested retail price. One large discount chain begins to sell the blender for $26 and asks you to cut the price to them to $17.50. Because of that chain's large sales, your production and profits are up. You will earn even higher profits if you cut the price to them to $17.50—a possible violation of the Robinson-Patman Act. Should you cut the price for the chain? What if the chain says that it will cut its retail price to $25.50 if you cut the price to $17.50?

CHAPTER 20

Securities Regulation

Merrill Lynch and Goldman, Sachs both earn about one billion dollars a year in fees from arranging the sale of (underwriting) new stocks and bonds. That is only a fraction of their income, since much of the companies' business involves assisting in trades of existing securities and other asset management functions. While the United States no longer leads the world in the production of many goods, such as televisions, the sophistication of financial services is unrivaled. Each year, American investment firms put together and sell hundreds of billions of dollars worth of new U.S. and foreign securities.

The size of financial markets and the complex transactions produce some spectacular litigation involving huge sums—and lead people who do not understand securities markets to think something shady might be going on. As stock market crashes have shown, investor confidence in financial institutions is important to the nation's financial solvency. The Securities and Exchange Commission (SEC) is important as the primary regulator of U.S. securities markets. Most nations look to the SEC for leadership in how to regulate, but not damage, the quality of the major sources of support for financing business operations. This chapter looks at the workings and legal control of some of the key elements of the securities industry.

Corporate Finance and Early Regulation

The sale of securities is the primary source of corporate finance. The efficient operation of the securities markets is vital to the economy. Business operations are financed by securities, and retirement pension funds are invested in securities.

SECURITIES AND CORPORATE FINANCE

Broadly defined, a *security* is a written document that provides evidence of *debt*—such as a corporate note or bond—or of *equity ownership*—such as a certificate of preferred or common stock. Securities have no intrinsic value in themselves—issuers can create them for virtually nothing. Thus, securities represent value in something else. For example, the value of a corporation's stock depends on the expected future profitability of the corporation as reflected in the price investors are willing to pay for that stock.

Debt

The capital needs of a corporation can be financed through debt or equity. *Debt financing* involves selling bonds or borrowing money. A debt instrument issued by a corporation, such as a bond, usually specifies the following:

1. Amount of the debt
2. Length of the debt period
3. Debt repayment method
4. Rate of interest charged to the sum borrowed

Thus, debt financing means incurring a liability. A corporation can sell ten million dollars worth of bonds to the public, promise to redeem the bonds in one year, and pay the bondholders 7 percent interest on the sum borrowed. In addition, bondholders usually can trade debt instruments. Most purchases and sales are handled by professional bond traders, such as Merrill Lynch.

Equity

Equity financing involves raising funds through the sale of company stock. It is called equity financing because a purchaser of shares of stock gains an ownership, or equitable, interest in the corporation. Shareholders have a claim on a portion of the future profits (if any) of the corporation. Unlike with debt financing, a company has no liability to repay shareholders the amount they have invested. For example, a corporation may issue one million shares of common stock at a price of $10 per share to raise $10 million to finance operations. Each share represents a right to one-millionth of the future profits of the corporation or to one-millionth of the value of the company if it is sold or dissolved.

Investors buy shares in the corporation if they think the profits will be sufficient to provide them a competitive rate of return on their investment. The officers of the corporation are under an obligation to make reasonable efforts to make a profit. As in the case of bonds, unless prohibited by contract, stock can be traded. A trade can be directly between two parties, but most trades are handled by a broker through a stock exchange.

Most people in the United States invest in securities, often indirectly through their pension plans or directly to help fund major expenses, such as their children's education. Trillions of dollar worth of securities exist in the United States, about half of which are in publicly traded stock, while the rest are in debt such as government bonds.

ORIGINS OF SECURITIES REGULATION

Public concern with investment sales fraud led to state legislation regulating the issuance and sale of securities. The first securities statute was enacted by the state of Kansas in 1911. State securities laws became known as *blue sky laws*, a term attributed to a Supreme Court opinion describing the purpose of state securities laws as attempting to prevent the "speculative schemes which would have no more basis than so many feet of blue sky." Supposedly, promoters had gone door-to-door selling worthless securities to unsuspecting Kansas farmers. Later—after their money and the promoter were gone—the farmers discovered that the securities had nothing more substantial backing them than the blue sky.

Beginnings of Federal Regulation

Federal regulation of securities began during a time of economic catastrophe. The stock market had crashed in 1929, and the crash was followed by the Great Depression. Over one-quarter of all jobs disappeared, and national income fell by one-third. Many people incorrectly blamed the depression on the stock market crash of 1929. In fact, the market was correctly forecasting the depression of the 1930s. Nevertheless, there was a common belief that manipulators on Wall Street needed to be controlled. Congress enacted a number of statutes in the 1930s.

Most important are the Securities Act of 1933 and the Securities Exchange Act of 1934. The 1933 Act regulates the initial public offerings of securities. The Act's basic objectives are to require that investors be provided with material information about new securities offered for public sale and to prevent misrepresentation and fraud in the sale of those securities. The 1934 Act extended federal securities regulation to cover trading in securities that were already issued. The Act imposes disclosure requirements on corporations that have issued publicly held securities. It also provides for the regulation of securities markets and professionals.

The Securities and Exchange Commission

The *Securities and Exchange Commission* (*SEC*) is the agency charged with the responsibility for the enforcement and administration of the federal securities laws (see www.sec.gov). The Securities Exchange Act of 1934 provides that the SEC has five members appointed by the president for five-year terms. One is appointed as chairman. The SEC's staff is composed of attorneys, accountants, financial analysts and examiners, and other professionals. The staff is divided into divisions and offices—including thirteen regional offices around the country.

Defining a Security

Although Congress often provides vague mandates to regulators—forcing the courts and the regulatory agencies to define the terms and the scope of the legislation—this was not the case in defining the term *security* in the 1933 Act. Congress provided a detailed definition that goes beyond investments called "stocks" and "bonds." According to the 1933 Act, *security* includes

> any note, stock, treasury stock, bond, debenture, evidence of indebtedness, certificate of interest or participation in any profit-sharing agreement, collateral-trust certificate, preorganization certificate or subscription, transferable share, investment contract, voting-trust certificate, certificate of deposit for a security, fractional undivided interest in oil, gas, or other mineral rights, or, in general, any interest or instrument commonly known as a

"security," or any certificate of interest of participation in, temporary or interim certificate for, receipt for, guarantee of, or warrant or right to subscribe to or purchase, any of the foregoing.

Despite this detailed definition of a security, both the courts and the SEC look to the economic realities of an investment transaction to determine whether it is a security. As the Supreme Court noted in *United Housing Foundation* v. *Forman* (1975):

> We reject . . . any suggestion that the present transaction, evidenced by the sale of shares called *stock*, must be considered a security transaction simply because the statutory definition of a security includes the words "any . . . stock."

That is, just because something is called a stock does not mean it is a security that falls within the jurisdiction of the federal security laws. Similarly, other things with names not included in the list written by Congress are securities.

SUPREME COURT'S *HOWEY* TEST

If an investment instrument is a security, it must comply with the legal requirements imposed on securities issuers. Note that investors have incentives to sue to have the court declare that an investment instrument is a security. If an investment instrument is a security, investors have a higher degree of legal protection than that given to investments not qualifying as securities. In *Howey*, the Supreme Court established a test to determine when an investment instrument is a security for the purposes of federal regulation.

Securities and Exchange Commission v. W. J. Howey Company
United States Supreme Court
328 U.S. 293, 66 S.Ct. 1100 (1946)

CASE BACKGROUND *Howey owned large tracts of land in central Florida, including hundreds of acres of citrus groves. Half the groves were offered for sale to the public. Prospective buyers were offered title to citrus grove acreage and a service contract under which Howey would cultivate, harvest, and sell the citrus grown on each parcel. Most investors in the citrus land lived outside Florida and bought the service contract.*

The SEC sued Howey, claiming that the sale of the acreage and service contracts was a security that should have been registered with the SEC before being offered for sale to the public. The district court and the court of appeals found for Howey. The SEC appealed to the Supreme Court.

CASE DECISION Murphy, Justice.

* * *

The legal issue in this case turns upon a determination of whether, under the circumstances, the land sales contract, the warranty deed and the service contract together constitute an "investment contract" within the meaning of §2(1). An affirmative answer brings into operation the registration requirements of . . . §5(a), the 1933 Securities Act.

* * *

In other words, an investment contract for purposes of the Securities Act means a contract, transaction or scheme whereby a person invests his money in a common enterprise and is led to expect profits solely from the efforts of the promoter of a third party, it being immaterial whether the shares in the enterprise are evidenced by formal certificates or by nominal interests in the physical assets employed in the enterprise.

* * *

The transactions in this case clearly involve investment contracts as so defined. The respondent companies are offering something more than fee simple interest in land, something different from a farm or orchard coupled with management services. They are offering an opportunity to contribute money and to share in the profits of a large citrus fruit enterprise managed and partly owned by respondents. They are offering this opportunity to persons who reside in distant localities and who lack the equipment and experience requisite to the cultivation, harvesting and marketing of the citrus products. Such persons have no desire to occupy the land or to develop it themselves; they are attracted solely by the prospects of a return on their investment.

* * *

Thus all the elements of a profit-seeking business venture are present here. The investors provide the capital and share in the earnings and profits; the promoters manage, control and operate the enterprise. It follows that the arrangements whereby the investors' interests are made manifest involve investment contracts, regardless of the legal terminology in which such contracts are clothed. The investment contracts in this instance take the form of land sales contracts, warranty deeds and service contracts which respondents offer to prospective investors. And respondents' failure to abide by the statutory and administrative rules in making such offerings, even though the failure results from a bona fide mistake as to the law, cannot be sanctioned under the Act.

* * *

We reject the suggestion of the Circuit Court of Appeals that an investment contract is necessarily missing where the enterprise is not speculative or promotional in character and where the tangible interest which is sold has intrinsic value independent of the success of the enterprise as a whole. The test is whether the scheme involves an investment of money in a common enterprise with profits to come solely from the efforts of others. If that test be satisfied, it is immaterial whether the enterprise is speculative or non-speculative or whether there is a sale of property with or without intrinsic value. The statutory policy of affording broad protection to investors is not to be thwarted by unrealistic and irrelevant formulae.

Reversed.

QUESTIONS FOR ANALYSIS

1. Suppose Howey had sold the plots of land to numerous investors but had not offered to manage the land as citrus groves. Would the land still have been a security?
2. Justice Frankfurter, in a dissenting opinion, noted that 20 percent of the land purchasers did not sign a management contract with Howey, since such signing was voluntary and not required to make a land purchase. Did the Supreme Court majority seem to violate their own test for what constitutes a security?

The test developed by the Court in *Howey* has been applied countless times since the case was decided. The *Howey* test holds that for an investment instrument to be classified as a security for the purpose of federal regulation, it must contain four basic elements:

1. The investment of money
2. In a common enterprise
3. With an expectation of profits
4. Generated by the efforts of persons other than the investors

Defining the Four Elements

The first element, *the investment of money*, requires that an investor turn over some money to someone else for investment purposes. The second element, *in a common enterprise*, means that the investment is not the property of an investor, such as an investor's own business or automobile. Rather, an investor's capital has been pooled with other investors' money so that each investor owns an undivided interest in the investment. An investor who owns Ford stock, for example, does not have the right to go to a Ford factory and demand an automobile or other property equal in value to the money the investor invested in the company. An investor has a claim only to a share of future earnings as established in the contract that accompanied the security. Even though stock owners (or shareholders) own a portion of the company, they own an *undivided interest* in the company. That is, the shareholders cannot divide company property among themselves unless they agree to liquidate (sell) the company.

The third and fourth elements, *the expectation that profits will be generated by the efforts of persons other than the investor*, require that an investor not have direct control over the work that makes the investment a success or failure. The SEC and the courts have taken a liberal view of the requirement that the profits be generated by other persons, ruling that a security still exists when most of the efforts to produce the profits are by other persons. Thus, the president of a corporation who purchases shares of the corporation's stock has purchased a security because most of the profits of the corporation are generated by the work of others.

Applying the Securities Definition

Since many investments go bad, there are numerous suits claiming violations of securities law. For a claim to be tried under the standards imposed by the federal securities laws, the investment instrument must meet the *Howey* test of a security. In various cases, lower courts have changed the scope of the *Howey* test, but the Supreme Court consistently returns to it. In *Reves*, the Court again discussed the *Howey* test.

Reves v. Ernst & Young
United States Supreme Court
494 U.S. 56, 110 S.Ct. 945 (1990)

CASE BACKGROUND *Farmer's Cooperative of Arkansas and Oklahoma (Co-Op) sold promissory notes not backed by collateral or insurance to raise money to support business operations. The notes paid above-market rates of interest and were called an "investment program." Advertisements for the notes said "YOUR CO-OP has more than $11,000,000 in assets to stand behind your investments. The Investment is not Federal [sic] insured but it is . . . Safe . . . Secure . . . and available when you need it." When Co-Op filed for bankruptcy in 1984, over 1,600 people held notes worth $10 million.*

Reves and other note holders sued Ernst & Young, the firm that audited Co-Op's books, claiming that the accounting firm had failed to follow generally accepted accounting procedures in its audit, especially with respect to the value of Co-Op's assets. They claimed that if Ernst & Young had valued the assets properly, Co-Op's financial instability would have been obvious and the notes would not have been purchased. Hence, the accounting firm had violated the antifraud provisions of the securities laws.

The note holders won a $6.1 million judgment. The appeals court reversed, holding that the notes were not securities under the federal securities law. The note holders appealed to the Supreme Court.

CASE DECISION Marshall, Justice.

* * *

Congress' purpose in enacting the securities laws was to regulate *investments*, in whatever form they are made and by whatever name they are called.

* * *

An examination . . . makes clear . . . factors that this Court has held apply in deciding whether a transaction involves a "security." First, we examine the transaction to assess the motivations that would prompt a reasonable seller and buyer to enter into it. If the seller's purpose is to raise money for the general use of a business enterprise or to finance substantial investments and the buyer is interested primarily in the profit the note is expected to generate, the instrument is likely to be a "security." . . .

Second, we examine the "plan of distribution" of the instrument . . . to determine whether it is an instrument in which there is "common trading for speculation or investment,". . . . Third, we examine the reasonable expectations of the investing public: The Court will consider instruments to be "securities" on the basis of such public expectations. . . .

Finally, we examine whether some factor such as the existence of another regulatory scheme significantly reduces the risk of the instrument, thereby rendering application of the Securities Acts unnecessary.

We conclude, then, that in determining whether an instrument denominated a "note" is a "security," courts are to apply the version of the "family resemblance" test that we have articulated here: a note is presumed to be a "security," and that presumption may be rebutted only by a showing that the note bears a strong resemblance (in terms of the four factors we have identified) to one of the enumerated categories of instrument. If an instrument is not sufficiently similar to an item on the list, the decision whether another category should be added is to be made by examining the same factors.

Applying the family resemblance approach to this case, we have little difficulty in concluding that the notes at issue here are "securities." . . .

The Co-Op sold the notes in an effort to raise capital for its general business operations, and purchasers bought them in order to earn a profit in the form of interest. Indeed, one of the primary inducements offered purchasers was an interest rate constantly revised to keep it slightly above the rate paid by local banks and savings and loans. From both sides, then, the transaction is most naturally conceived as an investment in a business enterprise rather than as a purely commercial or consumer transaction.

As to the plan of distribution, the Co-Op offered the notes over an extended period to its 23,000 members, as well as to nonmembers, and more than 1,600 people held notes when the Co-Op filed for bankruptcy. . . .

The third factor—the public's reasonable perceptions—also supports a finding that the notes in this case are "securities." We have consistently identified the fundamental essence of a "security" to be its character as an "investment." The advertisements of the notes here characterized them as "investments," and there were no countervailing factors that would have led a reasonable person to question this characterization. In these circumstances, it would be reasonable for a prospective purchaser to take the Co-Op at its word.

Finally, we find no risk-reducing factor to suggest that these instruments are not in fact securities. The notes are uncollateralized and uninsured.

* * *

For the foregoing reasons, we conclude that the demand notes at issue here fall under the "note" category of instruments that are "securities" under the 1933 and 1934 Acts. . . . Accordingly, we reverse the judgment of the Court of Appeals and remand the case for further proceedings consistent with this opinion.

QUESTIONS FOR ANALYSIS

1. Since the list of items in the 1933 Act that defines securities says "any note," why is not every note a security?
2. Should the accounting firm be held responsible for the losses of the investors here? What if they did the audit in good faith, not knowing that the results would be used to promote the sale of the notes?

Securities Exempt from Regulation

Some securities are exempt from regulation. The most important securities exempted by both the 1933 and the 1934 Acts are debts issued or guaranteed by a government—federal, state, or local. The 1933 Act (but not the 1934 Act) also provides an exemption for securities issued by banks, religious and charitable organizations, insurance policies, and annuity contracts. Since most of these securities are subject to control by other federal agencies, such as the Federal Reserve System, there is another regulatory scheme to protect investors.

In general, an exempted security is not subject to the registration and disclosure requirements of the federal statutes. However, the security may be subject to the Acts' general antifraud and civil liability provisions.

Offering a Security to Investors

The 1933 Act, sometimes called the "truth in securities" law, requires that sellers of securities fully *disclose* to prospective investors all material information about a security, its issuers, and the intended use of the funds raised before the securities are sold to the public. *Material information* is all relevant information that an investor would want to know about a company—its background, its executives, and its plan of operation. Disclosure is accomplished by filing a registration statement with the SEC.

Registration is intended to provide investors with sufficient and accurate information on material facts concerning the securities that a company is proposing to sell. With that information, it is expected that investors can make a realistic appraisal of the merits of new securities offerings and make informed decisions about whether or not to buy the securities.

THE REGISTRATION STATEMENT

The *registration statement* for a new security offering has two parts. The first part is the *prospectus*—a document providing the legal offering of the sale of the security. The second part consists of the disclosure of detailed information in response to specific questions by the SEC.

The Prospectus

A prospectus (called Schedule A by the SEC) condenses the longer registration statement provided to the SEC and helps investors evaluate a security before purchase. The preliminary version of the prospectus is called a *red herring* (because of the red ink used on the first page). It is used by securities brokers to interest potential investors in a forthcoming offering. Every prospectus, preliminary or final, provides material information about:

- The security issuer's finances and business
- The purpose of the offering
- The plans for the funds collected
- The risks involved in the business venture
- The promoters' managerial experience and financial compensation
- Financial statements certified by independent public accountants

Regulation S-K

Unlike the prospectus, which is printed as a pamphlet, the second part of the registration statement consists of more detailed disclosure than is in the prospectus. The SEC spells out the requirements in *Regulation S-K.* More history on the issuers is required, especially about their financial background and past experience with securities. The SEC also requires additional information about the proposed business and the issuers. This information may be used by professional investment analysts who wish to study the offering in detail. The disclosure document is available for public inspection at the SEC.

REVIEW BY THE SEC

The SEC cannot rule on the *merits* of an offering (that is, the likelihood of success of the proposed business as estimated by the reviewing official), but it can require issuers to make high-risk factors clear in the prospectus so as to put buyers on notice. The registration becomes effective twenty days after filing, but if the SEC issues a *deficiency letter*, the issuer needs time to amend the filing to provide more detail in the registration materials. For example, if the proposed business involves something that strikes the examiner as strange, such as a peculiar financial arrangement, that fact may need to be highlighted.

The SEC can issue a *stop order* to prohibit sale of securities until the registration statement is amended to satisfy the examiners, but this rarely happens. This power can slow the registration process and may quash an offering thought undesirable by the SEC staff.

Shelf Registration

The SEC allows *shelf registration* of securities offerings by certain issuers. Shelf registration means that a company can register a new security offering, but all of the security need not be sold at one time. Rather, the securities can be put "on the shelf" to be sold when the time is right. Hence, if a company wants to sell $200 million of new stock over a two-year period, it need not sell the stock all at once or have separate registrations each time it wants to sell some of the stock. Shelf registration is popular with stock issuers because it allows them to raise capital at the most opportune times by having more flexibility.

Shelf registration is not available to first-time issuers. It is for companies with a track record of meeting SEC securities disclosure requirements and that meet certain financial standards. Once registration of the new stock offering is complete, the offerors must amend the registration statement to reflect changes in any of the information. The rule has reduced the cost of the registration process by eliminating the need for a company to register one stock offering after another.

The Costs of Registration

Even for small securities offerings, say for $5 million, the registration process is expensive. The prospective issuer must hire such professionals as an experienced securities attorney, a certified public accountant, and a printer for the prospectus. The bill may run $100,000, excluding the expense of hiring an *underwriter* (the investment banker, such as Goldman, Sachs or Morgan Stanley, that will market the securities).

Stock underwriting fees may be less than one percent of the value of a large stock offering sold to the public, but the fee may be as high as 10 percent for a small offering by an unknown company. To avoid some costs of the registration process and other regulations, one may consider selling the security through a transaction that makes the security exempt from the registration process.

EXEMPTIONS FROM REGISTRATION

Some securities, such as government bonds, are exempt from the securities laws. All other securities are subject to the securities laws, but they may qualify for an *exemption from registration*. Only the initial sale of the securities is exempt from registration; the securities are never exempt from the securities laws. The securities are exempt from registration only so long as they meet the requirements of the exemption. If a provision of the exemption is violated, the securities may lose their exemption and be subject to full registration. Also, even if a transaction qualifies for an exemption from federal registration, state securities laws must be checked. Some states have more stringent rules for exemptions, and registration at the state level may be required.

CYBERLAW

Securities Offerings on the Web

 There is no technological reason why new securities offerings cannot be posted on the web, and some have been. The Capital Markets Efficiency Act of 1996, which preempts state registration of offers to "qualified purchasers," provides an opportunity for such offerings to develop. They are much cheaper than the traditional offers presented on paper. But such offerings have been slow to come about.

Outdated state laws tend to block web offerings for categories not specifically covered by the 1996 Act. Such offerors must still comply with state-law paper requirements. Offerings covered by the 1996 law are private placements or fall under the accredited investor category. These are not easy to use by unknown firms trying to get their securities placed with low overhead cost. Since few people are used to looking at the web for new securities offerings, especially those with such a limited set of buyers, such efforts have not been all that successful. But, as with other areas of E-commerce, this more cost-effective offering method should become more common.

Private Placement

The 1933 Act provides that registration is not necessary for new securities not offered to the public. In some years, more money has been raised through *private placement* securities than through public offerings. The primary users of the exemption are those placing large blocks of securities with institutional investors—most often pension funds or insurance companies. For example, IBM might sell $250 million in new bonds directly to Prudential Insurance.

Regulation D To reduce the uncertainty of what will qualify as a private placement, the SEC adopted *Regulation D* to spell out the elements of private placement exemptions.

- *Accredited investors* are those presumed sophisticated enough to evaluate investment opportunities without the benefit of an SEC-approved prospectus and wealthy enough to bear the risk of loss if an investment goes bad. Accredited investors may participate in private placement offerings of securities. Institutions, such as banks and insurance companies, are accredited investors. The rule for individuals is that they have an annual income of at least $200,000 or a net worth of at least $1 million. Other investors are classified as unaccredited investors.
- Placements up to $5 million in securities can involve up to thirty-five unaccredited investors (and any number of accredited investors). Unaccredited investors must be provided information similar to that provided in a registration statement.
- Securities offerings of over $5 million may be made only to accredited investors to keep the private placement exemption.

The rules regarding such private placements are complex. Even though the offerings may be exempt from registration, there is usually a reporting requirement to the SEC about the offers, and the law requires that investors be given information (called a private-placement memorandum) similar to what they would have received in a prospectus. To prevent private placements from becoming a cheap

The Rich Get Rooked, Too

Tom Clancy, highly paid author of books such as *The Hunt for Red October*, was presented an investment opportunity that he was told was "extraordinarily safe and solid." Clancy invested $1.4 million with Goldie's Coin and Stamp Center. He was told that part of his investment, in gold coins and stamps, was guaranteed a 15 percent return. The rest of his funds, put in a stock fund run by Goldie's, was claimed to earn 30 percent a year. By 1995, Goldie's had only $408,000 left of the over $6 million invested by Clancy and others. Goldie's attorney said this was "just an issue of investments gone awry."

Source: *Associated Press* and *The Wall Street Journal*

way around the registration requirements of most public offerings, restrictions are placed on the resale of securities bought by investors in private placements, which can reduce their value.

Rule 144A Private placements are most common for large security issues—mostly bonds—that are sold to institutional investors. Rule 144A exempts U.S. and foreign security issuers from registration requirements for the sale of bonds and stocks to institutions with a portfolio of at least $100 million in securities. Further, securities issued to such large institutions may be traded among similarly qualified institutions without registration or disclosure requirements. In recent years, about one-third of all offerings—over $150 billion some years—have been sold under this registration exemption.

Regulation of Traded Securities

While the 1933 Act imposes *disclosure requirements* on corporations issuing new securities, the 1934 Act imposes disclosure requirements on securities that are publicly traded. If a security was originally registered under the 1933 Act, a security must be registered with the SEC under the 1934 Act. Even if exempt from registration under the 1933 Act, a security must be registered under the 1934 Act if it is listed on a securities exchange (New York Stock Exchange, etc.) or if it is traded *over the counter* (*OTC*) and the company has $5 million or more in assets and 500 or more shareholders.

Any company that has issued securities that are publicly traded is referred to as a *publicly held company* and is subject to the reporting requirements. A company that has fewer than 500 shareholders and does not allow its securities to be openly traded is called a *private company*. Its financial information is not available to the public. A company can go from being publicly held to private by buying up its stock so that it is held by fewer than 500 shareholders. A number of multibillion-dollar corporations are in this category, the most notable being RJR-Nabisco, which went private when its $25 billion in stock was all purchased by an investment group.

Disclosure requirements apply to more than 10,000 publicly held companies, most of which have securities traded in the OTC market. These companies must file reports on their securities. The most important report is the *10-K annual report*, an extensive audited financial statement similar in content to the information provided in the registration process under the 1933 Act. Companies must also file *quarterly 10-Q reports* with unaudited financial information and *8-K reports* whenever significant financial developments occur. As with initial securities registration, the purpose of these reports is to ensure disclosure of comprehensive financial information to investors.

PROXIES AND TENDER OFFERS

Besides setting the rules for how much information must be provided to current or prospective securities owners, the SEC sets certain requirements for handling stock out in the market. Most shares of stock, besides representing a claim on a share of the future profits of a company, carry voting rights used to elect boards of directors and to determine major issues facing the company that issued the stock. Shares of stock carry extra value because of voting rights, especially when major events such as a takeover occur. The SEC ensures that certain procedures are followed to ensure fair voting procedures.

Proxies

A *proxy* is permission given by shareholders to someone else to vote their shares on their behalf in the manner they instruct. Since it is not practical for stock owners to attend corporate meetings at which shareholders vote to approve major decisions, such as to merge with another company or elect the board of directors, shareholders are sent proxy statements to be voted on their behalf. Firms must provide shareholders with proxy statements—information about major proposed changes in the business. SEC regulations spell out the form and timing that proxy solicitations must take.

While most proxies are routine, such as voting for boards of directors or amendments to company bylaws, proxy fights can be used in a struggle over the future of the organization. For example, a proxy fight was waged to try to force USX to split into two separate companies, U.S. Steel and Marathon Oil. The board of directors was successful in opposing this move, but the vote was close on the issue, which was forced to a proxy vote by dissatisfied USX shareholders. Shareholders were offered the chance to stay with current management or to switch to another team that offered a different strategy for the future of the company.

Tender Offers

When one company attempts to take over another, it often uses a *tender offer.* Stock owners in the target company are offered stock in the acquiring company or cash in exchange for their stock. If successful, the acquiring company obtains enough stock to control the target company. Tender offers must be registered with the SEC, and certain procedures must be followed.

State Regulation of Takeovers As a part of their control of state corporation law, many states have passed statutes that set certain restrictions on tender offers. In the 1987 case *CTS Corp.* v. *Dynamics Corp. of America*, 481 U.S. 69, the Supreme Court upheld an Indiana statute that provides statutory defenses against takeovers. For example, even if a buyer has acquired over 50 percent of all company stock, the board of directors must still give approval to the takeover. Also, time limits are placed on how purchases of large blocks of stock must proceed. These laws are controversial because some critics claim that they are primarily used to protect local companies against out-of-state takeovers, which hurts shareholders if the company is poorly run.

Securities Fraud

The disclosure requirements do not prevent the sale or trading of securities in risky or poorly managed companies. Rather, the Acts help ensure the adequate and accurate disclosure of material facts concerning the securities of a publicly traded company. Failure to follow the disclosure requirements may result in suits for *securities fraud*. Some securities fraud cases arise from false and misleading information in the registration materials, but most arise from information during later disclosure, such as a 10-K annual report, or from public statements by corporate representatives.

BASIS FOR SECURITIES FRAUD

Because contractual obligations and rights are created in the sale of a security, an investor can rely on common-law fraud standards for protection. Investors who think they have been injured and would like to sue for damages often have difficulty establishing all elements of common-law fraud. Thus, injured investors generally rely on the antifraud provisions of the 1933 and 1934 Acts that hold that specific acts may produce statutory fraud.

Section 11 of the 1933 Act imposes civil liability for *misleading statements* or *material omissions* in securities registration material. Any person who buys a security covered by a registration statement that contains false or misleading information or that fails to include information that was important to a decision to purchase may sue to recover losses incurred in that purchase. For example, in the *Reves* case, the notes were not registered as securities but since the notes were held to be securities, investors could recover as a result of the misleading information they were given when they bought the notes.

In other words, liability may be imposed whether or not a security is registered. All securities are covered by the law of securities fraud. Since this standard was extended by the 1934 Act to cover misleading information in all disclosures required under that statute, investors have protection during the life of the security. Hence, securities fraud often arises as a result of misstatements by company officials or from insider trading.

Rule 10b-5

Section 10(b) of the 1934 Act makes it illegal for any person "to use or employ, in connection with the purchase or sale of any security registered on a national securities exchange or any security not so registered, any manipulative or deceptive device or contrivance in contravention of such rules and regulations as the Commission may prescribe. . . ." It provides the broadest base for bringing a securities fraud action, and it has come to be used in litigation more than any other part of the Act.

The SEC adopted Rule 10b-5 to enforce Section 10(b) of the 1934 Act. The rule is broad in scope:

> It shall be unlawful for any person, directly or indirectly, by the use of any means or instrumentality of interstate commerce, or of the mails, or of any facility of any national securities exchange,

1. To employ any device, scheme, or artifice to defraud;
2. To make any untrue statement of a material fact or to omit to state a material fact necessary in order to make the statements made, in the light of the circumstances under which they were made, not misleading; or
3. To engage in any act, practice, or course of business which operates or would operate as a fraud or deceit upon any person, in connection with the purchase or sale of any security.

The rule applies to all securities, registered or not. Since the rule does not state specific offenses, it has been left to the SEC and the courts to decide how strict the standards will be and what will constitute offenses.

LIABILITY FOR SECURITIES LAW VIOLATIONS

As we have seen, if an investor buys or sells a security after receiving inaccurate information about the security knowingly provided by the issuer, the investor may sue to recover damages (usually the difference in price between what the investor paid and what the security was worth when sold). The 1933 and 1934 Acts modify the common-law fraud action to make it easier for injured investors to recover.

The law allows injured investors to bring an action against all parties connected with the preparation of disclosure documents or other important information about the securities: directors of the company; the chief executive, financial, and accounting officers of the company; and accountants, lawyers, and other experts who helped prepare disclosure material. All parties are held to high standards of professional care, which is one reason for the high cost of preparing all disclosure materials. Everyone involved can be responsible for material omissions or misleading statements.

SEC Action

The SEC may also act against those alleged to be in violation of the securities law. Most SEC actions are remedial in nature, such as an injunction ordering someone not to do something again or to direct a company to issue corrected financial statements. Financial penalties are not common. While this may seem mild, the effect is not. Since the SEC action is public, the parties involved are exposed to public inspection. Injury to reputation in financial dealings can be very costly as other people are likely to shy away from future dealings. Further, SEC action may lead to private actions to recover losses attributed to the error in information that has been corrected.

The SEC can also recommend that the Department of Justice bring criminal charges against violators. To warrant a criminal action, the offender must have engaged in the perpetration of fraud in any offer or sale of securities. The criminal penalty may involve fines and imprisonment.

LIABILITY FOR MISSTATEMENTS

The securities statutes impose liability for *misstatements* or *omissions* about the financial status of a business that has publicly traded securities. Liability can be imposed on corporate officials or on those involved in preparing the information containing the misstatements. Securities fraud under Rule 10b-5 can be based on any relevant business document that contains material omissions or misstatements: accountant reports, SEC disclosure documents, press releases, or public statements by executives.

Misleading information that would reasonably affect investment decisions by current or prospective securities owners includes misinformation about the present financial status or the future prospects of the enterprise that would affect the price of the security. For example, overly optimistic statements by executives can cause favorable expectations about the future profits of a company, leading investors to bid up the price of the company's stock. When the statements are found to be false, the stock price falls, imposing losses on those who bought the stock on the basis of the positive statements. This is one of the most common grounds for private suits seeking damages based on a claim of securities fraud.

Directors and senior officers of businesses know they are legally responsible for the consequences of misstatements they make that cause the price of the securities issued by their company to rise or fall. Under the law of securities fraud, if investors lose money because of things not said (omissions) or because of misstatements that investors reasonably rely on, then there was *material misinformation* that caused the loss. The Supreme Court made that point clear in the *Basic* case.

Basic Inc. v. Levinson
United States Supreme Court
485 U.S. 224, 108 S.Ct. 978 (1988)

CASE BACKGROUND *Basic, a publicly traded company, began talks with Combustion in 1976 about the possibility of a merger. Basic made public statements in 1977 and 1978 denying that it was engaged in merger negotiations. On December 19, 1978, the Basic board endorsed Combustion's offer of $46 per share for Basic's common stock.*

Basic and its directors were sued by shareholders who had sold their stock before the merger announcement but after Basic's first statement in 1977 that there were no merger negotiations. The shareholders received less than $46 per share, which they claim was caused by false and misleading statements of Basic and its directors in violation of Section 10(b) of the 1934 Securities Exchange Act and of Rule 10b-5. That is, they sold their stock at lower prices than they would have received had the company told the truth about the merger talks. The district court held for Basic, finding that any misstatements were not material. The court of appeals reversed in favor of the shareholders. Basic appealed to the Supreme Court.

CASE DECISION Blackmun, Justice.

* * *

The [Supreme] Court . . . has defined a standard of materiality under the security laws, concluding . . . that "[a]n omitted fact is material if there is a substantial likelihood that a reasonable shareholder would consider it important. . . ." Acknowledging that cer-

tain information concerning corporate developments could well be of "dubious significance," the Court was careful not to set too low a standard of materiality; it was concerned that a minimal standard might bring an overabundance of information within its reach, and lead management "simply to bury the shareholders in an avalanche of trivial information—a result that is hardly conducive to informed decisionmaking." It further explained that to fulfill the materiality requirement "there must be a substantial likelihood that the disclosure of the omitted fact would have been viewed by the reasonable investor as having significantly altered the 'total mix' of information made available." We now expressly adopt [that] standard of materiality for the §10(b) and Rule 10b-5 context.

* * *

[I]n order to prevail on a Rule 10b-5 claim, a plaintiff must show that the statements were *misleading* as to a *material* fact. It is not enough that a statement is false or incomplete, if the misrepresented fact is otherwise insignificant. . . .

[M]ateriality depends on the significance the reasonable investor would place on the withheld or misrepresented information. The fact-specific inquiry we endorse here is consistent with the approach a number of courts have taken in assessing the materiality of merger negotiations.

* * *

We turn to the question of reliance and the fraud-on-the-market theory. Succinctly put:

The fraud on the market theory is based on the hypothesis that, in an open and developed securities market, the price of a company's stock is determined by the available material information regarding the company and its businesses. . . . Misleading statements will therefore defraud purchasers of stock even if the purchasers do not directly rely on the misstatements. . . . The causal connection between the defendants' fraud and the plaintiffs' purchase of stock in such a case is no less significant than in a case of direct reliance on misrepresentations.

. . . [W]e previously have dispensed with a requirement of positive proof of reliance, where a duty to disclose material information had been breached, concluding that the necessary nexus between the plaintiffs' injury and the defendant's wrongful conduct had been established. Similarly, we did not require proof that material omissions or misstatements in a proxy statement decisively affected voting, because the proxy solicitation itself, rather than the defect in the solicitation materials, served as an essential link in the transaction.

* * *

It has been noted that "it is hard to imagine that there ever is a buyer or seller who does not rely on market integrity. Who would knowingly roll the dice in a crooked crap game?" Indeed, nearly every court that has considered the proposition has concluded that where materially misleading statements have been disseminated into an impersonal, well-developed market for securities, the reliance of individual plaintiffs on the integrity of the market price may be presumed. Commentators generally have applauded the adoption of one variation or another of the fraud-on-the-market theory. An investor who buys or sells stock at the price set by the market does so in reliance on the integrity of that price. Because most publicly available information is reflected in market price, an investor's reliance on any public material misrepresentations, therefore, may be presumed for purposes of a Rule 10b-5 action.

The Court of Appeals found that Basic "made public, material misrepresentations and Levinson sold Basic stock in an impersonal, efficient market. Thus the class, as defined by the district court, has established the threshold facts for proving their loss." The court acknowledged that Basic may rebut proof of the elements giving rise to the presumption, or show that the misrepresentation in fact did not lead to a distortion of price or that an individual plaintiff traded or would have traded despite his knowing the statement was false.

* * *

CASE NOTE Defendants can rebut a claim of material misrepresentation by showing that the omission or misrepresentation was not material or did not affect the security price or that the plaintiff did not rely on the information in making a decision to buy or sell the security. Since this case, all investors similarly injured by misinformation that affects securities prices have a potential cause of action. Such cases are generally filed as class actions.

QUESTIONS FOR ANALYSIS

1. Since rumors about merger talks usually come out right away, should executives always admit that they are engaged in merger talks even if the possibility of a merger is remote? What problems could that cause?
2. How can security holders who were ignorant of what was going on later get involved in such litigation?

Safe Harbor

The Securities Litigation Reform Act of 1995 amended the securities law to protect companies from liability for predictions about profits and the likely success of its products so long as forecasts are accompanied by "meaningful cautionary statements identifying important factors that could cause actual results to differ materially from those in the forward-looking statement." This is called a *safe harbor* because it gives greater immunity from suit for corporate forecasts that turned out after the fact not to be accurate.

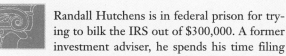

Pay Is OK, But the Food Is Terrible

Randall Hutchens is in federal prison for trying to bilk the IRS out of $300,000. A former investment adviser, he spends his time filing shareholder-fraud cases against companies in California small claims court, where the damages are limited to $5,000.

Rather than contest the claims, at least seventeen companies have paid settlements between $500 and $5,000, allowing Hutchens to collect over $30,000. His claims are bogus, especially since he never actually owned the stock involved. But the cost of hiring a California attorney to look into the securities fraud claims, based on alleged misinformation, is high enough that many companies just offer settlements.

Given that the prison provides Hutchens all the material he needs, his only expense is the small court filing fee.

Source: *The Wall Street Journal*

Federal Exclusivity

The intent of the 1995 Act to reduce the number of securities class-action suits of dubious merit did not have the desired effect in practice. Suits were filed in state courts under state securities statutes that tend to copy much of the language of the 1933 and 1934 Acts. Most class-action suits were brought by attorneys specializing in such litigation who would find a nominal plaintiff to be the head of a "class" of all affected investors. To prevent this skirting of federal law, President Clinton signed the Securities Litigation Uniform Standards Act of 1998, which requires securities suits involving nationally traded securities to be brought exclusively in federal court under federal law.

The 1998 Act prohibits the pursuit of a class action under the law of any state if the suit alleges: (a) an untrue statement or omission of a material fact in connection with the purchase or sale of a covered security; or (b) that the defendant used or employed any deceptive device or contrivance in connection with the purchase or sale of a covered security. All such suits must be filed in federal court.

LIABILITY FOR INSIDER TRADING

The most controversial application of Rule 10b-5 is its use to prohibit *insider trading*—the buying or selling of stock by persons who have access to information affecting the value of the stock that has not yet been revealed to the public. As the Supreme Court has noted, misappropriation of private information gives insiders an unfair advantage in the market over investors who do not have the information. It is illegal for an insider to trade on inside information until the information has been released to the public and the stock price has had time to adjust to the new information.

Corporate executives are the ones most likely to be affected by the rule, as they are most likely to have valuable information concerning the financial well-being of the company before the release of the information to the public. The SEC brings about forty such cases each year.

SEC Prosecution

The SEC may prosecute insiders—persons with access to nonpublic information—if the insiders trade to their benefit in the stock in question before the public has a chance to act on the information. For example, suppose an attorney working for General Electric found out in the process of normal work that GE would announce the sale of $1 billion worth of jet engines to Boeing in two days. Knowing that this good news would probably make GE stock rise, the attorney buys some GE stock before the public announcement. This is insider trading for which the attorney could be sued for all profits earned from the stock transaction.

What has not yet been fully resolved is to whom the rule against insider trading applies. If you are riding on the subway in New York and overhear two executives talking about something big about to happen to their company, you have just learned nonpublic information. Would it be illegal for you to trade on such information? For a while it looked as if that might be the case, but in 1980, the Supreme Court started to clarify the rules.

Supreme Court Interpretation

A printer at a company that printed financial documents read some confidential information. The printer traded in the stock of the company involved and made $30,000 in profits because of his access to inside information. The SEC charged the printer, Mr. Chiarella, with securities fraud, but the Supreme Court reversed the lower court conviction.

In the 1980 decision *Chiarella* v. *United States*, 445 U.S. 222, the Court said that Chiarella was not a corporate insider who owed a *fiduciary duty* to the shareholders of his company. He was an outsider who was lucky enough to learn inside information. He could be responsible only if his position has a requirement that he could not use such information. He may have had an unfair advantage over other stock traders, but it did not constitute securities fraud, said the Court. "He was not their [the corporation's] agent, he was not a fiduciary, he was not a person in whom the sellers had placed their trust and confidence. He was, in fact, a complete stranger who dealt with the sellers only through impersonal market transactions." The *Dirks* case further clarified liability for insider trading.

Dirks v. SEC
United States Supreme Court
463 U.S. 646, 103 S.Ct. 3255 (1983)

CASE BACKGROUND *Raymond Dirks worked for a broker-dealer firm in New York. His job was to study insurance firms to determine whether investors should buy their securities. A former officer of Equity Funding of America (the "tipper") told Dirks (the "tippee") that Equity Funding officers were engaged in fraud and thus the company's stock was overvalued. Dirks investigated and decided that the information appeared to be true. Dirks told his clients, who sold their holdings in Equity Funding, and he told a* Wall Street Journal *reporter. As*

Dirks's information spread, the price of Equity Funding stock fell from $26 to $15 per share. The New York Stock Exchange, sensing problems, suspended trading in the stock.

California insurance authorities and the SEC investigated and uncovered a major investment fraud. Besides investigating Equity Funding, the SEC charged Dirks with insider trading. That is, in his professional capacity he used knowledge not fully disclosed to the public. The SEC found Dirks guilty of insider trading. The court of appeals upheld the decision, ruling that any tippee (person who learns of inside information) must divulge the information to the public and not use it in any manner to trade in securities. The Supreme Court reviewed the decision.

CASE DECISION Powell, Justice.

* * *

Not "all breaches of fiduciary duty in connection with a securities transaction," . . . come within the ambit of Rule 10b-5. There must also be "manipulation or deception." In an inside-trading case this fraud derives from the "inherent unfairness involved where one takes advantage" of "information intended to be available only for a corporate purpose and not for the personal benefit of anyone." Thus, an insider will be liable under Rule 10b-5 for inside trading only where he fails to disclose material nonpublic information before trading on it and thus makes "secret profits."

* * *

Imposing a duty to disclose or abstain solely because a person knowingly receives material nonpublic information from an insider and trades on it could have an inhibiting influence on the role of market analysts, which the SEC itself recognizes is necessary to the preservation of a healthy market. It is commonplace for analysts to "ferret out and analyze information," and this often is done by meeting with and questioning corporate officers and others who are insiders. Any information that the analysts obtain normally may be the basis for judgments as to the market worth of a corporation's securities. The analyst's judgment in this respect is made available in market letters or otherwise to clients of the firm. It is the nature of this type of information, and indeed of the markets themselves, that such information cannot be made simultaneously available to all of the corporation's stockholders or the public generally.

The conclusion that recipients of inside information do not invariably acquire a duty to disclose or abstain does not mean that such tippees always are free to trade on the information. The need for a ban on some tippee trading is clear. Not only are insiders forbidden by their fiduciary relationship from personally using undisclosed corporate information to their advantage, but they may not give such information to an outsider for the same improper purpose of exploiting the information for their personal gain.

* * *

Determining whether an insider personally benefits from a particular disclosure, a question of fact, will not always be easy for courts. But it is essential, we think, to have a guiding principle for those whose daily activities must be limited and instructed by the SEC's inside-trading rules, and we believe that there must be a breach of the insider's fiduciary duty before the tippee inherits the duty to disclose or abstain. In contrast, the rule adopted by the SEC in this case would have no limiting principle.

Under the inside-trading and tipping rules set forth above, we find that there was no actionable violation by Dirks. It is disputed that Dirks himself was a stranger to Equity Funding, with no pre-existing fiduciary duty to its shareholders. He took no action, directly or indirectly, that induced the shareholders or officers of Equity Funding to repose trust or confidence in him. There was no expectation by Dirks' sources that he would keep their information in confidence. Nor did Dirks misappropriate or illegally obtain the information about Equity Funding. Unless the insiders breached their . . . duty to shareholders in disclosing the nonpublic information to Dirks, he breached no duty when he passed it on to investors as well as to *The Wall Street Journal.* . . . Dirks therefore could not have been "a participant after the fact in [an] insider's breach of a fiduciary duty."

We conclude that Dirks, in the circumstances of this case, had no duty to abstain from use of the inside information that he obtained. The judgment of the Court of Appeals therefore is Reversed.

CASE NOTE This decision limited the kinds of insider trading cases that the SEC could bring to cases involving the use of inside information by those with a fiduciary duty not to use such information.

QUESTIONS FOR ANALYSIS

1. Although Dirks did not own stock in Equity Funding, is it correct to say that he had no financial gain or loss at stake in revealing the inside information he knew?
2. Did shareholders in Equity Funding suffer losses from Dirks's giving the inside information to some investors, who then sold, driving the price down?

G-7 Country Approaches to Insider Trading

G-7 countries are the seven major industrial powers—Canada, France, Germany, Italy, Japan, the United Kingdom, and the United States. The United States has long had the strongest rules against insider trading, but the others are beginning to toughen.

In Canada, rules are set by the provinces. Ontario and British Columbia have rules similar to those of the United States and have exchanged information with the SEC about insider trading. Quebec has weak rules against insider trading.

The U.K. passed insider trading legislation in 1980 and brings about the same number of suits as does the SEC, given the size of the two nations. After a scandal involving high-ranking government officials, France adopted tough insider trading rules in 1989, giving the Commission des Operacions de Bourse much stronger powers than it had under older statutes.

Italy enacted its first insider trading law in 1991. Its first conviction from its regulatory agency, Consob, did not occur until 1994, a case that resulted in a fine of about $15,000. While the terms of the statute appear to be stringent, in practice, enforcement is minimal, and the law has significant loopholes.

Germany did not pass a law against insider trading until 1994. The law is enforced by a new agency, the Bundesaufsichtsamt fur den Wertpapierhandel, which obtained its first conviction in 1995.

Like Italy, Japan appears to have little interest in prosecuting insider trading. Such trading is weakly outlawed by some 1988 amendments to its 1948 Securities Exchange Act, but penalties are mild, and enforcement is minimal. It was not until the late 1990s that the Finance Ministry announced that it would not permit insider trading by Ministry officials with access to inside information.

The Supreme Court extended the possible application of insider trading laws in a 1997 case, *U.S. v. O'Hagan*, 521 U.S. 642. Attorney O'Hagen made a $4.3 million profit after buying shares in a firm involved in a takeover. O'Hagan was not working on the case, but he learned of the takeover from another attorney. Since O'Hagan did not represent the firm, he contended that he did not have a fiduciary duty not to use the inside information. The Supreme Court upheld O'Hagan's prison conviction, stating that trading done "on the basis of" insider information violates Rule 10b-5 as a misappropriation of information, even though he had no fiduciary duty.

Insider Trading Sanctions Act

The *Insider Trading Sanctions Act* of 1984 gave the SEC a statutory basis for prosecuting insider trading. The law does not define insider trading, but it gives the SEC authority to bring enforcement actions against violators who trade in securities while in possession of material nonpublic information. The courts may order violators to pay treble damages based on a measure of the illegal profit gained or the loss avoided by the insider trading. Those convicted of violations may also have to pay back illegal profits to those who suffered the losses, which effectively means quadruple damages. In addition, criminal penalties may be assessed.

This law was strengthened by the *Insider Trading and Securities Fraud Enforcement Act* of 1988, which increased the maximum fine to $1 million per criminal action for persons convicted of violating the law against insider trading and set the maximum prison term at ten years per violation. The fine against corporations was raised to $2.5 million per criminal violation, and the SEC is authorized to pay bounties (up to 10 percent of the penalty the government receives) to informants who give leads that produce insider trading convictions.

MAJOR INSIDER TRADING CASES

The SEC quickly applied its expanded powers in subsequent cases. A string of insider trading cases not only rocked the financial world but also became lead stories in regular news reporting.

Levine

The case involving Dennis Levine broke in 1986. Levine was a high-ranking officer in a major Wall Street firm. He specialized in helping firms merge. Hence, he had access to very valuable inside information that he knew was confidential but that he sold to others. Levine was sued by the SEC and arrested under a warrant obtained by the U.S. Attorney's Office. Cooperating with authorities, he provided information that helped the SEC bring insider trading charges against prominent lawyers and securities traders. Levine agreed to repay almost $13 million in illegal gains. That case led to even bigger fish—Ivan Boesky.

Boesky

In late 1986, the SEC sued Boesky. The complaint claimed that he purchased securities based on material nonpublic information provided by Dennis Levine as part of an organized trading scheme involving senior officers in prestigious investment firms. There is little wonder that Boesky earned the highest income on Wall Street in 1985. Boesky paid for nonpublic information on tender offers, mergers, and other business deals that greatly affect stock prices.

The SEC claimed that Boesky knew that all such information was confidential and had obtained it through breach of a fiduciary duty. For example, the SEC charged that Boesky paid Levine 5 percent of his profits earned on securities purchases and sales based on confidential information Levine gave him—some of which was obtained from other investment brokers who were also in on the deal. One firm was handling the forthcoming merger of Nabisco and RJ Reynolds. That created a fiduciary duty not to reveal that information or act on it for personal gain. However, those in a position of trust sold their valuable information, knowing that when word of the merger was made public the stock prices of the acquired company would rise.

Boesky agreed to pay $100 million in cash and assets. Half that amount was a civil penalty paid under the ITSA to the U.S. Treasury. The rest represented illegal gains and was placed in escrow for the benefit of investor claims. Boesky also agreed to an order barring him from any association with any broker, dealer, investment adviser, investment company, or municipal securities dealer. He also received a three-year prison sentence. Based on information Levine and Boesky provided, more cases were brought by the SEC in a continuing insider trading investigation. Kidder, Peabody & Co., New York securities dealers, agreed to pay $25 million in civil penalties in 1987 and to cooperate with the SEC in further investigations.

Drexel

Drexel Burnham Lambert Inc., one of the most innovative Wall Street firms of the 1980s, increased its business substantially through its "junk bond" (high-risk potentially high-yield bonds) operations headed by Michael Milken. Milken and

Drexel handled the issuance and marketing of about one-half of the nearly $140 billion worth of junk bonds issued through 1988.

In 1989, Drexel pleaded guilty to six felony counts of securities fraud and agreed to pay $650 million in fines and restitution. Drexel settled the case in part because of concern that if the company lost in court, under the Racketeer Influenced and Corrupt Organizations (RICO) law, it could have been assessed treble damages plus made subject to other litigation that would follow such a conviction. To help restructure the firm, Drexel then sold its public brokerage offices and hired a former SEC chairman to be its new chairman.

Milken

Having been indicted on ninety-eight counts of violations of the securities laws, Michael Milken pleaded guilty in 1990 to six felony counts. In 1992, he agreed to pay $200 million in fines to the government and $900 million in restitution to pay the claims of defrauded investors. The case against Milken had little to do with his fame for "junk bonds," which are legal, but involved his dealings with Boesky and others. Among the crimes he admitted to were

- Cheating Drexel's clients by falsely reporting to them the prices at which securities had been bought and sold, with his junk-bond department keeping the profits
- Helping a partner evade income taxes by manufacturing losses and gains from apparent stock transactions
- Conspiring with Boesky to keep secret records to hide the fact that Boesky was the owner of certain securities
- Secretly agreeing to buy stock from Boesky and hold it at Drexel so that Boesky could appear to have more capital on hand to meet certain SEC capital requirements

Sentenced to ten years in prison, Milken was released after two years and was barred from the securities industry.

The Investment Company Act

The *Investment Company Act (ICA)* of 1940 gives the SEC control over the structure of investment companies. It requires investment companies to register as such with the SEC, which then makes the companies subject to regulations of their activities and holds them liable to the SEC and to private parties for violations of the ICA.

INVESTMENT COMPANIES

An *investment company* is primarily in the business of investing or trading in securities. The ICA defines three types of investment companies: face-amount certificate companies, which issue debt securities paying a fixed return; unit investment trusts, offering a fixed portfolio of securities; and management companies, the most important type of investment company. Since passage of the National Securities Markets Improvement Act of 1996, all regulation is exclusively by the SEC.

Mutual Funds

The most common management company is the *open-end company*, generally known as a *mutual fund*. In 1980, $52 billion was invested in mutual funds. That has risen into the trillions now. Open-end companies offer no specific number of shares and can expand as long as people invest with them. The number of shares is reduced as investors redeem their shares. The money from these shares is invested in a portfolio of securities. The price of the shares is determined by the value of the portfolio divided by the number of shares sold to the public. This is the most common investment company because of the flexibility it offers to investors and portfolio managers.

There are two kinds of mutual funds: *load* and *no-load*. The former are sold to the public through a securities dealer and have a sales commission (load) of some percentage of the price. No-load funds are sold directly to the public through the mail with no sales commission. All funds charge an annual expense fee that covers costs of operation. The fee usually runs about one percent per year.

Investment companies that do not offer securities to the public but are involved in internal investing (such as banks, insurance companies, charitable foundations, and tax-exempt pension funds) are exempt from the regulations imposed on investment companies that deal with the public.

REGULATION OF INVESTMENT COMPANIES

Investment companies must register with the SEC, stating their investment policy and providing financial information. Annual reports and other information must be disclosed on a continuing basis. Capital requirements, including how much debt such companies may have, are set by the SEC. Payment of dividends to investors must equal at least 90 percent of the taxable ordinary income of the investment company. A company must invest in only those activities that it stated it would in its sales literature and policy statements.

Registration and Disclosure

Since investment companies sell securities, such as shares in mutual funds, to buy securities for investment purposes, their securities must be registered with the SEC. Hence, companies under the ICA are subject to the *registration and disclosure* requirements of the SEC for publicly traded securities. The sales literature used by mutual fund companies to promote their investment strategies to the public must be filed with the SEC for review. In general, no share of stock in an investment company may be sold for more than its current net asset value plus a maximum sales charge (load) of 8.5 percent.

Limiting Conflicts of Interest

To reduce possible *conflicts of interest*, there are restrictions on who may be on the board of directors of an investment company. At least 40 percent of the members of the board must be outsiders—persons with no direct business relationship with the company or its officers. The outsiders on the board are responsible for approving contracts with the investment advisers who are usually hired to manage the investment fund offered by the company. Further, investment companies may not use the funds invested with them for deals with any persons affiliated with the company. All deals are to be "arm's length."

Investment Advisers

Investment companies usually hire *investment advisers* to manage their operations. Investment advisers have several trillion dollars invested in their care. Registered investment advisers manage pension funds and the portfolios held by insurance companies and banks. According to the ICA, investment advisers are "deemed to have a fiduciary duty with respect to the receipt of compensation for services" rendered to investment companies. The standard fee paid to advisers to manage an investment company fund is 0.5 percent of the net assets of the funds each year.

The Investment Advisers Act

The *Investment Advisers Act* (*IAA*) defines *investment adviser* as a "person who, for compensation, engages in the business of advising others . . . as to the advisability of investing in, purchasing or selling securities." For example, investment advisers contract to direct the investment strategies of mutual funds. The regulations adopted by the SEC under the Act are a part of the regulation of professionals working in the securities industry.

Under the Investment Adviser Supervision Coordination Act, which became effective in 1997 and amended the IAA, an investment adviser may not register with the SEC unless it has at least $25 million under management or it is an investment adviser to a mutual fund. All other investment advisers are subject to state laws concerning record keeping, disclosure, and capital requirements. Hence, the SEC has primary responsibility for regulating larger advisers who are more likely to be involved in national money management, while the states have jurisdiction over smaller advisers more likely to be of a local nature.

BROKERS AND DEALERS

The IAA regulates *brokers* (persons engaged in the business of effecting transactions in securities for the account of others), *dealers* (persons engaged in the business of buying and selling securities for their own account), and *advisers* (persons engaged in the business of charging fees for investment advice). For simplicity, brokers, dealers, and investment advisers will all be referred to as *securities professionals*. Securities professionals must be registered with the SEC. Violations of SEC rules can lead to suspension or loss of the right to do business in the industry.

Professional Responsibility to Clients

Primary concerns of the SEC in regulating securities professionals are obligations to clients and possible conflicts of interest. The Supreme Court has held that broker-dealers must make known to their customers any possible conflicts or other information that is material to investment decisions. Professionals violate their duty when they charge excessive markups on securities above their market value to unsuspecting customers. Markups over 5 percent are difficult to justify, and those over 10 percent are not allowed under SEC guidelines.

Illegal practices include *churning*, whereby a broker who has control of a client's account buys and sells an excessive amount of stock to make money from the commissions earned on the transactions. Also illegal is *scalping*, whereby a professional buys stock for personal benefit, then urges investors to buy the stock so that the price will rise to the benefit of the professional.

Another concern of the SEC focuses on ensuring investors *adequate information* about available securities to make informed investment decisions. Generally, professionals violate the antifraud provisions of the regulations when they recommend securities without making adequate information available. Registered professionals may not deal in securities not registered under the securities laws. If the security is exempt from registration, the professional must have information about the security similar to the information that would be required of a registered security.

Rogue Traders

Investment firms are faced with the problem that their traders, of necessity, have access to large sums of money and, even with good intentions, can make trades that lead to disaster. Usually, the accounts of only a few clients are damaged. The firms cover such losses, but sometimes the losses are staggering. In recent years, several major cases came to light.

Barings PLC, a 233-year-old British investment company, collapsed in 1995 when one of its traders in Singapore, Nicholas Leeson, wrongly bet that the Japanese stock market would rise. The firm lost almost one billion dollars. Leeson was sentenced to over six years in prison in Singapore. Similarly, in 1995, a Daiwa Bank trader in New York, Toshihide Iguchi, was found to have hidden losses of almost two billion dollars from his trades in government bonds. Daiwa was expelled from the United States for hiding the losses, and Iguchi was convicted of criminal fraud. Trading firms have attempted to institute better controls over the limits within which their traders may operate.

INVESTMENT NEWSLETTERS

Investment advisers who violate securities laws may be suspended or barred from dispensing investment advice for compensation. While we usually think of an investment adviser who has stolen clients' funds or otherwise abused a fiduciary duty to a client as subject to SEC prosecution, does such regulation extend to the sale of investment advice via an investment newsletter? Numerous such newsletters exist, some publishers of which have made tens of millions of dollars dispensing investment advice in their newsletters. The Supreme Court, in *Lowe* v. *SEC*, held that investment newsletters are exempt from SEC regulation because of freedom of the press.

Stock Market Regulation

The volume and value of stock transactions have grown rapidly. They are about thirty times higher than they were in 1970. Since trillions of dollars are changing hands on the New York Stock Exchange and the other securities markets, investors want to be assured that proper safeguards are in place.

SELF-REGULATION OF SECURITIES MARKETS

The 1934 Securities Exchange Act allows private associations of securities professionals to set rules for professionals dealing in securities markets. Congress gave the SEC the power to monitor such self-regulating organizations, which include the stock exchanges, such as the New York Stock Exchange (NYSE), the American

JURIS **prudence?**

Sell! Whoops, I Mean Buy!

Many investors rely on advice from professionals who are presumed to investigate the soundness of companies and give careful thought to their future. Yet, *The Wall Street Journal* reports, investment firms show confusion at times, casting doubt on the value of their market research.

A report by the investment firm Lehman Brothers on the company Boston Chicken urged investors to buy, claiming that the price should rise to $30 per share. But on the following page, the report predicted that the stock price was likely to fall to $15 and advocated selling.

Similarly, a report by Prudential Securities listed twenty-nine "Single Best Ideas"—the stocks it recommended most highly to investors. But footnotes indicated that six of the stocks were rated poorly, and the company advocated selling them. Explanations for such oddities are vague. Asked to explain the seeming inconsistency, the head of Prudential's research said, "The arts and sciences are different."

Source: *The Wall Street Journal*

Stock Exchange (AMEX), the regional exchanges, and the over-the-counter (OTC) markets, the most important of which is the NASDAQ.

Rules for Exchange Members

The stock exchanges establish and enforce rules of conduct for their members. Some rules govern the operation of the exchange, how securities are listed, obligations of issuers of securities, who may handle certain transactions and in what manner, and how prices are set and reported. Other rules concern how member firms and their employees must qualify for membership to be allowed to handle various transactions. These rules include how investors' accounts are to be managed, the qualifications of dealers and brokers, limits on advertising, and other operations of securities firms. Governing the OTC market is the National Association of Securities Dealers (NASD), which sets rules of behavior for traders on the OTC market similar to the rules of the NYSE for its members.

Liability and Penalties

Punishment for violation of self-regulating organization rules can include suspension or expulsion from the organization, making transactions by the expelled member impossible. If an exchange knows that a member firm is violating the rules or the law and ignores such a violation, causing investors to lose money, it can be held liable for the losses. The potential liability and SEC pressure have given the exchanges an incentive to watch securities professionals for behavior that violates the standards.

REGULATION OF SECURITIES TRANSACTIONS

The SEC, in cooperation with the NASD, regulates the actions of securities professionals who handle the actual trading of securities. To reduce the number of problems, floor trading by professionals is strictly limited to registered experts, as is off-floor trading. The difference between these two types of trading is that one is done on the floor of a securities exchange, while the other is done elsewhere,

International Stock Markets

Trillions of dollars in equity (stock) are owned by millions of people around the world. The internationalization of markets and companies has forced many countries whose markets were nearly closed to noncitizens to open their markets to international investors. The result is an influx of money that boosts local economies. For example, before 1993, foreign ownership of companies in Finland, the poorest of the Scandinavian countries, was strictly limited. When the door was opened to foreign investment, the value of stock listed on the Finnish exchange grew from about $100 million to about $3.3 billion in one year. The inflow of foreign capital meant business expansion.

Other countries have developing securities markets, and many more would like to have them. Governments that used to try to control all capital flows have come to understand that it is difficult to stop capital from going to its best opportunities and that if they open their markets, they could benefit from capital inflows. From small

nations like Malaysia to large ones like Brazil, stock markets are being developed. Most nations adopt securities laws very similar to U.S. laws, because American securities markets have become world models.

Countries have difficulties developing stock markets when they have not had economic or political stability. Where governments seem perpetually unstable, most people are leery of risking their wealth in ventures the government could easily destroy or steal by simply changing the law. The size of a country has little to do with the development of equity markets. Hong Kong and Belgium have healthy markets because of their long-term political stability.

Stock markets frighten governments because they are a good measure of the wisdom of a government's economic policy. If a government implements policies that investors believe will injure the economy or reduce the rate of return on capital, stock prices will quickly fall as investors react to the news.

such as OTC. In either case, the professional securities dealers may not trade for their own advantage ahead of their customers.

Regulations also cover *specialist firms.* These firms generally do not deal directly with the public; rather, they handle transactions for brokers. Brokers may leave their customers' orders with the specialist to be filled when possible. For example, if a stock is currently selling for $21 a share and a stock owner is willing to sell at $22 dollars a share, the order may be left to be filled should the price rise to $22. Specialists also handle transactions that are unusual or difficult for most securities dealers to execute. SEC rules prohibit the specialists from exploiting their special position. Specialists may not deal for their own benefit in the orders left to execute. Since they are first to learn of price changes, they could buy and sell the stock left with them to take advantage of changes in stock prices.

ARBITRATION OF DISPUTES

When investors establish accounts with investment firms or stockbrokers, they usually sign a standard form that states that in the event of a dispute, the dispute must be arbitrated, not litigated. SEC rules govern the arbitration process, which is the primary dispute resolution mechanism for brokers and investors.

Under the regulations, the arbitration agreement must be pointed out to customers and explained. Arbitration boards appointed to settle disputes usually include one industry professional and two members of the public. Arbitrators from the public must provide details of their past ten years' activities, and they may not have worked for the securities industry for at least three years. Brokers must provide requested documents to investors before arbitration hearings. Although arbitration records are secret, the decisions are made public so that people have a better understanding about the process.

Supreme Court Support

The Supreme Court has upheld the binding nature of arbitration agreements. It will be an unusual case in which an investor will be allowed to litigate a dispute with a broker. The Court has held that the arbitration agreements apply to security fraud claims against brokers and that there is a "strong endorsement of the federal statutes favoring this method of resolving disputes."

Arbitration is generally much less expensive than litigation, and the results tend to be more certain because of the expertise of the arbitrators. Most of the thousands of arbitration cases filed annually are resolved in favor of the client. For example, in 1992 an American Arbitration Association panel ordered Prudential Securities to pay $1.4 million in damages, including $600,000 in punitive damages, for allowing its San Diego office to engage in excessive trading in an account of a retired couple. Three officers of the San Diego office were ordered to pay damages from $100,000 to $300,000.

Summary

- Securities include any (1) investment of money (2) in a common enterprise in which there is (3) an expectation of profits (4) from the efforts of persons other than the investors. This definition from the *Howey* case includes any investment device that meets these general criteria.
- Registration of new securities requires public disclosure of financial and managerial information and of future business plans with the SEC. Since the disclosure is complicated and mistakes can lead to serious legal consequences, skilled counsel is required.
- Securities that are sold under a private placement exemption do not have to be registered with the SEC prior to sale. Most securities sold this way are large bond issues sold directly to institutional investors, such as insurance companies. Some smaller stock offerings are sold in limited numbers to accredited (wealthy and sophisticated) investors to avoid the cost of registration. These securities are subject to SEC regulation after their sale.
- Companies that have publicly traded securities must file financial disclosure information with the SEC, including quarterly and annual reports. Production of these reports is costly and exposes a company's finances to the public, including competitors.
- Takeover attempts and proxy battles for control of a company are subject to SEC regulations, as are certain voting rights of shareholders.
- All securities are subject to the law concerning securities fraud, which arises from the common law of fraud. They are also subject to the securities statutes that are expressed by the SEC in Rule 10b-5, which applies to a wide range of activities related to the handling of securities.
- Liability may be imposed on securities issuers or corporate officials for misstatements in corporate documents, including statements to the media. Material information that misleads investors about a company and that causes profits in a security to be lost may be the basis of legal action. Executives and

those who work with sensitive financial matters must address company matters with a high degree of care.

- Insider trading can lead to criminal and civil prosecution under securities law as well as private liability. Liability is imposed when insiders violate a fiduciary duty. If one is in a position of trust that provides access to valuable information, one may not exploit the information for personal gain, since one has a duty to protect the information and use it for the benefit of those to whom the duty is owed—the shareholders.
- Securities professionals (brokers, dealers, and financial advisers) are regulated by the SEC and must meet certain financial requirements. Those who give investment advice only through an investment newsletter are not subject to regulation.
- Firms that trade securities for investors (brokerage firms), firms that make investments for investors (investment companies, such as mutual funds), and the stock exchanges are regulated by the SEC. Self-regulatory organizations impose rules on industry members that are subject to SEC approval. Violations of regulatory requirements are subject to civil and criminal penalties.

Issue

Should We Restrict Insider Trading?

Ivan Boesky and Michael Milken violated a fiduciary duty imposed by contract as well as by SEC regulation. Putting aside such cases, is it undesirable that corporate insiders trade on valuable information about their own company that they help to create? That is, do we not want executives to have strong financial incentives to maximize the profitability of their companies over time, thereby benefiting all shareholders? Some critics of the SEC claim that it is reducing market efficiency, not helping it, by attacking such insider trading. In this article, former SEC Commissioner Cox considers both sides of the arguments.

TWO VIEWS ON THE LAW OF INSIDER TRADING

Charles C. Cox

Copyright 1999, Charles C. Cox. Cox served as SEC commissioner from 1983–89. Currently, he is senior vice president of Lexecon, Inc., Chicago.

Opponents of insider trading maintain that insider trading destroys investor confidence in the stock market, particularly that of small investors. This, it is argued, causes

investors to move away from securities and decreases the usefulness of the securities market.

Proponents of insider trading, such as Henry G. Manne, George Mason University Law School, argue that insider trading should be allowed because it is socially beneficial. In particular, Manne contends that insider trading improves market efficiency by moving stock prices in the proper direction sooner than it would otherwise have occurred. Furthermore, Manne argues that insider trading is an efficient way to compensate innovative entrepreneurs. To use Professor Manne's language, he believes that "insider trading is the best, if not the only, method of adequately compensating corporate innovators."

Regardless of the position you take, no hard evidence exists to support either theory. To make a proper analysis, questions such as the following must be answered: Would the stock market be more efficient if insider trading were legal? If so, by how much? Does insider trading prevail over other methods of entrepreneurial compensation in countries where it is legal? Can evidence be produced to suggest that investor confidence and/or market liquidity is reduced by insider trading? These questions have not yet been answered. However, we should not assume that insider trading is always at work simply because price run-ups on stocks and other events are not fully explained by innocent reasons.

The fact that a handful of Wall Street investment bankers, arbitrageurs and even a prominent takeover attorney were caught with their hands in the till does not imply that most people in the business are corrupt. It does imply that, as watchdogs of Wall Street, the SEC is doing its job and that insider traders will be pursued and either enjoined or, where appropriate, referred to the Justice Department for criminal prosecution. While the SEC cannot claim to have stopped insider trading, it is clear that it has made progress in deterring insider trading activities.

Let us imagine for a moment that insider trading was not a violation of the securities laws. Imagine that the ability to profit from trades on material nonpublic information was available for corporations to use as a means of compensating managers and directors.

As I mentioned before, some commentators oppose the prohibitions on insider trading. They suggest that the decision to allow or prohibit insider trading should be left to the individual corporation. Suppose that we were to allow corporations to decide for themselves whether to permit insiders to trade on nonpublic information. It seems to me that if insider trading were legalized, we would probably end up about where we are at present. Most corporations would adopt a charter and bylaw provision prohibiting insider trading to protect their reputations.

Trades made by a corporation's employees based on corporate inside information would present a conflict of interest between the corporation's stockholders and the employees. If the corporation allowed its employees to profit from their special knowledge while at the same time allowing shareholders to continue trading, the shareholders would be at a definite disadvantage. The question remains—would a prohibition at the corporate level be effective?

Without regulatory laws, do you suppose the securities industry would enforce or monitor insider trading activities? Would companies that prohibit insider trading exercise aggressive monitoring to prevent it? I think not! Corporations do not have access to market surveillance that the government and the stock exchanges maintain. They would be unable to determine, with any degree of certainty, when one of their employees traded on inside information. You cannot rely on an employee's sense of honesty to come forward and admit to a highly profitable violation of company policy.

Moreover, corporations that discover employees who have violated company policy have a tendency to fire the violator without suing him. Consider a story in *The Wall Street Journal*. It concerned a man who had held accounting jobs at numerous companies and embezzled funds from all of them. When the embezzlement was discovered, each company fired the violator. None sued him, and some gave him good recommendations for a job at another company. This was the least costly way of dealing with the problem for each individual company, but not the least costly solution for the business community as a whole.

My point is that corporations faced with the difficult problem of monitoring and enforcing insider trading prohibitions would soon ask for help through the police power of government to enforce their rules. This is why SEC rules against insider trading would eventually evolve.

ISSUE QUESTIONS

1. During the 1980s, when insider trading cases involved prestigious Wall Street firms, the stock market continued to expand at above-average rates. Does this indicate that insider trading does not scare away investors and hurt the market?

2. If a few officers of a corporation know of an impending announcement that will cause the price of the stock in their company to rise and they engage in stock purchases before the news is made public and so make big gains when the stock price rises, who has been hurt? Is this not an efficient way to compensate the executives?

REVIEW AND DISCUSSION QUESTIONS

1. Define the following terms:

securities	proxies
debt	tender offers
equity	securities fraud
Howey test	misstatements
material information	insider trading
registration statement	investment company
exemptions from registration	mutual fund
disclosure requirements	investment adviser

2. What is the difference in the legal protection for purchasers of registered versus unregistered securities?

3. It is generally known that the information required by the SEC to be disclosed by various statutes is "stale" by the time it is available to the SEC. Does this necessarily mean that it has no value to investors?

4. What could an investment adviser do to profit abnormally at the expense of clients? Would such activities occur more often without SEC controls? Who has an incentive to limit such abuses?

CASE QUESTIONS

5. A developer announced that a new apartment building was to be constructed. To have first chance at a unit in the building, you would have to deposit $250 per room. Each room was called a share of stock in the building. If you wanted a six-room apartment, you had to buy six shares of stock and later pay the sale price or rental rate. The stock price was to be refunded at the time you sold your apartment or quit renting and left the building. You could not sell the stock directly to another person. Is this stock a security? [*United Housing Foundation* v. *Forman*, 421 U.S. 837, 95 S.Ct. 2051 (1975)]

6. PTL (Praise the Lord, or People That Love) was a nonprofit ministry run by James Bakker. Bakker and his wife Tammy had a TV show on which they discussed, among other things, the availability of "Lifetime Partnerships" in PTL that cost from $500 to $10,000. About 153,000 people bought the partnerships, contributing $158 million to the construction of Heritage USA, a Christian retreat center for families. According to the level contributed, purchasers were promised a short annual stay at a hotel at Heritage USA. Contributors were told that the number of partnerships sold was limited. However, the partnerships were oversold, and much of the money was spent on other facilities and lavish living. Was the sale of the partnerships securities fraud? [*Teague* v. *Bakker*, 35 F.3d 978 (4th Cir., 1994)]

7. For ten years, a certified public accounting firm audited the books of an investment company to prepare disclosure documents required by the SEC. The head of the firm was stealing investors' funds and rigging the books, and the accountants never found out. One day the head of the firm disappeared, leaving behind a mess and many unhappy investors. The investors sued the accounting firm to recover the money they lost, claiming that the firm was liable for securities fraud. Who won? [*Ernst & Ernst* v. *Hochfelder*, 425 U.S. 185, 96 S.Ct. 1375 (1976)]

8. Novell merged with WordPerfect by issuing Novell stock in exchange for WordPerfect stock. After the merge, Novell's stock fell 7 percent. Grossman sued in a class-action suit alleging false and misleading statements and omissions from

Novell, in the filing with the SEC related to the merger, that caused the stock price to be artificially inflated before the fall. Grossman cited statements from the company that the merger was "perhaps the smoothest of mergers in recent history" and that WordPerfect was "gaining market share . . . from less than 20% in 1992 to more than 40% today [1994]," and that the merger created a "compelling set of opportunities." Did the case have merit? [*Grossman v. Novell, Inc.*, 120 F.3d 1112 (10th Cir., 1997)]

9. Plains Resources' executives reported that the company found an unusually large natural gas field. As a result, the company's stock was bid up from $7.63 to $29 a share in a few months. Insiders were told that initial estimates were too high. They sold more than 30,000 shares of stock. Information about the lower estimates was then released, driving the price down to about $15. Shareholders sued, claiming that the executives traded on insider information and misled investors by not revealing bad information about the gas find more quickly. Was that securities fraud? [*Rubinstein v. Collins*, 20 F.3d 160 (5th Cir., 1994)]

10. A shareholder resolution called for a company to be more environmentally responsible. The corporation printed the resolution in the proxy statements it sent to shareholders before the annual meeting of the corporation. The proxy materials stated that the company opposed the resolution, claiming that it handles environmental matters "in an appropriate and timely manner" and is on the "forefront" of environmental protection. A shareholder sued, claiming that this was misleading information and that material omissions occurred because the company did not reveal that it had been accused of environmental offenses and had pleaded guilty to some felonies. The company claimed that the information was proper because the environmental problems were discussed in the company's annual report and were the subject of public news releases. Did the proxy statement issued by the company contain disclosure violations? [*United Paperworkers International Union* v. *International Paper Co.*, 985 F.2d 1190 (2d Cir., 1993)]

11. FIG was a registered broker-dealer and a member of the NASD. In hundreds of transactions, FIG sold securities to its customers at markups from 11.11 percent to 186.46 percent above its cost for such securities. The securities were not risky; the only issue was the markup on sale to investors. The NASD claimed that this was securities fraud and levied heavy fines on the company and placed restrictions on its trading activities. The SEC upheld that disciplinary action. FIG appealed, claiming that the SEC rule that markups over 5 percent are generally not allowed is arbitrary and capricious. Who wins? [*First Independence Group* v. *SEC*, 37 F.3d 30 (2d Cir., 1994)]

12. Several investors sued Merrill Lynch for securities fraud by charging excessive markups (that is, inflated prices and fees) and by failing to disclose either the prevailing market price of the bonds or the amount of the markups, which ran 4 percent to 10 percent on municipal bonds. The district court dismissed the case, holding that Rule 10b-5 was not violated because Merrill Lynch had no duty to disclose the markups. Did that decision hold on appeal? [*Grandon v. Merrill Lynch & Co., Inc.*, 147 F.3d 184 (2d Cir., 1998)]

POLICY QUESTIONS

13. The Securities Act of 1933 requires that a prospectus be given to all investors in securities before they purchase any security. Evidence is that investors pay little

or no attention to these documents. Does the existence of this requirement give investors a false sense of confidence that the investment must be okay because the SEC has reviewed a prospectus? If so, is the prospectus a waste of resources, and does it also perhaps have a negative effect?

14. Disputes between investors and their stockbrokers are usually settled by arbitration that is sponsored by the National Association of Securities Dealers or the New York Stock Exchange rather than by litigation in federal court. Arbitration panels grant millions of dollars in punitive damages each year. Members of the securities industry argue that this is improper—only actual damages should be awarded. Is the award of punitive damages by arbitration panels improper, and will it lead to an excessive number of claims being filed?

ETHICS QUESTIONS

15. You started the Triangular Frisbee Company as a small operation. When the product went over big, you decided to seek outside funding to build a larger company. Your lawyer explained to you the costs of SEC registration and securities disclosure in the case of a public stock offering. Your lawyer explains to you that you can avoid this by organizing as a corporation on the Caribbean island nation of Torlaga and selling stock in the corporation from there. U.S. investors simply buy your stock through a Torlaga stockbroker. This is much cheaper and quicker than U.S. registration. What are the pros and cons of this arrangement? Is it ethical to avoid compliance with American laws in this manner?

16. You overhear two executives, whom you recognize, discussing an important announcement that will be made public at 11 A.M. next Monday. The executives say that the announcement will make company stock "really shoot up." Obviously this is inside information that was not intended for your ears. Should you run to a stockbroker to buy all the stock in the company that you can? What if you knew the executives personally and they told you, "If I were you, I would buy all the stock in our company that you can before 11 A.M. on Monday"? What difference does it make whether they give the reason you should buy the stock (i.e., the inside information)? Presume you know that regardless of the legality of such transactions, there is no way you could get caught doing this?

17. Some investment newsletters have become very popular and made their publishers rich. There is no evidence that the newsletters have consistently outperformed the market. That is, the advice the newsletters sell could be had at a price near zero from investment firms such as Merrill Lynch. Is it ethical to write newsletters claiming to have unusual insights into the market? Is it ethical to write a book proclaiming a forthcoming economic catastrophe or some other nutty prediction? Some such authors have made a small fortune but have no liability for being completely wrong. Some people have lost large sums of money following the goofy advice of someone who claims to have special insights. Should the law hold such authors liable for their misinformation?

INTERNET ASSIGNMENT

After graduating from a prestigious law school, Shain went to work in the New York offices of Blackmon & Shannon, a nationally known litigation firm. Shain's first assignment was to conduct legal research regarding whether a prospective client, Rough Diamond, Inc., could recover treble damages under the antitrust laws from a rival company, Pickel & Brewery, Inc., a publicly owned company listed on the New York Stock Exchange. Shain's research was thorough and led to Blackmon & Shannon being retained to represent Rough Diamond in its antitrust case.

In the last weeks before Rough Diamond's antitrust suit was filed, while near-final drafts of the complaint were being reviewed by his supervisor and the client, Shain began trading in the soon-to-be defendant's stock. From his office at Blackmon & Shannon, Shain telephoned a stockbroker in New York, mailed her a personal check to open an account, and promptly started short selling Pickel & Brewery's stock by telephone. The same day Rough Diamond's antitrust suit was filed, Pickel & Brewery's stock price fell by 50 percent, where it remained. Shain's investment strategy yielded extraordinary gains.

Two weeks after the suit was filed, however, federal agents arrested Shain for mail fraud in violation of 18 U.S.C. §1341 (http://www.law.cornell. edu:80/uscode/18/1341.html), wire fraud in violation of 18 U.S.C. §1343 (http://www. law.cornell.edu:80/uscode/18/1343.html), and securities fraud in violation of §10(b) of the Securities Exchange Act of 1934, 15 U.S.C. §78j (http://www. law.cornell.edu:80/uscode/15/ch2B.html), and Rule 10b-5, 17 C.F.R. §240.10b-5 (http://www.law.uc.edu/CCCL/).

Shain's mail and wire fraud counts were based on his mail and wire communications with his broker. Shain's securities fraud counts were based on his misappropriation of Rough Diamond and Blackmon & Shannon's confidential information and its subsequent use in securities transactions. Shain was tried, convicted, fined and sentenced to prison by the United States District Court for the Southern District of New York. Will his convictions be upheld on appeal? See *United States* v. *Bryan*, United States Court of Appeals for the Fourth Circuit, No. 94-5124 (http://www.law.emory.edu/4circuit/). Would the result be different if Shain worked in Blackmon & Shannon's Alexandria, Virginia, offices? *Id.*

CHAPTER 21

The International Legal Environment of Business

Seawinds Limited was a Hong Kong corporation with its principal place of business in California. The successful shipping company owned three large container ships that operated primarily between the Far East and the United States. Seeking to expand, the company entered into shipping contracts with companies from Hong Kong, Singapore, Great Britain, the Netherlands, and the United States. Seawinds expected to develop into a major player in international shipping. Its expectations were never realized, and it sued the shippers for delivering only a small amount of goods for shipment, an alleged breach of contract. The contract specified that all disputes were to be brought before the Hong Kong courts and subject to the law of Hong Kong. However, the law of Hong Kong—compared to U.S. law—would not likely be favorable to Seawinds.

Was Seawinds obligated to bring the lawsuit in Hong Kong? Did all aspects of the dispute require the application of Hong Kong law? Was it possible to try those aspects of the dispute that were arguably outside the contract in U.S. courts under U.S. law?

These are some of the international legal issues that are the focus of this chapter on the international legal environment of business. The chapter begins with a discussion of the nature of the international business environment. It then considers the various ways that the U.S. government works to restrict imports and stimulate exports.

Next, it considers the business organizations that may be considered before becoming involved in an international venture. It then reviews the constraints imposed by the Foreign Corrupt Practices Act. Finally, the chapter discusses the nature of international contracting, insurance against loss, and procedures for the resolution of international disputes.

The Nature of International Business

With the technological improvements in transportation and communications, the nature of business has changed substantially. The percentage of U.S. gross domestic products involved in international trade has tripled in recent decades. Most businesses are affected by events originating in other countries. Crop failures in Argentina, political unrest within the Middle Eastern oil-producing countries, currency devaluations in Mexico, and shipping strikes in England can all have a significant impact on U.S. businesses.

THE INTERNATIONAL BUSINESS ENVIRONMENT

International business includes all business transactions that involve two or more countries. In addition to being involved with the movement of goods across national boundaries, international business involves the movement of services, capital, and personnel by multinational enterprises.

The *international business environment* involves more than just business transactions across national boundaries. It includes business activities that are affected by international business conditions and world events. For example, U.S. businesses that operate only in the domestic market often find themselves in direct competition with foreign manufacturers. Initially, the main source of foreign competition was from imported products. However, in the 1980s, foreign competitors began to build factories in this country to compete more directly with domestic businesses. The Japanese and Germans now compete directly with U.S. businesses in several domestic product markets, particularly automobiles.

Many U.S. industries had no intent to enter international business. But, as markets become global markets, those businesses are forced into international business. They must now be familiar with the international legal environment to maintain competitiveness.

RISKS IN INTERNATIONAL BUSINESS TRANSACTIONS

A principal distinction between domestic and international businesses is the special risks confronting the international business enterprise. Those risks include *financial, political,* and *regulatory risks.* They arise from a variety of sources, including differences between countries in currencies, language, business customs, legal systems, social philosophies, and national goals.

International risks require managerial supervision not common in domestic operations. Financial risks involve consideration of currency exchange rates and of differences in inflation and interest rates among countries. Political risks include the possibility of harsh treatment directed at foreign businesses by the government of the host nation. Political risk must be estimated years in advance if a business is considering investing significant sums in another country. The regulatory or legal risks arise from different legal systems and regulatory policies. Taken together, these risks significantly increase the difficulties of operating in international markets.

International Law

The international legal environment provides no system of laws or regulations for guiding business transactions between two countries. The legal environment consists of many laws and policies from all countries engaged in international commercial activity. As the *International Perspectives* throughout the text have illustrated, countries often differ dramatically in their legal philosophies, practices, and procedures. As a consequence, international businesses face a variety of legal uncertainties and conflicts.

HISTORY OF INTERNATIONAL LAW

Before the development of modern international laws and procedures, nations and merchants involved in international commerce established rules upon which trade was to be based. Early trade customs centered around the law of the sea. They provided, among other things, for rights of shipping in foreign ports, salvage rights, fishing rights, and freedom of passage.

International commercial codes date back as far as 1400 B.C. to Egyptian merchants involved in international trade. Merchants from other countries developed similar codes to provide some legal certainty in international transactions. In 700 B.C., for example, a code of international law had been developed on the Island of Rhodes in the Aegean Sea. The Greek and Roman civilizations both had well-developed codes of practice for international trade and diplomacy.

During the Middle Ages, principles embodied in the *lex mercatoria* (law merchant) arose from trading customs to govern commercial transactions throughout Europe. The law merchant conduct created a workable legal structure for the protection and encouragement of international transactions. The international commerce codes in use today are partly derived from codes reaching back many centuries.

SOURCES OF INTERNATIONAL LAW

The principal sources of international commercial law are the laws of the individual countries, the laws defined by trade agreements between countries, and the rules enacted by a worldwide or regional organization—such as the United Nations or the European Union (EU). There is, however, no international system of courts universally accepted for the purpose of resolving international conflicts between businesses or countries. International law can be pursued through (1) the International Court of Justice, (2) international arbitration, or (3) the courts of an individual country. However, the decisions of those tribunals can be enforced only if the parties or countries involved agree to be bound by them. An overview of some international and U.S. organizations affecting the international legal environment is provided in Exhibit 21.1.

INTERNATIONAL TRADE AGREEMENTS

Most countries seek to improve their economic relations through trade agreements that cover a variety of commercial problems. The intent is to improve the investment and trade climates among countries. For example, most industrialized countries have tax agreements to prevent double taxation of individuals and businesses. Two particularly important trade agreements for U.S. industry are the *North American Free Trade Agreement (NAFTA)* and the General Agreement on Tariffs and Trade, which created the World Trade Organization.

EXHIBIT 21.1

Selected Organizations Affecting the International Legal Environment

World Organizations

• United Nations (www.un.org)	Created as a peacekeeping body, the U.N. works to encourage international cooperation in a variety of areas. It has several departments that encourage world trade.
• World Bank (www.worldbank.org)	Promotes private foreign investment through loans and guarantees, and also provides technical and managerial assistance on large capital projects.
• International Monetary Fund (IMF) (www.imf.org)	Responsible for promoting international trade by working to promote the stability of currency exchange rates.
• World Trade Organization (WTO) (www.wto.org)	Reduces obstacles in international trade by establishing uniform tariff schedules that are accepted among its members. Replaced the General Agreement on Tariffs and Trades (GATT) in 1995.
• Commission on International Trade Law (www.un.or.at/uncitral)	Promotes uniformity in laws; discourages legal obstacles to trade.
• World Intellectual Property Organization (www.wipo.org)	Promotes protection of intellectual property worldwide.
• International Court of Justice (www.icj-cij.org)	Principal organ of the United Nations. It is located in the Netherlands and has jurisdiction over all cases brought to it, but only countries (not private parties) have standing.

United States Organizations

• International Trade Administration (ITA) (www.ita.doc.gov)	Part of the Department of Commerce. Developed to promote trade and to help American companies sell their products overseas. Provides companies with data, foreign license requirements, and other information.
• International Trade Commission (ITC) (www.usitc.gov)	Independent agency responsible for recommending trade restrictions to the President. Examines the impact of a subsidized foreign import on domestic industry.
• Court of International Trade (www.uscourts.gov)	Has jurisdiction to review findings of the ITC or ITA. Has jurisdiction over lawsuits against the United States regarding imports, tariffs, duties, or embargoes.
• Bureau of Export Administration (BEA) (www.bxa.gov)	Part of the Department of Commerce. Responsible for maintaining the Commodity Control List—good subject to export controls.
• United States Export-Import Bank (Eximbank) (www.exim.gov)	Provides loans and loan guarantees to foreign purchasers of goods exported from the United States. Mostly involved in heavy capital equipment projects and aircraft sales.
• Overseas Private Investment Corporation (OPIC) (www.opic.gov)	Provides insurance for U.S. projects that would be rejected by private insurers—largely projects in developing countries. Coverage protects against currency exchange problems, expropriation or confiscation, and war.
• United States Trade Representative (USTR) (www.ustr.gov)	Appointed by the President. Has authority to negotiate trade agreements on the behalf of the United States to reduce trade barriers, including the WTO.

North American Free Trade Agreement

NAFTA was signed by the governments of Canada, the United States, and Mexico in 1992. After being ratified by the legislatures in each of those countries, it went into effect in 1994. NAFTA reduces or eliminates tariffs and trade barriers on most North American trade. Although some tariffs were eliminated immediately, most tariffs are being phased out gradually through 2009. The industries most affected by NAFTA are agriculture, automobiles, pharmaceuticals, and textiles. In the end, the agreement creates the largest free trade area in the world, consisting of 360 million consumers.

In addition to having trade provisions, NAFTA provides for greater Mexican protection of U.S. and Canadian intellectual property. It calls for greater protection of the environment and ensures that the managers of U.S. companies do not use access to Mexico as a way to avoid U.S. environmental laws. NAFTA also provides for the creation of special panels to resolve disputes involving unfair trade practices, investment restrictions, and environmental issues. The activity spurred by NAFTA has generated interest to expand the reach of NAFTA to include other Latin American countries.

World Trade Organization

For forty-eight years, the *General Agreement of Tariffs and Trade (GATT)* worked to reduce trade barriers. GATT focused on key trade restrictions (largely import quotas and tariffs) and implemented its goals through the publication of tariff schedules to which countries agreed. Tariff schedules were developed periodically in multinational trade negotiations or *rounds*. In the most recent round (called the Uruguay Round), 124 nations participated.

GATT was replaced by the *World Trade Organization (WTO)*, one of the significant developments of the last round. Since 1995, the WTO has overseen the trade agreement and has worked to set up a dispute resolution system using three-person arbitration panels. The panels follow strict schedules for rendering decisions. Importantly, WTO member nations agreed they should not veto WTO decisions, as was the case under GATT.

The WTO trade agreement eventually will lower world tariffs by 40 percent. The United States, Japan, Canada, countries of the European Union, and other industrialized nations agreed to eliminate tariffs completely among themselves in ten industries:

Beer	Medical equipment
Construction equipment	Paper
Distilled spirits	Pharmaceuticals
Farm machinery	Steel
Furniture	Toys

The WTO also provides worldwide protection for intellectual property, providing seven years of protection for trademarks, twenty years for patents, and up to fifty years for copyrights. The parties also agreed to reduce or eliminate governmental subsidies on high-tech research and within the civil aviation and agriculture industries. Only in the film and television programming area was the United States not able to gain significant reductions in trade barriers by the Europeans. France was particularly adamant about maintaining the barrier because of its concerns about the domination of American films, music, and videos in Europe.

U.S. Import Restrictions and Promotions

Countries have long imposed restrictions on the importation and exportation of certain products and services. In addition, export laws and regulations are often enacted to encourage international business activity by domestic industries.

TAXES ON IMPORTS

Restrictions on imports generally are imposed to generate revenue for the government or to protect the country's domestic industries from foreign competition. Import licensing procedures, quotas, testing requirements, safety and manufacturing standards, government procurement policies, and complicated customs procedures are all means of regulating imports. The most common way to control imports into a country is through import tariffs.

Tariff Classes

A *tariff* is a duty or tax levied by a government on an imported good. Tariffs can be generally classified into two principal categories: *specific tariffs*, which impose a fixed tax or duty on each unit of a product, and *ad valorem tariffs*, which impose a tax as a percentage of the price of the product. Tariffs are either a revenue-generating device for the government or a way to protect domestic industries from foreign products. Businesses often argue that without a tariff, foreign products will force them out of the market. Workers will lose their jobs and the country will grow dependent on foreign businesses for supplies of products. Those arguing against tariffs assert that only through free trade will countries exploit their comparative advantage and increase their wealth.

In the United States, the duty imposed is published in the *tariff schedules*, which are applied by customs officials to all products entering U.S. ports. Customs officials classify products and determine the tariff rates when products enter the country. Any tariff imposed must be paid before the good may enter the country.

Most disputes arise over the classification of products under the tariff schedules. As the *Standard Brands* decision illustrates, the rate of duty can be significantly affected by a custom agent's decision on product classification.

Standard Brands Paint Co., Inc. v. United States
United States Court of Customs and Patent Appeals
511 F.2d 564 (1975)

CASE BACKGROUND *Standard Brands imported wooden picture frame moldings in different styles and lengths, each packaged separately. Standard Brands' customers would buy these parts and assemble a frame to the desired dimensions. The customs invoice on the imported merchandise read "Wooden Picture Frames" and was classified by customs agents under the Tariff Schedules as wood moldings. Customs assessed a duty of 17 percent ad valorem.*

Standard Brands claimed that the items should have been classified as "picture and mirror frames made of wood," which would have a duty of 12 percent. Standard Brands argued that the imported moldings were unassembled frames. Under the Doctrine of Entireties, these frames should be dutiable as entireties—that is, as "assembled" picture frames made of wood even though they were not assembled.

The U.S. Customs Court ruled against Standard Brands, holding that the merchandise had been classified properly. Standard Brands appealed to the U.S. Court of

Customs and Patent Appeals (now called the Court of Appeals for the Federal Circuit).

CASE DECISION   Baldwin, Justice.

* * *

Almost 50 years ago the Court of Customs Appeals stated as follows in *Altman & Co.* v. *United States:*

[I]f an importer brings into the country, at the same time, certain parts, which are designed to form, when joined or attached together, a complete article of commerce, and when it is further shown that the importer intends to so use them, these parts will be considered for tariff purposes as *entireties*, even though they may be unattached or inclosed in separate packages, and even though said parts might have a commercial value and be salable separately.

We do not agree with the Customs Court that the principle expressed in *Altman* is not applicable to the facts at bar because of an alleged failure to show an intent to either "use" or "treat" the imported merchandise as completed articles of commerce. Furthermore, *Altman* makes it clear that separate packaging of parts does not preclude the application of the doctrine of entireties.

The importer has merely given the consumer, when purchasing an unassembled picture frame, the opportunity to choose the size of picture frame he desires to assemble. This fact leads us to the basic problem—lack of a predictable relationship between the parts—which the Customs Court held to preclude the application of the doctrine of entireties to the imported merchandise.

We note that the "predictable relationship" referred to is only applicable to the size and not the shape of the frame to be assembled. The 45° mitered ends of the lengths of molding in each package make it readily apparent that only rectangular picture frames may be assembled. Thus, we are left with the question whether an unassembled 8″ × 10″ picture frame is a different article for classification purposes from an unassembled 10″ × 20″ picture frame. We think not. The imported merchandise is still basically picture frames.

* * *

Reversed.

QUESTIONS FOR ANALYSIS

1. What is the concept of "entireties" and why is it important to this case?
2. Why did the court believe that the unassembled frames were entireties?

Harmonized Tariff Schedules

The United States uses a *harmonized tariff schedule*, developed by a group of countries for the purpose of standardizing the ways in which goods are classified by customs officials worldwide. Under the system, each country uses the same six-digit codes to classify goods traded. The process greatly streamlines trade by eliminating language and usage differences between countries.

Bans on Certain Products

The entry of certain products may violate regulations. For example, certain explosives and weapons that raise national security concerns cannot legally be imported into this country. Illegal products, such as narcotics, violate domestic laws and cannot legally be imported. Products made from endangered species are prohibited from importation by environmental laws. Other items may not meet safety regulations or pollution requirements and cannot be imported.

Foreign automobiles that do not comply with U.S. safety and pollution regulations will not be cleared for importation. For example, Bill Gates, the president of Microsoft, tried to import a new Porsche 959 from Germany. Gates's 959 was the first Porsche of that model sold in the United States. Upon arrival at the U.S. port, the car was not allowed by customs officials to enter the country. According to Customs, that model Porsche had not been crash tested. Since its safety could not be verified, the car could not be imported.

IMPORT PRICE CONTROLS

Congress has given the Department of Commerce, through the *International Trade Administration (ITA)* and the *International Trade Commission (ITC)*, the ability to restrict imports. Specifically, these agencies are concerned with foreign companies that sell their products at prices lower in the U.S. market than in their home market (called dumping) or receive a subsidy from their government to lower costs of production. These agencies may restrict imports in the absence of dumping or subsidies. As international competition increases, some domestic industries and their workers face hardships. The ITC may temporarily restrict imports to give those industries an opportunity to adjust to the more competitive environment created by the lower trade barriers.

Antidumping Orders

Under both the WTO and U.S. antidumping laws, *dumping* "is the business practice of charging a lower price in the export market than in the home market, after taking into consideration important differences in the sale (such as credit terms and transportation) and the goods being sold." It was first prohibited in 1916, when Congress enacted the *Antidumping Duty Act*, which has been amended several times.

U.S. law provides that if it is determined that goods from a country are being dumped and domestic industries are injured, an antidumping order will be issued. Under such an order, the incoming goods will be subject to an antidumping duty (tax). The amount of the duty will be determined by comparing the market price in the home market with the price charged in the United States. The difference between the two prices determines the tariff to be applied to the price of the product when sold in the United States. This duty is paid to the Customs Service in a cash deposit at the port by the importer.

Duty orders generally remain in place until the importer can show three consecutive years of "fair market value" sales and Commerce is convinced that there is little likelihood of "less than fair market value" sales in the United States in the future. The *Empresa* decision considers the application of antidumping statutes to a Spanish company selling steel.

Empresa Nacional Siderurgica, S.A. v. United States
United States Court of International Trade
880 F. Supp. 876 (1995)

CASE BACKGROUND *On the basis of a complaint filed by eight domestic steelmakers, the Department of Commerce sought to determine whether Empresa Nacional Siderurgica (ENSIDESA) of Spain was dumping "certain cut-to-length carbon steel plate" in the United States. Commerce sent (ENSIDESA) an Antidumping Questionnaire requesting information on production costs and local market sales information.*

ENSIDESA requested several extensions until Commerce gave it a final response date. ENSIDESA informed Commerce that it would not respond, and Commerce, as required, designated it as "uncooperative." The designation allowed Commerce to use the best information available to make its dumping estimate. It determined that ENSIDESA was selling steel plate in the United States at half the price it sold for in Spain. After the ITC informed Commerce that domestic suppliers were being injured by imports from Spain, Commerce issued an Antidumping Order:

The Customs Service shall assess antidumping duties . . . on all entries of certain cut-to-length carbon steel plate from Spain. . . . of 105.61 percent ad valorem.

ENSIDESA appealed the determination of the Commerce Department that "imports of certain cut-to-length carbon steel plate from Spain were being sold in the U.S. at less than fair value."

CASE DECISION DiCarlo, Chief Judge.

* * *

ENSIDESA argues Commerce erred in denying ENSIDESA's request for [another] extension. . . . According to ENSIDESA, it had justifiable and compelling reasons for requesting the extension. . . . the steel industry in Spain was undergoing major restructuring and the resulting attrition of personnel impaired ENSIDESA's ability to respond to the [antidumping] Questionnaire.

* * *

Congress has imposed strict statutory deadlines upon Commerce in antidumping investigations. The statute mandates that Commerce issue its final determination within 75 days of the preliminary investigation. . . .

This investigation was but one of a large number of concurrent steel investigations that involved Commerce in "an unusually intensive and demanding period of work." To complete the large number of investigations within statutory time limits and allow Commerce time to verify submitted information, Commerce required parties to strictly observe the deadlines for submitting information. . . . Commerce was not obligated, by statute, regulation, or prior precedent, to further accommodate ENSIDESA.

* * *

ENSIDESA's failure to submit a response [to the questionnaire] deprived Commerce of necessary cost data, rendering Commerce unable to determine which home market sales, if any, could be used to determine fair market value. As Commerce was unable to calculate fair market value, it had no data to compare to the U.S. sales information. . . . Under the circumstances, Commerce could properly resort to . . . best information available.

In its Final Determination, Commerce designated ENSIDESA an "uncooperative respondent," due to ENSIDESA's failure to provide the cost of production information requested in [the antidumping] Questionnaire. . . .

ENSIDESA is a large and sophisticated company with a demonstrated ability to participate in an antidumping investigation. . . .

[ENSIDESA's] failure to provide cost of production information was not due to an "inability" to supply the information. Commerce's designation of ENSIDESA as uncooperative is supported by substantial evidence and otherwise in accordance with law.

The court finds Commerce's determination proper. The court denies ENSIDESA's request for judgment upon an agency record . . . and affirms Commerce's determination.

QUESTIONS FOR ANALYSIS

1. Antidumping cases have steadily risen over the years; what might contribute to that increase?
2. If the United States imposes such restrictions on sales in the United States, how are other countries likely to respond?

Countervailing Duties

In contrast to the focus of the antidumping laws on the prices private companies charge for their products in the United States, *countervailing duty laws* focus on the practices of foreign governments. Countervailing duties are designed to offset the subsidies provided by foreign governments to their industries that export to the United States. If the Commerce Department determines that a government is "providing, directly or indirectly, a subsidy with respect to the manufacture, production, or exportation of a class or kind of merchandise imported, or sold for importation into the U.S.," and the ITC determines that this injures a U.S. industry, countervailing duties (tariffs) are imposed in an amount equal to the net subsidy.

The kinds of subsidies that a government might provide include reductions in utility prices, low-interest loans, grants to cover operating losses or to subsidize research and development, and tax credits. The WTO does allow some governmental subsidies in selected areas. For example, within limits, governments may subsidize investments in pollution control equipment.

Certain Subsidies Allowed The action taken by Commerce depends on the department's relationship with the foreign government. If the government has a trade agreement with the United States, no countervailing duty is imposed unless the subsidy causes material injury to a domestic industry. If the government has no trade agreement with the United States, a countervailing duty will be imposed when that government gives a subsidy to a manufacturer or exporter.

Commerce requires that the government subsidy be reasonably specific to an industry. For example, the fact that the government of Mexico provided natural gas to all industrial users at below-market rates was found not to be specific enough to one industry to warrant a countervailing duty. In another case, a U.S. manufacturer filed a complaint about a subsidized loan program that a foreign government provided to a foreign competitor. Since Commerce found that the foreign competitor was the only company in the country getting the subsidy, it imposed a countervailing duty of 12.5 percent to offset the benefit of the loan subsidy.

Foreign Trade Zones and Duty-Free Ports

Foreign trade zones are areas where businesses can import goods without paying tariffs. Such zones encourage international business in that area. The zone itself is a secured area where goods may be processed, assembled, or warehoused. Tariffs are imposed only on the finished product (generally much less than those imposed on individual parts) and only when the product leaves the zone for sale in the domestic market. Products exported from the zone are generally not subject to import fees or tariffs.

Duty-free ports are ports of entry that do not assess duties or tariffs on products. Duty-free ports encourage the importation and sale of international goods within the country. Hong Kong is well known for such practices. Benefits to a country providing a duty-free port are the general encouragement of trade with other countries and the attraction of businesses and tourists to the country to purchase products free of duties and other fees.

EXPORT REGULATION AND PROMOTION

Most governments encourage the export of domestic products. They hope to stimulate employment and bring in foreign exchange from export sales. When the value of imports exceeds the value of exports, the country is said to be running a *trade deficit*. A chronic trade deficit can lead to long-term effects on the country's currency and standard of living. However, for reasons of national defense and foreign policy, governments may restrict exports of certain products.

The U.S. federal and state governments have a variety of activities to encourage U.S. companies to export. These efforts have been undertaken to reduce the trade deficit that the United States has been experiencing for over a decade. The U.S. merchandise trade deficit has averaged about $100 billion a year (that is, American consumers buy $100 billion more in foreign imported goods than American businesses sell to foreign consumers). Japan accounts for about half of that total, largely because of the importation of automobiles.

Federal Government Efforts

The Commerce Department is the major export-promotion agency. Primary responsibility for export promotion within Commerce falls upon the ITA. The ITA manages the U.S. Foreign Commercial Service, which employs commercial officers at major cities around the world and export counselors in district offices around the United States. At its overseas offices, referred to as Commercial Consulates, it works to encourage U.S. commercial activity by supplying U.S. product information, arranging business meetings with local firms, accompanying U.S. company representatives to meetings, and gathering local market information. The

JURIS **prudence?**

A Bargain—Only $29.35 for a Razor Blade!

 Some finance professors from Florida International University have questioned whether the trade deficit numbers are not inflated as a result of global money laundering via fake import/export invoices.

Professors Zdanowicz and Pak found ordinary telephones from Hong Kong "priced" at $2,400 each, salad dressing at $720 per bottle, smoke detectors at $653 each, and razor blades from Panama at $29.35 apiece. Similarly, they found underpriced export invoices: radial tires shipped to Colombia at $3.03 each, pianos to France at $38 each, and snowplows to Jamaica (!) at $267.70.

The professors' explanation is that the funds are transferred as the invoices assert, but the transferring is done for the purpose of money laundering to avoid paying income taxes. By making inflated payments to itself in another country, a business avoids U.S. taxes, and the transfer of funds is counted as a business expense. The professors estimate that the cost to the Treasury is about $40 billion a year in lost revenue. The Treasury "expressed interest" in the issue.

Source: *Forbes*

Commercial Consulates, for example, might assist a U.S. company in finding a foreign agent to distribute its products in a particular market. They also lead trade missions overseas each year and participate in hundreds of trade expositions.

The *Export Trading Company Act* allows U.S. companies to form trading companies similar to those in Japan. A large Japanese trading company will handle as many as 20,000 different products. This allows the trading companies to provide customers with better prices and quality control. Although the Export Trading Company Act provides an antitrust exemption, the exemption is too weak to encourage the development of large trading companies in the United States. Primarily small, single-product trading companies have been established under the act.

State Government Efforts

Many state governments have made efforts to encourage their industries to export. California, Florida, Illinois, Indiana, New York, and Washington have particularly well developed export-promotion programs. The purpose of the California Office of Export Development is to "strengthen the state's activities in marketing its agricultural, manufacturing, and service industries overseas. The office shall be responsible for conducting market research; disseminating trade leads; and sponsoring trade delegations, missions, marts, seminars, and other appropriate promotional events."

Several states have foreign development offices responsible for "assembling, publishing, and disseminating information about [the state's] products and services to potential foreign buyers in English and other appropriate languages." In addition, a few states offer export loan assistance and guarantees to small businesses interested in entering the export market.

Export Restrictions

Despite the desire to increase exports, the U.S. government imposes some restrictions on exports. The sale of a certain good may (1) injure domestic industry (for example, exporting a raw material in short supply), (2) jeopardize national security (for example, selling military hardware to the wrong country), or (3) conflict with national policy (for example, selling strategic goods to a country that the government has banned trade with because of terrorist activities). These restrictions are implemented through licensing requirements in the *Export Administration Act*.

Congress delegated the power to enforce export licenses to the Secretary of Commerce. Although Commerce has authority to impose licensing requirements, it can do so only according to strict standards. The standards reflect the tension between a desire to control exports of strategic goods for security reasons and the desire to encourage exports to reduce the trade deficit.

Licensing Agreements The Export Administration Act provides Commerce with the ability to require the following types of export licenses, depending on the good being exported:

1. A *validated license*, authorizing a specific export, issued upon application by the exporter
2. A *qualified general license*, authorizing multiple exports, issued upon application by the exporter
3. A *general license*, authorizing exports, without application by the exporter, and that applies to most U.S. goods intended for export
4. Other licenses as may assist in the implementation of the act

Commerce maintains a list—the *Commodity Control List*—of the goods subject to such licenses. The restrictions imposed depend upon the country to which goods are to be sent and the reason for the export restriction. Goods not on the list are subject to a general license, which requires little more than filing a Shipper's Export Declaration with Commerce.

A validated license is required for the export of goods on the list for national security reasons. Restrictions are imposed on a good "only to the extent necessary . . . to restrict the export of goods and technology which would make a significant contribution to the military potential of any other country or combination of countries which would prove detrimental to the national security of the United States." Such controls are imposed on military goods, computers, computer accessories, and certain materials considered to be strategic in the military sense.

Application to Reexported U.S. Goods Commerce's export licensing requirements also apply to the *reexport* of U.S. goods. That is, an export license is needed to ship U.S.-origin controlled goods from, say, India to Iran. The intent is to prohibit the shipment of sensitive goods from the United States first to a "safe" country and then to a controlled country. In this way, the Export Administration Act reaches beyond U.S. boundaries.

Penalty Provisions The penalties for violations of Commerce's licensing provisions include criminal and civil penalties and administrative sanctions. A person who "knowingly" violates the Act can be fined up to $50,000 or five times the value of the exports involved, whichever is greater, and receive up to five years in prison. A person who "willfully" violates the Act can be fined more and receive up to ten years in prison. A "willful" violation by a business can result in fines of up to one million dollars. Administrative sanctions can result in the suspension or revocation of an individual's or a business's authority to export. The extent of Commerce's authority in that regard is discussed in the *Moller-Butcher* decision.

Moller-Butcher v. U.S. Department of Commerce
United States Court of Appeals, District of Columbia Circuit
12 F.3d 249 (1994)

CASE BACKGROUND *Moller-Butcher founded M.E.S. Equipment, a U.S. corporation. From 1979 to 1981, M.E.S. exported semiconductor manufacturing equipment from the United States to Great Britain and Sweden. With Moller-Butcher's knowledge, the equipment was reexported to Bulgaria, Poland, and Romania. The items traded were controlled goods, classified as such by Commerce for national security reasons. Before exporting these items, Moller-Butcher was required to obtain a validated export license, but he did not do so. Commerce initiated a civil proceeding against him. Because Moller-Butcher did not respond to the charges, an administrative law judge (ALJ) at Commerce entered a default judgment that denied Moller-Butcher export privileges for twenty years.*

In 1990, Moller-Butcher filed a motion asking that his export privileges be reinstated. At a hearing before the ALJ, Moller-Butcher argued that the sanctions had ruined his business and that the government's interest in deterring export violations had been served. Commerce argued that the original sanctions were proper because Moller-Butcher had committed multiple violations and had falsified information. The ALJ sided with Moller-Butcher and reinstated his export privileges.

The Undersecretary of Commerce reviewed the ALJ's decision. She stated that only the Secretary had the authority to grant a sanction modification and declared the ALJ's decision merely "an advisory recommendation." The Undersecretary denied Moller-Butcher's motion for reinstatement, finding twenty years to be appropriate. Moller-Butcher appealed to the Court of Appeals.

CASE DECISION Edwards, Circuit Judge.

* * *

Moller-Butcher challenges the Under Secretary's decision on two grounds. First he argues that her order "reversed" the ALJ's decision to reduce his sanction, thereby exceeding the scope of her authority under [the Export Administration Act], which permits the Secretary only to "affirm, modify, or vacate" an ALJ's decision. Second, Moller-Butcher maintains that the Under Secretary's decision was arbitrary and capricious.

This is not a case in which Congress has remained silent on the breadth of our authority to review an agency decision. Rather, the plain language of [the Export Administration Act] confers and defines our jurisdiction, clearly limiting it to questions concerning the liability which occasioned the sanction at issue, not the sanction itself. . . . Because Moller-Butcher does not question his liability for the imposed sanction, we cannot entertain his challenge.

* * *

[The Export Administration Act] permits the Secretary to "vacate" a decision of the ALJ, and that is precisely what she has done—ordering, in effect, that the original sanction entered against Moller-Butcher be restored. . . .

For the reasons stated above, we lack jurisdiction to consider Moller-Butcher's substantive claims and therefore the petition is dismissed, leaving the Under Secretary's order undisturbed.

QUESTIONS FOR ANALYSIS

1. Why might Moller-Butcher have broken the law initially?
2. If American computer equipment had not been sold to the countries in question, the countries probably would have bought equipment from Japan or some other country. Why, then, should restrictions be imposed?

Business Organizations in Foreign Markets

United States businesses have used various ways to enter foreign markets. In general, they have two basic ways of selling products in foreign markets. A business can either export products manufactured in this country to the foreign country or manufacture products in the foreign country for distribution there.

Controlling International Pirates

 One of the most significant challenges facing a manager is deciding how to react to foreign manufacturers who pirate (copy) a company's products and then sell the product as authentic at lower prices than the real thing. Pirates cost U.S. industry more than $100 billion in lost sales every year.

Microsoft knows that pirates make copies of its Windows programs. After one three-month investigation, Microsoft led police to an apartment building in Taipei, Taiwan.

Police uncovered a sophisticated software pirating operation. In addition to finding the diskettes, they found flawless copies of the operation and installation manuals and of the hologram sticker intended to foil pirates. The number of copies on order at this one operation represented a lost revenue of $150 million to Microsoft, which sued the pirating company. In addition, the U.S. International Trade Commission issued a warning against Taiwan that Taiwan try to reduce pirating. If it fails, the United States could impose high tariffs on Taiwanese products entering the United States.

EXPORTING MANUFACTURED PRODUCTS

Companies initially entering international business generally prefer to export products manufactured domestically. Exporting is preferred because it requires relatively little investment on the part of the business and poses relatively lower risk than foreign manufacturing.

Businesses may export indirectly or directly. *Indirect exporting* involves using an exporter who sells the product in foreign markets for a U.S. manufacturer. The manufacturer may also sell to a foreign agent who is in the United States buying particular products for an overseas customer. *Direct exporting* usually involves developing an organization within the business that is responsible for export business. Initially, the company may ship directly to its overseas customers. Later, as business expands, the company may develop a marketing organization in its foreign markets and import products from its U.S. factory in its own name.

FOREIGN MANUFACTURING

Foreign manufacturing is generally motivated by a desire to reduce costs and enhance a business's ability to compete. Costs reduced by foreign manufacturing include shipping costs, labor expenses, and raw material costs. Operating in another country may also help secure long-term contracts to supply goods to producers in that country. In addition, foreign manufacturing may be a way to avoid import restrictions or tariffs imposed by the host country.

The management of several leading Japanese companies decided to move manufacturing facilities to the United States. They feared that Congress might impose high tariffs on Japanese products in an effort to reduce the U.S. trade deficit. Since products made by a Japanese business located in the United States are made in America, they are not subject to duties. Businesses considering foreign manufacturing have several options available to them, including the following:

- A wholly owned foreign subsidiary
- A joint venture

- A licensing agreement
- A franchise agreement
- Contract manufacturing

Wholly Owned Subsidiary

By doing foreign manufacturing through a *wholly owned subsidiary*, a business owns the facilities. A business may buy an existing facility or build a new one. Situations exist, however, in which complete ownership is not possible. Several countries impose limits on the percentage of ownership in a manufacturing facility held by foreigners.

Joint Venture

Through a *joint venture*, virtually any sharing of ownership with foreign partners is possible. For example, one party may supply the facilities, and the other party the technological skills required for the operation. Although a joint venture requires less investment by the company than does a wholly owned subsidiary, it can mean loss of managerial control. Many businesses engaging in commercial activity in China and Russia are doing so through joint ventures.

Licensing Agreement

A *licensing agreement* is a contract whereby one business—the *licensor*—grants another business—the licensee—access to its patents and other technologies. Licenses can be granted to cover the transfer of virtually any kind of expertise. The licensor is usually granted a royalty on sales. Allowing the licensee to use the business's trademark could help establish a worldwide reputation for the business. However, the licensing company needs to make sure that the licensing agreement is enforceable in the licensee's country.

Franchise Agreement

Franchising is a popular vehicle for establishing a foreign market presence. Franchising is a form of licensing. The franchisor (the supplier) grants the franchisee (the foreign dealer) the right to sell products or services in exchange for a fee. The most visible franchises are the fast-food restaurants: McDonald's, Pizza Hut, and Kentucky Fried Chicken have made major inroads as franchises. Other successful franchises include hotels (Holiday Inn), car rentals (Hertz), soft drinks (Coca-Cola), and business services (Muzak). The franchising company must work to make sure that the quality (and thus the reputation) of its products is maintained at overseas franchises.

Contract Manufacturing

Companies may contract for the production of certain products in foreign facilities. U.S. retailers, for example, have found it advantageous to contract for the production of clothing and other textile products in Malaysia, Korea, and China, where labor costs are lower than in the United States. The products are shipped to the United States for sale. Contract manufacturing has the advantage of requiring limited investment in production facilities.

Nike has made contract manufacturing an important part of its operations. Because the company does not own the manufacturing plants that produce its athletic shoes, production costs are variable costs rather than fixed costs. When demand for the products slows, management simply does not renew a manufacturing contract. The company does not have to worry about making payments on a plant that is not producing. The plant owners may contract with another company to stay in business.

Foreign Corrupt Practices Act

In contrast to the U.S. government and its relationship to businesses in the United States, governments in many countries are more directly involved in business activity. Favorable governmental action often is required before business transactions can be completed. As we noted at the beginning of the chapter, corruption is a worldwide problem. When action is at the discretion of a government official, the likelihood of corruption and bribery increases. This is not limited to less-developed nations.

In the United States, the *Foreign Corrupt Practices Act (FCPA)* prohibits U.S. companies and their agents from bribing foreign officials. The law was enacted in 1977 after exposure of cases in which U.S. corporations bribed foreign officials for favors. A study by the Securities and Exchange Commission found that the practice was widespread: More than 400 companies (117 of which were Fortune 500 companies) admitted to making substantial bribes to foreign officials.

CORRUPTION

In many countries, corruption is so common that normal business is nearly impossible. It is a major barrier to economic development, as few firms wish to bear the risks involved in dealing with corrupt officials. There are various services that measure risk of investment around the world. One measure comes from Transparency International (TI) (see www.transparency.de), an organization in Berlin founded by a former World Bank director who was infuriated at the inability of countries to grow because of corruption. Exhibit 21.2 shows some of TI's Corruption Perception Index, which is based on numerous surveys. A score of 10 indicates a corruption-free country; Denmark was the only country with such a ranking.

International Antibribery Movement

Until recently, the United States was the only country with a law that specifically addressed bribes paid to foreign officials. In late 1997, thirty-four nations signed a convention against corruption. All representatives agreed to present legislation to their national legislatures that would make bribery a crime, as it has been in the United States since 1977. In 1998, the U.S. Senate ratified the Convention on Combating Bribery of Foreign Officials in International Business Transactions. Other nations have not been quick to act, and, in some cases, enforcement remains another issue.

ANTIBRIBERY PROVISIONS

The antibribery provisions of the FCPA prohibit U.S. companies from "corruptly" paying or offering to pay a foreign official to gain assistance in obtaining or retaining business. The Act also prohibits payments to a person, such as a foreign agent, when the U.S. manager knows that the payment will go toward bribing a foreign official. The ability of a manager to know that a payment has been made by an agent is one of the more controversial aspects of the law.

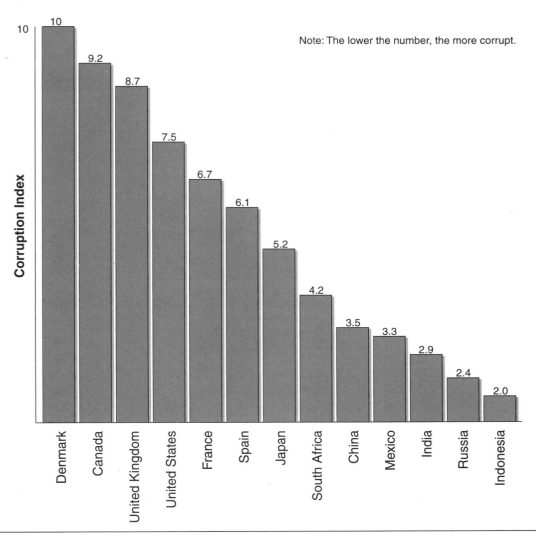

Note: The lower the number, the more corrupt.

Source: *Tramsparency International* and Göttingen University.

EXHIBIT 21.2

Corruption Perception Index

The Act recognizes that some governmental payments are necessary and routine. An exception exists for a "facilitating or expediting payment . . . the purpose of which is to expedite or secure the performance of a routine government action." Such "routine actions" normally include such services as processing visas and providing utilities or transportation services. However, because most such actions require some degree of discretion, it may be necessary to guess whether the action is "routine." Guess wrong, and the consequences could be serious. The basic test in determining whether a bribe is permissible focuses not on the person to whom payment is made but on the purpose for which payment is made. This is complicated by the fact that such payments are often made by local freight forwarders or other service providers without the knowledge of the U.S. manager.

Who Knows What?

The most controversial aspect of the antibribery provisions is the "knowing" requirement. Congress stated that "simple negligence" or "mere foolishness" should not be the basis for liability. The FCPA provides that the knowing requirement covers "any instance where any reasonable person would have realized the existence of the circumstances or result and the [individual] has consciously chosen not to ask about what he had reason to believe he would discover." Managers should be concerned about foreign agents who work on a commission basis. If it is later found that an agent's commission was used to make a payment to a government official, the U.S. government may review the payment to see whether management "knew" of the agent's bribe. The government will be particularly suspicious if the commission is disproportionate to the business service provided. Because the gray area of liability is large, most managers view the standard as too ambiguous. The act can have a chilling effect on investment decisions, particularly for small- and medium-sized companies.

ACCOUNTING REQUIREMENTS

The FCPA requires U.S. companies to "make and keep books, records, and accounts which, in reasonable detail, accurately and fairly reflect the transactions and dispositions of [their] assets." The FCPA also requires companies to "devise and maintain a system of internal accounting controls sufficient to provide reasonable assurances" that all transactions are authorized and that access to assets can be tracked. The accounting provisions were included in the Act in response to a study by the Securities and Exchange Commission that showed that many corporations maintained "slush funds" that were "off the books" to make bribes to foreign officials. The Act requires a "paper trail" that improves corporate accountability and allows detection of illegal payments to foreign government officials.

Penalties

The Department of Justice is responsible for criminal enforcement of the FCPA. A violation leads to fines up to $100,000 and imprisonment for up to five years for individuals. Corporations convicted of violations can incur fines of up to $2,000,000 per violation. An affirmative defense is that the payments made to foreign officials were intended to reimburse the officials for expenditures associated with tours of manufacturing facilities to demonstrate or explain the company's products.

International Contracts

As in domestic business agreements, the basis for any international agreement is the *international contract*. As we saw in Chapter 11, many sales of goods are under the CISG, but many contracts are not. Such contracts can differ significantly from domestic contracts in complexity and use of unusual provisions. International contracts often involve parties from differing cultural backgrounds who do not know each other at the outset of negotiations. The distance between the parties often complicates contract negotiation, substance, and performance. The differing languages, currencies, legal systems, and business customs of parties can affect the nature of the contract and influence the way it is written.

CULTURAL ASPECTS

A knowledge of and sensitivity to cultural differences is important in international contracting. In Japan, for example, *meishi*, or business cards, are exchanged at a first

International Business Is Soooo Stressful

 Gerald Finneran, managing director at the Trust Company of the West, was flying from Buenos Aires to New York when a flight attendant decided that Finneran had had enough to drink. "I was angry," he testified in court. He poured drinks on himself, threatened a flight attendant, shoved another one, dropped his pants, and defecated on the food-service cart.

Finneran's lawyer noted that Finneran is a "marvelously decent human being" who had flown more than 5 million miles without incident. Finneran testified that he "became annoyed" when the wine was stopped. Pleading guilty to a misdemeanor charge, he agreed to pay United Airlines $49,000 in damages, which included the cost of tickets that the airline refunded for nearby passengers.

Source: *Associated Press*

meeting, while in the United States, business cards may be exchanged at any time, usually after a meeting is over. In many countries, including China, hours may go by before the subject matter of the business concern is even mentioned. This is different from the U.S. approach, where the parties are forthright as to the purpose of the meeting.

A cultural impact on international agreements is the difference in language between the parties. Language itself should not be considered a barrier to an international contract. However, it is important that the terms of the contract are clearly defined in a language that all parties understand. Interpreters can be an integral part of the negotiations and the final draft of the contract where parties are not fluent in a common language.

The attitude toward relationships is another cultural difference. Many countries, including Japan, China, and many Latin American and European countries, have the cultural expectation that a relationship between contracting parties will be long-term. As a result, the negotiation process will be long, since it is necessary for the parties to know one another well before entering into a long-term relationship. Contracts based on trust and long-term expectations are often relatively short, with few contingencies expressly provided. The expectation is that problems can be worked out as they arise, with the parties working to maintain the underlying relationship.

FINANCIAL ASPECTS

To manage the financial risks that may arise in international contracts, care must be taken in specifying the method of payment. In addition, the parties may be concerned about removing profits from the countries in which they conduct their business.

Exchange Markets

In an international transaction, the seller often receives another country's currency. A business may want to exchange that currency into dollars. The exchange of money is not always simple. Exchange risk is the potential loss or profit that occurs between the time currency is acquired and the time it is exchanged for another currency. Suppose, for example, that U.S. Wine, Inc., enters a contract to buy French wines. The contract calls for the payment of three million French francs in 180 days. When the contract is signed, the exchange rate is 6.00 French francs to the dollar, or $500,000. Suppose that U.S. Wine waits 180 days before paying and the exchange rate falls to 5.00 francs to the dollar. U.S. Wine now must pay $600,000. Change in the exchange rate costs the company $100,000. To avoid such difficulties, businesses may require payment in dollars rather than in the currency of the other country.

Financial Instruments Used in International Contracts

International contracts often use special international financial devices. These devices either assure later payment or allow for the arrangement of credit when buyers are otherwise unable to come up with the cash necessary for the transaction. Various financial instruments are available to facilitate international transactions. One device commonly used is the letter of credit.

A *letter of credit* is an agreement or assurance by the bank of the buyer to pay a specified amount to the seller upon receipt of certain documents that prove that the goods have been shipped and that contractual obligations of the seller have been fulfilled. The usual documentation required includes a certificate of origin, an export license, a certificate of inspection, a bill of lading, a commercial invoice, and an insurance policy. Once the bank has received the required documentation, it releases payment to the seller. Exhibit 21.3 illustrates the route taken by a letter of credit and the documentation in an international business transaction between an Italian seller and an American buyer, each using its own bank.

Letters of credit can be either revocable or irrevocable. As the label attached to each implies, a *revocable letter of credit* may be withdrawn, while an *irrevocable letter of credit* may not be withdrawn before the specific date stated on it. Exhibit 21.4 is an example of an irrevocable letter of credit.

Repatriation of Monetary Profits

Repatriation of profits can be a concern to a party involved in an international transaction. *Repatriation* is the ability of a business to return money earned in the foreign country to its home country. The ability to repatriate is often regulated by a country's laws. Some countries restrict the amounts of local currencies that can be taken out of the country. The usual reasons for restrictions on repatriation involve concerns about a shortage in foreign currency reserves and a desire that money earned in the country be put back into the local economy.

SELECTED CLAUSES IN INTERNATIONAL CONTRACTS

The contract is the foundation of any international business venture. As with domestic contracts, care should be taken that the intent of the parties is fully represented by the contract. International contracts should be in writing, even if they only state the positions and goals of the parties. In some cases, standardized contracts may be used by the parties. When such standardized contracts are not available, the following clauses are often included.

Payment Clauses

The *payment clause* concerns the method and manner in which payment is to be received as well as the currency in which payment is to be made. Since some nations do not allow their currencies to leave the country, payments have special restrictive effects on the receiver of the currency. Those effects should be taken

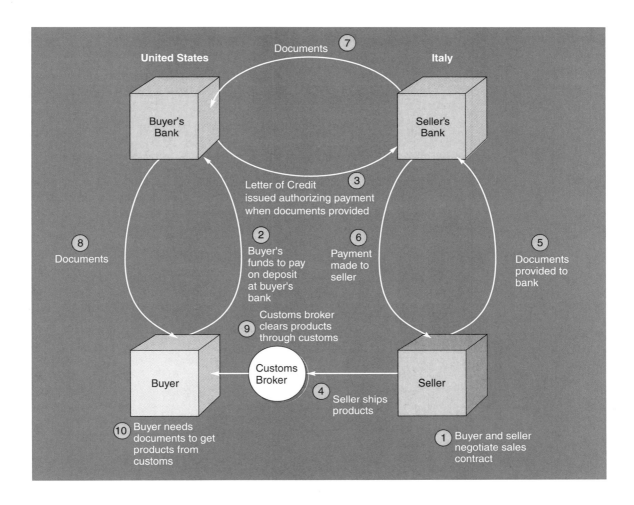

EXHIBIT 21.3

Letter of Credit in an International Transaction

into account when the contract is written. Problems with inflation and currency exchange risks, especially in unstable economies or in long-term agreements, should also be addressed in this contract clause. Unless specified in the contract, these are presumed to be an ordinary business risk.

Choice of Language Clause

Even when parties speak the same language, complex contractual terms may exceed the understanding of one of the parties when the contract is made in another country. A word or phrase in one language or country may not be readily translatable to another. Therefore, the contract should have a *choice of language clause*, which sets out the official language by which the contract is to be interpreted, as seen in Exhibit 21.5.

Force Majeure Clause

Force majeure is a French term meaning a "superior or irresistible force." Thus, it protects contracting parties from problems beyond their control. Traditionally, this clause was used to protect the parties from the consequences of a natural disaster that interfered with performance. The clause also protects the parties against

EXHIBIT 21.4

Example of an Irrevocable Letter of Credit

LETTER OF CREDIT—CONFIRMED, IRREVOCABLE

Western Reserve Bank Chicago, Illinois	Letter of Credit #59723 Issued on August 1, 2000
To: Exotica Company Dallas, Texas	From: Tiramisu Import Company Rome, Italy

Gentlemen:

We are instructed by Commercial Bank of Italy, Rome, Italy, to inform you that they have opened their irrevocable credit in favor of Tiramisu Import Company, Rome, Italy, for the sum in U.S. dollars not exceeding a total of about $55,000.00 (Fifty-five Thousand and 00/100 Dollars), available by your drafts on us, to be accompanied by:

1. Full Set On Board Negotiable Ocean Bills of Lading, stating: "Freight Prepaid" and made out to the order of Commercial Bank of Italy.
2. Insurance Policy or Certificate covering Marine and War Risk.
3. Packing List.
4. Commercial Invoice in triplicate:
   Covering 200 Pcs. 1025 Electric Espresso Coffee Machines
              200 Pcs. 750 Stove Top Espresso Coffee Makers
              350 Pcs. 420 Electric Pasta Makers
   Total Value $54,702.75 C.I.F. Rome, Italy
   Import Lic. No. 3792 Expires October 24, 2000
5. Shipper's Export Declaration.

   Partial Shipment Permitted. Transshipment Not Permitted.

   Merchandise must be shipped in SS *Mercaso*.

All documents must indicate Letter of Credit No. 59723, Import License No. 3792, expires October 24, 2000.

All drafts must be marked "Drawn under Letter of Credit No. 59723, issued by Western Reserve Bank. Drafts must be presented to this company not later than October 1, 2000."

This credit is subject to the Uniform Customs and Practices for Documentary Credits (1984 Revision) International Chamber of Commerce Publication No. 400.

We confirm the credit and thereby undertake that all drafts drawn and presented as above specified will be duly honored by us.

By
International Credit Department

---

unprecedented inflation or political upheavals. An illustration of a typical force majeure clause is given in Exhibit 21.6.

Forum Selection and Choice-of-Law Clauses

In international business, companies face additional uncertainties relative to domestic transactions. To reduce uncertainties in the event of a dispute, companies often put *forum selection* and *choice-of-law clauses* in their contracts. (Examples are given in Exhibit 21.7.) The forum may be in one place (Paris), and the law to be applied may be from another place (California). Commonly, the forum and the law to be applied are in agreement.

By selecting the court in which disputes are to be resolved and law that is to be applied, the possibility that the parties will go "forum shopping"—looking for the most favorable forum for the resolution of a dispute—is reduced. Forum selection clauses are generally presumed valid unless they deny one party an effective remedy, cause substantial inconvenience, are developed through fraud, or contravene

EXHIBIT 21.5

Choice of Language Clauses

Example of Choice of Language Clause with Arbitration Provision
This Agreement is signed in two (2) originals in the English language, which shall be regarded as the authoritative and official text. Any matters referred to arbitration will also be in the English language, which will be the official language used in arbitration.

Example of Choice of Language with Translation Provision
This Agreement is signed in two (2) originals in the French language, which shall be regarded as the authoritative and official text. Parties hereto agree to provide an official translation of this Agreement in the English language. This translation will be ratified by both parties, and it may be relied upon as being an accurate representation of the official form.

EXHIBIT 21.6

Example of Force Majeure Clause

The parties hereto shall not be liable for failure of performance hereunder if occasioned by war, declared or undeclared, fire, flood, interruption of transportation, inflation beyond the expected rate, embargo, accident, explosion, inability to procure or shortage of supply of materials, equipment, or production facilities, prohibition of import or export of goods covered hereby, governmental orders, regulations, restrictions, priorities or rationing by strike or lockout or other labor troubles interfering with production or transportation of such goods or with the supplies of raw materials entering into their production or any other cause beyond the control of the parties.

EXHIBIT 21.7

Forum Selection and Choice-of-Law Clauses

All claims and disputes arising out of or in relation to this contract shall be litigated before the courts of the city of Paris, France.
This contract shall be governed by the laws of the state of California, the country of the United States of America.

public policy. In some countries (for example, in Luxembourg), the clause and the contract both must be signed by the parties.

Frequently, forum selection and choice-of-law clauses are interrelated. The validity of one often reflects on the validity of the other. As a rule, choice-of-law provisions are valid if (1) the law chosen is from a place with a substantial relationship to the parties, and (2) the law is not contrary to a strong public policy of the place in which the lawsuit is brought.

LOSS OF INVESTMENT

International business is rarely undertaken without risk that the investment will be lost. Political upheavals, unstable monetary systems, changes in laws, and other problems associated with doing business with a developing country are some of the risks encountered. In addition, businesses must be concerned about governmental actions that can result in loss of investment through nationalization, expropriation, and confiscation. Companies can reduce some risks of loss through the purchase of insurance, but the price is high if the risk is high.

Nationalization

Nationalization occurs when a country takes over, or nationalizes, a foreign investment. The compensation paid by the government is often less than the true value

You Yanks Are Too Old for Us Hip Brits

Garland Denty worked for Smith Kline (a U.S. company) in Philadelphia, where he was Director of Manufacturing Operations/Technical Services, International. The firm had merged with Beecham and became SmithKline Beecham, a British corporation.

Denty was told he was to be promoted to Vice President of Technical Services/Plant Operations and transferred to England. But the company reversed its decision and told Denty he would not get the job because he was too old (at age 52). Denty sued for age discrimination.

The federal court tossed out Denty's suit. The Age Discrimination in Employment Act does not apply to employment decisions affecting U.S. employees that are made by foreign-owned companies regarding employment outside the United States.

Source: *Denty* v. *SmithKline Beecham*, 907 F.Supp. 879

of the business. Although such takeovers usually occur in less-developed nations, they are not limited to those countries. Nationalization has been seen in Iran, Saudi Arabia, and Venezuela. England, a highly developed country, has nationalized certain industries on and off over the years.

Expropriation and Confiscation

Expropriation is the action of a country in taking foreign property in accordance with international law. The general basis agreed upon by most countries for a valid expropriation is that prompt and adequate compensation be provided to the party whose property is taken. International law recognizes a country's right to expropriate the property of foreigners within its jurisdiction.

If a takeover is unlawful, it is a *confiscation*. The U.S. position has been that takings directed toward a particular nationality are discriminatory and are therefore considered confiscations rather than expropriations. The United States has responded to unlawful takings by denying certain rights under our laws to countries carrying out confiscations.

Insuring against Risk of Loss

An all-risk insurance policy can provide financial relief in the event of nationalization or upon the occurrence of a specific contract problem. Short-term private insurance usually lasts from three to five years and is available for most investments. Risks such as currency blockages, embargoes, and a government's arbitrary decision to recall letters of credit may be insured by such major insurers as Lloyds of London. In addition, sellers may obtain rejection insurance in the event that a buyer rejects a product for reasonable cause, such as spoilage at sea.

Some countries have government agencies to assist in insuring exporters from risk of loss. In the United States, for example, the *Overseas Private Investment Corporation (OPIC)* insures investors willing to invest in less-developed countries friendly to the United States. OPIC offers investors insurance against expropriation, currency inconvertibility, and damage from wars or revolutions.

International Dispute Resolution

World trade is in the trillions of dollars annually and growing rapidly. International disputes concerning contract performance are common. They may be due to unanticipated events, unforeseen difficulties in performance, or changes in the legal or political climate of a country that affect a contract. Whatever the basis of the problem, parties to international contracts seek assistance to resolve disputes and enforce their rights.

THE INTERNATIONAL COURT OF JUSTICE

Certain disputes may be taken to the *International Court of Justice (ICJ)* for resolution. The ICJ is headquartered at The Hague, Netherlands. It is a part of the United Nations. The ICJ has fifteen judges representing all of the world's major legal systems, with no two judges from the same country. The Court decides cases in accordance with Article 38 of the Court Statute, which provides the following:

1. The Court, whose function is to decide cases in accordance with international law for such disputes as are submitted to it, shall apply:
    a. International conventions, whether general or particular, establishing rules expressly recognized by the contesting parties;
    b. International custom, as evidence of a general practice accepted as law;
    c. The general principles of law recognized by civilized nations;
    d. Subject to the provisions of [statutes], judicial decisions and the teachings of the most highly qualified publicists of the various nations, as subsidiary means for the determination of the rules of law.
2. This provision shall not prejudice the power of the Court to decide a case *ex aequo et bono* (according to what is good and just), if the parties agree thereto.

Only nations have standing to go before the ICJ. Individuals and businesses have no standing to initiate a suit. Hence, countries, not the parties to a dispute, have complete discretion in deciding whether to pursue a claim. Suppose a country where an investor does business violates the law and damages the investor. The country in which the investor is a citizen has discretion to pursue or not to pursue the investor's claim by bringing suit against the other nation.

The court's decisions providing for monetary judgments or injunctive relief may be referred to the United Nations Security Council for enforcement. If the judgment is paid, however, the country need not distribute the payment to the wronged investor unless domestic laws require such a distribution. In the United States, such distributions are handled by the Foreign Claims Settlement Commission.

JUDICIAL LITIGATION

A party seeking to resolve an international contract dispute often seeks relief either in the court system at home or within the opposing party's country. Litigation is complicated because evidence, witnesses, and documents central to resolving the dispute are often located in two or more countries. In some instances, these difficulties may be overcome by treaties or conventions between the two countries.

Treaties or conventions may allow for proper notice of the suit to the foreign party involved, appropriate service of process, methods for documentation certification, and procedures for taking evidence.

If the action is commenced in a foreign court, the U.S. participant often encounters a judicial system very different from that in this country. Courts in some countries are influenced more by political pressures than are U.S. courts. In addition, some courts will not enforce contract provisions that may be enforceable in the United States but are against their public policy.

In this country, difficulty may arise in establishing proper jurisdiction over both parties to a dispute. U.S. courts require proof of "minimum contacts" within the country so that the court can have jurisdiction over a foreign defendant. (This is discussed in the *Harper-Wyman* decision.) The minimum contacts requirement can be met by a showing of the defendant's presence within U.S. territory; a residence in the United States; consent to the court's jurisdiction; carrying on of business within the court's jurisdiction; or participation in activities outside the country that have direct, substantial, or foreseeable effects within the country. Without jurisdiction, a U.S. court cannot help a party that may have been wronged in a dispute in another country.

Harper-Wyman Company v. In-Bond Contract Manufacturing, Inc., and Industrial Hase, S.A. de C.V.

United States District Court
1994 WL 22321 (N.D.Ill.)

CASE BACKGROUND *Harper-Wyman is a Delaware corporation with its principal place of business in Illinois. In-Bond Contract Manufacturing is a corporation with its registered office in the Cayman Islands. Industrial Hase, S.A. de C.V. is a Mexican corporation with its principal place of business in Ciudad Juarez, Mexico.*

Harper, In-Bond, and Hase were parties to an agreement negotiated and executed in Ciudad Juarez. Harper manufactures gas range parts in Illinois, which it shipped to the Hase plant in Mexico for assembly. (Harper contracted with In-Bond to complete the assembly work; In-Bond subcontracted the work to Hase.) Harper owns the equipment, has twenty-two employees, and maintains control of the parts and pieces in the Hase plant. Some assembled pieces are shipped directly to locations in Mexico. Seventy percent of the assembled pieces are shipped to El Paso, Texas, and then forwarded to Illinois for sale.

The dispute involved an increase that Hase wanted in the hourly labor charge. The request was based on an increase of labor costs mandated by a change in Mexican law. The agreement required good-faith negotiation of such disputes. During negotiations, Hase closed the plant and refused to turn over assembled pieces that belonged to Harper, allegedly costing Harper one million dollars. Harper sued In-Bond and Hase for damages in state court

in Illinois. In-Bond and Hase removed the case to federal court on the basis of diversity of citizenship and filed a motion to dismiss for lack of personal jurisdiction.

CASE DECISION Hart, District Judge.

* * *

As defendants point out, plaintiff initiated the relationship between it and the defendants. However, that relationship has continued for another nine years. Defendants, although located in Mexico, use equipment supplied by and owned by the Illinois plaintiff. Defendants have agreed to run the Mexican plant for the Illinois plaintiff under a contract that expressly provides that Illinois law controls. . . . During the nine years of the relationship, there have been a number of visits by employees of defendants to Illinois, both to discuss terms of the continuing relationship and to learn more about the operation and to be trained. During the relationship, defendants have also made frequent telephone calls and other communications to plaintiff in Illinois in order to discuss day-to-day management of the Mexican plant and parts being shipped and assembled. At this point in time, who initiated the relationship is no longer significant. Instead there is a substantial and ongoing relationship in which the parties work together closely in planning for and getting the parts assembled. By their conduct, defendants have evidenced an intent and desire to conduct an ongoing business relationship with an Illinois resident.

The . . . Agreement is a contract substantially connected with Illinois. It is a contract with an Illinois resident for the assembly of parts produced in Illinois and for assembly of a final product that generally is returned to Illinois. Plaintiff's claims arise from this contract. The fact that performance of the contract occurs outside Illinois does not prevent the contract from being substantially connected to Illinois.

* * *

The defendants in this case have already contractually agreed that Illinois law applies to plaintiff's claim. Therefore, it is not unfair to subject defendants to a foreign legal system; they have already agreed that a foreign law will apply. Also, the dispute between the parties was never whether defendants must pay a wage required by Mexican law, a subject of great interest to

Mexico. The parties dispute was whether plaintiff had to reimburse defendants for the increased wages, a more discrete dispute that does not directly involve Mexican labor law. The present dispute is whether the temporary shutdown was permissible under the parties' contract and whether defendants must pay plaintiff for damages they allegedly caused by the shutdown. The dispute centers around the assembly plant in Mexico and the parties' contract. It is probably correct to regard the dispute as being more connected to Mexico than to Illinois. However, for the reasons already stated, there is a substantial enough connection to Illinois to justify haling defendants into court in Illinois. Defendants' motion to dismiss will be denied.

QUESTIONS FOR ANALYSIS

1. What kind of clause did the parties leave out of their agreement that might have made it more clear where such a dispute would be tried in court?
2. What could Harper-Wyman do if Hase and In-Bond ignore the Illinois court?

ARBITRATION

Traditional judicial forums are not very effective in resolving most international commercial disagreements. Cost considerations, jurisdictional barriers, the length of time to litigate, legal uncertainties, and the inability of judicial systems to fashion appropriate relief encouraged the use of alternative dispute resolution techniques, especially *arbitration.*

Attempts by the international business community to standardize arbitral rules and procedures have resulted in the creation of organizations such as the United Nations Commission on International Trade Law, the International Chamber of Commerce, the American Arbitration Association, the Inter-American Commercial Arbitration Commission, and the London Court of Arbitration. These organizations have established rules to address issues concerning arbitration proceedings and awards. In more than fifty countries, including the United States, the enforcement of arbitral awards is facilitated by the 1958 United Nations Convention on the Recognition and Enforcement of Foreign Arbitral Awards. Federal district courts have jurisdiction to hear motions to confirm or challenge an international arbitration award involving a U.S. business.

DOCTRINE OF SOVEREIGN IMMUNITY

A foreign investor who suffers losses because of the expropriation of assets may consider suing to recover the losses. This litigation may take place in a country different from the country that expropriated the investment. However, the investor may be prohibited from obtaining relief through litigation by application of the doctrine of sovereign immunity.

In international law, the *doctrine of sovereign immunity* allows a court to give up its right to jurisdiction over foreign enterprises or countries. The doctrine is based on traditional notions that a sovereign should not be subject to litigation in a foreign court. As a result, investors may not be able to obtain relief in their country's court system.

Some countries restrict the doctrine's application in commercial circumstances. The *Foreign Sovereign Immunities Act* provides a uniform rule for the determination of sovereign immunity in legal actions in this country's courts. The Act provides the following:

> Under international law, [countries] are not immune from the jurisdiction of foreign courts insofar as their commercial activities are concerned, and their commercial property may be levied upon for the satisfaction of judgments rendered against them in connection with their commercial activities.

DOCTRINE OF ACT OF STATE

The *doctrine of act of state* is similar to the sovereign immunity doctrine in that it creates a bar to compensation by foreign investors who have sustained losses in host countries. Unlike the sovereign immunity doctrine, however, the doctrine of act of state may create a partial as well as a complete bar to a claim. The doctrine follows the principle that a country must respect the independence of other countries. The courts of one country may not judge the validity of the regulatory acts of another country's government in its own territory.

United States courts have upheld the doctrine, stating that, among other things, it ensures international harmony. Although the purpose of the doctrine is to avoid embarrassment to foreign relations, the practical effect is that a claimant seeking relief may be partially or totally barred from obtaining relief in the courts of a country where the doctrine applies.

Summary

- In contrast to the domestic market, the international market is characterized by additional financial, political, and regulatory risks. Those risks arise from differences among countries in currencies, language, business customs, legal and social philosophies, and national economic goals.
- The principal sources of international trade law are the laws of individual countries, the laws arising from trade agreements between countries, and the rules enacted by worldwide or regional trade organizations.
- To reduce trade barriers, most nations participated in the General Agreement on Tariffs and Trade (GATT), which resulted in the World Trade Organization, which now oversees some trade disputes.
- Most countries have import and export regulations. Import restrictions include import licensing requirements, import quotas, safety standards, government procurement policies, and customs procedures. To standardize tariff schedules and their application, most countries have adopted the harmonized tariff schedule to classify goods.
- The United States imposes prohibitions on the export of certain technologies that could be used by hostile nations or terrorists. The exportation of weapons and computers is monitored by the government.

- The most common international business arrangements are wholly owned subsidiaries, joint ventures, licensing agreements, franchise agreements, and contract manufacturing. The choice of business organization is influenced by the laws of a country, the purposes of the commercial venture, the financial resources of the parties, and the degree of managerial control desired by the company.

- The Foreign Corrupt Practices Act (FCPA) prohibits U.S. companies and their agents from bribing foreign officials. The FCPA makes the bribery of foreign officials a criminal offense and requires U.S. companies to establish internal accounting mechanisms to prevent such bribery. It is a criminal offense to make payments to foreign officials for the purpose of gaining business favor in a foreign country.

- To create an effective international contract, a business should consider differences in business customs, attitudes toward the contractual relationship, and language. Specific clauses in international contracts worthy of special consideration are the payment, choice of language, force majeure, and forum selection and choice-of-law clauses.

- Business in foreign countries may face special risks. Political upheavals, unstable monetary systems, dramatic changes in laws, and other problems associated with doing business with a developing country must be considered. Losses may occur through nationalization, expropriation, or confiscation of the foreign investment.

- Although most international trade occurs without incident, disputes sometimes arise concerning contract performance. Various national and international institutions may assist a business in effective dispute resolution. Those institutions include the International Court of Justice, judicial litigation in country court systems, and arbitration. The doctrines of sovereign immunity and act of state may create bars to recovery through the judicial system.

Issue

Are Bribery and Corruption Normal?

Payments from businesses to government officials for favor are not looked upon kindly, especially in the United States, but it is a normal part of business in much of the world. Even Germany, often seen as a model of proper relationships, has recently seen hundreds of cases filed against public officials and private parties for cash bribes and kickbacks. The United States has been viewed as a fuddy-duddy for subjecting its companies to the Foreign Corrupt Practices Act, but there may be a growing recognition that corruption goes beyond ethical concerns and usually means economic exploitation of innocent citizens.

POLITICAL CORRUPTION: THE GOOD, BAD AND UGLY

George Melloan

Reprinted with permission of *The Wall Street Journal*

© 1995 Dow Jones & Company, Inc. All rights reserved. Melloan is the International Deputy Editor of *The Wall Street Journal.*

Politicians regard the ladies and gentlemen of the press as predators hungrily eyeing the Achilles tendons of officeholders. Since public officials are so easily lured to cash-rich waterholes, journalists seldom lack for prey.

When I first arrived in Chicago to ply my trade some years back I mentioned with some approval the names of a local pol to a veteran copy editor. "He takes with both hands," my colleague snarled, thereby making a distinction between one-handed and two-handed grafters. As a young innocent, I had picked up a few broad hints of political corruption in Muncie, Indiana, including a newly elected county commissioner openly chortling, "to the victors belong the spoils." But Delaware County pols of that era were mostly one-handers. Kickbacks from suppliers of gravel to the county highway department were about the only loot available.

Which brings up the case of a man who ranks among the champion two-handers of history, Roh Tae Woo. The former president of South Korea, in a public apology, has admitted to amassing $653 million in a political slush fund and to having $242 million of that money still in his possession. The revelation, which carries the possibility of a jail term, has thrown Korean politics into a turmoil as charges fly back and forth that other high officials may have played similar games with the public trust.

Yet the most interesting thing about the Roh case is not the fact that Korea's thriving business tycoons were expected to pay generously for the good will of men in power. Tributes to local Caesars are common throughout Asia, even in once-admired Japan, Inc., where bribery scandals finally have weakened the grip on government of the Liberal Democratic Party. What is noteworthy about the Roh affair is that it dramatizes South Korea's move toward political maturity. It has progressed in a few short years from military dictatorship, where dirty secrets were never allowed to surface, to open democracy, where even a former general and head of state can be brought to book.

It's possible that a general theory can be derived from the Korean example. To wit, as countries grow richer, they develop a middle class that demands greater democracy and greater accountability from those who lead. So it is just possible that rapid economic development, which South Korea has enjoyed, carries a twofold benefit: greater wealth and better government. If so, that is a reason to be hopeful about the political future of Asia's rapidly growing states, Indonesia and China, for example.

Jim Rohwer, a former Economist editor who has just written a book called "Asia Rising," dropped by the Jour-

nal's offices in New York recently and offered some thoughts about Asian corruption. Without endorsing graft, he allows as how it may be a necessary evil in countries that do not yet have institutions for facilitating economic development. Bribes given by business investors for necessary approvals at least have the merit of getting things accomplished. Such practices, appalling as they may seem, may in some cases serve the public interest better than might be true if investors in new factories and jobs were unable to cut through red tape and bypass bureaucratic inertia.

Indeed, an oilfield equipment salesman I once met told me that doing business in China was far easier than in Russia because in China, greasing palms got results whereas the Russian practice was more akin to extortion, with no guarantee of any favors in return.

The acid test would seem to be whether a country enjoys growth or suffers stagnation. Bribe-taking facilitators can also be an aid to growth. But official corruption also can become a poison, destroying a people's trust in government and with it their own willingness to obey laws and deal fairly with each other. Scarce resources are misallocated to projects that are launched not because of their economic usefulness but because of opportunities for graft. Capital, amassed illegally, is exported out of the country to Swiss bank accounts. In short, graft can lead to a demoralization that destroys a nation's capacity for economic advancement.

Something like that happened in the Philippines under Ferdinand Marcos and the country is only now beginning to share in the Asian boom. Its current president, Fidel V. Ramos, has made war against corruption one of his highest priorities and that, along with opening the country up to foreign trade and investment, is beginning to pay off.

President Jiang Zemin of China also has launched an anti-corruption drive, but it is not clear whether this is a serious effort to curb the excesses of powerful party cadres and their families or is mainly a way to purge the president's rivals. Clearly, China still is far behind South Korea in its political and economic development. But there is a great deal of discussion among China watchers of what a new generation of Chinese officials might do. The best and brightest among China's 40-plus generation are men and women who have either at one time been Red Guards or suffered at their hands, but who also in many cases have studied at U.S. universities. They have seen both tyranny and democracy at work and presumably have drawn some conclusions. They also will be the core of China's middle class, which if it follows the Korean pattern, will be intolerant of abuses of political power.

But one unanswerable question is whether the future leaders of China will care enough about China and its people to respond well to pressures for political reform. There is a certain irony in the fact the Roh Tae Woo did in fact respond while he was president, starting the country down the road to democracy. Now, as Koreans demand new standards of accountability from their leaders, Roh has become a victim of his own good intentions. China's leaders may well see this as a warning, and become more intense in their desire to hold onto power at all costs.

But without putting too fine a point on it, the example of Korea, Japan, and the Philippines suggests less public tolerance of graft in a part of the world long noted for corruption. In western democracies, the U.S. for example, there is a public reaction against expanding government power, if the recent Republican sweep of Congress and state houses is any indication. Power breeds corruption. The world will never be free of politicians who "take with both hands," but these are encouraging signs.

ISSUE QUESTIONS

1. If American firms take a stance against paying bribes, perhaps because of the Foreign Corrupt Practices Act, does that not lead to a loss of jobs and business in the United States that just goes to other countries?

2. If corruption is a "way of life" in some countries and the citizens think of it as normal, is it the business of the United States to try to force American views of proper government behavior on another country?

REVIEW AND DISCUSSION QUESTIONS

1. Define the following terms:

   tariff   free trade zone
   harmonized tariff schedules letter of credit
   dumping   force majeure
   countervailing duty

2. Compare the merits of arbitration and judicial litigation as methods of dispute resolution in international trade.

CASE QUESTIONS

3. Dart (an American) planned to sell and ship to (then communist-controlled) Czechoslovakia wafer polishers used in making integrated circuits. Because the polishers were U.S.-origin goods, Dart told the importer to check at the Department of Commerce to see whether an export license would be required for the technically advanced equipment. The importer falsely told Dart that no license was required. The goods were seized by customs agents at the Los Angeles airport. Commerce charged Dart with attempting to violate the law by shipping without a license, threatening fines of $150,000 and a suspension of export privileges for fifteen years. Can you make an argument that Dart "knew or should have known" that such goods were subject to an export license? Is there another way that Dart could have handled the inquiry at Commerce? [*Dart* v. *U.S.*, 848 F.2d 217 (D. C. Cir., 1988)]

4. A Houston corporation contracted for a German corporation to tow a drilling rig from Louisiana to an area off Italy, where the Houston company was to drill wells. The contract provided that: "Any dispute arising must be treated before the London Court of Justice." While on its way to Italy, the rig was damaged by a

severe storm. The German tug towed the rig to Tampa, Florida, the nearest port. The Houston company sued in the U.S. District Court at Tampa, seeking $3,500,000 damages from the German company. Is the use of the American court proper in this situation? What effect would the contract clause have on the lawsuit? [*M/S Bremen* v. *Zapata Off-Shore Co.*, 92 S.Ct. 1907 (1972)]

5. Seawinds, a shipping company, was incorporated in Hong Kong with its principal place of business in California. It contracted with Nedlloyd Lines, a shipping company in the Netherlands, to "establish a joint venture company to carry on a transportation operation." The agreement had the following choice-of-law provision:

> This agreement shall be governed by and construed in accordance with Hong Kong law and each party hereby irrevocably submits to the nonexclusive jurisdiction and service of process of the Hong Kong courts.

Later, Seawinds sued in California state court, asserting that Nedlloyd had breached its duties under the contract by engaging in activities that led to the cancellation of charter hires essential to the joint venture's business and by making and then reneging on commitments to contribute additional capital. Nedlloyd responded that Seawinds had failed to state causes of action because Hong Kong law was to be applied. If the case is brought in California court, which law should be applied: that of Hong Kong or that of California? Does California have a substantial relationship to the parties or their transaction? Is there a reasonable basis for the selection of Hong Kong law by the parties in their original agreement? [*Nedlloyd Lines B.V.* v. *Superior Court (Seawinds Limited)*, 834 P.2d 1148 (Sup.Ct., Cal., 1992)]

6. Nettie Effron, a Florida resident, bought a sixteen-day cruise of the Brazilian coast from Sun Line Cruises. The cruise was on the *Stella Solaris*, owned by Sun Line Greece. The cruise ticket stated that "any action against the carrier must be brought only before the courts of Athens, Greece, to the jurisdiction of which the Passenger submits himself formally excluding the jurisdiction of all and other court or courts of any other country." Effron was injured when she fell while on the ship. She sued for damages in federal court in New York. Sun Line moved to have the case dismissed because of the forum selection clause in the ticket. The district court refused to dismiss; Sun Line appealed. What result? [*Effron* v. *Sun Line Cruises*, 67 F.3d 7 (2nd Cir., 1995)]

7. Liberty Bank issued an irrevocable letter of credit for its customer, Anderson-Prichard Oil. The credit was to be used to buy oil-well equipment from Tegtmeyer. The letter of credit was sent to the Bank of America, which issued its own letter of credit to the Union Bank of Switzerland. Anderson-Prichard and Liberty Bank refused payment of bills because of alleged differences between the documents and the letter of credit. One allegation was that the bill of lading was "foul" and "not clean"—that is, the printed words in the bill describing that the goods delivered would be "in apparent good order and condition" were crossed out by the carrier. Below these words was the typewritten insertion "ship not responsible for the kind and condition of merchandise," and in the body of the bill was a stamp stating "ship not responsible for rust." A second allegation was that the letter of credit called for new pipe but the certificates described the pipe as secondhand, and the pipe did not meet the expectations that Anderson-Prichard had for its quality. Should the court require payment by Anderson-Prichard and Liberty Bank? Discuss the letter of credit itself and the expectations of the parties and how that should affect the

court's decision. [*Bank of America* v. *Liberty National Bank & Trust Co.*, 116 F.Supp. 233 (W.D. Okla., 1953)]

8. Farr, a U.S. company, contracted to buy sugar from CAV, a Cuban company owned by U.S. citizens. Because the government of Cuba nationalized its sugar industry, including CAV, it demanded that payments for sugar already shipped must be made to the Banco Nacional de Cuba. At CAV's insistence that it was the rightful owner of the sugar and that the nationalization violated international law, Farr paid CAV. Banco Nacional sued to collect payment from Farr for the sugar delivered. The case went to the Supreme Court, where Banco Nacional was held to be correct. On what theory did the Supreme Court base this opinion? [*Banco Nacional de Cuba* v. *Sabbatino*, 84 S.Ct. 923 (1964)]

9. Chisholm & Company and the Bank of Jamaica agreed that Chisholm was to arrange lines of credit from a number of banks and to obtain ExIm Bank credit insurance. The Bank of Jamaica then "went around" Chisholm and dealt with ExIm Bank directly. It excluded Chisholm from receiving any benefit from the credit insurance that ExIm Bank provided. Chisholm sued the Bank of Jamaica. In its defense, the bank asserted that its actions were protected by sovereign immunity and the act of state doctrine. Were the bank's assertions correct? [*Chisholm & Company* v. *Bank of Jamaica*, 643 F.Supp. 1393 (S.D. Fla., 1986)]

POLICY QUESTIONS

10. Foreign ownership in U.S. properties has jumped in the past two decades. Foreigners own large tracts of farmland and urban real estate. Foreign investment in the United States is more than $1.5 trillion. Should we encourage or discourage foreign investments in this country? Are such investments adverse to our national security? Are there other alternatives to controlling foreign investments besides prohibiting or restricting foreign ownership?

11. What are the reasons that some countries allow items to enter duty free while other countries may require the same items to be subject to duties? What are the advantages and disadvantages of both approaches to international trade?

ETHICS QUESTIONS

12. In some circumstances, cultural expectations and business customs of a country may run counter to a person's ethical beliefs. What factors should people take into consideration when such a conflict arises and they are charged with making a business work within the cultural setting?

13. In some countries, it is expected that businesses will pay off government officials when negotiating a business transaction. Suppose it makes the difference between getting the contract and not getting the contract? If the payoff is not made, Foreign Corrupt Practices Act aside, a competitor would get the deal, and the American company that loses the deal would have to close a factory, putting 500 people out of work.

Case Analysis and Legal Research

The legal environment of business is often a student's first encounter with the law and the legal process. Legal citations, the organization of legal materials, and opinion analysis can be bewildering at first. This appendix provides a general explanation and overview of the important ingredients in legal research and analysis.

Reading a Legal Opinion

In resolving disputes, courts often report their decisions in written opinions. Decisions of appellate courts are most frequently reported. Usually only important decisions at the trial court level are reported. Through a written opinion, a judge explains the legal basis for the decision reached. Published opinions provide legal precedents in the common law.

An opinion can exceed one hundred pages and involve several complex issues. To assist in the analysis of an opinion, law students often prepare a summary of the opinion, called a case *brief*—essentially a digest or abstract of the opinion setting forth its most essential parts. Attorneys often write case briefs in researching a legal problem, particularly when a case involves a complicated situation or the dispute requires the court to consider several legal questions in reaching a resolution.

To brief an opinion, there is no formal or standard procedure. Here, we provide a basic approach to assist in briefing the opinions excerpted in this text. It is an effective way to study legal opinions.

Before you brief an opinion, read it carefully. Then separate the opinion into its five fundamental parts by asking yourself questions about those parts:

(1) A Statement of the Significant Facts
  Who is the plaintiff? The defendant?
  Who did what to whom?
  What relief is being sought from the court?

(2) A Statement of the Relevant Procedural Details
  Who prevailed in the lower court?
  Which party is appealing?

(3) A Statement of the Legal Issue in the Dispute
  What are the specific legal questions the court is being asked to address?

(4) A Statement of the Court's Decision

   How does the court respond to the question(s) posed to it?

   Does the plaintiff or the defendant prevail on the appeal?

(5) An Explanation of the Court's Reasoning

   Which is the legal basis for the court's decision?

This basic procedure is illustrated and described in the following opinion. Before examining the brief, read the actual opinion of the court (in the right-hand column). In the left-hand column is a commentary on the case opinion. Although an understanding of the law and legal terms used in the opinion is not essential to an understanding of the briefing process, most legal terms used in the opinion are defined in the glossary at the back of this text. As in the text, this opinion has been shortened by inserting * * * or . . . where material has been deleted. The essence is retained in the material that remains.

Dallas Parks v. George Steinbrenner and New York Yankees, Inc.

New York Supreme Court, Appellate Division, First Department

520 N.Y.2d 374 (1987)

BRIEF AND EXPLANATION. Begin by summarizing the essential facts in the opinion. In the text, the facts are summarized for you in the **Case Background** section provided with each opinion.

1. FACTS. Dallas Parks, the plaintiff, alleges that he was defamed by the defendant, George Steinbrenner, owner of the New York Yankees. The alleged defamation occurred when the defendant issued a press release criticizing Parks's abilities as an umpire. The plaintiff seeks damages on the grounds that the press release falsely attacked his abilities as an umpire.

The procedural history summarizes how the lower court(s) ruled on the dispute. In the text, the procedural history is summarized in the **Case Background** section.

2. PROCEDURAL HISTORY. The defendant argued that the press release represented a constitutionally protected expression of opinion. The Special Term (the lower court) disagreed, finding that although the press release expressed an opinion, it was not backed up by an adequate statement of the facts to support that opinion. The defendant appealed to the New York Supreme Court.

The legal issue in the opinion is the question the parties are asking the court to resolve. In some opinions, the opinion states exactly what the issue is that the court is being asked to resolve. In the text, the issue is generally found in our summary of the lower court's decision or from the stated contentions of the parties. In analyzing an opinion in the text, state

the issue in your own words to aid your understanding of the opinion.

Before Carro, J. P., and Kassal, Ellerin, Wallach, JJ.

MEMORANDUM DECISION. This action for defamation brings into play one of the most colorful of American traditions—the razzing of the umpire.

The plaintiff, Dallas Parks, served as an American League baseball umpire from 1979 through 1982. He alleges that he was defamed by George Steinbrenner, principal owner of the New York Yankees, when Steinbrenner on August 29, 1982, issued a press release, excerpts of which were published in newspapers throughout the United States, criticizing Park's abilities as an umpire. The press release, which was issued after the Yankees had played a two-game series with the Toronto Blue Jays in Toronto, Canada, on August 27th and 28th, at which Parks officiated, reads as follows:

Judging on his last two days' performance, my people tell me that he is not a capable umpire. He is a member of one of the finest crews umpiring in the American League today, but obviously he doesn't measure up.

We are making no excuse for the team's play this season, but this weekend our team has had several key injuries and for umpire Dallas Parks to throw two of our players out of ballgames in two days on plays he misjudges is "ludicrous."

This man, in my opinion, has had it in for the Yankees ever since I labeled him and several of the umpires as "scabs" because they worked the American League games in 1979 during the umpires' strike.

Parks must learn that the word scab is a commonly used phrase. It is in no way meant as a personal insult. However, because he worked during the strike for baseball management does not mean he should be protected by them and annually given a job he is not capable of handling.

3. **ISSUE.** Does the press release constitute a constitutionally protected statement of pure opinion?

> After stating the issue, state the court's decision, both procedural (e.g., judgment for the defendant) and substantive (a yes or no response to the issue presented).

4. **THE COURT'S DECISION.** Yes, the press release is a constitutionally protected expression of pure opinion. Judgment for the defendant; the Special Term's decision is reversed.

> The court's rationale is the heart of the opinion. The court will generally discuss the relevant law surrounding the question presented to it. Then the court will apply that law to the facts of the dispute before it. In reaching its decision, the court will explain its rationale—why and how it reached the conclusion that the facts in this dispute do or do not fall within the existing law. In the text, the court's rationale is presented in excerpts from the actual opinions in the **Case Decision** section.

5. **COURT'S RATIONALE.** A statement of pure opinion is a statement that is accompanied by the facts upon which it is based, or it does not imply that it is based on undisclosed facts.

Statements that constitute pure opinion whether false or libelous may not serve as the basis for an action for defamation.

In determining whether a statement is fact or opinion, consideration is given to what an average person hearing or reading the statement will take it to mean, the circumstances surrounding its use, and the way it is written.

The press release must be evaluated within the broader social context of baseball. It is an American tradition to verbally abuse umpires. In this context, the average reader would perceive the release as opinion and not fact. The release is the kind of statement that generally accompanies a voicing of displeasure at an umpire's calls.

The statement by the defendant represents the view of an owner of a baseball team that is doing poorly and who has chosen to vent his frustration by baiting the umpire.

There is no indication that defendant's opinions are based on some other undisclosed facts unknown to the reader.

This less than complimentary critical assessment appears to have been the "final straw" in the rhubarb that had long simmered between the umpire and the owner and

resulted in commencement of the instant action, against Steinbrenner and the Yankees, wherein plaintiff seeks damages for defamation on the ground that the press release falsely impugned his ability, competence, conduct and fairness as a baseball umpire.

In subsequently moving to dismiss the complaint for failure to state a cause of action, defendants argued that the press release represented a nonactionable constitutionally protected expression of opinion. While Special Term [lower court] found that the statement was "clearly expressed as an opinion," it nevertheless held that the complaint sufficiently pleaded a cause of action in defamation because the press release did not set forth an adequate statement of fact contained in the statement—i.e., that Parks expelled two Yankee players from the game—did "not in anyway support the opinions proffered" that plaintiff was incompetent and biased and, further, that no factual basis was set forth for the conclusory assertion that plaintiff misjudged plays.

We disagree with Special Term's assessment of the press release in question and find that it constituted a constitutionally protected expression of pure opinion.

In all defamation cases, the threshold issue which must be determined, as a matter of law, is whether the complained of statements constitute fact or opinion. If they fall within the ambit of "pure opinion," then even if false and libelous, and no matter how perjorative or pernicious they may be, such statements are safeguarded and may not serve as the basis for an action in defamation. A non-actionable "pure opinion" is defined as a statement of opinion which either is accompanied by a recitation of the facts upon which it is based, or, if not so accompanied, does not imply that it is based upon undisclosed facts. Alternatively, when a defamatory statement of opinion implies that it is based upon undisclosed detrimental facts which justify the opinion but are unknown to those reading or hearing it, it is a "mixed opinion" and actionable. Similarly actionable as a "mixed opinion" is a defamatory opinion which is ostensibly accompanied by a recitation of the underlying facts upon which the opinion is based, but those underlying facts are either falsely misrepresented or grossly distorted.

Determining whether particular statements, or particular words, express fact or opinion is ofttimes an exercise beset by the uncertainties engendered by the imprecision and varying nuance inherent in language. While mechanistic rules and rigid sets of criteria have been eschewed as inappropriate vehicles for the sensitive process of separating fact from opinion, reference to various general criteria has been found helpful in resolving the issue. Predominant among these is that the determination is to be made on the basis of what the average person hearing or reading the communication would take it to mean, and what significance is to be accorded the purpose of the words, the circumstances surrounding their use and the manner, tone and style with which they are used. An approach which was favorably commented upon in the *Steinhilber* case is that set forth by Judge Starr in his plurality opinion in *Ollman* v. *Evans* which enunciates four factors which should generally be considered in differentiating between fact and opinion. They are summarized . . . as follows:

(1) an assessment of whether the specific language in issue has a precise meaning which is readily understood or whether it is indefinite and ambiguous;

(2) a determination of whether the statement is capable of being objectively characterized as true or false;

(3) an examination of the full context of the communication in which the statement appears; and

(4) a consideration of the broader social context or setting surrounding the communication including the existence of any applicable customs or conventions which might signal to readers or listeners that what is being read or heard is likely to be opinion, not fact.

These factors have particular relevance to the statement here in issue which must be evaluated within the broader social context of a baseball club owner versus an umpire, and special attention should be accorded to whether there exist any customs and conventions regarding the status of an umpire in the great American pastime which would signal to readers that what is being read is likely to be opinion not fact.

* * *

From the late nineteenth century on, the baseball umpire has come to expect not only verbal abuse, but in many cases, physical attack as well, as part of the "robust debate" ingrained in the profession. . . .

Judges, too, have expressed their acceptance of this American tradition. In dismissing a minor league general manager's defamation action on other grounds, a federal court noted that harsh insults, especially those directed at an umpire, are accepted commonplace occurrences in baseball.

* * *

When Steinbrenner's remarks are viewed in this context, it is clear that they would be perceived by the average reader as a statement of opinion, and not fact. The negative characterizations of the plaintiff umpire as "not capable," that "he doesn't measure up," that he "misjudges" plays and that his decision to "throw two of our players out of ball games" was "ludicrous" are readily understood to be the kind of "rhetorical hyperbole" that generally accompany the communication of displeasure at an umpire's "calls." While the

subjective and emotional character of such sentiments is commonly recognized and construed as "opinion" rather than fact, that view is expressly emphasized upon a reading of the entire press release with its qualifying phrases of "my people tell me" immediately evident that the statement represents the view of the owner of an embattled baseball team who is obviously chafing at "the team's (poor) play this season", which has been exacerbated by a weekend of injuries and ejections of players, and who is venting his frustrations in the venerated American tradition of "baiting the umpire." Indeed, even if the assertions in the statement implying that plaintiff was incompetent and biased in performing his duties were to be viewed as statements of fact, it is questionable whether they could be construed as defamatory, i.e., exposing the plaintiff to public contempt, ridicule, aversion and disgrace and inducing an evil opinion of him in the minds of right thinking persons—in light of the generally "critical" attitudes which baseball umpires, in any event, ordinarily inspire in both the game's fans and its participants.

Although acknowledging that the statement in issue was "clearly expressed as opinion," Special Term held that it was actionable because the accompanying underlying facts were found by Special Term not to adequately support the opinions proffered. That one may dispute the conclusions drawn from the specified facts is not, however, the test. So long as the opinion is accompanied by a recitation of the facts upon which it is based it is deemed a "pure opinion" and is afforded complete immunity even though the facts do not support the opinion. The rationale for this broad protection of an expression of opinion accompanied by a recitation of the facts upon which it is based is that the reader has the opportunity to assess the basis upon which the opinion was reached in order to draw his or her own conclusions concerning its validity.

* * *

The reverence which the First Amendment accords to ideas has properly resulted in the determination that, "however pernicious an opinion may seem, we depend for its correction not on the conscience of judges and juries but on the competition of other ideas." Those competing ideas about baseball's arbiters will undoubtedly continue to abound aplenty both on the playing fields and in the sports columns, albeit not in the courtroom.

Accordingly, the Order, Supreme Court, Bronx County (Alfred J. Callahan, J.), entered May 9, 1986, which denied the defendants' motion to dismiss the complaint and supplemental complaint for failure to state a cause of action, should be reversed, on the law, and the complaint dismissed, without costs.

Finding the Law

There are several important sources of law in the United States, including the U.S. Constitution; case law established by the written opinions of judges; statutes enacted by legislative bodies; regulatory agency orders, opinions, and regulations; treatises; law reviews; and Restatements of Law. At one time or another, we reference these sources in explaining the laws making up the legal environment of business. This section provides a guide to reading a citation to a source of law. If you decide to study an aspect of the legal environment in more detail, this section provides guidance in locating appropriate material.

CASE LAW

The published judicial opinions of all federal courts and the appellate state courts are available in court reporters. As a rule, opinions appear in hardback volumes of the *Reporters* about a year after a court has delivered its decision. The opinions are available more quickly in paperback volumes published shortly after the case is decided, even more quickly through computer research services (such as *Westlaw* and *Lexis*), and in the form of "slip opinions," copies of a decision as soon as it is made public by the court.

Supreme Court decisions are published in *United States Reporter* (U.S.), *Supreme Court Reporter* (S.Ct.), *Lawyers' Edition of Supreme Court Reports* (L.Ed.), and *U.S. Law Week*. A citation reads as follows: *Arnett v. Kennedy*, 416 U.S. 134, 94 S.Ct. 1633 (1974). This tells us that Arnett appealed a decision of a lower court to the U.S. Supreme Court. In 1974, the Supreme Court heard the case, and its decision is reported in volume 416 of *United States Reporter* beginning on page 134 and in volume 94 of *Supreme Court Reporter* beginning on page 1633. A reference to a point cited on a particular page in that opinion might read 416 U.S. 134, 137, which means that the case begins on page 134 and the particular point referenced is on page 137. Decisions of U.S. Circuit Courts of Appeals are reported in *Federal Reporter* (F.), now in its third series (F.3d). The following is an example of a citation: *Easton Publishing Co. v. Federal Communications Commission*, 175 F.2d 344 (1949). The decision in this case can be found in volume 175 of *Federal Reporter* (second series), page 344. The decision was issued by the court in 1949.

Opinions of U.S. district courts that the judges decide to publish are reported in *Federal Supplement* (F.Supp.). An example is *Amalgamated Meat Cutters v. Connally*, 337 F.Supp. 737 (S.D.N.Y.1971). The decision can be found in volume 337 of *Federal Supplement* beginning on page 737. The case was decided by the federal district court in the southern district of New York in 1971.

State appellate court decisions are reported in regional reporters published by West Publishing Company. Decisions of the state supreme courts and courts of appeals for Arkansas, Kentucky, Missouri, Tennessee, and Texas, for example, are reported in *South Western Reporter* (S.W.). As shown in Exhibit A.1, other state court opinions are reported in *Atlantic Reporter* (A.), *North Eastern Reporter* (N.E.), *North Western Reporter* (N.W.), *Pacific Reporter* (P.), *South Eastern Reporter* (S.E.), and *Southern Reporter* (S.), all of which are in the second series (2d). Because they handle so many cases, California and New York have individual reporters, *New York Supplement* and *California Reporter*. Some states publish their own reporters in addition to the West series.

Statutory Law

Statutes—laws passed by Congress—are published in the *United States Code* (U.S.C.) and printed by the U.S. Government Printing Office. The U.S.C. contains the text of all laws

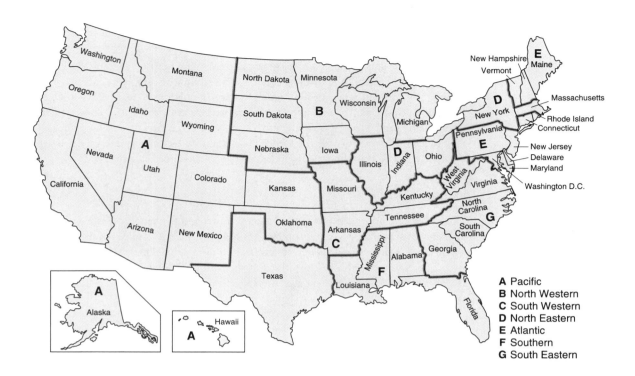

A Pacific
B North Western
C South Western
D North Eastern
E Atlantic
F Southern
G South Eastern

*National Reporter
System Map, Showing
the States Included in
Each Reporter Group*

passed by Congress and signed by the President. A reference to this source might read 40
U.S.C. §13.1 (volume 40, *United States Code*, section 13.1).

A very popular source of statutory law is the *United States Code Annotated* (U.S.C.A.). In
the U.S.C.A., each section of a statute contains helpful annotations that provide references
to the legislative history of the section and to court decisions using and interpreting it. A reference to this source might read 14 U.S.C.A. §45.3 (volume 14, *United States Code Annotated*,
section 45.3). In both the U.S.C. and the U.S.C.A., the laws are organized and integrated
into a pattern that makes them relatively easy to find and to read.

The U.S. Government Printing Office also publishes *Statutes at Large*, a chronological
list of all laws enacted by Congress. This list is not often used unless it is necessary to look
up a law that has just been passed by Congress but that is not yet reported in the U.S.C. or
U.S.C.A. A full citation might read: Voting Rights Act of 1965, Pub.L. No. 89—110, 79
Stat. 437, 42 U.S.C. §§1971, 1973. The Voting Rights Act of 1965 was the 110th *Public Law*
enacted by the 89th Congress and appears in volume 79 of *Statutes at Large*, section 437. In
addition, it appears in volume 42 of the U.S.C., sections 1971 and 1973. Also, remember that
there is often a difference between the number of the section in the statute as written by
Congress and the number of the section in the Code. For example, the "National Environmental Policy Act of 1969, §102, 42 U.S.C. §4332" means that section 102 of the statute as
passed by Congress is found in section 4332 of volume 42 of the U.S.C.

REGULATORY LAW

Regulations—rules passed by agencies subsequent to a congressional statute—are published
in the *Code of Federal Regulations* (C.F.R.). These regulations are intended to implement a
particular statute enacted by Congress. The C.F.R., revised annually, is organized by subject
matter and contains the text of regulations in effect as of the date of publication. A citation

reading 7 C.F.R. §912.65 refers to Title 7 of the *Code of Federal Regulations*, section 912.65. Different titles refer to different government agencies.

To keep up-to-date on new and proposed regulations, one needs to consult the *Federal Register* (Fed.Reg.). Printed five days a week by the U.S. Government Printing Office, the *Federal Register* lists all proposed regulations and all new and amended regulations. A citation might read 46 Fed.Reg. 26,501 (1981). This refers to volume 46 of the *Federal Register*, published in 1981, page 26,501, which has to do with a new environmental standard.

AGENCY ORDERS AND OPINION

Agency orders and opinions are official regulatory materials that go beyond the regulations. Orders may be issued by the top officials (e.g., the commissioners) of a regulatory agency, while opinions are generally issued by an agency's administrative law judge in adjudicatory hearings (discussed in Chapter 6). While agencies usually have official publications, the easiest way to find agency materials is to look in commercial reporters published by private companies such as Commerce Clearing House, Bureau of National Affairs, and Prentice-Hall. Each reporter covers a single topic, such as environmental law or federal tax law. The reporters are up-to-date and contain new regulations, orders, opinions, court decisions, and other materials of interest to anyone following regulations in a certain area. These reporters, which are usually large loose-leaf binders, cover hundreds of topics, such as chemical regulations, hazardous materials, transportation, noise regulations, collective bargaining negotiations, securities regulations, patents, and antitrust laws.

TREATISES, LAW REVIEWS, AND RESTATEMENTS OF THE LAW

Important secondary sources of law are legal treatises, law reviews, and Restatements of Law. Treatises generally cover one area or topic of law, summarizing the principles and rules dealing with the topic. An example of a treatise is W. Jaeger, *Williston on Contracts* (3d ed. 1957).

Law reviews, published by law schools and edited by law students, contain articles written by legal scholars, judges, and practitioners on virtually all aspects of the law. An example of a legal citation to a law review is Mark J. Roe, "Corporate Strategic Reaction to Mass Tort," 72 *Virginia Law Review* 1 (1986), which means that the article "Corporate Strategic Reaction to Mass Tort" written by Mark J. Roe can be found in volume 72 of *Virginia Law Review* beginning on page 1.

Like a treatise, a Restatement is limited in its coverage to a single area of law. Restatements are the consequence of intensive study on a specific topic by legal scholars, culminating in a written statement of the law. That statement will include rules stated in bold type—often referred to as "black-letter law"—along with explanatory comments. The rules presented are usually synthesized from opinions of the courts in all jurisdictions. An example is *Restatement (Second) of Torts*.

APPLICATION TO ENVIRONMENTAL LAW

In addition to all the general sources just discussed, helpful special sources of the law are available in any given area of law. In environmental law, there are, of course, the federal statutes in the *U.S. Code* and *U.S. Code Annotated*. In addition, a good single source for environmental statutes is *West's Selected Environmental Statutes—Educational Edition*, which contains the most important statutes and is updated annually to account for new laws and amendments to existing laws.

The federal regulations are found in *Title 40* of the *Code of Federal Regulations*. Because there are so many environmental regulations, the number of volumes (fifteen at last count) was second only to the number of volumes needed for IRS tax regulations. As regulations are proposed and then finalized (before they are entered in the *Code of Federal Regulation*), they are published in the *Federal Register*.

Reading the *Federal Register* is a task few enjoy, and it is not an efficient way to keep up on regulatory developments. To keep up on new legal events, one can consult the Bureau of National Affair's (BNA's) *Environmental Reporter*. Each week it has a "Current Developments" section. Indeed, the BNA publishes a *Daily Environmental Reporter* to keep on top of environmental stories on all fronts—state, federal, and international legal developments, as well as news events. Other publications, such as *Inside EPA* published by Inside Washington Publishers, monitors news inside the EPA and news affecting the EPA, such as what is being rumored in the White House or in Congress about the EPA. Such publications are a mixture of facts and rumors, often supplied by personnel in the agency.

Environmental law opinions appear in the various reporters, such as the *Federal Supplement*, but because it is hard to sort through all of the opinions that appear in the reporters to find the ones on environmental law, it is better to consult a reporter such as *Environmental Law Reporter* published monthly by the Environmental Law Institute. That reporter contains summaries of pending litigation, new cases, settlement agreements, and unpublished decisions, all in the environmental area.

Numerous environmental law treatises exist, published by different companies. They include *The Law of Environmental Protection* by Sheldon Novick, published by Clark Boardman. West Publishing Company's *Environmental Law* by William Rodgers is a well-known hornbook. An introductory level book is *A Practical Guide to Environmental Law* by David Sive and Frank Friedman, published by ALI-ABA, which also recently published *The Environmental Law Manual*, a collection of articles by experts on different areas of environmental law.

There are dozens of environmental journals and magazines. The Environmental Law Institute publishes *Environmental Forum*, devoted to recent policy developments. The American Bar Association Section of Natural Resources, Energy and Environmental Law publishes *Natural Resources & Environment*, which contains technical but short articles about new developments. The EPA publishes the easily read *EPA Journal*. A number of law journals are devoted to environmental law, including *Ecology Law Quarterly*, *Columbia Journal of Environmental Law*, and *Harvard Environmental Law Journal*.

Each year, the Environmental Law Institute and the American Bar Association host environmental law conferences at which leading experts talk about recent developments and forthcoming events. The conferences usually publish the papers presented. Many law schools and state bar associations hold environmental law conferences either regularly or on special occasions. There is no lack of materials—it's just a matter of tracking them down!

Legal Research and the Internet

Effective legal research has moved beyond the dusty stacks of law libraries and into the unbounded corridors of the Internet. While traditional means for researching and understanding the law remain functional, many legal resources once available only through books or expensive and comparatively limited on-line services, such as Westlaw or Lexis/Nexis, can now be found publicly and virtually without cost on almost any personal computer via the Internet. This appendix is intended to be an introductory guide to researching the law on this burgeoning medium. Students possessing only limited Internet skills will benefit most from the information in this appendix, although students with a deeper Internet experience can also learn from its particularly legal focus.

Understanding the Internet

The Internet, once only a loose network of computers designed to facilitate communications between academic institutions and between government offices, is now accessible to the general public. It is fast becoming an indispensable research and communications tool in most professions. Because of its complexity and fairly technical nature, many people do not understand its unusual and noncentralized architecture and, consequently, cannot fully reap its benefits.

A unique feature of the Internet as a publication medium is that no one person or group is in charge of its content. Every Internet user is a potential publisher. Thus, the Internet offers not only an enormous and continually expanding amount of information but also a managerie of essentially useless information, at least from the perspective of the self-interested and narrowly focused legal researcher. The key to understanding the Internet for the purposes of legal research lies in learning to navigate it, since knowing how to find useful law-related materials is more valuable than archiving all the available law—a futile endeavor for any individual, given the rate at which law-related Internet resources increase.

With the information in this appendix and a little exploration, students with an interest in the law, particularly as it relates to business and commerce, should be able to find what they seek.

Locating Legal Resources

One of the primary vehicles for finding law on the Internet is the World Wide Web, also known as WWW, or simply the Web. The main repositories of legal information on the Web are web sites built and maintained by law schools, the government (state and federal), and independent organizations with specialized interests.

The web is the multimedia porthole to the Internet, blending text, graphics, and sound to communicate information. It is monikered "the Web" because it is structured to connect one web site to another around the globe through hyperlinks, thus creating a virtual web of resources.

The basic Web unit is the "Web page," a file that can be displayed graphically via "Web browsers" (programs used to access the Web) and that contains information on a variety of subjects. Web pages typically include hyperlinks (usually displayed as bold, colored, or italicized text) which, when clicked with the mouse pointer, will bring the user to another page of related information often from the same web site or a web site located hundreds or even thousands of miles away. Thus, following these hyperlinks, or simply links, allows the user to retrieve pages in a seemingly infinite amount of information located all over the globe. For example, if the user was viewing the American Flag Home Page, a link for "The Star-Spangled Banner" would likely be present. By clicking the words *Star-Spangled Banner*, the words of the song would then load onto the screen. Clicking from page to page and from site to site in this manner is known as "surfing the web."

Accessing the Web involves either running a Web browser program on a computer connected to the Internet through a university or government Internet server or having a personal account with a commercial access provider. Typically, Web browsers are Windows-based programs that allow the user to search, view, and print the contents of Web pages. *Netscape Navigator*, the browser produced by Netscape Communications, is the best known Web browser and consistently is at the forefront of setting industry standards. It can be downloaded free for academic use (http://home.netscape.com/). In addition to having a Web browser capability, *Netscape* contains a suite of other useful applications, such as an E-mail reader and a newsgroup reader which, as explained later, are also invaluable tools for other forms of Internet legal research.

The initial strategy behind performing successful legal research on the Web is for the student to first visit a few sites that provide selection of useful links for starting—or perhaps completing—most recent missions. If a particular Web page does not provide the desired information outright, its links can often be followed until an appropriate site is found. If this surfing technique does not provide an answer, a keyword search should be performed using one of the Internet's many search engines, such as *Yahoo* (http://yahoo.com/) or *Alta Vista* (http://altavista. digital.com/).

LAW SCHOOL RESOURCES

Most law schools now have web sites offering their students and the public access to legal information on the Internet. These sites are the best place to begin most legal research projects. One of the most comprehensive law school sites is the *Cornell Law School's Legal Information Institute* (LII) (http://www.law.cornell.edu/). LII publishes electronic versions of core materials in numerous areas of the law. It organizes legal material residing elsewhere on the Internet by offering a detailed set of tables outlining legal materials by topic and by the type or source of linked documents. Case law available through Cornell's LII site includes full-text version of all Supreme Court decisions since 1990, decisions of the U.S. courts of appeals, and decisions of specific state courts. Statutory law accessible through LII includes the Uniform Commercial Code (including Official Comments), the Copyright Act, the Patent Act, and the Federal Trademark Act. LII also has a hypertext version of the full U.S. Code and a growing number of state statutes on the Internet.

Other law school web sites providing useful research aids are *Indiana University's Virtual Library* (http://www.law.indiana.edu), *Washburn University's Reflaw* (http://law.wuacc. edu/washlaw/reflaw//), and *Chicago-Kent College of Law* (http://www.kentlaw.edu/ lawlinks/index.html).

GOVERNMENT RESOURCES

The U.S. government, one of the early developers and chief users of the Internet, provides citizens with a wealth of searchable material that would normally require spending hours in a library or waiting weeks to receive by regular mail. As a result of its pioneering work and its public access mandate, the U.S. government produces web sites that are excellent sources for full-text versions of statutory law, agency orders, and economic data.

The *U.S. Government Printing Office's* web site is an invaluable repository (http://www.access.gpo.gov/). The Government Printing Office (GPO) prints, binds, and distributes the publications of the Congress as well as the executive departments and agencies of the federal government. Distribution is increasingly accomplished via electronic media in accordance with Public Law 103-40, the Government Printing Office Electronic Information Access Enhancement Act of 1993. The GPO is probably the best place to locate any published government document, including the *U.S. Code*. The *Federal Register*, the *Congressional Record*, and other documents are also available for a fee.

The *Library of Congress* Web site (http://www.loc.gov/) allows the student to find virtually any material in the Library's collections. The entire Library catalog is searchable through this web site. The Library makes federal legislative information freely available over the Internet pursuant to a directive from the 104th Congress via the *Thomas* World-Wide-Web-based system (http://thomas.loc.gov/). The first *Thomas* database made available over the Internet was *Bill Text*, followed shortly by *Congressional Record Text, Bill Summary & Status, Hot Bills, Congressional Record Index*, and the *Constitution*. Enhancements in data and search-and-display capabilities have been continuously added for each database. The next major database to come up under *Thomas* will be the full text of Committee reports.

Federal departments or agencies having web sites can be found using the *Federal Web Locator* run by the Villanova Center for Information Law and Policy (http:// www.law.vill.edu/FedAgency/fedwebloc.html). The mission of this site is to provide Internet users with a central location on the WWW for locating federal government information. The *Federal Web Locator* has an integrated search engine to facilitate the research process. This site is a good place to visit during any research project relating to agency orders or opinions.

INDEPENDENT SOURCES

Although academia and the government have a substantial Internet presence, particularly with regard to web-based legal research, most web sites are authored and maintained by for-profit and nonprofit corporations, organizations, and individuals. These sites often provide much of the same information and links found on law school and government sites, but they also frequently provide specialized information in interesting research niches.

Law firm web sites typically are not good legal research sites. Most law firms use the Internet primarily as a means of disseminating a firm's resumes, usually providing little more than the firm's mission statement, attorney biographies, and descriptions of the firm's areas of practice. A notable exception is the web site operated by *Oppendahl* (http://www.opphendahl.com), which provides the Internet's most comprehensive repository of intellectual property law resources (patent, copyright, trademark, and trade secret law) in addition to making information available about the firm itself.

Recently, law-related commercial sites have begun appearing on the Web. Increasingly, these sites are becoming good resources for locating material published in law-related magazines, newspapers, or journals and for finding electronic supplements to their print materials.

Commercial web sites can also serve as an alternative way for lawyers from around the world to contact each other, identify opposing counsel, and find support services such as court reporters and expert witnesses. *LawLinks.Com* (http://lawlinks.com/lawatty.html), *The Practicing Attorney's Home Page* (http://www.legalethics.com), *Legal dot Net* (http://legal.net), and *Lexis Counsel Connect* (http://www.counsel.com) are all sites worth visiting when performing cyber-research. Because these sites were designed to eventually generate revenue for their custodians through subscriptions and advertising, commercial web sites offer a fresh stream of insightful and valuable content, even if they are not always comprehensive.

Law journals and law-related newspapers vary in their usefulness to the legal researcher. Law journals on the Web typically provide only excerpts or abstracts of their contents. Archived copies are rarely searchable. Newspapers that serve the legal industry, however, have been quick to recognize that the Internet can be used as a vehicle to market their products and sell subscriptions. In turn, they provide full-text versions of selected articles that appeared in the printed versions of their publications. The legal researcher can explore these sites via keyword search and download articles for free. *Law Journal Extra!*, run by the triumvirate of the *National Law Journal*, *New York Law Journal*, and *Law Technology Product News* (http:/www.ljx.com/), is the premier web site in this category.

Occasionally, Internet enthusiasts not affiliated with any company or organization create very useful web sites. These individuals, facile enough with the Internet to develop their own personal home pages, usually have a good grasp of the Web's potential as a reference and communications tool. Individual attorneys often author Web pages that are effective resources for legal research because they have performed the iterative screening and distilling of the Internet's many law-related offerings and provide links to sites that are beneficial to their fellow members of the bar and laypeople alike.

These Web pages are sometimes difficult to locate using standard Internet search techniques because the searchable sections of the pages contain links to the author's hobbies, favorite vacation spots, and curriculum vitae as well as to law-related sites. A couple of personal home pages are worth mentioning that are dedicated to providing valuable direction to business and the law on the Internet. In particular, *Doc Steen's Law & Economics* (http://www.pic.net/~docsteen/law_econ.htm) page logically organizes essential links for anyone conducting research in law, economics, or business. Similarly, *The Law and Economics Site* (http://www-leland.stanford.edu/~trtanley/lawecon.html), edited by Tim Stanley, offers many of the same links as *Doc Steen* but adds the versatility of a search engine to extract resources from the site. Most personal Web pages such as these allow the user to contact the site's author by E-mail, opening up another valuable aspect of the Internet: communication and collaboration.

COMMUNICATION AND COLLABORATION

The Internet's flexibility allows the legal researcher to communicate directly with attorneys, professors, judges, and other professionals in the legal field wherever they may be located around the world. This contact is a worthy research device, as students can ask questions of legal professionals and receive insightful guidance on virtually any topic. E-mail and the Usenet newsgroups are the most popular methods used for Internet communication.

E-mail is one of the oldest and most widely used forms of personal communication on the Internet. Most of the millions of people who use the Internet have their own E-mail address and use it mainly to send and receive messages. However, E-mail is also a formidable resource for difficult research issues, and the legal researcher should take time to learn its scope. In its simplest form, E-mail is similar to traditional mail—known in Internet parlance as snail mail—in that it is based on user-to-user information exchanges. It differs from snail mail in that information ordinarily is sent and received nearly instantaneously. E-mail is most often simply text, but added value comes from its ability to transfer program files, pictures, and, indeed, virtually any form of electronic data. A beneficial E-mail feature is the availability of mailing lists, especially with regard to rapidly changing law or especially obscure questions. E-mail mailing lists are akin to subject-based newsletters or traditional bulletin boards that post information on specific topics. Mailing lists from virtual communities on the Internet, allowing participants to engage in ongoing dialogue via personal computers.

Joining E-mail lists is simple, requiring only a subscription to the list's server. Two of the most inclusive collections of law-related mailing lists are compiled by Lyonette Louis-Jacques at the *University of Chicago Law School* (http://www.lcp.com/The-Legal-List/ TLL-home.html). These sources provide exhaustive lists of discussion groups, announcements-only lists, electronic journals, and newsletters on virtually every legal topic on the Internet. Both sites also detail the protocol for subscribing, sending messages, and unsubscribing from the lists.

It is an Internet tradition that as mailing lists grow in popularity and use, they often are graduated to a usenet newsgroup. Presently, there are approximately 20,000 Usenet newsgroups. In essence, a newsgroup is a collection of publicly posted E-mail messages strung together by topic in "threads." Although some newsgroups are moderated, most are not, and users are free to post their messages or simply observe this electronic exchange of ideas and information. If a legal researcher has a particular question about any legal or business-related topic, a newsgroup probably exists with a member who has the expertise to assist in answering the query.

Participation in newsgroup dialogue requires the use of specific software that locates the particular group of interest, displays posted messages to the group, and posts new messages. Most of the new Web browsers, however, also include an integrated newsreader. Other non-Web newsreaders are available over the Internet for free or at a very modest cost.

Most newsgroup software supports keyword searches to locate appropriate groups and to search their contents. Newsgroup names are organized using conventions that suggest the theme of the various groups. For example, newsgroups beginning with "biz." are generally about business topics. These broad designations are followed in turn by a hierarchy of progressively more focused designators. Following the previous example, "biz.stocks" groups are limited to discussions about securities issues.

The Usenet newsgroups are a rich source for law-related information. Unfortunately, since "law" is not a newsgroup identifier, finding the helpful newsgroups is a bit of a challenge. Legal researchers should therefore consult *The Legal List*, previously mentioned, as their initial guide to law and business-related newsgroups.

Other Resources

Law is inextricably and recursively meshed with commerce. Decisions made in either area affect the other. Thus, it is important for legal researchers to acquire a facility with the business-related resources on the Internet.

Because the Internet is constantly hyped as the next great arena of commerce, businesses have blanketed it with information. While some of it is useful, most of it is of as much value as the junk mail pamphlets you receive in your snail mailbox or the billboards you see along highways. Really useful resources can be hard to separate from all the hype. Students should, however, explore the available company data and news media sources.

Business Information

Business success depends heavily on receiving the right information on the real-time basis. The Internet is helpful in this regard, and, accordingly, cyberspace may be replacing the breakfast table and the commuter train as the place where people review the latest happenings in the global marketplace. Two noteworthy examples of this transition are the Web-based versions of *The Wall Street Journal* and *The Financial Data Finder*, famous business publications that are valuable information fonts about the economy, corporations, finance, and business news.

The Wall Street Journal's web site, *Money & Investing Update* (http://update. wsj.com/), provides subscribers (still a free service as of this writing) with the same information as the famous print version but without the annoyance of ink-stained fingers. In addition to offering full-text articles, *Money & Investing* offers a feature named the Corporate Briefing Book, a name or ticker-searchable database of company backgrounds, financial performance, stock price history, recent WSJ articles, and press releases. The Briefing Book contains continually updated data on over 4,000 public companies. Any legal research on the Internet that requires business information should begin at this site.

Just as law schools often provide cyber-researchers with helpful legal links, many finance departments publish Web sites dedicated to business and finance. Ohio State University's Department of Finance maintains the *Financial Data Finder* web site (http://www.cob.ohiostate.edu/dept/fin/osudata.htm), an effectively organized site pointing to a far-reaching array of business and economic information. While this site provides no original content, its curators have sifted through the maelstrom of useless information on the Internet and posted only sites offering commercial substance.

Thousands of businesses, big and small, have Web pages offering their mission statements, product descriptions, and annual reports. Larger companies, like IBM (http://www.ibm.com), also post press releases and messages from the company executives. The truth is, however, that most corporate sites are primarily marketing tools. For the legal researcher, these sources sometimes provide corporate America's reactions to and opinions regarding specific government policy measures or rules of law. Many corporate sites provide an E-mail address for a company official. The legal researcher can use this to learn how a company or industry is affected by specific legal issues. With a little creativity, one can often acquire information unattainable through traditional research methods. The best way to find corporate web sites is through *Yahoo* (http://yahoo.com), the well-known Internet directory. *Yahoo* has compiled a searchable list on the Internet of thousands of companies, thus making their web sites available with merely a click of the mouse.

News Information

Legal news is important to people outside the legal profession. Recall, for example, the media attention paid to the Exxon *Valdez* suit, the spilled cup of McDonald's coffee, and recent tobacco litigation. Just as major television networks and newspapers employ reporters specifically assigned to cover the developments of the American justice system, they also dedicate sections of their web sites to delivering legal news and commentary to the Internet public. In some ways, gathering news over the Internet is more amenable to legal research than watching a television broadcast or leafing through a newspaper. Internet-based news sources constantly update their information. The ability to capture the latest information on a subject in near real time is a robust advantage for the legal researcher. Facts can be checked against new legal developments, and data can be verified up to the last minute. Also, much of the information disseminated over broadcast media is lost over the airwaves unless the legal researcher decides to purchase a videotape or a transcript. News sources on the Internet alleviate this problem by providing downloadable transcripts and video clips of stories. The best sources for news and information on televisions and print also set the place for their competition on the Internet.

CNN Interactive (http://www.cnn.com/) integrate the contents of the all-news network's cable broadcasts into a WWW site. News, sports, weather, business information, and legal updates arrive at this site almost as quickly as they happen. For certain newsworthy topics, CNN Interactive provides hyperlinks to other sites that provide in-depth analysis and supplemental information.

Many major newspapers provide electronic versions of their printed copy that are free, at least for now. Of particular interest are *The Chicago Tribune* and *The Boston Globe* web sites, which are fully searchable, although only for each day's content. The legal researcher should use these sites to keep updated on current events.

The Internet: A Dynamic and Indispensable Research Tool

The Internet can no longer be ignored as a legal research tool. Its expanding reservoir of resources is becoming easier to navigate as search methods become more sophisticated and practical. Using the Internet efficiently, however, requires one to scale a somewhat steep learning curve, the slope of which is elevated by a confusing host of legal resources and set of communications protocols and conventions. This section strives to flatten that curve for the legal researcher.

Perhaps even more important for legal researchers than mastering the techniques to navigating the Internet is gaining the ability to recognize useful information when it is culled from cyberspace. For example, an *Alta Vista* search for contract law will yield an unmanageable number of web sites to explore. If the researcher has a workable knowledge of some of the nuances of contract law, the search can be narrowed or the less helpful sites rejected immediately. In other words, to separate the wheat from the chaff, the researcher needs the ability to identify what chaff looks like. The Internet can be a wonderful learning instrument, but in the context of legal research, it helps to first have some level of expertise in the research subject.

Complete the Internet exercises at the end of each chapter and spend some time surfing the Net on your own. Using the resources suggested here as a beacon, over time you will build a customized list of your own favorite Internet information fonts. The Internet, however, is and will continue to be a work in progress. Web sites and newsgroups will debut, evolve, and disappear seemingly at random as the medium matures. This is a part of Internet reality. Once the astute legal researcher has acquired a basic set of cyberspace instincts and skills, he or she will be able to keep abreast of this truly dynamic medium.

The Constitution of the United States of America

PREAMBLE

We the People of the United States, in Order to form a more perfect Union, establish Justice, insure domestic Tranquility, provide for the common defence, promote the general Welfare, and secure the Blessings of Liberty to ourselves and our Posterity, do ordain and establish this Constitution for the United States of America.

ARTICLE I

Section 1. All legislative Powers herein granted shall be vested in a Congress of the United States, which shall consist of a Senate and House of Representatives.

Section 2. The House of Representatives shall be composed of Members chosen every second Year by the People of the several States, and the Electors in each State shall have the Qualifications requisite for Electors of the most numerous Branch of the State Legislature.

No Person shall be a Representative who shall not have attained to the Age of twenty five Years, and been seven Years a Citizen of the United States, and who shall not, when elected, be an Inhabitant of that State in which he shall be chosen.

Representatives and direct Taxes shall be apportioned among the several States which may be included within this Union, according to their respective Numbers, which shall be determined by adding to the whole Number of free Persons, including those bound to Service for a Term of Years, and excluding Indians not taxed, three fifths of all other Persons. The actual Enumeration shall be made within three Years after the first Meeting of the Congress of the United States, and within every subsequent Term of ten Years, in such Manner as they shall by Law direct. The number of Representatives shall not exceed one for every thirty Thousand, but each State shall have at Least one Representative; and until such enumeration shall be made, the State of New Hampshire shall be entitled to chuse three, Massachusetts eight, Rhode Island and Providence Plantations one, Connecticut five, New York six, New Jersey four, Pennsylvania eight, Delaware one, Maryland six, Virginia ten, North Carolina five, South Carolina five, and Georgia three.

When vacancies happen in the Representation from any State, the Executive Authority thereof shall issue Writs of Election to fill such vacancies.

The House of Representatives shall chuse their Speaker and other Officers; and shall have the sole Power of Impeachment.

Section 3. The Senate of the United States shall be composed of two Senators from each State, chosen by the Legislature thereof, for six Years; and each Senator shall have one Vote.

Immediately after they shall be assembled in Consequence of the first Election, they shall be divided as equally as may be into three Classes. The Seats of the Senators of the first Class shall be vacated at the Expiration of the second Year, of the second Class at the Expiration of the fourth Year, and of the third Class at the Expiration of the sixth Year, so that one third may be chosen every second Year; and if Vacancies happen by Resignation, or otherwise, during the Recess of the Legislature of any State, the Executive thereof may make temporary Appointments until the next Meeting of the Legislature, which shall then fill such Vacancies.

No Person shall be a Senator who shall not have attained to the Age of thirty Years, and been nine Years a Citizen of the United States, and who shall not, when elected, be an Inhabitant of that State for which he shall be chosen.

The Vice President of the United States shall be President of the Senate, but shall have no Vote, unless they be equally divided.

The Senate shall chuse their other Officers, and also a President pro tempore, in the Absence of the Vice President, or when he shall exercise the Office of President of the United States.

The Senate shall have the sole power to try all Impeachments. When sitting for that Purpose, they shall be on Oath or Affirmation. When the President of the United States is tried, the Chief Justice shall preside: And no Person shall be convicted without the Concurrence of two thirds of the Members present.

Judgment in Cases of Impeachment shall not extend further than to removal from Office, and disqualification to hold and enjoy any Office of honor, Trust or Profit under the United States: but the Party convicted shall nevertheless be liable and subject to Indictment, Trial, Judgment and Punishment, according to Law.

Section 4. The Times, Places and Manner of holding Elections for Senators and Representatives, shall be prescribed in each State by the Legislature thereof: but the Congress may at any time by Law make or alter such Regulations, except as to the Places of chusing Senators.

The Congress shall assemble at least once in every Year, and such Meeting shall be on the first Monday in December, unless they shall by Law appoint a different Day.

Section 5. Each House shall be the Judge of the Elections, Returns and Qualifications of its own Members, and a Majority of each shall constitute a Quorum to do Business; but a smaller Number may adjourn from day to day, and may be authorized to compel the Attendance of absent Members, in such Manner, and under such Penalties as each House may provide.

Each House may determine the Rules of its Proceedings, punish its Members for disorderly Behaviour, and, with the Concurrence of two thirds, expel a Member.

Each House shall keep a Journal of its Proceedings, and from time to time publish the same, excepting such Parts as may in their Judgment require Secrecy; and the Yeas and Nays of the Members of either House on any question shall, at the Desire of one fifth of those Present, be entered on the Journal.

Neither House, during the Session of Congress, shall, without the Consent of the other, adjourn for more than three days, nor to any other Place than that in which the two Houses shall be sitting.

Section 6. The Senators and Representatives shall receive a Compensation for their Services, to be ascertained by Law, and paid out of the Treasury of the United States. They shall in all Cases, except Treason, Felony and Breach of the Peace, be privileged from Arrest during their Attendance at the Session of their respective Houses, and in going to and returning from the same; and for any Speech or Debate in either House, they shall not be questioned in any other Place.

No Senator or Representative shall, during the Time for which he was elected, be appointed to any civil Office under the Authority of the United States, which shall have been created, or the Emoluments whereof shall have been encreased during such time; and no Person holding any Office under the United States, shall be a Member of either House during his Continuance in Office.

Section 7. All Bills for raising Revenue shall originate in the House of Representatives; but the Senate may propose or concur with Amendments as on other Bills.

Every Bill which shall have passed the House of Representatives and the Senate, shall, before it become a Law, be presented to the President of the United States; If he approve he shall sign it, but if not he shall return it, with his Objections to that House in which it shall have originated, who shall enter the Objections at large on their Journal, and proceed to reconsider it. If after such Reconsideration two thirds of that House shall agree to pass the Bill, it shall be sent, together with the Objections, to the other House, by which it shall likewise be reconsidered, and if approved by two thirds of that House, it shall become a Law. But in all such Cases the Votes of both Houses shall be determined by Yeas and Nays, and the Names of the Persons voting for and against the Bill shall be entered on the Journal of each House respectively. If any Bill shall not be returned by the President within ten Days (Sundays excepted) after it shall have been presented to him, the Same shall be a Law, in like Manner as if he had signed it, unless the Congress by their Adjournment prevent its Return, in which Case it shall not be a Law.

Every Order, Resolution, or Vote to which the Concurrence of the Senate and House of Representatives may be necessary (except on a question of Adjournment) shall be presented to the President of the United States; and before the Same shall take Effect, shall be approved by him, or being disapproved by him, shall be repassed by two thirds of the Senate and House of Representatives, according to the Rules and Limitations prescribed in the Case of a Bill.

Section 8. The Congress shall have Power to lay and collect Taxes, Duties, Imposts and Excises, to pay the Debts and provide for the common Defence and general Welfare of the United States; but all Duties, Imposts and Excises shall be uniform throughout the United States;

To borrow Money on the credit of the United States;

To regulate Commerce with foreign Nations, and among the several States, and with the Indian Tribes;

To establish an uniform Rule of Naturalization, and uniform Laws on the subject of Bankruptcies throughout the United States;

To coin Money, regulate the Value thereof, and of foreign Coin, and fix the Standard of Weights and Measures;

To provide for the Punishment of counterfeiting the Securities and current Coin of the United States;

To establish Post Offices and post Roads;

To promote the Progress of Science and useful Arts, by securing for limited Times to Authors and Inventors the exclusive Right to their respective Writings and Discoveries;

To constitute Tribunals inferior to the supreme Court;

To define and punish Piracies and Felonies committed on the high Seas, and Offenses against the Law of Nations;

To declare War, grant Letters of Marque and Reprisal, and make Rules concerning Captures on Land and Water;

To raise and support Armies, but no Appropriation of Money to that Use shall be for a longer Term than two Years;

To provide and maintain a Navy;

To make Rules for the Government and Regulation of the land and naval Forces;

To provide for calling forth the Militia to execute the Laws of the Union, suppress Insurrections and repel Invasions;

To provide for organizing, arming, and disciplining, the Militia, and for governing such Part of them as may be employed in the Service of the United States, reserving to the States respectively, the Appointment of the Officers, and the Authority of training the Militia according to the discipline prescribed by Congress;

To exercise exclusive Legislation in all Cases whatsoever, over such District (not exceeding ten Miles square) as may, by Cession of particular States, and the Acceptance of Congress, become the Seat of the Government of the United States, and to exercise like Authority over all Places purchased by the Consent of the Legislature of the State in which the Same shall be, for the Erection of Forts, Magazines, Arsenals, dock-Yards, and other needful Buildings;—And

To make all Laws which shall be necessary and proper for carrying into Execution the foregoing Powers, and all other Powers vested by this Constitution in the Government of the United States, or in any Department or Officer thereof.

Section 9. The Migration or Importation of such Persons as any of the States now existing shall think proper to admit, shall not be prohibited by the Congress prior to the Year one thousand eight hundred and eight, but a Tax or Duty may be imposed on such Importation, not exceeding ten dollars for each Person.

The Privilege of the Writ of Habeas Corpus shall not be suspended, unless when in Cases of Rebellion or Invasion the public Safety may require it.

No Bill of Attainder or ex post facto Law shall be passed.

No Capitation, or other direct, Tax shall be laid, unless in Proportion to the Census or Enumeration herein before directed to be taken.

No Tax or Duty shall be laid on Articles exported from any State.

No Preference shall be given by any Regulation of Commerce or Revenue to the Ports of one State over those of another; nor shall Vessels bound to, or from, one State, be obliged to enter, clear, or pay Duties in another.

No Money shall be drawn from the Treasury, but in Consequence of Appropriations made by Laws; and a regular Statement and Account of the Receipts and Expenditures of all public Money shall be published from time to time.

No Title of Nobility shall be granted by the United States: And no Person holding any Office of Profit or Trust under them, shall, without the Consent of the Congress, accept of any present, Emolument, Office, or Title, of any kind whatever, from any King, Prince, or foreign State.

Section 10. No State shall enter into any Treaty, Alliance, or Confederation; grant Letters of Marque and Reprisal; coin Money; emit Bills of Credit; make any Thing but gold and silver Coin a Tender in Payment of Debts; pass any Bill of Attainder, ex post facto Law, or Law impairing the Obligation of Contracts, or grant any Title of Nobility.

No State shall, without the Consent of the Congress, lay any Imposts or Duties on Imports or Exports, except what may be absolutely necessary for executing its inspection Laws: and the net Produce of all Duties and Imposts, laid by any State on Imports or

Exports, shall be for the Use of the Treasury of the United States; and all such Laws shall be subject to the Revision and Controul of the Congress.

No State shall, without the Consent of Congress, lay any Duty of Tonnage, keep Troops, or Ships of War in time of Peace, enter into any Agreement or Compact with another State, or with a foreign Power, or engage in War, unless actually invaded, or in such imminent Danger as will not admit of delay.

ARTICLE II

Section 1. The executive Power shall be vested in a President of the United States of America. He shall hold his Office during the Term of four Years, and, together with the Vice President, chosen for the same Term, be elected, as follows:

Each State shall appoint, in such Manner as the Legislature thereof may direct, a Number of Electors, equal to the whole Number of Senators and Representatives to which the State may be entitled in the Congress: but no Senator or Representative, or Person holding an Office of Trust or Profit under the United States, shall be appointed an Elector.

The Electors shall meet in their respective States, and vote by Ballot for two Persons, of whom one at least shall not be an Inhabitant of the same State with themselves. And they shall make a List of all the Persons voted for, and of the Number of Votes for each; which List they shall sign and certify, and transmit sealed to the Seat of the Government of the United States, directed to the President of the Senate. The President of the Senate shall, in the Presence of the Senate and House of Representatives, open all the Certificates, and the Votes shall then be counted. The Person having the greatest Number of Votes shall be the President, if such Number be a Majority of the whole Number of Electors appointed; and if there be more than one who have such Majority, and have an equal Number of Votes, then the House of Representatives shall immediately chuse by Ballot one of them for President; and if no Person have a Majority, then from the five highest on the List the said House shall in like Manner chuse the President. But in chusing the President, the Votes shall be taken by States, the Representation from each State having one Vote; a quorum for this Purpose shall consist of a Member or Members from two thirds of the States, and a Majority of all the States shall be necessary to a Choice. In every Case, after the Choice of the President, the Person having the greatest Number of Votes of the Electors shall be the Vice President. But if there should remain two or more who have equal Votes, the Senate shall chuse from them by Ballot the Vice President.

The Congress may determine the Time of chusing the Electors, and the Day on which they shall give their Votes; which Day shall be the same throughout the United States.

No Person except a natural born Citizen, or a Citizen of the United States, at the time of the Adoption of this Constitution, shall be eligible to the Office of President; neither shall any Person be eligible to that Office who shall not have attained to the Age of thirty five Years, and been fourteen Years a Resident within the United States.

In Case of the Removal of the President from Office, or of his Death, Resignation, or Inability to discharge the Powers and Duties of the said Office, the Same shall devolve on the Vice President, and the Congress may by Law provide for the Case of Removal, Death, Resignation or Inability, both of the President and Vice President, declaring what Officer shall then act as President, and such Officer shall act accordingly, until the Disability be removed, or a President shall be elected.

The President shall, at stated Times, receive for his Services, a Compensation, which shall neither be increased nor diminished during the Period for which he shall have been elected, and he shall not receive within that Period any other Emolument from the United States, or any of them.

Before he enter on the Execution of his Office, he shall take the following Oath or Affirmation:—"I do solemnly swear (or affirm) that I will faithfully execute the Office of President of the United States, and will to the best of my Ability, preserve, protect and defend the Constitution of the United States."

Section 2. The President shall be Commander in Chief of the Army and Navy of the United States, and of the Militia of the several States, when called into the actual Service of the United States; he may require the Opinion, in writing, of the principal Officer in each of the executive Departments, upon any Subject relating to the Duties of their respective Offices, and he shall have Power to grant Reprieves and Pardons for Offences against the United States, except in Cases of Impeachment.

He shall have Power, by and with the Advice and Consent of the Senate, to make Treaties, providing two thirds of the Senators present concur; and he shall nominate, and by and with the Advice and Consent of the Senate, shall appoint Ambassadors, other public Ministers and Consuls, Judges of the supreme Court, and all other Officers of the United States, whose Appointments are not herein otherwise provided for, and which shall be established by Law: but the Congress may by Law vest the Appointment of such inferior Officers, as they think proper, in the President alone, in the Courts of Law, or in the Heads of Departments.

The President shall have Power to fill up all Vacancies that may happen during the Recess of the Senate, by granting Commissions which shall expire at the End of their next Session.

Section 3. He shall from time to time give to the Congress Information of the State of the Union, and recommend to their Consideration such Measures as he shall judge necessary and expedient; he may, on extraordinary Occasions, convene both Houses, or either of them, and in Case of Disagreement between them, with Respect to the Time of Adjournment, he may adjourn them to such Time as he shall think proper; he shall receive Ambassadors and other public Ministers; he shall take Care that the Laws be faithfully executed, and shall Commission all the Officers of the United States.

Section 4. The President, Vice President and all civil Officers of the United States, shall be removed from Office on Impeachment for, and Conviction of, Treason, Bribery, or other high Crimes and Misdemeanors.

ARTICLE III

Section 1. The judicial Power of the United States, shall be vested in one supreme Court, and in such inferior Courts as the Congress may from time to time ordain and establish. The Judges, both of the supreme and inferior Courts, shall hold their Offices during good Behaviour, and shall, at stated Times, receive for their Services, a Compensation, which shall not be diminished during their Continuance in Office.

Section 2. The judicial Power shall extend to all Cases, in Law and Equity, arising under this Constitution, the Laws of the United States, and Treaties made, or which shall be made, under their Authority;—to all Cases affecting Ambassadors, other public Ministers and Consuls;—to all Cases of admiralty and maritime Jurisdiction;—to Controversies to which the United States shall be a Party;—to Controversies between two or more States;—between a State and Citizens of another State;—between Citizens of different States;—between Citizens of the same State claiming Lands under Grants of different States, and between a State, or the Citizens thereof, and foreign States, Citizens or Subjects.

In all Cases affecting Ambassadors, other public Ministers and Consuls, and those in which a State shall be Party, the supreme Court shall have original Jurisdiction. In all the other Cases before mentioned, the supreme Court shall have appellate Jurisdiction, both as to Law and Fact, with such Exceptions, and under such Regulations as the Congress shall make.

The Trial of all Crimes, except in Cases of Impeachment, shall be by Jury; and such Trial shall be held in the State where the said Crimes shall have been committed; but when not committed within any State, the Trial shall be at such Place or Places as the Congress may by Law have directed.

Section 3. Treason against the United States, shall consist only in levying War against them, or in adhering to their Enemies, giving them Aid and Comfort. No Person shall be convicted of Treason unless on the Testimony of two Witnesses to the same overt Act, or on Confession in open Court.

The Congress shall have Power to declare the Punishment of Treason, but no Attainder of Treason shall work Corruption of Blood, or Forfeiture except during the Life of the Person attainted.

ARTICLE IV

Section 1. Full Faith and Credit shall be given in each State to the public Acts, Records, and judicial Proceedings of every other State. And the Congress may by general Laws prescribe the Manner in which such Acts, Records and Proceedings shall be proved, and the Effect thereof.

Section 2. The Citizens of each State shall be entitled to all Privileges and Immunities of Citizens in the several States.

A Person charged in any State with Treason, Felony, or other Crime, who shall flee from Justice, and be found in another State, shall on Demand of the executive Authority of the State from which he fled, be delivered up, to be removed to the State having Jurisdiction of the Crime.

No Person held to Service or Labour in one State, under the Laws thereof, escaping into another, shall, in Consequence of any Law or Regulation therein, be discharged from such Service or Labour, but shall be delivered up on Claim of the Party to whom such Service or Labour may be due.

Section 3. New States may be admitted by the Congress into this Union; but no new State shall be formed or erected within the Jurisdiction of any other State; nor any State be formed by the Junction of two or more States, or Parts of States, without the Consent of the Legislatures of the States concerned as well as of the Congress.

The Congress shall have Power to dispose of and make all needful Rules and Regulations respecting the Territory or other Property belonging to the United States; and nothing in this Constitution shall be so construed as to Prejudice any Claims of the United States, or of any particular State.

Section 4. The United States shall guarantee to every State in this Union a Republican Form of the Government, and shall protect each of them against Invasion; and on Application of the Legislature, or of the Executive (when the Legislature cannot be convened) against domestic Violence.

ARTICLE V

The Congress, whenever two thirds of both Houses shall deem it necessary, shall propose Amendments to this Constitution, or, on the Application of the Legislatures of two thirds of the several States, shall call a Convention for proposing Amendments, which, in either Case, shall be valid to all Intents and Purposes, as Part of this Constitution, when ratified by the Legislatures of three fourths of the several States, or by Conventions in three fourths thereof, as the one or the other Mode of Ratification may be proposed by the Congress; Provided that no Amendment which may be made prior to the Year One thousand eight hundred and eight shall in any Manner affect the first and fourth Clauses in the Ninth Section of the first Article; and that no State, without its Consent, shall be deprived of its equal Suffrage in the Senate.

All Debts contracted and Engagements entered into, before the Adoption of this Constitution, shall be as valid against the United States under this Constitution, as under the Confederation.

This Constitution, and the Laws of the United States which shall be made in Pursuance thereof; and all Treaties made, or which shall be made, under the Authority of the United States, shall be the supreme Law of the Land; and the Judges in every State shall be bound thereby, any Thing in the Constitution or Laws of any State to the Contrary notwithstanding.

The Senators and Representatives before mentioned, and the Members of the several State Legislatures, and all executive and judicial Officers, both of the United States and of the several States, shall be bound by Oath or Affirmation, to support this Constitution; but no religious Test shall ever be required as a Qualification to any Office or public Trust under the United States.

ARTICLE VII

The Ratification of the Conventions of nine States, shall be sufficient for the Establishment of this Constitution between the States so ratifying the Same.

Amendment I [1791]
Congress shall make no law respecting an establishment of religion, or prohibiting the free exercise thereof; or abridging the freedom of speech, or the press; or the right of the people peaceably to assemble, and to petition the Government for a redress of grievances.

Amendment II [1791]
A well regulated Militia, being necessary to the security for a free State, the right of the people to keep and bear Arms, shall not be infringed.

Amendment III [1791]
No Soldier shall, in time of peace be quartered in any house, without the consent of the Owner, nor in time of war, but in a manner to be prescribed by law.

Amendment IV [1791]
The right of the people to be secure in their persons, houses, papers, and effects, against unreasonable searches and seizures, shall not be violated, and no Warrants shall issue, but upon probable cause, supported by Oath or affirmation, and particularly describing the place to be searched, and the persons or things to be seized.

Amendment V [1791]
No person shall be held to answer for a capital, or otherwise infamous crime, unless on a presentment or indictment of a Grand Jury, except in cases arising in the land or naval forces, or in the Militia, when in actual service in time of War or public danger; nor shall any person be subject for the same offence to be twice put in jeopardy of life or limb; nor

shall be compelled in any criminal case to be a witness against himself, nor be deprived of life, liberty, or property, without due process of law; nor shall private property be taken for public use, without just compensation.

Amendment VI [1791]

In all criminal prosecutions, the accused shall enjoy the right to a speedy and public trial, by an impartial jury of the State and district wherein the crime shall have been committed, which district shall have been previously ascertained by law, and to be informed of the nature and cause of the accusation; to be confronted with the Witnesses against him; to have compulsory process for obtaining witnesses in his favor, and to have the Assistance of counsel for his defence.

Amendment VII [1791]

In Suits at common law, where the value in controversy shall exceed twenty dollars, the right of trial by jury shall be preserved, and no fact tried by a jury, shall be otherwise re-examined in any Court of the United States, than according to the rules of the common law.

Amendment VIII [1791]

Excessive bail shall not be required, nor excessive fines imposed, nor cruel and unusual punishments inflicted.

Amendment IX [1791]

The enumeration in the Constitution, of certain rights, shall not be construed to deny or disparage others retained by the people.

Amendment X [1791]

The powers not delegated to the United States by the Constitution, nor prohibited by it to the States, are reserved to the States respectively, or to the people.

Amendment XI [1798]

The Judicial power of the United States shall not be construed to extend to any suit in law or equity, commenced or prosecuted against one of the United States by Citizens of another State, or by Citizens or Subjects of any Foreign State.

Amendment XII [1804]

The Electors shall meet in their respective states and vote by ballot for President and Vice-President, one of whom, at least, shall not be an inhabitant of the same state with themselves; they shall name in their ballots the person voted for as President, and in distinct ballots the person voted for as Vice-President, and they shall make distinct lists of all persons voted for as President, and of all persons voted for as Vice-President, and of the number of votes for each, which lists they shall sign and certify, and transmit sealed to the seat of the government of the United States, directed to the President of the Senate;—The President of the Senate shall, in the presence of the Senate and House of Representatives, open all the certificates and the votes shall then be counted;—The person having the greatest number of votes for President, shall be the President, if such number be a majority of the whole number of Electors appointed; and if no person have such majority, then from the persons having the highest numbers not exceeding three on the list of those voted for as President, the House of Representatives shall choose immediately, by ballot, the President. But in choosing the President, the votes shall be taken by states, the representation from each state having one vote; a quorum for this purpose shall consist of a member or members from two-thirds of the states, and a majority of all the states shall be necessary to a choice. And if the House of Representatives shall not choose a President whenever the right of choice shall devolve upon them, before the fourth day of March next following, then the Vice-President shall act as President, as in the case of the death or other constitutional disability of the President. The person having the greatest number of votes as Vice-President, shall be the Vice-President, if such number be a majority of the whole number of Electors appointed, and if no person have a majority, then from the two highest numbers on the list, the Senate shall choose the Vice-President; a quorum for the purpose shall consist of two-thirds of the whole number of Senators, and a majority of the whole number shall be necessary to a choice. But no person constitutionally ineligible to the office of President shall be eligible to that of the Vice-President of the United States.

Amendment XIII [1865]

Section 1. Neither slavery nor involuntary servitude, except as a punishment for crime whereof the party shall have been duly convicted, shall exist within the United States, or any place subject to their jurisdiction.

Section 2. Congress shall have power to enforce this article by appropriate legislation.

Amendment XIV [1868]

Section 1. All persons born or naturalized in the United States, and subject to the jurisdiction thereof, are citizens of the United States and of the State wherein they reside. No State shall make or enforce any law which shall abridge the privileges or immunities of citizens of the United States; nor shall any State deprive any person of life, liberty, or property, without due process of law; nor deny to any person within its jurisdiction the equal protection of the laws.

Section 2. Representatives shall be appointed among the several States according to their respective numbers, counting the whole number of persons in each State, excluding Indians not taxed. But when the right to vote at any election for the choice of electors for President and Vice President of the United States, Representatives in Congress, the Executive and Judicial officers of a State, or the members of the Legislature thereof, is denied to any of the male inhabitants of such State, being twenty-one years of age, and citizens of the United States, or in any way abridged, except for participation in rebellion, or other crime, the basis of representation therein shall be reduced in the proportion which the number of such male citizens shall bear to the whole number of male citizens twenty-one years of age in such State.

Section 3. No person shall be a Senator or Representative in Congress, or elector of President and Vice President, or hold any office, civil or military, under the United States, or under any State, who, having previously taken an oath, as a member of Congress, or as an officer of the United States, or as a member of any State legislature, or as an executive or judicial officer of any State, to support the Constitution of the United States, shall have engaged in insurrection or rebellion against the same, or given aid or comfort to the enemies thereof. But Congress may by a vote of two-thirds of each House, remove such disability.

Section 4. The validity of the public debt of the United States, authorized by law, including debts incurred for payment of pensions and bounties for services in suppressing insurrection or rebellion, shall not be questioned. But neither the United States nor any State shall assume or pay any debt or obligation incurred in aid of insurrection or rebellion against the United States, or any claim for the loss or emancipation of any slave; but all such debts, obligations and claims shall be held illegal and void.

Section 5. The Congress shall have power to enforce, by appropriate legislation, the provisions of this article.

Amendment XV [1870]

Section 1. The right of citizens of the United States to vote shall not be denied or abridged by the United States or by any State on account of race, color, or previous condition of servitude.

Section 2. The Congress shall have power to enforce this article by appropriate legislation.

Amendment XVI [1913]

The Congress shall have power to lay and collect taxes on incomes, from whatever source derived, without apportionment among the several States, and without regard to any census or enumeration.

Amendment XVII [1913]

The Senate of the United States shall be composed of two Senators from each State, elected by the people thereof, for six years; and each Senator shall have one vote. The electors in each State shall have the qualifications requisite for electors of the most numerous branch of the State legislatures.

When vacancies happen in the representation of any State in the Senate, the executive authority of each State shall issue writs of election to fill such vacancies; *Provided*, That the legislature of any State may empower the executive thereof to make temporary appointments until the people fill the vacancies by election as the legislature may direct.

This amendment shall not be so construed as to affect the election or term of any Senator chosen before it becomes valid as part of the Constitution.

Amendment XVIII [1919]

Section 1. After one year from the ratification of this article the manufacture, sale, or transportation of intoxicating liquors within, the importation thereof into, or the exportation thereof from the United States and all territory subject to the jurisdiction thereof for beverage purposes is hereby prohibited.

Section 2. The Congress and the several States shall have concurrent power to enforce this article by appropriate legislation.

Section 3. This article shall be inoperative unless it shall have been ratified as an amendment to the Constitution by the legislatures of the several States, as provided in the Constitution, within seven years from the date of the submission hereof to the States by the Congress.

Amendment XIX [1920]

The right of citizens of the United States to vote shall not be denied or abridged by the United States or by any State on account of sex.

Congress shall have power to enforce this article by appropriate legislation.

Amendment XX [1933]

Section 1. The terms of the President and Vice President shall end at noon on the 20th day of January, and the terms of Senators and Representatives at noon on the 3d day of January, of the years in which such terms would have ended if this article had not been ratified; and the terms of their successors shall then begin.

Section 2. The Congress shall assemble at least once every year, and such meeting shall begin at noon on the 3d day of January, unless they shall by law appoint a different day.

Section 3. If, at the time fixed for the beginning of the term of the President, the President elect shall have died, the Vice President elect shall become President. If a President shall not have been chosen before the time fixed for the beginning of his term, or if the President elect shall have failed to qualify, then the Vice President elect shall act as President until a President shall have qualified; and the Congress may by law provide for the case wherein neither a President elect nor a Vice President elect shall have qualified, declaring who shall then act as President, or the manner in which one who is to act shall be selected, and such person shall act accordingly until a President or Vice President shall have qualified.

Section 4. The Congress may by law provide for the case of the death of any of the persons from whom the House of Representatives may choose a President whenever the right of choice shall have devolved upon them, and for the case of the death of any of the persons from whom the Senate may choose a Vice President whenever the right of choice shall have devolved upon them.

Section 5. Sections 1 and 2 shall take effect on the 15th day of October following the ratification of this article.

Section 6. This article shall be inoperative unless it shall have been ratified as an amendment to the Constitution by the legislatures of three-fourths of the several States within seven years from the date of its submission.

Amendment XXI [1933]

Section 1. The eighteenth article of amendment to the Constitution of the United States is hereby repealed.

Section 2. The transportation or importation into any State, Territory, or possession of the United States for delivery or use therein of intoxicating liquors, in violation of the laws thereof, is hereby prohibited.

Section 3. This article shall be inoperative unless it shall have been ratified as an amendment to the Constitution by conventions in the several States, as provided in the Constitution, within seven years from the date of the submission hereof to the States by the Congress.

Amendment XXII [1951]

Section 1. No person shall be elected to the office of the President more than twice, and no person who has held the office of President, or acted as President, for more than two years of a term to which some other person was elected President shall be elected to the office of the President more than once. But this Article shall not apply to any person holding the office of President when this Article was proposed by the Congress, and shall not prevent any person who may be holding the office of President, or acting as President, during the term within which this Article becomes operative from holding the office of President or acting as President during the remainder of such term.

Section 2. This article shall be inoperative unless it shall have been ratified as an amendment to the Constitution by the legislatures of three-fourths of the several States within seven years from the date of its submission to the States by the Congress.

Amendment XXIII [1961]

Section 1. The District constituting the seat of Government of the United States shall appoint in such manner as the Congress may direct:

A number of electors of President and Vice President equal to the whole number of Senators and Representatives in Congress to which the District would be entitled if it were a State, but in no event more than the least populous State; they shall be in addition to those appointed by the States, but they shall be considered, for the purposes of the election of President and Vice President, to be electors appointed by a State; and they shall meet in the District and perform such duties as provided by the twelfth article of amendment.

Section 2. The Congress shall have power to enforce this article by appropriate legislation.

Amendment XXIV [1964]

Section 1. The right of citizens of the United States to vote in any primary or other election for President or Vice President, for electors for President or Vice President, or for Senator or Representative in Congress, shall not be denied or abridged by the United States or any State by reason of failure to pay any poll tax or other tax.

Section 2. The Congress shall have power to enforce this article by appropriate legislation.

Amendment XXV [1967]

Section 1. In case of the removal of the President from office or of his death or resignation, the Vice President shall become President.

Section 2. Whenever there is a vacancy in the office of the Vice President, the President shall nominate a Vice President who shall take office upon confirmation by a majority vote of both Houses of Congress.

Section 3. Whenever the President transmits to the President pro tempore of the Senate and the Speaker of the House of Representatives his written declaration that he is unable to discharge the powers and duties of his office, and until he transmits to them a written declaration to the contrary, such powers and duties shall be discharged by the Vice President as Acting President.

Section 4. Whenever the Vice President and a majority of either the principal officers of the executive departments or of such other body as Congress may by law provide, transmit to the President pro tempore of the Senate and the Speaker of the House of Representatives their written declaration that the President is unable to discharge the powers and duties of his office, the Vice President shall immediately assume the powers and duties of the office as Acting President.

Thereafter, when the President transmits to the President pro tempore of the Senate and the Speaker of the House of Representatives his written declaration that no inability exists, he shall resume the powers and duties of his office unless the Vice President and a majority of either the principal officers of the executive department or of such other body as Congress may by law provide, transmit within four days to the President pro tempore of the Senate and the Speaker of the House of Representatives their written declaration that the President is unable to discharge the powers and duties of his office. Thereupon Congress shall decide the issue, assembling within forty-eight hours for that purpose if not in session. If the Congress, within twenty-one days after receipt of the latter written declaration, or, if Congress is not in session, within twenty-one days after Congress is required to assemble, determines by two-thirds vote of both Houses that the President is unable to discharge the powers and duties of his office, the Vice President shall continue to discharge the same as Acting President; otherwise, the President shall resume the powers and duties of his office.

Amendment XXVI [1971]

Section 1. The right of citizens of the United States, who are eighteen years of age or older, to vote shall not be denied or abridged by the United States or by any State on account of age.

Section 2. The Congress shall have power to enforce this article by appropriate legislation.

Amendment XXVII [1992]

No law varying the compensation for the services of the senators and representatives shall take effect, until an election of representatives shall have intervened.

The Uniform Commercial Code (Excerpts)

ARTICLE 2. SALES

Part 1 **Short Title, General Construction and Subject Matter**

Section 2—101. **Short Title.**
This Article shall be known and may be cited as Uniform Commercial Code—Sales.

Section 2—102. **Scope; Certain Security and Other Transactions Excluded From This Article.**
Unless the context otherwise requires, this Article applies to transactions in goods; it does not apply to any transaction which although in the form of an unconditional contract to sell or present sale is intended to operate only as a security transaction nor does this Article impair or repeal any statute regulating sales to consumers, farmers or other specified classes of buyers.

Section 2—103. **Definitions and Index of Definitions.**
(1) In this Article unless the context otherwise requires
   (a) "Buyer" means a person who buys or contracts to buy goods.
   (b) "Good faith" in the case of a merchant means honesty in fact and the observance of reasonable commercial standards of fair dealing in the trade.
   (c) "Receipt" of goods means taking physical possession of them.
   (d) "Seller" means a person who sells or contracts to sell goods.

Section 2—104. **Definitions: "Merchant"; "Between Merchants"; "Financing Agency".**
(1) "Merchant" means a person who deals in goods of the kind or otherwise by his occupation holds himself out as having knowledge or skill peculiar to the practices or goods involved in the transaction or to whom such knowledge or skill may be attributed by his employment of an agent or broker or other intermediary who by his occupation holds himself out as having such knowledge or skill.
(2) "Financing agency" means a bank, finance company or other person who in the ordinary course of business makes advances against goods or documents of title or who by arrangement with either the seller or the buyer intervenes in ordinary course to make or collect payment due or claimed under the contract for sale, as by purchasing or paying the seller's draft or making advances against it or by merely taking it for collection whether or not documents of title accompany the draft. "Financing agency" includes also a bank or other person who

similarly intervenes between persons who are in the position of seller and buyer in respect to the goods (Section 2—707).

(3) "Between merchants" means in any transaction with respect to which both parties are chargable with the knowledge or skill of merchants.

Section 2—105. **Definitions: Transferability; "Goods"; "Future" Goods; "Lot"; "Commercial Unit".**

(1) "Goods" means all things (including specially manufactured goods) which are movable at the time of identification to the contract for sale other than the money in which the price is to be paid, investment securities (Article 8) and things in action. "Goods" also includes the unborn young of animals and growing crops and other identified things attached to realty as described in the section on goods to be severed from realty (Section 2—107).

(2) Goods must be both existing and identified before any interest in them can pass. Goods which are not both existing and identified are "future" goods. A purported present sale of future goods or of any interest therein operates as a contract to sell.

(3) There may be a sale of a part interest in existing identified goods.

(4) An undivided share in an identified bulk of fungible goods is sufficiently identified to be sold although the quantity of the bulk is not determined. Any agreed proportion of such a bulk or any quantity thereof agreed upon by number, weight or other measure may to the extent of the seller's interest in the bulk be sold to the buyer who then becomes an owner in common.

(5) "Lot" means a parcel or a single article which is the subject matter of a separate sale or delivery, whether or not it is sufficient to perform the contract.

(6) "Commercial unit" means such a unit of goods as by commercial usage is a single whole for purposes of sale and division of which materially impairs its character or value on the market or in use. A commercial unit may be a single article (as a machine) or a set of articles (as a suite of furniture or an assortment of sizes) or a quantity (as a bale, gross, or carload) or any other unit treated in use or in the relevant market as a single whole.

Section 2—106. **Definitions: "Contract"; "Agreement"; "Contract for Sale"; "Sale"; "Present Sale"; "Conforming" to Contract; "Termination"; "Cancellation".**

(1) In this Article unless the context otherwise requires "contract" and "agreement" are limited to those relating to the present or future sale of goods. "Contract for sale" includes both a present sale of goods and a contract to sell goods at a future time. A "sale" consists in the passing of title from the seller to the buyer for a price (Section 2—401). A "present sale" means a sale which is accomplished by the making of the contract.

(2) Goods or conduct including any part of a performance are "conforming" or conform to the contract when they are in accordance with the obligations under the contract.

(3) "Termination" occurs when either party pursuant to a power created by agreement or law puts an end to the contract otherwise than for its breach. On "termination" all obligations which are still executory on both sides are discharged but any right based on prior breach or performance survives.

(4) "Cancellation" occurs when either party puts an end to the contract for breach by the other and its effect is the same as that of "termination" except that the cancelling party also retains any remedy for breach of the whole contract or any unperformed balance.

Part 2 **Form, Formation and Readjustment of Contract**

Section 2—201. **Formal Requirements; Statute of Frauds.**

(1) Except as otherwise provided in this section a contract for the sale of goods for the price of $500 or more is not enforceable by way of action or defense unless there is some writing sufficient to indicate that a contract for sale has been made between the parties and signed by the party against whom enforcement is sought or by his authorized agent or broker. A

writing is not insufficient because it omits or incorrectly states a term agreed upon but the contract is not enforceable under this paragraph beyond the quantity of goods shown in such writing.

(2) Between merchants if within a reasonable time a writing in confirmation of the contract and sufficient against the sender is received and the party receiving it has reason to know its contents, its satisfies the requirements of subsection (1) against such party unless written notice of objection to its contents is given within ten days after it is received.

(3) A contract which does not satisfy the requirements of subsection (1) but which is valid in other respects is enforceable

  (a) if the goods are to be specially manufactured for the buyer and are not suitable for sale to others in the ordinary course of the seller's business and the seller, before notice of repudiation is received and under circumstances which reasonably indicate that the goods are for the buyer, has made either a substantial beginning of their manufacture or commitments for their procurement; or

  (b) if the party against whom enforcement is sought admits in his pleading, testimony or otherwise in court that a contract for sale was made, but the contract is not enforceable under this provision beyond the quantity of goods admitted; or

  (c) with respect to goods for which payment has been made and accepted or which have been received and accepted (Sec. 2—606).

Section 2—202. **Final Written Expression: Parol or Extrinsic Evidence.**

Terms with respect to which the confirmatory memoranda of the parties agree or which are otherwise set forth in a writing intended by the parties as a final expression of their agreement with respect to such terms as are included therein may not be contradicted by evidence of any prior agreement or of a contemporaneous oral agreement but may be explained or supplemented

  (a) by course of dealing or usage of trade (Section 1—205) or by course of performance (Section 2—208); and

  (b) by evidence of consistent additional terms unless the court finds the writing to have been intended also as a complete and exclusive statement of the terms of the agreement.

Section 2—203. **Seals Inoperative.**

The affixing of a seal to a writing evidencing a contract for sale or an offer to buy or sell goods does not constitute the writing a sealed instrument and the law with respect to sealed instruments does not apply to such a contract or offer.

Section 2—204. **Formation in General.**

(1) A contract for sale of goods may be made in any manner sufficient to show agreement, including conduct by both parties which recognizes the existence of such a contract.

(2) An agreement sufficient to constitute a contract for sale may be found even though the moment of its making is undetermined.

(3) Even though one or more terms are left open a contract for sale does not fail for indefiniteness if the parties have intended to make a contract and there is a reasonably certain basis for giving an appropriate remedy.

Section 2—205. **Firm Offers.**

An offer by a merchant to buy or sell goods in a signed writing which by its terms gives assurance that it will be held open is not revocable, for lack of consideration, during the time stated or if no time is stated for a reasonable time, but in no event may such period of irrevocability exceed three months; but any such term of assurance on a form supplied by the offeree must be separately signed by the offeror.

Section 2—206. **Offer and Acceptance in Formation of Contract.**

(1) Unless other unambiguously indicated by the language or circumstances

    (a) an offer to make a contract shall be construed as inviting acceptance in any manner and by any medium reasonable in the circumstances;

    (b) an order or other offer to buy goods for prompt or current shipment shall be construed as inviting acceptance either by a prompt promise to ship or by the prompt or current shipment of conforming or nonconforming goods, but such a shipment of nonconforming goods does not constitute an acceptance if the seller seasonably notifies the buyer that the shipment is offered only as an accommodation to the buyer.

(2) Where the beginning of a requested performance is a reasonable mode of acceptance an offeror who is not notified of acceptance within a reasonable time may treat the offer as having lapsed before acceptance.

Section 2—207. **Additional Terms in Acceptance or Confirmation.**

(1) A definite and seasonable expression of acceptance or a written confirmation which is sent within a reasonable time operates as an acceptance even though it states terms additional to or different from those offered or agreed upon, unless acceptance is expressly made conditional on assent to the additional or different terms.

(2) The additional terms are to be construed as proposals for addition to the contract. Between merchants such terms become part of the contract unless:

    (a) the offer expressly limits acceptance to the terms of the offer;

    (b) they materially alter it; or

    (c) notification of objection to them has already been given or is given within a reasonable time after notice of them is received.

(3) Conduct by both parties which recognizes the existence of a contract is sufficient to establish a contract for sale although the writings of the parties do not otherwise establish a contract. In such case the terms of the particular contract consist of those terms on which the writings of the parties agree, together with any supplementary terms incorporated under any other provisions of this Act.

Section 2—208. **Course of Performance or Practical Construction.**

(1) Where the contract for sale involves repeated occasions for performance by either party with knowledge of the nature of the performance and opportunity for objection to it by the other, any course of performance accepted or acquiesced in without objection shall be relevant to determine the meaning of the agreement.

(2) The express terms of the agreement and any such course of performance, as well as any course of dealing and usage of trade, shall be construed whenever reasonable as consistent with each other; but when such construction is unreasonable, express terms shall control course of performance and course of performance shall control both course of dealing and usage of trade (Section 1—205).

(3) Subject to the provisions of the next section on modification and waiver, such course of performance shall be relevant to show a waiver or modification of any term inconsistent with such course of performance.

Section 2—209. **Modification, Rescission and Waiver.**

(1) An agreement modifying a contract within this Article needs no consideration to be binding.

(2) A signed agreement which excludes modification or rescission except by a signed writing cannot be otherwise modified or rescinded, but except as between merchants such a requirement on a form supplied by the merchant must be separately signed by the other party.

(3) The requirements of the statute of frauds section of this Article (Section 2—201) must be satisfied if the contract as modified is within its provisions.

(4) Although an attempt at modification or rescission does not satisfy the requirements of subsection (2) or (3) it can operate as a waiver.

(5) A party who has made a waiver affecting an executory portion of the contract may retract the waiver by reasonable notification received by the other party that strict performance will be required of any term waived, unless the retraction would be unjust in view of a material change of position in reliance on the waiver.

Section 2—210. **Delegation of Performance; Assignment of Rights.**

(1) A party may perform his duty through a delegate unless otherwise agreed or unless the other party has a substantial interest in having his original promisor perform or control the acts required by the contract. No delegation of performance relieves the party delegating of any duty to perform or any liability for breach.

(2) Unless otherwise agreed all rights of either seller or buyer can be assigned except where the assignment would materially change the duty of the other party, or increase materially the burden or risk imposed on him by his contract, or impair materially his chance of obtaining return performance. A right to damages for breach of the whole contract or a right arising out of the assignor's due performance of his entire obligation can be assigned despite agreement otherwise.

(3) Unless the circumstances indicate the contrary a prohibition of assignment of "the contract" is to be construed as barring only the delegation to the assignee of the assignor's performance.

(4) An assignment of "the contract" or of "all my rights under the contract" or an assignment in similar general terms is an assignment of rights and unless the language or the circumstances (as in an assignment for security) indicate the contrary, it is a delegation of performance of the duties of the assignor and its acceptance by the assignee constitutes a promise by him to perform those duties. This promise is enforceable by either the assignor or the other party to the original contract.

(5) The other party may treat any assignment which delegates performance as creating reasonable grounds for insecurity and may without prejudice to his rights against the assignor demand assurances from the assignee (Section 2—609).

Part 3 **General Obligation and Construction of Contract**

Section 2—301. **General Obligations of Parties.**

The obligation of the seller is to transfer and deliver and that of the buyer is to accept and pay in accordance with the contract.

Section 2—302. **Unconscionable Contract or Clause.**

(1) If the court as a matter of law finds the contract or any clause of the contract to have been unconscionable at the time it was made the court may refuse to enforce the contract, or it may enforce the remainder of the contract without the unconscionable clause, or it may so limit the application of any unconscionable clause as to avoid any unconscionable result.

(2) When it is claimed or appears to the court that the contract or any clause thereof may be unconscionable the parties shall be afforded a reasonable opportunity to present evidence as to its commercial setting, purpose and effect to aid the court in making the determination.

Section 2—303. **Allocations or Division of Risks.**

Where this Article allocates a risk or a burden as between the parties "unless otherwise agreed", the agreement may not only shift the allocation but may also divide the risk or burden.

Section 2—304. **Price Payable in Money, Goods, Realty, or Otherwise.**

(1) The price can be made payable in money or otherwise. If it is payable in whole or in part in goods each party is a seller of the goods which he is to transfer.

(2) Even though all or part of the price is payable in an interest in realty the transfer of the goods and the seller's obligations with reference to them are subject to this Article, but not the transfer of the interest in realty or the transferor's obligations in connection therewith.

Section 2—305. **Open Price Term.**

(1) The parties if they so intend can conclude a contract for sale even though the price is not settled. In such a case the price is a reasonable price at the time for delivery if

    (a) nothing is said as to price; or

    (b) the price is left to be agreed by the parties and they fail to agree; or

    (c) the price is to be fixed in terms of some agreed market or other standard as set or recorded by a third person or agency and it is not so set or recorded.

(2) A price to be fixed by the seller or by the buyer means a price for him to fix in good faith.

(3) When a price left to be fixed otherwise than by agreement of the parties fails to be fixed through fault of one party the other may at his option treat the contract as cancelled or himself fix a reasonable price.

(4) Where, however, the parties intend not to be bound unless the price be fixed or agreed and it is not fixed or agreed there is no contract. In such a case the buyer must return any goods already received or if unable so to do must pay their reasonable value at the time of delivery and the seller must return any portion of the price paid on account.

Section 2—312. **Warranty of Title and Against Infringement; Buyer's Obligation Against Infringement.**

(1) Subject to subsection

(2) there is in a contract for sale a warranty by the seller that

    (a) the title conveyed shall be good, and its transfer rightful; and

    (b) the goods shall be delivered free from any security interest or other lien or encumbrance of which the buyer at the time of contracting has no knowledge.

(2) A warranty under subsection (1) will be excluded or modified only by specific language or by circumstances which give the buyer reason to know that the person selling does not claim title in himself or that he is purporting to sell only such right or title as he or a third person may have.

(3) Unless otherwise agreed a seller who is a merchant regularly dealing in goods of the kind warrants that the goods shall be delivered free of the rightful claim of any third person by way of infringement or the like but a buyer who furnishes specifications to the seller must hold the seller harmless against any such claim which arises out of compliance with the specifications.

Section 2—313. **Express Warranties by Affirmation, Promise, Description, Sample.**

(1) Express warranties by the seller are created as follows:

    (a) Any affirmation of fact or promise made by the seller to the buyer which relates to the goods and becomes part of the basis of the bargain creates an express warranty that the goods shall conform to the affirmation or promise.

    (b) Any description of the goods which is made part of the basis of the bargain creates an express warranty that the goods shall conform to the description.

    (c) Any sample or model which is made part of the basis of the bargain creates an express warranty that the whole of the goods shall conform to the sample or model.

(2) It is not necessary to the creation of an express warranty that the seller use formal words such as "warrant" or "guarantee" or that he have a specific intention to make a warranty, but an affirmation merely of the value of the goods or a statement purporting to be merely the seller's opinion or commendation of the goods does not create a warranty.

Section 2—314. **Implied Warranty: Merchantability; Usage of Trade.**

(1) Unless excluded or modified (Section 2—316), a warranty that the goods shall be merchantable is implied in a contract for their sale if the seller is a merchant with respect to

goods of that kind. Under this section the serving for value of food or drink to be consumed either on the premises or elsewhere is a sale.

(2) Goods to be merchantable must be at least such as

(a) pass without objection in the trade under the contract description; and

(b) in the case of fungible goods, are of fair average quality within the description; and

(c) are fit for the ordinary purposes for which such goods are used; and

(d) run, within the variations permitted by the agreement, of even kind, quality and quantity within each unit and among all units involved; and

(e) are adequately contained, packaged, and labeled as the agreement may require; and

(f) conform to the promises or affirmations of fact made on the container or label if any.

(3) Unless excluded or modified (Section 2—316) other implied warranties may arise from course of dealing or usage of trade.

Section 2—315. **Implied Warranty: Fitness for Particular Purpose.**

Where the seller at the time of contracting has reason to know any particular purpose for which the goods are required and that the buyer is relying on the seller's skill or judgment to select or furnish suitable goods, there is unless excluded or modified under the next section an implied warranty that the goods shall be fit for such purpose.

Section 2—316. **Exclusion or Modification of Warranties.**

(1) Words or conduct relevant to the creation of an express warranty and words or conduct tending to negate or limit warranty shall be construed wherever reasonable as consistent with each other; but subject to the provisions of this Article on parol or extrinsic evidence (Section 2—202) negation or limitation is inoperative to the extent that such construction is unreasonable.

(2) Subject to subsection (3), to exclude or modify the implied warranty of merchantability or any part of it the language must mention merchantability and in case of a writing must be conspicuous, and to exclude or modify any implied warranty of fitness the exclusion must be by a writing and conspicuous. Language to exclude all implied warranties of fitness is sufficient if it states, for example, that "There are no warranties which extend beyond the description on the face hereof."

(3) Notwithstanding subsection (2)

(a) unless the circumstances indicate otherwise, all implied warranties are excluded by expressions like "as is", "with all faults" or other language which in common understanding calls the buyer's attention to the exclusion of warranties and makes plain that there is no implied warranty; and

(b) when the buyer before entering into the contract has examined the goods or the sample or model as fully as he desired or has refused to examine the goods there is no implied warranty with regard to defects which an examination ought in the circumstances to have revealed to him; and

(c) an implied warranty can also be excluded or modified by course of dealing or course of performance or usage of trade.

(4) Remedies for breach of warranty can be limited in accordance with the provisions of this Article on liquidation or limitation of damages and on contractual modification of remedy (Sections 2—718 and 2—719).

Section 2—317. **Cumulation and Conflict of Warranties Express or Implied.**

Warranties whether express or implied shall be construed as consistent with each other and as cumulative, but if such construction is unreasonable the intention of the parties shall determine which warranty is dominant. In ascertaining that intention the following rules apply:

(a) Exact or technical specifications displace an inconsistent sample or model or general language of description.

(b) A sample from an existing bulk displaces inconsistent general language of description.

(c) Express warranties displace inconsistent implied warranties other than an implied warranty of fitness for a particular purpose.

Section 2—318. **Third Party Beneficiaries of Warranties Express or Implied.**
Note: If this Act is introduced in the Congress of the United States this section should be omitted. (States to select one alternative.)

Alternative A

A seller's warranty whether express or implied extends to any natural person who is in the family or household of his buyer or who is a guest in his home if it is reasonable to expect that such person may use, consume or be affected by the goods and who is injured in person by breach of the warranty. A seller may not exclude or limit the operation of this section.

Alternative B

A seller's warranty whether express or implied extends to any natural person who may reasonably be expected to use, consume or be affected by the goods and who is injured in person by breach of the warranty. A seller may not exclude or limit the operation of this section.

Alternative C

A seller's warranty whether express or implied extends to any person who may reasonably be expected to use, consume or be affected by the goods and who is injured by breach of the warranty. A seller may not exclude or limit the operation of this section with respect to injury to the person of an individual to whom the warranty extends. As amended 1966.

Part 4 **Title, Creditors and Good Faith Purchasers**

Section 2—401. **Passing of Title; Reservation for Security; Limited Application of This Section.**
Each provision of this Article with regard to the rights, obligations and remedies of the seller, the buyer, purchasers or other third parties applies irrespective of title to the goods except where the provision refers to such title. Insofar as situations are not covered by the other provisions of this Article and matters concerning title became material the following rules apply:

(1) Title to goods cannot pass under a contract for sale prior to their identification to the contract (Section 2—501), and unless otherwise explicitly agreed the buyer acquires by their identification a special property as limited by this Act. Any retention or reservation by the seller of the title (property) in goods shipped or delivered to the buyer is limited in effect to a reservation of a security interest. Subject to these provisions and to the provisions of the Article on Secured Transactions (Article 9), title to goods passes from the seller to the buyer in any manner and on any conditions explicitly agreed on by the parties.

(2) Unless otherwise explicitly agreed title passes to the buyer at the time and place at which the seller completes his performance with reference to the physical delivery of the goods, despite any reservation of a security interest and even though a document of title is to be delivered at a different time or place; and in particular and despite any reservation of a security interest by the bill of lading

(a) if the contract requires or authorizes the seller to send the goods to the buyer but does not require him to deliver them at destination, title passes to the buyer at the time and place of shipment; but

(b) if the contract requires delivery at destination, title passes on tender there.

(3) Unless otherwise explicitly agreed where delivery is to be made without moving the goods,

   (a) if the seller is to deliver a document of title, title passes at the time when and the place where he delivers such documents; or

   (b) if the goods are at the time of contracting already identified and no documents are to be delivered, title passes at the time and place of contracting.

(4) A rejection or other refusal by the buyer to receive or retain the goods, whether or not justified, or a justified revocation of acceptance revests title to the goods in the seller. Such revesting occurs by operation of law and is not a "sale".

Part 5 Performance

Section 2—507. **Effect of Seller's Tender; Delivery on Condition.**

(1) Tender of delivery is a condition to the buyer's duty to accept the goods and, unless otherwise agreed, to his duty to pay for them. Tender entitles the seller to acceptance of the goods and to payment according to the contract.

(2) Where payment is due and demanded on the delivery to the buyer of goods or documents of title, his right as against the seller to retain or dispose of them is conditional upon his making the payment due.

Section 2—508. **Cure by Seller of Improper Tender or Delivery; Replacement.**

(1) Where any tender or delivery by the seller is rejected because non-conforming and the time for performance has not yet expired, the seller may seasonably notify the buyer of his intention to cure and may then within the contract time make a conforming delivery.

(2) Where the buyer rejects a non-conforming tender which the seller had reasonable grounds to believe would be acceptable with or without money allowance the seller may if he seasonably notifies the buyer have a further reasonable time to substitute a conforming tender.

Section 2—511. **Tender of Payment by Buyer; Payment by Check.**

(1) Unless otherwise agreed tender of payment is a condition to the seller's duty to tender and complete any delivery.

(2) Tender of payment is sufficient when made by any means or in any manner current in the ordinary course of business unless the seller demands payment in legal tender and gives any extension of time reasonably necessary to procure it.

(3) Subject to the provisions of this Act on the effect of an instrument on an obligation (Section 3—802), payment by check is conditional and is defeated as between the parties by dishonor of the check on due presentment.

Section 2—512. **Payment by Buyer Before Inspection.**

(1) Where the contract requires payment before inspection non-conformity of the goods does not excuse the buyer from so making payment unless

   (a) the non-conformity appears without inspection; or

   (b) despite tender of the required documents the circumstances would justify injunction against honor under the provisions of this Act (Section 5—114).

(2) Payment pursuant to subsection (1) does not constitute an acceptance of goods or impair the buyer's right to inspect or any of his remedies.

Section 2—513. **Buyer's Right to Inspection of Goods.**

(1) Unless otherwise agreed and subject to subsection (3), where goods are tendered or delivered or identified to the contract for sale, the buyer has a right before payment or acceptance to inspect them at any reasonable place and time and in any reasonable manner. When the seller is required or authorized to send the goods to the buyer, the inspection may be after their arrival.

(2) Expenses of inspection must be borne by the buyer but may be recovered from the seller if the goods do not conform and are rejected.

(3) Unless otherwise agreed and subject to the provisions of this Article on C.I.F. contracts (subsection (3) of Section 2—321), the buyer is not entitled to inspect the goods before payment of the price when the contract provides

(a) for delivery "C.O.D." or on other like terms; or

(b) for payment against documents of title, except where such payment is due only after the goods are to become available for inspection.

(4) A place or method of inspection fixed by the parties is presumed to be exclusive but unless otherwise expressly agreed it does not postpone identification or shift the place for delivery or for passing the risk of loss. If compliance becomes impossible, inspection shall be as provided in this section unless the place or method fixed was clearly intended as an indispensable condition failure of which avoids the contract.

Part 6—Breach, Repudiation and Excuse

Section 2—601. **Buyer's Rights on Improper Delivery.**

Subject to the provisions of this Article on breach in installment contracts (Section 2—612) and unless otherwise agreed under the sections on contractual limitations of remedy (Sections 2—718 and 2—719), if the goods or the tender of delivery fail in any respect to conform to the contract, the buyer may

(a) reject the whole; or

(b) accept the whole; or

(c) accept any commercial unit or units and reject the rest.

Section 2—602. **Manner and Effect of Rightful Rejection.**

(1) Rejection of goods must be within a reasonable time after their delivery or tender. It is ineffective unless the buyer seasonably notifies the seller.

(2) Subject to the provisions of the two following sections on rejected goods (Sections 2—603 and 2—604),

(a) after rejection any exercise of ownership by the buyer with respect to any commercial unit is wrongful as against the seller; and

(b) if the buyer has before rejection taken physical possession of goods in which he does not have a security interest under the provisions of this Article (subsection (3) of Section 2—711), he is under a duty after rejection to hold them with reasonable care at the seller's disposition for a time sufficient to permit the seller to remove them; but

(c) the buyer has no further obligations with regard to goods rightfully rejected.

(3) The seller's rights with respect to goods wrongfully rejected are governed by the provisions of this Article on Seller's remedies in general (Section 2—703).

Section 2—606. **What Constitutes Acceptance of Goods.**

(1) Acceptance of goods occurs when the buyer

(a) after a reasonable opportunity to inspect the goods signifies to the seller that the goods are conforming or that he will take or retain them in spite of their non-conformity; or

(b) fails to make an effective rejection (subsection (1) of Section 2—602), but such acceptance does not occur until the buyer has had a reasonable opportunity to inspect them; or

(c) does any act inconsistent with the seller's ownership; but if such act is wrongful as against the seller it is an acceptance only if ratified by him.

(2) Acceptance of a part of any commercial unit is acceptance of that entire unit.

Section 2—607. **Effect of Acceptance; Notice of Breach; Burden of Establishing Breach After Acceptance; Notice of Claim or Litigation to Person Answerable Over.**

(1) The buyer must pay at the contract rate for any goods accepted.

(2) Acceptance of goods by the buyer precludes rejection of the goods accepted and if made with knowledge of a non-conformity cannot be revoked because of it unless the acceptance was on the reasonable assumption that the non-conformity would be seasonably cured but acceptance does not of itself impair any other remedy provided by this Article for non-conformity.

(3) Where a tender has been accepted

(a) the buyer must within a reasonable time after he discovers or should have discovered any breach notify the seller of breach or be barred from any remedy; and

(b) if the claim is one for infringement or the like (subsection (3) of Section 2—312) and the buyer is sued as a result of such a breach he must so notify the seller within a reasonable time after he receives notice of the litigation or be barred from any remedy over for liability established by the litigation.

(4) The burden is on the buyer to establish any breach with respect to the goods accepted.

(5) Where the buyer is sued for breach of a warranty or other obligation for which his seller is answerable over

(a) he may give his seller written notice of the litigation. If the notice states that the seller may come in and defend and that if the seller does not do so he will be bound in any action against him by his buyer by any determination of fact common to the two litigations, then unless the seller after seasonable receipt of the notice does come in and defend he is so bound.

(b) if the claim is one for infringement or the like (subsection (3) of Section 2—312) the original seller may demand in writing that his buyer turn over to him control of the litigation including settlement or else be barred from any remedy over and if he also agrees to bear all expense and to satisfy any adverse judgment, then unless the buyer after seasonable receipt of the demand does turn over control the buyer is so barred.

(6) The provisions of subsections (3), (4) and (5) apply to any obligation of a buyer to hold the seller harmless against infringement or the like (subsection (3) of Section 2—312).

Section 2—608. **Revocation of Acceptance in Whole or in Part.**

(1) The buyer may revoke his acceptance of a lot or commercial unit whose non-conformity substantially impairs its value to him if he has accepted it

(a) on the reasonable assumption that its non-conformity would be cured and it has not been seasonably cured; or

(b) without discovery of such non-conformity if his acceptance was reasonably induced either by the difficulty of discovery before acceptance or by the seller's assurances.

(2) Revocation of acceptance must occur within a reasonable time after the buyer discovers or should have discovered the ground for it and before any substantial change in condition of the goods which is not caused by their own defects. It is not effective until the buyer notifies the seller of it.

(3) A buyer who so revokes has the same rights and duties with regard to the goods involved as if he had rejected them.

Section 2—609. **Right to Adequate Assurance of Performance.**

(1) A contract for sale imposes an obligation on each party that the other's expectation of receiving due performance will not be impaired. When reasonable grounds for insecurity arise with respect to the performance of either party the other may in writing demand adequate assurance of due performance and until he receives such assurance may if commercially reasonable suspend any performance for which he has not already received the agreed return.

(2) Between merchants the reasonableness of grounds for insecurity and the adequacy of any assurance offered shall be determined according to commercial standards.

(3) Acceptance of any improper delivery or payment does not prejudice the party's right to demand adequate assurance of future performance.

(4) After receipt of a justified demand failure to provide within a reasonable time not exceeding thirty days such assurance of due performance as is adequate under the circumstances of the particular case is a repudiation of the contract.

Section 2—612. "Installment Contract"; Breach.

(1) An "installment contract" is one which requires or authorizes the delivery of goods in separate lots to be separately accepted, even though the contract contains a clause "each delivery is a separate contract" or its equivalent.

(2) The buyer may reject any installment which is non-conforming if the non-conformity substantially impairs the value of that installment and cannot be cured or if the non-conformity is a defect in the required documents; but if the non-conformity does not fall within subsection (3) and the seller gives adequate assurance of its cure the buyer must accept that installment.

(3) Whenever non-conformity or default with respect to one or more installments substantially impairs the value of the whole contract there is a breach of the whole. But the aggrieved party reinstates the contract if he accepts a non-conforming installment without seasonably notifying of cancellation or if he brings an action with respect only to past installments or demands performance as to future installments.

Part 7 Remedies

Section 2—701. Remedies for Breach of Collateral Contracts Not Impaired.

Remedies for breach of any obligation or promise collateral or ancillary to a contract for sale are not impaired by the provisions of this Article.

Section 2—702. Seller's Remedies on Discovery of Buyer's Insolvency.

(1) Where the seller discovers the buyer to be insolvent he may refuse delivery except for cash including payment for all goods theretofore delivered under the contract, and stop delivery under this Article (Section 2—705).

(2) Where the seller discovers that the buyer has received goods on credit while insolvent he may reclaim the goods upon demand made within ten days after the receipt, but if misrepresentation of solvency has been made to the particular seller in writing within three months before delivery the ten day limitation does not apply. Except as provided in this subsection the seller may not base a right to reclaim goods on the buyer's fraudulent or innocent misrepresentation of solvency or of intent to pay.

(3) The seller's right to reclaim under subsection (2) is subject to the rights of a buyer in ordinary course or other good faith purchaser under this Article (Section 2—403). Successful reclamation of goods excludes all other remedies with respect to them.

Section 2—703. Seller's Remedies in General.

Where the buyer wrongfully rejects or revokes acceptance of goods or fails to make a payment due on or before delivery or repudiates with respect to a part or the whole, then with respect to any goods directly affected and, if the breach is of the whole contract (Section 2—612), then also with respect to the whole undelivered balance, the aggrieved seller may

(a) withhold delivery of such goods;

(b) stop delivery by any bailee as hereafter provided (Section 2—705);

(c) proceed under the next section respecting goods still unidentified to the contract;

(d) resell and recover damages as hereafter provided (Section 2—706);

(e) recover damages for non-acceptance (Section 2—708) or in a proper case the price (Section 2—709);

(f) cancel.

Section 2—708. **Seller's Damages for Non-Acceptance or Repudiation.**

(1) Subject to subsection (2) and to the provisions of this Article with respect to proof of market price (Section 2—723), the measure of damages for non-acceptance or repudiation by the buyer is the difference between the market price at the time and place for tender and the unpaid contract price together with any incidental damages provided in this Article (Section 2—710), but less expenses saved in consequence of the buyer's breach.

(2) If the measure of damages provided in subsection (1) is inadequate to put the seller in as good a position as performance would have done then the measure of damages is the profit (including reasonable overhead) which the seller would have made from full performance by the buyer, together with any incidental damages provided in this Article (Section 2—710), due allowance for costs reasonably incurred and due credit for payments or proceeds of resale.

Section 2—709. **Action for the Price.**

(1) When the buyer fails to pay the price as it becomes due the seller may recover, together with any incidental damages under the next section, the price

(a) of goods accepted or of conforming goods lost or damaged within a commercially reasonable time after risk of their loss has passed to the buyer; and

(b) of goods identified to the contract if the seller is unable after reasonable effort to resell them at a reasonable price or the circumstances reasonably indicate that such effort will be unavailing.

(2) Where the seller sues for the price he must hold for the buyer any goods which have been identified to the contract and are still in his control except that if resale becomes possible he may resell them at any time prior to the collection of the judgment. The net proceeds of any such resale must be credited to the buyer and payment of the judgment entitles him to any goods not resold.

(3) After the buyer has wrongfully rejected or revoked acceptance of the goods or has failed to make a payment due or has repudiated (Section 2—610), a seller who is held not entitled to the price under this section shall nevertheless be awarded damages for non-acceptance under the preceding section.

Section 2—710. **Seller's Incidental Damages.**

Incidental damages to an aggrieved seller include any commercially reasonable charges, expenses or commissions incurred in stopping delivery; in the transportation, care and custody of goods after the buyer's breach, in connection with return or resale of the goods or otherwise resulting from the breach.

Section 2—711. **Buyer's Remedies in General; Buyer's Security Interest in Rejected Goods.**

(1) Where the seller fails to make delivery or repudiates or the buyer rightfully rejects or justifiably revokes acceptance then with respect to any goods involved, and with respect to the whole if the breach goes to the whole contract (Section 2—612), the buyer may cancel and whether or not he has done so may in addition to recovering so much of the price as has been paid

(a) "cover" and have damages under the next section as to all the goods affected whether or not they have been identified to the contract; or

(b) recover damages for non-delivery as provided in this Article (Section 2—713).

(2) Where the seller fails to deliver or repudiates the buyer may also

 (a) if the goods have been identified recover them as provided in this Article (Section 2—502); or

 (b) in a proper case obtain specific performance or replevy the goods as provided in this Article (Section 2—716).

(3) On rightful rejection or justifiable revocation of acceptance a buyer has a security interest in goods in his possession or control for any payments made on their price and any expenses reasonably incurred in their inspection, receipt, transportation, care and custody and may hold such goods and resell them in like manner as an aggrieved seller (Section 2—706).

Section 2—712. "Cover"; Buyer's Procurement of Substitute Goods.

(1) After a breach within the preceding section the buyer may "cover" by making in good faith and without unreasonable delay any reasonable purchase of or contract to purchase goods in substitution for those due from the seller.

(2) The buyer may recover from the seller as damages the difference between the cost of cover and the contract price together with any incidental or consequential damages as hereinafter defined (Section 2—715), but less expenses saved in consequence of the seller's breach.

(3) Failure of the buyer to effect cover within this section does not bar him from any other remedy.

Section 2—713. Buyer's Damages for Non-Delivery or Repudiation.

(1) Subject to the provisions of this Article with respect to proof of market price (Section 2—723), the measure of damages for non-delivery or repudiation by the seller is the difference between the market price at the time when the buyer learned of the breach and the contract price together with any incidental and consequential damages provided in this Article (Section 2—715), but less expenses saved in consequence of the seller's breach.

(2) Market price is to be determined as of the place for tender or, in cases of rejection after arrival or revocation of acceptance, as of the place of arrival.

Section 2—714. Buyer's Damages for Breach in Regard to Accepted Goods.

(1) Where the buyer has accepted goods and given notification (subsection (3) of Section 2—607) he may recover as damages for any non-conformity of tender the loss resulting in the ordinary course of events from the seller's breach as determined in any manner which is reasonable.

(2) The measure of damages for breach of warranty is the difference at the time and place of acceptance between the value of the goods accepted and the value they would have had if they had been as warranted, unless special circumstances show proximate damages of a different amount.

(3) In a proper case any incidental and consequential damages under the next section may also be recovered.

Section 2—715. Buyer's Incidental and Consequential Damages.

(1) Incidental damages resulting from the seller's breach include expenses reasonably incurred in inspection, receipt, transportation and care and custody of goods rightfully rejected, any commercially reasonable charges, expenses or commissions in connection with effecting cover and any other reasonable expense incident to the delay or other breach.

(2) Consequential damages resulting from the seller's breach include

 (a) any loss resulting from general or particular requirements and needs of which the seller at the time of contracting had reason to know and which could not reasonably be prevented by cover or otherwise; and

 (b) injury to person or property proximately resulting from any breach of warranty.

ARTICLE 3. NEGOTIABLE INSTRUMENTS

Section 3—104. Form of Negotiable Instruments; "Draft"; "Check"; "Certificate of Deposit"; "Note".

(1) Any writing to be a negotiable instrument within this Article must
    (a) be signed by the maker or drawer; and
    (b) contain an unconditional promise or order to pay a sum certain in money and no other promise, order, obligation or power given by the maker or drawer except as authorized by this Article; and
    (c) be payable on demand or at a definite time; and
    (d) be payable to order or to bearer.

(2) A writing which complies with the requirements of this section is
    (a) a "draft" ("bill of exchange") if it is an order;
    (b) a "check" if it is a draft drawn on a bank and payable on demand;
    (c) a "certificate of deposit" if it is an acknowledgment by a bank receipt of money with an engagement to repay it;
    (d) a "note" if it is a promise other than a certificate of deposit.

(3) As used in other Articles of this Act, and as the context may require, the terms "draft", "check", "certificate of deposit" and "note" may refer to instruments which are not negotiable within this Article as well as to instruments which are so negotiable.

Section 3—105. When Promise or Order Unconditional.

(1) A promise or order otherwise unconditional is not made conditional by the fact that the instrument
    (a) is subject to implied or constructive conditions; or
    (b) states its consideration, whether performed or promised, or the transaction which gave rise to the instrument, or that the promise or order is made or the instrument matures in accordance with or "as per" such transaction; or
    (c) refers to or states that it arises out of a separate agreement or refers to a separate agreement for rights as to prepayment or acceleration; or
    (d) states that it is drawn under a letter of credit; or
    (e) states that it is secured, whether by mortgage, reservation of title or otherwise; or
    (f) indicates a particular account to be debited or any other fund or source from which reimbursement is expected; or
    (g) is limited to payment out of a particular fund or the proceeds of a particular source, if the instrument is issued by a government or governmental agency or unit; or
    (h) is limited to payment out of the entire assets of a partnership, unincorporated association, trust or estate by or on behalf of which the instrument is issued.

(2) A promise or order is not unconditional if the instrument
    (a) states that it is subject to or governed by any other agreement; or
    (b) states that it is to be paid only out of a particular fund or source except as provided in this section.

Section 3—106. Sum Certain.

(1) The sum payable is a sum certain even though it is to be paid
    (a) with stated interest or by stated installments; or
    (b) with stated different rates of interest before and after default or a specified date; or
    (c) with a stated discount or addition if paid before or after the date fixed for payment; or
    (d) with exchange or less exchange, whether at a fixed rate or at the current rate; or
    (e) with costs of collection or an attorney's fee or both upon default.

(2) Nothing in this section shall validate any term which is otherwise illegal.

Section 3—107. **Money.**

(1) An instrument is payable in money if the medium of exchange in which it is payable is money at the time the instrument is made. An instrument payable in "currency" or "current funds" is payable in money.

(2) A promise or order to pay a sum stated in a foreign currency is for a sum certain in money and, unless a different medium of payment is specified in the instrument, may be satisfied by payment of that number of dollars which the stated foreign currency will purchase at the buying sight rate for that currency on the day on which the instrument is payable or, if payable on demand, on the day of demand. If such an instrument specifies a foreign currency as the medium of payment the instrument is payable in that currency.

Section 3—108. **Payable on Demand.**

Instruments payable on demand include those payable at sight or on presentation and those in which no time for payment is stated.

Section 3—109. **Definite Time.**

(1) An instrument is payable at a definite time if by its terms it is payable

(a) on or before a stated date or at a fixed period after a stated date; or

(b) at a fixed period after sight; or

(c) at a definite time subject to any acceleration; or

(d) at a definite time subject to extension at the option of the holder, or to extension to a further definite time at the option of the maker or acceptor or automatically upon or after a specified act or event.

(2) An instrument which by its terms is otherwise payable only upon an act or event uncertain as to time of occurrence is not payable at a definite time even though the act or event has occurred.

Section 3—110. **Payable to Order.**

(1) An instrument is payable to order when by its terms it is payable to the order or assigns of any person therein specified with reasonable certainty, or to him or his order, or when it is conspicuously designated on its face as "exchange" or the like and names a payee. It may be payable to the order of

(a) the maker or drawer; or

(b) the drawee; or

(c) a payee who is not maker, drawer or drawee; or

(d) two or more payees together or in the alternative; or

(e) an estate, trust or fund, in which case it is payable to the order of the representative of such estate, trust or fund or his successors; or

(f) an office, or an officer by his title as such in which case it is payable to the principal but the incumbent of the office or his successors may act as if he or they were the holder; or

(g) a partnership or unincorporated association, in which case it is payable to the partnership or association and may be indorsed or transferred by any person thereto authorized.

(2) An instrument not payable to order is not made so payable by such words as "payable upon return of this instrument properly indorsed."

(3) An instrument made payable both to order and to bearer is payable to order unless the bearer words are handwritten or typewritten.

Section 3—111. **Payable to Bearer.**

An instrument is payable to bearer when by its terms it is payable to

(a) bearer or the order of bearer; or

(b) a specified person or bearer; or

(c) "cash" or the order of "cash", or any other indication which does not purport to designate a specific payee.

Part 2 **Transfer and Negotiation**

Section 3—201. **Transfer: Right to Indorsement.**

(1) Transfer of an instrument vests in the transferee such rights as the transferor has therein, except that a transferee who has himself been a party to any fraud or illegality affecting the instrument or who as a prior holder had notice of a defense or claim against it cannot improve his position by taking from a later holder in due course.

(2) A transfer of a security interest in an instrument vests the foregoing rights in the transferee to the extent of the interest transferred.

(3) Unless otherwise agreed any transfer for value of an instrument not then payable to bearer gives the transferee the specifically enforceable right to have the unqualified indorsement of the transferor. Negotiation takes effect only when the indorsement is made and until that time there is no presumption that the transferee is the owner.

Section 3—202. **Negotiation.**

(1) Negotiation is the transfer of an instrument in such form that the transferee becomes a holder. If the instrument is payable to order it is negotiated by delivery with any necessary indorsement; if payable to bearer it is negotiated by delivery.

(2) An indorsement must be written by or on behalf of the holder and on the instrument or on a paper so firmly affixed thereto as to become a part thereof.

(3) An indorsement is effective for negotiation only when it conveys the entire instrument or any unpaid residue. If it purports to be of less it operates only as a partial assignment.

(4) Words of assignment, condition, waiver, guaranty, limitation or disclaimer of liability and the like accompanying an indorsement do not affect its character as an indorsement.

National Labor Relations Act (Excerpts)

* * *

Rights of Employees

Section 7. Employees shall have the right to self-organization, to form, join, or assist labor organizations, to bargain collectively through representatives of their own choosing, and to engage in other concerted activities for the purpose of collective bargaining or other mutual aid or protection, and shall also have the right to refrain from any or all of such activities requiring membership in a labor organization as a condition of employment as authorized in section 8(a)(3).

Unfair Labor Practices

Section 8. (a) It shall be an unfair labor practice for an employer—

(1) to interfere with, restrain, or coerce employees in the exercise of the rights guaranteed in section 7;

(2) to dominate or interfere with the formation or administration of any labor organization or contribute financial or other support to it: *Provided*, That . . . an employer shall not be prohibited from permitting employees to confer with him during working hours without loss of time or pay;

(3) by discrimination in regard to hire or tenure of employment or any term or condition of employment to encourage or discourage membership in any labor organization. . . .

(4) to discharge or otherwise discriminate against an employee because he has filed charges or given testimony under this Act;

(5) to refuse to bargain collectively with the representatives of his employees, subject to the provisions of section 9(a).

(b) It shall be an unfair labor practice for a labor organization or its agents—

(1) to restrain or coerce (A) employees in the exercise of the rights guaranteed in section 7: *Provided*, That this paragraph shall not impair the right of a labor organization to prescribe its own rules with respect to the acquisition or retention of membership therein; or (B) an employer in the selection of his representatives for the purposes of collective bargaining or the adjustment of grievances;

(2) to cause or attempt to cause an employer to discriminate against an employee . . . or to discriminate against an employee with respect to whom membership in such organization

has been denied or terminated on some ground other than his failure to tender the periodic dues and the initiation fees uniformly required as a condition of acquiring or retaining membership;

(3) to refuse to bargain collectively with an employer, provided it is the representative of his employees subject to the provisions of section 9(a);

(4) (i) to engage in, or to induce or encourage any individual employed by any person engaged in commerce or in an industry affecting commerce to engage in, a strike or a refusal in the course of his employment to use, manufacture, process, transport, or otherwise handle or work on any goods, articles, materials, or commodities or to perform any services; or (ii) to threaten, coerce, or restrain any person engaged in commerce or in an industry affecting commerce, where in either case an object thereof is—

(A) forcing or requiring any employer or self-employed person to join any labor or employer organization or to enter into any agreement which is prohibited by section 8(e);

(B) forcing or requiring any person to cease using, selling, handling, transporting, or otherwise dealing in the products of any other producer, processor, or manufacturer, or to cease doing business with any other person, or forcing or requiring any other employer to recognize or bargain with a labor organization as the representative of his employees unless such labor organization has been certified as the representative of such employees under the provisions of section 9: *Provided*, That nothing contained in this clause (B) shall be construed to make unlawful, where not otherwise unlawful, any primary strike or primary picketing;

(C) forcing or requiring any employer to recognize or bargain with a particular labor organization as the representative of his employees if another labor organization has been certified as the representative of such employees under the provisions of section 9;

(D) forcing or requiring any employer to assign particular work to employees in a particular labor organization or in a particular trade, craft, or class rather than to employees in another labor organization or in another trade, craft, or class, unless such employer is failing to conform to an order or certification of the Board determining the bargaining representative for employees performing such work:

Provided, That nothing contained in this subsection (b) shall be construed to make unlawful a refusal by any person to enter upon the premises of any employer (other than his own employer), if the employees of such employer are engaged in a strike ratified or approved by a representative of such employees whom such employer is required to recognize under this Act: *Provided further*, that for the purposes of this paragraph (4) only, nothing contained in such paragraph shall be construed to prohibit publicity, other than picketing, for the purpose of truthfully advising the public, including consumers and members of a labor organization, that a product or products are produced by an employer with whom the labor organization has a primary dispute and are distributed by another employer, as long as such publicity does not have an effect of inducing any individual employed by any person other than the primary employer in the course of his employment to refuse to pick up, deliver, or transport any goods, or not to perform any services, at the establishment of the employer engaged in such distribution:

(5) to require of employees covered by an agreement authorized under subsection (a)(3) the payment, as a condition precedent to becoming a member of such organization, of a fee in an amount which the Board finds excessive or discriminatory under all the circumstances. In making such a finding, the Board shall consider, among other relevant factors, the practices and customs of labor organizations in the particular industry, and the wages currently paid to the employees affected;

(6) to cause or attempt to cause an employer to pay or deliver or agree to pay or deliver any money or other thing of value, in the nature of an exaction, for services which are not performed or not to be performed; and

(7) to picket or cause to be picketed, or threaten to picket or cause to be picketed, any employer where an object thereof is forcing or requiring an employer to recognize or bargain with a labor organization as the representative of his employees, or forcing or requiring the employees of an employer to accept or select such labor organization as their collective bargaining representative, unless such labor organization is currently certified as the representative of such employees:

(A) where the employer has lawfully recognized in accordance with this Act any other labor organization and a question concerning representation may not appropriately be raised under section 9(c) of this Act;

(B) where within the preceding twelve months a valid election under section 9(c) of this Act has been conducted, or

(C) where such picketing has been conducted without a petition under section 9(c) being filed within a reasonable period of time not to exceed thirty days from the commencement of such picketing. . . .

Nothing in this paragraph (7) shall be construed to permit any act which would otherwise be an unfair labor practice under this section 8(b).

(c) The expressing of any views, argument, or opinion, or the dissemination thereof, whether in written, printed, graphic, or visual form, shall not constitute or be evidence of an unfair labor practice under any of the provisions of this Act, if such expression contains no threat of reprisal or force or promise of benefit.

(d) For the purposes of this section, to bargain collectively is the performance of the mutual obligation of the employer and the representative of the employees to meet at reasonable times and confer in good faith with respect to wages, hours, and other terms and conditions of employment, or the negotiation of an agreement, or any question arising thereunder, and the execution of a written contract incorporating any agreement reached if requested by either party, but such obligation does not compel either party to agree to a proposal or require the making of a concession. . . .

(e) It shall be an unfair labor practice for any labor organization and any employer to enter into any contract or agreement, express or implied, whereby such employer ceases or refrains or agrees to cease or refrain from handling, using, selling, transporting, or otherwise dealing in any of the products of any other employer, or to cease doing business with any other person, and any contract or agreement entered into heretofore or hereafter containing such an agreement shall be to such extent unenforceable and void. . . .

REPRESENTATIVES AND ELECTIONS

Section 9. (a) Representatives designated or selected for the purposes of collective bargaining by the majority of the employees in a unit appropriate for such purposes, shall be the exclusive representative of all the employees in such unit for the purposes of collective bargaining in respect to rates of pay, wages, hours of employment, or other conditions of employment: *Provided*, That any individual employee or a group of employees shall have the right at any time to present grievances to their employer and to have such grievances adjusted, without the intervention of the bargaining representative, as long as the adjustment is not inconsistent with the terms of a collective-bargaining contract or agreement then in effect: *Provided further*, That the bargaining representative has been given opportunity to be present at such adjustment.

(b) The Board shall decide in each case whether, in order to assure to employees the fullest freedom in exercising the rights guaranteed by this Act, the unit appropriate for the purposes of collective bargaining shall be the employer unit, craft unit, plant unit, or subdivision thereof. . . .

(c) (1)Whenever a petition shall have been filed, in accordance with such regulations as may be prescribed by the Board—

(A) by an employee or group of employees or an individual or labor organization acting in their behalf, alleging that a substantial number of employees (i) wish to be represented for collective bargaining and that their employer declines to recognize their representative as the representative defined in section 9(a), or (ii) assert that the individual or labor organization, which has been certified or is being currently recognized by their employer as the bargaining representative, is no longer a representative as defined in section 9(a); or

(B) by an employer, alleging that one or more individual or labor organizations have presented to him a claim to be recognized as the representative defined in section 9(a); the Board shall investigate such petition and if it has reasonable cause to believe that a question of representation affecting commerce exists shall provide for an appropriate hearing upon due notice. Such hearing may be conducted by an officer or employee of the regional office, who shall not make any recommendations with respect thereto. If the Board finds upon the record of such hearing that such a question of representation exists, it shall direct an election by secret ballot and shall certify the results thereof.

(2) In determining whether or not a question of representation affecting commerce exists, the same regulations and rules of decision shall apply irrespective of the identity of the persons filing the petition or the kind of relief sought and in no case shall the Board deny a labor organization a place on the ballot by reason of an order with respect to such labor organization or its predecessor not issued in conformity with section 10(c).

(3) No election shall be directed in any bargaining unit or any subdivision within which, in the preceding twelve-month period, a valid election shall have been held. Employees engaged in an economic strike who are not entitled to reinstatement shall be eligible to vote under such regulations as the Board shall find are consistent with the purposes and provisions of this Act in any election conducted within twelve months after the commencement of the strike. In any election where none of the choices on the ballot receives a majority, a run-off shall be conducted, the ballot providing for a selection between the two choices receiving the largest and second largest number of valid votes cast in the election.

(4) Nothing in this section shall be construed to prohibit the waiving of hearings by stipulation for the purpose of a consent election in conformity with regulations and rules of decision of the Board.

(5) In determining whether a unit is appropriate for the purposes specified in subsection (b) the extent to which the employees have organized shall not be controlling.

(d) Whenever an order of the Board made pursuant to section 10(c) is based in whole or in part upon facts certified following an investigation pursuant to subsection (c) of this section and there is a petition for the enforcement or review of such order, such certification and the record of such investigation shall be included in the transcript of the entire record required to be filed under section 10(e) or 10(f), and thereupon the decree of the court enforcing, modifying, or setting aside in whole or in part the order of the Board shall be made and entered upon the pleadings, testimony, and proceedings set forth in such transcript.

(e) (1) Upon the filing with the Board, by 30 per centum or more of the employees in a bargaining unit covered by an agreement between their employer and a labor organization made pursuant to section 8(a)(3), of a petition alleging they desire that such authority be rescinded, the Board shall take a secret ballot of the employees in such unit, and shall certify the results thereof to such labor organization and to the employer.

(2) No election shall be conducted pursuant to this subsection in any bargaining unit or any subdivision within which, in the preceding twelve-month period, a valid election shall have been held.

* * *

Title VII of Civil Rights Act of 1964 (Excerpts)

Definitions

Section 701. (j) The term "religion" includes all aspects of religious observance and practice, as well as belief, unless an employer demonstrates that he is unable to reasonably accommodate to an employee's or prospective employee's religious observance or practice without undue hardship on the conduct of the employer's business.

(k) The terms "because of sex" or "on the basis of sex" include, but are not limited to, because of or on the basis of pregnancy, childbirth or related medical conditions; and women affected by pregnancy, childbirth, or related medical conditions shall be treated the same for all employment-related purposes, including receipt of benefits under fringe benefit programs, as other persons not so affected but similar in their ability or inability to work, and nothing in Section 703(h) of this title shall be interpreted to permit otherwise. This subsection shall not require an employer to pay for health insurance benefits for abortion, except where the life of the mother would be endangered if the fetus were carried to term, or except where medical complications have arisen from an abortion: *Provided*, That nothing herein shall preclude an employer from providing abortion benefits or otherwise effect bargaining agreements in regard to abortion.

Discrimination Because of Race, Color, Religion, Sex, or National Origin

Section 703. (a) It shall be unlawful employment practice for an employer—
(1) to fail or refuse to hire or to discharge any individual, or otherwise to discriminate against any individual with respect to his compensation, terms, conditions, or privileges of employment, because of such individual's race, color, religion, sex, or national origin; or
(2) to limit, segregate, or classify his employees or applicants for employment in any way which would deprive or tend to deprive any individual of employment opportunities or otherwise adversely affect his status as an employee, because of such individual's race, color, religion, sex, or national origin.

(b) It shall be unlawful employment practice for an employment agency to fail or refuse to refer for employment, or otherwise to discriminate against, an individual because of his race, color, religion, sex, or national origin, or to classify or refer for employment any individual on the basis of his race, color, religion, sex, or national origin.

(c) It shall be an unlawful employment practice for a labor organization—

(1) to exclude or to expel from its membership, or otherwise to discriminate against, any individual because of his race, color, religion, sex, or national origin;

(2) to limit, segregate, or classify its membership or applicants for membership or to classify or fail or refuse to refer for employment any individual, in any way which would deprive or tend to deprive any individual of employment opportunities, or would limit such employment opportunities or otherwise adversely affect his status as an employee or as an applicant for employment, because of such individual's race, color, religion, sex, or national origin; or

(3) to cause or attempt to cause an employer to discriminate against an individual in violation of this section.

(d) It shall be an unlawful employment practice for any employer, labor organization, or joint labor-management committee controlling apprenticeship or other training or retraining, including on-the-job training programs to discriminate against any individual because of his race, color, religion, sex, or national origin in admission to, or employment in, any program established to provide apprenticeship or other training.

(e) Notwithstanding any other provision of this title, (1) it shall not be an unlawful employment practice for an employer to hire and employ employees, for an employment agency to classify, or refer for employment any individual, or for any employer, labor organization, or joint labor-management committee controlling apprenticeship or other training or retraining programs to admit or employ any individual in any such program, on the basis of his religion, sex, or national origin in those certain instances where religion, sex, or national origin is a bona fide occupational qualification reasonably necessary to the normal operation of that particular business or enterprise, and (2) it shall not be an unlawful employment practice for a school, college, university, or other educational institution or institution of learning to hire and employ employees of a particular religion if such school, college, university, or other educational institution or institution of learning is, in whole or in substantial part, owned, supported, controlled, or managed by a particular religion or by a particular religious corporation, association, or society, or if the curriculum of such school, college, university, or other educational institution or institution of learning is directed toward the propagation of a particular religion.

* * *

(h) Notwithstanding any other provision of this title, it shall not be an unlawful employment practice for an employer to apply different standards of compensation, or different terms, conditions, or privileges of employment pursuant to a bona fide seniority or merit system, or a system which measures earnings by quantity or quality of production or to employees who work in different locations, provided that such differences are not the results of an intention to discriminate because of race, color, religion, sex, or national origin; nor shall it be an unlawful employment practice for an employer to give and to act upon the results of any professionally developed ability test provided that such test, its administration or action upon the results is not designed, intended, or used to discriminate because of race, color, religion, sex, or national origin. It shall not be an unlawful employment practice under this title for any employer to differentiate upon the basis of sex in determining the amount of wages or compensation paid or to be paid to employees of such employer if such differentiation is authorized by the provision of Section 6(d) of the Fair Labor Standards Act of 1938 as amended (29 U.S.C. 206(d)).

(i) Nothing contained in this title shall apply to any business or enterprise on or near an Indian reservation with respect to any publicly announced employment practice of such business or enterprise under which a preferential treatment is given to any individual because he is an Indian living on or near a reservation.

(j) Nothing contained in this title shall be interpreted to require any employer, employment agency, labor organization, or joint labor-management committee subject to this title to grant preferential treatment to any individual or to any group because of the race, color, religion, sex, or national origin of such individual or group on account of an imbalance which may exist with respect to the total number or percentage of persons of any race, color, religion, sex, or national origin employed by any employer, referred or classified for employment by any employment agency or labor organization, admitted to membership or classified by any labor organization, or admitted to, or employed in, any apprenticeship or other training program, in comparison with the total number or percentage of persons of such race, color, religion, sex, or national origin in any community, State, section, or other area, or in the available work force in any community, State, section, or other area.

Other Unlawful Employment Practices

Section 704. (a) It shall be an unlawful employment practice for an employer to discriminate against any of his employees or applicants for employment, for an employment agency, or joint labor-management committee controlling apprenticeship or other training or retraining, including on-the-job training programs, to discriminate against any individual, or for a labor organization to discriminate against any member thereof or applicant for membership, because he has opposed any practice, made an unlawful employment practice by this title, or because he has made a charge, testified, assisted, or participated in any manner in an investigation, proceeding, or hearing under this title.

(b) It shall be an unlawful employment practice for an employer, labor organization, employment agency, or joint labor-management committee controlling apprenticeship or other training or retraining, including on-the-job training programs, to print or cause to be printed or published any notice or advertisement relating to employment by such an employer or membership in or any classification or referral for employment by such a labor organization, or relating to any classification or referral for employment by such an employment agency, or relating to admission to, or employment in, any program established to provide apprenticeship or other training by such a joint labor-management committee indicating any preference, limitation, specification, or discrimination, based on race, color, religion, sex, or national origin, except that such a notice or advertisement may indicate a preference, limitation, specification, or discrimination based on religion, sex, or national origin when religion, sex, or national origin is a bona fide occupational qualification for employment.

Americans with Disabilities Act (Excerpts)

(8) Qualified individual with a disability. The term "qualified individual with a disability" means an individual with a disability who, with or without reasonable accommodation, can perform the essential functions of the employment position that such individual holds or desires. For the purposes of this title, consideration shall be given to the employer's judgment as to what functions of a job are essential, and if an employer has prepared a written description before advertising or interviewing applicants for the job, this description shall be considered evidence of the essential functions of the job.

(9) Reasonable Accommodation. The term "reasonable accommodation" may include—

(A) making existing facilities used by employees readily accessible to and usable by individuals with disabilities; and

(B) job restructuring, part-time or modified work schedules, reassignment to a vacant position, acquisition or modification of equipment or devices, appropriate adjustment or modifications of examinations, training materials or policies, the provision of qualified readers or interpreters, and other similar accommodations for individuals with disabilities.

(10) Undue Hardship.

(A) In general: The term "undue hardship" means an action requiring significant difficulty or expense, when considered in light of the factors set forth in subparagraph (B).

(B) Factors to be considered: In determining whether an accommodation would impose an undue hardship on a covered entity, factors to be considered include—

(i) the nature and cost of accommodation needed under this Act;

(ii) the overall financial resources of the facility or facilities involved in the provision of the reasonable accommodation; the number of persons employed at such facility; the effect on expenses and resources, or the impact otherwise of such accommodation upon the operation of the facility;

(iii) the overall financial resources of the covered entity; the overall size of the business of a covered entity with respect to the number of its employees; the number, type, and location of its facilities; and

(iv) the type of operation or operations of the covered entity, including the composition, structure, and functions of the workforce of such entity; the geographic separateness, administrative, or fiscal relationship of the facility or facilities in question to the covered entity.

Section 102. Discrimination.

(a) General Rule. No covered entity shall discriminate against a qualified individual with a disability because of the disability of such individual in regard to job application procedures, the hiring, advancement, or discharge of employees, employee compensation, job training, and other terms, conditions, and privileges of employment.

(b) Construction. As used in subsection (a), the term "discriminate" includes—

(1) limiting, segregating, or classifying a job applicant or employee in a way that adversely affects the opportunities or status of such applicant or employee because of the disability of such applicant or employee;

(2) participating in a contractual or other arrangement or relationship that has the effect of subjecting a covered entity's qualified applicant or employee with a disability to the discrimination prohibited by this title (such relationship includes a relationship with an employment or referral agency, labor union, an organization providing fringe benefits to an employee of the covered entity, or an organization providing training and apprenticeship programs);

(3) utilizing standards, criteria, or methods of administration—

(A) that have the effect of discrimination on the basis of disability; or

(B) that perpetuate the discrimination of others who are subject to common administrative control;

(4) excluding or otherwise denying equal jobs or benefits to a qualified individual because of the known disability of an individual with whom the qualified individual is known to have a relationship or association;

(5) (A) not making reasonable accommodations to the known physical or mental limitations of an otherwise qualified individual with a disability who is an applicant or employee, unless such covered entity can demonstrate that the accommodation would impose an undue hardship on the operation of the business of such covered entity; or

(B) denying employment opportunities to a job applicant or employee who is an otherwise qualified individual with a disability, if such denial is based on the need of such covered entity to make reasonable accommodation to the physical or mental impairments of the employee or applicant;

(6) using qualification standards, employment tests or other selection criteria that screen out or tend to screen out an individual with a disability or a class of individuals with disabilities unless the standard, test or other selection criteria, as used by the covered entity, is shown to be job-related for the position in question and is consistent with business necessity; and

(7) failing to select and administer tests concerning employment in the most effective manner to ensure that, when such test is administered to a job applicant or employee who has a disability that impairs sensory, manual, or speaking skills, such test results accurately reflect the skills, aptitude, or whatever other factor of such applicant or employee that such test purports to measure, rather than reflecting the impaired sensory, manual, or speaking skills of such employee or applicant (except where such skills are the factors that the test purports to measure).

Section 104. Illegal Use of Drugs and Alcohol.

(b) Rules of Construction. Nothing in subsection (a) shall be construed to exclude as a qualified individual with a disability an individual who—

(1) has successfully completed a supervised drug rehabilitation program and is no longer engaging in the illegal use of drugs, or has otherwise been rehabilitated successfully and is no longer engaging in such use;

(2) is participating in a supervised rehabilitation program and is no longer engaging in such use; or

(3) is erroneously regarded as engaging in such use, but is not engaging in such use;

except that it shall not be a violation of this Act for a covered entity to adopt or administer reasonable policies or procedures, including but not limited to drug testing, designed to ensure that an individual described in paragraph (1) or (2) is no longer engaging in the illegal use of drugs.

The Antitrust Statutes (Excerpts)

SHERMAN ACT

Restraints of Trade Prohibited

Section 1—Trusts, etc., in restraint of trade illegal; penalty. Every contract, combination in the form of trust or otherwise, or conspiracy, in restraint of trade or commerce among the several States, or with foreign nations, is declared to be illegal. Every person who shall make any contract or engage in any combination or conspiracy declared by sections 1 to 7 of this title to be illegal shall be deemed guilty of a felony, and, on conviction thereof, shall be punished by fine not exceeding $10,000,000 if a corporation, or if any other person, $350,000, or by imprisonment not exceeding three years, or both said punishments, in the discretion of the court.

Section 2—Monopolizing trade a felony; penalty. Every person who shall monopolize, or attempt to monopolize, or combine or conspire with any other person or persons, to monopolize any part of the trade or commerce among the several States, or with foreign nations, shall be deemed guilty of a felony, and, on conviction thereof, shall be punished by fine not exceeding $10,000,000 if a corporation, or, if any other person, $350,000, or by imprisonment not exceeding three years, or by both said punishments, in the discretion of the court.

CLAYTON ACT

Refusals to Deal

Section 3—Sale, etc., on agreement not to use goods of competitor. It shall be unlawful for any person engaged in commerce, in the course of such commerce, to lease or make a sale or contract for sale of goods, wares, merchandise, machinery, supplies, or other commodities, whether patented or unpatented, for use, consumption, or resale within the United States or any Territory thereof or the District of Columbia or any insular possession or other place under the jurisdiction of the United States, or fix a price charged thereof, or discount from, or rebate upon, such price, on the condition, agreement, or understanding that the lessee or purchaser thereof shall not use or deal in the goods, wares, merchandise, machinery, supplies, or other commodities of a competitor or competitors of the lessor or seller, where the effect of such lease, sale, or contract for sale or such condition, agreement or understanding may be to substantially lessen competition or tend to create a monopoly in any line of commerce.

Private Suits

Section 4—Suits by persons injured; amount of recovery. Any person who shall be injured in this business or property by reason of anything forbidden in the antitrust laws may sue therefor in any district court of the United States in the district in which the defendant resides or is found or has an agent, without respect to the amount in controversy, and shall recover threefold the damages by him sustained, and the cost of suit, including a reasonable attorney's fee. . . .

Mergers

Section 7—Acquisition by one corporation of stock of another. No corporation engaged in commerce shall acquire, directly or indirectly, the whole or any part of the stock or other share capital and no corporation subject to the jurisdiction of the Federal Trade Commission shall acquire the whole or any part of the assets of another corporation engaged also in commerce, where in any line of commerce in any section of the country, the effect of such acquisition may be substantially to lessen competition, or to tend to create a monopoly.

No corporation shall acquire, directly or indirectly, the whole or any part of the stock or other share capital and no corporation subject to the jurisdiction of the Federal Trade Commission shall acquire the whole or any part of the assets of one or more corporations engaged in commerce, where in any line of commerce in any section of the country, the effect of such acquisition, of such stocks or assets, or of the use of such stock by the voting or granting of proxies or otherwise, may be substantially to lessen competition, or to tend to create a monopoly.

This section shall not apply to corporations purchasing such stock solely for investment and not using the same by voting or otherwise to bring about, or in attempting to bring about, the substantial lessening of competition. Nor shall anything contained in this section prevent a corporation engaged in commerce from causing the formation of subsidiary corporations for the actual carrying on of their immediate lawful business, or the natural and legitimate branches or extensions thereof, or from owning and holding all or part of the stock of such subsidiary corporations, when the effect of such formation is not to substantially lessen competition.

Interlocking Directorates

Section 8—Interlocking directorates and officers. No person at the same time shall be a director in any two or more corporations, any one of which has capital, surplus, and undivided profits aggregating more than $1,000,000, engaged in whole or in part in commerce, other than banks, banking associations, trust companies, and common carriers subject to the Act to regulate commerce approved February fourth, eighteen hundred and eighty-seven, if such corporations are or shall have been theretofore, by virtue of their business and location or operation, competitors, so that the elimination of competition by agreement between them would constitute a violation of any of the provisions of any of the antitrust laws. The eligibility of a director under the foregoing provision shall be determined by the aggregate amount of the capital, surplus, and undivided profits, exclusive of dividends declared but not paid to stockholders, at the end of the fiscal year of said corporation next preceding the election of directors, and when a director has been elected in accordance with the provisions of this Act it shall be lawful for him to continue as such for one year thereafter.

FEDERAL TRADE COMMISSION ACT

Unfair Methods of Competition Prohibited

Section 5—Unfair methods of competition unlawful; prevention by Commission—declaration. Declaration of unlawfulness; power to prohibit unfair practices.

(a) (1) Unfair methods of competition in or affecting commerce, and unfair or deceptive acts or practices in or affecting commerce, are declared unlawful. . . .

(b) Any person, partnership, or corporation who violates an order of the Commission to cease and desist after it has become final, and while such order is in effect, shall forfeit and pay to the United States a civil penalty of not more than $5,000 for each violation, which shall accrue to the United States and may be recovered in a civil action brought by the Attorney General of the United States. Each separate violation of such an order shall be a separate offense, except that in the case of a violation through continuing failure or neglect to obey a final order of the Commission each day of continuance of such failure or neglect shall be deemed a separate offense.

ROBINSON-PATMAN ACT (AN AMENDMENT TO THE CLAYTON ACT)

Price Discrimination; Cost Justification; Changing Conditions

Section 2—Discrimination in price, services, or facilities.

(a) Price; selection of customers.

It shall be unlawful for any person engaged in commerce, in the course of such commerce, either directly or indirectly, to discriminate in price between different purchases of commodities of like grade and quality, where either or any of the purchasers involved in such discrimination are in commerce, where such commodities are sold for use, consumption, or resale within the United States or any Territory thereof or the District of Columbia or any insular possession or other place under the jurisdiction of the United States, and where the effect of such discrimination may be substantially to lessen competition or tend to create a monopoly in any line of commerce, or to injure, destroy, or prevent competition with any person who either grants or knowingly receives the benefit of such discrimination, or with customers of either of them: *Provided,* That nothing herein contained shall prevent differentials which make only due allowance for differences in the cost of manufacture, sale, or delivery resulting from the differing methods or quantities in which such commodities are to such purchasers sold or delivered: *Provided, however,* That the Federal Trade Commission may, after due investigation and hearing to all interested parties, fix and establish quantity limits, and revise the same as it finds necessary as to particular commodities or classes of commodities, where it finds that available purchasers in greater quantities are so few as to render differentials on account thereof unjustly discriminatory or promotive of monopoly in any line of commerce; and the foregoing shall then not be construed to permit differentials based on differences in quantities greater than those so fixed and established: *And provided further,* That nothing herein contained shall prevent persons engaged in selling goods, wares, or merchandise in commerce from selecting their own customers in bona fide transactions and not in restraint of trade: *And provided further,* That nothing herein contained shall prevent price chages from time to time where in response to changing conditions affecting the market for or the marketability of the goods concerned, such as but not limited to actual or imminent deterioration of perishable goods, obsolescence of seasonal goods, distress sales under court process, or sales in good faith in discontinuance of business in the goods concerned.

Meeting Competition

(b) Burden of rebutting prima-facie case of discrimination.

Upon proof being made, at any hearing on a complaint under this section, that there has been discrimination in price or services or facilities furnished, the burden of rebutting the prima-facie case thus made by showing justification shall be upon the person charged with a violation of this section, and unless justification shall be affirmatively shown, the Commission is authorized to issue an order terminating the discrimination: *Provided, however,* That nothing herein contained shall prevent a seller rebutting the prima-facie case thus made by showing that his lower price or the furnishing of services or facilities to any purchaser or purchasers was made in good faith to meet an equally low price of a competitor, or the services or facilities furnished by a competitor.

Brokerage Payments

(c) Payment or acceptance of commission, brokerage or other compensation.

It shall be unlawful for any person engaged in commerce, in the course of such commerce, to pay or grant, or to receive or accept, anything of value as a commission, brokerage, or other compensation, or any allowance of discount in lieu thereof, except for services rendered in connection with the sale or purchase of goods, wares, or merchandise, either to the other party to such transaction or to an agent, representative, or other intermediary therein where such intermediary is acting in fact for or in behalf, or is subject to the direct or indirect control, of any party to such transaction other than the person by whom such compensation is so granted or paid.

Promotional Allowances

(d) Payment for services or facilities for processing or sale.

It shall be unlawful for any person engaged in commerce to pay or contract for the payment of anything of value to or for the benefit of a customer of such person in the course of such commerce as compensation or in consideration for any services or facilities furnished by or through such customer in connection with the processing, handling, sale, or offering for sale of any products or commodities manufactured, sold, or offered for sale by such person, unless such payment of consideration is available on proportionally equal terms to all other customers competing in the distribution of such products or commodities.

Promotional Services

(e) Furnishing services or facilities for processing, handling, etc.

It shall be unlawful for any person to discriminate in favor of one purchaser against another purchaser or purchasers of a commodity bought for resale, with or without processing, or by contracting to furnish or furnishing, or by contributing to the furnishing of, any services or facilities connected with the processing, handling, sale, or offering for sale of such commodity so purchased upon terms not accorded to all purchasers on proportionally equal terms.

Buyer Discrimination

(f) Knowingly inducing or receiving discriminatory price.

It shall be unlawful for any person engaged in commerce, in the course of such commerce, knowingly to induce or receive a discrimination in price which is prohibited by this section.

Predatory Practices

Section 3—Discrimination in rebates, discounts, or advertising service charges; underselling in particular localities; penalties. It shall be unlawful for any person engaged in commerce, in the course of such commerce, to be a party to, or assist in, any transaction of sale, or contract to sell, which discriminates to his knowledge against competitors of the purchaser, in that, any discount, rebate, allowance, or advertising service charge is granted to the purchaser over and above any discount, rebate, allowance, or advertising service charge available at the time of such transaction to said competitors in respect of a sale of goods of like grade, quality, and quantity; to sell, or contract to sell, goods in any part of the United States at prices lower than those exacted by said person elsewhere in the United States for the purpose of destroying competition, or eliminating a competitor in such part of the United States; or, to sell, or contract to sell, goods at unreasonably lower prices for the purpose of destroying competition or eliminating a competitor.

Securities Statutes (Excerpts)

SECURITIES ACT OF 1933

Definitions

Section 2. When used in this title, unless the context requires—

(1) The term "security" means any note, stock, treasury stock, bond, debenture, evidence of indebtedness, certificate of interest or participation in any profit-sharing agreement, collateral-trust certificate, preorganization certificate or subscription, transferable share, investment contract, voting-trust certificate, certificate of deposit for a security, fractional undivided interest in oil, gas, or other mineral rights, any put, call, straddle, option, or privilege on any security, certificate of deposit, or group or index of securities (including any interest therein or based on the value thereof), or any put, call, straddle, option, or privilege entered into on a national securities exchange relating to foreign currency, or, in general, any interest or participation in, temporary or interim certificate for, receipt for, guarantee of, or warrant or right to subscribe to or purchase, any of the foregoing.

Exempted Securities

Section 3. (a) Except as hereinafter expressly provided the provisions of this title shall not apply to any of the following classes of securities:

* * *

(2) Any security issued or guaranteed by the United States or any territory thereof, or by the District of Columbia, or by any State of the United States, or by any political subdivision of a State or Territory, or by any public instrumentality of one or more States or Territories, or by any person controlled or supervised by and acting as an instrumentality of the Government of the United States pursuant to authority granted by the Congress of the United States; or any certificate of deposit for any of the foregoing; or any security issued or guaranteed by any bank; or any security issued by or representing an interest in or a direct obligation of a Federal Reserve Bank. . . .

(3) Any note, draft, bill of exchange, or banker's acceptance which arises out of a current transaction or the proceeds of which have been or are to be used for current transactions, and which has a maturity at the time of issuance of not exceeding nine months, exclusive of days of grace, or any renewal thereof the maturity of which is likewise limited;

(4) Any security issued by a person organized and operated exclusively for religious, educational, benevolent, fraternal, charitable, or reformatory purposes and not for pecuniary

profit, and no part of the net earnings of which inures to the benefit of any person, private stockholder, or individual; . . .

Exempted Transactions

Section 4. The provisions of section 5 shall not apply to—

(1) transactions by any person other than an issuer, underwriter, or dealer.

(2) transactions by an issuer not involving any public offering.

(3) transactions by a dealer (including an underwriter no longer acting as an underwriter in respect of the security involved in such transactions), except—

> (A) transactions taking place prior to the expiration of forty days after the first date upon which the security was bona fide offered to the public by the issuer or by or through an underwriter,

> (B) transactions in a security as to which a registration statement has been filed taking place prior to the expiration of forty days after the effective date of such registration statement or prior to the expiration of forty days after the first date upon which the security was bona fide offered to the public by the issuer or by or through an underwriter after such effective date, whichever is later (excluding in the computation of such forty days any time during which a stop order issued under section 8 is in effect as to the security), or such shorter period as the Commission may specify by rules and regulations or order, and

> (C) transactions as to the securities constituting the whole or a part of an unsold allotment to or subscription by such dealer as a participant in the distribution of such securities by the issuer or by or through an underwriter.

With respect to transactions referred to in clause (B), if securities of the issuer have not previously been sold pursuant to an earlier effective registration statement the applicable period, instead of forty days, shall be ninety days, or such shorter period as the Commission may specify by rules and regulations or order.

(4) brokers' transactions, executed upon customers' orders on any exchange or in the over-the-counter market but not the solicitation of such orders.

(6) transactions involving offers or sales by an issuer solely to one or more accredited investors, if the aggregate offering price of an issue of securities offered in reliance on this paragraph does not exceed the amount allowed under section 3(b) of this title, if there is no advertising or public solicitation in connection with the transaction by the issuer or anyone acting on the issuer's behalf, and if the issuer files such notice with the Commission as the Commission shall prescribe.

Prohibitions Relating to Interstate Commerce and the Mails

Section 5. (a) Unless a registration statement is in effect as to a security, it shall be unlawful for any person, directly or indirectly—

(1) to make use of any means or instruments of transportation or communication in interstate commerce or of the mails to sell such security through the use or medium of any prospectus or otherwise; or

(2) to carry or cause to be carried through the mails or in interstate commerce, by any means or instruments of transportation, any such security for the purpose of sale or for delivery after sale.

(b) It shall be unlawful for any person, directly or indirectly—

(1) to make use of any means or instruments of transportation or communication in interstate commerce or of the mails to carry or transmit any prospectus relating to any security with respect to which a registration statement has been filed under this title, unless such prospectus meets the requirements of section 10, or

(2) to carry or to cause to be carried through the mails or in interstate commerce any such security for the purpose of sale or for delivery after sale, unless accompanied or preceded by a prospectus that meets the requirements of subsection (a) of section 10.

(c) It shall be unlawful for any person, directly, or indirectly, to make use of any means or instruments of transportation or communication in interstate commerce or of the mails to offer to sell or offer to buy through the use or medium of any prospectus or otherwise any security, unless a registration statement has been filed as to such security, or while the registration statement is the subject of a refusal order or stop order or (prior to the effective date of the registration statement) any public proceeding of examination under section 8.

SECURITIES EXCHANGE ACT OF 1934

Definitions and Application of Title

Section 3. (a) When used in this title, unless the context otherwise requires—

* * *

(4) The term "broker" means any person engaged in the business of effecting transactions in securities for the account of others, but does not include a bank.

(5) The term "dealer" means any person engaged in the business of buying and selling securities for his own account, through a broker or otherwise, but does not include a bank, or any person insofar as he buys or sells securities for his own account, either individually or in some fiduciary capacity, but not as part of a regular business.

* * *

(7) The term "director" means any director of a corporation or any person performing similar functions with respect to any organization, whether incorporated or unincorporated.

(8) The term "issuer" means any person who issues or proposes to issue any security; except that with respect to certificates of deposit for securities, voting-trust certificates, or collateral-trust certificates, or with respect to certificates of interest or shares in an unincorporated investment trust not having a board of directors or the fixed, restricted management, or unit type, the term "issuer" means the person or persons performing the acts and assuming the duties of depositor or manager pursuant to the provisions of the trust or other agreement or instrument under which such securities are issued; and except that with respect to equipment-trust certificates or like securities, the term "issuer" means the person by whom the equipment or property is, or is to be, used.

(9) The term "person" means a natural person, company, government, or political subdivision, agency, or instrumentality of a government.

Regulation of the Use of Manipulative and Deceptive Devices

Section 10. It shall be unlawful for any person, directly or indirectly, by the use of any means or instrumentality of interstate commerce or of the mails, or of any facility of any national securities exchange—

(a) To effect a short sale, or to use or employ any stop-loss order in connection with the purchase or sale, of any security registered on a national securities exchange, in contravention of such rules and regulations as the Commission may prescribe as necessary or appropriate in the public interest or for the protection of investors.

(b) To use or employ, in connection with the purchase or sale of any security registered on a national securities exchange or any security not so registered, any manipulative or deceptive device or contrivance in contravention of such rules and regulations as the Commission may prescribe as necessary or appropriate in the public interest or for the protection of investors.

Glossary

Abnormally dangerous activity *see* ultrahazardous activity.

Absolute liability liability for an act or activity that causes harm or injury even though the alleged wrongdoer was not at fault.

Acceptance the offeree's notification or expression to the offeror that he agrees to be bound by the terms of the offeror's proposal, thereby creating a contract. The trend is to allow acceptance by any means that reasonably notifies the offeror of the acceptance.

Accord in a debtor/creditor relationship, an agreement between the parties to settle a dispute for some partial payment. The creditor has a right of action against the debtor.

Accord and satisfaction in a debtor/creditor relationship, an agreement between the parties to settle a dispute, and subsequent payment. The agreement is an accord because the creditor has a right of action against the debtor. Accord and satisfaction is complete when payment has been tendered.

Account receivable a debt that arises in the course of business that is not supported by negotiable paper; for example, the charge accounts at a department store.

Actual authority power of an agent to bind a principal; the power is from an express or an implied agreement between principal and agent.

Adjudication the legal process of resolving a dispute.

Adjudicatory hearing in administrative law, a formal process involving a regulatory agency and the private parties involved in a complaint; procedures are more informal than a court trial, but protect due process rights.

Administrative agency a governmental bureau established by Congress (or the president) to execute certain functions of Congress. Agencies transact government business and may write and enforce regulations under the authority of Congress or the president.

Administrative law rules and regulations established by administrative agencies to execute the functions given them by Congress or the president; also the law that governs how agencies must operate.

Adversary system of justice a legal system in which the parties to a dispute present their own arguments and are responsible for asserting their legal rights.

Affirmative action employment programs, often mandated by federal law, to remedy discriminatory employment practices affecting racial minorities and women. Programs seek to remedy past patterns of discrimination and discrimination that results from facially neutral employment practices.

Affirmative defense defendant's response to plaintiff's claim that attacks the plaintiff's legal right to bring the action rather than attacking the truth of the claim. An example of an affirmative defense is the running of the statute of limitations.

Agency a relationship between two persons, by explicit or implicit agreement, where one (the agent) may act on behalf of the other (the principal) and bind the principal by words and actions.

Agency order in administrative law, a statement by a regulatory agency, under its powers granted by Congress and subject to procedural requirements, to inform parties subject to the rules what they must do to comply with a rule they are violating.

Agency regulation in administrative law, a rule issued by a regulatory agency, under its powers granted by Congress and subject to procedural requirements that detail the legal obligations of affected parties.

Agency shop in labor law, a unionized work-place where employees who are not union members must pay agency fees to the union for being the sole bargaining agent for all employees; illegal in states that have right-to-work laws.

Agent a person authorized to act for or to represent another, called the principal.

Agreement a "meeting of the minds"; a mutual understanding between the parties as to the substance of a contract.

Agreement (U.C.C.) means the bargain of the parties in fact as found in their language or by implication from other circumstances including course of dealing or usage of trade or course of performance as provided in the U.C.C.

Alternative dispute resolution a process by which the parties to a dispute resolve it through a mechanism other than litigation in court. Alternative dispute resolution includes arbitration, negotiation, and mediation.

Ambient air under the Clean Air Act, ambient air is the air outside of buildings or other enclosures.

Amicus curiae a party not directly involved in the litigation but who participates as a friend of the court, usually by submitting briefs in favor of one position at the appellate level.

Amount in controversy the damages claimed or the relief demanded by the injured party in a dispute.

Answer the response of a defendant to the plaintiff's complaint, denying in part or in whole the charges made by the plaintiff.

Anticipatory breach the assertion by a party to a contract that she will not perform a future obligation as required by the contract.

Antitrust federal and state statutes to protect commerce from certain restraints of trade, such as price fixing and monopolization.

Apparent authority that authority a reasonable person would assume an agent possesses in light of the principal's conduct.

Appeal requesting removal from a court of a decided or an adjudicated case to a court of appellate jurisdiction for the purpose of obtaining a review of the decision.

Appellant the party, either the plaintiff or the defendant, who invokes the appellate jurisdiction of a superior court.

Appellate jurisdiction the power of a court to revise or correct the proceedings in a case already acted upon by a lower court or administrative agency.

Appellee the party against whom an appeal is taken.

Arbiter in an arbitration proceeding, the person granted the authority to decide a controversy.

Arbitrary and capricious a judgment or decision, by an administrative agency or judge, which is without basis in fact or in law. Such a decision is often referred to as being without a rational basis.

Arbitration a means of settling disputes between parties when they submit the matter to a neutral third party of their choosing, who resolves the dispute by issuing a binding award. A popular alternative to the court system for resolving disputes due to lower cost and greater speed.

Articles of incorporation under state law, a document that every new corporation must file providing information about the name, address, and purpose of the corporation, as well as a statement about the stock that may be issued and the names of the principal officers.

Artificial seniority in employment discrimination law, a remedy that may be granted giving minority or women workers extra years of work credit to make up for past acts of discrimination by their employer.

Artisan's lien a possessory lien given as security for payment to a person who has made improvements to another person's property. The statutory right of an artisan to keep possession of the object that she has worked on until paid for the work.

Assault any word or action intended to cause another to be in fear of immediate physical harm.

Assault and battery intentionally causing another to anticipate immediate physical harm through some threat and then carrying out the threatened activity.

Assumption of risk common law doctrine under which a plaintiff may not recover for the injuries or damages that result from an activity in which the plaintiff willingly participated. A defense used by the defendant in negligence case when the plaintiff had knowledge of the danger, voluntarily exposed himself to the danger, and was injured.

Attachment the legal process of seizing another's property in accordance with a writ or judicial order for the purpose of security satisfaction of a judgment to be rendered.

Attachment (U.C.C.) when the requirements of a security interest (agreement, value, and conveyable rights in the collateral) exist, the security agreement becomes enforceable between parties and is said to attach.

Attainment areas under the Clean Air Act, areas that meet federal standards for major pollutants; they are designated "prevention of significant deterioration areas," because they will not be allowed to become more polluted.

Authorization card a card signed by an employee at a worksite targeted for possible unionization; the card authorizes the union to request that an election be held to determine if all workers will be represented by the union.

Back pay compensation for past economic losses (lost wages and fringe benefits) caused by an employer's discriminatory employment practices, such as, for example, limiting promotion opportunities for older workers.

Balance of payments an official accounting that records a country's foreign transactions; exports are recorded as credits and imports as debits.

Bankruptcy a proceeding under the law that is initiated by an insolvent individual or business (a voluntary bankruptcy), or by creditors (an involuntary bankruptcy) seeking to have the insolvent's assets distributed among the creditors and to then discharge the insolvent from further obligation or to reorganize the insolvent's debt structure.

Bankruptcy trustee in bankruptcy proceedings the person given authority to manage the assets of the bankrupt for the benefit of the creditors.

Bargaining agent the union recognized and certified by the National Labor Relations Board, upon election by a majority of the workers, to be the exclusive representative of employees in a bargaining unit (worksite) to determine working conditions and wages.

Battery the intentional unallowed touching of another. The "touching" may involve a mere touch that is offensive, or an act of violence that causes serious injury.

Bearer (U.C.C.) the person in possession of an instrument, document of title, or certificated security payable to bearer or indorsed in blank.

Beyond a reasonable doubt in criminal law, the general rule that for a judge or jury to find a defendant guilty there can be no significant doubt that the defendant violated a criminal statute.

Bilateral contract a contract formed by the mutual exchange of promises of the parties.

Bill of exchange an unconditional order in writing, addressed by one person to another, signed by the person giving it, requiring the person to whom it is addressed to pay on demand or at a fixed or determinable future date a certain sum of money. Same as a draft under the U.C.C.

Bill of lading (U.C.C.) a document evidencing the receipt of goods for shipment issued by one engaged in the business of transporting goods; includes an airbill.

Blue Sky laws name given to state laws that regulate the offer and sale of securities.

Bona fide occupational qualification (BFOQ) employment in particular jobs may not be limited to persons of a particular sex or religion unless the employer can show that sex or religion is an actual qualification for performing the job. Not permitted on the basis of race.

Bond an evidence of debt carrying a specified amount (principal), schedule of interest payments, and a date for redemption of the face value of the bond.

Bondholders creditors of a business, whose evidence of debt is a bond issued by the business.

Boycott an effort to organize a group to not deal with some party, such as a group of retailers refusing to buy products from manufacturers who do certain things not liked by the retailers, or a group of labor unions agreeing not to handle any products made by a certain company.

Breach of contract failure, without a legal excuse, of a promisor to perform the terms agreed to in a contract.

Bribery the offering, giving, receiving, or soliciting of something of value for the purpose of influencing the action of an official in the discharge of public or legal duties.

Brief an appellate brief is a written document, prepared by an attorney, to be the basis for an appeal of a case to an appellate court. It contains the points of law the attorney wants to establish, with the arguments and authorities to support that view.

Bubble concept under the Clean Air Act, when a polluting facility or a geographic area is treated as a single pollution source, in which one may build additional polluting facilities so long as total pollution is lowered within the "bubble."

Business judgment rule a principle of corporate law under which a court will not challenge the business decisions of a corporate officer or director made with ordinary care and in good faith.

Business necessity justification for an otherwise prohibited discriminatory employment practice based on employer's proof that (1) the otherwise prohibited employment practice is essential for the safety and efficiency of the business, and (2) no reasonable alternative with a lesser impact exists.

Business tort a noncontractual breach of a legal duty by a business resulting in damages or injury to another; includes certain torts that can only occur in business situations.

Bylaws in corporation law, the rules that regulate and govern the internal operations of a corporation with respect to directors, shareholders, and officers rights and duties.

Cartel a combination of independent producers in an industry attempting to limit competition by acting together to fix prices, divide markets, or restrict entry into the industry.

Cause in fact an act or omission without which an event would not have occurred. Courts express this in the form of a rule commonly referred to as the "but for" rule: the injury to a person would not have happened but for the conduct of the wrongdoer.

Cause of action the facts that give rise to a person's legal right of redress against another.

Caveat emptor Latin for "let the buyer beware."

Cease and desist order an order by an administrative agency or a court prohibiting a firm from conducting activities that the agency or court deems illegal.

Challenge for cause challenge by an attorney to a prospective juror for which some cause or reason is asserted.

Charter *see* corporate charter.

Citizen-suit provisions in regulatory law, a right provided by Congress for private citizens to bring a suit before a federal court to force compliance with the law passed by Congress; in some instances, the cost of the suit is borne by the government or the defendant if the private party wins the case.

Civil law (1) laws, written or unwritten, that specify the duties that exist between and among people, as opposed to criminal matters. (2) Codified or statutory law, used in many Western European countries and Japan, as distinguished from the common or judge-made law used in England and the United States.

Closed shop a worksite where one must be a union member before obtaining work.

Closing argument oral presentation to the jury by the attorneys after the plaintiff and defendant have stated their cases and before the judge charges the jury.

Collateral property pledged as a secondary security for the satisfaction of a debt in the event the debtor does not repay as expected.

Collective bargaining the process by which a union and an employer arrive at and enforce agreements regarding employment of workers represented by a union.

Commerce clause that part of the U. S. Constitution that gives Congress the power to regulate interstate commerce; the basis of much federal regulation.

Commercial speech expressions made by businesses about commercial matters or about political matters; the First Amendment protects most truthful speech in this category.

Common law law developed by American and English courts by decisions in cases. Unlike statutes, it is not passed by a legislative body and is not a specific set of rules; rather, it must be interpreted from the many decisions that have been written over time.

Common stock the shares of ownership in a corporation having the lowest priority with regard to payment of dividends and distribution of the corporation's assets upon dissolution.

Community property property owned in common by husband and wife.

Comparative negligence a defense to negligence whereby the plaintiff's damages are reduced by the proportion his fault bears to the total injury he has suffered.

Compensatory damages a sum awarded to an injured party that is equivalent to her actual damages or injuries sustained. The rationale is to restore the injured party to the position she was in before the injury.

Complaint the initial pleading by the plaintiff in a civil action that informs the defendant of the material facts on which the plaintiff bases the lawsuit.

Concentration in antitrust law, the percent of market share (usually sales volume) that one or more firms control in a given product or geographic market; used as a measure of the degree of competition within a market.

Concentration ratio fraction of total market sales made by a specified number of an industry's largest firms. Four-firm and eight-firm concentration ratios are the most frequently used.

Concerted activity in labor law, actions by employees, such as a strike or other mutual activity that furthers their employment interests, protected by the National Labor Relations Act.

Concurrent jurisdiction when two different courts are each empowered to deal with the subject matter at issue in a dispute.

Concurring opinion at the appellate court level, an opinion filed by one or more of the justices in which the justices agree with the majority opinion but states separate views or reasons for the decision.

Condition a provision in a contract providing that upon the occurrence of some event the obligations of the parties will be set in motion, suspended, or terminated.

Condition precedent in a contract, a condition that must be met before the other party's obligations arise.

Condition subsequent in a contract, a condition which, if met, discharges the obligations of the other party.

Confiscation the act whereby a sovereign takes private property without a proper public purpose or just compensation.

Conflict of laws body of law establishing the circumstances in which a state or federal court shall apply the laws of another state, rather than the laws of the state in which it is sitting, to decide a case before it.

Conglomerate merger a merger between two companies that do not compete with or purchase from each other.

Consent a voluntary agreement, implied or expressed, to submit to a proposition or act of another.

Consent decree a judgment entered by consent of the parties and approval of a court, whereby the defendant agrees to stop alleged illegal activity without admitting guilt or wrongdoing. Often used to settle complaints by regulatory agencies.

Consideration in a contract, the thing of value bargained for in exchange for a promise; the inducement or motivation to a contract; the element that keeps the contract from being gratuitous and, therefore, makes it legally binding on the parties.

Consignment the act or process of depositing goods to be sold in the custody of a third party.

Constitution the fundamental law of a nation; a written document establishing the powers of the government and its basic structure; the controlling authority over all other law.

Constructive notice information or understanding that is equivalent to a formal notice of facts that a person using proper diligence would be expected to know.

Consumer expectation test in tort law, as applied to products, the level of safe performance an ordinary consumer could expect from a product under the circumstances.

Consumer reports often called credit reports; files maintained by companies concerning consumers' credit history and evidence of income and debt; sold for legitimate business purposes.

Contempt of court any act that obstructs a court in the administration of justice, or that is calculated to lessen the court's authority.

Contract a legal relationship consisting of the rights and duties of contracting parties; a promise or set of promises constituting an agreement between the parties that gives each a legal duty to the other and also the right to seek a remedy for the breach of those duties. The elements of a contract include agreement, consideration, legal capacity, lawful subject matter, and genuine consent.

Contract (U.C.C.) the total legal obligation which results from the parties' agreement as affected by the U.C.C. and any other applicable rules of law.

Contract clause the statement in the constitution that "No State shall . . . pass any . . . Law impairing the Obligation of Contracts. . . ." Arises primary when a state attempts to reduce its obligations created by contracts with private parties.

Contractual capacity the mental capacity required by law for a party entering into a contract to be bound by that contract. Generally, minors, intoxicated persons, and the insane lack capacity to contract.

Contributory negligence as a complete defense to negligence, an act or a failure to act that produces a lack of reasonable care on the part of the plaintiff that is the proximate cause of the injury incurred.

Conversion the unauthorized taking of property, permanently or temporarily, that deprives its rightful owner of its lawful use.

Cooperative two or more persons or enterprises that act through a common agent to achieve a common objective.

Copyright a grant to an author or a publisher of an exclusive right to print, reprint, publish, copy, and sell literary work, musical compositions, works of art, and motion pictures for the life of the author plus an additional fifty years.

Corporate charter a certificate issued by a state government recognizing the existence of a corporation as a legal entity; it is issued automatically upon filing the information required by state law and payment of a fee.

Corporate social responsibility the belief that businesses have a duty to society that goes beyond obeying the law and maximizing profits.

Corporation a business organized under the laws of a state that allow an artificial legal being to exist for purposes of doing business in its name.

Cost-benefit analysis computing the costs of an activity compared to the estimated monetary value of the benefits from the activity.

Cost justification in antitrust law, a defense available in price discrimination (Robinson-Patman) cases to show that a buyer was offered a good at a lower price than another buyer because of differences in the costs of serving the two customers.

Counterclaim a claim a defendant asserts against the plaintiff.

Counteroffer an offeree's response to an offeror rejecting the offeror's original offer and at the same time making a new offer.

Covenant an agreement between two or more parties in which one or more of the parties pledges that some duty or obligation is or is not to be done.

Craft union a union organized on the basis of a specified set of skills or occupations.

Credit rating an opinion as to the reliability of a person in paying debts.

Credit report a report made by a consumer reporting agency concerning the financial condition and credit character of a person or business.

Creditor a person to whom a debt is owed by a debtor.

Crime a violation of the law that is punishable by the state or nation. Crimes are classified as felonies and misdemeanors.

Criminal law governs or defines legal wrongs, or crimes, committed against society. Wrongdoers are punished for violating the rules of society. A person found guilty of a criminal offense is usually fined or imprisoned.

Cross complaint during the pleadings, a claim the defendant asserts against the plaintiff. *See* also counterclaim.

Cross examination examination by the attorney representing the adverse party after the other party has examined her witness.

Cruel and unusual punishment punishment that is disproportionate to the offense and is a shock to the moral sense of the community; prohibited by the Eighth Amendment.

Damages money compensation sought or awarded as a remedy for a breach of contract or for tortious acts.

Debt a sum of money due by an express agreement.

Debt collection agency a business that is paid to or buys the right to collect the debts owed by consumers to a business.

Debtor a person who owes a debt to a creditor.

Debt securities an obligation of a corporation, usually in the form of a bond, issued for a certain value at a certain rate of interest to be repaid at a certain time.

Deception in consumer protection law, a claim, practice, or omission likely to mislead a reasonable consumer and cause the consumer to suffer a loss.

Decertification a process by which employees vote to withdraw their consent to union representation; an election is conducted by the National Labor Relations Board.

Deed a conveyance of realty; a writing signed by a grantor, whereby title to realty is transferred from one to another.

Defamation an intentional false communication, either published or publicly spoken, that injures another's reputation or good name.

Default the omission or failure to perform a contractual duty to fulfill a promise or discharge an obligation to pay interest or principal on a debt when due. Under the U.C.C., when default occurs may be defined by the parties to the agreement.

Default judgment judgment entered against a party who failed to appear in court to defend against a claim brought by another party.

Defendant the party against whom an action or lawsuit is brought.

Defense that offered and alleged by a defendant as a reason in law or fact why the plaintiff should not recover, or recover less than what she seeks.

Delaney clause the portion of the Food, Drug and Cosmetic Act that any food additive that is found to cause cancer in animals may not be marketed.

Delegation the legal transfer of power and authority to another to perform duties.

Delegation of powers the constitutional right of Congress to authorize government agencies to perform certain legal duties.

Demurrer an older term for a motion to dismiss a claim for failure to state a cause of action. *See* motion to dismiss.

Deposition sworn testimony—written or oral—of a person taken outside the court.

Design defect in products liability litigation, a claim that a consumer suffered an injury because a safer product design was not used.

Detrimental reliance *see* promissory estoppel.

Direct examination the initial examination of a witness by the party on whose behalf the witness has been called.

Directed verdict verdict granted by the court on the grounds that the jury could reasonably reach only one conclusion on the basis of the evidence presented during the trial.

Discharge the termination of one's obligation. Under contract law, discharge occurs either when the parties have performed their obligations in the contract, or when events, the conduct of the parties, or the operation of law releases parties from performing.

Disclosure requirements in securities law, the revealing of financial and other information relevant to investors considering buying securities; the requirement that sufficient information be provided prospective investors so that they can make an informed evaluation of a security.

Discovery the process by which the parties to a lawsuit gather information from each other to reduce the scope of what will be presented in court; process is determined by rules of procedure and may be limited by the court hearing the case.

Discrimination illegal treatment of a person or group (intentional or unintentional) based on race, color, national origin, religion, sex, disability or age. This includes the failure to remedy the effects of past discrimination.

Disparagement a false communication that injures a person in his business or profession.

Disparate impact in employment discrimination law, when an apparently neutral rule regarding hiring or treatment of employees works to discriminate against a protected class of employees.

Disparate treatment differential treatment of employees or applicants on the basis of their race, color, religion, sex, national origin, or age (for example, when applicants of a particular race are required to pass tests not required of other applicants).

Dissenting opinion an opinion written by one or more appellate judges or justices explaining why they disagree with the decision of the majority of the court in a given case.

Diversity of citizenship an action in which the plaintiff and the defendant are citizens of different states.

Dividend a distribution to corporate shareholders in proportion to the number of shares held.

Due care the degree of care that a reasonable person can be expected to exercise to avoid harm reasonably foreseeable if such care is not taken.

Due process constitutional limitation requiring that a person has a right not to be deprived of life, liberty, or property without a fair and just hearing.

Effluent charge a fee, fine, or tax imposed on a polluting activity.

Electronic fund transfer monetary transactions made electronically (telephone, computer).

Embezzlement statutory offense when a person fraudulently appropriates for her own use the property or money entrusted to her by another.

Eminent domain the power of the government to take private property for public use for fair compensation.

Emission offset under the Clean Air Act, a requirement that for a polluting facility to be built or expanded, the owner may be required to reduce certain pollutants by as much or more than the new pollution to be generated; this may be done by paying other polluters to reduce emissions.

Emotional distress a tort action for damages to compensate a person for mental injury suffered due to another's actions.

Employee handbooks manuals issued by employers to inform employees of their duties and rights as employees; often used as evidence of an employment contract that must be followed by both parties.

Employment-at-will a doctrine under the common law providing that unless otherwise explicitly stated an employment contract was for an indefinite term and could be terminated at any time by either party without notice.

Enabling statute legislative enactment granting power to an administrative agency.

En banc legal proceedings before or by the court as a whole rather than before or by a single judge, or a panel of judges.

Endangered species in environmental law, a list of animals and plants declared by the government to be in danger of becoming extinct; violators may be prosecuted for killing endangered animals or plants or injuring their habitat.

Environmental Impact Statement statements required by National Environmental Protection Act of agencies when they make recommendations concerning proposed legislation or other federal activity that significantly affects the quality of the environment.

Equal protection clause Section 1 of the Fourteenth Amendment to the Constitution, providing that states treat all persons subject to state laws in a similar manner.

"No State shall . . . deny to any person within its jurisdiction the equal protection of the laws."

Equitable remedy the means by which a court enforces a right adjudicated in equity or prevents or redresses the violation of such a right. Remedies include specific performance, injunction, recission, reformation and declaratory judgment.

Equity (1) in securities law, an ownership claim on a business interest; usually a security with no repayment terms; (2) a legal system that operates alongside the "law," and is concerned with achieving justice in cases when courts of law are incompetent to act.

Estoppel a principle that provides that a person is barred from denying or alleging certain facts because of that person's previous conduct, allegation, or denial.

Ethics the duties which a member of society owes to other members.

Evidence in procedural law, the legal matters—oral, written or physical testimony—that may be presented at a trial or at other legal proceeding for use in resolving a dispute.

Excise tax a tax on the sale of a good. A specific tax is a fixed tax per unit of the good sold. An ad valorem tax is a fixed percentage of the value of the good. *See* tariff.

Exclusive dealing contract an agreement between two firms to deal only with each other for certain products or services.

Exclusive jurisdiction the power of a court over a particular subject matter as provided by statute to the exclusion of other courts.

Exculpatory contract a contract that releases one of the parties from liability for their wrongdoings.

Executed contract a contract that has been fully performed by the parties.

Executive order under powers granted by the Constitution, or by Congress in legislation, an order by the president to establish or enforce a legal requirement.

Executory contract a contract that has not been performed by the parties.

Exemplary damages *see* punitive damages.

Exemptions from registration in securities law, provisions that allow certain securities to be sold without meeting the usual registration requirements with the Securities and Exchange Commission; does not exempt the securities from other aspects of securities laws.

Exhaustion of administrative remedies a doctrine providing that in instances when a statute provides an administrative remedy, relief must be sought through all appropriate agency channels before a court can act to consider other relief.

Ex parte Latin for "by one party."

Expert witness a witness with professional training or skill in helping evaluate evidence in a case.

Export products manufactured in one country, and then shipped and sold in another.

Express authority in agency law, when an agent has clear authority, verbal or written, to act on behalf of a principal for certain matters.

Express contract a contract that is oral or written, as opposed to being implied from the conduct of the parties (*see* implied contract).

Express warranty a promise, in addition to an underlying sales agreement, that goes beyond the terms of the sales agreement and under which the promisor assures the description, performance, or quality of the goods.

Expropriation the taking of a privately-owned property by a government. Governments are required to, but at times do not pay compensation for such takings.

Ex rel (Ex relatione) Latin for "on the relation or information."

Externalities effects, good or bad, on parties not directly involved in the production or use of a product. Pollution is an example of a bad effect, or negative externality.

Failing firm defense in antitrust law, a rule that firms may be allowed to merge that would not be allowed to do so otherwise because one of the firms is in danger of going out of business anyway.

Failure to warn in products liability cases, when a producer is found liable in tort for not warning consumers of dangers the producer knew existed or should have known existed.

Fair use the right of persons other than the owner of copyrighted material to use it in a reasonable manner without the consent of the owner; factors include the purpose of the use, the extent of the use, and the economic effect of the use.

False imprisonment the intentional detention or restraint of an individual by another.

Featherbedding a practice, under a union rule, in which the number of employees used, or the amount of time taken, to perform a job is unnecessarily high.

Federal question a question in a case in which one of the parties, usually the plaintiff, is asserting a right based on a federal law.

Fellow-servant rule a rule that precludes an injured employee from recovering from his employer when the injury results from the negligent conduct of a fellow employee.

Felony a serious class of crime (such as rape, murder, or robbery) that may be punishable by death or imprisonment in excess of one year.

Fiduciary a person having a duty, generally created by his own undertaking, to act in good faith for the benefit of another in matters related to that undertaking. A fiduciary duty is the highest standard of duty implied by law.

Firm offer (U.C.C.) a signed writing by a merchant promising to keep an offer open. In contrast to an option, a firm offer does not require consideration to make the offer irrevocable.

Floating lien a security interest retained in collateral even when the collateral changes in character, classification, or location. An inventory loan in which the lender receives a security interest or general claim on a company's inventory. Under the U.C.C., such security is not only in inventory or accounts of the debtor at the time of the original loan, but also in after-acquired inventory or accounts.

Foreign exchange rate the price of a country's currency stated in terms of the currency of another country.

Foreseeable dangers in tort law, the duty to reasonably anticipate when an injury is likely to result from certain acts or failure to act to protect others.

Forgery the false making, or the material altering, of a document with the intent to defraud.

Franchise a contract between a parent company (franchisor) and an operating company (franchisee) to allow the franchisee to run a business with the brand name of the parent company, so long as the terms of the contract concerning methods of operation are followed.

Fraud an intentional misrepresentation of a material fact designed to induce the person receiving the miscommunication to rely upon it to her detriment, so that a loss is suffered.

Free trade when all goods and services can be freely imported and exported without special taxes or restrictions being imposed.

Free trade zone areas where foreign merchandise may be brought without formal customs entry and payment of duty for most legal purposes including storage, grading, sampling, manufacturing, cleaning, or packaging. Duties are paid when the products enter the domestic market.

Fringe benefits medical, accident, and life insurance; retirement benefits; profit sharing; bonus plans; leave; and other terms and conditions of employment other than wage or salary compensation.

Full warranty defined by the Magnuson-Moss Warranty Act as an unlimited warranty for repairs or product replacement for problems that arise with a product within the warranty period.

Garnishment a legal process by which a creditor appropriates a debtor's wages, or property in the hands of a third party.

General creditor a lender with no lien or security to assist in the payment of his debt or claim.

General jurisdiction a power of a court to hear all controversies that may be brought before it.

General partner a partner in a limited partnership or any partner in a general partnership who accepts, or has imposed by law, personal liability for all debts of the partnership.

General verdict a verdict whereby the jury finds either for the plaintiff or the defendant in general terms.

Geographic market in antitrust law, the area in the country in which a business has market power.

Golden parachute a severance agreement a manager of a corporation negotiates in return for withdrawing opposition to a tender offer.

Good faith (U.C.C.) honesty in fact in the conduct or transaction in question.

Gratuitous agent an agent who volunteers services without an agreement or expectation of compensation, but whose voluntary consent creates the rights and liabilities of the agency relationship.

Grievance in labor law, a complaint filed by an employer or a union regarding failure to comply with terms of a collective bargaining agreement or to negotiate in good faith; also a dispute resolution procedure that workers must follow if represented by a union.

Guarantor one who makes a guaranty. Person who becomes secondarily liable for another's debt; in contrast to a surety who is primarily liable with the debtor. One who promises to answer for the debt in case of default.

Guaranty a collateral agreement for performance of another's undertaking. An agreement in which the guarantor agrees to satisfy the debt of a debtor, only if the debtor fails to repay the debt (secondary liability).

Guardian a person appointed to act on behalf of a person lacking ability to perform legal acts, to acquire legal rights, or incur legal liabilities.

Hazardous waste a substance that may cause or contribute to an increase in mortality or pose a hazard to human health or the environment when improperly treated.

Hearsay evidence not derived from the personal knowledge of the witness, but from what the witness has heard others say. Hearsay evidence is allowed only in special cases.

Hispanic legally, a person of Mexican, Puerto Rican, Cuban, Central or South American or other Spanish culture or origin, regardless of race.

Horizontal business arrangement an agreement among firms operating at the same level of business in the same market.

Horizontal merger a merger between two companies that compete in the same product market.

Horizontal price fixing price fixing among competitors; an agreement among competitors to charge noncompetitive prices.

Horizontal restraint of trade anti-competitive action by businesses at the same level of operation. Rival firms that come together by agreement in an attempt to restrain trade by restricting output and raising prices is called a *cartel*.

Hot cargo agreement an agreement between an employer and a union when the employer agrees to refrain from handling, using, selling, transporting or dealing in any products of an employer the union has labeled as unfair or "hot."

Howey test the rule established by the Supreme Court to determine what a security is under the federal securities law: an investment of money, in a common enterprise, with the expectation that profits will be generated by the efforts of others.

Hung jury a jury so divided in opinion that it cannot agree upon a verdict.

Identification (U.C.C.) the process of specifying the actual goods that are covered by a contract.

Implied authority in agency law, when the right of an agent to act on behalf of a principal is inferred from past actions or from the current position of the agent.

Implied contract a contract formed on the basis of the conduct of the parties.

Implied warranty an unwritten, unexpressed promise or guarantee that a court infers to exist and that accompanies a good.

Import a product manufactured in another country, then shipped to and sold in this country.

Impossibility of performance a doctrine used to discharge the obligations of parties to a contract when an event—such a law being passed that makes the contract illegal or the subject matter of the contract is destroyed (called objective impossibility)—makes performance "impossible" for one or both parties.

Indictment a formal written charge issued by a grand jury asserting that the named person has committed a crime.

Infringement in patent, copyright, and trademark law, the unauthorized use or imitation of another's recognized right to the property involved.

Injunction an order issued by a court that restrains a person or business from doing some act or orders the person to do something.

In personam jurisdiction the power the court has over the person(s) involved in the action.

In rem jurisdiction an action taken by a court against the property of the defendant.

Insider an officer or other person who has information not yet available to the general public concerning the future profits or losses of a corporation.

Insider trading the buying or selling of securities of a firm by persons who have information about the firm not yet available to the public and who expect to make a profit through those transactions.

Insolvency the financial state of a person or business when debts and liabilities exceed the value of assets.

Intangible asset property that is a "right" such as a patent, copyright or trademark, or one that is lacking physical evidence, such as goodwill in a firm.

Intangible property property that has no value because of its physical being but is evidence of value, such as securities, promissory notes, copyrights, patents, and certain contracts.

Intellectual property property recognized at law that arises from mental processes, such as inventions and works of art.

Intentional tort a wrong committed upon the person or property of another where the actor is expressly or impliedly judged to have intended to commit the act that led to the injury.

Interbrand competition competition among various brands of a particular product.

Interference with business relationship a tort in which a defendant commits an intentional and unjustified interference with a plaintiff's valid business dealings that inflicts monetary damage.

Interference with contractual relationship a tort in which there is a valid contract, the defendant knew of the contract but intentionally caused a breach of the contract, resulting in damages to the plaintiff.

International law those laws governing the legal relations between nations.

Interpretative rules statements issued by administrative agencies that explain how the agency understands its statutory authority to operate; these may be advisory or binding.

Interrogatories in the discovery process, a set of written questions for a witness or a party for which written answers are prepared with assistance of counsel and signed under oath.

Interstate commerce the carrying on of commercial activity that affects business in more than one state.

Intervening conduct in tort, an independent cause that comes between the original wrongful act and the injury that relieves liability that would otherwise exist for the original act; a legal break in the causal connection.

Intraband competition competition among retailers in the sales of a particular brand of product.

Invasion of privacy in tort, the encroachment on the right of a person to their solitude, the appropriation of a person's reputation for commercial purposes, or the public disclosure of facts that the person had a legal right to keep private.

Investigatory hearing in administrative law, when an agency uses rulemaking authority granted by Congress to gather information, on the public record, needed to determine the desirability of proposed rules.

Investment advisers Under securities law, a "person who, for compensation, engages in the business of advising others . . . as to the advisability of investing in, purchasing or selling securities. . . ." This includes securities brokers and dealers.

Investment company any corporation in business to own and hold the stock of other corporations.

Involuntary bankruptcy a bankruptcy proceeding against an insolvent debtor that is initiated by creditors.

Jeopardy a person is said to be in jeopardy when she is charged with a crime before a court. The constitutional doctrine of *double jeopardy* prohibits a person from being prosecuted twice in the same court for the same offense.

Joint and several liability liability that a person or business either shares with other tortfeasors or bears individually.

Joint liability liability that is owed to a third party by two or more other parties together.

Joint stock company a partnership in which the capital is divided, or agreed to be divided, into shares so as to be transferable without the express consent of the other partners.

Joint venture the participation of two companies jointly in a third enterprise. Generally, both companies contribute assets and share risks.

Judgment the official decision of a court of law upon the rights and claims of the parties to an action litigated in and submitted to the court for its determination.

Judgment lien a lien binding the real estate of a judgment debtor, in favor of the judgment holder, and giving the latter a right to levy on the property for the satisfaction of his judgment to the exclusion of others.

Judgment notwithstanding the verdict judgment entered by the court for a party following a jury verdict for the other party.

Judicial review authority of a court to reexamine a dispute considered and decided previously by a lower court or by an administrative agency.

Junior creditor a creditor whose claim against a debtor arose at a later date than that of the claim held by another creditor with the same or superior priority. A creditor whose claim ranks below other creditors with regard to priority to the debtors property.

Jurisdiction the right of a court or other body to hear a case and render a judgment.

Jurisdiction over the person power of a court to lawfully bind a party involved in a dispute before it.

Jurisdiction over the subject power of a court to lawfully affect the thing or issue in dispute.

Jurisprudence the science or philosophy of law.

Just compensation clause the portion of the Fifth Amendment that states "nor shall private property be taken for public use, without just compensation." The requirement that when the government uses its power to force a private party to give up a property interest, fair market value should be paid.

Kefauver amendment the portion of the Food, Drug and Cosmetic Act that requires the Food and Drug Administration to approve drugs only after their safety and effectiveness have been established.

Laissez faire French for "let do;" a policy implying the absence of government intervention in a market economy.

Law enforceable rules of conduct set forth by a government to be followed by the citizens of the society.

Law merchant in commercial law, the rules devised by merchants in Europe over several centuries to govern their trade; many of these rules were formally adopted into law.

Leading question a question by an attorney in a trial that instructs the witness how to answer or provides the desired answer.

Legal capacity the right to be able to enter into legal matters that may be restricted by age, mental ability, or other requirements established at common law or by statute.

Legal cause *see* proximate cause.

Legal ethics practice and customs among members of the legal profession, involving their moral and professional duties toward one another, clients, and the courts.

Legislative history the history of a statute consisting of the legislative committee reports and transcripts of debates in the legislature. Often used by a court in interpreting the terms and provisions of a statute.

Letter of credit a written document in which the party issuing the document—usually a bank—promises to pay third parties in accordance with the terms of the document.

Levy a seizure; the process by which a state official is empowered by writ or other court directive to seize or control a judgment debtor's property to satisfy a judgment.

Liability a general term referring to possible or actual responsibility; when one is bound by law or equity to be accountable for some act; in product liability, it is in reference to the obligation to pay for damages for which the manufacturer has been held responsible.

Libel a defamation that is in the form of a printing, a writing, pictures, or a broadcast on radio or television.

Lien a claim or encumbrance on property for payment of some debt, obligation or duty. Qualified right that a creditor has in or over specific property of a debtor as security for the debt or for performance of some act. Right to retain property for payment of a debt.

Lien creditor a creditor who has acquired a lien on certain property by attachment, levy or other judicial means.

Limited liability the fact that shareholders of a corporation are not liable for the debts of the corporation beyond the amount of money they have invested in the corporation.

Limited or special jurisdiction power of a court to hear a particular cause which can be exercised only under the limitations and circumstances prescribed by statute.

Limited partner a partner in a limited partnership whose liability for partnership debts is limited to the amount of his contribution to the partnership.

Limited partnership a business organization consisting of one or more general partners who manage and contribute assets to the business and who are personally liable for the debts of the business, and one or more limited partners who contribute assets only and are liable only up to the amount of that contribution.

Limited warranty under the Magnuson-Moss Warranty Act, any product sold with less than a full warranty has what is defined as a limited warranty, the terms of which must be explained in writing.

Liquidated damages amounts specified in a contract to be paid in the event of a breach. They represent a reasonable estimation by the parties of the damages that will occur in the event of breach.

Liquidated debt a debt for a known or determinable amount of money that can not be disputed by either the debtor or the creditor.

Liquidation the sale of the assets of a debtor, the proceeds from which are distributed to the creditors, with any remaining balance going to the debtor.

Lockout refusal by an employer to allow employees to work.

Long-arm statute a state statute permitting courts to obtain personal jurisdiction over nonresidents as long as the requirements of the statute are met.

Malice the intentional doing of a wrongful act, without a legal excuse, with the intent to inflict injury.

Mandatory subjects of bargaining under the National Labor Relations Act, all terms and conditions of employment that must be discussed by employers and unions or an unfair labor practice occurs.

Manifest system in environmental and occupational safety law, the requirement that certain chemicals have documentation concerning their production, distribution, and disposal to ensure proper handling and disposal of toxic substances.

Margin requirement the fraction of a price of a stock that must be paid in cash, while putting up the stock as security against a loan for the balance.

Market failure failure of an unregulated market to achieve socially optimal results. Sources include monopolies and externalities.

Market power in antitrust law, the ability to raise prices significantly above the competitive level without losing much business.

Market share the percentage of a market, by sales volume of a product nationally or in a geographic area, that is controlled by a firm.

Market share liability when plaintiff is unable to determine which manufacturer of a product caused her injury, the court may assign liability to all firms in the industry on the basis of their shares of the product market.

Maturity the due date of a financial instrument.

Mechanic's lien a claim under state law to secure priority of payments for the value of work performed and materials supplied in building on or improving land and buildings.

Mediation a form of alternative dispute resolution when a third party is hired by parties to a dispute with the intent to persuade them to settle their dispute.

Meeting competition in antitrust law, a defense in price discrimination (Robinson-Patman) cases, when a firm shows that prices were cut to meet the prices of competitors.

Mens rea Latin for "the state of mind" of the actor.

Mental distress *see* emotional distress.

Merchantability in commercial law, the notion that goods are "reasonably fit for the ordinary purposes for which such goods are used."

Merger a contract through which one firm acquires the assets and liabilities of another firm.

Merit regulations state securities law provision that in some states allows a securities commissioner to decide if a proposed security offering is "too risky" to be sold to the public in that state.

Minorities persons classified as black (not of Hispanic origin), Hispanic, Asian, Pacific Islander, American Indian, or Alaskan native.

Misdemeanors a lessor crime, that is neither a felony nor treason, punishable by a fine and/or imprisonment in other than state or federal penitentiaries.

Misrepresentation words or conduct by a person to another that, under the circumstances, amounts to a false statement.

Misstatements in securities law, liability may be imposed on those responsible for issuing information about securities that misleads a reasonable investor in investment decisions to her detriment.

Mistrial a trial that cannot stand in law because the court lacks jurisdiction, because of juror misconduct, or because of disregard for some other procedural requirement.

Mitigation of damages doctrine that imposes a duty upon an injured party to exercise reasonable diligence in attempting to minimize damages after being injured.

Mobile source under the Clean Air Act, a pollution source such as automobiles, trucks, and airplanes.

Monopoly a market structure in which the output of an industry is controlled by a single seller or a group of sellers making joint decisions regarding production and price.

Moral principles social rules that categorize different actions as right or wrong.

Morals generally accepted standards of right and wrong in a society.

Mortgage an interest in real property created by a written instrument providing security for the payment of a debt. In many states, a mortgage is a lien; it is a pledge or security of particular property to help insure payment of a debt or other obligation.

Mortgagee party who holds or receives a mortgage; the creditor.

Mortgagor one who, having all or part of title to real property, pledges the property in writing for a particular purpose, such as to secure a debt; the party who mortgages property; the debtor.

Motion the formal way an attorney submits a proposed measure for the consideration and action of the court.

Motion to dismiss a request that a complaint be dismissed because it does not state a claim for which the law provides a remedy, or is in some other way legally deficient.

National Ambient Air Quality Standards federal standards under the Clean Air Act that set the maximum concentration levels in the atmosphere for several air pollutants.

National Priority List contaminated sites, as determined by the Environmental Protection Agency under the Superfund law, that must be cleaned up and returned to nearly original condition.

National Uniform Effluent Standards federal standards under the Clean Water Act that set the water pollution effluent standards for every industry that discharges liquid wastes into the nation's waterways.

Natural monopoly an industry characterized by economies of scale so large that one business can supply the entire market most efficiently.

Necessary and proper clause the part of the U.S. Constitution that gives Congress the authority to use various powers to execute its functions under the Constitution.

Negligence the failure to do something that a reasonable person, guided by the ordinary considerations that regulate human affairs, would do, or the doing of something that a reasonable person would not do.

Negotiation the deliberation over the terms and conditions of a proposed agreement, or a form of alternative dispute resolution to resolve a dispute and avoid litigation.

Nominal damages a damage award whereby a court recognizes that the plaintiff has suffered a breach of duty, but has not suffered any actual financial loss or injury as a result. Plaintiff's recovery for such breaches is often as little as a dollar.

Nonattainment area under the Clean Air Act, an area in which the air quality for certain pollutants fails to meet the national ambient air quality standards.

Nonpoint sources under the Clean Water Act, sources of pollution that are diverse, such as urban and agricultural runoff from rainstorms.

Novation an agreement between the parties to a contract to discharge one of the parties and create a new contract with another party to be responsible for the discharged party's obligations.

Nuisance an unreasonable and substantial interference with the use and enjoyment of another's land (*private nuisance*); an unreasonable or substantial interference with a right held in common by members of the general public (*public nuisance*).

Occupational licensure requirements at the state level that for one to practice a certain profession one must meet certain educational or experience guidelines, pass an entry examination, and must show evidence of continuing education accomplishments.

Offer a proposal to do or refrain from doing some specified thing by a party called the offeror to another called the offeree. The proposal creates in the offeree a legal power to bind the offeror to the terms of the proposal by accepting the offer.

Offeree the party to whom an offer is made.

Offeror the party making an offer to another party to enter into a contract.

Open account credit extended by a seller to a buyer that permits buyer to make purchases without security.

Opening argument oral presentations made to the jury by the attorneys before the parties present their cases.

Original jurisdiction power of a court to take a lawsuit at its beginning, try it, and pass judgment upon the law and facts.

Out-of-court settlement an agreement by the parties in a case to resolve the matter before a determination by the court.

Over-the-counter market a stock market for securities generally not sold in large daily volumes so that they are not listed on a stock exchange, such as the New York Stock Exchange; a securities market created by stockbrokers who relay information to a central location about offers to buy or sell certain amounts of a stock.

Parol in French and Latin, spoken or oral.

Parol evidence rule a rule that prohibits the introduction into a lawsuit of oral evidence that contradicts the terms of a written contract intended to be the final and complete expression of the agreement between the parties.

Partnership a business owned by two or more persons that is not organized as a corporation.

Par value stock stock that has been assigned a specific value by the corporation's board of directors.

Patent a grant from the government conveying and securing for an inventor the exclusive right to make, use, and sell an invention for twenty years from the time of application.

Per curiam opinion Latin for "by the court." A per curiam opinion expresses the view of the court as a whole in contrast to an opinion authored by one member of the court.

Perfection of security interest in a secured transaction, the process by which a security interest is protected against competing claims to the collateral. It usually requires the secured party to give notice of the interest by filing it in the appropriate government office, usually the secretary of state.

Perfect tender rule at common law, seller's offer of delivery must conform to every detail of contract with buyer; under the U.C.C. parties may agree to limit the operation of this rule or the seller may cure a defective tender if the time for performance has not ended, the seller notifies the buyer quickly of intent to cure defect, or the seller repairs or replaces defective goods within performance time limits.

Performance in contract law, the fulfilling of obligations or promises according to the terms agreed to or specified by parties to a contract. Complete performance of those obligations or promises by both parties discharges the contract.

Periodic disclosure in securities law, requirements that issuers of most publicly held securities file monthly, quarterly, and annual reports with the Securities and Exchange Commission.

Per se Latin for "in itself" or "taken alone"; as in the per se rule in antitrust, whereby the facts alone are enough to lead to conviction of the defendants.

Personal property physical, moveable property other than real estate.

Personal service in the pleadings stage, personal service of the complaint is accomplished by physically delivering it to the defendant.

Piercing the corporate veil a court's act of ignoring the legal existence of a corporation and holding the corporation's officers personally liable for their wrongful acts done in the name of the corporation.

Plaintiff the party who initiates a lawsuit.

Pleadings statements of the plaintiff and the defendant that detail their facts, allegations, and defenses, that create the issues of the lawsuit.

Point source under the Clean Water Act, any definitive place of discharge of a water pollutant such as pipes, ditches, or channels.

Political speech in constitutional law, speech that concerns political, as opposed to commercial, matters; given a high level of protection by the First Amendment.

Pollution the release of substances into the air, water, or land that cause physical change.

Possessory lien a lien in which the creditor has the right to the possession of specific property until a debt is satisfied or an obligation is performed.

Potential competition in antitrust law, consideration given to the degree of competitiveness that exists in a market because of the possibility that firms not now in the market will enter it and compete with existing producers.

Power of attorney a document authorizing another person to act as one's agent or attorney with respect to the matters stated in the document.

Precedent a decision in a case that is used to guide decisions in later cases with similar fact situations.

Predatory pricing in antitrust law, pricing below an accepted measure of cost (such as average variable cost) to drive competitors from the market in the short run to reduce competition in the long run.

Preferred stock class of stock that has priority over common stock both as to payment of dividends and to distribution of the corporation's assets upon dissolutionment.

Preponderance of the evidence in civil trials, the burden of persuasion to win a verdict requires that the plaintiff prove its claim by having the majority or bulk of the evidence on its side.

Presumption means the trier of fact must find the existence of the fact presumed unless and until evidence is introduced which would support a finding of its nonexistence.

Prevention of significant deterioration area under the Clean Air Act, an area where the air quality is better than required by the national ambient air standards; such as national parks and wilderness areas. Air quality is not allowed to fall.

Price discrimination in antitrust law, charging different prices to different customers for the same product without a cost justification for the price difference.

Prima facie Latin for "at first sight." Something presumed to be true until disproved by contrary evidence.

Primary boycott in labor law, a union action that tries to convince people not to deal with an employer with which the union has a grievance.

Principal in an agency relationship, a person who, by explicit or implicit agreement, authorizes an agent to act on his behalf and perform acts that will be binding on the principal.

Principal (credit transactions) an amount of money borrowed or invested. The capital sum of a debt or obligation, distinguished from interest or other additions to it.

Principal (suretyship) the person primarily liable, for whose performance of her obligation the surety has become bound.

Private law a classification of law, generally denoting laws that affect relationships between people.

Private nuisance in tort law, when an activity reduces the right of one person, or a small number of persons, to enjoy property without unreasonable interference.

Private property right an individual economic interest supported by the law.

Privilege in tort law, the ability to act contrary to another's legal right without that party having legal redress for the consequences of that act; usually raised as a defense.

Privity a legal relationship between parties, such as between parties to a contract.

Privity of contract the immediate relationship that exists between the parties to a contract.

Probable cause reasonable ground to believe the existence of facts warranting the undertaking of certain actions, such as the arrest or search of a person.

Procedural law the rules of the court system that deal with the manner in which lawsuits are initiated and go forward. Court systems generally have rules regarding pleadings, process, evidence, and practice.

Product market in antitrust law, the product market includes all products that can be reasonably substituted by consumers for the product of the business under investigation.

Program trading the trading of stock on stock exchanges through the use of computers programmed to buy and sell at specified prices and other conditions.

Promise a statement or declaration that binds the party making it (the promisor) to do or refrain from doing a particular act or thing. The party to whom the declaration is made (the promisee) has a right to demand or expect the performance of the act or thing.

Promissee party to whom a promise is made.

Promisor party who makes a promise.

Promissory estoppel a doctrine that allows promises to be enforced in the absence of consideration if a promise is made which the promisor reasonably expects will induce action or forbearance on the part of the promisee and, which in fact, does cause such action or forbearance to the detriment of the promisee.

Promulgation an administrative order that causes an agency law or regulation to become known and obligatory.

Proprietorship a business owned by a person that is not organized as a corporation.

Prospectus under securities law, a pamphlet that must be produced for distribution to prospective buyers of securities that contains information about the background of the security being offered.

Protected class under Title VII of the Civil Rights Act of 1964, those groups the law seeks to protect, including groups based on race, sex, national origin, religion, and color.

Proximate cause in tort law, the action of the defendant that produces the plaintiff's injuries; without which the injury or damage in question would not have existed.

Proxy giving another person the right to vote one's vote on one's behalf; in stock votes when a person gives another the right to vote in a certain manner, such as for candidates for board of directors.

Public law a classification of law, generally denoting laws that affect relationships between people and their governments.

Public nuisance in tort law, when an activity reduces the right of the public in general to enjoy property without unreasonable interference.

Punitive damages compensation awarded to a plaintiff beyond actual damages; awarded to punish the defendant for doing a particularly offensive act.

Purchase money security interest a secured interest created when a buyer uses the money of a lender to make a purchase and gives the lender a security interest in the property purchased.

Quasi-contract a contract imposed by law, in the absence of an actual contract, to prevent unjust enrichment. A contract implied in law.

Quasi in rem jurisdiction a proceeding brought against the defendant personally, but when the defendant's interest in property serves as the basis of the court's jurisdiction.

Ratification in contract law, the act of accepting responsibility for a previous act that would not constitute an enforceable contractual obligation but for the ratification. Ratification causes the obligation to be binding as if it were valid and enforceable in the first place.

Real property land, the products of land (such as timber), and property that cannot be moved (such as houses).

Reasonable accommodation in employment discrimination law, the requirement that employers take steps that are not very costly to make employment possible for persons with disabilities.

Reasonable care the degree of care that a person of ordinary prudence would use in the same or similar circumstances or in the same line of business.

Reasonable person the standard which one must observe to avoid liability for negligence; often includes the duty to foresee harm that could result from certain actions.

Rebuttal during the trial stage, when evidence is given by one party to refute evidence introduced by the other party.

Recission in contract law, agreement of the parties to cancel a contract without performance; as a remedy, the cancellation of a contract by a court, the effect is as if the contract had never been made.

Red herring in securities law, a prospectus that has not yet been approved by the Securities Exchange Commission. It has a red border on its front to signal to interested parties that it is not yet approved for final distribution; used as an advertising device.

Registration statements in securities law, the financial information that must be filed with the Securities and Exchange Commission for review prior to the sale of securities to the public.

Regulation Z a rule issued by the Federal Reserve Board to implement the Truth-in-Lending Act requiring systematic disclosure of the costs associated with credit transactions.

Rejoinder during the trial stage, the defendant's answer to the plaintiff's rebuttal.

Remand the act of an appellate court in sending a case back to trial court ordering it to take action according to its decision. The order usually requires a new trial or limited hearings on specified subject matter.

Remedy the legal means by which a right is enforced or the violation of a right is prevented or compensated.

Removal jurisdiction the power to remove a case from one court system to another.

Repatriation the process used to transfer assets or earnings from a host nation to another nation.

Reply during the pleading stage, plaintiff's response to the defendant's answer to the plaintiff's original complaint.

Representation election in labor law, when at least thirty percent of workers in a current or proposed bargaining unit sign a request to have an election to determine if all workers in that workplace will be represented by a particular union.

Repudiation a rejection, disclaimer, or renunciation of a contract before performance is due, but which does not operate as an anticipatory breach unless the promisee elects to treat the rejection as a breach and brings a suit for damages.

Res Latin for "a thing" or "things."

Resale price maintenance when a manufacturer or wholesaler sets the price of a good at the next level, such as at the retail level; if the price set is not charged by the retailer, the manufacturer or wholesaler will no longer sell the good to the retailer.

Res ispa loquitor Latin for "the thing speaks for itself;" given the facts presented, it is clear that the defendant's actions were negligent and were the proximate cause of the injury incurred.

Res judicata a rule that prohibits the same dispute between two parties from being relitigated by a court after final judgment has been entered and all appeals exhausted.

Respondeat superior doctrine of vicarious liability under which an employer is held liable for the wrongful acts of his employees committed within the scope of their employment.

Respondent the party, plaintiff or defendant, that won in a lower court but must now respond to the appeal of the case by the losing party, the appellant.

Restraint of trade any contract, agreement, or combination that eliminates or restricts competition.

Reverse a decision by an appellate court that overturns or vacates the judgment of a lower court.

Revocation the recall of some power, authority, or thing granted; in contract law, the withdrawal by the offeree of an offer that had been valid until withdrawn.

Right-to-work law state laws that prohibit unions from forcing employees who do not want to pay union dues or agency fees, to pay such dues or fees even if the employees are represented by the union under a collective bargaining agreement.

Riparian at common law, relating to the bank of a river or stream; the owner of land bounded by a river or body of water has the right to reasonably use the water next to the land or that passes over the land.

Rule making in administrative law, the procedures that agencies must follow when issuing rules to interpret or enforce the statutory authority they were granted by Congress.

Rule of reason in antitrust law, the court considers all facts and decides whether what was done was reasonable and did not harm competition in net; compare to the per se rule.

Sales contract under the U.C.C. "the passing of title from the seller to the buyer for a price."

Sanction a penalty used to provide incentives to obey the law or rules and regulations.

Satisfaction the performance of a substituted obligation in return for the discharge of the original obligation.

Scienter Latin for "knowingly;" usually meaning that the defendant knew that the act in question was illegal.

Secondary boycott a union's refusal to handle products of or work for a secondary company with whom the union has no dispute; purpose is to force that company to stop doing business with another company with which the union has a dispute.

Second lien a lien that ranks after a first lien on the same property (such as a second mortgage) and is entitled to satisfaction out of the proceeds of the sale of the property after the first lien is satisfied.

Secured creditors a person who has loaned money to another and has a legally recognized interest in the property of the debtor until fulfillment of the terms of the debt agreement.

Secured transaction any transaction, regardless of form, intended to create a security interest in personal property, including goods, documents, and other intangible property.

Securities debt or equity instruments that, in securities law, are evidence of a contribution of money by a group of investors into a common enterprise that will be operated for profit by professional managers.

Securities fraud in securities law, the statutory basis for charging anyone involved in the issuance or trading of securities with fraud, which is usually due to misleading issuance of information or failure to disclose material information that causes investors to suffer losses.

Security interest interest in property obtained under a security agreement. An interest in property that allows the property to be sold on default to satisfy the obligation for which the security interest is given. A mortgage grants a security interest in real property.

Self-incrimination the rule that a witness is not bound to give testimony that would incriminate him with respect to a criminal act.

Service of process in the pleadings stage, the delivery of the complaint to the defendant either to her personally or, in most jurisdictions, by leaving it with a responsible person at her place of residence.

Shareholder the owner of one or more shares of stock in a corporation.

Shelf registration a Securities and Exchange Commission rule that allows certain companies to file a single registration statement for the future sale of securities. This registration allows the company to react quickly to favorable market conditions.

Short-swing profits profits made by an insider on the purchase and sale of stock of a corporation within a six-month period.

Sight draft a draft payable upon proper presentment.

Slander an oral defamation of one's reputation or good name.

Sole proprietorship *see* proprietorship.

Sophisticated purchaser in tort law, a defense that when a manufacturer sells a product to a sophisticated buyer, such as another manufacturer, the purchaser is responsible for instructing its employees about the dangers in using the product.

Sovereign a person, body, or nation in which independent and supreme authority is vested.

Sovereign immunity the doctrine under which a nonsovereign party is precluded from engaging in a legal action against a sovereign party, unless the sovereign gives its consent.

Special damages in contract law, damages not contemplated by the parties at the time the contract is made. To be recoverable, they must flow directly and immediately from the breach of contract, and must be reasonably foreseeable.

Specific performance an equitable remedy, whereby the court orders a party to a contract to perform his duties under the contract. Usually granted when money damages are inadequate as a remedy and the subject matter of the contract is unique.

Standing the right to sue in a particular court.

Stare decisis the use of precedent by courts; the use of prior decisions to guide decision making in cases before the courts.

State implementation plans under the Clean Air Act, a requirement that each state prepare, under Environmental Protection Agency supervision, a plan to control certain air pollutants by certain dates to meet national air quality standards.

Stationary sources under the Clean Air Act, a nonmoving source of pollution such as a factory or an electrical power plant.

Statute a law enacted by a legislative body.

Statute of Frauds a statutory requirement that certain types of contracts be in writing to be enforceable.

Statute of limitations a statute setting maximum time periods, from the occurrence of an event, during which certain actions can be brought or rights enforced. If an action is not filed before the expiration of that time period, the statute bars the use of the courts for recovery.

Statutory law laws enacted by a legislative body.

Stock equity securities that evidence an ownership interest in a corporation.

Strict liability a legal theory that imposes responsibility for damages regardless of the existence of negligence; in tort law, any good sold that has a defect that causes injury leads to the imposition of liability.

Strike a work stoppage by employees for the purpose of coercing their employer to give in to their demands.

Subrogation the substitution of one party in place of another with respect to a lawful claim, so that the party substituted succeeds to the rights of the other in relation to the debt or claim and its rights and remedies.

Subsidy a government monetary grant to a favored industry.

Substantial factor test a standard adopted in several states in place of proximate cause; a jury may hold a defendant liable in tort if it finds that defendant's conduct was a major cause of the injury in question.

Substantial performance a doctrine that recognizes that a party that performs a contract, but with a slight deviation from the contract's terms, is entitled to the contract price less any damages caused by the deviation.

Substantive law law that defines the rights and duties of persons to each other, as opposed to procedural law, which is law that defines the manner in which rights and duties may be enforced.

Substantive rules administrative rulings based on statutory authority granted an agency by Congress; the rules have the same legal force as statutes passed by Congress.

Substituted service a form of service other than personal service, such as service by mail or by publication in a newspaper.

Summary judgment a judgment entered by a trial court as a matter of law when no genuine issue of law is found to exist.

Summons process through which a court notifies and compels a defendant to a lawsuit to appear and answer a complaint.

Sunset laws a statute that requires periodic review for the continued existence of an administrative agency; the legislature must take positive steps to allow the agency to continue to exist by a certain date.

Superfund in environmental law, the Comprehensive Environmental Response, Compensation, and Liability Act (CERCLA) is called Superfund; it concerns requirements about when hazardous waste sites must be cleaned up and who is liable for the costs.

Superseding cause the act of a third party, or an outside force, that intervenes to prevent a defendant from being liable for harm to another due to negligence.

Surety one who undertakes to pay money or otherwise act in the event that her principal fails to pay or act as promised. A surety is usually bound with her principal by the same contract, executed at the same time and for the same consideration. Under the U.C.C., this includes a guarantor. However, liability of guarantor, depending on state law, is secondary and collateral, whereas liability of surety is primary and direct.

Suretyship the relationship among three parties in which one party (the surety) guarantees payment of a debtor's debt owed to a creditor or acts as a co-debtor.

Syndicates a business association made of parties for the purpose of carrying out some particular business transaction in which the members are mutually interested.

Takings clause *see* just compensation clause.

Tangible property property that has physical form and substance, such as real estate and goods.

Tariff a tax imposed on imported goods by the government to encourage domestic industry, or to raising revenues. *See* excise tax.

Tax incentive a government taxing policy intended to encourage a particular activity.

Tender offer an offer open to current stockholders to buy a stock at a certain price; offer may be contingent upon receiving a certain amount of stock before any purchase is completed or may be an open offer; a method used to obtain enough stock to control a corporation.

Termination in contract law, the ending of an offer or contract, usually without liability.

Territorial allocation in antitrust law, the boundaries specified by contract or other agreement in which a wholesaler or retailer may sell a product.

Territorial jurisdiction territory over which a court has jurisdiction. The authority of any court is generally limited to its territorial boundaries. *See* long-arm statute.

Tie-in sale in antitrust law, the requirement that if one product or service is purchased then another product or service must also be purchased, even if it is not desired by the customer.

Title generally, the legal right of ownership; under the U.C.C. title is determined by rules regarding identification of goods, the risk of loss of goods, and insurable interest in the goods.

Tort an injury or wrong committed with or without force to another person or to his property; a civil wrong that is a breach of a legal duty owed by the person who commits the tort to the victim of the tort.

Tortfeasor an individual or business that commits a tort.

Toxic pollutants a pollutant that may cause an increase in mortality or serious illness.

Trade dress intellectual property protected by trademark law and the Lanham Act that concerns the total appearance and image of products and of service establishments, including shape, size, graphics and color.

Trademark a distinctive design, logo, mark, or word that a business can register with a government agency for its exclusive use in identifying its product or itself in the marketplace.

Trade name a word or symbol that has become sufficiently associated with a product over a period of time that it has lost its primary meaning and has acquired a secondary meaning; once so established, the company has a right to bring a legal action against those who infringe on the protection provided the trade name.

Trade regulation rules administrative rulings by the Federal Trade Commission or other agencies that hold certain practices to be illegal or create standards that must be met by sellers of certain products or services.

Trade secret in tort law, valuable, confidential data, usually in the form of formulas, processes, and other forms of information not patented, or not patentable, that are developed and owned by a business.

Treble damages a money damage award allowable under some statutes that is determined by multiplying the jury's actual damage award by three.

Trespass an unauthorized intrusion upon the property rights of another.

Trial a judicial examination of a dispute between two or more parties under the appropriate laws by a court or other appropriate tribunal that has jurisdiction.

Trial de novo Latin for "a new" trial, or retrial at an appellate court in which the entire case is examined as though no trial had occurred.

Trustee a person who has legal title in some property (such as the property of a bankrupt business) held in trust for the benefit of another person (the beneficiary).

Tying arrangements an agreement between a buyer and a seller in which the buyer of a specific product is obligated to purchase another good. *See* tie-in sale.

Ultrahazardous activity in tort law, a rule that when an activity "necessarily involves a risk of serious harm," such as the use of explosives or toxic chemicals, that strict liability will be imposed when any harm is caused to other persons or property.

Unconscionable contract a contract, or a clause in a contract, that is grossly unfair to one of the parties because of stronger bargaining powers of the other party; usually held to be void as against public policy.

Underwriter a professional firm that handles the marketing of a security to the public; it either buys all of a new security offering and then sells it to the public, or takes a commission on the securities it actually sells.

Undue influence the misuse of one's position of confidence or relationship with another individual to overcome that person's free will, thereby taking advantage of that person to affect decisions.

Unenforceable contract a contract that was once valid but, because of a subsequent illegality, will not be enforced by the courts.

Unfair labor practice in labor law, a wide range of actions that violate the right of workers to organize and engage in collective activities or violate the rights of employers to be free from practices defined as illegal under the National Labor Relations Act.

Unfair methods of competition under the Federal Trade Commission Act, a range of business practices found to violate the public interest; they may be based on fraud, deception, or a violation of public policy because competition is injured.

Unfairness in consumer protection law, a charge under Section 5 of the Federal Trade Commission Act that a business practice causes harm to consumers that they cannot reasonably avoid.

Uniform Commerical Code a statute passed in similar form by the states that sets many rules of commercial sales agreements and negotiable debt instruments.

Unilateral contract an offer or promise of an offeror that is binding only after completed performance by the offeree. The offeree's completed performance serves as acceptance of the offer and performance of the contract.

Union an association of workers that is authorized to represent them in bargaining with their employers.

Union certification in labor law, when a majority of the workers at a workplace vote to have a union be their collective bargaining agent, the National Labor Relations Board certifies the legal standing of the union for that purpose.

Union shop a place of employment where one must be a union member before obtaining employment or must become a union member after obtaining employment.

Unknown hazard in products liability, a claim that tort liability should be assigned to a producer for injuries suffered by a consumer due to a defect or hazard in a product that was not known by the producer at the time the product was made.

Unliquidated debt a disputed debt; a debt that has not been reduced to some specific amount.

Usury laws statutes that prohibit finance charges (interest and other forms of compensation for loaning money) above a certain level for debt.

Valid contract a contract in which all of the elements of a contract are present and, therefore, is enforceable at law by the parties.

Venue the geographic area in which an action is tried and from which the jury is selected.

Vertical merger a merger of two business firms, one of which is the supplier of the other.

Vertical price-fixing an agreement between a supplier and a distributor, relating to the price at which the distributor will resell the supplier's product.

Vertical restraint of trade in antitrust law, contracts or combinations which reduce or eliminate competition among firms in the production, distribution and sale of some good.

Vesting under the Employee Retirement Income Security Act, the requirement that pension benefits become the property of workers after a specific number of years of service to an employer.

Vicarious liability liability that arises from the actions of another person who is in a legal relationship with the party upon whom liability is being imposed.

Void contract a contract that does not exist at law; a contract having no legal force or binding effect.

Voidable contract a contract that is valid, but which may be legally voided at the option of one of the parties.

Voidable preference a preference given to one creditor over another by a bankrupt person or business, usually manifested by a payment to that creditor just prior to the bankruptcy declaration, that may be set aside by the trustee in bankruptcy.

Voir dire literally, to "speak the truth." In the trial stage, preliminary examination of a juror in which the attorneys and the court attempt to determine bias, incompetency, and interest.

Voluntary bankruptcy a bankruptcy proceeding that is initiated by the debtor.

Waiver an express or implied relinquishment of a legal right.

Warrant a judicial authorization for the performance of an act that would otherwise be illegal.

Warranty an assurance or guaranty, either express in the form of a statement by a seller of goods, or implied by law, having reference to and ensuring the character, quality, or fitness of purpose of the goods.

Warranty of title in general, the duty of a seller to provide good title or legal right of ownership of goods to the buyer; under the U.C.C., specific warranty rights are provided when title to goods pass.

Wetlands in environmental law, land covered by water at least a part of the year; exact coverage by various environmental statutes is still unresolved.

Whistle blower an employee who alerts the authorities to the fact that her employer is undertaking an activity that is contrary to the law.

Winding up process of settling the accounts and liquidating the assets of a partnership or corporation for the purpose of dissolving the concern.

Worker's compensation laws state statutes that provide for awards to workers or their dependents if a worker incurs an injury or an illness in the course of employment. Under such laws, the worker is freed from bringing a legal action to prove negligence by the employer.

Writ a mandatory precept issued by a court of justice.

Writ of certiorari an order by an appellate court used when the court has discretion whether or not to hear an appeal from a lower court. If appeal is granted, the writ orders the lower court to certify the record and send it to the higher court which then has the discretion to hear the appeal. If the writ is denied, the judgment of the lower court stands.

Writ of execution a writ to put into force the judgment of a court.

Yellow-dog contract an agreement between an employer and an employee under which the employee agrees not to join a union and that if he joins a union there is a breach of contract and the employee is dismissed.

Index